Handbook of Research on Emerging Advancements and Technologies in Software Engineering

Imran Ghani
Universiti Teknologi Malaysia, Malaysia

Wan Mohd Nasir Wan Kadir
Universiti Teknologi Malaysia, Malaysia

Mohammad Nazir Ahmad
Universiti Teknologi Malaysia, Malaysia

A volume in the Advances in Systems Analysis, Software Engineering, and High Performance Computing (ASASEHPC) Book Series

An Imprint of IGI Global

Managing Director:	Lindsay Johnston
Production Editor:	Jennifer Yoder
Development Editor:	Allison McGinniss
Acquisitions Editor:	Kayla Wolfe
Typesetter:	Michael Brehm
Cover Design:	Jason Mull

Published in the United States of America by
Engineering Science Reference (an imprint of IGI Global)
701 E. Chocolate Avenue
Hershey PA 17033
Tel: 717-533-8845
Fax: 717-533-8661
E-mail: cust@igi-global.com
Web site: http://www.igi-global.com

Library of Congress Cataloging-in-Publication Data

Handbook of research on emerging advancements and technologies in software engineering / Imran Ghani, Wan Mohd Nasir Wan Kadir, and Mohammad Nazir Ahmad,
editors.
 pages cm
 "Topics covered: Advanced Architectures; Model-Driven Development; Project Management; Re-Engineering; Requirement Engineering; Service-Oriented Software Engineering; Social Systems; Software Evolution; Testing, Analysis, and Refinement"--Title page verso.
 Includes bibliographical references and index.
 ISBN 978-1-4666-6026-7 (hardcover) -- ISBN 978-1-4666-6027-4 (ebook) -- ISBN 978-1-4666-6029-8 (print & perpetual access) 1. Software engineering--Research. I. Ghani, Imran, 1975- II. Kadir, Wan Mohd Nasir Wan, 1971- III. Ahmad, Mohammad Nazir, 1976-
 QA76.758.H355 2014
 005.1072--dc23
                                        2014006870

This book is published in the IGI Global book series Advances in Systems Analysis, Software Engineering, and High Performance Computing (ASASEHPC) (ISSN: 2327-3453; eISSN: 2327-3461)

British Cataloguing in Publication Data
A Cataloguing in Publication record for this book is available from the British Library.

For electronic access to this publication, please contact: eresources@igi-global.com.

Advances in Systems Analysis, Software Engineering, and High Performance Computing (ASASEHPC) Book Series

Vijayan Sugumaran
Oakland University, USA

ISSN: 2327-3453
EISSN: 2327-3461

MISSION

The theory and practice of computing applications and distributed systems has emerged as one of the key areas of research driving innovations in business, engineering, and science. The fields of software engineering, systems analysis, and high performance computing offer a wide range of applications and solutions in solving computational problems for any modern organization.

The **Advances in Systems Analysis, Software Engineering, and High Performance Computing (ASASEHPC) Book Series** brings together research in the areas of distributed computing, systems and software engineering, high performance computing, and service science. This collection of publications is useful for academics, researchers, and practitioners seeking the latest practices and knowledge in this field.

COVERAGE

- Computer Graphics
- Computer Networking
- Computer System Analysis
- Distributed Cloud Computing
- Enterprise Information Systems
- Metadata and Semantic Web
- Parallel Architectures
- Performance Modeling
- Software Engineering
- Virtual Data Systems

IGI Global is currently accepting manuscripts for publication within this series. To submit a proposal for a volume in this series, please contact our Acquisition Editors at Acquisitions@igi-global.com or visit: http://www.igi-global.com/publish/.

Titles in this Series

For a list of additional titles in this series, please visit: www.igi-global.com

Handbook of Research on High Performance and Cloud Computing in Scientific Research and Education
Marijana Despotović-Zrakić (University of Belgrade, Serbia) Veljko Milutinović (University of Belgrade, Serbia) and Aleksandar Belić (University of Belgrade, Serbia)
Information Science Reference • copyright 2014 • 476pp • H/C (ISBN: 9781466657847) • US $325.00 (our price)

Agile Estimation Techniques and Innovative Approaches to Software Process Improvement
Ricardo Colomo-Palacios (Østfold University College, Norway) Jose Antonio Calvo-Manzano Villalón (Universidad Politécnica De Madrid, Spain) Antonio de Amescua Seco (Universidad Carlos III de Madrid, Spain) and Tomás San Feliu Gilabert (Universidad Politécnica De Madrid, Spain)
Information Science Reference • copyright 2014 • 399pp • H/C (ISBN: 9781466651821) • US $215.00 (our price)

Enabling the New Era of Cloud Computing Data Security, Transfer, and Management
Yushi Shen (Microsoft, USA) Yale Li (Microsoft, USA) Ling Wu (EMC, USA) Shaofeng Liu (Microsoft, USA) and Qian Wen (Endronic Corp, USA)
Information Science Reference • copyright 2014 • 336pp • H/C (ISBN: 9781466648012) • US $195.00 (our price)

Theory and Application of Multi-Formalism Modeling
Marco Gribaudo (Politecnico di Milano, Italy) and Mauro Iacono (Seconda Università degli Studi di Napoli, Italy)
Information Science Reference • copyright 2014 • 314pp • H/C (ISBN: 9781466646599) • US $195.00 (our price)

Pervasive Cloud Computing Technologies Future Outlooks and Interdisciplinary Perspectives
Lucio Grandinetti (University of Calabria, Italy) Ornella Pisacane (Polytechnic University of Marche, Italy) and Mehdi Sheikhalishahi (University of Calabria, Italy)
Information Science Reference • copyright 2014 • 325pp • H/C (ISBN: 9781466646834) • US $190.00 (our price)

Communication Infrastructures for Cloud Computing
Hussein T. Mouftah (University of Ottawa, Canada) and Burak Kantarci (University of Ottawa, Canada)
Information Science Reference • copyright 2014 • 583pp • H/C (ISBN: 9781466645226) • US $195.00 (our price)

Organizational, Legal, and Technological Dimensions of Information System Administration
Irene Maria Portela (Polytechnic Institute of Cávado and Ave, Portugal) and Fernando Almeida (Polytechnic Institute of Gaya, Portugal)
Information Science Reference • copyright 2014 • 321pp • H/C (ISBN: 9781466645264) • US $195.00 (our price)

DISSEMINATOR of KNOWLEDGE

www.igi-global.com

701 E. Chocolate Ave., Hershey, PA 17033
Order online at www.igi-global.com or call 717-533-8845 x100
To place a standing order for titles released in this series, contact: cust@igi-global.com
Mon-Fri 8:00 am - 5:00 pm (est) or fax 24 hours a day 717-533-8661

Editorial Advisory Board

List of Contributors

Table of Contents

Section 3
Model-Driven Development

Detailed Table of Contents

Section 1
Software Requirements

If software requirements are not right, companies will not end up with the software they need. This chapter discusses the various levels and types of requirements that need to be defined, the benefits of having the right software requirements, the stakeholders of the software requirements and getting them involved in the process, requirements activities throughout the software development life cycle, and techniques for eliciting, analyzing, specifying, and validating software requirements.

Requirements Engineering (RE) is the most crucial process within software development projects. In order to prepare skilled requirements engineers, Requirements Engineering Education (REE) needs to be provided to students at the university level before they become software engineers and part of the workforce. However, RE is considered the most difficult subject within the software engineering curriculum for students to learn and for lecturers to teach due to its uncertain nature. This chapter examines the current and potential areas for research within REE. It first presents the current status of REE provided in universities and the REE problems reported in the literature that lead us to the potential research problems in REE. The REE teaching approaches proposed by researchers are then elaborated. The proposed approaches are mapped back to address the REE problems. The chapter closes with recommended directions for future REE research.

Chapter 3

Sabrina Ahmad, Universiti Teknikal Malaysia Melaka, Malaysia
Noor Azilah Muda, Universiti Teknikal Malaysia Melaka, Malaysia
Maslita Abd. Aziz, Universiti Teknikal Malaysia Melaka, Malaysia
Emaliana Kasmuri, Universiti Teknikal Malaysia Melaka, Malaysia

Requirements elicitation is accepted as one of the most crucial stages in software engineering, as it addresses the critical problem of designing the right software for the stakeholder. It is seldom technical difficulties that cause problems in the process of requirements elicitation but rather human factors, especially communication. This chapter presents the requirements elicitation experience with the industry and the lessons learnt throughout the process. It highlights the requirements elicitation best practices and alternative options during the process. It also discusses the issues concerning communication disparity between the stakeholders, which may affect the software development project as a whole. The outcome of the requirements elicitation process experience is reported and analysed for future improvement.

Section 2
Software Design and Construction

Chapter 4

Abdelhamid Abdelhadi Mansor, University of Khartoum, Sudan
Wan Mohd Nasir Wan Kadir, Universiti Teknologi Malaysia, Malaysia

Coordination is becoming an increasingly important paradigm for systems design and implementation. With multiple languages and models for coordination emerging, it is interesting to compare different models and understand their strengths and weaknesses find common semantic models and develop mappings between formalisms. This will help us to gain a deeper insight into coordination concepts and applications, and also to establish a set of features/criteria for defining and comparing coordination models. In this chapter, the authors present the current work on modelling coordination based on the coordination features. The findings show that software elements have three distinct types of coordination needs—technical, temporal, and process—and that these needs vary with the member's role; geographic distance has a negative effect on coordination, but is mitigated by shared knowledge of the team and presence awareness; and shared task knowledge is more important for coordination among collocated members. The authors articulate propositions for future research in this area based on the analysis.

Chapter 5

Wei-Chih Huang, Imperial College London, UK
William Knottenbelt, Imperial College London, UK

As the variety of execution environments and application contexts increases exponentially, modern software is often repeatedly refactored to meet ever-changing non-functional requirements. Although programmer effort can be reduced through the use of standardised libraries, software adjustment for scalability, reliability, and performance remains a time-consuming and manual job that requires high levels of expertise. Previous research has proposed three broad classes of techniques to overcome these difficulties in specific application domains: probabilistic techniques, out of core storage, and parallelism. However, due to limited cross-pollination of knowledge between domains, the same or very similar techniques have been reinvented all over again, and the application of techniques still requires manual effort. This chapter introduces the vision of self-adaptive scalable resource-efficient software that is able to reconfigure itself with little other than programmer-specified Service-Level Objectives and a description of the resource constraints of the current execution environment. The approach is designed to be low-overhead from the programmer's perspective – indeed a naïve implementation should suffice. To illustrate the vision, the authors have implemented in C++ a prototype library of self-adaptive containers, which dynamically adjust themselves to meet non-functional requirements at run time and which automatically deploy mitigating techniques when resource limits are reached. The authors describe the architecture of the library and the functionality of each component, as well as the process of self-adaptation. They explore the potential of the library in the context of a case study, which shows that the library can allow a naïve program to accept large-scale input and become resource-aware with very little programmer overhead.

Chapter 6

Liguo Yu, Indiana University – South Bend, USA
Srini Ramaswamy, BU Power Generation at ABB, India

Design patterns are standardized solutions to commonly encountered problems using the object-oriented programming paradigm. Applying design patterns can speed up software development processes through the reuse of tested, proven templates, or development paradigms. Accordingly, design patterns have been widely used in software industry to build modern software programs. However, as different design patterns are introduced to solve different design problems, they are not necessarily superior to alternative solutions, with respect to all aspects of software design. One major concern is that the inappropriate use of design patterns may unnecessarily increase program complexity, such as class structural quality. Theoretical analysis of the effect of design patterns on software complexity has been widely performed. However, little work is reported to empirically study how design patterns might affect class structural quality. This chapter studies six components from five open-source Java projects and empirically investigates if design patterns can affect class structural quality. The chapter finds that pattern-involved classes are more complex than pattern-free classes and recommends the cautious use of design patterns to avoid unnecessary increases in class complexity and decrease in class structural quality.

Chapter 7

Furkh Zeshan, COMSATS Institute of Information Technology (CIIT), Pakistan
Radziah Mohamad, Universiti Teknologi Malaysia
Mohammad Nazir Ahmad, Universiti Teknologi Malaysia

Embedded systems are supporting the trend of moving away from centralised, high-cost products towards low-cost and high-volume products; yet, the non-functional constraints and the device heterogeneity can lead to system complexity. In this regard, Service-Oriented Architecture (SOA) is the best methodology for developing a loosely coupled, dynamic, flexible, distributed, and cost-effective application. SOA relies heavily on services, and the Semantic Web, as the advanced form of the Web, handles the application complexity and heterogeneity with the help of ontology. With an ever-increasing number of similar Web services in UDDI, a functional description of Web services is not sufficient for the discovery process. It is also difficult to rank the similar services based on their functionality. Therefore, the Quality of Service (QoS) description of Web services plays an important role in ranking services within many similar functional services. Context-awareness has been widely studied in embedded and real-time systems and can also play an important role in service ranking as an additional set of criteria. In addition, it can enhance human-computer interaction with the help of ontologies in distributed and heterogeneous environments. In order to address the issues involved in ranking similar services based on the QoS and context-awareness, the authors propose a service discovery framework for distributed embedded real-time systems in this chapter. The proposed framework considers user priorities, QoS, and the context-awareness to enable the user to select the best service among many functional similar services.

Chapter 8

Arsène Sabas, Université de Montréal, Canada
Subash Shankar, City University of New York (CUNY), USA
Virginie Wiels, ONERA – The French Aerospace Lab, France
John-Jules Ch. Meyer, Universiteit Utrecht, The Netherlands
Michel Boyer, Université de Montréal, Canada

Aspect-Oriented (AO) Technology is a post-object-oriented technology used to overcome limitations of Object-Oriented (OO) Technology, such as the cross-cutting concern problem. Aspect-Oriented Programming (AOP) also offers modularity and traceability benefits. Yet, reasoning, specification, and verification of AO systems present unique challenges, especially as such systems evolve over time. Consequently, formal modular reasoning of such systems is highly attractive as it enables tractable evolution, otherwise necessitating that the entire system be re-examined each time a component is changed or is added. The aspect interactions problem is also an open issue in the AOP area. To deal with this problem, the authors choose to use Category Theory (CT) and Algebraic Specification (AS) techniques. In this chapter, the authors present an aspect-oriented specification and verification approach. The approach is expressive and allows for formal modular reasoning.

Section 3
Model-Driven Development

Chapter 9

Rita Suzana Pitangueira Maciel, Federal University of Bahia, Brazil
Ana Patrícia F. Magalhães Mascarenhas, Federal University of Bahia, Brazil
Ramon Araújo Gomes, Federal University of Bahia, Brazil
João Pedro D. B. de Queiroz, Federal University of Bahia, Brazil

The adoption of Model-Driven Development (MDD) is increasing and it is widely recognized as an important approach for building software systems. In addition to traditional development process models, an MDD process requires the selection of metamodels and mapping rules for the generation of the transformation chain which produces models and application code. However, existing support tools and transformation engines for MDD do not address different kinds of software process activities, such as application modeling and testing, to guide the developers. Furthermore, they do not enable process modeling nor the (semi) automated execution of activities during process enactment. MoDErNE (Model Driven Process-Centered Software Engineering Environment) uses process-centered software engineering environment concepts to improve MDD process specification and enactment by using a metamodeling foundation. This chapter presents model driven development concept issues and the MoDErNE approach and environment. MoDErNE aims to facilitate MDD process specification and enactment.

Chapter 10
A Model-Driven Solution for the Automatic Generation of Executable Code from Business
Process Models 213
Javier Fabra, University of Zaragoza, Spain
Valeria de Castro, Rey Juan Carlos University, Spain
Verónica Andrea Bollati, Rey Juan Carlos University, Spain
Pedro Álvarez, University of Zaragoza, Spain
Esperanza Marcos, Rey Juan Carlos University, Spain

The business goals of an enterprise process are traced to business process models with the aim of being carried out during the execution stage. The automatic translation from these models to fully executable code that can be simulated and round-trip engineered is still an open challenge in the Business Process Management field. Model-driven Engineering has proposed a set of methodologies to solve the existing gap between business analysts and software developers, but the expected results have not been reached yet. In order to rise to this challenge, in this chapter the authors propose a solution based on the integration of three previous proposals: SOD-M, DENEB, and MeTAGeM. On the one hand, SOD-M is a model-driven method for the development of service-oriented systems. Business analysts can use SOD-M to transform their business goals into composition service models, a type of model that represents business processes. On the other hand, DENEB is a platform for the development and execution of flexible business processes, represented by means of workflow models. The authors' approach focuses on the automatic transformation of SOD-M models to DENEB workflow models, resulting in a business process that is coded by a class of high-level Petri-nets, and it is directly executable in DENEB. The model transformation process has been automated using the MeTAGeM tool, which automatically generates the set of ATL rules required to transform SOD-M models to DENEB workflows. Finally, the integration of the three proposals has been illustrated by means of a real system related to the management of medical images.

Chapter 11
Modeling Platform-Independent and Platform-Specific Service Architectures with UML and the
ArchiMeDeS Framework 254
Marcos López-Sanz, Rey Juan Carlos University, Spain
Esperanza Marcos, Rey Juan Carlos University, Spain

Service-oriented architectures have, over the last decade, gradually become more important. The vast diversity of implementation and support platforms for this kind of architecture increases the complexity of the processes used to develop service-based systems. The task of specifying service architectures can be eased by following a model-driven approach and the appropriate model notations. In this chapter, the authors explore the architectural properties of the service-oriented paradigm and present part of a framework for the specification of service-oriented software architectures. The main idea is to use the separation into different abstraction levels fostered by the MDA proposal and tackle the software architecture specification progressively, stepping from conceptual to platform-specific levels. This chapter particularly concentrates upon describing UML profiles for the PIM and PSM levels of service-oriented architectural models, along with their corresponding metamodels. The use of the proposed profiles is illustrated in a case study in which the proposed profiles are implemented.

Section 4
Agile Methods

Chapter 12

Roy Morien, Naresuan University Language Centre, Thailand

Massive failures of software development projects have been recorded in the literature, and particularly in the popular press, over the years. Yet, rarely if ever have we seen any objective, detailed analysis of the causes of these failures. Indeed, we usually can only surmise how the projects were managed or what the development methodology or approach was. This chapter analyses some aspects of software development projects and development methodologies in terms of the success or failure potential of these methodologies. The conclusion arrived at is that the system development methodologies handed down since the late 1970s as the preferred development approach, generally known as Structured Methodologies, based on the Structured Design Life Cycle methodology (SDLC), bear the seeds of their own failure. It is asserted that they cannot succeed because of the inherent nature and assumptions embedded in those methodologies. After some analysis of these assumptions, considered to be highly flawed and unworkable, the now not so recently published Agile Development methodologies are discussed and proffered as a workable and inherently successful approach to software system development.

Chapter 13

Imran Ghani, Universiti Teknologi Malaysia, Malaysia
Adila Firdaus Bt Arbain, Universiti Teknologi Malaysia, Malaysia
Zulkarnain Azham, Universiti Teknologi Malaysia, Malaysia
Nor Izzaty Yasin, Universiti Teknologi Malaysia, Malaysia
Seung Ryul Jeong, Kookmin University, South Korea

Agile methodologies have gained recognition in recent years as being efficient development processes through their quick delivery of software, even under time constraints. Agile methodologies consist of a few process models that have their own criteria in helping different types of projects. However, agile methods such as Scrum, Feature-Driven Development (FDD), and eXtreme Programming (XP) have been criticized due to the lack of availability of security elements in their various phases, resulting in the development of unsecure software. Thus, the authors propose the idea of a set of security-focused elements to enhance the existing agile models. In this chapter, the findings of the related research and the highlights of improved agile models after the integration of security are presented.

Chapter 14

Eran Rubin, Holon Institute of Technology, Israel
Hillel Rubin, Israel Institute of Technology (Technion), Israel

Agile processes emphasize operational system code rather than its documentation. Ironically, however, some traditional documentation artefacts come to support system-stakeholders interaction, which is another core aspect of agile development processes. In this chapter, the authors examine the relationship between system development and knowledge documentation. They develop an approach that enables incorporating domain documentation to agile development while keeping the processes adaptive. The authors also provide a system design that actively uses domain knowledge documentation.

Section 5
Software Quality and Testing

Chapter 15

J. A. Pavlich-Mariscal, Pontificia Universidad Javeriana, Colombia
S. Berhe, University of Connecticut, USA
A. De la Rosa Algarín, University of Connecticut, USA
S. Demurjian, University of Connecticut, USA

This chapter explores a secure software engineering approach that spans functional (object-oriented), collaborative (sharing), and information (Web modeling and exchange) concerns in support of role-based (RBAC), discretionary (DAC), and mandatory (MAC) access control. By extending UML with security diagrams for RBAC, DAC, and MAC, we are able to design an application with all of its concerns, and not defer security to a later time in the design process that could have significant impact and require potentially wide-ranging changes to a nearly completed design. Through its early inclusion in the software design process, security concerns can be part of the application design process, providing separate abstractions for security via new UML diagrams. From these new UML diagrams, it is then possible to generate security policies and enforcement code for RBAC, DAC, and MAC, which separates security from the application. This modeling and generation allows security changes to have less of an impact on an application. The end result is a secure software engineering approach within a UML context that is capable of modeling an application's functional, collaborative, and information concerns. This is explored in this chapter.

Chapter 16

William G. Tuohey, Dublin City University, Ireland

Many years of effort have been expended by experienced practitioners and academic experts in developing software engineering standards. Organizations should see it as a positive advantage—rather than as a costly negative necessity—when they are required to develop software to a recognized standard. A genuine, constructive program of measures to ensure compliance with an objective standard will achieve development process improvements that would otherwise be difficult to motivate and bring to fruition. This chapter provides an overview and comparison of a number of software engineering standards specific to safety-critical and regulated sectors. It goes on to describe implications and benefits that flow from these standards. Informed by current software engineering research, suggestions are made for effective practical application of the standards, both at individual project and at organizational level.

Chapter 17

José C. Delgado, Instituto Superior Técnico, Universidade de Lisboa, Portugal

One of the most fundamental aspects of software engineering is the ability of software artifacts, namely programs, to interact and to produce applications that are more complex. This is known as interoperability, but, in most cases, it is dealt with at the syntactic level only. This chapter analyzes the interoperability problem from the point of view of abstract software artifacts and proposes a multidimensional framework that not only structures the description of these artifacts but also provides insight into the details of the interaction between them. The framework has four dimensions (lifecycle, concreteness level, concerns, and version). To support and characterize the interaction between artifacts, this chapter uses the concepts of compliance and conformance, which can establish partial interoperability between the artifacts. This reduces coupling while still allowing the required interoperability, which increases adaptability and changeability according to metrics that are proposed and contributes to a sustainable interoperability.

Chapter 18

In line with the advancement of hardware technology and increasing consumer demands for new functionalities and innovations, software applications grew tremendously in term of size over the last decade. This sudden increase in size has a profound impact as far as testing is concerned. Here, more and more unwanted interactions among software systems components, hardware, and operating system are to be expected, rendering increased possibility of faults. To address this issue, many useful interaction-based testing techniques (termed t-way strategies) have been developed in the literature. As an effort to promote awareness and encourage its usage, this chapter surveys the current state-of-the-art and reviews the state-of-practices in the field. In particular, unlike earlier work, this chapter also highlights the different possible adoptions of t-way strategies including uniform interaction, variable strength interaction, and input-output-based relation, that is, to help test engineers make informed decision on the actual use of t-way strategies.

The foundation of any software testing process is test scenario generation. This is because it forecasts the expected output of a system under development by extracting the artifacts expressed in any of the Unified Modeling Language (UML) diagrams, which are eventually used as the basis for software testing. Class diagrams are UML structural diagrams that describe a system by displaying its classes, attributes, and the relationships between them. Existing class diagram-based test scenario generation techniques only extract data variables and functions, which leads to incomprehensible or vague test scenarios. Consequently, this chapter aims to develop an improved technique that automatically generates test scenarios by reading, extracting, and interpreting the sets of objects that share attributes, operations, relationships, and semantics in a class diagram. From the performance evaluation, the proposed model-based technique is efficiently able to read, interpret, and generate scenarios from all the descriptive links of a class diagram.

Section 6
Software Quality Measurement

Chapter 20

Mohd Adham Isa, Universiti Teknologi Malaysia, Malaysia
Dayang Norhayati Abang Jawawi, Universiti Teknologi Malaysia, Malaysia

In recent years, reliability assessment is an essential process in system quality assessments. However, the best practice of software engineering for reliability analysis is not yet of its matured stage. The existing works are only capable to explicitly apply a small portion of reliability analysis in a standard software development process. In addition, an existing reliability assessment is based on an assumption provided by domain experts. This assumption is often exposed to errors. An effective reliability assessment should be based on reliability requirements that could be quantitatively estimated using metrics. The reliability requirements can be visualized using reliability model. However, existing reliability models are not expressive enough and do not provide consistence-modeling mechanism to allow developers to estimate reliability parameter values. Consequently, the reliability estimation using those parameters is usually oversimplified. With this situation, the inconsistency problem could happen between different estimation stages. In this chapter, a new Model-Based Reliability Estimation (MBRE) methodology is developed. The methodology consists of reliability model and reliability estimation model. The methodology provides a systematic way to estimate system reliability, emphasizing the reliability model for producing reliability parameters which will be used by the reliability estimation model. These models are built upon the timing properties, which is the primary input value for reliability assessment.

Chapter 21

Manjula Peiris, Indiana University Purdue University Indianapolis (IUPUI), USA
James H. Hill, Indiana University Purdue University Indianapolis (IUPUI), USA

This chapter discusses how to adapt system execution traces to support analysis of software system performance properties, such as end-to-end response time, throughput, and service time. This is important because system execution traces contain complete snapshots of a systems execution—making them useful artifacts for analyzing software system performance properties. Unfortunately, if system execution traces do not contain the required properties, then analysis of performance properties is hard. In this chapter, the authors discuss: (1) what properties are required to analysis performance properties in a system execution trace; (2) different approaches for injecting the required properties into a system execution trace to support performance analysis; and (3) show, by example, the solution for one approach that does not require modifying the original source code of the system that produced the system execution.

Chapter 22

Al-Fahim Mubarak-Ali, Universiti Teknologi Malaysia, Malaysia
Shahida Sulaiman, Universiti Teknologi Malaysia, Malaysia
Sharifah Mashita Syed-Mohamad, Universiti Sains Malaysia, Malaysia
Zhenchang Xing, Nanyang Technological University, Singapore

Code clone is a portion of codes that contains some similarities in the same software regardless of changes made to the specific code such as removal of white spaces and comments, changes in code syntactic, and addition or removal of code. Over the years, many approaches and tools for code clone detection have been proposed. Most of these approaches and tools have managed to detect and analyze code clones that occur in large software. In this chapter, the authors aim to provide a comparative study on current state-of-the-art in code clone detection approaches and models together with their corresponding tools. They then perform an empirical evaluation on the selected code clone detection tool and organize the large amount of information in a more systematic way. The authors begin with explaining background concepts of code clone terminology. A comparison is done to find out strengths and weaknesses of existing approaches, models, and tools. Based on the comparison done, they then select a tool to be evaluated in two dimensions, which are the amount of detected clones and run time performance of the tool. The result of the study shows that there are various terminologies used for code clone. In addition, the empirical evaluation implies that the selected tool (enhanced generic pipeline model) gives a better code clone output and runtime performance as compared to its generic counterpart.

Chapter 23

Golnoush Abaei, University Technology Malaysia, Malaysia
Ali Selamat, University Technology Malaysia, Malaysia

Quality assurance tasks such as testing, verification and validation, fault tolerance, and fault prediction play a major role in software engineering activities. Fault prediction approaches are used when a software company needs to deliver a finished product while it has limited time and budget for testing it. In such cases, identifying and testing parts of the system that are more defect prone is reasonable. In fact, prediction models are mainly used for improving software quality and exploiting available resources. Software fault prediction is studied in this chapter based on different criteria that matters in this research field. Usually, there are certain issues that need to be taken care of such as different machine-learning techniques, artificial intelligence classifiers, variety of software metrics, distinctive performance evaluation metrics, and some statistical analysis. In this chapter, the authors present a roadmap for those researchers who are interested in working in this area. They illustrate problems along with objectives related to each mentioned criterion, which could assist researchers to build the finest software fault prediction model.

Chapter 24

Rudolf Ramler, Software Competence Center Hagenberg, Austria
Johannes Himmelbauer, Software Competence Center Hagenberg, Austria
Thomas Natschläger, Software Competence Center Hagenberg, Austria

The information about which modules of a future version of a software system will be defect-prone is a valuable planning aid for quality managers and testers. Defect prediction promises to indicate these defect-prone modules. In this chapter, building a defect prediction model from data is characterized as an instance of a data-mining task, and key questions and consequences arising when establishing defect prediction in a large software development project are discussed. Special emphasis is put on discussions on how to choose a learning algorithm, select features from different data sources, deal with noise and data quality issues, as well as model evaluation for evolving systems. These discussions are accompanied by insights and experiences gained by projects on data mining and defect prediction in the context of large software systems conducted by the authors over the last couple of years. One of these projects has been selected to serve as an illustrative use case throughout the chapter.

Section 7
Software Management and Evolution

Chapter 25

RuQian Lu, Chinese Academy of Sciences, China & Peking University, China
Zhi Jin, Peking University, China & Chinese Academy of Sciences, China

The first part of this chapter reviews the origin of knowware-based software engineering. It originates from the authors' experiences in finding new techniques for knowledge-based software engineering while performing PROMIS, a continuing project series from the 1990s. The key point of PROMIS is to generate applications automatically by separating the development of domain knowledge from that of software architecture, with an important innovation of acquiring and summarizing domain knowledge automatically based on the pseudo-natural language understanding techniques. However, during PROMIS development, the authors did not find an appropriate form for the separated domain knowledge. The second part of the chapter briefly describes how the authors came to the concept of knowware. They stated that the essence of knowware is its capacity as a commercialized form of domain knowledge. It is also the third major component of IT after hardware and software. The third part of the chapter introduces the basic concepts of knowware and knowware engineering. Three life cycle models of knowware engineering and the design of corresponding knowware implementations are given. The fourth part of the chapter introduces object-oriented mixware engineering. In the fifth part of the chapter, two recent applications of knowware technique regarding smart room and Web search are reported. As a further development of PROMIS, the sixth part of the chapter discusses knowware-based redesign of its framework. In the seventh part of the chapter, the authors discuss automatic application generation and domain knowledge modeling on the J2EE platform, which combines techniques of PROMIS, knowware, and J2EE, and the development and deployment framework (i.e. PROMIS/KW**).

Chapter 26

Renato Lima Novais, Federal Institute of Bahia, Brazil
Manoel Gomes de Mendonça Neto, Fraunhofer Project Center for Software and Systems
Engineering at UFBA, Brazil

Software Visualization is the field of Software Engineering that aims to help people to understand software through the use of visual resources. It can be effectively used to analyze and understand the large amount of data produced during software evolution. Several Software Evolution Visualization (SEV) approaches have been proposed. The goals of the proposed approaches are varied, and they try to help programmers and managers to deal with software evolution in their daily software activities. Despite their goals, their applicability in real development scenarios is questionable. In this chapter, the authors discuss the current state of the art and challenges in software evolution visualization, presenting issues and problems related to the area, and they propose some solutions and recommendations to circumvent them. Finally, the authors discuss some research directions for the SEV domain.

Foreword

A major goal of today's software industry is to develop high-quality software on time and within budget. High quality always means that the delivered software satisfies all of its requirements. Hence, software development poses significant technical challenges for practitioners, managers, and researchers.

Software engineering as a research discipline aims to offer industry-strength methods, tools, processes, and languages to support organizations to develop high-quality software. To achieve this goal, practitioners and researchers have to collaborate and exchange experience and new and innovative ideas.

This book contributes to this goal as it reflects the pragmatic notion of software development as an engineering discipline. The authors—from academia and industry—present selected topics of a variety of important software engineering topics such as requirements engineering, software design, software quality and testing, secure software development, model-driven development, agile development methods, and software quality measurement. Interestingly, software management and software evolution is also covered. Both topics are extremely important and challenging in industry, but they are often neglected in textbooks and software engineering curricula.

All in all, the presented topics make the very different facets of software engineering approachable to researchers, practitioners, and students. Readers of this book will gain a solid appreciation of the rich scope and the diversity of software engineering.

From my point of view, the chapters on software design, model-driven development, and software quality are especially remarkable, as they provide impressive examples of problems that illustrate the delicacies and challenges that software engineers must confront.

The book presents in a thorough and readable manner current and relevant software engineering topics. It contains results that have not been published yet. For me, it was a source of new and interesting ideas as it goes far beyond my expectations. It undoubtedly contributes to establishing software engineering as a mature engineering discipline.

Horst Lichter
RWTH Aachen University, Germany

Horst Lichter is a Professor of Computer Science and Head of the research group Software Construction at RWTH Aachen University. He received a diploma degree in Computer Science and Economics from Technical University Kaiserslautern, Germany. Afterwards, he was a Research Assistant at ETH Zurich and the University of Stuttgart, where he obtained his Ph.D. Following this, he worked as Project Manager at Union Bank of Switzerland Zurich and later as Scientist at ABB Corporate Research, Heidelberg, Germany. He has organized many international workshops and conferences and is member of IEEE, GI, and SI.

Preface

In the last six decades, many advanced software engineering approaches, techniques, and tools have been introduced to solve various problems related to the development and maintenance of complex large-scale software systems. Some of these advancements have been applied to practice with various degrees of success, including the acceptance of some methods and tools as *de facto* technologies by software industries. For example, with the introduction of the advanced CASE tools, developers are able to reduce the time to market and minimise the errors made during the software development stage.

Software systems play a major role in contemporary society and penetrate almost all aspects of modern life, ranging from social network systems to safety-critical systems. Although many advancements have been made in software engineering, there are emerging challenges in software engineering due to the increasing complexity of user requirements and operating environments. The produced software is sometimes unable to fulfill user requirements, delivered late or delivered at an unacceptable quality, and unable to cope with requirement changes after certain periods of time. This book highlights some significant research on emerging advancements and technologies in software engineering.

The aim of this book is to present some of the advances in software engineering research and practice. In Section 1, the authors discuss several topics related to software requirements. Understanding the software requirements is an important task in identifying the correct requirements for a large and complex software system.

Section 1 discusses the issues and new approaches in requirements engineering, which is one of the important topics in software engineering. The authors share their experiences obtained from real-life projects:

- "What, Why, Who, When and How of Software Requirements": Linda Westfall provides an exhaustive coverage of the major elements of requirements engineering such as the definition of software requirements, the benefits of having the right requirements, and the requirements engineering process. This chapter provides a quick guide to quality software requirements.
- "Critical Issues in Requirements Engineering Education" – Rafia Naz Memon, Rodina Ahmad, and Siti Salwah Salim investigate the current state of requirements engineering education and identify the issues in teaching software engineering. Based on the identified issues, the authors recommend the suitable teaching approaches and propose potential topics for further research in requirements engineering education.
- "When the Wisdom of Communication is Vital during the Requirements Elicitation Process: Lessons Learnt through Industry Experience" – Sabrina Ahmad, Noor Azilah Muda, Maslita Abd. Aziz, and Emaliana Kasmuri present the lessons learnt from the application of the requirement elicitation process for three different government agencies. The authors highlight the best practices in requirements elicitation and suggest alternative options during the process.

Section 2 presents the advancements in software design and construction. The chapters cover a number of issues related to model coordination, quality-of-service in relation to code bases, limitations of design patterns, service discovery in real-time systems, and the verification and specification of aspect-oriented systems:

- "State-of-the-Art Concepts and Future Directions in Modelling Coordination" – Abdelhamid Abdelhadi Mansor and Wan M. N. Wan-Kadir present the current work on modelling coordination based on the coordination features. The chapter shows that recent research has yielded significant contributions to coordination models and languages, and to the capture of QoS requirements as first class aspects in open distributed software. The authors emphasise that the impact of coordination models on the engineering of complex systems will have profound implications for methodologies and software processes, as well as for related research.

- "Low-Overhead Development of Scalable Resource-Efficient Software Systems" – Wei-Chih Huang and William Knottenbelt criticise the use of traditional software engineering pipelines that leads to either a small code base which cannot guarantee quality-of-service or multiple manually-optimised code bases, which are hard to maintain. The vision of this chapter is to propose a means to achieve both: a small, easily maintained code base, together with automated mechanisms to support improved quality-of-service delivery at run-time according to the specific execution environment and application context.

- "An Empirical Study of the Effect of Design Patterns on Class Structural Quality" – Liguo Yu and Srini Ramaswamy discuss how the inappropriate use of design patterns may unnecessarily increase program complexity, such as class structural quality. This chapter studies six components from five open-source Java projects and empirically investigates if the design patterns can affect the class structural quality. The authors find that pattern-involved classes are more complex than pattern-free classes, and recommend the cautious use of design patterns to avoid unnecessary increases in class complexity and decreases in class structural quality.

- "Service Discovery Framework for Distributed Embedded Real-Time Systems" – Furkh Zeshan, Radziah Mohamad, and Mohammad Nazir Ahmad present a framework for distributed embedded real-time systems for the automatic discovery of services based on the context and quality-of-service information. The proposed framework enables the user to efficiently and automatically search the services running on the embedded devices. The results of the experiment indicate the significance of the proposed work.

- "An Algebraic Approach for the Specification and Verification of Aspect-Oriented Systems" – Arsène Sabas, Subash Shankar, Virginie Wiels, John-Jules Ch. Meyer, and Michel Boyer present an algebraic specification approach which proposes a solution to the lack of modular formal reasoning, specification, and verification of aspect-oriented systems. This approach is based on category theory and algebraic specification techniques due to their formality, their modularity benefits, and their high levels of abstraction. The authors also present a prevention mechanism for three aspect fault types that can cause undesirable behaviours in an aspect-oriented system.

The chapters in Section 3 present recent advancements in model-driven development, which is one of the widely accepted approaches in software engineering. The authors aim to improve the specification and model transformation process:

- "Supporting Model-Driven Development: Key Concepts and Support Approaches" – Rita Suzana Pitangueira Maciel, Ana Patrícia F. Magalhães Mascarenhas, Ramon Araújo Gomes, and João Pedro D. B. de Queiroz provide an overview of the model-driven development process and propose an approach to support the model-driven software process, which they call the Model-Driven Process-Centered Software Engineering Environment (MoDErNE). MoDErNE consists of a metamodel and tool that facilitate the integrated specification and enactment of model-driven software processes.
- "A Model-Driven Solution for the Automatic Generation of Executable Code from Business Process Models" – Javier Fabra, Valeria de Castro, Verónica Andrea Bollati, Pedro Álvarez, and Esperanza Marcos integrate the service-oriented development method and a framework for the development and execution of business processes for the automatic code generation of applications based on service-oriented architecture applications. They also develop an automated tool to support the model transformation.
- "Modelling Platform-Independent and Platform-Specific Service Architectures with UML and the ArchiMeDeS Framework" – Marcos López Sanz and Esperanza Marcos propose UML profiles that consist of a set of metamodels that can be used in the modelling of service-oriented software. Their framework is used to systematically guide the model transformation processes using the proposed UML profiles. The feasibility of the proposed approach is validated using the GESiMED case study.

Section 4 presents the advancements in agile methods including security concerns, knowledge documentation, and project size issues:

- "Back to Basics: In Support of Agile Development" – Roy Morien provides insights into the factors causing failure or leading to success in a software project. The author discusses the issues related to the common misunderstanding of "project size." The author also criticises the traditional waterfall approach and emphasises the need to adopt the agile approach.
- "Integrating Security into Agile Models: Scrum, Feature-Driven Development, and eXtreme Programming" – Imran Ghani, Adila Firdaus Bt Arbain, Zulkarnain Azham, Nor Izzaty Yasin, and Seung Ryul Jeung report the performance of intensive studies into the suitability of original agile methods for developing secure software. Their studies conclude that the original agile methods such as Scrum, feature-driven development, and eXtreme Programming do not properly guide the agile teams to develop secure software.
- "Agile Development Processes and Knowledge Documentation" – Eran Rubin and Hillel Rubin discuss and highlight the importance of documentation for agile development. The authors propose an active documentation approach that attempts to overcome the key limitation of agile methods, which is the "lack of documentation." With the help of their active approach, agile methods can incorporate agile documentation.

Section 5 presents the recent advancements in software quality and testing, including test scenario generation, and highlights the importance of regulations and compliance:

- "An Integrated Secure Software Engineering Approach for Functional, Collaborative, and Information Concerns" – J.A. Pavlich-Mariscal, Steve Berhe, A. De la Rosa Algarín, and S. Demurjian explore a secure software engineering approach that spans functional (object-oriented), collaborative (sharing), and information (Web modelling and exchange) concerns in support of role-based, discretionary, and mandatory access control. Their findings illustrate that the proposed modelling and generation allows security changes to have less of an impact on an application.

- "Lessons from Practices and Standards in Safety-Critical and Regulated Sectors" – William G. Tuohey provides a comprehensive overview and comparison of a number of software engineering standards specific to safety-critical and regulated sectors. The author emphasises that Software Level C of RTCA/DO-178C (2011) represents a good baseline standard for software developments. A number of high priority improvement measures are identified in the chapter, the early implementation of which is likely to maximise the primary benefit of return on the investment in software process improvement.

- "The Role of Compliance and Conformance in Software Engineering" – José C. Delgado discusses the importance of compliance and conformance as the fundamental concepts for the interoperability problem of software artifacts. The author proposes a multidimensional framework and argues that the use of compliance and conformance can help establish partial interoperability among software artifacts.

- "T-Way Testing Strategies: Issues, Challenges, and Practices" – Kamal Z. Zamli, Abdul Rahman Al-Sewari, Mohammed I. Younis, and Rozmie Razif Othman emphasise the importance of software testing due to the increased possibility of faults in software. The authors review the fundamental elements of T-Way testing strategies and highlight the issues relevant to the current state-of-the-art and the current practices in the field.

- "An Improved Model-Based Technique for Generating Test Scenarios from UML Class Diagrams" – Oluwatolani Oluwagbemi and Hishammuddin Asmuni discuss the importance of test scenario generation. The authors propose a novel approach that automatically generates test scenarios by extracting the attributes, operations, and semantics of a class diagram. The authors present the performance evaluation of the proposed approach, leading to significant improvement in the generation of test scenarios.

Section 6 presents advancements in software quality measurement. Due to the increasing complexity of software, it is important for software quality to be measured early in the lifecycle. The measurement results are crucial in supporting decision-making at the various levels of development.

- "A Methodology for Model-Based Reliability Estimation" – Muhammad Adham Isa and Dayang Norhayati Abang Jawawi argue that existing reliability models are not expressive enough and do not provide adequate consistence-modelling mechanisms to allow developers to estimate the reliability parameter values. Consequently, the reliability estimation using those parameters is usually oversimplified. The authors propose a model-based reliability estimation methodology that supports the reliability estimation during the design stage. The methodology consists of a detailed description of the estimation process and the employed reliability model.

- "Non-Intrusive Adaptation of System Execution Traces for Performance Analysis of Software Systems" – Manjula Peiris and James H. Hill present the non-intrusive performance analysis approach based on information from the system execution traces. They propose a framework called the System Execution Trace Adaptation Framework that obtains the required properties by adapting system execution traces and the corresponding dataflow model. The proposed approach is successfully applied in two selected case studies (i.e., Apache ANT and DAnCE).

- "Code Clone Detection and Analysis in Open Source Applications" – Al-Fahim Mubarak-Ali, Shahida Sulaiman, Sharifah Mashita Syed-Mohamad, and Zhencang Xing review the existing code clone detection approaches and tools. They perform an empirical evaluation of two code clone detection tools, namely the generic pipeline model and the enhanced generic pipeline model, on three selected open source applications.

- "Important Issues in Software Fault Prediction: A Road Map" – Golnoush Abaei and Ali Selamat present an overview of the issues in software fault prediction and highlight the research challenges in this area. The authors present a general scheme of the steps that any researcher faces when he/she wants to conduct software fault prediction work. Different parameters such as software metrics, machine-learning techniques, and performance evaluation metrics are illustrated and compared in order to highlight the factors that have an effect on building the finest prediction models.

- "Building Defect Prediction Models in Practice" – Rudolf Ramler, Johannes Himmelbauer, and Thomas Natschläger present a defect prediction model and discuss the application of the prediction model in a real-world project. The authors provide rich discussion and insights gained by their recent experiences in data mining and defect prediction projects in the context of large software systems. One of these projects serves as an illustrative use-case throughout the chapter.

Section 7 presents the advancements in software management and evolution, including knowledge-based software engineering and software evolution visualization.

- "Knowware-Based Software Engineering: An Overview of its Origin, Essence, Core Techniques, and Future Development" – RuQian Lu and Zhi Jin propose the concept of knowledge-based software engineering called "Knowware-based software engineering." The concept originates in their experiences in finding new techniques for knowledge-based software engineering while performing PROMIS. The key point of PROMIS is to automatically generate applications by separating the development of domain knowledge. This is achieved by automatically acquiring and summarising domain knowledge based on the pseudo-natural language.

- "Software Evolution Visualisation: Status, Challenges, and Research Directions" – Renato Lima Novais and Manoel Gomes de Mendonça Neto perform an exhaustive study and discuss the current state-of-the-art and challenges in software evolution visualisation. The authors provide useful guidelines, solutions, and recommendations to circumvent the problems in this area.

This book is designed to be used by software engineers, developers, quality-assurance personnel, testers, researchers, teachers, coaches, and students of software engineering. This is a handbook on software engineering for practitioners or researchers at all levels of expertise from the novice to the expert.

In the preparation of this book, we received many high quality contributions in response to our call for chapters. The number of contributions indicates that software engineering is a very promising area in research and is a sign of continuous improvement in practice. We are very grateful for the contributions and would like to thank all the authors for their efforts.

Imran Ghani
Universiti Teknologi Malaysia, Malaysia

Wan Mohd Nasir Wan Kadir
Universiti Teknologi Malaysia, Malaysia

Mohd Nazir Ahmad
Universiti Teknologi Malaysia, Malaysia

Section 1
Software Requirements

Chapter 1
What, Why, Who, When, and How of Software Requirements

Linda Westfall
Westfall Team, Inc., USA

ABSTRACT

If software requirements are not right, companies will not end up with the software they need. This chapter discusses the various levels and types of requirements that need to be defined, the benefits of having the right software requirements, the stakeholders of the software requirements and getting them involved in the process, requirements activities throughout the software development life cycle, and techniques for eliciting, analyzing, specifying, and validating software requirements.

WHAT

Requirements are the agreement between the supplier of the software and its customers, users, and other stakeholders about capabilities and attributes of the software product. The requirements define the "what" of a software product:

- What the software must do to add value or utility for its stakeholders. These functional requirements define the capabilities of the software product.
- What the software must be to add value for its stakeholders. These quality attributes and nonfunctional requirements define the characteristics, properties, or qualities that the software product must possess. They also define how well the product performs its functions.
- What limitations there are on the choices that developers have when implementing the software. The external interface definitions and other design constraints define these limitations.

Types of Requirements: Most software practitioners just talk about "the requirements". However, by recognizing that there are different levels and types of requirements, as illustrated in Figure 1, we can gain a better understanding of what information we need to elicit, analyze, specify, and validate when we define our software requirements.

Business Requirements define the business problems to be solved or the business opportuni-

DOI: 10.4018/978-1-4666-6026-7.ch001

Figure 1. Levels and types of requirements

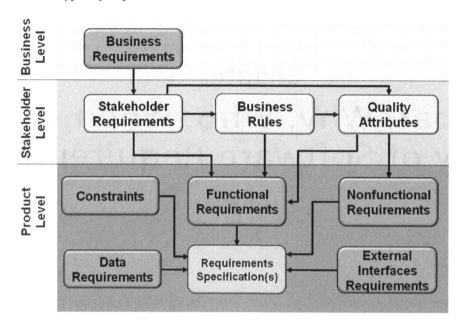

ties to be addressed by the software product. In general, the business requirements define why the software product is being developed. Business requirements are typically stated in terms of the objectives of the customer or organization requesting the development of the software. For example, a business requirement for an automated gas station system might state "Drivers can pay for their gas purchases at the pump without interaction with the Gas Station Attendant".

Stakeholder Requirements look at the functionality of the software product from the stakeholder's perspective. They define what the software has to do in order for the users and other stakeholders to accomplish their objectives (or in the case of "unfriendly" stakeholders, such as hackers, to keep them from accomplishing their objectives). Multiple stakeholder-level requirements may be needed in order to fulfill a single business requirement.

For example, the business requirement that allows the Driver to pay for gas at the pump might translate into multiple stakeholder requirements from different stakeholder perspectives:

- **Driver's Perspective:**
  - The Driver can swipe a credit or debit card.
  - The Driver can enter a security PIN number.
  - The Driver can request/receive a receipt at the pump.
- **Gas Station Owner's Perspective:**
  - The Owner can have the credit or debit card validated by the bank before gas is dispensed.
  - The Owner can have the final purchase price credited to their merchant account.
  - The Owner can change the price of gas.
- **Gas Station Attendant's Perspective:**
  - The Attendant can poll each pump from inside the station to determine the amount and price of gas pumped on the current transaction.
  - The Attendant is alerted of any errors during the pumping process.

The product's *functional requirements* define what the software must do to meet the stakeholder level requirements. If a programmer is told to "validate the credit card with the bank", that programmer would typically need additional information before the programmer could program that function. Multiple functional level requirements may be needed to fulfill a single stakeholder requirement. For example, the requirements that the Driver can swipe a credit card might translate into multiple functional requirements including requirements for the software to:

- Prompt the Driver to put a credit/debit card into the reader
- Detect that the card has been inserted
- Prompt the Driver to remove credit/debit card
- Determine if the card was incorrectly read and prompt the Driver to swipe the card again
- Parse the information from the magnetic strip on the card, and so on

As opposed to the business requirements, *business rules* are the specific policies, standards, practices, regulations, and guidelines that define how the stakeholders are allowed to conduct business and/or interact with the software (and are therefore considered stakeholder-level requirements). The software product must adhere to these rules in order to function appropriately within the business domain. Examples of business rules for the automated gas station system might include: which credit card types are accepted, a maximum on the dollar amount of gas pumped per transaction, tax amount to be charged, or government regulations.

Stakeholder-level *quality attributes* are characteristics or properties that define the software product's quality. Sometimes called the "ilities," quality attributes include characteristics desired by the customers and users like:

- **Usability:** The ease with which a user can operate or learn to operate software.
- **Reliability:** The extent to which the software can perform its functions without failure for a specified period of time under specified conditions.
- **Availability:** The extent to which the software or a service is available for use
- **Performance:** The levels of performance, such as capacity, throughput, and response times, that are required from the software.
- **Efficiency:** The extent to which the software can perform its functions while utilizing minimal amounts of computing resources, such as memory, or disk space).
- **Security:** The probability that an attack of a specific type will be detected, repelled or handled by the software.
- **Safety:** The ability to use the software without adverse impact to individual, property, the environment, or society.
- **Interoperability:** The degree to which the software functions properly and shares resources with other software applications or hardware operating in the same environment.
- **Accuracy:** The extent to which the software provides precision in calculations and outputs.
- **Accessibility:** The degree to which the software is available to as many people as possible (the ability to access). Accessibility is often focused on people with special needs or disabilities.
- **Flexibility:** The ease with which the software can be modified or customized by the user.
- **Robustness (Fault-Tolerance):** The extent to which the software can handle invalid inputs or other faults from interfacing entities like hardware, other software applications, the operating system, or data files.

Quality attributes also include characteristics desired by the suppliers and distributors of the software such as:

- **Installability:** The ease with which the software product can be installed on the target platform.
- **Maintainability**: The ease with which the software or one of its components can be modified.
- **Reusability:** The extent to which one or more components of a software product can be reused when developing other software products.
- **Portability:** The effort required to migrate the software to a different platform or environment.
- **Supportability:** The ease with which technical support or a help desk can configure, monitor, support and correct the software once it is in operations.

A *quality attribute* may translate into product-level functional requirements for the software that specify what functionality must exist to meet the quality attribute. For example, an "easy to use" stakeholder requirement might translate into an online help functional requirement. A quality attribute may also translate into product-level nonfunctional requirements that specify the characteristics the software must possess in order to meet that attribute. For example, an "easy to use" requirement might translate into nonfunctional requirements for response times to user commands, or report requests.

External interface requirements define the requirements for the information flow across shared interfaces to hardware, users, and other software applications outside the boundaries of the software product being developed. For example, there may be external interface requirements on what to communicate with the Credit Card Company in order to validate the credit card.

The *constraints* define any other restrictions imposed on the choices that the supplier can make when designing and developing the software. For example, there may be a requirement that the completed software use no more than fifty percent of available system memory or disk space in order to allow room for future enhancements without requiring hardware upgrades. There may also be requirements to use specific encryption methodologies when storing credit card information.

The *data requirements* define the specific data items or data structures that must be included as part of the software product. For example, the pay at the gas pump system might have requirements for saving transaction history information including the date/time of the transaction, the pump number, gallons pumped, price, bank confirmation codes, and so on.

The software may be part of a much larger system that includes other components. In this case, the business and stakeholder-level requirements feed into the product requirements at the system level. The system architecture then allocates requirements from the set of system requirements downward into the software, hardware, and manual operations components.

Requirements Specifications: All of these different levels and types of requirements must be captured in some type of specification. However, the form and format of that specification may vary greatly depending on the needs of supplier organization and the product stakeholders. To illustrate this, mechanisms for specifying the requirements might include:

- All of the different levels and types of requirements combined into a single requirements specification. For example, section 1 of the specification might be business level requirements, section 2 stakeholder level requirements with subsections for stakeholder requirements, business rules and quality attributes, and sections 3 through *n* include product level requirements for each of the major subsystems of the product.

- Separate specification documents for different types and levels of requirements. For example, the business level requirements might be specified in a project charter or business plan, the stakeholder requirements in a Concept of Operations or Marketing Requirements document and the product level requirements may be split between multiple documents including System Requirements Specification, Software Requirements Specification, one or more External Interface Specifications and even a Data Dictionary as appropriate.

- In the Scrum/Agile community, business requirements may be specified in a product vision, stakeholder requirements may be on User Story cards or further refined into use cases, and product level requirements may be captured directly into test cases without intermediate "requirements specification" in the traditional sense.

- In fact, if the organization is using a requirements management tool, there may be little to no hardcopy specification of the requirements. Each requirement may be captured as a data element in the tool. In more sophisticated tools, hyperlinks between data elements can be used to specifying the traceability between business, stakeholder, and product level requirements.

WHY

The following quote from Fredrick Brooks illustrates why requirements are so important:

The hardest part of building a software system is deciding precisely what to build. No other part of the conceptual work is as difficult as establishing the detailed technical requirements, including all of the interfaces to people, to machines, and to other software systems. No other part of the work so cripples the resulting system if done wrong. No other part is more difficult to rectify later. (Brooks 1995)

Eliciting, analyzing, and writing good requirements are the most difficult parts of software engineering. Therefore, to quote Karl Wiegers (Wiegers 2004), "If you don't get the requirements right, it doesn't matter how well you do anything else." Without good requirements, we can end up doing a perfect job of building the wrong product.

There are many requirements issues that can have a negative impact on software development projects and products if we don't do a good job of defining our software requirements.

Incomplete Requirements: If the requirements are incomplete, we end up building a software product that does not meet all of the stakeholder's needs. There is a direct relationship between customer satisfaction and the quality and completeness of the requirements. When requirements are elicited, the customer will explicitly state some of their requirements. For example, a prospective customer will state their preferences for the make, model, options, and gas mileage when shopping for a car. The customer will be dissatisfied (and buy a car elsewhere) if their stated requirements are not met. When most of their stated requirements can be met, the customer will consider doing business with the suppliers.

There are basic requirements in most products that customers expect the product to have. These requirements are assumed by the customer and are typically not explicitly stated. For example, customers expect a car to have a windshield, windshield wipers, and a steering wheel. Typically a customer wouldn't ask for those particular features while shopping for a car. However, the absence of these basic (unstated or assumed) requirements in the final product will dramatically increase a customer's dissatisfaction.

Lastly, there are innovative requirements, which are requirements that customers are unaware that they want but that they love when they see them. For example, remember when cup holders in cars were first introduced? Suppliers need to be forward thinking so that their software continues to excite the customer and their products maintain technical leadership. It should be remembered, however, that today's innovations are tomorrow's expectations. If innovative requirements are not included release after release, the resulting product will fall behind in technical leadership and eventually become antiquated.

In addition, if practitioners miss a stakeholder group or if they do not get the stakeholders involved in the requirements process, they can end up with gaps between the specified requirements and the stakeholder's actual needs for intended use.

Requirements Churn: Requirements churn refers to changes in the requirements after they are initially agreed to and baselined. Some of this change is a part of refining the developers' understanding as they develop the software. Changes also occur because of changes in the environment or in the stakeholder's needs over time that occur as a natural part of a project of any significant duration.

Unnecessary requirements churn occurs because of missing requirements that should have been included in the original specification or because of poorly written or ambiguous requirements. These are the types of requirements churn that good requirement engineering practices will help avoid.

Requirements Errors: Requirements errors account for 70 percent to 85 percent of the rework costs on a software project (Wiegers 2003). If a requirements defect is found during the requirements phase and it costs one unit to fix (for example, three engineering hours, or $500) the cost of fixing that same defect will typically increase as it is found later and later in the life cycle. In fact, studies show that it can cost more than 100 times more to fix a requirements defect if it is not found until after the software is released to the field.

Gold Plating: Another waste of resources occurs when gold plating is added to the software. Gold plating can take place when a developer adds functionality to the software that was not in the requirements specification but that the programmer believes "the stakeholders will just love" without putting that functionality through the requirements engineering process. Stakeholders may or may not want the new functionality. If they don't, the cost of developing it is a waste. Cycling these "good ideas" through the requirements engineering process helps ensure that they truly are something that's needed in the product so that gold plating does not occur.

A second kind of gold plating comes from the customers and users. For example, if practitioners ask the users "what they want" rather than "what they need to be able to do with the system," they may end up with a wish list of nice-to-haves or things that they might want sometime in the future but do not really need right now. This second type of gold plating is a good reason to prioritize the requirements and focus resources on the most important requirements first.

Gold plating can result in wasting resources on implementing functionality that is not of real value or that's never actually used. It also creates the risk that defects in that part of the functionality will cause reliability problems for the rest of the software. The requirements define the scope of the software that is being developed. Without a clear picture of that scope, estimates of the project schedule, cost, and quality will be less accurate.

WHO

One of the generic practices of the Software Engineering Institute's Capability Maturity Model Integration (CMMI) for Development (SEI 2006) is to "identify and involve relevant stakeholders." Nowhere is that more true than in the software requirements engineering processes. Stakeholders are individuals who affect or are affected by the

Figure 2. Software product stakeholders

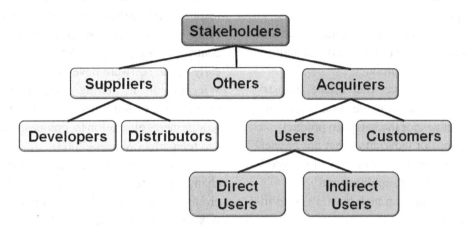

software product and therefore have some level of influence over the requirements for that software product. The software requirements engineering process provides the best opportunity to consider all of the various stakeholder's interest in context with one another. As illustrated in Figure 2, there are three main categories of software product stakeholders: the acquirers of the software product, the suppliers of the software product, and other stakeholders.

The *acquirer stakeholder* category can be divided into two major groups. First there are the *customers* who request, purchase, and/or pay for the software product in order to meet their business objectives. The second group is the *users*, also called end-users, who actually use the product directly or use the product indirectly by receiving reports, outputs, or other information generated by the product. The users can also be subdivided into *direct users* who actually interact with the software or system and indirect users who use the information that comes out of the software or system but never actually interact with it. For example, for the automated gas station system, the Drivers, Gas Station Owner, and Gas Station Attendant would be direct users while the Accountant or Corporate Headquarters Executive who use the reports from the system would be indirect users.

The suppliers of the software product include individuals and teams that:

- Are part of the organization that develops the software product,
- Are part of the organizations that distribute the software product, and
- Are involved in other product delivery methods (for example, outsourcing).

The development stakeholders may include requirements analyst, designers, coders, testers, technical publications, program/project management, marketing and others. If the software is part of a larger system, hardware designers and developers may also be stakeholders in the software requirements. The distributor stakeholders may include in-house release management and/or technical support team or external organizations like value added resellers or acquirers who incorporate the purchased software into their systems.

There may also be other stakeholders interested in the requirements. Examples of other requirements stakeholders include:

- Business owner, executives or senior managers,
- Product or program manager,
- Sales and marketing,

- Business shareholders on both the acquirer and supplier side,
- Lawmakers or regulatory agencies that create laws, regulations and standards that impact the software product,
- Other organizations that create industry standards or guidelines or define industry best practices for the software product,
- Any groups or individuals that are impacted by the actions or decisions of the product's acquirers or suppliers, and
- Society at large can also have a vested interest in the software.

Step 1: Identify the Stakeholders

Identifying and considering the needs of all of the different stakeholders can help prevent software product requirements from being overlooked. For example, if a company is creating a payroll system and it does not consider charities as one of its stakeholders, it might not include the requirements for the software to:

- Allow the payees to specify from one to three charitable deductions
- Withhold charitable deductions from payee's checks each pay period
- Report current and year-to-date charitable deductions on payee's pay slip
- Print a check to each charity for the accumulated amount deducted from payees

The requirements analyst will never know as much about a stakeholder's work as that stakeholder. By identifying and involving key stakeholders, the analyst gains access to their experience base and domain knowledge. The analyst's job is then to analyze, expand on, synthesize, resolve conflicts in, and combine the inputs from all the stakeholders into an organized set of requirements at the appropriate level of abstraction for the target audience.

Identifying the stakeholders and getting them involved in the requirements engineering process brings different perspectives to the table, and contribute to a more complete set of requirements early in the software development life cycle. As Wiegers puts it, getting stakeholders involved eliminates the need for two of the most ineffective requirements elicitation techniques: clairvoyance and telepathy (Wiegers 2003).

Many individuals are uncomfortable with change and therefore resist it. New software products typically mean changing the way some stakeholders will perform part or all of their jobs. Obtaining stakeholder input and participation gets them involved in the change based on their needs. Involved stakeholders are more likely to buy-in to the completed work, which can create "ownership" and make them champions for the change within their stakeholder community. This can be beneficial in the transition of the new product, process or project into the stakeholder's environment.

The first step in identifying the stakeholders is to make sure that we consider all of the potential stakeholders. The following checklist can help in identifying potential stakeholders:

- What different types or groups of people will use the software product?
- Who performs, is involved in, or manages the business activities supported by the software product?
- Whose job will be impacted by the introduction of the new software product?
- Who will receive the reports, outputs, or other information from the software product?
- Who will pay for the software product?
- Who will select the software product or its supplier?
- If the software product fails, who could be impacted?
- Who will be involved in developing, distributing, supporting, and maintaining the software product?

- Who knows about the hardware, other software, or databases that interface with this software product?
- Who established the laws, regulations, or standards governing the product and/or business activities supported by the software product?
- Who establishes industry standards or guidelines or define industry best practices for the software product and/or business activities supported by the software product?
- Who should be kept from using the software product or from using certain functions/data in the software?
- Who does this software product solve problems for?
- Who does this software product create problems for?
- Who does not want the software product to be successful?

Step 2: Prune the Stakeholder List

It is almost impossible when developing a software product to actively involve all of the potential stakeholders. The needs of stakeholders may also contradict each other, for example, the need to keep unfriendly hackers from breaking into the payroll software conflicts with the accountant's need for quick and easy access to the software. Therefore, decisions need to be made about how to determine which stakeholders have higher priorities so that appropriate trade-offs can be made. Once all of the stakeholders have been identified, the second step is to prune the stakeholder list by sorting stakeholders into categories of:

- **Must include:** This stakeholder must be included in requirements engineering activities.
- **Like to include:** This stakeholder will only be included in requirements engineering activities if time allows.

- **Ignore:** This stakeholder will not be directly included in requirements engineering activities.

It should be noted that while "ignore" (and potentially "like to include") stakeholders may not directly participate in the requirements engineering activities, their requirements are not ignored. We must ensure that these stakeholder's requirements are obtained. For example, for the automated gas station system, we may decide to ignore the corporate headquarters stakeholder (an indirect user type stakeholder) but during interviews with the gas station owners, we elicit information about all of the reports and other information that must be sent to corporate headquarters.

Step 3: Stakeholder Participation Plan

The third step is to decide who will represent that stakeholder group and to decide when and how they will participate in the requirements process.

For each included stakeholder group we must decide who will represent that stakeholder group in the requirements engineering activities. There are three main choices:

- **Representative:** Select a stakeholder champion to represent the group of stakeholders. For example, if there are multiple testers who will be testing the product, the lead tester might be selected to represent this stakeholder group. The lead tester would then participate in the requirements engineering activities and be responsible for gathering inputs from other testers and managing communication with them.
- **Sample:** For large stakeholder groups or for groups where direct access is limited, sampling may be appropriate. In this case, it would be necessary to devise a sampling plan for obtaining inputs from a representative set of stakeholders in that particu-

lar group. For example, if the gas station company had several thousand Attendants, it may decide to take a sample set of Attendants to interview about their needs for the automated gas station software.

- **Exhaustive:** If the stakeholder group is small or if it is critical enough to the success of the system, it may be necessary to obtain the input from every member of that stakeholder group. For example, if the software product has only a single customer or a small set of customers it might be important to obtain input from each of the customers.

The second decision is to determine when and how each included stakeholder group needs to participate in the activities. Are they going to participate throughout the entire product life cycle, process or project or only at specific times? What activities are they going to participate in? For example, a stakeholder's input may be gathered during the definition of the process, but that stakeholder might not be involved in the peer review of that definition or be part of the ongoing process change approval authority. For product requirements development, one stakeholder might just be interviewed during requirements elicitation activities, while another key stakeholder is considered part of the requirements development team and participates in:

- Requirements elicitation as an active participant in facilitated requirements workshops.
- Requirements analysis by evaluating use cases and requirements models.
- Requirements specification by documenting part of the requirements.
- Requirements verification by peer reviewing the requirements specification.
- Requirements management as a member of the requirements change control board.

WHEN

Requirements development encompasses all the activities involved in identifying, capturing, and agreeing upon the requirements. Requirements development includes the definition and integration of the business level, stakeholder level, and product level requirements. The majority of the requirements development activities occur during the early concept and requirements phases of the life cycle, as illustrated in Figure 3. Continued elaboration of the requirements, however, can progress into the later phase of the software development life cycle.

Requirements management encompasses all of the activities involved in requesting changes to the baselined requirements, performing impact analysis for the requested changes, approving or disapproving those changes, and implementing the approved changes. Requirements management also includes the activities used for ensuring that all work products and project plans are kept consistent as well as tracking the status of the requirements as the software development process progresses. Requirements management is an ongoing activity throughout the software development life cycle.

The implemented software product is validated against its requirements throughout the life cycle but this validation is emphasized during the testing phases to identify and correct defects and to provide confidence that the product meets those requirements.

Requirements engineering is an iterative process. Practitioners must first develop the business requirements and baseline them. The business requirements are input into the development of the user-level requirements. Based on that effort, practitioners may discover gaps in their business requirements that result in further refinement. They can then use the information they gain from refining the business requirements for further update of the user-level requirements. The business and user-level requirements feed into the definition of the product-level requirements. This may lead

Figure 3. Requirements and the software development cycle

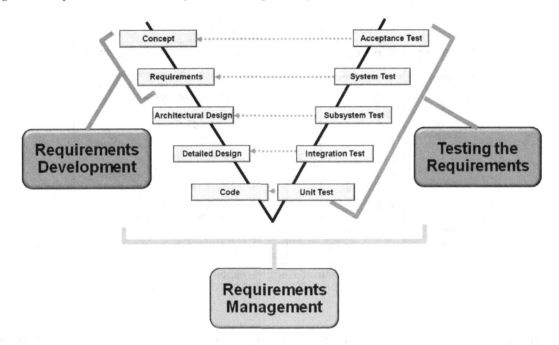

to further refinement of the business and user-level requirements. The product requirements are then input into the software design and development process, which may uncover implicit requirements or the need for further refinement of the business, user, and product-level requirements.

HOW

Software requirements engineering is a disciplined, process-oriented approach to the definition, documentation, and maintenance of software requirements throughout the software development life cycle. As illustrated in Figure 4, software requirements engineering is made up of two major processes: requirements development and requirements management.

Requirements Development: Requirements development encompasses all of the activities involved in eliciting, analyzing, specifying, and validating the requirements. Requirements development is an iterative process. It is unlikely that

you will go through the steps of the process in a one-shot, linear fashion. For example, the requirements analyst may talk to a stakeholder and elicit information, then analyze what that stakeholder said. The analyst may go back to that stakeholder for clarification and then document that revised understanding as part of the requirements specification. The analyst may then go on to talk to another stakeholder or hold a joint requirements workshop with several stakeholder representatives. A prototype may then be built and shown to a focus group. Based on the information gained, the analyst documents additional requirements in the specification and holds a requirements walkthrough to validate that set of requirements. The analyst then moves on to eliciting the requirements for the next feature, and so on.

The *requirements elicitation* step includes activities involved in identifying the requirement's stakeholders, selecting representatives from each stakeholder class, and determining the needs of each class of stakeholders. The *requirements analysis* step includes taking stakeholder needs

Figure 4. Requirements engineering process

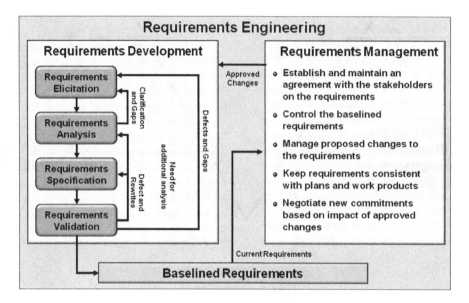

and refining them with further levels of detail. It also includes representing the requirements in various forms including prototypes and models, establishing priorities, analyzing feasibility, looking for gaps that identify missing requirements, and identifying and resolving conflicts between various stakeholder needs. The knowledge gained in the analysis step may necessitate iterations with the elicitation step. As clarification is needed, conflicts between requirements are explored, or missing requirements are identified. During the *requirements specification* step, the requirements are documented so that they can be communicated to all the product stakeholders. The last step in the requirements development process is *requirements validation*. This step ensures that requirements are well written, complete, and will satisfy the stakeholder's needs. Validation may lead to the iteration of other steps in the requirements development process because of identified defects, gaps, missing information, incomplete analysis, needed clarification, or other issues.

The requirements development process does not assume any specific software development life cycle model. In fact, requirements development

may be iterative and/or incremental, as illustrated in Figure 5. Whether the project defines all of the requirements at once, in small groups or even one requirement at a time, each requirement or set of requirements must be defined and baselined before software development can build that part of the software.

Requirements Elicitation Techniques: The requirements elicitation process is the information-gathering step in the requirements development process. Many different techniques may be used to elicit requirements, including:

- **Stakeholder Interviews:** "One of the most important and most straightforward requirements elicitation techniques is the interview, a simple, direct technique that can be used in virtually every situation" (Leffingwell 2000). Interviews are an excellent mechanism for obtaining detailed information from another person.
- **Focus Groups:** Focus groups are small groups of selected stakeholders that represent "typical" stakeholders in the type or types of stakeholders we need input from.

Figure 5. Iterative requirements engineering process

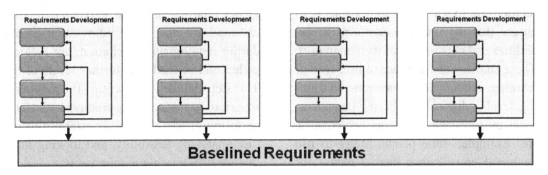

These groups can be particularly valuable if the software product has a large and/or very diverse customer/user base. The group should also be fairly homogeneous. For example, the gas purchaser stakeholder group might need to be divided into several focus groups that separate family car drivers from drivers of 18-wheelers from fleet drivers (taxis or military vehicles). The focus group stakeholders are brought together in a meeting to discuss one or more aspects of the requirements for the software product. While the members of a focus group typically don't have any decision making authority, their input into the requirements elicitation process can be valuable.

- **Facilitated Requirements Workshops:** Facilitated requirements workshops bring together cross-functional groups of stakeholders to produce specific software requirements work products. By bringing together the appropriate stakeholders, facilitated requirements workshops can help streamline communications while identifying and resolving requirements issues between affected parties. This can reduce the time it takes to elicit the requirements and produce higher-quality requirements work products. These workshops focus on team building and concepts of collaboration, which promotes a sense of shared ownership of the deliverables and resulting prod-

uct. The team synergy can also reduce the risk of missing requirements.

- **Observations of Current Work Processes:** This can include site visits where the users are observed performing their actual jobs, or the observation of users in a simulated environment (for example, using a prototype).

- **Questionnaires and Surveys:** Surveys can be sent to stakeholders to obtain their opinions or input into the requirements process. Previously conducted customer satisfaction surveys and/or marketing surveys may also include valuable requirements information.

- **Benchmarking:** Benchmarking is a process used to identify, understand, adapt, and adopt good practices from others, anywhere in the world. Benchmarking helps an organization improve the performance of its processes, projects, products, and/or services. Benchmarking can be used to elicit good practice product attributes. For example, when I define requirements for a user interface, I spend time surfing the web looking for both good and bad interfaces that I can benchmark to improve my requirements.

- **Human Factors Studies:** Human factors studies consider the ways in which the human users of a software system will interact with that system and its environment. The purpose of doing human factors studies in relationship to software requirements is to ensure that the software conforms to the abilities and capabilities of its human user. These studies consider ease of use, ease of learning, ergonomics, education and training levels, physical handicaps, languages, local customs/culture, usage preferences, (for example, some people prefer to use keyboard entry rather than a mouse, or certain screen color combinations may be aesthetically displeasing), and so on. The study of human factors can be particularly important where the potential exists for possible human errors to cause safety concerns, for example, where performing tasks out of sequence might cause unsafe conditions.

- **Document Studies:** Sometimes the requirements have already been written down or can be identified from some other form of documentation. For example, there may already be a detailed specification on how the software must interface with an existing piece of hardware, or a report may already exist that is being created manually, and the software just needs to duplicate its contents and layout. As appropriate, requirements elicitation should consider studies of documentation, including:
  - Industry standards, laws, and/or regulations
  - Product literature (one's own or the competition's)
  - Process documentation and work instructions
  - Change requests, problem reports, or help-desk tickets
  - Lessons learned from prior projects or products
  - Reports and other deliverables from the existing systems

Requirements Analysis: During the requirements analysis step the stakeholder's needs, assumptions, and other information identified during requirements elicitation, are melded together and refined into further levels of detail. This step includes representing the requirements in various forms including prototypes and models, performing trade-off analysis, establishing priorities, analyzing feasibility, and looking for gaps that identify missing requirements.

Utilizing models to aid in the requirements analysis process can be particularly beneficial because models:

- Present a summary view of requirements.
- Help decompose business- and user-level requirements into product-level requirements.
- Aid in communications, "a picture is worth 1000 words."
- Act as a transition between requirements and design.
- Aid in the identification of:
  - Requirements defects.
  - Missing requirements.
  - Non-value-added requirements.

The information gained in the analysis step may necessitate iteration with the elicitation step as clarification is needed, conflicts between requirements are explored, or missing requirements are identified. The requirements are formally documented during the specification step so they can be communicated to the product stakeholders.

Requirements Specification: As mentioned earlier, requirements specification can take one of many forms, including one or more documents or data items in a requirements management database. In its simplest form, the requirements specification may simply be a To-Do list, such as items in a scrum product backlog, elements in a spreadsheet, or documented on sticky notes and index cards displayed on the project's war room wall.

One good practice for requirements specification is to have predefined requirements specification templates (or checklists if requirements do not take the form of documents). Templates allow the requirements analyst to focus on content instead of forma. Templates/checklists can help ensure that key items are not overlooked as the requirements are being documented. For example, if assumptions are not documented, they may lead to future misunderstandings or other problems. Templates/checklists are also great tools for propagating lessons learned by updating the template/checklist to include the lesson so it is not repeated on the next project.

Requirements Validation: The last step in the requirements development process is to validate the requirements to ensure that they are well written, complete, and will satisfy the customer needs. As stated earlier, validation may lead to the iteration of other steps in the requirements development process because of identified defects, gaps, missing information, incomplete analysis, ambiguity, or other issues.

One of the primary tools for requirements validation is to conduct formal peer reviews of the requirements specification documents before they are baselined. Empirical evidence from many different companies shows that peer reviewing the requirements documentation has the highest return on investment of any defect detection activity. The peer review process should look at the requirements specification as a whole to ensure that it is:

- **Complete:** The requirements document includes all of the necessary requirements information. For example, the Software Requirements Specification (SRS) includes all the functions and nonfunctional requirements, constraints, external interface requirements, and data requirements that must be satisfied.
- **Consistent:** Internal conflicts do not exist between requirements in the document that result in the requirements contradict-

ing each other. The requirements also do not conflict with higher-level requirements including business, user, or system-level requirements. Terminology should also be used consistently within the document, for example:
  - A word has the same meaning every time it is used.
  - Two different words are not used to mean the same thing.
- **Modifiable:** The requirements document is organized and written in a manner that will facilitate making future change, for example:
  - Nonredundant: Each requirement is stated in only one place.
  - Changeable: Each requirement can be changed without excessive impact on other requirements.

The peer review process should also look at each individual requirement to ensure that it is:

- **Unambiguous:** Each requirement statement should have only one interpretation, and each requirement should be specified in a coherent, easy-to-understand manner. For example, many word that end in "ly" such as user-friendly and automatically are ambiguous.
- **Concise:** Each requirement should be stated in short, specific, action-oriented language.
- **Finite:** The requirement should not be stated in an open-ended manner. For example, words like "all," "every," and "throughout" should be avoided in requirements statements.
- **Measurable:** Specific, measurable limits or values should be stated for each requirement as appropriate. For example, many word that end in "ly" such as quickly or that end in "ize" such as, maximize, mini-

mize and optimize do not specify specific measurable values.

- **Feasible:** The requirement can be implemented using available technologies, techniques, tools, resources, and personnel within the specified cost and schedule constraints.

- **Testable:** There exists a reasonably cost-effective way to determine that the software satisfies the requirement.

- **Traceable:** Each requirement should be traceable back to its source for example, user-level requirements, system-level requirements, standard, and enhancement request. It should also be specified in a manner that allows traceability forward into the design, implementation, and tests.

Another major tool for validating the requirements is to start writing the test cases for functional (black box) testing of the software. Since functional testing only requires knowledge of the requirements and not of the internals of the software product, practitioners can start writing

test cases against the requirements as soon as the requirements are written. The major advantage to writing the functional test cases early in the life cycle is that it will uncover defects in the requirements. Writing test cases early may result in some rework if the requirements change, but the cost of that rework will be more than offset by the savings, resulting from finding and fixing more requirements defects earlier.

Requirements Management: Requirements management starts with getting stakeholder buy-in to the baselined requirements. After one or more iterations through the software requirements development process, part or all of the requirements are deemed "good enough" to baseline and become the basis for software planning, design, and development. The requirements will never be perfect, analysts can always add more refinement and gather additional input, but there is a possibility that these actions will not actually improve the requirements. At some point, the law of diminishing returns starts to apply, where the additional information is simply not worth the additional effort to obtain it. Requirements

Figure 6. Bi-directional traceability

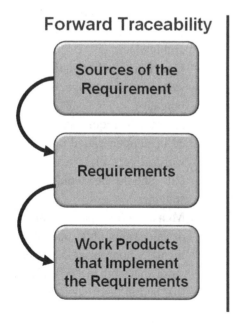
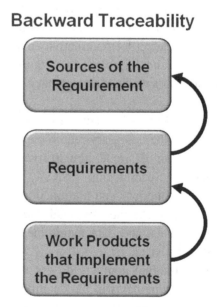

baselining is a business decision that should be based on risk assessment. Are the requirements "good enough" to proceed with development, remembering that the developers will continue to obtain valuable information as they implement the software, which can be fed back into requirements updates and enhancements at a future date.

Requirements management includes the activities performed to ensure that all work products and project plans are kept consistent and tracking the status of the requirements as the project progresses through the software development process. Requirements management ensures that the requirements are actually built into the software being developed. Requirements management also encompasses all of the activities involved in requesting changes to the baselined requirements, performing impact analysis for the requested changes, approving or disapproving those changes, and ensuring the implementation of approved changes.

One of the primary tools of requirements management is bi-directional traceability, as illustrated in Figure 6. Traceability is used to track the relationship between each unique product-level requirement and its source. For example, a product requirement might trace from a business need, through a user request, a business rule, or quality attribute or to some other source. Traceability is also used to track the relationship between each unique product-level requirement and the work products to which that requirement is allocated. For example, a single product-level requirement might trace to one or more software architectural elements, detailed design elements, objects/classes, code units, tests (at the unit, integration, system, acceptation or other test level), user or operational documentation topics, training materials, and/or even to people or manual processes that implement that requirement.

CONCLUSION

We must understand the different types and levels of requirements to do a good job of requirements engineering. Building high quality software requires an understanding of the benefits of having good requirements so that adequate resources and time are dedicated to the requirements engineering process throughout the software development life cycle. Doing requirements engineering correctly requires an interdisciplinary approach that considers the needs of multiple stakeholder groups. It also requires expertise in the various skills of requirements engineering including requirements elicitation, requirements analysis, requirements specification, requirements validation, and requirements management.

REFERENCES

Brooks, F. (1995). Mythical man-month: Essays on software engineering (20th Ann. Ed.). Reading, MA: Addison-Wesley.

Carnegie Mellon University Software Engineering Institute. (n.d.). *Capability Maturity Model Integration (CMMI®) for Development, Version 1.2* (CMU/SEI-2006-TR-008, ESC-TR-2006-008). Retrieved from www.sei.cmu.edu

Leffingwell & Widrig. (2000). *Managing Software Requirements: A Unified Approach*. Addison-Wesley.

Wiegers, K. E. (2003). *Software Requirements* (2nd ed.). Redmond, WA: Microsoft Press.

Wiegers, K. E. (2004). *In Search of Excellent Requirements*. Retrieved from www.processimpact.com

ADDITIONAL READING

Leffingwell, D. (2011). Agile Software Requirements: Lean Requirements Practices for Teams, Programs, and the Enterprise. Upper Saddle River, NJ: Addison-Wesley.

Gause, D., & Weinberg, G. (1989). Exploring Requirements, Quality Before Design. New York, NY: Dorset House Publishing.

Gause, D., & Weinberg, G. (1989). Exploring Requirements, Quality Before Design. New York, NY: Dorset House Publishing.

Robertson, S., & Robertson, J. (2012). Mastering the Requirements Process (3rd ed.). Harlow, England: Addison-Wesley.

Gottesdiener, E. (2002). Requirements by Collaboration. Boston: Addison-Wesley.

Sommerville, I., & Sawyer, P. (1997). *Requirements Engineering: A Good Practice Guide*. John Wiley & Sons: Chichester.

Thayer, R. H., & Dorfman, M. (2000). *Software Requirements Engineering* (2nd ed.). Los Alamitos, CA: IEEE Computer Society Press.

Young, R. (2004). The Requirements Engineering Handbook. Boston: Artech House.

Cohn, M. (2004). *User Stories Applied: For Agile Software Development*. Boston: Addison-Wesley.

Cockburn, A. (2001). Writing Effective Use Cases. Boston: Addison-Wesley.

KEY TERMS AND DEFINITIONS

Change Control: The formal process by which a change to a baselined system or its requirements or components is proposed, evaluated, approved, differed or rejected, scheduled, tracked and verified.

Requirements Analysis: All of the activities involved in identifying and resolving gaps and conflicts in the stakeholder requirements and refining those stakeholder requirements into the detailed product requirements.

Requirements Development: All of the involved in requirements elicitation, analysis, specification and validation.

Requirements Elicitation: All of the activities involved in gathering the information upon which the requirements are based including identifying the requirement's stakeholders, selecting stakeholder representatives and determining the needs of each class of stakeholders.

Requirements Management: All of the activities involved in ensuring that the requirements are built into the software product, in maintaining consistency between the requirements, other software work product and the project plans, and performing change control on the baselined requirements.

Requirements Specification: All of the activities involved in formally documenting the requirements so that they can be communicated to customers, users, development, and other stakeholders.

Requirements Validation: All of the activities involved in ensuring that the requirements are well written, complete, maintainable, measureable, unambiguous, finite and will satisfy the stakeholder and business objectives.

Chapter 2
Critical Issues in Requirements Engineering Education

Rafia Naz Memon
University of Malaya, Malaysia

Rodina Ahmad
University of Malaya, Malaysia

Siti Salwah Salim
University of Malaya, Malaysia

ABSTRACT

Requirements Engineering (RE) is the most crucial process within software development projects. In order to prepare skilled requirements engineers, Requirements Engineering Education (REE) needs to be provided to students at the university level before they become software engineers and part of the workforce. However, RE is considered the most difficult subject within the software engineering curriculum for students to learn and for lecturers to teach due to its uncertain nature. This chapter examines the current and potential areas for research within REE. It first presents the current status of REE provided in universities and the REE problems reported in the literature that lead us to the potential research problems in REE. The REE teaching approaches proposed by researchers are then elaborated. The proposed approaches are mapped back to address the REE problems. The chapter closes with recommended directions for future REE research.

1. INTRODUCTION

Requirements Engineering (RE) process is perceived as one of the most critical activities within software development projects because many projects fail due to RE problems. RE is about capturing the requirements of customers and analysing, modelling and validating those requirements and presenting them in a software requirements specification, which is the final output within the RE process. The software is then developed based on these specified requirements.

Failure to identify these requirements accurately will result in failure to meet the project goals and satisfy the customers. Hence, ensuring effective RE process is a great challenge not only

DOI: 10.4018/978-1-4666-6026-7.ch002

to the software industries but also to the academic world who is responsible for educating future requirements engineers. In order to prepare skilled requirements engineers, Requirements Engineering Education (REE) needs to be provided to students at university level before they become software developers and part of the workforce (Berenbach, 2005).

The purpose of REE is to teach students the relevant concepts and skills that they need to perform RE, as well as enabling them to practise performing RE activities while working on software development projects. Unfortunately, in most computer science or software engineering programmes, RE topics is not given a high priority and most programmes only allocate a small amount of credit hours to it. On top of that, due to its uncertain nature, students are only exposed to its theoretical concepts and lack practice. Additionally, lecturers may find the subject challenging to teach, specifically in finding the best way to prepare students for the RE activities within limited resources. Moreover, a requirements engineer's job is not an alluring job like a project manager or an architect's; this job is sometimes considered as dead-end and boring. In spite of all these drawbacks, RE is a vital part of software development life cycle (Berenbach, 2005). Due to the lack of RE topics in most academic programmes, software developers have to learn the RE activities during the job (Jiang, Eberlein, & Far, 2005). This circumstance makes most software developers lacking in RE skills and knowledge.

Besides that, current Software Engineering programmes still utilize the traditional methods of teaching basic RE concepts of processes, models and methodologies. Unfortunately, through typical lectures, students may not be able to learn the skills that the industry requires (Beatty & Agouridas, 2007). REE should be aimed at achieving the industrial relevance so that students will be able to cope with large scale software develop-

ment projects, and the challenges and proven techniques related to industrial development of software (Wohlin & Regnell, 1999).

Even though there is an increasing emphasis on RE in university curriculum for undergraduate as well as postgraduate students, only very few published work on improving the teaching of RE (Callele & Makaroff, 2006) has been visible. The most important challenge in REE is to equip students with sufficient skills to perform RE activities within the limited time and resources available at learning institutions (Yusop, Mehboob, & Zowghi, 2007). In order to meet that challenge, it is imperative to identify an enhanced pedagogical approach to incorporate a learner-centred design in the development of curriculum and instructional strategies, to develop a general and flexible curriculum framework along with the supporting materials, and to exploit new technologies for on-campus learning (Adroin, 2000).

This chapter highlights the current status of REE problems and proposes a list of suggestions for future research in REE. The chapter starts with a general overview of RE and REE, and then presents the REE offered at different universities and the recommended RE model curriculum and teaching strategies (in Section 2). Section 3 highlights the potential research problems in REE, while Section 4 presents the proposed pedagogical approaches that can be used to address the REE problems. In Section 5, a list of suggestions is proposed that highlights the future directions of REE research. Section 6 concludes the chapter.

2. CURRENT STATUS OF REQUIREMENTS ENGINEERING EDUCATION

This section presents an overview of RE and REE, and presents the REE offered in different countries together with researchers views on it.

2.1 Requirements Engineering

RE is the first phase of the development lifecycle, and all subsequent phases are dependent on it. This makes the RE phase crucial. The RE phase involves gathering information on customers' needs and clarifying them, or in the clearest possible terms, the problem that the product is expected to solve (Melonfire, 2007). The requirements engineering process involves examining the present work process in order to devise the best possible product to help with that work. As an outcome of this process, a requirements specification is produced which is a complete description of the functionality and the behaviour of the product (Robertson & Robertson, 1999). This section presents the definitions and main activities of the RE phase.

2.1.1 Definition

RE is an inherently complex discipline and has been broadly recognized as critical to a development project success (Beatty & Agouridas, 2007). A requirement is defined as "a property that must be exhibited in order to solve some real-world problem", whereas the term Requirements Engineering refers to the "systematic handling of requirements" (Abran, Moore, Bourque, Dupuis, & Tripp, 2004). The final output of RE is the software requirements specification (SRS), which is defined as: "A document that clearly and precisely describes each of the essential requirements (functions, performance, design constraints, and quality attributes) of the software and external interfaces" (Thayer, Bailin, & Dorfman, 1997).

Having defined requirements and SRS, the following definitions of RE are given: 1) A systematic approach to eliciting, organizing, and documenting the requirements of a system, and 2) a process that establishes and maintains agreement between the customer and the project team on the changing requirements of the system" (Wahono, 2003).

2.1.2 Requirements Engineering Activities

The RE phase consists of the following five core activities.

2.1.2.1 Requirements Elicitation

Requirements elicitation is a process of "identifying needs and bridging the disparities among the involved communities for the purpose of defining and distilling requirements to meet the constraints of these communities" (SEI, 1991). The most difficult part of this activity is to ensure effective communication between various stakeholders and the elicitation of tacit knowledge. The requirements in this phase are still largely unprocessed, unstructured and may contain many irrelevancies, inconsistencies and omissions (Jiang, 2005).

2.1.2.2 Requirements Analysis and Modelling

The Requirements Analysis and Modelling process is a combination of two activities which are requirements analysis and requirements modelling. During requirements analysis, requirements are reviewed and analysed, whereas during requirements modelling, requirements are modelled to resolve possible conflicts by negotiation between stakeholders (Jiang, 2005).

2.1.2.3 Requirements Documentation

Requirements documentation is the process of documenting the agreed requirements at an appropriate level of detail in the most suitable notation based on a well-defined document structure. This process has a very close relationship with requirements management (Jiang, 2005).

2.1.2.4 Requirements Verification and Validation

Requirements verification and validation (V&V) is the process of examining the requirements document to ensure that it is unambiguous, consistent and complete, and that the stakeholders are satisfied with the final requirements specification (Jiang, 2005). The task of verification is to check whether the requirements comply with given constraints, and are consistent, complete and unambiguous. This is usually done by formal verifications or inspections. The task of validation is to certify that the specified requirements comply with the given user and customer intentions. This means that the requirements need to be expressed in a notation that is understandable by the customer (Eberlein, 1997).

2.1.2.5 Requirements Management

Requirements management is the process of identifying, organizing, documenting and tracking changing requirements in a project as well as the impact of these changes. It is an on-going task throughout the whole RE process and might span the whole software lifecycle (Jiang, 2005). The management includes issues such as information storage, organization, traceability, analysis, visualization and documentation (Eberlein, 1997).

Figure 1 summarizes the information on each RE activity. The rectangular boxes present the RE activities, while the input and output of each activity are shown through labelled arrows. The output of every activity is the input of the next activity. The most common techniques of each activity are shown by the ovals connected to that activity. As requirements management is the activity that covers the overall RE process, it is

Figure 1. Requirements engineering activities

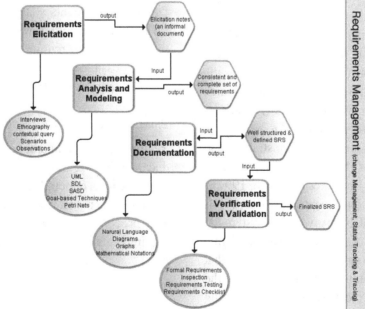

shown by the large rectangle at the right covering all other activities.

2.2 Requirements Engineering Education

This section presents the background studies on REE in different contexts. First, REE will be defined, and then RE courses offered in the Computer Science/Information Technology/Software Engineering (CS/IT/SE) curriculum will be discussed. Finally, recommendations from the Association for Computing Machinery (ACM) and Institute of Electrical and Electronic Engineers (IEEE) regarding the RE course content and teaching strategies will be presented.

2.2.1 Definition

Based on the descriptions of REE provided by (Rosca, 2000), (Svahnberg & Gorschek, 2005), UTS information Technology Handbook (UTS), and (Al-Ani & Yusop, 2004), it can be concluded that "the purpose of REE is to teach students the basic concepts and skills they need to perform RE, as well as enabling them to practise performing RE activities while working on real projects".

2.2.2 RE in the CS/IT/SE Curriculum

RE is being offered to students in different ways in universities, depending on the university's programme structure. The most common method involves offering RE to undergraduate students as a core subject or as an elective subject, or as a common topic in SE curriculum, or it may be embedded in other related courses or in a final year project as part of a CS/IT/SE programme. In order to observe the current RE course offerings, a random sample of prospectuses from a few universities in the UK, the USA, Australia, Malaysia and Canada has been examined. These examples are presented in Table 1.

From these examples, it can be seen that in most BSc SE programmes, RE is offered as a core module, while some of these programmes also include RE as an elective module so that students are equipped with a set of RE concepts (e.g., elicitation, analysis, modelling, documentation, verification, conflict resolution, team communication, problem identification etc.), RE tools (e.g., IBM Rational, RequisitePro, the Organisation Modelling Environment (OME) etc.) and RE techniques (e.g., dealing with incomplete requirements provided by the customer, changes to the customer's requirements, involving the customer in each phase of the project, etc.). However, in most BSc CS and BSc IT programmes, RE is taught as a topic as part of a course which only exposes students to a few fundamental RE concepts and activities.

2.2.3 Recommended RE Courses and Teaching Strategies from the ACM and IEEE Education Board

Traditionally, RE educators have developed courses based on the required textbooks, as well as academic and/or trade publications, and have then delivered these courses to students primarily in traditional classroom environments as part of the CS/IT/SE degree programmes (Davis, Hickey, & Chamillard, 2005).

In order to help educators and universities to design and deliver a suitable curriculum, the ACM Education Board and the IEEE Computer Society Educational Activities Board have recommended core SE topics and guidelines for delivery in a report entitled "Software Engineering 2004 – Curriculum Guidelines for Undergraduate Degree Programs in Software Engineering" (LeBlanc, Sobel, Diaz-Herrera, & Hilburn, 2006).

2.2.3.1 Recommended Model Curriculum

The section entitled "Software Modelling and Analysis" of the aforementioned report (LeB-

Table 1. RE courses at different universities

No.	Country	University	Programme	Core	Elective	Topics
01	UK	City University London	BSc SE [a]		√	
		University College London	BSc CS [b]			√
		Manchester University	BSc CS			√
		University of Birmingham	BSc CS			√
02	USA	Stanford University	BSc CS			√
		Florida Institute of Technology	BSc SE	√		
		Milwaukee School of Engineering	BSc SE	√		
		Columbus State University	BSc CS			√
		Carnegie Mellon University	BSc CS			√
03	Australia	Curtin University of Technology	BSc IT [c]			√
			BSc SE	√		
		University of New South Wales	BSc SE	√		
		University of Wollongong	BSc SE		√	
		University of Newcastle	BSc SE	√		
04	Malaysia	University of Malaya	BSc SE	√		
		University of Putra Malaysia	BSc SE	√		
		The National University of Malaysia	BSc IT			√
05	Canada	University of Toronto	BSc SE	√		
		University of Waterloo	BSc SE	√		
		University of Ontario Institute of Technology	BSc SE	√		

[a]Bachelor of Science in Software Engineering
[b]Bachelor of Science in Computer Science
[c]Bachelor of Science in Information Technology

lanc et al., 2006) includes the complete core RE curriculum that is presented in Table 2. This recommended curriculum consists of four units, and each unit consists of essential, desirable and optional topics. The essential topics are the parts of the core curriculum that professional SE teachers agree are necessary for anyone wishing to obtain an undergraduate degree in this field. These sections are denoted with the letter E. Desirable topics are not core subjects, but should be included in the core programmes if possible; otherwise they should be considered as elective topics. These topics are denoted with the letter D. Optional topics should be considered as elective only, and are denoted with the letter O.

This recommended curriculum was specially designed to support the development of under-graduate RE courses, and can be considered as a basis to design RE programmes for universities offering RE courses. Depending on their programme structure and the available resources, universities can include advanced topics in addition to this core curriculum.

Overall, 75% of the recommended curriculum consists of essential topics, including RE definitions, RE processes, basic RE concepts, requirements elicitation techniques, requirements analysis and modelling techniques, requirements documentation techniques, requirements verification and validation techniques, and techniques for

Table 2. Core curriculum recommended by the ACM and IEEE

Units	Topics	E, D, O
1. Requirements fundamentals	*1. Definition of requirements (e.g., product, project, constraints, system boundaries, external, internal, etc.)*	E
	2. Requirements process	E
	3. Layers/levels of requirements (e.g., needs, goals, user requirements, system requirements, software requirements, etc.)	E
	4. Requirements characteristics (e.g., testable, unambiguous, consistent, correct, traceable, priority, etc.)	E
	5. Managing changing requirements	E
	6. Requirements management (e.g., consistency management, release planning, reuse, etc.)	E
	7. Interaction between requirements and architecture	E
	8. Relationship of requirements to SE, human-centred design, etc.	D
	9. Wicked problems (e.g., ill-structured problems, problems with many solutions, etc.)	D
	10. Commercial Off The Shelf (COTS) as a constraint	D
2. Eliciting requirements	*1. Elicitation sources (e.g., stakeholders, domain experts, operational and organisational environments, etc.)*	E
	2. Elicitation techniques (e.g., interviews, questionnaires, surveys, prototypes, use cases, observation, participatory techniques, etc.)	E
	3. Advanced techniques (e.g., ethnography, knowledge elicitation, etc.)	O
3. Requirements specification & documentation	*1. Requirements documentation basics (e.g., types, audience, structure, quality, attributes, standards, etc.)*	E
	2. Software requirements specification	E
	3. Specification languages (e.g., structured English, UML, formal languages such as Z, VDM, SCR, RSML, etc.)	E
4. Requirements validation	*1. Reviews and inspection*	E
	2. Prototyping to validate requirements (summative prototyping)	E
	3. Acceptance test design	E
	4. Validating product quality attributes	E
	5. Formal requirements analysis	D

dealing with RE challenges in industry. A further 17% of the recommended curriculum consists of desirable topics; these topics are related to the relationship between RE and SE, RE problem analysis and structuring, RE constraints etc. These are supporting RE topics that, if combined with the essential topics, can provide in-depth RE knowledge to students. The overall percentage of essential and desirable topics in the core curriculum indicates that they are very important, and that one of the reasons for the problems facing educators and students in teaching and studying RE could be the lack of these topics in the curriculum. Advanced RE techniques are included as optional topics, which constitute 8% of the

model curriculum. Depending on their programme structure and available resources, universities can include advanced topics in addition to the core curriculum.

2.2.3.2 Recommended RE Teaching Strategies

Alongside the core curriculum, guidelines for curriculum delivery are also provided in the same report (LeBlanc et al., 2006). This report states that the most common approach to teaching SE material is the use of lectures supported by laboratory sessions or tutorials. The dominant delivery method in most higher education institutions today is classroom-type instruction, in which the instructor presents material to a class using lectures or lecture/discussion presentation techniques, which may be augmented by appropriate laboratory work. However, the report (LeBlanc et al., 2006) recommends that SE education in the 21st century needs to move beyond the lecture format, as alternative approaches can help students learn more effectively. Therefore, we should consider a variety of approaches to teaching and learning other than those which are currently in use. Some of the recommended strategies that might be considered for supplementing, or in certain cases, even largely replacing the lecture format include *problem-based learning* (teaching students to solve customers' implicit and explicit problems through practice and examples), *just-in-time learning* (teaching fundamental material immediately before teaching the application of the same material), *learning by failure* (students are given a task that they will have difficulty with and are then taught methods that will enable them to carry out the task more easily in the future) and *self-study materials* (students work through problems in their own time, including on-line and computer-based learning).

Researchers have also reported their view on RE teaching strategies used in universities. (Nguyen, Armarego, & Swatman, 2002) in their study found that the requirements process, as described in the literature and therefore taught at universities, does not match the real needs of industry. This is because the REE provided to students still includes the traditional teaching methods. However, students do not learn the skills that industry requires through typical lectures. According to (Davis et al., 2005) due to the disconnect between education and practice, educators are still using traditional methods of delivering RE course and are unable to identify those best practices from a myriad of RE research results which should be incorporated into their courses.

(Beatty & Agouridas, 2007) suggested that learning through doing is more effective than learning through being told, and that students should be taught to work on different problematic situations which are similar to those they will encounter in industry.

It can therefore be concluded that both educators and students are facing many problems with regards to teaching and studying RE because of the deficiencies in the current approaches to teaching RE.

3. CRITICAL ISSUES IN TEACHING REQUIREMENTS ENGINEERING

RE is considered as the most difficult stage of software development for students to learn and for lecturers to teach (Gibson, 2000). Despite being a relatively new field in Software Engineering, it has attracted the attention of both academics and practitioners because it is one of the most critical, difficult and problematic phase of software development. At present, academic institutions are working on producing more people who can perform the role of a Requirements Engineer but the gap between what the industry needs and what the graduates learn from the RE courses is still very vast (Scheinholtz, 2007).

The REE currently provided to students still incorporates the traditional methods of teaching basic concepts of processes, models and methodologies. However, through typical lectures, students are not able to equip themselves with the skills that the industry requires (Beatty & Agouridas, 2007). REE should be aimed at achieving industrial relevance so that students will be able to cope with large scale software development projects, and the challenges and proven techniques related to industrial development of software (Wohlin & Regnell, 1999). A typical industrial project has two to four thousand requirements, whereas a RE project in academic programs is usually very simple in order to keep the material manageable and not to overwhelm the students. However, students should learn to manage scale before they are placed in difficult situation i.e. the industry (Berenbach, 2005). (Regev, Gause, & Wegmann, 2009) suggested that for teaching RE, a curriculum is required in which the students do internships in the middle of their studies in order to get the experiences required to fully appreciate and understand the RE practices. (Beatty & Agouridas, 2007) suggested that there is a need to teach students how to use justifiable assumptions where the information is incomplete and how to integrate the required knowledge and skills. Students should understand the effect of poor requirements on projects that can lead them to an in depth understanding of RE. Also, learning through doing is more effective than learning through being told. Students should be taught to work on different problematic situations similar to those that they will encounter in the industry (Beatty & Agouridas, 2007).

Despite these efforts, problems in REE are frequently acknowledged within the REE community and reported in several studies such as (Beatty & Agouridas, 2007; Connor, Buchan, & Petrova, 2009; Hoffmann, 2008; Memon, Ahmad, & Salim, 2010; Zowghi, 2009) etc. In the literature, researchers have presented a significant number of REE problems in universities, as well as those RE problems in industry that can be addressed by providing proper REE in universities. An integrated view of REE problems was developed in a previous study (Memon, Salim, & Ahmad, 2013) which presents the collection of REE problems. Most of the REE problems presented in the integrated view are further discussed in the following section.

3.1 Software Practitioners do not Possess Sufficient Understanding of RE Techniques

In the software engineering areas, many RE techniques were introduced to cater for various

and differing project circumstances. There is a need for practitioners to be able to choose one or a combination of these techniques to be used based on the characteristics of a project. However, practitioners are usually unable to understand these techniques and their particular use, which results in the selection of a technique which may not be suitable for a particular project. This is a typical problem and is reported by many researchers because the successful completion of the RE process depends so much on selecting the right techniques for the right circumstances.

3.2 Lack of Emphasis on Teaching Communication Skills

Requirements elicitation is the first and important step of the RE process. To be able to perform this process efficiently, a requirements engineer must be equipped with the necessary communication skills. He must be able to communicate with a wide range of people from different backgrounds and goals, and should be able to ask them the right questions at the right time in order to capture their real needs. Unfortunately as reported by the researchers, there is a lack of communication skills that is required in order to perform well during the elicitation process which has led to a communication barrier between the developers and customers. Teaching these skills is very important but difficult to do; students need to understand the importance of these skills and should be aware of the need for collaboration in RE.

3.3 Lack of Emphasis on Teaching Problem Structuring and Analysis Skills

Most problems stated by customers are usually incomplete and ill-structured. Analysing and structuring these problems before solving them is an important RE issue, but has been given less attention when teaching RE. As a result, newly graduated software practitioners are unable to analyze the informal representation of problems and to structure these problems from the real-world mess. Therefore there is a need to explicitly teach this issue in REE.

3.4 Lack of Skills to Deal with Incomplete Requirements

The requirements elicited from stakeholders are usually incomplete and need to be iteratively elicited to get the full picture of the requirements. Therefore, it is a challenge for software practitioners to structure, analyze and work on these incomplete requirements. To have the ability to deal with incomplete requirements is very important and is reported by many researchers in RE literature. Subsequently, there is a need to equip software practitioners on how to deal with incomplete requirements.

3.5 Lack of Customer Involvement

RE is a phase that requires customers or stakeholders to be involved during the RE process to ensure that the project captures the right requirements and the stakeholders have the right expectation for the project. Most projects may face difficulties in getting the customers involved. Therefore, practitioners should be made aware and be given the necessary skills to get the customers involved in the project as much as possible to ensure the project's success.

3.6 Lack of Skills to Deal with Unrealistic Customer Expectations

During requirements elicitation, practitioners always try to get as many requirements as possible. A stakeholder on the other hand, might omit those requirements that are too obvious in his opinion. Also, often the requirements provided by stakeholders are unrealistic and difficult to implement within the provided time and resources. Understanding these unspoken issues and unrealistic

customer expectations proves very difficult for practitioners, thus they should have the necessary skills to deal with them.

3.7 Lack of Skills to Deal with Changing Requirements

During the software development process, the customers' requirements keep on changing and it becomes difficult for practitioners to deal with these changing requirements as the project moves from the initial to the later stages of development. Therefore, the practitioners must be equipped with the necessary skills to deal with the changing requirements.

3.8 Lack of Students' Awareness on the Importance of RE

Many students perceive RE as a boring subject due to its uncertain and complex nature. They prefer to work as a software programmer rather than an analyst or a requirements engineer. However, students should be made aware of the importance of the RE phase in any software development project. At the same time, educators should make use of interesting means to engage students in the learning process. Educators should emphasize on practice to achieve the desired practical work in RE because students may fail to see the point in spending much time in order to understand the business requirements. Also, the course should be designed in a way that develops students' interest in RE.

3.9 Lack of Skills to Deal with Various RE Process Challenges

During product development, practitioners have to deal with a number of RE process challenges such as ambiguity, uncertainty, confusion, fear, time pressure, collaboration, and corporate politics, along with the issues discussed above. Therefore the practitioners must be able to deal with these challenges.

3.10 Lack of Emphasis on Teaching Basic RE Concepts and Tools

The primary purpose of teaching RE is to introduce students to the process of RE, and to the methods and tools available for eliciting, analysing, specifying, validating and managing requirements. In the literature, researchers have presented the problems that students and lecturers faced in studying and teaching basic RE skills. These problems need to be addressed in order to provide students with the foundations of RE before they are taught other RE skills.

3.11 Lack of RE Skills

Due to the lack of REE in universities, students are left with a lack of RE skills. The literature presented many of the skills that are lacking such as the ability of practitioners to resolve conflicts, define scope, facilitate decisions, define expected system behaviour in a combination of user, systems and data states, and produce outputs suitable for a diverse audience, insufficient rigor, perceived impracticability, lack of awareness, increased short-term cost, current practices lag best practices, and lack of maturity and guidance These skills need to be provided in REE.

3.12 Lack of Providing Industrial Experience in REE

RE is the most important and difficult phase of software development life cycle, but students cannot understand its importance. They may not be able to cope with large scale software development until and unless they are provided with the organizational experience in REE. This aspect of REE is very important and researchers emphasized that REE should be relevant to industrial practices

so that the students may be able to cope with the challenges related to software development.

3.13 Light Coverage of RE Material in University Programmes

In most software engineering programmes in universities, RE is taught as a complete and independent course. Unfortunately, due to a lack of proper course outlines and practical experiences, RE is not taught in depth. Hence, students have only some vague knowledge through lectures. Due to this limitation in REE, software developers have to learn RE practices on the job which results in many problems. Therefore, proper course outlines, skills and resources are needed to teach students the required RE concepts, techniques and skills to enable them to become good requirements engineers in the near future.

3.14 Lack of Emphasis on Teaching the Skills to Produce Good Quality Requirements Specifications

RE is the first phase of software development cycle and the requirements specification is the final output of the RE process. It is the first point of reference for the following activities in the development cycle. The problem facing practitioners is the poor quality of the end product such as missing or ambiguously presented or misinterpreted information, poor representation, untestable statements of requirements, and redundant information. In REE, students should be provided with the skills and practice of writing good quality requirements specifications. The students must learn not only to write good quality specifications but they should also be able to use and update it at later development stages.

Among the above problems, a few problems are related to RE curriculum (faced by students and educators in teaching and learning RE in universities). These problems are the light coverage of RE material in university programmes, the lack of providing industrial experience in REE, the lack of students' awareness on the importance of RE, the lack of emphasis on teaching basic RE concepts and tools, the lack of emphasis on teaching communication skills, the lack of emphasis on teaching the skills to produce good quality requirements specifications and the lack of emphasis on teaching problem structuring and analysis skills. The other problems are related to RE practices (faced by practitioners in industry that can be addressed by providing REE in universities), which include the problem of software practitioners not possessing sufficient understanding of RE techniques, the lack of RE skills, the lack of skills to deal with various RE process challenges, the lack of skills to deal with changing requirements, the lack of skills to deal with unrealistic customer expectations, the lack of customer involvement, the lack of skills to deal with incomplete requirements

and the lack of RE skills. However due to the fact that the problems in RE practice occur due to the lack of REE in university, we can say that the RE problems in industry are dependent on the REE problems in universities. Table 3 shows the dependency of RE problems in industry on each one of the REE problems in university.

Due to the dependency of RE problems in the industry on REE problems in universities, it is obvious that if the REE problems are addressed, they may have a positive impact on the RE problems in industries. Therefore, the REE problems in universities need to be addressed in further REE research. These problems are therefore considered as potential research problems in REE. However the problem of a "lack of students' awareness on the importance of RE" only require didactic skills, hence can be omitted from the list of potential research problems in REE.

Table 3. The dependency of RE problems in industry to REE problems in universities

No.	REE problems in universities	RE dependent problems
1.	Light coverage of RE material in university programmes	■ Software practitioners do not possess sufficient understanding of RE techniques ■ Lack of RE skills ● Lack of skills to deal with various RE process challenges
2.	Lack of providing industrial experience in REE	● Lack of skills to deal with changing requirements ● Lack of skills to deal with unrealistic customer expectations ■ Lack of customer involvement ● Lack of skills to deal with incomplete requirements ● Lack of skills to deal with various RE process challenges
3.	Lack of students' awareness on the importance of RE	■ Software practitioners do not possess sufficient understanding of RE techniques ■ Lack of RE skills
4.	Lack of emphasis on teaching basic RE concepts and tools	■ Software practitioners do not possess sufficient understanding of RE techniques ■ Lack of RE skills
5.	Lack of emphasis on teaching communication skills	■ Lack of customer involvement
6.	Lack of emphasis on teaching the skills to produce good quality requirements specifications	■ Software practitioners do not possess sufficient understanding of RE techniques ■ Lack of RE skills
7.	Lack of emphasis on teaching problem structuring and analysis skills	■ Lack of customer involvement ■ Lack of skill to deal with unrealistic customer expectations

4. PROPOSED TEACHING APPROACHES FOR REQUIREMENTS ENGINEERING EDUCATION

Researchers and universities are encouraged to experiment various approaches for teaching RE in order to make the RE course more effective and to address the above issues. Some educationist and researchers have shared their experiences and suggestions on utilizing a variety of approaches which might be useful to us. These proposed approaches are presented below. The problems these approaches likely to address (from those presented in section 3) and success of each approach towards addressing those problems are also discussed.

4.1 Simulation

(Regev et al., 2009) designed a course that used an active, affective, experiential pedagogy giving students the opportunity to experience a simulated work environment in order to provide organizational experience to students in REE. The course was designed based on Kolb's experiential learning cycle of concrete experience, reflective observation, abstract conceptualization, and active experimentation. Based on this model, students use a game to simulate a business case, and then discuss the problems faced in the game.

(Smith & Gotel, 2007) designed and educationally used a board game to introduce organizations to basic RE good practices in order to effectively introduce these practices into small novice organizations where RE experience and the resources (i.e., time and money) for developing this competency is limited. This game-based approach intended to teach RE good practices to novice requirements engineers by reinforcing a small set of lessons as players accumulate and discharge project responsibilities.

These two researchers have successfully used simulation to teach RE course with emphasis on providing industrial experience while teaching RE. From potential REE research problems, the simulation approach likely to address the following problems of *providing industrial experience in REE, lack of emphasis on teaching communication skills and lack of emphasis on teaching skills to produce good quality requirements specifications.*

4.2 Role Playing

(Gabrysiak, Giese, Seibel, & Neumann, 2010) presented an approach of incorporating virtual stakeholders into REE to introduce a semantic gap between software engineering students and these virtual stakeholders. The students of non-software engineering disciplines played the role of virtual stakeholders. They embedded REE within software engineering lecture for undergraduate students. The preparation guidelines on how to set up the requirements elicitation and validation sessions with virtual stakeholders were provided. This also includes instructions for these virtual stakeholders on how to behave when asked divergent questions they were either not prepared for or forgot the answers to.

(Rosca, 2000) reported on a RE course as a component of the curriculum for the Masters in Software Engineering program at Monmouth University which introduced students to the process, methods and tools specific to this area, and the corresponding software quality issues in which students actively participate in their learning by playing different roles for eliciting requirements, collaboratively improve the quality of their standard requirements documents, or share their particular expertise with their teams when performing object-oriented analysis.

(Damian, Al-Ani, Cubranic, & Robles, 2005) taught a course in a collaboration of three universities in disparate locations, time zones and culture. The students from these three locations played the roles of a client and a developer, and experienced the iterative development of a requirements specification in global projects (Learning by doing approach). The course consisted of lectures which were carried out separately at two universities. A two hour laboratory session per week offered students the opportunity to participate in a global team to collaborate on a project.

(Zowghi, 2009) shared the experience of teaching an online postgraduate RE subject to first year students of Master of Software Engineering located in Iran. Role playing was used here as a pedagogical tool to give students a greater appreciation of issues and problems associated with RE in quasi-real settings in order to deal with RE-related problems faced by project teams such as the communication barrier that exists between developers and customers, the ability to choose the most effective analysis and modelling techniques suited to solving the problem at hand and the poor quality of the end product of RE.

(Al-Ani & Yusop, 2004) reported a RE course offered to students at the Faculty of Information Technology in the University of Technology, Sydney through role-playing and peer assessment within a group environment with the aim to create an environment in which the students play a more active role in the learning process by transforming them from recipients of information to active participants. This course was offered to both undergraduate and postgraduate students.

Role playing is an effective and widely used technique in RE courses (Kilicay-Ergin & Laplante, 2013). It is successfully used by various researchers with emphasis on providing communication skills to students while teaching them RE concepts. From potential REE research problems, the role playing approach likely to address the following problems of *providing industrial experience in REE and lack of emphasis on teaching communication skills.*

4.3 Researchers' Teaching Experiences Based on Various Approaches

(Kilicay-Ergin & Laplante, 2013) presented an online graduate RE course offered at Penn State World Campus. The target population was working professionals, i.e. globally distributed graduate students who have various learning styles and work constraints. All the course materials were provided on a lesson-by-lesson basis via the course Website, Microsoft Word documents (.doc), or Portable Document Format (PDF) documents. To alleviate students' feelings of isolation, the course was designed to emphasize social interaction among classmates.

(Mohan & Chenoweth, 2011) reported their experiences in constructing a curriculum that utilizes a three tier model of learning that provides students with hands-on experience on the various facets of requirements elicitation and management. The three tier model includes tier 1 - In-class Elicitation, tier 2 - Elicitation via Homework Projects and tier 3 - Elicitation through Junior Design. According to them, this curriculum can be integrated into an existing course on software engineering, software requirements or the senior capstone experience.

(Davis et al., 2005) proposed a framework to integrate RE research and education in order to improve performance. They developed a course module based on their proposed framework for educating practitioners, and defined and evaluated a phased, online delivery mechanism for course content that interleaves education, research and practice activities to enhance learning, and facilitates implementation of RE best practices.

(Gibson, 2000) emphasized the need for formality in RE and used formal methods for teaching RE, and also examined particular problems of teaching formal RE. The main goals of the formal RE part of the course were: teaching principles, teaching (requirements) engineering as a process of compromise, giving an overview of standard formal techniques and methods, and teaching students how to evaluate tools and techniques with respect to different problem domains.

(Callele & Makaroff, 2006) reported the experience of teaching RE to second year Computer Science class that familiarized the students with the approaches to problem solving, development methodologies and development tools, and gave the students an opportunity to engage in these activities with the purpose of broadening their view of software development. The course is presented in a combined lecture and mandatory laboratory format with significant support provided by the faculty, lab instructors, and other students via a discussion board. In this course, the authors have used the traditional methods of teaching the basic skills of RE and by presenting the responses of students.

(Barnes, Gause, & Way, 2008) shared class room experiences, successes and challenges in teaching the unknown and unknowable of RE and offered students a combination of lightweight and easy-to-apply approaches to address the unknown and unknowable of systems requirements. According to them, when designing a course with the intention of allowing students to experience a "real world" design scenario, a major challenge is making the course feel "real enough" by including lots of unknowns and even a significant amount of potentially unknowable design issues so that students will intimately feel and experience the unknown and unknowable of systems design and RE, and therefore are more likely to remember and retain critical skills for the workplace.

(Madhavji & Miller, 2005) incorporated an investigative study in RE course to prepare students for a career in industry, scientific research and policy making in undergraduate science education. In an attempt to understand investigation-based education, they let the students experience engineering of requirements in different contexts. One group of students elicited requirements for a new version of a system in the presence of the

existing architecture of the system and its set of requirements; while the second group elicited requirements only in the presence of the old requirements i.e. without access to the described architecture so as to let them find out for themselves whether or not there were any differences between the two groups in their decision making, solution approaches, assumptions and properties of requirements elicited.

(Huijs, Sikkel, & Wieringa, 2005) shared an experiment of teaching RE by integrating it in several courses and also challenging the students by using authentic cases taken from business practices. According to them, complex skills such as RE cannot be learned at once but need repetition and improvement based on reflection, therefore they have chosen to integrate RE as an explicit part in different courses.

(Svahnberg & Gorschek, 2005) proposed a software engineering master level RE course aimed towards mature students who have some form of practical software development project experience so that the students are able to relate the theory, skills, and techniques taught during the course to their own practical experiences. The aim of the course was to prepare students for practice that involves giving them an accurate view of reality as well as giving them the tools and the critical mind-set needed to perform and improve on RE practices in industry. The lectures and discussion seminars were used as teaching tools.

(Connor et al., 2009) designed and delivered a Masters course in Software RE to overcome some of the issues that have caused the research-practice gap. By encouraging students to share their experiences in a peer learning environment, it was aimed at improving the shared understanding between the students and researchers in order to increase the potential for effective collaborations, whilst simultaneously developing the RE skill sets of the enrolled students. The course emphasized on project-based learning in which students were engaged and were active learners. In addition, the course was taught using short lectures, group activities, online discussion and activities, and assignments.

Through these various approaches, researchers have successfully delivered RE concepts to students. All potential REE problems can be addressed by effectively adopting the various approaches used by researchers.

4.4 Short Courses

(Beatty & Agouridas, 2007) reported the experience of RE training in industry intended for practitioners. It was an eight hour course, all taught in one day. The content of the course covered methods to elicit requirements, discussed strengths, weaknesses and the important techniques for each elicitation methods, taught the necessary skills to prepare practitioners on how to apply models during the elicitation process and how to take effective notes.

(Lami, 2005) reported a short (16 hours) course on practical software engineering aimed at teaching practical skills related to software engineering. This course focused on the skills related to the RE discipline (for instance, the realisation of complete, unambiguous requirement documents, or the requirement change management) and was intended for undergraduate students.

(Hoffmann, 2008) proposed a way to instruct soft facts in RE using improvisation theatre techniques to help the participants to experience the human factor. Transforming the idea of improvisation to RE means not having a prefabricated solution in mind, or not being afraid of asking so called stupid or obvious questions in order to find out hidden assumptions.

In addition to full term RE course, these short courses helped researchers to enhance students' RE skills.

From potential REE research problems, teaching RE concepts though short courses likely to address the problems of *lack of emphasis on teaching communication skills and lack of emphasis on teaching basic RE concepts and tools.*

4.5 The Proposed Teaching Approaches to Address REE Problems

The proposed teaching approaches come from the research results of the researchers. We believe that by adopting these proposed approaches along with the traditional approaches (such as lectures, labs, assignments etc) for teaching RE course, it can help in addressing many of the REE problems. Figure 2 summarizes the traditional and proposed approaches and presents them with the REE problems to show that they can help in addressing these problems.

5. FUTURE DIRECTIONS OF REQUIREMENTS ENGINEERING EDUCATION RESEARCH

It is suggested that the RE course should not be confined to just its techniques and tools. The future research in REE can be extended and moved in many directions. A few suggestions are presented here to help REE researchers. Among the potential research areas include:

- Creating more creative approaches to enrich software engineering students to experience real world problems.
- Developing more interactive projects that can provide students with the required RE skills and knowledge.
- Developing more learning workbench for RE students to share experiences, resources and discuss practical problems.
- Developing teaching methods that make use of web resources in enriching students with project ideas.
- Developing approaches to teach cognitive skills required for RE process.
- Enhancing existing techniques for eliciting requirements from disabled or elderly people.

Figure 2. Potential research problems in REE and the teaching approaches that can be used to address these problems

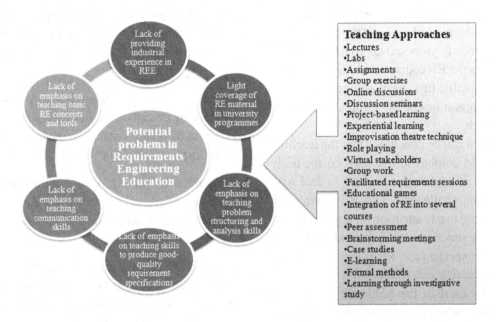

- Creating more learning or teaching models for RE process and activities.
- Embed more domain application within RE course, such as:
  - Application of RE techniques in e-learning system development
  - Application of RE techniques in web-based system development
  - Application of RE techniques in embedded systems
  - Application of RE techniques in critical systems
- Developing more appropriate and up-to-date learning tools to teach students the RE process.
- Designing more practical activities in the RE course to make it more useful and effective such as:
  - Focus group sessions
  - Game based activities to emulate the process of negotiations.

6. SUMMARY AND CONCLUSION

Preparing skilled software engineers who are equipped with the right RE skills has become crucial to ensure success in the software project development. REE should be effectively delivered to students in universities. The recommended curriculum by ACM Education Board and the IEEE Computer Society Educational Activities Board was especially designed to support the development of undergraduate RE courses, and can be considered as a basis to design RE programmes for universities offering RE courses. However, it was observed that educators and students are facing many problems with regards to teaching and studying RE because of the deficiencies in the current approaches to teaching RE. Although researchers have worked on addressing many of the REE problems, the present literature shows that many of the mentioned problems are not yet solved. In order to provide more rectification for

REE problems, this study gathers many suggestions on the ways of teaching RE. The suggested teaching approaches are presented along with the REE problems to highlight the necessity of introducing newly proposed approaches to effectively deliver the RE course and address the REE problems. Finally, this study also contributes to the list of suggestions on the future directions of REE research.

In short, it can be concluded that the teaching of RE should emphasise not only on the basic elements or skills, but also on how to deal with emerging RE challenges. The RE curriculum designers need to pay attention on improving current teaching practices, and to provide industrial or practical experience in REE. It is also crucial to transfer the research results from the research world to be used in the academic institutions and software industries. The student's interest in RE field has to be nurtured so that they become motivated to choose this as a leading profession.

REFERENCES

Abran, A., Moore, J. W., Bourque, P., Dupuis, R., & Tripp, L. L. (2004). *Guide to the software engineering body of knowledge: 2004 version.* IEEE Computer Society.

Adroin, W. R. (2000). Developing and deploying software engineering courseware in an adaptable curriculum framework. In *Proceedings of the 22nd international conference on Software engineering.* New York, NY: Academic Press.

Al-Ani, B., & Yusop, N. (2004). Role-playing, group work and other ambitious teaching methods in a large requirements engineering course. In *Proceedings of 11th IEEE International Conference and Workshop on the Engineering of Computer-Based Systems (ECBS '04).* IEEE. doi:10.1109/ECBS.2004.1316712

Barnes, R. J., Gause, D. C., & Way, E. C. (2008). Teaching the Unknown and the Unknowable in Requirements Engineering Education. In *Proceedings of Requirements Engineering Education and Training.* doi: doi:10.1109/REET.2008.6

Beatty, J., & Agouridas, V. (2007). Developing Requirements Engineering Skills: A Case Study in Training Practitioners. In *Proceedings of International Workshop on Requirements Engineering and Training (REET2007).* India Habitat Centre.

Berenbach, B. (2005). A hole in the curriculum. In *Proceedings of Workshop on Requirements Engineering Education and Training.* Paris: Academic Press.

Callele, D., & Makaroff, D. (2006). Teaching requirements engineering to an unsuspecting audience. *ACM SIGCSE Bulletin, 38*(1), 433–437. doi:10.1145/1124706.1121475

Connor, A. M., Buchan, J., & Petrova, K. (2009). Bridging the Research-Practice Gap in Requirements Engineering through Effective Teaching and Peer Learning. In *Proceedings of Sixth International Conference on Information Technology: New Generations.* doi: 10.1109/ITNG.2009.134

Damian, D., Al-Ani, B., Cubranic, D., & Robles, L. (2005). Teaching Requirements Engineering in Global Software Development: A report on a three-University collaboration. In *Proceedings of Workshop on Requirements Engineering Education and Training.* Paris: Academic Press.

Davis, A. M., Hickey, A. M., & Chamillard, A. T. (2005). Moving Beyond the Classroom: Integrating Requirements Engineering Research & Education to Improve Practice. In *Proceedings of Workshop on Requirements Engineering Education and Training.* Paris: Academic Press.

Eberlein. (1997). *Requirements Acquisition and Specification for Telecommunication Services.* (PhD Thesis). University of Wales, Swansea, UK.

Gabrysiak, G. Seibel, & Neumann. (2010). Teaching requirements engineering with virtual stakeholders without software engineering knowledge. In *Proceedings of 5th International Workshop on Requirements Engineering Education and Training (REET)*. doi:10.1109/REET.2010.5633109

Gibson, J. P. (2000). Formal requirements engineering: Learning from the students. In *Proceedings of Software Engineering Conference*. Academic Press.

Hoffmann, A. (2008). Teaching Soft Facts in Requirements Engineering Using Improvisation Theatre Techniques. In *Proceedings of Third international workshop on Multimedia and Enjoyable Requirements Engineering - Beyond Mere Descriptions and with More Fun and Games*. Barcelona: Academic Press.

Huijs, C., Sikkel, K., & Wieringa, R. (2005). Mission 2 Solution: Requirements Engineering Education as Central Theme in the BIT Programme. In *Proceedings of Workshop on Requirements Engineering Education and Training*. Paris: Academic Press.

Jiang, L. (2005). *A framework for the requirements engineering process development*. (Ph.D. Thesis). University of Calgary, Calgary, Canada.

Jiang, L., Eberlein, A., & Far, B. H. (2005). Combining Requirements Engineering Techniques– Theory and Case Study. In *Proceedings of 12th IEEE International Conference and Workshops on the Engineering of Computer-Based Systems (ECBS'05)*. doi:10.1109/ECBS.2005.25

Kilicay-Ergin, & Laplante. (2013). An Online Graduate Requirements Engineering Course. *IEEE Transactions on Education, 56*(2), 208–216. doi:10.1109/TE.2012.2208461

Lami, G. (2005). Teaching Requirements Engineering in the Small: an Under-graduate Course Experience. In *Proceedings of Workshop on Requirements Engineering Education and Training*. Paris: Academic Press.

LeBlanc. Sobel, Diaz-Herrera, & Hilburn. (2006). Software engineering 2004: curriculum guidelines for undergraduate degree programs in software engineering. In *Proceedings of ACM/IEEE-CS Joint Task Force on Computing Curricula*. IEEE Computer Society.

Madhavji, N. H., & Miller, J. (2005). Investigation-based Requirements Engineering Education. In *Proceedings of Workshop on Requirements Engineering Education and Training*. Paris: Academic Press.

Melonfire, C. (2007). *Five common errors in requirements analysis (and how to avoid them)*. Retrieved 25th Nov. 2011, from http://www.techrepublic.com/article/five-common-errors-in-requirements-analysis-and-how-to-avoid-them/6146544

Memon, R. N., Ahmad, R., & Salim, S. S. (2010). Problems in requirements engineering education: a survey. In *Proceedings of FIT '10*. FIT.

Memon, R. N., Salim, S. S., & Ahmad, R. (2013). *Analysis and classification of problems associated with requirements engineering education: Towards an integrated view*. Arabian Journal for Science and Engineering.

Mohan, & Chenoweth. (2011). Teaching requirements engineering to undergraduate students. In *Proceedings of the 42nd ACM Technical Symposium on Computer Science Education*. Dallas, TX: ACM.

Nguyen, L., Armarego, J., & Swatman, P. (2002). Understanding Requirements Engineering: a Challenge for Practice and Education. *School Working Papers Series 2002*.

Regev, G., Gause, D. C., & Wegmann, A. (2009). Experiential learning approach for requirements engineering education. *Requirements Engineering*, *14*(4), 269–287. doi:10.1007/s00766-009-0084-x

Robertson, S., & Robertson, J. (1999). *Mastering the requirements process*. ACM Press.

Rosca, D. (2000). An active/collaborative approach in teaching requirementsengineering. In Proceedings of 30th Annual Frontiers in Education. doi: doi:10.1109/FIE.2000.897606

Scheinholtz, L. A. (2007). What Are Employers Really Looking For? In *Proceedings of Requirements Engineering Education and Training*. Academic Press.

SEI. (1991). Software Engineering Institute Requirements Engineering Project. In *Proceedings of Requirements Engineering and Analysis Workshop*. Carnegie Mellon University.

Smith, R., & Gotel, O. (2007). RE-O-POLY: A Game to Introduce Lightweight Requirements Engineering Good Practices. In *Proceedings of International Workshop on Requirements Engineering and Training*. India Habitat Center.

Svahnberg, M., & Gorschek, T. (2005). Multiperspective Requirements Engineering Education with focus on Industry Relevance. In *Proceedings of the Workshop on Requirements Engineering Education & Training*. Paris: Academic Press.

Thayer, R. H., Bailin, S. C., & Dorfman, M. (1997). *Software Requirements Engineerings*. IEEE Computer Society Press.

UTS. (2011, May). Retrieved from http://www.handbook.uts.edu.au/subjects/32550.html

Wahono, R. S. (2003). Analyzing requirements engineering problems. In *Proceedings of IECI Japan Workshop*. IECI.

Wohlin, C., & Regnell, B. (1999). Achieving industrial relevance in software engineering education. In *Proceedings of 12th Conference on Software Engineering Education and Training*. New Orleans, LA: Academic Press.

Yusop, N., Mehboob, Z., & Zowghi, D. (2007). The Role of Conducting Stakeholder Meetings in Requirements Engineering Training. In *Proceedings of Requirements Engineering Education & Training*. Academic Press.

Zowghi, D. (2009). Teaching Requirements Engineering to the Baháí Students in Iran who are Denied of Higher Education. In *Proceedings of Fourth International Workshop on Requirements Engineering Education and Training* (REET). IEEE Computer Society.

ADDITIONAL READING

Al-Rawas, A., & Easterbrook, S. (1996). *Communication problems in requirements engineering: a field study*. Cognitive science research paper-University of Sussex Csrp.

Ali, M. R. (2006). Imparting effective software engineering education. *ACM SIGSOFT Software Engineering Notes*, *31*(4), 3. doi:10.1145/1142958.1142960

Armarego, J., & Minor, O. (2005). Studio Learning of Requirements: towards aligning teaching to practitioner needs. *In Proceedings of International workshop on Requirements Engineering Education & Training*, Paris.

Auriol, G., Baron, C., & Fourniols, J. Y. (2008). Teaching requirements skills within the context of a physical engineering project. *In Proceedings of Requirements Engineering Education and Training, 2008. REET, 08*, 6–11.

Bagert, D. J. (1998). A model for the software engineering component of a computer science curriculum. *Information and Software Technology, 40*(4), 195–201. doi:10.1016/S0950-5849(98)00039-1

Bernhart, M., Grechenig, T., Hetzl, J., & Zuser, W. (2006). Dimensions of software engineering course design. *In Proceedings of the 28th International Conference on Software Engineering,* New York, NY, USA, 667- 672.

Cheng, B. H. C., & Atlee, J. M. (2007). Research directions in requirements engineering. *In Proceedings of Future of Software Engineering (FOSE'07).* Pages 285-303

Dawson, R. (2000). Twenty dirty tricks to train software engineers. In *Proceedings of the 22nd international conference on Software engineering,* New York, NY, USA.

Dick, M., Postema, M., & Miller, J. (2001). Improving student performance in software engineering practice. *In Proceedings of International Conference on Software Engineering Education and Training (CSEE&T'01),* Charlotte, NC USA.

Faulk, S. R. (2000). Achieving industrial relevance with academic excellence: lessons from the Oregon Master of Software engineering. *In Proceedings of 22nd International Conference on Software Engineering,* New York, NY, USA, 293-302.

Fernandes, J. M., Machado, R. J., & Seidman, S. B. (2009). A Requirements Engineering and Management Training Course for Software Development Professionals. *In Proceedings of 22nd Conference on Software Engineering Education and Training (CSEET '09),* Hyderabad, Andhra Pradesh, 20-25.

Ford, G. (1990). 1990 SEI Report on Undergraduate Software Engineering Education: Technical Report SEI-90-TR-3, *Software Engineering Institute,* Carnegie Mellon University, Pittsburgh, Pennsylvania.

Ghezzi, C., & Mandrioli, D. (2006). The challenges of software engineering education. *Software Engineering Education in the Modern age. Lecture Notes in Computer Science, 4309,* 115–127. doi:10.1007/11949374_8

Hilburn, T. B., Hislop, G., Bagert, D. J., Lutz, M., Mengel, S., & McCracken, M. (1999). Guidance for the development of software engineering education programs. *Journal of Systems and Software, 49*(2-3), 163–169. doi:10.1016/S0164-1212(99)00092-8

IEEE Computer Society Washington, DC, USA Curran, W. S. (2003). Teaching software engineering in the computer science curriculum. *ACM SIGCSE Bulletin, 35*(4), 75.

Karunasekera, S., & Bedse, K. (2007). Preparing software engineering graduates for an industry career. In *Proceedings of the 20th Conference on Software Engineering Education & Training, 97*(106), 3-5. doi:10.1109/CSEET.2007.39

Maidantchik, C., Montoni, M., & Santos, G. (2002). Learning organizational knowledge: an evolutionary proposal for requirements engineering. *In Proceedings of the 14th international conference on Software engineering and knowledge engineering (SEKE '02),* New York, NY, USA, 151-157.

Memon, R. N., Salim, S. S., & Ahmad, R. (2012). Identifying Research Gaps in Requirements Engineering Education: An Analysis of a Conceptual Model and Survey Results. *In Proceedings of the IEEE Conference on Open Systems 2012,* Kuala Lumpur, Malaysia.

Minor, O., & Armarego, J. (2005). Requirements Engineering: a Close Look at Industry Needs and Model Curricula. *Australasian Journal of Information Systems, 13*(1), 192.

Naz, H., & Khokhar, M. N. (2009). Critical Requirements Engineering Issues & their Solution. *In Proceedings of International Conference on Computer Modeling and Simulation (ICCMS'09), 218*(222), 20-22. doi:10.1109/ICCMS.2009.50

Nguyen, L., & Swatman, P. A. (2003). Managing the requirements engineering process. *Requirements Engineering, 8*(1), 55–68. doi:10.1007/s00766-002-0136-y

Pears, A., Seidman, S., Eney, C., Kinnunen, P., & Malmi, L. (2005). Constructing a core literature for computing education research. *ACM SIGCSE Bulletin, 37*(4), 161. doi:10.1145/1113847.1113893

Regev, G., Gause, D. C., & Wegmann, A. (2008). Requirements Engineering Education in the 21st Century, An Experiential Learning Approach. *In Proceedings of 16th IEEE International Requirements Engineering,* Catalunya.

Rogers, D., Stratton, M. J., & King, R. E. (1999). *Manufacturing Education Plan: 1999 Critical Competency Gaps.* Dearborn, Mich.: Society of Manufacturing Engineers.

Schön, D. A. (1987). *Educating the reflective practitioner: Toward a new design for teaching and learning in the professions.* Jossey-Bass San Francisco.

Smith, R. (2009). Gameplay to introduce and reinforce requirements engineering good practices. *PhD Thesis,* Pace University, New York, United States. Retrieved from http://proquest.umi.com/pqdweb?did=1853239111&Fmt=7&clientId=18803&RQT=309&VName=PQD

Stiller, E., & LeBlanc, C. (2002). Effective software engineering pedagogy. *Journal of Computing Sciences in Colleges, 17*(6), 124–134.

Walden, J., & Frank, C. E. (2006). Secure software engineering teaching modules. *In Proceedings of the 3rd annual conference on Information security curriculum development.* pp. 19-23

Welch, H. L. (2007). Teaching a service course in software engineering. In *Proceedings of the 37th annual frontiers in education conference-global engineering: knowledge without borders, opportunities without passports* (FIE'07), *F4B-6*(F4B-11), 10-13. doi:10.1109/FIE.2007.4418062

KEY TERMS AND DEFINITIONS

Requirements Engineering: RE is about capturing the requirements of customers and analysing, modelling and validating those requirements and presenting them in a software requirements specification, which is the final output within the RE process. The software is then developed based on these specified requirements.

Requirements Engineering Education: The education provided to teach students the basic concepts and skills they need to perform requirements engineering, as well as enabling them to practise performing requirements engineering activities while working on real projects.

Requirements Engineering Education Problems: The issues related to requirements engineering curriculum that cause problems for stuents and lecturers in understanding and teaching RE concepts and activitities.

RE Teaching Strategies: The approaches used by educators to deliver for requirements engineering curriculum to students in requirements engineering course.

Software Engineering: The discipline that applies the principles of engineering to design, develop, test, maintain and evaluate the software.

Chapter 3

When the Wisdom of Communication is Vital During the Requirements Elicitation Process:
Lessons Learnt through Industry Experience

Sabrina Ahmad
Universiti Teknikal Malaysia Melaka, Malaysia

Noor Azilah Muda
Universiti Teknikal Malaysia Melaka, Malaysia

Maslita Abd. Aziz
Universiti Teknikal Malaysia Melaka, Malaysia

Emaliana Kasmuri
Universiti Teknikal Malaysia Melaka, Malaysia

ABSTRACT

Requirements elicitation is accepted as one of the most crucial stages in software engineering, as it addresses the critical problem of designing the right software for the stakeholder. It is seldom technical difficulties that cause problems in the process of requirements elicitation but rather human factors, especially communication. This chapter presents the requirements elicitation experience with the industry and the lessons learnt throughout the process. It highlights the requirements elicitation best practices and alternative options during the process. It also discusses the issues concerning communication disparity between the stakeholders, which may affect the software development project as a whole. The outcome of the requirements elicitation process experience is reported and analysed for future improvement.

DOI: 10.4018/978-1-4666-6026-7.ch003

INTRODUCTION

Requirements elicitation is a process to systematically extract and identify the requirements of the system from multiple stakeholders, the system's environment, feasibility studies, market analyses, business plans, analyses of competing products and domain knowledge. Obtaining the right requirements is crucial. This is because the requirements define what the stakeholders needed from it, as well as what the system must do in order to satisfy that need. They are the basis for every project. In addition, requirements that are agreed by the system stakeholders provide the basis for planning the development of a system and its acceptance on completion. The requirements also set the scope of projects, and, hence, are inputs to project planning. In addition, the requirements define what the software should do, and, therefore, affect the time and resources needed to develop the software. With such a responsibility, it is important to conduct proper requirements elicitation best practice for the sake of a successful software development project.

The process of requirements elicitation is never straight forward. It is ideal if the stakeholder is able to comply with the system analyst's query with one absolute answer. It is excellent if all requirements can be retrieved through a one-time effort using one technique, and, it is helpful if all the needed artefacts are complete and available for reference. The 'if' is impossible in most cases, and, therefore, requirements engineering (RE) best practice is crucial to ensure the continuity of the software development life cycle and to produce a quality product.

The main focus of this chapter is the experience sharing during the requirements elicitation process with industry. It highlights the obstacles faced during the process and the action path deployed to either rectify the situation or otherwise minimize the impact on the project. The central issue of the requirements elicitation dilemma forwarded in this chapter is communication. Based on the experience with industry, communication happens to be the most critical factor in the success or failure of the process and software development project as a whole. It is also a medium to gain trust and to establish a long-term relationship with the stakeholders. In addition, RE best practices are presented in line with the discussion rose from the industry experience.

The RE process is both important and crucial to the software development project. It moulds the shape of the entire project, determines the path it will follow through and influence the value of the end product. Human factors play a vital role in ensuring the success of the RE process in which the art of communication is the central point. Effective communication links all the necessary knowledge from the different sources and unfolds untold information to be utilized for the sake of the software project.

REQUIREMENTS ENGINEERING BEST PRACTICES

The focus of this chapter is the beginning stage of RE, which specifically looks at the requirements elicitation practice. However, an overview of RE is presented in this sub-section to provide a complete picture of where requirements elicitation fits in.

RE is the process of discovering, documenting and managing the requirements for a computer-based system. Common RE activities (Mulla and Girase, 2012) include elicitation, interpretation and structuring (analysis and documentation), negotiation, verification and validation, change management and requirements tracing. Alternatively, it is stated that there are only four generic, high level RE process activities (Sommerville, 2004). These are a system feasibility study, the requirements elicitation and analysis, requirements specification and requirements validation. In addition, requirements management is introduced to manage requirements change. A feasibility study is a focused study that recommends whether or not it is worth carrying on with the RE process. If the feasibility study approves the continuation of the system development, the requirements elicitation and analysis process is used to identify the application domain, what services the system should provide, the required performance of the system and the system constraints. Then, the requirements will be further detailed and documented in the requirements specification process. Subsequently, requirements will be validated. The validation concerns the ability of the requirements statements to actually define the system to be in line with the stakeholder's wants. The reason for this is that a change to the requirements usually means that the system design and implementation must also be changed and that the system must be re-tested. In addition, the requirements for large software systems are always changing due to the diverse user community, the changes in the business, technical environment and the potential conflicts between the end users and stakeholders. Thus, requirements management is needed to understand and to control the changes to the system requirements.

Requirements and Quality

Boehm pioneered the field of software engineering economics saying "the cost of repairing defects rises exponentially the later they are found in the software life cycle" (Boehm, 1981). He found that the cost of fixing errors increased exponentially the later the errors were detected in the development life cycle because the artefacts within a serial process are built upon each other. Also, the average cost increases exponentially after the defects are detected because the development continues upon an unstable foundation. This means that there is a possibility that the software being developed has been based on either unwanted or wrong requirements. The requirements provided by the

stakeholders are usually not the real requirements. Additional analysis is required to determine the real needs and expectations of the stakeholders. This is because the stakeholders vary widely in their understanding of fundamental business process and their ability to explain the requirements. In addition, stakeholders usually describe the requirements with the implicit knowledge of their own work, which might lead to unrevealed important information.

The consequences of having low quality requirements are many and varied. There is ample evidence around us of systems that failed because the requirements were not properly organized. A workable and fully functional system might be abandoned and useless if it is not the system that users want or need. In terms of requirements, quality usually refers to conformance to the user needs and expectations or "fitness for purpose". The requirements are of good quality if they satisfy the stakeholders and in doing so ensure that the needs of all the stakeholders are taken into account.

The Attitude Towards RE

The RE process is usually neglected and attributed as not being important by the software development team. Even though the failure to get the requirements right costs a lot, there are projects that still skip RE entirely and call their 'wise guess' of stakeholders needs, requirements. Several others call their initial design a requirement specification. In general, many projects do several simple things to handle requirements. They have a list of requirements in databases for easy cross referencing, they develop a prototype based on high level requirements plus their assumptions, they handle conflicts when they occur, and they ask the stakeholders questions from time to time when they need more information. Based on such an unstructured process or no process at all, it is common for projects to be delayed or incur additional cost.

The RE Process

The statement that there is 'No Silver Bullet' in software engineering is also valid in RE. This is due to the nature of the discipline, which is flexible and influenced by people. There is no single process that is right for all organizations or works well for all types of software projects. Each organization must develop its own process that is appropriate for the type of system it develops, its organizational culture, and the ability of the people involved in the RE process. However, very few organizations have an explicitly-defined and standardized RE process. Usually the people involved in the process decide what to do and when to do it, what information they need, and what tools they should use. It is believed that such an immature situation can be improved over time and by the organization paying more attention to RE, as the criticality of requirements is obvious.

A process is important because it defines the activities, and, ultimately, documents the outputs obtained. It basically gives an overview on what needs to be done, when it takes place, how it happens and who is responsible. Time and cost can be saved by reusing the same process when the same things need to be repeated in other projects in the future. In addition, through having a defined and documented process there is the opportunity for continuous improvement. The users of any process are likely to have some ideas and suggestions about the current process to make it even better.

Fundamentally, the requirements process should address the common activities:

- **Identifying Business and Stakeholders' Needs:** This activity involves understanding the business objectives and how a particular software project fits in. A key factor in the success of the system to be developed is the degree to which it supports the business requirements and assists the organization to achieve them. The stake-

holders' needs should include all the key stakeholders concerns to represent various perspectives of the organization. It should also describe both functional and non-functional requirements.

- **Analysing and Defining the Requirements:** The high level requirements need to be analysed and carefully defined as different stakeholders might describe the same thing in a different way or different things in the same way. It is important to remove conflicts and to state the requirements in a way that enables all the key stakeholders to understand the same thing.

- **Specifying the Requirements Statements:** The high level requirements are defined in precise detail and stated clearly in the specification document.

- **Prioritizing Requirements:** Prioritization is important due to the resource constraints. There is the possibility that not all the stated requirements can be fulfilled due to the limited time schedule and cost. In addition, not all requirements are of equal importance; some are essential and a must for the system, some are important to complete the system, some are nice to have and some requirements are additional features that can wait for the next version. Prioritization gives the opportunity to address the highest priority first, and the possibility of providing a later release of the product to address the lower priority needs.

- **Tracking and managing requirements:** Software projects need the ability to undertake the traceability of the requirements to the other artefacts of the project. This is important to locate where in the system each requirement is addressed and satisfied.

- **Verifying and validating requirements:** The most important part of all is the verification and validation of the requirements. This is to ensure that the system developed is in accordance with the stated requirements specification and the system delivered meets the stakeholders' expectations.

Referring to the above stated RE activities, it is obvious that almost all the activities need the ability for strong communication in order to grasp the essence of the requirements. For instance, in order to understand the needs of the business and stakeholders, the right questions need to be asked to the right stakeholders. How does requirements elicitation produce fruitful results if not by appropriate communication skills? The communication during requirements elicitation is not merely talking to each other but beyond that, all parties need to cooperate among themselves to contribute significant knowledge for the purpose of achieving successful system development. In the discipline of software engineering, the use of documents and models is a common communication mechanism to encourage understanding between all parties (Hickey and Davis, 2004). In relation to that, the statements from the various stakeholders may differ from each other. This is due to the individual perceptions and perspectives, which need to be resolved during the process. Again, the wisdom of communication is vital to obtain and to confirm the accuracy of the statements of requirements. The next section explains the role of communication and why it is important during the requirements elicitation process.

THE ROLE OF COMMUNICATION

Requirements elicitation is a process to extract and gather information about the stakeholders' needs and propose a new system. The important factor that determines the success of this process is the communication skills possessed by the stakeholder and the developer. Thus, communication plays an important role at the beginning of the software development process.

The success of requirements elicitation is very much dependent on effective communication between the developer and the stakeholder (Davis et al., 2006b). It is a process of information movement from the stakeholder to the developer and verified by the developer to the stakeholder. The information flows have to be agreed between two parties. The degree of acceptance by both parties is dependent on their understanding and perception, as well as the assumptions made by both. The ultimate success of requirements elicitation is when the requirement meets the stakeholders' needs (Coughlan and Macredie, 2002). However, this is very challenging due to the many factors that contribute to the success or failure of communication between these two parties. Among the commonly identified factors, are when the stakeholder has difficulty in stating their needs for the system, which results in misinterpretation by the developer or the perception that the stakeholder is inconsistent.

Many researchers have found that failure to communicate the requirements effectively is one of the common problems, which leads to poor software requirements (Mohd Zin and Che Pa, 2009). The effect of poor software requirements will result in revisiting the software requirements and design, budget overrun, untimely deliverables, poor quality of the system, dissatisfied stakeholders and project failure.

Types of Communication

The stakeholder and the developer communicate in various ways depending upon the message and the context. The choice of the type of communication affects the effectiveness of the communication. Two common communication techniques are used in the requirements elicitation process – verbal and non-verbal (Muqeem and Beg, 2012) – and an effective communication session is when both parties are able to understand and interpret both.

Verbal communication is the most chosen technique to capture the requirements from the stakeholder. Verbal communication consists of oral communication and written communication. The most common approach for verbal communication is face-to-face conversation. Usually the developer will hold a face-to-face meeting session after the project has kicked-off. The face-to-face meeting could be done in a room where the stakeholder and developer gather and sit in a common place. However, if the stakeholders are geographically dispersed, technology, such as telephone or video conferencing, can be used. The main success factor of verbal communication is the choice of the spoken language. The conversation should use a language that is understood by most of the members participating in the meeting. In the event that any of the members cannot understand, an interpreter is needed to correctly translate the message in the context of the discussion. Other than that, the success of verbal communication is factored from the fluency of the speaker, the choice of words, the volume and the pitch. Oral communication is the quickest way to receive feedback (Che Pa and Mohd Zin, 2011).

Written communication consists of either the stakeholder or developer expressing the content that needs be conveyed using characters and symbols. Written messages can be transmitted via emails, reports, memos or letters. The factors that contribute to the success of written communication are the clarity of the content using the correct terms, selection of vocabulary and usage of grammar.

Non-verbal communication is using wordless messages. This technique uses body language, gestures, posture and facial expressions to convey the message, which help in gaining a clearer understanding of the requirements (Che Pa and Mohd Zin, 2011). Non-verbal communication complements verbal communication.

The style of the communication depends on the formality chosen for the verbal communication (Mohd Zin and Che Pa, 2009). The styles include both formal and informal. Formal communication consists of certain rules and ethics, which need to be adhered to by all team members, and is set in a professional and official environment. In contrast, an informal style is conducted in a more social and relaxed environment that helps the bonding between the stakeholder and the developer.

Communication Challenges in Requirements Elicitation

The communication challenges differ from one project to another even for similar projects. (Che Pa and Mohd Zin, 2011) identified five communication challenges, as shown in Figure 1. However, this section will only address two with regard to the communication aspect; that is, communication skill and medium of communication.

In any part of the requirements elicitation process, it is acknowledged by many researchers that communication skills play a vital role in ensuring the success of the process and compliance of the proposed system to the user requirements. The delivery of information from both parties might not be organized due to the weakness in communication skills. There are underlying challenges in each process of RE. The ability of the developers to understand the business and stakeholders' needs is crucial because this stage will shape the requirement landscape of the project. The developers might start with document analysis, followed by numerous interviews with the stakeholders. Although it is very helpful if the developer is provided with a complete document about the organization's business process and stakeholders' concerns, this seldom happens. The business processes of organizations are complex and difficult to understand. Therefore, many developers opt for interviews or meetings to clarify their understanding. However, this process becomes more challenging when there are many discrepancies between the actual and the documented process, the incorrect appointment of stakeholders and owners of the business process due to the organiza-

Figure 1. Communication challenges
(Taken from Che Pa and Mohd Zin, 2011)

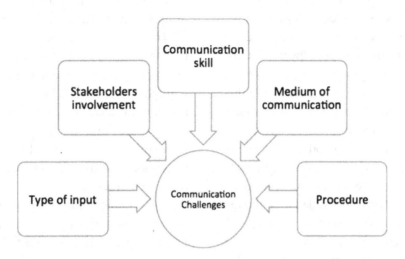

tional political issues, uncommitted stakeholders, stakeholders are not clear about the position of the project with organizational needs and a conflict of concerns among the stakeholders for shared processes. When such challenges arise, many techniques are used to clear the ambiguity, such as diagrams, flowcharts, process walkthrough, observation and workshops, in an effort to obtain the real requirements. Intellectual assumptions are used by the developers for irresolvable conflicts of requirements and stakeholders' concerns, which can be derived from the project's requirement database. Thoughts and ideas might not be properly articulated and sorted because of weak verbal, presentation, logic or written skills. The developer finds it difficult to understand their needs when there is an inherent weakness in the information delivery. Thus, information is not consistent. Ambiguity is one of the major factors that affect the quality of the requirement. This has to be solved by both sides. The developer has to highlight to the stakeholder the ambiguousness of the information while the stakeholder should be instructive to clear any ambiguity.

The developers have a tendency to write specification documents using technical language, which

the stakeholders find very intimidating. Apart from the incorrect choice of words, the stakeholders are not able to map the requirements to the business process due to the proposed changes. Even though screen prototypes are introduced to the stakeholder, they might be distracted by the new look of the system, which they feel does not represent their business process. The model should provide a seamless transition from the business process to the screen prototype so that the stakeholder can easily map it. This is due to the weakness of the design chosen by the developer to communicate the requirements.

The architecture and software design are concluded separately before the requirements are obtained. As a result, the developer fails to explain and convince the stakeholders that all the requirements have different priority due to various constraints because from the stakeholder's viewpoint all the requirements are equally important and must be delivered.

The selection of medium for communication is important for ensuring the effectiveness of the communication process in requirements elicitation. The medium of communication is used as a platform to exchange information either in oral or written form. The criticality of these challenges lies in the usage of the platform and the stakeholders' responsiveness. Some technology does not work well due to the culture of the organization of the stakeholders or developers, the trend of the technology and user exposure to the technology, which contributes to the late response from either the developer to the stakeholder or vice versa. Information communicated via an electronic platform is not accessible to both parties due to file corruption or access rights not being given to them. Information retrieved is sometimes through an informal session and unrecorded even though it is considered as highly important. Dealing with a change in management leads to information inconsistency due to the various concerns that have to be addressed by the developer.

Determinants of Successful Communication for Requirements Elicitation

The success of a software project is determined by the system complying with the user requirements. This shows that requirements elicitation is a very crucial process. The success of requirements elicitation is attributed to effective communication between the stakeholder and the developer (Davis et al., 2006a).

The communication process includes cognitive aspects, personalities, techniques and tools (Coughlan and Macredie, 2002). These are four essential elements for successful communication. The cognitive aspect is the understanding of the problem and the domain knowledge for the existing and the proposed system. This includes the underlying business process, constraints of the current system that hinder the efficiency of the organization, user expectations of the proposed system and the terminology used by the users to describe the system. These constitute the information that needs to be conveyed from the stakeholder to the developer or extracted by the developer from the stakeholder. A common understanding must

be established between the stakeholder and the developer so that they are able to communicate using the same language.

The term 'personalities' refers to the interpersonal skills, culture, experience and values owned by the stakeholder and the developer (Coughlan and Macredie, 2002). The ability to provide complete and unambiguous information helps to accelerate the process of requirements elicitation. The selection of the communication technique influences the choice of tools that are made to extract, record and gather the information. The choice of techniques and tools is very dependent on the type of project, developer familiarity and user comfort. Communication should happen both ways for the stakeholder and the developer.

REQUIREMENTS ELICITATION PROCESS: THE EXPERIENCE

Introduction

In this work, the requirements elicitation process is between the Government Agencies and the Consultant Team that are responsible for handling the software requirement before the development phase starts. RE is part of the Software Engineering domain that provides solutions to deal with the stakeholders' requirements through software development. RE, as defined by the IEEE Standard Glossary of Software Engineering Technology (IEEE, 1990), is a potential or a stipulation of a solution needed by a user to solve a problem or achieve an objective. The potential or the stipulation of a solution is needed or possessed by a system or a system component to satisfy formal documents or contracts or standards or specifications established earlier when the RE process begins.

RE considers important aspects, such as the sources of the software requirements and the techniques used to gather the requirements. This is important as it is the beginning or the first step in developing a mutual understanding between stakeholders (in our case the government agencies) and the developer (the consultant team) of the software problem that requires a solution. RE is a human activity in which stakeholders are identified and the relationship between the stakeholder and the development team is established. It is necessary to have good communication terms between both parties – the software users and the software engineers – in practicing good software requirement. The requirements specialist (the consultant team) acts as a mediator between the software users (or stakeholders) and the developer (software engineer) to ensure that both the users and the developers understand the needs from both sides.

The common methods or techniques commonly applied by the requirements specialist in the RE process are interviews, document analysis, prototyping and many others. In this work, the consultant team acts as the requirements specialist using methods, such as interviews, to interview the software users to obtain detailed requirements of the software needed. The team also uses the document analysis method to obtain information from the documents prepared previously. The document could be the previous user manuals, system requirement specification (SRS) or the rules and guidelines the company has set up regarding the software development process. Details of the activities or techniques for requirements elicitation are explained in the following part.

Techniques of Requirements Elicitation Applied

The main difficulty in requirements elicitation is how to efficiently gather requirements that accurately embody what the user desires (Tiwari et al., 2012). It is challenging to collect the requirements from the owner of the system rather than the end user as the user might only understand the process

and not the problems contributed from the process (Chang et al., 2009).

This work examines three agencies that provide services to the public: (i) agency that deals with housing development (agency A); (ii) agency that deals with land management (agency B) and; (iii) agency that deals with business establishment (agency C).

Interviews

The usual method is via interviews (Lauesen, 2002), and the most important aspect is to correctly identify the stakeholder (Pacheco and Garcia, 2012). The stakeholder refers to anyone who has a direct or indirect influence on the system, the end user and anyone who will be affected by the change (Sommerville, 2011). A mixture of stakeholders is involved in completing the requirements elicitation including the section leader, unit leader and operators. This arrangement of diverse background is important for the outcome but may be hindered by inappropriate personnel (Coughlan et al., 2003). This was true when identifying requirements with agency C, which was dominated by the unit leader.

Nevertheless, the requirements elicitation omits the participation of the end user, which affects the analysis of requirements. This is because the requirements from the service owner who provides the service are different from the requirements of the end user who uses the service. Therefore, it is important to interview a mixture of shareholders as it will contribute to strengthening the requirements elicitation (Mishra et al., 2008).

The common types of interview are closed and open interviews (Robertson and Robertson, 1999). This study gives greater preference to open interviews as all the agencies have an in-house system and are familiar with the concept of automated service. Furthermore, the questions asked are a mix of structured and unstructured questions.

Document Analysis

In order to understand the business process beforehand, the team studied the SRS of the current system. To further comprehend the process, guidelines for the end users were also studied. The team was also given the user manual of the current system and were permitted to interact with the current system.

Prototyping

Interfaces

The user interface design has to be clear, easy to understand as well as easy to use (Galitz, 2007), especially for the end users who are generally the public who have a different level of computer literacy. The general rules of building the interfaces are agreed as the project integrates diverse services oriented to the government agencies as well as statutory bodies (refer Figure 2). The rules are simplified into four basic guidelines that are based on how the end users perceive, think, learn

and act (Shneiderman et al., 2009). Firstly, the user interface design is more towards a conversation rather than an interrogation as most of the information asked requires the end users to provide honest and valid information. This is because it is hard to validate the accuracy of some of the information unless it is given by the end users. Therefore, the labelling or wording used is subtle and relaxed.

Secondly, the order of the labels is arranged logically so that the user can subconsciously anticipate what is required next. Furthermore, where possible, the arrangement of labels is mapped similar to the previous forms the users are familiar with. This is because the user perception is influenced by their previous experience of dealing with the agencies and the context or aim of what service they require.

Thirdly, related information is grouped together so that the end users are more focussed on completing the task at hand. Therefore, white spaces and indentations are used to indicate the relationship of the labels to prevent the user second guessing what they should do (Krug, 2005). For example, the

Figure 2. Example of the interface design

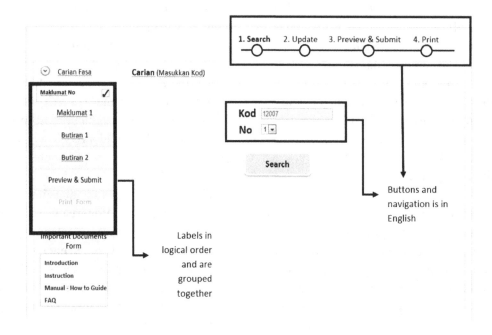

postal address constitutes information breakdowns to make it a full address, therefore the postcode, city, town and state are indented after the postal address label.

Lastly, the default buttons and navigation are written in English. Although the national language is Malay, it is appropriate for certain terms to be written in English, especially in computer terminology. This is to avoid confusion, because if the terms are translated into Malay there would be a lot of variation that would lead to misinterpretation.

Wireframe

Wireframe is an important stage to screen design, which is useful to attract the attention of users when interacting with the interface (Shneiderman et al., 2009). Conveying the design layout via wireframe is practical as it allows the designer to visualize the idea rather than describe it. The layout and interaction is interrelated and easily understood and independent of colour or font because what needs to stand out should be obvious for the user to identify. Nevertheless for this experience, a few of the stakeholders insist on a coloured wireframe in order for them to appreciate the layout design. The layout of the wireframe is divided into (i) Step Navigation; (ii) Left bar Navigation; (iii) Labels and Fields; (iv) Buttons; and (v) For Reference.

The first item in the layout is the step navigation, which is located at the top right of the interface to allow the user to move sequentially through the processes or pages, as shown in Figure 3. The general title for each agency is selected to indicate each main process as the navigation points and numbered accordingly. In order to emphasise the current process, the title is bolded with shadow text and the colour red is used to capture the user's attention. A filled red circle is used to show the previous process that the user has done but not necessarily completed. The print process is optional based on the agency's policy in allowing the form to be printed or not.

Figure 3. Step navigation

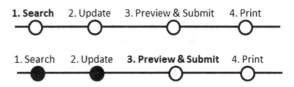

The second item in the layout is the left bar navigation, which explains the details of the activities of the step navigation, as shown in Figure 4. The left bar navigation consists of a combination of sections and buttons for current activity, next activity, preview and print, send online and important documents. The section indicating current activity is in white with a special icon. Each section is divided into other subtitles and the right or correct icon to represent the completed activity while the in progress subtitle is bolded and in orange. To distinguish the difference between the current and next activity, the background of the section is in grey. The listed sections are not interrelated as the user can choose which section to proceed with first; as if the section is incomplete the right or correct icon will appear. Nevertheless, if the process requires all the sections to be completed, the title will be grey and non-clickable, such as submission of the form (send online).

The third item in the layout is the labels and fields, as shown in Figure 5. The labels are left aligned, especially for long sentences or complex forms while for short sentences right aligned is used. The labels should maintain the usage of sentence case and a colon is inserted at the end of each label. The length of each input field must match the expected input so that no input is hidden from the user's view. The tool tip is located for further explanation where necessary. A red asterisk is a well-known indicator for the required fields but the explanation of the red asterisk is also provided in plain or simple explanation.

The fourth item in the layout comprises the buttons (as shown in Figure 6); where the system needs the user to proceed to the next page the but-

Figure 4. Left bar navigation

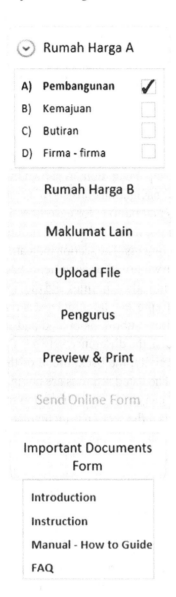

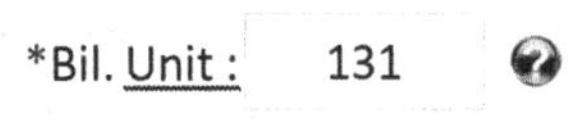

Figure 6. Buttons

ton is labelled as Save and Next. This is to ensure that the information has been saved and that the user can continue to the next process. The buttons are aligned to the left-hand end of the text boxes to show uniformity and consistency.

The last item in the layout is the reference or summary section, as shown in Figure 7. The reference section is placed at the top right under the step navigation and is produced where necessary. It is a prefilled text and the displayed information is extracted from the user input so that as the user keeps on inserting the needed information, the summary of the input is shown. It is easier for the user to keep track of what has been inserted as each user has multiple projects to be updated into the system. For example a user can handle more than one housing project and each development

Figure 7. Reference section

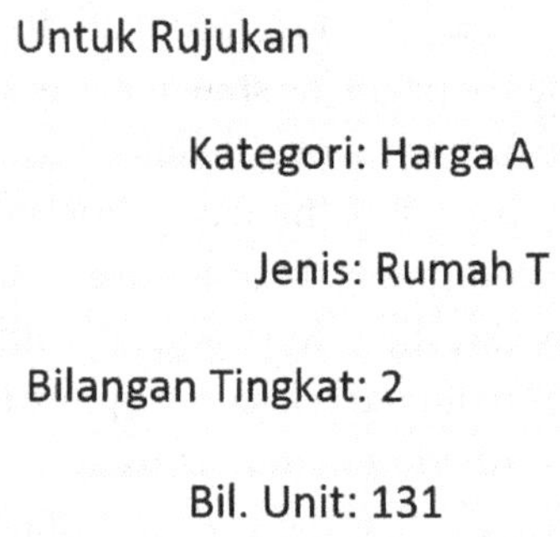

Untuk Rujukan

Kategori: Harga A

Jenis: Rumah T

Bilangan Tingkat: 2

Bil. Unit: 131

Figure 5. Labels and fields

*Bil. <u>Unit :</u>   131   ❷

must be recorded in the system. Nevertheless, the section could cause difficulties for modern screen readers and fail in the usability and accessibility test. This is because WCAG 2.0 suggested that the prefilled text input should be removed (W3C, 2008).

Communication Activities

The communication activities in requirements elicitation depend very much on the degree, structure and quality of communication between the developers and stakeholders (Coughlan and Macredie, 2002). The degree of the communications is related to the level of users' involvement in the process of eliciting the requirements. The structure of the communications provides a baseline of outcomes expected from the process while the quality of the activities measures the positive outputs gained from the process. The participation of users and stakeholders in the development process is very important as it reliably determines the success of the requirements elicitation process, which needs a shared understanding through cooperation and negotiation between both parties (Hartwick and Barki, 2001). The work follows the suggested communication activities. In addition to the three communication activities, each decision made in each meeting was formally documented and reviewed by the agencies.

- **Knowledge Acquisition:** The first communication activity in requirements elicitation is to acquire knowledge. Usually, a relationship is established between the stakeholder and the developer to achieve a shared understanding or common overview of the needed application. In this work, workshops were held for the purpose of knowledge acquisition. The series of sessions were divided into two parts starting with (i) the interpretation from the developer, followed by (ii) the clarification from the agency. The information gathering was initiated by the developer because the team constructed the preliminary understanding through the existing automated system, and, later, the agency could clarify or highlight what needed to be corrected or added. The developer then prepared the requirements document, which was submitted to the stakeholders for approval.

- **Knowledge Negotiation:** The second communication activity is knowledge negotiation. The negotiations are necessary to define the requirements gathered to achieve a mutual understanding between the stakeholder and the developer in terms of the scope and capabilities of the future system. In this work, negotiations occurred to ensure that all the requirements documented were finalized and completed before the development phase started. The negotiations were crucial because the project required integration and sharing of data between agencies. The negotiations ended up with Agency A and B being willing to proceed with the idea while Agency C set a few restrictions.

- **Stakeholder Acceptance:** The third communication activity is to seal an agreement concerning the agreed requirements statements. This occurs when both parties achieve a mutual understanding concerning the scope of the project and the impact of the application to be developed on the organization. In this work, a review session using the walkthrough method was conducted. An immediate acceptance or acceptance with amendment was expected at the end of the review. The review sessions witnessed immediate acceptance with one agency and acceptance with minor amendment with another agency. However, there was one agency which kept postponing the agreement. Once finalized and accepted, the developer started the development work.

The success of the communication activities can simply be measured by looking at the levels of acceptance from the stakeholders' viewpoint once the process has gone through the three communication activities. However, a number of pitfalls occurred while trying to apply effective communications to achieve consensus between the stakeholders and the developer. The main pitfall identified in the process is discussed in the communication issues section.

Communication Issues

The communication issues in requirements elicitation are the challenges that should be seriously looked into. It has been stated (Che Pa and Mohd Zin, 2011) that the communication challenges can be categorized under five issues – the type of input, personalities involved, communication skills, medium of communication and procedures. The problems relating to type of input might be caused by the ambiguity of information delivered with the scope and the requirement of the information being frequently changed. While the problem of information is ambiguous and changing, the person involved also contributes to the problem, as some of the information delivered and received might be beyond their field of expertise. Without adequate expertise, the person responsible to deliver the information will lack focus and work without enough concentration. This will then cause the developer to assume the information received is not consistent and ambiguous, and definitely not enough to proceed to the next level of work.

The medium used to deliver the information can also contribute to the problem. The often used mediums in the process are telephones, emails, face-to-face appointments and meetings. Problems like misinterpretation of the information, late response, not enough information and not consistent are the common problems that occur relating to the medium used. The procedures established to deal with the changing information or inconsistent

information delivered also play a major role in the process. Changes in the requirements or scope of the software developed are common issues in the requirement engineering field. These frequent changes can also affect the information delivered, which later exacerbate the problems.

Based on our experience, explained below are the issues that occurred and how we handled the situation. For the purpose of explanation, the issues are explained according to five categories:

1. **Type of Input:** The information given was sometimes ambiguous, confusing, redundant, and changed inconsistently. Sometimes, it even introduced new information and caused a change in the project scope. During the sessions with the stakeholders, the information given kept on changing and became even more frustrating when different sessions were attended by different individuals. This was especially true with Agency C. Although they came from the same department and have a similar job scope, the input delivered was not the same, and the information was often ambiguous. The inconsistencies also created confusion and problems to the developer, which later prolonged the process. In order to handle the changes, the developer requested to meet the same stakeholders in each session to avoid conflicting information being delivered. It was also requested that the input must be approved by the head of department.

2. **Personalities Involved:** The stakeholder responsible for delivering the information and the developer who received the information were not always in the 'same boat'. This usually led to a lack of cooperation, lack of participation and commitment. They also became less tolerant and lacked the ability to handle conflicts. In order to reduce the risk of personality issues, the developer summarized all the information gathered

throughout the sessions in the form of a short presentation before the session ended. The short presentation was presented to the stakeholders with the purpose being to confirm the information, and, if possible, to achieve a mutual understanding.

3. **Communication Skills:** A lack of communication skills leads to the inability to deliver information proactively and instructively. It may also cause a problem for both parties to understand the same thing when presenting the information gathered. In this work, communication materials, such as documents and presentation slides, were used to assist the stakeholders to understand the requirement statements. In addition, wireframe, graphics and an interface prototype were also utilized to enhance the communication ability. In addition, in an effort to avoid a breakdown in communications, the developer used layman terms throughout the sessions with the stakeholders.

4. **Medium of Communication:** The main medium of communication was face-to-face meetings. Emails and phone calls were also adopted as alternative communication channels. Problems like late response to emails; technical errors, such as unable to access the attached files via email; misinterpretation of the information; inconsistent information and also unrecorded information contributed to the problems. In order to handle these problems, the coordinator of the project sent out frequent reminders to both the developers and the stakeholders to respond and give feedback through email as soon as possible to resolve the dispute. Sometimes phone calls were the best means of providing an immediate response if there were urgent matters that needed attention from both parties.

5. **Procedures:** One of the weaknesses during the process was the absence of a requirements change procedure. It was even more

difficult when the stakeholders claimed that they were not making any changes but only stated the right requirements statements. The boundary of the two processes – elicitation and conformance – were not clear, especially with Agency C when they refused to sign off on an agreement even after they agreed with the requirements statements during the exit review. The situation caused the requirements elicitation process works to come to a halt without being able to move forward.

The communication challenges need to be handled appropriately as they contribute to the failure of the requirements elicitation process. This is very important to ensure the success of the entire software development life cycle. The next section highlights the success story.

Requirements Elicitation Success Story

The success of requirements elicitation for agency A and B is mainly because the initial objectives were agreed and understood by all the stakeholders. The initial objectives were integrating the individual system from each agency into the national level portal so that most of the data could be shared among the agencies. Meanwhile, agency C is very peculiar in respect of data sharing as it deals with policies or Acts of Law. In addition, C claimed that the data ownership is legally theirs. The selection of the stakeholders is also one of the contributions to the success of the requirements elicitation. The stakeholders from A and B comprise the people who handle the process on a daily basis, meaning that they really understand what needs to be highlighted when the process is translated into a system. In contrast, C prefers to work in a large team and the final say is generally from the leader or the key person. In theory, a large team should provide a better understanding of the requirements; however, the key person controlled the situation and made the others under her to keep quiet. The requirements elicitation was also delayed whenever the key person was absent or late even though the daily operations were being done by others.

The experience shows that when the stakeholder understands the system they will support their operation in a systematic manner, especially in reducing the end users complaints about filling in the necessary forms. This is because every recommendation suggested to help the end user was comprehended and appreciated by A and B. However, Agency C did not realize the effort and insisted on maintaining the previous approach of asking for information from the end users. This was because the study did not include the end user's experience of using the previous system; hence, the study lacked data for requirements elicitation. The challenge here is to change the perspective of interacting with the system in order for improvement.

LESSONS LEARNT

Based on the requirements elicitation experience with the three agencies, listed below are the lessons learnt:

No Silver Bullet

It is true that there is no single process or technique or approach that works well for all the requirements in the elicitation scenario. Even though the three agencies are based in the same country and have a similarity in terms of culture and language, it does not guarantee that the same approach is workable in all agencies. In our case, the project aimed to improve the end user experience through a one stop portal governed by the government. The end users were not only the agencies involved to manage the business process but also the civilians who use the services. There was one agency that was very proud of its own work and resisted changing the way they do their work. The changes

were necessary to standardize the process with other agencies for services accessed through the same portal. In addition, the improvement focused on the civilians' experience to promote a paperless government in the long-run. The problems occurred when the requirements elicitation process kept repeating by itself changing minor things without being able to move forward. In our opinion, the body that has the highest authority needs to provide an extensive explanation to the agency that they need to go with the flow as the effort involves many agencies and consideration of changing the current process is essential.

Expect the Unexpected

In theory, a review is one of the methods to exit one process and to move on to another. In our case, after a review was done and documents were signed, the agency was allowed to log a complaint stating that they disagreed with the requirements document and asked for rework. As our party was bound to an agreement with the authority, our team had no choice but to do as requested. The requirements document improvement session was stressful as many new requirements and changes to the requirements were introduced. This was due to the new faces introduced by the agency's side and because they had not been involved since the beginning. Therefore, in terms of requirements elicitation one needs to be ready for such situations.

Dare to Say No

The old saying 'the customer is always right' is not always true. A customer or a stakeholder usually states what they want and only a few of them really state what they need. It is the responsibility of the technical people to explain, and, if possible, to persuade the stakeholder to see the real picture for their own benefit. Therefore, it is important to learn to say no in a professional and acceptable way to allow good progress of the project.

CONCLUSION

This chapter presents the experience of conducting the requirements elicitation process with government agencies in order to produce Software Requirements Specification (SRS). The focus of discussion concerns the importance of communication between all the parties involved during the process in order to produce reliable software requirements. In addition, this chapter provides an overview of requirements engineering best practices and the role of communication in the requirements elicitation process.

The central part of the chapter elaborates on the elicitation process experienced by the authors. It starts with the explanation of the techniques applied with the medium of communication used during the process. It also discusses the communication activities, which involved workshops and meetings for the purpose of knowledge acquisition, knowledge negotiation and stakeholders' acceptance. This is then followed by the discussion of communication issues, which highlights the difficulties faced during the process and explanations concerning how the situation was handled. In addition, the success story is also provided towards the end of the section. Then, the lessons learnt presents three main points that were discovered during the process that are also expected to provide a guide for other practitioners.

Technical skills and fully automated requirements tools are not able to assist the software project team to obtain adequate requirements to fulfil the satisfaction of the stakeholders. This is the unique feature of engineering requirements as it involves a lot of human dynamics. The human dynamics include the communication skills, culture, problem solving skills, leadership and response ability. The right skill is needed to handle various situations with different types of user throughout the elicitation process. The most crucial skill is communication as it plays a vital role in delivering and accepting information from both parties – software project team and stakehold-

ers. Sometimes it is just a few words that make things happen. Conversely, it is possible that the wrong words used in the wrong place will cost the software project a fortune. The ability to ask the right questions to the right person at the right moment is not a coincidence, rather, the ability is developed throughout the experience of eliciting requirements.

REFERENCES

Boehm, B. (1981). *Software Engineering Economics*. Prentice Hall.

Chang, G., Suihuai, Y., Gangjun, Y., & Weiwei, W. (2009). A collaborative requirements elicitation approach based on scenario. In *Proceedings of IEEE 10th International Conference on Computer-Aided Industrial Design & Conceptual Design*, (pp. 2213-2216). Wenzhou, China: IEEE Computer Society.

Che Pa, N., & Mohd Zin, A. (2011). Requirement Elicitation: Identifying the Communication Challenges between Developer and Customer. *International Journal on New Computer Architecture and their Applications, 1*, 371-383.

Coughlan, J., Lycett, M., & Macredie, R. D. (2003). Communication Issues in Requirements Elicitation: A Content Analysis of Stakeholder Experiences. *Information and Software Technology, 45*, 525–537. doi:10.1016/S0950-5849(03)00032-6

Coughlan, J., & Macredie, M. (2002). Effective Communication in Requirements Elicitation: A Comparison of Methodologies. *Requirements Engineering, 7*, 47–60. doi:10.1007/s007660200004

Davis, A., Dieste, O., Hickey, A., Juristo, N., & Moreno, A. M. (2006a). Effectiveness of Requirements Elicitation Techniques: Empirical Results Derived from a Systematic Review. In *Proceedings of Requirements Engineering, 14th IEEE International Conference* (pp. 179-188). IEEE. http://dx.doi.org/10.1109/RE.2006.17

Davis, C. J., Fuller, R. M., Tremblay, M. C., & Berndt, D. J. (2006b). Communication Challenges in Requirements Elicitation and The Use of the Repertory Grid Technique. *Journal of Computer Information Systems, 47*, 78–86.

Galitz, W. O. (2007). *The Essential Guide to User Interface Design: An Introduction to GUI Design Principles and Techniques*. Wiley.

Hartwick, J., & Barki, H. (2001). Communication as a Dimension of User Participation. *IEEE Transactions on Professional Communication, 44*, 21–36. doi:10.1109/47.911130

Hickey, A. M., & Davis, A. M. (2004). A Unified Model of Requirements Elicitation. *Journal of Management Information Systems, 20*, 65–84.

IEEE. (1990). *IEEE Standard Glossary for Software Engineering Terminology*. IEEE Standard 610.12-1990.

Krug, S. (2005). *Don't Make Me Think: A Common Sense Approach to Web Usability* (2nd ed.). New Riders.

Lauesen, S. (2002). *Software Requirements: Styles and Techniques*. US: Addison-Wesley.

Mishra, D., Mishra, A., & Yazici, A. (2008). Successful Requirement Elicitation by Combining Requirement Engineering Techniques. In *First International Conference on the Applications of Digital Information and Web Technologies, 2008. ICADIWT 2008.* (pp.258-263). Ostrava: IEEE Computer Society. http://dx.doi.org/10.1109/ICADIWT.2008.4664355

Mohd Zin, A., & Che Pa, N. (2009). Measuring Communication Gap in Software Requirements Elicitation Process. In *Proceedings of 8th WSEAS International Conference on Software Engineering, Parallel and Distributed Systems* (pp. 66-71). Cambridge, UK: World Scientific and Engineering Academy and Society (WSEAS).

Mulla, N., & Girase, S. (2012). Comparison of Various Elicitation Techniques and Requirement Prioritisation Techniques. *International Journal of Engineering Research & Technology, 1*, 1–7.

Muqeem, M., & Beg, M. R. (2012). NVC Based Model for Selecting Effective Requirement Elicitation Technique. [IJSEA]. *International Journal of Software Engineering & Applications, 3*, 157–165. doi:10.5121/ijsea.2012.3513

Pacheco, C., & Garcia, I. (2012). A Systematic Literature Review of Stakeholder Identification Methods in Requirements Elicitation. *Journal of Systems and Software, 85*, 2171–2181. doi:10.1016/j.jss.2012.04.075

Robertson, S., & Robertson, J. (1999). *Mastering the Requirements Process*. Harlow, UK: Addison-Wesley.

Shneiderman, B., Plaisant, C., Cohen, M., & Jacobs, S. (2009). *Designing the User Interface: Strategies for Effective Human-Computer Interaction* (5th ed.). Prentice Hall.

Sommerville, I. (2004). *Software Engineering* (7th ed.). Addison-Wesley.

Sommerville, I. (2011). *Software Engineering* (9th ed.). Pearson.

Tiwari, S., Rathore, S. S., & Gupta, A. (2012). Selecting Requirement Elicitation Techniques for Software Projects. In *Proceedings of Sixth International Conference on Software Engineering (CONSEG)*, (pp. 1-10). IEEE Computer Society. http://dx.doi.org/10.1109/CONSEG.2012.6349486.

W3C. (2008). *Web Content Accessibility Guidelines (WCAG) 2.0*. Retrieved 16 August 2013, from http://www.w3.org/TR/WCAG/

KEY TERMS AND DEFINITIONS

Conflict: To come into collision or disagreement; be contradictory, at variance, or in opposition.

Effective Communication: Effective communication occurs when a desired effect is the result of intentional or unintentional information sharing, which is interpreted between multiple entities and acted on in a desired way.

Requirements: A condition or capability needed by a user to solve a problem or achieve an objective.

Requirements Elicitation: Requirements elicitation means gathering requirements or discovering requirements.

Requirements Engineering: Requirements engineering is the process, which enables us to systematically determine the requirements for a software product.

Stakeholder: A stakeholder of a system is a person or an organization that has an (direct or indirect) influence on the requirements of the system.

Walkthrough: Walkthrough is a form of software (requirements) peer review in which all interested parties sit together and go through the requirements statements, raise issues, give comments and finally agreed on the requirements (maybe subject to amendment).

Section 2
Software Design and Construction

Chapter 4

State-of-the Art Concepts and Future Directions in Modelling Coordination

Abdelhamid Abdelhadi Mansor
University of Khartoum, Sudan

Wan Mohd Nasir Wan Kadir
Universiti Teknologi Malaysia, Malaysia

ABSTRACT

Coordination is becoming an increasingly important paradigm for systems design and implementation. With multiple languages and models for coordination emerging, it is interesting to compare different models and understand their strengths and weaknesses find common semantic models and develop mappings between formalisms. This will help us to gain a deeper insight into coordination concepts and applications, and also to establish a set of features/criteria for defining and comparing coordination models. In this chapter, the authors present the current work on modelling coordination based on the coordination features. The findings show that software elements have three distinct types of coordination needs—technical, temporal, and process—and that these needs vary with the member's role; geographic distance has a negative effect on coordination, but is mitigated by shared knowledge of the team and presence awareness; and shared task knowledge is more important for coordination among collocated members. The authors articulate propositions for future research in this area based on the analysis.

INTRODUCTION

Coordination is the harmonious adjustment or interaction of different things to achieve a goal or effect (Canal et al., 2005). Coordination languages and models are being developed to address the problem of managing the interactions among concurrent and distributed processes (De Vries et al., 2009). The underlying principle is the separation of computations by components and their interactions (Colman & Han, 2005; Gesbert et al., 2007). To achieve correct coordination (Zhu, 2008), rather than only considering dependency relations between multiple adaptations, this approach further focuses on dependency relations between managers at runtime. This work considers

DOI: 10.4018/978-1-4666-6026-7.ch004

a number of features including specification to identify and measure achievement of managerial goals to insure that the modelling provides mechanisms for structuring or modularising coordination activities and to verify that coordinated managers do not have any explicit action that may affect the coordination (Nogueira et al., 2012; Wang et al., 2012).

Coordination is a central issue in software agent systems in particular, and in distributed artificial intelligence (DAI) in general (Nwana et al., 1996). However, it has also been studied by researchers in diverse disciplines in the social sciences, including organization theory, political science, social psychology, anthropology, law and sociology. For example, organization theorists have investigated the co-ordination of systems of human beings, from small groups to large formal organizations. Economists have studied coordination in markets of separate profit-maximising firms (Haruna, 2012). Even biological systems appear to be coordinated though individual cells or 'agents' act independently and in a seemingly non-purposeful fashion. Human brains exhibit coordinated behaviour from apparently 'random' behaviours of very simple neurones. Essentially, co-ordination is a process in which agents engage in order to ensure a community of individual agents acts in a coherent manner.

Coordination is important in software development because it leads to benefits such as cost savings, shorter development cycles, and better-integrated products (Omicini & Viroli, 2011; Wang et al., 2012). Team cognition research suggests that members coordinate through team knowledge, but this perspective has only been investigated in real-time collocated tasks and we know little about which types of team knowledge best help coordination in the most geographically distributed software work. In this field study, we investigate the coordination needs of software teams, how team knowledge affects coordination, and how this effect is influenced by geographic dispersion.

In this chapter we introduce definitions, advantages and disadvantages of coordination from different views. Some examples will be used to discuss and clarify the concepts of coordination. The aim of this chapter is to discuss about what coordination is, the different kinds of coordination that can be demanded by a system, and the relationships, differences and similarities between coordination and other fields such as adaptation. Moreover, the section started discussing about what is software coordination in a broad sense. Thus, thinking about what coordination is, the first emerging question is what kind of coordination can be adapted in a software system.

BACKGROUND

Coordination languages and models are being developed to address the problem of managing the interactions among concurrent and distributed processes (Nogueira et al., 2012). The underlying principle is the separation of computations by components and their interactions (Colman & Han, 2005; Gesbert et al., 2007). To achieve correct coordination, rather than only considering dependency relations between multiple adaptations, this approach further focuses on dependency relations between managers at run-time.

There are a number of works in autonomic system and formal methods with different kinds of models that have been proposed. Actor model was used in various methods for modelling open, concurrent and distributed systems, in which actors interact and coordinate system tasks through messages. However, a review of the literature suggests that a few researchers have considered higher level coordination between managers before a decision has been made, so that qualitative demands can be specified and realized by utilizing the power of coordination models.

The underlying computation model of concurrency, developed by Dinges and Agha (2012), is based on the actor model of distributed objects interacting via asynchronous message passing. The model describes the reason that the actor model is suitable for exploiting large-scale parallelism in order to address divergence and deadlock that come as a result of the concurrent execution of independent transactions. Because the concurrency in actors is constrained by the availability of hardware resources and by the logical-dependence inherent in the computation, this model uses asynchronous message-passing thus pipelining the dynamic creation of actors. Furthermore, actors are dynamically reconfigurable and can model shared resources with changing local states in addition to the capability of actors to permit dynamic deadlock detection and removal. Tuple Centers Spread over Network (TuCSoN) (Omicini & Zambonelli, 1998, 1999) is a control-driven model based on mobile agents. The model takes decentralization into account by distributing communication abstractions (tuple centers) to the Internet nodes. TuCSoN environment node provides its local communication space and produces its own local coordination rules. This model enables flexible cooperation between agents over space and time, and allows easy handling of the many issues critical to Internet applications, such as heterogeneity and dynamicity of the execution environments.

Cruz and Ducasse (1999) proposed a coordination model called CoLaS for the specification of the coordination aspect in concurrent object-oriented systems based on active objects. CoLaS is based on the notion of a Coordination Group dividing the whole distributed system into coordination groups and targeting the scalability issues of the distributed systems through such groups. Each group is an entity that specifies controls and enforces the coordination of groups of collaborating active objects, and takes care of an independent set of coordination policies.

Meseguer and Talcott (2002) proposed a generic formal model of reflective distributed object computation based on rewriting logic, called Reflective Russian Dolls (RRD) (Meseguer & Talcott, 2006). The model combines logical reflection and structuring of distributed objects to provide a general layered coordination model. Each layer (meta-object) controls the communication and the execution of objects in the layer below. As in RRC, the objects being coordinated are actor-like objects thus making this model suitable to develop formal specifications of interaction as well as architectural and behavioral aspects of distributed object-based systems. Arbab (2004) proposed a channel-based coordination model called Reo for component composition based on calculus channel composition. Each channel has two ends (source and sink) and is composed of simplest channels with defined behaviors. A channel may be synchronous when the pair of operations can only succeed atomically, otherwise it is asynchronous. In Reo there is no shared global memory. Coordination in Reo is imposed by a manager on connected actors by determining when data can be accepted on input ports and when it can be taken from output ports thereby blocking actors attempting to send or receive until the operation is available. The decision to connect to a port is made by the manager; but once connected; the manager has no control over how the data is routed.

Talcott et al. (2006) proposed an actor-based coordination model called Actor-Role-Coordination (ARC), to facilitate open distributed embedded (ODE) system design and development. In ARC, a manager controls message delivery in the system according to a given global policy. Further on point, in ARC, model dynamicity was not a main concern for synchronizers since it directly addresses the potential behavioral volatility of coordinated actors. In an autonomic environment (Huebscher & McCann, 2008), there are a number of proposals to capture Quality of Service (QoS) requirements as first class aspects in openly distributed software and autonomic environments such as developed by Khakpour et al. (2010) and Ren (2006). The common feature of these works is that they have decoupled the coordination layer from the functional layer to decrease the complexity of the verification procedure and to address the system's QoS requirements.

Khakpour et al. (2011) present a formal model named PobSAM, which is composed of a collection of autonomous managers and managed actors. In PobSAM, managers use suitable policies as a mechanism to direct and adapt the behavior of managed actors. Moreover, a manager has a set of configurations including two types of policies: governing and adaptive. To adapt system behavior in response to the changes, the managers switch among different configurations during runtime. However, in PobSAM, autonomous managers use policies to coordinate actors to achieve system goals and there is no coordination among autonomous managers considered.

Wang et al. (2012) present a coordination space based resource-centered dynamic coordination model. Their model divided software systems into three kinds of entities. The first contains computation entities that include role, actors and services; second coordinators that include communication, resource and service coordinators. Third, the coordination space contains computation description, resource description, environment description and registry. When new computation entities interact with the system, they must login and logout of the registry. A change of computation entities at runtime causes an automatic modification of information in the space. This approach is capable of changing the requirement and environment. However, these authors do not discuss the requirement conflicts statically but have taken into account the resource conflict at runtime. Also, a decentralised coordination model based on an effective feedback mechanism is proposed (Nogueira et al., 2012) to reduce the time and complexity of the necessary interactions among nodes until a collective adaptation behavior is determined. Additionally, this model supposes the system should be able to maintain a global feasible QoS level while allowing individual nodes

to autonomously adapt under different constraints of resource availability and input quality. The model puts forth by Wang and colleagues, is faster to achieve a globally acceptable result because it requires fewer messages exchanged. However, the kinds of communication in the model require more discussion to identify the critical situations and the most effective policies relating to various domains. The paper assumes that every node in the system is trusted. However, in distributed systems this will not always be the case.

Mansor et al. (2011) present a modelling of PobMC. The presented model is composed of three layers Actors, Connectors and Coordinators/managers. These three layers will address autonomic systems adaptability and scalability, and treat autonomic systems as a composition of concurrent computation and coerced coordination. The PobMC allows the coordination between managers, and the monitoring of system environments to detect policy errors at compile time and during execution. The coordination constraints are transparently imposed on actors through message manipulations, which are carried out by the Connectors and Coordinators. These messages support the coordination between managers by allowing all relevant parties to access other connector variables that reflect the state of others within the structure.

ILLUSTRATIVE CASE STUDY

The Smart Mall System (SMALLS) allows users to navigate their location in the mall. The users should be able to query the place to where they are heading such as baby area, shoes area, food area, banking services area, etc. The system directs a user how to find the location. SMALLS operation can be summarized as follows. Each user carries a mobile device, such as a Smartphone, as well as a wireless sensor. Additionally, locations in the environment shopping or services area are associated with its own wireless sensors. The sensors determine which area is closest to the user at a given moment and passes this information to a server, which provides specific Web services for an individual object.

SMALLS must adapt its behaviour according to the changes of the environment. To achieve this aim, this work supposes that the system runs in normal, vacation and failure modes and in each context it enforces various sets of policies to adapt to the current conditions. For the reason of area, these authors have only identify policies defined for sensing a control module while the system runs in normal or failure modes.

In this SMALLS scenario, there are some identical clients (Smart Phones SP) that need some specific service, which is provided by three identical servers as shown in Figure 1. Each client sends requests to the corresponding manager (which plays the role of a load-balancer), instead of communicating directly with the servers. The responsibility of a manager is to distribute the incoming requests evenly among the servers. As a result, the servers receive an equal number of service requests. After finishing the requested service, the servers reply directly to the clients. Then the clients may ask for service again.

Figure 1. Communication graph for the SMALLS example

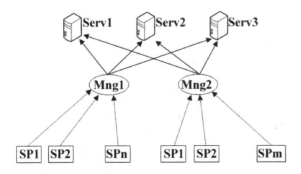

COORDINATION FEATURES

Coordination languages (Colman & Han, 2005) and models are being developed to address the problem of managing the interactions among concurrent and distributed processes. The underlying principle is separation of computations by components and their interactions. In our study of the most prominent works of coordination we considered a number of features which are representing some dimensions in the design space. Such features will be used to review the current state-of-the art.

Coordination is the harmonious adjustment or interaction of different things to achieve a goal or effect. Coordination languages and models are being developed to address the problem of managing the interactions among concurrent and distributed processes. The underlying principle is the separation of computations by components and their interactions (Colman & Han, 2005; Gesbert et al., 2007). To achieve correct coordination, rather than only considering dependency relations between multiple adaptations, this approach further focuses on dependency relations between managers at runtime. This paper considers a number of features including: specification to identify and measure achievement of managerial goals, to insure that the modelling provides mechanisms for structuring or modularising coordination activities and to verify that coordinated managers do not have any explicit action that may affect the coordination.

The main features differentiating this proposed modelling from existing work include: first, the separation of component coordination logic from its business logic, this will increase system flexibility and scalability, unlike most approaches in which the coordination logic is hard-wired into the business logic (Agha, 1985; Wang et al., 2012). Second, achieving correct coordination, such like PobMC which focuses on dependency relations between managers at run-time, rather than only considering dependency relations between multiple coordinated entities. Third, while most of the research focuses on coordination between actors (Arbab, 2004; Khakpour et al., 2010; Meseguer & Talcott, 2002; Ren et al., 2006), few works proposed the coordination between managers adding additional connectors variables and eliminating what occurs in the actors layer, see Figure 2.

Because of the essential dynamic nature of the SMALLS environment, the underlying actors could be both dynamic and extensive in number. The stability, flexibility and scalability of coordination policies is difficult to maintain if coordination is based on these numerous and highly dynamic actors (Ren et al., 2006). Then the anticipated behaviour of such an environment should be monitored through collaboration between managers in PobSAM and PobMC. Thus, PobMC allows end users to adapt to unforeseen situations by simply defining a new set of policies.

Policies are high-level specifications that can be defined and loaded dynamically (Lupu & Sloman, 1999). SMALLS policies can be changed to control the system behaviour dynamically, which will alter the behaviour of the arrangement consequently. Therefore, the policy-based design of system improves the flexibility and supports the long-term evolution of the system. Thus, PobMC provides the capability to adapt to unforeseen situations by defining a new set of policies and this feature is allowed without modifying the low-level system code.

As shown in Figure 2 the connectors bridge the gap between actors and the coordinators and may therefore be viewed as active from both sides. From the actor layer side, the job is to receive and provide messages sent from coordinators to the corresponding actors. From the coordinators layer side, the connectors play two roles (i) manage and coordinate actors without requiring detailed knowledge of the individual actor that is accessing the connectors' variables, and (ii) enable the coordination between different managers involved in the coordinators' layer by accessing different connectors through the coordinator.

Scalability is important for adaptive software in order to prevent a difficult evolution in addition to increasing total throughput under an increased load when resources (typically hardware) are added (Mansor et al., 2012). Due to this complexity in the scale of the Information Technology (IT) Ecosystem, scalability became a significant feature in the design of such systems. PobMC Hierarchical logic allows users to build the system hierarchically from adaptive components thus enhancing the scalability of the system. In a centralized approach the scalability is limited because a single controller is responsible for collecting and processing the control information. Since Hierarchical both PobMC and ARC are distributed in terms of controllers, see Figure. 2 and Figure 3, the self-coordinator manager interacts with other managers to achieve specific goals for immediate

Figure 2. Higher level hierarchal representation

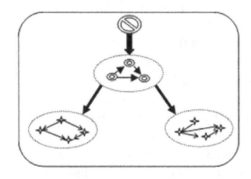 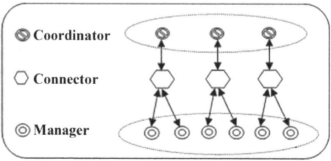

Figure 3. SMALLS architecture graph

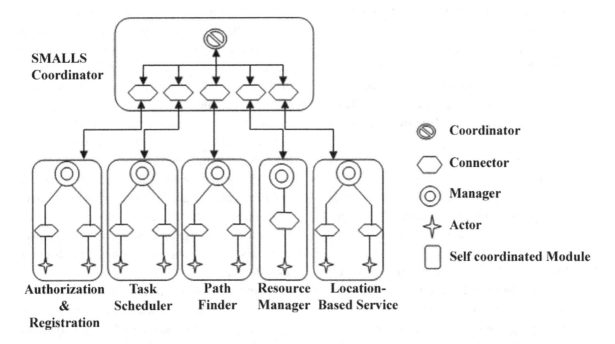

higher-level self-adaptive PobMC. Each manager is responsible for collecting the control information to be processed locally. Therefore, the local control points in a PobMC make it scale well in terms of size. Moreover, since a manager collects and processes information locally, it improves performance.

In both PobSAM and PobMC, coordination among managers is coerced through message passing and scalability requirements are fulfilled by the forced coordination transparent to the managers. A high level instruction for schedulers is required when a message must be moved to the beginning of a job queue, blocked, or postponed. Moreover, messages in the manager's space need to be manipulated to satisfy coordination requirements. Coordinators are responsible for harmonizing system scalability requirements among different connectors. Furthermore, coordinators are able to observe events through the managerial activities. Thus, the coordinators may change states and enact different coordination constraints on the responsible managers.

COORDINATION LANGUAGES

Coordination languages (Nogueira et al., 2012) and models are being developed to address the problem of managing the interactions among concurrent and distributed processes. The underlying principle is the separation of computations by components and their interactions (Colman & Han, 2005; Gesbert et al., 2007). To achieve correct coordination, rather than only considering dependency relations among multiple coordinated components. In this chapter the advantages of coordination languages will be discussed based on the current state-of-the art.

While coordination can be defined as above, without making assumptions about the ways to achieve it, building a practical language for representing coordination can not be done without clearly stating such assumptions as its foundation. The assumptions on which coordination language is to be developed are as follows.

1. Autonomous system managers have their own plans according to which they pursue their goals.
2. Being aware of the multi-managers environment they are in, managers plans explicitly represent interactions with other managers. Without loss of generality, it is assumed that this interaction takes place by exchanging messages.
3. Managers cannot predict the exact behavior of other agents, but they can delimitate classes of alternative behaviors that can be expected. As a consequence, managers plans are conditional over possible actions/reactions of other managers.
4. Managers plans may be incomplete or inaccurate and the knowledge to extend or correct them may become available only during execution. For this reason, managers are able to extend and modify their plans during execution.

In the context of distributed application, correctness and validity of single processes does not imply the correctness of the whole system. In such systems, the communication between the processes is of a high importance. These communications can be implemented within the process but the maintenance of such built-in communications can be a problem. However, communications and interactions protocols can be specified using coordination languages.

Reo is a coordination language designed and proposed by Arbab (2004). A typical Reo model consists of connectors. A more complex connector can be built up using simpler connectors. In each channel there exist a number of Channels and Nodes. Two nodes communicate through a channel which has two ends. A channel end can be source or sink depending on accepting or dispensing data into / out of its channel. The behaviour of a channel specifies how the channel affect the data flow through its ends which defined by its type. An effect of this type can be,

for example, the content, the conditions for loss, and/or creation of data go through the channel ends, or the atomicity, exclusion, order, and/or timing of their passage. There is no limitation on the behaviour of a channel. Therefore, new types of channels can be used simultaneously with other channels in a model.

Coordination models and languages have gone through an amazing evolution process over the years. From closed to open systems, from parallel computing to multi-agent systems and from database integration to knowledge intensive environments, coordination abstractions and technologies have gained in relevance and power in those scenarios where complexity has become a key factor.

Complex computational systems of today intelligent, knowledge-intensive, pervasive, self-organizing systems could be seen as the dynamic ensemble of a large number of distributed components, heterogeneous in nature, structure and behaviour, put together somehow so as to build up a coherent overall system behaviour. Roughly speaking, that 'somehow' is typically the key issue in the research for abstractions, models, technologies and methodologies for the engineering of complex systems. In spite of their origin in the context of closed and parallel systems, coordination models and languages (Arbab, 2004; Baier et al., 2006) are likely to play a key role there.

Tuple-based models (Rossi et al., 2001) represent the main class of space-based coordination models, where communication and coordination occur through a shared data space as in the case of blackboard systems (Corkill, 1991). A shared communication space, whose life is independent of the interacting components, is the conceptual basis for generative communication (Lee & Stotts, 2012): as such, it represents the essential environment abstraction for the support of openness in distributed systems. In fact, the very idea of a coordination abstraction persisting along with the messages exchanged is the essential prerequisite for a system where components may come and go at run-time, and provides for time uncoupling, which makes it possible to conceive and design patterns of interaction that could survive the potential erraticism of component behaviour.

Nevertheless, the ancestor of all tuple-based models that is, LINDA (Capmbell, 1997; Busi et al., 2000), where components communicate and synchronise by exchanging tuples through a shared tuple space was first conceived to support parallel computation in closed systems, at least with no apparent concern for open systems. However, Gelernter and Carriero (1992) were soon aware of the conceptual consequences of the introduction of an environment abstraction devoted to the management of the agent interaction space: computation and coordination there conceived as the governing of interaction (Wegner, 1997) were to be considered as two orthogonal dimensions of computer-based systems, to be handled that is, analysed, modelled, designed, programmed in an independent way, by adopting suitable abstractions and mechanisms.

Although suspensive semantics of coordination primitives is an essential mechanism for LINDA and its derivatives (requests for tuples by components are served only when tuples matching the request template are actually available in the tuple space), other features of tuple-based models would pave the way for the coordination of complex systems. First of all, a tuple is an ordered collection of possibly heterogeneous knowledge chunks. Therefore, in short, synchronisation based on the availability of tuples essentially means synchronisation based on the availability of structured knowledge of some sort. As such, tuple-based coordination is first of all knowledge-based coordination, where tuple spaces are possibly interpreted as knowledge repositories. In addition, tuple spaces are accessed associatively: queries specify tuple templates that match tuples based on their structure and the data they contain. On the one hand, this provides for complete uncoupling in communication: information neither on the sender nor on the structure of the share

space is required for a message to be received. On the other hand, the possibility to synchronise over a partial representation of knowledge (the tuple template) is a fundamental feature in all the contexts where information is often vague, inaccurate, incomplete or partially specified, as is typical in knowledge-intensive systems. Even more, in logic tuple-space models, such as Shared Prolog (Brogi & Ciancarini, 1991) and ReSpecT (Omicini & Viroli, 2011), components coordinate through first-order tuples, and tuple spaces are first-order logic theories, thus pushing further the interpretation of the shared communication space as a knowledge repository used for component coordination.

Finally, two other features characterise tuple-based models as they descend from the original LINDA ancestor: distribution and expressiveness of the coordination abstractions—termed as 're-shaping the coordination media' and 'programming the coordination rules', respectively, by Busi et al. (2001). On the one hand, distribution is essential for any complex system: so, in the same way as components of a distributed system are spread all over the system topology, multiple tuple spaces fill the system environment, providing for distributed coordination abstractions as in JavaSpaces (Freeman et al., 1999) and TSpaces (Wyckoff et al., 1998) and paving the way towards pervasive coordination systems. The ability to express the environment topology in a distributed setting is then essential for supporting the coordination of local interaction as well as of mobile components, as in LIME (Murphy et al., 2006) and KLAIM (De Nicola et al., 1998).

On the other hand, expressiveness of coordination media often needs to be tailored to the complexity and peculiarity of the specific coordinated system. Therefore, a number of LINDA derivatives focus on the programmability of the tuple space, in order to make it possible to explicitly express the rules of coordination, and to embed them within the coordination abstraction as in the case of Law-Governed Interaction

(Minsky & Ungureanu, 2000), MARS (Cabri et al., 2000) and ReSpecT (Omicini & Denti, 2001). There, arbitrarily complex coordination policies can in principle be associated with each of the coordination media, which can be individually programmed so as to embed either global or local coordination policies, as required by the specific coordinated systems. Finally, the ability to define arbitrarily complex coordination policies and to embed them within the coordination media should in principle be coupled with the ability to capture and react to arbitrary environment events—as in the case of Situated ReSpecT (Casadei & Omicini, 2009) thus providing for the level of situatedness typically required by coordination in pervasive computational environments.

ON THE USE OF FORMAL METHODS

Formal methods (Bandara, et al., 2005; Li et al., 2006) are known to be mandatory when a non-ambiguous description of systems is needed, or when these systems are required to be validated for security matters. Within the context of CBSE, it is commonly agreed that the current state of the art has given a solution to coordination issues at the signature level, being now the turn for the upper levels of scalability, and in particular, for the behavioural level. To provide context we give a brief introduction to rewriting logic and the Reflective Russian Dolls (RRD) model of distributed object reflection.

Rewriting logic (Meseguer, 1992) is a logical formalism designed for modelling and reasoning about concurrent and distributed systems (Martı-Oliet & Meseguer, 2002). It is based on two simple ideas: states of a system are represented as elements of an algebraic data type; and the behavior of a system is given by local transitions between states described by rewrite rules. A rewrite rule has the form $t \Rightarrow t_0$ if c where t and t_0 are terms representing a local part of the system state, and c is a condition on the variables of t. This rule says that when the system has a subcomponent matching t, such that c holds, that subcomponent can evolve to t_0, possibly concurrently with changes described by rules matching other parts of the system state. The process of application of rewrite rules generates computations (also thought of as deductions). Maude (Clavel, et al., 2003) is a formal language and tool set based on rewriting logic used for developing, prototyping, and analyzing formal specifications.

Reflective Russian Dolls (RRD) is a generic formal model of distributed object reflection based on rewriting logic. The model combines logical reflection with a structuring of distributed objects as nested configurations of meta-objects (a la Russian Dolls) that can reason about and control their sub-objects. This model can be used to develop formal specifications of interaction as well as architectural and behavioral aspects of distributed object-based systems. For example, the Internet is not really a flat network, but a network of networks, having different network domains that may not be directly accessible except through specific gateways, firewalls, and so on. As another example, a multimedia server is a nested collection of resource manager objects (load balancing, admission control, object placement, and so on) and an execution environment object that coordinates execution of contained objects generating media streams.

For the purpose of specifying and modelling coordination we use two broad classes of meta-object-coordinators and customizers. A coordinator has a distinguished attribute that holds a nested configuration of objects and messages and controls delivery of messages in its contained configuration. A customizer contains a single object and is used to locally manage object meta-data and adapt the objects communication.

The work of the author in the field of component coordination and adaptation falls in the research stream that advocates the application of formal methods, in particular of process algebras, to describe the interactive behaviour of software systems. As already mentioned, several authors have proposed to extend current IDLs in order to deal with behavioural aspects of component interfaces. The use of finite state machines (FSM) to describe the behaviour of software components is proposed for instance in (Cho et al., 1998; Magee et al., 1999; Yellin & Strom, 1997). The main advantage of FSM is that their simplicity allows an efficient verification of protocol compatibility. On the other hand, this same simplicity is a severe expressiveness bound for modelling complex open distributed systems.

Process algebras feature more expressive descriptions of protocols, enable more sophisticated analysis of concurrent systems (Najm et al., 1999; Szyperski, 2002), and support system simulation and formal derivation of safety and liveness properties. In particular, the calculus differently from FSM and other algebras like CCS is able to model some relevant features for component-based open systems, like local and global choices, dynamic creation of new processes, and dynamic reorganization of network topology. The usefulness of calculus has been illustrated for describing component models like COM (Feijs, 1999) and CORBA (Gaspari & Zavattaro, 1999), and architecture description languages like Darwin (Baumgartner et al., 2004).

However, the main drawback of using process algebras for software specification is related to the inherent complexity of the analysis. In order to manage this complexity, behaviour interfaces have to be described in an abstract and modular way. Modularity is achieved by the partition of the interface in several roles each one describing the a partial view of component behaviour, as seen from a particular partner involved in the interaction. Abstraction, can be provided by the use of behavioural types —such as session types (Honda et al., 1998), instead of full process algebras. The ultimate objective of employing behavioural types is to provide a basic means to describe complex interaction behaviour with clarity and discipline at a high-level of abstraction, together with a formal

basis for analysis and verification. Behavioural types are supported by a rigorous type discipline, thus featuring a powerful type checking mechanism of component behaviour. Moreover, the use of types —instead of processes— to represent behaviour features the possibility of describing recursive behaviour while maintaining the analysis tractable.

A general discussion of the issues of component interconnection, mismatch and adaptation is reported in (Bosch, 1998; Ducasse & Richner, 1997; Feijs, 1999), while formal approaches to detecting interaction mismatches are presented for instance in (Allen & Garlan, 1997; Canal et al., 2001; Compare et al., 1999). The problem of software adaptation was specifically addressed by the work of Yellin and Strom (Yellin & Strom, 1997), which constitutes the starting point for our work. They use finite state grammars to specify interaction protocols between components, to define a relation of compatibility, and to address the task of (semi)automatic adaptor generation.

The outstanding paper of Yellin and Strom is probably one of the starting works in this field. However, some significant limitations of their approach are related with the expressiveness of the notation used. For instance, there is no possibility of representing internal choices, parallel composition of behaviours, or the creation of new processes. Furthermore, the architecture of the systems being described is static, and they do not deal with issues such as reorganizing the communication topology of systems, a possibility which immediately becomes available when using more expressive foundations, like session-types or the calculus.

Another closely related work is that of Reussner (2001), who proposes the extension of interfaces with FSM in order to check correct composition and also to adapt non-compatible components. Protocols are divided into two views: the services the component offers, and those it requires from its environment. In their proposal, these two views are orthogonal, i.e. each time a service is invoked in a component it results the same sequence of external invocations, though this usually depends on the internal state of the component. It should be also noticed that only method invocation is considered, while in a more general setting other forms of interaction should be addressed. Finally, adaptation is considered in this work as restriction of behaviour; if the environment does not offer all the resources required, the component is restricted to offer a subset of its services, but no other forms of adaptation (like name translation, or treatment of protocol mismatch) is considered.

Also similar in goals and approach is the work of Inverardi and Tivoli (2001), who address the automatic synthesis of connectors in COM/DCOM environments. Their approach assumes a layered system architecture in which the connectors/adaptors play the role of data buses carrying and translating messages between components located in adjacent layers. The formal approach used in their proposal guarantees deadlock-free interactions between components. However, the capability of adaptation achieved is limited to the (immediate) translation of message names between component interfaces, and for instance their connectors cannot act as buffers, temporarily storing messages to be transmitted later, and therefore adapting bigger behavioural mismatch between the components involved.

FUTURE RESEARCH DIRECTIONS

There are many challenges in developing coordination capabilities for a software system. The major challenge deals with consistency preservation to avoid undesirable transient behaviour. Whatever functionality change to be enforced, it should result in a correctly operating system. When some situations require coordinated adaptations of multiple system components it is important to have coordination mechanisms to maintain a globally consistent state.

Another interesting direction is to consider notions of composition of coordination requirements or of coordinators. Several notions of composition for container meta-objects exist that can be explored. In addition, composition based on policy composition is another possibility. Here we can consider composition with policies other than coordination, such as security.

Finally, coordination that involves explicit time or use of resources is of interest. For this, the semantic model will need to be extended appropriately.

Instead of treating coordination objects or communications as meta-level entities, the concept of hierarchal directors which encapsulate coordination among a cast of actors is introduced. However, the cast is not based on roles or behaviors. The directors are regular actors in the sense that the directors do not have the capability of intercepting messages. Nevertheless, a director represents a group of actors when the group interfaces with other groups. In particular, when a message is targeted to an actor within a group, the message must first be routed to the director of the group, and then routed to the director's director, and so forth. The message is dispatched to the target actor only after all directors on the hierarchical path have approved. As we stated above, such a hierarchical model avoids the special runtime support required by a meta-level approach; however, the price paid for such simplicity is the coordination transparency. Furthermore, as the hierarchical model does not put a limit on the depth of a director tree, it is possible for a simple message dispatch to require many levels of potentially expensive routing and approval.

There are several other more specific issues concern modelling of coordination. These issues do not have to be considered only as problems or challenges, but also as a good opportunity for opening promising research directions:

Formal Methods

As shown, there is a big research effort being put in the field of automatic, dynamic software adaptation and coordination, going further the mere signature adaptation provided by currently available commercial component platforms, and addressing the more complex behavioural adaptation. However, there is also some interesting issues still open, deserving future research.

First of all, many of the works in the literature of coordination model among them author's own works, deal with adapting behaviour (i.e. the protocols that the components follow in their interactions), rather than functionality (i.e. the actual semantics of the computations associated to these interactions).

However, solving all pending issues in the behavioural level will allow components to interact successfully, but cannot ensure at all the correctness of the system. In fact, behavioural specifications are deprived from the semantic information of the messages exchanged that is, the functionality actually carried by a component when the operation corresponding to a received message is invoked. Hence, behavioural adaptation is useless if the mapping between interface specifications is wrong or meaningless.

Rigorous description of component functionality can be achieved by means of contracts, using pre- and post-conditions for describing the semantics of component's services. Hence, we would know beforehand whether we can use a given component within a certain context. However, in case that semantic mismatch is detected, some issues arise: (i) under which circumstances would it be possible to adapt the functionality that a component offers to that required by its context? (ii) would these contract descriptions be enough for deriving a "semantic adaptor"? and (iii) if not, what other kind of information should be included in the interfaces in order to achieve automatic adaptation?

Formal methods can be used to do the following:

1. Programs development; this has been dubbed formal methods lite. This may be the most cost-effective option in many cases.
2. Formal development and formal verification in order to produce a program in a more formal manner. For example, proofs of properties or refinement from the specification to a program may be undertaken. This may be most appropriate in high-integrity systems involving safety or security.
3. Theorem proves to undertake fully formal machine-checked proofs. This can be very expensive and is only practically worthwhile if the cost of mistakes is extremely high (e.g., in critical parts of microprocessor design).

However, formal methods are unacceptable to users. The fact is that formal methods help users understand what they are getting. To realize this benefit, the formal specification must be more comprehensible to the user. This is achieved mainly by paraphrasing the specification into natural language. Furthermore, formal methods require highly trained mathematicians. The fact is that mathematics for specification is easy. A much higher level of mathematical skill is needed if you intend to go beyond formal specification and carry out a fully formal development that includes proofs. Therefore, competent people who can cope with the necessary mathematical manipulations are the ones who must carry out safety-critical projects. Of course, the same is true of bridge building.

Beside these skills challenges, formal methods replace traditional engineering design methods. One of the major criticisms against formal methods is that they fail to support many of the methodological aspects of the more traditional structured-development methods. This statement is partially true of some types of formal methods. Structured-development methods using a model such as Bohem's spiral model generally support all stages of the system.

Furthermore, today, a major area of research is integration of structured and formal methods. The result is that two views of the system are presented. Approaches to method integration vary from running structured and formal methods in parallel, to formally specifying transformations from structured-method notations to formal specification languages.

We conclude that in order to facilitate the technology-transfer process from formal-methods research to practice, more real links between the industry and the academia are required.

- Also, the successful use of formal methods must be better publicized
- More research is required to further develop the use of formal methods.
- Formal methods are not a panacea, but one method among many.

Coordination Languages

The main problems to be solved by a language designer are, data structures and types, which data structures are allowed in the tuples?. Matching rules for operations in the Tuple Space, how is defined the matching operation?. Control of tuple operations, which kind of control structures can be used with particular model operations? (for instance, backtracking is difficult to implement in a distributed setting). And the definition of eval, which is the semantics of new processes/agents? Which code and data of the parent process they can refer to? How many active threads can be included in a tuple? How do they synchronize?.

In this chapter, we adopted the software engineering notion of the coordination model discussed in Omicini (2001). Accordingly, a coordination model works as the source of the abstractions and metaphors required to shape the space of component interactions in complex computational systems. Along this line, we briefly recapitulated the evolution of coordination models in the last 25 years from closed, parallel systems towards open, intelligent, knowledge intensive, pervasive and self-organizing systems.

From the very beginning (Gelernter & Carriero, 1992), literature on coordination models promoted the separation between computation and coordination as two orthogonal dimensions in the modelling and engineering of complex computational systems (Wegner, 1997). According to this view, systems are built out of a (possibly huge) number of (possibly heterogeneous) computational components put together by means of environment abstractions, the coordination media, explicitly meant to govern the space of component interaction. The separation between computational and coordination components is at the core of the evolution of coordination models towards complex systems. Therefore, for instance, by exploiting the expressiveness of coordination abstractions, systems could be provided with social intelligence independently of the component intelligence, as in stigmergic coordination. However (possibly diverging), individual goals of autonomous components could be reconciled to achieve a global system goal without harming the autonomy of components as in multi-agent systems. The tuple space abstraction constituted the basic brick for such evolution, promoting generative communication and uncoupled coordination. Then, its many developments towards distributedness, reactiveness, situatedness, time-dependence, probabilistic behaviour, etc. made coordination models rich enough to be possibly exploited as the sources for metaphors, patterns and mechanisms for complex systems such as knowledge-intensive, pervasive and self-organising systems.

Finally, a huge number of technical challenges are waiting to be faced by researchers engaged in the development of coordination middleware and infrastructures, by means of which the effectiveness of coordination-based approaches is going to be actually put to test against many complex, real-world application scenarios. Among the many challenges, we could mention the integration of organisational and security models in the coordination setting; the full development and testing of nature-inspired coordination models; the definition of knowledge-oriented coordination models and languages embodying international standards; the construction of light-weight coordination technologies for pervasive scenarios; and, finally, the design of rich coordination frameworks providing developers with a complete and expressive set of tools to harness the intricacy of engineering the space of interaction in complex computational systems.

CONCLUSION

In this chapter, we present the current work on modelling coordination based on the coordination features. The chapter shows that recent research has yielded significant contributions on coordination models and languages, and to capture QoS requirements as first class aspects in open distributed software. However, few proposals have considered interpreting QoS requirements as coordination constraints so that qualitative demands can be specified and realized by utilizing the power of coordination models.

An obvious direction of future work is to develop refinement rules that guarantee preservation of requirements satisfaction for different classes of policy. Are there general principles for deriving a distributed coordination protocol? Can the localization transformation sketched for the case of group communication be generalized?

Future directions of research are likely to further deepen the novel theoretical settings discussed here like the one of self-organising semantic coordination, possibly devising original and even unexpected ones. In addition, the impact of coordination models on the engineering of complex systems is going to have profound implications on methodologies and software processes and on related research as well.

Three distinct types of coordination needs—technical, temporal, and process—and that these needs vary with the members' role; geographic distance has a negative effect on coordination, but is mitigated by shared knowledge of the team and presence awareness; and shared task knowledge is more important for coordination among collocated members.

REFERENCES

Agha, G. A. (1985). *Actors: A model of concurrent computation in distributed systems*. The MIT Press.

Allen, R., & Garlan, D. (1997). A formal basis for architectural connection. [TOSEM]. *ACM Transactions on Software Engineering and Methodology*, *6*(3), 213–249. doi:10.1145/258077.258078

Arbab, F. (2004). Reo: A channel-based coordination model for component composition. *Mathematical Structures in Computer Science*, *14*(3), 329–366. doi:10.1017/S0960129504004153

Baier, C., Sirjani, M., Arbab, F., & Rutten, J. (2006). Modelling component connectors in Reo by constraint automata. *Science of Computer Programming*, *61*(2), 75–113. doi:10.1016/j.scico.2005.10.008

Bandara, A., Lupu, E., Russo, A., Dulay, N., Sloman, M., & Flegkas, P. (2005). *Policy refinement for DiffServ quality of service management*. Paper presented at the 2005 9th IFIP/IEEE International Symposium on Integrated Network Management. Nice, France.

Baumgartner, P., Fuchs, A., & Tinelli, C. (2004). *Darwin: A theorem prover for the model evolution calculus*. Paper presented at the IJCAR Workshop on Empirically Successful First Order Reasoning (ESFOR (aka S4)), Electronic Notes in Theoretical Computer Science. New York, NY.

Bosch, J. (1998). Adapting object-oriented components. In *Object-Oriented Technologys* (pp. 379–383). Springer. doi:10.1007/3-540-69687-3_77

Brogi, A., & Ciancarini, P. (1991). The concurrent language, shared prolog. [TOPLAS]. *ACM Transactions on Programming Languages and Systems*, *13*(1), 99–123. doi:10.1145/114005.102807

Busi, N., Gorrieri, R., & Zavattaro, G. (2000). On the expressiveness of Linda coordination primitives. *Information and Computation*, *156*(1), 90–121. doi:10.1006/inco.1999.2823

Cabri, G., Leonardi, L., & Zambonelli, F. (2000). MARS: A programmable coordination architecture for mobile agents. *Internet Computing, IEEE*, *4*(4), 26–35. doi:10.1109/4236.865084

Canal, C., Murillo, J. M., & Poizat, P. (2005). Coordination and adaptation techniques for software entities. In *Object-oriented technology* (pp. 133–147). Springer. doi:10.1007/978-3-540-30554-5_13

Canal, C., Pimentel, E., & Troya, J. M. (2001). Compatibility and inheritance in software architectures. *Science of Computer Programming*, *41*(2), 105–138. doi:10.1016/S0167-6423(01)00002-8

Capmbell, D. (1997). *Implementing algorithmic skeletons for generative communication with linda*. Report-University of York Department of Computer Science YCS.

Casadei, M., & Omicini, A. (2009). Situated tuple centres in ReSpecT. In *Proceedings of the ACM Symposium on Applied Computing* (pp. 1361-1368). ACM.

Cho, I. H., McGregor, J. D., & Krause, L. (1998). A protocol based approach to specifying interoperability between objects. In *Proceedings of Technology of Object-Oriented Languages* (pp. 84–96). IEEE.

Clavel, M., Durán, F., Eker, S., Lincoln, P., Martı-Oliet, N., Meseguer, J., et al. (2003). *Maude 2.0 Manual*. Retrieved from http://maude.cs.uiuc.edu

Colman, A., & Han, J. (2005). *Coordination systems in role-based adaptive software*. Paper presented at the 7th International Conference on Coordination Models and Languages, COORDINATION 2005. Namur, Belgium.

Compare, D., Inverardi, P., & Wolf, A. L. (1999). Uncovering architectural mismatch in component behavior. *Science of Computer Programming*, *33*(2), 101–131. doi:10.1016/S0167-6423(98)00006-9

Corkill, D. D. (1991). Blackboard systems. *AI Expert*, *6*(9), 40–47.

Cruz, J. C., & Ducasse, S. (1999). A group based approach for coordinating active objects. In *Coordinatio Languages and Models* (pp. 355–370). Springer. doi:10.1007/3-540-48919-3_25

De Nicola, R., Ferrari, G. L., & Pugliese, R. (1998). KLAIM: A kernel language for agents interaction and mobility. *Software Engineering. IEEE Transactions on*, *24*(5), 315–330.

De Vries, W., Meyer, J. C., De Boer, F., & Van der Hoek, W. (2009). A coordination language for agents interacting in distributed plan-execute cycles. *International Journal of Reasoning-based Intelligent Systems*, *1*(1), 4–17. doi:10.1504/IJRIS.2009.026713

Dinges, P., & Agha, G. (2012). Scoped synchronization constraints for large scale actor systems. In *Coordination Models and Languages* (pp. 89–103). Springer. doi:10.1007/978-3-642-30829-1_7

Ducasse, S., & Richner, T. (1997). Executable connectors: Towards reusable design elements. *ACM SIGSOFT Software Engineering Notes*, *22*(6), 483–499. doi:10.1145/267896.267928

Feijs, L. M. (1999). Modelling Microsoft COM using π-calculus. In *Proceedings of FM'99—Formal Methods* (pp. 1343-1363). Springer.

Freeman, E., Hupfer, S., & Arnold, K. (1999). *JavaSpaces principles, patterns, and practice.* Addison-Wesley Professional.

Gaspari, M., & Zavattaro, G. (1999). A Process Algebraic Specication of the New Asynchronous CORBA Messaging Service? In *Proceedings of ECOOP'99—Object-Oriented Programming* (pp. 495-518). Springer.

Gelernter, D., & Carriero, N. (1992). Coordination languages and their significance. *Communications of the ACM, 35*(2), 96–107. doi:10.1145/129630.376083

Gesbert, D., Kiani, S. G., & Gjendemsjo, A. (2007). Adaptation, coordination, and distributed resource allocation in interference-limited wireless networks. *Proceedings of the IEEE, 95*(12), 2393–2409. doi:10.1109/JPROC.2007.907125

Haruna, S. (2012). A Unified Theory of the Behaviour of Profit-maximising, Labour-managed and Joint-Stock Firms Operating under Uncertainty: A Comment. *The Economic Journal, 95*(380), 1093–1094. doi:10.2307/2233269

Honda, K., Vasconcelos, V. T., & Kubo, M. (1998). Language primitives and type discipline for structured communication-based programming. In *Programming Languages and Systems* (pp. 122–138). Springer. doi:10.1007/BFb0053567

Huebscher, M. C., & McCann, J. A. (2008). A survey of autonomic computing—degrees, models, and applications. [CSUR]. *ACM Computing Surveys, 40*(3), 7–13. doi:10.1145/1380584.1380585

Inverardi, P., & Tivoli, M. (2001). Automatic synthesis of deadlock free connectors for com/dcom applications. *ACM SIGSOFT Software Engineering Notes, 26*(5), 121–131. doi:10.1145/503271.503227

Khakpour, N., Jalili, S., Talcott, C., Sirjani, M., & Mousavi, M. R. (2010). PobSAM: policy-based managing of actors in self-adaptive systems. *Electronic Notes in Theoretical Computer Science, 263*, 129–143. doi:10.1016/j.entcs.2010.05.008

Khakpour, N., Khosravi, R., Sirjani, M., & Jalili, S. (2010). *Formal analysis of policy-based self-adaptive systems.* Paper presented at the 25th Annual ACM Symposium on Applied Computing. Sierre, Switzerland.

Lee, K. L., & Stotts, D. (2012). Composition of bioinformatics model federations using communication aspects. In *Proceedings of Bioinformatics and Biomedicine (BIBM), 2012 IEEE International Conference on* (pp. 1-5). IEEE.

Li, X., Kang, H., Harrington, P., & Thomas, J. (2006). *Autonomic and trusted computing paradigms.* Paper presented at the Thrid International Conference on Autonomic and Trusted Computing. Wuhan, China.

Lupu, E. C., & Sloman, M. (1999). Conflicts in policy-based distributed systems management. *IEEE Transactions on Software Engineering, 25*(6), 852–869. doi:10.1109/32.824414

Magee, J., Kramer, J., & Giannakopoulou, D. (1999). Behaviour analysis of software architectures. In Software Architecture (pp. 35-49). Springer US.

Mansor, A., Kadir, W. M. N. W., Anwar, T., & Elyas, H. (2012). Policy-based Approach to Detect and Resolve Policy Conflict for Static and Dynamic Architecture. *Journal of Theoretical and Applied Information Technology, 37*(2), 268–278.

Mansor, A. A., Kadir, W. M. W., & Elias, H. (2011). Policy-based approach for dynamic architectural adaptation: A case study on location-based system. In *Proceedings of Software Engineering (MySEC), 2011 5th Malaysian Conference in* (pp. 171-176). IEEE.

Martı-Oliet, N., & Meseguer, J. (2002). Rewriting logic: Roadmap and bibliography. *Theoretical Computer Science, 285*(2), 121–154. doi:10.1016/S0304-3975(01)00357-7

Meseguer, J. (1992). Conditional rewriting logic as a unified model of concurrency. *Theoretical Computer Science, 96*(1), 73–155. doi:10.1016/0304-3975(92)90182-F

Meseguer, J., & Talcott, C. (2002). Semantic models for distributed object reflection. *Lecture Notes in Computer Science*, 1–36. doi:10.1007/3-540-47993-7_1

Meseguer, J., & Talcott, C. (2006). Semantic models for distributed object reflection. In *Proceedings of ECOOP 2002—Object-Oriented Programming* (pp. 1-36). Springer.

Minsky, N. (2005). *Law governed interaction (lgi): A distributed coordination and control mechanism.* Department of Computer Science, Rutgers University.

Murphy, A. L., Picco, G. P., & Roman, G.-C. (2006). LIME: A coordination model and middleware supporting mobility of hosts and agents. [TOSEM]. *ACM Transactions on Software Engineering and Methodology, 15*(3), 279–328. doi:10.1145/1151695.1151698

Najm, E., Nimour, A., & Stefani, J. B. (1999). Infinite types for distributed object interfaces. In Formal Methods for Open Object-Based Distributed Systems (pp. 353-369). Springer US.

Nogueira, L., Pinho, L. M., & Coelho, J. (2012). A feedback-based decentralised coordination model for distributed open real-time systems. *Journal of Systems and Software, 85*(9), 2145–2159. doi:10.1016/j.jss.2012.04.033

Nwana, H. S., Lee, L. C., & Jennings, N. R. (1996). Coordination in software agent systems. *British Telecom Technical Journal, 14*(4), 79–88.

Omicini, A. (2001). *Coordination of Internet agents: Models, technologies, and applications.* Springer. doi:10.1007/978-3-662-04401-8

Omicini, A., & Viroli, M. (2011). Coordination models and languages: From parallel computing to self-organisation. *The Knowledge Engineering Review, 26*(1), 53–59. doi:10.1017/S026988891000041X

Omicini, A., & Zambonelli, F. (1998). TuCSoN: a coordination model for mobile information agents. In *Proceedings of the 1st Workshop on Innovative Internet Information Systems* (Vol. 138). Academic Press.

Omicini, A., & Zambonelli, F. (1999). Tuple centres for the coordination of Internet agents. In *Proceedings of the 1999 ACM symposium on Applied computing* (pp. 183-190). ACM.

Papadopoulos, G. A., & Arbab, F. (1998). Coordination models and languages. *Advances in Computers, 46*, 329–400. doi:10.1016/S0065-2458(08)60208-9

Ren, S., Yu, Y., Chen, N., Marth, K., Poirot, P. E., & Shen, L. (2006). Actors, roles and coordinators—a coordination model for open distributed and embedded systems. In *Coordination Models and Languages* (pp. 247–265). Springer. doi:10.1007/11767954_16

Reussner, R. H. (2001). Enhanced component interfaces to support dynamic adaption and extension. In *Proceedings of the 34th Annual Hawaii International Conference on* (pp. 10-20). IEEE.

Rossi, D., Cabri, G., & Denti, E. (2001). Tuple-based technologies for coordination. In *Coordination of Internet agents* (pp. 83–109). Springer. doi:10.1007/978-3-662-04401-8_4

Scheu, H., & Marquardt, W. (2011). Sensitivity-based coordination in distributed model predictive control. *Journal of Process Control, 21*(5), 715–728. doi:10.1016/j.jprocont.2011.01.013

Szyperski, C. (1998). *Component software: Beyond object-oriented programming.* Harlow, UK: Addison-Wesley.

Talcott, C. L. (2006). Coordination models based on a formal model of distributed object reflection. *Electronic Notes in Theoretical Computer Science, 150*(1), 143–157. doi:10.1016/j.entcs.2005.12.028

Wang, C., Zheng, X., & Tu, X. (2012). A Coordination Space Based Resource-Centered Dynamic Coordination Approach to Software Systems. In *Proceedings of Advances in Computer Science and Information Engineering* (pp. 655–660). Academic Press. doi:10.1007/978-3-642-30126-1_103

Wegner, P. (1997). Why interaction is more powerful than algorithms. *Communications of the ACM, 40*(5), 80–91. doi:10.1145/253769.253801

Wyckoff, P., McLaughry, S. W., Lehman, T. J., & Ford, D. A. (1998). T spaces. *IBM Systems Journal, 37*(3), 454–474. doi:10.1147/sj.373.0454

Yellin, D. M., & Strom, R. E. (1997). Protocol specifications and component adaptors. [TOPLAS]. *ACM Transactions on Programming Languages and Systems, 19*(2), 292–333. doi:10.1145/244795.244801

Zhu, H. (2008). Role-based systems are autonomic. In *Proceedings of Cognitive Informatics* (pp. 144–152). IEEE.

ADDITIONAL READING

Ciancarini, P. (1996). Coordination models and languages as software integrators. [CSUR]. *ACM Computing Surveys, 28*(2), 300–302. doi:10.1145/234528.234732

Clarke, E. M., & Wing, J. M. (1996). Formal methods: State of the art and future directions. [CSUR]. *ACM Computing Surveys, 28*(4), 626–643. doi:10.1145/242223.242257

Craigen, D., Gerhart, S., & Ralston, T. (1993). An international survey of industrial applications of formal methods. In Z User Workshop, London 1992 (pp. 1-5). Springer London.

Gelernter, D., & Carriero, N. (1992). Coordination languages and their significance. *Communications of the ACM, 35*(2). doi:10.1145/129630.129635

Giese, H., Graf, J., & Wirtz, G. (1998). Modelling distributed software systems with object coordination nets. In Software Engineering for Parallel and Distributed Systems, 1998. Proceedings. International Symposium on (pp. 39-49). IEEE.

Pettersson, P. (1999). *Modelling and verification of real-time systems using timed automata: theory and practice. Department of Computer systems.* Univ.

KEY TERMS AND DEFINITIONS

Autonomic System: The self-managing characteristics of distributed computing resources, adapting to unpredictable changes while hiding intrinsic complexity to operators and users. Started by IBM in 2001, this initiative ultimately aims to develop computer systems capable of self-management, to overcome the rapidly growing complexity of computing systems management, and to reduce the barrier that complexity poses to further growth.

Coordination: A managerial function refers to the act of organizing, makes different activities interlink and work together for a goal or effect to fulfill desired goals.

Formal Methods: The application of a fairly broad variety of theoretical computer science fundamentals, in particular logic calculi, formal languages, automata theory, and program semantics, but also type systems and algebraic data types to problems in software and hardware specification and verification.

Formal Verification: The process of checking whether a design satisfies some system properties (requirements). In order to formally verify a design, it must first be converted into a simpler "verifiable" format. The design is specified as a set of interacting systems; each has a finite number of configurations, called states. States and transition between states constitute Finite State Machines (FSMs). The entire system is an FSM, which can be obtained by composing the FSMs associated with each component. Hence the first step in verification consists of obtaining a complete FSM description of the system. Given a present state (or current configuration), the next state (or successive configuration) of an FSM can be written as a function of its present state and inputs (transition function or transition relation).

Managers: Software entities that are playing vital roles in managing actors, planning for future actions and controlling their tasks in order to meet achieve the system objectives.

Modelling: The representation of a real world object or system in a mathematical framework. In such way software tools can be used to imitate the operation of the real world system over time so that inferences can be drawn about potential future outcomes.

Software Adaptation: The use of adaptor-specific computational entities guaranteeing that software components will interact in the right way not only at the signature level, but also at the behavioural, semantic and service levels.

Chapter 5
Low–Overhead Development of Scalable Resource–Efficient Software Systems

Wei-Chih Huang
Imperial College London, UK

William Knottenbelt
Imperial College London, UK

ABSTRACT

As the variety of execution environments and application contexts increases exponentially, modern software is often repeatedly refactored to meet ever-changing non-functional requirements. Although programmer effort can be reduced through the use of standardised libraries, software adjustment for scalability, reliability, and performance remains a time-consuming and manual job that requires high levels of expertise. Previous research has proposed three broad classes of techniques to overcome these difficulties in specific application domains: probabilistic techniques, out of core storage, and parallelism. However, due to limited cross-pollination of knowledge between domains, the same or very similar techniques have been reinvented all over again, and the application of techniques still requires manual effort. This chapter introduces the vision of self-adaptive scalable resource-efficient software that is able to reconfigure itself with little other than programmer-specified Service-Level Objectives and a description of the resource constraints of the current execution environment. The approach is designed to be low-overhead from the programmer's perspective – indeed a naïve implementation should suffice. To illustrate the vision, the authors have implemented in C++ a prototype library of self-adaptive containers, which dynamically adjust themselves to meet non-functional requirements at run time and which automatically deploy mitigating techniques when resource limits are reached. The authors describe the architecture of the library and the functionality of each component, as well as the process of self-adaptation. They explore the potential of the library in the context of a case study, which shows that the library can allow a naïve program to accept large-scale input and become resource-aware with very little programmer overhead.

DOI: 10.4018/978-1-4666-6026-7.ch005

1. INTRODUCTION

Modern software engineers are faced with an explosion in the number of execution environments in which their applications might execute (e.g. smartphone, tablet, laptop, server, etc.). In each of these potential execution environments, each class of application is subject to different resource constraints and may also be subject to different Quality of Service (QoS) requirements. Consider Figure 1, which presents the importance of three common QoS parameters (performance, memory efficiency, and reliability) in different application contexts and execution environments. For example, when a game is operated on a game console, the game's performance should be at a very high level to meet players' expectations, possibly leading to the use of more memory space and higher electric power consumption. By contrast, if the game is executed on a smartphone, lower performance may be tolerated to save battery power and to use less memory space. Similarly, if a web browser runs on a smartphone, due to high usage frequency of the web browser and limited memory space of the smartphone, high performance with low memory consumption is expected. But when the web browser is executed

on a server or a game console, the demand of high performance with low memory consumption is not required because these two platforms can provide sufficient memory space and are not frequently used to surf the internet.

It is a major challenge to write software capable of maintaining QoS in every possible execution environment and application context, especially in the face of bursty and/or high-intensity workloads that may frequently stretch or exceed resource limitations. To avoid unacceptable degradations in the quality of user experience, it is necessary to implement mechanisms for scalability, robustness and intelligent resource exploitation. Even if sound software engineering principles are applied to maximise software reuse, there are major barriers to the application of traditional software development techniques in light of these challenges. Specifically, significant manual reimplementation and refactoring must be carried out for each execution environment, and substantial levels of programmer expertise is necessary.

To address this situation, we propose a self-adaptive framework for "intelligent" software which adapts at run-time to the resource constraints of its present execution environment, as well as automatically scaling up to handle large input sizes,

Figure 1. The importance of QoS requirements on different application contexts and execution environments

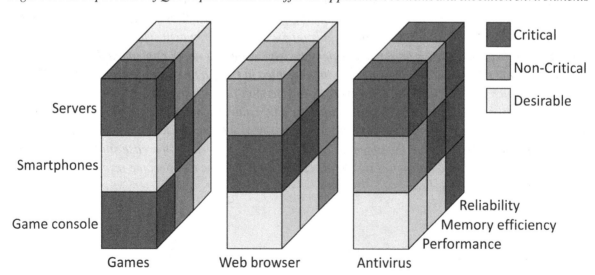

all the while respecting non-functional Quality of Service requirements. Ideally, the method of developing such software should be as close to that of developing ordinary software as possible, in order to reduce required levels of expertise and programmer effort. Our framework focuses on containers, whose underlying data structures differ in performance, memory consumption, and reliability, as they are critical to QoS requirements. Dynamic and automatic selection of underlying data structures can enable software to change its resource usage at run time, which releases programmers from reimplementing software.

The present chapter is motivated by the observation of the reinvention of similar techniques for scalability, robustness and intelligent resource exploitation across different application domains. Table 1 shows a real example, which demonstrates that in order to deal with large-scale input, five different application domains have adopted the techniques of out-of-core storage, probabilistic data structures, and parallelism. The first application domain, explicit state-space exploration, which is based on a breadth-first search core, is the key primary step in either the model checking or performance analysis of concurrent systems. The

Table 1. The application domains and the techniques they applied

Application Domains	Applied Techniques		
	Out-of-Core Storage	Probabilistic Data Structures	Parallelism
Explicit state-space exploration	(Deavours & Sanders, 1997) (Knottenbelt & Harrison, 1999) (Bell & Haverkort, 2001) (Kwiatkowska & Mehmood, 2002) (Bingham, et al., 2010)	(Holzmann, 1988) (Wolper & Leroy, 1993) (Stern & Dill, 1995) (Knottenbelt, 2000) (Haverkort, Bell, & Bohnenkamp, 1999) (Bingham, et al., 2010) (Saad, Zilio, & Berthomieu, 2010)	(Caselli, Conte, & Marenzoni, 1995) (Allmaier & Horton, 1997) (Ciardo, Gluckman, & Nicol, 1998) (Knottenbelt, 2000) (Edelkamp & Sulewski, 2010) (Bingham, et al., 2010) (Saad, et al., 2010)
DNA sequence assembly	(Cook & Zilles, 2009) (Kundeti, Rajasekaran, Dinh, Vaughn, & Thapar, 2010) (Y. Li et al., 2012)	(Melsted & Pritchard, 2011) (Pell et al., 2012) (Chikhi & Rizk, 2012)	(Butler et al., 2008) (Jackson, Regennitter, Yang, Schnable, & Aluru, 2010) (Kundeti, et al., 2010) (Liu, Schmidt, & Maskell, 2011)
Route planning / motion planning	(Edelkamp & Schrodl, 2000) (Goldberg & Werneck, 2005) (Sanders, Schultes, & Vetter, 2008) (T. Li, Yang, & Lian, 2012)	(Jing, Zhengang, Liying, & Fei, 2009) (Wewetzer, Scheuermann, Lübke, & Mauve, 2009) (Jiang, Ji, Wang, Zhu, & Cheng, 2013)	(Witkowski, 1983) (Gudaitis, Lamont, & Terzuoli, 1995) (Delling, Katz, & Pajor, 2012)
Visualisation	(Chiang & Silva, 1999) (Cignoni, Montani, Rocchini, & Scopigno, 2003) (Vo, Silva, Scheidegger, & Pascucci, 2012)		(Upson et al., 1989) (Abram & Treinish, 1995) (Meredith, Ahern, Pugmire, & Sisneros, 2012)
Similarity search	(Gionis, Indyk, & Motwani, 1999) (Fogaras & Rácz, 2005) (Bawa, Condie, & Ganesan, 2005) (H. Wang & Liu, 2012)	(Bhattacharya, Kashyap, & Parthasarathy, 2005) (Krishnamurthy et al., 2007) (Ren, Wang, & Wang, 2012) (C. Wang, Ren, Yu, & Urs, 2012) (Abram & Treinish, 1995) (Zhao, Tang, & Ye, 2012)	(Galper & Brutlag, 1990) (Berchtold, Böhm, Braunmüller, Keim, & Kriegel, 1997) (Teodoro, Valle, Mariano, Torres, & Meira, 2011) (Alabduljalil, Tang, & Yang, 2013)

major issue regarding this domain is the explosion of states, which results in shortage of primary memory. Through the use of these techniques, the supported capability has been improved from ~ 10^5 states to ~ 10^{10} states (Bingham et al., 2010).

The second application domain, DNA sequence assembly, involves DNA fragment aligning and merging. De Bruijn graphs (Idury & Waterman, 1995), which were proposed to assemble genome sequences from a set of overlapping reads, have been incorporated into the Euler (Pevzner, Tang, & Waterman, 2001) and Velvet (Zerbino & Birney, 2008) software packages. However, they consume huge amounts of memory during the execution, which restricts their capability when assembling large genomes. The adoption of the same three techniques mentioned above (see Table 1) has driven the assembly capability from organisms with 10^6 base pairs (e.g. simple virus) to organisms with 10^9 base pairs (e.g. humans) (Chikhi & Rizk, 2012).

The third application domain, route planning, refers to the computation of the most effective route between two geographical locations. Its well-known application is GPS devices, which guide drivers by calculated routes to destinations. The typical memory hierarchy of these kinds of devices is composed of faster but limited primary memory and slower but sufficient out-of-core memory (e.g. flash memory, memory card), which causes similar problems to those which occur in explicit state-space exploration and DNA sequence assembly. The proposed research listed in Table 1 contributes to the improvement of a navigation system with approximately 30 million nodes from 3735-MB primary memory consumption and 329-second query time (Goldberg & Werneck, 2005) to 548-MB primary memory consumption and 42-second query time (Sanders, et al., 2008).

The fourth application domain, visualisation, refers to a technique which expresses data in the form of images, diagrams, or animations. If the size of data is too large, they cannot be loaded into primary memory and it would take considerable

time to process them. Hence, a part of the data are moved to external storage, and the algorithms visualising the data are parallelised to improve performance. In so doing, the layout computation time of the Happy Buddha data set (Levoy, 2011), which comes from the 3D scanning of the Happy Buddha statue and has approximately 0.5 million vertices as well as one million triangles, is lessened from 71 second to 0.4 second (Vo, et al., 2012).

The final application domain, similarity search, is used to find out the data closest to each other among a data library in the context of a given query, and is applied in many fields such as multimedia, chemistry and biology. Based on the size of a data library, data might be stored in external memory, which generates large numbers of I/O operations. To improve performance, some researchers invented parallel methods, others tried to reduce primary memory consumption while others sought to exploit efficient external memory accesses. Take protein similarity search on a 20 giga-base pairs dataset for example. The running time was reduced from approximately 3 weeks to 5 hours, and the required memory dropped from 8 GB to 2 GB (Zhao, et al., 2012). In summary, the applied techniques adopted in these application domains exhibit lots of commonality (e.g. the technique of probabilistic data structures commonly adopts Bloom filters or their variants); yet in each domain the techniques have to date been manually applied at great implementation cost by individual research teams.

In this work, we introduce the framework of self-adaptive software, which can dynamically adapt to execution environments and automatically deploy required techniques. Self-adaptation pertaining to software brings the following benefits to people involved in software development, management, and usage. From the perspective of programmers, they are relieved of the tedium of reimplementing software. This enables programmers to concentrate on algorithm development, safe in the knowledge that peripheral concerns will be taken care of by self-adaptation mechanisms

(Lalanda, McCann, & Diaconescu, 2013). From a manager's point of view, the barriers to creation of robust scalable resource-efficient software are dramatically lowered (Kramer & Magee, 2007). In addition, managers can easily administer software since there is only a single version of software which can be applied to all platforms. Furthermore, the requirement for very high skilled programmers is reduced. From end-users' perspective, they get an improved user experience from a non-functional point of view (Salehie & Tahvildari, 2009). Their access to software on a multitude of different platforms is also improved. Despite these benefits, self-adaptive software brings new challenges in terms of the overhead of self-adaptation and debugging (Salehie & Tahvildari, 2009). The design of self-adaptation mechanisms should be sophisticated because a poor design may cause software to spend too much time adjusting itself. And because self-adaptation is triggered at run time and controlled by complicated mechanisms, programmers cannot easily trace software flow when software does not behave as expected.

To illustrate the use of our work concretely, we propose the use of self-adaptive containers, which support most functionalities of existing container libraries, but adjust themselves at run time to satisfy non-functional requirements, and automatically deploy efficient out-of-core storage, probabilistic data structures when necessary, and parallelism (although the latter is not yet implemented in our prototype implementation). Each container instance can be assigned desired Service Level Objectives (SLOs) including maximum response times, maximum in-core memory consumption, and minimum reliability in WSLA (Keller & Ludwig, 2003) format, which can avoid ambiguity among SLOs. When any SLO is violated, the library can dynamically adapt its use of data structures through the self-adaptive mechanism embedded in the library. The library features tight functionality specifications in order to optimise non-functional requirements as well. Thus, the library provides a ready route to scalable

QoS-aware applications with low programmer overhead.

The remainder of this chapter is organised as follows. Section 2 briefly introduces background knowledge including containers and the extension of conventional container libraries, autonomic computing and reference models for building autonomic systems, QoS specification languages, and probabilistic data structures. Section 3 describes our self-adaptive container library, and a case study. Section 4 presents future directions for self-adaptive containers, and Section 5 concludes.

2. BACKGROUND AND RELATED WORK

This section will introduce the techniques that we adopt to build scalable resource-efficient software. They include the concepts of containers and autonomic/self-adaptive computing. To solidify the two concepts, their implementations are introduced as well. Additionally, mechanisms for QoS specification and probabilistic data structures are presented to define programmer-specified Service Level Objectives and boost scalability, respectively.

2.1 Containers and Extension of Conventional Container Libraries

Containers are collections of objects of the same data type. They are used for storing data which can be accessed through member functions (or interfaces) and are implemented as template classes, which avoids duplicate codes of different data types. In the Standard Template Library (STL) (Musser, Derge, & Saini, 2001), containers can be divided into three groups: sequence containers, associative containers, and container adaptors. Sequence containers, including *deque, list,* and *vector,* maintain the order of inserted elements, whose positions can be specified by developers. Associative containers, including *set, multiset, map*, and *multimap*, keep inserted elements in a predefined order, which means user-defined classes should provide their equal functions. Container adaptors are interfaces on top of sequence containers. For example, a queue is implemented through *deque* by default, but it can also exploit *list* as its underlying sequence container. In the Java Collection Framework (JCF) (Watt & Brown, 2001), containers comprise collections and maps. The collections contain two groups: Lists and Sets. The list group, including *ArrayList* and *LinkedList*, are similar to *vector* and *list* in STL and maintain inserted elements in the order in which they are inserted. The set group, which is composed of *HashSet*, *TreeSet*, and *EnumSet*, maintains inserted elements according to a predefined order. The maps (*HashMap*, *TreeMap*, and *EnumMap*) store keys and their corresponding values according to a predefined order.

The standardised libraries such as STL and JCF are designed for general purpose contexts, where all functionalities are always ready to be supplied, which restricts the possibility of optimisation. Additionally, they are not designed to be aware of non-functional requirements, which causes the software implemented through them to have to be refactored when execution environments and application contexts change. Furthermore, their current functionalities are not sufficient to deal with data in high-capacity contexts (e.g. data which have to be manipulated in out-of-core memory, parallel environments, or probabilistic data structures). Hence, several extensions of conventional libraries have been proposed to address these shortcomings. We list some of them written in C++ and Java in Table 2. As can be seen in the table, the Parallel Standard Template Library (Johnson & Gannon, 1997), STAPL (Buss, Papadopoulos, Pearce, & Smith, 2010), MCSTL (Singler, Sanders, & Putze, 2007), Smart Data Structure (Eastep, Wingate, & Agarwal, 2011), MapDB (Kotek, 2013), and the Parallel Java library (Kaminsky, 2007) intend to help programmers more easily develop parallel programs. Among them, Smart Data Structure can dynamically adjust algorithms and algorithm parameters to improve performance. Also, STXXL (Dementiev, Kettner, & Sanders, 2008), Boost (Karlsson, 2005), and Jaguar (Welsh & Culler, 1999) provide a means to efficiently access out-of-core memory. Boost and Guava (Bourrillion &

Table 2. The enhanced functionalities of existing libraries

		Enhanced Functionalities			
	Language	Out-of-Core Storage	Parallelism	Probabilistic Data Structures	Self-Adaptation
Parallel Standard Template Library	C++		×		
STAPL	C++		×		
STXXL	C++	×	×		
MCSTL	C++		×		
Smart Data Structure	C++		×		×
Boost	C++	×		×	
MapDB	Java		×		
Jaguar project	Java	×			
Parallel Java Library	Java		×		
Guava	Java			×	

Levy, 2014) include probabilistic data structures, such as Bloom filters. Although these libraries attempt to boost the functionalities of STL and JCF, compared with our library, programmer effort and expertise of developing large-input software is relatively higher. Even if Smart Data Structure can perform self-adaptations at run time, its ability of self-adaptation is restricted, which means it can only be applied in parallel environments. Moreover, none of these libraries can be assigned SLOs, which increases the complexity of changing execution environments.

2.2 Autonomic Computing and Reference Models for Building Self-Adaptive Systems

The foundations of the study of modern self-adaptive systems arose in the late 1990s and early 2000s, when IBM coined the term autonomic computing (Horn, 2001). Nowadays many researchers use the notions of "self-adaptive systems", "self-managing systems" and "autonomic systems" interchangeably (Huebscher & McCann, 2008). The term autonomic computing was inspired by human autonomic nervous systems, which control people's bodies without the explicit awareness of their brains (e.g. heart rate and body temperature). In the context of IT systems, an autonomic system is one which attempts to deliver good service levels while sparing administrators the trouble of system operations and maintenance. The definitions of autonomic computing's four properties, self-configuring, self-optimising, self-healing, and self-protecting, are listed as follows:

- **Self-Configuring:** The ability to automatically adjust itself in accordance with high-level policies.
- **Self-Optimising:** The ability to assess the current performance and continuously try to improve it.
- **Self-Healing:** The ability to detect, analyse, and repair faults.

- **Self-Protecting:** The ability to be aware of potential threats in order to defend against them.

To construct systems equipped with these properties, the systems should embed autonomic managers, which control managed resources. The autonomic managers contain control loops (Ganek & Corbi, 2003), sensors and effectors. The control loops monitor managed resources through the sensors, compare their impacts and changes with the expectations of resource usage (e.g. policies, history logs), decide if adaptation actions should be taken, and then execute them through the effectors.

A stockpile of research related to autonomic computing has been conducted with a view to building self-managing systems. Salehie and Tahvildari (Salehie & Tahvildari, 2009) categorised related work according to their own taxonomy. Their taxonomy is composed of a hierarchy of levels. In each level, one question related to *where*, *when*, *what*, *why*, *who* or *how* is asked to decide which of the levels a piece of research falls into e.g. which part of the system can be changed? (*where*), when can the system be changed? (*when*), what resources can be adjusted? (*what*), why is self-adaption needed? (*why*), who is responsible for system changes? (*who*), and how is the adaptation applied? (*how*). According to Salehie and Tahvildari's classification method, our library's adaptation actions belong to the *strong* class, the reason being that the adaptation actions reconfigure the underlying data structure to meet non-functional requirements.

While Salehie and Tahvildari introduced their methodology to classify proposed research efforts, Huebscher and McCann (Huebscher & McCann, 2008) defined four elements: *Support*, *Core*, *Autonomous*, and *Autonomic*, to measure the degree of autonomicity. Based on their metrics, our proposed library is classified as *Autonomic*, which takes into account high-level objectives. In Khalid et al.'s work (Khalid, Haye, Khan,

& Shamail, 2009), the existing frameworks, architectures, and techniques are reviewed and classified according to application domains. In addition, they also identified adopted autonomic techniques based on autonomic computing's four properties. In accordance with Khalid et al.'s taxonomy, our self-adaptive container library is a technique which implements the *self-configuring* and *self-optimising* properties.

To build autonomic systems, some well-known reference models are proposed. In 2003, IBM proposed the MAPE-K control loop (Kephart & Chess, 2003), which represents a cycle constructed by five functions: Monitor, Analyze, Plan, Execute, and Knowledge. The Monitor function observes and collects information from managed resources (e.g. hardware resources). This information is then passed to the Analyze function to decide if changes are necessary based on the data stored in Knowledge function. If changes are required, a change request is formed and sent to the Plan function, which proposes the actions necessary to achieve goals or objectives. After that, the Execute function adjusts managed resources according to the change plan from the Plan function. The Knowledge function stores data (e.g. policies, metrics, logs) which are generated by the Monitor function, updated by the Execute function and shared by the Monitor, Analyze, Plan, and Execute functions.

After MAPE-K was proposed, Garlan et al. introduced Rainbow (Garlan, Cheng, Huang, Schmerl, & Steenkiste, 2004), an architecture-based self-adaptive system framework. The characteristic of Rainbow is its external self-adaptive mechanism, which claims to work more effectively with regard to problem detection and reuse across different execution environments than do internal mechanisms. Rainbow's framework contains system-specific adaptation knowledge and adaptation infrastructure, which is comprised of three layers: system, translation, and architecture. The system-specific adaptation knowledge, which provides the target system's operational model

to ensure the adaptation infrastructure's behavior goes as expected, includes resource constraints, adaptation strategies, and information related to target systems such as component types and properties. At the system layer of the adaptation infrastructure, a series of system APIs (e.g. probes, effectors, resource recovery) are implemented. These APIs are used to monitor and measure system states, perform adaptation actions, and find new resources. At the architecture layer, the system states reported from probes are examined to determine if an adaptation should be taken. Finally, the translation layer provides mapping between the architecture layer and the system layer.

Similar to Rainbow, a self-adaptive framework called Zanshin (Souza, 2012), whose self-adaptive mechanism is also independent of target systems, was put forward by Souza. In the Zanshin framework, the target system is supposed to be equipped with the ability to record the state changes of requirements. Hence, the Zanshin framework can receive both logs which record when requirement states change and awareness requirements, which are requirements describing other requirements' run-time statuses (e.g. a service which should be satisfied 90% of the time). When logs and awareness requirements are received by the Monitor component in the framework, they are checked to decide if the Adapt component should be triggered to execute requirement evolution operations. The latter are executed based on requirements defining desired strategies (e.g. if requirement S cannot be satisfied, it can be replaced by S'). The action of the Adapt component can be further divided into two steps. Desired strategies are selected by the Event-Condition-Action-based adaptation component and then executed by the qualitative reconfiguration component.

2.3 Mechanisms for QoS Specification

The concept of quality-of-service originated from networking and has now been applied in many domains. When specifying QoS, it is crucial to represent QoS parameters in a precise and rigorous way. QoS specification languages, therefore, are introduced to define metrics of QoS parameters and Service Level Agreements (SLAs) unambiguously. Many QoS specification languages have been proposed, and we will recap four well-known QoS languages, namely WSLA (Keller & Ludwig, 2003), WS-Agreement (Andrieux et al., 2004), SLAng (Lamanna, Skene, & Emmerich, 2003), and Performance Trees (Suto, Bradley, & Knottenbelt, 2006).

Web service level agreement (WSLA) language is an XML-based language used for monitoring and measuring QoS parameters, and negotiating SLAs. A WSLA specification is made up of three sections: Parties, Service Description, and Obligations. The Parties section defines who is involved in the agreement, divided further into signatory parties and supporting parties. The Service Description section specifies the QoS parameters of interest and the way they are measured. Two parameters, SLAParameter and Metric, are used in this section. The former represents the QoS parameters of interest such as response times, and the latter indicates how to measure them. The final section, Obligations, describes the Service Level Objectives, which are compared with their corresponding SLAParameters, and action guarantees, which are triggered to give a particular notification or perform a control activity when a Service Level Objective is not met.

Web service agreement specification (WS-Agreement) (Andrieux, et al., 2004) is an XML schema whose objective is to create guarantee terms between service providers and service customers during service provisioning. It contains two sections: Context and Terms. The Context section, which is similar to the Parties section of WSLA, defines the participants of this agreement. The Terms section, which specifies functional and non-functional requirements, is composed of Service Description Terms and Guarantee Terms. The Service Definition Terms describe the func-

tionalities of services, and the Guarantee Terms define the guarantees of service qualities related to the functionalities described in the Service Description Terms section.

SLAng (Lamanna, et al., 2003) is also an XML-based language for describing the QoS properties of SLAs. Its major functionality is similar to other SLA specification languages, but it claims three differences. First, it can be applied not only to web services but also to domains such as Internet Service Provision, Application Service Provision, and Storage Service Provision. Second, SLAng is designed with practicality and monitorability in mind, such that constraints can only be placed on activities that can be observed by contracting parties. Third, the formally defined semantics of SLAng, which can check the consistency of SLAs, focuses on service and client behaviour.

Compared with the above-mentioned QoS specification languages, Performance Trees (Suto, et al., 2006) are an alternative which provides a more intuitive way of defining QoS parameters. Performance trees represent performance queries as tree structures containing nodes and connecting arcs. Nodes can be divided into two kinds: operation nodes and value nodes. The former represent performance-related functions, and the latter are used to store literal information associated with the performance query (e.g. set of states, actions, numerical/Boolean constants). One benefit of adopting Performance Trees to define QoS is that the structures of Performance Trees can be easily generated and analysed through the use of the *PIPE2* (Dingle, Knottenbelt, & Suto, 2009) software tool.

Our library chooses WSLA to specify QoS requirements due to three reasons. First, WSLA is an XML-based standard, which makes QoS requirements more easily parsed and validated. Second, it can define desired resources, specify how to measure them, and compare the target resources with SLOs. Third, it does not have to define hard QoS guarantees because our library attempts to fulfill QoS requirements but does not guarantee that they can be 100% satisfied.

2.4 Probabilistic Data Structures

Probabilistic data structures are data structures influenced by random factors; this might entail random constructions of data structures (e.g. skip lists) or highly compressed data representations subject to random collisions that might lead to an error in retrieval results. The most well-known probabilistic data structure is the Bloom filters (Bloom, 1970). These are memory-efficient data structures which provide insertion operations and test-for-membership operations. They are constructed by k hash functions (h_1, h_2, ..., h_k with range $[0,m-1]$) and an m-bit storage array (B) whose initial values are 0. With insertion of an element i, the positions of $h_1(i)$, $h_2(i)$, ..., $h_k(i)$ in the m-bit array are set to 1. When membership of an element j is tested, the element is considered to exist if and only if $\prod_{i=1}^{k} B\left[h_i\left(j\right)\right] = 1$. The major benefit of Bloom filters is memory efficiency because they do not actually store inserted elements. In addition, the time complexity of insertion operations and test-for-membership operations is related to the number of hash functions but not related to the number of stored elements, which enhances performance when manipulating elements. However, there are two drawbacks to Bloom filters, which prompt the introduction of their two variants, counting Bloom filters (Fan, Cao, Almeida, & Broder, 2000) and sparse Bloom filters (Knottenbelt, 2000).

Counting Bloom filters add deletion operations to the standard Bloom filters. Instead of using m-bit arrays, counting Bloom filters adopt arrays (C) with m positions, each of which contains a counter. With insertion of an element i, 1 is added to the values of $C[h_1(i)]$, $C[h_2(i)]$, ..., $C[h_k(i)]$. Deletions are performed with 1 deducted from the values of $C[h_1(i)]$, $C[h_2(i)]$, ..., $C[h_k(i)]$. Despite deletion operations, counting Bloom filters may result in a new drawback - false negatives, when counters have overflows.

Although the standard Bloom filters can save memory space, they are not reliable when too many elements are inserted; they also require a static preallocation of known size. Sparse Bloom filters solve these drawbacks by growing dynamically and storing only the set of positions whose values are 1. In this chapter, we will introduce an improved sparse Bloom filter in section 3.4. as one potential data structure that can be deployed to provide insertion and test-for-membership functionalities for containers in an efficient manner.

3. THE FRAMEWORK OF THE SELF-ADAPTIVE CONTAINER LIBRARY AND IMPLEMENTATION

This section introduces our self-adaptive container library, which intends to reduce programmer overhead with regards to change of execution environments as well as application contexts and to provide a straightforward means to specify and maintain QoS requirements under heavy load. Our method is centered on containers because they are a universally-deployed and fundamental tool for building all kinds of software and the efficiency of their operations are critical to software's non-functional behaviour. We also believe that the use of our self-adaptive containers can reduce the learning time required when building self-adaptive software.

3.1 Self-Adaptive Containers

The architecture of our container library is depicted in Figure 2. As can be seen, our library consists of two major components: the Application Programming Interface (API) and the Self-Adaptive Unit (SAU).

The API is a channel through which programmers send commands to and obtain operation

Figure 2. The architecture of the self-adaptive container library

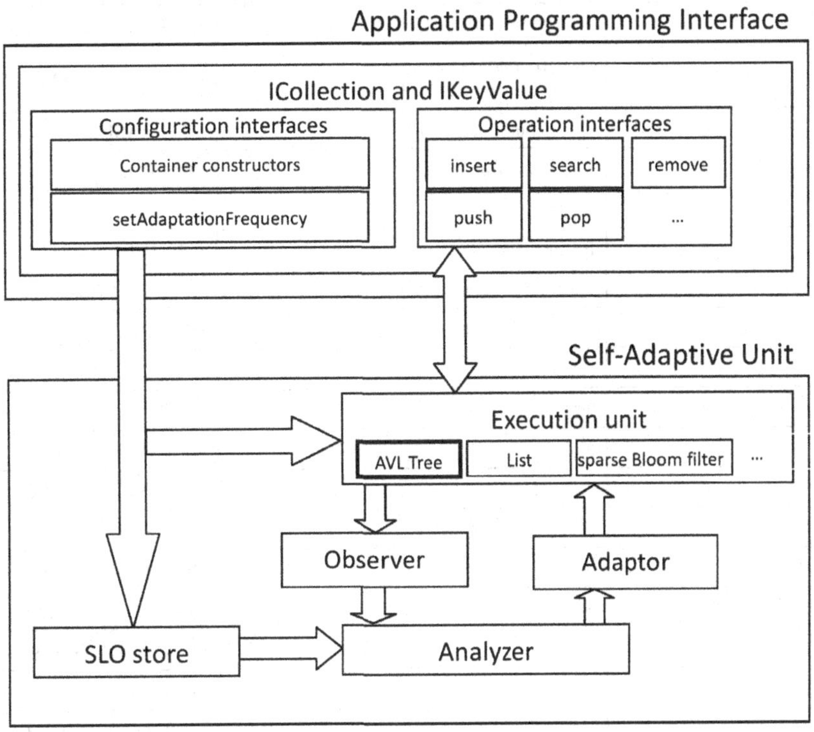

results from the SAU. Its primary constituents are the *ICollection* class, which subsumes the functionalities of the *vector*, *list*, *set*, *multiset*, *stack*, and *queue* STL classes, and the *IKeyValue* class, which subsumes the functionalities of *map* and *multimap* STL classes. The interfaces supported by *ICollection* and *IKeyValue* can be divided into two categories: operation interfaces and configuration interfaces, based on their functionalities. Operation interfaces provide the ability to specify support for commonly-used operations such as *insert*, *search*, and *remove*. All the currently supported operation interfaces and their corresponding operation descriptors are listed in Table 3. The purpose of these operation descriptors, whose definitions are shown in Table 4, is to provide tight functionality specifications that will help the library choose a suitable data structure to fulfil functional and non-functional requirements at run time. To configure required

functionalities in a succinct manner, the combined operation descriptors shown in Table 5 are also provided. Configuration interfaces control the SAU by means of container constructors and the method *setAdaptionFrequency*, which provides one means to control the frequency with which the library invokes self-adaptation operations.

The usage of container constructors is demonstrated as follows:

ICollection<T> (op_desc, SLO_file[, freq])

and

IKeyValue<K, V> (op_desc, SLO_file[, freq]).

The three parameters indicate required functionalities (*op_desc*), the path of an XML file containing desired SLOs (*SLO_file*), and the frequency with which self-adaptive mechanism

Table 3. The supported methods of ICollection and IKeyValue and involved operation descriptors

ICollection<T> Methods	IKeyValue<K, V> Methods	Involved Operation Descriptors
insert (const T& x)	insert(const std::pair<K, V>T& x)	OP_INSERT
insert (iterator position, const T& x)	insert(iterator position, const std::pair<K, V>& x)	OP_INSERT I OP_ITERTOR
erase (const T& x)	erase(const K& x)	OP_ERASE
find (const T& x)	find(const K& x)	OP_FIND
search (const T& x)	search(const K& x)	OP_SEARCH
begin(), end()	begin(), end()	OP_ITERATOR
operator++, operator*	operator++, operator*	OP_ITERATOR
operator[]	operator[]	OP_INDEX
size()	size()	
empty()	empty()	
push_front	N/A	OP_INSERT_FRONT
push_back	N/A	OP_INSERT_BACK
pop_front	N/A	OP_ERASE_FRONT
pop_back	N/A	OP_ERASE_BACK
push	N/A	OP_INSERT_FRONT (queue)
		OP_INSERT_BACK (stack)
pop	N/A	OP_ERASE_FRONT (queue)
		OP_ERASE_BACK (stack)

Table 4. The definition of operation descriptors

Operation Descriptor		Definition
OP_INSERT		Insertion
OP_ERASE		Deletion
OP_SEARCH		Search (existence)
OP_INDEX		Direct index-based access
OP_ITERATOR		Iterator support
OP_FIND (= OP_SEARCH I OP_ITERATOR)		Find (retrieval)
OP_MULTI		Duplicate elements support
OP_RAM		Primary memory access
OP_RELIABILITY		Reliability calculation
OP_FRONT	OP_INSERT_FRONT	Front insertion
	OP_ERASE_FRONT	Front deletion
OP_BACK	OP_INSERT_BACK	Back insertion
	OP_ERASE_BACK	Back deletion

Table 5. Combined operation descriptors

Container Behavior	Representative Descriptor	Involved Operation Descriptors
Vector	OP_VECTOR	OP_INSERT I OP_ERASE I OP_SEARCH I OP_ITERATOR I OP_BACK I OP_INDEX
List	OP_LIST	OP_INSERT I OP_ERASE I OP_SEARCH I OP_ITERATOR I OP_BACK I OP_FRONT
Queue	OP_QUEUE	OP_INSERT_BACK I OP_ERASE_FRONT
Stack	OP_STACK	OP_INSERT_FRONT I OP_ERASE_FRONT
Set	OP_SET	OP_INSERT I OP_ERASE I OP_SEARCH I OP_ITERATOR
Map	OP_MAP	OP_INSERT I OP_ERASE I OP_SEARCH I OP_ITERATOR
Multiset	OP_MULTISET	OP_INSERT I OP_ERASE I OP_SEARCH I OP_ITERATOR I OP_MULTI
Multimap	OP_MULTIMAP	OP_INSERT I OP_ERASE I OP_SEARCH I OP_ITERATOR I OP_MULTI

is activated (*freq*). The content of the *SLO_file* is described in WSLA format, where *MeasurementURIs* are required to specify measurements of the target operations. We adopt Uniform Resource Name (URN) scheme to describe these as follows:

urn:*ContainerClass*:*ResourceName*:*Operation Descriptor.*

Here *ContainerClass* may be ICollection or IKeyValue. *ResourceName* indicates the target resource. The available resource names are listed in Table 6. *OperationDescriptor* is used to provide further information about *ResourceName*. For example, *ResponseTime* can be associated with insertion time, search time, and deletion time, which can be specified via OP_INSERT, OP_SEARCH, and OP_ERASE, respectively. The final parameter (*freq*) determines the frequency of self-adaptation operations. Different values of *freq* may affect response times, as discussed in Huang & Knottenbelt, 2013. Essentially there is an optimal value of *freq* which is high enough to be responsive in terms of adaptation but low enough not to exhibit too much overhead.

The SAU performs the operations laid down by the operation interfaces and activates its self-adaptive mechanism as necessary. It is composed

Table 6. The available resource names

Resource Name	Definition
RAM	Primary memory consumption
Response Time	The response time of a certain operation
Reliability	The container's reliability

of an SLO store, an Execution unit, an Observer, an Analyzer, and an Adaptor. The SLO store holds all Service Level Objectives as specified via the configuration interfaces. The SLO includes per operation response time (insertion time, search time, and deletion time), maximum primary memory usage, and reliability, which for probabilistic data structures is defined as the probability that every inserted element is mapped to a unique key (Knottenbelt, 2000). The metrics of desired SLOs are described in the following section. The Execution unit carries out container manipulation commands sent by the operation interfaces through the access of the currently used data structure. The Observer monitors the Execution unit to measure each operation's response time, primary memory consumption, and reliability where appropriate. The operation profile is then reported to the Analyzer, which decides if the Adaptor is triggered to perform an adaptation action. While the Adaptor is activated, it adjusts the underlying data structures in the Execution unit.

3.2 SLO Metrics

SLOs might be related to maximum operation response times, maximum primary memory usage, or minimum acceptable reliability. For response times, they can be defined as soft requirements, which means that a certain percentage of response times can be above a response time target without violating the SLO. All SLOs are specified in WSLA format, which helps programmers clearly define desired SLOs and prevents ambiguity. An example of how to express SLOs for our self-adaptive containers in WSLA format is shown in Huang & Knottenbelt, 2013.

3.3 Self-Adaptive Mechanism

A self-adaptive mechanism is a cycle (Rohr et al., 2006) formed by an observation phase (i.e. Observer), an analysis phase (i.e. Analyzer), and an adaptation phase (i.e. Adaptor). It is activated periodically after completion of container operations according to the container's current adaptation frequency. The self-adaptive cycle starts from the Observer, which measures relevant SLO metrics (e.g. response times, memory usage, and reliability). After that, the operation profile is reported to the Analyzer, which compares it with the expectations of the SLOs in the SLO store. If either no SLO is violated or an adaptation cannot improve the violated SLO, the self-adaptive mechanism terminates. Otherwise, the Adaptor is invoked to adjust the underlying data structures in the Execution unit.

With the Analyzer examining if any SLO is violated, a possible result is that not all SLOs can be satisfied simultaneously. In some extreme cases, none of them can be achieved. To deal with these situations, the SLOs are assigned priorities in their order of declaration. Hence, when SLOs are violated, the Analyzer will try to find an adaptation which can satisfy the violated SLOs or reduce the degree to which they are violated, without violating currently-satisfied SLOs with higher priority.

Based on the nature of the violated SLOs, three adaptation actions may be taken. If they are related to performance, the underlying data structure may be subdivided. Subdivision can reduce operation response times but causes two side effects. The first one is the increase of memory consumption, and the second one is the improvement of reliability (when a probabilistic data structure is used and a reliability requirement is specified). If memory-related SLOs are violated, there are two possible actions. One is the deployment of out-of-core storage, which results in the sharp decrease of performance and the drop of reliability. The other action is the adoption of probabilistic data structures when the acceptable reliability is less than 100%. Finally, if the violated SLOs are related to reliability, the underlying data structures are also subdivided to enhance reliability. This, too, expends memory space and boosts performance.

3.4 Probabilistic Container Data Structures

In this work, we propose an improved sparse Bloom filter as one of the many data structures potentially adopted by the library. The purpose of embedding the improved sparse Bloom filter in our library is to increase (where possible) its scalability and capacity through more efficient use of CPU and memory. It can only be utilised when reliability requirements are less than 100%. In addition, it can interact with out-of-core storage if iterator-based operations are required. The structure of the improved sparse Bloom filter consists of a forest of AVL trees, whose number can be dynamically adjusted to trade off performance, memory efficiency, and reliability, and of hash functions which exploit the CityHash function library (Pike & Alakuijala, 2013). The CityHash function library can, according to reliability requirements, generate 32, 64, 128, and 256 bit hash keys from arbitrary data. When it is necessary to store duplicate data (e.g. multiset), a sparse counting Bloom filter (Bonomi, Mitzenmacher, Panigrahy, Singh, & Varghese, 2006; Rottenstreich, Kanizo, & Keslassy, 2012) is used to provide essential functionalities.

3.5 A Case Study

The case study chosen to demonstrate the library's ability is a breadth-first search (BFS), which is the core algorithm of explicit state-space exploration. Figure 3 displays a naïve implementation of BFS and the program adopting our library. As can be seen, the only difference between the two programs is the declaration of variables. To observe the library's run-time behaviour under different orders of SLOs, the following SLOs are transformed into a WSLA-format file (*ExploredSLOs.xml*, as shown in Figure 3, specified in the second parameter of *explored*), the full contents of which can be seen in Huang & Knottenbelt, 2013:

1. 90% of insertion times should be less than 1000 ns, and 85% of search times should be less than 1200 ns.
2. Reliability should be higher than 0.99.
3. Memory consumption should be no more than 7.5 GB

Furthermore, *unexplored*'s SLO, which specifies that the maximum primary memory consumption is 40 MB, is defined in *unExploredSLOs.xml*.

In order to evaluate the performance, memory consumption, and reliability of our library, the same algorithm (BFS) was executed using an AVL tree, a STL set, a standard Bloom filter, and our library, which was assigned the above SLOs in order of declaration. Figure 4 depicts the average insertion times and search times of conventional data structures and our library. It illustrates that our library yields better performance than conventional data structures. This figure also shows the sudden increase of our library's insertion time and search time. That is because our library needs to adjust its data structures to meet the SLOs.

Figure 3. The naïve breadth-first search (left) and the breadth-first search adopting our library (right)

```
void bfs (Graph G, State s)
{
    queue<State> unexplored;
    set<State> explored;

    unexplored.push(s);
    explored.insert(s);
    while (!unexplored.empty()) {
        State next = unexplored.front();
        unexplored.pop();
        State *w = G.first_edge(next);
        for (; w ; w = G.next_edge(next)) {
            if (!explored.search(*w)) {
                unexplored.push(*w);
                explored.insert(*w);
            }
        }
    }
}
```

```
void bfs (Graph G, State s)
{
    ICollection<State> unexplored(OP_QUEUE, "UnexploredSLOs.xml");
    ICollection<State> explored (OP_INSERT|OP_SEARCH, "ExploredSLOs.xml", 100);

    unexplored.push(s);
    explored.insert(s);
    while (!unexplored.empty()) {
        State next = unexplored.front();
        unexplored.pop();
        State *w = G.first_edge(next);
        for (; w ; w = G.next_edge(next)) {
            if (!explored.search(*w)) {
                unexplored.push(*w);
                explored.insert(*w);
            }
        }
    }
}
```

Figure 4. The average insertion and search times of the AVL tree, the standard Bloom filter, the STL set, and our library

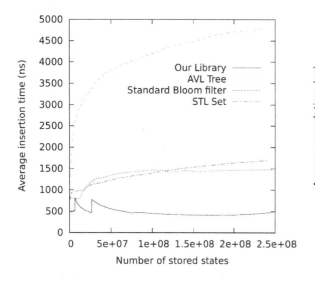

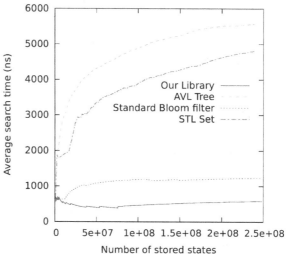

Figure 5 illustrates the memory consumptions of the AVL tree, the STL set, the standard Bloom filter, and our library. Our library used an order of magnitude less memory space than the AVL tree and the STL set. In other words, our library can accept larger input sizes than the two data structures. Although our library was not as memory efficient as the standard Bloom filter, its reliability was higher.

When given different SLO priorities (by declaring them in different orders), our library's average insertion times and average search times are shown in Figure 6. As can be seen, when performance-related SLOs had the highest priority, our library would achieve considerably lower insertion times and search times. By contrast, when the priority of memory consumption (MemRelPer or MemPerRel) was the highest in order, the insertion times and search times sharply rose when the memory quota was reached. That was because our library frequently accessed out-of-core memory.

The library's memory consumption conditions under the six priority orders and reliability changes are depicted in Figure 7. The memory space changes of our library illustrated three kinds

Figure 5. The memory usages of the AVL tree, the standard Bloom filter, the STL set, and our library

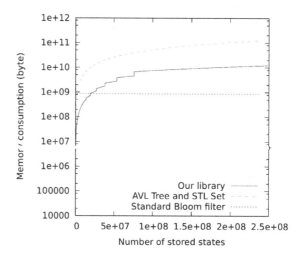

of behaviour. First, when the priority of memory consumption was the highest, the consumed memory space was the least. On the contrary, when the priority of memory consumption was lower than that of reliability and performance, our library would consume more memory space to enhance reliability and performance. Second, when memory consumption reached its limit,

Figure 6. The average insertion and search times under different SLO priorities

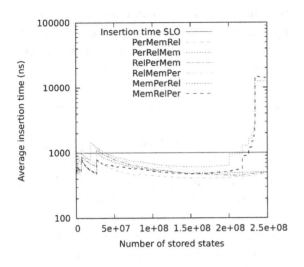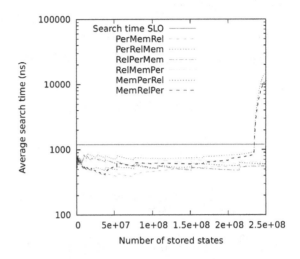

MemRelPer and MemPerRel would reduce the number of currently-used AVL trees to save memory space. Once the number of AVL trees could not be reduced, an out-of-core technique was triggered to store states on disk. Third, when the number of stored states reached about 100 million, PerMemRel stopped increasing the number of AVL trees but PerRelMem did not. That was because the priority of memory consumption in the former case was higher than that of reliability. As a result, when the actual reliability was lower than the required reliability, PerMemRel would not enhance reliability to protect the memory quota.

The changes of our library's reliability are shown in the right-handed side of Figure 7, which indicates that when reliability had the highest priority, our library adapted its data structure to maintain a desirable reliability – over 0.99. This figure also makes clear that when reliability was the lowest in order of priority, the library's reliability would deteriorate as stored states increased.

Figure 7. The reliability and memory consumption changes under different SLO priorities

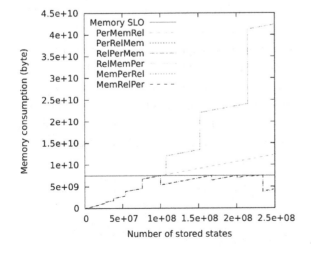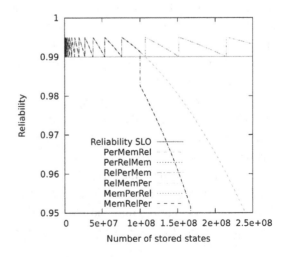

Figure 8. Memory consumptions of naïve queue and intelligent queue

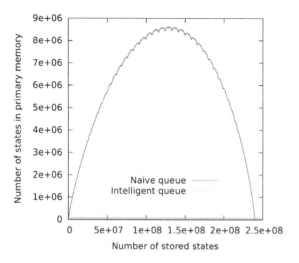

The difference of *unexplored*'s (the queue for storing unexplored states) primary memory usage is demonstrated in Figure 8. As displayed in the figure, the queue adopting our library consumed 40 MB primary memory, which amounted to a mere 1% memory consumption of the naïve implementation.

4. FUTURE RESEARCH DIRECTIONS

The case study has shown that self-adaptive containers can effectively achieve programmer-specified Service Level Objectives at run time. However, it also brings drawbacks to testing and debugging. All of our library's adaptations happen at execution time, which increases the difficulty of tracing program flow. Hence, when software does not behave as programmers expect, it is hard to find the root cause. To overcome this challenge, the library should provide an option which enables the action of recording software status (e.g. data in the primary memory, the previously used data structure) when an adaptation is taken. Additionally, adaptations may cause performance bottlenecks if our library expends too much time on changing data structures. This may be improved by tuning the adaptation frequency and parallelising adaptation actions across different cores and/or processors within a single system or different machines in distributed environments.

Our current focus on container libraries allows us to improve on the low-level complexity and resource usage of many applications, but we cannot address the problem of the use of fundamentally inefficient algorithms at higher program levels. One promising approach that might help relates to the automated detection and correction of performance anti-patterns. Compared to software design patterns (Gamma, Johnson, Vlissides, & Helm, 1994), which provide templates for good solutions to design problems, anti-patterns (Brown, Malveau, McCormick, & Mowbray, 1998) are templates for bad practices which are virtually guaranteed to lead to undesirable non-functional behaviour. According to Smaalder's work (Smaalders, 2006), significant performance improvements can result from modifications of algorithms. If automated correction of performance anti-patterns were to become feasible in the future it would further push the frontiers of intelligent self-adaptive software.

Another future direction limited to the scope of our current approach is to consider different ways to carry out the multi-objective optimisation when presented with multiple SLOs. The technique our library currently uses is the lexicographic method (Marler & Arora, 2004), which means each SLO is addressed one at a time in accordance with their importance (priority). Other multi-objective optimisation methods could be used with our library which combines multiple SLOs into single objective functions, either as a weighted product or a weighted sum. We would then be able to explicitly trade off multiple SLOs simultaneously in a rigorous way.

5. CONCLUSION

As the number of execution environments and application contexts explodes, the use of traditional software engineering pipelines leads to one of two scenarios: either there is a small code base which cannot guarantee quality-of-service or there are multiple manually-optimised code bases which are hard to maintain. The vision of this chapter has been to propose a means to achieve both: a small easily-maintained code base together with automated mechanisms to support improved quality-of-service delivery at run-time according to the specific execution environment and application context. Self-adaption has played a central role in achieving this vision, which has been concretely demonstrated using a prototype self-adaptive C++ container library. Our experience has shown us that some barriers to practical adoption remain: especially those related to debugging and the guaranteeing of system correctness in the face of self-adapting data structures. Further, the problem of attempting to satisfy simultaneously multiple QoS objectives subject to resource constraints is not a trivial one, and indeed may sometimes be impossible to achieve. The best way to provide best-quality degraded service in this context remains an open problem, and opens up one of many future directions for research.

REFERENCES

Abram, G., & Treinish, L. (1995). An extended data-flow architecture for data analysis and visualization. In *Proceedings of the 6th Conference on Visualization* (pp. 263-270). Atlanta, GA: IEEE Computer Society.

Alabduljalil, M. A., Tang, X., & Yang, T. (2013). Optimizing parallel algorithms for all pairs similarity search. In *Proceedings of the sixth ACM International Conference on Web Search and Data Mmining* (pp. 203-212). Rome, Italy: ACM.

Allmaier, S. C., & Horton, G. (1997). Parallel shared-memory state-space exploration in stochastic modeling. In *Proceedings of the 4th International Symposium on Solving Irregularly Structured Problems in Parallel* (pp. 207-218). Paderborn, Germany: Springer-Verlag.

Andrieux, A., Czajkowski, K., Dan, A., Keahey, K., Ludwig, H., & Nakata, T. et al. (2004). *Web Services Agreement Specification (WS-Agreement)*. Academic Press.

Bawa, M., Condie, T., & Ganesan, P. (2005). LSH forest: Self-tuning indexes for similarity search. In *Proceedings of the 14th International Conference on World Wide Web* (pp. 651-660). Chiba, Japan: ACM.

Bell, A., & Haverkort, B. R. (2001). Serial and parallel out-of-core solution of linear systems arising from generalised stochastic Petri nets. In *Procdings of High Performance Computing 2001* (pp. 181–200). Copenhagen, Denmark: Springer-Verlag.

Berchtold, S., Böhm, C., Braunmüller, B., Keim, D. A., & Kriegel, H.-P. (1997). Fast parallel similarity search in multimedia databases. In *Proceedings of the 1997 ACM SIGMOD International Conference on Management of Data* (pp. 1-12). Tucson, AZ: ACM.

Bhattacharya, I., Kashyap, S. R., & Parthasarathy, S. (2005). Similarity searching in peer-to-peer databases. In *Proceedings of the 25th IEEE International Conference on Distributed Computing Systems* (pp. 329-338). Columbus, OH: IEEE Computer Society.

Bingham, B., Bingham, J., Paula, F. M. D., Erickson, J., Singh, G., & Reitblatt, M. (2010). Industrial strength distributed explicit state model checking. In *Proceedings of the 2010 9th International Workshop on Parallel and Distributed Methods in Verification, and second International Workshop on High Performance Computational Systems Biology* (pp. 28-36). Enschede, The Netherlands: IEEE Computer Society.

Bloom, B. H. (1970). Space/time trade-offs in hash coding with allowable errors. *Communications of the ACM, 13*(7), 422–426. doi:10.1145/362686.362692

Bonomi, F., Mitzenmacher, M., Panigrahy, R., Singh, S., & Varghese, G. (2006). An improved construction for counting Bloom filters. In *Proceedings of the 14th Conference on Annual European Symposium* (vol. 14, pp. 684-695). Zurich, Switzerland: Springer-Verlag.

Bourrillion, K., & Levy, J. (2014). *Guava project.* Retrieved February 4, 2014, from https://code.google.com/p/guava-libraries/

Brown, W. J., Malveau, R. C., McCormick, H. W. S., & Mowbray, T. J. (1998). *AntiPatterns: Refactoring software architectures, and projects in crisis.* Hoboken, NJ: John Wiley and Sons, Inc.

Buss, A., Papadopoulos, H. I., Pearce, O., & Smith, T. (2010). STAPL: Standard template adaptive parallel library. In *Proceedings of the 3rd Annual Haifa Experimental Systems Conference* (pp. 1-10). Haifa, Israel: ACM.

Butler, J., MacCallum, I., Kleber, M., Shlyakhter, I. A., Belmonte, M. K., & Lander, E. S. et al. (2008). ALLPATHS: De novo assembly of whole-genome shotgun microreads. *Genome Research, 18*(5), 810–820. doi:10.1101/gr.7337908 PMID:18340039

Caselli, S., Conte, G., & Marenzoni, P. (1995). Parallel state space exploration for GSPN models. In *Proceedings of the 16th International Conference on Application and Theory of Petri Nets* (pp. 181-200). Turin, Italy: Springer-Verlag.

Chiang, Y.-J., & Silva, C. T. (1999). External memory techniques for isosurface extraction in scientific visualization. In J. M. Abello, & J. S. Vitter (Eds.), *External memory algorithms* (pp. 247–277). American Mathematical Society.

Chikhi, R., & Rizk, G. (2012). Space-efficient and exact de Bruijn graph representation based on a Bloom filter. In *Proceedings of the 12th International Conference on Algorithms in Bioinformatics* (pp. 236-248). Ljubljana, Slovenia: Springer-Verlag.

Ciardo, G., Gluckman, J., & Nicol, D. (1998). Distributed state-space generation of discrete-state stochastic models. *INFORMS Journal on Computing, 10*(1), 82–93. doi:10.1287/ijoc.10.1.82

Cignoni, P., Montani, C., Rocchini, C., & Scopigno, R. (2003). External memory management and simplification of huge meshes. *IEEE Transactions on Visualization and Computer Graphics, 9*(4), 525–537. doi:10.1109/TVCG.2003.1260746

Cook, J. J., & Zilles, C. B. (2009). Characterizing and optimizing the memory footprint of de novo short read DNA sequence assembly. In *Proceedings of the IEEE International Symposium on Performance Analysis of Systems and Software* (pp. 143-152). Boston, MA: IEEE Computer Society.

Deavours, D. D., & Sanders, W. H. (1997). An efficient disk-based tool for solving very large Markov models. *Performance Evaluation, 33*(1), 67–84. doi:10.1016/S0166-5316(98)00010-8

Delling, D., Katz, B., & Pajor, T. (2012). Parallel computation of best connections in public transportation networks. *Journal of Experimental Algorithmics, 17*, 4.1-:4.26.

Dementiev, R., Kettner, L., & Sanders, P. (2008). STXXL: Standard template library for XXL data sets. *Journal of Software- Practice & Experience, 38*(6), 589-637.

Dingle, N. J., Knottenbelt, W. J., & Suto, T. (2009). PIPE2: A tool for the performance evaluation of generalised stochastic Petri nets. *SIGMETRICS Performance Evaluation Review, 36*(4), 34–39. doi:10.1145/1530873.1530881

Eastep, J., Wingate, D., & Agarwal, A. (2011). Smart data structures: An online machine learning approach to multicore data structures. In *Proceedings of the 8th ACM International Conference on Autonomic Computing* (pp. 11-20). Karlsruhe, Germany: ACM.

Edelkamp, S., & Schrodl, S. (2000). Localizing A*. In *Proceedings of the 7th National Conference on Artificial Intelligence and 12th Conference on Innovative Applications of Artificial Intelligence* (pp. 885-890). Austin, TX: The MIT Press.

Edelkamp, S., & Sulewski, D. (2010). Efficient explicit-state model checking on general purpose graphics processors. In *Proceedings of the 17th International SPIN Conference on Model Checking Software* (pp. 106-123). Enschede, The Netherlands: Springer-Verlag.

Fan, L., Cao, P., Almeida, J., & Broder, A. Z. (2000). Summary cache: A scalable wide-area web cache sharing protocol. *IEEE/ACM Transactions on Networking, 8*(3), 281–293. doi:10.1109/90.851975

Fogaras, D., & Rácz, B. (2005). Scaling link-based similarity search. In *Proceedings of the 14th International Conference on World Wide Web (pp.* 641-650). Chiba, Japan: ACM.

Galper, A. R., & Brutlag, D. L. (1990). *Parallel similarity Search and Alignment with the Dynamic Programming Method (Tech. Rep.).* Academic Press.

Gamma, E., Johnson, R., Vlissides, J., & Helm, R. (1994). *Design patterns: Elements of reusable object-oriented software.* Reading, MA: Addison-Wesley Professional.

Ganek, A. G., & Corbi, T. A. (2003). The dawning of the autonomic computing era. *IBM Systems Journal, 42*(1), 5–18. doi:10.1147/sj.421.0005

Garlan, D., Cheng, S.-W., Huang, A.-C., Schmerl, B., & Steenkiste, P. (2004). Rainbow: Architecture-based self-adaptation with reusable infrastructure. *Computer, 37*(10), 46–54. doi:10.1109/MC.2004.175

Gionis, A., Indyk, P., & Motwani, R. (1999). Similarity search in high dimensions via hashing. In *Proceedings of the 25th International Conference on Very Large Data Bases* (pp. 518-529). Edinburgh, UK: Morgan Kaufmann Publishers Inc.

Goldberg, A. V., & Werneck, R. F. (2005). Computing point-to-point shortest paths from external memory. In *Proceedings of the 7h Workshop on Algorithm Engineering and Experiments* (pp. 26-40). Vancouver, Canada: SIAM.

Gudaitis, M. S., Lamont, G. B., & Terzuoli, A. J. (1995). Multicriteria vehicle route-planning using parallel A * search. In *Proceedings of the 1995 ACM Symposium on Applied Computing* (pp. 171-176). Nashville, TN: ACM.

Haverkort, B., Bell, A., & Bohnenkamp, H. (1999). On the efficient sequential and distributed generation of very large Markov chains from stochastic Petri nets. In *Proceedings of the 8th International Workshop on Petri Nets and Performance Models* (pp. 12-21). Zaragoza, Spain: Presnsas Universitarias de Zaragoza.

Holzmann, G. J. (1988). An improved protocol reachability analysis technique. *Software, Practice & Experience, 18*(2), 137–161. doi:10.1002/spe.4380180203

Horn, P. (2001). *Autonomic computing: IBM's perspective on the state of information technology.* Academic Press.

Huebscher, M. C., & McCann, J. A. (2008). A survey of autonomic computing- degrees, models, and applications. *ACM Computing Surveys, 40*(3), 1–28. doi:10.1145/1380584.1380585

Idury, R. M., & Waterman, M. S. (1995). A new algorithm for DNA sequence assembly. *Journal of Computational Biology, 2*(2), 291–306. doi:10.1089/cmb.1995.2.291 PMID:7497130

Jackson, B. G., Regennitter, M., Yang, X., Schnable, P. S., & Aluru, S. (2010). Parallel de novo assembly of large genomes from high-throughput short reads. In *Proceedings of the 27th IEEE International Symposium on Parallel & Distributed Processing* (pp. 1-10). Atlanta, GA: IEEE Computer Society.

Jiang, P., Ji, Y., Wang, X., Zhu, J., & Cheng, Y. (2013). Design of a Multiple Bloom Filter for Distributed Navigation Routing. *IEEE Transactions on Systems, Man, and Cybernetics: Systems,* (99), 1-7.

Jing, C., Zhengang, N., Liying, L., & Fei, Y. (2009). Research and Application on Bloom Filter in Routing Planning for Indoor Robot Navigation System. In *Proceedings of Pacific-Asia Conference on Circuits, Communications and Systems (PACCS '09)* (pp. 244-247). Chengdu, China: IEEE Computer Society.

Johnson, E., & Gannon, D. (1997). HPC++: Experiments with the parallel standard template library. In *Proceedings of 11th international conference on Supercomputing* (pp. 124-131). Vienna, Austria: ACM.

Kaminsky, A. (2007). Parallel Java: A Unified API for Shared Memory and Cluster Parallel Programming in 100% Java. In *Proceedings of 21st IEEE International Parallel and Distributed Processing Symposium (IPDPS 2007)* (pp. 1-8). Long Beach, CA: IEEE Computer Society.

Karlsson, B. (2005). *Beyond the C++ Standard Library: An Introduction to Boost.* Reading, MA: Addison-Wesley.

Keller, A., & Ludwig, H. (2003). The WSLA framework: Specifying and monitoring service level agreements for web services. *Journal of Network and Systems Management, 11*(1), 57–81. doi:10.1023/A:1022445108617

Kephart, J. O., & Chess, D. M. (2003). The vision of autonomic computing. *Computer, 36*(1), 41–50. doi:10.1109/MC.2003.1160055

Khalid, A., Haye, M. A., Khan, M. J., & Shamail, S. (2009). Survey of Frameworks, Architectures and Techniques in Autonomic Computing. In *Proceedings of 2009 5th International Conference on Autonomic and Autonomous Systems* (pp. 220-225). Valencia, Spain: IEEE Computer Society.

Knottenbelt, W. J. (2000). *Performance Analysis of Large Markov Models.* (Unpublished PhD Thesis). Imperial College of Science, Technology and Medicine.

Knottenbelt, W. J., & Harrison, P. G. (1999). Distributed Disk-based Solution Techniques for Large Markov Models. In *Proceedings of 3rd International Workshop on the Numerical Solution of Markov Chains* (pp. 58-75). Zaragoza, Spain: Presnsas Universitarias de Zaragoza.

Kotek, J. (2013). *MapDB.* Retrieved February 18, 2014, from http://www.mapdb.org/

Kramer, J., & Magee, J. (2007). Self-managed systems: An architectural challenge. In *Proceedings of the Conference on The Future of Software Engineering* (pp. 259-268). Minneapolis, MN: IEEE Computer Society.

Krishnamurthy, P., Buhler, J., Chamberlain, R., Franklin, M., Gyang, K., & Jacob, A. et al. (2007). Biosequence similarity search on the mercury system. *The Journal of VLSI Signal Processing Systems for Signal, Image, and Video Technology, 49*(1), 101–121. doi:10.1007/s11265-007-0087-0 PMID:18846267

Kundeti, V. K., Rajasekaran, S., Dinh, H., Vaughn, M., & Thapar, V. (2010). Efficient parallel and out of core algorithms for constructing large bi-directed de Bruijn graphs. *BMC Bioinformatics, 11*(1), 560. doi:10.1186/1471-2105-11-560 PMID:21078174

Kwiatkowska, M. Z., & Mehmood, R. (2002). Out-of-core solution of large linear systems of equations arising from stochastic modelling. In *Proceedings of the Second Joint International Workshop on Process Algebra and Probabilistic Methods, Performance Modeling and Verification* (pp. 135-151). Copenhagen, Denmark: Springer-Verlag.

Lalanda, P., McCann, J. A., & Diaconescu, A. (2013). *Autonomic computing: Principles, design and implementation.* Berlin: Springer. doi:10.1007/978-1-4471-5007-7

Lamanna, D. D., Skene, J., & Emmerich, W. (2003). SLAng: A language for defining service level agreements. In *Proceedings of the 9th IEEE Workshop on Future Trends of Distributed Computing Systems* (pp. 100-106). San Juan, Puerto Rico: IEEE Computer Society.

Levoy, M. (2011). *The Stanford 3D scanning repository.* Retrieved September 2, 2013, from http://www-graphics.stanford.edu/data/3Dscanrep/

Li, T., Yang, D., & Lian, X. (2012). Road crosses high locality sorting for navigation route planning. *Recent Advances in Computer Science and Information Engineering, 124,* 497–502. doi:10.1007/978-3-642-25781-0_74

Li, Y., Kamousi, P., Han, F., Yang, S., Yan, X., & Suri, S. (2012). Memory efficient de Bruijn graph construction. *CoRR.*

Liu, Y., Schmidt, B., & Maskell, D. L. (2011). Parallelized short read assembly of large genomes using de Bruijn graphs. *BMC Bioinformatics, 12,* 354. doi:10.1186/1471-2105-12-354 PMID:21867511

Marler, R. T., & Arora, J. S. (2004). Survey of multi-objective optimization methods for engineering. *Structural and Multidisciplinary Optimization, 26*(6), 369–395. doi:10.1007/s00158-003-0368-6

Melsted, P., & Pritchard, J. K. (2011). Efficient counting of k-mers in DNA sequences using a Bloom filter. *BMC Bioinformatics, 333.* doi:10.1186/1471-2105-12-333 PMID:21831268

Meredith, J., Ahern, S., Pugmire, D., & Sisneros, R. (2012). EAVL: The Extreme-scale Analysis and Visualization Library. In *Proceedings of the Eurographics Symposium on Parallel Graphics and Visualization (EGPGV)* (pp. 21-30). Cagliari, Italy: Eurographics Association.

Musser, D. R., Derge, G. J., & Saini, A. (2001). *Stl Tutorial and Reference Guide: C++ Programming with the Standard Template Library.* Boston: Addison-Wesley.

Pell, J., Hintze, A., Canino-Koning, R., Howe, A., Tiedje, J. M., & Brown, C. T. (2012). Scaling metagenome sequence assembly with probabilistic de Bruijn graphs. In *Proceedings of the National Academy of Sciences* (pp. 13:272-213:277). PNAS.

Pevzner, P. A., Tang, H., & Waterman, M. S. (2001). An Eulerian path approach to DNA fragment assembly. In *Proceedings of the National Academy of Sciences* (pp. 9748-9753). PNAS.

Pike, G., & Alakuijala, J. (2013). *CityHash.* Retrieved June, 2013, from https://code.google.com/p/cityhash/

Ren, K., Wang, C., & Wang, Q. (2012). Toward secure and effective data utilization in public cloud. *IEEE Network, 26*(6), 69–74. doi:10.1109/MNET.2012.6375896

Rohr, M., Giesecke, S., Hasselbring, W., Hiel, M., Heuvel, W.-J. V. D., & Weigand, H. (2006). A classification scheme for self-adaptation research. In *Proceedings of International Conference on Self-Organization and Autonomous Systems*. Erfurt, Germany: Academic Press.

Rottenstreich, O., Kanizo, Y., & Keslassy, I. (2012). The variable-increment counting Bloom filter. In *Proceedings of the 31st Annual IEEE International Conference on Computer Communications* (pp. 1880-1888). Orlando, FL: IEEE Computer Society.

Saad, R. T., Zilio, S. D., & Berthomieu, B. (2010). A general lock-free algorithm for parallel state space construction. In *Proceedings of the 2010 9th International Workshop on Parallel and Distributed Methods in Verification, and second International Workshop on High Performance Computational Systems Biology* (pp. 8-16). Enschede, The Netherlands: IEEE Computer Society.

Salehie, M., & Tahvildari, L. (2009). Self-adaptive software: Landscape and research challenges. *ACM Transactions on Autonomous and Adaptive Systems, 4*(2), 1–42. doi:10.1145/1516533.1516538

Sanders, P., Schultes, D., & Vetter, C. (2008). Mobile route planning. In *Proceedings of ESA 2008* (LNCS), (vol. 5193, pp. 732-743). Berlin: Springer.

Singler, J., Sanders, P., & Putze, F. (2007). MC-STL: The multi-core standard template library. In *Proceedings of the 13th International Euro-Par Conference on Parallel Processing* (pp. 682-694). Rennes, France: Springer-Verlag.

Smaalders, B. (2006). Performance anti-patterns. *Queue - Performance, 4*(1), 44-50.

Souza, V. E. S. (2012). *Requirements-based software system adaptation*. (Unpublished PhD Thesis). University of Trento.

Stern, U., & Dill, D. L. (1995). Improved probabilistic verification by hash compaction. In *Proceedings of the IFIP WG 10.5 Advanced Research Working Conference on Correct Hardware Design and Verification Methods* (pp. 206-224). Frankfurt, Germany: Springer-Verlag.

Suto, T., Bradley, J. T., & Knottenbelt, W. J. (2006). Performance trees: A new approach to quantitative performance specification. In *Proceedings of the 14th IEEE International Symposium on Modeling, Analysis, and Simulation of Computer and Telecommunication Systems* (pp. 303-313). Monterey, CA: IEEE Computer Society.

Teodoro, G., Valle, E., Mariano, N., Torres, R., & Meira, W. J. (2011). Adaptive parallel approximate similarity search for responsive multimedia retrieval. In *Proceedings of the 20th ACM International Conference on Information and Knowledge Management* (pp. 495-504). Glasgow, UK: ACM.

Upson, C., Thomas Faulhaber, J., Kamins, D., Laidlaw, D. H., Schlegel, D., & Vroom, J. et al. (1989). The application visualization system: A computational environment for scientific visualization. *IEEE Computer Graphics and Applications, 9*(4), 30–42. doi:10.1109/38.31462

Vo, H. T., Silva, C. T., Scheidegger, L. F., & Pascucci, V. (2012). Simple and efficient mesh layout with space-filling curves. *Journal of Graphics Tools, 6*(1), 25–39. doi:10.1080/2151237X.2012.641828

Wang, C., Ren, K., Yu, S., & Urs, K. M. R. (2012). Achieving usable and privacy-assured similarity search over outsourced cloud data. [Orlando, FL: IEEE Computer Society.]. *Proceedings - IEEE INFOCOM, 2012*, 451–459.

Wang, H., & Liu, K. (2012). User oriented trajectory similarity search. In *Proceedings of the ACM SIGKDD International Workshop on Urban Computing* (pp. 103-110). Beijing, China: ACM.

Watt, D. A., & Brown, D. (2001). *Java collections: An introduction to abstract data types, data structures and algorithms*. New York, NY: John Wiley & Sons, Inc.

Welsh, M., & Culler, D. (1999). Jaguar: Enabling efficient communication and I/O in Java. *Concurrency (Chichester, England)*, *12*(7), 519–538. doi:10.1002/1096-9128(200005)12:7<519::AID-CPE497>3.0.CO;2-M

Wewetzer, C., Scheuermann, B., Lübke, A., & Mauve, M. (2009). Content registration in VANETs - saving bandwidth through node cooperation. In *Proceedings of the 34th IEEE Conference on Local Computer Networks* (pp. 661-668). Zurich, Switzerland: IEEE Computer Society.

Witkowski, C. M. (1983). A parallel processor algorithm for robot route planning. In *Proceedings of the 8th International Joint Conference on Artificial Intelligence* (pp. 827-829). Karlsruhe, Germany: Morgan Kaufmann Publishers Inc.

Wolper, P., & Leroy, D. (1993). Reliable hashing without collision detection. In *Proceedings of the 5th International Conference on Computer Aided Verification* (pp. 59-70). Elounda, Greece: Springer-Verlag.

Zerbino, D. R., & Birney, E. (2008). Velvet: Algorithms for de novo short read assembly using de Bruijn graphs. *Genome Research*, *18*(5), 821–829. doi:10.1101/gr.074492.107 PMID:18349386

Zhao, Y., Tang, H., & Ye, Y. (2012). RAPSearch2: A fast and memory-efficient protein similarity search tool for next-generation sequencing data. *Bioinformatics (Oxford, England)*, *28*(1), 125–126. doi:10.1093/bioinformatics/btr595 PMID:22039206

KEY TERMS AND DEFINITIONS

Container: An data structure that holds a set of other objects. In many standardised libraries, container classes feature member functions to manipulate and access the held objects.

Out-of-Core Algorithm: An algorithm which exploits external storage in order to support large data volumes that cannot be supported by primary memory.

Probabilistic Data Structure: A data structure which exploits randomness to boost its efficiency, for example skip lists and Bloom filters. In the case of Bloom filters, the results of certain operations may be incorrect with a small probability.

Quality of Service: An objective characterisation of the performance levels delivered to users by a system or service. Ideally, a system should maintain QoS at or above some minimum level.

Resource-Aware System: A system which has the ability to monitor its resource usage and to dynamically manage resources according to user-specified constraints.

Self-Adaptive System: A system which can automatically reconfigure itself in response to changes in its environment.

Service Level Objective: A measurable QoS-related target, defined jointly by service providers and customers.

Standard Template Library: A C++ software library that provides commonly-used containers and algorithms to simplify software design.

Chapter 6

An Empirical Study of the Effect of Design Patterns on Class Structural Quality

Liguo Yu
Indiana University – South Bend, USA

Srini Ramaswamy
BU Power Generation at ABB, India

ABSTRACT

Design patterns are standardized solutions to commonly encountered problems using the object-oriented programming paradigm. Applying design patterns can speed up software development processes through the reuse of tested, proven templates, or development paradigms. Accordingly, design patterns have been widely used in software industry to build modern software programs. However, as different design patterns are introduced to solve different design problems, they are not necessarily superior to alternative solutions, with respect to all aspects of software design. One major concern is that the inappropriate use of design patterns may unnecessarily increase program complexity, such as class structural quality. Theoretical analysis of the effect of design patterns on software complexity has been widely performed. However, little work is reported to empirically study how design patterns might affect class structural quality. This chapter studies six components from five open-source Java projects and empirically investigates if design patterns can affect class structural quality. The chapter finds that pattern-involved classes are more complex than pattern-free classes and recommends the cautious use of design patterns to avoid unnecessary increases in class complexity and decrease in class structural quality.

1. INTRODUCTION

Design patterns are standardized experience-based solutions for commonly recurring object-oriented design problems (McNatt & Bieman, 2001; Shalloway & Trott, 2005). The use of design patterns can provide several advantages, such as increasing reusability, modularity, and quality of a program. Design patterns can also improve the consistency between program design and program implementation and help achieve better coordination between the design and the implementation teams (Hash-

DOI: 10.4018/978-1-4666-6026-7.ch006

eminejad & Jalili, 2012). Since the introduction of design patterns (Gamma et al., 1995), software developers and researchers have identified over 20 patterns, many of which have been widely used in object-oriented programs. A recent study found that design patterns have also been widely used in open-source programs (Ampatzoglou et al., 2011a), which greatly facilitated the rapid growth and distribution of open-source projects.

Although design patterns can provide tested, proven solutions to representative and oft-occurring software design problems, they are not necessarily the best of class solutions with respect to software quality. First, while design patterns could be used to solve certain design problems, they might introduce new problems and reduce the system quality (Ampatzoglou et al., 2011a). Second, the use of design patterns should be context-based; an inappropriate use of design patterns could increase the system complexity and accordingly reduce software quality (Ampatzoglou et al., 2011b). To address this issue, extensive research has been performed in this area to study how design patterns can affect software quality, including reusability and maintainability (Ampatzoglou et al., 2011a; Ampatzoglou et al., 2011b). For example, theoretical analysis has been performed on several design patterns to see how they might affect complexity measurements (Huston, 2001). However, little work has been reported to empirically investigate the relationship between design patterns and software design quality.

This chapter presents a case study to investigate the relationship between class structural quality and design patterns. The study is performed on six open-source java components, which range from small to large applications. The class structural quality measurements of pattern-involved classes and pattern-free classes are calculated and compared.

The remainder of the chapter is organized as follows. Section 2 reviews related work in the quality analysis of design patterns. Section 3 presents the background knowledge of this study.

Section 4 describes the data source and the data mining process. Section 5 presents the analysis and the results. Threats to validity are discussed in Section 6. Conclusions and future work appear in Section 7.

2. LITERATURE REVIEW

Because of the widespread use of design patterns in object-oriented software development, a large body of intensive research in this area has been published. For example, design patterns have been used to study the maintenance and evolution of software systems. Fushida et al. (2007) used pattern detection tools to study the change history of JUnit from the viewpoint of design pattern evolutions. Hsueh et al. (2011) proposed a method to evaluate how design patterns can effectively affect software evolution.

The work that is directly related to our study is to analyze the relationship between design patterns and software quality (Ampatzoglou & Chatzigeorgiou, 2007; Di Penta et al., 2008; Prechelt et al., 2001). For example, Zheng and Harper (2010) surveyed some concurrency design patterns and illustrated the relationship between concurrency design patterns and software quality attributes. Their study presented a mapping between concurrency design patterns and software performance and modifiability. Sandhu et al. (2008) proposed a set of quality metrics for various design patterns. Their study aimed to build high quality product through using high quality reusable design patterns.

Although extensive work has been reported, there are still no conclusive findings reported. Some studies showed that design patterns could reduce software complexity (Lange & Nakamura, 1995), and accordingly increase product quality. Some other studies found that design patterns could unintentionally increase software complexity (Wendorff, 2001; Bieman et al., 2002; Bieman et al., 2003) and potentially reduce software quality;

which raises concerns about the wide use of design patterns in the software industry: some patterns might be used unwisely and inappropriately.

Recent studies supporting the argument that design patterns can reduce program complexity are reported by Aydinoz (2006) and Turk (2009). In his master thesis, Aydinoz found that refactoring an object-oriented program with design patterns can reduce its complexity measures, such as WMC (weighted method per class), CBO (coupling between objects), and RFC (response for a class). Similarly, in Turk's master thesis, an experiment was designed to investigate the effect of design patterns on class attributes of an object-oriented program. He found design patterns can improve most maintainability predicting metrics. The drawback is that both studies were performed on 'school' projects, which were implemented specifically for the experiments.

A negative report about using design patterns is given by Khomh and Gueheneuc (2008) and Khomh et al. (2008), where they presented an empirical study of the impact of design patterns on quality attributes of a software program. These quality attributes are correlated with software maintenance and evolution. Their study found that design patterns affect several quality attributes of a program negatively. Based on their findings, they suggested that design patterns should be used with caution during development because these patterns may actually impede maintenance and evolution.

Software quality has often aroused different meanings with respect to different properties, such as readability, maintainability, and reusability. In all these different measurements, complexity metrics are the most commonly used and have been proved to be directly related to other quality measurements (Cartwright & Shepperd, 2000). There are many software complexity metrics, such as coupling metrics and cohesion metrics. Various complexity metrics have been used to measure and evaluate different design patterns. For example, Hsueh et al. (2008) performed a theoretical analysis of the design patterns based on the QMOOD (quality model of object oriented design) model. They found some patterns are polymorphism-improver, hierarchy-improver, and abstraction-improver. They also found that not all design patterns are quality improvers. For example, the singleton design pattern is proposed to resolve a specific design or programming problem, not for quality improvement. Therefore, the singleton design pattern is more like a problem-solver, instead of a quality improver.

Chidamber and Kemerer (1994)'s metrics suite is the most popular complexity metrics for object-oriented programs. Several studies have been reported to use these metrics to measure the complexity of design pattern-involved classes. For example, Huston (2001) theoretically analyzed the effect of design patterns on class metric scores. Specifically, he studied three design patterns: mediator, bridge, and visitor, and compared the complexity scores of these design patterns and the alternative non-pattern solutions. The results showed that the usage of these design patterns could improve design quality such as reducing the average NOC (number of children) measurements.

Recent studies in this line of research are reported by Ampatzoglou et al. (2012). In their studies, they proposed and illustrated a methodology for comparing the quality attributes of design patterns to the quality attributes of alternative non-pattern design solutions using an analytical method. The study suggested that the decision of applying a design pattern is usually a trade-off, because patterns are not universally good or bad. Patterns typically improve certain aspects of software quality, while they might weaken some other aspects of software quality. In another study (Ampatzoglou, 2011a), they investigated the reusability of design patterns in open-source projects, where reusability metric is constructed based on complexity measurements. The study found that design patterns are widely used and reused in open-source projects.

To summarize, although intensive work has been reported to study the complexity of design patterns, most of such work is done through theoretical analysis. The reported empirical studies were performed on self-designed experiments. The work that is most similar to the study presented in this chapter is reported by Khomh et al. (2009), who studied the roles of design patterns across several open-source projects. To our knowledge, no empirical work has been performed to study the class structural quality of design patterns in real-world projects. Our study intends to fill this research gap by providing empirical evidence about the effect of design patterns on real-world software class quality measurements.

3. BACKGROUND

Related background knowledge for this study, which investigates the relationship between design patterns and software class structural quality in object-oriented programs, is addressed in this section.

3.1. Chidamber and Kemerer Metrics Suite

The complexity metrics suite used in this study is proposed by Chidamber & Kemerer (1994). This metrics suite was introduced for measuring the class complexity of object-oriented programs. Since then, it has become one of the most popular metrics suites in software industry. The original version of the Chidamber & Kemerer metrics suite consists of 6 metrics: WMC (weighted methods per class), DIT (depth of inheritance tree), NOC (number of children), CBO (coupling between object classes), RFC (response for a class) and LCOM (lack of cohesion in methods). Besides Chidamber & Kemerer metrics suite, other two object-oriented metrics are also used in this study. They are Ca (afferent couplings) and NPM (number of public methods) (Martin, 2003). These metrics are listed in Table 1 and are in general, collectively termed as class structural quality metrics.

It is worth noting that a high value of class structural quality measurements indicates a low quality, while a low value of class structural quality measurements indicates a high quality.

Table 1. Class structural quality metrics used in this study

Name	Description
WMC	Number of methods defined in a class
DIT	Maximum inheritance path from a class to the root class
NOC	Number of immediate sub-classes of a class
CBO	Number of classes to which a class is coupled
RFC	Number of methods in a class plus number of remote methods directly called by methods of the class
LCOM	Number of pairs of methods in a class that do not share any data members of the class minus number of pairs of methods in the class that share some data members of the class; negative value will be converted to 0
Ca	Number of other classes that depends on a class
NPM	Number of public methods defined in a class

3.2. Design Patterns

The design patterns analyzed in this study are described in Table 2. Certainly, there could be other design patterns in the projects we analyzed. However, due to the limitation of the pattern detection tool, we can only identify these 13 design patterns.

4. DATA SOURCE AND DATA MINING PROCESS

In this study, five open-source java projects are analyzed: Apache Ant[2], Apache Tomcat[3], Eclipse java IDE[4], JUnit[5], and Stripes[6]. Because the size of Eclipse java IDE is too big to be handled by our pattern detection tool, only two packages are analyzed in this study. They are UI and Core. The

details of these six java components are described in Table 3. It can be seen that our selections of java open-source components represent a wide size range of projects (247KB to 10 MB).

The binary distributions of these six java components are downloaded and the class files are extracted. For every class file, 8 metrics (WCM, DIT, NOC, CBO, RFC, LCOM, Ca, and NPM) described in Section 3 are measured using Java CASE tool CKJM[7]. Design pattern detection is an important part in our study. There are many tools available (Vokac, 2004; Vokac et al., 2004; Gueheneuc & Antoniol, 2008; De Lucia et al., 2009; Smith & Stotts, 2003; Gueheneuc et al., 2004; Heuzeroth et al., 2003). In this study, we choose the tool implemented by Tsantalis et al. (2006) and Chatzigeorgiou et al. (2006). This tool is based on graph theory and similarity scoring. It can be used to detect the 13 design patterns listed

Table 2. Design patterns analyzed in this study[1] (Gamma et al., 1995)

Name	Description
Adapter	Convert the interface of a class into another interface clients expect. An adapter lets classes work together that could not otherwise because of incompatible interfaces. The enterprise integration pattern equivalent is the translator.
Command	Encapsulate a request as an object, thereby letting you parameterize clients with different requests, queue or log requests, and support undoable operations.
Composite	Compose objects into tree structures to represent part-whole hierarchies. Composite lets clients treat individual objects and compositions of objects uniformly.
Decorator	Attach additional responsibilities to an object dynamically keeping the same interface. Decorators provide a flexible alternative to subclassing for extending functionality.
Factory method	Define an interface for creating an object, but let subclasses decide which class to instantiate. Factory Method lets a class defer instantiation to subclasses.
Observer	Define a one-to-many dependency between objects where a state change in one object results in all its dependents being notified and updated automatically.
Prototype	Specify the kinds of objects to create using a prototypical instance, and create new objects by copying this prototype.
Proxy	Provide a surrogate or placeholder for another object to control access to it.
Singleton	Ensure a class has only one instance, and provide a global point of access to it.
State	Allow an object to alter its behavior when it's internal state changes. The object will appear to change its class.
Strategy	Define a family of algorithms, encapsulate each one, and make them interchangeable. Strategy lets the algorithm vary independently from clients that use it.
Template method	Define the skeleton of an algorithm in an operation, deferring some steps to subclasses. Template method lets subclasses redefine certain steps of an algorithm without changing the algorithm's structure.
Visitor	Represent an operation to be performed on the elements of an object structure. Visitor lets you define a new operation without changing the classes of the elements on which it operates.

Table 3. Six Java components analyzed in this study

Name	Version	Jar file size
Apache Ant	1.8.3	3.24 MB
Apache Tomcat	7.0.20	10.09 MB
Eclipse java IDE Core package	3.7.2	2.38 MB
Eclipse java IDE UI package	3.7.2	9.85 MB
JUnit	4.10	247.23 KB
Stripes library	1.5.6	636.36 KB

Table 4. Number of classes and number of design patterns in the six Java components

Java components	Number of classes	Number of patterns
Apache Ant	1276	196
Apache Tomcat	2577	378
Eclipse java IDE Core package	1368	421
Eclipse java IDE UI package	6059	590
JUnit	234	62
Stripes library	353	45

in Table 2 in a Java program[8]. Because the tool uses the graph theory and similarity scoring, it cannot differentiate (1) adapter pattern from command pattern, and (2) state pattern from strategy pattern. Therefore, for each class, we identify whether it is involved in any of the 11 different patterns: adapter/command, composite, decorator, factory method, observer, prototype, proxy, singleton, state/strategy, template method, and visitor.

5. Analysis and Results

Table 4 lists the number of Java classes and the number of design patterns detected in the six open-source Java components. We can see that four components (Apache Ant, Apache Tomcat, Eclipse Core, and Eclipse UI) are relatively much larger than the other two components (JUnit and Stripes). Details about the number of different design patterns detected in different components are listed in Table 5.

Figure 1 illustrates the number of different design patterns detected in all six components. It can be seen that in the open-source projects studied here, the adapter/command, state/strategy, singleton, and template method are the most popular design patterns; while composite and proxy are not as popular as other design patterns. In the following subsections, we will study the effect of design patterns on class structural quality measurements.

5.1 Detailed Effect

In each of the six Java components, classes are divided into different groups according to the number of design patterns they are involved with. For example, classes in Ant are divided into 7 groups, because the number of design patterns related with a class is found to be 0, 1, 2, 3, 4, 5, and 7. For Stripes, the number of patterns related to a class is found to be 0, 1, 2, and 3 and accordingly, its classes are divided into 4 groups

To study the effect of design patterns on class structural quality measurements, for each group of classes in each component, the eight metrics are measured and the results are summarized in Table 6 through Table 13, where an empty entry indicates no classes in that group. Table 6 shows the mean values and median values of WMC (weighted method per class) in each group of the six components. It can be seen that in Eclipse Core, the mean and median measurements of WMC increase as more design patterns are involved in a class. Other components have similar trends about WMC measurements.

Table 7 shows the mean values and median values of DIT (depth of inheritance tree) in each group of the six components. Table 8 shows the measurements of NOC (number of children); Table 9 shows the measurements of CBO (coupling between objects); Table 10 shows the measurements of RFC (response for class); Table 11 shows

Table 5. The number of design patterns detected in each component

Pattern	Ant	Tomcat	Eclipse Core	Eclipse UI	JUnit	Stripes
Adapter/Command	54	87	166	167	15	22
Composite	2	2	3	1	1	0
Decorator	6	25	15	6	11	0
Factory method	4	12	35	15	4	1
Observer	3	12	5	14	1	0
Prototype	13	28	23	2	0	0
Proxy	4	7	4	3	1	0
Singleton	27	66	31	103	6	7
State/Strategy	56	91	95	176	14	11
Template method	27	47	41	103	9	4
Visitor	0	1	3	0	0	0

Figure 1. The number of different design patterns detected in all six components

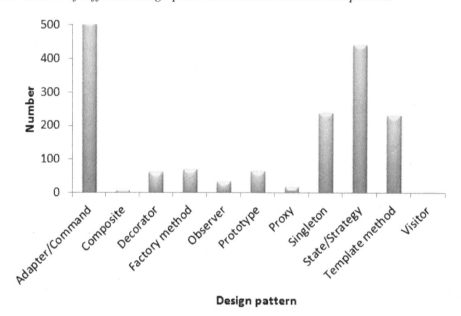

the measurements of LCOM (lack of cohesion of methods); Table 12 shows the measurements of Ca (afferent couplings); and Table 13 shows the measurements of NPM (number of public methods). We can see that in all these tables, all the class structural quality metrics follow similar trends: the mean and median values increase as more design patterns are involved in a class.

In Table 6 through Table 13, Group 0 (0 patterns are involved) classes are pattern-free classes; Groups 1-7 (1-7 patterns are involved) classes are pattern-involved classes. It can be seen that in general, pattern-involved classes have greater mean and median values of complexity measurements than pattern-free classes, which means they have lower class structural quality measurement.

Table 6. The mean and median values of WMC measurement of classes of different groups that are involved with different number of design patterns

		Group (number of patterns involved in a class)							
		0	**1**	**2**	**3**	**4**	**5**	**6**	**7**
Ant	mean	7.3	12.9	17.8	34.5	78.0	38.0		3.0
	median	4.5	6.0	8.5	18.0	78.0	38.0		3.0
Tomcat	mean	8.8	16.3	23.7	28.3	32.0	32.0		
	median	5.0	8.0	14.5	18.0	27.5	32.0		
Eclipse Core	mean	6.4	7.6	13.2	22.5	43.3		131.0	
	median	4	4	10	16	26		131	
Eclipse UI	mean	5.5	9.5	19.7	45.2	49.0	60.5	46.0	
	median	2	6	12	31	48.0	60.5	46.0	
JUnit	mean	4.7	6.3	5.8	9.5	7.0			
	median	3.0	4.0	2.0	6.0	7.0			
Stripes	mean	7.9	7.8	12.3	36.0				
	median	5.0	4.0	10.0	36.0				

Table 7. The mean and median values of DIT measurement of classes of different groups that are involved with different number of design patterns

		Number of patterns involved in a class							
		0	**1**	**2**	**3**	**4**	**5**	**6**	**7**
Ant	mean	2.3	2.0	2.2	2.6	4.0	5.0		1.0
	median	2.0	2.0	2.0	3.0	4.0	5.0		1.0
Tomcat	mean	1.8	1.8	1.9	1.5	1.9	3.5		
	median	1.0	1.0	1.0	1.0	1.5	3.5		
Eclipse Core	mean	1.7	1.5	1.9	1.9	2.0		2.0	
	median	1.0	1.0	1.0	1.0	2.0		2.0	
Eclipse UI	mean	2.0	2.0	2.0	1.7	3.0	2.0	1.0	
	median	1.0	1.0	1.0	1.0	4.0	2.0	1.0	
JUnit	mean	1.8	1.6	1.5	1.3	1.0			
	median	2.0	1.5	1.5	1.0	1.0			
Stripes	mean	1.8	1.3	1.0	3.0				
	median	1.0	1.0	1.0	3.0				

5.2 Quantitative Analysis

To systematically study the effect of design patterns on class structural quality. The eight metrics are combined together to define a combined class metric. First, we define normalized measurement.

Definition 1: *A normalized structural quality measurement of a class is defined as the ratio of the measurement over the largest measurement of this metric of any classes within the same component.*

Table 8. The mean and median values of NOC measurement of classes of different groups that are involved with different number of design patterns

		Number of patterns involved in a class							
		0	**1**	**2**	**3**	**4**	**5**	**6**	**7**
Ant	mean	0.3	1.5	0.8	0.8	1	2		0
	median	0	0	0	0	1	2		0
Tomcat	mean	0.2	0.6	0.8	1.2	5.0	8.5		
	median	0.0	0.0	0.0	0.0	3	8.5		
Eclipse Core	mean	0.2	0.3	0.6	1.2	0.8		2.0	
	median	0.0	0.0	0.0	0.0	0.0		2.0	
Eclipse UI	mean	0.1	0.6	1.3	1.1	1.4	2.0	5.0	
	median	0.0	0.0	0.0	0.0	1.0	2.0	5.0	
JUnit	mean	0.2	0.5	1.3	3.3	4.0			
	median	0.0	0.0	0.0	3.5	4.0			
Stripes	mean	0.2	0.1	0.3	11.0				
	median	0.0	0.0	0.0	11.0				

Table 9. The mean and median values of CBO measurement of classes of different groups that are involved with different number of design patterns

		Number of patterns involved in a class							
		0	**1**	**2**	**3**	**4**	**5**	**6**	**7**
Ant	mean	4.0	6.3	7.9	13.1	44	13		0
	median	3.0	4.0	5.5	7.0	44	12		0
Tomcat	mean	3.8	8.0	11.4	12.7	14.4	32.0		
	median	2	4	7	8	14	32		
Eclipse Core	mean	4.8	7.6	11.7	14.4	25.1		76.0	
	median	3.0	5.0	9.0	11.0	13.5		76.0	
Eclipse UI	mean	7.8	11.5	21.2	47.1	51.2	35.0	13.0	
	median	5.0	7.0	12.0	32.0	32.0	35.0	13.0	
JUnit	mean	2.8	4.3	3.5	8.3	6.0			
	median	2.0	3.0	3.0	4.0	6.0			
Stripes	mean	2.7	5.6	11.0	21.0				
	median	1.0	3.0	9.0	21.0				

Based on this definition, a normalized measurement could have a value in the range of [0, 1], where 0 means this class has the smallest value of a metric (highest quality) in this component and 1 indicates this class has the largest value of a metric (lowest quality) in this component. Next, we define a combined metric.

Definition 2: *A combined structural quality metric of a class is defined as the summation of*

Table 10. The mean and median values of RFC measurement of classes of different groups that are involved with different number of design patterns

		Number of patterns involved in a class							
		0	1	2	3	4	5	6	7
Ant	mean	22.4	37.9	48.2	84.8	269	86		3
	median	14.0	18.0	30.5	53.0	269	86		3
Tomcat	mean	22.6	43.0	61.2	76.4	62.1	81.0		
	median	12	25	37	45	46.5	81		
Eclipse Core	mean	16.7	20.9	36.4	49.6	108.5		388.0	
	median	9.0	11.0	23.0	36.0	59.5		388.0	
Eclipse UI	mean	17.6	30.0	57.9	137.6	143.0	151.5	74.0	
	median	9.0	15.0	33.5	93.0	107.0	151.5	74.0	
JUnit	mean	11.5	15.5	13.8	21.7	12.0			
	median	6.0	9.0	8.5	14.5	12.0			
Stripes	mean	22.3	25.3	45.6	110.0				
	median	14.0	12.0	19.0	110.0				

Table 11. The mean and median values of LCOM measurement of classes of different groups that are involved with different number of design patterns

		Number of patterns involved in a class							
		0	1	2	3	4	5	6	7
Ant	mean	30.7	148.0	298.6	1047.7	2471.0	407.0		3.0
	median	2	6.0	15.5	103.0	2471.0	407.0		3.0
Tomcat	mean	60.7	612.0	587.5	619.7	659	470.5		
	median	1	6	27.5	102	430.5	470.5		
Eclipse Core	mean	28.6	40.6	101.3	271.8	1345.9		6467.0	
	median	1.0	0.0	19.0	64.0	235.5		6467.0	
Eclipse UI	mean	35.4	76.2	349.6	1701.2	1205.2	1379.0	1017.0	
	median	0.0	4.0	51.5	371.0	1068.0	1379.0	1017.0	
JUnit	mean	18.5	31.1	27.6	77.8	19.0			
	median	0.0	3.0	1.0	14.0	19.0			
Stripes	mean	55.1	52.6	115.9	600.0				
	median	3.0	4.0	39.0	600.0				

normalized structural quality measurements of WMC, DIT, NOC, CBO, RFC, LCOM, Ca, and NPM of this class.

The reason we provide these two definitions is to make it easy to investigate the correlations between class structural quality and design patterns. Based on these definitions, we can see that combined structural quality metric of a class

Table 12. The mean and median values of Ca measurement of classes of different groups that are involved with different number of design patterns

		Number of patterns involved in a class							
		0	1	2	3	4	5	6	7
Ant	mean	2.9	7.4	11.6	48.8	5.0	6.0		85.0
	median	1.0	2.0	5.0	4.0	5.0	6.0		85.0
Tomcat	mean	3.3	7.2	9.6	26.2	54.4	67.0		
	median	1.0	2	4	7	37	67		
Eclipse Core	mean	3.6	4.1	8.1	22.3	32.4		31.0	
	median	1.0	1.0	4.0	11.0	11.0		31.0	
Eclipse UI	mean	3.1	7.7	24.2	18.6	14.8	36.5	43.0	
	median	1.0	3.0	7.5	10.0	16.0	36.5	43.0	
JUnit	mean	2.2	3.2	10.3	10.7	12.0			
	median	1.0	2.0	1.0	8.0	12.0			
Stripes	mean	2.5	5.6	8.3	19.0				
	median	1.0	2.0	3.0	19.0				

Table 13. The mean and median values of NPM measurement of classes of different groups that are involved with different number of design patterns

		Number of patterns involved in a class							
		0	1	2	3	4	5	6	7
Ant	mean	5.5	8.8	13.5	26.3	36.0	30.0		3.0
	median	4.0	5.0	7.0	14.0	36.0	30.0		3.0
Tomcat	mean	7.2	12.4	19.1	22.5	28.8	28.0		
	median	4.0	6.0	9.0	11.0	26.0	28.0		
Eclipse Core	mean	4.6	5.1	8.0	15.1	30.1		111.0	
	median	3.0	2.0	6.0	12.0	15.5		111.0	
Eclipse UI	mean	3.2	5.2	10.9	20.2	18.2	43.0	42.0	
	median	1.0	3.0	8.0	16.0	17.0	43.0	42.0	
JUnit	mean	3.1	3.9	4.3	5.0	6.0			
	median	2.0	2.0	2.0	4.5	6.0			
Stripes	mean	6.3	5.6	6.6	26.0				
	median	4.0	3.0	5.0	26.0				

could have values in the range of [0, 8], where 0 indicates this class has a lowest complexity measurement (highest quality measurement) and 8 indicates that this class has a highest complexity measurement (lowest quality measurement).

It should be noted that both normalized class structural quality measurement and combined class structural quality metric are relative values within the same components. We cannot use these values to compare the complexity of classes across different components.

Figure 2 shows the distributions of classes with different measurements of combined structural quality metric in Ant (Figure 2a), Tomcat (Figure 2b), Eclipse Core (Figure 2c), Eclipse UI (Figure 2d), JUnit (Figure 2e), and Stripes (Figure 2f). It can be seen that for large projects (Ant, Toncat, Eclipse Core, and Eclipse UI), they generally follow the power-law distribution: frequency of classes increases as the measurement decreases or as the quality increases, which means more classes tend to have high structural quality. However, for small projects (JUnit and Stripes), the power-law distribution is not clear.

Figure 3 shows the boxplots of combined structural quality metric of different groups of classes in the six components, where each group contains the classes that are involved in the same number of design patterns. The bold line within the box indicates the median. The box spans the central 50 percent of the data. The lines attached to the box denote the standard range. The circles indicate the data points that are out of the lower standard range. The asterisks indicate the data points that are out of the higher standard range. From Figure 3, we can see that in general the combined metric increases (the quality decreases) with the number of patterns the class is involved.

Figure 2. Distributions of classes with different measurements of combined class structural quality metric in (a) Ant; (b) Tomcat; (c) Eclipse Core; (d) Eclipse UI; (e) JUnit; and (f) Stripes

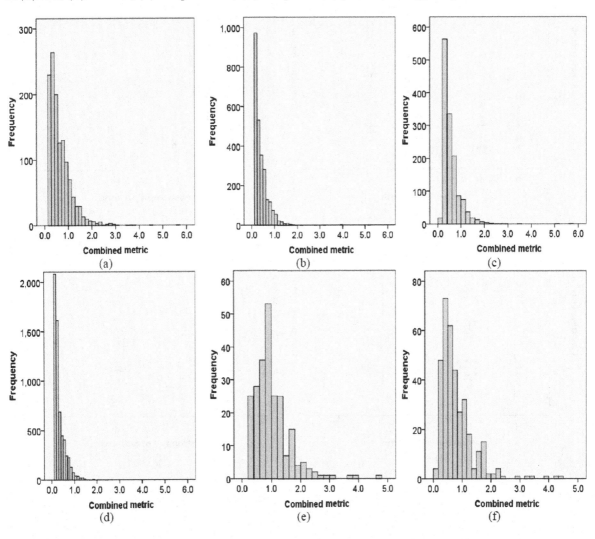

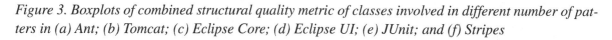

Figure 3. Boxplots of combined structural quality metric of classes involved in different number of patterns in (a) Ant; (b) Tomcat; (c) Eclipse Core; (d) Eclipse UI; (e) JUnit; and (f) Stripes

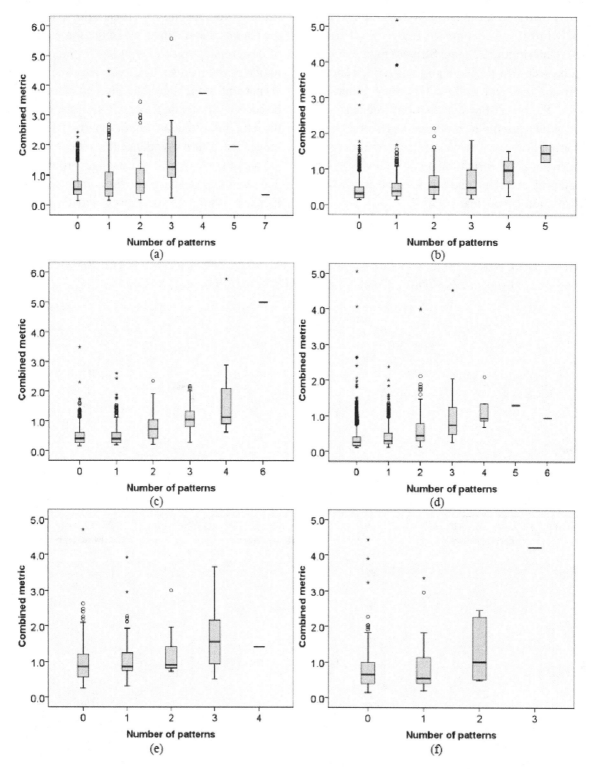

In Figure 3, to reiterate, Group 0 (0 patterns are involved) classes are pattern-free classes; Groups 1-7 (1-7 patterns are involved) classes are pattern-involved classes. To clearly see the measurement differences between pattern-free classes and pattern-involved classes, the data are re-summarized in Figure 4, which compares the mean and median values of combined structural quality metric between pattern-free classes and pattern-involved classes. Again, we can see that in general, pattern-involved classes have greater mean and median values of complexity measurements than pattern-free classes, which indicates their lower quality.

To see if the combined structural quality metric values of pattern-free classes and pattern-involved classes are significantly different, one-way ANOVA tests and Kruskal-Walli tests are performed to compare differences between the mean values of pattern-free classes and pattern-involved classes. Although one-way ANOVA tests could tolerate the violations of normality assumption well, Kruskal-Walli tests are more robust against normality assumption. Therefore, both tests are performed and the results are listed in Table 14 and Table 15 for comparisons. Similar results could be seen in Table 14 and Table 15: in four components (Ant, Tomcat, Eclipse Core, and Eclipse UI), the mean values of combined metric between pattern-free classes and pattern-involved classes are significantly different at the 0.001 level; in one component (JUnit), the mean values of combined metric between pattern-free classes and pattern-involved classes are signifi-

Figure 4. Comparison of combined structural quality metric of pattern-free classes and pattern-involved classes

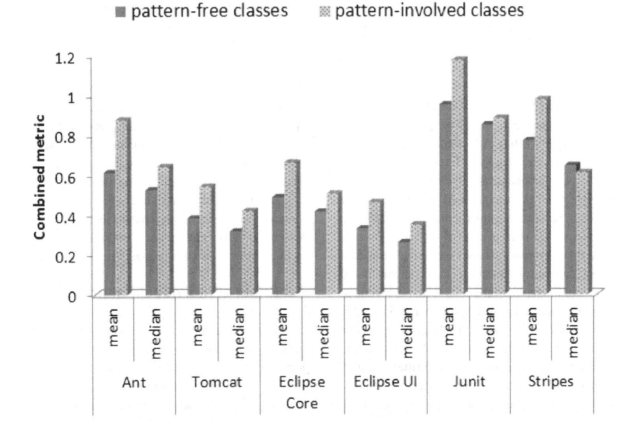

Table 14. ANOVA tests of combined metric values between pattern-free classes and pattern-involved classes

	Ant	Tomcat	Eclipse Core	Eclipse UI	JUnit	Stripes
F value	15.59	117.71	62.32	185.67	6.478	6.197
Significance	<0.001	<0.001	<0.001	<0.001	0.012	0.013
Number of classes	1276	2577	1368	6959	234	353

Table 15. Kruskal-Walli tests of combined metric values between pattern-free classes and pattern-involved classes

	Ant	Tomcat	Eclipse Core	Eclipse UI	JUnit	Stripes
Chi-Square	15.59	108.29	36.64	169.89	4.386	1.16
Significance	0.001	<0.001	<0.001	<0.001	0.036	0.28
Number of classes	1276	2577	1368	6959	234	353

Table 16. The Correlation tests of number of design patterns and combined metric

	Ant	Tomcat	Eclipse Core	Eclipse UI	JUnit	Stripes
Correlation coefficient (r)	0.106	0.212	0.238	0.173	0.155	0.068
Significance (p)	<0.001	<0.001	<0.001	<0.001	0.018	0.205
Number of classes (N)	1276	2577	1368	6059	234	353

cantly different at the 0.05 level; in one component (Stripes), the mean values of combined metric between pattern-free classes and pattern-involved classes are significantly different at the 0.5 level.

To further quantitatively study the effect of design patterns on combined structural quality metric, Spearman's rank correlation tests are performed on data of each component. In each test, there are two variables measured from each class: number of patterns a class is involved and the combined structural quality metric of this class. The results of the tests are summarized in Table 16. It can be seen that in four large components, significant correlations at the 0.001 level are found between the number of patterns and the combined metric. In JUnit, the correlation significance is at the 0.05 level, which is also significant. In Stripes, the correlation significance is at the 0.5 level, which is conventionally considered insignificant.

Based on our analysis, we can see that design patterns do have an effect on class complexity and structural quality. If a class is involved in more design patterns, it is more likely to have a large value of complexity measurement, which indicates a lower quality. This effect is more observable in large projects with over one thousand classes.

5.3 Effect of Individual Patterns

So far, we have analyzed the effect of the 13 design patterns as a whole. Because these 13 design patterns could target on different design problems, provide different design solutions, and introduce different relations into the program, their effect

Figure 5. The effect of each design pattern on each class structural quality metric (highlighted cell indicates the effect is significant; blank cell indicates the effect is insignificant)

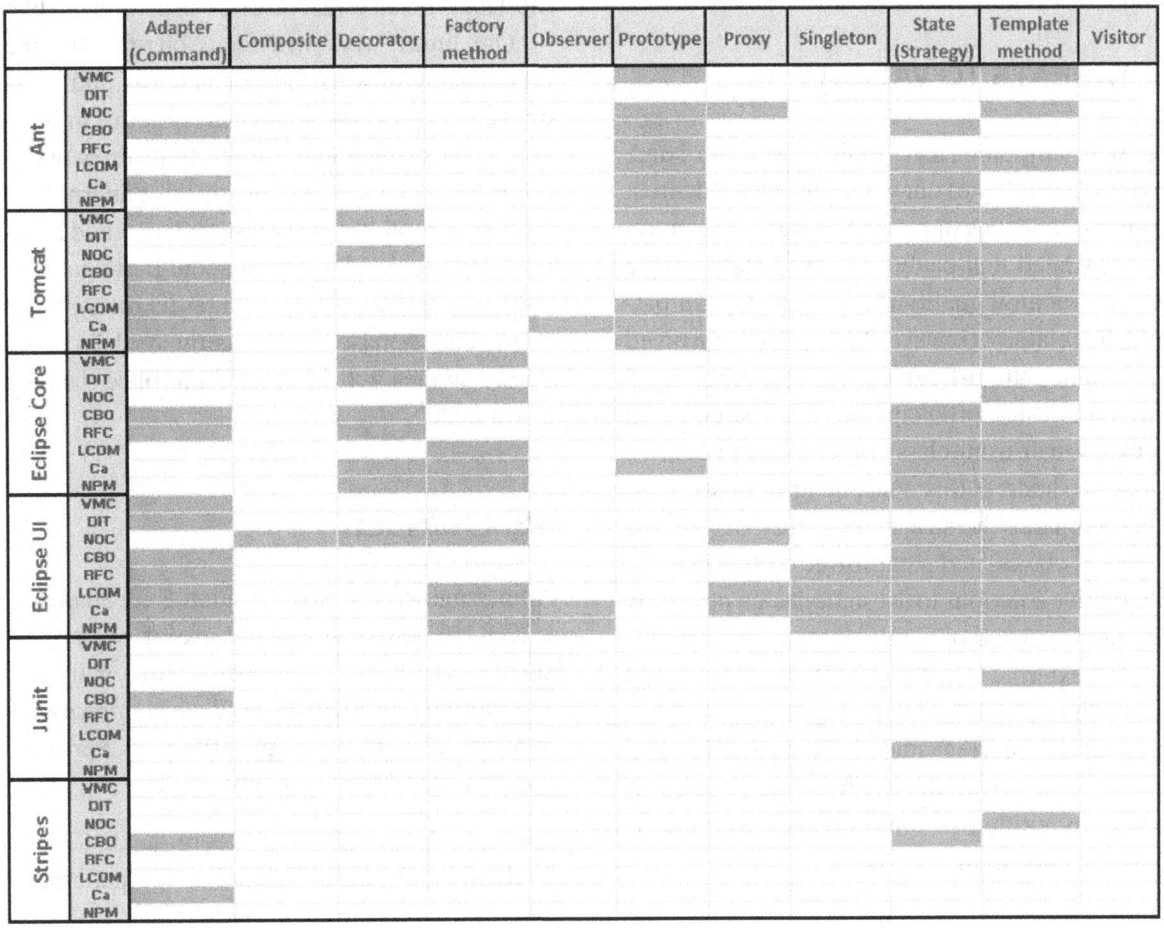

on class structural quality could be different. To see how different design patterns might affect the metrics measurement, using Spearman test, we study the correlation between each class structural quality metric and each deign pattern in the six Java components. The results are summarized in Figure 5.

In Figure 5, if the p-value of Spearman's rank correlation is less than 0.0001, the corresponding cell will be highlighted. Otherwise, the corresponding cell will be left blank. From the figure, we can see that adapter/command pattern, state/strategy pattern, and template method pattern have the most significant effect on class structural quality; prototype pattern, decorator pattern, and factory method pattern have moderate effect on class structural quality; singleton pattern, proxy pattern, observer pattern, and composite pattern have little effect on class structural quality; while visitor pattern have almost no effect.

From Figure 1, we also see that the three most common design patterns in the six Java components are adapter/command, state/strategy, and template method and the two least common design patterns are visitor and composite. These observations match Spearman's rank correlation test results illustrated in Figure 5. Due to the limitation of the data used, we cannot conclude in general that the greater use of design pattern implies a greater effect on class structural quality.

However, our analysis of the 6 Java components supports this argument.

6. THREATS TO VALIDITY

As with any empirical studies, there are some threats to validity of our work. The internal threat comes from the design of the research. Our study demonstrated that pattern-involved classes have lower structural quality measurements than pattern-free classes. However, these pattern-involved classes and pattern-free classes could have targeted different design problems. It might be unfair to compare them using class structural quality metrics alone. To address this issue, an ideal experiment that compares the structural quality of pattern-involved classes and pattern-free classes that are alternative solutions to the same design problems should be carried out in the future.

The external threat to the validity of the study is that this work might not be applicable to other systems. Our current study is performed on Java projects. To extend the findings of this study to programs written in other object-oriented languages, more studies are needed.

7. CONCLUSION AND FUTURE WORK

In this study, we investigated the effect of design patterns on class structural quality measurement. Six components from five open-source Java projects were analyzed. Our study empirically demonstrated that the use of design patterns could increase program complexity, and accordingly, reduce class structural quality. Our study also found that the greater the use of design patterns, the more significant could be their effect on class structural quality. Specifically, in the five Java projects we studied, we found adapter/command,

state/strategy, and template method are the three most commonly seen design patterns and have the most significant effect on class structural quality.

Our future work will focus on studying the relationship between design patterns and class quality on other object-oriented systems. In addition, an investigation of the relationship between the roles played by classes in the patterns and class structural quality measurement could be an interesting topic. However, we could not figure out a way to represent and measure the roles played by the classes based on currently available data. Future studies will be carried out once the data is available.

REFERENCES

Ampatzoglou, A., Charalampidou, S., & Stamelos, I. (2011b). Investigating the use of object–oriented design patterns in open–source software: A case study. In *Evaluation of novel approaches to software engineering* (pp. 106–120). Springer. doi:10.1007/978-3-642-23391-3_8

Ampatzoglou, A., & Chatzigeorgiou, A. (2007). Evaluation of object–oriented design patterns in game development. *Information and Software Technology*, *49*(5), 445–454. doi:10.1016/j. infsof.2006.07.003

Ampatzoglou, A., Frantzeskou, G., & Stamelos, I. (2012). A methodology to assess the impact of design patterns on software quality. *Information and Software Technology*, *54*(4), 331–346. doi:10.1016/j.infsof.2011.10.006

Ampatzoglou, A., Kritikos, A., Kakarontzas, G., & Stamelos, I. (2011a). An empirical investigation on the reusability of design patterns and software packages. *Journal of Systems and Software*, *84*(12), 2265–2283. doi:10.1016/j. jss.2011.06.047

Aydınoz, B. (2006). *The effect of design patterns on object–oriented metrics and software error–proneness*. (Master thesis). Middle East Technological University, Turkey.

Bieman, J. M., Alexander, R., Munger, P. W., III, & Meunier, E. (2002). Software design quality: Style and substance. In *Proceedings of ICSE Workshop on Software Quality*. Orlando, FL: ACM.

Bieman, J. M., Straw, G., Wang, H., Munger, P. W., & Alexander, R. T. (2003). Design patterns and change proneness: An examination of five evolving systems. In *Proceedings of the 9th International Software Metrics Symposium* (pp. 40–49). Sydney, Australia: IEEE.

Cartwright, M., & Shepperd, M. (2000). An empirical investigation of an object–oriented software system. *IEEE Transactions on Software Engineering, 26*(8), 786–796. doi:10.1109/32.879814

Chatzigeorgiou, A., Tsantalis, N., & Stephanides, G. (2006). Application of graph theory to OO software engineering. In *Proceedings of the 2006 International Workshop on Interdisciplinary Software Engineering Research* (pp. 29–36). Shanghai, China: ACM.

Chidamber, S. R., & Kemerer, C. F. (1994). A metrics suite for object oriented design. *IEEE Transactions on Software Engineering, 20*(6), 476–493. doi:10.1109/32.295895

Di Penta, M., Cerulo, L., Guéhéneuc, Y. G., & Antoniol, G. (2008). An empirical study of the relationships between design pattern roles and class change proneness. In *Proceedings of 24th IEEE International Conference on software Maintenance* (pp. 217–226). Beijing, China: IEEE.

Fushida, K., Kawaguchi, S., & Iida, H. (2007). A method to investigate software evolutions using design pattern detection tool. In *Proceedings of the 1st International Workshop on Software Patterns and Quality* (pp. 11–16). Academic Press.

Gamma, E., Helm, R., Johnson, R., & Vlissides, J. (1995). *Design patterns: Elements of reusable object–oriented software*. Reading, MA: Addison–Wesley.

Gueheneuc, Y. G., & Antoniol, G. (2008). Demima: A multilayered approach for design pattern identification. *IEEE Transactions on Software Engineering, 34*(5), 667–684. doi:10.1109/TSE.2008.48

Gueheneuc, Y. G., Sahraoui, H., & Zaidi, F. (2004). Fingerprinting design patterns. In *Proceedings of the 11th Working Conference on Reverse Engineering* (pp. 172–181). Delft, The Netherlands: IEEE.

Hasheminejad, S. M. H., & Jalili, S. (2012). Design patterns selection: An automatic two–phase method. *Journal of Systems and Software, 85*(2), 408–424. doi:10.1016/j.jss.2011.08.031

Heuzeroth, D., Holl, T., Hogstrom, G., & Lowe, W. (2003). Automatic design pattern detection. In *Proceedings of the 11th IEEE International Workshop on Program Comprehension* (pp. 94–103). Portland, OR: IEEE.

Hsueh, N. L., Chu, P. H., & Chu, W. (2008). A quantitative approach for evaluating the quality of design patterns. *Journal of Systems and Software, 81*(8), 1430–1439. doi:10.1016/j.jss.2007.11.724

Hsueh, N. L., Wen, L. C., Ting, D. H., Chu, W., Chang, C. H., & Koong, C. S. (2011). An approach for evaluating the effectiveness of design patterns in software evolution. In *Proceedings of the 35th Annual Computer Software and Applications Conference Workshops* (pp. 315–320). Munich, Germany: IEEE.

Huston, B. (2001). The effects of design pattern application on metric scores. *Journal of Systems and Software, 58*(3), 261–269. doi:10.1016/S0164-1212(01)00043-7

Khomh, F., & Gueheneuc, Y. G. (2008). Do design patterns impact software quality positively? In *Proceedings of the 12th European Conference on Software Maintenance and Reengineering* (pp. 274–278). Athens, Greece: IEEE.

Khomh, F., Gueheneuc, Y. G., & Antoniol, G. (2009). Playing roles in design patterns: An empirical descriptive and analytic study. In *Proceedings of the 25th International Conference on Software Maintenance* (pp. 83–92). Edmonton, Canada: IEEE.

Khomh, F., Gueheneuc, Y. G., & Team, P. (2008). *An empirical study of design patterns and software quality* (Technical report 1315). University of Montreal.

Lange, D. B., & Nakamura, Y. (1995). Interactive visualization of design patterns can help in framework understanding. *ACM Sigplan Notices, 30*(10), 342–357. doi:10.1145/217839.217874

Lucia, A. D., Deufemia, V., Gravino, C., & Risi, M. (2009). Design pattern recovery through visual language parsing and source code analysis. *Journal of Systems and Software, 82*(7), 1177–1193. doi:10.1016/j.jss.2009.02.012

Martin, R. C. (2003). *Agile software development: Principles, patterns, and practices.* Prentice Hall.

McNatt, W. B., & Bieman, J. M. (2001). Coupling of design patterns: Common practices and their benefits. In *Proceedings of the 25th Annual International Computer Software and Applications Conference* (pp. 574–579). Chicago, IL: IEEE.

Prechelt, L., Unger, B., Tichy, W. F., Brossler, P., & Votta, L. G. (2001). A controlled experiment in maintenance: Comparing design patterns to simpler solutions. *IEEE Transactions on Software Engineering, 27*(12), 1134–1144. doi:10.1109/32.988711

Sandhu, P., Singh, P., & Verma, A. A. (2008). Evaluating quality of software systems by design patterns detection. In *Proceedings of International Conference on Advanced Computer Theory and Engineering* (pp. 3–7). Singapore: IEEE.

Shalloway, A., & Trott, J. (2005). *Design patterns explained: A new perspective on object–oriented design.* Reading, MA: Addison–Wesley.

Smith, J. M., & Stotts, D. (2003). SPQR: Flexible automated design pattern extraction from source code. In *Proceedings of the 18th IEEE International Conference on Automated Software Engineering* (pp. 215–224). Montreal, Canada: IEEE.

Tsantalis, N., Chatzigeorgiou, A., Stephanides, G., & Halkidis, S. T. (2006). Design pattern detection using similarity scoring. *IEEE Transactions on Software Engineering, 32*(11), 896–909. doi:10.1109/TSE.2006.112

Turk, T. (2009). *The effect of software design patterns on object–oriented software quality and maintainability.* (Master thesis). Middle East Technological University, Turkey.

Vokac, M. (2004). Defect frequency and design patterns: An empirical study of industrial code. *IEEE Transactions on Software Engineering, 30*(12), 904–917. doi:10.1109/TSE.2004.99

Vokac, M., Tichy, W., Sjoberg, D. I., Arisholm, E., & Aldrin, M. (2004). A controlled experiment comparing the maintainability of programs designed with and without design patterns—A replication in a real programming environment. *Empirical Software Engineering, 9*(3), 149–195. doi:10.1023/B:EMSE.0000027778.69251.1f

Wendorff, P. (2001). Assessment of design patterns during software reengineering: Lessons learned from a large commercial project. In *Proceedings of the 5th European Conference on Software Maintenance and Reengineering Conference* (pp. 77–84). Lisbon, Portugal: IEEE.

Zheng, J., & Harper, K. E. (2010). Concurrency design patterns, software quality attributes and their tactics. In *Proceedings of the 3rd International Workshop on Multicore Software Engineering* (pp. 40–47). Cape Town, South Africa: ACM.

KEY TERMS AND DEFINITIONS

Class Complexity: The measurement of class structure and its inter-dependencies with other classes. Class complexity has been shown to have direct relations with software quality.

Class Structural Quality: A measure of the design quality of object-oriented software system.

Design Pattern: A standard object-oriented solution to a common software design problem.

Empirical Study: A scientific method that uses experienced or experimental data to obtain knowledge and understanding of the target system.

Open Source Project: A software project whose source code is freely available for use and study under certain license.

Software Quality: The measurement of readability, usability, maintainability, reusability, and error-proneness of a software product.

ENDNOTES

[1] http://en.wikipedia.org/wiki/Software_design_pattern
[2] http://ant.apache.org/
[3] http://tomcat.apache.org/
[4] http://www.eclipse.org/
[5] http://www.junit.org/
[6] http://www.stripesframework.org/display/stripes/Home
[7] http://www.spinellis.gr/sw/ckjm/
[8] http://java.uom.gr/~nikos/pattern-detection.html

Chapter 7
Service Discovery Framework for Distributed Embedded Real–Time Systems

Furkh Zeshan
COMSATS Institute of Information Technology (CIIT), Pakistan

Radziah Mohamad
Universiti Teknologi Malaysia

Mohammad Nazir Ahmad
Universiti Teknologi Malaysia

ABSTRACT

Embedded systems are supporting the trend of moving away from centralised, high-cost products towards low-cost and high-volume products; yet, the non-functional constraints and the device heterogeneity can lead to system complexity. In this regard, Service-Oriented Architecture (SOA) is the best methodology for developing a loosely coupled, dynamic, flexible, distributed, and cost-effective application. SOA relies heavily on services, and the Semantic Web, as the advanced form of the Web, handles the application complexity and heterogeneity with the help of ontology. With an ever-increasing number of similar Web services in UDDI, a functional description of Web services is not sufficient for the discovery process. It is also difficult to rank the similar services based on their functionality. Therefore, the Quality of Service (QoS) description of Web services plays an important role in ranking services within many similar functional services. Context-awareness has been widely studied in embedded and real-time systems and can also play an important role in service ranking as an additional set of criteria. In addition, it can enhance human-computer interaction with the help of ontologies in distributed and heterogeneous environments. In order to address the issues involved in ranking similar services based on the QoS and context-awareness, the authors propose a service discovery framework for distributed embedded real-time systems in this chapter. The proposed framework considers user priorities, QoS, and the context-awareness to enable the user to select the best service among many functional similar services.

DOI: 10.4018/978-1-4666-6026-7.ch007

INTRODUCTION

According to the Internet of Things vision (Fleisch et al., 2005), the majority of devices will soon have communication and computation capabilities which users will apply to connect, interact and cooperate with the surrounding environment. In this dynamic environment, service-based systems will provide a good groundwork for a new type of real-world aware applications. In such an environment, efficiency will depend on the heterogeneous networked embedded devices and the challenge is how to discover the best real-world services for their integration into applications.

Heterogeneity in terms of programming language, operating platform and data management standards restricts the ability of devices to interact with each other: if two devices speak different languages, have different operating platforms or data management standards, then the data provided by one device cannot be interpreted correctly by the other. Therefore, in the dynamic environment of devices, heterogeneity restricts the understanding of the capabilities of the devices and the proper discovery and use of these devices.

In this regard, Service-Oriented Architecture (SOA) with the help of semantic web technology provides the base on which to properly address these restrictions as it enables different devices to work together by exposing their functionalities to others as services. The combination of the semantic web and ontologies (that present the concepts in a formal way by eliminating the terminological heterogeneity and enable the use of reasoning tools for knowledge discovery) allows the binding of data semantics along with the data for ease of sharing and correct interpretation.

In order to develop dynamic, flexible, distributed and cost-effective applications, service-oriented computing can be used. The web services can handle the complexity and heterogeneity with the help of ontology. Services are the entities which enable users to access the capabilities through pre-defined interfaces in accordance with the policies and constraints which are part of the description of that service (Estefan et al., 2008). Services are platform-independent and can be accessed through the internet. The most significant aspect of the web, due to which the overheads of companies have reduced and business is flourishing, is its role as facilitator in service outsourcing (Medjahed et al., 2003; Tsur et al., 2001). The service deployment model can be applied to any application component in order to make it a service. Services are well-defined, self-described and reusable software components that can be used over the web using the most silent and stable technologies such as the SOAP communication framework, Web Services Description Language (WSDL) and Universal Description Discovery Integration (UDDI) (which provides a mechanism to clients to find services (Bellwood et al., 2002)) (Curbera et al., 2002). A service is a set of related functions that can be accessed through programming over the web (Tsur et al., 2001). The key feature of the web services is that they are loosely coupled, allowing ad-hoc and dynamic binding and reusable software components and the key challenge is to find (discover) the best service for solving the particular problem.

With an ever-increasing number of functionally similar web services in the central repository, merely functional descriptions of web services are not sufficient for the discovery process. Therefore, we need Quality of Service (QoS) descriptions of services as an additional set of criteria to select the best service among many similar functionality services. However, the traditional UDDI lacks QoS descriptions, so it is difficult to rank the similar services by their functionality only. To solve this problem, some researchers have tried to add the QoS information during the service discovery process (Ran, 2003; Tran et al., 2009; Yao et al., 2008). However, the syntactic descriptions of QoS are not adequate, since the service providers and requesters may use different concepts, scales and measurements. Hence, the provision of QoS semantics is necessary in web service discovery in order to satisfy users' needs and to determine whether the service is the most suitable for the requesters' needs.

Over the last two decades, researchers have considered context-awareness for enhancing human-computer interaction by providing applications with context information (Dey et al., 2001; Schilit et al., 1994; Want et al., 1992) while in recent years, ontologies have been playing an important role in embedded and real-time computing. Therefore, context-awareness can also play an important role in service ranking as an additional set of criteria which enables the selection of the most suitable service among the functional similar services. The work of Bettini et al. (2009) and Strang et al. (2004) has emerged as an important tool for context modelling and to integrate, share and reuse context knowledge from distributed and heterogeneous sources of information.

In this paper, we present an ontology-based service discovery framework which uses QoS, application and context ontologies for modelling the user request and a service-matching algorithm. The proposed service-matching framework also considers the associated priorities with the requirements of the requester during the service-ranking process. The framework has the ability to extend and adapt the vocabulary used to describe services and to utilise the existing concepts defined in the QoS / context ontology to obtain the inferential benefits of logical reasoning over such descriptions. Such benefits are necessary within dynamic and evolving environments.

The remainder of the paper is organised as follows. The next section presents some of the most important requirements for service discovery frameworks; next, the details of the proposed service discovery framework are presented. The following sections discuss the web service discovery process and the evaluation results. Finally, we conclude the overall paper in the last section.

REQUIREMENTS FOR SERVICE DISCOVERY FRAMEWORKS

The development of successful embedded real-time systems depends on the correct specification of the relevant requirements. This section focuses on the general requirement specifications for embedded real-time systems related to the context-awareness and quality of services that we have considered in our work. In our opinion, this is a minimum set of the important requirements that a framework must satisfy for the effective, efficient and automatic discovery of services in the distributed embedded real-time environment. The details of these requirements are given below.

- **Context-awareness:** Context-awareness is the information related to the data produced by the service. For example, generally, the information related to the temperature measurement service (device) describes when and where the data was produced by the service; without this description, the produced data is meaningless. In service discovery, the user context and service context are compared with each other so as to fetch services of relevance with the aid of context-awareness.
- **Quality of Service:** With an ever-increasing number of similar web services in UDDI, a merely functional description of web services is not sufficient for the discovery process. It is also difficult to rank the similar services based on their functionality. Therefore, the QoS description of web services plays an important role in ranking services within many similar functional services.
- **Prioritisation:** In the case of similar values for the metrics of a candidate service, a user must be allowed to assign values to the metrics to get the best result according to his or her requirements.

- **Extensibility:** Extensibility is a concept of software engineering applied to software systems to deal with how to avoid errors by adding functionality in the system in the future. In the case of an application server for the semantic web, extensibility deals with the XML parsers or validators that support the XML schema data types, RDF stores, tools that map the relational databases to the RDF schema ontologies, ontology stores and OWL reasoners (Oberle et al.,2004).

- **Correctness:** In a real-time system, the concreteness of the system behaviour not only depends on the logical results of the computations, but also on the physical instant at which these results are produced. Normally, the determination of the correctness of a specific input is performed in the business logic layer against the business rules.

- **Dynamicity:** In the real world, services in terms of devices are highly dynamic and they continually degrade, disappear and re-appear. This implies the need for the automated and immediate (dynamic) discovery of services as well as their effective management.

- **Clarity:** Clarity means the ontology is understandable by domain experts and is intended for shared conceptualisation.

- **Modularity:** This requirement allows for adapting the context / QoS ontology for different domains and applications.

- **Automation:** Automation enables the web services to be selected dynamically at runtime with minimal user intervention and has the effect of accelerating the process. Automation reduces the time spent in order to create a weighted list of services. It eliminates human errors and reduces the overall cost of the process.

- **Approximate matching:** For effective service discovery, it is necessary for any approach to return the service that meets the user requirements but if no service is found exactly according to the user defined criteria, the approach should return the approximate results to the user.

- **Advanced categorisation:** The service-matching approach should categorise the found results based on the similarity score. It may be beneficial for the requester.

RELATED WORK

Due to the continuous increase of functionally similar services in the central repository, the demand for the efficient retrieval of services based on a set of required QoS criteria is also increased. In this regard, many researchers have presented service discovery frameworks to address the limitations discussed above. In this section, we provide a brief overview of the existing work on service-based frameworks that we divide into two categories: QoS-based frameworks, and context-aware frameworks.

QoS-Based Service Discovery Frameworks

Baocai et al. (2010) proposed a QoS ontology-based framework for the automatic discovery, composition and execution of web services using semantic descriptions. The ontology is a general purpose ontology for describing the QoS attributes of the web service using the semantic description of the web services. The framework can resolve the issue of the interoperability of QoS descriptions and can improve the efficiency for users in finding the best services. The QoS ontology uses OWL-S to describe its specifications.

Ma et al. (2008) proposed a semantic QoS-aware framework for semantic web service discovery. The framework is based on three layers. In the first layer, semantic matchmaking is performed through Description Logic (DL) reasoning for the purpose of examining the compatibility of the concepts involved from both sides (demand and offer). In the second layer, the QoS conditions are translated as the declarative constraints and user Constraint Programming (CP) to find the satisfying values. In the third layer, optimisation of the global utility function is used to get the optimised result.

Chua et al. (2007) presented a visualisation framework in which the service discovery and selection are performed based on the QoS attributes in a visual context. The visualisation enables users to interact positively with the information. This technique has not been widely used in the process of web service discovery and selection. The framework considers the graphical user interface design criteria and design patterns in the service discovery process as a visual context. The framework also considers the priorities of users in the discovery process.

The semantic web service discovery framework proposed by Ayadi et al. (2011) uses the functional and non-functional requirements of the user to select the most appropriate service. The authors used a canonical web service model (in which other semantic frameworks can be linked through semantic mapping) for the flexible matching of services. The model is based on deductive techniques which relax the query constraints (based on semantic descriptions and domain knowledge) for the enhancement of the search space of candidate services. A ranking process in the framework is performed based on the priority weights assigned by the users to a set of non-functional attributes.

Zhao et al. (2010) presented a multi-source QoS collection-based framework. This framework can collect, aggregate and store the QoS data of different web services. This framework can construct a QoS model to support the computation of QoS. An experiment was performed to demonstrate the flexibility of the framework, wherein the service requester's QoS data collection approach was implemented using WSDL and the Java mapping data structure while the service provider's QoS

data collection approach was implemented using the handler method.

Li et al. (2009) proposed a framework consisting of an ontology-based QoS meta-model and the Web Service Modeling Ontology (WSMO). The WSMO-QoS framework is based on the web service execution environment (WSMX) and has two parts, namely, the core part and the expansion part. In the core part, service matching is performed at three levels (basic information matching, IOPE matching and QoS matching); in the expansion part, services are rated based on the QoS score and the feedback from a third-party organisation, and the score is returned to the service requester.

Context-Aware Service Discovery Frameworks

The framework proposed by Zhu et al. (2010) is based on the three-layer pervasive semantic service-matching algorithm. Service matchmaking in the framework is performed on service capability (input/output, preconditions/effects) and the non-capability (QoS) description. In response to the user's request, the algorithm matches the request against all services by means of the service category, input/output and required QoS and finally identifies the desired service. The whole matchmaking procedure is based on the semantic filter while the QoS matching is performed by the type of parameter. The algorithm finally returns the ordered list based on the user-defined preferences for the web service.

The COnTag (Arabshian et al., 2012) is a framework for a personalised ontology-based context-aware data search based on the general concepts of PeCMan (Daenen et al., 2010) and GloServ (Arabshian et al., 2007), the global service discovery system. The framework uses additional information on data coming from the users and resources other than the tagged keywords for query optimisation. Researchers used the extended Newman tag ontology (Ayers et al., 2005) to map the knowledge obtained from the user, tag and the resource onto a hybrid hierarchical peer-to-peer network. This extended ontology combines the flat tag registration and querying with ontology-based tag registration and queries.

The framework in (Santos et al., 2009) consists of a goal-based service ontology (to define domain specifications), a set of domain ontologies and a service-matching algorithm. After defining the goal, the client submits the goal to the platform, then the matching algorithm searches for services that can fulfill the client's goal. The platform also uses the client's contextual information as inputs in the search for services, resulting in reduced interaction with the client. The researchers has (Santos et al., 2009) used the task descriptions and concrete realisation of activities for the support of the dynamic service discovery. This framework is based on the assumption that the existing domain and task ontologies are defined by the domain experts. It is noted that the researchers tested the framework with a limited amount of services and ontology concepts.

Based on the above review and analysis, it appears that research on QoS and context-aware frameworks focusing on the most neglected requirements, namely, advanced categorisation, approximate matching, automatic, extensibility, prioritisation and correctness, would be highly beneficial for the industry.

SERVICE DISCOVERY FRAMEWORK FOR DISTRIBUTED EMBEDDED REAL-TIME SYSTEMS

Due to the continuous increase of functionally similar services in the central repository, the demand for an automatic and efficient retrieval of services based on a set of required QoS criteria is also increasing. To deal with the automatic discovery of web services, we propose a framework (SDFD) that enables the user to create a query based on the ontology concepts and provides a rigorous algorithm discovery service from a service

repository based on the user-defined query. The framework consists of the following components:

- Ontology repository,
- Context repository,
- Service repository,
- Constraints solving engine (ECLIPSe), and
- Pellet as ontology reasoner.

This framework consists of the service repository where advertised services are stored, the context base where the context descriptions of the devices/agents are stored, and the ontology base where the QoS, domain and application ontologies are stored.

Figure 1 presents the service discovery framework. Figure 2 presents the workflow of the framework, with each step in the workflow described in more detail as follows:

- **Step 1:** In the initial stage, the relevant requester needs to input the detailed request into the system, including the employee roles, schedule, timing and resources. The framework supports the service requester to query services through an interface aligned with the classes and the data-type of the ontologies provided through the Protégé editor (Fergerson et al., 2000).
- **Step 2:** Once the request becomes consistent, the request will be converted into a constraint satisfaction problem (CSP) using XSLT and is checked for its solution through the ECLIPSe engine.
- **Step 3:** If the CSP is satisfiable, then the request will be converted into a SPARQL query, which is similar to the SELECT query as it retrieves the services from the service repository in which any of the request concepts are present.
- **Step 4:** The semantic similarity measurement and ranking is performed through the service-matching and ranking component.

Figure 1. Service discovery framework

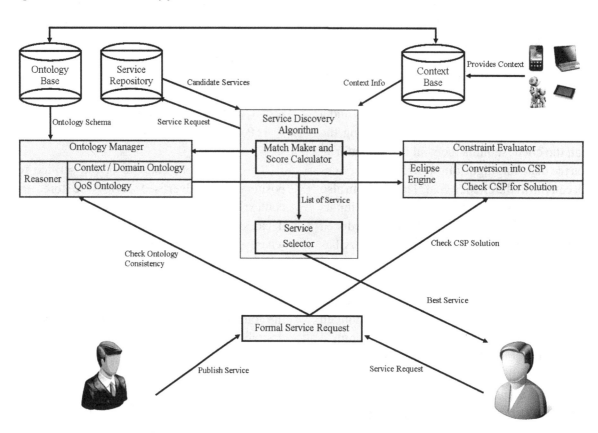

Constraint Programming

Constraint programming is a study of computational models and systems based on constraints. Constraint programming uses constraints to state the problem declaratively without specifying the computational method to implement them. A problem in CP is expressed in a set of constraints called a constraint satisfaction problem. A CSP consists of variables V, a set of domain values D and a set of constraints C. The solution for any CSP is the assignment of values from D to each variable V until it does not violate the constraint C and the solution space of CSP is a set of all solutions. A CSP is satisfiable if the solution space is not empty. CP is becoming a standard method for modelling problems based on its strong theoretical foundations which can solve hard problems.

Web Service Discovery

A web service discovery task receives a query as an input as well as a service registry consisting of service descriptions, and returns a list of matched services as the output. A user request specifies the non-functional requirements of the requested services. Context and QoS parameters can be used to rank services according to non-functional criteria or to restrict the quality of the requested services. The main principle is the use of the similarity measures which can exist between ontology terms. There exist several approaches and algorithms which can be performed in order to apply the comparison and similarity measures. The request formulation is done by using the defined ontology which plays the canonical modelling role.

Figure 2. Request process of SDFD

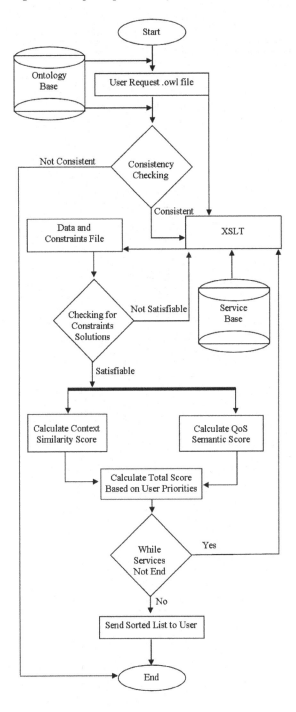

Context-Aware Concept Matching

During the process of service discovery, the first phase is called the matchmaking process where the context descriptions of the web services are matched with the user request. The output of the context description matchmaking phase is four types of lists, namely, the super, exact, partial and fail match lists. The super match list contains the services which satisfy all of the required context constraints; these are the highest level results. The second category of results is the exact match list (the second level of list), the partial match list is the third level of list, while the last category of results is the fail match list. The fail match list contains the results that do not satisfy the constraints of the requester (user).

The second phase of the service discovery is a selection process whereby the lists are sorted according to the calculated scores of the services. The context-aware web service discovery algorithm is presented in Figure 3, and discussed in more detail below. The details of the notions used in the algorithm are presented in Table 1.

The context of any service is defined by factors such as its location, role and status. In order to determine the closeness between the concepts of the offer and the demand, the description logic reasoner can be used to find the subsumption relation between these two concepts. These rules are as follows:

$ContxMatch(O, D) = (O = D) \lor (O \subseteq D) \lor (D \subseteq O)$
Where

$(O = D) = (O.IsNumeric \land D.IsNumeric)$
$\land (O.value = D.value)$
$(D \subseteq O) = (O.IsNamedConcept \land$
$D.IsNamedConcept) \land (O.level \leq D.level)$
$(O \subseteq D) = (O.IsNamedConcept \land$
$D.IsNamedConcept) \land (O.level \geq D.level)$

Figure 3. Service categorisation process

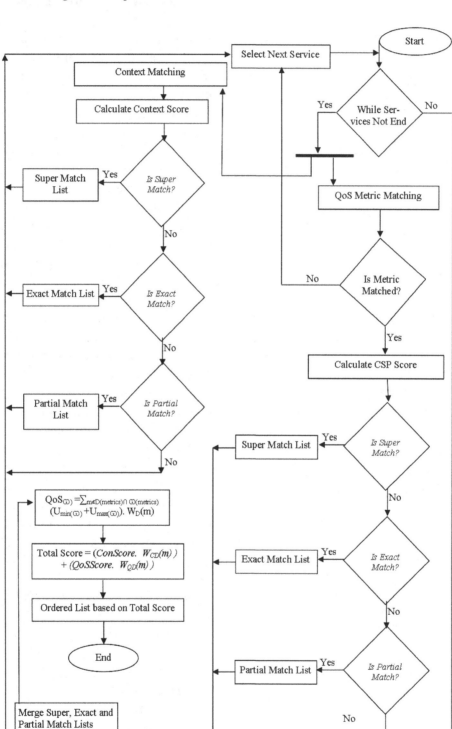

Table 1. Notation description

Notation	Description
$W_{D(attrib)}$	Weight of demanding attribute
Parent(C)	Function to move C to its parent
O_i	i[th] offer
D	Demanding attributes of service
s_D	Score of demand
s^i_O	Score of ith offer
p^i_{s1}	Best service score of ith offered service
p^i_{s2}	Worst service score of ith offered service
$S_{charAtrib}$	Score of named attribute
$S_{numAtrib}$	Score of numeric attribute
CCU/PICU	Special types of intensive care unit (ICU)

QoS Metric Matching

Cortes (Estefan et al., 2008) proposed the conformance metric for matchmaking which is mathematically expressed by the following equation:

$$conformance\ (O_i, D) \Leftrightarrow S\ (P^O_i \wedge \neg\ P^D) = false$$

The above equation can be written as:

$$conformance\ (O_i, D) \Leftrightarrow S\ (P^O_i \wedge \neg\ P^D) = false$$
$$\Leftrightarrow S\ (P^O_i \wedge \neg\ (C^D_1 \wedge C^D_2 \wedge.....\wedge C^D_{2M})) = false$$
$$\Leftrightarrow S\ (P^O_i \wedge (\neg\ C^D_1 \vee \neg\ C^D_2 \vee.....\vee \neg\ C^D_{2M})) = false$$
$$\Leftrightarrow S\ ((P^O_i \wedge \neg\ C^D_1) \vee (P^O_i \wedge \neg\ C^D_2) \vee.....\vee (P^O_i \wedge \neg\ C^D_{2M})) = false$$
$$\Leftrightarrow (S\ (P^O_i \wedge \neg\ C^D_1) = false) \wedge (S\ (P^O_i \wedge \neg\ C^D_2) = false) \wedge.....\wedge (S\ (P^O_i \wedge \neg\ C^D_{2M}) = false)$$

This matchmaking process takes two constraint satisfaction problems of the offers and demands as an input and produces the four types (super, exact, partial and fail) of lists, where S is a function which returns true if the CSP is satisfiable, and is otherwise false. The equivalence of two QoS metric descriptions will be assessed based on the following rules where it is supposed that the

QoS metric descriptions are expressed in OWL-Q (Kritikos et al., 2006). Each rule corresponds to the different type of metric matching, while the last rule is recursive:

$$match\ (M_1, M_2)\ rrm\ (M_1, M_2) \vee rcm(M_1, M_2) \vee ccm(M_1, M_2)$$
$$sm(M_1, M_2)\ svm\ (M_1.scale, M_2.scale, M_1.type, M_2.type) \wedge$$
$$M_1.object = M_2.object \wedge M_1.measures = M_2.measures$$
$$rrm\ (M_1, M_2)\ ResourceMetric(M_1) \wedge ResourceMetric(M_2) \wedge sm(M_1, M_2)$$
$$rcm\ (M_1, M_2)\ ResourceMetric(M_1) \wedge CompositeMetric(M_2) \wedge sm(M_1, M_2) \wedge$$
$$M_2.derivedFrom \cap CompositeMetric = \varnothing \wedge \neg\exists\ V \in M_2.derivedFrom\ match\ (M_1, V)$$
$$ccm\ (M_1, M_2)\ CompositeMetric(M_1) \wedge CompositeMetric(M_2) \wedge sm(M_1, M_2) \wedge$$
$$msm(M_1.derivedFrom, M_2.derivedFrom) \wedge \neg\ solve\ CSP\ (M_1.derivedFrom, M_2.derivedFrom, M_1.measuredBy - M_2.measuredBy\ != 0)$$

In the above given rules, M_1 and M_2 are two metrics where $svm(M_1.scale, M_2.scale, M_1.type, M_2.type)$ and it is concluded that the scale and type of both metrics are the same, while the rule $msm(M_1.derivedFrom, M_2.derivedFrom)$ matches the derived list of the first metric M_1 with the list of metric M_2. The method $solve\ CSP\ (M_1.derivedFrom, M_2.derivedFrom, M_1.measuredBy - M_2.measuredBy != 0)$ solves the CSP defined over the metric lists of M1 and M2 with the help of the $M_1.measuredBy - M_2.measuredBy != 0$ equation. This procedure returns true if the solution exists, and is otherwise false.

Calculating Context Similarity Score

Concepts in the request or offer may be either named or numbers (Hentenryck et al., 1996). In the first category, an ontology reasoner will be used to calculate the similarity (using taxonomic relation) by subsumption relation. In this category, the relation between the demand and the offer may fall into four sub-categories. In the first category, if two concepts (demand and offer; both numbers) are exactly equal then the similarity score will be equal to 1. Otherwise, the score will be calculated based on the following formula:

$$S_{numAtrib} = 1-((Demand - Offer) / Demand)$$

If the demand (in case of a named concept) is at a higher level in the same branch of taxonomy tree as compared to the offer, then its score will be calculated based on the following formula:

$$Level_O = \sum Level(O)$$
$$If\ Level(D) < Level(O)$$
$$S_{charAtrib} = (CountAttributes(D) / CountAttributes(O))$$

where *CountAttributes(O)* denotes the total number of attributes of classes *O* and *D*.

Service Categorisation

The constraint satisfaction problems of the offers and demands are given in Table 3. Based on the given problems, the minimum and maximum utility assessment of the offers and demands is computed using the formula given below while the computed values can be seen in Table 4.

$$U_{max(\omega)} = max_{(\omega)} \sum_{m \in D(metrics) \cap \omega(metrics)} U(m)WD_{(}m)$$
$$U_{min(\omega)} = min_{(\omega)} \sum_{m \in D(metrics) \cap \omega(metrics)} U(m)WD_{(}m)$$

where $U(m) = m - m_{min} / m_{max} - m_{min}$ is a utility function that assigns the unique value to a metric m from a set [0, 1]. m_{max} and m_{min} are the maximum and minimum values that the metric *m* can take. $W_D(m)$ is the weight of metric *m* of demand D. The overall utility assessment is calculated based on the following formula:

$$U_\omega = a.U_{max} + b.\ U_{min}$$
where $0 \leq a, b < 1$ and $a + b = 1$.

For each offer CSP *Pi*, we compute the preferences p^i_{s1} and p^i_{s2} of its worst s^i_1 and best s^i_2 solution, respectively, and then we consider four cases, as described next.

The constraint satisfaction problems of the offers and demands are given in Table 2. Based on the given problems, the final score of the offers and demands is computed using the formula given below while the computed values can be seen in Table 6:

$$s^i_j = \sum(S_{j(charAtrib)} + S_{j(numAtrib)})\ W_D(attrib_j)$$
where $W_D(attrib_j)$ is the weight of attribute $_j$ of demand D.

For each offer CSP S_i, we compute the preferences s^i_j and then we consider the four cases of a super match, exact match, partial match and fail match, as described below.

Super Match

If a CSP of an advertisement contains more variables than the CSP of the request then it is a super match. It is the best type of match wherein the QoS advertisement not only satisfies the QoS constraints but also provides more QoS constraints. This match can be expressed as follows:

$$If\ (((p^i_{s1} \geq p^D_{s1}) \wedge (p^i_{s2} > p^D_{s2}) \vee (p^i_{s1} \geq p^D_{s2}))\ or\ (s^i_O \geq s_D))$$

Exact Match

If a CSP of an advertisement contains the same number of variables and score as the CSP of the request then the advertisement is called an exact match. This type of match is the second most preferable match which completely satisfies all of the QoS request constraints. This match can be expressed as follows:

$$If\ ((p^i_{s1} \geq p^D_{s1}) \wedge (p^i_{s2} \leq p^D_{s2})\ or\ (s^i_O = s_D))$$

Partial Match

If a CSP of an advertisement does not contain all of the variables of the CSP of the request then it is a partial match. This is the next level of preferred results as it contains those QoS advertisements that satisfy the QoS request only for the QoS metrics that appear in both types of specifications. This match can be expressed as follows:

$$If\ (p^i_{s2} > p^D_{s1}) \wedge (p^i_{s1} < p^D_{s1})\ or\ ((s^i_O \geq s_D * .4) \wedge (s^i_O < s_D))$$

Fail Match

If a CSP of an advertisement does not contain any of the variables of the CSP of the request then it is a fail match. In this case, the user must further alter the categorisation of his or her constraints. This match can be expressed as follows:

$$If\ ((p^i_{s2} \leq p^D_{s1})\ or\ (s^i_O < s_D * .4))$$

Service Ranking

The ranking of services that satisfy the user request based on the suitability (score) may be beneficial for the requester. This is especially important in the absence of exact matches; the requester might be interested to consider the service among the rest which meet most of the requirements. The matchmaking engine performs this task based on the calculated scores of the offers. The final score of the services presented in the super, exact and partial lists is calculated with the help of the following formula:

$$Final\ Score = \sum (S_{j(charAttrib)}\ W_D(attrib) + S_{j(numAttrib)}\ W_D(attrib))$$

The score of the quality attributes will be calculated with the help of the following formula:

$$Total_{(\omega)} = \sum_{m \in D(metrics) \cap \omega(metrics)} (Um_{in(\omega)} + Um_{ax(\omega)}) \cdot WD_{(}m)$$

where $U_{min(\omega)}$ is the minimum and maximum weighted score of the service.

Finally, the lists are sorted based on their final score and returned to the requester. By providing a sorted list of the best possible matches, the service requester is supported in choosing the best context-aware offer according to his or her preferences, which are expressed by a list associating the weighted sum of the scores. The algorithm in the present study uses the weights method involving the requester's preferences (priorities) for ranking the similar functional services. The proposed mechanism considers the requester's multiple context requirements for the selection of web services.

Algorithm at a Glance

The algorithm proposed in this study considers the context QoS information for the calculation of the similarity score. This algorithm produces four types of results, namely, super matches, exact matches, partial matches and failed matches, in decreasing order of significance. The algorithm presented in this study provides an approximate matching mechanism which is executed after the user request is found consistent and relevant CSP are satisfiable. The matching process then begins and the score is assigned to the services depending on the similarity between the offer and the request. The similarity score depends on the semantic deviation between the offer and request. Once all of the offers are compared and scored, the offers are categorised into super, exact, partial and fail groups on the basis of the score they have received. The service selector component of the framework then returns the ordered list of offers to the requester along with the rankings. (see Box 1)

Box 1.

```
While service list L not end
        While QoS attributes of a service S from L not end
          Calculate MinScore using utility function
          Calculate MaxScore using utility function
        End while
        Calculate TotalMinScore for all attribute of service S
        Calculate TotalMaxScore for all attribute of service S
        Calculate QoSTotalScore by summing up MinScore and MinScore of each
          attribute and multiplying with the user assigned priority wait.
        While Context attributes of a service S from L not end
                If attribute is the named concept
                        If the concepts are not disjoint
                                Calculate the similarity score based on the utility
                                  function provided
                    If the attribute is the numbered
                                Calculate the similarity score based on the utility
                                  function provided and value type direction
        Calculate ConTotalScore of the service based on the user assigned
          priority waits to the concepts.
        Categorize services according to the categorization formulas
        End while
        Calculate GrandTotal by multiplying and summing up the QoSTotalScore
          and ConTotalScore with the user assigned waits.
        Return the sorted list of services to the user.
End while
```

EVALUATION

The service discovery system has three phases: request consistency checking, context evaluator, and service matchmaking and ranking. After the successful completion of these phases, the system shows the details of the final search result. In the first step, the user provides the query which consists of two parts. The first part consists of the context parameters, and the second part consists of the QoS parameters. After checking the consistency of the query, the query is converted into constraint satisfaction problems to check their solutions. Details of the converted parts of the query into relevant constraint satisfaction problems

are given in Table 2 and Table 3. In the next step, the service matchmaker matches the requested parameters with the published parameters of the services and produces the discovery results. Finally, the discovery results are sorted and the best result is returned to the user.

In this part of the work we also use a part of an application ontology (Figure 4) (Zeshan et al., 2012) along with the context ontology presented above in Figure 1 in order to create the request. It is assumed that the class of Location has five attributes, the Hospital class has twelve attributes, the ICU class has fifteen attributes, the PICU class has nineteen attributes and the CCU class has seventeen attributes.

Table 2. CSP context constraints of offers and demand

Service Id	Activity Description ↑	Status ↑	Remaining Battery Life ↑	Remaining Mem. Space ↑	Deadline ↓	Location Description ↑
O1	X4 = Body temperature measurement	X5 = 1	X6 ≥ 51	X7 ≥ 57	X8 ≤ 7	X9 = Clinic
O2	X4 = Body temperature measurement	X5 = 1	X6 ≥ 65	X7 ≥ 53	X8 ≤ 9	X9 = Hospital
O3	X4 = Heartbeat measurement	X5 = 1	X6 ≥ 79	X7 ≥ 88	X8 ≤ 10	X9 = Ward
O4	X4 = Body temperature measurement	X5 = 1	X6 ≥ 61	X7 ≥ 51	X8 ≤ 8	X9 = Hospital
O5	X4 = Body temperature measurement	X5 = 1	X6 ≥ 76	X7 ≥ 67	X8 ≤ 7	X9 = CCU
O6	X4 = Body temperature measurement	X5 = 1	X6 ≥ 57	X7 ≥ 55	X8 ≤ 11	X9 = Clinic
D	X4 = Body temperature measurement	X5 = 1	X6 ≥ 95	X7 ≥ 90	X8 ≤ 2	X9 = CCU

Table 3. CSP QoS constraints of the offers and demand

Service ID	Response Time	Throughput	Reliability
O_1	X1 ≤ 7 ∧	X2 ≤ 60 ∧ X2 ≥ 40 ∧	X3 ≥ .95
O_2	X1 ≤ 5 ∧	X2 ≤ 50 ∧ X2 ≥ 40 ∧	X3 ≥ .95
O_3	X1 ≤ 11 ∧	X2 ≤ 70 ∧ X2 ≥ 40 ∧	X3 ≥ .98
O_4	X1 ≤ 14 ∧	X2 ≤ 60 ∧ X2 ≥ 40 ∧	X3 ≥ .98
O_5	X1 ≤ 12 ∧	X2 ≤ 70 ∧ X2 ≥ 40 ∧	X3 ≥ .95
O_6	X1 ≤ 10 ∧	X2 ≤ 60 ∧ X2 ≥ 50 ∧	X3 ≥ .94
D	X1 ≤ 15 ∧	X2 ≤ 60 ∧ X2 ≥ 40 ∧	X3 ≥ .99

Suppose the service requester sends the following request:

Query – Looking for a service for measuring temperature measurement of patient in CCU with device status ON, remaining battery greater than or equal to 95%, remaining memory space greater than or equal to 90% and deadline less than or equal to 2 seconds whereas the required reliability is 99%, throughput between 40 to 60 seconds while response time less than 15 seconds.

In order to perform our QoS and context-aware ranking and selection algorithm, we consider a small set of seven context-aware and QoS services. We use a random number generator to create the context and QoS variable values for our services. Table 3 presents the constraint satisfaction problems of the QoS parameters of web service advertisements and the demand constraints.

It is assumed the requester provides the weights to the metrics as follows: a = .7; b = .3; Response Time (X1) = .3; Throughput (X2) = .2; Reliability (X3) = .4; Activity = .5; Location = .3; Deadline = .2; In addition, it is assumed that the following utility functions have been used by the request for calculating the values of the QoS variables: Ufx1 = (16 - X1) / 16; Ufx2 = (X2 - 30) / 70; Ufx3 = (X3 - .9) / .1

After computing the QoS and context constraint satisfaction problems, the matchmaking process checks the satisfiability and produces the following four lists:

Super = [∅];
Exact = [O1, O4, O2];
Partial = [O3, O5, O6];
Final List = [O1, O4, O2, O3, O5, O6]; then,
Ordered Final List = [O3, O2, O4, O1, O6, O5].

The basic aim of the selection process is to facilitate the web service requester to choose the best QoS and context-aware service according to his or her requirements. In this regard, we use the following formula to calculate the final score of the offers of the final ordered list given above:

$$Total_{(\omega)} = \sum_{m \in D(metrics) \cap \omega(metrics)} (Um_{in(\omega)} + Um_{ax(\omega)} \cdot WD_{(}m)$$

Figure 4. Part of application ontology

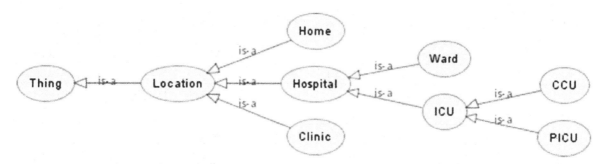

Table 4. CSP computed values of QoS variables

Service ID	Response Time		Throughput		Reliability				Total Score
	Min	Max	Min	Max	Min	Max	Min	Max	
O_1	0.16875	0.16875	0.02857	0.08571	0.20	0.48	0.397	0.735	0.498
O_2	0.20625	0.20625	0.02857	0.05714	0.20	0.48	0.435	0.743	0.527
O_3	0.09375	0.09375	0.02857	0.11429	0.32	0.64	0.442	0.848	0.564
O_4	0.03750	0.03750	0.02857	0.08571	0.32	0.64	0.386	0.763	0.499
O_5	0.07500	0.07500	0.02857	0.11429	0.20	0.48	0.304	0.669	0.413
O_6	0.11250	0.11250	0.05714	0.08571	0.16	0.44	0.330	0.638	0.422
D_1	0.01875	0.01875	0.02857	0.08571	0.36	0.68	0.407	0.785	0.520

The calculated final scores according to the above-mentioned formula are presented in Table 5.

Using the above-calculated total weights, the ordered list is as follows:

Ordered List = [O3, O4, O2, O1, O5, O6].

This list is presented in more detail in Table 6 along with the QoS and context information. Table 3 presents the computed context scores of the offers and the demand based on the formulas presented above.

Based on the calculated score and the criteria discussed above, the services are categorised as follows:

Super match list = [∅];
Exact match list = [∅];

Partial match list = [O1, O2, O3, O4, O5, O6];
Fail match list = [∅];
Final ordered match list = [O5, O2, O4, O3, O6, O1].

It is also supposed that the requester's most preferred category of services is context-awareness while the least one is QoS, hence the requester assigns the priorities to these categories as follows: Context awareness = 0.7; QoS = 0.3.

Based on these priorities and the total scores of QoS and context-awareness (Table 5 and Table 6), the final computed scores of the services are given in Table 7.

Ordered List: [O5, O2, O4, O3, O1, O6]

Table 5. CSP computed values of QoS variables with priorities

Service ID	Response Time	Throughput	Reliability	Total Weight
O_1	0.10125	0.022857143	0.272	0.3963
O_2	0.12375	0.017142857	0.272	0.4129
O_3	0.05625	0.028571429	0.384	0.4688
O_4	0.02250	0.022857143	0.384	0.4294
O_5	0.04500	0.028571429	0.272	0.3456
O_6	0.06750	0.028571429	0.240	0.3361
D_1	0.01125	0.022857143	0.416	0.4501

Table 6. Context similarity scores of services

Service ID	Activity Description	Status	Remaining Battery Life	Remaining Mem. Space	Deadline	Location Description	Total Weighted Score
O1	1	1	0.537	0.633	0.286	0.00	2.73
O2	1	1	0.684	0.589	0.222	0.71	3.03
O3	0	1	0.832	0.978	0.200	0.00	2.85
O4	1	1	0.642	0.567	0.250	0.71	2.97
O5	1	1	0.800	0.744	0.286	1.00	3.40
O6	1	1	0.600	0.611	0.182	0.00	2.75
D	1	1	1.000	1.000	1.000	1.00	4.00

Table 7. Context similarity scores of services

Service ID	QoS Score	Context Score	Total Weighted Score
O_1	0.498	2.73	2.060
O_2	0.527	3.03	2.279
O_3	0.564	2.85	2.164
O_4	0.499	2.97	2.229
O_5	0.413	3.40	2.504
O_6	0.422	2.75	2.052
D_1	0.520	4.00	2.956

The basic aim of the selection process is to facilitate the web service requester to choose the best context-aware service according to his or her requirements. In this study, we evaluate the obtained results of the experiments against the human perception. From this step, O5 from the results of Table 3 is returned to the requester as it meets most of the requirements of the requester, while O2 is the second best service which meets most of the user requirements, while O6 is the least preferred service.

COMPARATIVE EVALUATION

In order to evaluate the existing frameworks for web service discovery against the defined criteria, we selected fourteen studies and divided these studies into two groups (seven studies in each group): QoS-based frameworks, and context-aware frameworks. Similarly, we divided the evaluation criteria into two groups (each group consisting of six requirements): design-based criteria, and process-related criteria. Table 8 presents the observed data of these studies.

By analysing the results in Figure 5 (consisting of the data presented in Table 8) carefully, we concluded that the framework proposed by Baocai et al. (2010) is the most mature framework because it fulfills eight requirements out of 12; hence, its contribution to meeting the defined requirements is 66%. It also meets the highest design-based requirements out of all the participating frameworks, with a 100% contribution to fulfilling the design-based criteria. Similarly, the framework proposed by Liang et al. (2012) meets the highest process-related requirements (83%), whereas the framework proposed by Zhao et al. (2010) does not meet any process-related requirements.

From the results presented in Figure 6, it is observed that the modularity requirement from the group of design-based criteria is the most fulfilled requirement, whereas the advanced categorisation requirement from the group of process-related criteria is the least fulfilled requirement in the studied frameworks. It is also observed that five requirements (advanced categorisation, approximate matching, automation, extensibility, prioritisation, and correctness) which are mostly related to the process-related criteria are the least considered requirements in the frameworks. The

Table 8. Comparison of service discovery frameworks

Framework	Design-Based Criteria						Process-Based Criteria					
	Clarity	OWL-S	Automation	Extensibility	Modularity	Quality of Service	Dynamicity	Prioritisation	Correctness	Context-awareness	Approximate matching	Advanced categorisation
Baocai et al. (2010)	√	√	√	√	√	√		√	√			
Ma et al. (2008)	√	√		√	√	√			√			
Chua et al. (2007)	√				√	√		√	√			
Ayadi et al. (2011)	√		√			√		√			√	
Zhao et al. (2010)				√	√	√						
Li et al. (2009)	√				√	√	√					
Zhu et al. (2010)		√			√	√		√				
Arabshian et al. (2012)		√						√	√	√		
Santos et al. (2009)	√				√			√		√		
Suraci et al. (2007)		√			√					√		
Qi et al. (2007)		√		√	√			√		√	√	
Gu et al. (2008)					√			√		√		
Liang et al. (2012)			√		√		√	√	√	√	√	
Daniele et al. (2009)	√				√			√		√	√	√
SDFD	√	√	√	√	√	√	√	√	√	√	√	√

Figure 5. Framework evaluation based on evaluation criteria

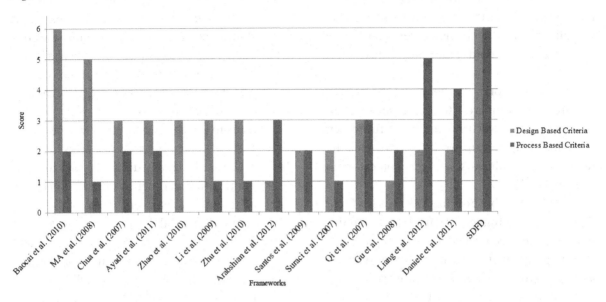

Figure 6. Comparison of framework evaluation criteria

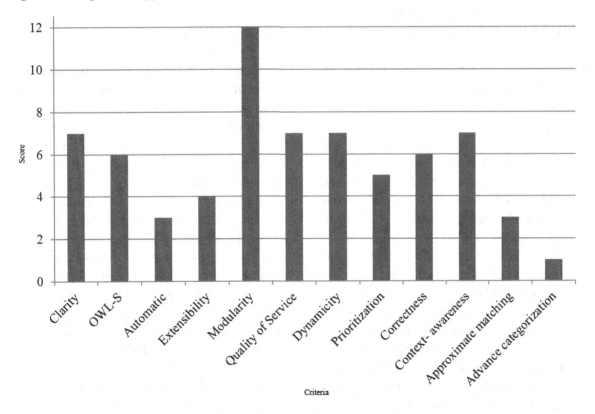

total percentage of the fulfillment of these requirements is 33%. From the analysis it is also observed that almost equal efforts have been made by the researchers in the field of QoS and context-aware frameworks.

QoS frameworks are shown to be slightly matured as compared to the context-aware frameworks because the requirement fulfillment score for the QoS frameworks is 51%, while the requirement fulfillment score for the context-aware frameworks is 49%.

Based on the above detailed analysis it is found that most of the frameworks neglect the requirements of advanced categorisation, approximate matching, automation, extensibility, prioritisation and correctness, whereas the proposed framework (SDFD) addresses all these requirements successfully.

LIMITATIONS AND FUTURE RESEARCH DIRECTIONS

This section discusses the limitations of our work and suggests some valuable future research directions, as follows:

- Tools could be developed to help users to create requests from ontologies by converting the requests into .owl files for reasoning and into CSP variables for checking their satisfiability and then finally converting all variables into a SPARQL query.
- To make SDFD more generic, the evolution of an ontology based on the new concepts should be considered in the ontology and, thus, added to the modelling language.
- To determine the impact of the use of the SDFD on the service discovery activity, testing in a real-world application should be considered. Testing in real-world applications was beyond the scope of the current work. More formal experiments with the method could be conducted to evaluate

more precisely the gains in the productivity of the development team. In the current study, only informal experiments were conducted and conclusions were reached based on the requesting developers' opinions.

- The lack of integration of accessibility tools within the service discovery process tends to leave accessibility assessment procedures to quality assurance tasks.
- There are still many difficult issues to solve in the future in order to meet the objective of automated discovery. In this regard, our approach should be extended to a more general form of ontology properties and inference rules in relation to the reasoning aspect in the approach. In addition, user-friendly tools adapted for the reuse of existing web services in an ontology-based approach would be highly beneficial.

CONCLUSION

The trend to use smaller, more intelligent and cost-effective embedded real-time systems continues, resulting in much greater functionality and complexity. In the last decade, practitioners have begun to use server and desk-top technology in the development of embedded systems. These systems are being increasingly connected with the help of wireless networks including the internet. In order to operate and maintain such complex systems, SOA, which relies heavily on web services, can be the best methodology. The semantic web, the advanced form of the normal web, handles the system complexity with the help of ontologies. Web service discovery, ranking and selection processes based on context and QoS information have remained hot topics for researchers since the start of the semantic web. Context-awareness, which is closely related to embedded systems, can play an important role in service ranking. Context-awareness and QoS can be used in the service selection process among many functionally similar services as a set of criteria to enable the requester to select the most suitable service among similar functional services. In this paper, we have presented a framework for distributed embedded real-time systems for the automatic discovery of services based on the context and QoS information. The proposed framework enables the user to efficiently and automatically search the services running on the embedded devices. The results of the experiment indicate the significance of our work.

REFERENCES

Arabshian, K., Dickmann, C., & Schulzrinne, H. (2007). *Service composition in an ontology-based global service discovery system (Technical report)*. New York: Columbia University.

Arabshian, K., & Troy, C. (2012). *COnTag: A Framework for Personalized Context-aware Search of Ontology-based Tagged Data*. Paper presented at the 19th International Conference on Web Services 2012. New York, NY.

Ayadi, N. Y., & Mohamed, B. A. (2011). An Enhanced Framework for Semantic Web Service Discovery. *Lecture Notes in Business Information Processing*, *82*, 53–67. doi:10.1007/978-3-642-21547-6_5

Ayers, D., Newman, R., & Russell, S. (2005). *Tag ontology*. Retrieved from http://www.holygoat.co.uk/owl/redwood/0.1/tags/

Baocai, Y., Huirong, Y., Pengbin, F., Liheng, G., & Mingli, L. (2010). *A Framework and QoS Based Web Services Discovery*. IEEE. doi:10.1109/ICSESS.2010.5552261

Bellwood, T., Clément, L., Ehnebuske, D., Hately, A., Hondo, M., Husband, Y. L., et al. (2002). *Article*. Retrieved from http://uddi.org/pubs/uddi-v3.00-published-20020719.htm

Bettini, C., Brdiczka, O., Henricksen, K., Indulska, J., Nicklas, D., Ranganathan, A., & Riboni, D. (2009). A Survey of Context Modelling and reasoning Techniques. *Pervasive and Mobile Computing*. PMID:20161031

Chua, F. F., Hao, Y., & Soo, D. K. (2007). *A Visualization Framework for Web Service Discovery and Selection Based on Quality of Service*. Paper presented at the Asia-Pacific Services Computing Conference 2007. Shanghai, China.

Curbera, F., Duftler, M., Khalaf, R., Nagy, W., Mukhi, N., & Weerawarana, S. (2002). Unraveling the Web services web: An introduction to SOAP, WSDL, and UDDI. *Internet Computing, IEEE*, *6*, 86–93. doi:10.1109/4236.991449

Daenen, K., Theeten, B., Vanderfeesten, D., Vrancken, B., Waegeman, E., & Moons, J. et al. (2010). The personal internet. *Bell Labs Technical Journal*, *15*(1), 3–21. doi:10.1002/bltj.20421

Daniele, L. M., Silva, E., Pires, L. F., & Sinderen, M. (2009). A SOA-Based Platform-Specific Framework for Context-Aware Mobile Applications. *Lecture Notes in Business Information Processing*, *38*, 25–37. doi:10.1007/978-3-642-04750-3_3

Dey, A. K., & Abowd, G. D. (2001). Towards a better understanding of context and context awareness. In *Proceedings of the workshop on the What, Who, Where, When and how of Context Awareness*. ACM Press.

Estefan, J. A., Laskey, K., McCabe, F. G., & Thornton, D. (2008). *Reference Architecture for Service Oriented Architecture Version 1.0*. Academic Press.

Fensel, D., Lassila, O., Harmelen, F., Horrocks, I., Hendler, J., & McGuinness, J. (2000). The Semantic Web and its Languages. *IEEE Intelligent Systems*, 67–73.

Fergerson, R. W., Noy, N. F., & Musen, M. A. (2000). The knowledge model of protégé 2000: Combining interoperability and flexibility. In R. Dieng (Ed.), *Proceedings of the 12th EKAW Conference*, (pp. 17–32). Springer-Verlag.

Fleisch, E., & Mattern, F. (2005). *Das Internet der Dinge. Ubiquitous Computing und RFID in der Praxis: Visionen, Technologien, Anwendungen, Handlungsanleitungen*. Springer-Verlag. doi:10.1007/3-540-28299-8

Gu, X., Shi, H., & Ye, J. (2008). A Hierarchical Service Discovery Framework for Ubiquitous Computing. In *Proceedings of Third International Conference on Pervasive Computing and Applications*. ICPCA.

Hentenryck, P. V., & Saraswat, V. (1996). Strategic directions in constraint programming. *ACM Computing Surveys*, *28*(4).

Jakkilinki, R., Sharda, N., & Ahmad, I. (2005). Ontology-Based Intelligent Tourism Information Systems: An overview of Development Methodology and Applications. In *Proceedings of Tourism Enterprise Strategies – 2005*. Melbourne, Australia: Academic Press.

Kritikos, K., & Plexousakis, D. (2006). Semantic QoS Metric Matching. In *Proc. of European Conf. on Web Services*. IEEE Computer.

Li, S., & Juan, Z. (2009). *The WSMO-QoS Semantic Web Service Discovery Framework*. Paper presented at the International Conference on Computational Intelligence and Software Engineering, CiSE 2009. New York, NY.

Liang, Y., Zhou, X., Yu, Z., Wang, H., & Guo, B. (2012). A context-aware multimedia service scheduling framework in smart homes. *EURASIP Journal on Wireless Communications and Networking*. doi:10.1186/1687-1499-2012-67

Ma, Q., Hao, W., Ying, L., Guotong, X., & Feng, L. (2008). *A Semantic QoS-Aware Discovery Framework for Web Services*. Paper presented at the International Conference on Web Services 2008. New York, NY.

Medjahed, B., Bouguettaya, A., & Elmagarmid, A. K. (2003). Composing Web services on the Semantic Web. *The VLDB Journal*, *12*, 333–351. doi:10.1007/s00778-003-0101-5

Oberle, D., Volz, R., Motik, B., & Staab, S. (2004). An extensible ontology software environment. In *Handbook on Ontologies*. Springer. doi:10.1007/978-3-540-24750-0_15

Qi, Y., & Guo-Xing, S. (2007). *Context-Aware Service Discovery in Pervasive Computing Environments*. Paper presented at the Third International Conference on Semantics, Knowledge and Grid, 2007. New York, NY.

Ran, S. P. (2003). A model for Web services discovery with QoS. *ACM SIGecom Exchanges*, *4*(1), 1–10. doi:10.1145/844357.844360

Santos, L. O. B. S., & Eduardo, G. ̧. Alves, S., Lu'ıs, F., P., & Marten, V. S. (2009). *Towards a Goal-Based Service Framework for Dynamic Service Discovery and Composition*. Paper presented at the Sixth International Conference on Information Technology: New Generations 2009. New York, NY.

Schilit, B. N., Adams, N. W. R., & Roy, W. (1994). Context-Aware Computing Applications. In *Proceedings of the 1994 First Workshop on Mobile Computing Systems and Applications*. IEEE Computer Society.

Strang, T., & Linnhoff-Popien, C. (2004). A Context-Modelling survey. In *Proceedings of First International Workshop on Advanced Context Modelling, Reasoning and Management*. UbiComp.

Suraci, V., Mignanti, S., & Aiuto, A. (2007). *Context-aware Semantic Service Discovery*. Paper presented at the 16th IST, Mobile and Wireless Communications Summit. New York, NY.

Tran, V. X., Tsuji, H., & Masuda, R. (2009). A new QoS ontology and its QoS-based ranking algorithm for Web services. *Simulation Modelling Practice and Theory*, *17*, 1378–1398. doi:10.1016/j.simpat.2009.06.010

Tsur, S., Abiteboul, S., Agrawal, R., Dayal, U., Klein, J., & Weikum, G. (2001). Are Web Services the Next Revolution in e-Commerce? (Panel). In *Proceedings of the 27th International Conference on Very Large Data Bases*. Morgan Kaufmann Publishers Inc.

Want, R., Hpper, A., Falcao, V., & Gibbons, J. (1992). The Active Badge Location System. *ACM Transactions on Information Systems*, 91–102. doi:10.1145/128756.128759

Yao, S. J., Chen, C. X., Dang, L. M., & Liu, W. (2008). Design of QoS ontology about dynamic web service selection. *Computer Engineering and Design*, *29*(6), 1500–1548.

Zeshan, F., & Radziah, M. (2012). Medical Ontology in the Dynamic Healthcare Environment. *Procedia Computer Science*, *10*, 340–348. doi:10.1016/j.procs.2012.06.045

Zhao, J., Lingshuang, S., Zhiwen, C., & Bing, X. (2010). *A Flexible Multi-Source Web Service's QoS Acquisition Framework and Implementation*. Paper presented at the Symposia and Workshops on Ubiquitous, Autonomic and Trusted Computing 2010. New York, NY.

Zhu, Y., & Xiao-Hua, M. (2010). *A Framework for Service Discovery in Pervasive Computing*. Paper presented at the 2nd International Conference on Information Engineering and Computer Science (ICIECS). New York, NY.

KEY TERMS AND DEFINITIONS

Ontology: Ontology is an explicit formal specification of how to represent the device objects, concepts and other entities that are assumed to exist in some area of interest and the relationships that hold among them (Jakkilinki *et al.*, 2005). Ontologies provide metadata schema, along with the vocabulary of the concepts used in annotation.

Semantic Web: The Semantic Web is the extension to the existing Web which gives a well-defined meaning to Web resources by describing and annotating them with a suitable language. Semantic Web by using ontologies provides a shared vocabulary for the specification of device and service information. Semantic web uses semantic annotation to facilitate the software / intelligent agents to process the data (Fensel et al., 2000).

Web Service: Web Services are a software system designed to support interoperable machine-to-machine interaction over a network. It uses SOAP protocol and XML messages to receive request and offer responses. The key feature of the web services is that they are loosely coupled, allows ad-hoc and dynamic binding and are reusable software components.

Chapter 8
An Algebraic Approach for the Specification and the Verification of Aspect–Oriented Systems

Arsène Sabas
Université de Montréal, Canada

Subash Shankar
City University of New York (CUNY), USA

Virginie Wiels
ONERA – The French Aerospace Lab, France

John-Jules Ch. Meyer
Universiteit Utrecht, The Netherlands

Michel Boyer
Université de Montréal, Canada

ABSTRACT

Aspect-Oriented (AO) Technology is a post-object-oriented technology used to overcome limitations of Object-Oriented (OO) Technology, such as the cross-cutting concern problem. Aspect-Oriented Programming (AOP) also offers modularity and traceability benefits. Yet, reasoning, specification, and verification of AO systems present unique challenges, especially as such systems evolve over time. Consequently, formal modular reasoning of such systems is highly attractive as it enables tractable evolution, otherwise necessitating that the entire system be re-examined each time a component is changed or is added. The aspect interactions problem is also an open issue in the AOP area. To deal with this problem, the authors choose to use Category Theory (CT) and Algebraic Specification (AS) techniques. In this chapter, the authors present an aspect-oriented specification and verification approach. The approach is expressive and allows for formal modular reasoning.

DOI: 10.4018/978-1-4666-6026-7.ch008

1 INTRODUCTION

Aspect-Oriented Programming has emerged in recent years as a new paradigm that provides a set of concepts that allow programmers to modularize their applications in order to provide better Separation of Concerns (SoC). Thanks to AOP, programmers can implement different concerns in well-defined entities called aspects by breaking the inherent dependencies that can exist between the different program modules. By using AOP, programmers thus increase the maintainability and the readability of their programs. AOP, giving rise to programming languages such as AspectJ Kiczales et al. (1997), evolved from a programming activity to a full-blown software engineering process, having the goals of preserving modularity and traceability, which are two important properties of high-quality software.

Yet, there are also many challenges in AO Technology. Reasoning, specification, and verification of AO programs present unique challenges especially as such programs evolve over time. Consequently, modular reasoning of such programs is highly attractive as it enables tractable evolution, which would otherwise require that the entire program be re-examined each time a component is changed or is added. It is well known in the literature, however, that modular reasoning about AO programs is difficult due to the fact that the applied aspects often alter the behavior of the base components Khatchadourian et al. (2008). The same modular reasoning difficulties are also present in the specification and verification phases of software development processes. To the best of our knowledge, AO modular specification and verification is a poorly studied subject and constitutes an interesting open research field.

Aspect interaction is also a major concern in the aspect-oriented community. Detection and resolution of undesirable aspect interactions is an important open research field and we believe that formal models are needed to handle unexpected interactions. Most AO verification approaches are based on a strategy of detection and correction. Although these detection approaches are relevant for AO software reliability, we believe that they are time and cost consuming. It is good to detect and correct system failures, but it is better to first prevent them; consequently, we advocate a prevention policy to be integrated at the specification phase. We believe indeed that this will make the verification phase timeless and costless.

To help reason about AO systems, the use of formal methods becomes desirable. Formal methods are essential to support quality, modifiability and reusability by formal concepts for data abstraction and modularity Ehrig et al. (1992). We believe that CT and AS can help us achieve these goals. CT is a good and powerful tool for the modularization of system components which can be considered as objects of a category. It introduces the notion of morphism, which can be used as a means to study and to implement interactions within these components. Moreover, it has construction operators that allow to structurally compose these components to form the complete system. To deal with the resolution of undesirable interactions between aspects and base components, we decided to rely on CT and AS to model and verify AO systems. By using CT, we can take advantage of the structure of a system specification to carry out the verification task and to infer some desirable properties on the global system. The principle of this modular verification is as follows: for a morphism m: $MOD_1 \rightarrow MOD_2$, if a property P is true in MOD_1, then $m(P)$ is true in MOD_2. For example, suppose we want to prove a property (by model-checking or a theorem proving technique) on the module MOD_S representing the entire system and we have the morphisms $MOD_3 \rightarrow MOD_S$ and $MOD_4 \rightarrow MOD_S$. This property may result from the conjunction of two lemmas; each lemma may be proved in the smallest modules (MOD_3 and MOD_4) and then translated to MOD_S.

The main contributions of this chapter are the following:

1. Extension of Algebraic Specification Technique to Aspect Orientation.
2. Development of a weaving algorithm using the co-limit concept of category theory.
3. Modular formal specification and verification of AO systems.
4. Development of a prevention policy to avoid undesirable aspect interactions. The best strategy of handling conflicts is to prevent conflicts from happening.

Next, we apply our approach to an industrial case study to validate our framework. This case study is a Pratt & Whitney Canada (an aerospace company) Pratt (2013) project.

2 BACKGROUND

2.1 Algebraic Specification

AS was based on specifying data types in a way similar to that used for the study of different algebraic structures, such as groups, rings, etc. AS of an algebra is a syntactical representation of that algebra. It is obtained by associating to each element of the algebra a symbol. Finite syntactical representations are very important in computer science Ehrig & Mahr (1985). AS is constituted of two parts: 1) a signature that defines the vocabulary required to define the second part, and 2) a body, a set of axioms that describes the behavior of the specification. A logic can be used to set up these axioms.

2.2 Category Theory

Current software development methods, namely object-oriented ones, typically model the universe as a society of interacting objects. Complexity does not necessarily arise from the computational or algorithmic nature of systems, but results from the fact that their behavior can only be explained

as emerging from the interconnections that are established between their components Fiadeiro (2005). CT is a good toolbox that can be used to model software systems by focusing not only on the components of these systems, but especially on the interactions between these components. The following definitions come from the work of Barr and Wells Barr & Wells (1999) and Fiadeiro Fiadeiro (2005).

Definition 2.1: *Graph. A graph G is a quadruple $\langle G_0, G_1, s, t \rangle$ where: G_0 is a collection of nodes; G_1 is a collection of edges; $s: G_1 \to G_0$ is a function (source); $t: G_1 \to G_0$ is a function (target). For $f \in G_1$, we write $f: X \to Y$ to indicate $s(f) = X$ and $t(f) = Y$.*

Definition 2.2: *Paths in a Graph. Let $k > 0$. In a graph $G = \langle G_0, G_1, s, t \rangle$, a path from a node X to a node Y of length k is a sequence $(f_1, f_2, ..., f_k)$ of (not necessarily distinct) arrows for which:*
- $s(f_k) = X$,
- $t(f_i) = s(f_{i-1})$ for $i = 2, ..., k$, and
- $t(f_1) = Y$.

By convention, for each node X there is a unique path of length 0 from X to X that is denoted (). It is called the empty path at X. The set of paths of length k in a graph G is denoted G_k. Hence:
- G_0 *corresponds to the collection of nodes.*
- G_1 *corresponds to the collection of arrows.*
- G_2 *corresponds to the collection of composable pairs of arrows.*

Definition 2.3: *Category. A category C is a graph $\langle C_0, C_1, s, t \rangle$ together with two functions $c: C_2 \to C_1$ and $u: C_0 \to C_1$ with properties 1 through 4 below. The elements of C_0 are called objects and those of C_1 are called morphisms or arrows. The function c is called composition, and if (g, f) is a composable pair, $c(g, f)$ is written $g \circ f$ and is called the composite of g and f. If X is an object of C, $u(X)$ is denoted Id_X which is called the identity of the object X.*

1. $s(g \circ f) = s(f)$ *and* $t(g \circ f) = t(g)$.
2. *For all* $f, g, h \in C_1$, $(h \circ g) \circ f = h \circ (g \circ f)$ *whenever either side is defined.*
3. $s(Id_X) = t(Id_X) = X$.
4. *If* $f: X \to Y$, *then* $f \circ Id_X = Id_Y \circ f = f$.

Definition 2.4: *Pushout. In a category C, a pushout of a pair of morphisms f: $X \to Y$ and g: $X \to Z$ is an object W and a pair of morphisms p: $Y \to W$ and q: $Z \to W$ such that* $p \circ f = q \circ g$, *and for all object W^t and all morphisms p^t: $Y \to W^t$ and q^t: $Z \to W^t$ such that $p^t \circ f = q^t \circ g$, there is a unique morphism u: $W \to W^t$ such that $u \circ q = q^t$ and $u \circ p = p^t$.*

Pushout is an example of the co-limit notion in CT. There are many other examples. This notion of co-limit has a constructor role. We can use the concept of co-limit to compose two modules and obtain the third module. A category is (finitely) cocomplete if all (finite) diagrams have colimits.

2.3 Aspect Oriented Technology

Aspect-oriented programming is a relatively new programming paradigm that allows for the separation of concerns, especially, separation of crosscutting concerns. Crosscutting concerns are concerns which are spread out over multiple modules, or intermixed with other concerns. AOP allows better modularity, cohesion, understandability, maintainability, and evolvability of a program or system. Yet, aspect-oriented programming brings new challenges, ideas, and concepts. We define some of these concepts.

- **Joinpoint:** A well-defined point in the execution of a program, which is used to define the dynamic structure of a crosscutting concern.
- **Pointcut:** A set of patterns that are used to select joinpoints.
- **Advice:** A method-like construct that contains additional behavior to be added at the

matched joinpoint. There are four kinds of advices: before advice, after advice, around advice, and InsteadOf advice: (1) Before advice: executes its body before executing the body of the matched joinpoint; (2) After advice: executes its body after executing the body of the matched joinpoint; (3) Around advice: surrounds the matched joinpoint; (4) InsteadOf advice: replaces the execution of the matched joinpoint body.

- **Aspect:** A construct that encapsu- lates a crosscutting concern. Aspects are similar to class in OO programming.
- **Aspect Weaving:** The process by which behavior of aspects are merged into the original byte-code. It is worth to note that the concepts of Aspect-Oriented Modeling (AOM) are similar to the ones of AOP.

2.4 Related Work

2.4.1 Aspect Oriented Modeling and Verification Approaches

Most aspect modeling approaches (AOM) (for example ones in Stein et al. (2002); Pawlak et al. (2002); Baniassad & Clarke (2004); Jacobson & Ng (2005); Cottenier et al. (2007); France et al. (2004); Whittle & Jayaraman (2007); Qaisar et al. (2013)) we studied are based on UML, and one cannot formally verify the systems built by these approaches due to UML's lack of formal semantics. Lightweight Formal Analysis of Aspect Oriented Models Nakajima & Tamai (2004) is an approach that applies role-based modeling to aspect-oriented modeling, and then uses Alloy to describe role-based aspect models. Although Alloy allows formal verification, we did not notice any verification step in the paper we read, and Alloy can only verify small models. None of the approaches we have studied use as formalisms the AS and the CT (see the advantages of using these formalisms in sections 1, 2.1, 2.2). The future work presented in Khatchadourian et al. (2008) is a little bit similar to our goal. There are formal works such as the one in Skipper (2004); Walker et al. (2003) which act at the implementation level but we are dealing with the specification and verification phases of the software development process. Moreover, our framework is intended to be programming language independent.

The paper Fox (2005) presents a formal abstraction of an aspect and constructs for component compo- sition. Their aspect abstraction is close to our aspect signature concrete definition. This aspect abstraction seems to not take into account the fact that an aspect can affect other aspects. We believe that a specification of an aspect should show in a compact way not only the related classes and methods, but also where the aspect crosscuts a given related class. By using the concept of module specification, our abstraction level is higher than theirs. Our weaving process is based on the concept of co-limit. The co-limit notion has some properties described in section 4.2. These properties are required in the weaving process in AOSD.

There are some verification approaches (for example ones in Xu et al. (2007); Mostefaoui (2008); Storzer et al. (2003); Goldman & Katz. (2006); Katz & Katz (2008); Khatchadourian et al. (2008); Cui et al. (2013)), but these generally focus on one or two specific undesirable aspect interactions, rather than the full complement of such interactions. Also, these verification approaches are based on conflict detection, contrary to our approach which is based firstly on a prevention strategy and thereafter on a detection and correction strategy if it is necessary.

2.4.2 Work of Wiels

We decided to use Wiels' work Wiels (1997); Michel & Wiels (1997) because of the modularity benefits offered by her approach at the specification and verification levels. Moreover, this approach is supported by the MOKA tool that we

can use and extend to aspect-oriented concepts. The proposed approach combines algebraic modules and a temporal logic of action. This temporal logic of action is a combination of linear temporal logic and dynamic logic. She adapted the calculus of modules proposed by Ehrig and Mahr Ehrig & Mahr (1990), by using her logic to describe the behavior of the module parts, and construction op- erators defined by Ehrig and Mahr to compose modules. Wiels' approach is motivated by the need to import the modularity concepts of object-oriented programming (OOP) into formal specification and verification phases. Our goal is to import AOP modularity concepts into formal specification and verification phases. AOP is an extension of OOP. Our approach is an extension of Wiels' approach, with the main differences being: our approach is intended for AOS while her approach is for OOS; we use a combination of temporal, dynamic, and deontic logics while she uses temporal and dynamic logics.

3 ASPECT ORIENTED ALGEBRAIC APPROACH

In AO Technology, system components can be aspect or class components, which use data structures. Aspect components, class components, and abstract data types are described by aspect, class, and abstract data type module specifications, respectively. As in Wiels' approach, there are three levels of a system description in our approach: (1) a system is described by modules that are interconnected by morphisms and on which composition operations can be performed; (2) a module is composed of four specifications linked by specification morphisms; (3) each specification consists of a vocabulary part and a set of formulae describing the behavior and the constraints of this specification. The formulae are written with the logic L_A (see section 3.1). We equip module specifications with a prevention policy consisting a set of properties expressing the societal life of the components. These properties are expressed by our logic in the form of societal norms forbidding the undesirable interactions and behaviors that a component could have. Any violation of these norms will be penalized.

3.1 Logic L$_A$

We propose a logic L_A which will be used to specify behavioral properties and societal life of aspect-oriented system components. The logic L_A includes modalities of three other logics: (1) linear temporal logic (LTL) Manna & Pnueli (1992) to reason on the time (2) (first-order) dynamic logic (FDL) Harel et al. (2000) to reason explicitly on actions or computer programs and properties (LTL cannot explicitly reason on actions); (3) deontic logic Wright (1951) to specify the social life of system components. L_A contains other modalities corresponding to the aspect modifiers **Before**, **After**, **Around**, and **InsteadOf**.

Others have shown that such a combination (LTL + Dynamic Logic + Deontic Logic) is adequate for systems specification Khosla & Maibaum (1987) because it can distinguish between description and pre-scription of behavior. Action prescriptions are meant to convey when actions may or must occur, via the deontic concepts of allowed or required action. The description is achieved by the traditional pre and post condition style description of actions. This then allows us to state when actions may and must happen as opposed to just describing the effects of such actions Khosla & Maibaum (1987).

We give an informal meaning of formulae of L_A.

- $X \varphi$ means that φ will hold in the next state.
- $G\varphi$ means that φ holds in the current state and will always hold in the future state.
- $F \varphi$ means that there exists a future state in which φ holds.
- $\phi \cup \psi$ means that ϕ holds until ψ holds.

- $[\alpha]\beta$ is an action which means that immediately after each execution of the action α, the action β must be executed (necessity).
- $< \alpha > \beta$ is an action which means that it is possible to execute the action α and reach a state in which the action β has to be executed (possibility).
- $\alpha; \beta$ means that the action α is executed first followed by the execution of β (sequential composition).
- $\alpha \vee \beta$ means that the action α or β is executed non deterministically (non-deterministic choice).
- $\alpha \wedge \beta$ means that the actions α and β are executed simultaneously (parallel composition).
- α^* means that the action α is executed sequentially n times (n $\geq$ 0) (non-deterministic iteration).
- $\neg\alpha$ is an action indicating that the action α is not executed.
- $I \alpha$ means that it is forbidden to execute the action α, otherwise there will be a sanction represented by a constant action V.
- $O\alpha$ means that it is obligatory to execute the action α, otherwise there will be a reparation represented by a constant action V.
- $O_k \alpha$ means that it is obligatory to execute the action α before the date k, k being a positive integer.
- $P \alpha$ means that it is permissible to execute action α .
- $[\alpha]\varphi$ is a formula meaning that the formula φ holds after all execution of the action α (necessity).
- $< \alpha > \varphi$ is a formula meaning that it is possible to execute the action α and reach a state in which the formula φ holds (possibility).
- $\varphi \rightarrow \alpha/\beta$ means that if φ holds in the current state, then the action α is executed otherwise the action β is executed (conditional). It is worth pointing out that $\varphi \rightarrow \alpha/\beta$ is not

the same as the formula $\varphi \to \alpha$ because the latter is somewhat problematic, since we don't know its status when φ does not hold.

- $\varphi?$ is an action which tests if the formula φ is true. If φ is true, then proceed, otherwise fail (test). Dynamic logic associates to every proposition φ an action $\varphi?$ called a test. If φ holds, the test $\varphi?$ acts as a skip, changing nothing while allowing the action to move on. If φ is false, $\varphi?$ acts as an "abort".

In the following four formulae, $(B_e\varphi)\alpha$, $(A_f\varphi)\alpha$, $(A_r\varphi)\alpha_1, \alpha_2$ and $(I_o\varphi)\alpha$, φ is an atomic proposition meaning that a joinpoint jp is reached.

- $(B_e\varphi)\alpha$ is a formula which means that just before each state s where the formula φ is true, the action α is obliged to be executed (before). We read $(B_e\varphi)\alpha$: before φ α.
- $(A_f\varphi)\alpha$ is a formula which means that immediately after each state s where the formula φ is true, the action α is obliged to be executed (after). We read $(A_f\varphi)\alpha$: after φ α.
- $(A_r\varphi)\alpha_1, \alpha_2$ is a formula which means that in each state s where the formula φ is true, α_1 is obliged to be executed immediately before and α_2 immediately after the action that should be executed in s (Around). We read $(A_r\varphi)\alpha_1, \alpha_2$: around φ α_1, α_2.
- $(I_o\varphi)\alpha$ is a formula which means that in each state s where the formula φ is true, the action α is obliged to be executed instead of the action (encapsulated in the body of the joinpoint jp) that should be executed in s (InsteadOf). We read $(I_o\varphi)\alpha$: instead of φ α.

The semantics assumes given a set J (of joinpoints) and two functions defined on J; the function

$fj: J \to A$

$jp >\to fj(jp)$

that associates to a joinpoint jp, the action $fj(jp)$ encapsulated in the body of jp (A is a set of actions); the function

$pr: J \to \Phi_0$

$jp >\to$ "jp is reached"

that associates to a joinpoint jp, the (atomic) proposition "the joinpoint jp is reached" (Φ_0 is a set of atomic propositions) such as:

$pr(jp_1 \| jp_2) = pr(jp_1) \vee pr(jp_2)$ and

$pr(jp_1 \&\& jp_2) = pr(jp_1) \wedge pr(jp_2)$.

For example, if $np = jp_1 jp_2$ then,

$(B_e pr(np))\beta \equiv (B_e pr(jp_1))\beta \vee (B_e pr(jp_2))\beta$ and

$(B_e pr(jp_i))\beta \equiv G(pr(jp_i) \to O(\beta; fj(jp_i); T?)/T?)$

We show that L_A is sound and complete. The complete development of this logic can be found in Sabas(2012). We think that what is given here suffices to understand this chapter.

3.2 Specifications

Since components of a system can be aspects or classes, we have to consider aspect and class specifica-tions. These components use data types; this led us to consider abstract data type (ADT) specification. The definitions of these kinds of specification are based on work of Ehrig and Mahr Ehrig & Mahr (1985). Ehrig and Mahr's work is an equational theory while our work is a logical theory.

Figure 1. Pattern of an ADT Specification (Concrete definition)

```
SPEC_ADT Specification Name
Sorts          ⟨list of sorts name⟩

Subsorts       ⟨list of subsorts relations⟩

Actions        ⟨operation signatures setting out the names and the sorts of
                 the parameters of the operations and the return sort⟩

Axioms         ⟨operations properties⟩

Theorems       ⟨possible theorems⟩
End Specification Name
```

3.2.1 Specification of an Abstract Data Type

The two basic notions in computer science are the notions of operations and data. Data structures and data types are fundamental concepts of programming and specification of software systems. A set of operations is associated to each abstract data type, making it an algebra. We can thus define the specification of this algebra. Figure 1 defines the pattern of an ADT specification.

The pattern of an *ADT specification* is composed of:

1. a header with reserved word **SPEC_ADT** followed by the specification name.
2. a field **Sorts** which lists the imported sorts plus the sort corresponding to the current ADT. For exam- ple, if the name of the ADT specification is Bool, the sort of Bool is noted by bool.
3. a field **Subsorts** lists the subsort relations of the specification under consideration. In order to model sort inclusions and coercions, we equip the specification with a partial order relation $\leq$ over the set of sorts. Thus, overloading is supported and operations are allowed to be sub-sort polymorphic. Hence, we increase the expressiveness of our algebraic specification.

4. a field **Actions** which contains the operation signatures of the ADT. It also contains the constructors. Actions could be partial or total operations. We choose the term Action to conform to our logic L_A.
5. a field **Axioms** which defines the semantics of the operations by defining a set of axioms that characterize the behavior of the ADT. These axioms written with our logic L_A could be formulae or positive conditional equations of the form: *Conditions $\Rightarrow$ equation.*
6. a **Theorems** field contains possible formulas which are assumed to be true. These formulas are generally consequences derived from the axioms.
7. the specification ends with the reserved word **END** followed by the specification name.

Thus, our specification pattern defines a class of partial order-sorted algebras (because of the subsort relation).

3.2.2 Specification of a Class

Although AS was originally intended for describing data types, it soon grew into a formal specification technique aiming to cover the whole specification phase within the software development process Ehrig et al. (1992). Large systems are usually decomposed into sub-systems which are developed independently. Sub-systems are often defined as a set of abstract data types or object classes. A class is used to model the behavior of objects.

We are modeling computer programs as algebras. A specification defines a set of algebras (computer programs). Thus, classes can be described by AS techniques. By doing this, algebraic specifications could be rendered more suitable for large applications on the one hand, and computer programs could be supported by specifications with well-defined semantics on the other hand.

The pattern of a Class specification is defined as the pattern of an ADT (Figure 1) with the following additional fields:

1. a field **States** gives the list of the attribute signatures of the class instances. These attributes determine at a given time the state of an class instance or object. The template of an attribute signature is at: $s_1 s_2 ... s_n \rightarrow s$ with $n \geq 0$; at is the name of the attribute; $s_1, s_2, ..., s_n$ denote optional parameter sorts while s denotes the range sort of the attribute. In programming terms, an attribute symbol which has no arguments corresponds to a program variable, whereas those with arguments can be associated with more complex data structures such as arrays.
2. the field **Initial** gives the initial state of an object or default values of the attributes.
3. a field **Prescription Axioms** which defines properties describing what the system should do, or proscribing the violation of desired properties, i.e., undesirable interactions.

and in which the header is replaced by the reserved word **SPEC_CLASS**.

3.2.3 Specification of an Aspect

Aspects are a class-like constructs. Like classes, aspects can have attributes (states) and methods; in addition they encapsulate the remaining components of quantified statements: conditions are specified by point-cut expressions and actions are specified by method-like constructs called advice Shaker & Peters (2005) (see section 2.3). A pointcut is a predicate that matches JoinPoints. More precisely, a pointcut is a relationship from JoinPoint $\rightarrow$ boolean, where the domain of the relationship is all possible JoinPoints Berg et al. (2005). Thus, we specify an aspect by using algebraic specification technique. The pattern of an Aspect specification is defined as the pattern of a Class with the following additional fields:

1. **Pointcut** field lists the pointcut signatures inside the aspect. A pointcut signature is comprised of its name, the sorts (types) of its optional parameter sorts (source, target, and arguments of the joinpoints), and the result sort bool (boolean sort). The template of a pointcut signature is pc: $s_1 s_2 ... s_n \rightarrow$ bool with $n \geq 0$.
2. **Pointcut Axioms** define the joinpoints contained in the pointcut expressions. In other words, they describe the selection action of the pointcuts.
3. **Advice Axioms** give the advice descriptions using the logic L_A.

and in which the header is replaced by the reserved word **SPEC_ASPECT**. Examples can be found in section 4.4.

3.2.4 Abstract Syntax of a Specification

The abstract syntax definition is needed to manipulate specifications, for instance to define semantics of specifications and module specifications. In general, an algebraic specification consists of three parts:

1. A signature, consisting of sort names and functions symbols, from which one can build data terms. Each function symbol f is of the form (signature or interface) $f: s_1 s_2 ...$

$s_n \to s$ for some $n \geq 0$, where $s_1, s_2, \ldots s_n, s$ are sort names; f is said to have arity $s_1, s_2, \ldots s_n$, result sort (or co-arity) s, and rank (or declaration) $(s_1 \, s_2 \ldots s_n, s)$. This means that if $d_1, d_2, \ldots d_n$ are data terms of sorts $s_1, s_2, \ldots s_n$ respectively, then $f(d_1, d_2, \ldots d_n)$ is a data term of sort s. If $n = 0$, that is $f{:}\to s$, we use the abbreviation $f{:}\ s$ and f is a constant; $f{:}\ s$ can be written $f{:}\ \lambda \to s$ where λ is the empty string of sorts. If S is a set of sorts, then we note S^* the set of all strings of elements of S (S^* is the free monoid over S). If $\omega = s_1 \, s_2 \ldots s_n$, $\omega \in S^*$, we can note $f{:}\ \omega \to s$. The set of all function symbols $f{:}\ \omega \to s$ with $\omega \in S^*$ is noted $\Omega_{\omega, s}$.

2. For each sort *s,* a countable infinite set of data variables of sort *s.*

3. A set of axioms, i.e., equations $d = e$ between data terms (possibly containing data variables) of same sort, which induces an equality relation on data terms.

We define our signature as an ordered sorted signature Goguen (1992), because of the benefits (polymor- phism, overloading, error detection, partial operation, etc.). A signature defines the specific vocabulary symbols that are relevant for the description of the specification. A signature or interface defines the bound- aries (limits) of the specification representing a component. The components of a system will interact via this interface, enforcing the principle of the encapsulation. When we reason about a component, we must use only the vocabulary of that component.

Classes are described on the basis of conventional data type specifications. The basic difference between data values as instances of data types and objects as instances of object classes is that values are regarded as stateless items while objects are associated with an inherent notion of state. A Class specification consists of a signature (defining the specific vocabulary symbols that are relevant for the description of the class instances), and a collection of formulae of the language generated

from the signature. A difference between a class and an ADT is that an instance of a class can have states while an ADT does not.

Like classes, aspects can have attributes (whose values at a given time determine their states), methods, pointcut expressions, and advices. Thus aspects are described on the basis of conventional data type specifications, with the notions of state, point-cut, and advice.

The details of these definitions can be found in Sabas (2012). Due to space limitations, we do not give these definitions in this chapter.

3.3 Specification Morphism

A morphism between two objects (in general) specifies the way these two objects interact with each other. The meaning of this interaction or relationship is up to the user or system speci- fier. The focus that CT puts on morphisms as structure-preserving mappings is paramount for software architectures because it is the morphisms that determine the nature of the interconnections that can be established between objects (system components). As a structure-preserving mapping, a morphism between two objects is defined in such a way that we can consider one of them a component of the second one Fiadeiro (2005).

Globally, the morphisms translate the vocabu- lary of one specification into the vocabulary of another, preserving the theorems. A signature morphism (a vocabulary mapping) maps the sorts and operations from one specification to another, and must preserve the rank (input and output sorts) of each operation. A specification morphism is a signature morphism for which each axiom of the first specification maps to a theorem of the second specification. An ADT specification mor- phism is defined as an equational specification morphism Ehrig & Mahr (1985) that preserves the partial order and the axioms. We extend this in the natural way to define class specification morphisms, aspect specification morphisms, and aspect-class specification morphisms (due to the space limitation, the details of these definitions can be found in Sabas (2012)).

3.4 Module Specification and Morphism

3.4.1 Module Specification

Modules can be seen as the basic building blocks being used for modularization, which is one of the main principles in software development. We don't fundamentally modify the definition of Ehrig and Mahr in Ehrig & Mahr (1990). A module specification MOD is structured in four algebraic specifications, called parameter (PAR), import interface (IMP), export interface (EXP) and body (BOD), which are combined by inclusions or other specification morphisms: e: PAR → EXP; i: PAR → IMP; v: EXP → BOD; s: IMP → BOD such that $v \circ e = s \circ i$. The import interface identifies those resources which are to be provided by other modules and used in the modules body for construction of resources to be exported. The export interface is the visible part which must be known to use this module in connection with other modules. The parameter part is the intersection of import and export parts. It contains the possible parameters of the module. The body part defines the construction of the resources declared in the export interface using those declared in the import interface. This part may also contain auxiliary sorts and operations which do not belong to any other part of the module but depend on the particular choice of construction. The body part is not visible from the outside of the module.

Definition 3.1: *ADT Module Specification. An ADT module specification is a module specification in which PAR, IMP, EXP, BOD are ADT specifications and morphisms are ADT specification morphisms.*

Definition 3.2: *Class Module Specification. A Class module specification is a module specifi-* cation in which PAR, IM, EXP, BOD are Class specifications and morphisms are Class specification morphisms.

Definition 3.3: *Aspect Module Specification. An aspect module specification is a module specification in which PAR, IMP, EXP, BOD are Aspect specifications and morphisms are Aspect specification morphisms.*

3.4.2 Module Morphism

Definition 3.4: *Module morphism. A module morphism m: $MOD_1 \to MOD_2$ is a 4-tuple $m = (m_p, m_e, m_i, m_b)$ of specification morphisms with m_p: $PAR_1 \to PAR_2$, m_e: $EXP_1 \to EXP_2$, m_i: $IMP_1 \to IMP_2$, and m_b: $BOD_1 \to BOD_2$ such that: $m_e \circ e_1 = e_2 \circ m_p$ $m_i \circ i_1 = i_2 \circ m_p$ $m_b \circ v_1 = v_2 \circ m_e$ $m_b \circ s_1 = s_2 \circ m_i$*

In other words, a module morphism forms a graph such that from any node A to another B, the result will be the same regardless of the path. If MOD_1 and MOD_2 are ADT (resp. Class, Aspect) module specifications, then m_p, m_e, m_i, m_b are ADT (resp. Class, Aspect) specification morphisms and m is a ADT (resp. Class, Aspect) module morphism. If MOD_1 is an aspect module specification and MOD_2 is a class module specification, then m_p, m_e, m_i, m_b are aspect-class specification morphisms and m is an Aspect-Class module morphism.

3.4.3 Category of Module Specifications

One of our main motivations for using category theory is that it allows for composing two or more modules to result in a larger module. In "Categorical Manifesto" Goguen (1991), Goguen asserts several "dogmas", each of which suggests a use for a particular categorical construction. The dogma for the section on "Colimits" says:

Given a species of structure, say widgets, then the result of interconnecting a system of widgets to form a super-widget corresponds to taking the colimit of the diagram of widgets in which the morphisms show how they are interconnected.

Roughly speaking, what this means is that category theory prescribes a way in which one can depict each widget as a dot, and the relations that describe how they interconnect as arrows. The resulting diagram has a precise interpretation, and by applying the categorical operation called "colimit" to it, one can derive a description of the "super-widget" thus formed. Many computer scientists have used this idea to give a precise semantics to specification languages: to describe exactly how combining specifications of parts of a system results in a specification of the entire system Paine (2007). To be able to perform such operations on a category, we have to show that this category is finitely co-complete.

Theorem 3.1: *Let* $\mathbf{CAT}_{Mod}$ *be the set of all ADT, Class and Aspect module specifications and their different morphisms of a system.* $\mathbf{CAT}_{Mod}$ *is a finitely co-complete category.*

The proof of this theorem can be found in Sabas (2012). A consequence of this theorem is that we can calculate the co-limit of any finite diagram of the system.

At the semantics level, we chose to use a loose semantics because it is natural and simple. This semantics uses algebras and the logic L_A (defined in chapter 3.1). A semantics of a module specification is defined as a set of deontic models that validate the axioms of this module specification. These deontic models differ from more conventional ones, for example one in Ehrig & Mahr (1990, 1985) where semantics is defined by an interface semantics (constituted of categories of parameter, import, and export with two functors), a construction semantics (defined by a free functor from the category of import models to the category of body models), and a behavior semantics represented by a functor between the categories of import and export models. We think that this semantics is too complex. Our model has advantages that allow us to formalize information like error recovery through corrective action or sanctions if desired. Moreover, it integrates our prevention mechanism which will allow avoiding undesirable behaviors in aspect-oriented systems. In this structure, we can distinguish between description and prescription of behavior. We are not able to give all the machineries of this semantics, due to the space limitation. Details of this semantics can be found in Sabas (2012).

4 MODULE INTERCONNECTION

Module interconnections define the way modules interact with each other or how they are tied together. Module interconnections form the architectural structure of a modular system which can be viewed as a larger module itself. Interconnections of algebraic module specifications are explicitly declared by specification morphisms which express how resources in the interfaces and the parameter part are matched Ehrig & Mahr (1990). Four types of interconnection have been defined and used in Ehrig & Mahr (1990); Wiels (1997): client/server relationship, share relationship, actualization relationship, and extension. For each of the four relationships, construction operators have been defined to realize the interconnection associated. Construction operators allow us to compose two modules to obtain a new one. In aspect-oriented system development, we need a fifth relationship, weaving, that links an aspect module to a (base) class module.

We develop an algorithm that takes an aspect module and a class module as inputs, and outputs an augmented module. Our algorithm represents the operator of the weaving relation and it is based on the notion of co-limits and the union operator. Figure 2 shows the union of the modules MOD_1 and MOD_2. MOD_0 denotes the shared submodule of MOD_1 and MOD_2. Arrows represent the mod-

Figure 2. Union Operator

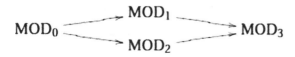

ule specification morphisms. Union of module specifications is defined componentwise by the notion of pushout, which is a co-limit. MOD_3 denotes the output of the union of the modules MOD_1 and MOD_2 with shared submodule MOD_0. MOD_3 is written $MOD_3 = MOD_1 + MOD_0 MOD_2$.

4.1 Ordered Module Specification

The weaving introduces an order through the advice concept.

Definition 4.1: *Let $\langle X, \leq_o \rangle$ be a partial order set. If $x \leq_o y$ and $x /= y$, then we write $x <_o y$ and we say that x is a predecessor of y. $x \leq_o y$ means that $x <_o y$ or $x = y$. If $x \leq_o y$ and if $y \leq_o z$, we say that y is between x and z. If $x <_o y$ and if $y <_o z$, we say that y is strictly between x and z. If $x <_o y$ and if there is no element strictly between x and y, we say that x is an immediate predecessor of y, or y is the immediate successor of x and we write $x <_o^i y$.*

Definition 4.2: *Ordered signature. Let Σ be an algebraic signature. Σ is an ordered signature iff there is an order $\leq_o$ defined over Σ such as in the above definition 4.1.*

Definition 4.3: *Ordered specification. An algebraic specification SPEC is ordered iff its signature is an ordered signature with an order $\leq_o$, and the set of axioms is ordered by $\leq_o$.*

Definition 4.4: *Ordered module specification. A module specification is ordered iff its four algebraic specifications are ordered.*

4.2 Weaving Algorithm

Weaving is the predominant notion of model combination in Aspect Oriented Software Development (AOSD) Filman et al. (2005). Weaving uses a binary strategy because a weaver weaves an aspect into the base component at a time. Binary strategies allow merging two models at a time. To merge more than two models, the result of merging two models is considered as a new model and then merged with another model. The weaving process is a kind of the model merging. In our formalism, models are aspect-class module specifications and aspect-class relationships are structure-preserving mappings, i.e. aspect-class morphisms. The mappings express ways in which the structure of one module maps onto that of another. Model merging has some requirement criteria which are Sabetzadeh (2008):

- **Non-redundancy**: Only one copy of the common parts is included in the merged model.
- **Completeness**: Merge should not lose information, i.e., it should represent all the source models completely.
- **Minimality**: Merge should not introduce information that is not present in or implied by the source models.
- **Semantic Preservation**: Merge should support the expression and preservation of semantic properties.

For example, if models are expressed as state machines, one may want to preserve their temporal behaviors to ensure that the merge properly captures the intended meaning of the source models.

The weaving operator we describe in this section is based on category concepts and union operator, which use the notion of colimit. The colimit of an interconnection diagram is a new object, called the colimiting object, together with a family of mappings, one from each object in the diagram onto the colimiting object. Since each mapping expresses how the internal structure of its source object is mapped onto that of its destination object, the colimit expresses the merge of all the objects in the interconnection diagram. Furthermore, the colimit respects the mappings in the diagram: The intuition here is that the image of each object in the colimit is the same, no matter which path through the mappings in the diagram is followed. By definition, the colimit is also minimal; it merges the objects in the diagram without adding anything essentially new. Hence, the use of the notion of colimit is an advantage of our weaving formalism because the merging requirements quoted above, which are present in the notion of colimit, are also required in the weaving process in AOSD.

Suppose we want to weave a class component and an aspect component. Let the class component be represented by the module specification $MOD_c = \langle PAR_c, EXP_c, IMP_c, BOD_c \rangle$ and the aspect component by $MOD_a = \langle PAR_a, EXP_a, IMP_a, BOD_a \rangle$. We first define a connector module specification which contains the common part of the aspect and the class module specifications. Then, we specify through morphisms how this connector is embedded in the source modules. Afterwards, we apply the weaving algorithm to compute the augmented module. Let $MOD_s = \langle PAR_s, EXP_s, IMP_s, BOD_s \rangle$ be the connector (shared) module specification, $f: MOD_s \rightarrow MOD_a$ and $g: MOD_s \rightarrow MOD_c$ the morphisms between the connector module and the aspect and class modules respectively. Denoting the weaving operator as w, we write $MOD_w = MOD_a \, w \, MOD_c$ and we read MOD_w is the woven module of MOD_a and MOD_c. Let $MOD_w = (PAR_w, EXP_w, IMP_w, BOD_w)$ be the augmented module specification. We note an advice of an aspect as $Ad = \langle mod, TJ, \alpha \rangle$ where:

- mod is the modifier of the advice Ad . mod belongs to the set MODIFIER = {before, after, around, insteadOf}
- *TJ* is a multiset of the joinpoints containing in the pointcut of the advice *Ad* ;

- α is an action representing the body of the advice;

Ad.mod gives the modifier mod of the advice, Ad.TJ gives TJ, and Ad.α gives α. We denote the set of all advices of an aspect by TAD. For an aspect A, A.TAD gives this set TAD. The weaving algorithm starts by computing the union (using union operator) of the module specifications MOD_a and MOD_c (line 2). If the aspect does not contain any advice, MOD_a is empty and the augmented module MOD_w is equal to MOD_u (line 4). For each advice in the aspect module, we consider the four kinds of the advice. For example, if the advice type is *before*, for each joinpoint *jp* related to this advice, if *jp* is selected (line 9) and the apparition of *jp* is before the apparition of the advice body in M_u, we permute this joinpoint and this advice body (line 10) s.t. the advice body is the immediate predecessor of the joinpoint. The algorithm does the same thing for the *after* and around advices. For around advice, α_1 is the action inserted before *jp* and α_2 the action after *jp*. For the *insteadOf* advice, we replace all occurrences of the selected joinpoints by the advice body (line 26). At line 29, we remove all pointcut and advice elements (e.g., pointcut names, advice names) except selected joinpoints and advice bodies. At line 30, we replace the selected joinpoints by their associated actions by using the function *fj*: $J \rightarrow A$ that associates to a joinpoint *jp*, the action *fj(jp)* encapsulated in the body of *jp* ; *J* is a set of joinponts and *A* a set of actions.

Let *T* be a multiset containing all (matching) joinpoints between an aspect module and a class module. $M^t = replaceAll(M, T, \alpha)$ is the replacement in the module *M of* all occurrences of each element of *T* by the action α .

Our algorithm works because union operation works. Many research proposals have explored different mechanisms for specifying and weaving aspects into UML design models (for instance one in Nouh et al. (2010)), while others have used UML models and graph transformation. The advantage of our weaving approach over these approaches is the use of colimit concepts with the above properties, which allow a formal modular reasoning.

4.3 The Definition of the Connector Module

If we want to merge two modules, A and B, that overlap in some way, we can express the overlap as a third module, C, with mappings C to each of A and B (three-way merging technique). C is called the *connector module*. Our weaving operator is also based on this three-way merging technique. A connector module specification $MOD_s = \langle PAR_s, EXP_s, IMP_s, BOD_s \rangle$ does not provide any service; it is just a link between an aspect module $MOD_a = \langle PAR_a, EXP_a, IMP_a, BOD_a \rangle$ and a class module $MOD_c = \langle PAR_c, EXP_c, IMP_c, BOD_c \rangle$. MOD_s is a shared submodule of MOD_a and MOD_c. We define BOD_s as a part containing only auxiliary elements. These auxiliary elements are joinpoint bodies contained in MOD_a, which are included in MOD_c.

$$PAR_s = PAR_a \cap PAR_c \; EXP_s = EXP_a \cap EXP_c \; IMP_s = IMP_a \cap IMP_c$$

$$BOD_s = (BOD_a \cap BOD_c \cap \{ jp \in Ad.TJ, \forall Ad \in MOD_a.TAD\}) \cup \{shared\ sorts\}.$$ The four specification morphisms are inclusion morphisms.

The two module specification morphisms $f: MOD_s \to MOD_a$ and $g: MOD_s \to MOD_c$ are inclusion morphisms, i.e., $f(x) = x$ and $g(x) = x$. For clarity purpose, we add a field **Joinpoints** to the pattern of an aspect specification. This field will contain all joinpoints of the aspect component.

4.4 Example

We give an example to illustrate, without great details, the weaving algorithm. This example is taken from Nagy et al. (2004). The example consists of a simple personnel management system.

The *Employee* class, shown in Figure 3, forms an important part of the system. The method of this class *increaseSalary()* uses its argument to compute a new salary.

This example has been constructed as a scenario that introduces new requirements at each step. Applying the principle of separation of concerns, each of these requirements is represented by aspects that will be woven on the same JoinPoint (as well as others), after the execution of the method *increaseSalary()* of the *Employee* class.

As a first step, the company introduces a logging system to monitor the change of salaries. This fea-ture is represented by the *MonitorSalary* aspect. This aspect prints a notification whenever a salary has been changed. This could include information about the employee and the type of salary change. For the sake of simplicity, we only give this first step and present the body part of the module specification of the components Employee, MonitorSalary.

The axiom in the Figure 4 means that after performing increaseSalary action, the output should be greater than the input.

The advise axiom of the Figure 5 means that each time the JoinPoint call(em.increaseSalary(int)) is se-lected by the pointcut salaryChange(em.salary), immediately after this JoinPoint, the action mo.print should be performed.

Let $MOD_s = \langle PAR_s, EXP_s, IMP_s, BOD_s \rangle$ be the connector module of the MonitorSalary module and Employee module. Figure 6 shows the body part of the connector module. By applying the algorithm 1, we first compute M_u and then MOD_w. The body part of the module MOD_w is giving by the Figure 7.

5 ASPECT PREVENTION MECHANISM

The interaction between aspects and classes may introduce a variety of bug hazards into the system. Detection and resolution of undesirable aspect

Algorithm 1.Weaving Algorithm

```
1: Begin weaving
2:    M_u ← MOD_a +(MOD_s, f, g) MOD_c
3: if MOD_a .TAD = 0 then
4:       MOD_w ← M_u
5: end if
6: for all Ad in MOD_a .TAD do
7:      if Ad.mod = before then
8:           for all jp in Ad.TJ do
9:                if jp ∈ MOD_s then
10:                    permut jp and Ad.α s.t. Ad.α <_o fj(jp)
11:               end if
12:          end for
13:     else if Ad.mod = after then
14:          for all jp in Ad.TJ do
15:               if jp ∈ MOD_s then
16:                    permut jp and Ad.α s.t. fj(jp)<_o^i  Ad.α
17:               end if
18:          end for
19:     else if Ad.mod = around then
20:           for all jp in Ad.TJ do
21:                if jp ∈ MOD_s then
22:                    permut jp and Ad.α = α_1 α_2 s.t. α_1 <_o fj(jp) <_o α_2
23:               end if
24:           end for
25:     else
26:          M_u ← replaceAll(M_u, Ad.TJ, Ad.α)
27:     end if
28: end for
29: remove from M_u, pointcut and advice elements, except selected joinpoints
    and advice bodies related to base module.
30: replace in M_u selected joinpoints jp by their associated actions fj(jp) .
31: MOD_w  ← M_u
32: End weaving
```

Algorithm 2. Function replaceAll

```
1: Begin replaceAll(M, T, α) { M = ⟨PAR, EXP, IMP, BOD⟩ }
2: for all e in T do
3:      if e is in PAR ∪ EXP ∪ IMP ∪ BOD then
4:          replace e by α in M
5:      end if
6: end for
7: End replaceAll
```

Figure 3. The Employee class and its superimposed aspects

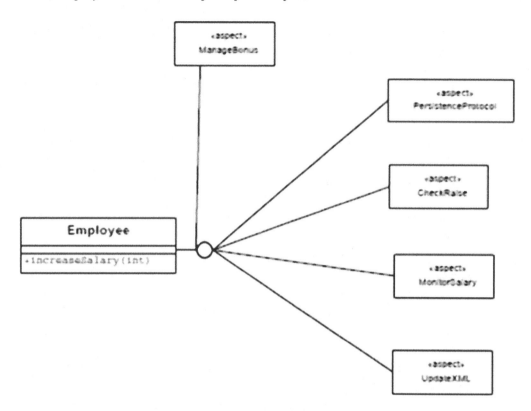

interactions is an important open research field. Most aspect-oriented verification approaches are based on a detection and correction strategy. Although these detection approaches are relevant for aspect-oriented software reliability, we believe that they are time-consuming and costly.

The best strategy for handling conflicts is to prevent conflicts from happening. We can convince ourselves by making an analogy to the medicine, where experts and governments prefer to place more emphasis on measures to prevent disease. The same analogy could be observed in avionics where MRO (maintenance, repair, and overhaul) activities put more emphasis on preventive actions than corrective actions for flight quality and reliable aircraft. The spirit of our work is similar to one of Intrusion Prevention Systems.

An aspect fault model developed in Alexander et al. (2004) lists the main fault types that can arise in aspect-oriented applications due to the

aspect integration into the base systems. Existing verification approaches can detect only one or two of these fault types. To the best of our knowledge, there are no existing methods or tools capable of taking all of them into account. An aspect verification approach survey Katz (2005) also points this out. There is a lack of efficient mechanisms for dealing with aspect interactions, and which can take most of these aspect fault types into account. The logic L_A helps us to specify system components with a prevention mechanism. This prevention mechanism will prevent most of the undesirable aspect interactions characterized by the fault classes developed in Alexander et al. (2004). In this section, we deal with three of these aspect fault types

Figure 4. Specification of Class Employee (body part)

```
SPEC-CLASS   Employee
  Sorts :  employee, int, string
  States :
     name :  string  →  string
     id :  int  →  int
     department :  string  →  string
     salary :  int  →  int
  Actions :
     increaseSalary :  int  →  int
  Axioms :  x :  int
     ∀x,  [increaseSalary(x)](increaseSalary(x) > x)
End  Employee
```

Figure 5. Specification of Aspect MonitorSalary (body part)

```
SPEC–ASPECT   MonitorSalary
  Sorts :  monitorSalary, int, employee, string, bool
  Joinpoints :  em : employee
       call(em.increseSalary(int))
  Pointcuts
  salaryChange : int  →  bool
  Actions :
  print : string  →  string
  Pointcut Axioms :     x : int, em : employee
  ∀x, em,
  salaryChange(x) : pr(call(em.increaseSalary(int)))
  Advice Axioms :  x : int, s : string, mo : monitoSalary
  ∀ s, x, em, mo
  (A_f pr(salaryChange(x))) mo.print)
End  MonitorSalary
```

Figure 6. Specification of the Connector Module (Body part)

```
SPEC–CLASS  BOD_S
   Sorts :  int , employee
   Joinpoints :  em : employe ,
       call(em.increseSalary(int))
End  BOD_S
```

5.1 Incorrect Strength in Pointcut Patterns

According to Lemos et al. (2006), a pointcut can

Figure 7. Module specification MOD_w (Body Part)

```
SPEC–ASPECT   BOD_w
  Sorts :  employee, int, monitorSalary, string, bool
  States :
     name : string  →  string
     id : int  →  int
     department : string  →  string
     salary : int  →  int
  Actions :
     increaseSalary : int  →  int
     print : string  →  string
  Axioms :  x :  int
     ∀x, [increaseSalary(x)](increaseSalary(x) > x)
End  BOD_w
```

be wrong in the following ways; it can:

1. select a set of joinpoints which has some intersection with the adequate set but also selects other joinpoints (i.e., selects some of the intended joinpoints but also some unintended points);
2. select a different set, with no intersection with the adequate set of joinpoints (i.e., selects none of the intended joinpoints);
3. select a bigger set than the adequate set of joinpoints (i.e., selects all the intended joinpoints and also unintended ones);
4. select a smaller set than the adequate set of joinpoints (i.e., selects some of the intended joinpoints, but not all).

5.2 Failure to Establish Expected Post-Conditions

Aspects can cause changes in the flow of control of a class's code (a class of the base program). Such a change in flow of control can result in a class (core concern) not being able to fulfill the post-conditions of its class contract. The clients of core concerns expect those concerns to behave according to their contracts. A client has the responsibility to ensure that a method precondition holds prior to calling the method. Given that the precondition is ensured, the client can reasonably assume that the method's postcondition will be satisfied. Clients expect method post-conditions to be satisfied regardless of whether or not aspects are woven into the concern. Hence the behavioral contracts of the concern should hold after the weaving process. Thus, for correct behavior, woven advice must allow methods in core concerns to satisfy their post-conditions. Defining advice that does not cause behavioral contracts to be broken in all likely weave contexts, and with all likely combinations of aspects will be a difficult challenge for aspect developers, and a likely source of errors.

5.3 Failure to Preserve State Invariants

A concern's behavior is defined in terms of a physical representation of its state, and methods that act on that state. The integration of an aspect into the base program can introduce new methods and instance variables into the core concerns (classes). Thus, this integration can introduce new states and can cause the classes to violate their state invariants. In addition to establishing their post-conditions, methods must also ensure that state invariants are satisfied. Ensuring that weaving does not cause violations of state invariants is another difficult challenge for aspect developers, and another source of errors.

We defined a model for the prevention policy of each of these fault types. The collection of these models represents our prevention mechanism for a given aspect application. To define a model for the prevention policy of a fault type, we can follow these three steps:

1. Define the requirements or constraints for a given application.
2. Formalize each constraint by using the logic L_A.
3. Define a coordination aspect module which will contain mainly these formalized constraints under the field Prescription Axioms.

This coordination aspect module is unique for a given aspect application and records information about all aspect modules which are present in the application and also the classes. It can contain other elements such as mechanisms that add and remove dynamically an aspect to and from the application, respectively. The set of its advices contains at least the action T?, an action which changes nothing. This coordination aspect module is responsible for the management of the aspect scheduling or ordering at the shared JoinPoints. This module concept reinforces the separation of concerns principle of aspect technology and therefore improves the modularity principle.

5.4 Model of "Incorrect Strength in Pointcut Patterns"

We assume that the specifier has correctly determined the joinpoints with regard to each advice and the related base component. For a pointcut $PC = \{jp_i, i \in \{1, 2, ..., n\}\}$ related to a base component BP and advice α of an aspect A, we can state the following lines:

1. if $jp \notin PC$ (i.e., if the joinpoint jp is not in the pointcut) or $\neg pr(jp)$ (i.e., if jp has not been selected), it is forbidden to perform action α at jp. This sentence avoids the cases of superset or overset selection of joinpoints.
2. The formulae $O(pr(jp))$? for all $jp \in PC$ (which means jp has to be selected if $jp \in PC$) avoid the cases of subset or underset selection of joinpoints.

In the following, we use the abbreviations:

* $(B, pr(jp))\alpha$ for $G(\neg pr(jp) \rightarrow I (\alpha; ff(jp))/T$?) Before advice case.
* $(A, pr(jp))\alpha$ for $G(\neg pr(jp) \rightarrow I (ff(jp); \alpha)/T$?) After advice case.

- $(I_I\ pr(jp))\alpha$ for $G(\neg pr(jp) \rightarrow I\ ((I\ fj(jp));$ $\alpha)/T$?) Instead Of advice case.

The formulae $(B_I\ pr(jp))\alpha$, $(A_I\ pr(jp))\alpha$, and $(I_I\ pr(jp))\alpha$ pertain to the above point 1. In other words, $(B_I\ pr(jp))\alpha$ means that in any state, if jp is not selected then, it is forbidden to perform action α followed by the action encapsulated in the body of the joinpoint jp. $(A_I\ pr(jp))\alpha$ means that in any state, if jp is not selected then, it is forbidden to perform the action encapsulated in the body of the joinpoint jp followed by the action α. $(I_I\ pr(jp))\alpha$ means that in any state, if jp is not selected then, it is forbidden to replace the action encapsulated in the body of the joinpoint jp by the action α.

Thus, the prevention policy of the *Incorrect Strength in Pointcut Patterns* fault type will be the following set of formulae in the coordination aspect module under the Prescription Axioms field:

$(U_{i \in K1}\ \{(B_I\ pr(jp_i))\alpha \cup O(pr(jp_i))?\})$

$\cup\ (U_{i \in K2}\ \{(A_I\ pr(jp_i))\alpha \cup O(pr(jp_i))?\})$

$\cup\ (U_{i \in K3}\ \{(I_I\ pr(jp_i))\alpha \cup O(pr(jp_i))?\})$

$\cup\ (U_{i \in K4}\ \{((B_I\ pr(jp_i))\alpha_1 \wedge (A_I\ pr(jp_i))\alpha_2) \cup O(pr(jp_i))?\})$

K_i is the set of the joinpoints related to each advice case. Note that K_i may be empty for some i. The meaning of each formula of this set is defined in the above lines.

5.5 Model of "Failure to Establish Expected Post-Conditions"

Method preconditions are assertions that must hold when the execution of the method starts. Method post-conditions are assertions that must hold immediately after the execution of the method ends. To prevent the occurrence of this fault type in an aspect oriented system, we have to analyze the effect of the execution of the advice on the context of the client class, i.e., the effect of the advice body at each selected joinpoint of the client class.

Representation of an Action: We can represent an action (a program) α as Hoare clauses, i.e., $\{\phi\}\alpha\{\psi\}$, where $\phi = Pre(\alpha)$ is the precondition of α and $\psi = Post(\alpha)$ its postcondition. If α does not have any precondition, then α can be written $\{T\}\alpha\{\psi\}$ where T is the boolean true value. In our logic L_A, $\{\phi\}\alpha\{\psi\}$ can be represented by $\phi \rightarrow ([\alpha]O(\psi?))/T?$.

Representation of a Joinpoint: A joinpoint jp can be represented by $\{\phi\}fj(jp)\{\psi\}$ where $fj(jp)$ is the action encapsulated in jp, ϕ is the precondition of this action, and ψ its postcondition. Thus, in L_A, jp can be represented by $\phi \rightarrow ([fj(jp)]O(\psi?))/T?$.

Prevention Mechanism: In our analysis, we distinguish four cases: one case for each advice type (Before, After, Around, InsteadOf). We notice that the reasoning is the same for all these four cases. In this chapter, we show this analysis with Before advice. A Before advice is written in the logic L_A as $(B_e\ pr(np))\beta$ where np is a pointcut expression, and β is the body of the advice. Assume that $np = jp_1 \| jp_2$ (we can do the same thing if np contains an arbitrary number n of joinpoints). Let jp_i be represented by $\phi_i \rightarrow ([fj(jp_i)]O(\psi_i?))/T?$, $i \in \{1, 2\}$. We know that $(B_e\ pr(np))\beta \equiv (B_e\ pr(jp_1))\beta \vee (B_e\ pr(jp_2))\beta$ and $(B_e\ pr(jp_i))\beta \equiv G(pr(jp_i) \rightarrow O(\beta; fj(jp_i);\ T\ ?)/T\ ?)$. The prevention policy of the *Failure to establish expected post-conditions* fault type will be the set of these following formulae in the coordination aspect module under the Prescription Axioms field: $\phi_i \rightarrow ([fj(jp_i)]O(\psi_i?))/T?$ for all joinpoints jp_i in a aspect oriented system. This formula means that after each time the action $fj(jp_i)$ is performed, the postcondition ψ_i must be satisfied. If $np = jp_1\ \&\&\ jp_2$, the reasoning is the same as in the case where $np = jp_1 \| jp_2$.

5.6 Model of "Failure to Preserve State Invariants"

Generally speaking, the aspects of crosscutting concerns alter the control flows defined in the core concern. From the perspective of state models of system behavior, they not only modify the state-transition relations but also possibly introduce extra states in the state models of objects defined by their classes. This can affect or even change the behavior of objects specified by the base programs Xu et al. (2005). State invariants are formulas that are trues in all states of an correct execution. The prevention policy for this fault type is a set of the following formulae in the coordination aspect module under the Prescription Axioms field: $GO(p?)$ for all state invariants p in a aspect oriented system. G is the always modality of our logic and O the obligation modality. $GO(p?)$ means that the invariant p must hold in all states.

5.7 Examples

We will use two examples to illustrate our prevention mechanism. The first one is for *Incorrect Strength in Pointcut Patterns* fault type and the second one is for other fault types in this chapter. The first example shows that our approach can be applied to a real application; while the second one (even though it is a simple example) is adequate for these fault types.

The first example is taken from Xu & Wong (2008). This example consists of a greeting card purchase subsystem of an online shopping application. The subsystem consists of 12 classes, 3 aspects and 398 lines of code. The application supports flexible business rules for a variety of greeting cards. The price of a card in a purchase depends on the card type and the quantity of the cards. The cards are categorized as holiday cards, birthday cards, valentine cards, etc. Different types of cards have different unit price, minimum quantity of cards for discount, and discounted unit price. Discounted unit price is available only

when the quantity is greater than the required minimum. There are numerous base classes (core functional concerns) in this example: *Card, Price, HolidayCardPrice, BirthdayCardPrice, ValentineCardPrice, Purchase, Transaction*; but we consider only two classes Card and Purchase to illustrate the prevention model of *Incorrect Strength in Pointcut Patterns* fault type. A card has information such as code and price. A purchase includes a particular type of card and the quantity of the cards. The aspect we consider here is *AccessControl* aspect. This aspect is responsible for distinguishing legal and illegal access to sensitive data, such as price information. A password-based access control has been used for security check. Figure 8 shows a class/aspect diagram with the two classes: *Purchase* and *Card*. Each class has a JoinPoint collected by pointcut expression *priceMonitor* in aspect *AccessControl*, which facilitates communication between Purchase and Card objects. The *priceMonitor* pointcut is associated with an InsteadOf advice which checks if the caller is authorized. If so, the caller may proceed to invoke getPrice; otherwise the access is denied. Thus, advice action $= \alpha \vee \beta$, where $\alpha =$ [authorize?] getPrice $\beta = [(\neg$authorize$)?]$denyAccess

α is the action that executes getPrice each time the caller is authorized. denyAccess is the action that denies access to the caller. β is the action that denies access to the caller each time he is not authorized. The prevention policy related to this fault type for this subsystem depicted in the Figure 8 consists of the following prescription axiom defined in a coordination aspect module:

$(I_1 pr($withincode(* Purchase.getCharge()) &&

call(* Card.getPrice()))))$\alpha \vee \beta$

since,

$(I_o pr($withincode(* Purchase.getCharge()) &&

call(* Card.getPrice()))))$\alpha \vee \beta$

Figure 8. The class/aspect diagram for card purchasing

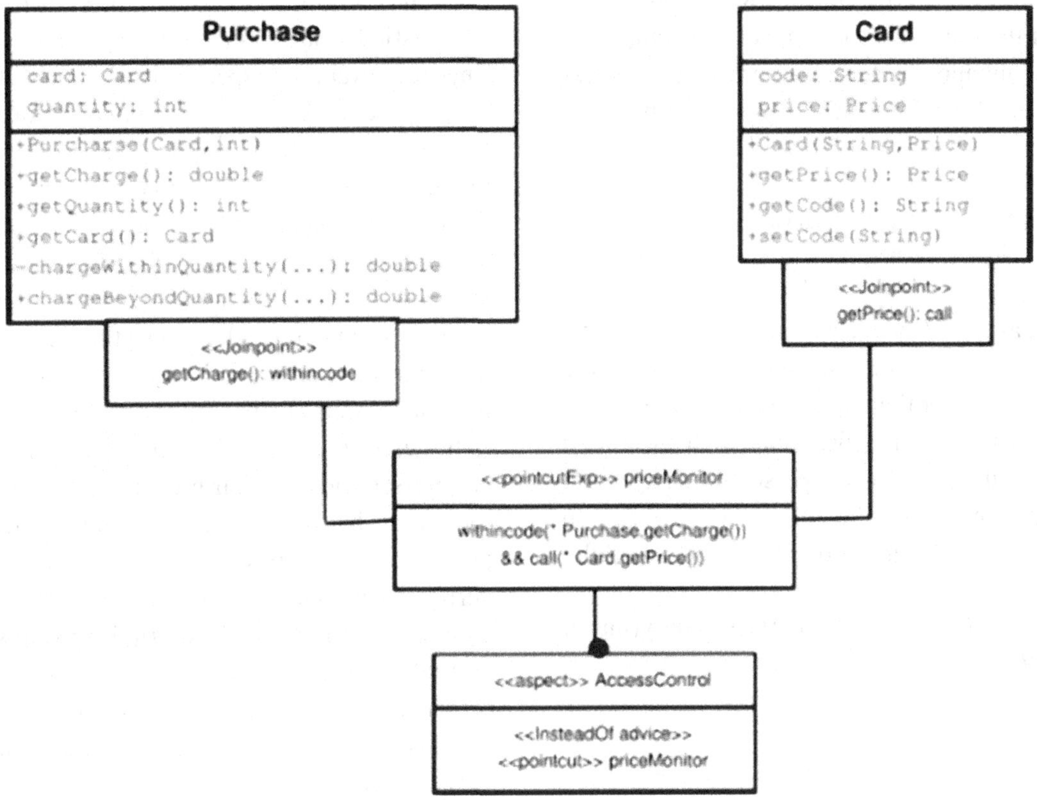

will be defined in aspect *AccessControl*. The first formula says that in any state, if the joinpoint *within- code(*Purchase.getCharge())* && call(* Card.getPrice()) is not selected then, it is forbidden to replace action encapsulated in the body of this joinpoint by the action $\alpha \vee \beta$. The second formula is an instead advice axiom. It means that in each state s where the joinpoint *withincode(* Purchase.getCharge())* && call(* Card.getPrice()) is selected, the action $\alpha \vee \beta$ is obliged to be executed instead of the action (encapsulated in the body of this joinpoint) that should be executed in s.

We use the example shown in Figure 3 (see section 4.4) to describe how to define the prevention policy for *Failure to Establish Expected Post-Conditions* and *Failure to Preserve State Invariants* fault types in aspect-oriented systems.

The precondition ϕ and postcondition ψ of the method *increaseSalary()* are

ϕ: the employee has worked one more year

$-$ *newSalary = oldSalary + ΔSalary*

ψ: $-$ the employee is happy

We are interested in the aspect *ManageBonus*. This aspect manages attributions of the bonus and penalties to the employees. If the performance of an employee is higher than a threshold value t_1, *ManageBonus* adds a + bonus to the salary of this employee. But, if the employee performance is less than a threshold valuer t_2, *ManageBonus* adds a -bonus to the salary of this employee. The only advice method of the aspect *ManageBonus* which is applied before the joinpoint *execution(Employee.*

increaseSalary(int)), is *addBonus(int b)*. The aspect *ManageBonus* may break down the postcondition of the joinpoint body in a case an employee will be unhappy because his performance is less than the threshold valuer t_2. Besides, Employee class has a state invariant p

p: an employee's salary cannot be higher than his/her manager's salary

The aspect *ManageBonus* may break down this invariant in a case the new salary of the employee becomes greater than his manager's salary.

The prevention policy related to these two aspect fault types for this personal management system consists of the following prescription axioms defined in a coordination aspect module:

$\phi \rightarrow$ ([fj (execution(em.increaseSalary(int)))] $O(\psi?))/T?$

and

$GO(p?)$

em is an instance of Employee class. The first formula says that after each execution of the method *increaseSalary(int)*, the postcondition ψ must be satisfied. The second formula says that the invariant p must always be satisfied.

Concerning the verification, proving that the specified object (module) has a certain property consists of proving that the property is a logical consequence of the axioms of the specification. The aim of a modular verification is to provide the possibility of reusing properties of components when the specifications of the components are themselves reused when building larger systems. The strategy is to prove locally a property at the level of the specification of a component and use it as lemma when reasoning about global properties of a system.

In this case, it is even a very simple importation because the property is an axiom. Indeed, suppose that we want, for instance, to verify that at any time, the constraints (3) and (4) described above are satisfied in our personnel management system. These constraints are specified in the coordination aspect, under the field Prescription Axioms. To guaranty that these formulae (3) and (4) are not violated in the system, it suffices to weave at first (before weaving any other aspect) the coordination aspect into the base module Employee. By weaving the coordination aspect into the base module Employee, all prescription axioms of this coordination Aspect become theorems of the modular system, by the weaving operator which is basically based on the colimit concept. The colimit satisfies the four properties described in section 1. Thus (by using the modular verification principle described in section 1), if we want to verify an invariant p is satisfied, we just need to check that the associated prescription axioms, i.e., GO(p?) is a theorem in the modular system. The presence of these prescription axioms provides means to regulate the societal life of aspects and classes 'actions in the modular system environment. It is interesting to exploit the structure of specifications to verify properties in a modular way and it is easier to prove a property on a smaller specification that on a larger one.

6 CONCLUSION AND FUTURE WORK

In this chapter, we have presented an algebraic specification approach which proposed a solution to the lack of modular formal reasoning, specification, and verification of (AO) systems. This approach is based on CT and AS due to their formality, their modularity benefits, and their high level of abstraction. Our weaving operation uses the concepts of colimit which allows a modular formal reasoning. A modular formal reasoning would significantly help in alleviating the complexity of software models and application code, as well as reducing development costs and maintenance time.

We also present a prevention mechanism for three aspect fault types that can cause undesirable behaviors in an aspect-oriented system. Most of the aspect-oriented verification approaches are based on a detection and correction strategy, contrary to our approach which is based firstly on a prevention strategy and then on a correction strategy if it is necessary.

We validated our approach by means of an industrial case study. This case study entitled "NextGen MRO Instructions Application" has been proposed by Pratt & Whitney Canada Pratt (2013). This case study shows that our approach can be applied to a real life application. It is a large project and its development cannot be presented in this chapter. Details of this can be found in Sabas (2012).

For future work, we plan to extend to aspect concepts the tool MOKA developed by the team of Wiels (1997); Michel & Wiels (1997) to do some verification tasks.

ACKNOWLEDGMENT

This research work is supported by FQRNT (Fonds Québécois de la Recherche sur la Nature et les Technologies). We thank Michael Barr for his useful comments on this work.

REFERENCES

Alexander, R., Bieman, J., & Andrews, A. (2004). *Towards the systematic testing of aspect oriented pro- grams*. Tech. Rep. CS-4-105, Colorado State University.

Baniassad, E., & Clarke, S. (2004). Theme: An approach for aspect-oriented analysis and design. In *Proc. of 26th International Conference on Software Engineering (ICSE'04)*. Edinburgh, UK: ICSE.

Barr, M., & Wells, C. (1999). *Category Theory for Computing Science*. Les Publications CRM.

Berg, K., Conejero, J. M., & Chitchyan, R. (2005). *AOSD ontology 1.0: Public ontology of aspect orientation*. Tech. Rep. AOSD-Europe-UT-01, Report of the EU Network of Excellence on AOSD.

Cottenier, T., Berg, A., & Elrad, T. (2007). The motorola WEAVR: Model weaving in a large industrial context. In *Proc. of the 6th Int. Conf. on Aspect-Oriented Software Development (AOSD'07)*. Vancouver, Canada: AOSD.

Cui, Z., Wang, L., Liu, X., Bu, L., Zhao, J., & Li, X. (2013). Verifying aspect-oriented activity diagrams against crosscutting properties. *International Journal of Software Engineering and Knowledge Engineering*, *23*(5). doi:10.1142/S0218194013400123

Ehrig, H., & Mahr, B. (1985). *Fundamentals of Algebraic Specification 1: Equations and Initial Semantics*. Springer-Verlag. doi:10.1007/978-3-642-69962-7

Ehrig, H., & Mahr, B. (1990). *Fundamentals of algebraic specification 2: module specifications and constraints*. Springer-Verlag. doi:10.1007/978-3-642-61284-8

Ehrig, H., Mahr, B., & Orejas, F. (1992). Introduction to algebraic specification: Part 1: Formal methods for software development. *The Computer Journal*, *35*, 468–477. doi:10.1093/comjnl/35.5.468

Fiadeiro, J. L. (2005). *Categories for Software Engineering*. Springer.

Filman, R. E., Elrad, T., Clarke, S., & Aksit, M. (2005). *Aspect-Oriented Software Development*. Boston: Addison-Wesley.

Fox, J. (2005). A formal foundation for aspect oriented software development. In *Proceedings of Memoria del XIV Con- greso Internacional de Computacion CIC*. IPN.

France, R., Ray, I., Georg, G., & Ghosh, S. (2004). Aspect-oriented approach to early design modelling. In *Proc. of the 6th Int. Conf. on Aspect Oriented Software Development (AOSD'07)*. Vancouver, Canada: IEE Proceedings Software.

Goguen, J. A. (1991). A categorical manifesto. In *Mathematical Structures in Computer Science* (pp. 49–67). Academic Press.

Goguen, J. A. (1992). Order-sorted algebra 1: Equational deduction for multiple inheritance, overloading, exceptions and partial operations. *Theoretical Computer Science, 105*, 217–273. doi:10.1016/0304-3975(92)90302-V

Goldman, M., & Katz, S. (2006). Modular generic verification of LTL properties for aspects. In *Proc. of Foundations of Aspect Languages Workshop* (FOAL06), (pp. 17–24). Bonn, Germany: FOAL.

Harel, D., Kozen, D., & Tiuryn, J. (2000). *Dynamic Logic*. The MIT Press.

Jacobson, J., & Ng, P. (2005). *Aspect-Oriented Software Development with Use Cases*. Addison-Wesley.

Katz, E., & Katz, S. (2008). Incremental analysis of interference among aspects. In *Proc. of Foundations of Aspect Languages Workshop* (FOAL08). Brussels, Belgium: FOAL.

Katz, S. (2005). *A survey of verification and static analysis for aspects*. Tech. Rep. Part of Milestone M8.1. Formal Methods Laboratory of AOSD-Europe.

Khatchadourian, R., Dovland, J., & Soundarajan, N. (2008). Enforcing behavioral constraints in evolving aspect-oriented programs. In *Proceedings of the 7th International Workshop on Foundations of Aspect-Oriented Languages* (FOAL'08). Brussels, Belgium: FOAL.

Khosla, S., & Maibaum, T. (1987). The prescription and description of state based systems. In B. Banieqbal, H. Barringer, & A. Pnueli (Eds.), *Temporal Logic in Specification, (LNCS)*, ((Vol. 398, pp. 243–294). London, UK: Springer-Verlag. doi:10.1007/3-540-51803-7_30

Kiczales, G., Lamping, J., Mendhekar, A., Maeda, C., Lopes, C. V., Loingtier, J., & Irwin, J. (1997). Aspect oriented programming. In *Proceedings of the 11th European Conference on Object-Oriented Programming ECOOP*. Jyväskylä, Finland: Springer.

Lemos, O. A. L., Ferrari, F. C., Masiero, P. C., & Lopes, C. V. (2006). Testing aspect-oriented programming pointcut descriptors. In *Proceedings of the 2nd workshop on Testing aspect-oriented programs, in conjunction with the International Symposium on Software Testing and Analysis (ISSTA'06)*. Portland, MN: ISSTA.

Manna, Z., & Pnueli, A. (1992). *The Temporal Logic of Reactive and Concurrent Systems: Specification*. Springer-Verlag. doi:10.1007/978-1-4612-0931-7

Michel, P., & Wiels, V. (1997). A framework for modular formal specification and verification. In *Proceedings of Formal Methods Europe 97*. Academic Press. doi:10.1007/3-540-63533-5_28

Mostefaoui, F. (2008). *Un cadre formel pour le développement orienté aspect: Modélisation et vérification des interactions dues aux aspects*. (Ph.D. thesis). Université de Montréal.

Nagy, I., Bergmans, L., & Aksit, M. (2004). Declarative aspect composition. In *Software-engineering Properties of Languages for Aspect Technologies, SPLAT!* Lancaster, UK: AOSD.

Nakajima, S., & Tamai, T. (2004). Lightweight formal analysis of aspect oriented models. In *Proceedings of Workshop on Aspect Oriented Modeling at UML*. UML.

Nouh, M., Ziarati, R., Mouheb, D., Alhadidi, D., Debbabi, M., Wang, L., & Pourzandi, M. (2010). Aspect weaver: A model transformation approach for uml models. In Proceedings of *the 2010 Conference of the Center for Advanced Studies on Collaborative Research (CASCON '10)*. ACM Press.

Paine, J. (2007). *Make category theory intuitive!* Retrieved from http://www.j-paine.org/make_category_theory_intuitive.html

Pawlak, R., Duchien, L., Florin, G., Legond-Aubry, F., Seinturier, L., & Martelli, L. (2002). A UML notation for aspect oriented software design. In *Proc. of the 1st Workshop on Aspect Oriented Modeling with UML* (AOSD'02). Enschede, The Netherlands: AOSD.

Pratt. (2013). *Pratt & Whitney Canada*. Retrieved from http://www.pwc.ca/

Qaisar, Z. H., Anwar, N., & Rehman, S. U. (2013). Using UML Behavioral Model to Support Aspect Oriented Model. *Journal of Software Engineering and Applications, 6*.

Sabas, A. (2012). *A Categorical Framework for the Specification and the Verification of Aspect Oriented Systems*. (Ph.D. thesis). Université de Montréal.

Sabetzadeh, M. (2008). *Merging and Consistency Checking of Distributed Models*. (Ph.D. thesis). University of Toronto.

Shaker, P., & Peters, D. K. (2005). An introduction to aspect oriented software development. In *Proc. of Newfoundland Electrical and Computer Engineering Conference*. IEEE.

Skipper, M. C. (2004). *Formal Models for Aspect-Oriented Software Development*. (Ph.D. thesis). Imperial College London.

Stein, D., Hanenberg, S., & Unland, R. (2002). A UML-based aspect oriented design notation for aspect. In *Proceedings of Aspect Oriented Software Development (AOSD 2002)*. AOSD.

Storzer, M., Krinke, J., & Breu, S. (2003). Trace analysis for aspect application. In Proceedings of Analysis of Aspect Oriented Software (AAOS). ECOOP.

Walker, D., Zdancewic, S., & Ligatti, J. (2003). A theory of aspects. In *Proceedings of the 8th ACM SIGPLAN International Conference on Functional Programming (ICFP'03)*. ACM Press.

Whittle, J., & Jayaraman, P. K. (2007). Mata: A tool for aspect-oriented modeling based on graph transfor- mation. In *Proceedings of MoDELS Workshops 2007*. Nashville, TN: MoDELS.

Wiels, V. (1997). *Modularité pour la conception et la validation formelles de systèmes*. (Ph.D. thesis). ENSAE-ONERA/CERT/DERI, Toulouse, France.

Wright, G. H. V. (1951). Deontic logic. *Mind, 60*, 1–15. doi:10.1093/mind/LX.237.1

Xu, D., Alsmadi, I., & Xu, W. (2007). Model checking aspect oriented design specification. In *Proceedings of 31st Annual International Computer Software and Applications Conference*. Beijing, China: Compsac.

Xu, D., & Wong, W. E. (2008). Testing aspect-oriented programs with UML design models. *International Journal of Software Engineering and Knowledge Engineering, 18*, 413–437. doi:10.1142/S0218194008003672

Xu, D., Xu, W., & Nygard, K. (2005). A state-based approach to testing aspect oriented programs. In *Proc. of the 17th International Conference on Software Engineering and Knowledge Engineering*, (pp. 188–197). Academic Press.

KEY TERMS AND DEFINITIONS

Aspect: A program abstraction that defines a cross-cutting concern. It includes the definition of a pointcut and the advice associated with that concern.

Deontic Logic: A formal system that attempts to capture the essential logical features of obligation, permission and related concepts.

Dynamic Logic: A modal logic for reasoning about computer programs or complex dynamic behavior.

Joinpoint: A point in the base program where a hook is placed to combine objects and aspects.

Modular Reasoning: Being able to make decisions about a module while looking only at its implementation, its interface and the interfaces of modules referenced in its implementation or interface.

Specification: A kind of description which expresses in a given language what properties a system must satisfy. The best way of expressing a specification is to use a mathematical notation, in which case we talk about a formal specification.

Verification: Software verification is a broader and more complex discipline of software engineering the goal of which is to assure that software fully satisfies all the expected requirements.

Weaving: The integration of an aspect behavior at the specified joinpoints by an aspect weaver.

Section 3
Model-Driven Development

Chapter 9
Supporting Model–Driven Development:
Key Concepts and Support Approaches

Rita Suzana Pitangueira Maciel
Federal University of Bahia, Brazil

Ana Patrícia F. Magalhães Mascarenhas
Federal University of Bahia, Brazil

Ramon Araújo Gomes
Federal University of Bahia, Brazil

João Pedro D. B. de Queiroz
Federal University of Bahia, Brazil

ABSTRACT

The adoption of Model-Driven Development (MDD) is increasing and it is widely recognized as an important approach for building software systems. In addition to traditional development process models, an MDD process requires the selection of metamodels and mapping rules for the generation of the transformation chain which produces models and application code. However, existing support tools and transformation engines for MDD do not address different kinds of software process activities, such as application modeling and testing, to guide the developers. Furthermore, they do not enable process modeling nor the (semi) automated execution of activities during process enactment. MoDErNE (Model Driven Process-Centered Software Engineering Environment) uses process-centered software engineering environment concepts to improve MDD process specification and enactment by using a metamodeling foundation. This chapter presents model driven development concept issues and the MoDErNE approach and environment. MoDErNE aims to facilitate MDD process specification and enactment.

DOI: 10.4018/978-1-4666-6026-7.ch009

INTRODUCTION

Model Driven Development (MDD) is an approach that is primarily concerned with reducing the gap between problem and solution spaces. More specifically, the application of MDD relies on software implementation domains through the use of technologies that support systematic transformation of problem-level abstraction in software implementations (France & Rumpe, 2007). System models are not only used for system documentation, but they actually serve as a basis for the implementation phase. Each activity in the development process requires a number of input models that produce further models as output. This way the development of an application can be viewed as a set of transformations that lead to the final system. MDD has changed not only the way systems are built but also the way they are tested (Mussa et al., 2009). Model Driven Testing (MDT) (Blaker et al., 2007) is an approach based on MDD in which tests can be generated from development models in an automated way through the use of transformations. One of the most well-known initiatives in this scenario is Model-Driven Architecture (MDA) proposed by the Object Management Group (OMG) (OMG, 2003). MDA relies on several OMG standards to apply MDD concepts. As MDA is an MDD realization, in this text we use only the MDD acronym for software processes that use this approach, including those which follow OMG standards.

Unlike traditional development process models (Rational Unified Process (RUP), eXtreme Programming (XP), Open/UP, etc.), an MDD process requires the selection of metamodels and mapping rules for the generation of the transformation chain which produces models and application code. In this context, if modeling and transformation tasks are not properly performed, the desired final code will not be reached. Existing research in MDD practice has revealed the importance of software processes and suitable tools, concluding that they are crucial for the use of the MDD approach in industry (Hutchinson, Rouncefield, & Whittle, 2011).

The techniques to apply Model-Driven Engineering (MDE) correctly depend on tool support and integration in the software process project (Hutchinson, Rouncefield, & Whittle, 2011; Hutchinson et al., 2011). Many tools have been designed to support MDD. These environments usually have a specific focus on a transformation strategy or transformation engine in order to automatically generate models, codes and test cases from a variety of models. However, current MDD supporting tools are basically interested in defining and executing transformations which produce code and deployment artifacts from models (e.g. AndroMDA, BluAge and others) for a specific part of the software life cycle or for a specific domain. Indeed, other activities in a software process are usually not considered. They do not focus on the software process specification, neglecting support for the integration of different process specification activities into the software development process phases. On the other hand, tools for process modeling and specification (e.g. Eclipse Platform Foundation – EPF) lack integration to modeling tools and model transformation engines. This scenario does not help software engineers who want to use MDD as a main software development approach or to adapt existing software processes.

There have been attempts to integrate process design and enactment (Bispo et al., 2010). Environments called PSEEs (Process-Centered Software Engineering Environment) with different characteristics, features and contexts (Alves, Machado, & Ramalho, 2008; Baker et al., 2007) have been proposed. However, most of them have shortcomings regarding process enactment. Some of them are enactable but proprietary and use a non-standard Process Modeling Language (PML) (Magalhães et al., 2011). In some cases they have a restricted focus on the management view of a software development process alone (Gomes et al., 2011). PSEE concepts can be applied to support the enactment peculiarities of an MDD process, i.e. an integrated environment including modeling and metamodeling, definition and execution of model transformations.

This paper presents MoDErNE (Model Driven Process-Centered Software Engineering Environment) which is an environment for model driven development that uses process centered concepts to aid the adoption of MDD. The environment is based on the MDD and MDT approaches for both system development and testing using SPEM (Software and Systems Process Engineering Metamodel) (OMG, 2008) concepts. Based on metamodels, model-driven processes can be instantiated. Therefore this instance, a specific process model, can be enacted several times in different software development projects.

By using and combining process-centered software engineering concepts and a model-driven approach, MoDErNE offers an environment that supports model-driven software process specification and enactment properly. It is an environment where different strategies for modeling and transformation tasks can be specified and used in an appropriate sequence and in an integrated way to assist and facilitate the use of the MDD approach in software processes.

The MoDErNE approach was initially proposed in (Maciel, Gomes, & Silva, 2011). The first version of this tool, named Transforms (Silva et al.,2009), was only able to support software development tasks. Currently it comprises two modules with complementary features: a Process Editor and a Process Executor. In the Process Editor process models can be specified using a specialization of the SPEM metamodel as well as several kinds of software development, testing and management activities. In the Process Executor, it is possible to enact the processes previously specified in the Process Editor using UML (Unified Modeling Language) diagrams and transformations.

This chapter is organized as follows: Initially the background to model driven development

is presented; Section 2 presents related work; Section 3 describes MoDErNE, the proposed solution; Section 4 focuses on case studies used to evaluate MoDErNE. Section 5 presents future research directions and Section 6 presents final remarks and future work.

MODEL DRIVEN DEVELOPMENT BACKGROUND

Model Driven Development (MDD) is a paradigm where models are the first-class artifacts in software development: the focus of the development changes from code to models. High abstract level models are transformed automatically / semi-automatically through a transformation chain in low abstract level models until code generation. In this approach certain concepts have to be well understood, such as model, metamodels, metametamodels, profiles, transformations and so on.

A model is a collection of elements that describe a system. Models are specified in a modeling language that comprises three basic elements: (i) the abstract syntax, with language structures and combinations thereof; (ii) the concrete syntax, which describes the language representation; and (iii) the semantic, with the meaning of the language elements (Bambrilla, Cabot, & Wimmer, 2012). In an MDD context languages can be formalized using metamodels. Therefore, metamodels describe the modeling language constructors, their relationships, constraints and modeling rules, and models are instances of these metamodels.

The most widely known and used modeling language is the Unified Modeling Language (UML) which can be used to specify many kinds of systems. However, there are some situations in which it is difficult to express specific aspects of a system using a general purpose language. In such cases it is necessary to use domain specific languages (DSL). A DSL is a language defined with an appropriate syntax and semantic to support a specific domain. For example, we can use Meta Object Facility (MOF) to create a DSL suitable for the web domain. It is also possible to create a DSL specializing UML concepts and defining new constraints to serve a domain, preserving the UML metamodel. A UML specialization is called a profile.

At the core of MDD there is a transformation chain that encapsulates the knowledge and strategies required to transform models. Essentially, transformations are programs that receive input models and produce output models (Model2Model transformation) or produce text files (Model2Text transformation) (Bambrilla, Cabot, & Wimmer, 2012). These models are specified according to metamodels. Similarly, metamodels are specified according to a metametamodel (Mellor, 2004). Models should reflect a conformity relationship with their metamodel. A model is conformed to its metamodel if it is syntactically correct and meets the constraints imposed by the metamodel.

A transformation comprises a set of rules that describes how an input model can be transformed into the output model. Transformations are described using specific transformation languages such as ATL (Atlas Transformation Language) and QVT (Query/View/Transformation). These languages can be expressed at a metamodel level enabling the creation of transformations as models.

Figure 1 illustrates the concepts related to the creation and execution of a transformation. The input model of the transformation (*mi*) is in conformance with is conforms to the metamodel MM_s (source metamodel), which is also is in conformance with conforms to the metametamodel *MMM*. Analogously, the output model (*mo*) is defined in conformance with conformed to the metamodel *MMt* (target metamodel), which is in conformance with the metametamodel *MMM*. The transformation *T* is modeled in conformance with the metamodel *MMt*, which represents a transformation language and comprises a set of rules that relates the elements of *MMs* to the elements of *MMt*. The execution of the transformation by an engine receives *mi* and produces *mo* according to the defined rules of *T*.

Transformations are classified in endogenous if the source and target metamodels are the same, and exogenous if they are different. Transformations are also classified as horizontal if input and output modes are at the same abstract level; or vertical if input and output models are at different abstract levels.

The transformation chain must preserve the conformity and correction of the generated models through each development process phase: the generation of a correct code depends on the models involved.

MDD Process

The development of a software requires the adoption of a development process that defines which activities are expected to be executed, when to perform them and by whom. It is also necessary to identify the tools to be used and the format of the documents to be created and manipulated.

MDD, like other development approaches, also requires the adoption of a development process. However, existing processes (e.g. RUP and XP) are not appropriate for this context. MDD processes should have extra activities, artifacts and roles (e.g. it is necessary to define metamodels, develop the transformation chain and specify metamodeling activities). Therefore it is necessary to specify the processes specific for this approach using software modeling strategies.

Software process modeling should facilitate the communication, understanding, reutilization, evolution, management and standardization of the process (Humprey & Kelner, 1989). A process is said to be enacted when a development team follows the process model definitions during the development life cycle. Processes can be described using PMLs, a particular language to model and describe software processes. The most well known PML is the OMG standard SPEM 2.0.

Figure 1. Relationship between metamodel and model in a model transformation (adapted from (Bézivin et al.,2006))

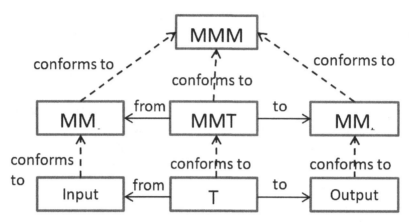

Over the years some environments have been proposed to support various types of activities involved in software development and the literature usually refers to such environments as PSEEs (Process-centered Software Engineering Environments) (Gregor et al., 2001; Ambriola, Conrasi, & Fuggeta, 1997). By using PSEEs a process has to be modeled first and then it can be enacted in several projects. During process enactment, software developers are reminded of activities which have to be carried out, automatic activities may be executed without human interaction and consistencies among documents are facilitated. This is especially important in an MDD approach because the models produced in the software specification are transformed from one development phase to another until code generation.

MoDErNe aims to support an MDD process using some PSEE features. The MoDErNe Environment presented in this chapter enables the specification of processes according to the MDD approach necessities and the enactment of these processes using SPEM as a PML: Developers follow process model descriptions, performing several kinds of activities including creating models and transforming them into other models until code.

Model Driven Architecture (MDA)

Model Driven Development (MDA) is an OMG proposal for the MDD approach. The main goal of MDA is to increase portability, interoperability and productivity in software development given that concepts are more stable than technology and business concepts are technology free.

MDA standardizes the models at three levels: Computational Independent Model (CIM); Platform Independent Model (PIM); and Platform Specific Model (PSM). From PSM, code on a specific platform is generated (Figure 2).

In the CIM model business necessities are identified. After that, in the PIM model a computational solution is defined for the system and finally at the PSM level this solution is mapped to a desired platform (Mellor, 2004). It is possible to map a PIM model in different PSM models and then generate code on many platforms. The models generated at each of these levels (CIM, PIM and PSM) are instances of the correspondence metamodels.

The MDA transformation chain comprises transformations from CIM to PIM, from PIM to PSM and from PSM to code (Figure 2). The design of these transformations consists of the definition of transformation rules mapping the elements

Figure 2. Life cycle of an MDA application

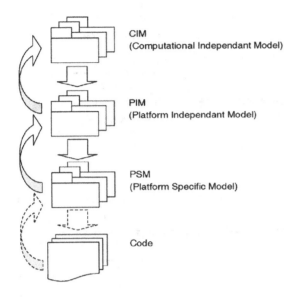

of the source metamodels to the elements of the target metamodels (e.g. CIM to PIM transformation contains the rules to map elements of CIM metamodels to elements of PIM metamodels). Therefore, a transformation engine receives a model as input (e.g. CIM model) and executes the transformation (e.g. CIM to PIM transformation) generating an output model (e.g. PIM model).

With the MoDErNe Environment presented in this chapter it is possible to specify and enact a process according to the MDA architecture (e.g. process phases are specialized in CIM, PIM, PSM and Code).

Model Driven Testing (MDT)

Due to the increasing complexity of systems today, software testing has become a very important activity in Software Engineering. Testing is recognized in both academic and industrial environments as an essential activity for system quality assurance.

As well as for system development, models can be used to improve software testing activities. Model Based Testing (MBT) (Weber et al., 2009) is a model driven approach that proposes

that software test cases can be generated automatically/semi-automatically from system development models. This automation can reduce errors in the creation of test cases and thus increase the efficiency of the testing process.

MBT itself can provide many benefits and innovations for software testing activities. However, it is well known that for a testing process to be considered complete it must involve much more than only test case generation. Like the development process, the testing process also encompasses activities such as planning, design and implementation (IEEE, 2008). Models could be used to support all these tasks.

Model Driven Testing (MDT) is an MBT extension which considers that all testing artifacts should be conceived as models (Baker et al., 2007). It brings the MDD philosophy to system testing and proposes that models should be the first-class artifacts for testing activities too. For OMG, as well as MDA, MDT uses the concept of abstraction levels, which classifies the models in platform independent and platform specific models. Therefore, according to the MDT approach, testing models can be defined independent of the system and testing target platforms and be refined until code generation. This results in the early integration of development and testing activities. By doing this, design mistakes and implementation faults can be detected at an early stage of the process, potentially reducing time and cost.

Figure 3 shows the MDA abstraction levels applied to MDT. The horizontal arrows represent the transformations that generate testing models from system development models. The testing models can be obtained from both platform independent and platform specific models. The vertical arrows represent the transformations between abstraction levels. Like system development models, Platform Specific Testing Models (PSTM) can be obtained from Platform Independent Testing Models (PITM) and test code can be generated from both PITM and PSTM.

Figure 3. System development and testing model transformations

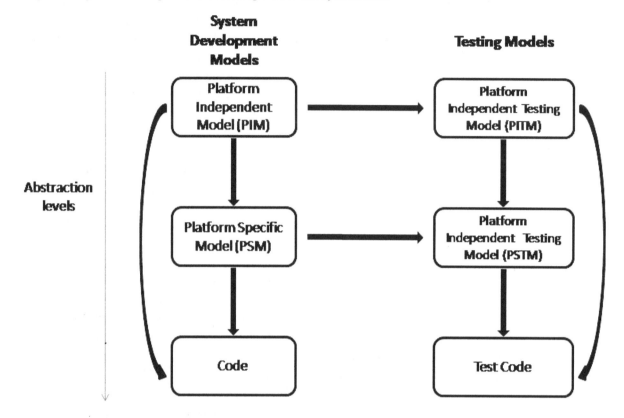

UML is currently the most popular modeling language used in the software community. However, UML itself can not represent all the testing aspects necessary to make a complete testing model. Therefore OMG has defined the UML Testing Profile (UTP) (OMG, 2005) to facilitate the design, visualization, specification, construction and documentation of functional testing artifacts. It is a profile that extends the UML modeling language in order to represent specific aspects of testing, enabling the automatic generation of test cases from testing models. UTP is completely independent of any technology and therefore is used to create platform independent testing models.

UTP defines concepts to represent both the static and dynamic aspects of the testing artifacts. It is subdivided in four complementary parts: i) Test Architecture, which defines concepts related to the elements, the structure and the configura-

tion used in the testing project ii) Test Behaviour, used to represent the test cases and their behaviour iii) Test Data, which defines the concepts used to describe the data used to test the software and iv) Time Concepts, which define concepts that constrain and control test behavior regarding aspects of time. Each part encompasses a set of concepts which are important for the testing activities.

Many approaches have emerged to give support to MDT. Most of them (Hartmann, Vieira, & Axel, 2004; Wang & Zhang, 2003; Mingsong, Xiaokang, & Xuandong, 2006; Bouquet et al., 2008) consist of methods to generate test cases from system models in order to increase automation in testing activities. Others, like (Alves, Machado, & Ramalho, 2008), focus on other important aspects of an MDT process, such as its integration with a model driven development process. The MoDErNe approach presented in this chapter integrates UTP in the MDD process specification enabling the definition of specific test activities. The enactment of these activities generates test cases from the application models.

Strategies to Perform Model Driven Development

In recent years a number of research initiatives related to MDD have emerged. We can divide these into two categories which we shall explain in this section: processes and methodologies for MDD; and languages and tools for model transformation. We also describe some related work about PSEEs and how their legacy concepts connect to our tool environment.

Processes and Methodologies for MDD

Several methods for MDD have been proposed in the literature. Some of these include an MDA process for middleware specific services (Maciel, Silva, & Mascarenhas, 2006), an MDD process for web applications (Koch, 2006), an MDA methodology for e-learning systems (Wang & Zhang, 2003), fault tolerance distributed software families (Guelfi et al., 2003), KobrA (Atkinson et al., 2001) a method for the development of component-based software with model driven techniques. The MDD approach for software development has not only changed the way software systems are built and maintained but also the way they are tested. In this context, several works have been proposed concerning Model Driven Testing (MDT). Most of them (Hartmann, Vieira, & Axel, 2004; Yuan et al., 2008; Mingsong, Xiaokang, & Xuandong, 2006; Bouquet et al., 2008) propose methods to generate test cases from system models in order to increase automation in testing activities. In (Javed, Strooper, & Watson, 2007), for instance, the authors generate test models from system models using use case and activity diagrams, annotations and transformation rules to derive the test cases.

However, most of the approaches for MDD and MDT processes and methodologies are defined using non-standard notation and language. They are specified imprecisely in natural language with supplementary pictures and diagrams. In fact, there is a lack of consistent terminology as there is no unified language to specify MDD processes. Ad hoc notations and different concepts are used to define the activities and artifacts for the software development life cycle. In addition, each methodology focuses on a specific application domain and several of them comprise only one specific software project phase (e.g. architectural design, testing, etc.). All of this hampers software development. Software process modeling using unified and consistent terminology should facilitate understanding, reutilization, management and standardization of the process (Humprey & Kelner, 1989).

Languages and Tools for Model Transformation

Model transformation support tools play an important role in software development activities and in the model-driven development context this is no different. It is essential due to the intrinsic need for automatic model transformation and code generation. Therefore organizations which follow a model-driven approach also have to use a supporting tool to automate their transformations, even partially. The process for model-driven development must therefore be accomplished with some tool support; otherwise it could become unfeasible (Hutchinson, Rouncefield, & Whittle, 2011).

Transformation is an essential activity for model-driven development and many of the approaches in the literature focus on this task. Several languages for model transformation specification have been proposed as well as a number of transformation engines to carry out the transformations. At present, there is a variety of open source and proprietary MDD languages with different characteristics and features, such as ATL (Atlas Transformation Language) and QVT (Query/View/Transformation) for model-to-model transformation, and MOFScript and Acceleo for model-to-text transformation.

Other environments enable system modeling and provide predetermined transformations for specific platforms, programming languages and also for a specific phase in the software development life cycle (requirement, architecture, codification, etc.). For example AndroMDA is an environment which follows the MDA approach and provides transformations from platform independent models (PIM) to the Java EE (Java Enterprise Edition) platform. The transformations are provided in so called cartridges and are added as plug-ins for the AndroMDA environment. Another example is Blu Age, which is a proprietary tool that claims to facilitate the migration of legacy systems. The tool can extract platform independent models from legacy system code and provides transformation to generate code for a different platform, such as Java EE or .NET. WebRatio is another proprietary tool used to develop web applications. It uses BPMN (Business Process Management Notation) and WebML (Web Modeling Language) to represent the business logic and system requirements and then generates java code for the Java EE platform. Other MDD tools can be easily found on the web, such as in http://www.modelbased.net/.

In spite of the high number of MDD tools already proposed as well as those used both in academia and industry, most focus primarily on model transformation execution, i.e. they define and execute transformations which produce code and deployment artifacts from models. They are therefore used for specific tasks and do not cover the whole development process life cycle. A development process involves other important tasks which should be carried out during the process enactment such as requirement analysis, testing, manual tasks etc. rather than just doing model transformations. Recently, SPEM4MDE (Samba, Lbath, & Coullet, 2011) has been proposed. Like

MoDErNE, the SPEM4MDE approach uses SPEM as PML and its tool also has a Process Editor and Process Enactment modules. For instance, the focus of the SPEM4MDE approach relies on transformation definition and execution. The environment does not support MDA and MDT specificities and its does not have several of the desired features for a PSEE, such as management tasks. Although transformations are an important aspect in MDE processes, it is only a part of these processes. A supporting tool must cover several and different aspects of MDE processes.

Recent studies into MDE practice reveal some issues that should be addressed (Hutchinson, Rouncefield, & Whittle, 2011; Hutchinson et al., 2011; Mohagheghi & Dehlen, 2008). Successful MDE adoption appears to require a progressive and iterative approach because it is usually adopted gradually, in specific stages or tasks of a software development process (testing, coding, etc.). Despite the fact that software processes are recognized as being important in successfully applying MDE, the proposed model-driven methods or processes were considered unsuitable for use by the participants of these studies. Additionally, much effort is required to develop new transformations or customize existing ones (Hutchinson et al., 2011). Some findings point to specific issues with regard to MDE tools, for example, they are expensive or need to be used in specific ways (Hutchinson, Rouncefield, & Whittle, 2011). The decision to adopt an MDE approach is not made with much understanding of the process changes required (Hutchinson et al., 2011).

PSEE is a process centered environment which gives support to various types of activities during the software development life cycle. It provides many services for software developers by modeling and enacting software processes. Interest in the PSEE approach is not new. While the first generation of PSEE environments and their characteristics were revised in (Arbaoui et al., 2002) and (Gruhn, 2002), the latest generation (after 2003) proposed in the last ten years were analyzed in (Reza & Raman, 2012). Initially, some PSEE desired requirements included process modeling through a PML, process model enactment, process tasks ordering, process evolution, management and documentation. Several environments have been proposed (Cass et al.,2000; Weber et al., 2009; Zamli, Mat, & Khamis, 2005) however, they have limitations in supporting process enactment and integrating different kinds of tools. To solve PSEE integration problems, (Gruhn, 2002) proposed the use of middleware platforms as a solution.

Although a middleware platform approach was proposed as a solution for any kind of software process, modern PSEEs still tend to focus on a software process specific for a domain (e.g. for web application, model-driven, software product lines). The common functionalities of the latest PSEEs (e.g. SPACE (Weber et al., 2009), VRML (Zamli, Mat, & Khamis, 2005), WebApSEE (Lima et al., 2006), Transforms (Silva, et al., 2009), etc.). (Reza & Raman, 2012) are: interactive assistance throughout software development, automation of routine and labor-intensive tasks and invocation and control of software development tools, process flexibility during the enactment and software team distribution. However, they fail to provide security and mobility features. Besides these general functionalities, an MDD focused PSEE should allow users to represent MDD related process elements, such as transformation and model artifacts. Furthermore, it should provide an enactment environment that supports both system modeling and model transformation, which are essential activities within the MDD context. To the best of our knowledge, there is no such environment available neither in academia nor in industry.

Currently MDD tools do not have process-centered features as they are not designed for achieve this, and current PSEEs do not address specific features for MDD processes. We believe that it is important to have a tool which can help to define the activities, artifacts and roles of the software development process within the MDD context as well as integrate different approaches

and tools that automate model and transformation tasks and thus support the process enactment properly.

Our work presents an environment that supports both process modeling and enactment for the MDD process context. In the model driven approach strategy, system models are metamodel instances. Our approach uses this same strategy for software process specification. It comprises a set of metamodels to provide a standard notation to specify a software process allowing the explicit representation of MDD related elements, such as models and model transformations. Process element descriptions are placed at the metamodel level, and consequently process models become instances of these metamodels. The approach has several other PSEE characteristics adapted for the MDD context, such as (semi) automation support for process activities, a collaborative environment and integration with other MDD related tools.

MoDErNE: Model Driven Process-Centered Software Engineering Environment

MoDErNE is an approach and tool which supports the specification and enactment of model-driven software processes in an integrated way using process-centered software engineering concepts. Figure 4 gives an overview of the MoDErNE environment. MoDErNE has two main goals: process specification, through the Process Editor Module; and process enactment, through the Process Executor Module.

The Process Editor comprises a UML profile editor; a transformation rule editor; and process publication. The Process Executor comprises process enactment in collaborative way following the previous process specification; UML modeling editor; and transformation execution for code generation.

The MDD process specification includes definitions of management, development and testing processes. These definitions follow a set

Figure 4. MoDErNE's main functionalities

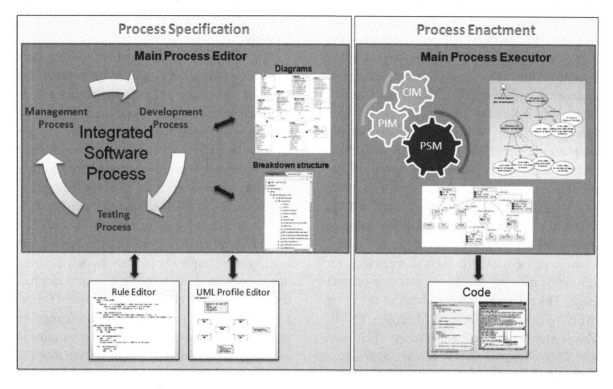

of metamodels based on SPEM 2.0. The result of this is that MDD process models, which can be expressed as an SPEM instance and which use UML as a modeling language, may use this environment as a support tool. Additionally, we extended SPEM to adapt them to the MDA context, e.g. Computation Independent Model (CIM), Platform Independent Model (PIM) and Platform Specific Model (PSM) concepts.

The process is represented by models, which are instances of these metamodels and they are basically made in UML diagrams. The process may be modeled by: (i) a class diagram, to show the process elements in a visual representation; (ii) an activity diagram to model phase/iteration sequence and their specific tasks (iii) a use case diagram to map responsibilities through associations between roles and tasks. As well as this, a work breakdown structure is also available for those who prefer a hierarchical visualization.

The Process Editor enables the creation of reusable software engineering best practice libraries. For example, some of methodologies proposed and cited in section 2 could be specified as a library and libraries can be used for: web applications, real-time systems, testing services, etc. These libraries comprise elements such as tasks, steps, roles and produced/consumed artifacts (i.e. UML models and transformation rules) for the process specification. The definition of a new process begins by selecting library elements and organizing them in terms of *phases* and *iterations*, besides the common process elements (i.e. phases, tasks and roles). MDD processes need some new definitions such as model transformation and profiles. These definitions are supported as the environment provides a transformation rule editor (ATL, MOFScript and QVT for instance) and a UML profile editor respectively. Process definitions are stored in a repository to be later enacted by the Process Executor module.

To exemplify the use of the Process Editor, let us consider a company that their developers wants to adapt their RUP process for the MDD approach. In the process editor the reusable elements should be specified such as *disciplines* (e.g. *Requirements and Analyze & Design*), *tasks* (e.g. *define requirements*, *define scope* and so on), the *workproducts* involved (e.g. *use case model*, *class model*) and the performed *roles* (e.g. *system analyst*). Dynamic definitions should also be specified such the *phases* (*inception*, *elaboration*, *construction* and *transition phases*) and *iterations* (e.g. the *elaboration phase* has two *iterations*) using the *tasks* previewed modeled. Besides these definitions, MDD processes require other specifications. It is also necessary to develop the appropriate transformations for the process and select the source and target profiles. (e.g. we can develop a transformation to transform inception phase model the first version of elaboration the phase model). These activities also involve new *roles* (e.g. *process specifier*, *transformation specifier* and *transformation developer*) that only exist in MDD processes. The resulting process, named RUPMDD, is then organized into two different libraries: (i) *Ruplib* and (ii) *inception2elaboration*. *Ruplib* keeps the RUP process definition and *inception2elaboration* keeps the ATL transformations files and UML profiles that enable the model transformations from one phase to another. The specification of the sequence in which process *tasks* from these two libraries must be performed are also defined using MoDErNE Process Editor support.

The main goal of the Process Executor is the enactment of a process previously specified in the Editor and stored in the repository. *Phases*, *iterations* and their *tasks* follow in the sequence specified in the process editor. The execution of these *tasks* is managed by the Executor showing the *task* status that indicates if the *task* is finished, in progress, pending, etc. The Process Executor integrates modeling and runs transformation tools. When executing a modeling *task*, a modeling editor

(i.e. UML2Tools) is available with the appropriate diagram elements and profiles specified for the *task*. When executing a transformation *task*, a transformation tool is presented (i.e. MOFScript or ATL engine) to run the rules specified in the process. Following the sequence of the process *tasks* the developer can create his/her models and transform them until code generation. Any other modeling tool can be used and then the XMI (XML Metadata Interchange) file should be imported as input in a transformation rule. As the process comprises validation tasks, test cases may also be generated for software validation.

MoDErNE also allows the development team to work collaboratively to build a software system. When starting software development a team is defined according to the *roles* specified for the process and associated to each *task*. Each person in this team can execute different *tasks* at the same time during process enactment.

Any kind of *task* may be specified for the process and will be available in the sequence when enacted. However, only modeling *tasks* (producing UML workproducts) or transformation *tasks* (related to transformation workproducts) are associated to the UML editor and transformation engines. Using our example of the RUPMDD process, the Process Executor shows the *inception*, *elaboration*, *construction* and *transition phases* sequentially with their *iterations* and *tasks*. When a user (associated to a specific role) selects a *task* to perform, the appropriate tool is shown according to the Process Editor specification. For example, when the systems analyst performs the *define requirements task*, a UML editor is automatically opened with the appropriate metamodel for the use case diagram specification. When a *transformation task* is selected, the associated transformation is executed, and so on.

The following sections explain our approach in greater detail. Section 3.1 focuses on the metamodeling foundations on which MoDErNE is based. Section 3.2 explains the tool architecture and section 3.3 details its main modules and functionalities.

MoDErNE's Metamodels

In this section we present the metamodels on which MoDErNE is based and that represent software processes that use MDD techniques. They make the modeling and instantiation of MDD, MDT and management processes elements explicit and have specialized semantics that facilitate automated support during the process enactment. Just as metamodels are used to describe application models of the same domain, they can also describe the models of software processes that guide the development of these applications. Therefore, our main goal is to provide a mechanism with a metamodeling foundation in order to create an effective way to support a model-driven development process specification and enactment.

According to the OMG model layers shown in Figure 5, a specific software development project is located at level M0, i.e. the layer where a development team works on a project enacting a process which is specified at the level above (M1). RUP, XP and other processes are situated at M1. Process models at M1 are designed according to a process metamodel (i.e. a metalanguage to specify process models) which corresponds to level M2. For instance, SPEM was used to design the well-known RUP process model. As highlighted in Figure 5, our approach is located at level M2. Thus, an MDD process model (located at level M1) can be designed and will be available for the development of new projects at level M0. Consequently, any process definition modeled at M1 can be used during the process enactment in M0 providing specific features according to its specification. The definition of MDD, MDT and management process concepts at metamodel level (M2) is important to provide a meaningful way to design software processes with explicit characteristics of these kinds of processes. The specified semantic for each element is important

because it will be used in the process enactment (i.e. use the profile associated to a specific phase to validate the input models, associate a transformation engine to a transformation rule artifact, etc.).

Our approach is composed of a set of metamodels, based on SPEM 2.0, which refer to each aspect of a software process (development, testing or management) in an MDD context. According to SPEM, software process specification should be divided into two dimensions: static concepts, which are made up of *disciplines*, *tasks*, *steps*, *roles* and *workproducts*, forming what they call *Method Content*; and dynamic concepts, which include *phases*, *iterations* and *task uses*, forming the so-called *Process*.

The *Method Content* involves co-related elements that can be reused in many process models. We specialize a *Method Content* in three different types, representing the various processes needed in a software development lifecycle: the *CoreMethodContent,* which represents general MDD development process elements; the *MethodContentForTesting,* which describes testing process elements following the MDT approach; and the *ManagementMethodContent,* which focuses on project management based on Project Management Body of Knowledge (PMBOK).

It is therefore possible to specify the development, testing and management processes independently. This can increase the potential reuse of one kind of process (development, testing or management) with others different processes. For instance, the same testing process (specified in the *MethodContentForTesting*) could be used with many different development processes (located in the *CoreMethodContent*). This independent process specification can also facilitate the work of independent teams for development, testing and project management.

After modeling each process independently, they have to be integrated in a unified process that covers all software development aspects (Figure 6).

As explained before, the *Process* is used to represent dynamic aspects of software processes,

Figure 5. OMG Model layers

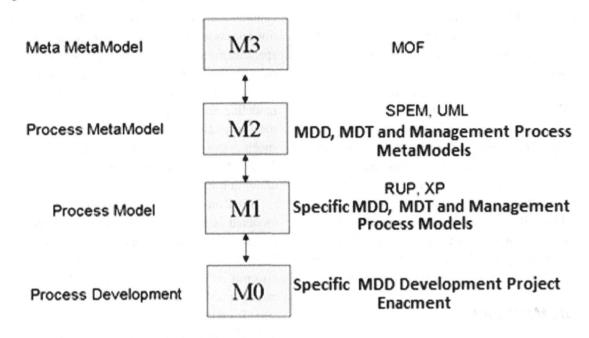

Figure 6. Software process integration

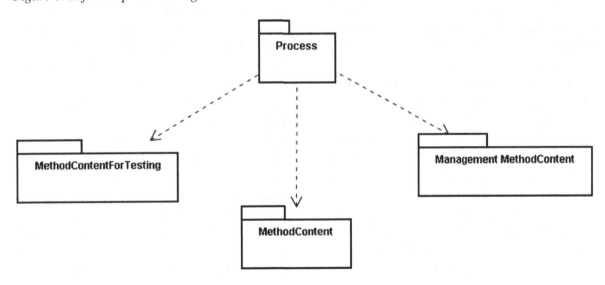

such as *phases* and *iterations*. It references the static elements defined in a *MethodContent* package to perform a complete process specification. A software process instantiated in a *Process* package can use elements of different kinds of *Method Contents*. Thus, the *Process* package is respon-

sible for process integration, selecting elements of each *Method Content* and distributing them to the *phases* and *iterations* of a process instance.

A model-driven development process called OpenUP/MDD (OpenUP, 2006) is a variation of the Open Unified Process for MDD. This process was specified according to the SPEM 2.0 standard using the EPF tool, which is an environment for software process modeling following SPEM. As a result, OpenUP/MDD is an instance (i.e. a metamodel instance) of the SPEM metamodel. Unlike OpenUP/MDD we decided to add the MDD concepts at the metamodel level.

Our hypothesis is that by using metamodeling techniques to describe several aspects of software processes, they can be integrated in a flexible manner enabling better software process specification and enactment.

The following subsections explain the Core metamodel and metamodel for testing that is part of our approach. Due to lack of space, the management metamodel will not be presented.

Core Metamodel

The use of MDD requires process definitions associated with modeling activities and transformation rules to compose the transformation chain. These elements are not usually found (explicitly) in traditional software development processes. Therefore, we selected some of the SPEM 2.0 concepts and specialized them in order to cover specific aspects of the MDD context. Again, it is important to highlight that our hypothesis focuses on the explicit modeling and instantiation of process elements with specialized semantics which can facilitate process design and enactment. The core metamodel is illustrated in Figure 7.

As explained before, the *MethodContent* package represents the process static elements. A *Discipline* groups a set of related *Tasks* that are performed by *Roles*. A *Role* defines the responsibilities of an individual or a group of individuals. A *Task* may comprise many *Steps* to describe meaningful work. During the process enactment, *Workproducts* as input and output artifacts can be consumed/produced. In this approach a *Workproduct* can be specialized into four kinds of artifacts: a *UML model*, transformed/generated during the process enactment; a *Transformation*, for any kind

of transformation; a *Transformation Rule*, which contains the rules for automatic model transformation and code generation; an *Extra Model*, textual specifications or supplementary notation necessary for the project; and a *Profile*, which gives additional and specialized semantics for system modeling according to a specific application domain or platform. *Tasks* are also performed in a specific *tool* (Modeling Tool or Transformation Tool) which can be modeling tools (e.g. magic draw) or transformation tools (e.g. ATL engine).

Based on static definitions many processes are modeled using metamodel dynamic concepts. A *Process* may comprise many *Phases* specialized in *modeling CIM, PIM, PSM (OMG, 2003)* and also in *Codification*. Moreover, an *Extra Phase* can be specified representing an additional stage apart from modeling and codification. The modeling *phases* can be associated with *profiles* to support modeling *tasks*. Each *Phase* can contain one or more *Iterations* that specify the TaskUses necessary to carry out a *task*.

According to this metamodel, in MoDErNE an MDD process can be diagrammatically specified by the construction of three kinds of UML diagrams (class, use case and activity diagrams), following the concepts of the metamodel. It is therefore possible to model classes named as *Software Architecture Definition* or *Service Interface Design* and associate these classes to a PIM phase stereotype, according to the MDD process characteristics. Furthermore, a *Transformation Rule artifact*, modeled as a class named *UseCaseToClass*, which maps use case elements into class, can be associated to another element stereotyped as *Transformation* to form, for example, a transformation chain.

Metamodel for Testing

A specific metamodel for testing processes has been built to enable the explicit definition of process elements concerning model-driven testing within an MDD process. It is based on several

Figure 7. Core metamodel (adapted from (Maciel, Silva, & Mascarenhas, 2006))

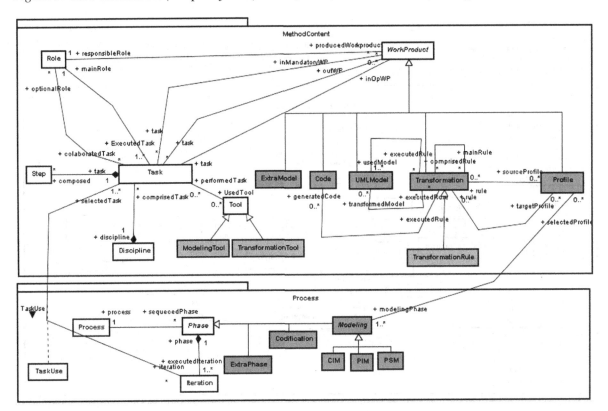

concepts from an IEEE (Institute of Electrical and Electronics Engineers) Standard (IEEE, 2008). The IEEE Standard was chosen because it proposes a complete testing process and documentation with test activities for each part of the software life cycle.

The metamodel for Testing is illustrated in Figure 8. Some meta-classes were specialized from the Core Metamodel (Figure 8). They include concepts which can be treated specifically for testing specification, and also some of them can be handled in model transformations. *Task, Role* and *Workproduct* are concepts that belong to the *Method Content* package of the *Core* Metamodel, making the connections between both metamodels. The associations and/or generalizations with the concepts of the *Method Content* package complement the comprehension of the metamodel for testing.

A *TestingTask* is a kind of *Task* which is constrained by the OCL (Object Constraint Language) rules described at the top of Figure 8. The leftmost OCL rule indicates that a *TestingTask* must have as input or output at least one *workproduct* which is a *TestingWorkProduct*. The rightmost OCL rule requires that the main *Role*, responsible for *TestingTask* execution, must be a *TestingRole*, which is a role in the process especially involved in testing activities.

A *TestingWorkProduct*, an artifact for testing, can be generated or consumed by a *TestingTask*. The *TestPlans*, for instance, are documents that contain the planning information related to the test, such as the schedule of its implementation and execution, and they are usually developed in the early phases of the process. The *TestCases* represent the code that is going to execute the system in order to find errors. *TestDesign* and *TestProcedure*

Figure 8. Metamodel for testing (adapted from(Maciel, Gomes, & Silva, 2011))

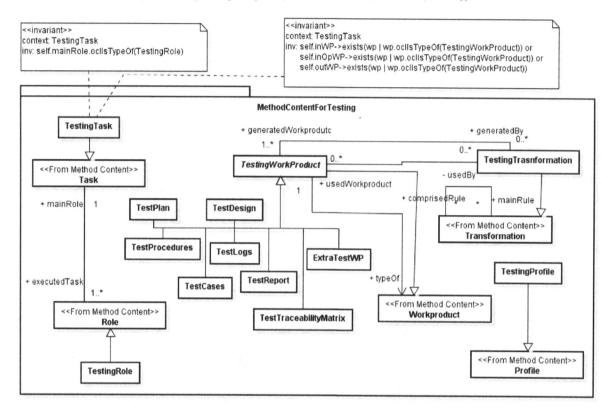

represent the structural and behavioral aspects of the test respectively and there are testing model artifacts adapted to MDT context. *TestReport* and *TestLog* are *workproducts* produced after the execution of the tests to document the results. *TestTraceabilityMatrix* track what requirements are being tested by a test case and *ExtraTestWP* represents extra documentation occasionally needed by the test activities.

The *Transformation* class of the Core metamodel was extended to the *TestingTransformation class*. This allows exclusive treatment when transformations are carried out for MDT. *Transformation rules* for MDT should generate at least a *TestingWorkProduct*, using a *TestingProfile* or not, which can define specific modeling notation for modeling tests, such as U2TP (UML 2.0 Testing Profile) (OMG, 2005).

As we explained before, a *Process* package can use more than one *Method Content* for

distinct purposes. It is important to note that the test metamodel was modeled as a SPEM Method Content which can be reused in several different software processes.

MoDErNE's Architecture

Based on the previously explained metamodels, MoDErNE has been developed to support MDD development testing and management process modeling and enactment. MoDErNE's general architecture is shown in Figure 9. The tool contains two main modules with complementary resources, namely the Process Editor and the Process Executor components. The Process Editor is responsible for the process specification following the conceptual metamodels. The Process Executor supports the enactment of the processes previously specified in the Process Editor.

The two main components communicate with each other through a repository which is a relational database (MySQL database). Either the process models, created in the Process Editor, or the artifacts such as the application models created during the development lifecycle in the Process Executor remain in this repository.

A client-server architecture style is used to provide collaborative enactment of the process. A RMI (Remote Method Invocation) based component (Server) communicates various instances of the Process Executor to the same repository. This repository is accessed and controlled by the PersistenceControl component. By using the Process Executor, developers can persist models, code and other artifacts and make them accessible to other team members. This collaborative environment plays an important role as software team distribution and cooperation is one of the key functionalities that should be provided by PSEEs.

The main modules are implemented as RCP (Rich Client Platform) products on the Eclipse platform. It is therefore possible to use Eclipse's graphic widgets as well as some of the several plug-ins developed for this platform, such as: ATL and QVT for model-to-model transformation rule editing and execution; MOFScript, for the editing and execution of model-to-text transformation rules; GMF (Graphical Modeling Framework) for the customized diagram graphic editor creation and generation; EMF (Eclipse Modeling Framework), for modeling and automatic code generation of process models, which are based on the metamodels; and UML2Tools and PapyrusUML, which are both plug-ins for the modeling of profiles and other UML artifacts. As an Eclipse RCP product, MoDErNE also provides extension points that can be used to expand support to the process enactment by integrating other useful Eclipse plug-ins to the environment.

Figure 9. MoDErNE's general architecture (adapted from (Gomes, et al., 2011))

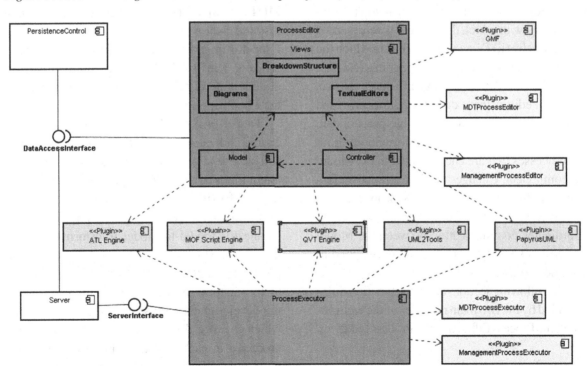

Based on the metamodels and on the specified process, the tool identifies the element type and calls the correct plugin to support an activity. MDT support as well as project management support is provided as an Eclipse plug-in. Therefore, the user can choose whether to have testing and management support or not. There are four plug-ins (Figure 9 - lighter grayscale) in the MoDErNE: MDTProcessEditor MDTProcessExecutor, ManagementProcessEditor, ManagementProcessExecutor, ATLEngine, Mof Script Engine, QVT Engine, UML2tools and PapyrusUML.

The Management Process Editor extends the Process Editor functionalities, enabling the modeling and editing of testing and management processes respectively; and the MDTProcessExecutor and the Management Process Executor extend the Process Executor functionalities in order to support the enactment of the MDT and management processes previously created in the Process Editor.

The Process Editor component uses a MVC (Model View Controller) pattern. The Editor provides three different means of specifying and visualizing process elements: (i) Breakdown Structure is a view in which the process is represented as a hierarchy (ii) Diagrams is a view in which the process is represented by UML diagrams (classes, use cases or activities) (iii) Textual Editors consists of a set of editors that extend the editors provided by the Eclipse Platform and enable process data editing. These views reflect information about the processes that are encapsulated in the Model subcomponent. Changes made in a process class diagram, for example, are thus propagated to the other views. The Controller subcomponent coordinates communication between the Model and Views so that different views correspond to a single Model element.

The following sections detail the functionalities provided by the two main modules of the environment: the Process Editor and the Process Executor.

MoDErNE Modules

The following sections detail each of these modules using the Integrated Process as an example. This process uses the specification of the MDA process for middleware specific services proposed in (Maciel, Silva, & Mascarenhas, 2006) and the MDT process proposed in (Maciel, Gomes, & Silva, 2011). The goal of this MDA process is to develop middleware services in Java EE or CCM (CORBA Component Model) platforms based on application functional requirements. Initially, this process was defined in an ad hoc manner and then specified using MoDErNE metamodels. The MDT process generates test cases for JUnit platform from UML models stereotyped using the U2TP profile.

The Integrated Process specification uses two reusable libraries (SPEM method content) named *Middleware Service Develop*, with only strategies for the development of middleware services, an instance of the Core Metamodel (section 3.1.1); and model driven test, with only strategies for software validation and test generation, based on the MDT metamodel (section 3.1.2). Its specification is stored in the repository to be used by the Process Executor in several other software development projects. The Process Executor section illustrates the Integrated Process enactment in a case study for a bank application.

To perform the Integrated Process specification and enactment without MoDErNE, the software development team had to use some different kinds of tools: (i) for process specification (e.g. EPF) (ii) UML editor diagram according to metamodel stereotypes process needs (iii) an engine for model-to-model transformation (iv) model-to-text transformation engine, and (v) for process management. In MoDErNE, in addition to the features of each tool mentioned above, the development team will have a repository in which to store the artifacts that were used and produced in each task available. Moreover, the process specification works as a support for task delegation among project members as well as a guide for task sequence and workproducts required for each task.

MoDErNE Process Editor

To specify a new process, the first step is to select existing method content or define new method content with the *disciplines*, *tasks*, *roles* and *workproducts* that will be used in the process definition. After this, processes can be specified. A process can use all method content elements or only some of them.

Figure 10 shows the method content *Model Driven Test* with elements defined for the *Test Implementation Discipline*. It illustrates how class diagrams can be used to represent the method content elements and their relationships. In the figure there is a *discipline* called *Test Implementation* which comprises a set of *tasks* such as *Generate Component Test Cases* and *Execute Component Test*. It also shows the input and output *workproducts* which are used and generated by each *task*. For example, *Generate Component Test Cases task* uses as input *Test Design* and *TestModelToTestCode workproducts* and, as output *ComponentTest* Case. The available class editor shows a tool pallet with the Core and Testing metamodel concepts to be used in the edition of the process. It is important to note that each element is stereotyped according to these metamodels. This allows us to give specific treatment to such elements. For instance, the tool can recognize that the *TestModelToTestCode* artifact is a transformation rule (as it is stereotyped as *TestingTransformation*) and then provides users with the integrated ATL environments for rule creation and edition. Transformations developed outside MoDErNE can be used if they were developed in ATL, QVT of MOFScript languages and thus their transformation code can be imported as a Transformation artifact.

Figure 11 illustrates the Process Editor screen which is divided into four sections. Pane box (A) presents the process being edited, the Integrated Process, its breakdown structure and elements (*tasks*, *roles*, *workproducts*, etc.). In pane (A) we can see two different *MethodContents*: the *Middleware Specific Services MethodContent*, which has elements concerning the development process, and the *Model Driven TestMethodContentForTesting*, which comprises the elements regarding the testing process, such as testing roles (*Test Analyst*, *Test Modeler* and *Tester*) and testing *workproducts* (*Component Test Design, Component Test Case*, etc.), as well as certain artifacts related to it, such as the UML 2.0 Testing profile (U2TP). Panes (B) and (D) correspond to visual modeling areas in which the user can create and edit process elements through UML diagrams. Pane (B) illustrates a use case diagram, used to assign responsibilities to the various process *roles*. In the example shown in Pane (B), a *Domain Analyst* is responsible for the *Review Generated BP Composition, Decompose Process* and *Transform BP (CIM) for CCA (PIM)* process *tasks*. Pane (D), on the other hand, contains an activity diagram which represents the activity flow of one process iteration. This represents the sequence of activities of the *Technology Modeling* iteration required to generate code from the PSM Model and the application unit test cases using ATL Language. It contains two main flows: one comprises *Review Generated PSM* and *Generate Code tasks* regarding the development process; and the other contains *Generate Component Test Design, Generate Component Test Procedures* and *Generate Component Test Cases tasks*, which are testing activities. Panes (C) and (E) contain option palettes which support the creation of the process models, instances of the extended SPEM metamodels from section 3.1.

MoDErNE Process Executor

The first activity when initiating a new project is to select a process from the repository. The entire environment is configured according to the process definition: phases, iterations and tasks are organized in a hierarchical structure ready

Figure 10. Method Content class diagram example

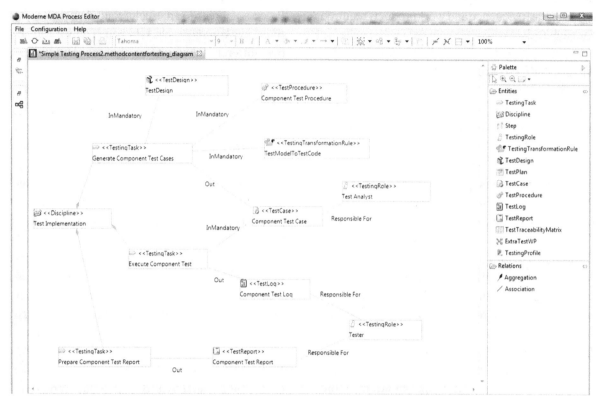

Figure 11. Process Editor

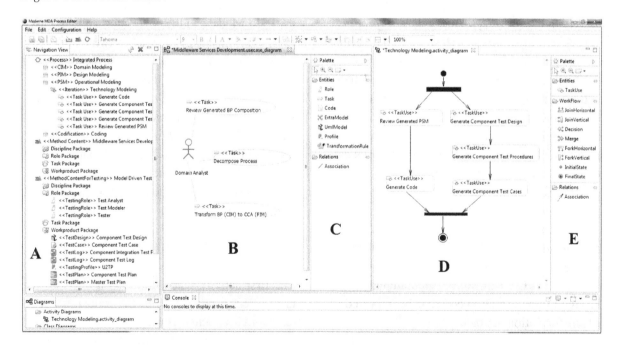

Figure 12. Process Executor

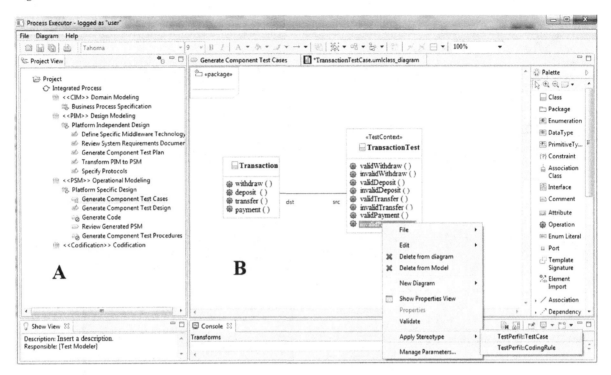

for use. Figure 12 illustrates an Executor screen for the bank application development project. It is divided into two panes. Pane (A) contains the process previously specified in the Editor (Figure 10 and 11) and selected for the project. In this area, the project manager can assign roles to other users enabling access control to the tasks. This will be used to control the collaborative development of the project.

Although all the tasks in the specified process can be visualized by each member of the development team, task execution is individual. Role definition is used to manage the collaborative project controlling access to each task by each specific role. Different people may work on the same project at the same time but on different tasks.

Furthermore, the tasks have an icon that indicates whether they are being performed ( ), have already been done ( ), have not yet started but are ready to start ( ), or have not started and depend on another task that has not yet been finished ( ).

Pane (B) consists of the modeling environment in which the developer can create the application models. According to the workproduct stereotype specified for each task in the process specification, MoDErNE associates and makes the necessary tool available to support the task being performed. For example, in Figure 12 (B), the user is performing the *GenerateComponent-TestCase* task. This task was specified to produce a workproduct stereotyped as a TestDesign (as can be seen in Figure 12), which is an UMLModel. Therefore, MoDErNE opens a UML class editor for the *TransactionTestCaseclass* diagram modeling. The UML profiles specified in the process in the Editor are automatically available to use in the Executor and its stereotypes can be applied by the developer while the diagrams are being created. U2TP (UML 2.0 Testing Profile), a profile for system testing, is available in the environment and whenever a testing task is performed it is enabled, allowing users to annotate their models with the stereotypes of the profile. This feature is

Figure 13. MoDErNE's support for model transformations

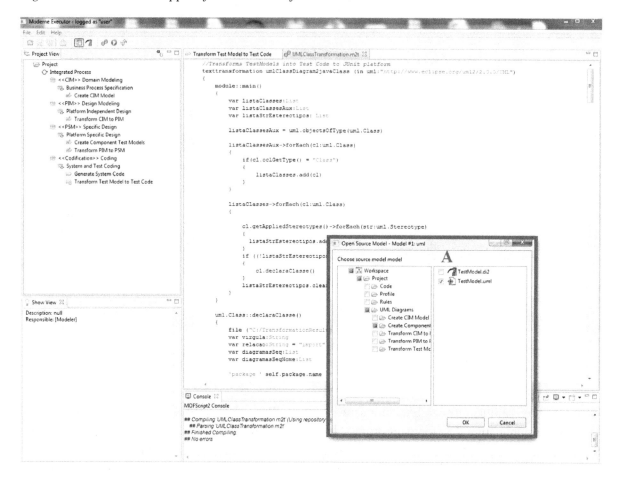

possible because an *UMLModel workproduct* can be associated to a *Profileworkproduct* according to the Core metamodel (see Figure 12 pop-up).

In the Figure10 example, unit test cases are being modeled and the user can apply U2TP defined stereotypes. These test case models can later be transformed into JUnit test case codes for the JUnit platform.

Figure 13 illustrates MoDErNE's support for model transformation enactment. Whenever the performed tasks are associated to a workproduct stereotyped as a Transformation, the correct transformation engine is automatically shown to the user. The transformation engine receives as input a previously created model and generates as output another model (in low abstraction level)

or a specific code to compose an application that is under development. The example in Figure 13 exemplifies a MOFScript transformation rule (UMLClassTransformation.m2t) to generate test code from test models. The user selects the previously created input model and then executes the transformation generating the testing code.

CASE STUDIES

This section presents our latest work on the evaluation of our environment through case studies that have been carried out. Evaluating software process specification and enactment is not an easy task due to the complexity of the usage scenarios.

In general, many people enact on processes but few of them specify or model a software process.

In order to evaluate our approach and tool we have carried out different case studies in recent years in different contexts and scenarios. Our aim was to see if it was possible to specify MDD and MDT processes and understand and enact these processes using our approach and tool.

Except in the first case study we used some GQM-based (Goal-Question and Metric) assessment techniques. For the case studies we establish a main goal, pose some questions, draw up a scale for questions, answers and metrics concerning the goal. Each case study can encompass one or more scenarios. When the case study ended, a questionnaire was applied. Then the answers were recorded and analyzed. After each experiment we analyzed the artifacts produced in the process specification and enactment tasks.

Previous Case studies were detailed in (Maciel et al., 2006) and demonstrate our approach and tool feasibility. It is important to highlight that we have performed one case with a real company. Our latest case studies have encompassed different kinds of MDD and MDT scenarios: process specification, understanding a previously specified process and process enactment using the MoDErNE Envi-

ronment. Case Studies for Management process context have not been performed yet as these functionalities are still undergoing validation.

Case Study 1: MDD Process Authoring and Enactment

In this case study, the goal was to evaluate the applicability of the MoDErNE tool. This case encompasses two different scenarios. The first scenario was to verify MoDErNE Process Editor in relation its support for process specification and the second was to verify the MoDErNE Process Executor with regard to its support for process enactment.

The participants in this study were fourteen graduates working in the industry. Most of them were systems analysts working for software factories and banks.

First of all, we gave them some lectures about MDD concepts, technologies and also provided training on our approach and tool totaling 16 hours divided into 4 days in one week (4h/day). The questionnaire which was answered individually by each participant was divided in two parts: the first concerning the MoDErNE Process Editor regarding process specification and modeling;

Table 1. GQM summary for assessing MoDErNE Process specification

Goal	Question	Metric
(G1) Verify the applicability of the MoDErNE environment for process specification.	**(Q1.1)** Is it possible to clearly define the sequence of phases?	**(M1.1)** Degree of ease and comprehension to define process phases
	(Q1.2) Is it possible to clearly define the tasks?	**(M1.2)** Degree of ease and comprehension to define process tasks
	(Q1.3) Is it possible to clearly define the roles involved in each task?	**(M1.3)** Degree of ease and comprehension to define process roles and associate them with tasks
	(Q1.4) Is it possible to clearly define the workproducts and their (input/output) associations with the tasks?	**(M1.4)** Degree of ease and comprehension to define workproducts and associate them with tasks
	(Q1.5) Does the MoDErNE tool support process specification properly?	**(M1.5.1)** Degree of effort to put in the process specification using our tool
		(M1.5.2) Time spent on processes specification
		(M1.5.3) Degree of expected effort in the next process specification

and the second regarding the MoDErNE Process Executor.

Scenario 1: Assessing the Authoring of an MDD Process in MoDErNE Editor

In this case study scenario, our goal was also to evaluate the applicability of the MoDErNE environment regarding the MDD process specification without our intervention. We organized the students into 4 groups and asked them to specify an MDD process from their experience at work using the MoDErNE Process Editor. We gave them a deadline, but the specification time was not restricted. They had all the time they needed to organize themselves in their group to do the job and deliver the process. After the process specification the resulting process models were checked.

After process delivery, we also applied a questionnaire and started analyzing the process specification. The questionnaire had a total of 15 questions related to the (GQM) method for the generation of necessary metrics concerning our initial goals, some of which are detailed in Table 1. A GQM question can be related to one or more questionnaire answers, while the answer to a question is related to a GQM metric for a question. For metric measures, the answers with a rating scale were used (e.g. some effort, high effort, low effort, etc.). The collected results and our analysis are presented below.

The following figures show some results from questions regarding tool support in the MDD process specification. The charts in Figures 14, 15 and 16 show some results from the questionnaire. The first one (Figure 14) shows the answers to questions about the simplicity of defining tasks, roles, workproducts and phases, and are related to questions Q1.1 to Q1.4 from Table 1. The scale for the answer was 5 – Easily, 4 – Reasonably, 3 – Satisfactorily, but with some difficulty, 2 – Inadequate, 1 – Could not.

Most of the participants' answers demonstrated that it was possible to define all the process elements (Figure 14) despite many never having worked with the MDD approach, and some of them not having worked with a previously defined process. Besides the aspects discussed from the results summarized in the above charts and from analyzing the process models resulting from the experiment, it was also possible to observe that all the processes defined by the participants had well-defined modeling (CIM, PIM and PSM) and codification phases, including tasks and steps, role assignment, associated *workproducts* and also transformation rules. Therefore, it can be concluded that our approach and tool enabled process definition with the expected characteristics

Figure 14. Answers about the simplicity of defining tasks, roles, workproducts and phases

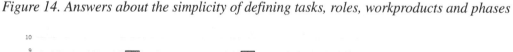
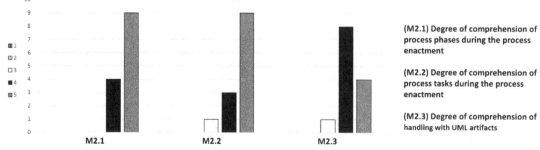

(M2.1) Degree of comprehension of process phases during the process enactment

(M2.2) Degree of comprehension of process tasks during the process enactment

(M2.3) Degree of comprehension of handling with UML artifacts

Figure 15. (a) Time and (b) Effort spent on process specification

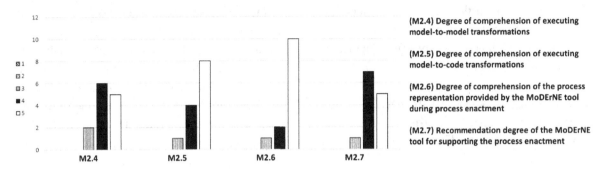

(M2.4) Degree of comprehension of executing model-to-model transformations

(M2.5) Degree of comprehension of executing model-to-code transformations

(M2.6) Degree of comprehension of the process representation provided by the MoDErNE tool during process enactment

(M2.7) Recommendation degree of the MoDErNE tool for supporting the process enactment

Figure 16. Answers about phases and task visualization and understanding

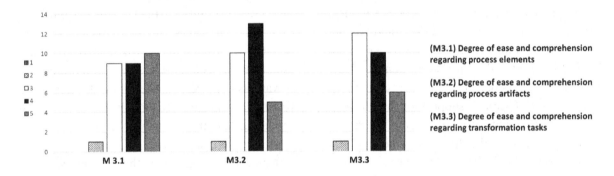

(M3.1) Degree of ease and comprehension regarding process elements

(M3.2) Degree of ease and comprehension regarding process artifacts

(M3.3) Degree of ease and comprehension regarding transformation tasks

of a traditional software process while also adding the peculiarities of an MDD process.

Figure 15 shows the results regarding adequate support for the MDD processes specification aspects in MoDErNE (Table 1, Q1.5, M1.5.1 and M1.5.2). To measure these aspects we asked three questions about the time and effort taken to perform the process specification tasks.

Figure 15(a) indicates that half of the participants spent less than eight hours in their group meetings for the process specification. Less than half spent more than eight hours and two participants did not answer the question. Figure 15(b) indicates that more than half of them considered that it took little effort while 42% of the participants thought it took considerable effort.

Regarding the degree of expected effort in the next process specification (M1.5.3), most of the participants (93%) agreed that the effort put into the process specification would not be repeated

in the future if they used the MoDErNE environment for specifying the new process. That is, the time spent learning the approach and tool would not be repeated. We also should consider that the process definitions in the method content remain available for reuse which will possibly reduce time and future effort in process specifications.

Some participants had difficulty understanding some process definitions as presented in the tool, however, none of them rated the process comprehension as presented in the tool negatively. The effort put into the process specification is valuable but necessary. Most of them classified such effort as reasonable but not enough to rate it as a negative point. Besides, part of that effort would not be repeated on future occasions when using the tool.

Considering such aspects as (i) the training time for both MDD approach and tool, (ii) students inexperience with process specification tasks, (iii) the resulting process models were well formed according to the XMI (XML Metadata Interchange) format, we can say that MoDErNE facilitated the MDD process specification task in the experimental scenario.

Scenario 2: Assessing an MDD Process Enactment in the MoDErNE Process Executor

In this scenario our goal was to evaluate the applicability of the MoDErNE environment regarding the MDD process enactment. A key point in the MDD process enactment is to produce models according the metamodel stereotypes and execute the transformations properly. Developers must know the exact task sequence to generate correct models and code. The case study goal was to observe MoDErNE's support for these tasks.

The participants were the same as in the first experiment in the third case study. In this experiment each participant had to enact several tasks (modeling and transformation) from the

MDA process for middleware service modeling to implement services for a school library management application. These services had to have operations to support book loans, namely, borrow a book, return a book, apply a fine, include, delete and update a book. The questionnaire had a total of 15 questions like the previous one described. These questions were related to GQM method for the generation of necessary questions and metrics concerning our goals, of which eight are detailed in Table 2. For the first six questions we used the following scale for participants to rate the issues: 5 – Easily, 4 – Reasonably, 3 - Satisfactorily, but with some difficulty, 2 – Inadequate, 1 - Could not.

Figure 16 shows the participants' answers about process phases and task visualization and understanding (Q2.1 to Q2.3). Most answered that it was easy and reasonable. They also answered that it was easy and reasonably easy to perform modeling and transformation tasks during the process enactment (Figure 17, Q2.4 through Q2.5). After process enactment, the artifacts (models and code) were checked. One participant failed

Table 2. GQM summary for assessing MoDErNE process enactment

(G2) Verify the applicability of the MoDErNE tool for process enactment.	**(Q2.1)** Is it possible to visualize and understand the process phases during the process enactment supported by the MoDErNE tool?	**(M2.1)** Degree of comprehension of process phases during the process enactment
	(Q2.2) Is it possible to visualize and understand the process tasks during the process enactment supported by the MoDErNE tool?	**(M2.2)** Degree of comprehension of process tasks during the process enactment
	(Q2.3) Is it possible to clearly create, edit and visualize the UML artifacts produced during the process?	**(M2.3)** Degree of comprehension of handling with UML artifacts
	(Q2.4) Is it possible to clearly execute the model-to-model transformations during the process enactment?	**(M2.4)** Degree of comprehension of executing model-to-model transformations
	(Q2.5) Is it possible to clearly execute the model-to-code transformations during the process enactment?	**(M2.5)** Degree of comprehension of executing model-to-code transformations
	(Q2.6) Is the process representation provided by the MoDErNE tool during the process enactment easy to understand?	**(M2.6)** Degree of comprehension of the process representation provided by the MoDErNE tool during process enactment
	(Q2.7) What is your general impression of the MoDErNE tool for the process enactment?	**(M2.7)** Recommendation degree of the MoDErNE tool for supporting the processes enactment.

Figure 17. Answers about transformation tasks, process representation and general impressions

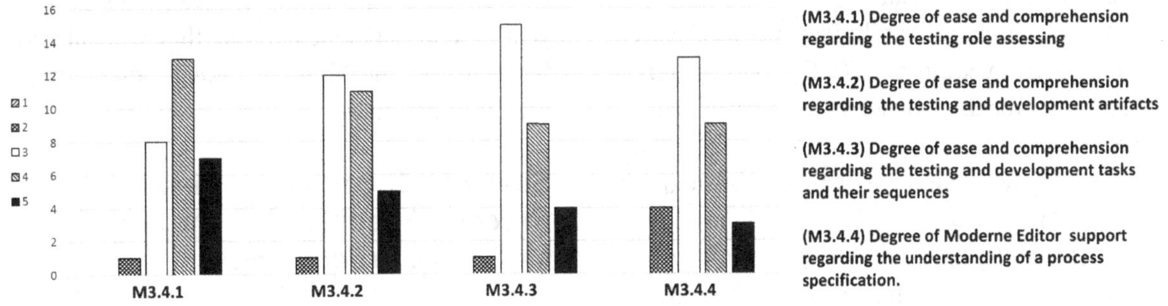

(M3.4.1) Degree of ease and comprehension regarding the testing role assessing

(M3.4.2) Degree of ease and comprehension regarding the testing and development artifacts

(M3.4.3) Degree of ease and comprehension regarding the testing and development tasks and their sequences

(M3.4.4) Degree of Moderne Editor support regarding the understanding of a process specification.

to generate the models correctly and therefore it was not possible to generate service code.

Q 2.6 (Figure 17) shows the answers about the MoDErNE process representation. As explained in section 3, process elements can be visualized through UML diagrams or breakdown structures. While UML diagrams give more details about tasks and artifacts, it is easier to find and access process elements in a breakdown structure.

The last question, regarding their general impression of MoDErNE (Q 2.7 of Figure 17) we used a different scale: 5 - Extremely positive, 4 - Positive with few restrictions, 3 - Positive, but with important restrictions, 2 - Negative. A few positive points I could find, 1 - Extremely negative. I did not see a positive side. The majority evaluated the MoDErNE tool support for process enactment extremely positively or positively with some restrictions. Some open answers show that there were some bugs in the tool presented.

Considering that the participants in the experiment were new to the model-driven approach and the service models and the code were correct, we can say that MoDErNE facilitated the MDA process enactment tasks in this case study scenario.

Case Study 2: MDD and MDT Process Understanding and Enactment

In this case study we had the largest number of participants: twenty-nine. We set up a scenario to observe the tool support for a process that used both MDD and MDT techniques. The case study encompassed two scenarios: (i) one to understand a process previously specified in the MoDErNE Editor and (ii) the second to enact this process in the MoDErNE Executor.

The process used in this case study was an abbreviated version of the MDA process for middleware service modeling in which new tasks to test the service were included. The new resulting process contained only modeling, transformation and testing tasks. The specified process contained eight tasks for modeling, implementation and testing of middleware services, 4 of which were transformation tasks (CIM-PIM, PIM-PSM, PSM-code, Test Model → JUnit). In this case, the domain being modeled was for a banking application with operations for withdrawal, deposit and obtaining account balances.

The case study was divided into four moments. Initially a one and a half hour lecture was given highlighting MoDErNE's features, showing examples of use. Then the participants had to use the MoDErNE Process Editor followed by the

MoDErNE Process Executor and finally they had to answer the questionnaire.

The questionnaire was divided into three parts with a total of 25 questions. The first part with five questions was designed to identify the participants' experience and professional profiles. The other questions were about the metrics established for the experiment using GQM. The scale used was 5 – Easily, 4 – Reasonably, 3 – Satisfactorily, but with some difficulty, 2 – Inadequate, 1 – Could not.

The participants were students and staff invited from two different universities: the Federal University of Bahia (UFBA) and the Federal University of Campina Grande (UFCG). With regard to their

experience, sixty percent described themselves as systems analysts with experience from four to six years. Eighty percent said that they were already familiar with the MDD approach, but had never used it in practice.

Scenario 1: Understanding a Process Specification through MoDErNE Process Editor

In the first scenario from the first case study described here, participants browsed through the process specification in the MoDErNE Editor in order to understand the process elements and the

Table 3. GQM summary for assessing MoDErNE Process specification

Goal	Question	Metric
(G3) Verify the understanding of a previously specified process in the MoDErNE tool	**(Q3.1)** Is it possible to clearly identify the process phases, task and roles?	**(M3.1)** Degree of eases and comprehension regarding process elements
	(Q3.2) Is it possible to clearly identify the artifacts input and output?	**(M3.2)** Degree of ease and comprehension regarding process artifacts
	(Q3.3) Is it possible to clearly identify the transformation tasks?	**(M3.3)** Degree of ease and comprehension regarding transformation tasks
	(Q3.4) Does MoDErNE Editor tool support MDD and MDT process specification properly?	**(M3.4.1)** Degree of ease and comprehension regarding the testing role assessing
		(M3.4.2) Degree of ease and comprehension regarding the testing and development artifacts
		(M3.4.3) Degree of ease and comprehension regarding the testing and development tasks and their sequences
		(M3.4.4) Degree of MoDErNE Editor support regarding the understanding of a process specification.

Figure 18. Answers about process element comprehension

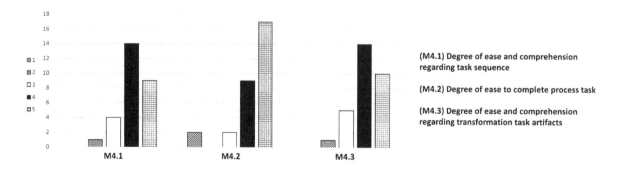

(M4.1) Degree of ease and comprehension regarding task sequence

(M4.2) Degree of ease to complete process task

(M4.3) Degree of ease and comprehension regarding transformation task artifacts

Figure 19. Answers about implementing and testing process elements comprehension

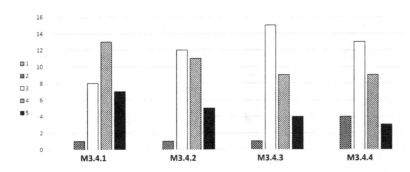

(M3.4.1) Degree of ease and comprehension regarding the testing role assessing

(M3.4.2) Degree of ease and comprehension regarding the testing and development artifacts

(M3.4.3) Degree of ease and comprehension regarding the testing and development tasks and their sequences

(M3.4.4) Degree of Moderne Editor support regarding the understanding of a process specification.

task that they would perform later. Soon after completing each experiment, the participants answered a questionnaire available on the web. Table 3 shows the questions and corresponding metrics.

Figure 18 shows the answers to questions Q3.1 to Q3.3 in Table 3. Although it was the participants first contact with MoDErNE, they answered that they did not have difficulty identifying the phase, tasks, roles, workproducts and transformation rule process elements. As the process mixes both implementation and testing tasks we wanted to observe if the participants could distinguish the testing tasks from the others. Figure 19 shows the answers about these aspects (Q3.4 question 4), most answered that this distinction could be made.

From the answers it can be said that the MoDErNE Editor made the understanding of the implementation and testing activities in this

case study possible. While they were browsing the process specification some doubts arose, for example, where to find the button to generate some workflow task diagram. This observation and other similar ones indicate that we have to improve our graphic interface in order to make it more user-friendly.

Scenario 2: Assessing Testing and Development Software Process Tasks through MoDErNE Executor

After the process description and brief contact we wanted to observe if the participants would be able to perform the assigned tasks. First the participants had to create the CIM model of the application, which contains the business process representation. Then, they had to execute the first tasks related to the transformation chain, making

Table 4. GQM summary for assessing MoDErNE Process Enactment

Goal	Question	Metric
(G4)Verify the applicability of the MoDErNE Executor module for process enactment for integrated process.	(Q4.1)Is it possible to follow the task sequence?	(M4.1) Degree of ease and comprehension regarding task sequence
	(Q4.2) Is it possible to perform all the process tasks?	(M4.2) Degree of ease to complete process task
	(Q4.3) Is it possible to clearly visualize the transformation task input and output artifacts?	(M4.3) Degree of ease and comprehension regarding transformation task artifacts
	(Q4.4)Does MoDErNE environment support MDD and MDT process enactment properly?	(M4.4.1) impression for process enactment facilitation
		(M4.4.2) Possibility of carrying out the process without the tool.

Figure 20. Answers about the process task enactment

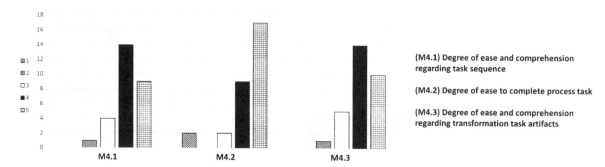

(M4.1) Degree of ease and comprehension regarding task sequence

(M4.2) Degree of ease to complete process task

(M4.3) Degree of ease and comprehension regarding transformation task artifacts

CIM to PIM and PIM to PSM transformations. On completion of the PIM to PSM transformations, the participants had to execute the first testing activity which was to create models stereotyped with U2TP to represent the unit test cases with the PSM model as input. This test case generates the application's unit test case codes for the JUnit platform by a MOFScript transformation rule. The last task was to generate the application code by applying another MOFScript transformation to the PSM model which had previously been generated.

In the text we did not detail the MDT technique to adopt in the processes. The participants performed the modeling tasks, model to model and model to code transformation tasks without our intervention. However, to perform the transformation testing task a template of a model test artifact was given to the participants. They had to complete the model with U2TP stereotypes and then had to perform the transformations to generate the test cases for the JUnit platform. After this, they had to answer the questionnaire presented in Table 4.

Figure 20 shows the answers to questions Q4.1 to Q4.3 in Table 4. Most participants could follow the task sequence and performed all the tasks and visualized the artifacts associated to the transformation tasks. Two participants could not perform all the tasks. One of them reported that they could not perform the testing tasks. Another could not finish the process specification browsing activity on time, therefore he did not perform any task. During the process task enactment, some

questions were asked about the correctness of the models. Participants were a little insecure about performing transformation tasks without being sure that their models were correct. The Modeling task has some tool support for UML profile stereotype application. If a UML diagram has an associated profile, by clicking the right button on the mouse, one stereotype from a list can be chosen. This shows the only stereotype that can be applied to each UML diagram element. However, the participants wanted to check not only that the diagram was "syntactically correct" but also about its semantic correctness. At the time they were informed that they could see this semantic correctness after the transformation task, if the output model or code was generated correctly. However, in a longer transformation chain, an error in a stereotype application could be hard to find.

Regarding their impressions about the process enactment (M 4.4.1) most participants (87%) agreed that MoDErNE tool makes the process execution easier and 96.7% of them agreed that they would not have been able to execute the process without MoDErNE's help (M 4.4.2). It can be said that this tool supported MDD and MDT process enactment properly in this case study.

Case Studies: Lessons Learned and Study Constraints

The MDD approach has been used in our research laboratory in various projects (Bispo et al., 2010;

Maciel & ferraz, 2005; Magalhães et al., 2011). Initially we specified a process in a completely ad-hoc way, using natural language. After much research, trying to use and adapt some tools for our process transformation without success, an engine using the Java language to perform the transformations was developed. With our experience in the specification and use of MDD processes and studies that indicate the need for adequate processes and tools as a key point to facilitate the use of MDD, MoDErNE was proposed and developed.

The case studies were designed to evaluate specific aspects of model-driven development using MoDErNE: (i) the specification and enactment of a process, (ii) the integration and use of different strategies for testing and model driven languages and transformation engines, (iii) the understanding of previously specified process.

The first three case studies showed positive results in the specification and implementation of model-driven processes while the fourth shows positive results regarding process understanding using MoDErNE tool. Process enactment also obtained positive results. It is important to highlight that in one case study the proposed scenario is related to the integration of two different strategies in the same process. Despite this, the participants could understand the process, distinguished development and testing activities as well as executing them.

Empirical assessment usually takes into account the amount of data collected from the subjects. However, in the case of a process specification activity it is difficult to involve a high number of people in the experiments. There are few professionals in organizations involved in this kind of work. In general, many people enact on processes but few specify or model a software process. This observation was identified in our previous studies and it is also confirmed here. Empirical assessment in this area facilitates more qualitative analysis than quantitative analysis. Therefore, in the assessment of the process enactment it is easier to collect larger amounts of data,

facilitating better quantitative analysis in contrast to assessing process specification. Furthermore, in real scenarios developers perform specific tasks (requirement elicitation, programming, testing, etc.) in a software process, few are involved in different types of tasks. In addition, the MDT and MDD approaches require skills not yet required in traditional process software.

Additionally, metrics to assess the process enactment are more mature in the literature and are also easier to apply in the software industry, they include metrics to evaluate productivity and cost. Nevertheless, metrics to assess process modeling and specification (apart from its enactment) need further development.

We should also highlight that the conclusions obtained from our studies are restricted to the particular set of participants. In other words, our analysis regarding the advantages and drawbacks of using our approach and tool can not be directly generalized to other contexts. However, these studies have allowed us to make useful assessments about whether the specification and enactment of MDD processes with a supporting tool is worth studying further. In addition, the studies have also allowed us to make a useful evaluation of the applicability of the MoDErNE tool concerning the specification and enactment of MDD processes, and this can be a starting point for other assessments.

FUTURE RESEARCH DIRECTIONS

Software development is not a trivial task. In this context, some software supports carrying out software development activities as they automate and systematize the work. Software development focusing on coding does not achieve the results of process productivity and product quality. Although modeling activity helps the understanding of the system and potentially improves product quality, it can be costly when models are only used as an artifact for documentation without relating to the system code. If there is no relation between system's code and its models, code will be the only updated software artifact after several evolutions. The complexity of today's software requires mechanisms that help developers to understand software architecture and information to continue to evolve properly.

The MDE approach is helping this scenario as it proposes automation of software process activities, as models and codes are generated through transformations. Thus, these artifacts are still related and updated, facilitating software evolution.

Despite being a very promising for some software engineering issues and the fact that it has attracted great interest from academia, MDE is currently little used in practice by industry. Much remains to be done to promote its widespread use. Support tools are essential to MDE, but the first generation of these tools have failed to give adequate support.

Transformation engines are difficult to customize and have little flexibility to fit in software development processes that are currently used in companies, while the development of transformation requires expertise not yet widely available in the market. Research proposing strategies to facilitate transformation implementation, bi-directional transformations and traceability among artifacts through transformation chain will certainly be of great help to the use of this approach by industry.

CONCLUSION

This chapter presented MoDErNE, an environment that supports software process modeling and enactment based on SPEM 2 concepts for the MDD approach. In MoDErNE, the software process should be specified as an instance of metamodels that describes software process elements that make MDD and MDT concepts

explicit. MoDErNE possesses several tools to support different kinds of activities in the MDD and MDT process context. The MDD requires some developer skills, which are not yet widely used in traditional software processes (metamodeling, transformations, etc.). Supporting tools play an important part in establishing MDD use in industry on a wider scale.

In MoDErNE, once a process is specified, it could be used in the development of several different application projects. Different methods and techniques can be specified and integrated into a single process description and then customized to its own needs. Using our environment the software process specification has the same conceptual and notational framework. The proposed metamodels become a point of convergence for process integration, specification and enactment. This facilitates the understanding of models both by development teams and by software process automation. Using MDD and process-centered software engineering concepts in a combined way can help software process systematization and automation. In this scenario, we expect that software processes can be used as software itself. As software, it has a specification and automated support for performing tasks. Final users (developers) can run these tasks several times, at different moments to achieve business process goals, which in this context is the development of an application.

Although the management metamodel is integrated in the environment, its functionalities are under validation and it was not possible to include them in the recent case studies. Several case studies were performed and it was possible to verify the applicability of our environment. As future work, we are planning to conduct case studies with different software processes proposed in the literature, broadening the scope of evaluation for different MDD approaches.

REFERENCES

Alves, E. L. G., Machado, P. D. L., & Ramalho, F. (2008). Uma abordagem integrada para desenvolvimento e teste dirigido por modelos. In *Proceedings of the 2nd Brazilian Workshop on Systematic and Automated Software Testing* (pp. 74–83). Campinas.

Ambriola, V., Conradi, R., & Fuggetta, A. (1997). Assessing Process-centered Software Engineering Environments. *ACM Transaction on Software Engineering and Methodoloty, 283-328.*

Arbaoui, S. et al. (2002). A comparative review of Process-Centered Software Engineering Environments. *Annals of Software Engineering, 14.*

Atkinson, C., Fraunhofer, I., Kaiserslautern Paech, B., Reinhold, J., & Sander, T. (2001). Developing and applying component-based model-driven architectures. In *Proceedings of the Enterprise Distributed Object Computing Conference (EDOC '01)*. Seattle, WA: EDOC.

Baker, P., Dai, Z., Grabowski, J., Haugen, O., Schieferdecker, I., & Williams, C. (2007). *Model-driven testing: Using UML testing profile.* New York: Springer-Verlag New York Inc.

Bézivin, J., Buttner, F., Gagolla, M., & Jouault, F. Kurtev, & Lindow, A. (2006). Model Transformations? Transformation Models? Berlin: Springer-Verlag.

Bispo, C. P., Maciel, R. S. P., David, J., Ribeiro, I., & Conceição, R. (2010). Applying a Model-Driven Process for a Collaborative Service-Oriented Architecture. In *Proceedings of the 14th International Conference on Computer Supported Cooperative Work in Design* (pp. 378-383). Shangai, China: Academic Press.

Bouquet, F., Grandpierre, C., Legeard, B., & Peureux, F. (2008). A test generation solution to automate software testing. In *Proceedings of the 3rd international workshop on Automation of software test* (pp. 45-48). Leipzig, Germany: Academic Press.

Brambilla, M., Cabot, J., & Wimmer, M. (2012). *Model-driven software Engineering in Practice.* Morgan & Claypool Publichers.

Cass, A. G., Lerner, B. S., Sutton, S. M., McCall, E. K., Wise, A., & Osterweil, L. J. (2000). Little-JIL/Juliette: A Process Definition Language and Interpreter. In *Proceedings of the 22nd International Conference on Software Engineering.* Limerick, Ireland: Academic Press.

Engels, G., Schäfer, W., Balzer, R., & Gruhn, V. (2001). Process-centered software engineering environments: academic and industrial perspectives. In *Proceedings of the 23rd International Conference on Software Engineering (ICSE '01)* (pp. 671-673). Washington, DC: IEEE Computer Society.

France, R., & Rumpe, B. (2007). Model-driven development of complex software: A research roadmap. In *Proceedings of Future of Software 2007 (FOSE'07)* (pp. 35-54). Washington, DC: IEEE Computer Society.

Gomes, R., Maciel, R., Silva, B., Silva, F., & Magalhães, A. (2011). MoDErNE: Model Driven Process Centered Software Engineering Environment. In *Proceedings of the II Brazilian Conference on Software: Theory and Practice, Tools Session.* São Paulo. Brazil: Academic Press.

Gruhn, V. (2002). Process-Centered Software Engineering Environments: A Brief History and Future Challenges. *Annals of Software Engineering, 14,* 363–382. doi:10.1023/A:1020522111961

Guelfi, N., et al. (2003). DRIP Catalyst: An MDE/MDA Method for Fault-tolerant Distributed Software Families Development. In *Proceedings of the Workshop on Best Practices for Model Driven Software Development.* Academic Press.

Hartmann, J., Vieira, M., & Axel Ruder, H. (2004). *UML-based test generation and execution* (White paper). Siemens Corporate Research.

Humprey, W., & Kelner, M. (1989). *Software Modeling: Principles of Entity Process Models*. Carnegie Mellon University.

Hutchinson, J., Rouncefield, M., & Whittle, J. (2011). Model-driven Engineering practices in industry. In *Proceedings of the 33rd International Conference on Software Engineering (ICSE '11)* (pp. 633-642). Waikiki, HI: IEEE.

Hutchinson, J., Whittle, J., Rouncefield, M., & Kristoffersen, S. (2011). Empirical assessment of MDE in industry. In *Proceedings of the 33rd International Conference on Software Engineering (ICSE '11)* (pp. 471-480). Waikiki, HI: ICSE.

IEEE. (2008). *IEEE Standard for Software and System Test Documentation (IEEE Std 829-2008)*. IEEE Computer Society.

Javed, A., Strooper, P., & Watson, G. (2007). Automated generation of test cases using modeldriven architecture. In *Proceedings of the 2nd International Workshop on Automation of Software Test (AST)*. Minneapolis, MN: AST.

Koch, N. (2006). Transformation Techniques in the Model-Driven Development Process of UWE. In *Proceedings of the 6th International Conference on Web Engineering*. Palo Alto, CA: ACM.

Lima, A., et al. (2006). Gerência Flexível de Processos de Software com o Ambiente WebAPSEE. In *Proceedings of the 20th Brazilian Symposium on Software Engineering*. Florianópolis, Brasil: Academic Press.

Maciel, R., Gomes, R., & Silva, B. (2011). On the Use of Model-Driven Test Process Specification and Enactment by Metamodelling Foundation. In *Proceedings of the International Conference Applied Computing* (pp. 51-58). Rio de Janeiro, Brazil: Academic Press.

Maciel, R., Silva, B., Magalhães, A. P., & Rosa, N. (2009). An integrated approach for model driven process modeling and enactment. In *Proceedings of the XXIII Software Engineering Brazilian Symposium* (pp. 104-114). Fortaleza, Brazil: Academic Press.

Maciel, R., Silva, B. C., & Mascarenhas, L. A. (2006). An Edoc-based Approach for Specific Middleware Services Development. In *Proceedings of the 4th Workshop on Computer Based Systems* (pp. 135–143). Postdam, Germany: Academic Press.

Maciel, R. S. P., & Ferraz, C. (2005). InterDoc: Reference Architecture for Interoperable Services in Collaborative Writing Environments. In *Proceedings of 9th International Conference on Computer Supported Cooperative Work in Design (CSCWD 2005)* (pp. 289-295). Coventry, UK: CSCWD.

Magalhães, A. P., David, J. M. N., Maciel, R. S. P., Silva, B. C., & Silva, F. A. (2011). Modden: An Integrated Approach for Model Driven Development and Software Product Line Processes. In *Proceedings of the V Brazilian Symposium on Software Components, Architectures and Reuse (SBCARS 2011)* (pp. 21-30). Sao Paulo, Brazil: SBCARS.

Mellor, S. et al. (2004). *MDA Distilled*. Addison Wesley.

Mingsong, C., Xiaokang, Q., & Xuandong, L. (2006). Automatic test case generation for UML activity diagrams. In *Proceedings of the International Workshop on Automation of software test* (pp. 2-8). Shangai, China: Academic Press.

Mohagheghi, P., & Dehlen, V. (n.d.). Where Is the Proof? - A Review of Experiences from Applying MDE in Industry. In *Proceedings of the 4th European conference on Model Driven Architecture*, (pp. 432-443). Berlin, Germany: Springer-Verlag.

Mussa, M., Ouchani, S., Sammane, W., & Hamou-Lhadj, A. (2009). A survey of model-driven testing techniques. In *Proceedings of Ninth International Conference on Quality Software* (pp. 167-172). Jeju, South Korea: Academic Press.

OMG. (2003). *MDA Guide: Version 1.0.1*. Retrieved from omg/2003-06-01

OMG. (2005). *UML 2.0 Testing Profile, Final Adopted Specification Version 1.0*. Retrived July, 2005, from http://www.omg.org/spec/UTP/1.0/ IEEE 2008

OMG. (2008). *Software Process Engineering Metamodel Specification, Version 2.0*. OMG.

Open, U. P. (2008). *OpenUP component – MDD*. Retrieved from http://www.eclipse.org/epf/openup_component/mdd. php

Reza, M., & Raman, R. (2012). An Analytical Review of Process-Centered Software Engineering Environments. In *Proceedings of the 19th International Conference and Workshops on Engineering of Computer-Based Systems* (pp. 64-73). Novi Sabi, Serbia: Academic Press.

Samba, D., Lbath, R., & Coulette, B. (2011). Specification and Implementation of SPEM-4MDE, a metamodel for MDE software processes. In *Proceedings of the 23rd International Conference on Software Engineering Knowledge Engineering (SEKE'2011)* (pp. 646-653). Miami Beach, FL: SEKE.

Silva, B. C., Magalhães, A. P., Maciel, R. S. P., Martins, N., & Nogueira, L. (2009). Transforms: Um Ambiente de Apoio a Modelagem e Execução de Processos de Software Dirigido por Modelos. In *Proceedings of the XXIII Brazilian Symposium on Software Engineering, Tools Session*. Fortaleza, Brazil: Academic Press.

Wang, H., & Zhang, D. (2003). MDA-based Development of E-Learning System. In *Proceedings of the 27th International Computer Software and Applications Conference* (pp. 684-689). IEEE Press.

Weber, S., Emrich, A., Broschart, J., Ras, E., & Ünalan, Ö. (2009). Supporting Software Development Teams with a Semantic Process and Artifact-oriented Collaboration Environment. In *Proceedings of the Collaboration and Knowledge Sharing in Software Development Teams*. Kaiserslautern, Germany: Academic Press.

Yuan, Q., Wu, J., Liu, C., & Zhang, Z. (2008). A model driven approach toward business process test case generation. In *Proceedings of the 10th International Symposium on Web Site Evolution (WSE)* (pp. 41–44). Beijing, China: WSE.

Zamli, K. Z., Mat Isa, N. A., & Khamis, N. (2005). The Design And Implementation Of The VRPML Support Environments. *Malaysian Journal of Computer Science*, *18*(1), 57–69.

ADDITIONAL READING

Basili, V., Caldiera, G., & Rombach, H. (1994). *The Goal Question Metric Approach*. Retrieved 2008-11-12.

El-far, I. K., |& Whittaker, J. A. (2001). *Model-based software testing*. Encyclopedia on Software Engineering.

Solingen, R., & Berghout, E. (1999). *The Goal/Question/Metric Method*. McGraw-Hill Education.

(2006). Taba Workstation: Supporting Software Process Deployment Based on CMMI and MR-MPS.BR. In Montoni, M. et al. (Eds.), *Proceedings of Product-Focused Software Process Improvement* (pp. 249–262). Springer.

KEY TERMS AND DEFINITIONS

MDA: The OMG's particular vision of MDD and thus relies on the use of OMG standards.

MDE: A software development methodology which focuses on creating and exploiting domain models, rather than on the computing concepts.

Metamodel: The language and processes from which to form a model.

Model-Driven Development: A development paradigm that uses models as the primary artifact of the development process.

Model-Driven Testing: A model-based testing that follows Model Driven Engineering paradigm.

Process Centered Software Engineering: A comprehensive theoretical basis for the purpose of understanding, describing and enhancing specific software process.

Profile: A generic extension mechanism for customizing UML models for particular domains and platforms.

Software Process: A framework for a set of Key Process Areas (KPAs) that must be established for effective delivery of software engineering technology.

Software Process Model: An abstraction of the actual process which is being described.

Transformation: Generating a model from another, using a set of transformation rules that describe how this model can be transformed.

Chapter 10
A Model–Driven Solution for the Automatic Generation of Executable Code from Business Process Models

Javier Fabra
University of Zaragoza, Spain

Verónica Andrea Bollati
Rey Juan Carlos University, Spain

Valeria de Castro
Rey Juan Carlos University, Spain

Pedro Álvarez
University of Zaragoza, Spain

Esperanza Marcos
Rey Juan Carlos University, Spain

ABSTRACT

The business goals of an enterprise process are traced to business process models with the aim of being carried out during the execution stage. The automatic translation from these models to fully executable code that can be simulated and round-trip engineered is still an open challenge in the Business Process Management field. Model-driven Engineering has proposed a set of methodologies to solve the existing gap between business analysts and software developers, but the expected results have not been reached yet. In order to rise to this challenge, in this chapter the authors propose a solution based on the integration of three previous proposals: SOD-M, DENEB, and MeTAGeM. On the one hand, SOD-M is a model-driven method for the development of service-oriented systems. Business analysts can use SOD-M to transform their business goals into composition service models, a type of model that represents business processes. On the other hand, DENEB is a platform for the development and execution of flexible business processes, represented by means of workflow models. The authors' approach focuses on the automatic transformation of SOD-M models to DENEB workflow models, resulting in a business process that is coded by a class of high-level Petri-nets, and it is directly executable in DENEB. The model transformation process has been automated using the MeTAGeM tool, which automatically generates the set of ATL rules required to transform SOD-M models to DENEB workflows. Finally, the integration of the three proposals has been illustrated by means of a real system related to the management of medical images.

DOI: 10.4018/978-1-4666-6026-7.ch010

1. INTRODUCTION

In recent years, rapid development in the field of Web service technologies and Service-Oriented Computing (SOC) has created an interest in the area of Business Process Management (BPM) (Watson, 2008). BPM has broadened to become a set of technologies and standards for the design, execution, administration and monitoring of business processes, and also as a way of dealing with frequent changes in business and value chains (Watson, 2008; Havey, 2005). In conceptual terms, a business process is a defined set of activities that represents the steps required to achieve a business objective (OMG, 2011). In BPM terminology, an activity can be seen as the work of a person, an internal system, a service provided by an external entity or the process of a partner company.

The motivation in BPM and Service Oriented Architectures (SOA) areas has also led to the emergence of several languages for the design and implementation of such processes. The Web Services Business Process Execution Language, WS-BPEL (BPEL, 2011), is a standard language widely used for the specification of executable business processes. However, WS-BPEL and most of the current existing approaches for the specification of processes have some relevant problems: i) it is difficult for business analysts to use them in the early stages of the development process (Verner, 2004) (analysis and modeling stages); ii) they are dependent on a specific implementation technology (more specifically, on the Web service technology) and, finally, iii) the lack of formal semantics that permit process analysis. These problems increase the gap between business analysts and software developers, which leads to serious limitations in the BPM field.

The evolution of the Business Process Model and Notation standard, BPMN 2.0 (OMG, 2011), was published as a future means to reduce this gap. The informal formalization of the execution semantics for all BPMN elements and the independence of specific implementation tech-

nologies proposed by the specification will solve the first two problems associated with previous approaches. Nevertheless, this promising proposal lacks formal semantics and needs time to mature. The aforementioned gap is, therefore, still open.

In order to overcome these limitations, the Web Engineering field has proposed a set of methodologies that make it easier to develop service-oriented systems based on current technologies. Model-driven Development (MDD) is a development methodology that is principally characterized by the use of models as a product (Selic, 2003). MDD is a subset of Model-driven Engineering (MDE) (Schmidt, 2006) because, as the E in MDE suggests, MDE goes beyond pure development activities and encompasses the other model-based tasks of a complete software engineering process (Ameller, 2009). Model-driven Architecture (MDA) (Miller & Mukerji, 2003) is the particular MDD methodology defined by the Object Management Group (OMG) and therefore relies on the use of OMG standards. More specifically, MDA offers an open, vendor neutral approach with which to master technological changes and provides a conceptual structure for: (i) specifying a system independently of the platform that supports it; (ii) choosing a particular platform for the system; (iii) specifying a system including platforms details; and (iv) transforming the system specification into the corresponding code for a particular target platform (i.e., moving the system specification to the technological one). Therefore, the two most relevant features of MDD methodologies are: the provision of models with which to cover the different stages involved in the design of a system, and the definition of models which are explicitly separated from implementation technologies and execution platform details.

However, after several years of the popularization of MDA proposals and the appearance of many MDD approaches for software development, the usefulness of these approaches is questionable (Selic, 2003). The main controversy is related to the lack of support in the automatic generation of code from models. Ideally, technological frameworks should be able to transform models into executable code and then execute the resulting code without human intervention (Selic, 2008). Automatic code generation has traditionally been restricted to the generation of code skeletons and fragments, requiring human intervention to complete them. In order to overcome the limitation imposed by this kind of automation, modeling and implementation languages should converge to facilitate the generation of complete programs. Moreover, the code generated could also be used for the automatic verification of models on a computer. This signifies checking that the requirements fulfill the business goals and that there are no undesirable properties in the models. From an empirical point of view, model verification can be based on the simulation of generated programs (Selic, 2003). Nevertheless, more powerful and formal analysis methods and techniques should be integrated into MDA approaches to verify a system's model (model checking or logical inference, for instance). Code generation therefore emerges as a key element if the usefulness of MDA solutions is to be achieved in different stages of the development of a software system.

In this work we present a solution for the automatic generation of executable code from business process models. The resulting code is generated without human intervention and it is directly executable by a concrete business workflow engine. More specifically, our solution integrates three previous approaches: SOD-M, DENEB, and MeTAGeM. From the point of view of MDD, the Service-Oriented Development Method, SOD-M (De Castro et al., 2009), defines a model-driven method for the development of service-oriented information systems. The key concept in SOD-M is the use of composition service models, which are equivalent to business process models, to represent the Platform independent Model (PIM) level of a system. On the other hand, from an execution point of view, the platform for the Development and Execution of iNteroperable dynamic wEB

processes, DENEB (Fabra et al., 2011), provides an environment for the deployment and execution of business processes. Our integration proposal therefore consists of automatically translating SOD-M composition models into business processes that are directly executable by DENEB. With regard to existing approaches our proposal presents three relevant contributions in connection with the resulting business processes: firstly, they are completely generated without human intervention; secondly, they can integrate a wide variety of implementation technologies (not only Web services); and, finally, they have formal semantics (a class of high-level Petri-nets has been used to code DENEB processes), and could therefore be analyzed by using formal analysis techniques (Ibáñez et al., 2008a, 2008b).

In order to transform the SOD-M models automatically to DENEB processes we have used the MeTAGeM framework (Bollati, et. al., 2013). This framework has been built from the integration of existing projects supported by Eclipse (Eclipse, 2011), such the ATLAS Transformation Language (ATL) (Jouault & Kurtev, 2005) and the Eclipse Modeling Framework (EMF) (Biermann et al., 2008; Steinberg et al., 2008). From a functional point of view, MeTAGeM allows us to define models in different Domain Specific Languages (DSLs), to specify high-level and language-independent model transformations, and, finally, to generate the set of rules required to execute automatically model transformations.

The remainder of this chapter is structured as follows. Section 2 presents the main work related to the BPM modeling area, the execution of business processes and code generation from business process models. In Section 3, the foundations of the underlying approaches are introduced. The proposed model-driven solution in this work is sketched in Section 4, and their implementation by means of the MeTAGeM tool is presented in Section 5. Further details about Domain-Specific Languages (DSL) and about the generation of the model transformation implemented in this work are also presented in that section. The application of the proposal is then illustrated in Section 6 by means of a real use case related to the management of medical images. Finally, Section 7 concludes the chapter and addresses our future work.

2. BACKGROUND

In this section the role of MDA in the BPM–SOA combination is presented, and the key points in which MDA helps and improves in the whole process are described. Several BPM standards have been proposed for their application to the different levels of MDA in order to enhance its benefits. The most relevant ones, and the most important transformation approaches to generate executable business process models, are also depicted here.

2.1. The Role of MDA in the BPM and SOA Combination

Service-oriented development has recently become one of the major research topics in the field of software engineering, which has even led to the appearance of a new and emerging discipline called Service Engineering (SE). Service Engineering aims to bring together the benefits of SOA and BPM initiatives. The BPM and SOA combination has been proposed as the best approach to achieve a closed alignment between business processes and IT resources. This combination enables the rapid development of agile processes that can respond to changes in business requirements.

However, BPM and SOA represent two different initiatives. BPM is mainly a management discipline and strategy that endorses the idea that a business can be modeled in terms of its end-to-end processes which cut across organizational and system boundaries. These processes are then represented in a manner that computers can understand and process (Brunswick, 2008; Frye, 2006). On the other hand, SOA looks for a better business process alignment with service protocols, legacy applica-

tions and software components, i.e., it comprises an organizational paradigm that is supported by the underlying IT infrastructure. Moreover, BPM is a business driven, project-oriented and top-down approach, whereas SOA uses an IT-driven, enterprise infrastructure-oriented one. SOA can also be a top-down (when based on portfolio management and service analysis and design) or a bottom-up approach (Kamoun, 2007). Finally, BPM reuses process models, whereas SOA reuses service implementations, being more dependent on technological issues.

Fortunately, BPM and SOA have evolved over time to be applied together, becoming two sides of the same coin (Frye, 2006). SOA assists in BPM proliferation, allowing processes modeled using BPM tools to be implemented quickly using the loosely coupled and agile infrastructure of SOA. On the other hand, BPM provides SOA with a wide and strong business-case, facilitating the close alignment between business and IT. The combination of BPM and SOA would reduce the investment, development and maintenance costs, since both initiatives encourage the loose coupling and spreading of internal and external applications across a distributed technology platform (Selic, 2008).

The OMG group has recently proposed the use of its MDA architecture as a means to model processes and services based on a platform-independent approach (OMG, 2010; Miller & Mukerji, 2003). According to Watson (2008), the convergence of SE with MDE represents one of the most important frameworks to hold out the promise of rapid and accurate development of software that serves software users' goals. By using MDA, complete SOA solutions can be developed through models, thus avoiding investment in specific technologies and protocols (De Castro et al., 2006). The Service Oriented Architecture SIG group (SOA ABSIG) coordinates the SOA standardization efforts between the OMG and other SOA standards groups such as the W3C, OASIS or the Open Group (OMG, 2009). Its aims are to promote a faster adoption of SOA-specific modeling approaches and best practices and to support an MDA approach to SOA that links architectural, business and technological views of services.

2.2. BPM Standards Applied to MDA

MDA proposes the use of different models to represent the different points of view of a system, from the higher abstraction level to the concrete technological level, namely: Computation Independent Model level (CIM), Platform Independent Model (PIM) level and Platform Specific Model (PSM) level (Miller & Mukerji, 2003). In the specific case of BPM, several business process-related language proposals have been proposed in relation to the different MDA stages (Ko et al., 2009; Roser & Bauer, 2005).

At the top level (CIM level), the Business Process Modeling Notation v1.1 (BPMN) standard is generally used (BPMN 1.1, 2008). BPMN became the predominant notation standard with which to graphically depict process models thanks to the merging of the BPM initiative into the OMG group. This merging came about as a result of the overlapping scope of BPMN and UML activity diagrams. BPMN provides a graphical notation that is easy for all the participants in the business process, from business analysts to developers, to understand. It specifies business process diagrams by means of flows, events, activities and results. Business decisions and forks can also be modeled by means of gateways. BPMN activities can be elementary tasks or sub-processes. BPMN also allows the participants involved in the process to be modeled by means of pools. In these pools, activities can be organized and categorized by means of lanes, although the use of these elements is left to the modeler's discretion. Several approaches have proposed the application of certain transformation techniques in order to obtain a UML equivalent model from a BPMN model and the corresponding code which that model implements (Harmon, 2004).

The BPMN specification has recently evolved from version 1.2 (between 2008 and 2009) to the latest version in 2010, BPMN 2.0 (OMG, 2011). This new version contains many significant changes, principally regarding execution semantics and choreography, and also important modifications in conformance, swimlanes, dataobjects, subprocesses and events. The specification has been rebuilt and now differentiates process modeling, process execution, BPEL process execution and choreography modeling. An extensibility mechanism has been defined for both process model extensions and graphical extensions. Another major innovation is that it extends the definition of human interactions. BPMN 2.0 therefore represents one of the most serious and suitable candidates for model description at CIM level. Finally, the ARIS language is also applied to the CIM level, providing a graphical notation that is supported by the ARIS Toolset (ARIS Design Platform, 2007).

At the PIM level, the Business Process Definition Metamodel (BPDM) provides a graphical notation when used in conjunction with UML (Ko et al., 2009). BPDM has been proposed as a standard by the OMG. The J2EE SUN standard, which represents the basis of most Web applications, can also be used to obtain a graphical notation when used in conjunction with UML (Johnson, 2002).

The Business Process Modeling Language (BPML) (Arkin, 2002), the Electronic Business using eXtensible Markup Language (commonly known as e-business XML, or formally ebXML) (Walsh, 2002), WS-BPEL (BPEL, 2011) and the Web Services Choreography Description Language (WS-CDL) (Ko et al., 2009) are normally used to represent the PSM abstraction level. The popularity of BPML has been outperformed with the widespread adoption of XPDL and BPMD as interchange and serialization formats (Verner, 2004). SOA foundation standards are required to achieve a Model-driven Development in BPM tools. Without them, BPM would become slow and expensive. Several languages for the design and execution of business processes based on

Web services have appeared. Some examples are XLANG (Thatte, 2001), the Web Services Flow Language (WSFL) (Leymann, 2001) or WS-BPEL (BPEL, 2011). More specifically, WS-BPEL is recognized as one of the most common SOA orchestration languages. WS-BPEL is used to describe the execution logic of Web services by defining their control flow and providing a means to share the context among the different architectures partners. The use of WS-BPEL signifies that those business processes, which integrate a Web service collection in the same process flow, can be constructed. The result is an interoperable, robust and standard-based SOA solution. WS-BPEL is based on several XMLbased specifications such as WSDL 1.1, XML Schema 1.0, XPath1.0 and XSLT 1.0 (BPEL, 2011). WSDL messages and XML Schemas provide the data model used by the processes described using WS-BPEL, whereas XPath and XSLT support data management.

WS-BPEL also provides several extension mechanisms in order to easily adapt new versions of these standards, principally those related to XPath and XML-based standards. Curiously, several vendors do not use WS-BPEL as an execution language, but as an import/export interchange language (Sandy, 2006).

WS-BPEL and BPMN 1.2 are sometimes thought to be similar. Nevertheless, BPMN 1.2 is used in a different development stage to WS-BPEL, specifically when the business process is being designed and improved, whereas BPEL is used to implement it. Obviously, these two phases have completely different requirements (Dikmans, 2008). Moreover, business analysts use BPMN 1.2 and technical analysts and programmers use WS-BPEL. Each of them uses different paradigms and is focused on different aspects and issues when modeling a process. BPMN 1.2 and WS-BPEL were not originally intended to work together. From a standardization point of view, this represents an important gap that should be solved before processes can be modeled and deployed within a BPM-MDA unified framework.

However, the publication of BPMN 2.0 has changed this differentiation. Moreover, BPMN 2.0 is intended to replace WS-BPEL, although some steps must be taken in this area if such a task is to be achieved. BPMN 2.0 still has some issues, such as semantics of non-executable models, model portability, graphics interchange or simulation properties (Silverás, 2011). There are also some problems with support to prior versions, and the validation tools are still rather immature. The portability of BPMN 2.0 process models is a desirable and achievable goal that business analysts have expected. However, the existence of multiple schemas and separate graphics complicates validation, and the graphic portability in existing tools is becoming more difficult. BPMN 2.0 plus WS-BPEL does not therefore solve the portability problem for business analysts, and there are still some differences between both standards. However, it is clear that in recent years the evolution of BPMN 2.0 has overcome the limitations and differences of its previous version compared to WS-BPEL.

2.3. Generating Executable Business Processes from Models

A key aspect in a standard-based description of a business process is the generation of source code to implement it in a semiautomatic manner, i.e., with minimum human intervention. This would allow business analysts to generate a process model that could then be translated into an implementation language. At this stage, software developers may be able to complete the process implementation compliant with the analysts' requirements. The use of BPM standards aims to ease this process. However, the main weakness of most of the BPM standards presented is the difficulty involved in their use by business analysts during the early stages of the development process (Verner, 2004). In most cases, these standards only address those processes that are composed exclusively of Web services; they do not have a graphical rendering;

they do not usually include a framework to perform a top-down design and they do not provide capabilities for process analysis. Therefore, the transformation from high-level business process modeling, which is generally only carried out by business analysts, into a composition language which implements those business processes with Web services is not a trivial matter.

In White (2005), the authors provide a set of rules with which to generate the corresponding code between a BPMN 1.1 process model and its corresponding WS-BPEL executable process. To do this, the object diagrams and their properties are dissected and then mapped into the appropriate WS-BPEL elements. A BPMN 1.1 diagram therefore attains gets a double utility/finality: to provide the business process from the perspective of the business-level view, and to allow executable code to be generated in WS-BPEL. This work describes the transformation process by means of examples, making a distinction between graph structures (flow element) and WS-BPEL blocks (sequence element). However, it does not provide any methodology or implementation to perform this transformation in an automatic manner. Indeed, the features of a tool able to model an annotated BPMN 1.x process with the information required to perform the transformation are depicted, but the tool is not developed. The transformation of BPMN 1.x into BPEL is also carried out using the Oracle Business Process Analysis Suite in Dikmans (2008). This tool is complementary to the Oracle Business Process Management Suite, and can be used to formally model the business architecture of an organization using the BPMN notation. The differences between both BPMN 1.x and WS-BPEL are identified and analyzed, and a transformation process is depicted. However, when using this method some semantic differences exist between BPMN 1.x and the final WS-BPEL models. The use of this proposal should therefore be limited to technical and simple models (with a few services) and it could not be applied to more complex requirement scenarios. With regard to

BPMN 2.0, the interesting work presented in Dijkman (2010) depicts the development of precise execution semantics for a subset of BPMN 2.0 using graph rewrite rules. The justification of using these rules is the strong relation between the execution semantic rules that are informally specified in the 2.0 standard and their formalization. The authors propose two different transformations. The first is from BPMN 2.0 to the workflow system YAWL (van der Aalst & ter Hofstede, 2005), thus allowing models to be executed in workflows. The other is to the Petri net formalism (Murata, 1989), which allow BPMN 2.0 models to be formally analyzed.

The XML Process Definition Language, XPDL, defines an XML schema to specify the declarative part of workflow/business processes (Hrastnik, 2004). XPDL permits the graphic representation of business processes, specifying attributes such as roles, activity description, timers, Web service invocations, etc. The aim of XPDL is to store and allow the exchange of BPMN process diagrams. It offers a standard means to represent processes and to import/export them to/from any editor that is compliant with the standard. XPDL 2.0 has the extensions needed to represent all the aspects of BPMN. In Palmer (2006), an interesting approach that integrates BPMN 1.0, XPDL and WS-BPEL is presented. The starting point is a BPMN 1.0 model, and the partial diagrams are stored as XPDL during the design stage (in the case of XPDL 2.0 this is immediate). These parts are then translated into WS-BPEL, and a complete transformation process is provided. However, this process is limited to data exchange, since human interactions cannot be modeled in WS-BPEL. This task cannot be carried out without the use of specific and vendor-dependent modules. The WebML approach offers a Web-based perspective and allows business processes to be specified according to the BPMN notation, and these are then transformed from the BPMN notation to WebML hypertext diagrams (Brambilla, 2006). These diagrams then allow the fast generation of skeletons that implement the specified business process. However, these skeletons are not suitable for the implementation of the whole process, and a developer must therefore complete the code with the remainder and specific implementation details.

Some other proposals are based on UML, such as (Brambilla, 2006; Johnson, 2002), and others define their own models, as in Selic (2008) and De Castro et al. (2009). The main advantage of these proposals is that they are generally supported by modeling tools that include modules for automatic code generation from those models to Web Service composition languages (for example, OptimalJ and ArcStyler (Butler Group, 2003)). However, these proposals contemplate isolated models that cannot be easily and automatically mapped on a final target platform. The proposal used in this work allows us to obtain a service composition model that can be almost directly or automatically mapped onto executable languages.

The UML 2.0 modeling activity notation has been widely criticized because of its similarities to the BPMN notation (Unified Modeling Language, 2011). Although UML covers activity modeling, class modeling, state machine modeling and more, a model of a business process described using UML is not a model of software, but is still a model of a business process. However, the Executable UML approach (also called xtUML or xUML) supports the specification of PIM models and their compilation into PSMs (Mellor & Balcer, 2002). Other approaches have also proposed the generation of XPDL specifications from UML activity diagrams (Guelfi & Mammar, 2006; Jiang et al., 2003; van der Aalst, 2004).

Finally, the OMG has collected a comprehensive list of successful histories (vendors and products) when performing direct transformations from PIM to PSM models (OMG and MDA, 2011).

As shown in this section, MDA serves as a bridge between BPM and SOA. The use of MDA allows processes and services to be modeled by following a model-based approach, along with the generation of platform-independent process models. The use of BPM standards when applied

to MDA also helps in the business process alignment when developing a SOA solution. However, it is clear that the use of these standards creates a serious gap in the development stages. These standards are principally difficult for business analysts to be used in the early stages of the development process. Moreover, several limitations exist in the semi-automatic generation of executable code for the process descriptions provided. These limitations are generally related to the generation of code skeletons that must be completed by software engineers in later stages. A few approaches allow a complete process implementation to be generated. However, these approaches normally produce solutions that are composed exclusively of Web services, which is not normally the business analyst's aim, as occurs for example in the case of WS-BPEL.

3. UNDERLYING APPROACHES

This section introduces both the SOD-M and DENEB approaches integrated into this work and it depicts the key concepts behind their integration.

3.1. SOD-M: Service-Oriented Development Method

SOD-M defines a service-oriented approach for the development of information systems (IS) (De Castro et al., 2009, 2011). Its main characteristics are the provision of a set of guidelines with which to build IS based exclusively on services. SOD-M proposes the use of services as first-class objects for the whole process of the IS development. This approach facilitates the development of service-oriented applications, along with their implementation using current technologies such as Web services.

The method provided in SOD-M follows an MDA-based approach. It proposes a set of models that cover from the highest level of abstraction of the MDA, the CIM level, to the PIM and PSM levels. SOD-M provides the benefits related to the alignment of high-level business processes with the application of current technologies to deploy the Service-Oriented paradigm by means of different mapping rules between the models (De Castro et al., 2006).

SOD-M focuses on the development of behavioral aspects of IS and defines the guidelines needed to build behavioral models from high-level business modeling. The method is part of a larger MDA framework called MIDAS (Marcos et al., 2006) in which other aspects such as content (Vara et al., 2009) and hypertext (Cáceres et al., 2006) are considered. Content models are thus derived from a domain model defined at CIM level, and hypertext models are derived by taking into account the content models (which contain data that need to be shown) and the behavioral models (which contain the steps and functionalities needed to carry out specifics tasks).

The concepts used in SOD-M to model the behavior of an IS are organized from two different points of view. On the one hand, the business view focuses on the features and requirements of the business in which the IS will be built. On the other hand, the information system view focuses on the functionalities and processes which need

to be implemented in the IS in order to satisfy the business requirements. Figure 1 depicts the modeling process of SOD-M. It includes models that correspond with: (i) the three different abstraction levels considered by MDA: CIM, PIM and PSM; and (ii) SOD-M views: business and information system views.

As is shown in Figure 1, the SOD-M model-driven process begins by building the high-level computational independent models and enables specific models for a service platform to be obtained as a result.

For the sake of simplicity, in this work we shall focus on the composition service model of SOD-M (highlighted in Figure 1). The composition service model is the model that will be taken as input for the transformation process to generate the corresponding workflow model that will be executed in the DENEB platform. Note that SOD-M proposes representing this model by using the UML activity diagram technique (Unified Modeling Language, 2011). The main reason for using the UML activity diagram notation instead of BPMN is because the latter is basically a software development method, whereas UML is a standard notation that is well known by software developers. As is argued in White (2004), in which BPMN

Figure 1. SOD-M development process

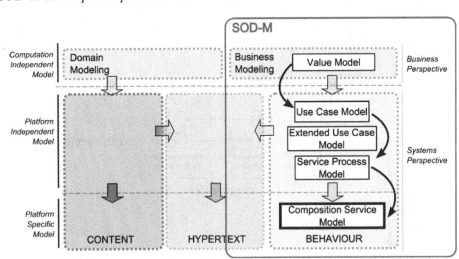

and UML activity diagrams are compared in terms of workflow patterns, although both notations are very similar and represent views of the same metamodel, the main differences between the two diagrams consist of the users' targets. The BPMN notation was created for business people, while the UML activity diagram is a standard notation for software (IS) development. A more detailed description of the other different SOD-M models can be found in De Castro et al. (2009). A more detailed description of the composition service model, its elements and the metamodel will be presented in Section 4.1.

3.2. DENEB: Business Processes Based on the Conversational Approach

DENEB is an open, flexible, extensible and adaptive framework for the development and execution of interoperable dynamic Web processes (Fabra et al., 2006, 2011). In DENEB, *processes* are composed of a set of tasks to be executed, and these tasks are arranged according to a specified set of ordering constraints. DENEB processes are described and executed using workflow technology, in terms of which is usually called *business logic*. On the other hand, the execution of each task usually corresponds to the invocation of either a particular internal process or published service. The specification of the correct sequences of messages exchanged among communicating entities is referred to as an *interaction protocol*. In DENEB, these protocols are organized as a set of roles. A *role* is the part of the protocol that a participant process or service must execute. In an interaction protocol, many alternative and valid sequences of messages often exist, each of which triggers one action or another. The execution of one of these possible sequences is called a conversation.

Figure 2 shows an abstraction of a business process executed by DENEB. The process consists of a workflow that implements its business logic. If a task needs to interact with an external service (let us say task *t3*, for instance), the process must execute the required role in order to interact with the selected service. A service registry may be used beforehand to discover the role specification. The sending and receiving of messages (denoted by *S* and *R*, respectively) by the process during the role execution are encapsulated as a part of the task. Nevertheless, a clear and explicit separation between the business logic aspects (that is, the workflow) and the interaction aspects (that is, the roles) is kept in order to achieve flexible service integration. Consequently, the same workflow

Figure 2. Abstraction of a business process executed by DENEB

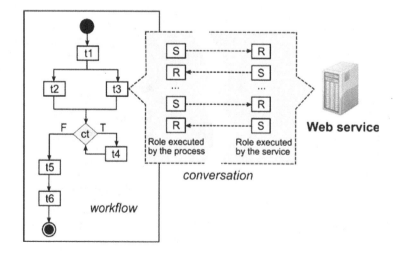

could execute the roles of alternative candidate services for each specific task. This methodology for the design of business processes is called the conversational approach (Hanson et al., 2002).

Both the workflows and roles executed in DENEB are implemented using Reference nets, a subclass of high-level Petri nets belonging to the Nets-within-Nets paradigm in which tokens in the system net can be references to other nets, thus making it possible for different tokens to point to the same instance (Kummer, 2001). Reference nets are described internally by means of the Petri Net Markup Language, PNML, an XML-based standard language for the interchange of Petri nets, and they are directly executable by means of the Renew tool (Billington et al., 2003; Kummer et al., 2003). DENEB also allows PNML descriptions of both workflows and protocols to be imported, and their acquisition at runtime (Fabra et al., 2011).

3.3. The Operating Environment of DENEB

DENEB has been built as a SOA-based platform that is able to execute business processes that are compliant with the previous description. The architectural model of DENEB uncouples business logic aspects from interaction logic aspects (workflows and their related protocol roles, respectively).

Figure 3 depicts an overview of the DENEB architecture. Note that these architectural guidelines correspond with the requirements of the conversational approach. The core of the platform consists of three main components: a *workflow engine*, a *conversation engine* and a *message broker*. The workflow engine executes the business logic of processes, whereas the conversation engine executes their corresponding interaction roles. Both engines communicate in order to exchange information between a workflow and its roles (such as parameters for the service invocation or results from external invocations). The message broker is responsible for supporting this commu-

Figure 3. SOA-based architecture of DENEB

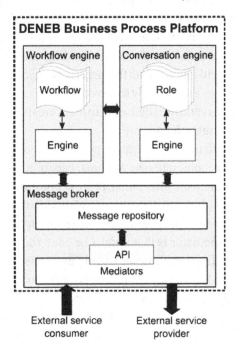

nication and coordinating interactions by means of an internal message repository in which normal messages or control/synchronization messages can be stored. From a design point of view, the broker infrastructure facilitates the independence and decoupling in time of the engines. Different implementations of engines could be plugged into the broker infrastructure and they would cooperate by means of the exchange messages using a common and defined format (Fabra et al., 2007).

Additionally, the message broker is responsible for the management of communication with external services. *Mediators* provide all the means needed to send and receive messages using different transport protocols and message formats. They also serve to isolate the business process model from the details of particular protocols, such as SOAP, RPC, HTTP, and SMTP, thus enabling communication with external entities that use a wide variety of communication technologies. Internally, the conversation engine executes the roles, and mediators communicate and are accessed through the message repository. When a role needs to communicate with an external service, it stores a tagged message in the repository. This means that this message will be taken and processed by the corresponding mediator, which will interact with the target service. Service responses are similarly received and processed by mediators and then delivered to the corresponding role through the repository.

Mediators represent a powerful tool with which to integrate new features, capabilities and functionalities into DENEB in a non-intrusive manner (that is, without having to modify the core of the platform). The only requirement for adding a new mediator is that it must be compliant with a predefined API. Some examples of mediators used in DENEB are an encapsulated business rule engine (BRE) to extend the executing platform with decision-making features, a security component to allow secure communications using a PKI schema, or a new component for supporting human–user interactions during the execution of business processes.

Finally, from an implementation point of view, Reference nets (Kummer, 2001) were used to implement the workflow and conversational engines, along with a distributed message broker based on the Linda coordination model (Carriero & Gelernter, 1989), called DRLinda (Fabra et al., 2007). The lifecycle of business processes (deployment, initiation, execution, interaction and termination), their corresponding conversations and the capabilities and functionalities described above are also managed using Reference nets. We should stress that the same formalism has been used to design/implement the business processes and its runtime environment: the DENEB platform itself.

3.4. Why to Integrate DENEB with SOD-M?

SOD-M and DENEB provide several individual contributions on different levels of the software development lifecycle. On the one hand, SOD-M addresses the main problem of typical languages

for business process specification: their limitations when being used in the early stages of the software development process by business analysts. SOD-M provides a top-down design framework along with capabilities for the process analysis. Its method provides a composition service model, starting from the user requirements, which specifies the services required to achieve a common business goal. On the other hand, DENEB provides an infrastructure for the execution of processes composed of services and different interaction technologies; it has a graphical rendering interface; and it provides a flexible and easily extensible mechanism to support the dynamic capabilities of processes (Fabra et al., 2011). DENEB uses the formalism of the Nets-within-Nets that facilitates the representation of executable workflows and protocols by following the conversational approach. This design approach improves the flexibility in the development of processes and decouples business and interaction logic.

The objective of our proposal is to integrate both existing approaches in order to provide a complete framework for the analysis, design, development and execution of business processes. This integration is based on the ability to generate executable code (more specifically, executable DENEB processes) from SOD-M composition service models. Compared to existing approaches, this represents an innovative integration work, since the resulting processes are generated without human intervention, they are fully and directly executable, and they have formal semantics that can be used for their verification (as will be detailed in Section 6). The transformation from high-level business process models, which is generally carried out by business analysts, to a composition language that implements these business processes is not a trivial matter. However, as shown in this work, this process can be achieved more easily by means of the definition of models at different levels of abstraction and the use of model transformation techniques. In order to support the model transformation, we have used the MeTAGeM tool with the purpose of implementing business processes that can be executed directly in the DENEB platform, and starting from previous models proposed by SOD-M, in particular from the Composition Service Model.

Additionally, it is important to remark that existing approaches are based on standards for the specification and implementation of business processes. These standards and Web service technologies are strongly connected (WS-BPEL is a good example of this connection). Regarding this issue, our proposal for integration is more flexible than existing approaches. The use of DENEB makes it possible for executable processes to communicate not only with Web services, but also with any external entity that is accessible via the network (a GRID system, for instance). What is more, from the point of view of SOD-M, these interactions could be easily modeled using executable activities in composition service models. Our integration therefore results in a unique, extensible and flexible framework that covers all development stages.

3.5. How to Integrate DENEB with SOD-M?

The integration of DENEB and SOD-M has been supported by MeTAGeM (Bollati, et. al., 2013). This tool applies the MDE principles to the development of model transformations, this is, it aims at model transformations as models (Bézivin, et. al, 2005). MeTAGeM provides a language to specify high-level model transformations without taking into account the language used for programming these transformations. Users can model transformations between elements of metamodels and then generate automatically the code (in different languages such as ATL, for instance) required for carrying out these model transformations.

MeTAGeM distinguishes four levels of abstraction in the model-driven development of model transformations. These coincide with the levels typically identified in the MDA proposal (PIM, PSM and Code) plus the inclusion of a Platform Dependent Model (PDM) level that could be seen as a specialization of the PSM level (OMG, 2001):

- Firstly, at PIM level, we define a model called the *Platform Independent Transformation* (PIT). This model collects the relations between the elements of the source and target metamodels without considering the technology or the paradigm that will be chosen to implement the transformation. This first model may be carried out by the developer using the interface provided by MeTAGeM, which is based on the use of weaving models (Didonet Del Fabro et al., 2006).

- Then, a new model at the PSM level is generated, the *Platform Specific Transformation for Hybrid approach* (PST-H), which combines the previous specifications with the details of a specific style of programming. In particular, the first version of MeTAGeM supports only a hybrid style, although others programming styles such as the imperative or declarative ones are to being added in the future (Bollati et al., 2013).

- In the next step the model of the transformation for the specific programming languages (those following the programming style chosen in the previous PSM level) are generated. We refer to this model as *Platform Dependent Transformation*, PDT. Currently, MeTAGeM supports two hybrid languages for model transformation: ATL (Jouault, et. al, 2008), which is the one chosen in our case, and also RubyTL (Sanchez et al., 2006).

- Finally, the *code* that implements the transformation is obtained from the previous model. This *code* can be also seen as a model with the minimum abstraction level by means of extractor/injector mechanisms.

It is important to point out that although each step of the process is automated in MeTAGeM by means of model transformations, the user can refine these models using the editors provided by MeTAGeM.

As will be shown in the next sections, the methodology and models proposed by MeTAGeM have guided the transformation from SOD-M composition service models to DENEB workflows. MeTAGeM allowed us to automate the integration of both proposals. In this case, ATL has been the model transformation language selected to code the gluing between SOD-M and DENEB.

4. AN OVERVIEW OF THE MODEL TRANSFORMATION PROCESS

As was previously mentioned, in this work we have defined a model-based solution for the automatic generation of executable business processes. This solution integrates two previous proposals, SOD-M and DENEB. The objective is the generation of a DENEB workflow starting from a SOD-M composition service model. However, it is relevant to emphasize that the composition service model is not modeled from scratch, but it is obtained as a result of a general process defined by SOD-M in which a set of models are built following a service-oriented approach.

Let us now concentrate on the description of the model transformation process proposed in this work. Figure 4 shows the main elements of the process. Firstly, the methodology provided by SOD-M is used to transform and model the business goals into a Composition Service Model. The semantic of this type of models are defined by its corresponding metamodel (*CompServiceMetamodel*). In a similar way, the metamodel of DENEB processes also have been defined (*WorkflowMetamodel*). The model editors needed to support the graphical representation of these metamodels have been developed using EMF in accordance to the proposal of (Vara & Marcos,

2012). Then, the model transformation needed to carry out the mappings between both SOD-M and DENEB metamodels has been implemented using ATL transformation rules. The implementation of rules (*CompService2Workflow*) has been automated by means of the use of MeTAGeM. As a result of the model transformation process, an instance of a workflow model and its related protocol models are obtained starting form a particular instance of a composition service model. Both the resulting workflow and the protocols are coded using DENEB high-level Petri nets. The workflow represents the business logic modeled in the composition service model, whereas protocols implement the interaction logic (which is normally linked to service invocations and interactions). The resulting net instances are then directly executable in the DENEB platform.

In the next subsections the two metamodels defined in our model-driven method and the mapping rules defined to support their transformation will be detailed. The automation of this transformation will be presented in the next section.

4.1. Describing the Semantics of the Involved Models

Figure 5 depicts the specification of composition service metamodel proposed by SOD-M (at the top) and the conformance relation with regard to a composition service model (at the bottom). Although this model will be detailed in Section 6 when the use case is introduced, it is shown here because it comprises most of the main components of the metamodel. The composition service model represents a workflow needed to carry out a business service; identifying those entities that collaborate in the business processes and the actions that each of them performs. As was previously stated, this model is represented using the UML activity diagram technique. Thus, as can be seen in Figure 5, the metamodel includes typical modeling elements of the activity diagram such as *ActivityNodes*, *InitialNodes* and

Figure 4. General overview of the proposed model-driven solution

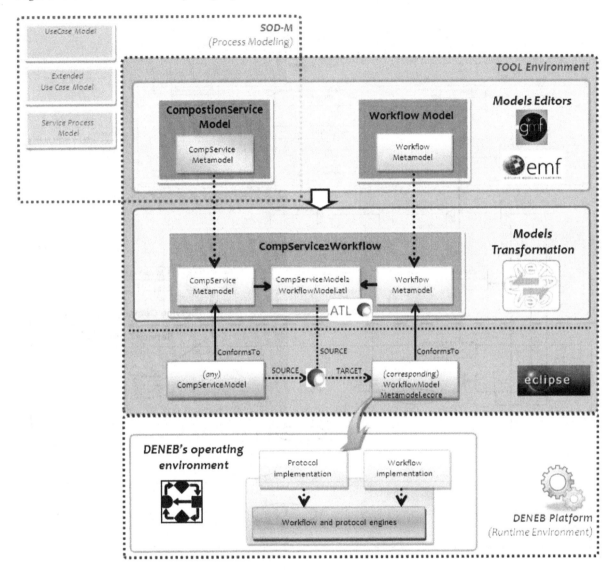

FinalNodes, DecisionNodes, etc., along with new elements defined by SOD-M such as Collaborators, *ServiceActivities* and Actions. Some of the metarelations between the metamodel and the depicted model are represented by the highlighted dashed boxes and arrows in Figure 5. Note that for the sake of clarity, only some, and not all of the metarelations are shown.

Let us now describe the main elements of the composition service model. Collaborator elements represent those entities that collaborate in the business processes by performing some of the required actions, and are displayed as a partition in the activity diagram. A collaborator can be either internal or external to the system being modeled. When the collaborator of the business is external to the system, the attribute *IsExternal* of the collaborator is set to *true*.

Actions, a kind of *ExecutableNode*, are represented in the model as an activity. Each Action identified in the model describes a fundamental behavior unit that represents some type of transfor-

Figure 5. Conformance and meta relations with regard to the composition service metamodel

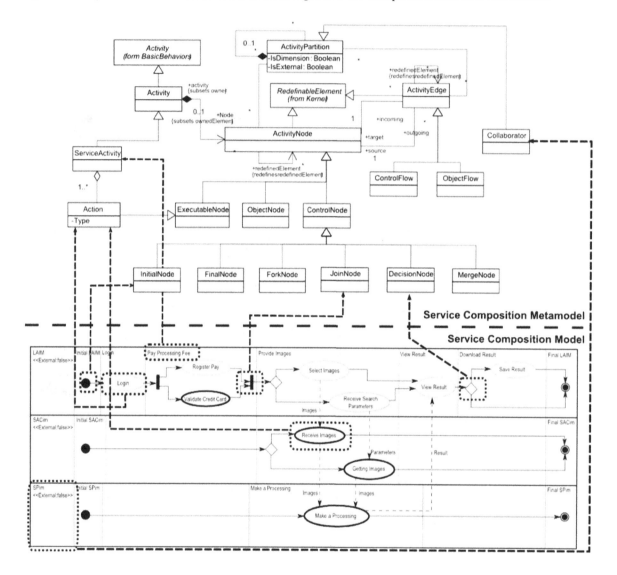

mation or processing in the system being modeled. There are two types of action: (i) a *WebService* (attribute Type is WS); and (ii) a simple operation that is not supported by a Web Service, called an *ActivityOperation* (attribute Type is AOP). The *WebService* element (highlighted in bold type in Figure 5) specifies those activities that are or will be supported by Web services, depending upon whether they are implemented or not. A *WebService* element has as a tagged value that contains the set of operations it performs and the

information required to achieve the Web service invocation on a concrete platform (endpoint, operation name, input and output parameters). The *ServiceActivity* element is an activity that must be carried out as part of a business service and is composed of one or more executable nodes.

As the same manner, Figure 6 depicts the specification of DENEB's workflow metamodel and the conformance relation with a simple workflow model. This model depicts a simple task for which a new conversation is instantiated. Some data is

Figure 6. Conformance and meta relations with regard to the DENEB's workflow metamodel

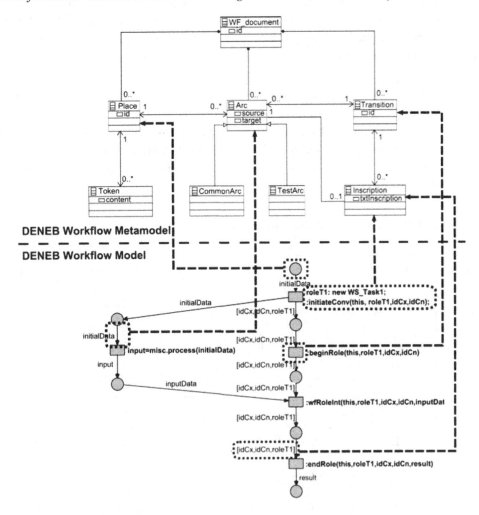

exchanged with it by means of the processing of the input data and through a *:wfRoleInt(..)* synchronization channel, and the result is eventually received from the executing conversation and stored in the final place. Note that Figure 6 only shows the workflow, and not the conversation. The meta-relations between the metamodel and the depicted model are highlighted by means of dashed boxes and arrows. Moreover, only the most important relations are linked in the figure, while the others are not. However, it would be highly intuitive to link the remaining relations. Like all models, the DENEB's workflow model is composed of a number of distinct modeling elements, which are compliant with the reference nets terminology: places, transitions, arcs and their corresponding text inscriptions. These different elements, along with the way in which they are related, are defined in the scope of the workflow metamodel.

4.2. A Rule-Based Mapping of Models

In order to develop a tool that allows us to automate the transformation process between models, in our case from the composition service model to the workflow model, it is necessary to define the corresponding set of mappings rules. Each rule specifies relations between elements of the source metamodel and elements of the target metamodel. The mappings have been defined in this work by following the method shown next step:

1. Mappings between models are defined using natural language.
2. These mappings are structured by collecting them in a set of rules, again expressed in natural language.

3. Mapping rules are implemented using one of the existing model transformation approaches. In this case we have chosen the ATL Language.

Table 1 shows the mappings defined between the composition service model (source) and the workflow model (target) in a set of mapping rules defined in natural language. In order to clarify the description of the mappings, we have specified

Table 1. SOD-M to DENEB model transformation rules

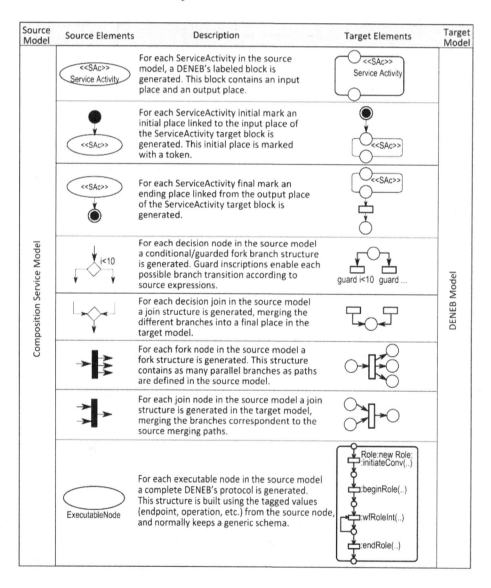

that elements in the source and target models are affected by each transformation, and have also provided some partial diagrams that will help the reader to understand the rules.

Since the use of SOD-M executable nodes represents an outstanding difference with regard to other transformation approaches, we shall focus on the translation of these executable nodes. They normally represent service invocations and are used to access an external service provider in the composition service model, but can also represent internal invocations to an object method or a human intervention, depending on the value of the type tag. We shall focus on the first case for the sake of simplicity.

From the point of view of DENEB, the translation of an executable node generates the following two results. First, the role net required executing the interaction with the invoked service. And second, a net skeleton is introduced in the workflow of the resulting DENEB process to initiate and manage the execution of the role net. On the other hand,

from an execution point of view, both nets will be executed in a coordinated manner by means of the synchronized firing of a set of special transitions. A detailed explanation of these transitions will be provided in the following example.

We shall now explain a specific example of translation. In this case the executable node represents a REST interaction with an external service to validate a credit card. The left-hand side of Figure 7 shows the net skeleton introduced in the workflow while the right-hand side shows the role net required for the interaction (the Role-REST mediator net). This role net is able to interact (by means of the message broker) with the REST mediator of DENEB that is responsible for invoking REST services. All the information required (endpoint, operation, parameters, etc.) has been specified in the executable node in the SOD-M composition service model.

A detailed explanation of the transitions of the resulting nets and the actions triggered by their execution is shown as follows. The role net is

Figure 7. Workflow-role (REST mediator) interaction in DENEB

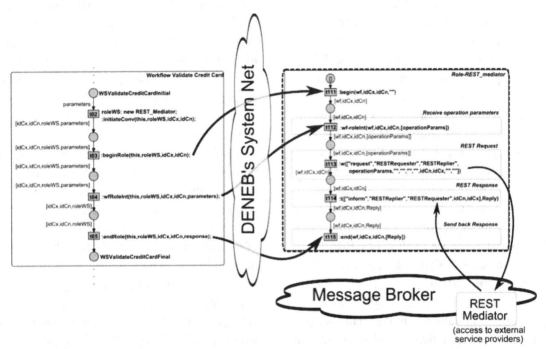

instantiated when the workflow fires a transition with the inscription *:initiateConv(..)*. In our example, this takes place by means of the transition *t02* in the workflow skeleton. The synchronized firing of transitions *:beginRole()* (*t03* and *t111* in the workflow and the role, respectively) then starts the role execution (in this case, a REST request to validate a credit card through the bank API). The necessary parameters (operation, URL, parameters) are passed from the workflow to the role by means of the *:wf-roleInt* synchronization channel inscribed in transitions *t04* and *t112*. These parameters will have the format of a tuple, such as [*"REST"*, *"validateCC"*, *"*https://ws.bank.com/rest/*"*, *"skey=xxxx"*, *"ccid=22678856445656"*, *"ccv=331"*, *"cardholder=John Doe"*]. The REST interaction is then executed in the role by means of the interaction with the REST mediator that is integrated into the message broker (transitions *t113* and *t114*). Finally, the result from the REST execution is sent back to the workflow by means of the synchronized firing of transitions *:endRole()* (*t115* and *t05* in the role and the workflow nets, respectively). This firing also ends the execution of the role. Further information about how mediators work can be found in Fabra and Álvarez (2010) and Fabra et al. (2011). It is supposed that the bank validation service will have established the format of the response message in its REST API, so no post-processing of the data sent back to the role is necessary.

Finally, it is also important to explain how the translation of guards from SOD-M to DENEB is carried out. Table 1 depicted an example in which the guards are translated from the SOD-M model to the DENEB's workflow. As was shown, DENEB requires all the variables involved to be bound to the input arcs of the guarded transition. In this approach we use a subset of XPath 1.0 to support expressions (XML Path Language, 1999; Fabra & Álvarez, 2010).

Expressions are normally codified as a text string by means of natural language. This string is then parsed and the equivalent XPath expression is generated. The subset considered here includes arithmetic operators ($+, -, *, \mathrm{div}, \mathrm{mod}$), relational operators ($=, !=, <=, <, >=, >$) and logic operators (and, or). Precedency and associativity is also established among these operators. Equivalence and comparison string operators are also available (*strcompare*, *strgt*, *strlt*). The resulting XPath expression can be directly evaluated in DENEB by means of its built-in XPath engine.

It would be also possible to include functions and external calls in the guard expression. However, in such a case the corresponding library must be provided to load the required functions or procedures into the DENEB framework. Additional aspects regarding the dynamic load and extension of the DENEB framework can be viewed in Fabra et al. (2011).

5. USING MeTAGeM TO AUTOMATE THE MODEL TRANSFORMATION

MeTAGeM provides the technological support to automate the transformation of our models. The tool includes the implementation of a set of Domain-Specific Languages (DSLs) (Mernik et al., 2005) to describe the involved models in our proposal, and the implementation of the required model transformation. For the development of the tool we followed an adaptation of the guidelines proposed in Vara and Marcos (2012) for the development of EMF-based toolkits. Figure 8 provides an overview of this process.

As is shown in Figure 8, the development process begins with the specification of -a first draft of- the *abstract syntax* of each DSL that will be bundled in the tool, one per each model as was previously detailed. The abstract syntax of a particular model is defined by means of its metamodel, which is described in terms of the Ecore metamodeling language (Gronback, 2009; Steinberg et al., 2008). The second step is to provide the DSLs with a *concrete syntax*, which means defining a graphical editor for each

Figure 8. Adaptation of the development process of DSL toolkit

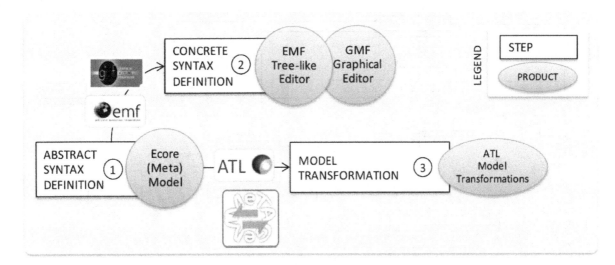

particular model (normally a tree-like interface). For this purpose, EMF and the Graphical Modeling Framework (GMF) are used. In our solution, we have generated graphical editors for both the SOD-M composition service model and for the DENEB's workflow mode. The corresponding generated DSLs will be depicted in Section 5.1.

At this point of the development process, there exist isolated versions of the DSLs to be bundled in the tool. Therefore, the next step is to connect them by means of a set of *model transformations*. In this work, we have used MeTAGeM to implement the model transformations using the ATL language. Such transformations are presented in Section 5.2.

5.1. Implementation of the DSLs

Let us now present the abstract and concrete syntaxes for the two DSLs involved in this work.

5.1.1. SOD-M Composition Service Model DSL

Following the process shown in Figure 8, the first step is to define the abstract syntax of the DSL. Figure 9 depicts the abstract syntax of the

Composition Service metamodel, defined by means of an Ecore, and which is a simplified Essential MOF (EMOF) implementation (Gronback, 2009). It is important to remark that during the implementation of the metamodel using Ecore, and due to its underlying XML nature, the initial metamodel of any model has to be modified (the metamodels defined from Ecore must include a root element, for instance). As shown in Figure 9, unlike the metamodel presented in Figure 5, the *CompositionService* metamodel includes the *CompositionofService* metaclass, which is the root element. *ActivityPartition*, *Activity* and *ActivityEdge* metaclasses compose then the *CompositionofService* metaclass. These metaclasses are defined as abstract types and are a specialization of *NamedElement*.

The *ActivityPartition* metaclass is specialized in the *Collaborator* metaclass, which is used to represent those entities that collaborate in the business processes by performing some of the required actions. The *ServiceActivity* metaclass is a type of *Activity* that must be carried out as part of a business service and it is composed of one or more actions (*Action* metaclass). As was explained in Section 4, the *Action* elements in the model could be of two different types: *WebService*

Figure 9. Abstract syntax of the composition service metamodel

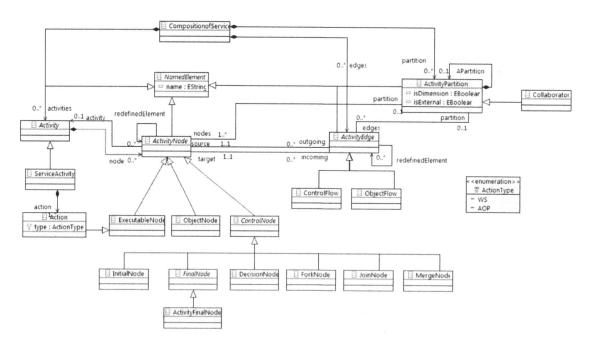

(WS) or *ActivityOperation* (AOP). To represent those types in the Ecore, it is necessary to create an enumerated type with two possible values (see *ActionType* enumeration in Figure 9).

After defining the abstract syntax of the Composition Service model DSL, the next step is to define the *concrete* syntax, in other words, the tree-like or graphical editor that allows users to represent the concepts of the metamodels previously defined. The editor of the composition service model represents a very important aspect in easing the task of handling and building instances of models. Following the proposal of (Vara & Marcos, 2012) we have implemented a tree-editor for the representation of composition service models using EMF. Due to the generic nature of EMF tree-based editors they do not fit always into the specific nature of the DSLs (as happens in the case of the Composition Service model, which is essentially an Activity Diagram). Therefore, in order to enable to depict graphically the models in an UML-like fashion, the graphical editor was developed using GMF. Figure 10 shows

a screenshot of the tree-view (on the left-hand side) and the graphical-view (on the right-hand side). The tree-editor allows an instance of a Composition Service model to be built following a tree-based hierarchical methodology. This is sometimes more useful for testing and debugging, or simply to set specific parameters. Furthermore, the graphical editor provides developers with a palette to facilitate the construction of instances. Note how certain internal details, such as the specification of the type of action depicted in Figure 10, can easily be established as WS or AOP in both views.

5.1.2. DENEB Workflow Model DSL

Figure 11 depicts the abstract syntax DENEB's workflow metamodel by means of its corresponding Ecore metamodel. As is shown, the metaclass *WF_document* is the root element of the metamodel, and is composed by *Place*, *Arc* and *Transition* metaclasses. The Arc metaclass is defined as an abstract metaclass and it is specialized by the CommonArc and TestArc metaclasses.

Figure 10. Partial view of the composition service model editor

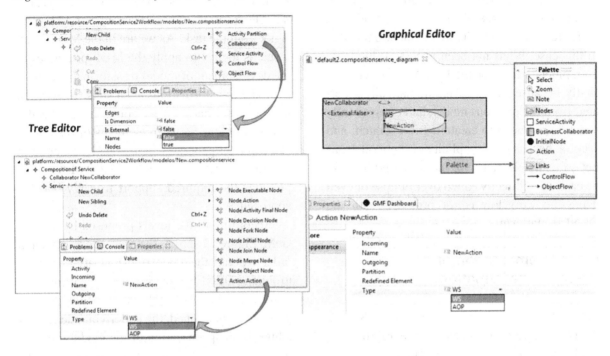

Figure 11. Abstract syntax of workflow metamodel

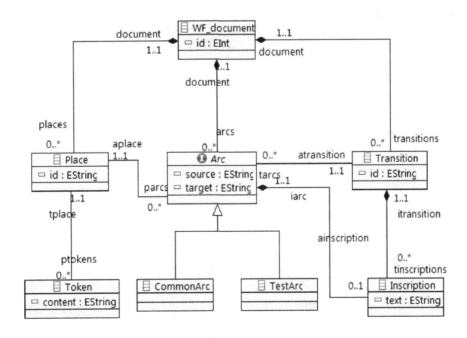

The concrete syntax for this model was created following a tree-like style. A screenshot is presented in Figure 12. It is worth mentioning that in this case, it has not been necessary to create a graphical editor for the DSL for two reasons: firstly, because this model is automatically generated from the previous model, and consequently users do not need to create it from scratch; and second, because the simplicity of the models, as not so many elements are included and it could be easily and directly edited over Eclipse or even using the workflow editor provided with the DENEB platform.

5.2. Implementation of the Model Transformations

Following the process described in Figure 8, once the DSLs have been created, the next step is the implementation of specific model transformations.

In our case we have decided to codify them using the ATL language. The codification of ATL rules is not a simple task. As we are in the MDE field, it seems logical to apply the MDE principles to the development of model transformations: look at model transformations as models (Bézivin et. al, 2005). In that way, we could model specific transformations between elements of metamodels, and then generate automatically the code of the transformation in any language. MeTAGeM provides the required support to carry out this approach.

According to the levels proposed by MeTA-GeM, Figure 13 depicts the process carried out in order to obtain the model transformations needed to obtain a DENEB Workflow model starting from a SOD-M Composition Service model. As was previously mentioned, the underlying idea is that a high-level specification of the model transformations is subsequently refined into lower-level

Figure 12. Partial view of the tree-like workflow model editor

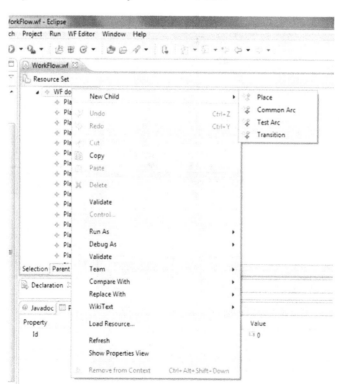

Figure 13. Development process of the 'Composition Service to Workflow' ATL transformation with MeTAGeM

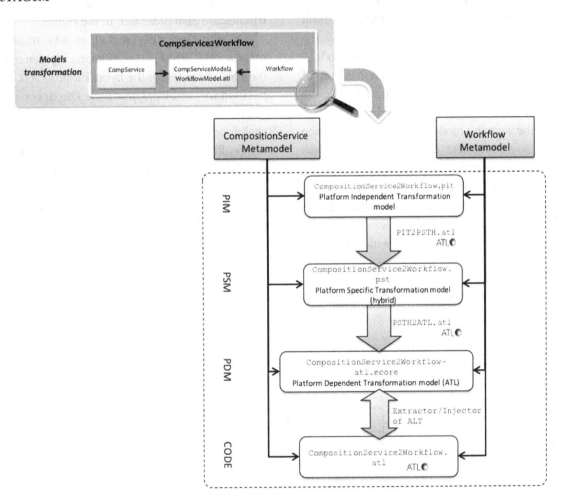

models until they can be used to semi-automatically generate the code implementing the model transformations (ATL, in our case).

Considering the mapping rules previously depicted in Table 1 and following the MeTAGeM process, we have defined a PIT model that collects the correspondences between the elements of the Composition Service and the Workflow metamodels (*CompositionService2Workflow.pit*). In order to create this model, the user defines a new weaving model where the correspondences between elements of the source and target metamodels are collected (in our case, from the Composition Service Metamodel to the Workflow Metamodel). For each correspondence specified in Table 1, the designer adds an object to the weaving model instantiating the corresponding metaclass of the source metamodel (the *ServiceComposition* metamodel depicted in Figure 9) to the type of correspondence from those collected in the target metamodel (the *Workflow* metamodel depicted in Figure 11).

Figure 14 shows a view of the Platform Independent Transformation model *CompService-2Workflow,* obtained with MeTAGeM. As can be seen in the top part of the figure, the interface presents three different panels: the one on the left depicts the elements of the *CompositionService* metamodel, the right one shows the elements of the *Workflow* metamodel, and the panel in the middle is the weaving model, whose objects represent the different correspondences specified by the user between the source and target metamodels. The first rule of Table 1 is illustrated in the top of Figure 13. An *OneToMany* relation between the *ServiceActivity* element and *Place* elements is created in the weaving model. Such correspondence has one source element (*ServiceActivity*) and two target elements (showed as *Out Element Place* in Figure 14). The lower part of Figure 14 focuses on the high-level binding between the names of both elements: name attribute of the *Service Activity* and the *Id* attribute of the *Place*, which indicates

that the name of places will be the same as the service activity. The *properties tab* for both attributes are also presented in the figure.

Once this model is created, an ATL transformation (PIT2PSTH.atl) automatically generates the PST-H model for the hybrid approach (*CompositionService2Workflow.pst*). The upper-right corner of Figure 15 shows a partial overview of such model (the upper-left corner shows the corresponding PIT model introduced previously). For each relation between the elements specified in the PIT model a *Rule* element is generated in the PST-H model. In particular, the bottom part of the figure shows the relation between a *ServiceActivity2Places* of the PIT model and the

Figure 14. CompService2Workflow platform independent transformation model

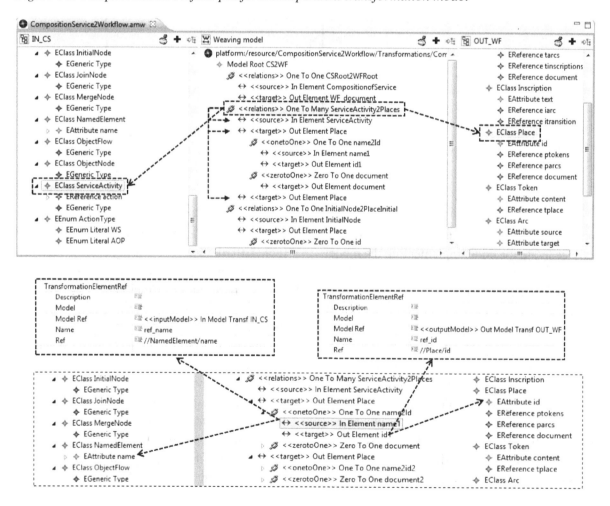

Figure 15. CompService2Workflow platform specific (hybrid) transformation model

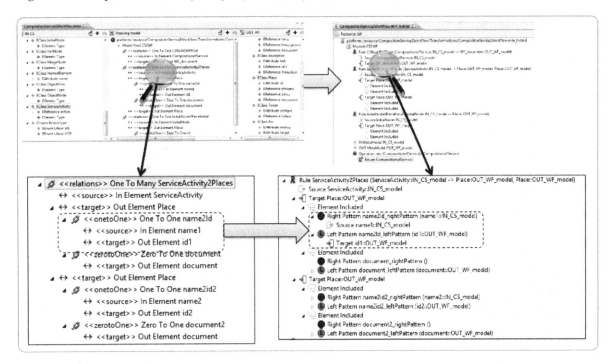

element that maps it in the PST-H model, the *ServiceActivity2Places rule*.

Similarly to the case of the PIT model, the developer may refine the PST-H model (modifying some of the rules generated or adding new elements, for instance).

The following step in MeTAGeM is to generate a transformation model for a particular language, the PDT model for ATL (*CompositionService-2Workflow-atl.ecore*) in our case. To do this, the transformation *PSTH2ATL.atl* consumes the previous model and automatically generates the model for ATL, which is depicted on the upper-right part of Figure 16. The bottom half of the figure focuses on the *ServiceActivity2Place* mapping. In this case, the object rule of the PST-H model, whose property is *Main*, takes the value *true* and it is then mapped into a *Matched Rule* object in the target model (transformation model for ATL).

Finally, once the model for the ATL language has been obtained, MeTAGeM uses a textual extractor/injector that allows serializing the previous model in the final ATL source code that implements the model transformation (*CompService-2Workflow.atl*). This step is illustrated in Figure 17.

6. CASE STUDY

In this section, our model-driven proposal is shown by means of its application to a real use case. First, the Composition Service Model DSL was used in order to build the initial SOD-M composition service model. The ATL transformation rules automatically generated by means of MeTAGeM depicted in the previous section were then applied to generate the DENEB workflow model. Eventually, these models (represented as DENEB nets) were imported and executed in the DENEB platform. The use case is presented first and the DENEB nets generated and the correspondence of their elements with the source composition service model are then described. Finally, some

Figure 16. CompService2Workflow platform dependent transformation model for ATL

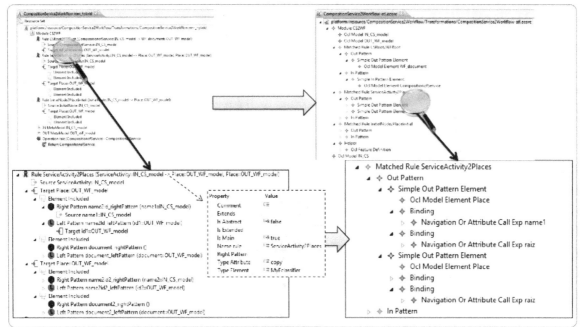

Figure 17. Generation of the CompService2Workflow ATL code

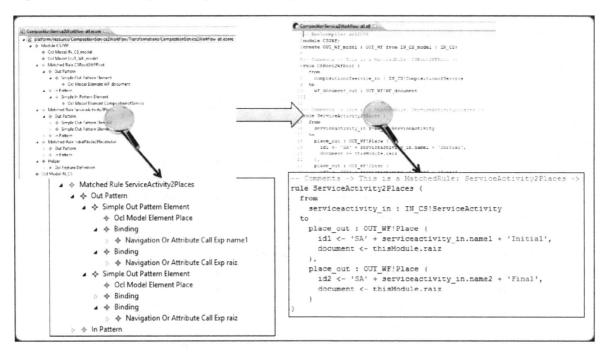

of the ATL rules involved in the transformation process are detailed.

6.1. Scenario

The case study presented in this chapter consists of a Web IS for medical image management and processing called GesIMED, which has been developed in collaboration with the GTEBIM research group at Rey Juan Carlos University (RJCU) (Tamames et al., 2007; GesIMED System, 2008).

Nowadays, medical image modalities such as Positron Emission Tomography (PET) and Functional Magnetic Resonance Imaging (FMRI) allow images of quantitative and qualitative cerebral activity to be obtained. Neuroscience researchers, particularly those working in clinical fields such as neuroradiology, neurology, neuropsychiatry and neuropsychology, carry out FMRI and PET studies. The first step towards achieving their work is to obtain the required images. They then process them using different techniques, and in very different manners related to improvement, correction and statistical analysis.

GesIMED is a Web IS, which has been successfully deployed in several medical, and research centers in Madrid, Spain, facilitating the work of neuroscientists and clinicians. Its objective is to provide neuroscience researchers with (a) an easy-to-access historical medical image store and (b) a duly standardized method for processing and analyzing the images. It also stores both the original and the processed images in a database. Figure 18 shows a layout of the GesIMED system.

Neuroscience researchers are offered three specific services:

- **Storage Service:** The storage service is implemented by a database that stores the images and the results of the processes performed on them. Neuroscience researchers may access and consult them using different criteria (such as study, and pathology) for diagnostic purposes, research or even teaching.

- **Processing Service:** Neuroscience researchers are offered two kinds of processing: analysis and segmentation. The former consists of the measurement of physical and physiological parameters, while the latter refers to image segmentation. A typical example of image segmentation would be the extraction of the bone's part from a radiological image. Researchers can request to process a set of images stored in the database or upload new medical images to be processed.

- **Visualization Service:** The visualization service provides image reconstruction processes (for example, the creation of 3D images from 2D images) and multimodality functions (such as the creation of both anatomical and functional image views within a single image). Researchers can follow the

Figure 18. Layout of GesIMED system

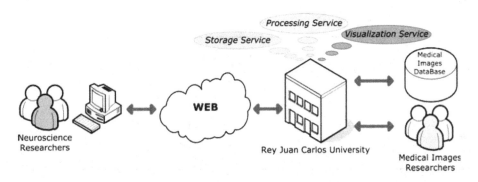

same procedures as in the processing service, to request visualizations of medical images stored in the database or to upload new images in order to view them later.

This case study has already been fully modeled using the SOD-M method in previous works (Tamames et al., 2007; De Castro et al., 2009). In this work we shall only present the composition service model, along with the resulting workflow model that was generated from the transformation process. This workflow model can be imported to the DENEB framework and executed without additional transformations. Both models for the case study are first described, and the implemented model transformation result is then presented.

6.2. Models

Figure 19 shows the composition service model of the GesIMED case that represents the composition process of the different activities needed to carry out the obtained processed images business service. This model was built by taking the elements identified in a previous service process model, along with certain elements identified in the value model (such as business actors) as input.

As shown, the composition service model contains three different collaborators: the *LAIM*, the processing service (*SPim*), and the storage service (*SACim*). The LAIM collaborator is divided into several service activities. First, a login is required to access the business service. Once the user's credentials have been verified, the *Pay Processing Fee* SAc starts a parallel processing: the payment is registered in the system (*Register Pay* action) and the information from the credit card is validated (*Validate Credit Card* action). When this has finished, there are two different possibilities depicted in the *Provide Images* SAc. On the one hand, the user can select a set of images in order to retrieve them (*Select Images*). On the other hand, the user can specify certain search parameters in order to obtain the selected images (*Receive Search Parameters*). These two actions exchange some information with the actions contained in the SACim collaborator (Receive Images and Getting Images, respectively), which will interact with the Make a Processing action in the SPim collaborator. As a result, the data generated will be obtained by means of the View Result action, and the user has the option of choosing to download and save this information or simply to exit from the process.

The validate credit card executable node represents a Web service since it is already a standard Web service provided by several organizations. Moreover, the activities performed by both the

Figure 19. Composition service model for the business service obtain processed images

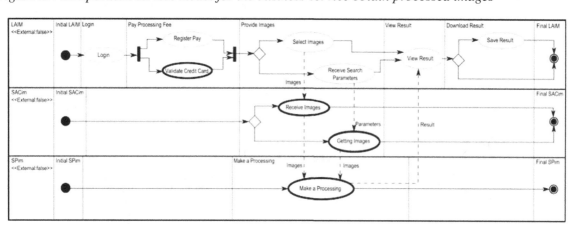

SPim and the SACim are represented as Web services, since their behavior is related to the communication between the central server of the application and the different services provided by them. As was previously described in Section 4, these types of nodes have a tagged value that contains the set of operations they perform and the information required to achieve the Web service invocation on a concrete platform (endpoint, operation name, input and output parameters).

An extract (corresponding to the *Initial LAIM*, *Login* and *Pay Processing Fee* SACs) from the result of the transformation of the LAIM collaborator for the obtained processed images process is depicted in Figure 20. This is the resulting DENEB workflow as seen in the tool once it has been imported. A layout schema filter is applied in order to beautify the net, thus producing a printable net but without altering its execution

capabilities. Figure 20 also shows the elements corresponding to the register pay activity operation and the validate credit card Web service elements in the composition service model. The credit card validation service is the most interesting, since it depicts the service-oriented capabilities of the approach presented in this work.

Let us now concentrate on the case shown in Figure 20. First, the *Pay Processing Fee* service activity generates a block in the workflow model labeled with the *«SAc» Pay Processing Fee inscription*. Then, both the register pay and the validate credit card elements contained in that activity generate the two corresponding blocks placed inside the *«SAc» Pay Processing Fee*. As is shown, DENEB workflows not only model the flow control of the execution, but must also follow a defined structure. These blocks contain a predefined structure that corresponds to a role

Figure 20. Workflow excerpt corresponding to the obtain processed images service, and generated as a result of the transformation process

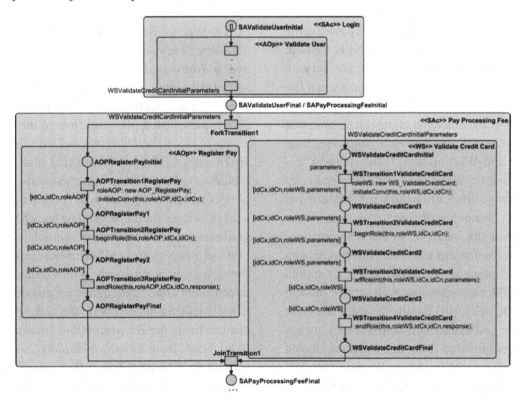

instantiation and a workflow-role interaction in DENEB.

Once the workflow model has been generated, it can be imported to the DENEB platform and directly executed. The workflow depicted in Figure 20 will be placed in the workflow engine and will start its execution firing the enabled transitions at each moment. As shown, the initial token mark is placed in the *Login* service activity, which will be the first task to be executed. Once the login has been completed, the *ForkTransition1* transition will fire, and two parallel branches will then be under execution, corresponding to the *register pay* activity operation and the *validate credit card* Web service, respectively.

All those activities that take place by following the conversational approach (that is, the interaction logic), must be instantiated in the workflow by means of what are denominated as the *synchronization channels* in DENEB's terminology. First, the corresponding role that must be played by the workflow is instantiated at runtime using the new *<rolename>* inscription (*AOPTransition1RegisterPay* and *WSTransition1ValidateCreditCard* transitions). The new instance is then passed to the system net, which is the core of DENEB, through the synchronized firing of transitions labeled with the *inscription:initiate Conv(..)*. The normal life cycle of the roles in DENEB is therefore the following: (i) start the execution of the instantiated role (channel *:beginRole(..)*, in *AOPTransition2RegisterPay* and *WSTransition2ValidateCreditCard* transitions); (ii) if required, workflows and roles can exchange information through the system net using the channel *:wfRoleInt(..)* as many times as required (for example, in the *WSTransition3ValidateCreditCard* transition, this mechanism is used to pass the parameters that are required to make the corresponding Web service invocation to the role); (iii) finally, the roles end their execution and return the final result by means of the synchronized firing of transitions labeled *:endRole(..)* (*AOPTransition3RegisterPay* and *WSTransition4ValidateCreditCard* transitions).

A more detailed description of the DENEB system net and the described synchronization channels, which are in charge of managing the workflow-role interactions, is provided in Fabra et al. (2006, 2011).

Let us now concentrate on the explicit separation between activity operations and Web service invocations inside the *Pay processing fee* service activity depicted in the workflow. Whereas the *Register pay* operation corresponds to an internal operation, the *Validate credit card* operation requires a Web service invocation. A protocol playing the role side of requester or invocator of a Web service has therefore been automatically generated. As previously described, this protocol is put into execution by the workflow when the corresponding branch is reached. First, the firing of the *WSTransition1ValidateCreditCard* transition creates a new instance of the protocol and initiates it. Figure 21 depicts, on the left, the protocol implementation generated to interact with the *Validate credit card* Web service using SOAP and, on the right, the corresponding excerpt of the workflow involved in the interaction.

The synchronized firing of the *WSTransition2ValidateCreditCard* transition (in the workflow) and the *Transition1RoleValidateCreditCard* transition (in the protocol) starts the protocol execution itself. The information related to the credit card data is passed from the workflow to the role by means of the *:wfRoleInt()* channel, thus firing the *WSTransition2ValidateCreditCard* and *Transition2RoleValidateCreditCard* transitions, respectively. Once this information has been passed, the workflow keeps the corresponding branch blocked until a response from the protocol is obtained. The protocol also performs a SOAP invocation through the message broker using the write and take directives in order to pass the required information to the SOAP mediator and to obtain the corresponding answer, firing the *Transition3RoleValidateCreditCard* and *Transition4RoleValidateCreditCard* transitions. The response is then passed to the workflow as an ending message by firing the

Figure 21. Corresponding protocol (on the left) for the validate credit card Web service activity in the workflow (on the right)

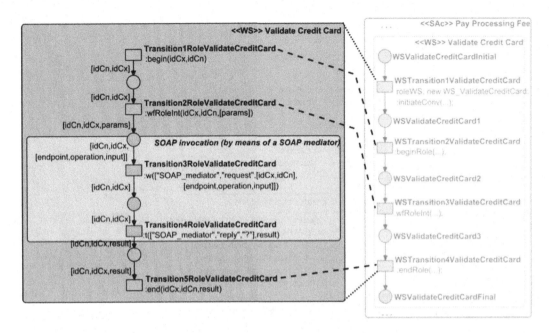

Transition5RoleValidateCreditCard transition, and the protocol ends its execution. Note that the error control branches have been hidden in order to clarify the presentation of the resulting nets. The workflow then receives the response from the protocol and resumes its execution, joining both execution branches by firing the *JoinTransition1* transition, and continuing the execution of the business process.

The skeleton generated in the workflow model remains the same for both SOAP or REST cases, and changes are only introduced in the corresponding role. As shown, neither the SOAP nor the REST roles contain any technological detail. This is owing to the use of the mediation system in the DENEB message broker. The SOAP and REST mediators allow this type of models to be produced, while avoiding such specific details, thus increasing flexibility and providing a very suitable mechanism to promote reusability and optimization.

Let us now briefly depict the case of the *Register Pay* action in the workflow depicted in

Figure 19. The code for this action must access an internal organizational resource, that is, a database, to register each payment that has been made. The workflow excerpt generated is almost equal to a service invocation, and also the corresponding role, which will interact with a database mediator. What is different in this case is the information exchanged between the workflow and the role. The corresponding mediator to access the database will require knowledge of the type of database, the query to be executed, the access policy information and the parameters of the query. DENEB provides a database mediator built on top of the Hibernate framework, thus supporting several database implementations using the same role. As has been shown, the capabilities of the DENEB framework allow us to provide a very flexible code for the implementation.

6.3. ATL Transformation Rules

Finally, let us now describe some of the ATL transformation rules involved in the previous

Figure 22. CompositionService2Workflow ATL code excerpt, ServiceActivity2Places rule

```
rule ServiceActivity2Places
{
    from
    s : CS!ServiceActivity
    to
    p1 : WF!Place
    (
        id <- 'SA' + s.name + 'Initial',
        document <- thisModule.raiz
    ),
    p2 : WF!Place
    (
        id <- 'SA' + s.name + 'Final',
        document <- thisModule.raiz
    )
}
```

description. Figures 22 and 23 illustrate the model transformation and show an excerpt from the *CompositionService2Workflow* ATL transformation plus a partial view of *Process Images Composition* Service and *Workflow* models.

Figure 22 shows how the source pattern in the *ServiceActivity2Places* rule matches all the *ServiceActivity* objects found in the source model (*CompositionService* model). The target pattern states that two *Place* objects are to be created in the target model (*Workflow* model) for each matching, one initial place and one final place in accordance with the transformation table depicted in Table 1. The *Id* identifier for each new place in the target model is built using the chain *SA +* *<ServiceActivity name> + <Initial or Final>*, thus generating unique names for these identifiers. The *document ← thismodule.raiz* instance is used to relate the *Place* element to the root element in the model (*WF document*). *Raiz* represents the root element and it is a *Helper*, codified in ATL, which

locates the root element in the target model, while *document* is the name of the relation between the *Place* element and the root.

For example, as is shown in Figure 22, the *ValidateUser* service activity contained in the Login AOP of the composition service model (Figure 19) corresponds to the excerpt contained in the *SAc Login* box in the generated workflow (top of Figure 20). As shown, two places have been generated: the initial place *SAValidateUserInitial* and the final place *SAValidateUserFinal* (which also corresponds to the *SAPayProcessingFeeInitial* initial SA place). The *ValidateUser* action is then contained between these two places in the target workflow model.

On the other hand, Figure 23 partially shows the *ActionWS2Places* rule for which some of the objects (places, transitions and inscription) are created in the target model for every Action object of type WS found in the source model. This ATL rule was responsible for the generation of the *WS*

Figure 23. CompositionService2Workflow ATL code excerpt, ActionWS2Places rule

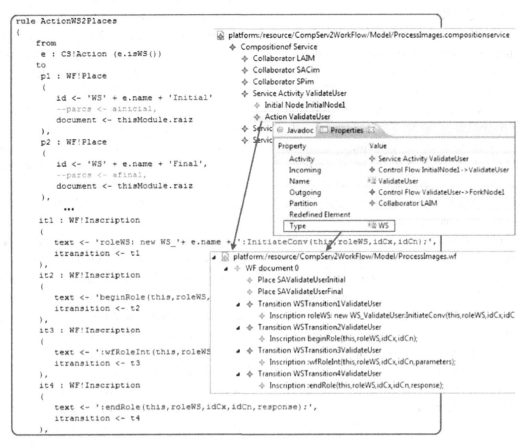

Validate Credit Card skeleton in the workflow (Figure 20) from the *ValidateCreditCard WS* action in the composition service model (Figure 19). As shown in Figure 23, and in accordance with the transformation rules depicted in Table 8, in the specific case of a WS action, a skeleton is automatically generated in the target workflow model. This skeleton is then configured with all the information required to instantiate a WS conversation, initiate it and play the participant's corresponding role. All the information regarding the WS is contained in the source SOD-M model. The way it is organized to play the corresponding role is achieved in the rule. The conversation corresponds to a pattern which interacts with the mediation system in DENEB, and which will process the required Web service interactions (a detailed overview of this interaction process was previously shown in Section 4).

As shown in this section, the application of the approach presented herein to the GesIMED real use case has resulted in the generation of the corresponding high-level Petri nets which model executable DENEB workflows and protocols automatically. This signifies that the SOD-M methodology was applied from a very early development stage in order to obtain the required models. The composition service model was used to apply the plug-ins developed in order to transform this model and generate the corresponding nets. These nets were then imported to the DENEB platform and consequently deployed and executed without any human intervention.

7. CONCLUSION AND FUTURE WORK

In this chapter we have presented a model-driven solution to automatically generate executable code from business process models. The proposal consists of the integration of SOD-M and DENEB by means of the MeTAGeM framework. More specifically, a set of ATL rules generated by MeTAGeM is executed in order to transform SOD-M composition service models to DENEB executable workflows. The result is a model-driven method for the analysis, design, development and execution of business processes that covers BPM solutions from the very early stages of their development to their deployment and execution. As part of this work we have provided a complete EMF-based tool supporting the method. The integration of both approaches is based on the automatic generation of code that is directly executable in DENEB. The contribution of our proposal is the ability to generate executable code without human intervention, as opposed to code skeletons or fragments. This solution frees business analysts and IT developers from the implementation, deployment and execution details of business processes.

Moreover, the resulting framework has been tested in a real case study, GesIMED, a Web IS for medical image management and processing. Business analysts have used the SOD-M methodology to specify their business goals and requirements. Both of them have been expressed in a composition service model, and a set of transformation rules has subsequently been applied in an executable DENEB process. Our solution permits the implementation (code programming) stage to be eliminated and eases the deployment of the resulting business process in the target execution environment. The cost of the development has therefore been reduced and deployment risks have been minimized.

On the other hand, as was mentioned in the introduction, the analysis of process models is another relevant challenge in the MDE field. In this respect, our approach has the advantage of using Petri nets to program executable processes. The mathematically sound foundation of Petri nets allows different analysis techniques to be integrated into our approach for the validation and verification of process models. Although these solutions are not within the scope of this chapter, we shall briefly discuss them and refer to our previous experience in the field of process analysis.

The analysis of models consists of checking whether the process modeled actually behaves as expected. Different techniques can be used for this purpose, such as simulation, enumeration or structure based analysis techniques. Simulation has traditionally been used for the validation of processes. In our approach, once a SOD-M model has been translated to a DENEB executable process, it can be simulated using the DENEB execution environment and its behavior can therefore be studied and analyzed. Moreover, the simulation capabilities of DENEB could be reused to analyze and improve the performance of the resulting process. Performance models for Petri nets could be integrated into our workflows and roles (Merseguer & Campos, 2004), for instance) to evaluate performance estimations of the process. On the other hand, we are also able to verify some behavioral properties of DENEB processes, in other words, to guarantee that processes are free of certain logical errors. In Ibáñez et al. (2011a) we proposed a method with which to verify whether a DENEB process can correctly interact with other processes so that the process terminates correctly. An implementation of this method could be directly integrated into the solution presented in this chapter. Other behavioral properties could be also checked by reusing the traditional verification techniques of Petri nets (Reisig et al., 2006; van der Aalst, 2000). (van Breugel et al., 2006) provides an interesting overview of the techniques and tools developed for Petri nets to be exploited in the verification of business processes modeled using the WS-BPEL standard.

Finally, in the near future we intend to increase the capabilities of our MDA framework to support semantic annotations of the SOD-M composition models. A given model, its activities, data, control structures and even the whole model will be semantically described using domain ontologies. This solution will be very interesting from an analytical point of view. In Ibáñez et al. (2011b) we proposed a new class of Petri nets, RDF Unary Petri nets (RDF-U-PN), to model semantic business processes, along with a methodology based on model checking techniques for the verification of their correctness and behavioral properties. Semantic SOD-M processes could be modeled using this Petri-net based formalism and then analyzed using the proposed method.

ACKNOWLEDGMENT

This work has been partially supported by the research projects TIN2010-17905 and TIN2011-22617, granted by the Spanish Ministry of Science and Innovation, by the Scientific and Technological Network on Service Science (TIN2011-15497-E), financed by the Spanish Ministry of Economy and Competitiveness, and also by the regional project DGAFSE, granted by the European Regional Development Fund (ERDF).

REFERENCES

Ameller, D. (2009). *Considering Non-functional Requirements in Model-Driven Engineering.* (Master Thesis). Universitat Politecnica de Catalunya, Departament de Llenguatges i Sistemes Informatics.

Arkin, A. (2002). *Business Process Modeling Language (BPML). Business Process Management Initiative.* BPMI.

Bézivin, J., Rumpe, B., Schürr, A., & Tratt, L. (2005). *Mandatory Example Specification.* Paper presented at CFP of the Model Transformations in Practice Workshop at MoDELS 2005. Montego Bay, Jamaica.

Biermann, E., Ermel, C., & Taentzer, G. (2008). *Precise Semantics of EMF Model Trans- formations by Graph Transformation.* Academic Press.

Billington, J., Christensen, S., van Hee, K. M., Kindler, E., Kummer, O., & Petrucci, L. (2003). The Petri net markup language: concepts technology, and tools. In *Proceedings of International Conference on Applications and Theory of Petri Nets – ATPN 2003,* (LNCS), (vol. 2679, pp. 483–505). Springer.

Bollati, V. A., Vara, J. M., Jimenez, A., & Marcos, E. (2013). Applying MDE to the (semi-) automatic development of model transformations. *Information and Software Technology, 55*(4), 699–718. doi:10.1016/j.infsof.2012.11.004

BPEL 2.0 Specification – OASIS. (2011). Retrieved from http://docs.oasis-open.org/wsbpel/

BPMN 1.1 – OMG Final Adopted Specification. (2008). Retrieved from http://www.omg.org/docs/formal/08-01-17.pdf

Brambilla, M. (2006). Generation of WebML Web application models from business process specifications. In *Proceedings of 6th International Conference on Web Engineering* (ICWE'06). ACM.

Brunswick, J. (2008). *Extending the Business Value of SOA through Business Process Management, Architect: SOA and BPM.* Academic Press.

Budinsky, F., Brodsky, S. A., & Merks, E. (2003). *Eclipse Modeling Framework.* Pearson Education.

Butler Group. (2003). *Application Development Strategies*. Author.

Cáceres, P., de Castro, V., Vara, J. M., & Marcos, E. (2006). Model transformations for hypertext modeling on web information systems. In *Proceedings of 2006 ACM symposium on Applied computing – SAC'06*. ACM.

Carriero, N., & Gelernter, D. (1989). Linda in context. *Communications of the ACM, 32*(4), 444–458. doi:10.1145/63334.63337

De Castro, V., Marcos, E., & Sanz, M. L. (2006). A model driven method for service composition modelling: A case study. *International Journal on Web Engineering Technology, 2*(4), 335–353. doi:10.1504/IJWET.2006.010419

De Castro, V., Marcos, E., & Vara, J. M. (2011). Applying CIM-to-PIM model transformations for the service-oriented development of information systems. *Information and Software Technology, 53*(19), 87–105. doi:10.1016/j.infsof.2010.09.002

De Castro, V., Marcos, E., & Wieringa, R. (2009). Towards a service-oriented MDA-based approach to the alignment of business processes with IT systems: From the business model to a web service composition model. *International Journal of Cooperative Information Systems, 18*(2), 225–260. doi:10.1142/S0218843009002038

Design Platform, A. R. I. S. (2007). *Getting Started with BPM*. Springer.

Didonet Del Fabro, M., Bézivin, J., & Valduriez, P. (2006). *Weaving Models with the Eclipse AMW plugin*. Paper presented at the Eclipse Modelling Symposium, Eclipse Summit Europe. Esslingen, Germany.

Didonet Del Fabro, M., & Valduriez, P. (2008). Towards the efficient development of model transformations using model weaving and matching transformations. *Software & Systems Modeling, 8*(3), 305–324. doi:10.1007/s10270-008-0094-z

Dijkman, R. (2010). BPMN 2.0 execution semantics formalized as graph rewrite rules. In *Proceedings of BPMN 2010*. BPMN.

Dikmans, L. (2008). *Transforming BPMN into BPEL: Why and How*. Oracle Technology network.

Eclipse. (2013). Retrieved from http://www.eclipse.org/

Fabra, J., & Álvarez, P. (2010). BPEL2DENEB: translation of BPEL processes to executable high-level petri nets. In *Proceedings of Fifth International Conference on Internet and Web Applications and Services – ICIW 2010*. IEEE Computer Society Press.

Fabra, J., Álvarez, P., Bañares, J., & Ezpeleta, J. (2006). A framework for the development and execution of horizontal protocols in open BPM systems. In *Proceedings of 4th International Conference on Business Process Management – BPM 2006* (LNCS). Springer Verlag.

Fabra, J., Álvarez, P., Bañares, J., & Ezpeleta, J. (2011). DENEB: a platform for the development and execution of interoperable dynamic web processes. *Concurrency and Computation*. doi:10.1002/cpe.1795 PMID:23335858

Fabra, J., Álvarez, P., & Ezpeleta, J. (2007). DRLinda: a distributed message broker for collaborative interactions among business processes. In *Proceedings of 8th International Conference on Electronic Commerce and Web Technologies – EC-Web'07* (LNCS), (vol. 4655, pp. 212-221). Springer Verlag.

Frye, C. (2006). BPM inside the belly of the SOA whale. *Web Services News*, 1–3.

GesIMED System. (2008). Retrieved from http://ariadna.escet.urjc.es/gesimed/

Gronback, R. C. (2009). *Eclipse modeling project: a domain-specific language toolkit*. Addison-Wesley Professional.

Guelfi, N., & Mammar, A. (2006). A formal framework to generate XPDL specifications from UML activity diagrams. In *Proceedings of 2006 ACM symposium on Applied computing – SAC'06*. ACM.

Hanson, J. E., Nandi, P., & Kumaran, S. (2002). Conversation support for business pro- cess integration. In *Proceedings of Sixth International Enterprise Distributed Object computing Conference – EDOC'02*. IEEE Computer Society.

Harmon, P. (2004). The OMG's model driven architecture and BPM. *Business Process Trends*, 1–3.

Havey, M. (2005). *Essential Business Process Modeling*. O'Reilly Media, Inc.

Hrastnik, P. (2004). Execution of business processes based on web services. *International Journal of Electronic Business*, *2*(5), 550–556. doi:10.1504/IJEB.2004.005886

Ibáñez, M., Álvarez, P., Bañares, J., & Ezpeleta, J. (2011). Control and data flow compatibility in the interaction between dynamic business processes. *Concurrency and Computation*, *23*(1), 57–85. doi:10.1002/cpe.1595

Ibáñez, M. J., Álvarez, P., Bañares, J. A., & Ezpeleta, J. (2011b). Analyzing Behavioral Properties of Semantic Business Processes with Parametric Data. *Concurrency and Computation*, *23*(5), 525–555. doi:10.1002/cpe.1661

Ibáñez, M. J., Álvarez, P., & Ezpeleta, J. (2008). Flow and data compatibility for the correct interaction among web processes. In *Proceedings of International Conference on Intelligent Agents, Web Technologies and Internet Commerce – IAWTIC 08*, (pp. 716–722). IAWTIC.

Ibáñez, M. J., Álvarez, P., & Ezpeleta, J. (2008). Checking necessary conditions for control and data flow compatibility between business and interaction logics in web processes. In *Proceedings of 6th IEEE European Conference on Web Services*, (pp. 92–101). IEEE.

Jiang, P., Mair, Q., & Newman, J. (2003). Using UML to design distributed collaborative workflows: from UML to XPDL. In *Proceedings of IEEE International Workshops on Enabling Technologies*. IEEE.

Johnson, R. (2002). *Expert One-on-One J2EE Design & Development*. Wrox Press Ltd.

Jouault, F., Allilaire, F., Bézivin, J., & Kurtev, I. (2008). ATL: A model transformation tool. *Science of Computer Programming*, *72*, 1–2, 31–39. doi:10.1016/j.scico.2007.08.002

Jouault, F., & Kurtev, I. (2005). Transforming models with ATL. In *Proceedings of MoDELS Satellite Events*, (pp. 128–138). MoDELS.

Kamoun, F. (2007). A roadmap towards the convergence of business process management and service oriented architecture. *Ubiquity*, 1–1.

Ko, R. K., Lee, S. S., & Lee, E. W. (2009). Business process management (BPM) standards: a survey. *Business Process Management Journal*, *15*(5). doi:10.1108/14637150910987937

Kummer, O. (2001). Introduction to Petri nets and reference nets. *Sozionik Aktuell*, *1*, 1–9.

Kummer, O., Wienberg, F., Duvigneau, M., Köhler, M., Moldt, D., & Rölke, H. (2003). Renew – the reference net workshop. In *Proceedings of 24th International Conference on Application and Theory of Petri Nets – ATPN 2003*, (pp. 99–102). ATPN.

Leymann, F. (2001). *Web Services Flow Language (WSFL 1.0)*. IBM.

Marcos, E., Acuña, C. J., & Cuesta, C. E. (2006). Integrating software architecture into a MDA framework. In *Proceedings of 3rd European Workshop on Software Architecture – EWSA* (LNCS), (vol. 4344, pp. 127-143). Springer.

Mellor, S. J., & Balcer, M. (2002). *Executable UML: A Foundation for Model-driven Architectures*. Addison-Wesley Longman Publishing Co.

Mellor, S. J., Clark, A. N., & Futagami, T. (2003). Model-driven development. *IEEE Software, 20,* 14–18. doi:10.1109/MS.2003.1231145

Mernik, M., Heering, J., & Sloane, A. M. (2005). When and how to develop domain-specific languages. *ACM Computing Surveys, 37*(4), 316–344. doi:10.1145/1118890.1118892

Merseguer, J., & Campos, J. (2004). Software performance modelling using UML and petri nets. *Lecture Notes in Computer Science, 2965,* 265–289. doi:10.1007/978-3-540-24663-3_13

Miller, J., & Mukerji, J. (2003). *MDA Guide Version 1.0.1, Document number omg/2003- 06-01.* Retrieved from http://www.omg.com/mda

Murata, T. (1989). Petri nets: properties, analysis and applications. *Proceedings of the IEEE, 77,* 541–580. doi:10.1109/5.24143

Object Management Group. (2010). Retrieved from http://www.omg.org/

OMG. (2001). *Model Driven Architecture. A technical perspective.* OMG document-orm-sc/01-07-01.

OMG & MDA. (2011). *The Architecture of Choice for a Changing World.* Retrieved from http://www.omg.org/mda/productssuccess.htm

OMG BPMN 2.0 – OMG Formal Specification. (2011). Retrieved from http://www.omg.org/spec/BPMN/2.0/

OMG Service Oriented Architecture SIG – ABSIG. (2009). Retrieved from http://soa.omg.org/

Palmer, N. (2006). Understanding the BPMN–XPDL–BPEL value chain. *Business Integration Journal,* 54–55.

Path Language, X. M. L. XPath. (1999). *Version 1.0.* Retrieved from http://www.w3.org/TR/xpath/

Reisig, W., Fahland, D., Lohmann, N., Massuthe, P., Stahl, C., Weinberg, D., et al. (2006). Analysis techniques for service models. In *Proceedings of Second International Symposium on Leveraging Applications of Formal Methods, Verification and Validation, 2006* (ISoLA 2006). IEEE Computer Society.

Roser, S., & Bauer, B. (2005). A categorization of collaborative business process modeling techniques. In *Proceedings of Seventh IEEE International Conference on E-Commerce Technology Workshops – CECW'05.* IEEE Computer Society.

Sánchez Cuadrado, J., García Molina, J., & Menarguez Tortosa, M. (2006). *RubyTL: A Practical, Extensible Transformation Language.* Paper presented at the European Conference on Model Driven Architecture - Foundations and Applications (ECMDA-FA 2006). Bilbao, Spain.

Sandy, K. (2006). *BPM Think Tank. EbizQ.* Retrieved from http://www.ebizq.net/blogs/column2/archives/bpmthinktank2006/

Schmidt, D.C. (2006). Model-driven engineering. *IEEE Computer, 39* (2).

Selic, B. (2003). The pragmatics of Model-driven Development. *IEEE Software, 20*(5), 19–25. doi:10.1109/MS.2003.1231146

Selic, B. (2008). MDA manifestations upgrade. *The European Journal for the Informatics Professional, 9*(2), 12–16.

Silverás, B. (2011). *BPMS Watch.* Retrieved from http://www.brsilver.com/

Steinberg, D., Budinsky, F., Paternostro, M., & Merks, E. (2008). *EMF: Eclipse Modeling Framework.* Addison-Wesley Professional.

Tamames, J. A. H., Acuña, C. J., de Castro, V., Marcos, E., Sanz, M. L., & Malpica, N. (2007). Web-PACS for multicenter clinical trials. *IEEE Transactions on Information Technology in Biomedicine, 11*(1), 87–93. doi:10.1109/TITB.2006.879601 PMID:17249407

Thatte, S. (2001). *XLANG: Web Services for Business Process Design*. Microsoft.

Unified Modeling Language (UML). (2011). Retrieved from http://www.uml.org/

van Breugel, F., & Koshkina, M. (2006). *Models and Verification of BPEL*. Retrieved from http://www.cse.yorku.ca/franck/ research/drafts/tutorial.pdf

van der Aalst, W. M. P. (2000). Workflow verification: finding control-flow errors using petri-net-based techniques. In *Business Process Management, Models, Techniques, and Empirical Studies*. Springer-Verlag.

van der Aalst, W. M. P. (2004). Business process management demystified: a tutorial on models, systems and standards for workflow management. In Lectures on Concurrency and Petri Nets (LNCS), (vol. 3098, pp. 1-65). Springer-Verlag.

van der Aalst, W. M. P., & ter Hofstede, A. H. M. (2005). YAWL: Yet another workflow language. *Information Systems*, *30*(4), 245–275. doi:10.1016/j.is.2004.02.002

Vara, J. M., & Marcos, E. (2012). A framework for model-driven development of information systems: Technical decisions and lessons learned. *Journal of Systems and Software*, *85*(10), 2368–2384. doi:10.1016/j.jss.2012.04.080

Vara, J. M., Vela, B., Bollati, V. A., & Marcos, E. (2009). Supporting model-driven development of object-relational database schemas: a case study. In *Proceedings of 2nd International Conference on Theory and Practice of Model Transformations – ICMT'09*. Springer-Verlag.

Verner, L. (2004). BPM: the promise and the challenge. *Queue*, *2*(1), 82–91. doi:10.1145/984458.984503

Walsh, A. E. (2002). *Ebxml: The Technical Reports*. Prentice Hall.

Watson, A. (2008). A brief history of MDA, upgrade. *The European Journal for the Informatics Professional*, *9*(2), 7–11.

White, S. (2004). *Process Modelling Notations and Workflow Patterns*. IBM Corporation.

White, S. A. (2005). *Using BPMN to Model a BPEL Process*. IBM Corp.

KEY TERMS AND DEFINITIONS

DENEB: A platform for the development and execution of flexible business processes, represented by means of workflow models.

GesIMED: A Web information system for medical image management and processing.

Message Broker: The component responsible for supporting communication and coordinating interactions among parties by means of an internal message repository in which normal messages or control/synchronization messages can be stored.

MeTAGeM: A tool for the automatic generation of ATL rules required to transform SOD-M models to DENEB workflows.

Model Driven Architecture (MDA): A specific incarnation of MDE nowadays that defines three abstraction levels, namely Computer Independent, Platform Independent and Platform Specific Models (CIM, PIM and PSM), and promotes the use of OMG standards, like the UML, OCL, BPMN, etc. The principles of MDE emerged as a generalization of the Model Driven Architecture (MDA).

Model Driven Engineering (MDE): A new trend in software engineering whose main proposal is to focus on models rather than in computer programs. This way, models are used to raise the abstraction level at which software is conceived, developed, etc. and to increase the level of automation at any stage of the development process.

PNML: An XML-based standard language for the interchange of Petri nets.

SOD-M: A model-driven method for the development of service-oriented systems.

Chapter 11

Modeling Platform–Independent and Platform–Specific Service Architectures with UML and the ArchiMeDeS Framework

Marcos López-Sanz
Rey Juan Carlos University, Spain

Esperanza Marcos
Rey Juan Carlos University, Spain

ABSTRACT

Service-oriented architectures have, over the last decade, gradually become more important. The vast diversity of implementation and support platforms for this kind of architecture increases the complexity of the processes used to develop service-based systems. The task of specifying service architectures can be eased by following a model-driven approach and the appropriate model notations. In this chapter, the authors explore the architectural properties of the service-oriented paradigm and present part of a framework for the specification of service-oriented software architectures. The main idea is to use the separation into different abstraction levels fostered by the MDA proposal and tackle the software architecture specification progressively, stepping from conceptual to platform-specific levels. This chapter particularly concentrates upon describing UML profiles for the PIM and PSM levels of service-oriented architectural models, along with their corresponding metamodels. The use of the proposed profiles is illustrated in a case study in which the proposed profiles are implemented.

INTRODUCTION

The development of systems based on services has grown in importance over the last few years. The introduction of the service orientation principles into the business field (Krafzig et al., 2004), the

specification of new technological standards for services (W3C, 2011) or the usage of services as a basis in the construction of middleware systems (Foster and Kesselman, 1998) are among the main motivations. However, several problems have arisen throughout this evolution, among which

DOI: 10.4018/978-1-4666-6026-7.ch011

are issues such as the migration of the execution platform, the design and implementation of intricate lifecycles, the increase in the complexity of the development process and the lack of a precise definition for the concepts involved in SOA (*Service Oriented Architecture*) solutions.

Various actions can be taken to tackle these problems. We focus on two:

- The accomplishment of a study of the architectural principles governing the service-oriented designs. The architecture of a system reflects that system's structure and behavior, and how it evolves as time elapses. The architecture of a service-oriented system should also include features related to business processes and organizational aspects. The integration of business models, which has led to their rapid evolution and spreading, is one of the main benefits of SOA.

- The use of a methodological approach in order to reduce the complexity of the SOA development process. One of the current trends that is gaining most importance is the model-driven approach. The ideas behind the MDA (*Model-Driven Architecture*) proposal (Miller and Mukerji, 2003) can facilitate and improve the development of SOA solutions.

Service-oriented development methods based on the MDA principles and an architecture-centric method could consequently be used to solve the problems stated at the beginning. MDA conceives models as first class elements during system design and implementation, and establishes the separation of the development process into three abstraction levels, namely CIM (*Computation Independent Model*), PIM (*Platform Independent Model*) and PSM (*Platform Specific Model*). Its main feature, however, is the definition of mappings (model transformation rules) between the models defined at each level and between levels,

which makes the automation of the development process possible (Selic, 2003). In our case, the methodological framework that we use as a basis is ArchiMeDeS, a service-oriented framework for the model-driven specification of software architectures (López-Sanz and Marcos, 2012).

In previous research works (Marcos et al., 2006), we have made an in-depth study of the convenience of extending the MDA proposal in order to support the specification of the architectural modeling aspect within an MDE (*Model-Driven Engineering*) process. The conclusions of the aforementioned work have been used as a basis to develop a UML profile for the PIM and PSM levels within a process for service-oriented architectural modeling, which is presented in this chapter. We shall also present the corresponding metamodel comprising the semantic meaning and relationships associated with the elements defined in the profile. This is illustrated and validated through the use of a real-world case study: an extension for a Web Information System for medical image management called GESiMED (Acuña et al., 2008).

In order to place the research presented in context, we comment on some other works related to the topic shown in this chapter. We shall analyze proposals dealing with: the definition of the SOA principles (Aiello and Dustdar, 2006; Lublinsky, 2007; Papazoglou, 2008); UML profiles for service-based developments (Amir and Zeid, 2004; Wada et al., 2006; Zdun and Dustdar, 2007), and even the MDA principles when applied to SOA (Larrucea and Benguria, 2006).

The remainder of the chapter is structured as follows: Section 2 provides a general overview of the framework in which the research is framed, and positions our work with some other relevant works. Section 3 presents, firstly the concepts involved in the UML profile by means of depicting the associated meta-model and, secondly, a UML profile for the PIM and PSM levels of service-oriented architectural modeling, together with an illustrative case study. Section 4 discusses some future research directions related to the modeling and specification of service architectures. Finally, Section 5 presents the main conclusions of the work presented.

BACKGROUND

In this section we summarize the research context in which our proposal for modeling service-oriented architectures with UML is framed: ArchiMeDeS (López-Sanz and Marcos, 2012), a model-driven framework for the service-oriented development of software architectures. We shall also discuss some related works in order to establish a coherent background on the modeling of service architectures.

Research Context: Architecture-Centric Development

Figure 1 shows an overview of the global idea behind the global concept of architecture-centric development. Our proposal is to situate the system architecture in the middle of the development process and the remaining software concerns in the outer rings. It is thus possible to consider the architecture as the main artifact in a software development process. It not only provides the basic skeleton for the system, but also the basic guide which drives and facilitates the development itself by adding flexibility and adaptability (Gomaa, 2005; Alti et al., 2007; Broy, 2004). By developing systems in these ways it is possible to configure and improve the development process according to a particular system architecture. This implies that the elements that appear in the architecture will drive the creation of models or the definition of additional software concerns (Marcos et al., 2006). This signifies that when, for example, defining a service-oriented system, the modeling of a service-oriented architecture at the conceptual level, and thus independently of the platform on which the software will be executed,

will help software developers to determine what kind of elements need to be modeled; in this case, services, service compositions, service providers, service contracts, IT services, etc.

The ArchiMeDeS Framework

ArchiMeDeS (López-Sanz and Marcos, 2012) is a modeling framework that represents a coherent solution that can be used to architect the existing gap between a high-level perception of a system, in which the software solution is modeled conceptually and independently from the platform on which the software will be executed, to its low-level representation, where technological aspects determine the final shape of the system providing technical support to the previously identified entities and constraints.

ArchiMeDeS attains this goal with an integrated solution that follows the MDA approach for the specification of software architectures. Accordingly, and following the separation into abstraction levels fostered by MDA, several DSLs (*Domain Specific Languages*) with which to represent Software Architectures have been created: a DSL at the PIM level, to allow the specification of conceptual service architectures and architectural styles (López-Sanz et al., 2011), and various DSLs at the PSM level. This PSM level has been divided into two sublevels in order to reflect the commonalities of service platforms (*Platform-Dependent Model*, PDM) separately, in addition to the particularities of concrete service technologies (*Technology-Dependent Model*, TDM), for which an independent DSL has been designed for each of the technological approaches chosen (Web Services, Grid Services or REST Services).

Figure 2 shows a global overview of the model architecture, along with the different model transformations of the ArchiMeDeS framework.

In each case, both the abstract syntax (set of concepts used to build the model semantics) and the concrete syntax have been defined at either PIM or PSM level. For the semantics, the concepts

Figure 1. Global overview of the ArchiMeDeS framework

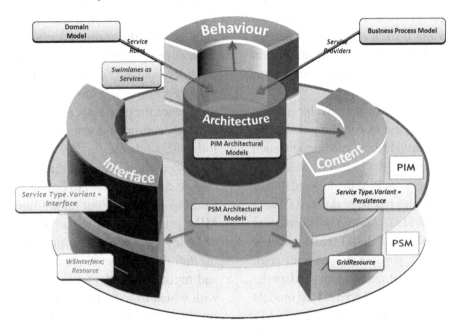

Figure 2. Global overview of the ArchiMeDeS framework

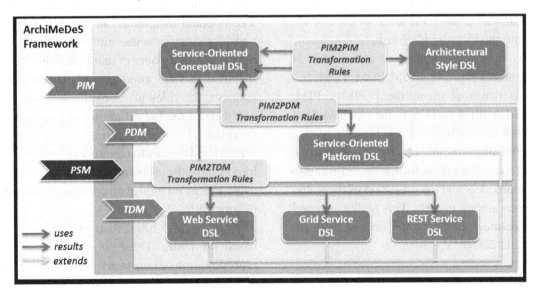

used are those contained within the SOC (*Service-Oriented Computing*) paradigm (Papazoglou, 2008). The software architectures modeled are consequently transformed into service-oriented artifacts, thus taking advantage of their features to represent the structural characteristics of a soft-

ware solution supporting the business processes required. This is done by placing the concepts in metamodels that allow the definition of service-oriented architectural models. The concrete syntax of each DSL is meanwhile represented by means of a UML-based notation. The goal is to provide a specific, adaptable and widely accepted notation for the representation of software artifacts. Moreover, by using UML it is possible to benefit from its extension mechanisms for the definition of personalized graphical models using the extension mechanisms defined by UML.

Several model transformations have been defined with the purpose of enriching the architectural models with additional information (such as that of architectural styles). On the one hand, a weaving process between PIM models and that of the architectural styles has been defined. Weaving models and ATL (*ATLAS Transformation Language*) (Jouault et al., 2008) transformation rules are used for this purpose (López-Sanz et al, 2011). On the other hand, and in order to adapt the architectural information gathered in PIM models to the particularities of service platforms, additional transformation rules have been specified, first in natural language and then implemented with ATL, between the PIM metamodel and every metamodel at the PSM level for each of the aforementioned service platforms.

Apart from the definition of metamodels at different abstraction levels (PIM, PDM, TDM) and the transformations among them (PIM-to-PIM, PIM-to-PDM/PIM-to-TDM), the ArchiMeDeS framework also includes a set of modeling tools. This toolkit allows the graphical editing of models, the validation of their conformance according to their metamodels and the execution of the transformations among models. This toolkit is based on the features offered by the Eclipse platform (Gronback, 2009).

Related Works

The model-driven development of SOA systems has been tackled by several other authors in the last few years. Baresi et al. (2003) propose the modeling and validation of Service-oriented architectures using UML to represent SOA static concepts, graph transformation rules to represent the behavior, and transition systems

to validate them. Although these authors use UML as an abstraction method to model the architecture, this proposal considers that any SOA development is built upon service clients, providers and service discovering agents. This vision constrains the scope in which SOA can be used, since the proposal cannot be generalized to other execution platforms apart from those that follow this scheme.

Heckel et al. (2003) use the proposal of Baresi et al. as a starting point to define a UML profile for SOA modeling, but taking into account the MDA principles, i.e., the separation of PIM and PSM levels. Their UML profile only permits the definition of two kinds of services (provider and registry) and does not include any facility with which to model semantic or constraint issues (when applied, for example, to exchanged messages).

Another work related to SOA modeling is that presented by Zhang et al. (2006) who define a component metamodel in which services are considered as first-class element. This proposal is also similar to ours in that it defines concepts included in our proposal such as the service contract, the roles given to the services in the contracts or the identification of pre- and post-conditions. However, the composition of services is restricted merely to choreographies and, most importantly, the problem of user interaction is not dealt with as no modeling component is defined to support it.

Wada et al. (2006) also present a solution based on UML. These authors focus on the representation of non-functional aspects and the definition of services, messages, connectors and pipes as the only first-class available elements. Another drawback of this proposal is that all the restrictions are gathered inside comments. This is an important inconvenience if we wish to automate the development process or to validate models.

Amir and Zeid (2004) discuss another UML profile proposal for SOA modeling. Following the principles of Web services, they define 5 different profiles, each of which is associated with a SOA concept: resource, service, message, policy and agent. This proposal is too close to the implementation technology and would not therefore be suitable for the development of a generic SOA system in which a platform exchange should take place.

Various other proposals originate from the enterprise research field. Papazoglou (2008), for example, makes a classification of the concepts involved in SOA development but from the viewpoint of the role given to each component. We consider this viewpoint by including a hierarchy of services in our metamodel. Moreover, their research is based on the Web Services principles. This circumstance also appears in other works from the enterprise research field such as those by Aiello and Dustdar (2006), Lublinsky (2007), Erl (2005), or Krafzig et al. (2004). This is mainly owing to the fact that they start from the definition of service (and SOA by extension) provided by the W3C, in which a service is defined as a stateless distributed entity. This represents a serious restriction when attempting to define the system architecture at a conceptual and platform independent level as in the PIM level of MDA.

The UML 2.0 profile created by IBM (Arsanjani et al., 2008) is one of the proposals that is closest to the content presented in this article. In this work, a generic model with the main concepts of the SOA paradigm is presented from a more conceptual viewpoint which is not so constrained to the Web Service concepts.

Many other proposals related to the definition of SOA architectures (Rennie and Misic, 2004; Kruger and Mathew, 2004) include the specification of ADLs (Architecture Description Languages) for the formal definition of architectures, but this topic is beyond the scope of this article. The latter (that by Kruger and Mathew) additionally defines a systematic development process based on sequence diagrams as graphical notation for the description of service architectures.

The proposal by Larrucea and Benguria (2006) is among the rare proposals that focus on the MDA approach for the specification of platform-independent service architectures we have found. These authors present a tool with which to obtain partial implementations from business models throughout the definition of an ad-hoc UML profile for business aspects, named POP*.

When considering concrete model-driven initiatives for the representation of platform-specific service-oriented architectures, there are some interesting works that are in some respects related to our proposal. . It is worth mentioning the modeling approach presented by the OMG in the form of the SoaML UML profile (OMG, 2009) whose main goal is to help architects to better describe the inner structures of SOA developments. As far as we are concerned, this language assumes some unusual premises in SOA, such as the fact that the participant (a mixture of service enactor and consumer) element is positioned as a central artifact of the modeling architecture rather than being the service itself, thus emphasizing role and contract as the most important concepts. On the contrary, we defend that it is the service, understood as the architectural component that collects the business logic, which must be the key element in the modeling of platform-specific service architectures.

PROPOSAL OF PIM-LEVEL UML PROFILE FOR SERVICE ARCHITECTURES

In this section we introduce our proposal for a UML profile to be used in the definition of the architecture model for service architectures at PIM level. We first describe the concepts in the UML profile using the associated metamodel, and we then go on to present the UML profile itself. The use of these profiles is illustrated with a case study which is described in the following section.

Figure 3. PIM level metamodel for service-oriented architectures

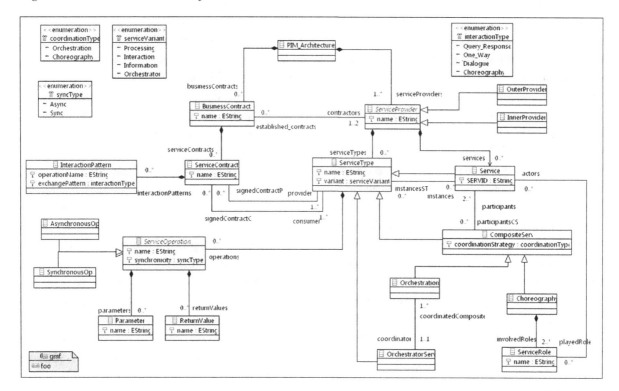

Concepts Involved in the Definition of the Profile

The set of concepts that appear in the PIM-level architecture metamodel depicted in Figure 3 are explained below:

Service Providers

Business organizations involved in business processes performed using services play a key role in the definition of the properties of the architectural elements. Service providers are the architectural elements that represent such organizations within the architectural model. Depending on whether they are internal to the system modeled (and therefore considered part of the software solution or external entities that collaborate to perform a specific task of value but not under its control) they will be modeled as *Inner Service Providers* or *Outer Service Providers*, respectively. An

association named *'business contract'* will be defined among them, and will contain the set of service contracts established among the services they contain.

Service Description

The main concepts that permit the description (and clear understanding) of a service are identified as service attributes. They are aligned with the vision of service provided by OASIS in their Reference Model (OASIS, 2007) and consist of the following properties:

- **SERVID Property:** This property allows a service to be placed within an architectural configuration and, therefore, the univocal identification of a service. The architectural concept of service can be understood from two complementary point of views: first, as actual services that entail the functionalities offered, hence our reference to 'service instances'; and second, as the functionality that is expected to be provided without identifying a concrete service exemplar, using the term 'service type' for that objective.

- **Service Operations:** Atomic functionalities offered by a service that collaborates to build a joint description of that service.
- **Service Role:** When a service acts by following a concrete role, its base behavior is modified to adapt it to the context in which the service participates. In this respect, the service offers a subgroup of the operations initially defined in its service type.

Service Taxonomy

In order to ease the identification of the responsibilities that each service may have in the business processes that the system aims to cover, a detailed service classification is recommended from the architectural point of view. At the PIM abstraction level, developers already know what the main function of a service is as part of the software solution, and this 'knowledge' is architectonically understood as a design decision agnostic of the underlying technology or platform.

In the PIM DSL defined by ArchiMeDeS all these variants are associated with a service in the form of a feature (named *variant* in the metamodel) comprising one or more of these values.

- **Processing:** Another kind of service that may be easily identified is that which is in charge of performing information processing or computation tasks.
- **Interaction:** Services may also serve as boundaries of the system. In this respect, services will be identified with the interaction value.
- **Information:** A service whose main purpose is to serve as an access point in which

to store information, independently of the storage strategy chosen.

- **Orchestration:** For services in charge of handling the flow of the business process defined for the system.

Service Composition

As already stated, the interactive collaboration among participants defines the way in which composition is understood within the service-oriented paradigm. The coordination scheme used to build up the composition allows a classification of service composition alternatives to be established:

- **Choreography:** One alternative is to consider an interacting environment among equivalent services. This 'equivalence' signifies that there is no service mastering over any other or directing the flow of information.
- **Orchestration:** When there is a special service in charge of directing the whole compound element, we refer to orchestrations. Such a service (*orchestrator*) knows the flow of service consumptions that must take place in order to accomplish the functionality desired.

Service Interaction

The way in which interaction among architectural elements is achieved is one of the key differences between service-orientation and other architectural paradigms. On the one hand, services are not encapsulated in composite elements; they are consumed by interacting agents to attain a specific goal. On the other hand, rather than using method invocation on an object reference, service orientation shifts the conversation to that of message passing. Finally, *service contracts* represent the interaction among services, and are understood as the tacit agreement reached to act in a particular manner and signed by the participant services.

Figure 4. Stereotypes defined in the PIM-level UML profile for service architectural modeling

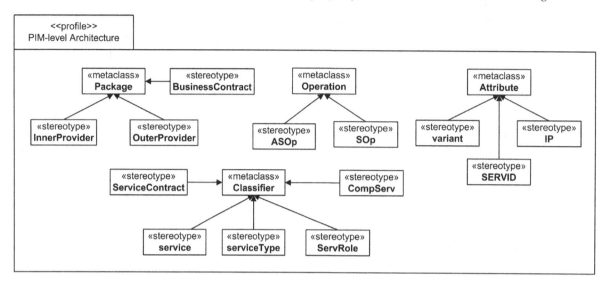

- **Service Contracts** represent architectural connectors, meaning point-to-point relationships between the services that 'sign' these contracts.

- **Interaction Patterns** are defined as 'operation name-interaction kind' pairs, the former element being a reference to the set of operations offered by the provider service and the latter being the kind of exchange pattern that will be followed when using that operation.

PIM-Level UML Profile for Service-Oriented Architectural Models

In this section we show the main stereotypes needed to represent the concepts described previously in a UML model for SOA. Figure 4 shows the main components of the profile created. The usage of each stereotype is then illustrated by means of a case study.

Table 1 lists all the stereotypes defined, in addition to the base UML metaclass from which they are derived and the tag used to represent each stereotype.

PROPOSAL OF PSM-LEVEL UML PROFILE FOR SERVICE ARCHITECTURES

The number of service platforms currently available signifies that any modeling initiative for platform-specific modeling must be able to cope with the potential diversity of implementation alternatives. We have accordingly opted to divide the PSM level into two independent sublayers: a PDM (*Platform-Dependent Model*) layer containing a DSL with which to reflect the commonalities of service platforms, and a TDM (*Technology-Dependent Model*) layer containing several DSLs with which to model the architecture of a system using service technologies based on web services (W3C, 2004), REST services (Fielding, 2000) and grid services (Foster et al., 2002). We are thus able to simultaneously model not only the architecture of concrete service technologies but also architectures based on different technologies. See Figure 5 for an overview of the PSM-level metamodel.

Although these platforms define and treat the architectural elements differently, a common set of concepts can be extracted from them. This

Table 1. Stereotypes of the UML profile for the PIM-level modeling of service architectures

Notation	Associated Concept	Base UML Metaclass	Meaning
<<innerProvider>>	Inner provider	Package	Provider of inner services
<<outerProvider>>	Outer provider	Package	External provider of services
<<businessContract>>	Business contract	Package	Business contract established between providers
<<Service>>	Service	Classifier	Architectural element representing an instance of a computational entity offering a certain capability
<<ServiceType>>	Service Type	Classifier	Architectural element representing an indefinite number of computational entities offering a certain capability
<<SERVID>>	SERVID	Attribute	Represents a unique identifier for a service
<<variant>>	Type of service	Attribute	Indicates the type of service (interaction, information, processing, orchestration)
<<ASOp>>	Asynchronous operation	Operation	Asynchronous atomic functionality offered by a service
<<SOp>>	Synchronous operation	Operation	Synchronous atomic functionality offered by a service
<<serviceContract>>	Service contract	Classifier	Acts as connector of services
<<IP>>	Interaction patter	Attribute	Indicates a pair operation name-exchange pattern to be fulfilled by contractor services
<<ServRole>>	Service role	Classifier	Identifies the role given to a service within a choreography
<<CompServ>>	Composite service	Classifier	Indicates that the architectural element is composed of several services

Figure 5. PSM level metamodel for service-oriented architectures

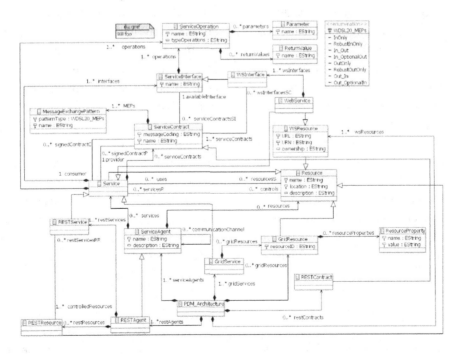

263

leads to the creation of a base metamodel that can be used as a kernel for any service-oriented platform, as has been explained previously. As a direct consequence, the PSM level of ArchiMeDeS also includes the PDM sublayer, which gathers all the concepts that the target service-oriented platforms have in common. This subdivision has been previously used in the context of grid service modeling in works such as that of Smith et al. (2006).Although this is still an ongoing research effort, the existence of the PDM layer also paves the way towards providing support for the platform migration of service-oriented systems.

Common Concepts (PDM Metamodel)

Service Agents

The services and resources in a service-oriented environment must be executed and managed by a physical entity. At lower levels, this job is accomplished by physical entities which are globally known as *service agents* (W3C, 2004). Service agents may be understood to be the elements that serve as the factual executing substrate of the services implemented over that substrate.

Architectonically speaking, service agents can be paired with the concepts of node or server, in the sense of acting as the deploying infrastructure over which services are executed and resources are positioned. The main difference with these elements is that the identification of service agents within architectural models may not refer solely to hardware components but, in contrast and from the point of view of the ArchiMeDeS framework, they may also represent software artifacts, thus allowing the tasks provided by a service under its charge to be performed.

Resources

RFC 2396 (Berners-Lee et al., 1998) defines a *resource* as 'anything that has identity'. This general definition covers any electronic entity that may be computationally described, managed and accessed (W3C, 2004). Elements such as a Web page, an image, a text file or a database storing information are therefore identified as resources. A processing facility, a computing platform (in the sense of an execution substrate) or any software artifact that can be used by any external entity in order to obtain a value derived from its interaction with the resource can also take this term. By following this definition, the consideration of any service implementation (based on whichever current service-related technology is being used) is easily acceptable as a special kind of resource. Depending on the technology or paradigm used to implement the resource, all its distinguishable properties will be defined jointly (think of a REST-compliant service for example) or separately in different software elements (e.g. a URL plus a WSDL document for the description of a Web Service). *Services* A service represents a piece of software that performs part of a business task that is clearly defined and implemented over a concrete platform. At a lower abstraction level, it is understood as a special kind of resource that, consequently, inherits all its properties. However, it differs from a resource in its purpose as part of a software solution. A service acts as an active entity in charge of performing a specific function in its context, either on its own or together with a specific resource. With regard to the possible relationships between services and resources, it is important to note that there are situations in which the consumption of the functionalities offered by a service requires the previous use of a resource (for example when a Web page permits access to a specific Web Service). The existence of this kind of contexts requires an explicit description of the relationships permitted between resources and services:

- **From Resources to Services:** Since resources are considered to be 'passive' elements within the architecture, these elements will provide only a standard means of referencing and accessing the capabilities defined by the service (e.g. a link to the service entry point or URL).

- **From Service to Resource:** Access may take many forms, including retrieving a representation of the resource, adding or modifying a representation of the resource, and deleting some or all representations of the resource.

Services, like architectural elements, define another concrete property: a well-known interface, which represents the boundary of a service such as the resource description element, with the difference that, in the case of a service, a service interface contains a description of the operations offered. *Service contracts* Interaction in service-oriented environments is accomplished by the active elements, that is, among services, through the exchange of messages (i.e., tokens of information). The conditions under which messages are exchanged are defined in an agreement signed by contractor services. The architectural element that defines all these conditions is known as a service contract. At the PIM abstraction level, a service contract represents the conditions under which a particular client could use the operations defined by a service. At the PDM level, in turn,

these conditions may define not only the message interaction pattern but, more consistently, the protocol used to encode the communication process, the message format used or the concrete interface of the provider service that the consumer will be able to use. This situation can be easily tracked within platforms such as Web services (in which a WSDL file includes both the message exchange pattern and a reference to the scheme that messages follow) and Grid Services (in which standards such as WS-Addressing permit the definition of the interconnection conditions).

Technology Specific Concepts (TDM Metamodels)

The PDM metamodel has been extended to support the modeling of some of the currently most wide-spread service technologies. We first focus on providing modeling support for web service technologies, and particularly the *Web Service Architecture* (WSA) initiative (W3C, 2004). In addition, since the WSA specification recommends the use of WSDL (W3C, 2007), we also rely on this standard to populate the properties of the architectural elements. The main concepts of the TDM DSL for web services are (see metamodel in Figure 6):

Figure 6. Concepts for modeling web service architectures

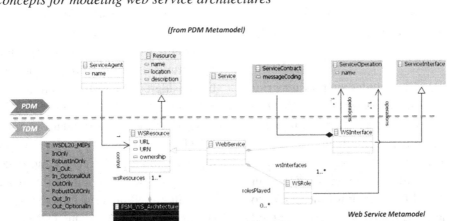

Figure 7. Concepts for modeling grid service architectures

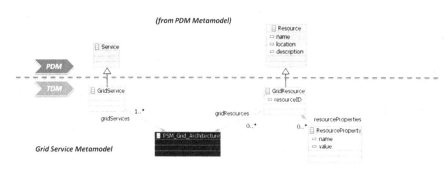

- **Resource:** Entities that have a *name*, may have reasonable representations (resource descriptions) and can be said to be owned.
- **Web Service:** Abstract resources that represent a capability of performing tasks from the point of view of provider entities and requester entities.
- **Service Interface:** The abstract boundary that a service exposes. This defines the types of messages and the message exchange patterns (MEPs) that are involved in interacting with the service.
- **Service Contract:** This element is inherited from the PDM metamodel and relies on the acceptance of the features and constraints defined as part of the service interface, hence the establishment of a relationship with this element.
- **Service Role:** This is played by a service and refers to the performance of choreographic interactions among services using some of the standard languages defined by the W3C.

Our proposal also includes support for grid-based architectures materialized in the TDM DSL for grid services. The history of grid computing shows the underlying technology evolved to adopt the web service technology as defined in the OGSA Architecture (Foster et al., 2002) but with a substantial difference: it was necessary to provide support for stateful services (understood

as grid resources), a fact that finally materialized in the WSRF specification (Graham et al., 2005). The concepts identified in the Architecture of grid environments based on grid services are described below (see view of metamodel in Figure 7):

- **Grid Service:** Any technological service that "virtualizes" the use of any existing element in the grid environment and that allows any facility managed in the Grid to be accessed (Foster et al., 2002).
- **Grid Resource:** Anything that can be virtualized within the scope of a grid environment and that has some specific properties. In our proposal, a grid resource represents the same concept as a WS-Resource as is defined by OASIS (Graham et al, 2005). The architectural element has been assigned a different name since the TDM DSL for web services already defines the concept of *WSResource*.

Finally we also provide support for REST architectures (Fielding, 2000). Although this might be considered as a restriction to the vision of the WSA initiative, it uses many of its principles, but usually relies on the standard operations of the HTTP protocol. It is also related to grid computing, since both grid services and REST services aim to provide a solution for the management of statefulness within service-oriented environments (Pautasso et al., 2008). Our TDM DSL for REST

Figure 8. Concepts for modeling REST service architectures

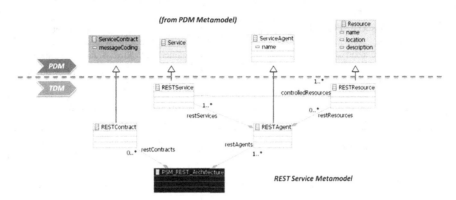

services defines several elements, which are shown in Figure 8 and explained below:

- **REST Agent:** Entities whose main purpose is to know what 'piece of code' (i.e., RESTService) should be executed when a request to a concrete URL is made.
- **REST Service:** The computational entities that actually respond to a client's request to access a resource.
- **REST Resource:** A conceptual mapping onto a set of entities and not the entity that corresponds to the values or state of a resource at a specific moment (Pautasso et al, 2008).
- **REST Contract:** The contract generally adopted for REST services is named a uniform contract and consists of the description of the URI defining the resource and the standard operation accompanying the resource.

PSM-Level UML Profile for Service-Oriented Architectural Models

In this section we show the main stereotypes needed to represent the concepts described previously in a UML model for SOA. Figure 9 shows the main components of the profile created. The

usage of each stereotype is then illustrated in the following section by means of a case study.

Table 2 lists all the stereotypes defined, along with the base UML metaclass from which they are derived and the tag used to represent each stereotype.

USING ARCHIMEDES AND UML PROFILES TO ARCHITECT THE GESIMED SYSTEM

In this section we briefly comment on the architectural models that have been used to verify the feasibility of the proposal and thus to refine the DSLs presented, in addition to checking the usefulness of the UML profiles described above.

Case Study Overview: The GESiMED System

The development of the entire ArchiMeDeS framework has been accomplished using a case study-based research method. In particular, the case study is based on the architectural modeling of the GESiMED system, an information system which permits the creation and maintenance of scientific studies for research in neuroscience (Hernández et al, 2006). This information system supports several business processes related

Table 2. Stereotypes of the UML profile for the PSM-level modeling of service architectures

Notation	Associated Concept	Base UML Metaclass	Meaning
<<*ServiceAgent*>>	Service agent	Package	Architectural elements understood as executing substrate
<<*Resource*>>	Resource	Classifier	Any electronic entity that can be computationally described
<<*Service*>>	Service	Classifier	Active entity in charge of performing a specific capability or function
<<*serviceContract*>>	Service contract	Classifier	Architectural element that defines the conditions under which communication among services takes place
<<*MEP*>>	Message Exchange Pattern	Attribute	Represents the way messages are exchanged as indicated in WSDL 1.1/2.0
<<*ServOp*>>	Service operation	Operation	Atomic functionality offered by a service
<<*ServiceInterface*>>	Service interface	Classifier	Indicates the boundary of a service
<<*WService*>>	Web Service	Classifier	Represents a Web Service according to WSA
<<*WSResource*>>	Web Service resource	Classifier	A resource accessed by a Web Service or that gains access to it
<<*WSInterface*>>	Web Service interface	Classifier	Indicates the boundary of a Web Service
<<*WSRole*>>	Web Service role	Classifier	The role played by a Web Service as indicated in its WSInterface
<<*RESTAgent*>>	REST agent	Package	A service agent capable of answering petitions made to REST services
<<*RESTService*>>	REST service	Classifier	Computational entity that responds to standard HTTP operations mapped onto REST enquiries
<<*RESTResource*>>	REST resource	Classifier	Conceptual mapping of a set of properties managed by a REST service
<<*RESTContract*>>	REST contract	Classifier	The set of standard HTTP operations available to query a REST service
<<*GridService*>>	Grid service	Classifier	A service implemented over a Grid infrastructure
<<*GridResource*>>	Grid resource	Classifier	A stateful entity accessed and managed by a Grid Service
<<*RP*>>	Grid resource property	Attribute	The individual properties that are enclosed within a Grid Resource

to that field of research: storage and retrieval of digital medical images, processing and result management of such images and medical image visualization (2D and 3D). A global overview of the working environment of this case study is shown in Figure 7.

In its origins, this system was implemented using a web engineering approach (not based on service technologies). That initial knowledge of the system served as a basis to tackle its reimplementation using service technologies. The functionality and requirements were expected to be the same

and, therefore, the conceptual modeling, but not the implementation technology.

The conceptual modeling of this case study is shown in Figure 8. This figure shows the PIM metamodel as it has been defined with the ArchiMeDeS tool (López-Sanz et al., 2012b) and using the stereotypes defined in the previously presented UML profiles. It is possible to observe the existence of two outer service providers (Massive Image Processing System and Secure Storage System) which are in charge of performing the image processing (comprising services executing

Figure 9. Stereotypes defined in the PSM-level UML profile for service architectural modeling

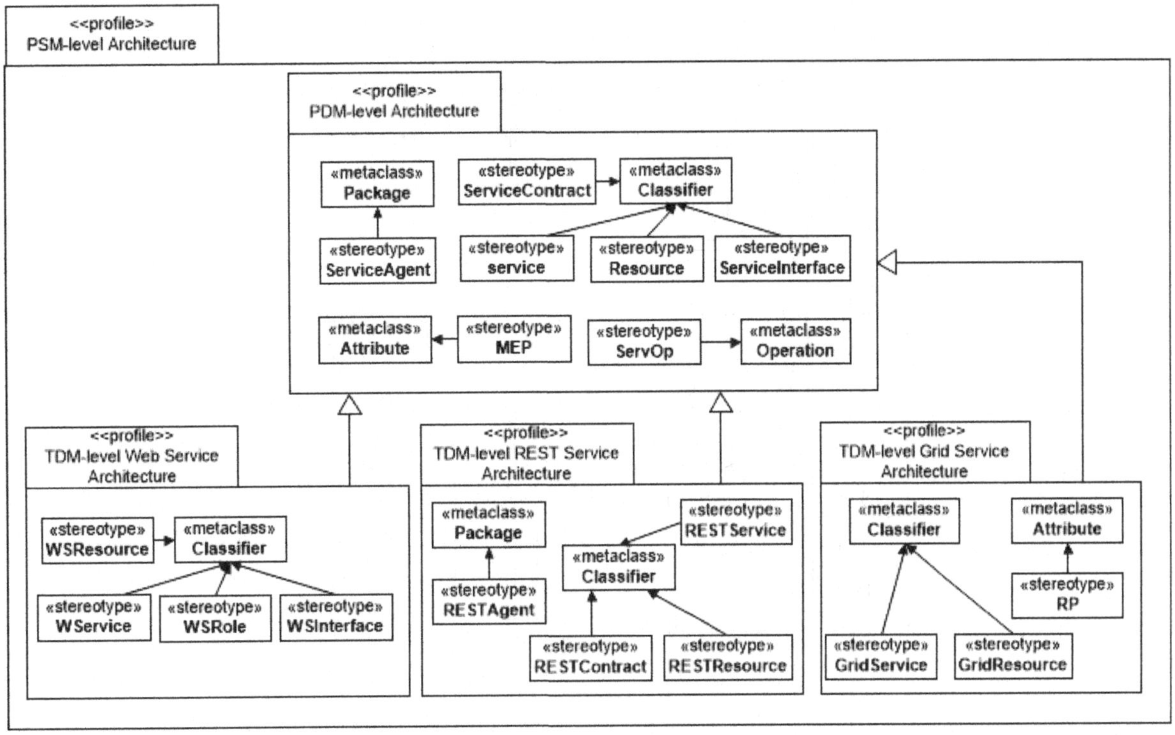

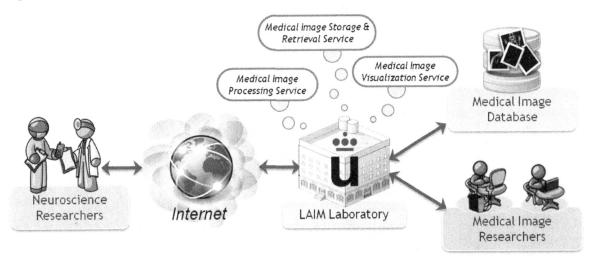

Figure 10. Overview of the GESiMED working environment

complex normalization algorithms) and the secure storage of the patients' images (in accordance with the current legislation on digital content management), respectively. It also includes the services that implement the functionalities required (such as a Front-End service for interaction purposes) and the service contracts established among them. In order to support the behavioral aspect of the

Figure 11. Complete GESiMEDPIM service-oriented architectural model

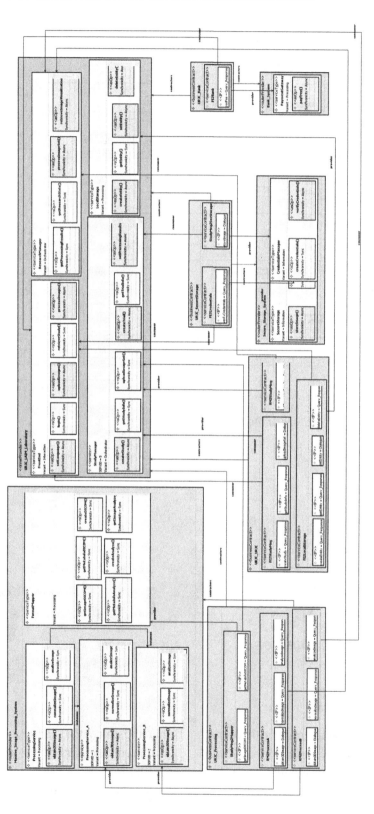

Figure 12. Fragment of the GESiMEDPSM service-oriented architectural model: PDM sample

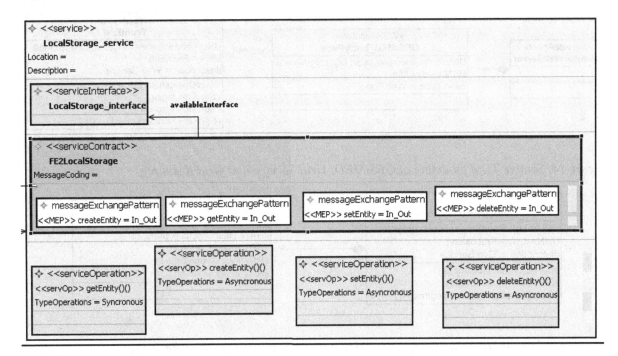

system under development, we take advantage of SOD-M (De Castro et al., 2009), a service-oriented method for the development of information systems that additionally allows the business needs and activities to be collected by means of different models (in particular, a value model and several business process models).

Modeling GESiMED at the PSM level allows us to benefit from the possibility of simultaneously specifying information about computational elements that can be implemented using different service technologies. For the sake of clarity, only some excerpts from the final PSM model are shown here. We provide examples to show the usability of each of the DSLs and UML profiles defined at PDM and TDM levels in different parts of that final PSM model (not shown here in its entirety owing to its size).

For example, the TDM architectural model for GESiMED uses the TDM DSL for web services to model the *FrontEnd* service and the resource that can access it (Figure 13). It additionally shows

the service agent in charge of its execution. This information shows that it is necessary to have a web page resource that allows access to a web service that performs a particular functionality. Note that this is the only information that can be extracted from the architectural model, a skeleton of the system source code or, more properly, a *protoarchitecture* of the system (Dardenne et al., 2003). Additional information is needed to implement either the web page or the web service itself. In the case of the web page, for instance, the modeling of the interface concern is encouraged.

The part of the GESiMED that benefits from the capabilities offered by the use of a grid computing platform is focused on the *ProcessingService* element and the related resources needed to compute tasks concerning image processing using specialized image normalization algorithms. Figure 14 shows a partial model of the GESiMED architecture focused on the modeling of the *ProcessingService* using the TDM DSL for grid services.

Figure 13. Sample TDM modeling of GESiMED: Web Services, Resources and Service Agents

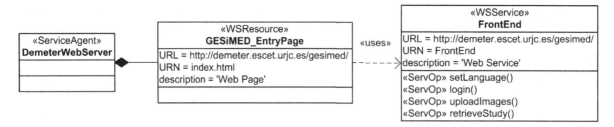

Figure 14. Sample TDM modeling of GESiMED: Grid Service and Grid Resource.

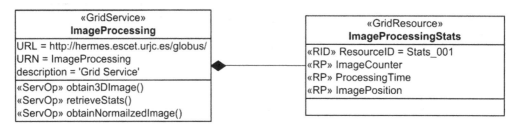

Figure 15. Sample TDM modeling of GESiMED: REST Service, Agent and Resource

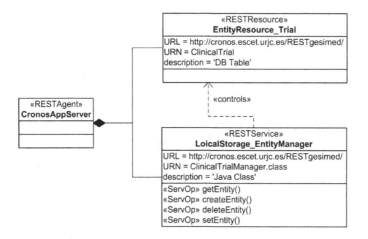

In order to illustrate the impact of using REST services on the system architecture, we shall focus on the *LocalStorage* service which permits the management of entities within the scope of the GESiMED system (Figure 15). The *LocalStorage_EntityManager* service conforms to the REST principles, by offering a standard set of operations that are available to access a concrete entity (in this case, a clinical trial): *getEntity* (GET opera-

tion), *setEntity* (POST), *createEntity* (PUT) and *deleteEntity* (DELETE).

CONCLUSION AND FUTURE LINES OF RESEARCH

The service-oriented paradigm is gaining importance in the software development field, principally because of the broadening of the fields in which it is being used and accepted as a guiding paradigm. Several problems, such as an increase in the complexity of the development process, have arisen as a result of this evolution. This has motivated the need to design new development methods to assist in the development process of service-oriented systems. Accordingly, in this chapter we have presented several UML profiles for the modeling of service architectures at the PIM and PSM levels of MDA. The concepts behind the profiles have also been presented by means of describing the corresponding metamodels.

Model-driven engineering approaches in general, and the MDA proposal in particular, have proven to be a great advance in service-oriented software development. The separation into abstract levels (CIM, PIM and PSM) and the definition of transformation rules between the models defined within these levels and among levels are the foundations of the MDA proposal. The application of the MDA principles to the SOA paradigm favors the development of solutions based on services, while the design of the architecture is a critical aspect in service-oriented developments since one of its main goals is to achieve flexible implementations of interacting software entities.

Although there are other proposals for the service-oriented system development, many of them consider Web Service principles as a basis and keep them apart from generic designs. Those which are sufficiently generic to avoid being fixed to a specific technology cannot usually be applied to MDA or do not use a high-level standard notation to assist during the development process. Practically none of the proposals that define UML profiles for SOA have a complete development method associated with them, and focus solely on the ways in which to represent the SOA principles and not on the entire development process. Finally, none of them allows the representation, as a first-class architectural element, of a component in charge of interacting with the user.

At this moment we are working on the specification of model transformation rules to support the migration between different service-oriented architectural models for different service execution platforms (Web Service, Grid, CORBA, agents, etc.). We also expect to provide a formal representation of the concepts outlined in this article by means of an ADL which will allow us to represent both the semantics shown in the metamodel and its restrictions.

ACKNOWLEDGMENT

This research has been partially funded by the Project MASAI (TIN-2011-22617) from the Spanish Ministry of Science and Innovation.

REFERENCES

Acuña, C., Marcos, E., de Castro, V., & Hernández, J. A. A. (2004). Web Information System for Medical Image Management. In *Proceedings of 5th International Symposium on Biological and Medical Data Analysis* (LNCS), (vol. 3337, pp. 49-59). Springer-Verlag.

Aiello, M., & Dustdar, S. (2006). Service Oriented Computing: Service Foundations. In *Proceedings of the Dagstuhl Seminar 2006*. Service Oriented Computing.

Alti, A., Khammaci, T., Smeda, A., & Bennouar, D. (2007). Integrating software architecture concepts into the MDA platform. In *Proceedings of ICSOFT'07* (SE), 2007. ICSOFT.

Amir, R., & Zeid, A. (2004). *A UML profile for service oriented architectures*. OOPSLA Companion. doi:10.1145/1028664.1028745

Arsanjani, A., Ghosh, S., Allam, A., Abdollah, T., Ganapathy, S., & Holley, K. (2008). SOMA: a method for developing service-oriented solutions. *IBM Systems Journal, 47*(3). doi:10.1147/sj.473.0377

Baresi, L., Heckel, R., Thone, S., & Varro, D. (2003). Modeling and validation of service-oriented architectures: Application vs. style. In *Proc. ESEC/FSE 2003*. Helsinki, Finland: ESEC/FSE.

Berners-Lee, T., Fielding, R., & Masinter, L. (1998). *Uniform Resource Identifiers (URI), Generic Syntax, IETF RFC 2396*. Retrieved from http://www.ietf.org/rfc/rfc2396.txt

Broy, M. (2004). Model Driven, Architecture-Centric Modeling in Software Development. In *Proceedings of 9th Intl. Conf. in Engineering Complex Computer Systems* (ICECCS'04), (pp. 3-12). IEEE Computer Society.

Dardenne, A., van Lamsweerde, A., & Fickas, S. (2003). Goal-directed Requirements Acquisition. *Science of Computer Programming, 20*(1-2), 3–50. doi:10.1016/0167-6423(93)90021-G

De Castro, V., Marcos, E., & Wieringa, R. (2009). Towards a service-oriented MDA-based approach to the alignment of business processes with IT systems: From the business model to a web service composition model. *International Journal of Cooperative Information Systems, 18*(2), 225–260. doi:10.1142/S0218843009002038

Erl, T. (2005). *Service-Oriented Architecture: Concepts, Technology, and Design.* Upper Saddle River, NJ: Prentice Hall PTR.

Fielding, R. T. (2000). *Architectural Styles and the Design of Network-Based Software Architectures*. (Ph.D. Thesis). University of California, Irvine, CA.

Foster, I., & Kesselman, C. (1998). *The Grid: Blueprint for a New Computing Infrastructure*. Morgan Kauffmann.

Foster, I., Kesselman, C., Nick, J., & Tuecke, S. (2002). *The Physiology of the Grid: An Open Grid Services Architecture for Distributed Systems Integration*. Open Grid Service Infrastructure WG, Global Grid Forum.

Gomaa, H. (2005). Architecture-Centric Evolution in Software Product Lines. In *Proceedings of ECOOP'2005 Workshop on Architecture-Centric Evolution* (ACE'2005). Glasgow, UK: ACE.

Graham, S., Karmarkar, A., Mischkinsky, J., Robinson, I., & Sedukhin, I. (2005). *Web Services Resource Framework 1.2*. OASIS WSRF-TC.

Gronback, R. C. (2009). *Eclipse Modeling Project: A Domain-Specific Language (DSL) Toolkit*. Addison-Wesley Professional.

Heckel, R., Küster, J., Thöne, S., & Voigt, H. (2003). *Towards a UML Profile for Service-Oriented Architectures*. Paper presented at the Workshop on Model Driven Architecture: Foundations and Applications (MDAFA '03). Enschede, The Netherlands.

Hernández, J. A., Acuña, C., de Castro, V., Marcos, E., López, M., & Malpica, N. A. (2006). WEB-PACS for multi-center clinical trials. *IEEE Transactions on Information Technology in Biomedicine, 11*(1), 87–93. doi:10.1109/TITB.2006.879601

Jouault, F., Allilaire, F., Bézivin, J., & Kurtev, I. (2008). ATL: A model transformation tool. *Science of Computer Programming, 72*(1-2), 31–39. doi:10.1016/j.scico.2007.08.002

Krafzig, D., Banke, K., & Slama, D. (2004). *Enterprise SOA Service Oriented Architecture Best Practices*. Upper Saddle River, NJ: Prentice Hall PTR.

Krüger, I. H., & Mathew, R. (2004). Systematic Development and Exploration of Service-Oriented Software Architectures. [WICSA.]. *Proceedings of WICSA, 2004*, 177–187.

Larrucea, X., & Benguria, G. (2006). Applying a Model Driven Approach to an E-Business Environment. In *Proceedings of the XV Jornadas de Ingeniería del Software y Bases de Datos* (JISBD 2006). Barcelona: JISBD.

López-Sanz, M., & Marcos, E. (2012).ArchiMe-DeS: A model-driven framework for the specification of service-oriented architectures. *Inf. Syst. 37*(3), 257-268. DOI=10.1016/j.is.2011.11.002

López Sanz, M., Marcos, E., Vara, J.M., Bollati, V., & Verde, J. (2012). *ArchiMeDeSTool: Especificación e Implementación de Modelos para el frameworkArchiMeDeS*. Reg. No.M-009008/2012. Date: 03/12/2012

López-Sanz, M., Vara, J. M., Marcos, E., & Cuesta, C. E. (2011). A Model-Driven Approach to Weave Architectural Styles into Service-Oriented Architectures. *International Journal on Cooperative Information Systems, 20*(2), 201–220. doi:10.1142/S0218843011002201

Lublinsky, B. (2007). *Defining SOA as an architectural style: Align your business model with technology*. Retrieved from http://www-128.ibm.com/developerworks/webservices/library/ar-soastyle/index.html

Marcos, E., Acuña, C. J., & Cuesta, C. E. (2006). Integrating Software Architecture into a MDA Framework. In *Proceedings of the Third European Workshop on Software Architectures* (EWSA 2006). Nantes, France: EWSA.

Miller, J., & Mukerji, J. (2003). *MDA Guide Version 1.0.1 (omg/03-06-01). Object Management Group*. OMG.

OASIS. (2007). *Reference Model for Service Oriented Architecture, Committee Draft 1.0*. Retrieved from http://www.oasis-open.org/committees/download.php/16587/wd-soa-rm-cd1ED.pdf

OMG. (2009). *Service Oriented Architecture Modeling Language (SoaML), FTF Beta 2*. Retrieved from http://www.omg.org/spec/SoaML/1.0/Beta2/PDF/

Papazoglou, M., Traverso, P., Dustdar, S., & Leymann, F. (2008). Service-Oriented Computing. Research Roadmap. *International Journal of Cooperative Information Systems, 17*(2), 223–255. doi:10.1142/S0218843008001816

Pautasso, C., Zimmermann, O., & Leymann, F. (2008). *RESTful Web Services vs. Big Web Services: Making the Right Architectural Decision*. Paper presented at 17th International World Wide Web Conference (WWW2008). Bejing, China.

Rennie, M. W., & Misic, V. B. (2004). *Towards a Service-Based Architecture Description Language (TR 04/08)*. University of Manitoba.

Selic, B. (2003). The pragmatics of Model-Driven development. *IEEE Software, 20*(5), 19–25. doi:10.1109/MS.2003.1231146

Smith, M., Friese, T., & Freisleben, B. (2006). Model driven development of service-oriented grid applications. In *Proceedings of the Advanced International Conference on Telecommunications and International Conference on Internet and Web Applications and Services* (AICT-ICIW'06). AICT-ICIW.

W3C. (2004). *Web Services Architecture (WSA)*. Retrieved from http://www.w3.org/TR/ws-arch/

W3C. (2007). *Web Services Description Language (WSDL) Version 2.0 Part 1: Core Language*. Retrieved from http://www.w3.org/TR/2007/REC-wsdl20-20070626

W3C. (2011). *Web Service Standards*. Retrieved from http://www.w3.org/2011/07/wspas-pr.html

Wada, H., Suzuki, J., & Oba, K. (2006). Modeling Non-Functional Aspects in Service Oriented Architecture. In *Proc. of the 2006 IEEE International Conference on Service Computing*. Chicago, IL: IEEE.

Zdun, U., & Dustdar, S. (2007). Model-Driven Integration of Process-Driven SOA Models. *International Journal of Business Process Integration and Management.*

Zhang, T., Ying, S., Cao, S., & Jia, X. (2006). A Modeling Framework for Service-Oriented Architecture. In *Proceedings of the Sixth International Conference on Quality Software* (QSIC 2006), (pp. 219-226). QSIC.

ADDITIONAL READING

Bézivin, J. (2004), In search of a Basic Principle for Model Driven Engineering, Novatica/Upgrade, vo.l.V, no. 2, pp. 21-24.

Bollati, V. A., Vara, J. M., Jimenez, A., & Marcos, E. (2012). Applying MDE to the (semi-) automatic development of model transformations. *Information and Software Technology.* doi: doi:10.1016/j.infsof.2012.11.004

Clark, T., Evans, A., Sammut, P., & Willans, J. (2008). Applied Metamodelling - A Foundation for Language Driven Development (2nd Ed.), http://itcentre.tvu.ac.uk/~clark/book.html

Clements, P. (1996) A Survey of Architecture Description Languages, 8th International Workshop on Software Specification and Design, Mar. 1996, pp. 16-25.

Clements, P., Bachmann, F., Bass, L., Garlan, D., Ivers, J., & Little, R. et al. (2002). *Documenting Software Architectures, Views and Beyond, Pearson Education, Inc.* Boston: Addison-Wesley.

De Roure, D. et al: The Semantic Grid: A Future e-Science Infrastructure, International Journal of Concurrency and Computation: Practice and Experience, 5. 2003.

Erl, T. (2004). *Service-Oriented Architecture: A Field Guide To Integrating XML and Web Services.* Upper Saddle River, NJ: Prentice Hall.

Fiadeiro, J. L., Lopes, A., & Bocchi, L. (2006). The SENSORIA Reference Modelling Language: Primitives for Service Description, available at www.sensoria-ist.edu.

IEEE-SA Standards Board. IEEE AWG. (2000). IEEE RP-1471-2000: Recommended Practice for Architectural Description for Software-Intensive Systems, IEEE Computer Society Press.

Josuttis, N. M. (2007). *SOA in Practice The Art of Distributed System Design.* O'Reilly.

Malavolta, I., Muccini, H., Pelliccione, P., & Tamburri, D. A. (2010). Providing Architectural Languages and Tools Interoperability through Model Transformation Technologies, IEEE Transactions on Software Engineering (TSE). *IEEE CS*, *36*(1), 119–140.

Mattsson, A., Lundell, B., Lings, B., & Fitzgerald, B. (2009). Linking model-driven development and software architecture: a case study. *IEEE Transactions on Software Engineering, 35*(1), 83–93. doi:10.1109/TSE.2008.87

Medvidovic, N., & Taylor, R. N. (2000). A classification and comparison framework for software architecture description languages. *IEEE Transactions on Software Engineering, 26*(1), 70–93. doi:10.1109/32.825767

Mernik, M., Heering, J., & Sloane, A. M. (2005). When and how to develop domain-specific languages. *ACM Computing Surveys, 37*(4), 316–344. doi:10.1145/1118890.1118892

NEXOF-RA Project Team. (2009). NEXOF-RA Model V2.0, Public Project Deliverable 6.2_v2.0, available from: http://www.nexof-ra.eu/?q=rep/term/140.

OMG. (2001). Model Driven Architecture (MDA), Document No. ormsc/2001-07-01, available at: http://www.omg.com/mda.

Open Service Oriented Architecture (OSOA) Collaboration. (2007). Service Component Architecture Project. http://www.osoa.org/.

Papazoglou, M. P. (2003). Service-oriented computing: concepts, characteristics and directions. Fourth International Conference on Web Information Systems Engineering (WISE'03), Roma, Italy, pp. 3–12.

Perovich, D., Bastarrica, M. C., & Rojas, C. (2009). Model-driven approach to software architecture design.Fouth International Workshop on Sharing and Reusing Architectural Knowledge, SHARK 2009, IEEE Computer Society, Vancouver, Canada, pp. 1–8.

Perry, D. E., & Wolf, A. L. (1992). Foundations for the study of software architecture. *ACM SIGSOFT Software Engineering Notes*, *17*(4), 40–52. doi:10.1145/141874.141884

Puder, A., Römer, K., & Pilhofer, F. (2011). *Distributed Systems Architecture: A Middleware Approach (The MK/OMG Press)*. Morgan Kaufmann.

Sanz, J. L. C., Ren, G., Glissmann, S., Spohrer, J., & Leung, Y. T. (2010). What is Business Architecture and how can it contribute to Service Science. Frontiers in Service Conference, Karlstad Sweden, June 2010.

Selic, B. (2008). MDA Manifestations, Upgrade. *The European Journal for the Informatics Professional*, *IX*(2), 12–16.

Sendall, S., & Kozaczynski, W. (2003, Sep.). Model Transformation: The Heart and Soul of Model-Driven Software Development. *IEEE Software*, *20*(5), 42–45. doi:10.1109/MS.2003.1231150

Shaw, M., & Garlan, D. (1996). *Software Architecture: Perspectives on an Emerging Discipline*. Prentice Hall.

Tanenbaum, A. S., & Van Steen, M. (2007). *Distributed Systems: Principles and Paradigms* (2nd ed.). Prentice-Hall.

The Open Group. (2003). The Open Group Architecture Framework (TOGAF) 8.1 Enterprise Ed., Doc Number: G051.

KEY TERMS AND DEFINITIONS

Architecture-Centric Development: Software development approach in which the description of the architecture is the heart and central concern of the process. The use of this approach permits the (abstract) architectural description to be checked, refined and designed in order to obtain more concrete descriptions that will be executed.

Domain-Specific Language (DSL): A language that is written to represent or describe terms and concepts within a specific domain. UML Profiles: An extension mechanism that allows standard semantics to be refined in a strictly additive manner, thus preventing them from contradicting standard semantics. These profiles provide a generic extension mechanism with which to customize UML models for particular domains and platforms.

Model-Driven Architecture (MDA): A software design approach for the development of software systems that is based on the provision of a set of guidelines for the structuring of software specifications in different abstraction levels. It uses models as first-class elements and fosters the definition of model transformation rules to progress in the software development.

Model-Driven Engineering (MDE): Refers to the systematic use of models as primary engineering artifacts throughout the engineering lifecycle. According to many authors, it offers a promising approach with which to address the inability of third-generation languages to alleviate the complexity of platforms and express domain concepts effectively.

Service-Oriented Architecture (SOA): A software design, software architecture design pattern and architectural style based on structured collections of discrete software entities with clearly defined capabilities, known as services, which collectively provide the complete functionality of a large software application.

Software Architecture: The fundamental concepts or properties of a system in its environment embodied in its elements, relationships, and in the principles of its design and evolution.

Section 4
Agile Methods

Chapter 12
Back to Basics:
In Support of Agile Development

Roy Morien
Naresuan University Language Centre, Thailand

ABSTRACT

Massive failures of software development projects have been recorded in the literature, and particularly in the popular press, over the years. Yet, rarely if ever have we seen any objective, detailed analysis of the causes of these failures. Indeed, we usually can only surmise how the projects were managed or what the development methodology or approach was. This chapter analyses some aspects of software development projects and development methodologies in terms of the success or failure potential of these methodologies. The conclusion arrived at is that the system development methodologies handed down since the late 1970s as the preferred development approach, generally known as Structured Methodologies, based on the Structured Design Life Cycle methodology (SDLC), bear the seeds of their own failure. It is asserted that they cannot succeed because of the inherent nature and assumptions embedded in those methodologies. After some analysis of these assumptions, considered to be highly flawed and unworkable, the now not so recently published Agile Development methodologies are discussed and proffered as a workable and inherently successful approach to software system development.

INTRODUCTION

The message in this chapter is simple, but presumably controversial to the extreme that it is almost ideological in the on-going 'methodologies' battle in the IT industry. This battle is between what may be termed the 'Heavyweight" methodologies, and the 'Lightweight' methodologies used in software system development and project management. Sometimes the 'heavyweight' methodologies are termed 'industrial strength methodologies',

emphasising their apparent strength in process control, especially in large systems development. The implication inherent in this terminology is that the 'lightweight' methodologies are weak and inappropriate to 'real world' large projects.

Notwithstanding this terminology, the message in this chapter is that the traditional approaches to software systems development, first published under the heading of Structured Design Lifecycle Approaches (SDLC) in the late 1970's (deMarco, 1979), (Yourdon & Constantine, 1979), (Gane &

DOI: 10.4018/978-1-4666-6026-7.ch012

Sarson, 1977) have over time proven to be at best flawed and at worst disastrous in ensuring successful system development outcomes. Yes, many systems have been developed that do work, but the contention is that even these 'successful' systems would have had more successful outcomes; lower cost, shorter development times, greater business value and better user acceptance if a 'lightweight' development approach had been applied.

That 'lightweight' approach is now generally known as Agile Development, and comes in various guises, such as Extreme Programming (Beck, 1999), Scrum (Schwaber & Beedle, 2001), Dynamic Systems Development Methodology (DSDM) (DSDM Consortium, 2012) to name the most prominent, and Evo (Gilb, 1976), to name one of the oldest. These methodologies all have their roots in development approaches such as Software Prototyping (Naumann & Jenkins, 1982), Rapid Development (RAD) (McConnell, 1996) and Rapid Application Development (Martin, 1991) of much earlier years.

ORGANIZATION OF THE CHAPTER

The chapter develops the theme that to gain support for the adoption of Agile methods in software system development and project management, it is necessary to identify and explain the weaknesses in the traditional development approaches to be able to counter the usual objections to Agile Methods. This is done in the sections discussing, and refuting, the idea of 'Big Systems' and the preferred development methods for such systems. The weaknesses and failure of the underlying assumptions supporting the traditional Waterfall Approach are then discussed.

This refutation of traditional development practice finishes with a discussion of the justifying Fear of Change that is still felt, even in the face of significant changes to all or most other development dimensions and the development of

a significant marketplace in development tools, application generators and the like.

The chapter continues into a description of what is seen as the true nature of software projects, as being 'people-centric', and 'learning organisations'. The thesis is that these types of group activities need to be managed differently to projects in civil engineering and construction, which seems to be the preferred paradigm for a 'project management', regardless of project type. More appropriate means of gathering and specifying requirements are addressed, as a lead in to a discussion on iterative and incremental methods, and the perceived benefits inherent in such approaches.

Finally, the chapter introduces a number of what may be called 'reference disciplines' in an attempt to provide an intellectual and theoretical underpinning to a development approach that has been largely promulgated based on practitioner experience, rather than having a principled and theoretical basis.

A contentious place to start this discussion is found in a recent government inquiry in the state of Queensland in Australia which investigated the substantial failure of the development of a payroll system for the Health Department in that state. In summary, the $5,000,000 inquiry looked at a project that initially was quoted as a development cost of about $6,200,000 and has apparently exceeded $2 billion in sunk cost and remediation costs, and operating costs blown out due to poor design causing substantial operating costs. This figure of $2 billion seems to have been modified to $1.2 billion in later announcements by the Queensland Premier, perhaps indicating the inability to estimate the actual cost. Substantial business disruption occurred due to the failure of the system to pay wages and salaries correctly to numerous employees that lead to street demonstrations by affected staff protesting the situation; such was the seriousness of the problem.

A search of the popular press and the technical and industry press reveals that this development disaster is certainly not the only one to have occurred. Many major software developments over the last 40 years have resulted in failed systems, with substantial to unbelievably enormous cost blowouts, and huge disruption to businesses; indeed, disruption to whole industries on occasion.

The author's interest in this particular disaster; that of a payroll system, a government payroll system, goes back to the late 1970's. At that time, and since, there have been similar disasters, on similar such systems, on at least 3 separate occasions. The first, in this author's knowledge, was a Commonwealth Public Service Commission effort in Canberra, about 1979, to develop a service-wide payroll system which cost some $35 million (at that time, well in excess of $100 million in 2014 dollars) and was ultimately abandoned and never saw the light of day. A similar situation occurred in about 1987 in the Western Australian Public Service with the development and ultimate abandonment of a payroll system. The cost of this failure is only remembered as substantial, without recalling the exact cost.

In contrast, the author has personal knowledge of and involvement in, the highly successful development of a payroll and personnel system for the building and construction industry in Western Australia. A PC based system was developed, using the Clipper(R) language, during the late 1980's. This system was characterised by the complexity of managing payroll in an industry with a multitude of industrial awards each with highly complex rules for paying allowances for all sorts of circumstances, such as wet weather allowance, weekend work, week day overtime, public holiday loadings and allowances, site allowances, dangerous conditions allowances, height allowances, location allowances, tea break allowances, shift penalties, union affiliation, job description and so on.

This contrast is included for the specific purpose of encouraging response, and surely retort, about the obvious difference between these systems. On the one hand we have some clearly 'big' systems being compared with a 'small' system. It is obvious, some would say, that developing a big system is much more complex than developing a small system.

This begs the question about what are the characteristics of a 'big' system, such that it is substantially more complex, and therefore more prone to development difficulties, than a' small' system. There is also the question about the best (and apparently necessary) project management approach and development methodology to be used in developing a 'big' system. It is to these 'big' systems that the 'industrial strength' development methods are seen to be best applied.

CHARACTERISTICS OF A 'BIG' SYSTEM

Bigness in software systems can be described in many ways:

1. the number of tables in the underlying database.
2. the size of the database, in terms of the number of records and overall number of megabytes.
3. the extent and complexity of the communication network that the system will operate in.
4. the number of on-line, interactive users who may be or will be attached to the system at any one time.
5. the number of code lines in the code base.
6. the length of time necessary to develop the system.
7. the complexity of the algorithms in the system.

We must also consider the actual project factors that make it a 'big' project as well.

8. size of the development team as a complexity factor in the development activity.
9. experience, expertise and competence of the development team.
10. familiarity with and expertise in the development tools and languages to be used.
11. Maturity of the development team in terms of experience working together as a team.

Of these, only complexity and development team size have considerable potential for development failure. All of the first 4 'bigness' factors can be handled outside the actual development project. For example, if the database is likely to have 1000 tables and an overall size of a terabyte, then the solution to this problem is the correct selection of a DBMS that can handle that number of tables and actual database size. If there will be a widespread network with the potential for hundreds of simultaneous on-line users, then the solution is the correct selection of networking equipment and a DBMS that can handle a high volume of server requests. Obviously the design of the database and the data access code must be constructed in such a way as to handle multi-user access correctly, and database accessing code, including SQL code, should be optimised. However, none of these matters adds significantly, if at all, to the complexity of the development of the software system.

In any case, a significant point about 'big systems', obvious but rarely stated is that regardless of the particular view of bigness, such systems are never developed as one large, amorphous chunk. A million lines of code is developed function by function, procedure by procedure, object by object, in parallel usually, but separately nonetheless. A 1000 table database is developed table by table, in parallel perhaps, but evolved separately, not as a single activity with a sudden, single outcome. So 'big' systems can be readily viewed as many

small systems being developed separately with convergence on an integrated outcome. This further detracts from the views discussed next regarding the preferred methodology for 'Big' systems development.

PREFERRED METHODOLOGY FOR 'BIG' SYSTEMS

It has usually been held that big systems require a well-structured and strictly managed development methodology; the 'industrial strength' methodology. This has usually been interpreted as being the linear or serially phased approaches popularised in the 1970's, referenced previously. These approaches or methodologies enshrine the principal that you must have a detailed understanding of the requirements before you start development. The first phase of the SDLC methodology is the 'Specification Phase'. This is followed in linear succession by the Design Phase then the Development Phase and finally the System Testing Phase.

By specifying and agreeing to all requirements, and extensively documenting them, at the start of the project, before design and development takes place, it is supposed that this comprises the 'fixed scope' of the system and therefore a detailed and accurate project plan can be developed, and subsequently implemented.

This approach to software development has been termed the 'Waterfall Method' from the diagrammatic representation of the phases. (see Figure 1).

PROBLEMS OF THE WATERFALL MODEL

Many developers and project leaders now question the Waterfall Model, and it is often suggested that it is a poor model of the software development process, and too often results in project failure. Why is this?

Figure 1. The standard waterfall model

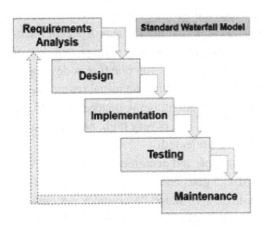

1. **Complete Requirements Up-Front:** It depends on a full, comprehensive, complete and detailed statement of requirements, from the Client, at the start of the project. This is considered necessary so that both Client and Developer know exactly what is to be done. They are trying to achieve certainty. The problem is that the Client cannot specify all requirements at the start. This fact has been established in almost every software project ever attempted. This is why we have elaborate Change Management Systems in place. This level of certainty just is not possible, so this underlying assumption fails!

2. **Unchanging Requirements:** The assumption is that the requirements specified at the start of the project will not change during the project's lifetime, and we can deliver a system that conforms to the requirements stated at the start. The problem is that requirements do change. Clients and developers both learn many new things as the project proceeds. Things Change! Also, often what was correct and necessary at the start of the project becomes unnecessary or irrelevant because of changes to the business activities. Indeed, the longer a development project goes on, the more likely it is that the end result is unacceptable, if based only on their initial

requirements, as specified. So this underlying assumption fails!

3. **Outdated Requirements:** To repeat; requirements do change. Like many things, they become stale while they sit on the shelf waiting to be developed. Research has shown that maybe as much as 60% of original requirements will change. This can be interpreted that 60% of the original time and effort in discovering and recording those requirements was a waste of time, money and effort. What a waste!

4. **No Adapting to New Circumstances:** By making a plan at the start, and 'sticking to the plan', the project leader is unable to take advantage of new circumstances, or is unable to adapt to changing situations as the project proceeds. The assumption is, also, that the original plan is 'correct and workable', and if it is not, then it is a failure of project management or a failure of planning. The problem is that circumstances do change. Clients and developers frequently wish to change the plan, to adapt the plan, often based on the project team's experience. So this underlying assumption fails!

5. **No Continuous Learning:** When there is the assumption that the original specification of requirements is correct, and if any change is requested it will be viewed as a negative impact on the project plan and scope, the project leader, the client, and the developers are being refused the opportunity to discover better requirements. No learning is allowed to take place and no lessons from team experience are allowed to be included in the on-going project activity. So this underlying assumption is damaging!

6. **Success Criteria Limited and Inappropriate:** The conventional and usual success criteria for software development projects managed under the SDLC approach are In Time, In Budget, In Scope. It is the

original projections or estimates made at the start of the project that are used in these assessments of success. But, when the success of the project is measured in terms of meeting the (original) deadline, meeting the (original) budget, and delivering the (original) specified scope of requirements, then the project is locked into a set of project success criteria, projections and plans that have almost always proven to be wrong. Delivery according to (original) scope, time and budget does not include any consideration of possible error at the start, and it also doesn't include quality, and business value of the software being delivered. So this underlying assumption is damaging! What also is missing from the success criteria of such projects is Value to the Business, and Acceptance by the Ultimate End-User. These, however, do seem to be contradictory to the acknowledged success criteria.

7. **Change Management Overhead:** As the project proceeds, any change requests are managed as if they are always potentially damaging to the project, and will have a negative impact on the project. Therefore, refusing to accept changes is considered to be an acceptable, if not a desirable, result of the 'change management' process. The potential result of this change management process is that every change refused moves the final delivered system one step further away from the desired and valuable system that is really needed at the time of delivery. This 'requirements gap' is at a maximum at the time of delivery and implementation, and may be so wide that the system is effectively useless. At best it may be acceptable only if there is an intention to start another 'project' for the purpose of applying all the changes to the delivered system. But this does not seem to be very reasonable or practical. So this underlying assumption is damaging!

Conclusion: Every foundation assumption of the Waterfall Project Management Model is wrong and / or damaging to the prospect of a successful development activity. The probability of the delivered system, even one that is developed in strict accordance with the initial requirements as stated by the client, being unacceptable to the contemporary users, is very high, and the system is likely to be rejected.

Criticism of, and disagreement with, the Waterfall Model goes back to its earliest times. Gilb (Tom Gilb, 1976) stated "A complex system will be most successful if it is implemented in small steps and if each step has a clear measure of successful achievement …" in 1976. Presumably Gilb was referring to 'big' systems in terms of their complexity.

THE FEAR OF CHANGE

In the 1970s and into the 1980s, any request for a change to the specifications or the already developed components of the system, was genuinely a matter of concern. The sparse development toolset, the difficulty of changing the database schema, the often scarce availability of computer time, meant that change was indeed to be assiduously avoided. There still seems to be this fear rampant in the IT industry today. Bold project management advice still seems to be to refuse change, to 'plan the work and work the plan'. Software project managers are exhorted to be tough on change. Consultants complain that it was the user changing the specification which made it impossible to meet the deadlines. This was quite clear in IBM's response to the criticism about the Queensland Health Department Payroll System debacle; "The successful delivery of the project was rendered near-impossible by the state failing to ... commit to a fixed scope."

So much has happened in software development since the late 1970s when the SDLC approaches to development were first published.

Today there is a huge marketplace in development tools that enable remarkably quick generation of functionality, and changes to aspects of the system, such as the database schema, are able to be done in minutes without even logged-on users noticing.

In fact, it is remarkable how almost every aspect of the IT industry has undergone such substantial and disruptive change in the last 30 years. Yet one major and surprising exception to this seems to be the systems development approach generally used (and taught in universities and colleges). All has changed, that is except the thinking by many practitioners about development methodologies; they remain embedded in 1979, while developing in 2014. They also still draw intellectual comfort from civil engineering and construction project management; a quite inappropriate paradigm.

Some important aspects of this fear of change need to be considered. There are three major areas of change:

- Changes are requested to as-yet undeveloped requirements. There is no change to already developed requirements. This should have no impact on the project progress, except to require a reassessment of the cost and possible completion date. It does, however, for traditional Project Managers imply failure under the traditional criteria for project success.

- Requested changes are often incremental, adding to the requirements, not contradicting or countermanding them. Again, it ought to have no impact on project progress but merely expands the scope, and affects the cost and completion time of the project. Under an agile project management regime this is seen as desirable as a learning exercise.

- Requested changes require 'back stepping' over previously completed work. The question must be asked, Why? The answer is probably (a) the wrong information was recorded at the start, or (b) someone has

learned more about their requirements. In an agile project, this would be 'learning by doing'; a wholly desirable outcome. Refusal to accept and implement these changes is unreasonable, implying that delivering wrong functionality is acceptable.

Regardless of the nature of the 'change', if it is refused, then the project outcome will be that much less useful or have that much less business value.

In any case the change is usually able to be made quickly and easily if the right portfolio of development tools has been selected. There is an enormous marketplace today for such tools that make development substantially faster, and makes change almost trivial, in most cases.

SPECIFYING REQUIREMENTS: WHEN AND HOW?

It would be nonsensical to say that it is not necessary to specify requirements. IBM, the primary contractors in the disastrous and horrendously expensive system failure of the Queensland Health Department Payroll System excused itself from full blame by blaming the client's failure to provide proper specifications. "The successful delivery of the project was rendered near-impossible by the state failing to properly articulate its requirements or commit to a fixed scope."

The real question here is not about the necessity for 'properly articulated requirements'. That goes without saying. The real question is twofold; when should those requirements be properly articulated, and secondly, how should they be properly articulated.

Traditional IT thinking usually turns towards voluminous written documents prepared during the initial Specifications Phase. This results in an enormous document that most users will not read in detail, and cannot verify as complete and correct. The sheer volume of the document predicates against this. Further, the impressiveness of the size and format of the document camouflages the fact that the requirements are usually, in fact, incomplete and not 'properly articulated'. It is a standard 'out' by the developer contractor to refer back to that document and often demand that the client show exactly where a specific 'requirement' is specified, and to claim that the system is complete in accordance with the 'spec'. On the other hand, the client often falls back on the complaint that 'surely you understood that this was implied in the our requests'. Finger pointing covers up the reality of the reasons for failure.

INCREMENTAL REQUIREMENTS SPECIFICATION

The author has coined the phrase, or question "Why do you need to know everything before you can do anything?" The fact is you do not need to! The incremental development of requirements specifications is perfectly feasible and controllable. What stands in the way of this being the usual way of discovering requirements is the often stated demand of the client to have a fixed price 'up front' for a project that is likely to have significant complications, and a development period of some years. The client does this in an attempt to have certainty of scope, certainty of cost, and certainty of development time. The fact that these have so often been demonstrated as being near impossible to attain only calls forth a more vocal demand next time for even stricter requirements elicitation 'up front'. This is akin to the blood sacrifices of superstitious tribes done to achieve favour with the Gods; a better harvest this year because we have sacrificed a rooster and sprinkled its blood on the rows of sown corn seed. If the harvest is poor, then the obvious solution is to sacrifice two roosters next season.

So how could, and should, requirements be elicited? According to the Agile Development methodologists, requirements can be elicited in sufficient detail at the start of the project to enable a broad and reasonably well understood scope of the system, and those requirements prioritised in accordance with concepts of business value. Albeit subjective, this should reflect the clients' view of what is most important and most valuable to them in the system. The developers can then estimate the development effort needed, and give an initial estimate of completion time and cost. As always, the iron law of prediction applies. As a well-known comedian once quipped 'Never make predictions, especially about the future'. Notwithstanding that this statement was made by a comedian, it is a reasonable warning against relying too much on the correctness and accuracy of predictions. The future is in fact unknowable; uncertainty is the hallmark characteristic of 'the future'.

As the project proceeds, all requests for change are added to this list of requirements, prioritised again in terms of business value and are estimated and a new set of outcomes decided. This new set of outcomes will state a new completion date, and a completion cost. If these are considered unacceptable by the client, then the requirements list can be paired back by dropping off the least important requirements. The clients can then see the impact of their changing requirements, and have almost immediate notice of the future dimensions of the development project, including estimated cost and probable completion date. It also implies that the user can see what can be delivered by the agreed date, and within the agreed budget, if those must stand unaltered.

Given the requirement to prioritise requested features, then another view of the set of requirements becomes clear. If the new estimated completion date, or budget, are seen as unacceptable, then the set of requested features can be pared back, dropping the least important features (as decided by the users).

In Agile Development terms this is called having a Product Backlog, which is a constantly updated set of requirements as yet unfulfilled, captured as User Stories.

A major factor in this thinking is that there will be no surprises in store as the delivery deadline approaches.

THE LIGHTWEIGHT APPROACH

What are the hallmarks of the lightweight approaches to system development? Primarily, these recognise and acknowledge that software system development is a people-oriented activity. A development activity is done by PEOPLE (for PEOPLE), using development TOOLS, while following a PROCESS, to produce a PRODUCT.

Developing software is a human and business activity. It is also a technical activity, but first, it is a 'human-centric' activity. Therefore, any development process will only be effective if it enables the people to perform at their best, and most creative. The development process must enable continuous learning, and enhance the capabilities of the developers. Project management must be people-management, first and foremost, and acknowledge that the people are well-trained, competent professionals, or are at least eager and willing to learn and become so. Developers will contribute the technical knowledge to the development project, and the client, or client representative, must contribute the business knowledge. This means that the developers, and the clients, must work closely together, and must recognise each other's abilities and knowledge. They must form a team!

The creation of, and availability of a substantial written Requirement Specification document actually can raise a barrier between developers and potential clients, rendering communication and interaction impractical, and even seen as unnecessary. This is therefore a substantial inhibitor of on-going learning. If the written Requirement Specification document is seen as the final record of requirements, then there is apparently no need for on-going collaboration or consultation. Therefore the view should be that the written Requirements Specification is actually a record of achievement and explanation rather than a blueprint for future work.

Drawing on a variety of sources (Agile Alliance,2007), (Agile Manifesto, 2003), (Cockburn, Alistair, 2004), (Cockburn, Alistair, 2006) and synthesising the definitions and suggested characteristics in those sources, Agile development is seen to have these characteristics:

- **People Focused:** (1) Collaborative: collaboration between developers and clients is continuous and continual, (2) Self-Organizing and Self-Managing Teams: Significant responsibility is handed to the team members, rather than a Project Manager, to decide on the work to be done in the next iteration.

- **Empirical and Adaptive:** Project management practices that have been published to support 'agile development' are described as 'empirical', 'adaptive', 'evolutionary' or 'experiential' rather than 'prescriptive', or 'pre-planned'.

- **Iterative:** Development is achieved through a series of short iterations each of which produces a useable enhancement to the system. This provides a frequent and regular feedback cycle, and opportunities for validation and verification of successful progress.

- **Incremental:** Development is achieved through a series of delivered increments to the system, each of which produces a fully developed, fully tested and certified extra feature or component of the system.

- **Evolutionary:** the system grows in size, the requirements in detail are continuously discovered, and are continually evolving during the development period.

- **Emergent:** the whole of the system is greater than the parts. The characteristics of the system emerge as parts are added.

- **Just-in-Time Requirements Elicitation:** Requirements are stated in detail 'just in time' to develop them, in the iteration in which those requirements will be implemented.
- **Knowledge-Based:** Development activity is decided upon by the knowledgeable, self-managing members of the team, with continual knowledge sharing about the product, the technology and the progress of the project. Learning and knowledge sharing are emphasized.
- **Client Driven, 'Pull-Based' development:** Only develop what is asked for by the Client, and only when the Client asks for it.

Agile methods emphasize project transparency, continual communication and collaboration between project partners.

THE VISION PHASE VS. THE ANALYSIS PHASE

At the start of a project, instead of trying immediately to delve into requirements in depth and detail, under the guise of being the Analysis Phase, an activity must take place that considers the general landscape of the development activity to come. This is often termed the Vision Phase. In this phase, many questions must be asked, and answered and the feasibility of the project is analysed.

- Do we have a senior manager who supports the project?
- What are the risks of the project? What must be done to overcome the risks?
- Who are the Users? What are their areas of interest?
- Is it valuable to the business? The Business Case?

- Is it feasible? Do we have the technology? Do we have the skills? Do we have the budget?
- What is the development budget? Is that reasonable and realistic?
- Do we all understand the business importance of the system?
- Do we understand the system complexity and overall scope?
- Are we all prepared to do the job and work as a team?
- Do we need training in the development environment confronting us.
- Will we get value for money from the system, for the budget?
- What are the project plan predictions; iterations, dates of releases, final completion date, Are they achievable?

Notice that this list uses the collective 'we' and 'us', and some of these questions are appropriate to the business side users, and some are appropriate to the technology side developers. This is done deliberately to emphasize the collective nature of this activity, involving both users and developers in close collaboration.

Following this, a sequence of development iterations is undertaken, called in Scrum 'sprints' given their characteristics as short periods of intense development with a given outcome in a given time, usually 2 weeks or up to a month.

Each sprint is accompanied by an empirical planning activity that keeps an up-to-date backlog of requirements, each prioritized according to perceived business value. Each requirement is estimated in terms of complexity, and the total development time is estimated, using the concept of team development velocity. At the end of each sprint, it is known, inasmuch as it can be known accurately, when the project finish date will be, the extent of the functionality that can be delivered by that finish date, and the corollary of that, the functionality that has been requested that cannot be completed by that finish date. Clients have all the information available to them to make decisions pertinent to the ongoing system development, and development budgets. This puts greater responsibility into the hands of the client in regard to the budget, the features to be implemented or dropped, the time scale acceptability.

QUALITY CONTROL AND QUALITY ASSURANCE FACTORS

One criticism considered almost mortal to the agile, iterative approaches is that, without an agreed upon, frozen specification at the start, there is no proper way to establish the quality parameters of the system, and to assess the quality of the developing system.

However, an analysis of the SDLC methodologies, which are based on what we may call 'large scale phases', shows that there are few real opportunities for QC and QA. In fact, it is assumed that there will be a major quality assessment phase at the end of the development process, in which presumably all defects will be discovered prior to delivery, and fixed.

This 'end of line' quality control is, frankly, too late! Its purpose is to discover defects, mainly. Isn't the day before delivery a little too late to be discovering defects? On the other hand, in an Iterative Development Approach, such as Scrum, there is an opportunity perhaps every two weeks to scrutinize the system 'so far' and discover defects. One clear and unbending intention of the Sprint in Scrum is to develop and deliver error-free code that implements a given requirement, and can be demonstrated to achieve this. Especially in Extreme Programming, concepts of Test Driven Development and Continuous Testing are fundamental practices.

It can be confidently stated that the Agile, Iterative Approaches both instigate greater and more searching Quality Control and Quality Assurance measures and practices, and enable that to be undertaken frequently in a systemic way, with timely feedback.

ATTENTION TO FAILURE

No one likes to fail! But isn't it better to fail sooner rather than later? For 'big' projects, designated 'big' by being multi-year in development, failure is usually acknowledged at the end of the development project. Hundreds of millions of dollars are written off, and often substantial business cost and damage is experienced. The fact seems to be that either nobody is able to identify the failure looming, or nobody is willing to acknowledge it. It is often a case of throwing good money after bad because of the attitude that 'it can be fixed before it is implemented'. This is often a cover-up to save the blushes of the decision makers. It is also called 'kicking the can down the road' by some.

But with an Agile, Iterative Approach, failure is always an option to be identified and considered on a regular and frequent basis; fortnightly or monthly. Entrenched in the philosophy of the Agile Approaches is the demand that progress be confirmed, validated and verified every step of the way. Each step is an iteration of perhaps two weeks duration. The worst case scenario is that an entire fortnight's or month's work may need to be written off, discarded! And that might involve only a single feature, or the work of only a single developer or small group of developers, not the whole iteration's total output of all the developers. How much better is that than writing off and abandoning 5 year's effort, and hundreds of millions of dollars.

INTELLECTUAL AND THEORETICAL SUPPORT FOR AGILE METHODOLOGIES

Apart from considerable experience over a career encompassing better than 35 years in software development, teaching and research, this author has attempted to identify supporting studies not directly referencing software development practices. The experience gained over 35 years allows the author to confidently discuss the failures of the structured approaches, and the almost inevitable successes of the agile approaches. It also appears that there has been very little research and intellectual support for the various methodologies, except what is based on 'experience', and the well established project management methods applied to Process Control Systems, construction and civil engineering, none of which are considered relevant in software development.

First, there is the concept of Chaordic Systems, a concept developed and published in the landmark book Birth of the Chaordic Age, Dee Hock coined the term 'chaordic' to describe 'the behavior of any self-governing organism, organization or system which harmoniously blends characteristics of order and chaos'. It is suggested here that the activity of software development, as a system, manifests those characteristics. Rubinstein & Firstenberg (1999) proffers a model of decision making behaviour that describes most compellingly the characteristics of chaordic systems, which software projects seem to be. It is this model; The Model of Concurrent Perception, that seems entirely appropriate to the activity of software development. The Model of Concurrent Perception 'moves us from questions to answers, from divergent perceptions to convergent perceptions, from individual creativity to team implementation, from abstract thinking to concrete action, from quick experimentation to quality results, from deliberate chaos to emergent order' and 'chaos should be deliberately created up front'. It is suggested that this is an almost perfect paradigm of software system development, reflecting the usually unremarked reality of that activity.

The concept and practice of the learning organization is amply discussed in Senge (Senge, 1990), referencing Peter Drucker who defined a learning organization being necessary because

'The function of the society of post-capitalist organisations … is to put knowledge to work … it must be organised for constant change'.

The Core Capabilities of a Learning Organization are discussed and summarised in Maani & Cavana (2007).

In discussing Team Learning, Senge (1990) states (at p.236) 'team learning (has) the need to think insightfully about complex issues ... to tap the potential of many minds'. Other statements about team learning include '... team learning involves mastering the practices of dialogue and discussion ... there is a free and creative exploration of complex and subtle issues ... '.

Lean production was a manufacturing methodology developed originally by the Toyota Motor Company. It is also known as the Toyota Production System. The goal of lean production and lean product development is stated as 'to get the right things to the right place at the right time, the first time, while minimizing waste and being open to change'. See Liker (2004), and Lean Thinking as appropriate to software development (Poppendieck & Poppendieck, 2003; Poppendieck & Poppendieck, 2006).

Leadership studies and case studies provide valuable input and insight into successful project leadership, rather than project management. One case study of a surprisingly successful venture identifies success factors, and attributes the success to:

- The inspirational leadership of the syndicate leader.
- The strong sense of community within the syndicate team.
- The openness of communication between team members.
- 'Customer'- led development – the sailors!
- The sustained rate of continual improvement (of the boat speed).
- The level of commitment and purpose by all participants.

When all of the reference disciplines are considered in terms of the Structured Development Approaches, it can be readily seen that they are missing from the intellectual and philosophical bases of that approach.

CONCLUSION

The Traditional Lifecycle Approaches (SDLC, Structured Development) are seen to be flawed and even fatal to the successful development of systems. The primary reference discipline of these approaches is Construction Engineering Project Management, which really has little to offer in 'soft'ware development. These failures in development are a matter of the public record, even if little analysis has ever been undertaken to properly identify the causes of those horrendous failures. This is why we must go Back to Basics to understand the flaws and damaging assumptions inherent in them.

On the other hand, there is significant practical support for the Agile Approaches, if not academic, intellectual and theoretical support.

Nonetheless, and unfortunately, the question still remains, 13 years after the term Agile Development came into being, and 40 years after its roots in Iterative and Incremental Development, and Software Prototyping, why isn't Agile the paradigm of choice, inevitably and unremarkably, for software development projects, large or small?

REFERENCES

Agile Alliance. (n.d.). Retrieved from http://www.agilealliance.org/show/1641

Agile Manifesto. (2003). Retrieved from http://agilemanifesto.org/

Beck, K. (1999). *Extreme Programming Explained: Embrace Change.* Addison-Wesley.

Cockburn, A. (2004). *Crystal Clear: A Human-Powered Methodology for Small Teams.* Addison-Wesley.

Cockburn, A. (2006). *Agile Software Development: The Cooperative Game.* Addison-Wesley.

deMarco, T. (1979). *Structured Analysis and System Specification.* Prentice Hall.

DSDM Consortium. (n.d.). Retrieved from http://www.dsdm.org/

Gane, C., & Sarson T. (1977). *Structured Systems Analysis: Tools and Techniques.* McDonnell Douglas Systems Integration Company.

Gilb, T. (1976). *Software Metrics.* Studentlitteratur AB.

Liker, J. K. (2004). *The Toyota Way.* McGraw-Hill.

Maani, K. E., & Cavana, R. Y. (2007). *Systems Thinking, Systems Dynamics – Managing Change and Complexity.* Pearson Education NZ.

Martin, J. (1991). *Rapid Application Development.* Prentice-Hall.

McConnell, S. (1996). *Rapid Development: Taming Wild Software Schedules.* Microsoft Press.

Naumann, J. D., & Jenkins, A. M. (1982). Prototyping: The New Paradigm for Systems Development. *Management Information Systems Quarterly, 6*(3). doi:10.2307/248654

Poppendieck, M., & Poppendieck, T. (2003). *Lean Software Development: An Agile Toolkit.* Addison-Wesley.

Poppendieck, M., & Poppendieck, T. (2006). *Implementing Lean Software Development: From Concept to Cash.* Addison-Wesley.

Rubinstein, M. F., & Firstenberg, I. R. (1999). *The Minding Organisation.* John Wiley & Sons.

Schwaber, K., & Beedle, M. (2001). *Agile Software Development with Scrum.* Prentice Hall.

Senge, P. M. (1990). *The Fifth Discipline – The Art & Practice of the Learning Organization.* Currency Doubleday.

Yourdon, E., & Constantine, L. (1979). *Structured Design.* Prentice Hall.

ADDITIONAL READING

Ambler, S. (2003). *Agile Database Techniques: Effective Strategies for the Agile Software Developer.* Wiley Application Development Series.

Beck, K. (2000). *Extreme Programming Explained: Embrace Change.* Addison-Wesley Professional.

Beck, K., & Fowler, M. (2001). *Planning Extreme Programming.* Addison-Wesley Professional.

Cohn, M. (2004). *User Stories Applied: For Agile Software Development.* Addison-Wesley.

Cohn, M. (2004). *Agile Project Management with Scrum.* Microsoft Professional.

Cohn, M. (2005). *Agile Estimating and Planning.* Prentice-Hall.

Gilb, T. (1988). *Principles Of Software Engineering Management.* Addison-Wesley.

Graham-Cumming, J. (2007), *The Agile Heartbeat, white paper,* Electric Cloud, Inc.

Highsmith, J. (2000), *Retiring Lifecycle Dinosaurs- Using Adaptive Software Development to meet the challenges of a high-speed, high-change environment,* Software Testing and Quality Engineering, www.stqemagazine.com

Highsmith, J. (2009). *Agile Project Management: Creating Innovative Products* (2nd ed.). Pearson Education.

Kniberg, H. (2007), *Scrum and XP from the Trenches,* InfoQ Enterprise Development Series, e-book at http://infoq.com/minibooks/ scrum-xp-fromthe-trenches.

Larman, C. (2004). *Agile & Iterative Development: A Managers Guide.* Addison-Wesley.

Liker, J. K. (1997). *Becoming Lean: Inside Stories of U.S. Manufacturers.* Productivity Press.

Morgan. (2002), *Applying Lean Principles to Product Development,* SAE Foundation for Science & Technology Education, http://www.sae. org/topics/leanfeb02.htm, accessed March 24, 2014

Solon, R. (2002). *Benchmarking the ROI for Software Process Improvement, The DoD SoftwareTech News, Nov.2002.* USA DoD.

Thomas, M. (2001). *IT Projects Sink or Swim.* British Computer Society Review.

KEY TERMS AND DEFINITIONS

Agile Development: A system development approach based on iterative activities and empirical project management and planning.

Chaordic Systems: A term used to describe a system process or organisational structure that combines and blends elements of chaos and order.

Lean Development: A development process where every step or phase in the development activity is scrutinised for its contribution to the end-product, and the elimination of waste in the product development process, to ensure efficient process flow.

Structured Design Lifecycle: A systems development approach based on rigorous initial definition of requirements and a linear stream of phases, including Analysis, Design, Construction and Testing. Considered to be ineffective and inefficient.

The Model of Concurrent Perception: A model of product development proposing that product development moves from an initial 'chaotic' activity involving individuals and various ideas to converge on an agreed design in an orderly fashion.

Chapter 13
Integrating Security into Agile Models:
Scrum, Feature–Driven Development (FDD), and eXtreme Programming (XP)

Imran Ghani
Universiti Teknologi Malaysia, Malaysia

Adila Firdaus Bt Arbain
Universiti Teknologi Malaysia, Malaysia

Zulkarnain Azham
Universiti Teknologi Malaysia, Malaysia

Nor Izzaty Yasin
Universiti Teknologi Malaysia, Malaysia

Seung Ryul Jeong
Kookmin University, South Korea

ABSTRACT

Agile methodologies have gained recognition in recent years as being efficient development processes through their quick delivery of software, even under time constraints. Agile methodologies consist of a few process models that have their own criteria in helping different types of projects. However, agile methods such as Scrum, Feature-Driven Development (FDD), and eXtreme Programming (XP) have been criticized due to the lack of availability of security elements in their various phases, resulting in the development of unsecure software. Thus, the authors propose the idea of a set of security-focused elements to enhance the existing agile models. In this chapter, the findings of the related research and the highlights of improved agile models after the integration of security are presented.

DOI: 10.4018/978-1-4666-6026-7.ch013

Figure 1. Scrum process model

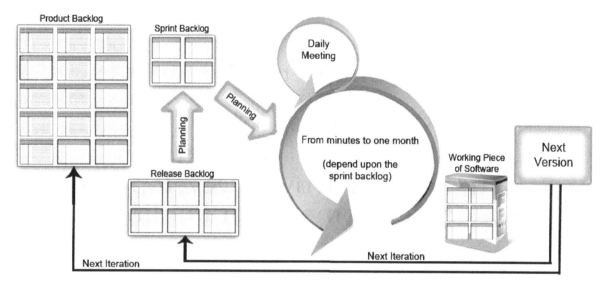

1. AGILE MODELS

1.1. Scrum

Scrum (Schwaber & Beedle, 2002) is an iterative, incremental software process, which is by far the most popular agile developmental process (Version one, 2006). Scrum can assist with small to medium size projects consisting of many subtasks that need to be done. In relation to the idea of iteration, decomposition to small tasks that group them in backlogs and daily meetings; scrum ensures that the process is simple and effective in delivering small and working software packages.

Figure 1 shows the processes of Scrum within a project. It starts with collecting the user stories (requirements) in product backlog; from this product backlog, a sprint backlog is then created. Each sprint will undergo development process while a daily scrum meeting will be held to evaluate the progress and hold discussions about any problems that may have arisen with the current sprint. After concluding the sprints, the finished sprint will become the potentially shippable product to the customer.

1.2. FDD

Even though people have always maintained that iterative processes do not require much planning (Hunt,2006), FDD has proven otherwise. By planning the building of the list of feature processes and subsequent planning by these feature processes, FDD has become well-known for its efficient project management processes. FDD is deemed suitable for small to large scale projects respectively.

Figure 2 shows the existing FDD process model that consists of 5 main phases. In the first phase, Develop an Overall model, the architect will seek to draw out the whole design of the system. The second phase is the creation of a Building a Feature list. This phase will identify a list of features for the whole set of systems. After acquiring a set of features, the project manager will then, specifically: plan the features based on the due dates; assign the feature to class owners and rank the features based on priority. The design of the feature sets will then be started in the Design by Feature phase. Lastly, the feature will be built incrementally by features designed in the Build by Features' phase.

Figure 2. Existing FDD process model

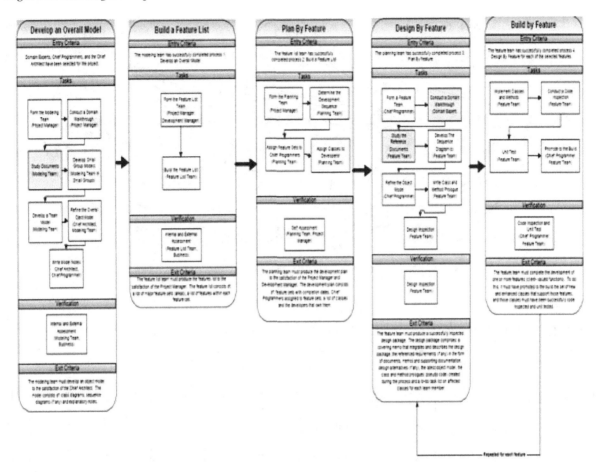

1.3. eXtreme Programming (XP)

eXtreme Programming (XP) methodology consists of a variety of practices and roles. However, in its original form or so called traditional XP method does not clearly defines that which role should adopt which practice. This confuses the XP team. In order to overcome this confusion, we have mapped the roles and XP practices, which we call role-based XP (Figure 3).

The XP practices are used by developers in creating the required software. XP developed the system in a more 'loose' fashion since XP does not have any specific standards processes that the development team should follow.

2. SOFTWARE SECURITY

Security principles (Julia at al., 2008) are the primary concepts which are used to determine appropriate levels of security in software. They are universal guidelines adopted by developers, project planners, practitioners and experts in the security field in order to mitigate risks in the phases of requirement, architecture, design, implementation, testing and maintenance. As illustrated in Table 1, research has been conducted proposing solutions that satisfy some or all of the security principles. The 'X' symbol is used when researchers have not mentioned the security principle; while the '$\sqrt{}$' symbol is used when it has been

Figure 3. XP practices and their mapping with the roles

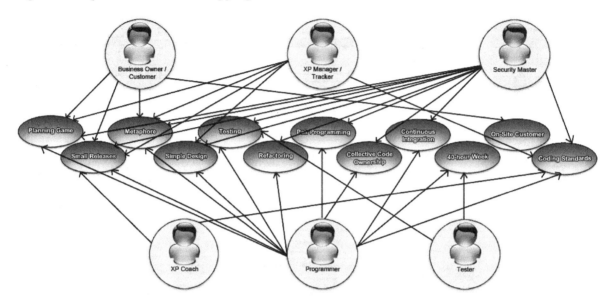

Table 1. Security principles

	Least privilege	Failing securely	Securing the weakest link	Defense in depth	Separation of privilege	Economy of mechanism	Least common mechanism	Reluctance to trust	Never assuming that your secrets are safe	Complete mediation	Psychological acceptability	Promoting privacy
Julia H. Allen et. al., 2009	√	√	√	√	√	√	√	√	√	√	√	√
OWASP, 2013	X	√	X	√	X	√	X	√	X	X	√	X
Viega, et al., 2001	√	√	√	√	√	√	√	√	√	√	√	√
Saltzeret al., 1975	√	√	X	X	√	√	√	X	X		√	X

mentioned in their work. For more information about security principles, see (Julia at al., 2008).

3. ENHANCED AGILE MODELS WITH SECURITY

After explaining each of the agile models and respective security attributes, this section will discuss the agile models that have been enhanced with security measurements. Each agile model will be explained as below.

3.1. Security and Enhanced Scrum

In this section, our previously proposed SB and its integration into the Scrum model is analyzed and the authors explain the overall enhanced Scrum model. As mentioned in Table 2, existing scrum does not offer a solution for the security issues

(Azham et al., 2011). Therefore, our aim is to merge two new elements into the existing Scrum. These are: 1) a new security component known as SB, and 2) a new role known as Security Master (SM). The SM is in charge of the SB during the Scrum lifecycle.

The enhanced Scrum model in Figure 4 has two additional components. These are:

1. A Security Backlog (SB) that manages security in Scrum.
2. A Security Master (SM) that handles security in Scrum and is in-charge of the SB.

As illustrated in Figures 4 and 5, the process flow is shown below.

1. The requirements are translated into product backlog and go through SB.

2. In this phase, the SM figures out certain features in the product backlog that require security attention.
3. The Security Master marks (dotted in illustrations) the selected features in the security backlog. The SM creates a document of its activity for use as a reference during the development and testing phases. The marked security concerns are noted in the sprint backlog for the attention of the developers.
4. Testing is verified in sprint phases by the security master.

Figure 6 displays SQL injection and buffer overflow attack possibilities identified by the SM. Since the agile method documentation needs to be as simple as that suggested in agile manifesto (Fowler & Highsmith 2001), the SB also helps to produce a simple but comprehensive document.

Figure 4. Enhanced Scrum process with additional SB and SM

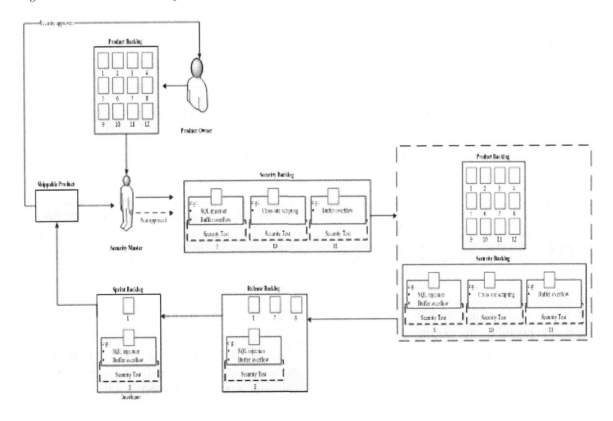

Figure 5. Security process in Scrum

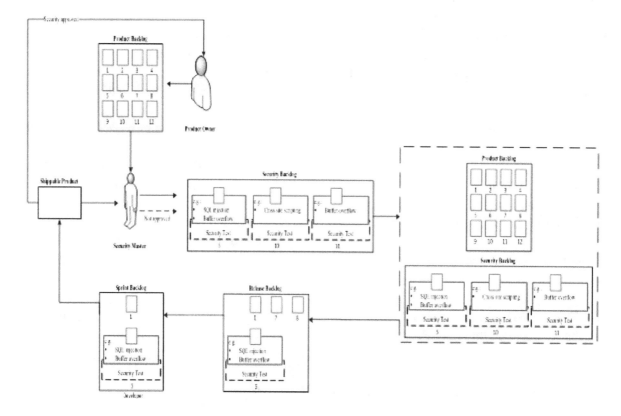

Table 2. Security Description in Each Phase (Azham et al., 2011)

Process	Description
Product Backlog	The Product Backlog is the master list of all functionality desired in the product. When using Scrum, it is not necessary to start a project with a lengthy, upfront effort to document all requirements. The documentation for security will be absent here because the team wishes to produce simple documentation.
Release Backlog	A release backlog is a subset of the product backlog that is planned to be delivered in the coming release. It is anticipated to partition the product backlog to provide a release backlog for each release. The release backlog is the subset of product requirements that will be delivered in a given release. The prioritized feature that will need to be released quickly will present a danger if it is not analyzed in the threat analysis phase.
Sprint Backlog	The sprint backlog is the list of tasks that the Scrum team is committing in order to complete the current sprint. Here, the time release has been decided, and any additions in the security part will be hard to manage in time.
Testing and shippable phase	In this phase, all products have been integrated and will be tested for a final analysis. When it comes to this phase, the security part will require a considerable amount of time and money to maintain.

At the same time, it attempts to provide clear information regarding the security risks.

3.2. Security and Enhanced FDD

After identifying the security related limitations in the existing FDD model (Firdaus, et al., 2013a), (Firdaus & Ghani., 2013b), we have attempted

Figure 6. Release backlog highlighted with security related features

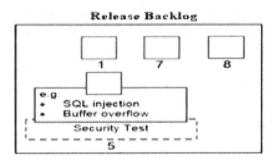

Figure 7. Build and design feature

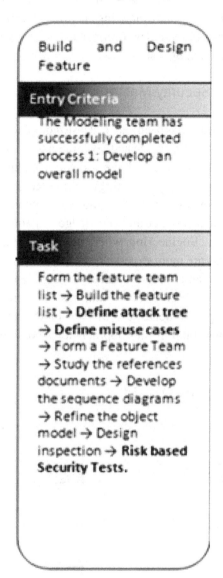

to propose a conceptual Secure Feature Driven Development (SFDD) model. In this enhanced FDD model, we made a number of changes as detailed below.

- The first change involves combining two existing phases, namely, Design by Feature phase and Build a Feature List into one comprehensive phase, specifically: Build and Design Features.
- The second change concerns the addition of new elements inside the phases; known as In-Phase Security.
- The third change refers to two additional phases named Build Security by Feature and Test Security by Feature. This feature is called After-Phase Security.
- The fourth change concerns the introduction of a new role called Security Master.

All of these new improvements in FDD methods are explained in the next- subsection. As we know, based on the existing FDD model there are 5 main phases. According to the case study, we have discovered that the Design by Feature phase should not be a stand-alone phase as it joins the Build a Feature List and becomes a new phase entitled Build and Design Features. There are two reasons for this, as explained below (Figure 7):

1. Based on the original model; after the building of the design, came the planning stage. Time can be saved if, both during and after the features are built, the feature can be directly designed and the implementation is planned based on the design. Better planning can be done if we can see the whole design of the feature.

2. This procedure is beneficial for a less experienced development team who may have less

experience in estimating time to develop the features just by looking at the list of features, as compared with considering the whole design of system.

3.2.1. Security Master

A case study has been undertaken to compare projects of undergraduate and postgraduate students. They were tasked with the project of building a secure software system using the same agile model, FDD. However, in this case study we compared the value of experience and knowledge and Software Security Engineering where the postgraduate students are more experienced in developing the software and in security knowledge. As a result, the software programme that has been created by the postgraduate students was more secured. It shows that if the development team consists of

people who have expertise in software security, we can produce secured software. That is why this study proposes a security role that we called Security Master. In this role, the minimum number of persons to be in security master is one. A case study on the undergraduate students shows that one person having Software Security knowledge in the team is enough to bring about awareness of security features in the system.

3.2.2 In-Phase Security

This technique includes any necessary security processes within the FDD phases (Figure 8). For example, after studying the documents in the Develop an Overall Model phase, we identify and link the business processes with the technical risks. By adding this method, we can identify all the risks for a system based only on the user requirements

Figure 8. SFDD model

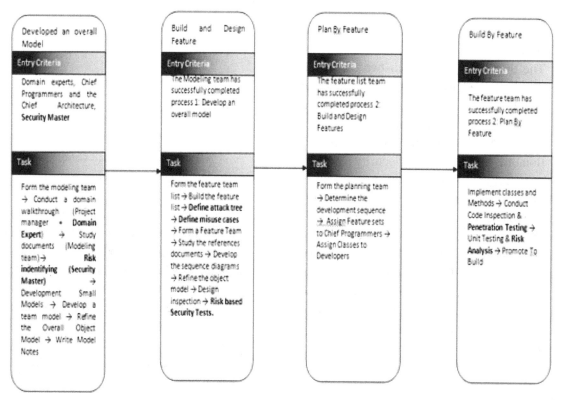

Figure 9. After phase security

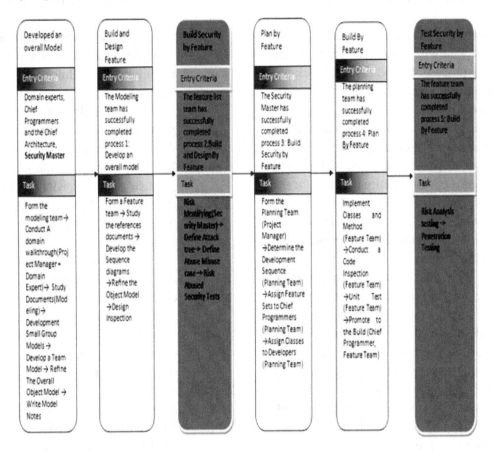

or the overall model. There are more additional processes that can be viewed in Figure 8and these have been highlighted in bold font.

3.2.3 After-Phase Security

Unlike the first technique, security has only been defined after a phase. In this way, we have proposed the Security by Feature phase after the Build and Design Features phase and Build by Feature phase respectively. Based on Figure 9, we can call these two phases: Security by Feature and Test security by feature. These two phases are suitable for newer and less experienced development teams, or team members that have the Software Security Engineering knowledge but cannot directly identify the security measurements. Further, this stage can be

dedicated to the job of Security Master. Therefore, there are six phases altogether, namely: Develop an Overall Model, Build and Design Features, Build Security by Feature, Plan by Feature, Build by Feature and Test Security by Feature.

Next, this book chapter will focus on the XP model in relation to improving or enhancing the process and practices involved with security measurements. As we know, XP is inter-linked with the collection of core values, principles and practices that provide a highly efficient and effective means of developing software. XP is also known as one of the agile methods which collaborate with customers for the whole development process. In addition, existing XP does not offer a solution for the security issues (Ghani &Yasin, 2013a), (Ghani, et al., 2013b).

3.3 Security and Enhanced XP

XP is known as one of a number of agile methods which collaborate with customers for the whole development process. In addition, XP includes both communication and feedback as interdependent process values which are essential for projects to achieve successful results. In each XP team, there are several different roles, each having its own unique responsibilities.Since XP is not a structured agile approach, hence it is hard for the team to understand that which practice should be adopted by which role. Thus, we developed role-based mapping-matrix that helps in mapping the roles and XP practices.

Table 3 shows the mapping between roles and practices of the existing XP methodology. The tick "$\sqrt{}$" shows the roles adopting relevant XP practices. It should be noticed that we have added a security layer in the XP mapping-matrix. This means that security should be considered as a part of each XP practice. In addition, a new role called "Security Master" has been introduced. Having the mapping available helps to ensure that the process of producing a secured system is completed. Based on the table above, there are five basic roles via twelve practices as shown. We now illustrate each stage of the role in further detail as follows:

3.3.1 XP Roles with Practices

1. **Customer/Business Owner**
   a. *Planning game:* Customer is one of the accompanying partners in XP team to, schedule user stories for current iteration, determine which features to implement next and collaborate with the technical team (programmer) in choosing a story card during the planning game (Aydal, et al 2006). According to the study by (Ge, et al 2007), this practice was important for teams (either customer or programmer)

in order to get the iteration off to a good start.
   b. *Small release:* This process enables customer evaluation of the business requirement fulfillment by using the acceptance test (Beck & Gamma,1998).
   c. *Metaphor:* Firstly, the customer will picture how the software looks in order to help programmers understand how the software should work in this practice (Dudziak, 1999). Following this, they will then work together until the end so the product does not deviate from the actual requirement.
   d. *On-site customer:* This means a special rule for a customer (usually a domain expert who is a potential user of the system). They will be part of the development team and therefore at the development "site" (Ge, et al 2007). (see Figure 10)

2. **Coach**
   a. *Small release:* Coach will monitor and ensure small releases will be issued to the development teams according to the schedule set. He will always lead the XP teams so that the project will not deviate from the original schedule.
   b. *Coding standard:* Determine which coding standard can be used in its organization. Each organization has its own style in describing the code. (see Figure 11)

3. **Manager/Tracker**
   a. *Planning game:* The manager will monitor every movement of the activities carried out by XP team in order to smooth the development process without encountering any problems. Accordingly, he should know all the movements of the group, distribution of tasks, and the schedule for whole process and user stories that will be determined by them (programmer

Table 3. XP-Mapping Matrix for mapping XP practices based on Roles (a security layer and Security Master role have been introduced in the Matrix)

	Planning Game	Small Releases	Metaphor	Simple Design	Testing	Refactoring	Pair Programming	Collective Code Ownership	Continuous Integration	40-Hour Week	On-Site Customer	Coding Standards
	SECURITY FOCUS PRACTICE											
Business Owner / Customer	✓	✓	✓								✓	
XP Coach		✓										✓
XP Manager / Tracker	✓	✓	✓	✓								✓
Programmer	✓	✓	✓	✓	✓	✓	✓	✓	✓	✓	✓	✓
Security Master	✓	✓	✓	✓	✓	✓	✓	✓	✓			✓
Testers					✓						✓	

Figure 10. Customer role process model

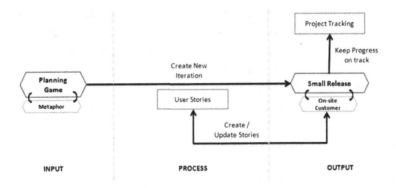

and customer) based on priorities and relevance.

b. *Small release:* Make sure the small release will be produced on time with 100 percent approval by customer. Otherwise, whatever is remaining will be communicated to the teams so as to determine how much time is left before the deadline.

c. *Metaphor:* Ensure the whole team has a shared understanding of the important elements of the product during the planning game until the finish of the development process. This practice is needed to produce effective architecture of the system.

d. *Small design:* Adoption of this practice will ensure that programmers will

Figure 11. Coach role process model

Figure 12. Manager role process model

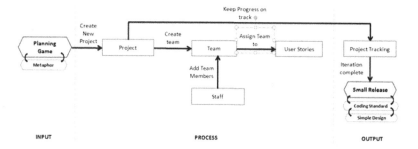

provide the simplest design that should be working in order to minimize time consumption.

e. *Continuous integration:* Ensure the team integrates the code immediately after finishing a certain task and after running the unit test correctly.

f. *Coding standard:* Ensure coding standards meet the requirements of the particular organization. If not, the conversion code executed by another programmer will be more difficult and increase time-consumption when changing back. (see Figure 12)

4. **Programmer**

a. *Planning game:* This involves having individuals signup for the tasks that are included at this stage. It helps to ensure that they are more responsible during implementation; thus leading to decreased number of errors in the time estimates (Ge et al, 2007).

b. *Small release:* This entails working on software to the customer's satisfaction and passing the acceptance test before a small release can be delivered (Wang, et al., 2008)

c. *Metaphor:* Actually, this practice addresses architecture directly. Reference to (Jensen, et al., 2006) shows that the purpose of metaphor is to guide all development with a simple shared story of how the whole system works using architecture. However, there are papers which have found that the metaphor concept is hard to grasp (Beck & Andres,2004).Meanwhile, excerpts from the book (Pitta &Fowler,2005)

Figure 13. Manager role process model

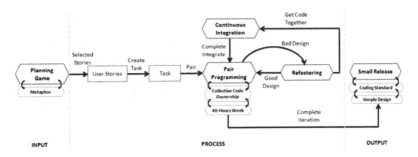

Figure 14. Tester role process model

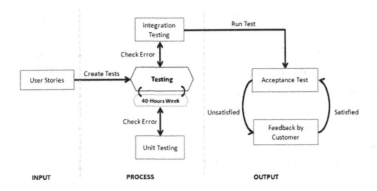

state that the metaphor is no longer a practice.

d. *Small design:* To achieve a stable and simple system structure, it is necessary to do the simplest thing that could possibly work. Thus, as we taught in (Aydal, et al 2006), the requirement is to state "Enough Design Up Front", and provide a continuous incremental design that is defined in terms of architecture and design models before any implementation can take place.

e. *Refactoring:* Refactoring means a continuous design improvement process such as: removal of duplication, reduction of coupling and an increase in cohesion. In addition, it is notable that this practice has the highest adoption rate according to survey data so as to see how practitioners perceive its potential benefits for project outcomes (Aydal, et al 2006).

f. *Pair programming:* Only programmers can use this practice. It helps them to double check any error and to ensure correct implementation of security in their system by review with another pair (Karlstrom, 2002). Moreover, experiments by conclude that pair programming reduces the time required to correctly perform change tasks and increases the percentage of correct solutions.

g. *Collective code ownership:* Any pair of programmers can improve any code at any time so there are no 'secure workspaces'. Rather, it helps in managing time and schedules and does not face

Figure 15. Security master role process model

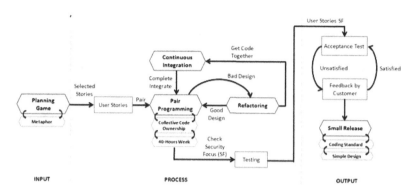

any difficulty while converting other people to in-charge in coding.

h. *Continuous integration:* Teams must keep the system fully integrated at all times. Thus, this practice will prevent errors at early stage which might not be detected during testing (Beck & Gamma, 1998).

i. *40-hours week:* Maintaining a schedule of 40 hours per week is very important for the productivity of system development. It also increases the quality of software as well as the provision of quality software. Otherwise, they must avoid overtime in order to ensure that team members can remain rested and motivated.

j. *Coding standard:* All codes in the system must use the same common coding standard to support collective code ownership. At the same time, the codes can be more consistent in how they are understood and can be edited by other programmers. (see Figure 13)

5. **Tester**

a. *Testing:* In XP, tests are written before the code is developed; this is also known as Test Driven Development (TDD) (Beck & Gamma, 1998). This practice helps programmers to produce codes with 100% test coverage more easily. Based on customer specifications, the customer acceptance test requires developers to provide the customer with the results of the acceptance tests along with demonstrations (Beck & Andres, 2004).

b. *40-hours week:* Teams must avoid overtime and maintain a schedule of 40 hour weeks. If a week work schedule of 40 hours is not maintained, the outcome will not be productive. The teams involved will be affected by work pressure and exhausted; this will be unproductive and ultimately decrease the quality of the software itself. (see Figure 14)

6. **Security Master**
One of the methods to improve security in the XP process involves proposing a security role and defining the process. In this method, the security roles are known as Security Master. Security Master will be responsible for any security measurements during the software developments. As shown in Figure 15, the process model for the Security Master role could be used as a guideline for this role being used during development.

4. CONCLUSION

After preliminary analysis, comparison, and collection of literature including journals, books, magazines and case studies, we were able to successfully identify the security issues related to the agile methods such as Scrum, FDD and XP. Through further research, we were able to discover the relationship between the security principles and security in each of these three agile models. Firstly, we introduced security roles and security backlogs to Scrum. Then, we improved the FDD by, specifically; introducing some new security processes based on the situation and new security roles in FDD. As for XP, it has been determined that we can improve this by a role-based approach on the practices in XP and also by the introduction of a security role. Team members who had experience using the agile model (team leaders, requirement engineers, developers and testers) evaluated whether agility was affected or not. Based on their evaluations, the studies show that agility was not negatively affected if security is added to the agile model.

REFERENCES

Aydal, E. G., Paige, R. F., Chivers, H., & Brooke, P. J. (2006). Security planning and refactoring in extreme programming. In *Proceedings of Extreme Programming and Agile Processes in Software Engineering* (pp. 154-163). Springer.

Azham, Z., Imran, G., & Ithnin, N. (2011). Security Backlog in Scrum Security Practices. In *Proceedings of 5th Malaysian Software Engineering Conference* (MySEC). MySEC.

Beck, K., & Gamma, E. (1998). Test infected: Programmers love writing tests. *Java Report*, *3*(7), 37–50.

Beck, K., & Andres, C. (2004). *Extreme programming explained: Embrace change*. Addison-Wesley Professional.

Firduas, A., Ghani, I., & Jeong, S. R. (2013a). *A Systematic Literature Review on Secure Software Development using Feature Driven Development (FDD) Agile Model*. Paper presented at the KSII The 8th Asia Pacific International Conference on Information Science and Technology. Korea.

Firduas, A., & Ghani, I. (2013b). *2nd International Conference on Informatics, Environment, Energy and Applications*. IEEA.

Ge, X., Paige, R. F., Polack, F., & Brooke, P. (2007). Extreme programming security practices. In *Agile Processes in Software Engineering and Extreme Programming* (pp. 226–230). Springer. doi:10.1007/978-3-540-73101-6_42

Hunt, J. (2006). *Agile software construction*. New York: Springer.

Imran, G., & Izaty, Y. (2013a). Software Security Engineering in Extreme Programming Methodology: A Systematic Literature Review. *Journal Sci-Int*, *25*(2), 215–221.

Imran, G., Izaty, Y., & Adila, F. (2013b). Role-Based Extreme Programming (Xp) For Secure Software Development. *Sci. Int. (Lahore)*, *25*(4), 1071–1074.

Jensen, R. Jensen, & Sonder, P. (2006). Architecture and Design in eXtreme Programming. Introducing 'Developer Stories' (LNCS), (vol. 4044, pp. 133–142). Berlin: Springer.

Julia, H. A. (Ed.). (2008). *Software Security Engineering: A Guide for Project Manager*. Addison Wesley Professional.

Julia, H. A., et al. (2009). *Making the business Case for Software Assurance*. Retrieved in 15 Apr 2010 from http://repository.cmu.edu/sei/29/

Karlstrom, D. (2002). *Introducing Extreme Programming - An Experience Report*. Paper presented at the Third International Conference on eXtreme Programming and Agile Processes in Software Engineering. New York, NY.

OWASP. (2013). Retrieved on 10 August 2013, https://www.owasp.org

Pitta, D. A., & Fowler, D. (2005). Online consumer communities and their value to new product developers. *Journal of Product and Brand Management*, *14*(5), 283–291. doi:10.1108/10610420510616313

Saltzer, J. H., & Schroeder, M. D. (1975). The protection of information in computer systems. *Proceedings of the IEEE*, *63*(9), 1278–1308. doi:10.1109/PROC.1975.9939

Schwaber, K., & Beedle, M. (2002). *Agilè Software Development with Scrum* (International Ed.). Pearson.

Versionone. (2006). *3rd Annual Survey: 2008, The State of Agile Development*. Retrieved October 13, 2012, from http://www.versionone.com

Viega, J., & McGraw, G. (2001). *Building secure software: how to avoid security problems the right way*. Pearson Education.

Wang, X., Wu, Z., & Zhao, M. (2008). The relationship between developers and customers in agile methodology. In *Proceedings of Computer Science and Information Technology* (pp. 566–572). IEEE. doi:10.1109/ICCSIT.2008.9

KEY TERMS AND DEFINITIONS

Agile Software Development: A software management and development approach that helps to create software quickly while addressing the issue of requirement change.

DSDM: This process model is also phase-based, which is normally used in resource constraints project.

FDD: This process model consists of 5 main phases.

Scrum: This is an iterative, incremental software process, which is by far the most popular agile developmental process.

Secure Software Development: A software management and development approach that focuses on software security throughout the development lifecycle from requirement, design, implementation, testing to maintenance.

Security Master: A team member in an agile team who ensures that security has been implemented throughout the development lifecycle from requirement, design, implementation, testing to maintenance.

XP: This methodology consists of a variety of practices. These practices are used by developers in creating the required software.

Chapter 14
Agile Development Processes and Knowledge Documentation

Eran Rubin
Holon Institute of Technology, Israel

Hillel Rubin
Israel Institute of Technology (Technion), Israel

ABSTRACT

Agile processes emphasize operational system code rather than its documentation. Ironically, however, some traditional documentation artefacts come to support system-stakeholders interaction, which is another core aspect of agile development processes. In this chapter, the authors examine the relationship between system development and knowledge documentation. They develop an approach that enables incorporating domain documentation to agile development while keeping the processes adaptive. The authors also provide a system design that actively uses domain knowledge documentation.

INTRODUCTION

Agile development processes come to enable a more flexible and adaptive system development process than the traditional development processes do (Maurer & Hellmann 2013, Fowler 2005).

Agile methods require less documentation for tasks, and promote implementation based on informal collaborations between system stakeholders (Fowler 2005). While traditional software engineering methods emphasize careful planning and design, agile methods emphasize the actual software implementation.

However, this shift of emphasis is not without cost. Documentation which is lost under agile development processes could have helped, among other things, to facilitate knowledge sharing and reduce knowledge loss when team members become unavailable (Abrahamsson et al. 2003). Indeed compromising on documentation is not a key point, but rather a consequence of the agile objective of being adaptive (Paetch et al. 2003), which agile methods attempt to overcome by significantly relying on constant collaboration between developers and users (Abrahamsson et al. 2003). While such approaches may well lead to the release of a system that fits customer needs, the knowledge extracted under such approaches will be hard to access after development is complete.

DOI: 10.4018/978-1-4666-6026-7.ch014

The premise of this chapter is that it should be possible to support documentation in agile development methods without compromising the agile manifesto. If documentation is adaptive, and if the documentation supports people collaboration rather than replacing it, then documentation can be well aligned with agile development principles.

In this work we discuss the kind of documentation that can support collaboration and the way to integrate such documentation in agile development. Namely, we propose a way of creating an adaptive system for documenting the knowledge necessary for the interaction and collaboration between system stakeholders.

Our approach provides agile documentation of domain knowledge gathered during systems analysis in traditional processes. Specifically, we provide an approach to document in agile processes the type of knowledge, which under traditional processes would have typically been documented during systems analysis. We aim to document this type of knowledge as the traditional system analysis stage is the stage in which all system stakeholders interact and a common understanding of the domain is established and documented. Therefore, in the traditional system analysis phase we are able to find documents supporting collaboration, which are missing in agile development processes. Although such documents are missing in agile processes, they have great potential to facilitate these processes' effectiveness. For example, Daneva et al (2013) point out that understanding requirements dependencies and vendor's domain knowledge is a key asset for setting up successful client-developer collaboration in agile methodologies.

Accordingly, we identify a set of collaboration supporting documents of the traditional development processes, and we establish a method to incorporate such documents in agile processes. Namely, since agile development emphasizes the reference to working system code, we develop a way of having the identified documentation as part of the executable system code. More specifically,

we suggest a system architectural design which enables adaptable documentation as part of the source code. We term our proposed system design Active Documentation Software Design (ADSD). Under this design, source code execution incorporates the execution of documentation statements, which in turn drive the processing of the system. Stated differently, with ADSD changes in the documentation change executable code and vice versa, changes in source code change the relevant documentation.

This chapter is developed as follows:

- The background describes the motivation for this work.
- The section "supporting agile documentation" elaborates on principles guiding the development of the architecture.
- The section "representation of domain knowledge in the system code" describes the architecture and the implementation of components for its support.
- The section "the ADSA system design" provides a description of experience in using and applying the architecture.
- Finally, come discussion and summary of the manuscript.

BACKGROUND

Traditionally, the design process gradually moves from the "problem space" to the "solution space" (Booch 1987). However, as different paradigms of programming emerged, the difference between the problem and solution domain became less and less distinct (Henderson-Sellers & Edwards 1990). Initially, programs did not exhibit problem level information that could be understood or modified. The programmer was not required to make a program understandable and modifiable, but rather programs were merely measured by their efficiency and whether they could accurately solve a specific problem. Presently, software engineering emphasizes that programs should be written to be understandable and maintainable. An important step in this direction was the introduction of Object Oriented Programming (OOP) paradigm, in which programmers are thinking more in terms of the problem domain (Abbot 1987).

The more source code related to the problem space, the more difficult it was to distinguish between design and implementation. For example, Heramann (1999) states that some studies (Coad and Yourdon 1991, Jacobson 1995) have pointed out that object oriented analysis refers only to domain objects, while object oriented design refers also to future system objects. He also mentions that other studies have not yet clearly distinguished between the designs (Rumbaugh et al. 1991, Shlaer et al. 1992).

Agile development methodologies emerged as a result of the difficulties described in the preceding paragraph, and they embrace the unique attributes of working code. In agile processes a minimum set of principles is provided rather than detailed development rules.

However, it is well understood that regardless of the processes used, systems cannot be developed without knowledge. In both agile and traditional approaches, during the processes known as requirements engineering, the development team must acquire the same information and the customer must make the same decisions about the system (Kovitz 2003). In this context, recently various methods and languages to support agile requirements engineering have been gaining increasing attention. For example, Ernst et al. (2013) propose the RE-KOMBINE requirements language. Helmy et al. (2012) propose an agile requirements elicitation method.

The requirements engineering process, however, assumes two major differences when comparing the agile approach and the traditional approach: 1) due to the difference in development practices, traditional development usually embodies the requirements in a written document, while agile development does not (Kovitz 2003), and 2)

the approaches differ in *when* requirements engineering should take place (Kovitz 2003). In agile development, requirements are built throughout the development process. Therefore, there are no models documenting acquired domain knowledge. Rather, knowledge is only found in code, test cases, and programmers' memory (Nawrocki et al. 2002).

Therefore, while agile processes and traditional processes need to use the same kind of knowledge to facilitate an effective development process, agile processes cannot reconcile its documentation with the agile principles. Instead of written documents, knowledge is usually gathered through informal questions and gestures (Sim and Gallardo-Valencia 2013). The agile approach suggests that source code is in fact the most relevant written design document. Blum (1996) states that "a program is not an object but rather it is a design of an object". Reeves (1992) claims that programming is designing software, and "the final source code is the real software design". While these arguments have merits, we cannot claim that source code and other design models created during the traditional development process are equivalent. Two major differences exist between these two concepts:

1. Source code is less accessible to different stakeholders in the organization than design documents are. Basically, only a professional programmer can understand the source code. Further, familiarity with the development environment is needed in order to navigate through the source code.

2. While there may be an overlap of information available in source code and other design documents, there are still many differences. For example, source code contains more information since it holds implementation related details. Such details include networking details, security issues, etc. On the other hand, in other respects source code contains less information due to differences in its semantic power. For example, most programming languages do not support the

explicit representation of roles, while roles are often found in early design documents.

Although domain knowledge is more difficult to reconcile there is evidence for its important role both in promoting methodology adoption (Senapathi and Srinivasan 2013) and for effective outcomes of its use (Daneva et al. 2013).

SUPPORTING AGILE DOCUMENTATION

Documentation Objectives

The background section has indicated that important documents, which are absent when using agile methods, are those created during the analysis phase in traditional development processes.

The concept of systems analysis has undergone some transformations over the years. Gradually reference to the systems analysis phase has shifted from "Systems Analysis" to "System Requirements Analysis" (e.g. Grady 2006), "Requirements Analysis" (e.g. Hay 2003), and most commonly today to "Requirements Engineering" (RE). There is no clear distinction between the different terms. However, it appears that in earlier days Systems Analysis referred to well defined processes leading to coherent development, and RE refers to methods for understanding and capturing organizational needs.

RE is concerned with interpreting and understanding stakeholders' terminology, viewpoints and goals (Nuseibeh & Easterbrook 2000). Therefore, models support all RE activities (Lamsweerde 2000). More specifically, in traditional development methods, RE processes incorporate the modeling of the existing domain as well as alternative hypothetical systems (Lamsweerde 2000). In the literature, these two types of models are often referred to as "conceptual models" and "system models" respectively.

Both conceptual models and system models are essential for the RE process - conceptual models for understanding the problem domain, and system models for generating requirements associated with the system. Conceptual models represent the problem understanding (Devedzic 2002), and facilitate understanding among various stakeholders in the organization (Mylopoulos & Borgida 1997).

Since the understanding of the application domain and alternative systems changes as development process propagates, both conceptual and system views are dynamic and evolving. In this respect, evolved system code naturally represents the most accurate *system* model. Therefore, as the agile movement has pointed out, the need for the original *system* models may be challenged. Nonetheless, this is not the case for *conceptual* models. As the understanding of the domain evolves, *conceptual* models are not accurately represented anywhere. Ironically, while conceptual models are lost in agile development methods, they could be highly relevant when using such methods. Agile development requires constant and efficient communication between all system stakeholders, which is the core purpose of conceptual models. Since our objective is to facilitate their documentation in agile processes, we examine the content of conceptual models.

Documentation Constructs

In order to enable agile documentation of conceptual knowledge we examine the core documentation constructs used when creating conceptual models under the traditional RE processes.

As stated by Nuseibeh & Easterbrook (2000), to a great extent the elicitation technique used during RE is driven by the choice of the modeling scheme, and vice versa. To this end, Nuseibeh & Easterbrook (2000) mention four general categories of modeling approaches used in RE: Data Modeling, Behavioural Modeling, Enterprise Modeling, and Domain Modeling.

In each of the four modeling approaches we identify a set of core modeling constructs, which are commonly used for communication about the domain. By enabling the use of these constructs in working implementation code, we wish to enable active documentation of the domain. Therefore, in the following subsections we review the core constructs used under each modeling approach.

It is important to note that the approaches are not mutually exclusive, but rather each approach takes a different view as to the aspects that should be emphasized to facilitate requirements elicitation. Data modeling approaches deal with understanding the information that needs to be stored, maintained, and managed by the information system. Behavioural modeling approaches deal with the dynamic or functional behaviour of stakeholders and systems. Enterprise modeling approaches deal with understanding an organization's structure, the business rules that affect its operation, and the goals, tasks and responsibilities of its members. Finally, domain modeling approaches deal with understanding the impact of the system on the domain, and the way it helps to control the domain.

Since the approaches are not mutually exclusive, the meaning of some of the core constructs used in different approaches may overlap with each other. Hence, to facilitate clear documentation of domain knowledge in Information Systems (IS) code, we compared the constructs and integrated them. This enables us to provide a set of constructs that do not overlap with one another, are well defined, and their inter-relationships are clearly understood. The core domain constructs identified in the different approaches are as follows:

Data Modeling

Data modeling aims at helping stakeholders make decisions about the type of information the developed system should represent. These models help communicate the correspondence between the information system and the real world (Nuseibeh & Easterbrook 2000).

The core domain aspects captured in the data modeling approaches are:

- **Entity:** A "thing" in the domain that can be distinctly identified.
- **Operations:** Services or tasks a thing can execute or perform.
- **Entity Sets/Entity Types:** A group of entities of the same type.
- **Relationship:** A relation between entities.
- **Relationship-Sets:** A relation between entity-sets.
- **Value Sets:** A range of values.
- **Attributes:** Mappings from entity sets or relationship sets to value sets.
- **Constraints:** Relationship sets and attributes can have cardinality constraints

Behavioural Modeling

Behavioural modeling approaches emphasize the system behaviour rather than the domain. Still, in the behavioural perspective, the attempt is to identify the events that occur in the real world, the information affected by their occurrence, and the functions that are invoked to cause this effect.

The core domain aspects captured in the behavioural modeling approaches are those defined for state-machine that can relate to the domain. Accordingly, the core behavioural domain aspects are:

- **States:** Represent the state of the domain.
- **Transition:** A state change from the source state to a destination state.
- **Preconditions/Postconditions:** Define what causes a transition and what the consequence of a transition is.
- **Activities:** Performed as long as the state is active.
- **Events:** Trigger transitions between states.

Goal Oriented/Business Enterprise Modeling Approaches

Enterprise modeling concerns the business along with its goals. Central to this modeling approach are actors and goals. An actor is an active entity that carries out actions to achieve goals (Kavakli & Loucopoulos 2003). In turn, different definitions are available for the term *goal*. However, in general all definitions reflect the idea that a goal is a state that is desired to achieve (Lamsweerde 2001) or a state of affairs in the world that the stakeholders would like to achieve (Liu & Yu 2001).

The additional domain aspects captured in goal oriented modeling approaches are:

- **Goal:** A state that actors want to bring about.
- **Goal Relations:** The relation between goals capturing where goals positively or negatively support other goals.
- **Actor:** An active entity that carries out actions to achieve goals.
- **Resource:** A passive entity.
- **Task:** Specifies a particular way of doing something.
- **Dependency:** A relationship in which one actor depends on another actor.

The Domain Knowledge Approach in Requirements Engineering

Domain modeling approaches highlight the need for a clear relationship between requirements and specifications (Zave & Jackson 1997). The view under this approach is that specifications together with relevant domain knowledge should be sufficient to guarantee that requirements are satisfied.

Viewing RE under the domain knowledge approach dates back to 1982 with the work of Dubois et al. (1986), and more recently, Problem Frames (Jackson 2001, Hall et al. 2005) reflect this point of view.

The uniqueness of the approach is in the clear attempt to distinguish between the system and the environment. With this, the domain constructs of the domain modeling approaches are (Jackson 2001, Chen et al. 2007):

- **Phenomenon:** An element of what we can observe in the world.
- **(Given) Domain:** A set of related phenomena that are usefully treated as a behavioral unit for some purpose.
- **Event:** An occurrence at some point in time, regarded as atomic and instantaneous.
- **State:** A relationship among two or more individuals that can be true at one time and false at another.
- **Value:** An individual that cannot undergo change over time. It is a kind of a phenomenon. The values in which we are interested are things represented by numbers and characters.

Integration

The preceding sections revealed that the four RE approaches emphasise modeling different parts of the domain. Therefore, each approach takes a different set of modeling constructs. However, the different approaches are not mutually exclusive, and the knowledge they aim to document may overlap. Consequentially, the constructs used to model the domain in the different approaches may overlap.

Under these circumstances the challenge is to provide a coherent and well defined set of constructs that will enable the representation of the domain knowledge gathered in any of the four RE approaches. We approach this task by referring to the Enterprise Ontology (Uschold et al. 1998).

In the Enterprise Ontology, Uschold et al. (1998) define a set of constructs that enable representing any phenomenon at the business domain. As such, their constructs are well defined, and the interrelations between them are made clear.

By corresponding between the constructs used in the four RE approaches and those of the Enterprise Ontology we are able to clearly distinguish between the core constructs, as well as identify their compositions and interrelations.

However, not all constructs used in the Enterprise Ontology are necessarily relevant for representing RE based domain knowledge (REDK). The REDK representation constructs are those naturally used to discuss and identify system requirements. The Enterprise Ontology, on the other hand, aims at representing anything in the domain, including elements that may not be captured in RE. Furthermore, it is not clear how the constructs identified in the previous section relate to Enterprise Ontology constructs. There is a need to identify which constructs in the Enterprise Ontology can be used to represent RE domain knowledge.

Hence, in this section we identify a subset of the constructs defined at the Enterprise Ontology; namely, the constructs that can be used to represent REDK. For this purpose we apply a mapping from the constructs identified in the four RE approaches to constructs defined at the Enterprise Ontology. The mapping is given in Table 1. The leftmost column of the table incorporates the Enterprise Ontology construct. Immediately following the table, the meanings of the constructs are provided.

The explanations taken from the Enterprise Ontology for the constructs of Table 1 are:

- **Entity:** A fundamental thing in the modeled domain.
- **Relationship:** The way that two or more entities can be associated with each other. Within a relationship, an entity may have a role (e.g. a Person may be a Customer in a Sale). Alternatively, an entity may be seen as an attribute of another entity (e.g. Date of birth of a Person).
- **Roles:** An entity may have a role reflecting its relationship with other entities. Some relationships are special in that they entail

some notion of doing or cognition. We refer to an entity involved in such relationships as an *actor*. Relationships among actors may entail some view (activity or cognition) for one of them. This view indicates the actor has an *actor role*.

- **Actors:** Certain roles in a relationship are special in that the playing of these roles entails doing or cognition. These are called actor roles. Entities playing such roles are called actors. Hence, if the role played by an entity entails some notion of doing (such as exposing services), or cognition (such as desiring a goal), the entity is an actor. Actors are active entities in the organization. An actor can either be a person, an organizational unit, or a machine which performs some activity.
- **Resources:** When an entity does not expose a notion of doing or cognition in any relationship it is a resource. A resource is the role of an entity in a relationship with an activity whereby the entity is or can be used or consumed during the performance of the activity.
- **Activities/Services:** Something done over a particular time interval. An activity has pre-conditions and effects, is performed by one or more doers, can be decomposed into more detailed sub activities, may entail the use or consumption of resources, can have authority requirements, and may have an owner.
- **State (of Affairs):** A state is some kind of situation that can be thought of as holding or being true. An attribute is a relationship between two entities (referred to as the 'attributed' and 'value' entities) where for any particular attributed entity the relationship may exist with only one value entity. A state of affairs is a situation characterized by any combination of entities that are in any number of relationships with one another.

Table 1. Requirements engineering domain knowledge constructs mapping

Concept	Goal Oriented	Data based	Behavioural	Domain Based
Entity		Entity		Phenomenon
Relationship		Relationship		
Actor	Actor [1] Agent[2]	Entity [3]	–	Part of Phenomena[4]
Role *(Actor Role)*	Role[5]	Relation[6] Role[7]	Operations	–
Goal / Subgoals *(Purpose)*	Achieve Goal/ Maintain Goal[8]	–	–	
Concept	Goal Oriented	Data based	Behavioural	Domain Based
Help Achieve	Subgoals[8] Goal Dependency[5]			
Service *(Activity)*	High level Task[5]	Operations/ Methods[9]	Activities	–
Resource	Resource[5]	Entity[6]		
Constraint *(Activity* *Specification)*	Cease Goal; Avoid Goal[8]	Constraints[6]	–	–
State and *attributes (State* *of Affairs)*	–	Value (is part of attributes)[6]	State[10]	State[12]
Pre-Condition	Pre-Condition is part of a Task and a Resource Dependency[5]		Events[12] Pre-Condition is part of Transition	Events[13]
Effect	Effect is part of a Task and Resource Dependency[5]		Post Conditions[12] Effect is part of Transition[14]	

References that provide examples for the entries of Table 1:
[1] e.g. Anton 1996
[2] e.g. Castro et al. 2002
[3] e.g. Rumbaugh et al. 1991
[4] e.g. Jackson 2001
[5] e.g. Yu & Mylopoulos 1994
[6] e.g. Chen 1976
[7] e.g. Halpin 1998
[8] e.g. Dardenne et al. 1993
[9] e.g. Coad & Yourdon 1991
[10] e.g. Petri 1962
[11] e.g. Zave & Jakson 1997
[12] e.g. Harel 1987
[13] e.g. Hall et al. 2005
[14] e.g. Petterson 1977

- **Purpose/Goals:** A goal is the role of a state whereby the actor wants, intends, or is responsible for the full or partial achievement of the state. A goal (achieve) is the realization of a state (of affairs).
- **Help Achieve:** A relationship between two States of affairs whereby one state of affairs contributes to or facilitates the achievement of the other state of affairs. The help achieve relationship is particularly important when the States of affairs are goals. In this case, the Help Achieve relationship may define a directed acyclic network of goals which gives rise to a notion of higher- and lower-level Purposes / Goals.

- **Constraints:** The Enterprise Ontology mentions three types of constraints: 1) Effect - A State that is brought about by an activity. 2) Pre-Condition- a state required to be true in order for the activity to be performed. 3) Restrictions on the range of activities in the universe.

- **Pre-Condition:** A state of affairs required to be true in order for the activity to be performed.

- **Effect:** A state of affairs that is brought about by an activity.

Based on this mapping, it can be seen that the Entity and Relationship constructs are more abstract, and under the REDK constructs domain, other constructs subsume them. Entities are subsumed by resources and actors. Relationships are subsumed by roles and attributes. We also note that pre-conditions and effects are often used together both in RE literature and in the Enterprise Ontology. Specifically, the two together are part of the definition of a service in the Enterprise Ontology, and relate to transitions and dependencies in the RE approach. Therefore we compose them under one construct – *Transition*.

Hence, based on the RE literature and the Enterprise Ontology, we have identified eight fundamental domain related constructs: *Actors, Roles, Resources, Services, Goals (that relate to Help-Achieves), Constraints, Transitions (Incorporating Preconditions and Effects) and States (Consisting of Attributes).*

REPRESENTATION OF DOMAIN KNOWLEDGE IN THE SYSTEM CODE

Following our identifying of the core constructs used for RE domain knowledge representation, we turn to the task of enabling agile use of those constructs. That is, we suggest an infrastructure in which the identified REDK constructs can be used by developers to represent domain knowledge in system code.

We propose accomplishing this by enhancing the traditional object oriented programming paradigm; namely, enabling using REDK constructs in object oriented code. This in turn, should enable system developers to directly document in code things such as specific actors, resources, roles, goals, services, and constraints from the organization's domain. Hence, using REDK constructs in system code enables explicit documentation of domain knowledge as part of the working code.

Therefore, we provide a new class base. Our class base to support the use of REDK constructs is depicted using UML notation at the lower part of Figure 1. These classes are related, by a one-to-one relationship, to the REDK representation constructs of Table 1. That is, each construct of Table 1, has a matching class in the figure. Therefore all constructs can be used to document domain knowledge. We see that similarly to the interrelations between REDK constructs reflected in Figure 1, each class can involve using other classes; therefore the association between classes at the bottom part of the figure. For example, since a role may include a service we see the association between the role and the service classes in the figure.

The top part of Figure 1 illustrates the use of our base classes to represent specific domain knowledge. The class above the horizontal line reflects specific domain knowledge linked by an "is-a" relationship to the REDK role construct at the lower part of the figure. We have termed the area above the horizontal line Domain Knowledge Representation Layer (DKRL). Specifically, Figure 1 shows that the meaning of the role *Student* in the domain is made explicit at the DKRL.

We note that knowledge represented using the REDK constructs is usually incorporated in the information system code. However, without explicit representation constructs this knowledge is eventually intertwined with other implementation elements. For example, under the Object Oriented

Figure 1. Conceptual subsystem base classes used when representing knowledge at DKRL

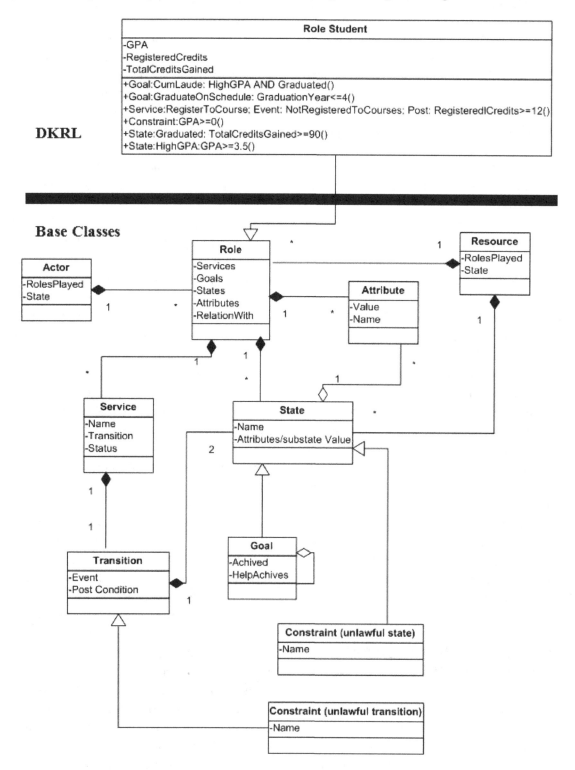

(OO) paradigm, actors, resources and roles, which are associated with the domain, may often have representation using the same construct (i.e. the class construct) in the final implementation code. Further, elements which have no domain meaning may be associated with domain related classes in the implementation code. For example, while a *student* in the domain typically does not incorporate any file handling services, the final implementation class may very well incorporate such services.

Therefore, in our approach we provide more than just means for using REDK representation constructs. We also provide a system design facilitating the separation of the represented REDK (i.e the DKRL) from other types of knowledge in the IS code. Hence, using REDK constructs under the suggested system design comes to facilitate the creation of domain models that reside at the DKRL. These domain models are part of the executable code, require minimal programming knowledge to understand, and are accessible to all system stakeholders.

THE ADSA SYSTEM DESIGN

We provide a system architectural design with a supporting mechanism which enables a physically isolated conceptual model to be used by other remote system components. We term this architectural design ADSA. Under ADSA the domain knowledge is separately located at what we term the *Conceptual Subsystem*, which includes an *Instance Base*. This domain mediated to other system components via a *Mediator Component*, and used by the *Processing Subsystem*. Formally we propose a system architecture comprising of four components (see Figure 2):

- **The Conceptual Subsystem (CS):** A subsystem implementing REDK knowledge. The source code of this subsystem includes explicit representation of REDK by utiliz-

ing the REDK representation constructs base classes. The knowledge incorporated in this subsystem can be used by processing subsystems, defined in the next paragraph.

- **The Processing Subsystems (PS):** A set of subsystems incorporating all other system related issues such as data type and structure information, service processing, algorithmic details, input/output operations, device interaction, and user interface aspects. Within the source code of these subsystems no segments would embed REDK.

- **The Instance Base (IB):** An instantiation of domain related elements, documented and coded at the Conceptual Subsystem. In other words, the IB incorporates instances of specific actors, roles and resources, of which knowledge needs to be used during runtime of the specific system. The source code defining these elements is found at the CS, and upon system execution the PS can instantiate these elements. Once instantiated these instances are found at the IB.

- **The Mediator Component (MC):** A component which incorporates all knowledge associated with interaction between the other components. This component does not include domain knowledge. It only facilitates the interaction between the PS and its IB.

Generally, under our proposed design, we facilitate a two way interaction channel between the processing subsystem and the conceptual subsystem. During system runtime, changing the state of an element related to documented domain knowledge is done through the conceptual subsystem. That is, the processing subsystem updates states related to the domain through the conceptual subsystem. Conversely, based on documented domain knowledge, the conceptual subsystem updates the processing subsystem once processing needs to be done.

319

Figure 2. System design and an example instance of use

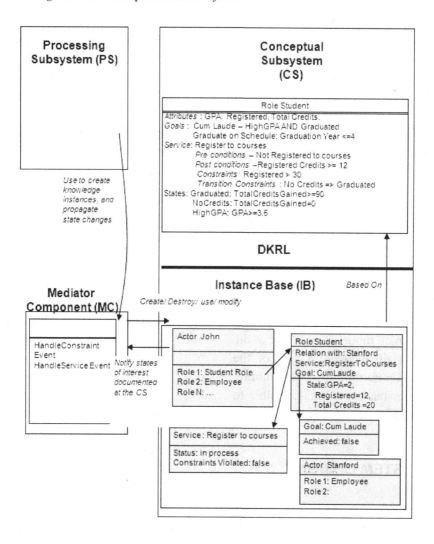

We have implemented system components to support such an interaction, and have used them on a case study of a student registration system, adapted from Barker and Palmer (2004). The new implementation fulfilled the same requirements and functionality, while abiding to the proposed system design using our implemented components. We illustrate the workings of our proposed system design based on this experience.

Briefly, the considered system handles tasks associated with student enrolment services. For example, the system enables enrolment into courses, a process students have to undertake if they are not registered to any course. During the student's enrolment process, the system enables students to keep track of their Grade Point Average (GPA), which helps them consider enrolling to particular courses. Students typically consider enrolling to courses which will enable them to complete their degree in time and improve their chances to complete it with honours.

Notably, being able to define the most basic system functionalities above, entails that considerable domain knowledge was accumulated:

1. Some of the people in the domain play the role of students.
2. In the domain, students have a GPA, a graduation year, and a total number of credits of courses in which they are currently enrolled.
3. In the domain, students desire to complete their degree cum laude.
4. In the domain, students desire to complete their degree within the timeframe of no more than 4 years.
5. In the domain, completion of degree cum laude requires a GPA greater than or equal to 3.5.
6. If someone in the domain is a student, he/she must always be registered to 12 points worth of credit courses. If this is not the case, the system needs to start the course registration processes.

Under our proposed design, all elements of the domain knowledge are explicitly documented at the Conceptual Subsystem. Figure 2 illustrates how this is done by using the REDK representation constructs.

Using the role representation construct, it is made clear that the student role entails having a GPA, a graduation year, and a total number of credits as the state-composing attributes. Further, using the goal construct, the two goals of students are documented. Next, using the service construct, the preconditions and post conditions of the course registration service are documented. Further, constraints are documented.

With domain knowledge documented at the DKRL, we now turn to describe how we support the interaction between the conceptual subsystem and the processing subsystem. In order to relate to the domain knowledge documented at the conceptual subsystem, the processing subsystem creates instances of the documented knowledge during runtime. In our example, the processing subsystem will create instances of actors and the student role which they play. These instances reside at the conceptual subsystem, and their

creation automatically derives the creation of other relevant instances; such as instances of the documented goals, services, and constraints of the student role. The area in which these instances reside is the *Instance Base* of the ADSA. In Figure 2 some of the created instances are depicted. These instances are shaded and can be found at the lower right part of the figure.

Whenever the processing subsystem needs to update states related to the created instances, the updates are done at the conceptual system. In our example, updates of a student's GPA or the number of credits in which a student is enrolled are done at the conceptual subsystem on the respective instance of the student role.

Once such updates are made at the conceptual subsystem, the conceptual subsystem examines relevant instances at the Instance Base. In this process, the conceptual subsystem identifies whether constraints have just been violated, whether goals have just been fulfilled, and whether services need to be performed.

In our example, once the GPA value changes, the system identifies whether the *HighGPA* state has been reached. Similarly, once the number of credits enrolled in changes, the conceptual subsystem identifies whether the *Not Registered to courses* state has become true. Arrival at one of these states will suggest that a service may needs to start, a constraint may have been violated, or a possible goal has been met. If indeed one of the latter occurs, the processing subsystem is notified via a complementary notification event. In our example, changing the GPA to an average higher than 3.5 may entail being *CumLaude*, if the student has also graduated. In such a case, the conceptual subsystem sends a notification event to the processing subsystem.

Hence, under ADSA, the processing subsystem is notified once an instance reaches a domain based situation of interest, which is documented at the Conceptual Subsystem. At the processing subsystem different implementations can be defined for the different events. For example, in a case of a violated constraint, an error message may be generated by the processing subsystem. Alternatively, when the 'event' state of a documented service is reached, the processing subsystem will execute the methods that should bring the object to service's documented post condition.

In our example, if a student is found to become *not registered to courses,* the notification event sent from the conceptual subsystem to the processing subsystem will trigger a registration process at the processing subsystem. This process will enable the student to use the system to register to new courses. Consequentially, during process execution, once the student's number of registered credits will reach a total greater than 12, the conceptual subsystem will identify that the post-condition state has been arrived at. In turn, identifying the arrival at the post-condition state triggers a new notification event to the processing subsystem; i.e. an event indicating that the service may have completed. Again, it is up to the processing subsystem to decide if and how to operate based on such an event. In our case, once such an event reaches the processing subsystem, the system indicates to the interacting student that the registration requirements have been met and no further registration to courses is needed.

This interaction between the conceptual subsystem and the processing subsystem is supported by a system component we term the *Mediating Component.* The component facilitates routing of notification events to the processing subsystem. In the figure, it can be seen that the component has procedures dedicated to handle notification events from the conceptual subsystem (such as, *HandelConstraintEvent*). These procedures activate the relevant methods at the processing subsystem as an outcome of the events.

DISCUSSION

In order to support explicit documentation of domain knowledge typically found in domain

models, the core constructs used in the different modeling approaches need to be clearly defined. In this work we have identified options of core constructs for domain models. However but our approach is not limited only to these constructs. Avenues for research progresses and new representation constructs are identified and their use can also be integrated. Extended representation constructs have been suggested in methodologies that evolved. The set of extended constructs which are relevant for representation may vary in different organizational settings. Other representation constructs can be incorporated by defining their meaning and their relations with the identified core constructs, and accordingly defining a respective core classes for use in IS code. In this respect, different views of what should be included as the set of *core* constructs for documentation may be suggested. We do not impose restrictions on which are the *core* constructs. Our method supports the inclusion and removal of constructs as needed, according to the organizational setting.

Our documentation approach is adaptive and fits within the context of agile development. According to Cockburn (2002) the agile manifesto incorporates four core values motivating agile software development practices. All values are kept when using the ADSD approach:

- Individuals and interactions over processes and tools.
- Working Software over comprehensive documentation.
- Customer collaboration over contract negotiation.
- Responding to change over following a plan.

SUMMARY

This study concerns documentation in agile development processes. Agile software development methods attempt to offer an answer to the eager business community asking for lightweight and nimbler software development processes (Abrahamsson et al. 2003). Agerfalk & Fitzgerald (2006) claim that these development methods differ significantly from the traditional plan-based approaches by emphasizing development productivity rather than the rigor process.

In a parallel venue, there is a general agreement the agile processes major disadvantage is in the loss of undocumented knowledge (Abrahamsson et al. 2003). Moreover, this knowledge is important to support communication, which is crucial in agile development (Korkala et al. 2006, Abrahamsson et al. 2002, Cockburn 2002). Furthermore, due to the general trend towards globalization, documentation becomes increasingly important since in physically separated development teams communication becomes even more difficult, especially in agile development processes (Herbsleb et al. 2002, Herbsleb & Mockus 2003). In this context, Parnas (2006) suggests that agile methods that try to avoid documentation should not be recommended.

Since agile processes take the general stand that true design can only be found in working source code, we have analyzed the relations between implementation and design documents. We have found that traditionally documented knowledge, which is not readily available in system source code, is the knowledge accumulated during the process of requirements engineering. Both agile RE and traditional RE processes come to help elicit user requirements. However, while traditional RE stresses rigid processes and documented domain knowledge, the agile processes forfeit domain documentation, assuming such documentation cannot effectively evolve.

By analyzing traditional RE processes we are able to extract the constructs facilitating documentation of domain knowledge. We suggest that agile documentation of domain knowledge is enabled by establishing means for using these documentation constructs as part of the system code. We also suggest an architectural design in which domain knowledge is represented explicitly and is isolated from other segments of code. Under this design, the documented domain knowledge drives the processing of the system at runtime.

Our method addresses consolidating agile processes with domain documentation. We have developed an *active* documentation approach, aimed at capturing the conceptual model of the domain. Conceptual models have been well recognized as facilitators of communication and domain understanding. Also, while system models are represented to different extents in actual implementation code, domain models are practically lost once implementation takes place.

This study identifies documentation constructs that are missed in agile processes and provides methods for incorporating their agile use. In this work we have identified the core constructs for domain models, but our approach is not limited only to these constructs. As research progresses and new representation constructs are identified, their use can be integrated as well. Further, the set of extended constructs which are relevant for representation may vary in different organizational settings. Other representation constructs can be incorporated by defining their meaning and their relations with the identified core constructs, and accordingly defining a respective core classes for use in IS code. In this respect, different views of what should be included as the set of *core* constructs for documentation may be suggested. We do not impose restrictions on which are the *core* constructs. Our method supports the inclusion and removal of constructs as needed, according to the organizational setting.

As the work presented in this chapter suggests that agile methods can incorporate agile documentation, many directions for future research can originate from it.

For example, examining other possible mechanisms and architectures to support the use of documentation constructs within working system code is a possible venue for future research. Empirical analysis of knowledge discovery process by developers and other organization members is another direction.

REFERENCES

Abbot, R. J. (1987). Knowledge abstraction. *Communications of the ACM, 30*(8), 664–671. doi:10.1145/27651.27652

Abrahamsson, P., Salo, O., Rankainen, J., & Warsta, J. (2002). *Agile Software Development Methods - Review and Analysis (VTT Publication 478)*. Oulu, Finland: VTT Electronics.

Abrahamsson, P., Warsta, J., Siponen, M. T., & Ronkainen, J. (2003). New directions on agile methods: a comparative analysis. In L.A. Clarke, L. Dillon, & W.F. Tichy (Eds.), *Proceedings of the 25ᵗʰ International Conference on Software Engineering,* (pp. 244-254), Portland, OR: IEEE Computer Society.

Agerfalk, P. J., & Fitzgerald, B. (2006). Flexible and distributed software processes: old petunias in new bowls? *Communications of the ACM, 49*(10), 27–34.

Agile Manifesto. (n.d.). Retrieved from http://www.agilemanifesto.org

Alford, M. W., & Lawson, J. T. (1979). *Software Requirements Engineering Methodology (Development)*. U.S. Air Force Rome Air Development Center.

Anton, A. (1996). Goal-based requirements analysis. In *Proceedings of the Second IEEE International Conference on Requirements Engineering (ICRE'96)* (pp. 136-144). Colorado Springs, CO: IEEE.

Balasubramaniam, R., Cao, L., Mohan, K., & Xu, P. (2006). How can distributed software development be agile? *Communications of the ACM, 49*(10), 41–46. doi:10.1145/1164394.1164418

Barker, J., & Palmer, G. (2004). *Beginning C# Objects: From Concepts to Code*. Berkeley, CA: Apress, University of California at Berkeley. doi:10.1007/978-1-4302-0691-0

Bennett, K., Cornelius, B., Munro, M., & Robson, D. (1991). Software Maintenance. In *Software Engineer's Reference Book*. Oxford, UK: Butterworlh-Heinemann. doi:10.1016/B978-0-7506-0813-8.50027-7

Blum, B. I. (1996). *Beyond Programming to a New Era of Design*. New York: Oxford University Press.

Booch, G. (1987). *Software Engineering with Ada*. Redwood, CA: Benjamin-Cummings.

Castro, J., Kolp, M., & Mylopoulos, J. (2002). Towards requirements-driven information systems engineering: the Tropos Project. *Information Systems, 27*(6), 365–389. doi:10.1016/S0306-4379(02)00012-1

Chen, P. P. (1976). The entity-relationship model-toward a unified view of data. *ACM Transactions on Database Systems, 1*(1), 9–36. doi:10.1145/320434.320440

Chen, X., Jin, Z., & Yi, L. (2007). An ontology of problem frames for guiding problem frame specification. In Z. Zhang, & J. Siekmann (Eds.), *Knowledge Science, Engineering and Management, Second International Conference,* (pp. 384-395). Berlin: Springer-Verlag.

Chung, L., Nixon, B. A., Yu, E., & Mylopoulos, J. (2000). *Non-Functional Requirements in Software Engineering*. New York: Springer Science. doi:10.1007/978-1-4615-5269-7

Clarke, S., Harrison, W., Ossher, H., & Tarr, P. (1999). Subject-oriented design. In *Towards Improved Alignment of Requirements, Design and Code* (pp. 325–337). New York: ACM.

Coad, P., & Yourdon, E. (1991). *Object-Oriented Analysis*. Upper Saddle River, NJ: Yourdon Press.

Cockburn, A. (2002). *Agile Software Development*. Boston, MA: Addison Wesley.

Daneva, M., Van Der Veen, E., Amrit, C., Ghaisas, S., Sikkel, K., & Kumar, R. et al. (2012). Agile requirements prioritization in large-scale outsourced system projects: An empirical study. *Journal of Systems and Software, 86*(5), 1333–1353. doi:10.1016/j.jss.2012.12.046

Dardenne, A., van Lamsweerde, A., & Fickas, S. (1993). Goal -directed requirements acquisition. *Science of Computer Programming, 20*(1-2), 3–50. doi:10.1016/0167-6423(93)90021-G

Davis, A. (1988). A Taxonomy for the early stages of the software development life cycle. *Journal of Systems and Software, 8*(4), 297–311. doi:10.1016/0164-1212(88)90013-1

Devedzic, V. (2002). Understanding ontological engineering. *Communications of the ACM, 45*(4), 136–144. doi:10.1145/505248.506002

Dubois, E., Hagelstein, J., Lahou, E., Rifaut, A., & Williams, F. (1986). A knowledge representation language for requirements engineering. *Proceedings of the IEEE, 74*(10), 1431–1444. doi:10.1109/PROC.1986.13644

Ernst, N. A., Borgida, A., Jureta, I. J., & Mylopoulos, J. (2013). Agile requirements engineering via paraconsistent reasoning. *Information Systems.*

Fowler, M. (2005). *The new methodology.* Retrieved June 18, 2013 from http://www.martinfowler.com/articles/newMethodology.html

Grady, J. O. (2006). *Systems Requirements Analysis.* Amsterdam: Elsevier.

Hall, J. G., Rapanotti, L., & Jackson, M. (2005). Problem frame semantics for software development. *Journal of Software and Systems Modeling, 4*(2), 189–198. doi:10.1007/s10270-004-0062-1

Halpin, T. (1998). Object role modeling (ORM/NIAM). In P. Bernus, K. Mertins, & G. Schmidt (Eds.), *Handbook of Architectures of Information Systems* (pp. 81–101). Berlin: Springer-Verlag.

Harel, D. (1987). Statecharts: A visual formalism for complex systems. *Science of Computer Programming, 8*(3), 231–274. doi:10.1016/0167-6423(87)90035-9

Hay, D. C. (2003). *Requirements Analysis: From Business Views to Architecture.* Upper Saddle River, NJ: Prentice Hall.

Helmy, W., Kamel, A., & Hegazy, O. (2012). Requirements Engineering Methodology in Agile Environment. [IJCSI]. *International Journal of Computer Science Issues, 9*(5), 293–300.

Henderson-Sellers, B., & Edwards, J. M. (1990). Object oriented systems life cycle. *Communications of the ACM, 33*(9), 142–159. doi:10.1145/83880.84529

Herbsleb, J. D., Atkins, D. L., Boyer, D. G., Handel, M., & Finholt, T. A. (2002). Introducing instant messaging and chat into the workplace. In *Proceedings of the ACM Conference on Computer-Human Interaction (CHI)* (pp. 171-178). Minneapolis, MN: ACM.

Herbsleb, J. D., & Mockus, A. (2003). An empirical study of speed and communication in globally distributed software development. *IEEE Transactions on Software Engineering, 29*(6), 481–494. doi:10.1109/TSE.2003.1205177

Hermann, K. (1999). Difficulties in the transition from OO analysis to design. *IEEE Software, 16*(5), 94–102. doi:10.1109/52.795107

Highsmith, J., & Cockburn, A. (2001). Agile software development: the business of innovation. *Computer, 34*(9), 120–122. doi:10.1109/2.947100

Jackson, M. A. (2001). *Problem Frames: Analyzing and Structuring Software Development Problems.* Boston, MA: Addison-Wesley.

Jacobson, I., & Christerson, M. (1995). A growing consensus on use cases. *Journal of Object-Oriented Programming, 8*(1), 15–19.

Kavakli, E., & Loucopoulos, P. (2003). Goal driven requirements engineering: evaluation of current methods. In *Proceedings of the 8th CAiSE/IFIP8.1 Workshop on Evaluation of Modeling Methods in Systems Analysis and Design, EMMSAD*. Velden, Austria: EMMSAD.

Kavakli, V. (2002). Goal oriented requirements engineering: a unifying framework. *Requirements Engineering Journal, 6*(4), 237–251. doi:10.1007/PL00010362

Korkala, M., Abrhamsson, P., & Kyllonen, P. (2006). A case study on the impact of customer communication on defects in agile software development. [AGILE.]. *Proceedings of AGILE, 2006*, 76–88.

Kovitz, B. (2003). Viewpoints: hidden skills that support phased and agile requirements engineering. *Requirements Engineering, 8*(2), 135–141. doi:10.1007/s00766-002-0162-9

Laitinen, K. (1992). Document classification for software quality systems. *ACM SIGSOFT Software Engineering Notes, 17*(4), 32–39. doi:10.1145/141874.141882

Laitinen, K. (1996). Estimating understandability of software documents. *ACM SIGSOFT Software Engineering Notes, 21*(4), 81–92. doi:10.1145/232069.232092

Lamsweerde, A. (2000). Requirements engineering in the year 2000: a research perspective. In *Proceedings of the 22nd International Conference on Software Engineering* (pp. 5-19). New York: ACM.

Lamsweerde, A. (2001). Goal-oriented requirements engineering: a guided tour. In *Proceedings of the 5th IEEE International Symposium on Requirements Engineering* (pp. 249-262). Toronto, Canada: IEEE.

Liu, L., & Yu, E. (2001). From requirements to architectural design – using goals and scenarios. In *Proceedings of from Software Requirements to Architectures Workshop (STRAW 2001)* (pp. 22-30). Toronto, Canada: ACM.

Loucopoulos, P., & Kavakli, V. (1997). Enterprise knowledge management and conceptual modeling. In *Proceedings of Workshop on Conceptual Modeling: Current Issues and Future Directions* (pp. 45-79). Los Angeles, CA: Springer-Verlag.

Maurer, F., & Hellmann, T. D. (2013). People-Centered Software Development: An Overview of Agile Methodologies. In *Proceedings of Software Engineering* (pp. 185–215). Berlin: Springer-Verlag. doi:10.1007/978-3-642-36054-1_7

Mylopoulos, J. (1992). Conceptual modeling and telos. In P. Locoupoulos, & R. Zicari (Eds.), *Conceptual Modeling, Databases and CASE* (pp. 49–68). New York: John Wiley and Sons.

Mylopoulos, J., Borgida, A., & Yu, E. (1997). Representing software engineering knowledge. *Automated Software Engineering, 4*(3), 291–317. doi:10.1023/A:1008627026003

Nakajo, T., & Kume, H. (1991). A case history analysis of software error cause-effect relationships. *Transactions on Software Engineering, 17*(8), 830–838. doi:10.1109/32.83917

Nawrocki, J., Jasiński, M., Walter, B., & Wojciechowski, A. (2002). Extreme programming modified: Embrace requirements engineering practices. In *Proceedings of the 10th Anniversary IEEE Joint International Conference on Requirements Engineering (RE'02)* (pp. 303-310). IEEE Computer Society.

Nuseibeh, B., & Easterbrook, S. (2000). Requirements engineering: a roadmap. In *Proceedings of the Conference on the Future of Software Engineering, (ICSE 2000)* (pp. 35-46). Limerick, Ireland: ACM.

Paetch, F., Eberlin, A., & Maurer, F. (2003). Requirement engineering and agile software development. In *Proceedings of the Twelfth IEEE International Workshops on Enabling Technologies (WETICE'03)* (pp. 308-313). IEEE Computer Society.

Parnas, D. (2006). Agile methods and GSD: the wrong solution to an old but real problem. *Communications of the ACM, 49*(10), 27–34.

Petri, C. A. (1962). *Kommunikation mit Automaten.* (PhD Dissertation). University of Bonn.

Petterson, J. (1977). Petri nets. *ACM Computing Surveys, 9*(3), 223–252. doi:10.1145/356698.356702

Reeves, J. W. (1992). What is software design?, *C++ Journal, 2*(2).

Rolland, C., & Prakash, N. (2000). From conceptual modelling to requirements engineering. *Annals of Software Engineering, 10*(1-4), 151–176. doi:10.1023/A:1018939700514

Rumbaugh, J., Blaha, M., Premerlani, W., Eddy, F., & Lorensen, W. (1991). *Object-Oriented Modeling and Design.* Upper Saddle River, NJ: Prentice-Hall.

Senapathi, M., & Srinivasan, A. (2012). Understanding post-adoptive agile usage: An exploratory cross-case analysis. *Journal of Systems and Software, 85*(6), 1255–1268. doi:10.1016/j.jss.2012.02.025

Shlaer, S., & Mellor, S. J. (1992). *Object Lifecycles: Modeling the World in States.* Upper Saddle River, NJ: Yourdon Press.

Sim, S. E., & Gallardo-Valencia, R. E. (2013). Performative and lexical knowledge sharing in agile requirements. In *Managing requirements knowledge* (pp. 199–219). Berlin: Springer-Verlag. doi:10.1007/978-3-642-34419-0_9

Sommerville, I. (1989). *Software Engineering.* Boston, MA: Addison-Wesley.

Turner, J. A. (1987). Understanding the elements of system design. In R. J. Boland Jr, & R. A. Hirschheim (Eds.), *Critical Issues in Information Systems Research* (pp. 97–111). New York: John Wiley.

Uschold, M., King, M., Moralee, S., & Zorgios, Y. (1998). The enterprise ontology. *The Knowledge Engineering Review, 13*(1), 31–89. doi:10.1017/S0269888998001088

Welsh, J., & Han, J. (1994). Software documents: concepts and tools. *Software - Concepts and Tools, 15*(1), 12-25.

Yu, E. S. K. (1997). Towards modeling and reasoning support for early-phase requirements engineering. In *Proceedings of Third IEEE International Symposium on Requirements Engineering RE97* (pp. 226-235). Annapolis, MD: IEEE Computer Society.

Yu, E. S. K. (2001). Agent-oriented modeling: software versus the world. In M.J. Wooldridge, G. Weiss, & P. Ciancarini (Eds.), *Agent-Oriented Software Engineering: Proceedings of the Second International Workshop (AOSE-2001),* (LNCS), (vol. 2222, pp. 206-225). Berlin: Springer-Verlag.

Yu, E. S. K., & Mylopoulos, J. (1994). Understanding why in software process modeling, analysis, and design. In *Proceedings of the 16th international Conference on Software Engineering* (pp. 159-168). Sorrento, Italy: IEEE Computer Society Press.

Zave, P., & Jackson, M. (1997). Four dark corners of requirements engineering. *ACM Transactions on Software Engineering and Methodology, 6*(1), 1–30. doi:10.1145/237432.237434

KEY TERMS AND DEFINITIONS

Agile Development: Incremental development methodologies where requirements and solutions evolve through collaboration and adaptation.

Conceptual Modeling: The act of devising a model capturing the problem domain.

Knowledge Management: The process of capturing, developing, sharing, and effectively using organizational knowledge.

Requirements Engineering: The process of formulating, documenting and maintaining software requirements.

System Documentation: Detailed information, in either written or computerized form, about a computer system, including its architecture, design, data flow, and programming logic.

Systems Analysis: The act of studying an activity, procedure or business, in order to define its goals or purposes and to discover operations and procedures for accomplishing them most efficiently.

Systems Design: The process of defining the architecture, components, modules, interfaces, and data for a system to fulfill its defined purpose and satisfy specified requirements.

Section 5
Software Quality and Testing

Chapter 15

An Integrated Secure Software Engineering Approach for Functional, Collaborative, and Information Concerns

J. A. Pavlich-Mariscal
Pontificia Universidad Javeriana, Colombia

S. Berhe
University of Connecticut, USA

A. De la Rosa Algarín
University of Connecticut, USA

S. Demurjian
University of Connecticut, USA

ABSTRACT

This chapter explores a secure software engineering approach that spans functional (object-oriented), collaborative (sharing), and information (Web modeling and exchange) concerns in support of role-based (RBAC), discretionary (DAC), and mandatory (MAC) access control. By extending UML with security diagrams for RBAC, DAC, and MAC, we are able to design an application with all of its concerns, and not defer security to a later time in the design process that could have significant impact and require potentially wide-ranging changes to a nearly completed design. Through its early inclusion in the software design process, security concerns can be part of the application design process, providing separate abstractions for security via new UML diagrams. From these new UML diagrams, it is then possible to generate security policies and enforcement code for RBAC, DAC, and MAC, which separates security from the application. This modeling and generation allows security changes to have less of an impact on an application. The end result is a secure software engineering approach within a UML context that is capable of modeling an application's functional, collaborative, and information concerns. This is explored in this chapter.

DOI: 10.4018/978-1-4666-6026-7.ch015

1 INTRODUCTION

The software development process has had significant improvements of the past forty plus years, from the introduction of the *waterfall model* (Winston, 1970) to the *iterative model* (Larman and Basili, 2002) in the late 70s to the *spiral model* (Boehm, 1986) in the mid-1980s to the *unified process model* (Scott, 2001) to the *agile development lifecycle* (Craig, 2003) in the early 21st century. Despite this progress, there remain many challenges when one attempts to design and develop large-scale applications, where there are a myriad of concerns such as user interfaces, server functionality, database support, logging and historical tracking, and secure information modeling, access, and enforcement. Rather than separation, there is often an entanglement of these different concerns, e.g., in an object-oriented application, code to read/write the database can be spread across multiple classes even if the database is abstracted via Hibernate. Also consider that security can be realized across the entire application, with security checks and enforcement at the GUI level, the server level, the database level, the network communications level, etc. All of these different concerns end up being tangled with one another, and spread out across the application's varied components. As a result, the traceability of security in terms of an application's functional, collaborative, and information concerns cannot be easily isolated; in such a situation, changes to the security policy often requires code-level alternations which are not acceptable in practice. The intent of this chapter is to elevate security to a primary and early priority in the software development process to provide a secure engineering approach that encompasses functional, collaborative, and information concerns.

To place this into a proper perspective, Figure 1 conceptualizes a secure software engineering approach for functional, collaborative, and information concerns via UML to visually model access control security. Over the past five years, our focus has been on extending UML with new diagrams that supports secure software engineering for role-based access control (RBAC) (Ferraiolo, et al., 2001), discretionary access control (DAC) (DoD, 1985), and mandatory access control (MAC) (Bell & LaPadula, 1976). In this chapter, we bring together our work for secure software engineering in three areas. First, from a functional perspective that focuses on object-oriented design, we have developed a framework of composable security features that preserves separation of security concerns from models to code through the extension of UML with new diagrams for RBAC, DAC, and MAC with the automatic generation of enforcement code in AspectJ that allowed the security definitions to be separated (untangled) from the code (Pavlich-Mariscal, 2005, 2010a, 2010b). Second, from a collaboration perspective, we have developed a framework for secure, obligated, coordinated, and dynamic collaboration that extends the RBAC to allow for the definition and enforcement of security for collaborative RBAC applicable to situations such as medical care where physicians from different specialties need to collaborate with one another to treat a patient in an effective and timely manner (Berhe, 2009, 2010, 2012); this work also defines new UML diagrams based on our functional work (Pavlich-Mariscal, 2005, 2010a, 2010b). Third, from an information perspective, we have defined and developed an XML security framework (De la Rosa Algarín, 2012, 2013a, 2013b) with new XML oriented UML diagrams that integrates RBAC, DAC, and MAC to further extend (Pavlich-Mariscal, 2005, 2010a, 2010b) by allowing the definition of security policies for XML for sharing and exchange of information in a secure manner via XACML. Our combined work promotes security as an integral part of a secure software engineering approach, while tracking software quality assurance in terms of the consistency of the security and non-security requirements.

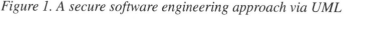

Figure 1. A secure software engineering approach via UML

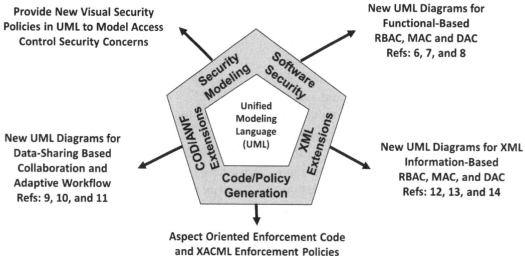

In this chapter, we will unify the aforementioned three security efforts as shown in Figure 1 to provide a secure software engineering process for functional, collaborative, and information modeling and design. From a functional perspective, our work (Pavlich-Mariscal, 2005, 2010a, 2010b) extended UML to represent RBAC, DAC, and MAC (see upper portion of Figure 2) via the introduction of the Role Slice Diagram, the User Diagram, the Delegation Diagram, and MAC extensions coupled with a Secure Subsystem Diagram (middle right hand side of Figure 2). The Secure Subsystem Diagram denotes the subset of an application's overall classes and methods that are restricted and require permissions to be in place for authorized users. The Role Slice Diagram denotes RBAC policies, providing the role slice, a stereotyped package that represents the permissions assigned to a role. A role slice uses method-based permissions to allow or deny users to access specific operations, regardless of the object to which it is applied. The Delegation Diagram can be utilized to represent all of the rules of delegation between roles. This diagram provides the *delegation slice*, a stereotyped package that contains all of the roles that a user can

delegate authority to another user, who may also be allowed to further delegate the role. The User Diagram uses stereotyped packages to denote users and stereotyped dependency relations to represent user-role assignments. MAC extensions enhance the previous three diagrams with sensitivity levels (e.g., confidential, secret, top secret) and their ordering relations to indicate classifications of methods, clearances of role slices, and, implicitly, to declare access constraints based in the relation between classifications and clearances. From an enforcement perspective, once defined, the diagrams are utilized to generate aspect-oriented enforcement code in AspectJ (bottom portion of Figure 2) that is able to verify, at runtime, whether the active user has a role with permissions over the protected method and grants or denies access accordingly. The end result is that aspects can effectively modularize access control concerns and enhance traceability from design to code.

The second part of our work (Berhe, 2009, 2010, 2012) (lower middle left of Figure 2) has focused on the extension of RBAC to define collaboration and sharing capabilities across a workflow. Collaborative computing has emerged in many domains, with users interacting with one

Figure 2. UML extensions for functional, collaborative, and information concerns

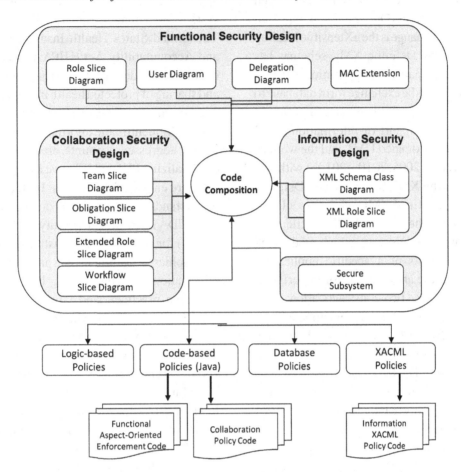

another towards some common goal. For example, in a health care setting, a patient's many providers (e.g., internist, cardiologist, physical therapist, etc.) need to interact with one another against a common set of data (patient's medical record). Unlike traditional security that defines separation of duty and mutual exclusion to prohibit what users can do, in a collaborative setting, the key is on defining when and how users collaborate. Thus, we have extended RBAC with a set of UML diagrams for collaboration on duty and adaptive workflow (COD/AWF) that interacts with our functional extensions in the top of Figure 2 (Pavlich-Mariscal, 2005, 2010a, 2010b). This includes the definition of four new UML diagrams: the extended Role Slice Diagram which defines

the roles and privileges for each user within each collaboration step; the Team Slice Diagram which defines the team members and their participation in the various collaboration steps; the Workflow Slice Diagram which defines the steps and connections among them for a given team and specific collaboration; and, the Obligation Slice Diagram which defines the required permissions and participations for a particular collaboration. In addition, we provide the mapping of these new UML based collaboration design-time diagrams to actual machine-readable code-based policies for runtime enforcement.

The third part of our work (De la Rosa Algarín, 2012, 2013a, 2013b) (middle right of Figure 2) has emphasized the control of information created by one application to be shared and/or exchanged with other applications. One dominant approach for information exchange is the eXtensible Markup Language (XML). Defining XML schemas has become an integral part of the application development process to handle exchange form database to server, from server to end user, among different databases, etc. In support of information-based security, we have extended UML and the work of (Pavlich-Mariscal, 2005, 2010a, 2010b) with two new diagrams: the XML Schema Class Diagram which models a defined XML schema as a UML class diagram via the use of a UML Profile; and, the XML Role Slice Diagram, which models the RBAC requirements of a specific application with respect to role and elements of the original XML schema. These two constructs allow us to automatically generate enforcement policies with the eXtensible Access Control Markup Language (XACML) via a mapping process between the XML Role-Slice Diagram and the XACML schema elements. In turn, these enforcement policies can be readily deployed into any security architecture that utilizes the XACML specification's processing model. With these two new UML diagrams augmented with the policy mapping process, a software engineer can consider and produce security enforcement code that targets information content by modeling the original XML schema (producing the XML Schema Class Diagram), augmenting it with security features with respect to the different roles and permissions (producing the XML Role Slice Diagram), and then automatically creating an enforcement policy with the mapping process (XACML).

To demonstrate the feasibility of the secure software engineering approach of this chapter, we leverage the health care domain that has a need to integrate multiple health information technology systems such as an Electronic Health Record (EHR) to store patient medical data, a personal health record to store patient data controlled by patient, a patient portal which is a practice management system for patients to communicate for

appointments, refills, and referrals, and, ancillary systems such imaging, laboratory, pharmacy, etc. The United States Health Insurance Portability and Accountability Act (HIPAA) provides a set of security guidelines in the usage, transmission, and sharing of protected health information (PHI); in e-commerce, there would be a need to protect personally identifiable information (PII) including names, addresses, accounts, credit card numbers, etc. Realizing PHI and PII must be part of a secure software engineering process. Further, the many XML standards (e.g., clinical document architecture (CDA) and the Continuity of Care Record (CCR)) for storage of administrative, patient demographics, and clinical data are used to support information exchange among hospitals, clinics, physician practices, and laboratories. As CDA and CCR XML documents are circulated among various systems and made available to particular users with specific needs (e.g., using a function via an API call), representing a collaboration via a shared application, or requiring information via an XML or database repository). In such a situation, secure software engineering must consider all of the APIs, XML repositories, and databases. This requires API level (functional), document-level (information), and interaction level (collaboration) access control in order to authorize users at different times based on criteria that include, but are not limited to, a user's role, time and value constraints on data, collaboration for sharing data, delegation of authority as privileges are passed among authorized users, etc.

The remainder of this chapter has six sections. Section 2 provides background on secure software engineering from functional, collaborative, and information perspectives. Section 3 introduces the work of (Pavlich-Mariscal, 2005, 2010a, 2010b) that extends UML with new diagrams to allow security to be modeled as a new separate concern for functional requirements. Section 4 details the work of (Berhe, 2009, 2010, 2012) that extends RBAC with new UML diagrams for collaboration on duty and adaptive workflow for sharing requirements of an application. Section 5 explores the work of (De la Rosa Algarín, 2012, 2013a, 2013b) for an XML framework of security that extends UML with XML-schema diagrams to handle the information requirements. Each of the Sections 3, 4, and 5 organizes the presentation by discussing the UML extensions for modeling security followed by the transition to the generation of security enforcement code or policies, which includes a case study using a medication management mobile application that has: a patient version to maintain information on medications, OTCs, supplements, etc., and the ability to authorize access to providers; and, a provider version to be able to view and comment on authorized patients and their medications. Using the material in Sections 3, 4, and 5, Section 6 presents a secure software engineering approach for the definition and enforcement of access control (RBAC, DAC, and MAC) for functional, collaborative, and information concerns integrated with a UML design; to provide an additional context for the utility of our work, we utilize a big-data application example that involves a facet of law enforcement, namely, the collection of data on motor vehicle crashes. Section 7 presents future trends in terms of emerging platforms for health information technologies that have the potential to further impact the secure software engineering process. Section 8 concludes the chapter.

2 BACKGROUND

This section provides background on secure software engineering and security for functional, collaborative, and information concerns. In the functional security area, there have been many research efforts that involve UML. SecureUML (Basin et al., 2006) is a modeling language to design security in distributed systems. This language is based in UML, extending its semantics and notation to support RBAC, and certain authorization constraints. The focus of this approach is to utilize

UML to specify access control as part of the main design of the application and then automatically generate access control infrastructures based on the design models. The approach defines a meta-model for SecureUML and details a methodology to integrate it into several design modeling languages. UMLSec, described in (Juerjens, 2005) and improved by (Zisman 2007) and (Popp et al., 2003), is an extension to UML that defines several new stereotypes towards formal security verification of elements such as: fair exchange to avoid cheating for any party in a 2-party transaction; secrecy and confidentiality of information (accessible only to the intended people); secure information flow to avoid partial leaking of sensitive information; and, secure communication links like encryption. AuthUML (Alghathbar 2007) models RBAC policies using use cases and Horn clauses to represent the access control information and to check its consistency. The approach of (Pavlich-Mariscal et al., 2010a) includes the definition of several new UML diagrams to represent different access control concerns (RBAC, MAC, and DAC), and a set of features that represent small subsets of an access control model. These features can then be composed to create custom access control policies.

In the collaborative security area, research has occurred in many areas. In terms of access control and collaboration, in (Tolone et al., 2003), a set of eight criteria (complexity, understandability, ease of use, applicability, groups of users, policy specification, policy enforcement, and granularity) critical for a collaborative environment are presented. The eight characteristics and their support are evaluated against seven access control models (Matrix, RBAC, TBAC, TMAC, C-TMAC, SAC, and Context-AW). This work demonstrates that collaboration capabilities are not primary goals in access control models. As given, the seven access control models do not support an integrated model for coordinated, obligated, secure, and team-based collaboration. Another related area is a distributed secure interoperability framework for collaboration environments (Sachpazidis 2008).

This framework presents a multi-system architecture in which different stakeholders with different privileges collaborate with one another towards optimizing monitoring prescription intake. With regard to collaboration, workflow, and security, the work of (Shehab et al., 2005) addressed security services that support inter-organizational collaborative enterprises, which may span multiple organizations. This work presents a framework for mediator-free collaboration. Similarly as in (Sachpazidis, 2008), this work focuses on inter-system collaboration, while our work focuses on early integration of collaboration requirements into the software engineering process. The work of (Kang et al., 2001) concentrates on workflows that are addressed from an access control perspective. This is an important aspect of our effort (Berhe, 2009, 2010, 2012), where workflow is also represented as collaboration steps with access control addressed at each step and for the overall workflow. The work in (Sun et al., 2005) proposes a model that integrates RBAC into workflows. In their approach, permissions, roles, cardinality, ancestors (pre-obligations), and a status value are assigned to activities (collaboration steps).

Finally, in the informational security area, one approach based on RBAC and UML is SecureUML (Lodderstedt et al., 2002) that combines a graphical notation for RBAC with constraints, where policies can be expressed using RBAC permissions with complex security requirements done with a combination of authorization constraints. A later effort (Mouelhi et al., 2008) presents a model-driven security approach for designers to set security requirements along with the system models to automatically generate an access control infrastructure. The approach combines UML with a security modeling language defining a set of modeling transformations; the former produces infrastructures for JavaBeans, and the latter can generate secure infrastructures for web applications. (Basin et al., 2006) utilizes the model-driven architecture paradigm to achieve security for e-government scenarios with inter-collaboration/

communication. This is achieved by describing security requirements at a high-level (models), with relevant "security artifacts" being automatically generated for target architectures, removing the otherwise present learning curve in specifying security requirements by domain experts with no technical know-how. In the approach presented in (De la Rosa Algarín et al., 2012, 2013a, 2013b), UML is leveraged to provide a secure information engineering approach for XML schemas and documents. By extending UML with new XML diagrams, an enforcement security policy in XACML can be generated and deployed for access control purposes (not unlike automatic code generation from UML class diagrams). By doing this, the approach scales to scenarios that involve a high volume of XML documents validated against a common schema.

3 FUNCTIONAL SECURITY

To better understand the perspective of our security solutions, it is important to review the five essential security dimensions in our previous work (Pavlich-Mariscal, Demurjian, & Michel, 2010a): access control models, visual notation, separation of concerns, traceability, and customizability. The *access control model* dimension encompasses mandatory access control (MAC) (Bell & LaPadula, 1976), discretionary access control (DAC) (DoD, 1985), and role-based access control (RBAC) (Ferraiolo, et al., 2001). MAC defines the objects that need protection and the subjects who are the individuals or other systems that require access to the information in the objects. Objects have classifications (e.g., Confidential, Secret, Top-Secret, etc.) that indicate the sensitivity level of the information they contain. Subjects have clearances that determine the set of objects to which they can access, based on the relationship between clearances and classifications. DAC specifies access to objects, based on the subjects to which the objects belong. A subject owns a set of objects. Owned objects can be accessed and modified discretionally by the subject. In addition, a subject can directly or indirectly pass that permission to another subject, unless it is restricted by a MAC policy, which is delegation (Liebrand et al., 2003). Our approach supports both *delegation of authority*, the ability to directly pass the permission to another subject, and *pass-on delegation authority*, the ability to allow to a second subject to further delegate a delegated authority. RBAC has a clear correspondence to the structure of information in organizations. Unlike MAC, which focuses on data, RBAC focuses on users. The essential element in RBAC is the role that represents a set of tasks that a user may perform in an organization, with the premise that the same role could be assigned to different users. While DAC assigns permissions directly to users (subjects), RBAC assigns permissions to roles. A role is assigned to a user, who obtains all of the permissions associated with the role (Ferraiolo, et al., 2001).

The second dimension, *visual notation*, provides a means to represent access control policies at a higher conceptual level. A visual notation facilitates the comprehension and development of an access control policy over time, since it can convey the essential information to designers. In this regard, widespread notations, such as UML do not provide explicit support for access control models. *Separation of concerns* (Parnas, 1972), our third dimension, is important not only for access control, but for the evolution of every concern in a software system. The premise is that in order to better understand and develop different concerns, including security, each concern should be adequately modularized. However, security is a concern that tends to be scattered throughout the application (e.g., access control code is usually included at each place where protection is required, such as at the beginning of methods) and tangled with other concerns (e.g., access control is usually tangled with the code that is being protected, which represents different concerns).

Our fourth dimension, *traceability*, is the ability to link requirements to design artifacts to the code parts that realize each requirement (Sommerville, 2006). In our work, the focus is on traceability from access control models to code. Traceability is directly influenced by separation of concerns. The better the separation of concerns, the better the traceability, since it is easier to identify the design and code artifacts associated to the same requirement. Our fifth and final dimension, *customizability*, is the ability to combine a set of primitive components to achieve different results (Pavlich-Mariscal, Demurjian, & Michel, 2010a). In our work, customizability is the ability to combine different access control models to satisfy different security requirements. Customizability is also facilitated by an adequate separation of concerns, since the boundaries of each primitive can be better defined, thus facilitating their composition. All of the above dimensions are important elements to address the ability to seamlessly create, understand, and evolve access control policies. The first part of this chapter addresses the five dimensions for functional security through a set of security extensions to UML to model different access control concerns and through a mapping to aspect-oriented security enforcement code. The remainder of this section describes the UML extensions to support security modeling of functional requirements in Section 3.1 followed by a discussion of the automatic generation of code via a mapping from UML in Section 3.2.

3.1 Functional Security Extensions to UML

To address the access control modeling, customizability, and visual notation dimensions, our work proposed a set of extensions to UML to model different access control concerns (Pavlich-Mariscal, Demurjian, & Michel, 2010a). This section describes the four extensions in the upper part of Figure 2, and the secure subsystem, which were conceived to address the five dimensions. To better understand the concepts, assume that designers are required to model a Virtual Chart Application (VCA) for healthcare (Kenny, 2008), which is intended to manage the medical history of a patient (e.g., demographics, vital statistics, medications, appointments, test history, test results, etc.) and is created from multiple sources (e.g., physician office, hospital, imaging center, etc.) to form a combined representation. For simplicity, the example only addresses a subset of VCA. Figure 3 has several diagrams, denoted from a to g, which show all of the proposed UML extensions for access control, namely: Secure Subsystem Diagram (a), Role Slice Diagram (b), User Diagram (c), Delegation Diagram (d), and MAC Extensions (e, f, and g). We examine each UML extension in turn.

The *Secure Subsystem Diagram (SSD)* denotes all of the resources in the system that requires protection, e.g., a subset of the classes and methods of an application like VCA. Figure 3a shows the secure subsystem for the VCA, represented as a package with the stereotype <<SecureSubsystem>>. The VCA may include several classes with different responsibilities. However, not all of the VCA's classes and methods require protection, since they may not access sensitive information, or they are classes that are not directly utilized by user interface layers in the application (e.g., private or protected methods). In this example, for simplicity, the Secure Subsystem Diagram contains only the class MedicalRecord with a set of methods to read and write different aspects of the patient's medical history. Classes and methods not shown in the SSD are assumed to be non-sensitive, thus they do not need protection.

Our second UML extension, the *Role Slice Diagram (RSD)*, provides a means to define permissions by role to the classes and methods that comprise the SSD. Figure 3b is an example RSD for the VCA, where each role is represented by a *role slice,* an artifact that contains all of the

methods and classes from SSD that are authorized for the corresponding role. Visually, a role slice is represented as a package with the stereotype <<RoleSlice>>. Role slices may inherit permissions from parent roles, denoted by the connection with the stereotype <<RoleInheritance>>. Permissions in a role slice are represented as methods with the stereotype <<pos>> or <<neg>>. The <<pos>> stereotype means that the method is a positive permission, i.e., it is explicitly allowed to that role. The <<neg>> stereotype means that the method is a negative permission, i.e., it is explicitly denied to that role.

Figure 3b illustrates BaseRole, Provider, Nurse, Physician, and Patient roles. BaseRole and Provider, denoted with the tag {abstract}, means that these roles cannot be assigned to users, but instead are utilized to contain permissions that are common to two or more roles. The BaseRole represents permissions that are shared by all of the descendant roles, with the Provider role defining shared permissions for its two descendant roles (Physician and Nurse). BaseRole has a collection of get methods to access information in the VCA (from the SSD in Figure 3a) and one set method related to billing. The Provider Role has the positive permission setMedicationHistory which is assgned to both Physician and Nurse through role inheritance. The Physician role is authorized to have access to the entire electronic health record (EHR) of the patient through the VCA via the BaseRole (read access via get methods) and Provider and Physician roles (write access via set methods). The Nurse role inherits all of the positive permissions from BaseRole and Provider, and has an additional positive method (setAppointmentHistory). Negative permissions can be used to override positive permissions in ancestor roles. For instance, while BaseRole is allowed to access method setBillingHistory, Patient is explicitly denied that permission. The negative permission in Patient overrides the positive one at BaseRole. Overall, the permissions of a given role slice is the union of the permissions directly

Figure 3. Example of UML extensions for access control

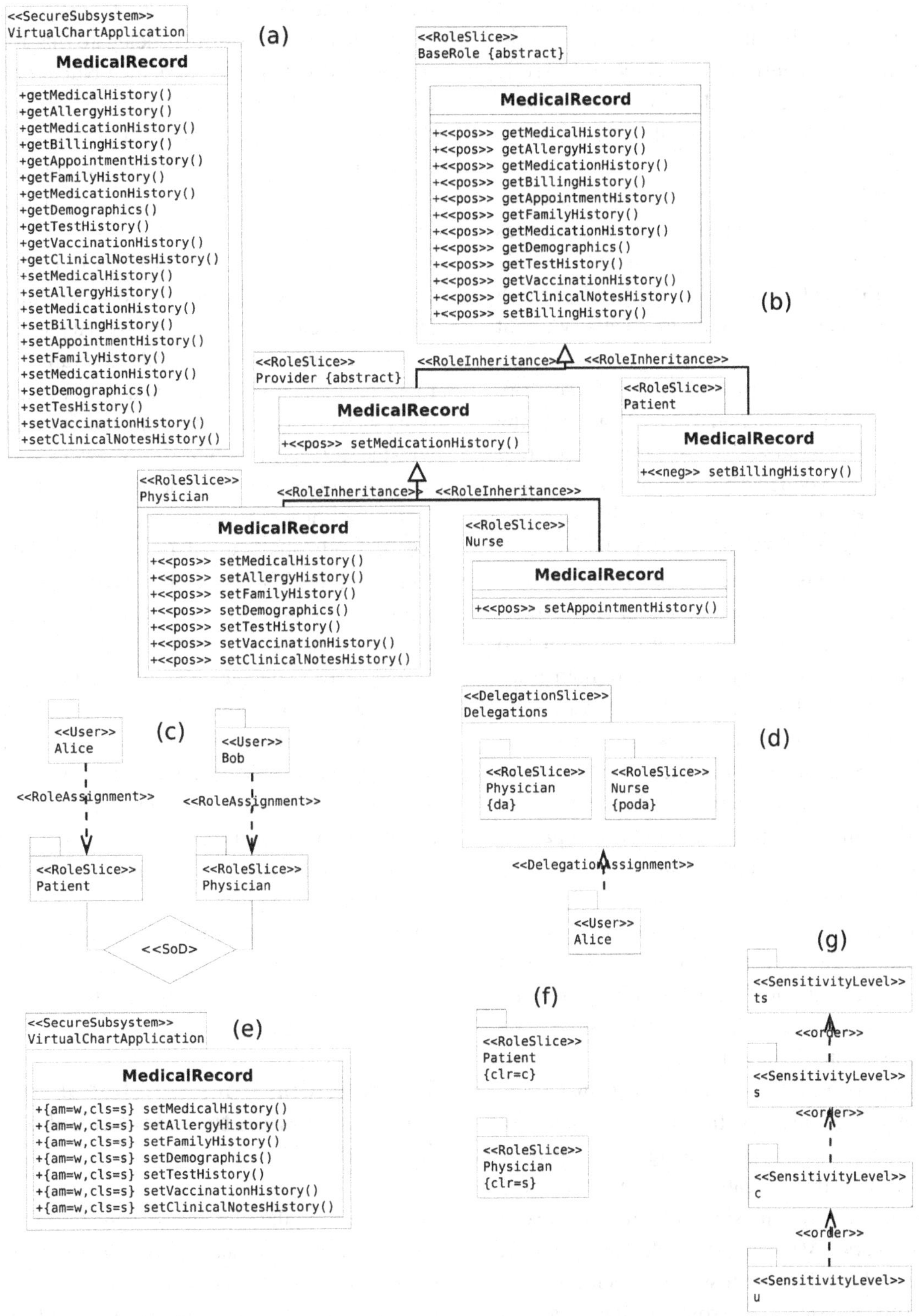

assigned to that role slice, with the permissions directly assigned to all of its ancestors and inherited down the RSD. For instance, Nurse has access to: setAppointmentHistory, which is directly assigned to Nurse; setMedicationHistory, which is assigned to Provider; and, all of the methods, assigned to BaseRole.

Our third UML extension, the *User Diagram,* shown in Figure 3c, focuses in denoting the roles assigned to each user in the system, with the role retaining the actual permissions. This approach allows a role's permissions to change without having to change each user that is assigned that role, easing the administrative process for security definition. A user is denoted as packages with the stereotype <<User>>. A user-role association is denoted as a dependency relation with the stereotype <<RoleAssignment>>. In this example, role slice Patient is assigned to user Alice and role slice Physician is assigned to user Bob. The user diagram also denotes Separation of Duty (SoD) constraints. A separation of duty between two roles means that a user cannot play both roles simultaneously. Pictorially, a SoD constraint is represented as an n-ary relation with the stereotype <<SoD>>. In the example, the roles Patient and Physician have a separation of duty constraint, providing the appropriate context that a patient cannot be his/her own physician.

Our fourth UML extension, shown in Figure 3d for VCA, is the delegation diagram that depicts all of the delegation constraints in an access control policy. The main artifact of this diagram is the delegation slice, a package with the stereotype <<DelegationSlice>> that represents the roles that a user may delegate to others; note that a user can only delegate a role that s/he is assigned to. These permissions can be assigned to specific users through the delegation assignment relation, a dependency relationship with the stereotype <<DelegationAssignment>>. In the example, the user Alice has permissions to delegate role Nurse and Physician. The role slice Physician has the tag {da}, which means that Alice has delega-

tion authority (da) over role Physician, i.e., Alice can delegate the role Physician to another user, but the latter cannot further delegate that role to another individual. The role slice Nurse has the tag {poda}, which means that Alice has pass-on delegation authority (pado) over role Nurse, i.e., Alice can delegate the role Nurse to another user and that user can further delegate that role to other individuals.

Lastly, to realize MAC policies in UML, we also provide several elements to represent classifications, clearances, and sensitivity levels in a policy. Figure 3g is a MAC diagram, which represents sensitivity levels and their order relations. Sensitivity levels are depicted as packages with the stereotype <<SensitivityLevel>>, while order relations are dependencies with the stereotype <<order>>. In the example, four levels are defined: unclassified (u), confidential (c), secret (s), and top-secret (ts). These sensitivity levels can be used to tag methods in the secure subsystem diagram to denote classifications, and in role slices to denote clearances. Figure 3e is a secure subsystem diagram with classifications in its methods. In this example, the cls tag indicates the classification of the method, which is secret for all of them. The am tag indicates the access mode to the method, which can be either read or write. In the example, all of the methods are tagged as write-methods. Figure 3f is a role-slice diagram with clearances. Each role slice has a clr tag that indicates the clearance of the corresponding role. In this example, Patient has confidential clearance, while Physician has secret clearance.

3.2 Transition from Functional Security Design to Automatically Generated Code

To properly realize an access control policy in an application, the access control design must be translated into its equivalent in code. In this regard, two of the dimensions discussed in the introduction of Section 3 must be taken into ac-

Figure 4. Basic security enforcement code

```
public void setMedicalHistory() {
        if (Session.isAuthorized(user, "setMedicalHistory")) {
                << Original Code of setMedicalHistory >>
        } else {
                throw new RuntimeException("Access denied to method setMedicalHistory");
        }
}
```

count: separation of concerns and traceability. *Separation of concerns* is important to properly modularize the system, facilitate distribution of tasks among developers, and above all, to improve the maintainability of the system (Parnas, 1972). Moreover, separation of concerns must be preserved from design models into code, in the sense that a generated code element must have a similar separation from other concerns as the corresponding access control diagrams (i.e., secure system, role slice, user, and delegation) are separated from standard UML diagrams (e.g., class, use-case, sequence, activity, etc.). Preserving separation of concerns in this way ensures that access control concerns are separated from other concerns both at the design and code. Therefore, it facilitates traceability of access control model elements to the parts that realize them in code. However, separating security concerns from the rest of the code is difficult, because security tends to be scattered across the code and tangled with other requirements (De-Win, 2004). For instance, one way to protect a Java method according to access control rules would be the code of Figure 4. In this example, method setMedicalHistory is being added in a conditional statement to realize security enforcement code which protects the method according to user permissions. This example is very simple, since the enforcement code is directly added to the method as an if-statement that verifies whether the logged user is authorized to access that method. If so, the code of the method is executed. Otherwise, an exception is raised and the access is denied.

To protect all of the methods in the system, similar code would have to be inserted at every method that requires protection. As a result, the security enforcement code is scattered throughout all of the methods that need access control and it is tangled with the code that is specific for each method. To address this problem, we proposed an approach based on aspect-oriented programming (Kiczales & Irwin, 1997) to enforce security in an application, shown in Figure 5. At the design level, designers create different access control diagrams by selecting each of their features (see Section 3.1 again). All of these diagrams are composed with one another into a custom access control policy. Aspect-oriented code is generated that realizes this policy in the form of aspects and classes that preserves the separation of concerns given at the design level to the realization of custom access control code at the implementation level, thereby achieving traceability. The aspect weaver and the compiler compose these components into the custom access control code for the application (Pavlich-Mariscal, Demurjian, & Michel, 2010b).

The main element of the generated code is the access control aspect show in Figure 6. Instead of manually inserting the enforcement code at each method, an aspect is created that weaves the enforcement code at every method belonging to the secure subsystem. In this example, the pointcut secSubs corresponds to all of the methods in the secure subsystem (only two join points are shown for space reasons). The advice that follows is executed before any method in the secure subsystem is executed. This advice obtains

Figure 5. Proposed approach to transition access control into enforcement code

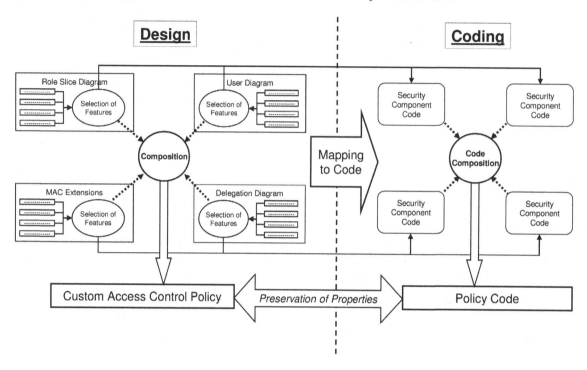

Figure 6. Access control aspect

```
public aspect AccessControl {
  pointcut secSubs() :
  execution(void MedicalRecord.setMedicalHistory(..)) ||
  execution(void MedicalRecord.setAllergyHistory(..)) ||
  ...);
  before(Object obj) : target(obj) && secSubs () {
    Method thisMethod = ((MethodSignature)  thisJoinPoint.getSignature()).getMethod();
    Object[] args = thisJoinPoint.getArgs();
    IOperation op = Policy.findOperation(thisMethod);
    if (!Session.isAuthorized(op, concatenate(obj, args))) { throw new RuntimeException("Access Denied: " + thisMethod);
    }
  }
  ...
}
```

the information about the method being executed (variable op), the object to which the method is executed (obj), and the arguments of the invocation (args). Then, the advice checks whether the active user is allowed to execute the method op over object obj, with arguments args. If not allowed, it throws a runtime exception and denies

access to the method. Otherwise, the execution of the method continues normally.

The mappings to code also include a set of code generation strategies for secure subsystems and the UML extensions. Figure 7 shows a portion of the generated code for the secure subsystem of the VCA, which is mapped to a class with the annotation @SecureSubsystem. Each class in the

Figure 7. Secure subsystem code

```
@SecureSubsystem
public interface VirtualChartApplicationSecureSubsystem {
        @ReferencedClass(MedicalRecord.class)
        interface MedicalRecord {
                @am(AM.WRITE) @cls(S.class) public void setMedicalHistory(...);
                @am(AM.WRITE) @cls(S.class) public void setAllergyHistory(...);
                ...
        }
}
```

secure subsystem maps to an interface with the annotation @ReferencedClass, which indicates the Java class that is being protected. This interface includes the methods being protected. Each of those methods includes the annotation @am to indicate the access mode (read or write) and the annotation @cls to indicate the classification of the method. Sensitivity levels map to an interface hierarchy, as shown in Figure 8, where the order relation between levels maps directly to interface inheritance. In the example, level C (confidential) is less secure than S (secret), thus interface C extends S. Similarly, role slices and delegation slices are directly mapped into interfaces. For instance, Figures 9 and 10 show portions of the code that realize the Nurse and Patient role slices, respectively.

Each role slice maps to an interface with the annotation @RoleSlice. Clearances are denoted with the annotation @clr. The interface contains a set of inner interfaces with the annotation @ReferencedClass which references the classes that are restricted by the corresponding role slice. The inner interfaces contain a set of methods annotated with @pos or @neg to denote positive or negative permissions, respectively. Interface Patient also has the annotation @SoD to indicate that it has separation of duty with the role slice Physician. Figure 11 is an example of the code generated from delegation slices. Delegation slices map to interfaces with the annotation @DelegationSlice

Figure 8. Sensitivity levels code

```
interface TS extends SensitivityLevel { }
interface S extends TS { }
interface C extends S { }
interface U extends C { }
```

Figure 9. Nurse role slice code

```
@RoleSlice
@clr(S.class)
public interface Nurse extends Provider {
        @ReferencedClass(MedicalRecord.class)
        public interface MedicalRecord {
                @pos public void setMedicationHistory(...);
        }
}
```

Figure 10. Patient role slice code

```
@RoleSlice
@clr(U.class)
@SoD(Physician.class)
public interface Patient extends BaseRole {
        @ReferencedClass(MedicalRecord.class)
        public interface MedicalRecord {
                @neg public void setBillingHistory(...);
        }
}
```

Figure 11. Delegation slice code

```
@DelegationSlice
public interface Delegations {
        @da interface Physician { }
        @poda interface Nurse { }
}
```

and contain inner interfaces, each one associated with the role slices allowed for that delegation slice. Inner interfaces are annotated with @da or @poda for delegation authority or pass-on delegation authority, respectively.

The above strategies to generate access control code have several important properties. First, the generated code is clearly isolated into specific modules. The access control aspect effectively modularizes enforcement code. The interfaces generated from access control diagrams (Figures 7-11) also belong to clearly identified modules. In other words, scattering of security code is effectively addressed. Second, the generated code is not mixed with non-access control concerns. The access control aspect contains only enforcement code. This code is not present anywhere else where other concerns are located. The interfaces generated from access control diagrams also contain only access control code and they are cohesive, in the sense that each interface contains only information associated to a specific artifact from the model level. For instance, the interface Nurse only contains the information from role slice Nurse, thereby eliminating tangling. Third, mappings to code are almost 1:1, which means that traceability is significantly improved. For instance, role slice Nurse from the design model is clearly traceable to the interface Nurse at the code level (Figure 9). Similarly, sensitivity levels from the MAC diagram are clearly traceable to the interfaces unclassified, confidential, secret, and top secret (U, C, S, and TS) at the code level. Overall, at the design level, access control modeling, visual notation, and customizability are addressed by our access control extensions to UML. At the code level, the mappings to code preserve separation of concerns and improve traceability.

4 COLLABORATIVE SECURITY

Collaborative computing is emerging a number of settings including: web portals such as Mediawiki and Sharepoint that facilitate interactions of stakeholders that are authoring, creating, and editing a shared content repository; collaborative software development tools such as Tigris and Git that turn the software development process into a truly shared activity; and, the health care setting where medical providers must interact and communicate with one another (and patients and their families) (Berhe et al., 2011; Abraham & Reddy, 2008; Agrawal et al., 2007). In the latter case, as a patient with a chronic condition transfers among different settings of care, there is increasing need to provide access to a patient's medical record that is stored in multiple locations and in different systems. The Virtual Chart Application (VCA) as introduced in Section 3 must be capable of limiting access while simultaneously promoting effective and timely collaborative treatment. Traditional RBAC approaches utilize *separation of duty, mutual exclusion,* and *cardinality constraints* (Ahn & Sandhu, 2000; Han et al., 2007) to limit what user can do. However, for collaborative health care, patient privacy and confidentiality must be protected while promoting and encouraging shared access of information by medical providers so that decisions can be made in a timely manner on the most up-to-date medical record of a patient.

Our prior work in this regard has been a model for obligated collaboration on duty and adaptive workflow (COD/AWF) (Berhe et al., 2009, 2010, 2011) that extends RBAC and UML with capabilities that include: secure collaboration to control access to data at the correct time (e.g., providers access a shared VCA); obligated collaboration which denotes individuals that must participate and how they interact towards a common goal (e.g., the internist, cardiologist, and radiologist who are all involved in treating the same patient); and, team-based collaboration, which defines the collaboration with multiple individuals toward a specific task (e.g., the team of medical providers and their interactions). This part of the chapter addresses collaboration security via extensions of the work in Section 3 and of UML to model collaborative structures and the interactions of individuals playing roles towards a common goal. The remainder of this section describes the UML extensions to support security modeling of collaboration requirements in Section 4.1 followed by a discussion of the automatic generation of

annotated code for enforcement via a mapping from UML in Section 4.2.

4.1 Collaboration Security Extensions to UML

This section describes our extensions to UML in support of collaboration of duty and adaptive workflow (COD/AWL). As shown in Figure 12, there are four new UML diagrams: the *collaboration workflow diagram* in Figure 12a which is in charge of defining the workflow requirements; the *extended role slice diagram* in Figure 12b which defines the roles and privileges for each collaboration step; the *collaboration obligation slice diagram* in Figure 12c which defines the

Figure 12. Four New UML Diagrams for collaboration of duty and adaptive workflow

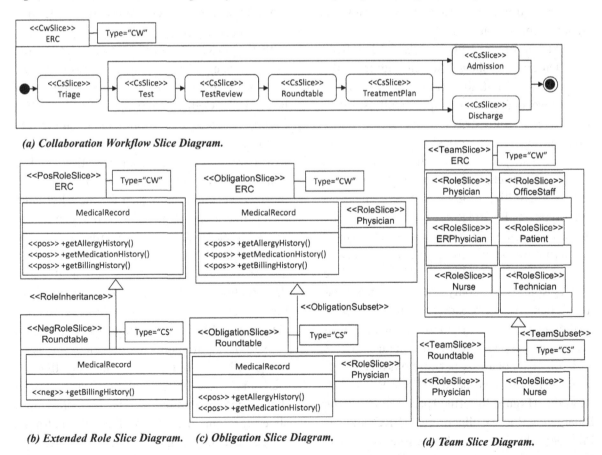

(a) Collaboration Workflow Slice Diagram.

(b) Extended Role Slice Diagram. *(c) Obligation Slice Diagram.*

(d) Team Slice Diagram.

required permissions and participations for a particular collaboration; and, the *collaboration team slice diagram* in Figure 12d which is in charge of defining teams. To begin, the *collaboration workflow diagram* in Figure 12a extends the UML activity diagram and allows the security engineer to focus only on interactions of a set of users playing roles through a set of collaboration steps as denoted by the <<CsSlice>> stereotype to represent each activity. Note that the set of activities in Figure 12a are each of type <<CsSlice>> which includes the steps Triage through TreatmentPlan with a linear flow, which can be forked in the last step to either Admit or Discharge a patient. The entire activity diagram for collaboration workflow is specialized using the <<CwSlice>> stereotype which serves as the second part (along with <<CsSlice>>), which via the type "CW" (collaboration workflow) can be associated with the other three diagrams in Figures 12b, 12c, and 12d.

Next, in Figure 12b, the Extended Role Slice Diagram is shown, which augments the one from Figure 3b to define permissions at a higher level of abstraction. Specifically, <<PosRoleSlice>> and <<NegRoleSlice>> (only positive/negative permissions allowed) can be applied to packages which contain classes which are restricted to only positive (negative) permissions utilizing the <<pos>> (<<neg>>) stereotype. <<PosRoleSlice>> only allows the specification of positive permissions and is used in the root role slice to set the scope of allowed privileges throughout the collaboration, while <<NegRoleSlice>> only allows the specification of negative permissions which is utilized to further restrict privileges in a particular collaboration step (CS). This insures that team members with roles cannot utilize permissions that are not permitted in the corresponding CS. The role slice diagram in Figure 3b defined permissions for the Emergency Room Collaboration (ERC) and has Provider, Physician, and Nurse role slices. The Nurse role slice negates getBillingHistory while

the Patient role slice negates all of the methods in the MedicalRecord class. During the collaboration, all of the activated permissions must be a subset of the allowed permissions which is modeled using <<RoleInheritance>>, so that the assigned permissions to the collaboration workflow (<<CwSlice>>) is represented as the root role slice (see Figure 12b), namely the MedicalRecord class.

The Obligation Slice Diagram shown in Figure 12c defines the set of permissions that must be activated and the set of roles that must participate in each collaboration step and in the overall collaboration workflow. These complement RBAC's separation of duty and cardinality constraints and model the obligation requirement (i.e., who is allowed to perform which method at which time) (Ahn & Sandhu, 2000). The <<ObligationSlice>> stereotype applies to packages that only contain obligated permissions and roles using <<obl>> obligation sets with the <<ObligationSubset>> relationship. For instance, during Triage, a Physician role must be present and the medication history must be read (getMedicationHistory in diagram 1 of Figure 3) before a decision is made on the way to continue with the patient treatment process. In Figure 12c, obligated participation implies that a role *must* activate *at least one* of the authorized permissions, which for the ERC team means that a physician is a role that can be obligated to participate. With regards to obligated permission activation, getMedicationHistory and getAllergyHistory *must* be activated before the collaboration terminates. Permissions from Figure 12b are used to constrain the role slice elements within the obligation slice. Permission activation requirements are modeled as classes along with their obligated permissions that are elements of the obligation slice marked using the <<obl>> stereotype. The root obligation slice represents the set of obligations that must be activated during the collaboration, while each collaboration step must fulfill a subset of the root obligation slice. To correctly link the obligation slices with the corresponding collaboration step, we utilize both the name of the obligation slice and its tagged note, which distinguishes between collaboration step slices and collaboration workflow obligation slices.

Finally, the team slice diagram in Figure 12d depicts a separate concern to capture permissions for a team. In the ERC example, each of the collaboration teams contains the specific role slices that are needed (see Figure 12b). Using the subset (<<TeamSubset>>) relationship for the team slice diagram, the root team slice represents the entire collaboration team and all of the CSs subset team members from this root team slice. A team slice is depicted as a UML package with the stereotype <<TeamSlice>>. This package contains a set of role slices. The <<TeamSlice>> diagram is used to define a team of <<RoleSlice>> members. For example, each collaboration step illustrated in Figure 12a (e.g., Triage, Lab Test, X-Ray Test, EKG Test, etc.) has its own team that participates in this context. To simplify the administration, we utilize the <<TeamSubset>> stereotype to indicate the parent-child relationship between two <<TeamSlice>> specialized packages. For permission activation, team membership allows a role to be authorized to a particular permission in the collaboration. The root team slice contains the set of roles that are allowed to participate throughout out the entire collaboration. To flag this setting, we utilize the tagged note which contains the stereotype <<CwSlice>> ERC which indicates that this team slice defines the underlying setting based on which sub-teams are defined for each of the collaboration steps. To indicate that a team slice corresponds to a collaboration step, the tagged note that contains the stereotype <<CsSlice>> with the corresponding collaboration step name. Both stereotypes (<<CwSlice>> and <<CsSlice>>) are used to match the teams with the other three diagrams in Figures 12a, 12b, and 12c.

4.2 Transition from Collaborative Security Design to Automatically Generated Policy Code

Once the COD/AWF requirements have been specified using UML as given in Section 4.1 and shown in Figures 12a to 12d, the next logical step is to generate code that can enforce the defined security policy for collaboration. To accomplish this, we utilize the meta-programming capabilities of the Java language to define the COD/AWF and RBAC policies that then are used to enforce their correct authorization. The main reason that we utilize Java is that its meta-programming capabilities provide a simple mechanism to define annotations, which allows additional semantic information to be assigned to any Java entity (e.g., variable, method, class, package, etc.). These annotations can be preprocessed before the compiler runs the code using the Java reflection library. Java expresses semantic meta-data using the character @ to signify an annotation. If the annotations are not read using meta-programming, the semantics of a program does not change. A summary of the annotations is given in Table 1 in order to allow the reader to more easily follow the discussion that maps from the diagrams of Figure 12 to annotated Java code.

First the team slice diagram from Figure 12d is mapped to the code given in Figure 13, using a public interface annotated with @TeamSlice. The interface name determines the collaboration workflow that the team belongs to. The team members are composed out of roles, which are defined within the roles interface. For each collaboration step, only a subset of the team members may be required. To specify the subset relationship between the entire collaboration and a particular collaboration step, we introduce the @TeamSubset annotation that allows only roles from the super set of roles specified in the entire collaboration workflow. This information is parameterized in the @TeamSubset annotation. In Figure 13, the entire collaboration team is composed out of six of

Table 1. Annotations for policy generation

@Pos:	The UML <<Pos>> stereotype defined during the design time, which states that the role is authorized to activate the method.
@Neg:	The UML <<Neg>> stereotype defined during the design time, which states that the role is not authorized to active the method.
@PosRoleSlice:	The UML <<PosRoleSlice>> stereotype defined during the design time, which states that this role slice can only have positive permissions.
@NegRoleSlice:	The UML <<NegRoleSlice>> stereotype defined during the design time, which states that this role slice can only have negative permissions.
@TeamSlice:	The UML <<NegRoleSlice>> stereotype defined during the design time, which states that this role slice can only have negative permissions (see @Neg annotation).
@TeamSubset:	The UML <<TeamSubset>> stereotype defined during the design time which states that a team may only be composed out of a subset of the parent team.
@Obl:	The UML <<Obl>> stereotype defined during the design time the set of permissions that must be activated and the set of roles that must participate.
@CollabWorkflowSlice:	The UML << CollabWorfklowSlice>> stereotype defined during the design time wraps the collaboration workflow specifying the set of collaboration step and their order for a particular collaboration.
@CollabSlice:	The UML <<CollabSlice>> stereotype defined during the design time, which specifies a collaboration step.
@NextCollabSlice:	The UML <<NextCollabSlice>> stereotype defined during the design time, which specifies the set of collaboration steps followed by a particular collaboration step.

the roles. Throughout the collaboration workflow, only those roles are allowed to participate. For the specific collaboration step named Roundtable, collaboration is limited to the nurse role and the physician role. The remaining four roles are not allowed to participate during the Roundtable collaboration step.

Second, the mapping between the extended role slice diagram from Figure 12b and the Java code in Figure 14 is equivalent with the role slice diagram presented in Section 3.1, except for one additional annotation. To satisfy the subset relationship between the collaboration workflow (root extended role slice) and the collaboration steps (child extended role slices), the @NegRoleSlice annotation is added. An interface with this annotation only allows negative permissions. For instance in Triage collaboration step, all of the methods from the parent extended roles are permitted except for the two methods related to appointment history and billing.

Third, the obligation slice in Figure 12c for the entire collaboration workflow and each collaboration step is mapped in Figure 15 to Java using the @ObligationSlice annotation. Similar as in the extended role slices, the subset relationship between the entire collaboration workflow and each of its collaboration steps is achieved using the @CodcSubset annotation. This dictates that only a subset of the obligations can be re-used. The obligated methods and roles are wrapped as public variables within the collaboration step/workflow interface. For example, during emergency room triage, the physician must check the allergy and medication history of the patient. After triage, if the patient is discharged, the office staff role must update the billing portion of the patient's medical record.

Finally, mapping of the Collaboration Workflow Slice Diagram in Figure 12a to Figure 16 in Java is accomplished by annotating the collaboration workflow with @CollabWorkflowSlice. Within the collaboration workflow, each collaboration step is defined as a separate interface and parameterizes the set of ensuing collaboration steps using the @NextCollabSlice annotation. The collaboration steps with an empty @Next-CollabSlice represents the last collaboration step in the collaboration workflow. In Figure 16, the interface Triage specifies that potential subsequent collaboration steps are limited to Test, Admission, and Discharge. During runtime, this information will be looked up to verify the clinical workflow.

5 INFORMATION SECURITY

The third aspect of our work with respect to software security focuses on the control of information created by an application that in turn is shared and/or exchanged with other applications. Information exchange can be achieved in multiple ways; efforts to structure data in order to provide a common processing model of information has resulted in the creation of formats such as the JavaScript Object Notation (JSON) and the eXtensible Markup Language (XML). The latter has emerged as the de facto standard for information exchange, with its use being leveraged for the creation of document standards to which information has to conform. For example, following the health care domain theme utilized throughout this chapter, standards such as the Continuity of Care Record (CCR) and Health Level 7's (HL7) Clinical Document Architecture (CDA) have been utilized to represent patient information in various care settings and situations. These standards are realized as XML schemas, which serve as a blueprint for the new document instances and as a validation agent for existing ones. The definition of XML schemas has become a necessary component of the software engineering process, usually with the purpose of handling exchange between the components that comprise an enterprise application.

With the purpose of supporting information-based security, our previous work (De la Rosa Algarín et. al, 2012, 2013a and 2013b) has extended

Figure 13. Mapping of team slice diagram to code

```
@TeamSlice
public interface ERC {
@ReferencedTeamClass(cod.Roles.class)
 public interface Roles {
  public interface Physician{};
  public interface OfficeStaff{};
  public interface ERPhysician{};
  public interface Patient{};
  public interface Nurse{};
  public interface Technician{};
 }
}
@TeamSlice
@TeamSubset(name="TeamSlice",value="ERC")
public interface Roundtable {
@ReferencedTeamClass(cod.Roles.class)
 public interface Roles {
  public interface Physician{};
  public interface Nurse{};
 }
}
```

Figure 14. Extended role slice diagram to code mapping

```
@PosRoleSlice
public interface ERC {
@ReferencedPermissionClass(cod.Emr.class)
public interface EMR {
 @pos public String getAllergyHistory();
 @pos public String getMedicationHistory();
 @pos public String getBillingHistory();
}
}
@NegRoleSlice
public interface Triage extends ERC {
@ReferencedPermissionClass(cod.Emr.class)
public interface EMR {
 @neg public String getBillingHistory();
}
}
```

the Unified Modeling Language (UML) with two new diagrams: an *XML Schema Class Diagram (XSCD)* to model a XML schema as a UML class diagram; and, an *XML Role Slice Diagram (XRSD)* to model RBAC requirements of a specific application with respect to the original XML

Figure 15. Obligation slice diagram to code mapping

```
@ObligationSlice
public interface EMC {
@ReferencedPermissionClass(cod.Emr.class)
public interface ERC {
 @obl public String getAllergyHistory();
 @obl public String getMedicationHistory();
 @obl public String getBillingHistory();
}
@ReferencedTeamClass(cod.Roles.class)
public interface Roles {
 @obl public interface Physician{};
 @obl public interface Nurse{};
}
}
```

Figure 16. Workflow slice diagram to code mapping

```
@CollabWorkflowSlice
public interface EMC {
@CollabSlice
@NextCollabSlice(name="CollabSlice", value="Test,
        Admission, Discharge")
@ReferencedCollabStepsClass(cod.CollabSteps.class)
public interface Triage{}
@CollabSlice
@NextCollabSlice(name="CollabSlice", value="")
@ReferencedCollabStepsClass(cod.CollabSteps.class)
public interface Admission{}
@CollabSlice
@NextCollabSlice(name="CollabSlice", value="")
@ReferencedCollabStepsClass(cod.CollabSteps.class)
public interface Discharge{}
}
```

schema. The definition of these two UML artifacts permits us to generate enforcement policies in the eXtensible Access Control Markup Language (XACML), which provides a common data and processing model for policy enforcement. This third part of this chapter addresses information security via extensions of the work in Section 3.1 and of UML to model the information structure (via XML schemas) at a level that allows abstract security policy definitions in UML from which XACML policies can be generated. The remainder of this section describes the UML extensions to

support security modeling of information requirements in Section 5.1 followed by a discussion of the automatic generation of annotated code for enforcement in XACML via a mapping from UML in Section 5.2.

5.1 Information Security Extensions to UML

XML schemas (and instances) exhibit a hierarchical structure as part of their specifications. Elements (nodes) can have sub-elements (children), and these can be of different types, such as xs:element, xs:complexType, etc. One approach to modeling with XML schemas is to represent them as UML diagrams (Bernauer et al., 2003; Vela et al., 2003). In our work the (De la Rosa Algarín et al., 2012), we extend UML with two new diagrams: the XML Schema Class Diagram (XSCD) to model the architecture, structure characteristics, element constraints, and relations of an XML schema; and, the *XML Role Slice Diagram (XRSD)* to model the role security requirements with respect to information, which contrasts to the method level focus of the role-slice diagram in Figures 3b and 12b. To begin, the XSCD that represents a given XML schema for an application will have a set of XSCDs (one corresponding to each XML schema) to support the definition of information security. Recall that XML schemas are characterized by a hierarchical structure with data type constraints. To handle the hierarchical nature of XML schemas, we represent each xs:complexType in the schema as a UML class with their respective UML stereotype. If an xs:element is a descendant of another schema concept, then this relation is represented as an equivalent class, denoted by a subclass relation in the class diagram. This holds true for xs:sequence, xs:simpleType, etc. XML schema extensions (xs:extension) are represented as associations between classes. Data-type cardinality requirements (minOccurs, maxOccurs) and constraints are represented with a generic <<constraint>> stereotype assigned to

Figure 17. Two New UML Diagrams for Information Security

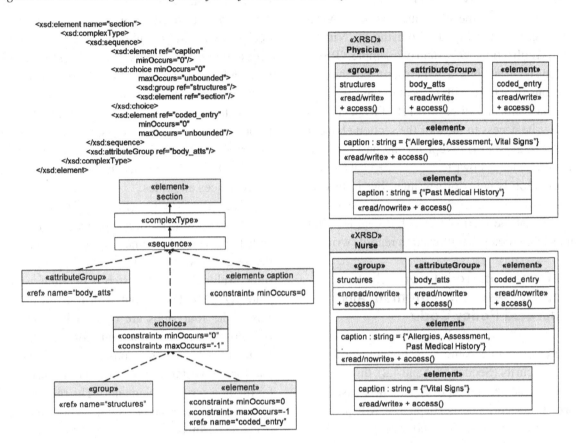

(a). XML Schema Segment (top) and XSCD (bottom).   *(b). XSRD Role Slice Diagram.*

the attribute. The xs:element type is respectively represented with a <<type>> stereotype to determine its type. Figure 17a shows the XSCD for the HL7's CDA "section" elements (upper left). Note that the hierarchical nature of the XML schema segments (upper left of Figure 17a) is maintained with class-subclass relations in the XSCD (lower left of Figure 17a), and the element constraints are set inside each respective element class.

After the XML schema utilized by the application is modeled and represented as a UML class diagram (with the XSCD), the next step is to model the security requirements of the application that are related to the information to be used. To model these requirements, the *XML Role Slice Diagram (XRSD* can be employed to represent

the way that each role targets information, which complements the approach from the RSDs in Sections 3.1 and 4.1 that are method based. We note that permissions on XML documents are read, no read, write, and no write. To represent these, we set stereotypes with the combination of permissions with respect to a role (4 total): <<read/write>>, <<read/nowrite>>, <<noread/write>>, and <<noread/nowrite>>, as shown for the XRSD in Figure 17b. Pictorially, the XRSD is an UML package via an <<XRSD>> stereotype, and class diagrams are members that represent each of the elements of the XML schema (form the XSCD) that need to be secured. These diagram segments, which are organized hierarchically depending on their position with respect to the XML schema tree, contain stereotypes that represent the operations permitted by the role being described. As an example, consider Figure 17b using the Virtual Chart Application (VCA) and two sample XRSDs for Physician and Nurse, which describes the permissions they have with respect to the "section" schema elements. In Figure 17b, Physician has read/write access to most of the section element (top of Figure 17a) except for the past medical history, which is nowrite (i.e., in medical record, information is never overwritten, but instead is added over time). Nurse has read access to the majority of the section element, except for vital signs, which they are allowed to record (write).

5.2 Transition from Information Security Design to Automatically Generated Policy Code

Following a similar path for functional and collaboration security (Sections 3.2 and 4.2), this section explores the generation from an UML-based information security design of an XACML instance enforcement policy. The end result is a policy that allows XML instances to be customized and delivered to users based on their role permissions, which has the benefit that the security privileges defined at a schema level do not impact the XML instances of an application. This means that when privileges and permissions evolve, updating the enforcement policy would just require a regeneration of the policy itself (unlike embedded security methods, which require the update of every existing instance), effectively providing separation of security concerns. Like XML schemas, the new UML diagrams XSCD and XRSD are leveraged as blueprints of the access-control policy for reading and writing permissions in a granular level. Each XRSD effectively describes the permission of a role, and the set of XRSDs for a given application is the set of roles and permissions for said application. To map an XRSD into an XACML policy, we utilize the policies' language structure and processing model. XACML policies consist

of a *PolicySet*, a *Policy*, and a *Rule*. An XACML *PolicySet* is utilized to make the authorization decision via a set of rules in order to allow for access control decisions. A *PolicySet* can contain multiple *Policy* structures, and each *Policy* contains the access control rules. As a result, the *Policy* structure acts as the smallest entity that can be presented to the security system for evaluation. To create an XACML Policy structure per each XRSD, Table 2 contains the general mapping equivalences and rules.

Given the XSCDs (Figure 17a) and their XRSDs (Figure 17b) for an application, it is possible to provide an automated process to generate the target XACML policy using the mapping rules (Table2). The first step is creating a template XACML Policy, but with four high level rules. The four rules are divided between the four possible permissions (one for the readable elements, one for the non-readable elements, one for the writable elements, and a fourth one for the non-writable elements). The resources of each of these rules and its single action (mapped from the permission) are associated with the tied permission stereotype of the XRSD. For example, in the Nurse XRSD in Figure 17b, all of the elements that have <<read/*>> would be mapped as resources to the rule with the mapped action of "read" (and effect Permit since it's an allowable permission). Those elements with a <<*/nowrite>> stereotype in turn would be added to the rule with the mapped action of "noread" and effect Deny. Naturally, all of the subjects of these rules are equal (the role), creating one policy with several rules for a given role. After the mapping processes between rules and XRSD elements/stereotypes are completed, sanitation can be performed. This sanitation verifies that all of the four rules contain at least one resource (element). If one of them does not, then the rule can be dropped. After this step is completed, the XACML Policy is finalized, shown in Figure 18, as a XACML rule for the Physician role. Note that the example shown has been condensed to

Table 2. XACML mapping equivalences and rules

Policy and Rule Descriptors and Structure:	Policy's *PolicyId* attribute value is the XRSD's *Role* value concatenated to *AccessControlPolicy*.
	Rule's *RuleId* attribute value is the XRSD's *Role* value concatenated to the XRSD's higher order element, also concatenated to *"ProductRule"*. If the permission stereotypes are not all positive or all negative (that is, at least once occurrence of read/nowrite or noread/write), the permission name is also concatenated to the *RuleId*.
	Rule's *Description* value is the XRSD's *Role* concatenated to *"Access Control Policy Rule"*.
	There are as many XACML *Rules* under a higher level *Target* element as there are permissions, unless all of the permission stereotypes in an XRSD are all-positive or all-negative.
Rule Target's Subject:	Only one XACML *Subject* and *SubjectMatch* per Rule.
	SubjectMatch's *MatchId* uses the function "string- equal" to evaluate the user's role as modeled in the XRSD.
	AttributeValue of the Subject is a string, and the value is the XRSD's *Role*.
	SubjectAttributeDesignator's AttributeId is the role attribute.
	While more than one *Rule* per Policy might exist, the *Subject* is equal in both cases. This means that the role to be considered for policy evaluation is the same for operations that are allowed or denied.
Rule Target's Actions:	One XACML *Action* per operation permitted exists. If the stereotypes of an XRSD are all-positive or all-negative, then both permissions are set as two actions under the same rule. Otherwise, one rule per permission is created (each one with an individual action).
	ActionMatch's MatchId uses the function "string- equal".
	ActionAttributeDesignator's AttributeId value is *action-write* or *action-read*.
	ActionMatch's Attributevalue is the permission, *read*, *write*, *noread*, *nowrite*, depending on the stereotypes of the XRSD.

the *subject*, *resource*, and *action* elements of the XACML schema. This segment represents one of the multiple rules (more specifically, the rule of not writing the Past Medical History element) that make the Physician policy.

6 A SECURE SOFTWARE ENGINEERING PROCESS

This section describes a secure software engineering process that spans across the functional, collaboration, and information security concerns for an application. As shown in Figure 19, our process provides a means to define a security policy using security diagrams and features to fully illustrate the creation of a custom security model, the composition of security features, and the security design for functional, collaboration, and information concerns. In Figure 19, the steps are numbered from 1 to 6, and will be referenced

when each concept is explained. To illustrate the secure software process in Figure 19, we leverage a big data application from the law enforcement/traffic domain where data collected from traffic crash reports that contain confidential information and access must be limited to authorized users and their respective roles. In effect, a traffic crash report system (CRS) big data application can be defined that would use hand-held and other devices to collect information on accidents (e.g., cars involved, people involved, location, specifics of actual accident, etc.) and would have as a backend a big data repository that can be queried by different stakeholders. This example is based on an actual crash report system in Connecticut that has data from over 20 years that has been a joint effort by faculty in the Civil & Environmental Engineering and Computer Science & Engineering faculty under the supervision of the State of Connecticut Department of Transportation. CRS serves as a means for researchers to collaboratively

Figure 18. The physician XRSD mapped to XACML

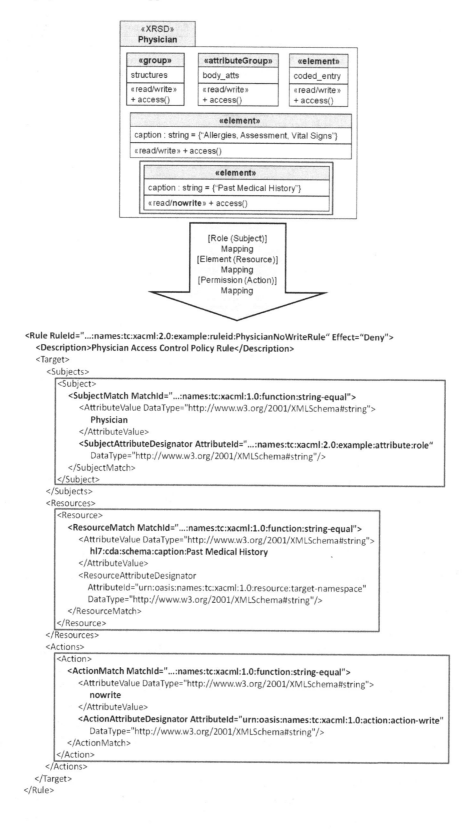

analyze the data for future crash prevention and other operational purposes. The example presented in this section has been excerpted from the Model Minimum Uniform Crash Criteria Guide (MMUCC) that defines an XML standard for data to be collected on traffic crashes to be stored in CRS.

To begin the process of Figure 19, software engineers create a requirements specification that serves as input to the (1) main security design.

Specifically, we assume that a class diagram for CRS has been developed as the output of step 1. This is shown in Figure 20, where a limited UML class diagram for CRS has: the CRS class that can write and read a crash history and share crash data; subclasses for tracking crashes on roads that are federal (FederalCRS), state (StateCRS), on local (LocalCRS); and, the InsuranceReporting class that allows insurance reporting information on the crash to be created and shared. Next, as part

Figure 19. Our secure software engineering process

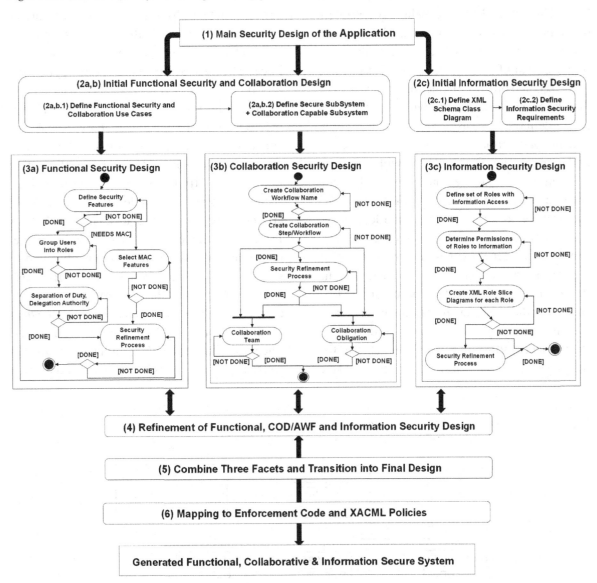

of an iterative process, designers create an initial security design of the application (steps 2a, b, and c). For functional and collaboration design, there is a need to define uses cases (steps 2a and b.1) as well as to define the secure subsystem diagram for the functional and collaboration concerns. The class diagram in Figure 20 will be utilized to define those methods that have the potential to be accessible to different users based on role. In this example, all of the classes and methods of Figure 20 are sensitive, thus they are all included in the Secure Subsystem Diagram in Figure 21a.

In addition to the class-based design, steps 2a, b, and c in Figure 19 will also include a description of the process and stakeholders involved in CRS at a high level coupled with a more detailed view of a scenario of usage to help guide later steps in the secure software engineering process. At a high level, each state has its own police or shared police with other towns. Accidents that occur in a municipality usually fall under the jurisdiction of the local office. Data collected will be entered in a central and shared regional, state, and federal crash report system that usually allows read and write access to officers at the same level (e.g., state officer to state crash report system). Accidents that happen on a state owned or interstate highway usually fall under the jurisdiction of the state police. Therefore, if a local officer arrives first and enters the crash data report, the local officer is obligated to share and hand over the data to the state officers and state troopers. This achieves the sharing or reports through system integration of the

local office's data with the state officer's system. Whenever there is a major accident and the local/state officers request federal help or whenever an accident happens between multiple states, the jurisdiction goes to the federal officers. In such use cases, data is often first collected by the local or state officers, and later shared with federal officers with write access. Researchers usually have read access to de-identified portions of the databases systems at the local, state, and federal level to query and analyze the collected big data.

At a more detailed level, a scenario could involve the following. On a Monday morning during rush hour, John Smith accidentally drives into Bob Doe's car and both cars have broken front tires and rear lights on the interstate highway I-84. Local officer Jackie Kerr while on her way to work, sees the accident and immediately rushes to the location, checks Bob's and John's health state, before starting the insurance and personal data collection, as well as information on the way that the accident happened. She enters the information into a hand-held traffic crash report system (CRS). A few moments later, state officer Neal Drake arrives and discusses the accident with Officer Jackie Kerr. Since the accident happened on an interstate highway, Officer Kerr is obligated to share the collected data via the local traffic crash report system so that the state officer can also access. Officer Neal Drake takes over the accident location and queries John Smith's accident history. The results show that Mr. Smith has a history of convicted car accidents in five states over the past

Figure 20. Limited class diagram of the CRS

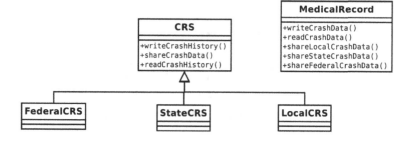

Figure 21. Various diagrams for the CRS access control policy

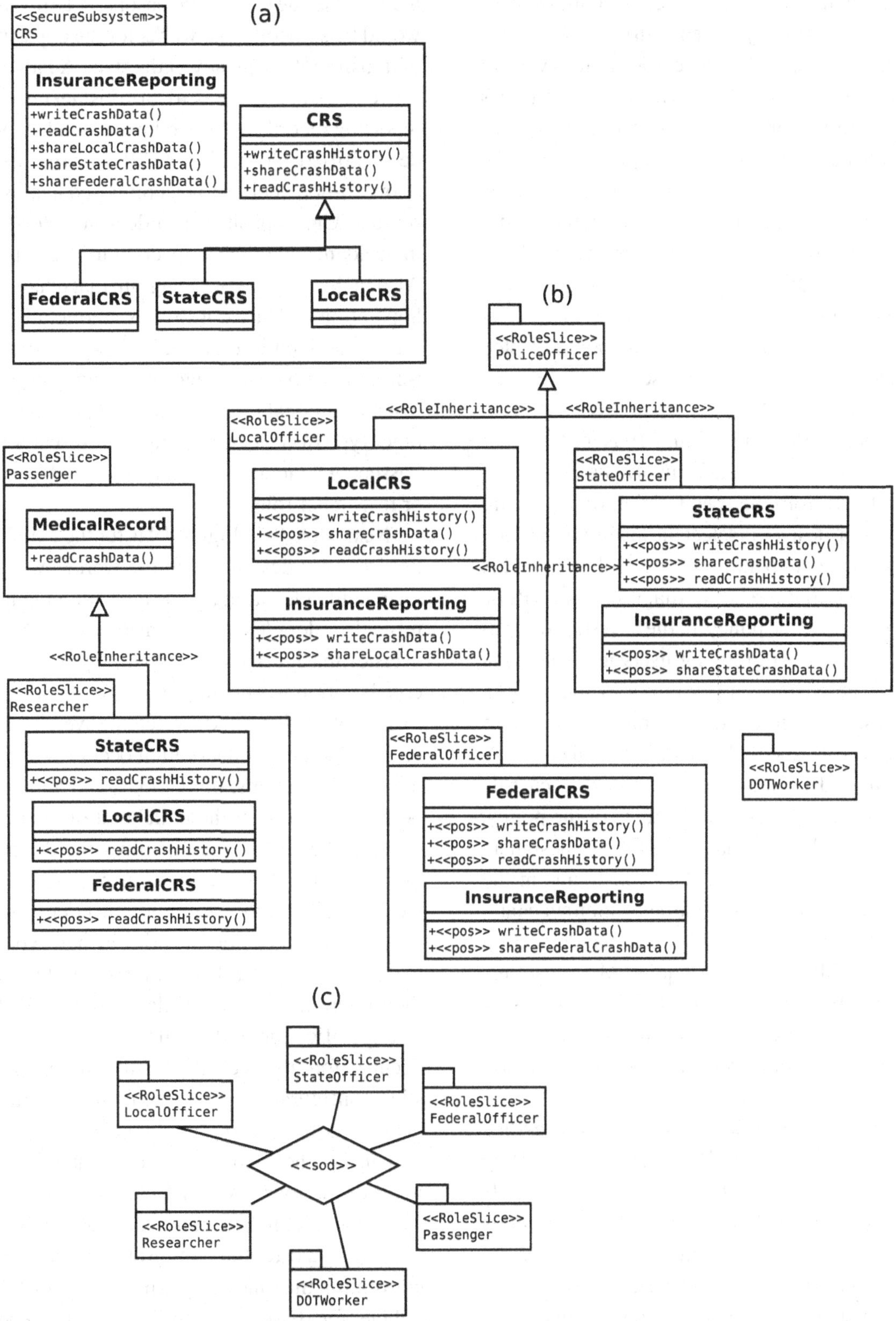

three years. Due to the multi-state car accident history, John Smith's collected accident information will be automatically shared with the federal crash report system read by Officer Ramona Tyler. In parallel, a researcher, Dr. Ervin Walsh, has access to the entire automatically updated de-identified CRS big data repository to query and analyze the data towards crash prevention. In order to make a decision on whether to charge John Smith or not in a legal court, Officers Kerr, Drake, and Tyler have a roundtable discussion about the crash. Using the high-level and detailed view of CRS as input, the functional (step 3a), collaboration (step 3b) and information (step 3c) security design can proceed in parallel.

To begin, Box 3a in Figure 19 is for the functional security design and involves a number of steps. First, from the specification of the secure subsystem, designers select the features they want to incorporate into the access control model. This is reflected in the security diagrams that will be used to specify the policy. In the next step, designers can then start grouping users into roles that denote their common privileges in the system. The result is a role slice diagram that contains only the role slices. Designers can also assign positive and negative permissions to each role slice to realize role-based features of the policy. Using the role slice diagram as input, designers can define separation of duty constraints in the user diagram, and also define delegation slices and delegation authority privileges in the delegation diagram. If the policy also requires MAC features, they can be incorporated into the diagrams as MAC extensions. The resulting policy can be further refined until designers decide it is ready to transition into code.

To illustrate Box 3a, in Figure 21b a role-slice diagram (RSD) of the CRS access control policy is defined. Role slices for LocalOfficer, StateOfficer, and FederalOfficer denote the permissions for each type of officer, which are, essentially, the ability to read, write, and share the crash history data registered in CRS, and also write insurance

reporting information in the system with denied read access due to privacy reasons. A DoTWorker would be someone that works for the department of transportation agency of the state. A Passenger can read his/her own crash data in his/her insurance reporting record. A Researcher can read all of the de-identified information in CRS with the intent to allow ad-hoc queries to be composed against the big-data CRS repository in order to look for trends in accidents and their impact on traffic patterns. Also in this step, a User Diagram that denotes the Separation of Duty constraints among all of the roles is defined in Figure 21c. No person with a role can assume any other role in the system. For instance a Local Officer cannot impersonate any other type of officer, passenger, or researcher. A Passenger cannot assume any type of officer role or researcher role.

Next, Box 3b in Figure 19 is for the collaboration security design where the workflow, steps, team, and delegation are defined and potentially refined via done/not done decision states. The first decision that must be made is with regards to which collaboration workflow is going to be designed. The collaboration workflow sets the overall context under which the collaboration occurs along with the specified teams, obligations, and authorized permissions. Given the collaboration workflow context, the second step involves the definition of all of the collaboration steps required in this workflow. This process requires different domain experts and stakeholders to bring in their expertise to define the set of collaboration steps along with their relationship into a collaboration workflow. The specification of the collaboration steps must occur before the security, teams, and obligation slice configuration, since the collaboration step happens in the context of a collaboration workflow, serving as the binding element that is utilized in all of the four new UML diagrams (extended role slice, a collaboration team, a collaboration workflow, and a collaboration obligation) with the convention that matching names imply matching policies for a particular step. As part of the security refinement process, collaboration step names are used in the other slices, while collaboration team and collaboration obligation have an input to an activity that parameterizes it, which expects a set of collaboration step names. After the role slices and the collaboration workflow is specified, the next step is the creation of obligation and team slice diagrams. The obligation slice diagram requires the permission set and the role set as an input. The team slice diagram requires the role set as an input.

Continuing with the CRS example, from a collaborative perspective in Box 3b, the order in which the officers work together follows a process that can be captured with the four diagrams shown in Figure 22. Specifically, the collabora-

tion workflow diagram in Figure 22a defines the workflow of the high-level detail of CRS stakeholders and their interactions, the extended role slice diagram in Figure 22b defines the roles and privileges for each collaboration step that build off of the role slice diagram of Figure 21b, the collaboration obligation slice diagram in Figure 22c defines the participation and permissions of CRS stakeholders, and, the collaboration team slice diagram in Figure 22d defines the CRS teams. When designing a system that is used in the traffic domain, obligated, coordinated, team-based and secure collaboration capabilities are an integral part from the early phases of the software engineering process.

Figure 22. Four UML Diagrams for collaboration of duty and adaptive workflow for CRS

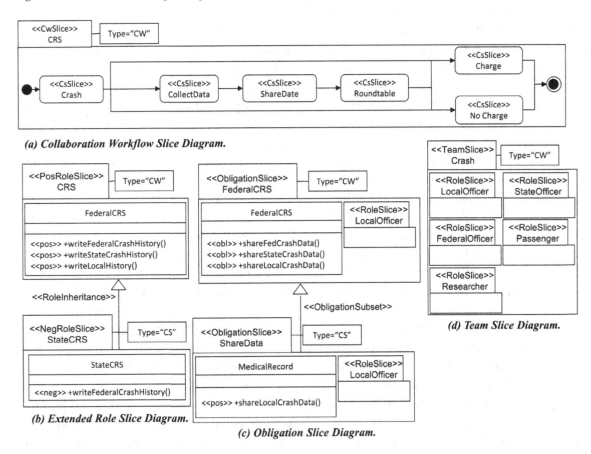

(a) Collaboration Workflow Slice Diagram.

(b) Extended Role Slice Diagram.

(c) Obligation Slice Diagram.

(d) Team Slice Diagram.

- **Team-Based Collaboration:** Local, state, and federal officers compose a team that work together to share and use the collected crash report data sets.
- **Coordinated Collaboration:** The order in which data is shared goes usually either from local to state to federal officers or reverse.
- **Obligated Collaboration:** If a major accident happens in an interstate highway, the local or state officers must inform the federal officers and share the collected data to determine future jurisdiction.
- **Secure Collaboration:** Depending on the context of the accident, read, write, or no access privileges are given to the three types of officers.

Collaboration can be effectively utilized in order to capture the interactions among the various stakeholders involved in the big data law enforcement/traffic domain application.

Finally, Box 3c in Figure 19 is for the information security design. By considering the roles that will interact with the different information structures of the application, the software engineer will select the role's permission with respect to information elements. These permissions, which are read and write (and their explicit opposites: no read and no write), are graphically described with respect to each role by the creation of the XML Role Slice Diagram (XRSDs). For example, if an application has 10 different roles, a total of 10 XRSDs will be created, each one representing the role's permissions with respect to the XML schema the application utilizes. Once these XRSDs are defined, if may also to perform a refinement process once all of the role slices and their potential interactions are defined. This feedback process permits software engineers to polish the roles and their information security permissions before an enforcement policy is created.

Picking up the CRS example again, the roles that are involved in collecting, reviewing, and analyzing the data include the officers at the local, state, and federal level as well as researchers, which are shown in Figures 21b and 22b, and can be expanded and refined as in Figure 23 for permissions and roles. Specifically, in Figure 23, the left-hand side indicates the roles, permissions, and entities (objects), the middle portion represents a PoliceOffice PSD, and the right portion represents a Researcher PSD (see Section 5.1). Box 3c can also be utilized to define the XRSDs. In support of this, from an information security perspective, the different roles that act upon the data might have different permissions (which could range from non-destructive operations, such as reading, to destructive operations, such as inserting or deleting) enforced in the information itself (see Figures 20 and 21). These permissions might be augmented with other security features, such as security levels from the MAC model. In these cases, collaboration might be a part of the information level security as well, where a role can be delegated to players in different layers of the operation, e.g., a state officer grating temporary access to a local officer to complete a task. This capability of information-level security can be granular as well. As shown in Figure 24, there are two XRSDs. Consider the role DoTWorker who works for the state transportation department and as a result may be part of the data acquisition process involving a traffic accident, particularly if it has occurred within a construction site. The DoT worker can have read/write permissions to the alcohol component of the MMCUU instances (MMCUU is an XML schema standard utilized for traffic accident information), but no write permission to the personal information of the parties involved. On the other hand, a PoliceOfficer would have read and write permissions to both these components of the CSR.

Over time, the processes of (steps 3a, b, c) in Figure 19 will eventually stabilize and lead to a consideration of the functional, collaboration, and information concerns that can be reconciled with one another in (step 4), and then combinable into

Figure 23. RBAC with basic operations applied to CRS

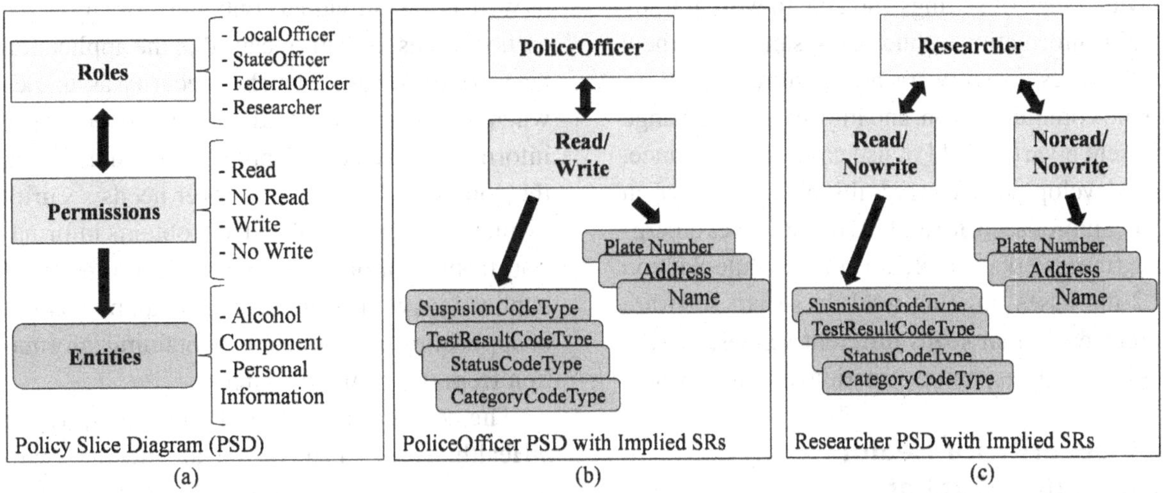

| Policy Slice Diagram (PSD) | PoliceOfficer PSD with Implied SRs | Researcher PSD with Implied SRs |
| (a) | (b) | (c) |

Figure 24. XML Role Slice Diagrams for Example Roles in the Law Enforcement Case Study

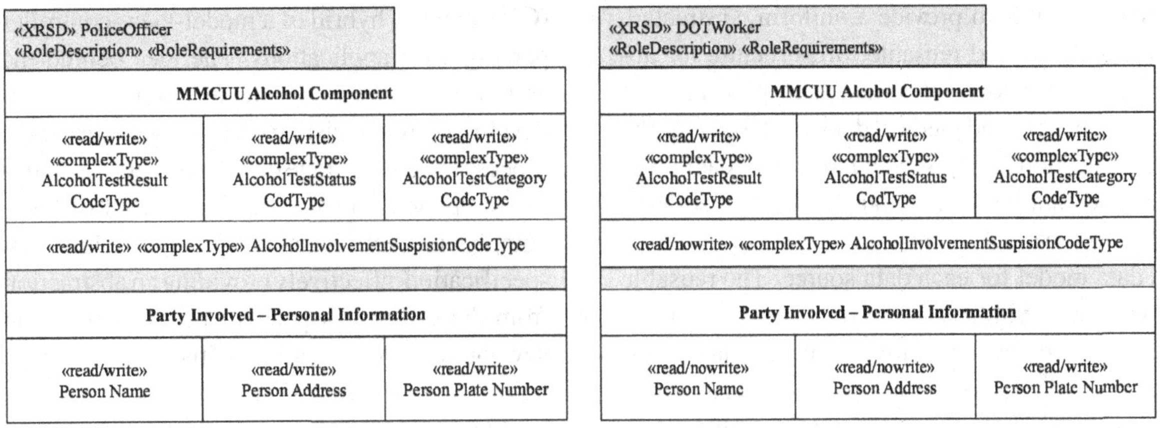

a single design instance (step 5). The combined design (step 5) satisfies the current iteration requirements, but it may be changed later to adapt to new requirements. A mapping procedure (step 6) translates the combined design (step 5) into security enforcement policies and code as a set of (step 6) to realize the enforcement mechanism for the application. Designers can further iterate over the design and repeat the whole process until the software is ready for deployment (last box on Fiugre.19).

7 FUTURE TRENDS

Future trends and research directions in secure software engineering are being influenced by the emergence of new standards, architectures, frameworks, and tools. The health care domain is full of approaches that strive to provide health information exchange (HIE) in order to support a more complete realization of patient data collected from multiple sources in real time to meet care needs. These new architectures and frameworks must be capable of achieving functional, collaborative, and information security concerns across a wide range of settings and able to work for any health information technology system. These new approaches to software architectures, development, communication, and information exchange present a varied field of use cases, maintenance, and development. Towards this objective, Section 7.1 explores security for HIE that involves emerging frameworks and architectures, while Section 7.2 discusses ongoing work in secure software engineering that spans different venues, certification agencies, and international organizations.

7.1 Security for Health Information Exchange

The Harvard University Sustainable Medical Applications, Reusable Technologies (SMART) Platform aims to provide a uniform, abstracted, well-defined and reusable infrastructure for application developers that want their applications to utilize patient and medical data of all types. At the specification level, SMART provides data owners and data source maintainers with a method to develop abstract containers that essentially define a data model for each data source. The reusable moniker of SMART comes from the fact that an application developed for a container that wraps around a data source, say A, can work in the same manner on another SMART container that wraps another data source, say B. The abstraction of data sources, A or B, into a container layer makes software development targets easier to maintain. For example, a SMART Container for an electronic health record would provide a common interface allowing the backend to integrate to different vendor products while providing the same front end to applications. In such an approach, it will be necessary to resolve not only data access issues but also address security concerns where the different patient data sources may have alternate security approaches. From a secure software engineering perspective, the SMART application developer will need to have some guarantee that the composition (union) of containers is secured as well as the individual containers for any of the authorized users. This means that the application layer needs to have a level of security assurance when considering isolated or interconnected (by information exchange) applications. In addition, the container (data source) layer needs security assurance when an isolated app obtains information from multiple sources or when a group of applications work in group (as a meta-application, or application of applications) obtaining information from one or more sources.

The second abstraction approach, Open *m*Health, is an open source architecture with modular components for health applications to be built from. These components, which come in the form of data visualization units (DVU), data processing units (DPU), and a cache unit (CU), create a hybrid of a model-view-controller paradigm for applications. The idea behind the architecture is to provide different end-point developers (e.g., visualization developers, data processors, data storage developers, etc.) a modular component to work on. In turn, all of these components work together using the architecture specification, effectively providing an abstraction from the different aspects of health application development. As an example of these components, a DPU might use insulin dosages and glucose readings with timestamps in conjunction with other patient information and analyze these units to provide some level of clinical decision support or other purpose. In contrast, a DVU can provide the means to display the results of a DPU analysis, and do so for different roles (e.g., a patient, a health provider, a researcher, etc.). Open mHealth provides the specifications on the way in which the different modular units should be developed, but localized security (as well as globalized) is not discussed. Any secure software engineering methodology for applications developed as one of the different modules in Open *m*Health must take into consideration that the original specification must be kept, regardless of the security requirements set. For example, a developer of a DPU can develop their own application and define their own security requirements, but the intercommunication aspect of the specification must not be broken. While another component might be denied access based on the security policy definitions, the communication component must be kept intact. This unavoidable constraint is necessary to maintain the original goal of the architecture itself. The two examples demonstrate that the health care domain presents secure software engineering challenges masked in existing abstraction solutions and architectures. Not only is it necessary to keep in mind the functional, collaborative, and information security aspects of an application, it is also necessary to keep in mind the way that some specifications provide constraints along with the complex challenges to the engineering process itself. Scenarios like meta-application security, modular intercommunicating component security, etc., must be considered in regards to the secure software engineering process.

Lastly, there are many ongoing efforts in the United States regarding health information exchange (HIE) for facilitating patient care by bringing together all of the patient data from multiple sources and for promoting data analysis against de-identified repositories. The DIRECT project provides a secure, scalable, and standards-based approach for HIE in support of making patient data available to providers, patients, clinics, hospitals, etc. Using this approach, information can be routed to the correct individuals at the required time with assurances in terms of authentication and a guarantee that the information has been routed to trusted recipients. Another effort is the Nationwide Health Information Network, which provides the policies, services, procedures, and standards that are necessary for secure information exchange of health care data. A third effort, Open Health Tools, is seeking to take a broader look at the integration of personal health care, healthcare delivery, and population health, in order to provide a solution that can respond to a wide range of needs includ-

ing: regularly scheduled patient care, emergency room treatment, disaster response, public health response, etc. Secure software engineering will play a significant role all of these efforts, in the development of the infrastructure that is necessary to link patient data from multiple repositories.

7.2 Focused Trends in Secure Software Engineering

The International Security Engineering Council (ISSECO) is an association with the main focus of software security. By focusing on the production of secure software, their goal is to provide and establish a secure information environment for all domains, users, etc. ISSECO's mission statement dictates that in order to create secure software, special knowledge about the software development lifecycle is a requirement. ISSECO notes that due to the development of the Internet, secure software engineering's importance has increased with respect to providing a desired level of software quality. With the ever-increasing amount of applications, all types of developers must take into consideration software security in order to maintain a level of trust from the customers. In support of this, ISSECO has standardized education and certification of skills for secure software development. These skills cover everything in the process of secure software production from the start to the end of the development lifecycle, including requirements engineering, trust modeling, threat modeling, secure coding, testing, and security response to the final code protection for deployed applications.

The European Network and Information Security Agency (ENISA) has several software engineering initiatives, including the monitoring of EU and international initiatives that aim to solve the issue of secure software engineering. ENISA organizes workshops with the purpose of bringing together different initiatives to foster collaboration and promote research and work efforts. Other goals of ENISA are the development of secure applications by providing security guidelines for the development of mobile (smartphone) applications. The third main objective of ENISA is the assessment of web standards for the next generation of technologies, including those drafted by the W3C and other organizations. In 2011, ENISA co-organized the Round Table session for Global Secure Initiatives – Beyond Awareness, at the OWASP APPSEC Europe 2011 Conference bringing together researchers and practitioners from the field of secure software engineering to discuss what could be done to ensure that valuable guidance and tools created for secure software engineering.

The Software Engineering Institute (SEI) at Carnegie Mellon has proposed the Security Quality Requirements Engineering (SQUARE) process. SQUARE consists of 9 steps to assist organizations and agencies in building the security and privacy aspects of software in the earliest stages of the engineering process. The benefit of using SQUARE is that organizations can predict schedules and costs of a more secure and consistent software component to address the current poor practice of security requirements defects that can cost from 10 to 200 times the amount to correct during the implementation process versus the cost during requirements specification. Another methodology, called software security measurement and analysis, aims to develop a risk-based approach for measuring and monitoring the security characteristics of software systems across the different steps of the application's lifecycle. This measurement and analysis approach has taken the form of the SEI Integrated Measurement and Analysis Framework that integrates collected performance data of modular software components, providing a consolidated view of the overall software performance. Also, there is the SEI Mission Risk Diagnostic process that is able to analyze a defined set of risk factors, providing decision makers with a benchmark of a software or system's latest state. Lastly, SEI also has a software assurance curriculum with a focus to identify a

core of knowledge necessary to develop a Master of Software Assurance degree (for educational institutions) and promote early specialization in software assurance and related areas.

8 CONCLUSION

The design, development, and deployment of software applications must fully embrace the definition and realization of security requirements in the earliest stages of the software design and development process. While software engineering at the design level is dominated by the utilization of the Unified Modeling Language (UML), this approach has a decided lack of consideration of security, which is a paramount concern in today's society. There exists a broad variety of security models that should be supported, including: role-based access control (RBAC) to allow privilege definitions to be geared towards a user's responsibilities and duties; discretionary access control (DAC) to allow a user to delegate authority in certain situations; and, mandatory access control (MAC) to strictly control access to information via security levels. However, their inclusion as part of the software engineering processed is often relegated as an afterthought, with little consideration given to security concerns. This chapter has addressed the need for secure software engineering of functional, collaborative, and information concerns via an extension of UML with RBAC, DAC, and MAC, allowing for applications to be defined to address security during early and all stages of the software development process. Towards this objective, this chapter has explored our extensions of UML for RBAC, DAC, and MAC, supporting the definition of functional, collaborative, and information concerns, as detailed in Sections 3, 4, and 5, respectively. This included both the modeling of RBAC, DAC, and MAC in the three concerns, as well as the automatic generation of security enforcement code and policies. To facilitate the presentation, we leveraged an example from the health care domain, where information must be collaboratively shared and exchanged in a secure manner. To place the work into its proper context, in Section 6, we detailed the secure software engineering process for the functional, collaborative, and information concerns, and we illustrated this process with a second example related to big data for law enforcement and the traffic domain. Future trends for secure software engineering in terms of emerging platforms and efforts that also span different venues, certification agencies, and international organizations, were explored in Section 7. Overall, we believe this chapter establishes a baseline for the inclusion of access control models in a secure software engineering process.

REFERENCES

Abraham, J., & Reddy, M. C. (2008). Moving patients around: a field study of coordination between clinical and non-clinical staff in hospitals. In *Proceedings of the 2008 ACM conference on Computer supported cooperative work* (pp. 225-228). ACM.

Agrawal, R., Grandison, T., Johnson, C., & Kiernan, J. (2007). Enabling the 21st century health care information technology revolution. *Communications of the ACM, 50*(2), 34–42. doi:10.1145/1216016.1216018

Ahn, G. J., & Sandhu, R. (2000). Role-based authorization constraints specification. [TISSEC]. *ACM Transactions on Information and System Security, 3*(4), 207–226. doi:10.1145/382912.382913

Alghathbar, K. (2007). Validating the enforcement of access control policies and separation of duty principle in requirement engineering. *Information and Software Technology, 49*(2), 142–157. doi:10.1016/j.infsof.2006.03.009

AppSecEU2011 – OWASP. (n.d.). Retrieved from https://www.owasp.org/index.php/AppSecEU2011

ASTM E2369 – 12 Standard Specification for Continuity of Care Record (CCR). (n.d.). Retrieved from http://www.astm.org/Standards/E2369.htm

Basin, D., Doser, J., & Lodderstedt, T. (2006). Model driven security: From UML models to access control infrastructures. [TOSEM]. *ACM Transactions on Software Engineering and Methodology, 15*(1), 39–91. doi:10.1145/1125808.1125810

Bell, D. E., & La Padula, L. J. (1976). *Secure computer system: Unified exposition and multics interpretation (No. MTR-2997-REV-1).* MITRE Corp.

Berhe, S. (2011). *A framework for secure, obligated, coordinated and dynamic collaboration that extends NIST RBAC.* University of Connecticut.

Berhe, S., Demurjian, S., & Agresta, T. (2009). Emerging trends in health care delivery: towards collaborative security for NIST RBAC. In *Data and Applications Security XXIII* (pp. 283–290). Springer. doi:10.1007/978-3-642-03007-9_19

Berhe, S., Demurjian, S., Gokhale, S., Pavlich-Mariscal, J., & Saripalle, R. (2011). Leveraging UML for security engineering and enforcement in a collaboration on duty and adaptive workflow model that extends NIST RBAC. In *Data and Applications Security and Privacy XXV* (pp. 293–300). Springer. doi:10.1007/978-3-642-22348-8_25

Berhe, S., Demurjian, S., Saripalle, R., Agresta, T., Liu, J., Cusano, A., & Gedarovich, J. (2010). Secure, obligated and coordinated collaboration in health care for the patient-centered medical home. In *Proceedings of AMIA Annual Symposium.* American Medical Informatics Association.

Bernauer, M., Kappel, G., & Kramler, G. (2004). *Representing XML schema in UML–A Comparison of Approaches.* Springer.

CDA – Hl7book. (n.d.). Retrieved from http://hl7book.net/index.php?title=CDA

Connecticut Crash Data Repository (Beta). (n.d.). Retrieved from http://www.ctcrash.uconn.edu/

Connecticut Transportation Safety Research Center | Connecticut Transportation Institute. (n.d.). Retrieved from http://www.cti.uconn.edu/connecticut-transportation-safety-research-center/

De la Rosa Algarín, A., Demurjian, S. A., Berhe, S., & Pavlich-Mariscal, J. A. (2012). A security framework for XML schemas and documents for healthcare. In *Proceedings of 2012 IEEE International Conference on Bioinformatics and Biomedicine Workshops (BIBMW)* (pp. 782-789). IEEE.

De la Rosa Algarín, A., Demurjian, S. A., Ziminski, T. B., Rivera Sanchez, Y. K., & Kuykendall, R. (2013). Securing XML with role-based access control: case study in health care. In A. Ruiz Martínez, F. Pereñíguez García, & R. Marín López (Eds.), *Architectures and Protocols for Secure Information Technology* (pp. 334–365). Academic Press. doi:10.4018/978-1-4666-4514-1.ch013

De la Rosa Algarín, A., Ziminski, T. B., Demurjian, S. A., Kuykendall, R., & Rivera Sánchez, Y. (2013). Defining and enforcing XACML role-based security policies within an XML security framework. In *Proceedings of 9th International Conference on Web Information Systems and Technologies* (pp. 16-25). Academic Press.

Direct Project – Best Practices for HISPs. (n.d.). Retrieved from http://wiki.directproject.org/Best+Practices+for+HISPs

Direct Project – Home. (n.d.). Retrieved from http://wiki.directproject.org/home

ENISA. (n.d.). Retrieved from http://www.enisa.europa.eu/

Ferraiolo, D. F., Sandhu, R., Gavrila, S., Kuhn, D. R., & Chandramouli, R. (2001). Proposed NIST standard for role-based access control. [TISSEC]. *ACM Transactions on Information and System Security*, 4(3), 224–274. doi:10.1145/501978.501980

Git. (n.d.). Retrieved from http://git-scm.com/

Han, M., Thiery, T., & Song, X. (2006). Managing exceptions in the medical workflow systems. In *Proceedings of the 28th international conference on Software engineering* (pp. 741-750). ACM.

Health Information Privacy. (n.d.). Retrieved from http://www.hhs.gov/ocr/privacy/

Home – SMART Platforms. (n.d.). Retrieved from http://smartplatforms.org/

ISSECO – Secure Software Engineering. (n.d.). Retrieved from http://www.isseco.org/

Kang, M. H., Park, J. S., & Froscher, J. N. (2001). Access control mechanisms for inter-organizational workflow. In *Proceedings of the 6th ACM symposium on Access control models and technologies* (pp. 66-74). ACM.

Kenny, P., Parsons, T., Gratch, J., & Rizzo, A. (2008). Virtual humans for assisted health care. In *Proceedings of the 1st t international conference on PErvasive Technologies Related to Assistive Environments.* ACM.

Kiczales, G., Lamping, J., Mendhekar, A., Maeda, C., Lopes, C., Loingtier, J. M., & Irwin, J. (1997). *Aspect-oriented programming.* Springer.

Liebrand, M., Ellis, H., Phillips, C., Demurjian, S., Ting, T. C., & Ellis, J. (2003). Role Delegation for a Resource-Based Security Model. In Research directions in data and applications security (pp. 37-48). Springer US.

Lodderstedt, T., Basin, D., & Doser, J. (2002). SecureUML: A UML-based modeling language for model-driven security. In « UML» 2002—The Unified Modeling Language (pp. 426-441). Springer.

MediaWiki. (n.d.). Retrieved from http://www.mediawiki.org/wiki/MediaWiki

Microsoft SharePoint – collaboration software – Office.com. (n.d.). Retrieved from http://office.microsoft.com/en-us/sharepoint/

MMUCC Guideline – Model Minimum Uniform Crash Criteria. (2012). Retrieved from http://mmucc.us/sites/default/files/MMUCC_4th_Ed.pdf

Mouelhi, T., Fleurey, F., Baudry, B., & Le Traon, Y. (2008). A model-based framework for security policy specification, deployment and testing. In *Model Driven Engineering Languages and Systems* (pp. 537–552). Springer. doi:10.1007/978-3-540-87875-9_38

Nationwide Health Information Network (NHIN). (n.d.). Retrieved from http://www.nist.gov/healthcare/testing/nhin.cfm

Open mHealth – Home. (n.d.). Retrieved from http://openmhealth.org/

OpenHealthTools – Home. (n.d.). Retrieved from http://www.openhealthtools.org/index.htm

Parnas, D. L. (1972). On the criteria to be used in decomposing systems into modules. *Communications of the ACM*, *15*(12), 1053–1058. doi:10.1145/361598.361623

Pavlich-Mariscal, J. A., Demurjian, S. A., & Michel, L. D. (2010). A framework of composable access control features: Preserving separation of access control concerns from models to code. *Computers & Security*, *29*(3), 350–379. doi:10.1016/j.cose.2009.11.005

Pavlich-Mariscal, J. A., Demurjian, S. A., & Michel, L. D. (2010). A framework for security assurance of access control enforcement code. *Computers & Security*, *29*(7), 770–784. doi:10.1016/j.cose.2010.03.004

Popp, G., Jurjens, J., Wimmel, G., & Breu, R. (2003). Security-critical system development with extended use cases. In *Proceedings of Software Engineering Conference*, (pp. 478-487). IEEE.

Sachpazidis, I., & Sakas, G. (2008). Medication intake assessment. In *Proceedings of the 1st international conference on Pervasive Technologies Related to Assistive Environments*. ACM.

Shehab, M., Bertino, E., & Ghafoor, A. (2005). Secure collaboration in mediator-free environments. In *Proceedings of the 12th ACM conference on Computer and communications security* (pp. 58-67). ACM.

Sommerville, I. (2006). *Software engineering*. Addison-Wesley.

SQUARE | Cybersecurity Engineering | The CERT Division. (n.d.). Retrieved from http://www.cert.org/cybersecurity-engineering/products-services/square.cfm

Sun, Y., Meng, X., Liu, S., & Pan, P. (2006). Flexible workflow incorporated with RBAC. In *Computer Supported Cooperative Work in Design II* (pp. 525–534). Springer. doi:10.1007/11686699_53

Tigris.org: Open Source Software Engineering. (n.d.). Retrieved from http://www.tigris.org/

Tolone, W., Ahn, G. J., Pai, T., & Hong, S. P. (2005). Access control in collaborative systems. [CSUR]. *ACM Computing Surveys*, *37*(1), 29–41. doi:10.1145/1057977.1057979

Vela, B., & Marcos, E. (2003). Extending UML to represent XML schemas. *CAiSE Short Paper Proceedings* (Vol. 74).

Zisman, A. (2007). A static verification framework for secure peer-to-peer applications. In *Internet and Web Applications and Services* (pp. 8–8). IEEE. doi:10.1109/ICIW.2007.11

KEY TERMS AND DEFINITIONS

Aspect-Oriented Programming (AOP): A programming paradigm which incorporates an additional modular unit, the aspect, which provides additional code that is automatically woven at specific points in the rest of the program by the compiler.

Continuity of Care Record (CCR): A document standard for health information typically used for Personal Health Records (PHR) with the intended purpose of information exchange. It provides a universal structure to the patient's information that can be utilized by different personal health records, applications and systems.

Discretionary Access Control (DAC): An access control model in which subjects have specific rights to access resources and can discretionarily give access privileges to other subjects to its own resources.

eXtensible Markup Language (XML): A structured language utilized for information exchange, standards and information validation via the use of schemas. Its extensibility allows developers and experts to design and implement common standards for the use across systems and domains.

eXtensible Access Control Markup Language (XACML): A security policy language designed from XML. Its specifications allow for a uniform policy language that can be enforced in heterogeneous systems. XACML policies can be enforced at a systems level, software level or information level, depending on the policies' targets and rules.

Health Insurance Portability and Accountability Act (HIPAA): HIPAA provides a US standard to protect the privacy of personal health information, including PHI.

Mandatory Access Control (MAC): An access control model in which objects have classifications that restrict their access. Only subjects with the adequate clearances can access those objects.

Protected Health Information (PHI): Under HIPAA, in clinical care and clinical research, PHI to date refers to a set of sensitive 18 data elements that must be protected or removed for deidentification purposes.

Role-Based Access Control (RBAC): An access control model in which permissions are assigned to roles, which in turn are assigned to users, who get all of the permissions of the assigned roles.

Chapter 16
Lessons from Practices and Standards in Safety–Critical and Regulated Sectors

William G. Tuohey
Dublin City University, Ireland

ABSTRACT

Many years of effort have been expended by experienced practitioners and academic experts in developing software engineering standards. Organizations should see it as a positive advantage—rather than as a costly negative necessity—when they are required to develop software to a recognized standard. A genuine, constructive program of measures to ensure compliance with an objective standard will achieve development process improvements that would otherwise be difficult to motivate and bring to fruition. This chapter provides an overview and comparison of a number of software engineering standards specific to safety-critical and regulated sectors. It goes on to describe implications and benefits that flow from these standards. Informed by current software engineering research, suggestions are made for effective practical application of the standards, both at individual project and at organizational level.

1. INTRODUCTION

Ten years ago, in a retrospective on data for 12,000 projects, Jones (2003) found that defect removal efficiency level was highest for "systems" software including safety-critical software, attributed in part to the use of reviews, inspections and intensive test activities; overall, good quality control was found to be the best indicator for project success. Since then, the world has become more and more dependent on software-intensive systems and there is a constant struggle to deal cost effectively with the great increase in system size and complexity while continuing to ensure safety (Larrucea, Combelles, & Favaro, 2013). Of course, most software is not safety-critical; indeed, "Nowadays, software is everywhere and is often built by relatively inexperienced programmers" (Abdulla & Leino, 2013) and "most programs today are written not by professional software developers" (Andrew et al., 2011). On the other hand, much software, including commercial applications, is built on top of middleware (Emmerich, Aoyama, & Sventek, 2008) which should certainly be well engineered.

DOI: 10.4018/978-1-4666-6026-7.ch016

This chapter is based on the belief that all software development can benefit from the experience of the safety-critical and similar communities, both in terms of successful past and present practices and in how future challenges are being tackled. The focus of the chapter is mainly on general practices and especially software engineering standards, but it is pointed out that there are many specific lessons to be learned also. For example, Durisic, Nilsson, Staron, and Hansson (2013) are concerned, for the automotive industry, with monitoring the impact on architecture of on-going changes but note that "…it is possible that the metrics are applicable to a wider range of software systems which rely on communication between different modules over multiplex buses". Apart from technical aspects, commercial benefits can be achieved by improving quality and, where applicable, regulatory practices in line with the criticality of the product (Meagher, Hashmi, & Tuohey, 2006).

There are very many published software engineering standards, some generic, some applicable within specific industrial sectors, some originating from particular procurement agencies, some developed by professional bodies, some relevant to certain categories of software (Tuohey, 2002). The multiplicity of standards, and the sometimes (necessarily) dry and legalistic style in which they are written, tend to make this material inaccessible to both software engineers and managers. Yet the standards may impose far-reaching constraints on day-to-day engineering work, on project procurement and management, and on an organization's commercial performance. This chapter presents a synthesis of a number of representative standards. This is achieved by first providing, with the aid of diagrams devised by the author, a somewhat detailed overview of the well known civil aviation standard RTCA/DO-178C (2011). It is hoped that this overview will be of practical utility to readers with particular interest in that standard. Next, more briefly, a selection of other standards is described in terms of their similarities and

differences with respect to that reference. It is believed that RTCA/DO-178C (2011) is a good point of reference in that it is mature, is used by a wide variety of development organizations, and is applicable to software of different levels of criticality. Remarks on the evolution of this standard from its predecessor RTCA/DO-178B (1992), to which backward compatibility was intended, are included in section 3.1.

Software engineering standards, together with supporting guidance and related material, constitute a considerable resource for the software developer. Some indications are provided in the chapter of the nature of the available material. A goal of the chapter is to provide practical suggestions on how to apply software engineering standards effectively. A particular effort is made to identify project- and organizational-level characteristics that follow from or are supportive of such standards. A key consideration is that measures taken should be effective and efficient.

Very often, software development takes place within a wider system development context. This is made explicit in some of the standards, especially those dealing with safety-related systems such as RTCA/DO-178C (2011) which, in comparison with RTCA/DO-178B (1992) and drawing especially on ARP4754A/ED-79A (2010), includes a significant amount of new material on the overall system. Evidently, this wider context may impact on or constrain how a software development is organized. While this chapter is mainly focused on purely software issues, some of these "wider" impacts are noted. In this context it is interesting to note the remark in Mashkoor and Jacquot (2011) that "by contrast [with older engineering disciplines] in software engineering, systems are sometimes developed by people with an incomplete knowledge of their particular domain".

In the past, rigorous software engineering standards were imposed mainly on certain kinds of software development, particularly those with safety impact or with stringent reliability requirements or of a clearly mission-critical nature (such as the on-board control of an unmanned satellite). However, the increasing use of software in all aspects of human activity means that the scope of the term "mission-critical" must be broadened. This is clear in the communications domain where software is increasingly used, for example, in financial transactions. In the particular case of civil aviation, the introduction of the aeronautical telecommunications network requires development of large amounts of communication software to certification standard. Consequently, there is a need to apply and extend what has been learned in applying strict software engineering standards in relatively specialized areas to much wider fields. This chapter is intended as a contribution to that effort.

Section 2 of the chapter provides context by outlining continuing challenges and current directions in software engineering. As a specific point of reference, it summarizes undesirable characteristics that are common within software development organizations, characteristics that can be removed or mitigated by effective use of software engineering standards. Section 3 provides an overview and comparison of selected standards. RTCA/DO-178C (2011) is treated in some detail, with more summary discussion of software standards for the space industry, for generic safety-related devices, for medical devices, and for defense. Section 3.3 provides a rough synthesis of the standards considered, including reference to current literature, and summarizes some business arguments for prioritizing certain of the processes that they address. Section 4 considers process improvement, informed by the preceding discussion of software engineering standards as well as by the research literature. Desirable organization characteristics are presented in section 4.1 and practical guidelines on how to achieve improvements are given in section 4.2. Section 5 identifies future and emerging trends with several references to current research literature. The final section highlights the main conclusions.

2. BACKGROUND

2.1 Context

Despite many advances, there remain considerable difficulties and challenges in the development of software. For example, in the context of methodologies for object oriented software, Ramsin and Paige (2008) identify the following problems:

1. *Requirements engineering is still the weak link, and requirements traceability is rarely supported …*
2. *Model inconsistency is a dire problem. UML has exacerbated the situation …*
3. *Integrated methodologies are too complex …*
4. *… agile methodologies are still not mature enough …*
5. *Seamless development … is not adequately appreciated …*

Reporting on traceability in submissions to the US Food and Drink Administration (FDA), Mäder, Jones, Zhang, and Cleland-Huang (2013) identified several problems including failure to explicitly formulate a Traceability Information Model (TIM), unclear definition of trace granularity, redundant traceability paths and trace information, failure to provide unique IDs across a project, important links missing, TIMs not included in information, poor presentation of large amounts of machine generated link data, and traceability as an afterthought. Clarifications of various aspects of traceability led to several changes in RTCA/DO-178C (2011) in comparison with its predecessor, an indication of the perceived importance of this topic. Cleland-Huang (2013) summarizes new challenges for requirements engineering due to the increased use of agile methods.

In the context of embedded systems, Sikora, Tenbergen, and Pohl (2012) identify problematic areas and open issues for requirements engineering under five headings: use of natural languages (important for legal contracts) versus models, support for high system complexity, quality assurance (verifiability, traceability, consistency), transition to architectural design, and interrelation with safety engineering. All but the last of these apply to all software systems.

Somewhat contrary to point (2) (above) of Ramsin and Paige (2008), Spinellis (2010) called for broad use of the UML notation and, while acknowledging the disparate ways in which UML is used, Dzidek, Arisholm, and Briand (2008) showed that working with a "good" UML tool during the software maintenance phase significantly increased the functional correctness of changes made.

Model-based software engineering is characterized by significantly greater levels of automation than traditional methods but its adoption has been disappointing due, according to Selic (2008), to problems of tool usability, interoperability and scalability but particularly to a "pervasive culture and psychology of traditional programming practice" that focuses on the programming process rather than on the end product and its usage. This seems consistent with weakness in requirements engineering, as observed above by Ramsin and Paige (2008), for example. In the same spirit, Jackson (2008) points out that the goal of software engineering tools should be to enable and support human understanding, particularly by reducing "perceived complexity" and "fragmentation-driven error". On a more positive note, Woodcock, Larsen, Bicarregui, and Fitzgerald (2009) found a "highly significant change" in that "the use of model checking has increased from 13% in the 1990s to 51% this decade".

As noted in section 1, in an analysis of 12,000 software projects from 1984 to 2003, Jones (2003) found that good quality control (use of QA teams, formal design and code inspections, pretest defect tracking) is the best overall indicator of a successful project. Such control is mandatory for many "critical" systems, as specified in related standards, but this is often not the case for many business function applications, nor for client-server and web-based applications.

2.2 Prior to Improvement: Typical Organizational Features

It is useful to recall, for later reference, some of the common problems that arise within software development organizations that have not undertaken a successful process improvement program. It would, of course, be an extreme case for an organization to exhibit all the problems in the following list:

1. Different groups with their own ways of working
2. Disparate tools and procedures (for example, in software design, inspections, releases)
3. Little effort to combine effectively people of different training, experience or expertise
4. Varying approaches to making use of existing company software or products
5. No agreed system of handling problems
6. Unsystematic approach to identifying and managing status of software and documentation
7. Individual projects show symptoms such as:
   a. Lack of effective traceability between project phases.
   b. Discrepancies between source code and design or other documentation.
   c. Tendency to proceed to implementation without firm requirements.
   d. Prevalence of the view that the "Main work is coding". In effect, use of the "code-and-fix" life cycle model with its attendant disadvantages of providing no means of identifying risks, assessing quality or identifying and eliminating anomalies early in the development process.
   e. Poor estimation of how much time and effort activities require.
   f. Inability to assess impact of changes.

3. OVERVIEW AND COMPARISON OF SELECTED STANDARDS

3.1 Software Considerations in Airborne Systems and Equipment Certification, RTCA/DO-178C

Document RTCA/DO-178B (1992) was until 2011, when it was replaced by RTCA/DO-178C (2011), the standard for development of airborne software in the Civil Aviation industry, for example see Avery (2011), Burger, Hummel, and Heinisch (2013), and Moy, Ledinot, Delseny, Wiels, and Monate (2013). As such its provisions have major *commercial* implications - without certification a system cannot "fly". Over the years, working group interpretations and clarifications have been produced on aspects of RTCA/DO-178B (1992) to assist in its application; some of these, in the form of Frequently Asked Questions (FAQs) and Discussion Papers (DPs), have now been revised and incorporated within the new standard RTCA/DO-178C (2011) while more appear in the supporting document RTCA/DO-248C (2011). In the context of software certification, the FAA has produced various documents on RTCA/DO-178B (1992), notably FAA Job Aid (1998) (revised 2004), a useful tool in applying aspects of the standard.

As noted in Pothon (2012), RTCA/DO-178C (2011) was intended to be backward compatible with its predecessor, and certainly not intended to "raise the bar" on what is required of software developer organizations. Also, as for its predecessor, it is objective-based and does not prescribe any particular software process (Daniels, 2011). Nevertheless, it was seen as important to update the standard so as to take advantage of advances in Software Engineering. Hence, three supplements have been produced, namely RTCA/DO-331 (2011), RTCA/DO-332 (2011), and RTCA/DO-333 (2011) which provide guidance, respectively, on Model-Based Development and Verification, Object-Oriented Technology and Related Tech-

niques, and Formal Methods. The continuing research focus on the use of models and on formal methods is noted elsewhere in this chapter. The intent is that additional supplements, in the same format and structure, may be produced in the future to accommodate further Software Engineering advances. Finally, as a further useful by-product, may be mentioned RTCA/DO-330 (2011) on "Software Tool Qualification Considerations".

As mentioned, in RTCA/DO-178C (2011) software is viewed as part of a wider system or equipment and the primary focus is on certifying that system or equipment. "System life cycle processes" result in the allocation of some of the system requirements to software. Also, as part of the "system life cycle processes", a system safety assessment process is carried out that categorizes software in terms of the consequences for the aircraft should the software behave anomalously. Five different categories or *levels* are identified according as anomalous software behaviour would cause or contribute to a failure of system function resulting, for the aircraft, in a condition of

- **Level A:** Catastrophic.
- **Level B:** Hazardous.
- **Level C:** Major.
- **Level D:** Minor.
- **Level E:** No Effect (i.e. No operational impact).

Six software processes (planning, development, verification, configuration management, quality assurance, certification liaison) are defined in RTCA/DO-178C (2011), and various objectives and outputs are identified for each process. Software levels are chiefly distinguished by the extent to which the objectives and outputs are applicable - this is defined explicitly by Tables A-1 to Table A-10 of Annex A ("Process objectives and outputs by software level") of RTCA/DO-178C (2011). A summary and comparison of the different levels is presented below; however,

Figure 1. Process summary for RTCA/DO-178C, software level D

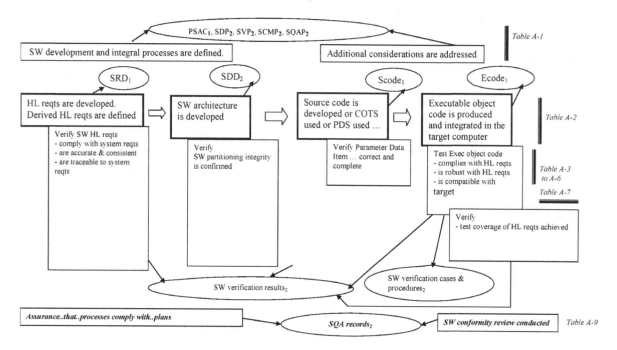

reference should be made to RTCA/DO-178C (2011) for complete details.

Guidelines are not offered in RTCA/DO-178C (2011) for Level E software, as by definition such software cannot impact on aircraft safety. A summary of the Level D software processes is provided in Figure 1 (apart from the software configuration management and certification processes, which are described separately in Figure 3). The following conventions and abbreviations are used:

- Rectangular boxes contain process objectives; ovals contain process outputs; block arrows show "flow" of development; other arrows relate objectives to corresponding outputs.
- Abutting/overlap of rectangles is used to link "verification" objectives with the activities they verify.
- "Table" references (to Annex A of RTCA/DO-178C (2011)) on right of the figure identify the process in question (A-

1: Planning, A.2: Development, A3: Verification (of software requirements), A4: Verification (of software design), A5: Verification of software coding & integration), A.6: Testing, A7: Verification (of verification), A9: Quality assurance).

- PSAC: Plan for software aspects of certification SDP, SVP, SCMP, SQAP: SW development, Verification, Configuration management, Quality assurance plans, respectively SRD, SDD: SW requirement and design data, respectively Scode, Ecode: Source and executable object code, respectively HL reqts: High-level requirements (similarly for LL in Figure 2).
- Subscripts 1, 2 denote, respectively, high & reduced degree of configuration control.
- "Additional considerations are addressed" could include *use of previously developed SW, tool qualification, alternative methods, product service history.*

Figure 2. Process summary for RTCA/DO-178C, software level C

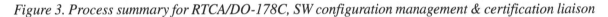

Figure 3. Process summary for RTCA/DO-178C, SW configuration management & certification liaison

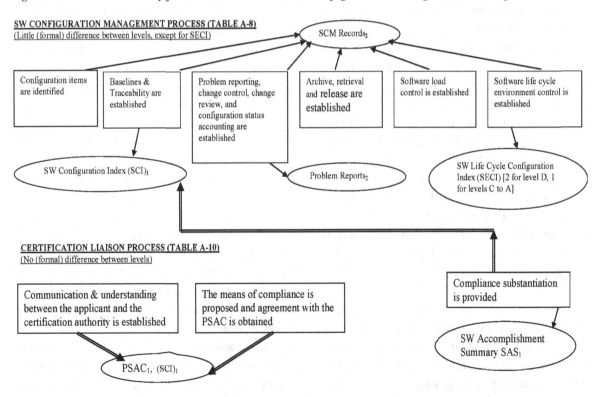

Figure 3 depicts the objectives and corresponding outputs for the software configuration management and certification liaison processes of RTCA/DO-178C (2011). For these processes, while there is little formal difference across software levels, there will, in practice, be major differences in terms of the depth of treatment.

The following aspects of RTCA/DO-178C (2011) Level D are highlighted:

- All 6 main software processes are present.
- There are no "mandatory" development standards, particularly for SW requirements, design and coding.
- The only "mandatory" tests are those to verify the (high) requirements stated in the SRD – no need for SW unit, SW integration, HW/SW integration or System tests *except* as needed to test these requirements.
- For non-test methods of verification (such as reviews or analyses) the focus is also on the SRD requirements. Apart from the specific objective of confirming SW partitioning integrity and a (new to RTCA/DO-178C (2011)) objective related to parameter data, there is no expressed need to use such methods to verify design or coding (for example, by code inspections).
- The possibility of using Commercial-Off-The-Shelf (COTS) software or Previously Developed Software (PDS), rather than developing new code, is allowed for.
- Verification of completeness of test coverage of SRD requirements is needed.
- Apart from SW quality assurance, there is no requirement for independence in satisfying process objectives.

Thus, for Level D software, attention is almost entirely on ensuring correct specification and complete verification of the high-level requirements. There are few explicit mandatory considerations to be taken account of regarding software design and implementation. In practice, of course, much depends on the chosen approach for handling high-level requirements; for example, whether very detailed analysis is performed in the requirements phase or deferred to the design phase.

Figure 2 provides a summary of the Level C software processes and is intended to facilitate comparison of Levels C and D. Additional requirements for level C over level D software are seen to include the following:

- Transition criteria, interrelationships, and sequencing among processes must be defined, as must the SW life cycle environment.
- Standards must be defined for SW requirements, design and coding.
- Tests must be extended to cover low level SW requirements.
- Non-test verification measures must be extended as follows to verify:
  ◦ SW plans and standards are consistent and coordinated.
  ◦ SRD (high level) requirements in greater depth than for Level D.
  ◦ SDD (low level) SW requirements, algorithm accuracy, SW architecture.
  ◦ Source code (typically including code inspections).
- Verification of process for production of executable code includes checks of test procedures & results, test coverage of low level requirements, and test coverage of SW structure (to an extent).

It can be seen that, for Level C software, there are many more verification measures than in Level D with the result that rather comprehensive visibility, tracing and checks are provided on the entire development process, and on planning and verification.

Diagrams similar to Figures 1 and 2 could be prepared to depict Levels B and A. The following summaries suffice for present purposes, however.

The main difference between levels C and B is the introduction of a requirement for independence in satisfying certain objectives. The specific additional requirements for level B over level C software are as follows:

- Plans, development standards, design data, and verification cases & procedures are required to be at a more stringent level of configuration control
- Tests against low level must be responsibility of independent personnel.
- Non-test verification measures must be extended to provide more thorough and independent checks of high- and low-level requirements, and of SW architecture and source code
- Extended checks of SW structure coverage; independent coverage checks
- SW QA extended to assure that process termination criteria are satisfied

Finally, a key difference between levels B and A is the introduction of even greater independence in satisfying verification objectives. Also, very complete checks on test coverage of SW structure are needed.

3.2 Other Software Engineering Standards (Not Comprehensive)

ESA Software Engineering Standards

The original ESA software engineering standards ESA PSS-05-0 (1991), "for all deliverable software implemented for the European Space Agency (ESA), either in house or by industry" provided a very clear and accessible definition of the "classical" approach to the conduct of software projects taking account, in particular, of "the software engineering standards published by the Institute of Electrical and Electronics Engineers (IEEE)". These have now been superseded by ESA ECSS-

-E--40 Part 1B (2003) and ESA ECSS--E--40 Part 2B (2005). A notable, and very useful element of ESA ECSS--E--40 Part 1B (2003) is the inclusion of "tailoring guidelines", taking account of technical, operational and management factors, to help decide what elements of the standard should be applied for a given project. For example, technical factors include novelty of the domain of application, complexity of the software and the system, criticality level, size of the software, reusability required of the software being developed, interface to system development projects, degree of use of COTS or existing software, maturity of the COTS and completeness or stability of the user requirements. It is clear that such factors arise in software projects of all kinds.

Functional Safety of Electrical/Electronic/Programmable ... Software Requirements, IEC 61508-3

Document IEC 61508-3 (1998) (edition 2, 2010) is one of eight parts of the IEC 61508 standard that is intended to set out "a generic approach for all safety lifecycle activities for systems comprised of electrical and/or electronic and/or programmable electronic components [E/E/PES] ... that are used to perform safety functions", and that has, as a major objective, facilitation of "the development of application sector standards". There are several sources of information on this standard, whose take-up and success appears to have been very considerable to date, available on the internet.

As in the case of RTCA/DO-178C (2011) software is categorized according to its criticality, in this case from SIL 1 (least critical) to SIL 4 (most critical), where SIL = Safety Integrity Level. Thus, SIL 1 corresponds roughly to Level D of RTCA/DO-178C (2011), SIL 2 to Level C, SIL 3 to Level B and SIL 4 to Level A; for completeness, one could envisage a level without operational impact (say SIL 0) corresponding to Level E of RTCA/DO-178C (2011). Unlike Level

D of RTCA/DO-178C (2011), there are explicit recommendations, across all SILs, for all the software development activities (architecture, design, coding, module testing, software integration testing, hardware/software integration testing). Also, coding standards are recommended for all SILs. The rigor required increases with the SIL number. It is noted that an overview of specific software engineering techniques and software measures referenced by IEC 61508-3 is provided in another part of the IEC 61508 standard.

FDA Guidance for Software Contained in Medical Devices

This item FDA (1998) (updated 2005) is one of a number of complementary FDA documents relating to software and medical devices; others are "General principles of software validation" and "Guidance for off-the-shelf software use in medical devices". The guidance in FDA (1998) "provides a discussion of the key elements of a pre-market medical device software submission [for regulatory review]" - "regulatory review" would correspond, approximately, to "certification review" in RTCA/DO-178C (2011) terms.

The term "level of concern", analogous to "software level" in RTCA/DO-178C (2011) and SIL in IEC 61508-3, is used in FDA (1998) "as an estimate of the severity of injury that a device could permit or inflict (directly or indirectly) on a patient or operator as a result of latent failures, design flaws, or using the medical device software". A rather clear procedure for "determining level of concern" is provided in Figure 2 of FDA (1998), from which a major, moderate or minor level of concern may result.

A table captioned "Documentation Based on Level of Concern" in FDA (1998) provides a contrast between the major, moderate and minor categories in terms of the software documentation to be provided to the regulatory reviewers (unlikely to be the total of the documentation produced). The corresponding table in the 2005 update appears not to be much different except notably that traceability analysis ("Traceability among requirements, specifications, identified hazards and mitigations, and Verification and Validation testing") is now made applicable for all levels of concern. From that table it can be seen that the requirements for software of "minor level of concern" are rather light. For example, they are less onerous than Level D of RTCA/DO-178C (2011) in terms of traceability and configuration control; however, as for Level D, the main focus is on requirement specification and corresponding verification (in this case by "functional test"). The requirements for "moderate" and "major" levels of concern" are more demanding, approximating, respectively, to Levels D and C of RTCA/DO-178C (2011) if independence in verification activities is not stressed.

Military Standard: Software Development and Documentation, MIL-STD 498

The purpose of MIL-STD-498 (1994) was "to establish uniform requirements for software development and documentation" in the context of U.S. defense contracts. While canceled in 1998, being replaced by the essentially identical EIA J-STD-016, it has continued in use outside of the military context, see Carrozza, Faella, Fucci, Pietrantuono, and Russo (2013) for example. At a minimum, this standard provides a comprehensive list of numbered points that can form the basis for agreement between software acquirer and developer, and subsequently can be used as a check for compliance. It is indicated in the standard that not all requirements may be applicable for a project, and some guidance is given on tailoring the standard to meet specific needs.

The core of MIL-STD-498 (1994) is a statement of "detailed requirements" broken down according to process. For example, requirements are stated for "System requirement analysis", "Software requirements analysis", "Software implementation and unit testing", "Software quality assurance" and so on. In fact, apart from the inclusion of system level activity, the processes considered are much as in Figure 2 of the present document (with some changes in nomenclature), that is, Level C of RTCA/DO-178C (2011). The requirements are rather high level and light on detailed technical guidance. However, attention is given to procedural and responsibility aspects such as the need for independence in some test work and in quality assurance.

An important and useful feature of MIL-STD-498 (1994) (similar to ESA ECSS--E--40 Part 2B (2005)) is that it is supported by several "Data Item Descriptions" (DIDs). The DIDs are essentially templates that provide detailed instructions on the expected content of the specific documents mandated by the standard.

Pharmaceuticals (Outline)

There is increasing automation using software-based systems in the pharmaceutical industry, with consequent increased regulation (see, for example, Meagher, Hashmi, and Tuohey (2006)). In response, the International Society for Pharmaceutical Engineering has published a related guide, GAMP4 (2001) and, more recently, GAMP5 (2008).

Railway (Outline)

The applicable standard, for software with safety impact, is EN 50128 (2011).

Nuclear (Outline)

Nevalainen, Halminen, Harju, and Johansson (2010) describe the issues arising for software certification in nuclear power plants. Further useful references are provided in Yoo, Jee, and Cha (2009).

3.3 Summary and Considerations for Application of the Standards

In the foregoing discussion of various software engineering standards RTCA/DO-178C (2011) was used as a reference against which to compare the other standards and, as such, described in rather greater detail. It was concluded that software level D, and particularly software level C of RTCA/DO-178C (2011) provide a useful, if coarse, means of characterising and distinguishing the standards considered. For highly critical software, software levels B and A of RTCA/DO-178C (2011) would be useful similarly as points of reference.

Software levels C and D have already been contrasted in section 3.1 but it is convenient to recall briefly their main similarities and differences and, in parallel, to note correspondences to key process areas (KPAs) of the Capability Maturity Model (CMM) (Paulk, Weber, Curtis, & Chrissis, 1995) – for the purpose of this chapter it is unnecessary to consider CMMI (CMM Integration). Comparison of Figures 1 and 2 shows that the software development and quality assurance processes (identified by Table A-2 and A-9, respectively, in these figures) are the same for software levels C and D. Similarly there is little difference for the software configuration management and certification liaison processes (see Figure 3). (The need in level D (and C) software for configuration management and quality assurance processes, and the importance given to software requirement management (definition, verification, change control) match closely to three of the six KPAs for CMM level 2). On the other hand, comparison of Figures 1 and 2 shows clear differences between levels C and D in the planning and verification processes. There are greater demands in level C on planning and control, on transition between project phases, on standards for performance of technical work, and on project coordination. In the verification process, there are significantly more objectives for level C in terms of more detailed testing but especially in pre-test verification activities (notably reviews and inspections) of requirements, design and source code. There are also several additional objectives related to "verification of verification", specifically addressing checking of test procedures, test results and of both requirement and design test coverage. (The more demanding requirements on the "planning" process for level C software are compatible with two further CMM level 2 KPAs (software project planning, software project tracking and oversight), while the introduction in level C of standards for performance of some technical work corresponds to (part of) the "software product engineering" KPA of CMM level 3. Finally, the introduction of several additional objectives in level C software for software verification, specifically for "non-test" verification activities, has a correspondence in the "peer review" KPA of CMM level 3.)

It is of practical concern to consider how software levels C and D "fit" in the context of investigations of the business case for software process improvements, particularly in terms of providing guidance on how to prioritise improvement measures. McGibbon (1999) provides a useful survey and summary of published literature on "success stories of cost savings resulting from software process improvements". The great majority of the literature surveyed by McGibbon report significant benefits due to <u>collective</u> software improvement measures, such as moving an organisation from CMM level 1 to level 2 - an analogous improvement at an individual project level would be to establish a capability to develop software to level D of RTCA/DO-178C (2011). Both primary (increased productivity, decreased rework) and secondary (more repeat business, reduced staff turnover, fewer release defects, etc) benefits are documented in McGibbon (1999). McGibbon also reports on the results of some <u>specific</u> process improvements and finds, in particular, very substantial benefits (better and earlier detection of errors, savings in test and integration, improved teamwork, etc) due to the introduction

of <u>inspections</u> ("formal processes that are intended to find defects in software and other products at or near the point of insertion"). This corresponds very well to the emphasis in level C software on "non-test" verification measures.

In Slaughter, Harter, and Krishnan (1998) there is a cost-benefit analysis of software quality improvements based on a detailed longitudinal (10 year) case study. A distinction is drawn in that paper between conformance costs of quality, further split between prevention costs (for example, arising from design reviews) and appraisal costs (for example, arising from (first time) code inspections and testing), and non-conformance costs of quality (due to all expenses incurred when things go wrong including all kinds of re-work). With reference to RTCA/DO-178C (2011), it is clear that there is a significant (but predictable) increase in conformance costs in going from level D to level C; the gain is that there will be a reduction in the (less predictable and less controllable) non-conformance costs. Slaughter, Harter, and Krishnan (1998) suggest that an organization should focus "on eliminating the major problems first" and "that much of the effect of quality improvement may be realized from the initial quality improvement efforts". For the particular case reported on, errors in job control language (JCL) were found to be the major source of defects so that a major initial effort was made to reduce such defects through measures including walkthroughs and mandatory use of JCL check software.

More recent work has, of course, been published on the business case for software process improvements, but the foregoing is a sufficient indication for present purposes. As a final, general point, it was found by Meagher, Hashmi, and Tuohey (2006) that "adopting and enhancing regulatory practices for existing or prospective suppliers of automated products into the pharmaceutical market can have significant business advantages in terms of both market share and competitiveness growth, and profit and sales improvement, above expectations".

RTCA/DO-178C (2011) and the other standards discussed in this chapter are focused primarily on the conduct of individual software projects. However, the importance of establishing a standardized, organization-wide approach to all software development activities is well recognized, for example Paulk et al. (1995). The following section discusses attributes of this wider context, within which particular, project-level software engineering standards can be applied.

4. SOLUTIONS AND RECOMMENDATIONS: SW ENGINEERING STANDARDS IN PROCESS IMPROVEMENT

4.1 Post Improvement: A Desirable State of Affairs?

Clearly, remedies should be put in place for the deficiencies listed in section 2.2. The following specific points are highlighted:

1. There should be a company-wide way of handling key aspects, particularly

    a. Problem reporting & corrective action; management of inconsistency, generally
    b. Configuration management (naming things, tracking, "publicising" status/ versions)
    c. Making releases to customers
    d. Ensuring a common look and feel to company outputs

Note: The importance of (a) and (b) is brought out in Jacobson (1992, p. 41) by the remark that "All larger systems will submit to changes during their life cycles. This fact must be considered in an industrial process approach to software engineering."

2. A standard, "tailorable" model for SW development projects should be in place. The model should be a practical and effective one:

    a. Taking account of the wider context, both technical and commercial, in which the organisation develops software. For example:

        ▪ A simple waterfall model is unlikely to suit the very common situation in which development of embedded software proceeds concurrently with development of its 'target' system; rather, some kind of evolutionary model is likely to be required, involving close cooperation between software and system developers. In a discussion of incrementally developed systems in Jacobson (1992), the point is made that "for the sequencing of development stages to be successful, it is essential to define stages which do not necessitate changing the results of earlier stages as the latter stages are introduced".

        ▪ At a technical level, in safety-related system developments, the importance of informing and involving software developers in the detail of system level issues is stressed in Leveson (1995), notably in sections 12.1.2 and 12.1.3.

        ▪ Commercially, it may be important that individual project plans take account of or be compatible with a company's financial reporting cycle.

    b. Embodying the applicable software engineering standards - as indicated in section 3 of this chapter, such standards specify the software development process in some detail, defining rules and guidelines to be observed to assure a satisfactory product in terms of technical scope and quality.

   c. Defining a practical, effective approach for the key *verification process*:

- Early planning (including agreement on acceptance criteria).
- Effective tracing between related activities.
- Adequate provision for reviews which, however, must be efficient; for example, a motivation for the tool environment presented by Arendt and Taentzer (2013) to relieve the effort in manual model reviews which are stated to be "very time consuming and error prone".
- Guidance on trade-off between schedule constraints and activity overlap (avoidance of excessive parallel activities).
- Support of the principle "*get it right first time*" to minimize leakage of errors to later reviews or tests.

   d. providing sound principles on how to carry out the inevitable trade-offs between what would be the ideal and what is sufficient for a project, subject to constraints on schedule and personnel.

3. The importance of the software requirements definition phase must be recognized and appropriate methods defined for requirement management, requirement analysis and requirement specification. In particular, a clear strategy should be in place to handle user (customer) requirements that are incomplete or immature.

4. There should be a common (organization-wide) set of tools & methods for various activities (requirements management, cod-

ing, design, testing, static analysis, ...). There should be openness to innovation & new ideas in the tools used but in a structured, efficient fashion - for example, for a project with very tight constraints it would be at least prudent to use techniques and tools that offer as little risk as possible from technical, cost and schedule perspectives.

5. Support should be provided for effective use of tools, including specific training and documentation. For example, guidance on the Ada language could indicate how it may be used in such a way that software integration activity is much abbreviated and such that detailed design and source code are almost identical. (See Jacobson (1992, p. 82) for a related discussion on integration testing of object-oriented systems).

Findings reported in Ropponen and Lyytinen (2000) provide an interesting perspective on the foregoing points. Based on a survey of project managers, the authors identify six components of software development risk and suggest ways of addressing them. The six risk components are "scheduling", "system functionality", "subcontracting", "requirements management", "resource usage and performance" and "personnel management". Methods of addressing these risks are categorized into "risk management practices" and "environmental contingencies", and it is found that the risks are impacted on differentially by these methods. In general, however, it is found that a mature, well-structured development process - as would follow from the points listed in this section - is of great importance in mitigating risk; specifically, the importance is brought out of conducting reviews before and during project execution, to cover both technical and project management decision-making. It is further found that risk is mitigated if the software developer has experience of the application area - this complements points made in this section regarding "taking account of the wider context ...". Generally, Ropponen and Lyytinen (2000) highlight the importance of including appropriate risk management measures as an integrated part of an organization's software development process.

4.2 Practical Guidelines to Achieve Improvement

Undesirable and desirable states of affairs were presented in sections 2.2 and 4.1, respectively. In this section some suggestions and indications are offered on how to bring about a "transformation" from the former to the latter. Note that in this chapter, the term Quality Management System (QMS) is used for the company-specific system that embodies an organization's approach to software engineering.

First, it should be seen as a major advantage if there are external requirements on an organization constraining it to develop software in accordance with a recognized standard such as RTCA/DO-178C (2011). Such requirements provide external pressure to bring about process improvements that could otherwise be difficult to achieve in the face of inevitable resistance and inertia. It is suggested that adoption of a suitable, specific software engineering standard, even where it is not mandatory, would be beneficial for an organization.

It is important to *prioritize those improvements that give organization-wide benefits within a relatively short time*. Summarizing from section 3.3, there should be in place:

1.   An effective *configuration/change management* system in place. It is suggested that all levels of staff, from trainee programmers to senior management should have access to this system, which should be straightforward to use, integrated as much as possible (for example, covering both software and documentation), and supported by adequate tools. A related priority is to establish a standard process for making releases. The importance of integrated configuration management

as a support for collaborative software development is discussed in Chu-Carroll and Sprenkle (2000).

2.   A *requirement management* process.
3.   A well-defined and sufficiently detailed process for *project planning & management*.
4.   An independent *quality assurance* function.
5.   An effective, efficient system for *peer reviews and code inspections*.
6.   *Technical standards & guidelines* for key areas (analysis, design, code).

There are many results from recent research that provide detailed guidance on how best to establish 1 to 6 and to put them into action. For example, Woodcock, Larsen, Bicarregui, and Fitzgerald (2009), in the context of adoption of formal approaches, note that "one of the main difficulties in engineering is the cost-effective choice of what to do and where. ... a formalism need not be applied in full depth to all components of an entire product and through all stages of its development, and this is what we see in practice. The various levels of rigor include the following:

- Best efforts to point out likely generic errors ...
- Near-guarantee that all potential errors of a certain class ... flagged ...
- Run-time checking of assertions ...
- Contractual programming, with assertions at major interfaces ...
- Lightweight formal methods"

The road ahead advocated by Ramsin and Paige (2008) for object-oriented methodologies (compactness, extensibility, traceability to requirements, consistency, testability of the artifacts from the start, tangibility of the artifacts, visible rationality) is clearly a good one for any methodology.

There is much current research in the areas of model building and model checking, including development of associated tools. Such tools should eventually replace or at least much improve manual processes; for example, Mattsson, Lundell, Lings, and Fitzgerald (2009) highlight "the heavy burden of manual reviews of architectural design rules described using natural languages". Păsăreanu (2011) provides an indication of the increasing availability of tools related to model checking, while Petrenko, Simao, and Maldonado (2012) report on model-based testing as offering testing techniques that are both rigorous and automatic. Queralt and Teniente (2012) presents an approach to verify and validate UML conceptual schemas. Maciel, Gomes, Magalhães, Silva, and Queiroz (2013) are concerned with improving the specification and enactment of model-driven development (MDD) processes by using process-centered software engineering concepts.

An essential practical aspect of setting up a QMS is the putting in place of materials needed in day to day engineering work (coding standards, procedures for carrying out code inspections and peer reviews, standards for test case generation and test implementation, guidance for use of tools such as compilers and code analyzers, document templates, etc). As indicated in section 3 there is, for published software engineering standards, a significant amount of both general and specific information on these topics that can be adapted for incorporation in a QMS.

In parallel to putting effective "coal-face" practices in place, it is essential to ensure that, at a higher level, the QMS is consistent with and supports the organization's strategic visions and plans. At this level, the ISO 9001 standard provides a useful and recognized QMS structure or template.

To summarize, it is important to establish a QMS that:

1. Has buy-in and active support from management.
2. Prioritizes areas that will maximize benefits (see (A) to (F), above).
3. Complies with relevant standards & is structured to facilitate "proof" of compliance;

is a good match to terminology, concepts, etc of relevant industry SW engineering standard(s) For example:

- Company level quality policy, regular senior quality meetings, main processes, etc – documented in a *Quality Manual*, based on ISO 9001 (1994) and/or CMM (Paulk et al., 1995)). For example, Kandt (2009) found that achievement of CMMI maturity level 3 contributed to reducing the number of defects and that it improved the assurance organization's effectiveness and efficiency, allowing more concentration on product assessments, and promoted less adversarial and more cooperative working relationships. Shull (2012) makes similar points on changing how "compliance assurance people" should work.
- Project level approach, guided by the CMM standard process Paulk et al. (1995) and/or RTCA/DO-178C (2011) and/or "SPICE" (ISO/IEC (1998/1999)) (and subsequent revisions) - documented in a *Projects Manual* (Martin, 1992).
- Lower level standards, specific procedures, document templates, etc consistent with RTCA/DO-178C (2011) and tailored from ESA ECSS--E--40 Part 1B (2003) and/or MIL-STD-498 (1994) or similar.

4. Preserves continuity (in product support) and conserves what works well of existing company standards and practices.
5. Supports re-use of previously developed software.
6. Ensures staff involvement in its production, review and maintenance.
7. Supports efficiency and avoids undue bureaucracy.
8. Promotes automation with appropriate tool usage.

9. Is supported by training programs, tutorials etc.
10. Is accessible and available to users (for example, through an organization's intranet).
11. Is flexible and open to (structured) future change and growth.

5. FUTURE RESEARCH DIRECTIONS

There has been much progress in learning how to develop software well in the past decades, as may be seen by consideration of elements 1 to 6 near beginning of Section 4.2. Some of these elements, particularly relating to management and supporting functions, are much better understood than before and good tool support is available. In more technical areas such as requirements engineering and verification, significant advances have been made but much remains to be done, including transforming research results and prototype tools into "industrial strength" technology.

In this regard, Ebert (2008) provides an interesting perspective on "software technology maturation" between 1983 and 2008. In particular, this author found that model driven development was (perhaps) starting to come into broader use but that formal development was still used to a limited extent only.

It is indeed the case that there is much current research on software models and some of this research has been cited earlier in the chapter. While different authors often have different concepts of what constitutes a model, Egyed (2011) presents a technology for incrementally detecting and tracking inconsistencies in software design models, which to date includes both UML (2 versions) and Matlab/Stateflow among others. Within UML and related modeling, Yue, Briand, and Labiche (2011) are concerned with how to reach the Platform Independent Model (PIM) after which the usual model driven architecture (MDA) principles are applicable. Lano and Kolahdouz-Rahimi (2013) is also an example of "main stream" MDA work, in this case making formal use of UML and Object Constraint Language (OCL).

Use of models has been reported in safety-critical and similarly demanding systems as, for example, Ferrari, Fantechi, Gnesi, and Magnani (2013) which is based on the use of Matlab; Yoo, Jee, and Cha (2009) which advocates the use of industrial strength formal methods and of visualization tools to facilitate use by domain experts; Carrozza, Faella, Fucci, Pietrantuono, and Rosso (2013); and Moy et al. (2013) which includes the interesting concept of "unit proof" as opposed to "unit test".

Jones and Müller-Olm (2011) in their preface to a special journal section on verification, model checking, and abstract interpretation make the important point that the overall goal to "provide mathematically well-founded techniques for sound semantic analysis". In this spirit, Hierons et al (2009) report on using formal specifications to support testing, viewing formal methods and testing as complementary with the idea of using formal model building support for test automation. Hatclif, Leavens, Leino, Müller, and Parkinson (2012) use now recognized ideas (preconditions, postconditions, invariants ...) to provide precise program specifications, to guide implementation, and to facilitate agreement between programmers in modular software development; the authors emphasize the advantages of formal specification languages. Finally, Abdulla and Leino (2013) describe key aspects and challenges of the "model checking and theorem proving category" of techniques for verification and validation.

Overall, key research thrusts are towards reliable automation of software development tasks as well as shifting development focus towards analysis at a higher level of abstraction. It is clear that there are lessons here also for software engineering educators.

6. CONCLUSION

This chapter has presented a comprehensive overview of the important civil aviation standard RTCA/DO-178C (2011) for airborne software and, with this as reference, has provided a comparative summary of a selection of other software engineering standards drawn from different industrial sectors. The content of these standards provided a basis and backdrop for a summary of what is undesirable and what is desirable in a software development organization's quality management system. Practical guidelines on how to put an effective quality management system in place were presented.

A specific conclusion is that Software Level C of RTCA/DO-178C (2011) represents a good baseline standard for software developments (aside from the certification process, which may not be relevant). A reasonable and achievable goal would be to build up a streamlined and uniform "Level C" capability throughout an organization. If this capability were in place, then it would be relatively easy to plan for and implement more demanding standards as needed within specific projects.

Achievement of a "Level C" or similar capability throughout an organization requires that an effective "quality management system" be put in place, reflecting the company's overall philosophy and approach, and embodying specific methods, work standards, templates, procedural steps, tools, training program and so on. Software engineering standards and associated documentation - guidelines, working group reports, and similar - provide much raw material from which to develop such quality management system items. A number of high priority improvement measures are identified in the chapter whose early implementation is likely both to maximize the primary benefit of return on the investment in software process improvement and also to give significant secondary benefits (such as repeat business and reduced staff turnover).

A major part of "conformance costs" are the costs incurred in carrying out peer reviews and code inspections, activities whose performance in practice is often less than optimal in terms of efficiency (both time and effort) and effectiveness. For example, there may be unsatisfactory integration with the configuration management process, too much reliance on "pencil and paper" methods, and a lack of follow-up to ensure that decisions have been implemented correctly. In addition to such research as that of van Genuchten, van Dijk, Scholten, and Vogel (2001) on supports for group work, it is hoped that the current intensive research on model building and model checking will yield major improvements in review effectiveness, accuracy and automation.

REFERENCES

Abdulla, P., & Leino, K. (2013). Tools for software verification. *International Journal on Software Tools and Technology Transfer*, *15*, 85–88. doi:10.1007/s10009-013-0270-5

Andrew, J., Abraham, R., Beckwith, L., Blackwell, A., Burnett, M., Erwig, M., ... Widenbeck, S. (2011). The state of the art in end-user software engineering. *ACM Computing Surveys, 43*(3), 21:1-21:35.

ARP4754A/ED-79A. (2010). *Guidelines for development of civil aircraft and systems*. SAE International & EUROCAE.

Arendt, T., & Taentzer, G. (2013). A tool environment for quality assurance based on the Eclipse modeling framework. *Automated Software Engineering*, *20*, 141–184. doi:10.1007/s10515-012-0114-7

Avery, D. (2011). The evolution of flight management systems. *IEEE Software*, *28*(1), 11–13. doi:10.1109/MS.2011.17

Burger, S., Hummel, O., & Heinisch, M. (2013). Airbus cabin software. *IEEE Software*, *30*(1), 21–25. doi:10.1109/MS.2013.2

Carrozza, G., Faella, M., Fucci, F., Pietrantuono, R., & Russo, S. (2013). Engineering air traffic control systems with a model-driven approach. *IEEE Software*, *30*(3), 42–48.

Chu-Carroll, M. C., & Sprenkle, S. (2000). Coven: Brewing better collaboration through software configuration management. *Software Engineering Notes*, *25*(6), 88–97. doi:10.1145/357474.355058

Cleland-Huang, J. (2013). Are requirements alive and kicking? *IEEE Software*, *30*(3), 13–15.

Daniels, D. (2011). Thoughts from the DO-178C Committee. In *Proceedings of 6th IET International Conference on System Safety*. IET.

Durisic, D., Nilsson, M., Staron, M., & Hansson, J. (2013). Measuring the impact of changes to the complexity and coupling properties of automotive software systems. *Journal of Systems and Software*, *86*, 1275–1293. doi:10.1016/j.jss.2012.12.021

Dzidek, W., Arisholm, E., & Briand, L. (2008). A realistic empirical evaluation of the costs and benefits of UML in software maintenance. *IEEE Transactions on Software Engineering*, *34*(3), 407–431. doi:10.1109/TSE.2008.15

Ebert, C. (2008). A brief history of software technology. *IEEE Software*, *25*(6), 22–25. doi:10.1109/MS.2008.141

Egyed, A. (2011). Automatically detecting and tracking inconsistencies in software design models. *IEEE Transactions on Software Engineering*, *37*(2), 188–204. doi:10.1109/TSE.2010.38

Emmerich, W., Aoyama, M., & Sventek, J. (2008). The impact of research on the development of middleware technology. *ACM Transactions on Software Engineering and Methodology*, *17*(4), 19:1-19:48.

EN 50128. (2011). *Railway applications - Communication, signalling and processing systems - Software for railway control and protection systems*. CENELEC.

ESA ECSS--E--40 Part 1B. (2003). *Software - Part 1: Principles and requirements*. European Space Agency (ESA).

ESA ECSS--E--40 Part 2B. (2005). *Software — Part 2: Document requirements definitions (DRDs)*. European Space Agency (ESA).

ESA PSS-05-0. (1991). *ESA software engineering standards. Issue 2*. European Space Agency (ESA). (superseded).

FDA. (1998). *Guidance for FDA reviewers and industry. Guidance for the content of pre-market submissions for software contained in medical devices. Version 1*. U.S. Department of health and human services, Food and Drink Administration (FDA), Center for devices and radiological health (CDRH), Office of device evaluation. (Updated 2005)

Ferrari, A., Fantechi, A., Gnesi, S., & Magnani, G. (2013). Model-based development and formal methods in the railway industry. *IEEE Software*, *30*(3), 28–34.

GAMP4. (2001). Good Automated Manufacturing Practice (GAMP) Guide for Validation of Automated Systems (4th ed.). International Society for Pharmaceutical Engineering (ISPE) (Updated as GAMP5 in 2008).

Hatclif, J., Leavens, G., Leino, K., Müller, P., & Parkinson, M. (2012). Behavioral interface specification languages. *ACM Computing Surveys*, *44*(3), 16:1-6:58.

Hierons, R., Bogdanov, K., Bowen, J., Cleaveland, R., Derrick, J., Dick, J., ... Zedan, H. (2009). Using formal specifications to support testing. *ACM Computing Surveys*, *41*(2), 9:1-9:76.

IEC 61508-3. (1998). *Functional safety of electrical/electronic/programmable electronic safety-related systems - Part 3: Software requirements.* International Electrotechnical Commission (IEC). (Second Ed.: 2010)

ISO/IEC TR 15504-1. (1998/1999). *Information technology -- Software process assessment (parts 1 to 9),* International Standards Organization (ISO)/ International Electrotechnical Commission (IEC) (Different parts have been updated in the past decade).

Jackson, M. (2008). Automated software engineering: supporting understanding. *Automated Software Engineering, 15*(3-4), 275–281. doi:10.1007/ s10515-008-0034-8

Jacobson, I. (1992). *Object-oriented software engineering: A use case driven approach.* Addison-Wesley.

FAA Job Aid. (1998). *Conducting software project reviews prior to certification.* Federal Aviation Authority (FAA). (Revised 2004)

Jones, C. (2003). Variations in software development practices. *IEEE Software, 20*(6), 22–27. doi:10.1109/MS.2003.1241362

Jones, N., & Müller-Olm, M. (2011). Preface to a special section on verification, model checking, and abstract interpretation. *International Journal on Software Tools and Technology Transfer, 13,* 491–493. doi:10.1007/s10009-011-0214-x

Kandt, R. (2009). Experiences in improving flight software development processes. *IEEE Software, 26*(3), 58–64. doi:10.1109/MS.2009.66

Lano, K., & Kolahdouz-Rahimi, S. (2013). Constraint-based specification of model transformations. *IEEE Software, 30*(3), 25–27.

Larrucea, X., Combelles, A., & Favaro, J. (2013). Safety-critical software. Guest editors' introduction. *Journal of Systems and Software, 86,* 412–436.

Leveson, N. G. (1995). *Safeware, system safety and computers.* Addison-Wesley.

Maciel, R., Gomes, R., Magalhães, A., Silva, B., & Queiroz, J. (2013). Supporting model-driven development using a process-centered engineering environment. *Automated Software Engineering, 20,* 427–461. doi:10.1007/s10515-013-0124-0

Mäder, P., Jones, P., Zhang, Y., & Cleland-Huang, J. (2013). Strategic traceability for safety-critical projects. *IEEE Software, 30*(3), 58–66. doi:10.1109/MS.2013.60

Martin, J.-P. (1992). *Qualité du logiciel et système qualité, l'industrialisation par la certification.* Masson.

Mashkoor, A., & Jacquot, J.-P. (2011). Utilizing Event-B for domain engineering: a critical analysis. *Requirements Engineering, 16,* 191–207. doi:10.1007/s00766-011-0120-5

Mattsson, A., Lundell, B., Lings, B., & Fitzgerald, B. (2009). Linking model-driven development and software architecture: A case study. *IEEE Transactions on Software Engineering, 35*(1), 83–93. doi:10.1109/TSE.2008.87

McGibbon, T. (1999). *A business case for software process improvement revised - measuring return on investment from software engineering and management.* Air Force Research Laboratory contract no. SP0700-98-4000.

Meagher, D., Hashmi, M., & Tuohey, W. (2006, November-December). Regulatory considerations and business implications for automated system suppliers. *Pharmaceutical Engineering,* 24-36.

MIL-STD-498. (1994). *Military Standard: Software development and documentation,* AMSC NO. N7069. US Department of Defense. (Cancelled but continues to be used).

Moy, Y., Ledinot, E., Delseny, H., Wiels, V., & Monate, B. (2013). Testing or formal verification: DO-178C alternatives and industrial experience. *IEEE Software, 30*(3), 50–57. doi:10.1109/MS.2013.43

Nevalainen, R., Halminen, J., Harju, H., & Johansson, M. (2010). Certification of Software in Safety-Critical I&C Systems of Nuclear Power Plants. In P. Tsvetkov (Ed.), *Nuclear Power*. InTech. doi:10.5772/9909

Păsăreanu, C. (2011). New results in software model checking and analysis. *International Journal on Software Tools and Technology Transfer, 13*, 1–2. doi:10.1007/s10009-010-0178-2

Paulk, M., Weber, C., Curtis, B., & Chrissis, M. (1995). *The Capability Maturity Model: Guidelines for improvement of the software process*. Addison-Wesley.

Petrenko, A., Simao, A., & Maldonado, J. (2012). Model-based testing of software and systems: Recent advance and challenges. *International Journal on Software Tools and Technology Transfer, 14*, 383–386. doi:10.1007/s10009-012-0240-3

Pothon, F. (2012). *DO-178C/ED-12C versus DO-178B/ED-12B: Changes and Improvements*. ACG Solutions.

Queralt, A., & Teniente, E. (2012). Verification and validation of UML conceptual schemas with OCL constraints. *ACM Transactions on Software Engineering and Methodology, 21*(2), 13:1-13:41.

Ramsin, R., & Paige, R. (2008). Process-centered review of object oriented software development methodologies. *ACM Computing Surveys, 40*(1), 3:1-3:89.

Ropponen, J., & Lyytinen, K. (2000). Components of software development risk: How to address them? A Project Manager survey. *IEEE Transactions on Software Engineering, 26*(2), 98–112. doi:10.1109/32.841112

RTCA/DO-178B. (1992). *Software considerations in airborne systems and equipment Certification*. RTCA Inc. [EUROCAE document number: ED-12B]

RTCA/DO-178C. (2011). *Software considerations in airborne systems and equipment Certification*. RTCA Inc. [EUROCAE document number: ED-12C]

RTCA/DO-248C. (2011). *Supporting Information for DO-178C and DO-278A*. RTCA Inc. [EUROCAE document number: ED-94C]

RTCA/DO-330. (2011). *Software Tool Qualification Considerations*. RTCA Inc. [EUROCAE document number: ED-215]

RTCA/DO-331. (2011). *Model-Based Development and Verification Supplement to DO-178C and DO-278*. RTCA Inc. [EUROCAE document number: ED-218]

RTCA/DO-332. (2011). *Object-Oriented Technology and Related Techniques Supplement to DO-178C and DO-278A*. RTCA Inc. [EUROCAE document number: ED-217]

RTCA/DO-333. (2011). *Formal Methods Supplement to DO-178C and DO-278A*. RTCA Inc. [EUROCAE document number: ED-216]

Selic, B. (2008). Personal reflections on automation, programming culture, and model-based software engineering. *Automated Software Engineering, 15*(3-4), 379–391. doi:10.1007/s10515-008-0035-7

Shull, F. (2012). Disbanding the process police: new visions for assuring compliance. *IEEE Software, 29*(3), 3–6. doi:10.1109/MS.2012.58

Sikora, E., Tenbergen, B., & Pohl, K. (2012). Industry needs and research directions in requirements engineering for embedded systems. *Requirements Engineering, 17*, 57–78. doi:10.1007/s00766-011-0144-x

Slaughter, S., Harter, D., & Krishnan, M. (1998). Evaluating the cost of software quality. *Communications of the ACM, 41*(8), 67–73. doi:10.1145/280324.280335

Spinellis, D. (2010). UML everywhere. *IEEE Software, 27*(5), 90–91. doi:10.1109/MS.2010.131

Tuohey, W. (2002). Benefits and effective application of software engineering standards. *Software Quality Journal, 10*, 47–68. doi:10.1023/A:1015772816632

van Genuchten, M., van Dijk, C., Scholten, H., & Vogel, D. (2001). Using group support systems for software inspections. *IEEE Software, 18*(3), 60–65. doi:10.1109/52.922727

Woodcock, J., Larsen, P., Bicarregui, J., & Fitzgerald, J. (2009). Formal methods: practice and experience. *ACM Computing Surveys, 41*(4), 19:1-19:36.

Yoo, J., Jee, E., & Cha, S. (2009). Formal modeling and verification of safety-critical software. *IEEE Software, 26*(3), 42–49. doi:10.1109/MS.2009.67

Yue, T., Briand, L., & Labiche, Y. (2011). A systematic review of transformation approaches between user requirements and analysis models. *Requirements Engineering, 16*, 75–99. doi:10.1007/s00766-010-0111-y

ADDITIONAL READING

Bensalem, S., Legay, A., & Bozga, M. (2013). Rigorous embedded design: challenges and perspectives. *International Journal on Software Tools and Technology Transfer, 15*, 149–154. doi:10.1007/s10009-013-0271-4

Bernardi, S., Merseguer, J., & Petriu, D. (2012). Dependability modeling and analysis of software systems specified with UML. ACM Surveys, 45(1), 48 pages.

Braude, E., & Bernstein, M. (2011). *Software engineering. Modern approaches* (2nd ed.). Wiley.

Bruegge, B., & Dutoit, A. (2010). *Object-oriented software engineering*. Pearson.

DeMarco, T. (2009). Software engineering: an idea whose time has come and gone? *IEEE Software, 26*(4), 95–96. doi:10.1109/MS.2009.101

Dunn, W. (2003). Designing safety-critical computer systems. *IEEE Computer, 36*(11), 40–46. doi:10.1109/MC.2003.1244533

Gandhi, R., Lee, S. (2011). Discovering multidimensional correlations among regulatory requirements to understand risk. *ACM transactions on Software Engineering and Methodology, 20*(4), 16:1-16:37.

Gomes, A., Mota, A., Sampaio, A., Ferri, F., & Watanabe, E. (2012). Constructive model-based analysis for safety assessment. *International Journal on Software Tools and Technology Transfer, 14*, 673–702. doi:10.1007/s10009-012-0238-x

Hayhurst, K., Holloway, C., Dorsey, C., Knight, J., Leveson, N., McCormick, G., & Yang, J. (1998). Streamlining software aspects of certification: Technical team report on the first industry workshop, *NASA/TM-1998-207648*.

Heineman, G., & Councill, W. (Eds.). (2001). *Component-based software engineering*. Addison-Wesley.

Hoare, C., Misra, J. (2009). Preface to special issue on software verification. *ACM Computing Surveys, 41*(4), 18:1-18:3.

Hoare, C., Misra, J., Leavens, G., Shankar, N. (2009). The verified software initiative: a manifesto. *ACM Computing Surveys, 41*(4), 22:1-22:8.

Jhala, R., Majumdar, R. (2009). Software model checking. *ACM Computing Surveys, 41*(4), 21:1-21:54.

Kernighan, B. (2008). Sometimes the old ways are best. *IEEE Software*, *25*(6), 18–19. doi:10.1109/MS.2008.161

Kleppe, A., Warmer, J., & Bast, W. (2003). *MDA explained*. Addison-Wesley.

McDaniel, P., & Nuseibeh, B. (2008). Guest editors' introduction: special section on software engineering for secure systems. *IEEE Transactions on Software Engineering*, *34*(1), 3–4. doi:10.1109/TSE.2008.10

McGregor, J., Muthig, D., Yoshimura, K., & Jensen, P. (2010). Guest editors' introduction: successful software product line practices. *IEEE Software*, *27*(3), 16–21. doi:10.1109/MS.2010.74

Shankar, N. (2009). Automated deduction for verification. *ACM Computing Surveys*, *41*(4), 20:1-20:56.

Sommerville, I. (2011). *Software Engineering* (9th ed.). Pearson.

Tiwana, A. (2008). Impact of classes of development coordination tools on software development performance: a multinational empirical study. *ACM transactions on Software Engineering and Methodology*, *17*(2), 11:1-11:47.

Tondel, I., Jaatun, M., & Meland, P. (2008). Security requirements for the rest of us: a survey. *IEEE Software*, *25*(1), 20–27. doi:10.1109/MS.2008.19

Van Lamsweerde, A. (2009). *Requirements engineering*. Wiley.

Van Vliet, H. (2004). *Software engineering. Principles and practice* (2nd ed.). Wiley.

KEY TERMS AND DEFINITIONS

Criticality Level: Characterizes expected direct and indirect effects of incorrect behavior in terms of gravity.

Formal Methods: Methods that are machine-processable and that have well-defined syntax & semantics.

Quality Management System: Embodies an organization's approach to SW engineering.

Requirement (Software): Prescription enforced by software only.

Requirement (System): Prescription enforced by software with other components.

Software Model: An abstract representation of a software system.

Tailoring of Standards: Process by which individual requirements of a standard are evaluated and made applicable to a specific project.

Chapter 17
The Role of Compliance and Conformance in Software Engineering

José C. Delgado
Instituto Superior Técnico, Universidade de Lisboa, Portugal

ABSTRACT

One of the most fundamental aspects of software engineering is the ability of software artifacts, namely programs, to interact and to produce applications that are more complex. This is known as interoperability, but, in most cases, it is dealt with at the syntactic level only. This chapter analyzes the interoperability problem from the point of view of abstract software artifacts and proposes a multidimensional framework that not only structures the description of these artifacts but also provides insight into the details of the interaction between them. The framework has four dimensions (lifecycle, concreteness level, concerns, and version). To support and characterize the interaction between artifacts, this chapter uses the concepts of compliance and conformance, which can establish partial interoperability between the artifacts. This reduces coupling while still allowing the required interoperability, which increases adaptability and changeability according to metrics that are proposed and contributes to a sustainable interoperability.

INTRODUCTION

Software systems are neither monolithic nor self-contained, but rather composed of models, specifications and working modules that are interrelated and need to fit together, usually by design. Decomposing a complex problem into several simpler and smaller artifacts, in a divide & conquer approach, is a fundamental software engineering technique to deal with complexity and improve design characteristics such as reusability, agility, changeability, adaptability and reliability.

An artifact can be any entity related to software engineering such as a concept, a specification or a program. The relationships between artifacts are essential to accomplish the goals of the software system but, at the same time, they create dependencies and coupling between them that translate into constraints and partially hinder these characteristics.

DOI: 10.4018/978-1-4666-6026-7.ch017

Therefore, software engineering can be described as the application of engineering principles, methods and techniques to computer-based artifacts under *quality* and *sustainability* constraints. Quality means that the problem needs to be decomposed into the right artifacts and with the right relationships (satisfying the problem's specifications with a good architecture). Sustainability (Jardim-Goncalves, Popplewell & Grilo, 2012) means that changes in the problem specification or in its context should translate to incremental changes in the artifacts and their relationships, implemented at a faster rate than the changes that motivated them.

Quality and sustainability are not exclusive of software engineering. A car, for example, is a system with several thousand components that need to fit together perfectly, under the same constraints. What distinguishes software engineering is the fact that, in most cases, artifacts are virtual (easy to create and to destroy), very flexible and exhibit a high variability rate. A computer program can be changed in minutes or even seconds, which is certainly not the case of physical products such as cars.

This chapter concentrates on the sustainability side of software engineering and specifically in the relationships between software artifacts, in an attempt to improve the characteristics mentioned above. The basic tenets that we will use are:

- If an artifact *A* has no relationship with an artifact *B* (does not depend on it), then *B* can change freely without impacting *A*. This is good for sustainability. Ideally, all artifacts should be completely independent (decoupled from all other artifacts);
- Artifacts that have no relationship cannot cooperate, which means that no value comes from decomposing a system into artifacts. Any system needs that artifacts establish relationships and cooperate, somehow. This implies some coupling between some artifacts.

These are conflicting goals. The fundamental problem that we are trying to solve is how to get the best compromise, or *how to minimize coupling as much as possible while still satisfying the problem's specifications*.

Relationships between software artifacts can be established at various levels, such as:

- *Conceptual*, involving concepts such as strategies, goals and architectures. For example, different artifacts may cooperate towards some common goal or complementary goals;
- *Documental*, which pertains mainly to specifications. For example, a given artifact must use the features defined by some standard;
- *Design*, entailing the way artifacts are used to build a composed system. For example, any software development method will include a decomposition of the problem's specification and a composition of already existing artifacts (such as a software library), trying to match both approaches;
- *Operational*, in which working artifacts (such as software modules) interact by sending messages. The receiver of a message must be able to understand the content of a message and the intention of the sender in sending that message.

This means that relationships between artifacts are not limited to message based interaction but can occur at any stage of the artifacts' lifecycle, right from their conception, even if the artifact never becomes active and able to interact, such as a concept or a document.

At the operational level, in particular, it is also important to check whether artifacts can be bound together in a single application or are distributed, most likely in different computers and probably implemented in different programming languages. Solutions to support the interaction between these artifacts are different in both cases. The concept underlying meaningful relationships between artifacts that exchange messages is designated *interoperability* (Wang, Tolk & Wang, 2009), which can be decomposed into two other important concepts relating two artifacts, *A* and *B*:

- *Compliance*. If *A* sends a message to *B*, then *A* must *comply with* the requirements established by *B* to accept messages (informally, must use only the features that *B* provides in its interface);
- *Conformance*. If *B* wants to be able to receive and to understand a message from *A*, then *B* must *conform to* what *A* expects as the receiver of that message (informally, must implement all the features that *A* may use).

The main goals of this chapter are:

- To establish a foundation layer of concepts upon which the relationship between artifacts in the context of software engineering should be based, both in functional and non-functional terms;
- To contribute to the systematization of these concepts, by proposing a generic framework to describe artifacts and their relationships;
- To discuss the role and importance of these concepts in software engineering, namely with respect to concerns such as reusability, agility, changeability, adaptability and reliability.

This chapter is structured as follows. We start by establishing a generic model for software engineering artifacts and presenting a multidimensional framework to describe them. Next, we introduce a basic interoperability model and the compliance and conformance concepts. We discuss the applicability of these concepts in establishing partial interoperability and present metrics to assess adaptability and changeability

in a quantitative way. We also show how compliance and conformance also apply between passive artifacts, such as specifications. Finally, we provide hints on future research directions and draw some conclusions.

BACKGROUND

We are particularly interested in compliance and conformance as the foundation mechanisms to ensure interoperability. These concepts have been studied in specific contexts, such as choreography (Bravetti and Zavattaro, 2009; Diaz and Rodriguez, 2009), modeling (Kim and Shen, 2007; Kokash and Arbab, 2009), programming (Läufer, Baumgartner and Russo, 2000; Adriansyah, van Dongen and van der Aalst, 2010) and standards (Graydon et al., 2012).

Interoperability is as old as networking. When two or more artifacts need to interact, an interoperability problem arises. Interoperability has been studied in the most varied domains, such as enterprise collaboration (Jardim-Goncalves, Agostinho & Steiger-Garcao, 2012), e-government services (Gottschalk & Solli-Sæther, 2008), military operations (Wyatt, Griendling & Mavris, 2012), cloud computing (Loutas, Kamateri, Bosi & Tarabanis, 2011), healthcare applications (Weber-Jahnke, Peyton & Topaloglou, 2012), digital libraries (El Raheb et al, 2011) and metadata (Haslhofer & Klas, 2010).

Compliance and conformance constitute only a fraction of the aspects involved in interoperability, necessary conditions to achieve integration between interacting artifacts. Other aspects, such as levels of interoperability (syntactic, semantic, and so on) and non-functional issues, must be considered as well. In general, a framework is needed to organize and to systematize the various aspects which interoperability entails. A typical approach to deal with it is to consider several layers of abstraction and complexity, along a single dimension. Other frameworks consider several dimensions, to detail issues and concerns.

One of the first systematizations of distributed interoperability was accomplished by the Open Systems Interconnection (OSI) reference model (Li, Cui, Li & Zhang, 2011), which considers seven layers, from Physical medium to Application. This pertains mostly to communication issues, with the objective of sending data and reproducing it at the receiver. How that data is interpreted by the receiver and how it reacts to it is left unspecified, encompassed by the topmost layer, Application. Since interoperability must not only deal with data exchange but also meaningful use of information (ISO/IEC/IEEE, 2010), we need to detail the Application layer.

Peristeras & Tarabanis (2006) proposed a framework (C4IF) based on four layers: Connection (basic use of a channel), Communication (data formats), Consolidation (meaning through semantics) and Collaboration (through compatible processes). It simplifies the lower levels (distinguishing only connectivity and communication) and refines the application layer, distinguishing information semantics from behavior.

Stamper, Liu, Hafkamp & Ades (2000) applied *semiotics* (the study of signs, stemming from linguistics) to the field of information systems and proposed a semiotic ladder, a layered structure in which each layer builds on the previous one (just like a ladder) in increasingly higher levels of abstraction and complexity. Besides the usual syntax and semantics, the pragmatics concept was used to refer to the effect caused by the reception of a message by a receiver. Empirics refer to the lower levels that use the physical world, encompassing details that are well established and less relevant to the understanding of interoperability as a whole. The social world tackle the higher levels, in which people become more involved.

Wang, Tolk & Wang (2009) described the LCIM framework, which follows the semiotic ladder in essence, with the interesting addition of a dynamic layer, which considers evolution along the system lifecycle.

The European Interoperability Framework (EIF, 2010) was conceived as a broad framework for the interoperability of public services and establishes four main interoperability levels (legal, organizational, semantic and technical), with an upper political context that should ensure compatible visions and aligned priorities.

Monfelt, Pilemalm, Hallberg & Yngström (2011) proposed a more detailed framework, by refining the social layer of the semiotic ladder to take care of higher level issues, such as risk (SWOT analysis) and dependencies on social and organizational aspects. This extends the basic OSI reference model with another seven layers, refining the issues that the OSI model leaves unspecified. This includes an organizational layer that refers to the effect that a message will have (pragmatic meaning of the message) and an adaptation layer that refers to the semantics of the message.

Other interoperability frameworks, particularly those conceived for complex systems, such as enterprises, try to complete the scenario by considering more than one dimension of interoperability, such as:

- Berre et al (2007) described the ATHENA Interoperability Framework (AIF), which builds on previous research, including the IDEAS and INTEROP projects (Chen, Doumeingts & Vernadat, 2008). This is a framework developed mainly for enterprise integration, in three dimensions: conceptual, application development and technical;

- Chen (2006) also proposed an enterprise interoperability framework, based on three dimensions (concerns, barriers and approach), reflecting not a mere framework but also a barrier-driven method (Chen & Daclin, 2007). This framework was the basis for the CEN EN/ISO 11354-1 standard (ISO, 2011), Framework for Enterprise Interoperability (FEI);

- Morris et al (2004) proposed an interoperability framework (SOSI) that includes not only the operational dimension but also the programmatic and constructive dimensions, which pertain to prior stages in the systems' lifecycle, namely conception and design, respectively;
- Ostadzadeh & Fereidoon (2011) presented an interoperability framework conceived for ultra-large-scale systems. It includes interoperability aspects from the previous frameworks, while adding an enterprise framework dimension;
- The European project ENSEMBLE (Agostinho, Jardim-Goncalves & Steiger-Garcao, 2011) embodies an effort to formulate a science base for enterprise interoperability (Popplewell, 2011). This involves discovering which interoperability problems exist in domains related to interoperability, such as social, applied and formal sciences, and identifying which are the relevant scientific areas underlying interoperability.

Existing interoperability frameworks tend to build on existing integration technologies, such as XML, Web Services and REST, focusing on how to integrate complex systems by using them. Therefore, they focus more on mimicking the current stage of development of these technologies than on modelling the interoperability problem in its true dimensions, independently from specific technologies. This chapter proposes to contribute to change this scenario.

DESCRIBING SOFTWARE ENGINEERING ARTIFACTS

Active and Passive Artifacts

These artifacts can range from pure abstract concepts to binary code applications and even, by extension, to computer-based physical resources. In this chapter, we are not concerned with the specific characteristics of each of them, but rather with how they can fit together in a framework that can guide the pursuit of our fundamental goal, stated in the Introduction.

Therefore, we devised a model and framework that are generic enough to describe any artifact, although not all artifacts relate with each other in the same way. We consider two fundamental categories of artifacts:

- *Active*, which have an active electronic existence that enables them to interact by exchanging messages. In some form or another, most of these artifacts correspond to computer programs;
- *Passive*, which have a recognizable existence but do not interact with others by messages, such as a model, a standard or the documentation of a computer program. Although there is no operational interaction, there is still a relationship. For example, a computer program (an active artifact) may implement a model that obeys a standard and has a given documented specification. These relationships are usually established at the human level.

We start by dealing with active artifacts and will extend to the passive artifacts in section "Extending compliance and conformance from interoperability to compatibility".

A Generic Active Artifact Model

To build generic artifacts, we use very simple model, depicted in Figure 1. It includes only two main kinds of basic artifacts, resources and services, a composition mechanism for resources and an interaction mechanism for services. In its simplicity, it can be used to build any arbitrarily complex software engineering artifacts, through recursive composition.

Figure 1. A generic active artifact model

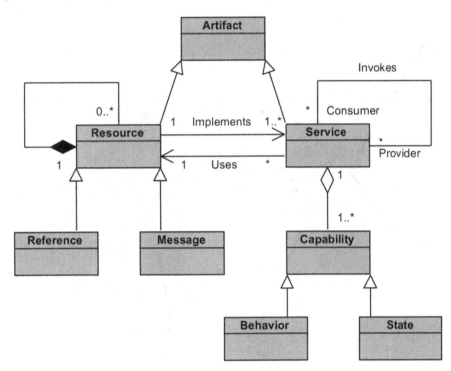

This model can be described in the following way:

- A *service* is a set of capabilities (involving behavior, state or both) that, as a whole, model some abstraction;
- A *resource* is the artifact providing the implementation of services and is either primitive or recursively composed of other resources. A resource implements at least one service (its *inherent service*), which exposes its inherent capabilities, but it can implement any number of other services;
- Services refer to each other by *references*, which are resources. Services interact by sending each other *messages*, which are also resources.
- Services engage in interactions in the roles of *consumer* and *provider*. The consumer sends a request message to the provider, which honors it and replies with a response message. All interactions relevant to the

context of this chapter occur between services;
- The inherent service of a resource exposes its basic capabilities, such as accessing state, invoking behavior or even dynamically deploying new services to that resource. The services implemented by a resource determine its set of capabilities.

Figure 2 illustrates this model, by considering two different computing contexts (two clouds) and the relationships between resources and services.

There are two resources, A and B, each with its own inherent service. In cloud *T*, a programmer invokes an operations in service A to deploy a new service, X. The resource is a virtual machine. In cloud *V*, another programmer develops, deploys and instantiates an application appliance that includes a resource B and a service Y that B implements. Service X then invokes service Y. A user (through a browser, for instance) invokes service X, but X could also be invoked by another service.

Figure 2. An example of application of the artifact model

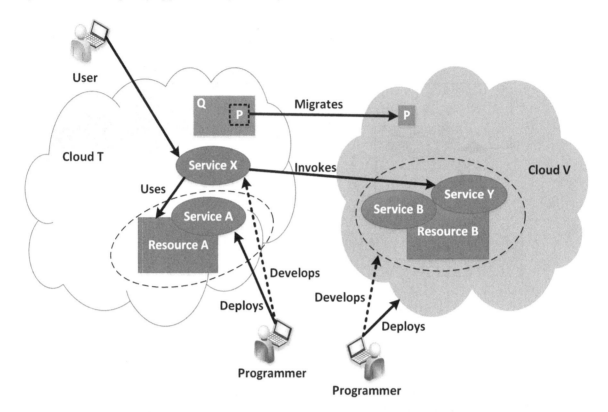

In cloud *T*, a resource *P* is a component of a container resource *Q*, but is migrated to the cloud *V*. This illustrates not only resource composition but also dynamic changes to resource composition trees. Resources can be created, destroyed or migrated.

References from a service to another will probably implement URIs, but not necessarily. Non-Internet networks, such as sensor networks, may use other addressing schemes and formats.

A Multidimensional Artifact Framework

The model of Figure 1 establishes the basic rules of artifact composition and interaction, but says very little regarding how artifacts are created and which are their characteristics. This section tries to shed some light on this matter by describing

a framework that organizes the characteristics of artifacts into orthogonal dimensions, to separate independent aspects and to provide a better understanding of artifacts.

We start by the fundamental dimension of any artifact, its lifecycle, which includes several stages that reflect different perspectives, from initial conception to final decommissioning. A software engineering method should animate the lifecycle, establishing guidelines on how the lifecycle should be traversed. There are many ways to organize the lifecycle and Figure 3 depicts our perspective, reflecting the stages most relevant for the purposes of this chapter. The loops support iteration of the lifecycle, to cater for changes and improvements.

The *architectural loop* is inspired by the Business Motivation Model (Malik, 2009) and laid around three main concepts:

Figure 3. Artifact lifecycle, with stages chained in changeability loops

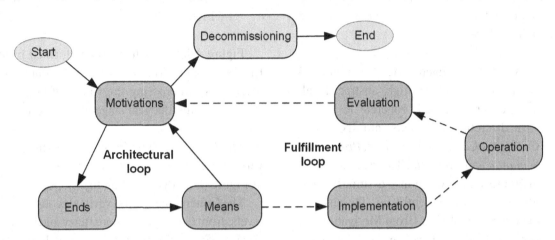

- *Motivations*, which emphasize the reasons behind the architectural decisions taken, in accordance with the specification of the problem that the artifact is designed to solve;
- *Ends*, which express the desires and expectations (e.g., goals and objectives) of the stakeholders for which the artifact is relevant;
- *Means*, which describe the mechanisms used to fulfill those expectations (e.g., actions).

These concepts embody three of the main questions about system development that were popularized by the Zachman framework (O'Rourke, Fishman & Selkow, 2003): *why* (motivations), *what* (ends) and *how* (means). The architectural loop should be iterated until a satisfactory specification exist for the outcome of each stage

The *fulfillment loop* in Figure 1 models subsequent stages and is based on the organization adopted by classical development methods, such as the Rational Unified Process (Kruchten, 2004):

- Ends and the Means of the architectural loop correspond roughly to the analysis and design stages of those methods;

- *Implementation* includes stages such as development, testing and deployment;
- *Operation* corresponds to animating (executing) the system;
- *Evaluation* measures KPIs (Key Performance Indicators) and assesses how well the system meets the expectations stemming from the motivations.

Iteration of the fulfillment loop goes back to Motivations, so that the artifact can be reconsidered again from the origin of the lifecycle. If the motivations are no longer deemed worthwhile, the lifecycle ends with the decommissioning of the artifact.

Figure 3 entails the first two dimensions (or axes) of our framework:

- *Lifecycle*, discretized into six stages. We consider only these (ignoring the Decommissioning stage), since they are the most relevant for our purposes;
- *Evolution*, discretized into versions, which stems from repeating the loops and expressing that the architecture can be successively changed and improved. Figure 5 illustrates this axis.

These axes are not enough to capture all the most important aspects and we need to consider two additional axes:

- **Concreteness:** Each stage in Figure 3 can be seen at a very high, abstract level, or at a very detailed, concrete level. We have discretized this axis into six levels: *Conceptual, Strategic, Tactical, Pragmatic, Semantic* and *Syntactic*. These are depicted in Figure 4. It is common to assume that the lifecycle axis itself embodies the abstract to concrete evolution (from Motivations to Implementation). However, we can have the Implementation stage at a conceptual level (ideas on how to do it) as well as the Motivations stage at an operational level (justification for the lowest level actions). Stages of the lifecycle and their level of concreteness are orthogonal concepts. This is why we have the Concreteness axis. In addition, we use *concreteness* instead of *abstraction* because, at the origin, each axis should correspond to a low level of detail (in what that axis is concerned). This means that, at the origin, the Concreteness axis should have a low value (which would not be the case if the designation of the axis was *abstraction*);
- **Concerns:** The focus words (*what, how, where, who, when, why*) in the Zachman framework (O'Rourke, Fishman & Selkow, 2003) are generic but do not address the entire focus range. Other questions are pertinent, such as *whence* (where from), *whither* (where to), *how much* (quantitative assessment) and *how well* (qualitative assessment). It is important to be able to express the dynamics of the architecture of the artifact, its quality (how good it is, quantitatively and qualitatively) and other concerns (performance, standards, security, reliability, and so on), both functional

and non-functional. This axis is illustrated by Figure 5.

Figure 4 lays down the plane formed by the Lifecycle and Concreteness axes. Each cell, resulting from crossing the values of both axes, represents one lifecycle stage at a given level of concreteness.

The Lifecycle axis (horizontal) exhibits one version (iteration) of the six main lifecycle stages of Figure 3, by disregarding the loops.

The Concreteness axis (vertical) considers six levels, from Conceptual, more fuzzy and abstract, down to Syntactic, more detailed and concrete. Each level in this axis is a refinement of the level above it, by including decisions that turn some abstract aspects into concrete ones. We consider these levels organized in two categories:

- *Decisions* taken, which define, structure and refine the characteristics of the artifact that we decide to include, at three levels:
  - The *Conceptual* level is the top view of the artifact and includes only global ideas;
  - The *Strategic* level details these ideas by taking usually long lasting decisions;
  - The *Tactical* level refines these decisions into shorter-term decisions. When considering the Evolution axis, tactical decisions are more prone to change than strategic ones;
- *Semiotics* (Chandler, 2007) is defined as the study of the relationship between signs (manifestations of concepts) and their interpretation (pragmatics), meaning (semantics) and representation (syntax). In this chapter, these designations are used in the following way:
  - The *Pragmatic* level expresses the outcome of using the artifact, most likely producing some effects, which

Figure 4. The Lifecycle and Concreteness plane

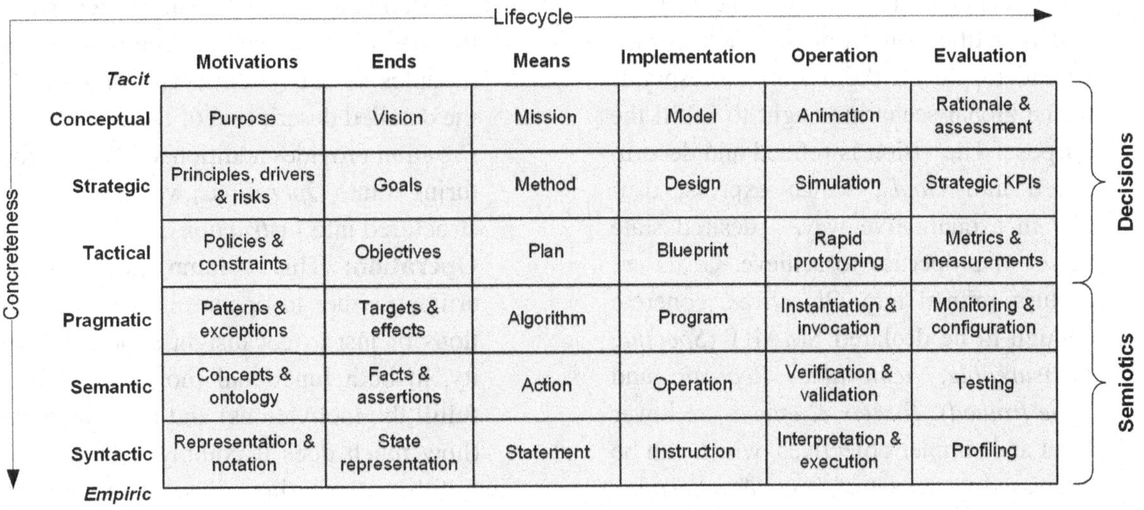

	Motivations	Ends	Means	Implementation	Operation	Evaluation	
Conceptual	Purpose	Vision	Mission	Model	Animation	Rationale & assessment	Decisions
Strategic	Principles, drivers & risks	Goals	Method	Design	Simulation	Strategic KPIs	Decisions
Tactical	Policies & constraints	Objectives	Plan	Blueprint	Rapid prototyping	Metrics & measurements	Decisions
Pragmatic	Patterns & exceptions	Targets & effects	Algorithm	Program	Instantiation & invocation	Monitoring & configuration	Semiotics
Semantic	Concepts & ontology	Facts & assertions	Action	Operation	Verification & validation	Testing	Semiotics
Syntactic	Representation & notation	State representation	Statement	Instruction	Interpretation & execution	Profiling	Semiotics

will depend on the context in which the artifact is used;

○ The *Semantic* level specifies the meaning of the artifact, using an ontology to describe the underlying concepts;

○ The *Syntactic* level deals with the representation of the artifacts, using some appropriate notation or programming language.

All these levels express a range between two opposite thresholds:

- **Tacit:** This is the highest level, above which concepts are too complex or too difficult to describe. It encompasses the tacit knowledge and know-how (Oguz & Sengün, 2011) of the people that conceived or manage the artifact, expressing their insight and implicit expectations and assumptions about the problem domain;

- **Empiric:** The lowest level, below which details are not relevant anymore and we settle for just using something that already exists and is known to work, such as a standard or a software library.

The plane in Figure 4, with each column and cells at each row, can be described in the following way:

- **Motivations:** This column is the result of requirements for the design of the artifact, acting as motivation and justification for the ensuing stages. At the top level, we have the *Purpose*, which reflects the essence and the reason for the existence of this artifact. The *Principles, drivers & risks* refine the *Purpose* by establishing not only the basic tenets that this artifact must obey but also the enablers and inhibitors that foster and limit the characteristics of the artifact (resulting probably from a SWOT analysis). The *Policies & constraints* perform a similar role, but at a lower level and with more detail, which in turn are refined into *Patterns & exceptions*, at the *Pragmatic* level. These are built with concepts, composed of others defined in the artifact's domain ontology, expressing the *Semantic* level. Concepts need to be represented by some notation, at the *Syntactic* level;

- **Ends:** This column corresponds to the expectations established for the artifact, under justification from the Motivations. At the top level, the *Vision* corresponds to the global scenario sought to fulfill the purpose. The vision is refined and decomposed into *Goals*, which express, usually in a qualitative way, a desired state or set of properties to achieve. Goals are in turn refined into *Objectives*, concrete enough to be declared SMART (*Specific, Measureable, Achievable, Realistic* and *Time framed*). *Targets & effects* are lower level and simpler objectives, which can be expressed as the set of *Facts & assertions* that define the state the artifact expected to be in. There must be some notation (a language, for example) that supports *State representation*, at the Syntactic level.

- **Means:** The cells in this column specify what needs to be done in order to meet the expectations, transforming the Motivations into Ends. The *Mission* is the top-level expression of the type of actions to carry out. The *Method* is a refinement of the mission by including the choice of an approach or paradigm. The method here refers to the high-level plan underlying a specific architecture and should not be mixed up with a software development method, which will be needed to traverse the artifact lifecycle. The *Plan* is a graph of steps that make the method concrete by choosing a set of techniques. The *Algorithm* is a set of actions that detail the plan by choosing the procedure to adopt. The *Action* is a coherent set of *Statements*, which are basic units of behavior;

- **Implementation:** This column specifies the tools, languages and procedures to provide an implementation of the Means, by transforming them into workable representations. The *Model* is an overall representation of the artifact, chosen to carry out

the mission and that is expressed in some notation, such as UML. The *Design* details the model, eventually structuring it into modules or subsystems. The *Blueprint* is the detailed description of the artifact. The *Program* provides additional details, structuring it into *Operations*, which in turn are structured into *Instructions*;

- **Operation:** This column exercises the artifact, either to operate it in real conditions or just to get insight about its quality, in both functional (how well does it fulfill the motivations) and non-functional (how much does it comply with a set of fulfillment criteria) terms. At the conceptual level, we can only imagine what will happen by *Animation* of scenarios and use cases (nevertheless, important to check global behavior). *Simulation* can abstract many details by using statistical models and still obtain meaningful insight into the behavior (in statistical terms). *Rapid prototyping* works with partial specifications (not statistical, but not fully implemented modules, either) and enables exercising some specific concerns (user interfaces, for instance). *Instantiation & invocation* correspond to exercising the completely implemented artifact, under real conditions, which involves *Verification & validation* of code and data semantics and *Interpretation & execution* of the code;

- **Evaluation:** This is the assessment of the Operation stage, so that changes and improvements can be introduced, if deemed necessary to better fulfill the purpose in the *Motivations* stage. At the top level, *Rationale & assessment* perform reasoning over the scenario and use case animation. *Simulation* provides the inputs to *Strategic KPIs*, which can be checked against the *Principles, drivers & risks* in *Motivations*. *Metrics & measurements* can check how well and how much the *Policies*

& constraints in *Motivations* are satisfied. *Monitoring & configuration* check events and serve as the basis for all higher-level evaluation procedures, assessing whether all *Patterns & exceptions* in *Motivations* are dealt with satisfactorily and causing reconfiguration of the artifact if not. At lower levels, monitoring must also perform *Testing* of semantic conditions and variables, as well as *Profiling* the interpretation or execution of instructions.

It is usual to consider a decision pipeline with strategic, tactical and operational levels. We did not include the latter in the Concreteness axis because we consider that an operational change does not entail a new version of the artifact but a mere change in configuration, something that must have been foreseen and allowed at the tactical level. These changes, if needed, are dealt with in the Evaluation column, at the Pragmatic level (Monitoring & configuration), looping back directly to the Operation column.

The Concerns axis expresses the various aspects under consideration in the artifact, both functional and non-functional and with a more qualitative or more quantitative emphasis, such as Social & legal issues, Organizational issues, Security, performance, and so on. The relevance of each concern depends on the artifact under consideration. Each concern corresponds to a Lifecycle and Concreteness plane.

The Evolution axis corresponds to a new batch of planes, expressing a new version of the artifact.

Figure 5 illustrates this multidimensional framework, with its various axes.

A method is needed to exercise the multidimensional interoperability framework, with the goal of designing, implementing or improving the artifact. The basic goal is to move every axis from its origin (essentially, ideas) to the other extreme, where everything is refined and established, eventually recycling the design through successive versions. The discussion of the method is outside the scope of this chapter.

THE INTERACTION BETWEEN ARTIFACTS

Now that we have a framework to describe artifacts, we need a framework to describe how active artifacts interact, by sending messages. We later show how the framework can cater for passive artifacts.

A Basic Interoperability Model

Artifacts are not made to stand alone. All artifacts have some form of interaction with another, which means that *interoperability* is one of the most fundamental issues that any artifact must deal with, in all its main slants, namely:

- Functionality (guaranteeing that one artifact understands the requests of another and reacts according to what is expected);
- Non-functional aspects (ensuring adequate service levels, resource management, security, and so on);
- Coupling (reducing it as much as possible, to avoid unnecessary dependencies);
- Reliability (maintaining interoperability, even in the presence of unanticipated failures);
- Adaptability (maintaining interoperability, even when interacting artifacts change their characteristics).

There is no universally accepted definition of interoperability, since its meaning can vary accordingly to the perspective, context and domain under consideration. Although limited to information, the 24765 standard (ISO/IEC/IEEE, 2010) provides the most cited definition of interoperability, as "the ability of two or more systems or components to exchange information and to use

Figure 5. The full framework, with Lifecycle, Concreteness, Concerns and Evolution axes

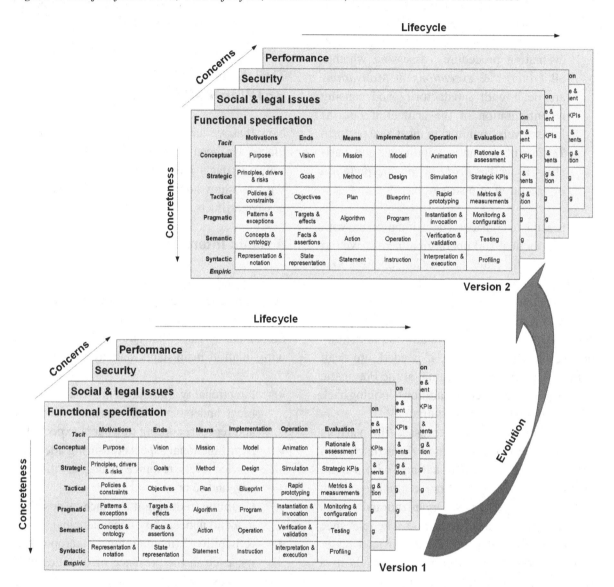

the information that has been exchanged". We can generalize this by defining interoperability as "the ability of two or more systems or components to exchange stimuli and to react to them according to some pattern or contract that fulfills all partners' expectations", but we need to detail what this really means.

Figure 6 illustrates a basic interaction scenario between two artifacts. An artifact *A*, in the role of consumer, sends a request to another artifact *B*, in the role of provider, which executes the request and eventually returns a response.

A and *B* are services implemented by two resources (or even by the same resource). Messages, requests or responses, are resources that migrate from the context of one service (the sender) to another (the receiver), becoming part of the structure of the resource that implements the receiver service.

Figure 6. Basic interaction between two artifacts, in the roles of consumer and provider. For simplicity, only the details of the provider are shown

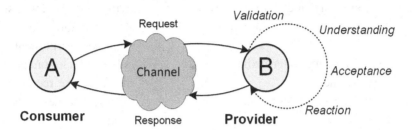

The goal of achieving such a simple interaction can be decomposed into the following objectives:

1. The request message reaches *B*, through an adequate channel, such as a network;
2. *B* validates the request, according to its requirements for requests;
3. *B* understands what *A* is requesting;
4. B is willing to accept and honor the request;
5. The reaction of *B* and the corresponding effects, as a consequence of honoring the request message are consistent with the expectations of *A* regarding that reaction;
6. The response message reaches *A* (probably through the same channel as the request message);
7. *A* validates the response, according to its requirements for the response;
8. *A* understands what *B* is responding;
9. *A* is willing to accept the response;
10. *A* accepts the response and reacts appropriately, as long as it is consistent with its expectations for that response.

This means that is not enough to send a request to a provider and hope that everything goes well (and the same regarding the response). We need to ensure that the request and response are validated and understood by the service that receives it.

In general, meaningfully sending a message (request and response reverse the sender and receiver roles) entails the following aspects:

- *Willingness* (objectives 4 and 9). Both sender and receiver are services and, by definition, are willing to accept requests and responses. However, non-functional aspects such as security can impose constraints;
- *Intent* (objectives 3 and 8). Sending the message must have a given intent, inherent to the interaction it belongs to and related to the motivation to interact and the goals to achieve with that interaction;
- *Content* (objectives 2 and 7). This concerns the generation and interpretation of the content of a message by the sender, expressed by some representation, in such a way that the receiver is also able to interpret it;
- *Transfer* (objectives 1 and 6). The message content needs to be successfully transferred from the context of the sender to the context of the receiver;
- *Reaction* (objectives 5 and 10). This concerns the reaction of the receiver upon reception of a message, which should produce effects according to the expectations of the sender.

The transfer aspects are usually the easiest to implement. The ability to transfer a message from the context of the sender to the context of the receiver requires *connectivity*, which can be seen at several levels, such as:

- *Message protocol*, which includes control information (for example, message type: request, response, etc.) and message payload (structured or just serialized as a byte stream);
- *Routing*, if required, with intermediate gateways that forward messages;
- *Communication*, the basic transfer of data with a network protocol;
- *Physics*, which includes communication equipment and physical level protocols.

To deal with the remaining aspects, ensuring interoperability, we need to resort to the artifact description framework depicted in Figures 4 and 5, in the following way:

- Willingness depends on the Concern planes (Figure 5). If concerns such as security, performance and levels of service impose constraints, then the receiver of a message needs to verify that the sender complied with those constraints (for example, if it is duly authorized to send messages to the receiver);
- The intent of the sender in sending a message is defined by the Ends and Motivations columns in Figure 4, which define what the sender wants to achieve and why, respectively. These must be acceptable to the receiver;
- The reaction of the receiver is specified by its Means column and must be in line with the expectations of the sender;
- For content, we need to keep in mind that:
  - A message is a resource (therefore, subject to the artifact framework);
  - Its Ends column reflects its state;
  - A service receives a message by assigning the message's content to the specification of the messages it is willing to accept, much like an actual argument is assigned to the formal argument of an invoked operation (in fact, the capabilities of services are usually discretized into operations, with their argument specifications);
  - Interoperability requires that this assignment (argument passing) is possible, which somehow indicates that the message received is in line with the type of messages that the receiver is expecting.

All these requirements and expectations entail coupling. Two completely decoupled and unrelated artifacts will not be able to understand each other messages. Therefore, some degree of previously agreed mutual knowledge is indispensable. The more they share with the other, the more integrated they are and interoperability becomes easier, but coupling also increases. This characteristic is known as *Integration*.

The interoperability between two artifacts can be seen in the perspective of each of the axes of the artifact framework, depicted in Figure 5:

- **Version:** Changing something can break interoperability. Ensuring that artifacts evolved while maintaining interoperability is a fundamental problem of software engineering;
- **Concerns:** Matching requirements and expectations against actual use must be achieved in all concern planes in Figure 5, not only on functional terms but also non-functional (security, quality of service, and so on). For example, a service provider can execute correctly a request but without the performance required by the consumer. In this case, interoperability is not achieved;
- **Lifecycle:** Coupling between two artifacts can be established by binding their lifecycles. The more stages are bound, the greater the coupling. This leads to a classification of artifact integration, discretized into the following values:

- ○ **Cooperative:** The artifacts need only establish a relationship in the Operation stage. This means that the provider can accept requests and honor them, but does not share procedures, goals or intentions of the consumer (and vice-versa). Integration is limited to these requests. This is typical of outsourcing contracts;
- ○ **Collaborative:** Each artifact has knowledge about the other's Means column and knows how it reacts to requests and responses, which means they can engage in a shared procedure. However, it does not know which are the goals and intentions of the interlocutor. This is typical of partnership arrangements;
- ○ **Aligned:** The interacting artifacts know about the goals of the other and can now share up to the Ends column. This usually corresponds to joint-ventures, in which interacting artifacts are aligned towards achieving common goals. But the motivations to engage in a joint-venture may be different or unknown;
- ○ **Coordinated:** The interacting artifacts now share all columns and are tightly integrated. This is typical of clusters of artifacts, under a joint governance, which can happen at very high level (such as enterprise information systems) or at low level (such as functions in a program).
- **Concreteness:** The interaction between two artifacts can be seen at various levels, from conceptual down to syntactic level, as depicted in Figure 4. For example, if we adopt a rapid prototyping approach, so that we can get a glimpse of how a system under design will behave, we will traverse the lifecycle of the system (and of its components) at the tactical level. Once a satis-

factory design is reached, the concreteness level can be increased (or the abstraction level lowered) until we reach the syntactic and empiric levels.

In practical cases, not all these combinations are used explicitly. In most software engineering activities, many aspects are dealt with in a tacit manner, which does not mean that they are not present, just assumed. At least, knowing that they exist helps to systematize thought, which is the main purpose of any framework.

Compliance and Conformance

In many cases, artifacts are made interoperable by design, i.e., conceived and implemented to work together. This can be seen in program development, in the design of classes and methods, as well as in distributed integration, using for example Web Services. In this case:

- Schemas are shared between interacting services, establishing coupling for all the possible values satisfying each schema, even if they are not actually used;
- Searching for an interoperable service is done by schema matching with *similarity* algorithms (Jeong, Lee, Cho & Lee, 2008) and ontology matching and mapping (Euzenat & Shvaiko, 2007). This does not ensure interoperability and manual adaptations are usually unavoidable.

The *interoperability* notion, as defined in this chapter, introduces a different perspective, stronger than similarity but weaker than commonality (resulting from using the same schemas and ontologies). The trick is to allow partial (instead of full) interoperability, by considering only the intersection between what the consumer needs and what the provider offers. If the latter subsumes the former, the degree of interoperability required by the consumer is feasible, regardless of whether the provider supports additional capabilities or not.

Interoperability (of a consumer with a provider) entails the following properties:

- *Compliance* (Kokash & Arbab, 2009). The consumer must satisfy (*comply with*) the requirements established by the provider to accept requests sent to it, without which these cannot be honored;
- *Conformance* (Kim & Shen, 2007; Adriansyah, van Dongen & van der Aalst, 2010). The provider must fulfill the expectations of the consumer regarding the effects of a request (including eventual responses), therefore being able to take the form of (*to conform to*) whatever the consumer expects it to be.

In full interoperability, the consumer can use all the provider's capabilities. In partial compatibility, the consumer uses only a subset of those capabilities, which means that compliance and conformance need only be ensured for that subset.

These properties are not commutative (e.g., if *A* complies with *B*, *B* does not necessarily comply with *A*) but are transitive (e.g., if *A* complies with *B* and *B* complies with *C*, then *A* complies with *C*).

Figure 7 illustrates this model. An artifact *A*, in the role of consumer, has been designed for full interoperability with artifact *B*, in the role of provider. *A* uses only the capabilities that *B* offers and *B* offers only the capabilities that *A* uses. Now, let us consider that we want to change the provider of *A* to artifact *X*, which has been designed for full compatibility with artifact *Y*, in the role of consumer. The problem is that *A* was designed to interact with a provider *B* and *X* was designed to expect a consumer *Y*. In other words, if we use *X* as a provider of *A*, *B* is how *A* views provider *X* and *Y* is how *X* views consumer *A*. How can *A* be made compatible with *X*, so that it becomes able to send it requests?

There are two necessary conditions:

Figure 7. Partial interoperability

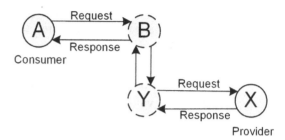

- *Compliance*. *B* must *comply with Y*. Since *A* complies with *B* and *Y* complies with *X*, this means that *A* complies with *X* and, therefore, *A* can use *X* as if it were *B*, as it was designed for;
- *Conformance*. *Y* must *conform to B*. Since *X* conforms to *Y* and *B* conforms to *A*, this means that *X* conforms to *A* and, therefore, *X* can replace (take the form of) *B* without *A* noticing it.

In this example, partial interoperability has been achieved by *subsumption*, with the set of capabilities that *A* uses as a subset of the set of capabilities offered by *X*. This inclusion relationship, without changing characteristics, is similar in nature to polymorphism used in many programming languages, but here in a potentially distributed context. It constitutes the basis for transitivity in compliance and conformance.

These properties are not commutative, since the roles of consumer and provider are different and asymmetric by nature. However, nothing prevents two interacting artifacts from switching roles in a symmetric way, by using and offering capabilities in a reciprocal fashion, which is typical of certain interaction protocols. These are just special cases.

The Usefulness of Compliance and Conformance

Compliance and conformance are general concepts, in terms of satisfying requirements and expectations, respectively, and can be applied to behavior, data or any other aspect of artifacts that somehow become related, at a high level of abstraction or at a low and detailed level. Wherever there is a relationship, compliance and conformance are present and can explain the degree of integration achieved.

Consider Figure 5 again, and in particular Figure 4, detailing the plane which describes life-cycle stages and concreteness levels. We say that an artifact *A* is *fully integrated* with artifact *B* if:

- Each cell of the Lifecycle-Concreteness plane in *A* complies with the corresponding cell of this plane in *B*, and each cell of the plane in *B* conforms to the corresponding cell of the plane in *A*;
- This is achieved for all the Concerns planes (including functional and non-functional concerns);
- This is achieved for the current versions of the artifacts.

This is equivalent to stating that compliance and conformance should hold for every corresponding aspect in artifacts *A* and *B*. Figure 8 illustrates this, with versioning omitted for simplicity.

Lower levels of integration can be achieved by relaxing some of these conditions, along each of the axes. This means considering them tacitly, instead of explicitly. For example:

- **Concerns:** Not all concerns are identically relevant. Security may require fulfilling every detail, but other concerns may have fuzzier rules, such as social and cultural issues, or vary dynamically, such as quality of service (in a best effort approach) or financial conditions (with dynamic optimizations);
- **Lifecycle:** The columns Implementation and Evaluation are less relevant to integration than the others, since different implementations can support the same opera-

tional specifications, and each artifact can be evaluated separately. Relaxing other columns leads to the integration scale with the values Cooperative, Collaborative, Aligned and Coordinated, as discussed in section "A basic interoperability model". The Operation column cannot be relaxed entirely, otherwise operational interaction will not be possible;

- **Concreteness:** By lowering the Tacit threshold (in Figure 4) and raising the Empiric threshold, we can adjust the levels of concreteness at which integration is considered. The most common case in programming is to deal explicitly with the syntactic level, with some incursions into higher levels in some columns (mostly Means and Implementation). Nevertheless, it also makes sense that integration at higher levels and at lower levels uses different technologies, by using APIs which raise the empiric level and hide the details of different implementations.

Note that compliance and conformance need not correspond to full interoperability. They only need to include the capabilities required by the specification of the artifacts.

The greatest advantage of partial compliance and conformance is the ability to tune up the right level of interoperability, achieving a balance between two opposing goals:

- Artifacts need to cooperate and therefore must share some set of specifications, so that information can flow between them, be properly understood and produce the intended effects;
- Shared specifications mean coupling and constraints to adaptability and changeability;

The more specifications are shared, the greater the coupling. Therefore, interoperability should

Figure 8. Artifact integration by compliance and conformance

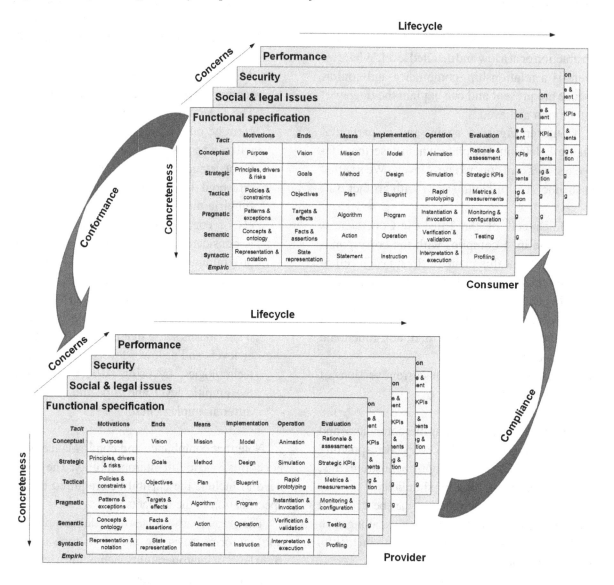

be reduced to the minimum compliance and conformance that are required and no more than that. On the other hand, an artifact that needs less compliance and/or less conformance has better chances of being able to participate with others in some choreography (Diaz and Rodriguez, 2009). This is an important aspect when discovering potential artifacts to interact with, during design.

To illustrate how compliance and conformance can promote adaptability and changeability, we now provide a way to quantify coupling and to show its impact.

An *adaptation* of an artifact is a set of changes made to that artifact to establish conformance with a new specification. This implicitly assumes that the artifact already exists and that the changes made correspond to a solution to bridge the differences between the previous and the new specification.

Adaptations can occur in any of the stages of the lifecycle of a service, at any concreteness level and involve any concern. An adaptation corresponds to a new version of the artifact. Figure 5 illustrates this.

Adaptations occurred during the operation stage are usually automatic and correspond to service *adaptiveness*, which expresses the capability of a service to adapt automatically and to reconfigure itself along time, within the limits of the flexibility of the operation stage. This is done with the help of the Monitoring & configuration cell in Figure 4, in the Evaluation column and Pragmatic row.

A*daptiveness* and *adaptability* (Delgado, 2012a) are different concepts. The latter expresses how easily a service can suffer a given adaptation at a given cell in the framework of Figure 5. As a metric, a value of 0 in adaptability means that the service cannot be adapted and is unable to conform to the new intended specification, due to some limitation, and a value of 1 means that the cost or effort of adaptation is zero. It depends essentially on two factors, defined quantitatively below:

- The *forward decoupling* D_F, the decoupling between the artifact and its provider. We use decoupling instead of coupling to reflect what we want to achieve;
- The *similarity* S between the specification of the artifact before and after the adaptation.

Adaptability *A* is directly proportional to these two factors:

$$A = D_F \cdot S \qquad (1)$$

This does not depend on which artifacts use the artifact being adapted and reflects only the ability (*can* it be adapted?) and the cost/effort to adapt it. The complementary adaptation question (*may* it be adapted?) is included in its *changeability* property *C* (Ross, Rhodes and Hastings, 2008), defined here as:

$$C = D_B \cdot D_F \cdot S \qquad (2)$$

or

$$C = D_B \cdot A \qquad (3)$$

in which D_B is the *backward decoupling* between the artifact being adapted and its consumers, expressing the impact of the adaptation of the artifact (which artifacts are affected). All these factors vary between 0 and 1. Any low value becomes dominant and imposes a low value on the changeability, which translates to a bad artifact architecture.

We use the artifact model of Figure 1, which states that resources can be recursively be composed of other resources and services are inseparable from and implemented by resources. Although not shown in this simple model, there must be a set of atomic resources (not composed of others), which the artifact ontology can be built upon. Therefore, there will be atomic and structured artifacts. We consider only the structural aspects and assume that adaptations and changes to atomic artifacts are also atomic.

Similarity between an artifact after adaptation and its previous specification is defined recursively in terms of the similarities of its components, as:

$$S = \begin{cases} 0 & changed\ atomic\ artifact \\ 1 & unchanged\ atomic\ artifact \\ \dfrac{\sum_{i \in T} S_i}{|T|} & structured\ artifact \end{cases}$$

$$(4)$$

where:

T - set of components of this artifact
S_i - similarity of component *i* (recursively) of the artifact

411

We define D_F (forward decoupling) of an artifact in the following way, in which the fraction represents the coupling (the sum of coupling and decoupling is 1 by definition):

$$D_F = 1 - \frac{\sum_{i \in P} \frac{Up_i}{Tp_i \cdot N_i}}{|P|} \qquad (5)$$

where:

P - Set of providers that this artifact uses

Up_i - Number of components that this artifact uses in provider i

Tp_i - Total number of components that provider i has

N_i - Number of providers this artifact complies with, in all uses of components of provider i by this artifact (that can replace provider i in what this artifact is concerned)

In the same manner, we define D_B (backward decoupling) of an artifact in the following way:

$$D_B = 1 - \frac{\sum_{i \in C} \frac{Uc_i}{Tc \cdot M}}{|C|} \qquad (6)$$

where:

C - Set of consumers that use that artifact as a provider

Uc_i - Number of components of this artifact that consumer i uses

Tc - Total number of components that this artifact has

M - Number of known artifacts that conform to this artifact and therefore can replace it

From (5), we conclude is that the existence of alternative providers to an artifact reduces its forward coupling and increases the forward de-coupling, because more artifact types (with which this artifact can comply) dilute the dependency.

In the same manner, from (6) we conclude that the existence of alternatives to this artifact as a provider reduces the system dependency on it, thereby reducing the impact this artifact may have on its potential consumers.

From (1) and (2), or (3), we conclude that adaptability and changeability increase with similarity (fewer changes are easier to carry out) and decoupling (less dependencies means less constraints). Reducing compliance and conformance to the minimum helps in increasing decoupling.

Reduced coupling also favor reusability (less constraints to reuse and broader base of applicability) and reliability (easier to find a replacement, since there are less requirements).

Extending Compliance and Conformance from Interoperability to Compatibility

We have defined interoperability as a meaningful exchange of messages, under compliance and conformance rules. This is valid only for active artifacts, which exchange messages. However, there are also passive artifacts, such as standards and other specifications, which do not exchange messages but with which other artifacts still establish compliance and conformance relationships.

To illustrate this, consider an artifact X that acts as consumer of a provider Y, in which both obey the clauses of an existing standard Z, with a specification S_Z. X and Y are active artifacts and their compliance and conformance can be described by Figure 7. Here, the specification of X (S_X) and the specification of Y (S_Y) are passive artifacts.

The relationship between S_X and S_Z can be described as:

- As a consumer, X will most likely use only a subset of the clauses of Z in the requests sent to Y;

- For each clause used, S_X must comply with what that clause requires from the consumer and should expect that the provider acts in conformance to what that clause determines for the provider.

The relationship between S_Y and S_Z can be described as:

- As a provider, Y must implement all the clauses of Z, in order to be able to honor any request that X may send;
- For each and every clause of Z, S_Y must conform to what that clause requires from the provider and should verify that the consumer acts in compliance with what that clause determines for the consumer.

There is no need to be a provider, but only a specification that must be obeyed, such as a law or a standard. Regulatory compliance is an example of this. Every organization is a consumer of that specification and must comply with its clauses.

Two notes on terminology:

- Interoperability is defined in terms of information exchange (as described in section "A basic interoperability model"). The term itself entails the concept of operation, which is exclusive of active artifacts. When passive artifacts are involved, we use the more generic designation of *compatibility*. The definition, in terms of capabilities, compliance and conformance is the same as for interoperability, with the exception that the set of capabilities can only include properties, definitions and other passive capabilities, but not the operations that provide the active part of artifacts;
- Many people use compliance and conformance interchangeably, in relation to standards and other specifications. The designation compliance is correct when the role performed is user or consumer (in

the context of that standard, as S_Z in the example above). When an artifact performs the role of server or provider, having to implement all the clauses of some standard or specification, the correct designation is conformance.

Passive artifacts still fit the framework of Figure 5. What happens is that not all cells are exercised. For example, a standard will not go beyond the Motivations and Ends columns, or the Means will be limited to the highest concreteness levels. In addition, not all concern planes will exist.

FUTURE RESEARCH DIRECTIONS

Compliance and conformance are basic concepts in interoperability and can be applied to all domains and levels of abstraction and complexity. Although work exists on its formal treatment in specific areas, such as choreographies (Adriansyah, van Dongen & van der Aalst, 2010), an encompassing and systematic study needs to be conducted on what is the formal meaning of compliance and conformance in each of the cells in Figure 5, building on previous work.

The interoperability framework presented in this chapter needs to be improved and made more complete, namely in the Concerns axis, to include additional concerns such as security and common domain-specific aspects and problems. Many have already been uncovered by other frameworks, namely by the project ENSEMBLE (Agostinho, Jardim-Goncalves & Steiger-Garcao, 2011; Jardim-Goncalves, Agostinho & Steiger-Garcao, 2012), which is systematizing the interoperability domain, establishing a scientific base for enterprise interoperability and developing an interoperability body of knowledge (Jardim-Goncalves *et al*, 2013).

The method to exercise the framework needs to be structured in a systematic way, with a comparative case study regarding other interoperability methods being used today, namely those that are part of specifications promoted by relevant bodies, such as the European Interoperability Framework (EIF, 2010) or standardized, such as the Framework for Enterprise Interoperability (ISO, 2011).

Cloud interoperability (Loutas, Kamateri, Bosi & Tarabanis, 2011) is a huge problem with ever increasingly importance. Cloud providers favor standardization but not homogeneity, since they need differentiation as a marketing argument. A study needs to be carried out on the suitability of compliance and conformance as a partial interoperability solution in cloud computing.

In spite of all its diversity, the Web is a homogenous network (all web devices use HTTP as the underlying protocol and text-based data description languages), with a very reliable backbone. This is not particularly suitable to newer networks and environments, such as the Internet of Things (Luigi, Iera & Morabito, 2010) and mesh network applications (Benyamina, Hafid & Gendreau, 2012), for which dynamic and adaptive protocols, as well as messages with binary formats, constitute a better match. The interoperability problem acquires completely new proportions and new solutions need to be envisaged, with particular emphasis on reliability in the context of *ad hoc* networks.

Current programming languages do not support structural compliance and conformance, in a way consistent with the artifact model described in Figure 1. Technologies based on Web Services and BPEL (or RESTful applications, for that matter) are not adequate to implement this model. Web Services do not include code nor structure, introducing relevant limitations in the WS-* stack with respect to the support of the *Motivations* (namely policies) and *Means* (namely, structural decomposition of goals and objectives). BPEL, like BPMN, is committed to the process paradigm. RESTful applications are strong in structure but weak in the information hiding and semantic gap principles.

We need a language and execution platform natively conceived for artifacts that combine resources and services. We have proposed a new architectural style, designated Structural Services (Delgado, 2012b), which combines the structural nature of REST with the service flexibility of SOA. We are developing a compiler and platform for a language (SIL – Service Implementation Language) (Delgado, 2013) to support natively this architectural style.

CONCLUSION

This chapter has discussed the importance of compliance and conformance as the foundational concepts for the interoperability problem in software engineering. What usually happens is that design interoperability mostly at the operation and syntactic levels, with higher abstraction levels and prior stages in the lifecycle of applications dealt with implicitly or manually, by resorting to documentation.

Frameworks are fundamental to get a better insight into the problem and a better grasp of how to organize the structure of possible solutions in a better way. This chapter adopted the following strategy:

- To define a model of generic artifacts, simply based on the idea that services expose capabilities and resources implement them. Using a model of resources and services (Figure 1) allowed us to describe all artifacts in the same, generic manner. We nevertheless distinguished artifacts into active and passive, due to their inherent differences in relationships (message-based for active artifacts and conceptual for passive artifacts);
- To systematize the description of artifacts, by developing a multidimensional framework, based on the lifecycle, levels of abstraction (or concreteness) and concerns. This framework supports the detailed description of any artifact, active or passive;

- To include interoperability in this framework, to express the relationship between artifacts, by considering the fundamental notions of compliance and conformance, asymmetric in nature;
- To analyze in detail what compliance and conformance mean, in the context of a single, basic interaction. Complex interactions can be obtained by structural composition;
- To discuss quantitative metrics that show how partial compliance and conformance can solve the fundamental interoperability problem: how to minimize coupling between artifacts while still maintaining the level of interoperability required by the artifacts under design.

Our main conclusion is that partial compliance and conformance constitute a better mechanism to ensure interoperability, because they provide lower coupling, than solutions today, which are either based on schema sharing or matching by similarity. In either case, coupling is established for the whole range of variability of the schema, even if only a part of that is actually used.

Although current software engineering tools and methods do not readily support this approach yet, we hope that this chapter makes a small contribution towards that goal.

REFERENCES

Adriansyah, A., van Dongen, B., & van der Aalst, W. (2010). Towards robust conformance checking. In *Business Process Management Workshops* (pp. 122–133). Springer.

Agostinho, C., Jardim-Goncalves, R., & Steiger-Garcao, A. (2011). Using neighboring domains towards setting the foundations for Enterprise Interoperability science. In *Proceedings of the International Symposium on Collaborative Enterprises* (CENT 2011). CENT.

Benyamina, D., Hafid, A., & Gendreau, M. (2012). Wireless Mesh Networks Design – A Survey. *IEEE Communications Surveys & Tutorials, 14*(2), 299–310. doi:10.1109/SURV.2011.042711.00007

Berre, A. et al. (2007). The ATHENA Interoperability Framework. In *Enterprise Interoperability II* (pp. 569–580). London, UK: Springer. doi:10.1007/978-1-84628-858-6_62

Bravetti, M., & Zavattaro, G. (2009). A theory of contracts for strong service compliance. *Journal of Mathematical Structures in Computer Science, 19*(3), 601–638. doi:10.1017/S0960129509007658

Chandler, D. (2007). *Semiotics: the basics.* New York: Routledge.

Chen, D. (2006). Enterprise interoperability framework. In *Open Interop Workshop on Enterprise Modelling and Ontologies for Interoperability.* Academic Press.

Chen, D., & Daclin, N. (2007). Barriers driven methodology for enterprise interoperability. In Establishing the Foundation of Collaborative Networks (pp. 453-460). Springer US.

Chen, D., Doumeingts, G., & Vernadat, F. (2008). Architectures for enterprise integration and interoperability: Past, present and future. *Computers in Industry, 59*(7), 647–659. doi:10.1016/j.compind.2007.12.016

Delgado, J. (2012a). Structural interoperability as a basis for service adaptability. In Adaptive Web Services for Modular and Reusable Software Development: Tactics and Solutions (pp. 33-59). IGI Global.

Delgado, J. (2012b). *Bridging the SOA and REST architectural styles. Migrating Legacy Applications: Challenges in Service Oriented Architecture and Cloud Computing Environments* (pp. 276–302). IGI Global. doi:10.4018/978-1-4666-2488-7.ch012

Delgado, J. (2013). Service Interoperability in the Internet of Things. In *Internet of Things and Inter-cooperative Computational Technologies for Collective Intelligence* (pp. 51–87). Springer. doi:10.1007/978-3-642-34952-2_3

Diaz, G., & Rodriguez, I. (2009). Automatically deriving choreography-conforming systems of services. In *Proceedings of IEEE International Conference on Services Computing* (pp. 9-16). IEEE Computer Society Press.

EIF. (2010). *European Interoperability Framework (EIF) for European Public Services, Annex 2 to the Communication from the Commission to the European Parliament, the Council, the European Economic and Social Committee and the Committee of Regions 'Towards interoperability for European public services'*. Retrieved July 26, 2013, from http://ec.europa.eu/isa/documents/isa_annex_ii_eif_en.pdf

Euzenat, J., & Shvaiko, P. (2007). *Ontology matching*. Berlin: Springer.

Graydon, P., Habli, I., Hawkins, R., Kelly, T., & Knight, J. (2012). Arguing Conformance. *IEEE Software*, *29*(3), 50–57. doi:10.1109/MS.2012.26

ISO. (2011). *CEN EN/ISO 11354-1, Advanced Automation Technologies and their Applications, Part 1: Framework for Enterprise Interoperability*. Geneva, Switzerland: International Standards Office.

ISO/IEC/IEEE. (2010). Systems and software engineering – Vocabulary. International Standard ISO/IEC/IEEE 24765:2010(E). First Ed. (pp. 186). Geneva, Switzerland.

Jardim-Goncalves, R., Agostinho, C., & Steiger-Garcao, A. (2012). A reference model for sustainable interoperability in networked enterprises: towards the foundation of EI science base. *International Journal of Computer Integrated Manufacturing*, *25*(10), 855–873. doi:10.1080/0951192X.2011.653831

Jardim-Goncalves, R., Grilo, A., Agostinho, C., Lampathaki, F., & Charalabidis, Y. (2013). Systematisation of Interoperability Body of Knowledge: the foundation for Enterprise Interoperability as a science. *Enterprise Information Systems*, *7*(1), 7–32. doi:10.1080/17517575.2012.684401

Jardim-Goncalves, R., Popplewell, K., & Grilo, A. (2012). Sustainable interoperability: The future of Internet based industrial enterprises. *Computers in Industry*, *63*(8), 731–738. doi:10.1016/j.compind.2012.08.016

Jeong, B., Lee, D., Cho, H., & Lee, J. (2008). A novel method for measuring semantic similarity for XML schema matching. *Expert Systems with Applications*, *34*, 1651–1658. doi:10.1016/j.eswa.2007.01.025

Kim, D., & Shen, W. (2007). An Approach to Evaluating Structural Pattern Conformance of UML Models. In *Proceedings of ACM Symposium on Applied Computing* (pp. 1404-1408). ACM Press.

Kokash, N., & Arbab, F. (2009). Formal Behavioral Modeling and Compliance Analysis for Service-Oriented Systems. In Formal Methods for Components and Objects, (LNCS), (vol. 5751, pp. 21-41). Springer-Verlag.

Kruchten, P. (2004). *The rational unified process: an introduction*. Pearson Education Inc.

Läufer, K., Baumgartner, G., & Russo, V. (2000). Safe Structural Conformance for Java. *The Computer Journal*, *43*(6), 469–481. doi:10.1093/comjnl/43.6.469

Li, Y., Cui, W., Li, D., & Zhang, R. (2011). Research based on OSI model. In *Proceedings of IEEE 3rd International Conference on Communication Software and Networks* (pp. 554-557). IEEE Computer Society Press.

Loutas, N., Kamateri, E., Bosi, F., & Tarabanis, K. (2011). Cloud computing interoperability: the state of play. In *Proceedings of International Conference on Cloud Computing Technology and Science* (pp. 752-757). IEEE Computer Society Press.

Luigi, A., Iera, A., & Morabito, G. (2010). The Internet of Things: A survey. *Computer Networks*, *54*(15), 2787–2805. doi:10.1016/j.comnet.2010.05.010

Malik, N. (2009). Toward an Enterprise Business Motivation Model. *The Architecture Journal*, *19*, 10–16.

Monfelt, Y., Pilemalm, S., Hallberg, J., & Yngström, L. (2011). The 14-layered framework for including social and organizational aspects in security management. *Information Management & Computer Security*, *19*(2), 124–133. doi:10.1108/09685221111143060

Morris, E., et al. (2004). *System of Systems Interoperability (SOSI), final report*. Retrieved July 26, 2013, from http://www.sei.cmu.edu/reports/04tr004.pdf

O'Rourke, C., Fishman, N., & Selkow, W. (2003). *Enterprise architecture using the Zachman framework*. Boston: Course Technology.

Oguz, F., & Sengün, A. (2011). Mystery of the unknown: revisiting tacit knowledge in the organizational literature. *Journal of Knowledge Management*, *15*(3), 445–461. doi:10.1108/13673271111137420

Ostadzadeh, S., & Fereidoon, S. (2011). An Architectural Framework for the Improvement of the Ultra-Large-Scale Systems Interoperability. In *Proceedings of International Conference on Software Engineering Research and Practice*. Las Vegas, NV: Academic Press.

Peristeras, V., & Tarabanis, K. (2006). The Connection, Communication, Consolidation, Collaboration Interoperability Framework (C4IF) For Information Systems Interoperability. *International Journal of Interoperability in Business Information Systems*, *1*(1), 61–72.

Popplewell, K. (2011). Towards the definition of a science base for enterprise interoperability: A European perspective. *Journal of Systemics, Cybernetics, and Informatics*, *9*(5), 6–11.

Ross, A., Rhodes, D., & Hastings, D. (2008). Defining changeability: Reconciling flexibility, adaptability, scalability, modifiability, and robustness for maintaining system lifecycle value. *Systems Engineering*, *11*(3), 246–262. doi:10.1002/sys.20098

Stamper, R., Liu, K., Hafkamp, M., & Ades, Y. (2000). Understanding the roles of signs and norms in organizations - A semiotic approach to information systems design. *Journal of Behaviour & Information Technology*, *19*(1), 15–27. doi:10.1080/014492900118768

Wang, W., Tolk, A., & Wang, W. (2009). The levels of conceptual interoperability model: Applying systems engineering principles to M&S. In *Spring Simulation Multiconference*. Society for Computer Simulation International.

ADDITIONAL READING

Athanasopoulos, G., Tsalgatidou, A., & Pantazoglou, M. (2006) Interoperability among Heterogeneous Services. In *International Conference on Services Computing* (pp. 174-181), IEEE Computer Society Press

Bell, M. (2008). *Service-Oriented Modeling: Service Analysis, Design, and Architecture*. New York: John Wiley & Sons.

Berkem, B. (2008). From the Business Motivation Model (BMM) to Service Oriented Architecture (SOA). *Journal of Object Technology, 7*(8), 57–70. doi:10.5381/jot.2008.7.8.c6

Dietz, J. (2006). *Enterprise Ontology: Theory and Methodology.* Springer-Verlag Berlin Heidelberg. doi:10.1007/3-540-33149-2

Earl, T. (2005). *Service-oriented architecture: concepts, technology and design.* Upper Saddle River, NJ: Pearson Education.

Earl, T. (2007). *SOA: Principles of Service Design.* Upper Saddle River, NJ: Prentice Hall PTR.

Earl, T. (2008). *Principles of service design.* Boston, MA: Pearson Education.

El Raheb, K. et al. (2011). Paving the Way for Interoperability in Digital Libraries: The DL.org Project. In A. Katsirikou, & C. Skiadas (Eds.), *New Trends in Qualitive and Quantitative Methods in Libraries* (pp. 345–352). Singapore: World Scientific Publishing Company.

Fewell, S., & Clark, T. (2003). Organisational interoperability: evaluation and further development of the OIM model. Defence Science And Technology Organisation. Edinburgh (Australia). Retrieved July 26, 2013, from http://www.dtic.mil/dtic/tr/fulltext/u2/a466378.pdf

Ford, T., Colombi, J., Graham, S., & Jacques, D. (2007) The interoperability score. In *Proceedings of the Fifth Annual Conference on Systems Engineering Research*, Hoboken, NJ.

Fricke, E., & Schulz, A. (2005). Design for changeability (DfC), Principles to enable changes in systems throughout their entire lifecycle. *Systems Engineering, 8*(4), 342–359. doi:10.1002/sys.20039

Ganguly, A., Nilchiani, R., & Farr, J. (2009). Evaluating agility in corporate enterprises. *International Journal of Production Economics, 118*(2), 410–423. doi:10.1016/j.ijpe.2008.12.009

Gehlert, A., Bramsiepe, N., & Pohl, K. (2008) Goal-Driven Alignment of Services and Business Requirements. In *International Workshop on Service-Oriented Computing Consequences for Engineering Requirements* (pp. 1-7), IEEE Computer Society Press.

Gottschalk, P., & Solli-Sæther, H. (2008). Stages of e-government interoperability. *Electronic Government. International Journal (Toronto, Ont.), 5*(3), 310–320.

Guédria, W., Chen, D., & Naudet, Y. (2009) A maturity model for enterprise interoperability. In Meersman, R., Herrero, P., & Dillon T. (Eds.) On the Move to Meaningful Internet Systems Workshops (pp. 216-225). Springer Berlin/Heidelberg.

Haslhofer, B., & Klas, W. (2010). A survey of techniques for achieving metadata interoperability. *ACM Computing Surveys, 42*(2), 7:1-37

Hoogervorst, J. (2004). Enterprise Architecture: Enabling Integration, Agility and Change. *International Journal of Cooperative Information Systems, 13*(3), 213–233. doi:10.1142/S021884300400095X

Hoogervorst, J. (2009). *Enterprise Governance and Enterprise Engineering.* Berlin: Springer-Verlag. doi:10.1007/978-3-540-92671-9

Juric, M., & Pant, K. (2008). *Business Process Driven SOA using BPMN and BPEL: From Business Process Modeling to Orchestration and Service Oriented Architecture.* Birmingham, UK: Packt Publishing.

Khadka, R., et al. (2011) Model-Driven Development of Service Compositions for Enterprise Interoperability. In van Sinderen, M., & Johnson, P. (Eds.), Lecture Notes in Business Information Processing, 76 (pp. 177-190), Springer Berlin Heidelberg.

Kingston, G., Fewell, S., & Richer, W. (2005). An organisational interoperability agility model. Defence Science And Technology Organisation. Edinburgh (Australia). Retrieved July 26, 2013, from http://www.dtic.mil/dtic/tr/fulltext/u2/a463924.pdf

Kurpjuweit, S., & Winter, R. (2009) Concern-oriented Business Architecture Engineering. In *ACM Symposium on Applied Computing* (pp. 265-272), ACM Press.

Lewis, G., Morris, E., Simanta, S., & Wrage, L. (2008) Why Standards Are Not Enough To Guarantee End-to-End Interoperability. In Ncube, C., & Carvallo, J. (Eds.) *Seventh International Conference on Composition-Based Software Systems* (pp. 164-173). IEEE Computer Society Press

Loutas, N., Peristeras, V., & Tarabanis, K. (2011). Towards a reference service model for the Web of Services. *Data & Knowledge Engineering*, *70*, 753–774. doi:10.1016/j.datak.2011.05.001

Markov, I., & Kowalkiewicz, M. (2008) Linking Business Goals to Process Models in Semantic Business Process Modeling. In *International Enterprise Distributed Object Computing Conference* (pp. 332-338), IEEE Computer Society Press.

Patten, K., Whitworth, B., Fjermestad, J., & Mahinda, E. (2005) Leading IT flexibility: anticipation, agility and adaptability. In Romano, N. (Ed.) *Proceedings of the 11th Americas Conference on Information Systems*, Omaha, NE, 11–14, Red Hook, NY: Curran Associates, Inc.

Perepletchikov, M., Ryan, C., Frampton, K., & Tari, Z. (2007) Coupling Metrics for Predicting Maintainability in Service-Oriented Designs. In *Australian Software Engineering Conference* (pp. 329-340), IEEE Computer Society Press.

Quartel, D., Engelsman, W., Jonkers, H., & van Sinderen, M. (2009) A goal-oriented requirements modelling language for enterprise architecture. In *International conference on Enterprise Distributed Object Computing* (pp. 1-11) IEEE Press.

Regev, G., & Wegmann, A. (2005) Where do goals come from: the underlying principles of goal-oriented requirements engineering. In *International Conference on Requirements Engineering* (pp. 353-362) IEEE Press.

Schekkerman, J. (2006). *How to survive in the jungle of enterprise architecture frameworks*. Bloomington: In Trafford Publishing.

Shroff, G. (2010). *Enterprise Cloud Computing: Technology, Architecture, Applications*. Cambridge, UK: Cambridge University Press. doi:10.1017/CBO9780511778476

Spohrer, J., Vargo, S., Caswell, N., & Maglio, P. (2008) The Service System is the Basic Abstraction of Service Science. In Sprague Jr., R. (Ed.) *41st Hawaii International Conference on System Sciences*. Big Island, Hawaii, 104, Washington, DC: IEEE Computer Society

Turnitsa, C. (2005). Extending the levels of conceptual interoperability model. In *IEEE Summer Computer Simulation Conference*. IEEE Computer Society Press

van der Aalst, W. (1999). Process-oriented architectures for electronic commerce and interorganizational workflow. *Information Systems*, *24*(8), 639–671. doi:10.1016/S0306-4379(00)00003-X

van Lamsweerde, A. (2001) Goal-Oriented Requirements Engineering- A Guided Tour. In *International Symposium on Requirements Engineering* (pp. 249-262), IEEE Computer Society Press.

Weber-Jahnke, J., Peyton, L., & Topaloglou, T. (2012). eHealth system interoperability. *Information Systems Frontiers*, *14*(1), 1–3. doi:10.1007/s10796-011-9319-8

Wyatt, E., Griendling, K., & Mavris, D. (2012) Addressing interoperability in military systems-of-systems architectures. In Beaulieu, A. (Ed.) *International Systems Conference* (pp. 1-8) IEEE Computer Society Press

Xu, X., Zhu, L., Kannengiesser, U., & Liu, Y. (2010). An Architectural Style for Process-Intensive Web Information Systems. In *Web Information Systems Engineering* (Vol. 6488, pp. 534–547). Lecture Notes in Computer Science Springer-Verlag Berlin Heidelberg. doi:10.1007/978-3-642-17616-6_47

Xu, X., Zhu, L., Liu, Y., & Staples, M. (2008) Resource-Oriented Architecture for Business Processes. In *Software Engineering Conference* (pp. 395-402), IEEE Computer Society Press.

KEY TERMS AND DEFINITIONS

Compatibility: Asymmetric property between a consumer *C* and a provider *P* (*C* is compatible with *P*) that holds if *C* is compliant with *P* and *P* is conformant to *C*.

Compliance: Asymmetric property between a consumer *C* and a provider *P* (*C* is compliant with *P*) that indicates that *C* satisfies all the requirements of *P* in terms of accepting requests.

Conformance: Asymmetric property between a provider *P* and a consumer *C* (*P* conforms to *C*)

that indicates that *P* fulfills all the expectations of *C* in terms of the effects caused by its requests.

Consumer: A role performed by an artifact *A* in an interaction with another *B*, which involves making a request to *B* and typically waiting for a response.

Interoperability framework: Set of principles, assumptions, rules and guidelines to analyze, to structure and to classify the concepts and concerns of interoperability.

Interoperability: A kind of compatibility in which compliance and conformance are assessed by exchanging messages between consumer and provider, during the Operation stage of their lifecycles (although they need to be designed in prior stages of the lifecycle).

Lifecycle: Set of stages that an artifact goes through, starting with a motivation to build it and ending with its decommissioning. Different versions of an artifact result from iterations of these stages, in which the artifact loops back to an earlier stage so that changes can be made.

Provider: A role performed by an artifact *B* in an interaction with another *A*, which involves waiting for a request from *A*, honoring it and typically sending a response to *A*.

Chapter 18
T–Way Testing Strategies:
Issues, Challenges, and Practices

Kamal Z. Zamli
Universiti Malaysia Pahang, Malaysia

AbdulRahman A. Alsewari
Universiti Malaysia Pahang, Malaysia

Mohammed I Younis
University of Baghdad, Iraq

ABSTRACT

In line with the advancement of hardware technology and increasing consumer demands for new functionalities and innovations, software applications grew tremendously in term of size over the last decade. This sudden increase in size has a profound impact as far as testing is concerned. Here, more and more unwanted interactions among software systems components, hardware, and operating system are to be expected, rendering increased possibility of faults. To address this issue, many useful interaction-based testing techniques (termed t-way strategies) have been developed in the literature. As an effort to promote awareness and encourage its usage, this chapter surveys the current state-of-the-art and reviews the state-of-practices in the field. In particular, unlike earlier work, this chapter also highlights the different possible adoptions of t-way strategies including uniform interaction, variable strength interaction, and input-output-based relation, that is, to help test engineers make informed decision on the actual use of t-way strategies.

1. INTRODUCTION

As an activity to ensure conformance and quality, software testing is an important phase in the software development lifecycle. Although desirable, exhaustive testing is practically impossible owing to the resource and timing constraints.

As a result, many sampling strategies have been developed including that of equivalence partitioning, boundary value, cause and effect graphing as well as decision table mapping. While these traditional static and dynamic sampling strategies are useful for fault detection and prevention, they are not sufficiently effective to tackle bugs due

DOI: 10.4018/978-1-4666-6026-7.ch018

to interaction. Addressing this issue, many t-way strategies (whereby t indicates the interaction strength) have been developed in the literature in the last 15 years. Here, t-way strategies help to search as well as to generate a set of test cases to complete the test suite that covers the required interaction strength at least once from a typically large space of possible test values.

Despite offering significant advantages in terms of test suite reduction (as well as testing costs), t-way testing strategies are not widely adopted in industry (Czerwonka, 2006). Thus, it is important to promote awareness as well as practical use of t-way strategies in order to encourage their applications as well as improve their acceptance within the mainstreams software testing community.

The remaining of this chapter is organized as follows. Section II highlights the fundamentals of t-way testing strategies. Section III surveys the existing t-way strategies. Section IV elaborates on the state-of-practice. Finally, Section V states our conclusion.

2. T-WAY TESTING FUNDAMENTALS

In general, t-way testing can be abstracted to a covering array. Throughout out this chapter, the symbols: p, v, and t are used to refer to number of parameters (or factor), values (or levels) and interaction strength for the covering array respectively. Earlier works suggested two definitions for describing the covering array (Cohen, 2004). The first definition is based on whether or not the numbers of values for each parameter are equal. If the number of values is equal (i.e. uniformly distributed), then the test suite is called Coverage Array (CA). Now, if the number of values in non-uniform, then the test suite is called Mixed Coverage Array (MCA). Unlike earlier work in the literature, this chapter unifies the CA and MCA notations in order to include that of variable

strength covering array (VCA), and input output based covering array (IOR).

Normally, the CA takes parameters of N, t, p, and v respectively (i.e. $CA(N, t, v^p)$). For example, $CA(9, 2, 2^4)$ represents a test suite consisting of 9x4 arrays (i.e. the rows represent the size of test cases (N), and the column represents the parameter (p)). Here, the test suite also covers pairwise interaction for a system with 4 2 valued parameter (see Figure 1). When the CA is the most optimal result, the covering array can be rewritten as $CAN(N, t, v^p)$.

Alternatively, MCA takes parameters of N, t, and Configuration (C). In this case, C captures the parameters and values of each configuration in the following format: $v_1^{p1} v_2^{p2}, \ldots v_n^{pn}$ indicating that there are p1 parameters with v1 values, p2 parameters with v2 values, and so on. For example, $MCA(8, 3, 2^3 1^1)$ indicates the test size of 8 which covers 3-way interaction. Here, the configuration takes 4 parameters: 3 2 valued parameter and 1 1 valued parameter (see Figure 2).

In the case of VCA, the parameter consists of N, t, C, and Set (S) (i.e. $VCA(N, t, C, S)$). Similar to MCA, N, t, and C carry the same meaning. Set S consists of a multi-set of disjoint covering array with strength larger t. For instance (see Figure 3), $VCA(12, 2, 3^2 2^2, (Zamli, et al., 2011))$ indicates the test size of 12 for pairwise interaction (with 2 3 valued parameter and 2 2 valued parameter) and 3-way interaction (with 1 3 valued parameter and 2 2 valued parameter).

Building from CA, MCA, and VCA notation, we can express Input Output based relation (IOR) as $IOR(N, R, C)$. Here, N and C take the same meaning given earlier whilst R represents a multi set of parameter relationship definition contributing towards the outputs. For example, for a 4 parameters system with 2 values, and each parameter will be assigned a number 0, 1, 2 and 3 respectively (see Figure 4). Assume two input-output relationships are involved in the outputs (i.e. the first, the second, and the third

Figure 1. CA (9,2,2⁴)

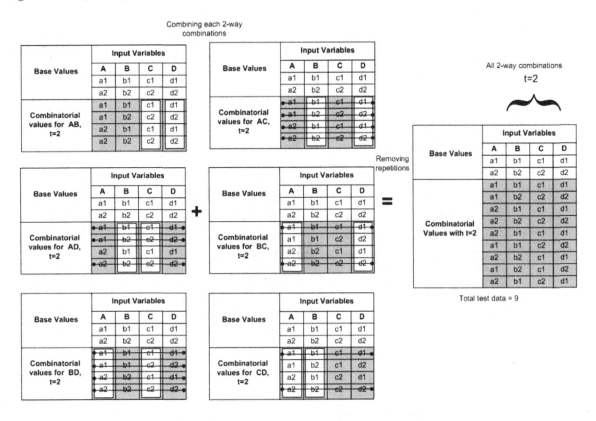

Figure 2. MCA (8,3,2³1¹)

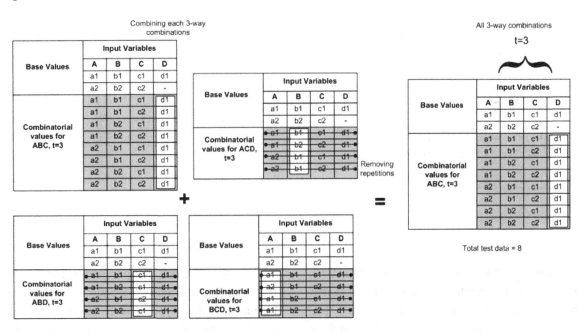

Figure 3. VCA (13,2,2⁴, {CA(3,2³)})

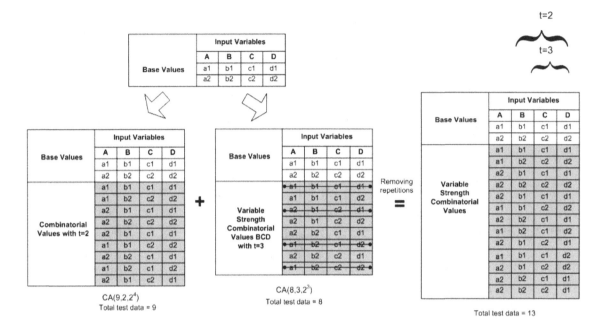

Figure 4. IOR (9, {{0,3}, {1,2}},4 ²)

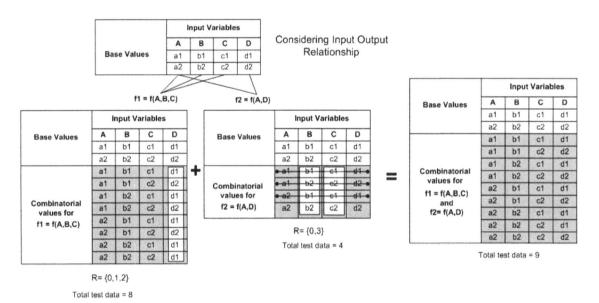

parameters for the first output as well as the first and the last parameter for the second output). Here, the relationship is written as R = {{0, 1, 2}, {0, 3}}. Considering the test size is 9, the complete notation for can be expressed as IOR (9, {{0,3}, {1,2}},4 ²).

Owing to the fact that parameter interactions may come in many number of ways, a question may be raised in which types of interaction are deemed effective for software testing consideration? Considering the fact that uniform strength, variable strength and IO relations can also be combined

Figure 5. Cooking knifes

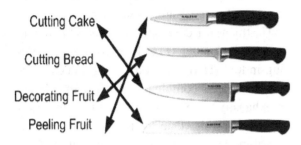

Cutting Cake

Cutting Bread

Decorating Fruit

Peeling Fruit

to cater for multiple interactions, there are at least 4 ways parameter may interact. To address this question, consider an analogy of cooking knifes (refer to Figure 5).

All knifes can work for general purpose cutting. However, they are not as effective as the specialized knife. For instance, the knife for cutting cake would not be as effective to peel fruit as the knife for peeling fruit! In this situation, it is the prerogative of the chefs to choose the right knife for the right job. Similarly, it is the test engineer's prerogative to understand the testing problem at hand. Based on his experiences on similar projects (and/or from other relevant observation and documentations), test engineer needs to pick the best type of interaction that would potentially maximize the detection of faults. As the rule of thumb:

- Uniform strength is suitable when testers have no knowledge on the effects of inputs on output(s).
- Cumulative strength/Variable strength is suitable in the case where testers have some knowledge on the contribution of particular parameters (but potentially limited knowledge on the effects of inputs on output(s)). Here, testers can relax interaction on overall strength (i.e. with t=2) but focus on (high strength) for specific interactions.
- IO based relations is suitable when testers can experimentally established the interaction effects of the parameters on the outputs (i.e. through design of experiments).

- Combinations of uniform, variable strength and IO based relations are suitable when the behaviour of the system under tests is well understood (i.e. in terms of each parameters contribution and input output relationship).

3. A SURVEY OF T-WAY STRATEGIES

Regarded as optimization problem, the search for optimum t-way set of test cases are NP hard process, i.e. an increase in the parameter size causes an exponential increase in the computational time as well as the problem complexity (Yu and Tai, 1998). For this reasons, many strategies have been developed for CA, MCA, VCA and IOR. While most strategies strive to find (near) optimal solutions within fast generation speed, no single strategy can claim dominance for every case (of p,v,t).

Obtaining optimum solution with fast generation speed are two sides of the same coin. As will be seen later, an optimal strategy in one that searches exhaustively for the most optimum possible solution in the expense of time. A fast strategy is one that search for an acceptable solution within a short period of time. To illustrate these two extremes, the next section surveys the current state-of-the-art on t-way strategies implementations.

Existing t-way strategies adopt either algebraic or computational approaches (Cohen, et al., 2003; Hartman and Raskin, 2004). Most algebraic approaches compute test sets directly by a mathematical function (Grindal, et al., 2005). As the name suggests, algebraic approaches are often based on the extensions of the mathematical methods for constructing Orthogonal Arrays (OAs)(Mandl, 1985). While proven to be useful, OA-based approaches are often too restrictive (i.e. typically requiring the parameter values to be uniform). Furthermore, apart from merely supporting pairwise (or 2-way) interactions, not all OA solutions can be found for t>2.

An improvement of OA-based approaches, called CA is developed as a result (Stevens and Mendelsohn, 1998). CA-based approaches are more flexible in the sense that it is independent of OA, i.e. a CA solution is possible to be found even without the existence of its OA solution. Some variations of the algebraic approach also exploit recursion in order to permit the construction of larger test sets from smaller ones (Williams, 2000). In addition, test sets are derived without performing any explicit enumeration of the combinations to be covered. Thus, the computations involved in algebraic approaches are typically small and extremely fast (Lei, et al., 2008).

As an improvement of CA, MCA is proposed to cater for the support for non-uniform parameter values (Cohen, 2004). Maity and Nayak, extend their CA strategy to generate some MCAs (Maity and Nayak, 2005). Colbourn et al. describe the construction of CAs and MCAs of Roux type (Colbourn, et al., 2006). In a nut shell, the construction of CAs or MCAs by means of pure algebraic approaches (i.e. without searching) can be achieved either by applying successive transformations to well-known array or by using a product of construction (Colbourn, et al., 2006). For this reason, algebraic approaches often impose restrictions on the system configurations to which they can be applied.

Unlike algebraic approaches, computational approaches often rely on the generation of all tuples and search the tuple space to generate the required test suite until all tuples have been covered (Klaib, et al., 2008; Zamli, et al., 2011). In general, computational based strategies can further be classified into two different categories based on the method used in generating the final test cases: one-test-at-a-time strategy and one-parameter-at-a-time strategy. In the case of one-test-at-a-time, the strategy often iterates all the pairs and generates a complete test case per iteration. Then, the strategy checks whether or not the generated test case is the best fit value (i.e. covering the most uncovered interaction) to be selected in the final test suite.

Hartman et al. developed the IBM's Intelligent Test Case Handler (ITCH) as an Eclipse Java plug-in tool (Hartman, et al., 2005). ITCH uses a sophisticated combinatorial algorithm based on exhaustive search to construct the test suites for t-way testing. Due to its exhaustive search algorithm, ITCH execution typically takes a long time and the results appear to be not optimized.

Jenkins developed a deterministic t-way generation strategy, called Jenny (Jenkins). Jenny adopts a greedy algorithm to produce a test suite in one-test-at-a time fashion. In Jenny, each feature has its own list of tuples. It starts out with 1-tuple (just the feature itself). When there are no tuple left to cover, Jenny goes to 2-tuples and so on. Hence, during generation instances, it is possible to have one feature still covering 2-tuples while another feature is already working on 3-tuples. This process goes on until all tuples are covered.

Complementary to the aforementioned work, significant efforts also involve extending existing pairwise strategies (e.g. in the case of AETG) to support *t*-way testing. AETG starts with all to be covered tuples and builds a test set one-test-at-a-time in each iteration until all tuples are covered (Cohen, et al., 1997).

Arshem developed a freeware Java-based t-way testing tool called Test Vector Generator (TVG) based on extension of AETG to support t-way testing (Arshem). Similar efforts are also undertaken by Bryce et al. to enhance AETG for t-way testing (Bryce and Colbourn, 2009).

Other variants of one-test-at-a-time strategy is based on artificial intelligent algorithms such as hill climbing, Tabu search (Zekaoui, 2006), Ant Colony Algorithm (ACA) (Shiba, et al., 2004), Simulated Annealing (SA) (Torres-Jimenez and Rodriguez-Tello, 2012), augmented annealing (Cohen, et al., 2008), Particle Swarm Optimization (Ahmed, et al., 2012) and Harmony Search Algorithm (Alsewari, et al., 2013; Alsewari and Zamli,

2012; Alsewari and Zamli, 2012). Briefly, these strategies start from some known test set. Then, a series of transformations were applied (starting from the known test set) until an optimum set is reached to cover all the interaction elements (Yan and Zhang, 2008). Although artificial intelligence based strategies produce smaller test size than most one-test-at-a-time strategies, they typically take longer time to complete. In addition, due to large search space, they can only support small parameters and values, typically, for t ≤3.

For VCA and IOR based one-test-at-a-time strategies, a number of works have also started to emerge. Union strategy (Schroeder, et al., 2002; Schroeder and Korel, 2000) generates the test suite for each output variable that cover all associated input interaction and then assign random value for all the 'don't care'. Then, the strategy finds the union of all test suites in order to reduce the number of generated test data.

Building from the Union Strategy, the Greedy strategy (Schroeder, et al., 2002) also generates the initial test suite that covered all associated input interaction by randomly selecting values for all don't care parameters. Nonetheless, unlike the Union strategy, the Greedy strategy picks only the unselected test case from the initial test suite which covers the most uncovered interactions as the final test suite. In this manner, the Greedy strategy often generates a more optimal test size than that of the Union Strategy.

Density strategy (Wang, et al., 2008) is based on the density concept, that is, the strategy starts with an empty test case and selects one requirement (i.e. the input-output relationships) with highest local density. Later, the strategy calculates global density for every interaction produced by the selected requirement. The interaction with highest global density will be selected in the final test suite. The whole process will start again until all interactions are covered.

In the case of one-parameter-at-a-time, the strategy constructs the test case incrementally

by horizontal extension until completion and then followed by vertical extension, if necessary. Here, the interaction coverage for each parameter extension is checked before the complete test case is generated. In-Parameter-Order strategy (IPO) strategy pioneers this approach. Later, IPO is generalized into IPOG (Lei, et al., 2007). A number of variants have also been developed to improve the IPOG's performance. These variants including: IPOG-D (Lei, et al., 2008), IPOF and IPOF2 (Forbes, et al., 2008).

Both IPOG and IPOG-D are deterministic strategies. Unlike IPOG, IPOG-D combines the IPOG strategy with an algebraic recursive construction, called D-construction, in order to reduce the number of tuples to be covered. In fact, Lei et al reported that when t=3, IPOG-D is degraded to the D-construction algebraic approach (Lei, et al., 2008). Here, when t>3, a minor version of IPOG is used to cover the uncovered tuples during D-construction. As such, IPOG-D tends to be faster than IPOG.

Unlike IPOG and IPOG-D, IPOF is a non-deterministic strategy. For this reason, IPOF produces a different test set in each run. Unlike IPOG, IPOF rearranges the rows during the horizontal extension in order to cover more tuples per horizontal extension. Results on the performance of IPOF with a small number of parameter values have been reported in (Forbes, et al., 2008). Similarly, a variant of IPOF, called IPOF2 (Forbes, et al., 2008) is also available, but it has been demonstrated with a small number of parameter values. Unlike IPOF, IPOF2 uses a heuristic technique to cover the tuples, allowing a faster execution time than that of IPOF but with a higher test set size.

Younis and Zamli proposed a strategy capable of supporting high interaction strength (i.e. for t>6) based on IPOG, called Modified-In-Parameter-Order-General (MIPOG) (Younis and Zamli, 2010). Like IPOG, MIPOG adopts the horizontal and vertical extensions in order to construct the desired test set. Unlike IPOG, MI-

POG optimizes both the horizontal and vertical extensions resulting into less test size than that of IPOG, (i.e., with the test size ratio ≤ 1). Three variants implementation of MIPOG algorithm are proposed; sequential implementation (MIPOG); concurrent and tightly coupled implementation (MC_MIPOG); and loosely coupled grid implementation (G_MIPOG).

Williams implemented a deterministic Java-based t-way test tool called TConfig (Test Configuration). TConfig consists of two strategies, namely RE (REcursive algorithm); for t=2 (Williams and Probert, 2001), and IPO (Williams, et al., 2003) for $2 \leq t \leq 6$. Williams reported that the RE failed to cover all tuples for t>2. For this reason, TConfig uses a minor version of IPO to cover the uncovered tuples in a greedy manner.

ParaOrder strategy (ParaOrder) and ReqOrder (Wang, et al., 2007) are one-parameter-at-time strategies that implements VCA and IOR. In ParaOrder, the initial test case is generated in-defined-order-of-parameter found. In the case of ReqOrder, the selection of initial test case does not necessarily follow the first defined input output relationships rather the selection is done based on the highest input output relationship coverage.

4. APPLICATIONS OF T-WAY TESTING STRATEGIES

Concerning its usage, a t-way minimization strategy has a wide range of applications. A significant efforts in the literature put focus on pairwise testing. Mandl adopts pairwise coverage using Orthogonal Latin Square (OLS) to testing an Ada compiler (Mandl, 1985). Berry reported that assessing of pairwise generation strategies in benchmark testing (Berry, 1992). Luo et al. and Cheung et al. apply pairwise strategies for Radio Frequency Identification (RFID) benchmarking (Cheung, et al., 2006; Luo, et al., 2006). Burr and Young demonstrate that pairwise testing achieves higher block and decision coverage than traditional methods for a commercial email system (Burr and Young, 1998). White and Almezen have also applied the technique to test Graphical User Interfaces (GUI) (White and Almezen, 2000). Berling and Runeson use interaction testing to identify real and false targets in target identification system (Berling and Runeson, 2003). Other applications of interaction testing include regression testing through the GUI (Memon and Soffa, 2003) and fault localization (Reorda, et al., 2005; Yilmaz, et al., 2006). In some class of system, pairwise testing appears to be adequate for achieving a good test coverage (Klaib, et al., 2008).

Chandra et al., Tang and Chen, and Boroday studied circuit testing in hardware environment, proposing test coverage that includes each 2^t of the input settings for each subset of t inputs (Boroday, 1998; Chandra, et al., 1983; Tang and Chen, 1984). Seroussi and Bshouti give a comprehensive treatment for circuit testing (Seroussi and Bshouty, 1988). In addition, Dumer examines the related question of isolating memory faults, and uses binary covering arrays (Dumer, 1989). Lazic and Velasevic employed interaction testing on modelling and simulation for automated target-tracking radar system (Lazic and Velasevic, 2004). Younis et al, considered the effectiveness of the pairwise strategy for fault detection in a parity checker circuit (Younis, et al., 2009).

Concerning the general application of t-way testing, much work has also been undertaken in the literature. Dunietz et al. demonstrate the need for higher order strength. In this case, Dunietz et al. demonstrates that significant block coverage is obtained when testing with two-way interactions, but higher strength is needed for good path coverage (Dunietz, et al., 1997). In other work, it is found that 100% of faults detectable by a relatively low degree of interaction, typically 4-way combinations (Kuhn, et al., 2004).

The National Institute of Standards and Technology (NIST) investigated the application of interaction testing for 4 application domains: medical devices, a Web browser, a HTTP server, and a NASA distributed database. It was reported that in the NASA study, 95% of the actual faults on the test software involve 4-way interaction (Kuhn, et al., 2008). In fact, according to the recommendation from NIST, almost all of the faults can be detected with 6-way interaction (Ellims, et al., 2008).

Another study by the *Software Development Technologies* (SDT) reports that an innovative company using a t-way strategy is able to reduce its system level test schedule by 68% and save 67% in labour costs associated with the testing as compared to a traditional company that adopts exhaustive testing (Wright, et al., 2009).

More recently, Younis and Zamli presented an approach to use interaction testing for t-way testing in reverse engineering of combinational circuit (Younis and Zamli, 2009). Unlike the NIST study, Younis and Zamli demonstrate the requirement of higher degree interaction test suite (i.e., t>6).

5. CONCLUSION

While much useful work has been done as far as t-way strategies are concerned, their adoption in the industry has not been widespread. For this reason, it is important to enhance awareness on the practical use of t-way strategies for software engineering communities alike.

ACKNOWLEDGMENT

This research is funded by the MOSTI's eScience Fund Grant [Project No: 01-01-16-SF0096]: Constrained T-Way Testing Strategy with Modified Condition/Decision Coverage.

REFERENCES

Ahmed, B. S., Zamli, K. Z., & Lim, C. P. (2012). Application of Particle Swarm Optimization to Uniform and Variable Strength Covering Array Construction. *Applied Soft Computing*, *12*, 1330–1347. doi:10.1016/j.asoc.2011.11.029

Alsewari, A.R.A., Khamis, N., & Zamli, K.Z. (2013). Greedy Interaction Elements Coverage Analysis for AI-Based T-Way Strategies. *Malaysian Journal of Computer Science, 26*.

Alsewari, A. R. A., & Zamli, K. Z. (2012). Design and implementation of a harmony-search-based variable-strength t-way testing strategy with constraints support. *Information and Software Technology*, *54*, 553–568. doi:10.1016/j.infsof.2012.01.002

Alsewari, A. R. A., & Zamli, K. Z. (2012). A Harmony Search Based Pairwise Sampling Strategy for Combinatorial Testing. *International Journal of the Physical Sciences*, *7*, 1062–1072.

Arshem, J. (n.d.). *Test Vector Generator Tool (TVG)*. Retrieved from http://sourceforge.net/projects/tvg

Berling, T., & Runeson, P. (2003). Efficient Evaluation of Multifactor Dependent System Performance Using Fractional Design. *IEEE Transactions on Software Engineering*, *29*, 769–781. doi:10.1109/TSE.2003.1232283

Berry, R. F. (1992). Computer Bench Mark Evaluation and Design of Experiments: A Case Study. *IEEE Transactions on Computers*, *41*, 1279–1289. doi:10.1109/12.166605

Boroday, S. Y. (1998). Determining Essential Arguments of Boolean Functions. In *Proceedings of the Conference on Industrial Mathematics* (ICIM '98). Taganrog, Russia: ICIM.

Bryce, R. C., & Colbourn, C. J. (2009). A Density-based Greedy Algorithm for Higher Strength Covering Arrays. *Software Testing, Verification, and Reliability, 19*, 37–53. doi:10.1002/stvr.393

Burr, K., & Young, W. (1998). Combinatorial Test Techniques: Table Based Automation, Test Generation and Code Coverage. In *Proceedings of the International Conference on Software Testing Analysis & Review (STAR)*. San Diego, CA: STAR.

Chandra, A. K. et al. (1983). On Sets of Boolean n-Vectors with All k-Projections Surjective. *Acta Informatica, 20*, 103–111. doi:10.1007/BF00264296

Cheung, S. C., et al. (2006). A Combinatorial Methodology for RFID Benchmarking. In *Proceedings of the 3rd RFID Academic Convocation in conjunction with the China International RFID Technology Development Conference & Exposition*. Shanghai, China: RFID.

Cohen, D. M. et al. (1997). The AETG System: An Approach to Testing based on Combinatorial Design. *IEEE Transactions on Software Engineering, 23*, 437–443. doi:10.1109/32.605761

Cohen, M. B. (2004). *Designing Test Suites for Software Interaction Testing*. (PhD Thesis). University of Auckland, Auckland, New Zealand.

Cohen, M. B., et al. (2003). Constructing Test Suites for Interaction Testing. In *Proceedings of the 25th IEEE International Conference on Software Engineering*. IEEE Computer Society.

Cohen, M. B., Colbourn, C. J., & Ling, A. C. H. (2008). Constructing Strength Three Covering Arrays with Augmented Annealing. *Discrete Mathematics, 308*, 2709–2722. doi:10.1016/j.disc.2006.06.036

Colbourn, C. J. et al. (2006a). Products of Mixed Covering Arrays of Strength Two. *Journal of Combinatorial Designs, 14*, 124–138. doi:10.1002/jcd.20065

Colbourn, C. J. et al. (2006b). Roux-Type Constructions for Covering Arrays of Strengths Three and Four. *Designs, Codes and Cryptography, 41*, 33–57. doi:10.1007/s10623-006-0020-8

Czerwonka, J. (2006). Pairwise testing in real world: Practical extensions to test case generator. In *Proceedings of 24th Pacific Northwest Software Quality Conference*. Portland, OR: Academic Press.

Dumer. (1989). Asymptotically Optimal Codes Correcting Memory Defects of Fixed Multiplicity. *Problemy Peredachi Informatskii, 25*, 3–20.

Dunietz, I. S., et al. (1997). Applying Design of Experiments to Software Testing. In *Proceedings of the International Conference on Software Engineering (ICSE '97)*. ACM Press.

Ellims, M., Ince, D., & Petre, M. (2008). The Effectiveness of T-Way Test Data Generation. *Springer LNCS 5219. SAFECOMP, 2008*, 16–29.

Forbes, M. et al. (2008). Refining the In-Parameter-Order Strategy for Constructing Covering Arrays. *Journal of Research of the National Institute of Standards and Technology, 113*, 287–297. doi:10.6028/jres.113.022

Grindal, M., Offutt, J., & Andler, S. (2005). Combination Testing Strategies: a Survey. *Software Testing, Verification, and Reliability, 15*, 167–199. doi:10.1002/stvr.319

Hartman, A., Klinger, T., & Raskin, L. (2005). *WHITCH: IBM Intelligent Test Configuration Handler*. IBM Haifa and Watson Research Laboratories.

Hartman, A., & Raskin, L. (2004). Problems and Algorithms for Covering Arrays. *Discrete Mathematics, 284*, 149–156. doi:10.1016/j.disc.2003.11.029

Jenkins, B. (n.d.). *Jenny Test Tool*. Retrieved from http://www.burtleburtle.net./bob/math/jenny.html

Klaib, M., et al. (2008). G2Way A Backtracking Strategy for Pairwise Test Data Generation. In *Proceeding of the 15th Asia-Pacific Software Engineering Conference APSEC '08'* (pp. 463-470). APSEC.

Klaib, M. F. J., et al. (2008). G2Way– A backtracking strategy for pairwise test data generation. In *Proceedings of the 15th Asia-Pacific Software Engineering Conference (APSEC 08)*. Beijing, China: APSEC.

Kuhn, D. R., Wallace, D. R., & Gallo, A. M. (2004). Software Fault Interactions and Implications for Software Testing. *IEEE Transactions on Software Engineering, 30*, 418–421. doi:10.1109/TSE.2004.24

Kuhn, R., Lei, Y., & Kacker, R. (2008). Practical Combinatorial Testing: Beyond Pairwise. *IEEE IT Professional, 10*, 19–23. doi:10.1109/MITP.2008.54

Lazic, L. J., & Velasevic, D. (2004). Applying Simulation and Design of Experiments to the Embedded Software Testing Process. *Software Testing, Verification, and Reliability, 14*, 257–282. doi:10.1002/stvr.299

Lei, Y., et al. (2007). IPOG: A General Strategy for T-Way Software Testing. In *Proceedings of the 14th Annual IEEE International Conference and Workshops on the Engineering of Computer-Based Systems (ECBS2007)*. IEEE Computer Society.

Lei, Y. et al. (2008). IPOG/IPOG-D: Efficient Test Generation for Multi-way Combinatorial Testing. *Software Testing, Verification, and Reliability, 18*, 125–148. doi:10.1002/stvr.381

Luo, Z., et al. (2006). RFID Middleware Benchmarking. In *Proceedings of the 3rd RFID Academic Convocation in conjunction with the China International RFID Technology Development Conference & Exposition*. Shanghai, China: RFID.

Maity, S., & Nayak, A. (2005). Improved Test Generation Algorithms for Pairwise Testing. In *Proceedings of the 16th IEEE International Symposium on Software Reliability Engineering (ISSRE 2005)*. IEEE Computer Society.

Mandl, R. (1985). Orthogonal Latin Squares: An Application of Experiment Design to Compiler Testing. *Communications of the ACM, 28*, 1054–1058. doi:10.1145/4372.4375

Memon, A. M., & Soffa, M. L. (2003). Regression Testing of GUIs. In *Proceedings of the 9th European Software Engineering Conference (ESEC) and the 11th ACM SIGSOFT International Symposium on the Foundations of Software Engineering (FSE-11)*. ACM Press.

Reorda, M. S., Peng, Z., & Violanate, M. (2005). *System-Level Test and Validation of Hardware/Software Systems*. Springer-Verlag. doi:10.1007/1-84628-145-8

Schroeder, P. J., Faherty, P., & Korel, B. (2002). Generating Expected Results for Automated Black-Box Testing. In *Proceedings of 17th IEEE International Conference on Automated Software Engineering (ASE'02)*. Edinburgh, UK: IEEE.

Schroeder, P. J., & Korel, B. (2000). Black-box Test Reduction Using Input-Output Analysis. In *Proceedings of the International Symposium on Software Testing and Analysis (ISSTA'00)*. Portland, OR: ISSTA.

Seroussi, G., & Bshouty, N. H. (1988). Vector Sets for Exhaustive Testing of Logic Circuits. *IEEE Transactions on Information Theory, 34*, 513–522. doi:10.1109/18.6031

Shiba, T., Tsuchiya, T., & Kikuno, T. (2004). Using Artificial Life Techniques to Generate Test Cases for Combinatorial Testing. In *Proceedings of the 28th Annual International Computer Software and Applications Conference (COMPSAC'04)*. IEEE Computer Society.

Stevens, B., & Mendelsohn, E. (1998). Efficient Software Testing Protocols. In *Proceedings of the 8th IBM Centre for Advanced Studies Conference (CASCON '98)*. IBM Press.

Tang, D. T., & Chen, C. L. (1984). Iterative Exhaustive Pattern Generation for Logic Testing. *IBM Journal of Research and Development, 28*, 212–219. doi:10.1147/rd.282.0212

Torres-Jimenez, J., & Rodriguez-Tello, E. (2012). New bounds for binary covering arrays using simulated annealing. *Information Sciences, 185*, 137–152. doi:10.1016/j.ins.2011.09.020

Wang, Z. Y., Nie, C. H., & Xu, B. W. (2007). Generating Combinatorial Test Suite for Interaction Relationship. In *Proceeding of the 4th International Workshop on Software Quality Assurance (SOQUA2007)*. Dubrovnik, Croatia: SOQUA.

Wang, Z. Y., Xu, B. W., & Nie, C. H. (2008). Greedy Heuristic Algorithms to Generate Variable Strength Combinatorial Test Suite. In *Proceedings of the 8th International Conference on Quality Software*. Oxford, UK: Academic Press.

White, L., & Almezen, H. (2000). Generating Test Cases for GUI Responsibilities Using Complete Interaction Sequences. In *Proceedings of the International Symposium on Software Reliability Engineering*. IEEE Computer Society Press.

Williams, A. W. (2000). Determination of Test Configurations for Pair-Wise Interaction Coverage. In *Proceedings of the 13th International Conference on the Testing of Communicating Systems (Testcom 2000)*. Ottawa, Canada: Testcom.

Williams, A. W., Ho, J. H., & Lareau, A. (2003). *TConfig Test Tool Version 2.1. School of Information Technology and Engineering (SITE)*. University of Ottawa. Retrieved from http://www.site.uottawa.ca/~awilliam

Williams, A. W., & Probert, R. L. (2001). A Measure for Component Interaction Test Coverage. In *Proceedings of the ACSI/IEEE International Conference on Computer Systems and Applications (AICCSA 2001)*. IEEE Computer Society.

Wright, J., Smith, J., & Shuller, S. (2009). *Development Technologies Introduction*. Software Development Technologies.

Yan, J., & Zhang, J. (2008). A Backtracking Search Tool for Constructing Combinatorial Test Suites. *Journal of Systems and Software, 81*, 1681–1693. doi:10.1016/j.jss.2008.02.034

Yilmaz, C., Cohen, M. B., & Porter, A. (2006). Covering Arrays for Efficient Fault Characterization in Complex Configuration Spaces. *IEEE Transactions on Software Engineering, 31*, 20–34. doi:10.1109/TSE.2006.8

Younis, M. I., & Zamli, K. Z. (2009). ITTW: T-Way Minimization Strategy Based on Intersection of Tuples. In *Proceedings of the IEEE Symposium in Industrial Electronics and Applications (ISIEA 2009)*. IEEE Press.

Younis, M. I., & Zamli, K. Z. (2010). MC-MIPOG: A Parallel t-Way Test Generation Strategy for Multicore Systems. *ETRI Journal, 32*, 73–82. doi:10.4218/etrij.10.0109.0266

Younis, M. I., Zamli, K. Z., & Isa, N. A. M. (2009). YZ Strategy for IC Testing. In *Proceedings of the 7th International Conference on Robotics, Vision, Signal Processing, & Power Applications (RoViSP 2009)*. Langkawi, Malyasia: RoViSP.

Yu, L., & Tai, K. C. (1998). In-parameter-order: a test generation strategy for pairwise testing. In *Proceedings of The 3rd IEEE International Symposium on High-Assurance Systems Engineering*. IEEE Computer Society.

Zamli, K. Z. et al. (2011). Design And Implementation of A T-Way Test Data Generation Strategy with Automated Execution Tool Support. *Information Sciences*, *181*, 1741–1758. doi:10.1016/j.ins.2011.01.002

Zekaoui, L. (2006). *Mixed Covering Arrays on Graphs and Tabu Search Algorithms*. (MSc Thesis). University of Ottawa, Ottawa, Canada.

KEY TERMS AND DEFINITIONS

Combinations of Uniform, Variable Strength and IO Based Relations: Hybrid consideration of interaction strength.

Cumulative/Variable Strength: More than one interaction strength is considered to different parameter interactions.

Covering/Mixed Covering Array: Formal mathematical description for expressing the covering of parameters for testing consideration.

IO Based Relations: The interaction considered is based on the input output behavior.

Strength: The interaction strength between the involved parameters (often denoted as t).

Uniform Strength: The same strength are adopted throughout all the parameter interactions.

Chapter 19
An Improved Model–Based Technique for Generating Test Scenarios from UML Class Diagrams

Oluwatolani Oluwagbemi
Universiti Teknologi Malaysia, Malaysia

Hishammuddin Asmuni
Universiti Teknologi Malaysia, Malaysia

ABSTRACT

The foundation of any software testing process is test scenario generation. This is because it forecasts the expected output of a system under development by extracting the artifacts expressed in any of the Unified Modeling Language (UML) diagrams, which are eventually used as the basis for software testing. Class diagrams are UML structural diagrams that describe a system by displaying its classes, attributes, and the relationships between them. Existing class diagram-based test scenario generation techniques only extract data variables and functions, which leads to incomprehensible or vague test scenarios. Consequently, this chapter aims to develop an improved technique that automatically generates test scenarios by reading, extracting, and interpreting the sets of objects that share attributes, operations, relationships, and semantics in a class diagram. From the performance evaluation, the proposed model-based technique is efficiently able to read, interpret, and generate scenarios from all the descriptive links of a class diagram.

INTRODUCTION

Model-based testing (MBT) is an approach used to assess the quality of software systems based on modeled requirements as captured during the requirements engineering phase of the system development life cycle processes (Prasanna & Chandran, 2009). MBT technique utilizes modeling tools used in representing stakeholder's requirements to extract artifacts and generate test scenarios (Machado & Sampaio, 2010). These modeling tools can be Unified Modeling Language

DOI: 10.4018/978-1-4666-6026-7.ch019

(UML), ArgoUML, Magic Draw or UML Rational Rose among others. Model-based software testing has to do with the creation of test cases from abstract software models which are eventually used to conduct software conformance testing (Sawant & Shah, 2011). Figure 1 depicts the processes involved in model-based software testing.

MBT consists of three basic flows of procedural events described as follows: (i) the modeling tool used in representing stakeholder's requirements (ii) the parser required to extract artifacts from the modeling diagram and (iii) a test case generation algorithm. From literature, most of the techniques for generating test cases in model-based software testing dwell on sequence, activity, state chart, and collaboration diagrams. Class diagram-based test scenario generation techniques are few. The reason may be due to the complexities associated with extracting all the attributes, classes, associations, generalizations, aggregations and compositions in class diagrams so as to generate comprehensive scenarios.

Figure 1. Model-based software testing process

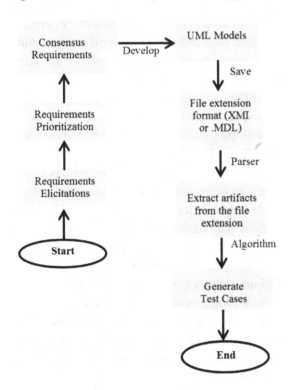

The major activities that take place during model-based testing as shown in Figure 1 are described below:

1. **Model Development:** This phase has to do with the construction of a UML-based diagram that reflects the specified or prioritized requirements using any of the modeling tools. The aim of this phase is to generate a test enabled model that will contain unambiguous artifacts required to generate test scenarios. In this research, the proposed technique was validated using ArgoUML tool because it is open source.

2. **Parser:** Once the modeled diagram is completed, the next task is to save it. UML stores its diagram in an .MDL file extension while ArgoUML stores its diagram in XMI file extensions for example. Therefore, a fundamental task in model-based software testing is the implementation of a parser that has a robust capacity of extracting artifacts from the file extensions of the relevant modeling tool. In this research, a parser was developed and implemented using Java programming language.

3. **Test Scenarios Generation:** These are derived from the parsed artifacts. The parsed artifacts are executed to generate and display test scenarios.

MBT enables testing processes to commence as soon as the requirement specifications and design documents are ready. It also reduces testing time since the testing and development processes can occur concurrently. Therefore, each output of a coding exercise can be compared to the generated test scenarios in order to determine whether the system under development is behaving as expected or not. With MBT, software systems are hardly rejected by stakeholders because each output of the development life cycle can be compared to the generated test scenarios to ensure conformance.

RELATED WORKS

There are many software testing techniques in the literature (Anand, Burke, Chen, Clark, Cohen, Grieskamp, Harman, Harrold & McMinn, 2013). However, existing software testing techniques have been identified to fall into one of the following categories (Anand et al., 2013):

1. Symbolic execution and program structural coverage testing;
2. Model-based testing;
3. Combinatorial testing;
4. Adaptive random testing as a variant of random testing;
5. Search-based testing.

It is therefore important to note that, this research focuses on model-based testing technique with precise emphasis on class diagrams.

A good number of researchers have developed new and different MBT techniques for deriving test cases from activity diagrams (Kundu, Sarma, Samanta & Mall, 2009; Linzhang, Jiesong, Xiaofeng, Jun, Xuandong & Guoliang, 2004; Mingsong, Xiaokang & Xuandong, 2006). Kundu et al.'s technique employed activity path coverage criterion to identify synchronization faults and faults in loops from activity diagrams. Linzhang et al. invented a new technique for deriving test cases from UML activity diagrams with the help of gray-box testing technique. Test scenarios were generated within a particular coverage criterion to avoid explosion of path in the loop. Mingsong et al. presented a test case generation approach from activity diagrams which haphazardly generated numerous arbitrary test cases but a program was implemented to trace those arbitrary test cases by simple path coverage criteria so as to obtain a compressed test suit that satisfies the test adequacy criteria. Also, an approach for generating test cases from behavioural UML diagrams (sequence and activity) has been developed (Swain & Mohapatra, 2010). They achieved their aim by transforming the diagrams into a graph and developed an algorithm to traverse and generate test cases from the graphs. Their approach reduced the number of generated test suits while achieving good test coverage criteria. Furthermore, techniques for generating test cases for object oriented software has been proposed (Shanti & Kumar, 2011). Genetic algorithm was used to achieve their aim while a parser was written in JAVA to extract all possible information from the saved .MDL file extension of the UML class diagram which was converted to a tree. They used the depth first search algorithm to generate test cases. More recent techniques dwelt on model-driven approach for generating test cases from UML's sequence, state and class diagrams at runtime (Lamancha, Reales, Polo & Caivano, 2013). They applied QVT and MOFScript to extract information from the diagrams and calculated the expected output of the software under test. Some techniques dealt with generating test cases for branch testing using genetic algorithm (Pachauri, 2013) while a novel technique for generating test cases from activity diagrams has been proposed using extension theory (Li, Li, He & Xiong, 2013). They used the Euler circuit algorithm to automatically generate test case in a reduced form while maintaining good adequacy criteria that is capable of detecting more software defects. There seems to be shortages of class diagram-based test case generation techniques in the literature. This could be due to the complexities associated with deriving test cases from class diagrams.

Although existing class diagram-based test case generation techniques demonstrate a high level of capabilities, some limitations still exist. A prominent limitation has to do with the inability of existing techniques to read and parse requirements from all the descriptive links of class diagrams. Various authors have developed models as well as algorithms that can read and parse information from one or two UML diagrams at runtime, all in a bid to enhance the model-based testing process. If efficient test case generation techniques are not developed, software engineers will surely have good excuses for boycotting requirements conformance testing. Therefore, the main objective of this research is to propose an improved technique that is capable of generating test scenarios from class diagrams with full coverage criteria.

MAIN FOCUS OF THE CHAPTER

The main focuses of this research are enumerated below:

1. To develop an enhanced parser that is capable of extracting artifacts from all the descriptive links of a class diagram;
2. To implement the parser using Java programming language;
3. To validate the parser using a relevant case study; and
4. Generate test scenarios from the case study.

PROPOSED TECHNIQUE

Given a software specifications document, a class diagram is created to represent the requirements of a proposed software system. ArgoUML saves its diagram in a .zargo file extension which is a zipped XML project file that contains the description of software requirements in XMI format. Our technique presents a parser that is capable of converting the XMI tags to generate a tree. The parser also has the capacity to read and interpret class diagrams and generate various nodes from the tree that stores the specified or categorized requirements. The generated nodes are mapped into various scenarios in line with the relationships of the classes in the diagram. Furthermore, an execution occurs to display results such as: attributes of the corresponding objects, classes, relations and arguments in the methods involved in the software development process. Figure 2 shows the diagrammatic illustration of the proposed technique.

As shown in Figure 2, a three-stage test case generation process is proposed. In Argo UML, a class diagram is drawn to reflect user's require-

Figure 2. Proposed technique

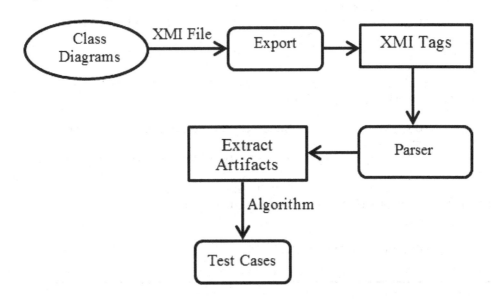

ments of a software application. In order to ensure accurate test scenario generation, the underlying artifacts that constitute a modeling diagram must be precise, consistent and unambiguous; otherwise, the resulting test scenarios may not produce the expected runtime behaviour of the proposed system. Thus, the class diagram is now transformed into XMI tags which store the extracted artifacts of the system under development. The reason for transforming class diagrams into XMI tags is to allow efficient and scalable parsing to execute. Furthermore, the pseudo-code proposed in the following section was employed to parse and generate test scenarios.

The concept of a parser in the context of this research work is based on reading artifacts from class diagrams; interpreting and converting them to another form based on some defined sets of rules for generating test scenarios. In simulating the token flow during model execution, the parser attempts to scan all the contents of the file path of the class diagram and stores the extracted ar-

tifacts in a stack for processing. The pseudo-code for the parser is described in Figure 3. Unlike conventional parsers, where test scenarios are generated randomly, the proposed parser visits all the descriptive links in a class diagram that describe one requirement or the other to generate test scenarios. Table 1 shows the test criteria for class diagrams.

The parser begins execution by considering all the component or object constraints in a class diagram and stores the parsed value in a cache member variable. All the conditions associated with the parsing process as spelt out in the pseudo-code must be met before the parsed values are finally stored in the stack. For example, all the strings been extracted from the class diagram must be lower cased and trimmed, after which test scenarios are generated in line with the corresponding semantics of the tokens stored at each node of the tree. At the moment, the pseudo-code deals with class diagrams which have various nodes and test scenarios generated based on the

Figure 3. Pseudo-code for the parser

```
/** Parses all component constraints and stores the parsed values in
the transient (cache) member varables.
      * @param constrMap The constraints as <code>String</code>s.
Strings <b>must be lower case and trimmed</b>
      * @return The parsed constraints. Never <code>null</code>.
      */public static Map<ComponentWrapper, CC>
parseComponentConstraints(Map<ComponentWrapper, String> constrMap)
    {
          HashMap<ComponentWrapper, CC> flowConstrMap = new
HashMap<ComponentWrapper, CC>();

          for (Iterator<Map.Entry<ComponentWrapper, String>> it =
constrMap.entrySet().iterator(); it.hasNext();) {
                Map.Entry<ComponentWrapper, String> entry =
it.next();
                flowConstrMap.put(entry.getKey(),
parseComponentConstraint(entry.getValue()));
          }

          return flowConstrMap;
    }
```

Table 1. Test criteria for class diagrams

Criteria	Description
Association End Multiplicity criterion	Given a test objective T with a corresponding class diagram CD, T should allow each multiplicity entity in CD to be created.
Generalization criterion	Given a test objective T with a corresponding class diagram CD, T should allow each entity defined in a generalization relationship to be created.
Class attributecriterion	Given a test objective T with a corresponding class diagram CD that contains a class C, T should allow a set of entity in each instance of class C to be created

visited nodes. To ensure accurate and satisfactory test results, iteration can occur to further search for unvisited nodes which are also trimmed to avoid redundant output. With this parser, test scenarios are automatically generated during iterations by recording the traces of the visited nodes starting from the initial node to the final node. At the end of the final execution, the generated test scenarios are evaluated against the specified test objectives.

In summary, the steps involved in generating test scenarios from class diagram are outlined below:

Step 1: Drawing Modeling Diagrams from the Project Description

Here, the description of the proposed software system is articulated via a class diagram in order to obtain the visualized consensus requirements by relevant stakeholders who have vested interest in the project.

Step 2: Generating XMI File

The ArgoUML modeling tool has the capacity of producing XMI file extensions from its diagrams which are easily transferable by installing the ArgoUML design tool. This tool also possesses the preference of exporting the UML diagram to zargo files which contain zipped XML files that generate XMI tags for the classes, attributes and other properties of the modeling diagrams used to generate test scenarios. An advantage of this approach is that, the XMI tags do not need further editing to extract the specified requirements for test scenario generation.

Step 3: Parsing the XMI File

A parser is developed to read XMI files emanating from the previous step in order to generate all the tags associated with each descriptive link of a class diagram. The information acquired from this phase is eventually used in generating test scenarios. This technique basically utilizes a tree-based Application Programming Interface (API) to form an in-memory tree representation of the XMI tags with nodes that provides classes and methods of the software under development for traversal.

Step 4: Generating Scenarios

The parsed XMI files from Step 3 serve as input for generating test scenarios. The nodes which store information such as artifacts parsed between two or more objects as well as the objects constraint languages of the information, if any, are executed to generate test scenarios by visiting each node at least once.

Step 5: Saving Generated Test Scenarios

After generating the test scenarios, there will be a need to save the files for reference purposes during requirement conformance testing, usually in a .txt extension file. At the end of the System

Development Life Cycle (SDLC) phases, software testers will require access to the generated test scenarios to determine the level of acceptability or compliance of the developed system.

IMPLEMENTATION

The steps and technique described above have been implemented with several lines of Java codes. As a result, a software tester can employ this tool to generate various test scenarios from class diagrams. To use this tool, the software tester obtains the required class diagram representing user's requirements and transforms the diagram into XMI tags by exporting the modeling file from the ArgoUML modeling environment. The tool receives the exported class diagram in XMI format and the necessary information is extracted when the tester hits the "Load XMI" button. At this stage, the parser is automatically activated to read and interpret the extracted information while the "Generate Button" is clicked for the display of generated scenarios based on the test criteria for class diagrams described in Table 1. All the extracted information is displayed on the right hand side of the snapshot and the "Classes", "Associations" and "Generalizations" folders are explored to view the generated test scenarios. The test scenarios generation tool was executed on a laptop, which has installed Windows 7, 1.86GHz CPU, and 2GB memory.

VALIDATION OF THE TECHNIQUE

The Automated Teller Machine (ATM) project requirements were adopted to validate and test the performance of the implemented technique. The ATM is meant to serve one customer at a time. To use an ATM, a customer is assumed to have obtained a valid card which is inserted into the machine to initiate any type of transaction. As soon as the card is inserted, a session is initiated which aims at verifying the card. If the verification is unsuccessful, the card is rejected but if it is successful, the card is accepted and the machine prompts the customer to insert his/her personal identification number (PIN) which is also verified by the bank. Once the PIN is verified, the customer will be required to perform the desired transaction. The card remains inside the machine until the customer confirms the completion of a transaction by terminating the process. In clear terms, the ATM machine is meant to provide the following sets of services which are also considered to be requirements.

1. **Cash Withdrawal:** A customer should be able withdraw cash within the amount limit.
2. **Cash Deposit:** A customer should also be able to deposit cash to any account connected to the card by entering the amount to be deposited into the machine and a message is displayed upon successful or unsuccessful transaction as the case may be.
3. **Money Transfer:** A customer should be able to effect transfer of funds from one customer to another.
4. **Balance Enquiry:** A customer should be able to check his/her balance at his/her own will.

From the above description, Figure 4 shows the class diagram of the ATM project, while Figure 5 displays the main interface of the implemented test scenario generation tool embedded with the improved parser for generating test scenarios. Figure 6 shows the extracted artifacts based on the descriptive links of a class diagram. The descriptive links include interface, attributes, operation, parameter, association, association end, generalization and dependency. Figure 7 shows the screenshot of the executed artifacts extracted from all of these links, which are synchronized to display the generated test scenarios. These scenarios are

Figure 4. Class diagram of the ATM project description

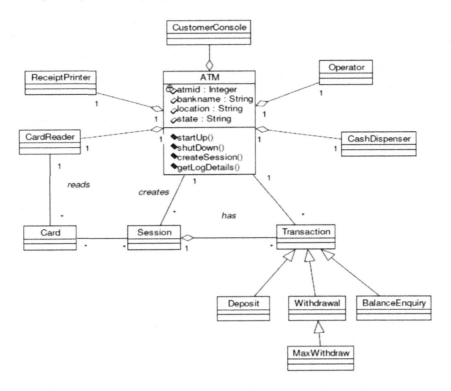

Figure 5. Main interface of the test case generation tool

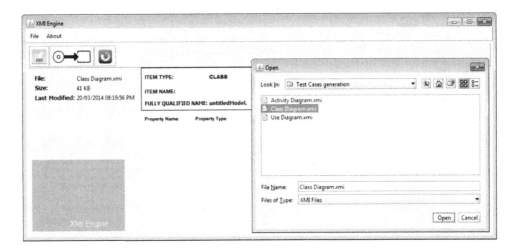

then used to perform requirements conformance testing at the end of the system development life cycle processes.

MATHEMATICAL MODEL FOR THE PROPOSED TECHNIQUE

Modeling has to do with a technique that enhances the assembly of components that constitute the

Figure 6. Extracted artifacts based on descriptive links of a class diagram

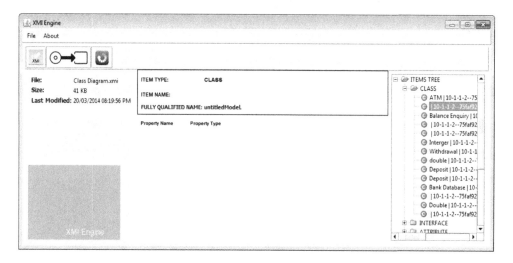

Figure 7. Displayed test case scenarios

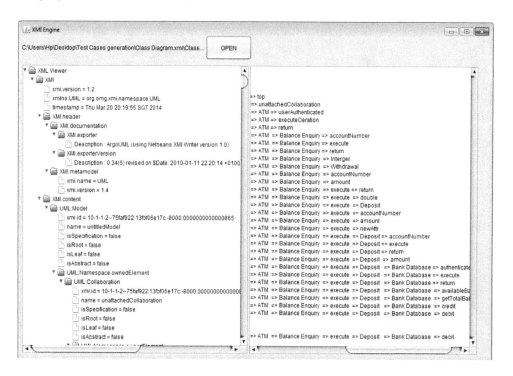

requirements of a proposed system articulated via any of the modeling diagrams. In this research, Class Diagram (*CD*) was used to generate test scenarios. Consequently, generating test scenarios from *CD* of specified requirements can be articulated by syntaxes consisting of four tuples described below:

CD = (C, A, RL, OP);

where: $C = \{c_1, c_2, c_3...c_n\}$, are finite sets of classes while $A = \{a_1, a_2, a_3...a_n\}$, are finite sets of attributes; $OP = \{op_1, op_2, op_3...op_n\}$ are finite sets of operations and $RL = \{rl_1, rl_2, rl_3...rl_n\}$, are finite sets of relationships between the entities in a class diagram.

Therefore, $CD \subseteq C \times A \times OP \times RL$ are sets of tuples that are contained in a class diagram. More precisely, an element $(C_1A_1OP_1C_2A_2OP_2....C_nA_nOP_n \cup RL) \in CD$ is an expression that represents the degree of membership of entities with respect to their relationships RL in a class diagram. The Relationships RL, Classes C, Attributes A, and Operations OP, forms the modeling description of an application domain articulated through a class diagram. A composite function is used to connect all the variables that are related when representing requirements with a class diagram. For instance, let $\otimes$ be a composition operator on all the relationships RL that exist between Classes C as defined earlier. During modeling, all the tuples are constituted as $\otimes$, which translate to an extended set of representations with respect to the composite operator defined as: $\otimes : CD \rightarrow CD^{\infty}$. With this composition operator imposed on the entities of the class diagram, the new sets of expressions can now be defined as: $\forall C_1A_1OP_1C_2A_2OP_2....C_nA_nOP_n \cup RL \in CD: (C_1A_1OP_1) \in RL \wedge (C_2A_2OP_2) \in RL \Rightarrow (C_1A_1OP_1 \times C_2A_2OP_2 \times C_nA_nOP_n \cup RL \otimes CD$. Once the number of classes are more than two which is usually the case, the set of 'n step' relationships, RL^n, is as follows: C_1, $C_{n-1}A_n \times OP_n \in CD \; \forall \; RL \in RL*: (C_1, C_{n-1}, RL_1) \, A_n \times OP_n \wedge (C_2, C_{n-2}, RL_2) \, A_n \times OP_n \in CD \Rightarrow (C_1C_2C_{n-1}C_{n-2}, RL_n, A_n \, OP_n, \otimes CD)$. The preceding expression is important because it optimizes the degree of membership of the attributes, relationship and other descriptive links associated with a class diagram. The formula to generate test scenarios is defined as follows:

Table 2. Experimental results

Case Study	Descriptive Links(DL)	Number of Extracted Artifacts (N)
ATM	Classes	38
	Interface	42
	Operation	14
	Parameter	13
	Model	6
	Association	38
	Association End	76
	Generalization	4
	Dependency	1
	Classifier role	4
	Total Extracted Items	236

$$TCG = \sum_{n=1}^{\infty} C \cup RL \otimes T \; ;$$

where C = *Numbers of classes*, RL = *Descriptive relationship of a class diagram* and T = *Test coverage* which must allow each possible class and relationships to be visited at least once.

EXPERIMENTAL RESULTS

We applied a real case to test the viability of the proposed test scenario generation tool. The case scenario involves the development of an automated teller machine. Table 2 summarizes the general description and numbers of extracted artifacts that were utilized by the proposed system in generating test scenarios. Figure 8 depicts the number of extracted artifacts used in generating scenarios by the proposed technique.

Figure 8. Extracted artifacts of the proposed system

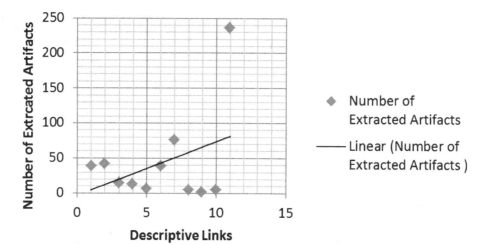

COMPARISON WITH RELATED WORKS

Most of the researches executed in class diagram-based test scenarios generation have been concatenated with one modeling diagram or the other (Sawant & Shah, 2011; Alhroob, Dahal & Hossain, 2010; Samuel, Mall & Kanth, 2007) which did not cover all the descriptive links of class diagrams. In contrast, we generate test scenarios automatically from class diagram with the feature of extracting all the information, attributes, relationships associated with all classes. To avoid redundancy of scenarios, the technique has the capacity of generating scenarios based on a single visit of each descriptive link. The proposed technique also supports iterations when requirements evolve. Furthermore, the prototype of the proposed test scenario generation technique has been implemented with Java programming language in company of a parser required to read, extract, interpret and generate test scenarios from ArgoUML class diagrams.

FUTURE RESEARCH DIRECTIONS

Software engineering discipline is fast becoming an enviable domain within the confines of computer science research as real world problems are addressed via well developed and computerized software systems. Software systems also serve as an indispensable catalyst for global business players in their quest to overtake and gain competitive edge over each other. This research will therefore help practitioners in their efforts to develop good quality systems for their clients. For software systems to satisfy stakeholder's requirements there is need to conduct requirement conformance testing at every stage of the development life cycle. Software testing has therefore become the most preferred technique for ensuring or guaranteeing the quality of software systems. However, the software testing process cannot be relied upon if accurate and comprehensive test cases are not generated. The essence of this research, therefore, was to propose means of generating test scenarios from UML class diagrams with full coverage criteria. In future work, we hope to develop an efficient test scenario generation technique that will be able to parse artifacts and generate test scenarios from all the various modeling diagrams and tools at runtime. Also, it will be expedient to test the proposed technique with large scale software requirements.

CONCLUSION

The aim of this research work was to develop an improved technique that is capable of reading and extracting information from UML class diagrams in order to generate test scenarios. The technique has been presented and validated using ATM project requirements. A class diagram that reflects the ATM project requirements was drawn which serves as input to the system. This technique does not need any adjustment or amendment in the diagram in order to parse artifacts from it to generate test scenarios. The technique was implemented and can be used as a tool during test scenario generation process. The tool is capable of automating the testing process. The implemented tool also reduces the time and complexities associated with generating test scenarios from class diagram. It assumes input in XMI format and display output in textual format.

REFERENCES

Alhroob, A., Dahal, K., & Hossain, A. (2010). Automatic test cases generation from software specifications modules. *Journal of e-Informatica Software Engineering, 4*(1), 109-121.

Anand, S., Burke, E. K., Chen, T. Y., Clark, J., Cohen, M. B., Grieskamp, W., & McMinn, P. (2013). An orchestrated survey of methodologies for automated software test case generation. *Journal of Systems and Software, 86*(8), 1978–2001. doi:10.1016/j.jss.2013.02.061

Kundu, D., Sarma, M., Samanta, D., & Mall, R. (2009). System testing for object-oriented systems with test case prioritization. *Software Testing. Verification and Reliability, 19*(4), 297–333. doi:10.1002/stvr.407

Lamancha, B. P., Reales, P., Polo, M., & Caivano, D. (2013). Model-Driven Test Code Generation. In *Evaluation of Novel Approaches to Software Engineering* (Vol. 275, pp. 155–168). Berlin: Springer. doi:10.1007/978-3-642-32341-6_11

Li, L., Li, X., He, T., & Xiong, J. (2013). Extenics-based Test Case Generation for UML Activity Diagram. *Procedia Computer Science, 17*, 1186–1193. doi:10.1016/j.procs.2013.05.151

Linzhang, W., Jiesong, Y., Xiaofeng, Y., Jun, H., Xuandong, L., & Guoliang, Z. (2004). Generating test cases from UML activity diagram based on gray-box method. In *Proceedings of Software Engineering Conference,* (vol. 55, pp. 284-291). IEEE.

Machado, P., & Sampaio, A. (2010). Automatic Test-Case Generation. In *Testing Techniques in Software Engineering* (Vol. 6153, pp. 59–103). Berlin: Springer. doi:10.1007/978-3-642-14335-9_3

Mingsong, C., Xiaokang, Q., & Xuandong, L. (2006). Automatic test case generation for UML activity diagrams. In *Proceedings of the 2006 International Workshop on Automation of Software Test* (pp. 2-8). New York, NY: ACM.

Pachauri, A. (2013). Automated test data generation for branch testing using genetic algorithm: An improved approach using branch ordering, memory and elitism. *Journal of Systems and Software, 86*(8), 1191–1208. doi:10.1016/j.jss.2012.11.045

Prasanna, M., & Chandran, K. R. (2009). Automatic test case generation for UML Object diagrams using Genetic Algorithm. *Int. J. Advance. Soft Comput. Appl, 1*(1), 19–32.

Samuel, P., Mall, R., & Kanth, P. (2007). Automatic test case generation from UML communication diagrams. *Information and Software Technology, 49*(2), 158–171. doi:10.1016/j.infsof.2006.04.001

Sawant, V., & Shah, K. (2011). Construction of test cases from UML models. In *Technology Systems and Management* (Vol. 145, pp. 61–68). Berlin: Springer Heidelberg. doi:10.1007/978-3-642-20209-4_9

Shanthi, A. V. K., & Kumar, D. G. M. (2011). Automated test cases generation for object oriented software. *Indian Journal of Computer Science and Engineering, 2*(4).

Swain, S. K., & Mohapatra, D. P. (2010). Test case generation from Behavioral UML Models. *International Journal of Computers and Applications, 6*(8), 5–11. doi:10.5120/1098-1436

ADDITIONAL READING

Aggarwal, M., & Sabharwal, S. (2012). Test case generation from UML state machine diagram: A survey. In *Computer and Communication Technology (ICCCT), 2012 Third International Conference: Vol.34.* (pp. 133-140). Allahabad: IEEE.

Ahmed, S. U., Sahare, S. A., & Ahmed, A. (2013). Automatic test case generation using collaboration UML diagrams. *World Journal of Science and Technology, 3*(1), 4–6.

Anbarasu, I. (2012). A Survey on Test Case Generation and Extraction of Reliable Test Cases. *International Journal of Computer Science & Applications, 1*(10).

Biswal, B. N., Nanda, P., & Mohapatra, D. P. (2008). A novel approach for scenario-based test case generation. In *Information Technology International Conference: Vol. 43.* (pp. 244-247). Bhubaneswar: IEEE.

Boghdady, P. N., Badr, N. L., Hashem, M., & Tolba, M. F. (2011). Test Case Generation and Test Data Extraction Techniques. *International Journal of Electrical & Computer Sciences, 11*(3).

Chen, M., Qiu, X., Xu, W., Wang, L., Zhao, J., & Li, X. (2009). UML activity diagram-based automatic test case generation for Java programs. *The Computer Journal, 52*(5), 545–556. doi:10.1093/comjnl/bxm057

Chen, T. Y., Kuo, F. C., Merkel, R. G., & Tse, T. H. (2010). Adaptive random testing: The art of test case diversity. *Journal of Systems and Software, 83*(1), 60–66. doi:10.1016/j.jss.2009.02.022

Dalal, S. R., Jain, A., Karunanithi, N., Leaton, J. M., Lott, C. M., Patton, G. C., & Horowitz, B. M. (1999). Model-based testing in practice. In *Proceedings of the 21st International Conference on Software Engineering: Vol. 1.* (pp. 285-294). New York, NY: ACM.

Dias-Neto, A. C., & Travassos, G. H. (2009). Model-based testing approaches selection for software projects. *Information and Software Technology, 51*(11), 1487–1504. doi:10.1016/j.infsof.2009.06.010

Escalona, M. J., Gutierrez, J. J., Mejías, M., Aragón, G., Ramos, I., Torres, J., & Domínguez, F. J. (2011). An overview on test generation from functional requirements. *Journal of Systems and Software, 84*(8), 1379–1393. doi:10.1016/j.jss.2011.03.051

Hasling, B., Goetz, H., & Beetz, K. (2008). Model based testing of system requirements using UML use case models. In *Software Testing, Verification, and Validation, 2008 1st international conference: Vol. 9.* (pp. 367-376). Lillehammer: IEEE.

Kaur, A., & Vig, V. (2012). Systematic review of automatic test case generation by UML diagrams. *International Journal of Engineering, 1*(6).

Kim, H., Kang, S., Baik, J., & Ko, I. (2007). Test cases generation from UML activity diagrams. In *Software Engineering, Artificial Intelligence, Networking, and Parallel/Distributed Computing, Eighth ACIS International Conference: Vol. 3.* (pp. 556-561). Qingdao: IEEE.

Patel, P., & Patel, N. N. (2012). Test case formation using UML activity diagram. *World Journal of Science and Technology, 2*(3).

Paulish, D. J., Kazmeier, J., & Rudorfer, A. (2009). *Software & systems requirements engineering: in practice.* New York: McGraw-Hill.

Prasanna, M., Chandran, K. R., & Thiruvenkadam, K. (2011). Automatic test case generation for UML collaboration diagrams. *Journal of the Institution of Electronics and Telecommunication Engineers, 57*(1), 77. doi:10.4103/0377-2063.78373

Reales Mateo, P., & Polo Usaola, M. (2013). Automated test generation for multi-state systems. In *Proceeding of the 15th Annual Conference on Genetic and Evolutionary Computation Companion: Vol. 1.* (pp. 211-212). New York, NY: ACM.

Sabharwal, S., Singh, S. K., Sabharwal, D., & Gabrani, A. (2010). An event-based approach to generate test scenarios. In *Computer and Communication Technology (ICCCT) International Conference: Vol. 10.* (pp. 551-556). Allahabad, Uttar Pradesh: IEEE.

Samuel, P., Mall, R., & Bothra, A. K. (2008). Automatic test case generation using unified modeling language (UML) state diagrams. *IET software, 2*(2), 79-93.

Sapna, P. G., & Mohanty, H. (2010). Automated test scenario selection based on levenshtein distance. In *Distributed Computing and Internet Technology* (pp. 255–266). Berlin: Springer Heidelberg.

Sarma, M., Kundu, D., & Mall, R. (2007). Automatic test case generation from UML sequence diagram. In *Advanced Computing and Communications, International Conference: Vol. 68.* (pp. 60-67). Guwahati, Assam: IEEE.

Shahamiri, S. R., Kadir, W. M. N. W., Ibrahim, S., & Hashim, S. Z. M. (2011). An automated framework for software test oracle. *Information and Software Technology, 53*(7), 774–788. doi:10.1016/j.infsof.2011.02.006

Sharma, A., & Singh, M. (2013). Generation of automated test cases using UML modeling. *International Journal of Engineering, 2*(4).

Shirole, M., Suthar, A., & Kumar, R. (2011). Generation of improved test cases from UML state diagram using genetic algorithm. In *Proceedings of the 4th India Software Engineering Conference: Vol. 4.* (pp. 125-134). New York, NY: ACM.

Singh, S. K., Sabharwal, S., & Gupta, J. P. (2012). A novel approach for deriving test scenarios and test cases from events. *Journal of Information Processing Systems, 8*(2), 213–240. doi:10.3745/JIPS.2012.8.2.213

Sun, C. A., Zhang, B., & Li, J. (2009, August). TSGen: A UML activity diagram-based test scenario generation tool. In *Computational Science and Engineering, International Conference on: Vol. 2.* (pp. 853-858). Vancouver, BC: IEEE.

Swain, R., Panthi, V., Behera, P. K., & Mohapatra, D. P. (2012). Automatic test case generation from UML state chart diagram. *International Journal of Computers and Applications, 42*(7), 26–36. doi:10.5120/5705-7756

Utting, M., Pretschner, A., & Legeard, B. (2012). A taxonomy of model-based testing approaches. *Software Testing. Verification and Reliability, 22*(5), 297–312. doi:10.1002/stvr.456

KEY TERMS AND DEFINITIONS

Class Diagrams: Diagrams used to depict objects or entities, attributes and the relationships of a proposed system.

Model: The blueprint or architectural plan of a proposed system.

Requirements: The expected functionalities and attributes of a proposed system.

Software Testing: The act of determining whether or not a system under test has performed in line with stakeholder's expectations.

Technique: A step by step procedures executed to address a specific problem.

Test Case Generations: The parsed artifacts of a system which is used as a yardstick to evaluate the performance of a proposed system.

Test Scenarios: Conditions that a proposed system must satisfy in order to ensure acceptance.

UML: Unified Modeling Language used to diagrammatically depict system requirements.

XMI: The conventional format for electronic metadata interchange between one or more components in order to achieve interoperability.

Section 6
Software Quality Measurement

Chapter 20
A Methodology for Model–Based Reliability Estimation

Mohd Adham Isa
Universiti Teknologi Malaysia, Malaysia

Dayang Norhayati Abang Jawawi
Universiti Teknologi Malaysia, Malaysia

ABSTRACT

In recent years, reliability assessment is an essential process in system quality assessments. However, the best practice of software engineering for reliability analysis is not yet of its matured stage. The existing works are only capable to explicitly apply a small portion of reliability analysis in a standard software development process. In addition, an existing reliability assessment is based on an assumption provided by domain experts. This assumption is often exposed to errors. An effective reliability assessment should be based on reliability requirements that could be quantitatively estimated using metrics. The reliability requirements can be visualized using reliability model. However, existing reliability models are not expressive enough and do not provide consistence-modeling mechanism to allow developers to estimate reliability parameter values. Consequently, the reliability estimation using those parameters is usually oversimplified. With this situation, the inconsistency problem could happen between different estimation stages. In this chapter, a new Model-Based Reliability Estimation (MBRE) methodology is developed. The methodology consists of reliability model and reliability estimation model. The methodology provides a systematic way to estimate system reliability, emphasizing the reliability model for producing reliability parameters which will be used by the reliability estimation model. These models are built upon the timing properties, which is the primary input value for reliability assessment.

INTRODUCTION

System software has become vastly more complicated in recent years, and ranges from e-commerce to industrial embedded systems, which support both functional and non-functional requirements of the system. In fact, the satisfaction of non-functional requirements or software quality, such as performance, reliability, security and adaptability, towards functional requirements are often treated as critical. Performance-sensitive systems are widely used to support various application domains, such as tele-

DOI: 10.4018/978-1-4666-6026-7.ch020

communications, embedded systems, and industrial control systems. The unreliability of such systems is often related to underperformance of systems and could affect the whole system. Therefore, it is largely necessary to ensure promising software quality from as early as possible in the design phase to satisfy today's demanding standards.

Software qualities generally can be defined as a combination of quality attributes of a system in a certain accepted degree (IEEE 1061, 1992). According to ISO 25000 (ISO/IEC, 2005), software quality is defined as a set of qualities of a system that satisfies the given system's requirements'. In recent years, several researchers and standard organizations have proposed the software quality taxonomy in order to define exactly which software quality is justified as being important for the software systems (McCall *et al.*, 1977; Boehm, 1978; Dromey, 1995; ISO 25000, 2005).

Among software quality attributes, considerable significance has been given to reliability attributes (Kramer and Volker, 1997). Software reliability is described as the capability of the system/component/services to perform a given task under a specific condition and time frame (IEC 9126-1, 2001). The system operation is said to be reliable when continuously operating with minimal failure. Software reliability generally acknowledges the probability that a system may fail within a certain period. The failure elements can be traced from the system's error and fault information (Eusgeld *et al.*, 2008). Faults in the system will impose a certain error that will lead to a system failure if no specific approach is applied to handle this matter. A system failure might be due to faults in implementation, unreliable system resources or misplaced system tasks (Salfner and Lenk, 2010; Valis and Bartlett, 2010). Therefore, wherever the operation of the system is disturbed, the consequences may result in an enormous risk to either people or the environment. On the other hand, the risk can be greatly reduced if an adequate reliability analysis is carried out before deploying the system (Krishna and Mall, 2010).

To quantify the reliability of a system, most traditional efforts are likely to be more interested in evaluating reliability analysis during system runtime (Yang *et al.*, 2009) because of its accurate analysis. However, this approach suffers from a few problems, in particular, an increase in effort and the costs involved in rectifying the problems (if the problems are visible) (Singh, 2011; Zio, 2009). Another approach that has gained importance to the reliability analysis is a model-based approach (Balsamo *et al.*, 2004; Immonen and Niemelä, 2007). The model-based approach at design phase could assist in estimating system reliability. It could therefore aid in identifying critical parts in the system that could cause a system failure and thus, use those results to further assess the design decision process. Therefore, it is suggested that the software reliability analysis should be made at design phase rather than during the implementation phase.

In recent years, existing works have appeared, in order to facilitate reliability estimation through design models (Brosch *et al.*, 2011, 2010; Distefano *et al.*, 2011; Gokhale and Trivedi, 2006; Spyrou *et al.*, 2008; Yacoub and Ammar, 2002). Thus, by facilitating the prior design models, developers can dynamically identify problems from a reliability point of view, hence reducing the risk after deploying the system. However, to successfully utilize the capability of the design model for reliability estimation purposes, a specific methodology is needed to systematically manage the design model for estimation analysis (Krka *et al.*, 2009). The previously mentioned works are mostly dominant in an ad-hoc process and haphazard implementation. In this sense, the flow of the information among the models is always loose and not consistent. It is therefore necessary to have a systematic methodology in place for model-based reliability estimation during the system development process. A systematic estimation is capable of fluidly organizing the reliability estimation by preserving the information flows from one model to another. The organization of the estimation process emphasizes the reliability information in the design model; hence, applying step-by-step transfer of those information details to the next models for estimation purposes. To support this argument, the existing methodology for reliability analysis, Software Reliability Engineering (SRE) (Lyu, 2007), also encourages a systematic methodology for reliability analysis, however, this is seen more in a wider coverage by including details from analysis to implementation phase. In this sense, the reliability estimation through design model is likely more necessary to systematically organize reliability estimation without losing any valuable reliability information throughout the process.

Generally, model-based reliability estimation methodology consists of three primary models, namely: reliability design model, reliability parameters model and reliability estimation model (Cheung et al., 2008; Krka et al., 2009). These models provide a strong coupling between each other to ensure that the correctness of the estimation result is preserved. However, existing methodologies often fail to provide a systematic estimation.

Some previous works have tried to obtain a systematic method of estimating the system reliability at design time. A wide range of target applications have been deployed, such as: component-based system (Brosch et al., 2011; Grassi et al., 2007), general system (Distefano et al., 2011; Petriu and Woodside, 2006; Yacoub et al., 2004; Yacoub et al., 2002) and healthcare (Spyrou et al., 2008). The success of model-based reliability estimation is dependent on the correlation between those models, as mentioned before. In the case of the reliability design model, some of the methodologies provide their own models (Brosch et al., 2011; Distefano et al., 2011; Grassi et al., 2007; Petriu and Woodside, 2006), but suffer some drawbacks in terms of ad-hoc process (Petriu and Woodside, 2006). Regarding the parameter estimation model, most works tend to obtain a real data set, whether through simulation (Gokhale, 2005; Meedeniya et al., 2011) or statistical testing (Song and Kang, 2009). However, obtaining such data is difficult, especially for a system under development. A few methodologies have provided a facility to produce their own reliability parameters specifications, such as (Spyrou et al., 2008; Yacoub and Ammar, 2002), but these are not implicitly derived from the reliability design model. Concerning the estimation model, some of the methodology has applied its own estimation model (Yacoub and Ammar, 2002), however most of them have employed an estimation model with a more isolated process (Distefano et al., 2011; Grassi et al., 2007; Petriu and Woodside, 2006). In this sense, the aforementioned problems may affect the level of model consistency when the time comes to trace back to a reliability parameter and reliability estimation model. Therefore, the need for an expressive reliability design model is inevitable in order to support systematic reliability estimation methodology, which, in turn, promotes a model consistency during the estimation process.

The main challenge to the problems alluded to can be divided into two primary issues, namely: model representation and model analysis. The model representation is aimed at determining how the reliability design model can express its context from the reliability point of view. Another issue is that of model analysis. This model is responsible for dealing with production of a reliability parameter specification from the reliability design model that will be used by the reliability estimation model. Both issues aim to address the issues of model expressiveness and model consistency, problems which will be explained in detail in the following sections.

BACKGROUND

A brief introduction on software quality model and current practice of reliability estimation are given.

Software Quality Model

The origin of reliability definition is actually derived from the definition of software quality. A general definition of software quality has been given by a number of 'gurus' in software quality areas where each researcher defines the software quality from differing views and aspects. Referring to Hoyer (2001), the learning curve of software quality can be classified into two major aspects, specifically:

1. *Product satisfaction* aims to take into account how the software quality could confirm a product specification and requirement as outlined by early product specification in its development life cycle.
2. *User satisfaction* aims at satisfying a product stakeholder(s) as to which software quality they intend to see in the final product.

Both aspects lead to the issue of quality satisfaction within software systems. From this standpoint, software quality attributes are further explored based on more systematic representation. Software quality attributes such as reliability, efficiency and reusability were obtained from the software systems requirements and were developed in more understandable ways.

The software quality can be represented as a measure to ensure that users are satisfied with the developed product and, at the same time, with the product itself in conformance with all the defined specifications. In recent years, many researchers have proposed a variety of software quality models to show the software quality attributes that might have a risk of being compromised in existing software systems. McCall (1977) developed a software quality model encompassing three perspectives, namely: product revision, product operations and product transition.

Product operation defines the quality of the software during software execution. During this phase, factors such as correctness, reliability, ef-

ficiency, integrity and usability are considered as highly capable of smoothing product operations. Product revision describes the capability of the software to be maintained, tested and evolved, while product transition aims at enabling software systems to be portable, reusable and interoperable.

A software quality attributes can be divided into two modes, namely, *execution* and *management* mode. Execution mode defines the quality of the software during operation time such as reliability, efficiency, usability and functionality, whereas management mode is all about the capability of the software to adapt into a new constraint for instance maintainability, portability, integrity, interoperability, testability, flexibility and reusability. These quality attributes is clearly very important to ensure a system stability and sustainability. However, in this chapter, the scope is to analyse software quality attributes during execution time. Since functionality and usability attributes are a likely "compulsory" attribute in the software systems, reliability and efficiency (from now refer to performance) attributes are our main concerns since these attributes have a significant impact upon the operation of software systems.

From Table 1, Boehm (1978) presented a quality model similar to that of McCall (1977), with the only difference being that Boehm (1978) focused more on sub-characteristics of maintainability quality. In addition, a model known as the Functionality, Usability, Reliability, Performance and Supportability Model (FURPS) (Grady, 1992) also addressed the same quality model as that of a previous quality model; while Dromey (1995) introduced a more specific quality model that interconnects close views between software product specifications and software quality attributes. With the emergence of software quality coverage, the International Organization for Standardization (ISO) has responded by producing a standard for software quality called ISO 25000 (2005). This standard is actually based on the quality models of Boehm (1978) and McCall (1977) respectively, but represents a more systematic definition for in-

Table 1. Software quality model classification

Attributes Mode	Software Quality Attributes	McCall	Boehm	FURPS	ISO 9126	Dromey	(Rawashdeh and Matalkah, 2006)
Execution Time	Reliability	√	√	√	√	√	√
	Efficiency	√	√	√	√	√	√
	Usability	√	√	√	√	√	√
	Functionality			√	√	√	√
Management	Maintainability	√	√	√	√	√	√
	Portability	√	√		√	√	
	Integrity	√	√				
	Interoperability	√					√
	Testability	√					√
	Flexibility	√	√	√			
	Reusability	√	√			√	

ternal and external software quality. Furthermore, recent works by Rawashdeh and Matalkah (2006) indicated that they do not intend to introduce a new quality model but rather, are more interested in classifying software quality attributes based on product and process specifications.

Software Reliability Engineering (SRE)

Software reliability comprises a significance portion of the software development lifecycle so as to produce a reliable software system. Such effort however, gives birth to the domain for software reliability assessment called Software Reliability Engineering (SRE). The system is said to be reliable when it has been run to assess functionality, with minimal errors, for a specified period of time and under certain conditions (IEEE, 1991). Software reliability needs to be evaluated during the development lifecycle so as to ensure the completeness of the system. SRE is an engineering process, which enables the measurement of reliability attributes through a specific process. A specific process includes the definition of, specifically: reliability objectives, operational profile, reliability design modelling

and measurement and reliability validation (Lyu, 2007). SRE is widely used nowadays (Musa, 2004) and has been implemented by numerous large organizations such as IBM and NASA.

Even though SRE has a history of success in implementation in various companies, the SRE still suffers from a number of shortcomings. According to Lyu (2007), the existing SRE has some flaws, which include:

1. SRE methodology using failure data for reliability analysis. Failure data only present after the system is deployed or during testing. Therefore, some problems that might be discovered could be troublesome for design changes.
2. Failure data is usually obtained from in-house testing. The data might be limited for real environment testing.

Some studies have been conducted to attempt to solve the flaws in (i) and (ii) respectively (Mohanta *et al.*, 2010; Gokhale and Trivedi, 2006) and yet, software reliability engineering still has limitations in many aspects (Gokhale, 2007; Zio, 2009; Singh *et al.*, 2011) such as:

1. **Modeling:** Architecture style that limit the use of multiple failure model into single reliability analysis that produce independence analysis for certain component/resources.

2. **Analysis:** Estimation result is produced from assumption that required to analyzing the system reliability. The lack of integration between UML based model and analysis model inherits the uncertainty quantification for model-based analysis.

System Reliability Estimation Methodology

The foundation of the model-based system reliability estimation (MBSRE) comes originally from SRE. The complete SRE process extends from analysis until implementation phase. On the other hand, parts of SRE investigate the model of the system for reliability purposes, especially at the design phase. To quantitatively estimate the system reliability based on models, the MBSRE methodology was developed. Even though there is no standard process for MBSRE, some researchers in studies by Krka *et al.* (2009) and Schneidewind (2009) have proposed a guideline on the nature of essential models in order to realize MBSRE methodology and how to execute it. Based on the previous works, some researchers have proposed a methodology for estimating the system reliability during design time (Brosch *et al.*, 2011; Ciancone *et al.*, 2013; Distefano *et al.*, 2011; Grassi *et al.*, 2007; Petriu and Woodside, 2006; Spyrou *et al.*, 2008).

Table 2 shows previous works having the guideline criteria as mentioned in Krka *et al.* (2009). The criteria contain the inclusion of three compulsory models to execute MBSRE, namely: *reliability design model*, *parameter estimation model* and *reliability estimation model*. To adequately compare the MBSRE in relation to specific needs, it was necessary to exclude the methodology that did not have these models from the comparison. In this sense, only the MBSRE methodology that offers these three models is investigated.

Table 2. The comparison of existing MBSRE methodology

Authors	Methodology	Reliability Model	Reliability Parameter model	Reliability estimation model	
				Implementation	Type
(Petriu & Woodside, 2006)	Not specifically defined	Core Scenario Model (CSM)	Not Available (parameters is considered known)	Isolated	EQ, LQN
(Grassi et al., 2007)	Process	KLAPER	Not Available (parameters is considered known)	Isolated	QN, Markov Chain
(Distefano et al., 2011)	Step	PCM	Simulation and testing	Isolated	Block Level Petri Net (BLPN)
(Brosch et al., 2011)	Step	Palladio	Simulation	Isolated	Markov chain
(Sherif M Yacoub & Ammar, 2002)	Step	Sequence Diagram	Estimated from usage profile	Composite	CDG
(V. Cortellessa, 2005)	Step	UML Use Case, Sequence and Deployment Diagram	Estimated from usage profile	Composite	Execution Graph
(Spyrou et al., 2008)	Step	UML Use Case and Activity Diagram, Customer Behavior Model Graph (CBMG)	Estimated from usage profile	Isolated	Markov Chain

The purpose of the comparison is to witness the advantages and any drawbacks of the existing methodology in terms of model consistency aspect. There are four main criteria for the comparison, specifically: *methodology, reliability design model, parameter estimation model* and *estimation model*. Research studies by Petriu and Woodside (2006) offer an ad-hoc process for performance analysis using integrated resources and scenarios. A specific reliability design model called CSM was constructed, which acts as a pivot model between the UML-based model and analysis model. This methodology assumes the existence of reliability parameter values from the existing data set. Further research studies by Brosch *et al.* (2011), Distefano *et al.* (2011) and Grassi *et al.* (2007) offer a systematic process for reliability analysis, in particular whether to use step or process. These methodologies have provided their own reliability design model and obtained the desired reliability parameter either using real data set (Grassi *et al.*, 2007) or through simulation (Brosch *et al.*, 2011; Distefano *et al.*, 2011). With regard to the estimation model, there are two approaches, namely, isolated or composite. The isolated approach (Brosch *et al.*, 2011; Distefano *et al.*, 2011; Grassi *et al.*, 2007; Petriu and Woodside, 2006; Spyrou *et al.*, 2008) was attempted but suffered a model consistency drawback. This appears to differentiate with the composite approach (Cortellessa *et al.*, 2011; Sherif Yacoub and Ammar, 2002), where this approach offers an estimation model that is suitable with the reliability design model they used. In this sense, model consistency is not an issue due to the fact that the whole process of estimation is originally derived from its own models (reliability design model, parameter estimation model, estimation model).

Benefits of Reliability Estimation at Design Phase

From Table 3, there are three approaches of software quality evaluation, namely, during design time, through simulation and during runtime. The main concern in this research is to estimate the system reliability before the system is deployed. Even though quality evaluation is more accurate during runtime and through simulation, but those approaches lack of in certain important criteria such as scale, feedback, predictable, time and cost to execute. In addition, if the quality problems are discovered during runtime evaluation, it is nearly not possible to rectify those problems in a short time. Quality evaluation during design time is likely more convenient in many aspects as shown in Table 3 and thus, provides more space to rectify the quality problems if exist.

CHALLENGES

Reliability Design Modeling

Incorporation of a reliability context into every aspect of a design principle is much needed for the purposes of reasoning of the system reliability during the development process (Lyu, 2007). With reference to (IEC 9126-1, 2001), system reliability is described as the capability of the system/component/services to perform a given task under constraints of a specific condition and time frame. From this definition, it is undeniable that the reliability contextual issues such as resource, timing and task play an important role in system reliability level. In addition, the reliability of the system depends not only on the system task, but also considers the availability of the resource of the system (Pietrantuono *et al.*, 2010). Even if any task of the system execution is free from failures, the lack of availability of resources due to an unexpected failure could nevertheless cause system failures (Hong and Gu, 2011). Therefore,

Table 3. The comparison of software quality evaluation approach

Criteria	Design Time	Simulation	Run Time
Model	Stochastic Process Queuing Network Petri Nets UML Based	NS-2 TOSSIM	Performance Monitor
Development Process	Early design phase	During Design phase	After implementation
Predictable	Very high	High	Very low
Cost	Low	High	Very High
Time	Short	Long	Long
Accuracy	Medium	High	Very High
Feedback	Very High	High	Low
Scale	High	Low	Low

the incorporation of these contexts into a design model as early as possible during the design phase could provide an insight as to what is the possible design problem relating to reliability (Mohamed and Zulkernine, 2010; Singh, 2011). Consequently, the needs of a design model having minimal flaws regarding reliability could avoid any additional efforts to rectify the system if a problem is discovered after deployment. Therefore, the challenges are, namely: how can the design model provide a view for reliability contexts (resource, timing and task) and, at the same time, provide an expressive model for the process of reliability estimation. The expressiveness of the model emphasized the availability and specificity respectively (Luck *et al.*, 2009). The expressiveness of the reliability design model specifies a high possible reliability context in a single model that makes this model available for analysis purposes. In this sense, the process for reliability estimation could still provide a view from the primary reliability context (resource, timing and task) together with support from the expressive reliability design model.

Many works have appeared recently using a model for reliability estimation. Works by Becker *et al.* (2009), Distefano *et al.* (2011), Grassi *et al.* (2007), Petriu and Woodside (2006) make an inclusion into the *Unified Modelling Language*

(UML) diagram using the UML profile. The UML profile provides a rich annotation for various domain applications. However, less effort has been devoted to relating the influence of timing, task and resource upon the level of system reliability. For instance, the Core Scenario Model (CSM) proposed by Petriu and Woodside (2006) is the intermediate model which poses the capability of identifying when the resource is acquired and released by the activity. Their definition of activity actually originates from the *Message* in a sequence diagram, which is annotated with the related timing requirements. However, when transforming the sequence diagram into this model, a timing requirement (which is available in the prior model), is completely ignored. Their capabilities only consider the allocation and usage of the resource for reliability estimation.

Moreover, in Distefano *et al.* (2004), the proposed model poses a similar concept as CSM, but the idea is to emphasize a system scenario so as to discover possible reliability problems in a scenario execution. However, this work only considers timing information but fails to relate it with a resource and task. In Grassi *et al.* (2007), for instance, the author has proposed a model called *Kernel Language for Performance and Reliability Analysis* (KLAPER). This model provides a performance and reliability estimation for a component-based system built on component behaviour. The inclusion of timing, task and resource in this model is attempted, but the details for timing failure information are not sufficient for reliability estimation purposes. Other works in Brosch *et al.* (2011) provide a Palladio component model, responsible for systematically performing reliability analysis with the inclusion of resource and task information, but ignoring a timing context. Other notable works that consider a timing context for reliability estimation can be found in Bernardi *et al.* (2011), Rohr *et al.* (2010) and Voeten *et al.* (2011); however, these are not specifically intended for a model-based approach.

Drawing this insight together, there is no doubt that the influence of timing, resource and task for reliability estimation is inevitable. The inclusion of these elements in the reliability design model could facilitate the process of reliability estimation. In fact, the existing modelling notation provided by UML profile for *Modelling and Analysis for Embedded Real Time System* (MARTE) and *Quality of Services and Fault Tolerance* (QoS/FT) is adequate for modelling notation. However, it is also limited by a certain constraint, especially for the expressiveness of the model towards timing concepts for reliability. The constraint may be solved by use of an analytical model such as Markov chain or Petri Nets, but suffers from a complexity issue within a model transformation process. Thus, the introduction of a new reliability design model could enhance the expressiveness of the reliability design model towards a reliability context, especially with regard to timing aspects. To conclude, the existing models lack two important criteria, namely: timing failure annotation and the influence of a resource and a task. To the best of our knowledge, existing works provide adequate information for system reliability but fail to express timing failure behaviour through system scenario. Moreover, most of the existing works fail to indicate the effect of the resource and task upon system reliability.

Provision of an expressive reliability design model may be useful for reliability estimation purposes. The expressiveness of the reliability design model allows the incorporation of reliability contexts (timing, resource, task, etc.) into a single design model. Hence, this implies an early estimation for reliability through model design and, thus, possible system failure information regarding system reliability could be obtained for further analysis.

Reliability Parameter Estimation

Estimating a reliability parameter for reliability estimation is difficult, especially during the design phase of a model (Schneidewind, 2009). The difficulty arises from lack of availability of failure data for the system. The acquisition of failure data usually occurs after system deployment, where the system is closely monitored and its failure data is collected during runtime. In order to estimate the failure data during the design phase, the models involved should be sufficiently expressive regarding reliability contexts and, at the same time, incorporated with additional artefacts in order to produce related reliability parameters. To realize this process, existing works emphasize the employment of a usage profile (Musa, 1993). The usage profiling of the system describes possible input values, call sequence behaviour and expected output of the system. In fact, early formal documentation for expressing system's behaviour could foresee any design flaws based on usage profile. Existing models, which only focus on the selection of these contexts, restrict meaningful acquisition of reliability parameters.

The capability of the integrated usage profile, failure model and reliability design model respectively to estimate the values for reliability parameters during the design phase could similarly avoid the problems of unavailability of failure data (Gokhale, 2007). The system usage profile (also known as operational profile) can provide pre-defined input values, which may explain the behaviour of the system. The list of input values may influence the behaviour of the system, as these input values may impose some pre-defined system requirements. The usage profile for the system under study can provide necessary details for a system reliability estimation process (Krka *et al.*, 2009), especially for a model-based system reliability analysis. The behaviour of the system is possible to be evaluated and estimated based on a pre-defined usage profile. In a usage profile, various assumptions could be made in order to investigate the system behaviour based on a series of input values that would be used during a system operational process in order to produce a necessary system output. The input values that may influence the behaviour of the system can be clearly defined, that is, involve reliability (Lai-shun *et al.*, 2011). Recent studies that utilize a usage profile for estimating or predicting reliability of the system can be found in Brosch *et al.* (2011), Brosch *et al.* (2011), Grassi *et al.* (2007), Sato and Trivedi (2007) and Sharma and Trivedi (2007).

However, many assumptions of a particular nature are often made by domain experts to assign reliability values to the system (Distefano *et al.*, 2011; Hamlet, 2009). This assumption often ignores the varying reliability combinations that cause failures. For instance, a particular resource reliability may be based on its period and utilization time (Bernardi *et al.*, 2011). However, the reliability of the resource may vary with the combination of various resources or tasks that are indirectly attached to that resource. Therefore, simplifying the process of assigning reliability values for the resources or task is doubtful with regard to effective reliability estimation.

In this sense, by having the reliability design model that contains most of the related reliability context, the acquisition of the reliability parameters is much easier, as it would have support from the usage profile and failure model. Hence, this indicates a real value of reliability parameters based on the design model, which will be used later by the estimation model for a further analysis.

Reliability Estimation Modeling

Many reliability estimation models have been proposed, inspired by the 'white-box approach', to estimate system reliability during design time (Gokhale *et al.*, 2004; Gokhale and Trivedi, 2006). The models, including those described in Cheung (1980), Hsu and Huang (2011), Lo *et al.* (2005) and Yacoub *et al.* (2004) consider the reliability of individual components and their transition. Traditionally, reliability values for components and transitions have been available, from either a usage profile or calculated using simulation or observation (Gokhale, 2005). Most existing models (Bai *et al.*, 2005; Baier *et al.*, 2010) adapt a Markov chain process by which to estimate the system. This assumes that the subsequent component failure is dependent on the current component, thus ignoring other component states within its structure.

However, most of the estimation models have neglected the influence of an execution environment (resource, task). The importance of correlation between system task and resource usage in scenario executions for reliability analysis can be found in Joseph (2011), Mohanta *et al.* (2010) and Pietrantuono *et al.* (2010). Other works were only addressed for the purposes of component interaction aspects (Su *et al.*, 2011; Yacoub and Ammar, 2002) and resource usage (Garousi *et al.*, 2008) respectively.

In relation to works relating to reliability estimation of a system based on components and its transition, it is worth describing the works of Cheung (1980), Hsu and Huang (2011), Lo *et al.* (2005) and Yacoub *et al.* (2004). The study in Yacoub *et al.* (2004) proposed the Component Dependency Graph (CDG) for analysing component interaction behaviour and its transition probability. However, this approach is not explicitly associated with the triggered *system task* that is used by the resources, and may cause inconvenience with regard to misuse of resources. This problem may suffer drawbacks that increase the probability of failure of the resources. Another work by Lo *et al.* (2005) considers the estimation of system reliability based on multiple input and output values. The estimation model is called the "Lo component-based reliability design model" (LCBRM) and the output of the result is determined by sensitivity analysis so as to determine the most sensitive parameters in relation to the estimation accuracy. Studies by Hsu and Huang, (2011) adapted a path-based model called adaptive reliability analysis. This model uses Adaptive Reliability Analysis Using Path Testing (ARAUPT) and estimates the reliability of a system based on a mixed structure (branch, loop and sequence) in order to determine the best scenario to be tested for reliability analysis. Another estimation model worthy of mention is Cheung's user-oriented reliability (CUORM) (Cheung, 1980) which estimates the reliability of the system with respect to user module reliability and covers heterogonous system structures such as pipeline, call-return and fault tolerance.

Aggregating this together, the influence of the execution environment (resource and task) is worth considering for estimating system reliability. The previously mentioned existing works mostly include only component and transition reliability as an ingredient for reliability estimation. In fact, the influence of system task in each component silently affects the transition from one component to another. On the other hand, the influence of system execution should also be considered for reliability estimation. This is because the estimation for every possible system execution could help to identify what aspect is the most reliable and, hence, foresee the effects of scenario complexity from a reliability level. Therefore, the criteria of estimation result should be driven by the following requirements, namely: the complexity of system scenario and the transition between components through task transition.

The Proposed Methodology

In this chapter, the *Model-Based System Reliability Estimation-PerFAM (MBSRE-PerFAM)* methodology is proposed. This methodology provides a systematic process by which to estimate the system reliability at design phase, supported by the models for a reliability estimation process. In general, the *MBSRE-PerFAM* methodology is represented using Software Process Engineering Model (SPEM), which is a standard process in the software engineering domain. The essential elements for model-based reliability estimation have been reported in (Gokhale and Trivedi, 2006; Krka et al., 2009) which provide the inclusion of three compulsory models, namely: reliability model, reliability parameters model and reliability estimation model. However, current methodologies offer an ad-hoc process for the practice of reliability estimation. In addition, the lack of model expressiveness and model consistency between those models subsequently restricts the systematic process for reliability estimation. This makes it essentially difficult to preserve model consistency, especially for the use of reliability parameters. As shown in Figure 1, the proposed methodology consists of one process, which is comprised of seven activities. Each activity consists of tasks, which essentially provide a detailed task list in terms of "*what to execute*" and "*what to produce*". The details of the activities and its task are described in the following sub-sections.

Establish the Context

As shown in Figure 2, this activity consists of two tasks, namely: *identify key system scenario* and identify *timing specification*. The domain experts, who are essentially responsible for the system description, will perform both tasks. Firstly, the key system scenario is identified. In general, the system usually comprises the whole array of scenarios, ranging from the simple to the critical. Each scenario represents its own goal

Figure 1. The MBSRE Methodology

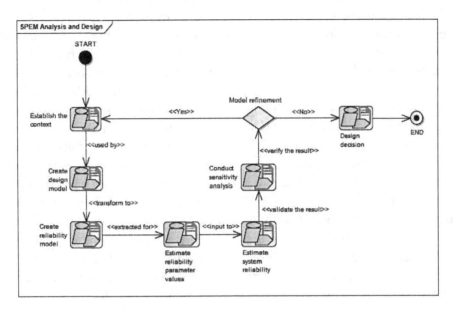

Figure 2. Step for establish the context activity

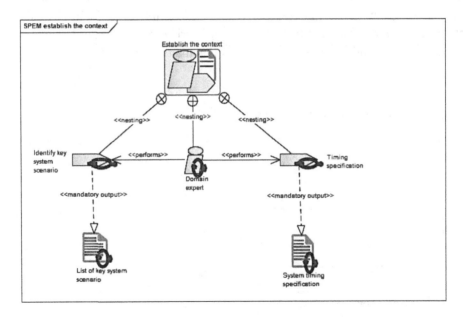

and behaviour, which lead to the success of the system. In this sense, being able to adequately estimate the reliability for the whole scenario of the system is nearly impossible, due to the state of space explosion problems. Therefore, the domain experts of the system are responsible for identifying which is the scenario that most affects a system and will consequently lead to system failure. With respect to the selected scenario, the domain experts will initially try to determine the system timing specification for each scenario, so as to jointly take into account the reliability parameters on the system scenario.

Create the Design Model

Once the critical system scenario and its timing specification are identified, the next activity is to translate that information into a system model. Figure 3 shows the second activity the created design model activity will carry out. The purpose of this activity is the creation of the *behaviour diagram* with *timing annotation* through tasks. To adequately represent the system scenario, the design model was designed using the UML sequence diagrams so as to define the key scenario of systems at a high level. Each sequence diagram represents a key scenario of the system, where the reliability associated with timing failure will be annotated and defined. The development of multiple sequence diagrams (SD) is considered independently of each other, assuming that each SD involves different timing failures. Each SD will

elaborate upon how the system may perform during message exchanges between resources. The input parameters and timing properties will be defined using the UML MARTE profile. More specifically, the Performance Analysis (PA) and Generic Quantitative Analysis Modelling (GQAM) will be used to annotate the related timing and resource requirements in detail.

To express the reliability contexts of the sequence diagrams in a detailed level, it is necessary to provide enrichment with a specific UML profile called MARTE. This profile provides a rich notation for reliability (timing, resource, etc.), as to where and how the timing and resource will be deployed and operate. In this sense, the adoption of reliability contexts only relates to the timing, resource and task that are associated with system scenarios. The developed sequence diagrams consist of the definition of a high-level system scenario of the timing properties associated with *Message* and *Resource*. In particular, each system scenario represents a key behaviour of the system that may influence the level of system reliability.

Figure 3. Step for create design model activity

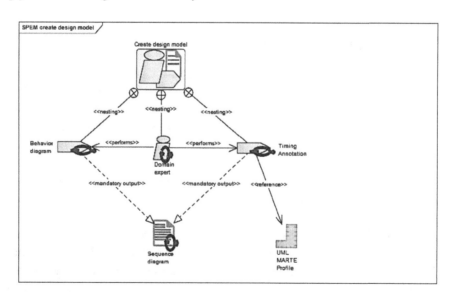

Figure 4. Access Control Scenario in BSS (Petriu & Woodside, 2006)

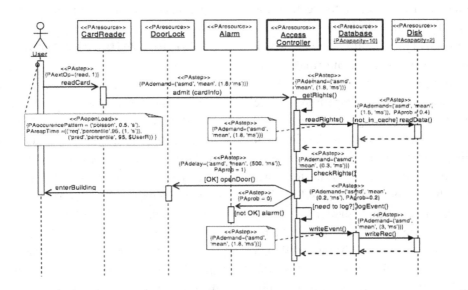

Figure 5. Step for create reliability design model activity

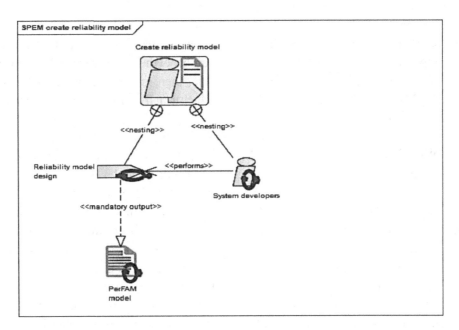

Each resource is associated with *period* time and *executionTime* for each *Message* when exchanging the information between resources. Figure 4 shows an example of sequence diagram from (Petriu & Woodside, 2006).

Create the Reliability Design Model

Indeed, in order to successfully represent the UML sequence diagram from the reliability point of view, a specific reliability model is needed that can expressively represent the reliability context as a single model. Therefore, in this section, the subsequent task as shown in Figure 5 provides the development of a reliability model, which has been developed using the information derived from the created design model. This model should provide a good insight for timing failure behaviour identification through call sequence and resource association. Before that, the development of a reliability model is based on a design model (UML sequence diagram) and the rules for transforming from the former to the latter is described specifically based on the target model (reliability model). The transformation rules such as Query, View and Transformation (QVT) from UML can be applied to define transformation rules from the former to the later model. The developed reliability model provides a scenario model for expressing the timing failure behaviour, associated in each *Activity*. For each *Activity* to seamlessly correlate with the resource that is being referenced, each resource also poses its own timing *period*. Figure 6 is an example the reliability design model called *Performability failure behaviour awareness metamodel* (PerFAM) for reliability design model (Isa, Jawawi, & Zaki, 2013).

Estimate Reliability Parameter Values

As shown in Figure 7, the estimation for reliability parameters consists of two tasks, namely, *estimate activity parameters* and *estimate resource parameters* with the support of a usage profile as mentioned in Chapter 6. These values are estimated with support provided from a failure distribution function that combines the timing requirements that have been annotated at *Activity* and *Resource*. The produced results are the probability or reliability values for the *Activity* and *Resource*. Such types of reliability values will be applied in the estimation model at a later step. Observe that this step will significantly affect the accuracy of estimation results at a later stage; the timing

properties in *Activity* can be changed according to the needs of the system scenario.

Estimate System Reliability

This activity as shown in Figure 8 provides an estimation of the system reliability previously identified with the selected system scenario to represent the whole system execution. The various analytical model for reliability estimation such as Petri Nets, graph theory and automata can be used to calculate the system reliability with the support of the reliability parameters specification produced in the previous step. The results produced in this step will be validated using a sensitivity analysis approach. This approach is adopted since the relevant failure data is not available.

Conduct Sensitivity Analysis

This activity as shown in Figure 9 is carried out when the real failure data is not available. The validity of the estimation result cannot be validated since there is a lack of important real failure data, which usually can be obtained after system deployment. Therefore, the sensitivity analysis identifies and evaluates the boundaries of estimation, in order to identify which system task or resources contribute to the level of system reliability. Such types of validation techniques are often used in reliability estimations for the system under study.

In order to ensure the accuracy of our approach, there are several aspects that need to be considered, one of them being *plausible behaviour*. Plausible behaviour handles the robustness of the model against a number of input parameters to the system. This means that plausible changes of the estimation result depend on a variation of input parameters to the system. However, in the current practice, reliability estimation is mostly done on a plausibility level that makes the validation of estimation results against measured values difficult to be implemented. The primary problem is the difficulty in measuring reliability values onto

Figure 6. The example of PerFAM model (Isa, Jawawi, & Zaki, 2013)

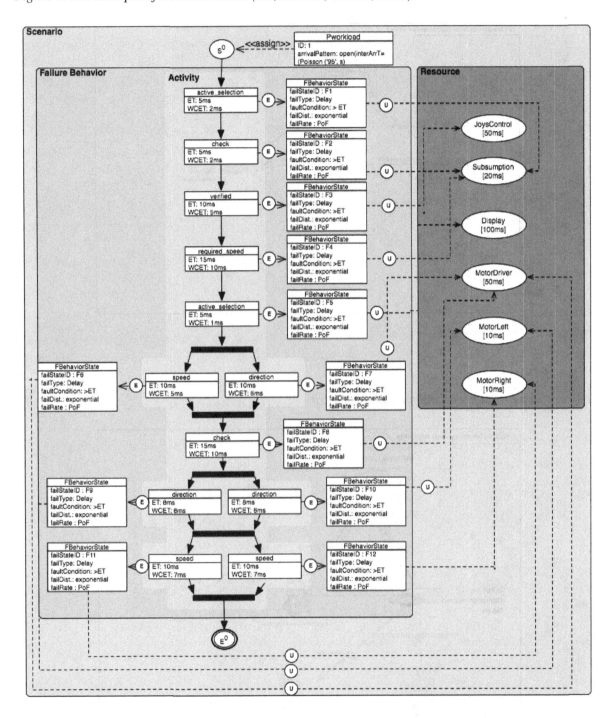

software. This difficulty could be overcome by using a statistical approach, thus enabling measurement of the reliability of the system before deployment. However, the lack of real failure data could hinder progress towards reliability measurements. Even if failure data is available, the input parameters are mostly not included as a result of measured system execution. Therefore, the only

Figure 7. Step for estimate reliability parameter values activity

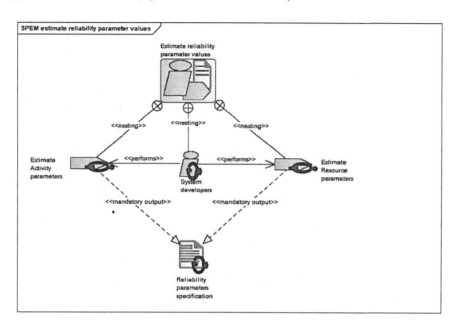

Figure 8. Step for estimate system reliability activity

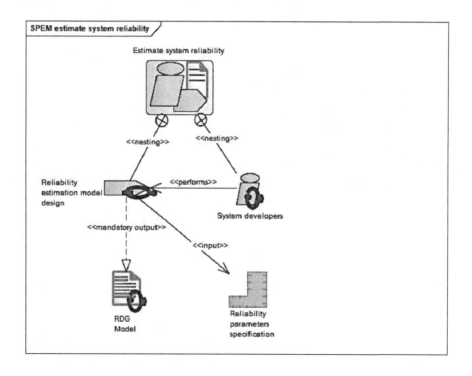

Figure 9. Step for conduct sensitivity analysis activity

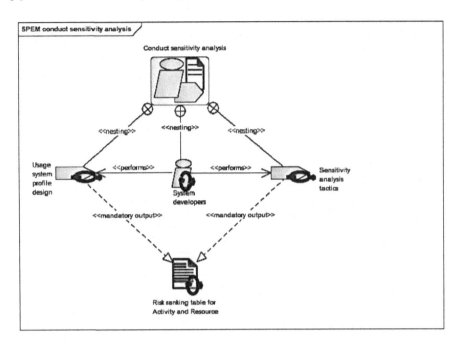

reliable approach by which to validate a software reliability design model is through plausibility. Existing previous works on reliability validation are compared in Brosch *et al.* (2011).

The sensitivity analysis is used to discover the effect of the system reliability, with a support form *usage system profile design* as well as the number of failures based on the input parameters in the system (time execution for activity and resource reliability). Similarly, a reliability design model was often validated by plausibility (input parameters are changed over time and their sensitivity on the result is observed) from previous works due to the shortcoming of failure data for system failure by applying *sensitivity analysis tactics*. This validation approach is well-suited to the usage profile method so as to rectify the abovementioned shortcomings.

Design Decision

As shown in Figure 10, the design decision activity consists of deciding whether the result of reli-

ability estimation is acceptable or not. To do this, the result from the sensitivity analysis procedure is required. The results are aimed at identifying the critical parts, both for resource and task. Both parts contain the reliability values that influence the level of system reliability. The design decision is provided in a form of general guidelines on how to modify and improve the design so as to increase the system reliability.

This guideline, that has to be applied in the design decision, give instruction on how to alleviate the identified critical resources and activities. Based on the previous step, the result of sensitivity analysis shows a different output for system failure when the delay was injected to both resource and activities timing.

When the critical element is a system resource, an alternative resource allocation could be studied for the design refinement in the UML sequence diagram (1). The resource is either reallocated to decrease its burden for utilization or readjusted the activities that attached to those resources (2). In the case of activities, the rectification can be done

Figure 10. Step for design decision activity

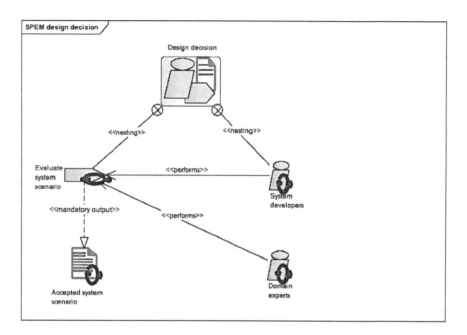

either to readjusted the timing that goes beyond the timing constraint or to re-draw the system scenario to give a balance among activities timing properties (3). After either of these changes has been done in the UML sequence diagram, the whole step has to be applied again to check the level of system reliability and its sensitivity results regarding on resource and activity (4).

FUTURE RESEARCH DIRECTIONS

The capability of models for visualizing and representing the system under development can be seen in the successful of UML modelling language. Indeed, this language has contributed to the world of system modeling. In this sense, this chapter has proposed a methodology for model-based estimation for reliability. The methodology utilized the models that are focusing on reliability point of view and estimate a possible reliability value for the system. From this standpoint, any mishap or design problems in system models can be traced and rectified before deployment.

In addition, to completely automate the whole process of reliability estimation, the implementation of a modeling and analysis tool is recommended so as to facilitate a developer to accelerate the estimation process. In this sense, a detailed model depicting transformation rules, semantics and syntax of the proposed models is needed. The modeling and analysis tools can be implemented using existing modeling frameworks such as Generic Modeling Environment (GME).

CONCLUSION

The systematic methodology for model-based system reliability estimation is proposed. The methodology context is the reliability design model, derived from UML sequence diagram, which is enriched with MARTE profile to capture the timing properties. The developed reliability design model is then produced the reliability parameters specifications that are beneficial for estimation purposes using the reliability estimation model. The result of system estimation is then validated with the sensitivity analysis approach as to identify a critical resources and activities that influence the level of system reliability. Later, the design decision is executed if the level of system reliability is not satisfied through model refinement. The simple guideline is provided on how to alleviate the identified critical resources and tasks in terms of timing and resource allocation.

In this chapter, the best practice of software engineering practices was applied (UML, profiling, model transformation) together with additional model for reliability to propose a systematic methodology for estimating the system reliability during design phase. The main contribution in this chapter is the systematic methodology for reliability estimation (MBSRE-PerFAM methodology) by following the standard process of model-based reliability estimation. This methodology can give a broad insight on how to systematically estimate the system reliability without losing its consistency regarding on reliability parameters.

REFERENCES

Alexander, D. (2003). Application of monte carlo simulations to system reliability analysis. In *Proceedings of the 20th International Pump Symposium*. Houston, TX: Academic Press.

Bai, C. G., Hu, Q. P., Xie, M., & Ng, S. H. (2005). Software failure prediction based on a Markov Bayesian network model. *Journal of Systems and Software*, 74(3), 275–282. doi:10.1016/j.jss.2004.02.028

Baier, C., Cloth, L., Haverkort, B. R., Hermanns, H., & Katoen, J. P. (2010). Performability assessment by model checking of Markov reward models. *Formal Methods in System Design*, 36(1), 1–36. doi:10.1007/s10703-009-0088-7

Balsamo, S., Di Marco, A., Inverardi, P., & Simeoni, M. (2004). Model-based performance prediction in software development: a survey. *IEEE Transactions on Software Engineering*, 30(5), 295–310. doi:10.1109/TSE.2004.9

Becker, S., Koziolek, H., & Reussner, R. (2009). The Palladio component model for model-driven performance prediction. *Journal of Systems and Software*, 82(1), 3–22. doi:10.1016/j.jss.2008.03.066

Bernardi, S., Campos, J., & Merseguer, J. (2011). Timing-failure risk assessment of UML design using Time Petri Net bound techniques. *Industrial Informatics. IEEE Transactions on*, 7(1), 90–104.

Brosch, F., Koziolek, H., & Buhnova, B. (2011). Architecture-Based Reliability Prediction with the Palladio Component Model. *IEEE Transactions on Software Engineering*, 38(6), 1319–1339. doi:10.1109/TSE.2011.94

Brosch, F., Koziolek, H., Buhnova, B., & Reussner, R. (2010). Parameterized reliability prediction for component-based software architectures. In *Research into Practice–Reality and Gaps* (pp. 36–51). Springer. doi:10.1007/978-3-642-13821-8_5

Cheung, L., Roshandel, R., Medvidovic, N., & Golubchik, L. (2008). Early prediction of software component reliability. In *Proceedings of the 30th international conference on Software engineering* (pp. 111–120). ACM.

Cheung, R. C. (1980). A User-Oriented Software Reliability Model. *IEEE Transactions on Software Engineering*, SE-6(2), 118–125. doi:10.1109/TSE.1980.234477

Ciancone, A., Drago, M. L., Filieri, A., Grassi, V., Koziolek, H., & Mirandola, R. (2013). The KlaperSuite framework for model-driven reliability analysis of component-based systems. *Software & Systems Modeling*, 1–22.

Ciardo, G., Miner, A. S., & Wan, M. (2009). Advanced features in SMART: the stochastic model checking analyzer for reliability and timing. *ACM SIGMETRICS Performance Evaluation Review, 36*(4), 58–63. doi:10.1145/1530873.1530885

Cortellessa, V., Di Marco, A., & Inverardi, P. (2011). Model-Based Software Performance Analysis. *Analysis*, 65–78.

Cortellessa, V., Goseva-Popstojanova, K., Appukkutty, K., Guedem, A. R., Hassan, A., Elnaggar, R., & Ammar, H. H. (2005). Model-based performance risk analysis. *Software Engineering. IEEE Transactions on, 31*(1), 3–20.

Distefano, S., Paci, D., Puliafito, A., & Scarpa, M. (2004). UML design and software performance modeling. [Springer.]. *Proceedings of Computer and Information Sciences-ISCIS, 2004*, 564–573.

Distefano, S., Scarpa, M., & Puliafito, A. (2011). From UML to Petri Nets: The PCM-Based Methodology. *IEEE Transactions on Software Engineering, 37*(1), 65–79. doi:10.1109/TSE.2010.10

Garousi, V., Briand, L. C., & Labiche, Y. (2008). A UML-based quantitative framework for early prediction of resource usage and load in distributed real-time systems. *Software & Systems Modeling, 8*(2), 275–302. doi:10.1007/s10270-008-0099-7

Gokhale, S. (2007). Architecture-Based Software Reliability Analysis: Overview and Limitations. *IEEE Transactions on Dependable and Secure Computing, 4*(1), 32–40. doi:10.1109/TDSC.2007.4

Gokhale, S. S. (2005). A simulation approach to structure-based software reliability analysis. *IEEE Transactions on Software Engineering, 31*(8), 643–656. doi:10.1109/TSE.2005.86

Gokhale, S. S., & Trivedi, K. S. (2006). Analytical Models for Architecture-Based Software Reliability Prediction: A Unification Framework. *IEEE Transactions on Reliability, 55*(4), 578–590. doi:10.1109/TR.2006.884587

Gokhale, S. S., Wong, W., Horgan, J. R., & Trivedi, K. S. (2004). An analytical approach to architecture-based software performance and reliability prediction. *Performance Evaluation, 58*(4), 391–412. doi:10.1016/j.peva.2004.04.003

Grassi, V., Mirandola, R., & Sabetta, A. (2007). Filling the gap between design and performance/reliability models of component-based systems: A model-driven approach. *Journal of Systems and Software, 80*(4), 528–558. doi:10.1016/j.jss.2006.07.023

Hamlet, D. (2009). Tools and experiments supporting a testing-based theory of component composition. [TOSEM]. *ACM Transactions on Software Engineering and Methodology, 18*(3), 12. doi:10.1145/1525880.1525885

Hong, D., Gu, T., & Baik, J. (2011). A UML model based white box reliability prediction to identify unreliable components. In *Proceedings of Secure Software Integration & Reliability Improvement Companion (SSIRI-C), 2011 5th International Conference on* (pp. 152-159). IEEE.

Hsu, C. J., & Huang, C. Y. (2011). An adaptive reliability analysis using path testing for complex component-based software systems. *Reliability. IEEE Transactions on, 60*(1), 158–170.

Immonen, A., & Niemelä, E. (2007). Survey of reliability and availability prediction methods from the viewpoint of software architecture. *Software & Systems Modeling, 7*(1), 49–65. doi:10.1007/s10270-006-0040-x

Isa, M. A., Jawawi, D. N. A., & Zaki, M. Z. (n.d.). Model-driven estimation approach for system reliability using integrated tasks and resources. *Software Quality Journal*, 1-37.

Joseph, S. (2011). A Model for Reliability Estimation of Software based Systems by Integrating Hardware and Software. *Science and Technology*, 26–29.

Krka, I., Edwards, G., Cheung, L., Golubchik, L., & Medvidovic, N. (2009). A comprehensive exploration of challenges in architecture-based reliability estimation. [Springer.]. *Proceedings of Architecting Dependable Systems, VI*, 202–227.

Lai-Shun, Z., Yan, H., & Zhong-Wen, L. (2011). Building Markov chain-based software reliability usage model with UML. In *Proceedings of Communication Software and Networks (ICCSN), 2011 IEEE 3rd International Conference on* (pp. 548-551). IEEE.

Lo, J. H., Huang, C. Y., Chen, I. Y., Kuo, S. Y., & Lyu, M. R. (2005). Reliability assessment and sensitivity analysis of software reliability growth modeling based on software module structure. *Journal of Systems and Software, 76*(1), 3–13. doi:10.1016/j.jss.2004.06.025

Lyu, M. R. (2007). Software reliability engineering: A roadmap. In *Proceedings of 2007 Future of Software Engineering* (pp. 153–170). IEEE Computer Society.

Meedeniya, I., Moser, I., Aleti, A., & Grunske, L. (2011). Architecture-based reliability evaluation under uncertainty. In *Proceedings of the Joint ACM SIGSOFT Conference--QoSA and ACM SIGSOFT symposium--ISARCS on Quality of software architectures--QoSA and architecting critical systems--ISARCS* (pp. 85-94). ACM.

Mohamed, A., & Zulkernine, M. (2010). A taxonomy of software architecture-based reliability efforts. In *Proceedings of the 2010 ICSE Workshop on Sharing and Reusing Architectural Knowledge* (pp. 44-51). ACM.

Mohanta, S., Vinod, G., Ghosh, A. K., & Mall, R. (2010). An approach for early prediction of software reliability. *ACM SIGSOFT Software Engineering Notes, 35*(6), 1–9. doi:10.1145/1874391.1874403

Musa, J. D. (1993). Operational profiles in software-reliability engineering. *Software, IEEE, 10*(2), 14–32. doi:10.1109/52.199724

Petriu, D. B., & Woodside, M. (2007). An intermediate metamodel with scenarios and resources for generating performance models from UML designs. *Software & Systems Modeling, 6*(2), 163–184. doi:10.1007/s10270-006-0026-8

Pietrantuono, R., Russo, S., & Trivedi, K. S. (2010). Software Reliability and Testing Time Allocation: An Architecture-Based Approach. *IEEE Transactions on Software Engineering, 36*(3), 323–337. doi:10.1109/TSE.2010.6

Rohr, M., van Hoorn, A., Hasselbring, W., Lübcke, M., & Alekseev, S. (2010). Workload-intensity-sensitive timing behavior analysis for distributed multi-user software systems. In *Proceedings of the first joint WOSP/SIPEW international conference on Performance engineering* (pp. 87-92). ACM.

Salfner, F., Lenk, M., & Malek, M. (2010). A survey of online failure prediction methods. [CSUR]. *ACM Computing Surveys, 42*(3), 10. doi:10.1145/1670679.1670680

Sato, N., & Trivedi, K. S. (2007). Accurate and efficient stochastic reliability analysis of composite services using their compact Markov reward model representations. In *Proceedings of Services Computing* (pp. 114–121). IEEE. doi:10.1109/SCC.2007.21

Schneidewind, N. F. (2009). Analysis of object-oriented software reliability model development. *Innovations in Systems and Software Engineering, 5*(4), 243–253. doi:10.1007/s11334-009-0097-0

Sharma, V., & Trivedi, K. (2007). Quantifying software performance, reliability and security: An architecture-based approach. *Journal of Systems and Software, 80*(4), 493–509. doi:10.1016/j.jss.2006.07.021

Singh, L. K. (2011). Software Reliability Early Prediction in Architectural Design Phase: Overview and Limitations. *Journal of Software Engineering and Applications, 4*(3), 181–186. doi:10.4236/jsea.2011.43020

Song, J., & Kang, W. H. (2009). System reliability and sensitivity under statistical dependence by matrix-based system reliability method. *Structural Safety*, *31*(2), 148–156. doi:10.1016/j.strusafe.2008.06.012

Spyrou, S., Bamidis, P. D., Maglaveras, N., Pangalos, G., & Pappas, C. (2008). A methodology for reliability analysis in health networks. *Information Technology in Biomedicine. IEEE Transactions on*, *12*(3), 377–386.

Su, X., Liu, H., Wu, Z., Yang, X., & Zuo, D. (2011). SA based software deployment reliability estimation considering component dependence. *Journal of Electronics (China)*, *28*(1), 118–125. doi:10.1007/s11767-011-0561-5

Valis, D., & Bartlett, L. (2010). The failure phenomenon: a critique. *International Journal of Performance Engineering*, *6*(2), 181–190.

Voeten, J., Hendriks, T., Theelen, B., Schuddemat, J., Suermondt, W. T., Gemei, J., & van Huët, C. (2011). Predicting Timing Performance of Advanced Mechatronics Control Systems. In *Proceedings of Computer Software and Applications Conference Workshops (COMPSACW), 2011 IEEE 35th Annual* (pp. 206-210). IEEE.

Yacoub, S., Cukic, B., & Ammar, H. H. (2004). A Scenario-Based Reliability Analysis Approach for Component-Based Software. *IEEE Transactions on Reliability*, *53*(4), 465–480. doi:10.1109/TR.2004.838034

Yacoub, S. M., & Ammar, H. H. (2002). A Methodology for Architecture-Level Reliability Risk Analysis. *IEEE Transactions on Software Engineering*, *28*(6), 529–547. doi:10.1109/TSE.2002.1010058

Yacoub, S. M., Ammar, H. H., & Robinson, T. (2002). A methodology for architectural-level risk assessment using dynamic metrics. In *Proceedings of Software Reliability Engineering* (pp. 210–221). IEEE.

Zio, E. (2009). Reliability engineering: Old problems and new challenges. *Reliability Engineering & System Safety*, *94*(2), 125–141. doi:10.1016/j.ress.2008.06.002

KEY TERMS AND DEFINITIONS

Estimation: An approximation or informal guesstimate that don't need for real measurement data validation.

Methodology: A framework that is structured, planned and consists of models to develop something.

Model: An abstract representation of a real world.

System Design: The process of defining the architecture, components, modules, interfaces, and data for a system to satisfy specified requirements.

System Quality Analysis: An assessment for evaluating the quality of the system.

System Reliability: A capability for a system to operate in a specific time and condition.

Systematic Process: An organized process to execute something.

Chapter 21
Non–Intrusive Adaptation of System Execution Traces for Performance Analysis of Software Systems

Manjula Peiris
Indiana University Purdue University Indianapolis (IUPUI), USA

James H. Hill
Indiana University Purdue University Indianapolis (IUPUI), USA

ABSTRACT

This chapter discusses how to adapt system execution traces to support analysis of software system performance properties, such as end-to-end response time, throughput, and service time. This is important because system execution traces contain complete snapshots of a systems execution—making them useful artifacts for analyzing software system performance properties. Unfortunately, if system execution traces do not contain the required properties, then analysis of performance properties is hard. In this chapter, the authors discuss: (1) what properties are required to analysis performance properties in a system execution trace; (2) different approaches for injecting the required properties into a system execution trace to support performance analysis; and (3) show, by example, the solution for one approach that does not require modifying the original source code of the system that produced the system execution.

1. INTRODUCTION

Challenges of using system execution traces for performance analysis. Software performance analysis is the process of analyzing performance properties (*e.g.* response time, service time, throughput) of a software system. Analyzing system execution traces is one technique used in

software performance analysis. System execution traces can be generated by (1) compiling the source code of the system with instrumentation code(Wolf & Mohr, 2003); (2) collecting the log messages while executing the instrumented system (Hill J., 2010); and (3) registering for certain events in the target system and generating messages whenever that event occurs (Mod & Murphy, 2001). The first

DOI: 10.4018/978-1-4666-6026-7.ch021

method is an intrusive method because it modifies the actual source code of the target system. Second and third methods are non-intrusive, because it does not require modifying the system's original source code.

Most of the existing approaches for using system execution traces to analyze software performance are based on intrusive methods(Wolf & Mohr, 2003). The main limitation with these approaches is it requires access to the system's source code. Other approaches for using system execution traces to analyze software performance are tightly coupled with system architecture and deployment (Mod & Murphy, 2001). Finally, approaches that are not architecture-dependent require system execution traces to be generated in a certain format (Salonen & Piilil, 2012)(Salonen & Piilil, 2012),(Nagaraj, Killian, & Neville, 2012). Moreover, such approaches are not trying to utilize system log messages, but rather enforce system developers to use provided logging mechanisms. This approach therefore requires system developers to change the underlying implementation for the purpose of performance analysis. The limitations discussed above make it *hard* to generalize existing approaches for different kinds of systems, and their generated system execution trace.

We have focused on using non-intrusive approaches, such as execution log messages for performance analysis, to overcome the current limitations of using intrusive system execution traces for software performance analysis. Rather than modifying the system's original source code, we focus on creating an intermediate model to abstract out the events in the system execution trace and the relations among log messages. Likewise, we assume generated log messages are not in a certain format.

The realization of our approach is in a tool called *Understanding Non-functional Intensions via Testing and Experimentation (UNITE)* (Hill & Schmidt, 2009). UNITE uses dataflow models to describe causality relationships between event types—not event instances—in the system. This

allows UNITE to operate at a higher level of abstraction that remains constant regardless of how the underlying software system is designed, implemented, and deployed (i.e., the mapping of software components to hardware components). The dataflow model is then used to process the system execution trace, and analyze performance properties.

Although it is possible to analyze performance properties via system execution traces using tools like UNITE, it is assumed that system execution traces contain several properties, e.g., identifiable keywords, unique message instances, enough variations among the same event types to support performance analysis. Moreover, the dataflow model must contain several properties, e.g., identifiable log formats and unique relations between different log formats. If planned early enough in the software lifecycle, it is possible to ensure these properties exist in both the dataflow model and generated system execution trace. Unfortunately, it is not possible to always ensure that these requirements are met.

This chapter therefore illustrates the following on adapting system execution traces and their dataflow models to contain properties required to analyze software system performance properties:

- How to adapt system execution traces and corresponding dataflow models to contain the properties required for supporting performance analysis using a framework we have developed called *System Execution Trace Adaptation Framework (SETAF)*;
- What are the different design alternatives—including their advantages and disadvantages—for adapting system execution traces to support performance analysis;
- How SETAF can be applied to system execution traces generated by different software systems; and
- A performance comparison of two different system execution trace adaptation techniques.

2. BACKGROUND

Before beginning the discussion on adapting system execution traces and dataflow models to support performance analysis, let us first understand existing techniques for validating software performance properties using system execution traces.

TimeToPic (Salonen & Piilil, 2012) is a tool that visualizes a system execution log. It also provides facilities to analyze different locations, such as points of interests in the visualization graph. This visualization graph can be used to analyze different performance properties. The main limitation in TimeToPic is it relies heavily on log message format. The developer has to either use the common message format TimeToPic has defined or implement the logger of the application using TimeToPic's logging API. This approach is easy to apply on newly developed systems, and hard to apply on existing systems.

Nagaraj et al. (Nagaraj, Killian, & Neville, 2012) used comparative analysis of execution logs to detect performance problems. Nagaraj et al. propose such a technique. In their approach, two execution logs—the baseline log and the erroneous log—are assumed to have performance related issues. Nagaraj's technique compares the erroneous log with the baseline log, and provides a report on the locations of performance problems. The main limitation of Nagaraj's approach is that the Perl scripts that process the execution logs must be modified each time when it encounters a new system. This is because the execution logs of different systems are heterogeneous in nature.

There are platform-dependent approaches. For example, StackMine developed by Han et al. (Han & Xie, 2012) uses stack traces collected by Microsoft ® application monitoring tools to debug performance. Their performance monitoring method sends traces only when the response time of a method is above a certain threshold.,

There are language- and architecture-dependent approaches. For example, previous research efforts have focused on proposing methods for performance monitoring in Enterprise Java Beans (EJB) applications (Mos, 2001)(Mania & Murphy, 2002)(Parsons, Mos, & and Murphy, 2006).

"Imperfectness" of system execution traces. There are other approaches that have attempted to find solutions to "imperfectness of system execution traces" problem. These efforts are mainly focused on functional issues of the software system in contrast to performance issues.

Cinque et al.(Cinque, Cotroneo, & and Pecchia, 2009) propose a technique to overcome the imperfectness of system execution traces. In their approach, they follow a minimal set of logging rules during design and implementation. For example, the main types of rules that Cinque proposes are enabling logging for service start/end events and interaction start/end events. Then, they use the generated system execution traces for dependability evaluation of complex software systems. Although this approach contributes to the generation of well-structured logs, it is hard to ensure that every system follows these rules.

Yang et al. (Yang, Evans, & and Bhardwaj, 2006) use system execution traces for dynamic inference. Yang accepts the fact that system execution traces are imperfect. Likewise, Yang uses coding conventions to prune large number of unimportant properties for developers. They, however, have not tried to use imperfect traces for software performance analysis.

3. MOTIVATION: UNITE AND IT'S LIMITATIONS

UNITE is a method and tool for analyzing system execution traces and validating software system performance properties. UNITE's analytical techniques are not tightly coupled to (1) system implementation *i.e.*, what technologies are used to implement the system, (2) system composition, *i.e.*, what components communicate with each other, and (3) deployment, *i.e.*, where components

Table 1. Example system execution trace of a distributed system

Time of Day	Hostname	Message
2013-02-25 06:16:20	Node2	Planner: sent event 2 at 120394465
2013-02-25 06:16:18	Node1	Config: sent event 1 at 120394455
2013-02-25 06:16:21	Node2	Planner: received event 2 at 120394476
2013-02-25 06:16:23	Node1	Config: received event 1 at 120394480
2013-02-25 06:16:25	Node3	Effector: sent event 3 at 120394488
2013-02-25 06:16:27	Node3	Effector: received event 3 at 120394502

are located. This is opposed to processing system execution traces using simple scripts where the scripts are typically hard-coded for a specific use case, system, and/or problem. Because it is important to understand UNITE to understand the adaptation of system execution traces, we will now describe the theory, technique and limitations in UNITE.

Theory and Technique of UNITE

Table 1 shows a trivial system execution trace generated from a distributed software system. The system execution trace is a collection of log messages. Each log message represents an event that has occurred in the system. It also has the time of the day and the host name where the event occurred.

When doing performance analysis using UNITE, system testers first have to identify what log messages to extract from the system execution trace. These log messages should contain metrics of interest that support desired performance analysis. Once the log messages are identified, software system testers convert the common log messages into log formats.

Definition: *A **log format** is a high-level representation of a log message that captures both the static and variable portions of its corresponding log message. The static portions are those that do not change between different log messages. The*

variable portions are those that change between different log messages.

Listing 1 shows the log formats that represent the different log messages of the trace shown in Table 1. As shown in this listing, each log format (*e.g.*, LF1 and LF2) contains static and variable portions. For example, LF1 contains the variables: *cmpid, eventid*, and *sent*. The *sent* variable is used to extract the sending time. The remaining variables in the log format are used for correlating messages, which is explained next.

A log format LF_i can have zero or more variables. We denote the set of variables of log format LF_i as V_i. Similarly, the set of variables of log format LF_j is V_j.

Definition: Causal relation. *$CR_{i,j}$ between two log formats LF_i and LF_j is denoted as $LF_i \rightarrow LF_j$ where LF_i is the cause log format and LF_j is the effect log format. This kind of a causal relation is also called a log format relation. A causal relation $CR_{i,j}$ can have zero or more variable relations.*

Variable relation. *$VR_{C,E}$ of a causal relation $CR_{i,j}$ is defined as $v_C = v_E$, where $v_C \in V_i$ and $v_E \in V_j$.*

A system execution trace can have many log formats, many causal relations between the log formats, and many variable relations for each causal relation. For the purpose of performance analysis, system testers can use subsets of the log

Listing 1. Log formats of the system execution trace shown in Table 1

```
LF1: {STRING cmpid} sent event {INT eventid} at {INT sent}
LF2: {STRING cmpid} received event {INT eventid} at {INT recv}
```

Listing 2. Dataflow model of the system execution trace shown in Table

```
Log Formats:
LF1: {STRING cmpid} sent event {INT evid} at {INT sent}
LF2: {STRING cmpid} received event {INT evid} at {INT recv}


Log Format Relations:
LF1 → LF2


Variable Relations:
LF1.cmpid = LF2.cmpid
LF1.evid = LF2.evid
```

formats, causal relations and variable relations. We call this a *dataflow model*.

Definition: Dataflow model. *DM = (LF, CR, VR) is defined as,*

- *A set LF of log formats where each log format represents a set of log messages useful for analyzing a performance property;*
- *A set CR of causal relations that specify order of occurrence and causality among the log formats LF; and*
- *A set VR of variable relations attached to causal relations CR.*

Like dataflow models in program analysis (Allen, 1976) that relate variables across different source lines, dataflow models in UNITE relate log format variables across different log messages (or application contexts). The dataflow model enables reconstruction of execution flows in the system (1) irrespective of system complexity and composition and (2) without a need for a global

clock to ensure causality (Mukesh & Niranjan, 1994). This is because the relations between the log formats preserve causality. For the system execution trace in Table 1, Listing 2 illustrates the dataflow model.

The dataflow model illustrated in Listing 2 is a high-level abstraction of the system execution trace being analyzed. Using this dataflow model and the system execution trace, UNITE creates a variable correlation table based on variables defined in the dataflow model.

Definition: Variable correlation table. *A set of tuples $(d_1, d_2, .., d_i, .., d_n)$ where each tuple $d_i(i \leq n)$ contains instance values for all the variables of log formats defined in the dataflow model.*

Our previous work on UNITE (Hill & Schmidt, 2009) illustrates an algorithm based on topological sorting a directed acyclic graph and constructing variable correlation table for a given system execution trace and a dataflow model. Because each tuple in the variable correlation table is an instance

Table 2. Variable correlation table for the dataflow model in Listing 1

LF1.cmpid	LF1.evid	LF1.sent	LF2.cmpid	LF2.evid	LF2.recv
Config	1	120394455	Config	1	120394480
Planner	2	120394465	Planner	2	120394476
Effector	3	120394488	Effector	3	120394502

of a variable relation in the dataflow model, it is important that log messages are processed in the correct order. This ordering is defined by reverse topological sorting the log formats in the dataflow model. By sorting the log formats in this manner, if we find an effect log message instance for a log format, then we should find the corresponding cause log message instance from the same system execution trace.

The reverse, however, is not always true. For example, there can exist a "sent" event without a "received" event. On the other hand, if there is a "received" event, then the corresponding "sent" event must exist in the same system execution trace. While processing the log messages in this order, UNITE populates the variable correlation table based on the values of the variables of each log message instance. For example, Table 2 shows the variable correlation table for the system execution trace in Table 1 and dataflow model in Listing 2.

The variable correlation table shown in Table 2 enables software system testers to analyze performance properties. For example, Listing 3 highlights the expression for evaluating average event round trip time.

Based on this expression, UNITE generates a SQL query that aggregate performance results captured from the variable correlation table. Likewise, if the aggregation function (*i.e.*, AVG) is removed from the expression, then UNITE will present the data trend for the performance property undergoing analysis. Lastly, UNITE provides

Listing 3. Performance property analysis equation

```
AVG(LF2.recv - LF1.sent)
```

facilities to group aggregated results—similar to grouping in SQL.

Situations where UNITE Only is Not Applicable

Although UNITE enables analysis of software system performance properties using system execution traces, we have observed the following situations where UNITE cannot be applied.

Situation 1: Correlating Log Formats that have Non-Unique Instances

The variable correlation table is a set of tuples and each tuple is a set of values for log format variables. We can define the subset of a tuple that does not represent time as F. UNITE assumes that the set F of any tuple in the variable correlation table to be unique (*i.e.*, any instance of a particular log format is different from any other instance of the same log format apart from the timestamps). This is called the *uniqueness* among the log messages.

As shown in Table 1 and Listing 1, the event ids are different in each log format. It, however, is possible that the uniqueness of an instance of a particular log format be broken. When this situation occurs, the relation between the two log messages is considered non-unique. Using UNITE alone in this kind of situation yields incorrect results.

Table 3 illustrates an example system execution trace for this situation. As shown in the table, different instances of the same log format are similar. Moreover the set F is not unique. It is therefore hard to know what start/finish messages are associated with each other without human intervention.

Table 3. Example system execution trace that does not contain unique ids

Time of Day	Hostname	Message
2011-02-25 12:00:55	Node1	Started doing task A at 12.00
2011-02-25 12:01:55	Node1	Finished doing task A at 12.01
2011-02-25 12:02:55	Node1	Started doing task A at 12.02
2011-02-25 12:03:55	Node1	Finished doing task A at 12.03

Table 4. System execution trace that contains hidden relations

Time of Day	Hostname	Message
2011-02-25 10:00:55	Node1	Initializing the system at 10.00
2011-02-25 10:10:55	Node1	Start Monitoring components at 10.10
2011-02-25 10:11:55	Node1	Finish Monitoring components at 10.11
2011-02-25 10:40:55	Node1	Shutting down the system at 10.40

When UNITE alone is used to analyze this kind of a system execution trace, it will yield incorrect results (see Section 5.2 for supporting results).

Situation 2: Correlating Log Formats with Hidden Relations

When there are repetitive events as shown in Table 1, it is easy to identify the relations between log formats. When there are no repetitive events, it is hard to identify relations between log formats. This is because there are no true variable parts (other than the log message time) for defining causality between log formats. When this occurs, we say the dataflow model and system execution trace contain *hidden relations*.

In the system execution trace in Table 4, time is a variable in each log format and each log message is unique, however, there is no explicit variable for determining causality between the log messages. The system execution trace in Table 4 therefore cannot be analyzed using UNITE.

Situation 3: Associating Values of Newly Added Log Format Variables

UNITE assumes that values for a given log format variable are populated using data from its corresponding log messages. Correlating log formats in Table 3 and Table 4, however, requires adding new log format variables to the dataflow model. In this situation, preserving the relationship between different log formats is also important. This process is sometimes as simple as adding a monotonically increasing id, but it requires coordinating values from other log messages. Unfortunately, there is no uniform way to associate data for the newly added log format variables in UNITE.

4. DESIGN AND IMPLEMENTATION OF SETAF

To address the issues mentioned in Section 3, we need to adapt system execution traces and its associated dataflow model. Because the system execution trace of one system defers from that of another system, the same adaptation technique cannot be used for each system execution trace.

We therefore cannot adhere to one adaptation technique and implement it in UNITE. Instead, testers need a framework that supports specifying different adaptations. We call this framework the *System Execution Trace Adaptation Framework (SETAF)*.

SETAF provides two main functionalities for adaptation of system execution traces:

1. It provides a domain specific language for software testers to write adaptation specifications. An adaptation specification captures the execution semantics of the system that are missing in the system execution trace.
2. It converts this domain specific language to a format that is compatible with UNITE. This allows UNITE to do the performance analysis while using the adaptations at runtime.

Defining the Adaptation Specification

An adaptation specification is required when the execution semantics are not reflected in the system execution trace. The adaptation specification captures what properties must be added to the dataflow model to support performance analysis. Each adaptation specification contains the following details:

- **Variables:** The variables keep the state of the current adaptation and assist with adapting the corresponding system execution trace. The variables are visible only to the adaptation specification, and not visible to UNITE.
- **Initialization:** The above-mentioned variables are initialized in this section.
- **Reset:** When UNITE starts processing each log format, the variables defined above may need to be rest. This section therefore contains the reset value for each variable.

- **Data points:** The data points are new columns added to UNITE's variable correlation table. For example, a data point named *LF1.uid* will become a column name in UNITE's variable correlation table. Finally, data points are used to create new relations in the dataflow model—thereby addressing Situation 1 described in Section 3.
- **Relations:** The Relations section inserts new causality relations among log formats into the dataflow model. These relations cannot be instantiated using the system execution trace because they are based on the data points added from the adaptation specification. For example, assume the following two data points named *LF1.uid* and *LF2.uid* are added to the dataflow model. This section is used to define that *LF1.uid* causes *LF2.uid*—thereby supporting correct analysis in Situation 2 described in Section 3.
- **Adaptation Code:** The adaptation code is where the domain-specific logic resides for the adaptation specification. This logic is based on the execution semantics of the system execution trace. The adaptation code defines logic only for the log formats that must undergo adaptation. Each segment dictates how to update variables in the dataflow model, as well as its own private variables—thereby helping UNITE to correctly analyze execution traces in situations similar to Situation 3 in Section 3.

SETAF in Action

To show the adaptation specification defined in SETAF, we are going to use a portion of an example system execution trace of Apache ANT (ant.apache.org), which is presented in Table 3. We selected Apache ANT because its adaptation specification is a simple example for illustrating the concepts previously discussed. We, however,

Listing 4. Dataflow model for ANT system execution trace

Log Formats:
```
LF1: Started doing task {STRING taskname} at {INT startTime}
LF2: Finished doing task {STRING taskname} at {INT finishTime}
```

Relations:
```
LF1.taskname = LF2.taskname
```

have applied SETAF to more complex examples and one of them is described in Section 5.

Apache ANT completes different tasks during a build process. A task finish event is the effect of a task start event. Using this domain knowledge of the system execution trace, Listing 4 illustrates the dataflow model for analyzing the execution time of each task in Apache ANT.

When repeating the same task, ANT uses the same task name in different log messages, which results in identical instances of LF1 and LF2 in the system execution trace. When UNITE is processing the system execution traces using the dataflow model shown in Listing 4, it first identifies all the log message instances of type LF2. Then for each message of that type, UNITE tries to find the corresponding LF1 message instance (*i.e.*, UNITE is trying to correlate the finish event of an ANT Task with the start event of the same task). As shown in the Listing 4, the only possible way to do this is using the *taskname*. Because *taskname* is not always different among different message instances, UNITE cannot do this correlation correctly. This is a situation similar to Situation 1 described in Section 3.

A log message representing the start of a task, however, is always preceded by a log message representing completion of the corresponding task. This knowledge can be used to write a SETAF specification that adapts ANT's dataflow model accordingly. Listing 5 highlights the adaptation pattern—written as a SETAF specification—to ensure correct analysis of ANT's system execution trace.

As shown in Listing 5, the first task in defining the adaptation specification is defining the variables needed to adapt the system execution trace. This information is captured in the section labeled *Variables*. For the adaptation specification of ANT, the variable named *id* maintains the state of the adaptation. The section labeled *Init* initializes the value to 0 and section labeled *Reset* resets the value of this variable to 0 each time a new log format is processed. Software system testers then use the *DataPoints* section to specify what data

Listing 5. Adaptation pattern specification for Apache ANT in SETAF

```
Variables: int id_;
Init:  id_ = 0;
Reset: id_ = 0;

DataPoints:
  int LF1.uid;
  int LF2.uid;

Relations:
  LF1.uid -> LF2.uid;

// Begin adaptation code section
On LF1:
  id_ = id_ + 1;
  [uid] = id_;

On LF2:
  id_ = id_ + 1;
  [uid] = id_;
```

points to be add to each log format. For example, two data points named *LF1.uid* and *LF2.uid*, which are of integer type, are injected into the dataflow model. These two variables are needed to ensure that the relations are unique between the two log formats named *LF1* and *LF2*.

The *Relations* section defines new relations that should be added to the dataflow model. As illustrated in Listing 5, the left side of the arrow represents the cause variable; whereas, the right side of the arrow represents the effect variable. This specification of the relations is similar to how existing relations are defined in UNITE.

The final part of the SETAF specification is defining the actual adaptation logic preserving the execution semantics of the system. As shown in Listing 5, the *uid* variable is assigned the current value of id in both *LF1* and *LF2*. In both *LF1* and *LF2* the state variable id is incremented. This ensures that the next occurrence of *LF1* is differentiated from the previous occurrence of *LF1*, as well as *LF2*. Finally, the variable inside the brackets "[]" represents log format variables in UNITE. Writing the variable inside brackets is used to differentiate the adapter state variables from UNITE's log format variables.

We extended UNITE to provide a configuration option for specifying the location of the adaptation specification, and a standard interface to support the functionality of the adaptation specification described above. The unified interface of UNITE defines three main methods: *update_log_format(), update_relations(), update_values()*. The implementations of these functions are defined in the adaptation specification. When there is an adaptation specification provided with a dataflow model, UNITE calls the three methods as follows:

1. **update_log_format.** UNITE wants SETAF to add data points defined in the adaptation specification to the dataflow model.
2. **update_relations.** When UNITE does not know about a particular data point that is specified in the original dataflow model, it

consults SETAF for the set of relations for those data points using this method.

3. **update_values.** This method is called during the population of variable correlation table. When UNITE cannot find the required values from the system execution trace.

Using the Adaptation Specification

As described in the above section, SETAF adapter specification is written in a domain specific language. This specification is then converted into an intermediate version that is compatible with UNITE. There are two possible techniques for this: compiled and interpreted. As shown in Figure 1 when using the compiled adapter technique, SETAF generates C++ source code using the adaptation specification. Software system testers then compile the auto-generated code into an external module. During the system execution trace analysis, UNITE loads the external module and invokes the methods above accordingly.

Listing 6 showcases the source code auto-generated for ANT's adapter based on the SETAF specification in Listing 5. As shown in this listing, the variables in the Variables section of the SETAF specification are mapped into private variables in the adapter. Likewise, the *DataPoints* in the specification are used inside the *update_log_format()* method. More specifically, these data points are used to create new log format variables.

Similarly, the *update_relations()* method uses the relations specified in the Relations section of the specification. This method is therefore responsible for creating new relations among log formats with respect to the new log format variables. The *update_values()* method does the actual adaptation. Each adaptation section in the SETAF specification (*i.e.*, On [name]) is given its own if statement based on the log format's unique name as defined in the dataflow model.

The identifier *SETAF::int32_vp()* represents a log format variable casting operator. It is needed because all the variables types in UNITE are de-

Figure 1. Performance analysis process when using SETAF compiled adapter technique

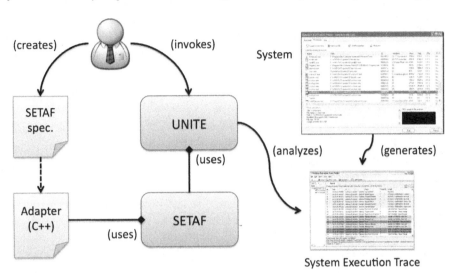

System Execution Trace

rived from a common variable type. This casting operator allows the system tester to narrow the generic variable type to its concrete variable type, such as an integer, to set its value accordingly. SETAF has log format variable casting operators for each variable type supported in UNITE. Lastly, UNITE uses SETAF to adapt the dataflow model as it processes the system execution trace.

The main limitation of the compiled adapter technique is the extra overhead of code generation and compilation. As shown in the Figure 2, interpreted adapter technique eliminates this overhead. When using this technique, UNITE loads the adaptation specification and SETAF builds an in-memory object model of the adapter. UNITE uses the in-memory object model to support analysis of the system execution trace. The interpreted adapter technique is easier to use because the overhead associated with compiling the adapter, such as obtaining UNITE libraries and setting up a development environment, are not present. We developed the compiled adapter technique because our initial intuition was that the compiled technique would have better performance. This is because UNITE calls the functionality for adaptation from a compiled module compared to

parsing the specification file and building an object model in the interpreted adapter. Section 5 shows a performance comparison of the two techniques to evaluate whether our intuition is correct.

5. EXPERIMENTAL RESULTS

The section presents two case studies of using SETAF with UNITE for analyzing performance properties of two open source software systems. The case studies are based on the system execution traces collected from following open-source software projects:

1. **Apache ANT.** Apache ANT, which was previously introduced in Section 4, is a widely used Java library
2. **Deployment And Configuration Engine (DAnCE).** DAnCE is an implementation of the Object Management Group Deployment & Configuration (D&C) specification for deploying and configuring component-based distributed systems(OMG).

Listing 6. Auto generated code for Apache ANT adapter

```
class Ant_Adapter: public CUTS_Log_Format_Adapter {
public:
  void init (void) { this->id_ = 0; }
  void reset (void) { this->id_ = 0; }
  void close (void) { delete this; }

  void update_log_format(CUTS_Log_Format * lfmt) {
    const string & name = lfmt->name ();

    if (name == "LF1")
      lfmt->add_variable ("uid", "int");
    else if (name == "LF2")
      lfmt->add_variable ("uid", "int");
  }
  void update_relations(CUTS_Log_Format * lfmt) {
    const string & name = lfmt->name ();

    if (name == "LF1")
      lfmt->add_relation ("LF2", "uid", "uid");
  }
   void update_values(Variable_Table & vars, CUTS_Log_Format * lfmt) {
    const ACE_CString & name = lfmt->name ();

    if (name == "LF1") {
      ++this->id_;
      SETAF::int32_vp (vars["uid"])->value (this->id_);
    }
    else if (name == "LF2") {
      ++this->id_;
      SETAF::int32_vp (vars["uid"])->value (this->id_);
    }
  }
private:
  int id_;
};
```

We used logging appenders and interceptors to collect system execution traces from the systems above, and store the execution traces in a database. We then used SETAF to adapt each stored system execution trace for performance analysis. The remainder of this section discusses our results from applying SETAF to the system execution traces.

Figure 2. Performance analysis process when using SETAF interpreter technique

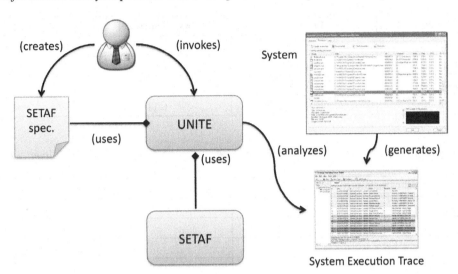

Case Study 1: Apache ANT

The correlation table constructed by UNITE when analyzing ANT's system execution trace without SETAF is shown in Table 5. The end goal was to measure the average execution time of each ANT task, which is accomplished by subtracting the *finishTime* from the *startTime*. Unfortunately, Table 5 produces incorrect results because some rows are not correlated correctly. For example, the first and third rows have a *startTime* that is greater than the *finishTime*. This means that the task finished before it actually started, which is not the case.

The reason for the incorrect correlation is the relations in the dataflow model are not unique (see Listing 4). More specifically, when UNITE processes the log formats in reverse topological order, it first populates the *finishTime* column. Then, UNITE uses a SQL UPDATE query to update the corresponding data value of the *startTime* column. In this case, UNITE can only do the correlation using the relation *LF1.task = LF2.task*. This causes UNITE to update multiple rows simultaneously, which results in negative values for the average execution time. (see Table 6)

Table 7 highlights the variable correlation table reconstructed by UNITE after using SETAF to apply the adaptation pattern during the reconstruction process. As shown in this table, *startTime* and *finishTime* are now correlated correctly because of the unique id added by SETAF. In this table, *startTime* is always less than *finishTime*, which is the expected result.

Table 8 illustrates the updated final results for analyzing task execution time after using SETAF to adapt the system execution trace as UNITE analyzed it. As shown in this table, all the service times for different ANT tasks have positive values. This is the expected analysis results.

Case Study 2: DAnCE

We used SETAF and UNITE to evaluate the amount of time it takes DAnCE to deploy a set of components to a given node. We used the BasicSP scenario provided with DAnCE for this case study. The BasicSP scenario has four different components mapped into four different nodes. We selected log format for key phases of the deployment process. We then manually constructed the corresponding dataflow model.

Table 5. Variable correlation table constructed by UNITE without SETAF for subset of Apache ANT's tasks

startTime (msec)	LF1.task	finishTime (msec)	LF2.task
1500	property	860	property
1500	property	1704	property
1516	available	1511	available
1516	available	1518	available

Table 6. IN correct performance analysis results for Apache ANT, when UNITE is used w/o SETAF

Task	Average Execution Time (msec)
available	-630.333333333333
delete	0.0
macrodef	140.0
mkdir	-25.125
path	297.0
patternset	-9.76923076923077
property	-241.4
Total evaluation time (sec)	0.11994

Table 7. Improved variable correlation table after using SETAF

LF1.uid	LF1.task	startTime	LF2.uid	LF2.task	finishTime
1	property	766	1	property	860
2	property	1500	2	property	1704
3	available	1500	3	available	1511
4	available	1516	4	available	1518

Table 8. Correct analysis of ANT task service times using SETAF

Task	Average Execution Time (msec)
available	93.6666666666667
delete	55.0
macrodef	79.0
mkdir	2.0
path	390.0
patternset	6.0
property	17.975
Total evaluation time of compiler technique (sec)	0.210
Total evaluation time of interpreter technique (sec)	0.220

Figure 3. Portion of the dataflow model for DAnCE system execution trace

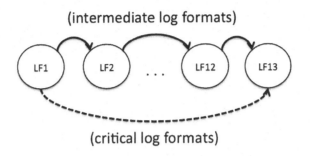

(intermediate log formats)

(critical log formats)

As shown in Figure 3, the dataflow model contains 13 different log formats (out of 50+ log formats) that depend on each other. The DAnCE deployment process can be divided into three main phases: (1) preparation phase; (2) start launching phase; and (3) finish launching phase. Each of these phases is driven by remote method calls between different components in DAnCE. The first 5 log formats represent the analysis of the preparation phase. The next 4 log formats represent the start-launching phase. The last 4 log formats represent the finish-launching phase. If software testers want to isolate different phases for performance testing, the tester can use log formats within each phase for that purpose. Because of different execution flows in DAnCE and its distributed functionality, it is not possible to use only the first and last log formats for analysis. Instead, each intermediate log format between the first and last log format must be considered to ensure correct correlation. Unfortunately, the relation between the intermediate log formats is not unique.

Listing 7 presents the SETAF specification for adapting DAnCE's generated system execution traces for analysis using UNITE. As illustrated in Listing 7, all the log formats in the SETAF specification for DAnCE, other than LF12 and LF13, use the private variable *planid*. The value of this private variable is set by LF12 because it is the first log format SETAF processes. Correlation of LF12 and LF13 is done using newly added id named *nodeid*. The instance counts of

this log format are kept in state variables *LF12. count* and *LF13.count*. These variables are used to populate the value of *LF12.nodeid* and *LF13. nodeid*, which allows us to differentiate similar instances of the same log format.

As shown in Table 9, we were not able to analyze DAnCE's system execution trace using only UNITE because some of the log formats were lacking variables parts to define causalities. When we used both UNITE and SETAF to analyze DAnCE's system execution trace, we learned that all four nodes take approximately equal time to deploy. More importantly, these results show that with careful analysis of the generated system execution trace, SETAF and UNITE can be used to analyze system execution traces without modifying existing source code.

Interpreted vs. Compiled Adaptation Techniques

We used following equation to compare the performance comparison of interpreted and compiled technique for adaptation.

Total Evaluation Time = Load Time + Process Time

In the compiled adapter, the load time is the amount of time taken to load the compiled adapter module. In the interpreted adapter, the load time is the amount of time taken to parse the adapter

Listing 7. SETAF adapter specification for DAnCE

```
Variables:
  string planid_;
  int lf12_count_, lf13_count_, nodeid_;

Init:
  lf12_count_ = lf13_count_ = nodeid_ = 0;

Reset:
  lf12_count_ = lf13_count_ = nodeid_ = 0;

DataPoints:
  string LF1.planid; string LF2.planid;
  string LF5.planid; string LF6.planid;
  string LF9.planid; string LF11.planid;
  int LF12.nodeid; int LF13.nodeid;

Relations:
  LF1.planid->LF2.planid; LF5.planid->LF6.planid;
  LF6.planid->LF7.planid; LF8.planid->LF9.planid;
  LF9.planid->LF10.planid; LF10.planid->LF11.planid;
  LF11.planid->LF12.planid; LF12.nodeid->LF13.nodeid;

// Begin adaptation code section
On LF1:
  [planid] = planid_;
On LF2:
  [planid] = planid_;
On LF5:
  [planid] = planid_;
On LF6:
  [planid] = planid_;
On LF9:
  [planid] = planid_;
On LF11:
  [planid] = planid_;
On LF12:
  [nodeid] = lf12_count_;
  lf12_count_ = lf12_count_ + 1;
  plan_id_ = [planid];
On LF13:
  [nodeid] = lf13_count_;
  lf13_count_ = lf13_count_ + 1;
```

Table 9. Results of applying SETAF and UNITE to measure the Deployment Time (DT) of DAnCE

Node	DT w/o SETAF	DT w/ SETAF (sec)
EC	N/A	5.0
BMDevice	N/A	5.0
BMClosedED	N/A	5.0
BMDisplay	N/A	5.1
Total evaluation time of compiler technique (sec)	N/A	0.237
Total evaluation time of interpreter technique (sec)	N/A	0.272

specification and create the object model that represents an adapter. In both cases, the process time is the amount of time taken to evaluate the dataflow model using either adapter

Figure 4 shows the load times for both the techniques. In addition to ANT and DAnCE we have applied SETAF to two other open source software applications—Apache Tomcat (http://tomcat.apache.org/) and Apache ActiveMQ (http://activemq.apache.org/). As shown in the figure, the compiled adapter has a much lower load time when compared to the interpreted adapter. This is expected because the interpreted adapter

has to parse the specification and build an object model at run-time. In the compiled adapter, this object model is already in binary form and UNITE only has to load the compiled adapter into memory.

The significant difference in load time is not contributing to the total evaluation time as shown in Figure 5. This is because total evaluation time for both techniques is dominated by the processing time (e.g., more than 96% as shown in Table 10). The reason for the dominance in processing time is the number of database operations executed during the analysis stage of UNITE.

Figure 4. Load time of SETAF interpreted compiled adapter

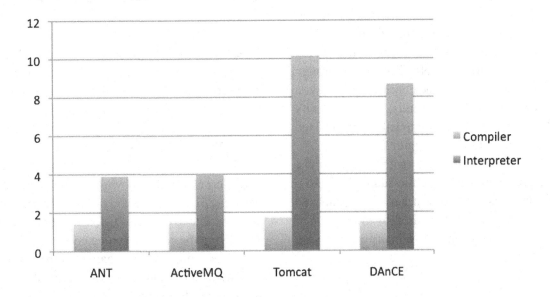

Figure 5. Total evaluation time of SETAF compiled and interpreted adapter techniques

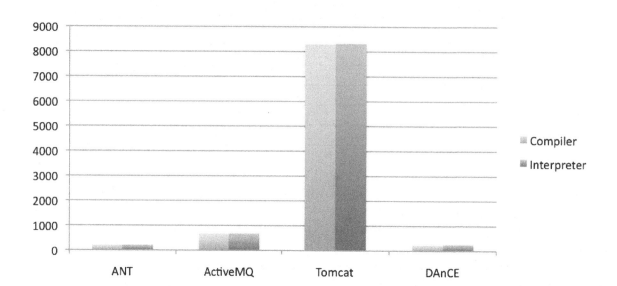

Table 10. Process time as a percentage of total evaluation time

Open-source Project	Size of the trace (KB)	Compiled Adapter	Interpreted Adapter
ANT	4032	99.33%	98.23%
ActiveMQ	2242	99.79%	99.41%
Tomcat	27880	99.97%	99.87%
DAnCE	576	99.36%	96.80%

For example, for each log format defined in the dataflow model UNITE must find all the corresponding log message instances (Hill et al. 2009), and extract values for the data points in each log format. This requires UNITE to iterate through the system execution trace each time it finds a new log format. Consequently, this complexity is the same for both the compiled and interpreted adapter, and reflected in Figure 5.

We therefore conclude that it is best to use the interpreted version of the adaptation specification. This is because it has similar runtime performance when compared to the compiled adapter specification, but the interpreted version is "easier" to use.

CONCLUSION AND FUTURE WORK

This chapter described the System Execution Trace Adaptation Framework (SETAF), which is a framework for adapting system execution traces for performance analysis. SETAF operates by allowing system testers to write adaptation pattern specifications for an existing system execution trace. The adaptation specifications can then be used with UNITE to analyze performance properties correctly. As shown in the results from applying SETAF to several open-source projects, it is possible to perform such adaptation without modifying the original source code.

Based on experience gained from applying SETAF to open-source software applications and systems, the following is a list of lessons learned and future research directions:

- **Automatically identifying the dataflow model from a system execution trace.** Complex software systems, such as distributed systems can easily generate system execution traces that are large in size. When the generated system execution trace is large, it is hard to identify a valid dataflow model—irrespective of the dataflow model having properties required for performance analysis. Future work therefore includes applying existing data mining techniques to assist in identifying the dataflow model—thereby easing complexities associated with the analysis. We have already proposed a technique to automate this process using frequent-sequence mining and evidence theory(Peiris & Hill, 2013). Furthermore, with adequate domain knowledge, data mining techniques can also be used to assist in locating adaptation patterns, which is a manual process.

- **Adaptation specification size does not have much impact on evaluation time of performance analysis.** As learned from the performance comparison of the compiled and interpreted adapters, total evaluation time depends on the number of log messages and the size of the dataflow model (*i.e.*, processing time). For example, total evaluation time for Apache Tomcat is greater than DAnCE even though DAnCE's adaptation specification is larger. This is because Apache Tomcat's system execution trace has more log messages when compared to DAnCE's system execution trace.

- **Making adaptation patterns reusable in performance analysis tools.** Apart from ANT and DAnCE system execution traces we have applied SETAF to other system execution traces of different software systems. After applying SETAF to other system execution traces, we learned that some adaptation patterns are reoccurring.

We therefore believe it is possible to make common adaptation pattern first-class entities in the adaptation specification. This will prevent developers from having to reinvent the adaptation pattern.

- **Real-time adaptation of system execution traces.** The current approach for adapting system execution traces is done offline. Adapting system execution traces in real-time for online analysis, however, will present several challenges—especially without compromising the existing system's performance properties. Future work will therefore investigate real-time adaptation capability of system execution traces to support online performance analysis.

SETAF and UNITE are integrated into the CUTS system execution modeling tool. All are freely available in open-source format for download from the following location: http://cuts.cs.iupui.edu.

REFERENCES

Allen, F. E. (1976). A program data flow analysis procedure. *Communications of the ACM*, 137. doi:10.1145/360018.360025

Breu, S., & Krinke, J. (2004). *Automated Software Engineering, 2004. Proceedings. 19th International Conference on*. IEEE.

Cinque, M., Cotroneo, D., & Pecchia, A. (2009). A Logging Approach for Effective Dependability Evaluation of Complex Systems. In *Proceedings of the 2009 Second International Conference on Dependability* (pp. 105-110). IEEE Computer Society.

Geimer, M., & Wolf, F. (2010). The Scalasca performance toolset architecture. *Concurrency and Computation*, 702–719.

Han, S., & Xie, T. (2012). Performance debugging in the large via mining millions of stack traces. In *Proceedings of the 2012 International Conference on Software Engineering* (pp. 145--155). IEEE.

Hill, J. (2010). Context-based Analysis of System Execution Traces for Validating Distributed Real-time and Embedded System Quality-of-Service Properties. In *Proceedings 16th IEEE International Conference on Embedded and Real-Time Computing Systems and Applications (RTCSA)* (pp. 92-101). Macau: IEEE.

Hill, J., & Schmidt, D. (2009). Unit Testing Non-functional Concerns of Component-based Distributed Systems. In *Proceedings of the 2nd International Conference on Software Testing, Verification, and Validation* (pp. 406-415). Denver, CO: IEEE.

Mania, D., & Murphy, J. (2002). Developing performance models from non-intrusive monitoring traces. In Proceeding of Information Technology and Telecommunications (IT&T). IT&T.

Mod, A., & Murphy, J. (2001). Performance monitoring of Java component-oriented distributed applications. In *Proc. IEEE 9th International Conference on Software, Telecommunications and Computer Networks (SoftCOM)* (pp. 9-12). IEEE.

Mos, A. A. (2001). Performance monitoring of Java component-oriented distributed applications. In *Proceedings of IEEE 9th International Conference on Software, Telecommunications and Computer Networks (SoftCOM)* (pp. 9--12). IEEE.

Mukesh, S., & Niranjan, G. (1994). *Advanced Concepts in Operating Systems*. McGraw-Hill, Inc.

Nagaraj, K., Killian, C., & Neville, J. (2012). Structured comparative analysis of systems logs to diagnose performance problems. In *Proceedings of Symposium on Networked Systems Design and Implementation*. USENIX Association.

OMG. (n.d.). *Deployment and Configuration Adopted Submission*. Retrieved from www.omg.org

Parsons, T., Mos, A., & Murphy, J. (2006). Non-intrusive end-to-end runtime path tracing for J2EE systems. *IEE Proceedings. Software*. doi:10.1049/ip-sen:20050069

Peiris, M., & Hill, J. (2013). Auto-Constructing Dataflow Models from System Execution Traces. In *Proceedings of 16th IEEE International Symposium on Object/Component/Service-Oriented Real-Time Distributed Computing*. Paderborn, Germany: IEEE.

Safyallah, H., & Sartipi, K. (2006). Dynamic Analysis of Software Systems using Execution Pattern Mining. In *Proceedings of the 14th IEEE International Conference on Program Comprehension* (pp. 84--88). IEEE.

Salonen, E., & Piilil, R. (2012). *Find the bug, Fix the bug, Do it fewer times (TimeToPic)*. Retrieved from http://www.timetopic.net/Pages/default.aspx

Schmidt, D. (1993). *The ADAPTIVE Communication Environment: An object-oriented network programming toolkit for developing communication software*. Academic Press.

Wolf, F., & Mohr, B. (2003). Automatic performance analysis of hybrid MPI/OpenMP applications. *Journal of Systems Architecture*, 702–719.

Wylie, B., Wolf, F., Mohr, B., & Geimer, M. (2007). Integrated runtime measurement summarization and selective event tracing for scalable parallel execution performance diagnosis. *Applied Parallel Computing. State of the Art in Scientific Computing*, 460--469.

Yang, J., Evans, D., & Bhardwaj, D. (2006). Perracotta: mining temporal API rules from imperfect traces. In *Proceedings of the 28th international conference on Software engineering* (pp. 282--291). ACM.

KEY TERMS AND DEFINITIONS

Adaptation: Enabling two different entities to work together without, changing any of them.

Adapter: The entity, which can be used to do the adaptation process.

Dataflow Model: A directed acyclic graph, which represents the cause-effect relationships in a system.

Intrusive Analysis: Analyzing a system without altering the source code for the sake of analysis.

Log Format: An abstract event type, which can represent one or more log messages in a system execution trace.

Log Format Relation: A cause-effect relation between logs formats.

Service Time: The time taken by the system to complete a pre-defined task.

System Execution Trace: Collection of messages generated by the system during its execution.

Chapter 22
Code Clone Detection and Analysis in Open Source Applications

Al-Fahim Mubarak-Ali
Universiti Teknologi Malaysia, Malaysia

Shahida Sulaiman
Universiti Teknologi Malaysia, Malaysia

Sharifah Mashita Syed-Mohamad
Universiti Sains Malaysia, Malaysia

Zhenchang Xing
Nanyang Technological University, Singapore

ABSTRACT

Code clone is a portion of codes that contains some similarities in the same software regardless of changes made to the specific code such as removal of white spaces and comments, changes in code syntactic, and addition or removal of code. Over the years, many approaches and tools for code clone detection have been proposed. Most of these approaches and tools have managed to detect and analyze code clones that occur in large software. In this chapter, the authors aim to provide a comparative study on current state-of-the-art in code clone detection approaches and models together with their corresponding tools. They then perform an empirical evaluation on the selected code clone detection tool and organize the large amount of information in a more systematic way. The authors begin with explaining background concepts of code clone terminology. A comparison is done to find out strengths and weaknesses of existing approaches, models, and tools. Based on the comparison done, they then select a tool to be evaluated in two dimensions, which are the amount of detected clones and run time performance of the tool. The result of the study shows that there are various terminologies used for code clone. In addition, the empirical evaluation implies that the selected tool (enhanced generic pipeline model) gives a better code clone output and runtime performance as compared to its generic counterpart.

DOI: 10.4018/978-1-4666-6026-7.ch022

INTRODUCTION

Software maintenance is an important phase in preserving quality and relevancy of software due to advances in technology. Maintenance of a software system is defined as a modification of software product after the implementation of the software to improve performance or to adapt the product to a modified environment (Ueda, Kamiya, Kusumoto, & Inoue, 2006). Software maintenance consumes a substantial amount of the software development life cycle costs. Maintainability is one of the issues in software maintenance. One of the factors that affects maintainability of software is code clone (Roy & Cordy, 2007). Code clone refers to similar copies of the same instances or fragments of source codes in software. Code clone also causes an increase in software maintenance cost. This happens due to frequent changes carried out on clone instances (Deissenboeck, Hummel, Juergens, Pfaehler, & Schaetz, 2010). If a source code in a program contains bugs, there is a possibility that other code clone contains the same bug that requires a fix. Hence, this increases maintenance work not only due to the increase of the number of code clone but also the number of bugs that exist in the code clone itself (Roy & Cordy, 2007).

Although code clone increases software maintenance tasks, software community also acknowledges it as a practice in software development. Software developers tend to clone the codes for various reasons. One of the reasons is to speed up the development process (Hou, Jacob, & Jablonski, 2009). This occurs especially when a new requirement is not fully understood and a similar piece of code is present in the software that is not designed for reuse. Programmers usually clone the code instead of adopting the costly redesigning approach. Other reasons of cloning a code during development includes the application of design pattern or implementation of the same requirement of a software (Gang, Xin, Zhenchang, & Wenyun, 2012).

Current code clone research focuses on the detection and analysis of code clones in order to help software developers in identifying code clones in source codes and reuse the source code in order to decrease the maintenance cost. Many approaches such as textual based comparison, token based comparison, and tree based comparison approaches are available to detect code clone. As software grows and becomes legacy, the complexity of these approaches to detect code clone increases, thus makes it more cumbersome to detect code clones.

The issues that occur in current code clone detection research include conflicting, less distinguished terminology and definition on types of code clone. Furthermore, the evaluation differs as most of the code clone detection tools have their own set of code clone definition that is used for evaluation purposes. Therefore, this chapter aims is to provide a comparative study on current state-of-the-art in clone detection approaches and tools, and also to perform an empirical evaluation on selected clone detection tools. In order to achieve this aim, this chapter focus three main aspects that are:

1. **Code Clone Terminology:** There are various terminologies and definitions regarding the type of code clone. This chapter attempts to unify existing terminologies and definitions. This chapter also looks into scenarios that contribute to code clone.

2. **Code Clone Detection Approaches and Models:** Various approaches and models have been proposed and implemented as code clone detection tools in order to detect code clone. This chapter aims to study the best approach or model that can be used for a comparative study. These approaches are compared and evaluated based on their strengths and weaknesses. Only tools that have a complete set of code clone detection process will be used for the evaluation process.

3. **Empirical Evaluation of Existing Approaches and Models:** This chapter looks into the state-of-the-art of code clone detection tools derived from (ii) by evaluating empirically the selected code clone detection tool using open source applications. The results are recorded and analyzed based on detected code clone and the tool performance.

BACKGROUND

As software evolves rapidly, maintaining software becomes costly. Many existing tools can detect and remove code clones. As software grows and becomes legacy, complexity of existing code clone detection techniques in detecting fully similar parts of source code increases (Bellon, Koschke, Antoniol, Krinke, & Merlo, 2007). This causes difficulties to detect code clones and increases maintainability of software. Code clone does not only give impacts on software maintenance cost but it also has other residing impacts to a software system. The impacts include (Roy & Cordy, 2007):

1. **Increase in Bug Propagation and New Bug Introduction:** If a code segment that contains a bug is reused by copy-and-paste technique without any changes, the bug of the original segment may remain in the pasted segments. Therefore, the probability of bug propagation increases in a system. Furthermore, new bugs might occur if the structure of duplicated code is reused without any changes.

2. **Contribution to Poor Design:** Due to the lack of good inheritance structure or abstraction, code cloning may cause bad design. Consequently, it makes the reuse of the inheritance or abstraction for future project implementation impossible. Thus, it badly affects maintainability of the software.

3. **Difficulty in Improving an Existing System:** In order to make an improvement to an existing system, additional time and attention are needed in understanding existing implemented code clone and concerns that need to be implemented. Therefore, it is difficult to add changes to the system.

4. **Increase in Resource Requirements:** Since code clone increases the size of a program, there is a need to upgrade hardware specifications. Furthermore, compilation time also has a detrimental effect on the edit-compile-test cycle, as it requires compilation of many codes in order to achieve the output.

Although code clone is known to increase software maintenance cost, code clone is also known to be advantageous in certain circumstances especially during software development. Apart from speeding up the development of the software (Hou et al., 2009) and the application of design pattern or same requirement of software (Gang et al., 2012), code clone is advantageous in the following examples of situations (Kapser & Godfrey, 2006) (Kapser & Godfrey, 2008):

1. Used as a method to address requirements changes.
2. During the use of templates in programming for certain programming paradigm.
3. The only solution left to enhance existing functionality that is limited by programming language and lacks of reuse and abstraction mechanism.
4. Efficiency consideration with regard to overhead of procedure calls.

Various techniques and approaches such as textual based comparison, metric based comparison, token based comparison and tree based comparison have been applied in detecting code clones (Koschke, Falke, & Frenzel, 2006). These approaches have been applied in several code clone detection tools such as CCFinder (Kamiya,

Kusumoto, & Inoue, 2002), DECKARD (Jiang, Misherghi, Su, & Glondu, 2007) and CloneTracker (Duala-Ekoko & Robillard, 2007). CCFinder (Kamiya et al., 2002) uses token based approach with combination of transformation rules. CloneTracker (Duala-Ekoko & Robillard, 2007) is an example of a tool that uses a combination of tree based comparison with dynamic programming while DECKARD (Jiang et al., 2007) uses combination of tree based comparison with tree matching technique. Another work introduces a generic pipeline model for code clone detection process (Biegel & Diehl, 2010a). Generic pipeline model is a flexible yet extensible code clone detection process that contains all required steps in a clone detection process. This model is implemented in a code clone detection tool called Java Code Clone Detection API (JCCD) (Biegel & Diehl, 2010b).

CODE CLONE DETECTION

Scenario and Terminology

There are three scenarios that contribute to cloning (Jarzabek & Xue, 2010). The first scenario is clones caused by poor design. These clones can be removed by replacing them with functions or through a refactoring process. However, technically there will be risks that might cause difficulty in the clone removal process. The second scenario is between long-lived clones and temporary clones (Jarzabek & Xue, 2010). Long-lived clones are clones that have existed in a program for a long time, while temporary clones only exist during the creation of the program. The third scenario is an essential clone that programmers cannot eliminate from their source codes. This scenario happens if the elimination of code clone affects quality of program. In addition, simplification is a prime reason for clone removal. Complexity of source code is due to the restriction of programming language or the adopted design techniques or approaches.

Code clone is the common terminology used, yet there are also other terminologies used to describe code clone. The most common terminology of code clone is categorized into three types: Type 1, Type and Type 3 (Koschke et al., 2006). Type 1 is an exact copy of code without modifications with exception to white space and comments. Type 2 identifies identical copy syntactically. It only allows changes to variable, type or function identifiers. Type 3 is a copy of code with further modifications. Modification involves statements that are changed, added, or removed.

Figure 1 shows the lifecycle of a code clone in software (Gang et al., 2012). Tentative clone is clones that are duplicated through copy, paste and modify method by developers in their own copy of software that is being developed. This clone is called as tentative clones as the developers have not completed a full solution of the software yet. The impact of tentative clone is local, as this does not affect other developers who are working on the same software. The tentative clone is optional to be removed and it is also merged with the baseline code of the software. The merged clones are called as baseline clone.

Accidental clones are clones that are introduced unintentionally by developers who are not aware of creating the clones. These clones might appear due to design pattern application or implementing the same requirement of software. Usually, accidental clones will be combined into the baseline code of software due to developers' unawareness. Thus, these accidental clones become baseline clones. Code clones that are inside the baseline of software will remain until it is removed or modified (Gang et al., 2012).

Other terminologies that refer to code clones include induced and temporal clones (Hou et al., 2009). Induced clones are clones that are purposely induced into a program for certain purposes such as for testing code clone detection approaches. Temporal clones are clones that occur temporarily during development during an execution of a program.

Figure 1. Lifecycle of a code clone (Gang et al., 2012)

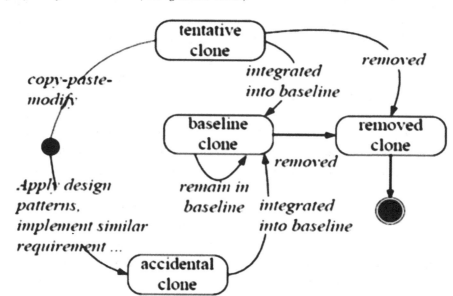

Although there are various terms used to define code clones, the variation in terminologies of code clones differs according to definitions of similarity and associated levels of allowed tolerance for different kinds and degrees of code clones (Bellon et al., 2007). In simple words, code clones can be said as fragments of source code that form clone pairs based on a given definition of similarity (Bellon et al., 2007). As a whole, a general definition of code clone refers to a portion of codes that contains some similarities with regard to the changes made to the codes such as removal of white spaces and comments, changes of code syntactic and addition or removal of code lines.

Existing Clone Detection Approaches and Models

Textual or string matching approach is the pioneer in code clone detection approach. It compares source code line by line. The line comparison is only done for lines that are in the same partition. Metric comparison is an enhanced approach of textual or string based comparison approach. Distance in the metric vectors is used instead of

code line for comparing purposes (Koschke et al., 2006).

Token-based comparison approach is done by dividing the line of source code into token sequences. The characterization of this token is done uniquely using a hash function (Koschke et al., 2006). A tool that uses this approach is CCFinder (Kamiya et al., 2002). CCFinder is a tool for code clone detection that adopts token base comparison technique. This tool uses combination of token-based comparison clone detecting technique and transformation rules. The first process in the tool is lexical analysis. This process divides the codes into sets of tokens based on the lexical rule of the programming language. Transformation is the second process in code detection using token-based approach. The tokenized code undergoes transformation using rules such as and parameter replacement step. The transformation rules are regularization of the identifier and identification of structures. In addition, the parameter replacement involves the replacement of each identifier that relates to types, variables, and constants with a special token. Then the transformed tokens undergo the third process, which is match detection. The last process includes formatting and converting each location of clone pair into line numbers as appear in the original source files.

Tree based comparison approach is a widely used approach after token based comparison approach. This approach uses partition sub trees of the abstract syntax tree of a program based on a hash function and then compare sub trees in the same partition through a few techniques such as tree matching or dynamic programming (Koschke et al., 2006). CloneTracker (Duala-Ekoko & Robillard, 2007) is an example of tool that uses this approach with dynamic programming. Clone-Tracker automatically tracks evolving code clones by using region descriptor. It uses abstract syntax tree in searching clones in clone region descriptors. Clone Region Descriptor (CRD) is an abstract description for the location of a clone region in code base. It represents the characteristics of each code block in which a clone region is nested. CRD is obtained through the output of clone detection tool. It contains set of code blocks that will be used in the analysis process. The drawback of this tool is the CRD needs a lot design modification that compromises the robustness and accuracy of code clone detection.

Apart from the detection approaches, models also has been used in detecting code clones. The generic pipeline is a model for code clone detection that uses a combination of processes to detect code clone. A new flexible yet extensible process for code clone detection contains all required steps in a clone detection process. There are five processes that are involved in this generic pipeline model (Biegel & Diehl, 2010a). The first process is the parsing process in the generic pipeline model. A process transforms source code into source units. Each source unit indicates the start and the end of a fragment in a source file. Representations of source units use sub trees of an Abstract Syntax Tree (AST). A source unit of the set of all source units, U, refers to a fragment of a source file f which starts at a certain position of a line and

ends at position of line *lend*. A source unit might be represented in many forms such as a sub tree of an AST, a line, a sub graph of a program dependence graph. The representation of a source unit is highly dependent on the approach that has been used. Furthermore, every approach requires different additional techniques like a line extractor, a lexer, or a parser.

The second process is the pre-processing process. It is a process to normalize source units and to add additional annotations to the source units. Normalization turns the source units into a regular form and makes different source units more similar. It uses AST as input and pre-processed AST as output. The third process is the pooling process. It is a process of grouping pre-processed AST source units into sets of groups according to defined characteristics based on criteria set by the user. The sets are called as pool. The user-defined criteria are characteristics that can be directly read from the source unit and its annotations without comparing it to another one. Source units, which are not in the same pool, are not considered candidates for similarity pairs. Comparing process is the fourth process and comes after the pooling process. It is a process of recursive comparison of source units in all pools using a divide and conquer strategy. Filtering is the final process in the generic pipeline model. This process is utilized in removing non-relevant candidate sets out of the result set.

The generic pipeline model is implemented using the Java Code Clone Detector or JCCD (Biegel & Diehl, 2010b). A flexible yet extensible code clone detection detects code clones in the Java source file only. Each process of the model is implemented separately and integrated with the JCCD. The advantage of this tool is that users can customize each process according to their needs. JCCD allows pipeline manipulation for large amount of source file per time yet this is done manually and causes bottleneck in the process code clone detection. The bottleneck causes decrease the runtime performance of the generic pipeline model.

An enhanced version was proposed to overcome the bottleneck issue in JCCD (Mubarak-Ali, Syed-Mohamed, & Sulaiman, 2011). The enhanced generic pipeline model implemented a process called concatenation process to overcome the bottleneck problem. Concatenation process is a process that speeds up the load processing by processing smaller part of source code files first before focusing on the large chunk of source code in a single pipeline. This concatenation process partially adopts parallel concatenation approach. Source codes in a source file are segmented iteratively based on function type, which is singular and nested type functions. This process ends when all the functions are segmented out and represented in the form of sub source files.

The generic clone model is a clone description model that defines existence of a clone in a program (Giesecke, 2007). The model allows separation of concerns among clone detection, description, and management using layers. This reduces the effort in the implementation of tools supporting these activities. There are two types of elements associated to the model. The first is the elements that correspond to system artifacts. The second elements are the artifacts that represent parts of the clone data that is generated by a clone detection algorithm based on the system artifacts. The highest level of representation of the model is called as project instance. An instance is structured into selection units and comparison units through a selection function and an enumeration function. This instance is then known as clone data. The clone data is aggregated at the top level in clone sets, which contains clone pairs. The clone pairs exist in two granularities that are the selection units and the comparison units. Clone pairs are grouped into clone sets by a presentation function. The clone sets used here are sets with a distinguished reference element to reduce redundancy in a clone set.

The implementation of this model works as a plug-in to Eclipse. Eclipse is an integrated development environment (IDE) that supports development of standalone programs and web applications. The advantage of this model is that it has a clear separation of the definition of clone detection process using layers. Furthermore, the main use of this model is to describe clones. The drawback of this model is that it focuses more on management of code clone that was driven by the operational aspects of code clone detection and removal. Furthermore, it is only available only as a plug-in for IDE rather than a separated tool for code clone detection. Table 1 shows the comparison of existing tools for code clone detection based on approaches and models.

EMPIRICAL EVALUATION ON OPEN SOURCE APPLICATIONS

This section includes the evaluation results and discussion, and threats to results validity.

Evaluation Results

Based on the comparison done, the study chose to evaluate Java Code Clone Detector (JCCD) tool that implements the generic pipeline model. The justification of the choice is due to JCCD consists of systematic process of code clone detection that adopts the generic pipeline model. The processes in the model can be evaluated segregately as compared to other tools; thus allowing more analysis to be done on each process that is applied in JCCD. The evaluation is also done on the enhanced version of the generic pipeline model (Mubarak-Ali et al., 2011) that implements the concatenation process. Three open source applications were used for evaluation purposes of both tools. JHotDraw 7.0.6 (JhotDraw, 2012), ANTLR 4 (Antlr, 2005) and SableCC (SableCc, 2009) were selected for this reason. JHotDraw 7.0.6 is an open source two-dimensional graphics

Table 1. Comparison of existing tools for code clone detection based on approaches and models

Tool	Approach/ Model	Strength	Weakness
CCFinder (Kamiya et al., 2002)	Token-based comparison	- Uses combination of transformation rules together with token. - Supports clone detection for million line of codes.	- Load processing is done only on large software and no automated process for load processing.
CloneTracker (Duala-Ekoko & Robillard, 2007)	Tree-based comparison	- automatically tracks evolving codes clones code by using region descriptor. -uses abstract syntax tree in searching clones in clone region descriptors.	- region descriptors need a lot of design modification that compromises the robustness and accuracy of code clone detection.
JCCD (Biegel & Diehl, 2010b)	Generic pipeline model	- a new flexible yet extensible code clone detection. - More freedom to the user to customize each process according to their needs.	- Non-efficient way to handle source files as an input as it leads to a decrease in its performance due to its pipeline limitation.
A plug-in in Eclipse (Giesecke, 2007)	Generic Clone Model	- A clear separation of clone detection process. - definition using layers. - A model that is used to describe clones.	- A framework that is more focused on management of code clone that was driven by the operational aspects of code clone detection and removal. - Available only as a plugin for IDE rather than a separate code clone detection tool.

framework for structured drawing editor tools. It contains 309 source files with 56697 lines of code. ANTLR is a multi-language parser generator that takes input from a specified programming language and generates output for a recognizer of targeted programming language. It contains 337 source files with 45904 lines of code. SableCC is also a parser generator but it generates fully featured object-oriented frameworks for building compilers, interpreters and other text parsers. It contains 198 source files with a total of 35586 lines of code. These applications have proven to have occurrences of clones in their source codes (Ishio et al. 2008). These open source applications use the Java programming language in their program development.

The result of the evaluation is shown in Table 2, while the result of runtime performance of the models is shown in Table 3. The evaluation was done in a lab environment setting using a workstation with the specification of 1.73GHz quad core CPU, 4GB of memory, and Windows 7 operating system.

There were 2322 clones detected in JHotDraw 7.0.6 using the generic pipeline model but the number of clones detected increased by 0.6% that is 2336 clones detected using the enhanced generic pipeline model. As for SableCC 3.2, there were 2072 clones detected using the generic pipeline model but an increase up to 0.57% that is 2084 clones detected when using the enhanced generic pipeline model. There were 326 clones detected in ANTLR 4 using the generic pipeline model but the number of clones detected increased by 1.2% (330 clones detected) using the enhanced generic pipeline model.

Based on the results shown in Table 3, all runtime performance showed a decrement in the enhanced generic pipeline model as compared to the generic pipeline model using SableCC 3.2. The run time of the parsing process is 859.02 ms by using the generic pipeline model but the run

Table 2. Result of detected clones

Application	Amount of Line of Code	Amount of Source File	Clone detected using Generic Pipeline Model	Clone detected using Enhanced Generic Pipeline Model
JHotDraw 7.0.6	56697	309	2322	2336
ANTLR 4	45904	337	2072	2084
SableCC 3.2	35586	198	326	330

Table 3. Result of run time performance

Process	Time (millisecond or ms)					
	JHotDraw 7.0.6		SableCC 3.2		ANTLR 4	
	Generic Pipeline Model	Enhanced Generic Pipeline Model	Generic Pipeline Model	Enhanced Generic Pipeline Model	Generic Pipeline Model	Enhanced Generic Pipeline Model
Concatenation process	-	522.00	-	151.00	-	455.00
Parsing	309.82	361.69	859.02	224.26	2785.90	218.86
Pre-processing	231.84	269.68	268.50	128.05	247.76	324.15
Pooling	960.98	937.69	78.43	58.85	847.70	391.62
Comparing	1181.25	314.20	817.17	611.67	21.02	55.02
Filtering	36.30	40.77	383.03	29.97	0.01	0.01
Overall	2720.19	2446.03	2406.15	1203.8	3902.57	1444.66

time decreased by 73.9% that is 224.26 ms using the enhanced generic pipeline model. As for the pre-processing process, the runtime is 268.50 ms when using the generic pipeline model but the run time decreased by 52.3% (128.05 ms) when using the enhanced generic pipeline model. The run time of the pooling process is 78.43 ms when using the generic pipeline model but the run time decreased by 30% (58.85 ms) when using the enhanced generic pipeline model. The run time of the fourth process, which is the comparing process, is 817.17 ms by using the generic pipeline model but the run time decreased by 25.1% (611.67 ms) when using the enhanced generic pipeline model. The run time of the final process, which is the filtering process, is 383.03 ms by using the generic pipeline model but the run time

decreased by 92.2% that is 29.97 ms when using the enhanced generic pipeline model.

The runtime process using the JHotDraw 7.0.6 showed an increment for the three processes, which are the parsing process, the pre-processing process, and the filtering process. The run time of the parsing process is 309.82 ms in JHotDraw 7.0.6 when using the generic pipeline model but the run time increased by 16% (361.69 ms) using the enhanced generic pipeline model. The run time of the pre-processing process is 231.84 ms in JHotDraw 7.0.6 when using the generic pipeline model but the run time increased 16.3% (269.68 ms) when using the enhanced generic pipeline model. As for the filtering process, the run time of this process is 36.30 ms in JHotDraw 7.0.6 when using the generic pipeline model but the run time increased by 11% to be 40.77 ms when using the enhanced generic pipeline model. The remaining two processes, which are the pooling, and comparing process showed a decrement in the runtime process. As for the pooling process, the runtime of this process is 960.98 ms in JHotDraw 7.0.6 when using the generic pipeline model but the run time decreased 2.4% (937.69 ms) when using the enhanced generic pipeline model. The run time of the comparing process is 1181.25 ms in JHotDraw 7.0.6 when using the generic pipeline model but the run time decreased 73.5% to 314.20 ms when using the enhanced generic pipeline model.

As for the ANTLR 4 runtime results, the run time process for parsing and pooling processes showed a decrement. The run time detected in parsing process is 2785.90 ms when using the generic pipeline model but the run time decreased 92.1% (218.86 ms) when using the enhanced generic pipeline model. As for the run time detected in the pooling process, it is 847.70 ms when using the generic pipeline model but the run time decreased by 53.8% (391.62 ms) when using the enhanced generic pipeline model. The second and the fourth process, which is the pre-processing and comparing process showed an increment in the runtime process. The run time detected in the pre-processing process is 247.76 ms when using the generic pipeline model but the run time increased by 30.8% (324.15 ms) when using the enhanced generic pipeline model. The run time detected in comparing process is 27.02 ms when using the generic pipeline model but the run time increased by 81.4% to be 55.02 ms when using the enhanced generic pipeline model. The runtime for the final process, which is the filtering process, showed no changes in the runtime process. The run time of the process remained 0.01 ms.

The overall runtime performance showed a decrement by using the tree open source applications. As for JHotDraw 7.0.6, the overall run time performance when using the generic pipeline model is 2720.19 ms but the run time decreased by 10.1% (2446.03 ms) when using the

enhanced generic pipeline model. The overall run time performance in SableCC 3.2c decreased by 49.9% from 2406.15 ms when using the generic pipeline model to 1203.8 ms when using the enhanced generic pipeline model. Finally, the overall run time detected in ANTLR 4 when using the generic pipeline model is 3902.57 ms (decreased by 62.9%) but the value is the same (1444.66 ms) when using the enhanced generic pipeline model. Based on the comparison done, it shows that the overall run time decreased for all the sample data. Therefore, this shows that the enhanced generic pipeline was able to reduce the overall run time as compared to the generic pipeline model.

Discussion

This section digests the derived results from the empirical evaluation. Based on the comparison done in the parsing process, it shows that the run time of the parsing process decreased for SableCC 3.2 and ANTLR 4 but increased for JHotDraw 7.0.6. The increase run time of the parsing process in JHotDraw 7.0.6 might be influenced by the length of code in a function for detected code clone. Since parsing is the process of producing source units by determining the start and the end point, it takes more time for functions that has lengthy lines of source code to be determined as source units. Therefore, the functions in JHotDraw 7.0.6 might have contained lengthy source codes that causing the run time to increase.

As for the pre-processing process, the run time of the pre-processing process decreased for SableCC 3.2 but increased for JHotDraw 7.0.6 and ANTLR 4. The amount of white spaces that exists in the source units and the process of adding additional notations to the source units might influence the increase run time of the parsing process in JHotDraw 7.0.6 and ANTLR 4. Since pre-processing is the process of normalizing and adding additional notations of source units, it takes more time for functions that has a lot of whitespaces and the use of additional annotations in normalizing the source units. Therefore, the source units in JHotDraw in 7.0.6 and ANTLR 4 might have contained a lot of white spaces that cause the run time to increase.

The results show that the run time of the comparing process decreased for JHotDraw 7.0.6 and SableCC 3.2 but increased for ANTLR 4. The increase in run time of the comparing process in ANTLR 4 might be due to the amount of pools exist in ANTLR 4. Since comparing is a recursive process of comparing pools to form similarity group, it takes more time for applications that has many pools. Therefore, many pools in ANTLR 4 could have contributed to the increase in the run time.

As for the filtering process, it shows that the run time of the filtering process increased for JHotDraw 7.0.6, decreased for SableCC 3.2 and has no change in ANTLR 4. The increase in run time of filtering process in JHotDraw 7.0.6 could be due to the amount of irrelevant clones in JHotDraw 7.0.6. Since filtering is a process that filters the similarity group in removing irrelevant code clone candidates, it takes more time for applications that has many irrelevant code clones to be removed. Thus, many irrelevant code clones in JHotDraw 7.0.6 could have caused the increase in the run time. As for ANTLR 4, the unchanged run time might be influenced by the minimal occurrence of irrelevant code clones.

Threats to Result Validity

The result of the evaluation shows that the enhanced generic pipeline model was able to detect more code clone and improve overall run time performance of the code clone detection. Yet, there are issues that might cause threats to the validity of the evaluation results. The issues are:

1. **Sample Selection:** Sample data used for the testing are open source applications since there is no standard sample data available for code clone detection. Furthermore, the amount of code clone and function existence are unknown in the open source applications which makes it difficult to know total code clones and total functions exist in the applications.

2. **Sample Size:** Sample size refers to the amount of source code lines and source code files exist in the sample data. Currently, the maximum sample size used for experimentation is 56000 lines of source codes with 337 of source code files. As shown in the results, the run time decreases for the used sample size. The results might vary for larger lines of source files and source code lines.

3. **Code Structures:** The code structure varies for each open source application due to various reasons such as coding convention, system architecture and coding styles used by the programmers. Therefore, the code clone structure is also affected due to the variant code structures.

4. **Hardware Specification:** The current workstation specification used for experiment enables the process that is limited to 400 source files or 60000 lines of codes per time. A higher memory and CPU workstation may give a better overall run time performance.

FUTURE RESEARCH DIRECTIONS

Code clone detection and analysis is a fast expanding research area in the research domain of software clone. Many studies have focused on improving code clone detection by introducing new or enhanced detection techniques or approaches and their tools. Such tools have supported software maintainers and developers in maintaining and developing software with the aim to reduce occurrences of clones in their software. Although code clone detection is critical, the trend is moving towards on how to manage clones or better known as software clone management (Koschke, Baxter, Michael Conradt, & Cordy, 2012). The aim of software clone management is to identify and organize existing clones, controlling growth and dispersal of clones, and avoiding clones as much as possible.

Code clone detection is part of the software clone management activities. Other activities involved in software clone management include correction, presentation and, prevention and compensation of the clones. Correction is an activity that is more related in removing clone from the software (Roy & Cordy, 2007). This activity is mainly focused on removing detected clones in software. Presentation is an activity that is concerned with the visualization of code clone results (Roy & Cordy, 2007). Some of visualization methods that have been used for the display of code clone results are Dotplots, Hasse diagrams, Polymetric views, tree maps, arc and bars diagrams, and strips diagrams (Roy & Cordy, 2007). These visualization methods give a better view of code clone results besides aiding programmers to analyze the code clone obtained in a better way. Prevention and compensation is an activity revolves in applying prevention control that is complemented with integration of problem mining approach in the prevention control (Roy & Cordy, 2007). It is a measure taken to detect code clone continuously while the code is being modified. Tools that adopt this activity are SHINOBI (Kawaguchi et al., 2009) and Clone Detective (Juergens, 2011).

CONCLUSION

This chapter has digested the terminology used in reference to code clones such as induced clones and temporal clones. Although there are various terms used for code clone reference, the most common code clone terminology used is categorized into three types. Type 1 is an exact copy of code without modifications with exception to white space and comments. Type 2 identifies identical copy syntactically. It only allows changes to vari-

able, type or function identifiers. Type 3 is a copy code with further modifications. Modification involves statements that are changed, added, or removed. This chapter has also compared various approaches and models that have been proposed and implemented as code clone detection tools. The most common approaches used in code clone detection are textual or string matching approach, metric based comparison, token based comparison approach and tree based comparison approach (Koschke et al., 2006). Generic pipeline model and generic clone model are models used in detecting clones. Based on the comparison done, generic pipeline model that is implemented in Java Code Clone Detector (JCCD) (Biegel & Diehl, 2010b) was chosen as a tool to be evaluated, as it is the state-of-the-art of code clone detection tool. It consists of systematic process of code clone detection. The empirical evaluation compared three open source applications, which are JHotDraw 7.0.6 (JhotDraw, 2012), ANTLR 4 (Antlr, 2005) and SableCC (SableCc, 2009) using the selected generic pipeline model and the enhanced generic pipeline model (Mubarak-Ali et al., 2011). The result shows that the enhanced generic pipeline model gives a better code clone output and run time performance as compared to the generic pipeline model.

REFERENCES

Antlr. (2005). ANTLR Parser Generator. *ANTLR v3*. Retrieved January 30, 2012, from http://www.antlr.org/files/100/www.antlr.org.html

Bellon, S., Koschke, R., Antoniol, G., Krinke, J., & Merlo, E. (2007). Comparison and evaluation of clone detection tools. *IEEE Transactions on Software Engineering*, *33*(9), 577–591. doi:10.1109/TSE.2007.70725

Biegel, B., & Diehl, S. (2010a). *Highly configurable and extensible code clone detection.* Paper presented at the 17th Working Conference on Reverse Engineering (WCRE). Beverly, MA.

Biegel, B., & Diehl, S. (2010b). *JCCD: a flexible and extensible API for implementing custom code clone detectors.* Paper presented at the IEEE/ACM International Conference on Automated Software Engineering (ASE '10). Antwerp, Belgium.

Deissenboeck, F., Hummel, B., Juergens, E., Pfaehler, M., & Schaetz, B. (2010). *Model clone detection in practice.* Paper presented at the 4th International Workshop on Software Clones (IWSC '10). Cape Town, South Africa.

Duala-Ekoko, E., & Robillard, M. P. (2007). Tracking code clones in evolving software. In *Proceedings of the 29th International Conference on Software Engineering* (ICSE '07). Minneapolis, MN: ICSE.

Gang, Z., Xin, P., Zhenchang, X., & Wenyun, Z. (2012). *Cloning practices: Why developers clone and what can be changed.* Paper presented at the 28th IEEE International Conference on Software Maintenance (ICSM). Trento, Italy.

Giesecke, S. (2007). Generic modeling of code clones. Dagstuhl, Germany: Internationales Begegnungs und Forschungszentrum Informatik (IBFI).

Hou, D., Jacob, F., & Jablonski, P. (2009). *Proactively managing copy-and-paste induced code clones.* Paper presented at the IEEE International Conference on Software Maintenance (ICSM 2009). Edmonton, Canada.

Jarzabek, S., & Xue, Y. (2010). *Are clones harmful for maintenance?* Paper presented at the 4th International Workshop on Software Clones (IWSC '10). Cape Town, South Africa.

JhotDraw. (2012). *JHotDraw 7.* Retrieved from http://www.randelshofer.ch/oop/jhotdraw/files/120/jhotdraw.html

Jiang, L., Misherghi, G., Su, Z., & Glondu, S. (2007). *DECKARD: Scalable and Accurate Tree-based Detection of Code Clones.* Paper presented at the 29th international conference on Software Engineering (ICSE '07). Minneapolis, MN.

Juergens, E. (2011). *Research in Cloning Beyond Code: A First Roadmap.* Paper presented at the 5th International Workshop on Software Clones (IWSC '11). Waikiki, HI.

Kamiya, T., Kusumoto, S., & Inoue, K. (2002). CCFinder: a multilinguistic token-based code clone detection system for large scale source code. *IEEE Transactions on Software Engineering, 28*(7), 654–670. doi:10.1109/TSE.2002.1019480

Kapser, C. J., & Godfrey, M. W. (2006). Supporting the analysis of clones in software systems. *Journal of Software Maintenance and Evolution: Research and Practice, 18*(2), 61–82. doi:10.1002/smr.327

Kapser, C. J., & Godfrey, M. W. (2008). Cloning considered harmful considered harmful: patterns of cloning in software. *Empirical Software Engineering, 13*(6), 645–692. doi:10.1007/s10664-008-9076-6

Kawaguchi, S., Yamashina, T., Uwano, H., Fushida, K., Kamei, Y., Nagura, M., & Iida, H. (2009). *SHINOBI: A Tool for Automatic Code Clone Detection in the IDE.* Paper presented at the 16th Working Conference on Reverse Engineering, 2009. New York, NY.

Koschke, R., Baxter, I. D., Michael Conradt, M., & Cordy, J. R. (2012). *Software Clone Management Towards Industrial Application.* Dagstuhl, Germany: Academic Press.

Koschke, R., Falke, R., & Frenzel, P. (2006). *Clone detection using abstract syntax suffix trees.* Paper presented at the 13th Working Conference on Reverse Engineering (WCRE '06). Benevento.

Mubarak-Ali, A.-F., Syed-Mohamed, S. M., & Sulaiman, S. (2011). *An Enhanced Generic Pipeline Model for Code Clone Detection.* Paper presented at the 5th Malaysian Software Engineering Conference (MySEC). Kuala Lumpur, Malaysia.

Roy, C. K., & Cordy, J. R. (2007). A Survey on Software Clone Detection Research. School of Computing TR 2007-541, Queen's University, 115.

SableCc. (2009). SableCC. *SableCC.* Retrieved Jan 30, 2012, from http://sablecc.org/

Ueda, Y., Kamiya, T., Kusumoto, S., & Inoue, K. (2006). Code clone analysis environment for supporting software development and maintenance. *Electronics and Communications in Japan (Part III Fundamental Electronic Science), 89*(11), 10–18. doi:10.1002/ecjc.20279

ADDITIONAL READING

Banks, R. (2011). Clone Detective for Visual Studio 2008: Richard Banks - Agile and.NET. Retrieved June 5, 2011, from http://www.richardbanks.org/2008/08/clone-detective-for-visual-studio-2008.html

Baxter, I. D., Yahin, A., Moura, L., Sant'Anna, M., & Bier, L. (1998). *Clone detection using abstract syntax trees.* The International Conference on Software Maintenance, Bethesda, MD.

Calefato, F., Lanubile, F., & Mallardo, T. (2004). Function clone detection in web applications: A semiautomated approach. *Journal of Web Engineering, 3,* 3–21.

Dang, Y., Ge, S., Huang, R., & Zhang, D. (2011). *Code clone detection experience at Microsoft.* The 5th International Workshop on Software Clones (IWSC '11), Waikiki, Honolulu, USA.

Deissenboeck, F., Hummel, B., Juergens, E., Schätz, B., Wagner, S., Girard, J. F., & Teuchert, S. (2008). *Clone detection in automotive model-based development.* The 30th International Conference on Software Engineering (ICSE '08), Leipzig, Germany.

Di Lucca, G. A., Di Penta, M., & Fasolino, A. R. (2002). *An approach to identify duplicated web pages.* The 26th International Computer Software and Applications Conference (COMPSAC 2002), Oxford, England.

Engelbertink, F., & Vogt, H. (2010). *How to save on software maintenance costs* (pp. 1–12). OMNEXT.

Frey, T., & Köppen, V. (2012). *Hypermodelling Live OLAP for Code Clone Recommendation.* The Tenth International Baltic Conference on Databases and Information Systems.

Girschick, M. (2006). Difference detection and visualization in UML class diagrams. *Technical University of Darmstadt Technical Report TUD-CS-2006-5.*

Göde. Nils, & Koschke, Rainer. (2009). *Incremental Clone Detection.* The 13th European Conference on Software Maintenance and Reengineering (CSMR '09), Kaiserslautern, Germany.

Higo, Y., Ueda, Y., Kamiya, T., Kusumoto, S., & Inoue, K. (2002). *On software maintenance process improvement based on code clone analysis.* The 4th International Conference on Product Focused Software Process Improvement (PROFES '02), Rovaniemi, Finland.

Hou, D., Jacob, F., & Jablonski, P. (2009). *Exploring the design space of proactive tool support for copy-and-paste programming.* The 2009 conference of the Centre for Advanced Studies on Collaborative Research (CASCON '09), Toronto, Ontario, Canada.

Hummel, B., Juergens, E., Heinemann, L., & Conradt, M. (2010). *Index-based code clone detection: incremental, distributed, scalable.* The IEEE International Conference on Software Maintenance (ICSM 2010), Timisoara.

Jiang, Z. M. (2006). *Visualizing and understanding code duplication in large software systems. (Master of Mathematics in Computer Science), University of Waterloo.* Waterloo, Ontario, Canada: Available from Google Scholar.

Johnson, J. H. (1993). *Identifying redundancy in source code using fingerprints.* The Conference of the Centre for Advanced Studies on Collaborative research: software engineering (CASCON '93), Toronto, Ontario, Canada.

Kontogiannis, K. A., DeMori, R., Merlo, E., Galler, M., & Bernstein, M. (1996). Pattern matching for clone and concept detection. *Automated Software Engineering, 3*(1), 77–108. doi:10.1007/BF00126960

Krinke, J. (2001). *Identifying similar code with program dependence graphs.* The 8th Working Conference on Reverse Engineering (WCRE'01), Suttgart, Germany.

Krinke, J., Gold, N., Jia, Y., & Binkley, D. (2010). *Cloning and copying between gnome projects.* The 7th IEEE Working Conference on Mining Software Repositories (MSR), Cape Town.

Lague, B., Proulx, D., Mayrand, J., Merlo, E. M., & Hudepohl, J. (1997). *Assessing the benefits of incorporating function clone detection in a development process.* The International Conference on Software Maintenance, Bari, Italy.

Leitao, A. M. (2004). Detection of redundant code using R 2 D 2. *Software Quality Journal, 12*(4), 361–382. doi:10.1023/B:SQJO.0000039793.31052.72

Liu, H., Ma, Z., & Shao, W. (2006). *Detecting Duplications in Sequence Diagrams Based on Suffix Tree.* The 13th Asia Pacific Software Engineering Conference (APSEC 2006), Kanpur, India.

Livieri, S., Higo, Y., Matsushita, M., & Inoue, K. (2007). *Analysis of the linux kernel evolution using code clone coverage.* The Proceedings of the Fourth International Workshop on Mining Software Repositories (MSR '07), Minneapolis, USA.

Monden, A., Nakae, D., Kamiya, T., Sato, S., & Matsumoto, K. (2002). *Software quality analysis by code clones in industrial legacy software.* The 8th IEEE Symposium on Software Metrics, Ottawa, Canada.

Pham, N. H., Nguyen, H. A., Nguyen, T. T., Al-Kofahi, J. M., & Nguyen, T. N. (2009). *Complete and accurate clone detection in graph-based models.* The IEEE 31st International Conference on Software Engineering (ICSE 2009) Vancouver, BC.

Rahman, F., Bird, C., & Devanbu, P. (2012). Clones: What is that smell? *Empirical Software Engineering, 17*(4-5), 503–530. doi:10.1007/s10664-011-9195-3

Roy, C. K., & Cordy, J. R. (2008). *Scenario-based comparison of clone detection techniques.* Paper presented at the The 16th IEEE International Conference on Program Comprehension (ICPC 2008), Amsterdam.

Störrle, H. (2010). *Towards clone detection in UML domain models.* The Fourth European Conference on Software Architecture: Companion Volume (ECSA '10), Copenhagen, Denmark.

Ueda, Y., Kamiya, T., Kusumoto, S., & Inoue, K. (2002). *Gemini: Maintenance support environment based on code clone analysis*. The 8th IEEE Symposium on Software Metrics, Ottawa, Canada.

Van Rysselberghe, F., & Demeyer, S. (2003). *Reconstruction of successful software evolution using clone detection*. The 6th International Workshop on Principles of Software Evolution, Helsinki, Finland.

Wahler, V., Seipel, D., Wolff, J., & Fischer, G. (2004). *Clone detection in source code by frequent itemset techniques*. The 4th IEEE International Workshop Source Code Analysis and Manipulation, Chicago, IL.

KEY TERMS AND DEFINITIONS

Code Clone: Identical or same copies of source code that appear in a program.

Code Clone Detection Approaches: Approaches to detect code clone.

Code Clone Models: Models to detect code clone.

Code Clone Scenario: Scenario that contributes to code clone occurrence.

Code Clone Terminology: Equivalent terms used to refer code clone.

Copy-and-Paste Technique: A technique that copies portion of source code and pasted in other part of the same program.

Software Clone Management: A domain that emphasizes on management of code clones.

Software Maintenance: A domain that emphasizes on maintenance of software.

Chapter 23
Important Issues in Software Fault Prediction:
A Road Map

Golnoush Abaei
University Technology Malaysia, Malaysia

Ali Selamat
University Technology Malaysia, Malaysia

ABSTRACT

Quality assurance tasks such as testing, verification and validation, fault tolerance, and fault prediction play a major role in software engineering activities. Fault prediction approaches are used when a software company needs to deliver a finished product while it has limited time and budget for testing it. In such cases, identifying and testing parts of the system that are more defect prone is reasonable. In fact, prediction models are mainly used for improving software quality and exploiting available resources. Software fault prediction is studied in this chapter based on different criteria that matters in this research field. Usually, there are certain issues that need to be taken care of such as different machine-learning techniques, artificial intelligence classifiers, variety of software metrics, distinctive performance evaluation metrics, and some statistical analysis. In this chapter, the authors present a roadmap for those researchers who are interested in working in this area. They illustrate problems along with objectives related to each mentioned criterion, which could assist researchers to build the finest software fault prediction model.

1. INTRODUCTION

As today's software grow rapidly in size and complexity, the prediction of software reliability plays a crucial role in a software development process (Catal, 2011). Software fault[1] is an error situation of the software system. The explicit and potential violation of security policies at runtime causes these faults because of wrong specification and inappropriate development of configuration (Dowd, MC Donald, & Schuh, 2007). Early detection of fault-prone software components could enable verification experts to concentrate their time and resources on the problematic areas of the system

DOI: 10.4018/978-1-4666-6026-7.ch023

under development. In fact, when limited budget and time do not allow for complete testing of an entire system, software managers can use predictors for software quality to focus on testing parts of the system that seems to be defect prone. So the defect prone trouble spots can then be examined in more detail by model checking and intensive testing. In fault prediction approaches, previous reported faulty data with the help of distinct metrics could identify the fault-prone modules. In addition, important information about location, number of faults and distribution of defects are extracted to improve test efficiency and software quality of the next version of the program. In other word, fault prone modules can be identified prior to system test by using these models. Application of defect predictors in software developments helps the managers allocate the resources such as time and effort more efficiently. It would also be cost effectively to test some certain section of the code (Calikli, Tosun, Bener, & Celik, 2009).

Area of software fault prediction still poses many challenges and unfortunately, none of the techniques proposed within the last decade has achieved widespread applicability in the software industry due to several reasons including the lack of software tools to automate this prediction process, the unwillingness to collect the fault data, and other practical problems (Catal, Sevim, & Diri, 2009).

According to (Catal & Diri, 2009b), analyzing and predicting defects are needed for three main purposes, firstly, for assessing project progress and plan defect detection activities for the project manager. Secondly, for evaluating product quality in order to assess the finished product, and thirdly, for improving capability and assessing process performance for process management.

Any fault prediction model could be built based on variety of learning methods, distinctive software metrics, and different performance evaluation metrics; each of them has its own challenges. We should mention that the type of applications that software metrics extracted from them could also

be varied. In this chapter, we reviewed all related parameters to build a finest prediction model. Although literature review paper (Catal, 2011) and many systematic literature review papers (Arisholm, Briand, & Johannessen, 2010; Catal & Diri, 2009b; T. Hall, Beecham, Bowes, & Counsell, 2011; Radjenović, Heričko, Torkar, & Živkovič, 2013) are available, but to our knowledge none of them has classified the fault prediction issues and challenges as we have done here. Figure 1 shows the overall structure of building any software fault prediction model. All problems and objectives related to each part of this diagram are discussed and reviewed throughout this chapter.

Often, fault prediction approaches are most suitable in less critical domains such as software packages and telecommunication companies. Anyhow, in limited time and budget and specially for testing different versions of the software that have been completely tested before, using software prediction model would be a good choice. One of the practical examples could be found in Chapter 24 entitled "Building Defect Prediction Models in Practice". Key questions and consequences arising when establishing defect prediction in a large software development project are answered in the mentioned chapter.

This chapter is organized as follows: section 2 presents background of the problem. Section 3 describes different fault prediction issues. Related works are presented in section 4. Section 5 presents fault prediction challenges and finally section 6 is conclusion.

2. BACKGROUND OF THE PROBLEM

Testing is the most popular method for defect detection in most of the software projects. However, when project's sizes grow in terms of both lines of code and effort spent, the task of testing becomes more difficult and costly. According to Bohem (1988), fault removal is considerably less costly when performed in the design phase

Figure 1. A general software fault prediction model scenario

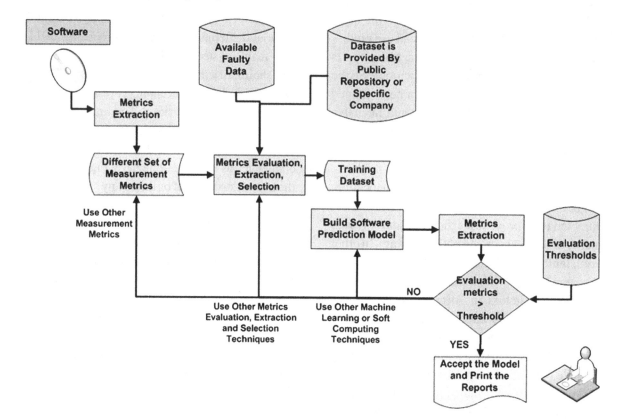

rather than after deployment. According to Menzies, Greenwald, & Frank (2007) any member in a review team which usually consists of 4 to 6 members, may inspect 8 to 20 lines of code per minute and the detection ratio during the review process is around 60%. Therefore, software fault prediction approaches are much more cost effective to detect software faults compared to software reviews (Catal, 2011).

Defective modules cause significant risk by decreasing customer fulfillment and by increasing the development and maintenance costs. Therefore, in software development life cycle, it is desirable to predict defected modules in early stages of software development. Effective risk prediction modules can improve software developer's ability to identify the defect prone modules and focus quality assurance activities such as testing and inspection (Koru and Liu, 2005b) on them.

However, identifying and locating defects in any software project is a difficult work, especially when project size grows, this task becomes more expensive and more sophisticated.

Some advantages of software fault prediction is listed as follows; reaching a highly dependable system, improving test process by focusing on fault prone modules, identifying refactoring candidates that are predicted as fault prone (Catal & Diri, 2009a), reduce the cost of testing and therefore the cost of development process, and finally delivering more accurate software in a shorter time.

The focus of this chapter is on three different issues that are very essential and inevitable in building any software fault prediction model which are, learning methods, software metrics, and performance evaluation metrics. These factors are explained and challenges based on the related literature reviews are presented in the following section. The content of this chapter could be a helpful material for those researchers who are interested to pursue their research in this area.

3. FAULT PREDICTION ISSUES

In this section, we describe the facts and issues that matter in building any fault prediction model. As you may see in Figure 2, a general scheme is given that contains important factors that need to be taken care of in this field. A brief explanation is given about each part in following sub sections.

3.1. Inclusion Criteria

We included papers in our study if the paper describes research on software fault prediction and software quality prediction. Papers with respect to their datasets, software metrics, learning techniques, and performance evaluation criteria have

been examined. The inclusion of papers is based on the similarity degree of the study with fault prediction research topic.

3.2. Software Metrics

Measurements help us to compare and capture quality in terms of some quantity, or to quantify the qualities so that we can choose correct steps and have progress. Software measures help in decision making in various life cycle phases. According to Ince (1990), software quality metrics are numerical measures that are extracted from a software project and are used to quantify some aspect of a software product. The software metric data gives us the values for specific variables to measure a specific module/function or the whole project. When combined with the weighted error/ defect data, this dataset becomes the input for a machine learning system. Studies show that design and code metrics, possibly focused with the

Figure 2. Software fault prediction issues

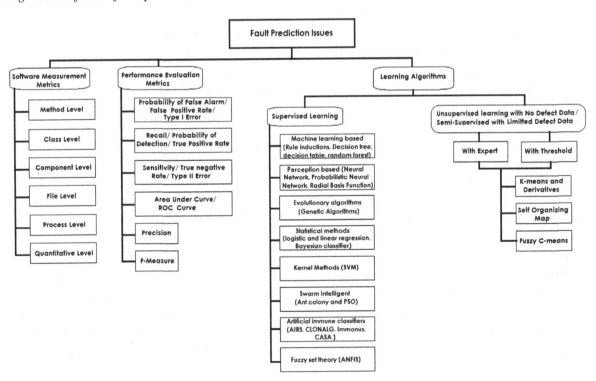

requirement metrics offer sufficient information for effective modeling (Jiang, Cukic, & Menzies, 2007). Some usage of software metrics are listed as follows:

1. How good is the design? Bad design is:
   ○ Hard to understand.
   ○ Hard to implemented.
   ○ Hard to maintain.
2. How complex is a code? Complex codes are:
   ○ Hard to understand.
   ○ Hard to test.
   ○ Hard to debug.
   ○ Hard to change.
3. How much effort will be required in each phase of design, implement, test, …

Evidence based software engineering is the process of collecting software metrics and using these metrics as a basis for constructing a model to help in the decision making process. Software metrics are mostly used for the purposes of product quality and process efficiency analysis and risk assessment for software projects. Software metrics have many benefits; one of the most noteworthy benefits is that they provide information for defect prediction. For example, metric analysis allows project managers to assess software risks.

There are different metrics classifications according to some studies (Boetticher, 2006), two common types of software metrics are project and product metrics. Project metrics refer to estimated time, money, or resource effort needed in completing a software project and product metrics are metrics extracted from software code and are frequently used for software defect predictions. Defect prediction models can be classified according to the metrics used and the process step in the software life cycle. Most of the defect models use the basic metrics such as complexity and size of the software. Analyses of measured metrics are good indicators of possible defects in the software being developed.

Currently there are numerous metrics for assessing software risks. The early researches on software metrics have focused their attention mostly on McCabe (1976), Halstead (1977) and lines of code (LOC) metrics. Some sets of metrics with brief information are listed in Appendix 1 to 5. As it is shown in Appendix 1 and according to the literatures, six different software metrics are usually used for building software fault prediction model. Deciding about the type of metrics sets that are used in prediction process is done based on the type of application, the programming language, development style, and other factors. These sets of metrics can also be used in combination with each other. They are method-level or static code metrics, class-level or package-level metrics, component-level metrics, file-level metrics, process-level metrics, and quantitative-level metrics. A detail explanation is given about class-level, method-level, and component level metrics in appendix 2, 3, and 4 respectively. It should be mentioned here that a new web-related metrics were introduced by (Giang, Kang, & Bae, 2010) which reflects the characteristics of the applications that are web-based, see Appendix 5.

According to the literatures (Catal & Diri, 2009b), method-level metrics are the most popular metrics that could be collected from structured programming as well as object-oriented programming. Class-level metrics are the second popular metrics that are used for object-oriented programming. Chidamber-Kemerer (CK) is the famous class-level metrics among others (Chidamber & Kemerer, 1994).

3.3. Machine Learning Algorithm

A learning system is defined as a system that is said to learn from experience with respect to some class of tasks and performance measure, such that its performance at these tasks improves with experience (Mitchell, 1997). In order to build a prediction model, we must have defect and measurement data collected from actual software development efforts to use as input to the learning algorithm. A trade-off usually exists between how well a model fits to its learning set and its prediction performance on additional dataset that is called test set. Therefore, we should evaluate a model's performance by comparing the predicted defectiveness of the module in a test set against their actual defectiveness (Koru and Liu, 2005a). Software quality problems can be formulated as learning processes and can be classified by the characters. It is possible to apply regular machine learning algorithms to come up with a probability distribution for errors analysis. Most of these machine-learning and statistical techniques are presented in Figure 2. Machine learning is also used to generate models of program properties that are known to cause errors, to classify and investigate the most relevant subsets of program properties for training and classification

The main idea behind the prediction models is to estimate the reliability of the system, and investigate the effect of design and testing process over number of defects. Since software problems can be formulated as learning processes and classified according to the characteristics of defect, regular machine learning algorithms are applicable to prepare a probability distribution and analyze errors (D. Zhang, 2000). According to Menzies, Greenwald, et al. (2007), the choice of learning method is far more important than which subset of available data is used for learning.

As mentioned above, to design a learning system, we need both training and test set, because of the absence of additional datasets, it is a common practice to use the portion of available data as learning set to build a model and use the remainder as the test set. One of the frequent solutions is using 10-fold cross validation. It partitioned the dataset into 10 equal portions. It uses each partition once as a test set to evaluate the model built using the remaining nine portions.

As it is shown in Figure 2, learning algorithms are classified in two main sections, supervised and unsupervised/semi-supervised learning. As stated earlier, all the software fault prediction studies use metrics and faulty data of previous software release to build fault prediction models, which is called supervised Learning approaches. Sometimes, the fault labels for modules are not available; for example, we might have a new project and therefore we do not have a faulty dataset, so usually in such cases unsupervised learning such as clustering techniques are used. The process of labeling each program module one at a time is a laborious, expensive, and time-consuming effort. Clustering is an appropriate choice for software quality analysis in the absence of fault-proneness labels or defect data (Seliya & Khoshgoftaar, 2007). There is another classification, which is known as semi-supervised approach. In this method, some of the modules are labeled and some are not. Seliya & Khoshgoftaar (2007) used a constrained-based k-means clustering that employ a software engineering expert's domain knowledge to iteratively label clusters in a semi-supervised procedure.

Name of the authors that used any of the learning approaches are listed next to each method in Appendix 7 for the sake of simplicity.

3.4. Performance Evaluation Metrics

Many statistical and machine learning techniques have been proposed to predict fault-proneness of program modules in software engineering. Choosing the "best" candidate among many available models involves performance assessment and detailed comparison, but these comparisons are not simple due to many performance evaluation metrics. Different measurements could give different evaluation results. So, we can conclude that the space of "best" predictors is brittle; minor change in a data and performance metrics selections can make different attributes appear most useful for defect prediction Menzies, Dekhtyar, et al. (2007) and some models more acceptable than others. List of the most popular performance evaluation metrics are presented in Appendix 6.

4. RELATED WORKS

Usually paper related to fault prediction studies focus on three major challenges. Two of them are learning approaches, and software metrics. Another challenging task is building software fault prediction model to identify the number of faults for each modules instead of just predicting whether the module is faulty or not faulty. The following three sub sections are classified according to the mentioned challenges.

4.1. Learners

Software fault prediction became one of the noteworthy research topics since 1990, and the number of research papers is doubled until year 2009 (Catal & Diri, 2009a). Many different machine learning techniques were used for building software fault prediction models such as genetic programming (Evett, Khoshgoftaar, Chien, & Allen, 1999), decision trees (Koprinska, Poon, Clark, & Chan, 2007), neural network (Thwin & Quah, 2005), naïve bayes (Menzies, Greenwald, et al., 2007), case-based reasoning (El Emam, Benlarbi, Goel, & Rai, 2001a), fuzzy logic (Yuan, Khoshgoftaar, Allen, & Ganesan, 2000), and the artificial immune recognition system algorithms in (Catal & Diri, 2007, 2009a). Brief explanations about some of these studies are presented in this section. We should mention here that, most of the research papers used more than one learner for building a prediction model.

Koru and Liu (2005b) have applied the J48, K-Star and random forest algorithms on public NASA datasets to construct fault prediction model based on 21 method-level with f-measures as an evaluation performance metrics.

Menzies, Greenwald, et al. (2007) have conducted an experiment with the help of several data mining algorithms on public NASA datasets using method-level metrics and evaluated the results using probability of detection (PD), probability of false alarm (PF) and balance parameter metrics. They used log-transformation with info-gain filters before applying the algorithms and they claim that fault prediction using naïve bayes performed better than the J48 algorithm. Menzies, Dekhtyar, Distefano, & Greenwald (2007) argued that since some models with low precision performed well, using it as a reliable parameter for performance evaluation is not good.

Shafi, Hassan, Arshaq, Khan, & Shamail (2008) were used two other datasets from PROMISE repository, JEditData and AR3. They applied 30 different techniques on them and showed that classification via regression and locally weighted learning (LWL) are better than the other techniques. They chose precision, recall, and accuracy as evaluation performance metrics.

Catal and Diri (2009a) have used some machine learning techniques such as random forest; they also applied artificial immune recognition system on five NASA datasets and used accuracy and area under receiver operating characteristic curves (AUC) as for evaluation purpose.

Turhan and Bener (2009) have used probability of detection (PD), probability of false alarm (PF) and balance parameter. The results indicated that independence assumption in naïve bayes algorithm is not detrimental with principal component analysis (PCA) pre-processing.

Alsmadi and Najadat (2011) have developed the prediction algorithm based on studying statistics of the whole dataset and each attributes. They proposed a technique to evaluate the correlation between numerical values and categorical variables of fault prone dataset to be able to automatically predict faulty modules based on attribute's values.

Sandhu, Singh, & Budhija (2011) claimed that, the prediction of different level of severity or impact of faults in object oriented software systems with noise can be done satisfactory by using density-based spatial clustering; they used KC1 from NASA public dataset.

Turhan, Kocak, & Bener (2009) analyzed 25 projects of the largest GSM operator in Turkey, Turkcell, to predict defect before the testing phase. They used a defect prediction model that is based on static code attributes such as lines of code, Halstead and McCabe. They suggested that at least 70% of the defects could be detected by inspecting only 6% of the code using a naïve bayes model and 3% of the code using call graph based ranking (CGBR) framework.

Yin, Luo, & Guo (2011) proposed the framework that integrate testing and fault prediction for unit testing. They applied artificial immune network (aiNet) to extract and simplify data from the modules that have gone through testing process.

Yuan et al. (2000) used fuzzy subtractive clustering to predict the number of faults and then they applied module-order modeling to check whether modules were fault prone or not. Subtractive clustering can produce the fuzzy interference rule automatically through the training process. When relationship in a data cannot be modeled by one linear equation, this approach is used as a multiple linear relationships for various regions of the input space.

Pandey, & Goyal (2010a), proposed a model which predicts the fault density at the end of each phase of software development life cycle based on relevant metrics in each phase. They selected totally ten metrics from all the phases and the output of the model were fault densities at the end of each cycle. Fuzzy profile of metrics was developed by human experts to express their evaluation and the characteristics of the metrics. They also utilized the classification capability of data mining techniques and knowledge stored in software metrics to classify the software module as fault-prone or not fault-prone in the KC2 dataset form repository of NASA. Later, Pandey, & Goyal (2010b) applied ID3 algorithm and extracted the rules from the decision tree, and integrated the

model with fuzzy inference system to either classify the modules as fault-prone or not fault-prone for the target data. The model is also able to rank the fault-prone module based on its degree of fault-proneness.

Arisholm et al. (2010) systematically compared fault prediction models based on three different modeling criteria which, one of them was based on three different learning techniques that were C4.5, neural network, and logistic regression. Two more modeling criteria were software metrics and evaluation performance metrics variations. They claimed that what is considered the best model is highly dependent on the criteria that are used to evaluate and compare the models.

D'Ambros, Lanza, & Robbes (2012) presented a benchmark by conducting three sets of experiment, first based on comparing the same modeling approaches across different systems, second based on observing whether differences in performance are statistically significant by using different sets of software metrics, and finally investigating the stability of approaches across different learners which were decision trees, naïve bayes, and generalized linear logistic regression. They compared the prediction models based on binary classification, ranking based on defects, and effort-aware ranking based on defect density.

4.2. Software Metrics

Different studies show different results, which means that the use of metrics to predict design quality during development is still vague. For any developing software, significant amounts of resources must be dedicated to maintain the quality of those systems. Many researches (Basili, Briand, & Melo, 1996; Chidamber & Kemerer, 1994; Gyimothy, Ferenc, & Siket, 2005; Subramanyam & Krishnan, 2003; Wilkie & Kitchenham, 2000) showed that some metrics such as CBO, RFC, WMC, DIT, and NOC are significant predictors of class error proneness and there is a relationship between these metrics and various quality factors.

Some researchers such as Fenton and Pfleeger (1998) found a high correlation between McCabe's cyclomatic (v(g)) and lines of code. Some studies (Cartwright & Shepperd, 2000) recognized that the parts of the system that used inheritance were three times more error prone than the parts that did not use inheritance. Elish, Al-Yafei, & Al-Mulhem (2011) evaluated and compared three suites of package-level metrics (Martin, MOOD, and CK) empirically in predicting the number of pre-release and post-release faults in packages of object oriented systems through a case study of Eclipse. They have constructed seven different multivariate linear regression models using different combinations of the three suites across three releases of Eclipse. The results indicate that the prediction models that include subset of Martin metrics achieved competitive accuracy

Giang et al. (2010), stated that although current fault prediction models can be applied for web application software as well, but they do not consider certain characteristics of these applications. They mentioned three important web characteristics as interaction of many state-of-the-art technologies, high priority requirement for user interfaces and hyperlink-based structure. They used Li, Alaeddine, & Tian (2010) web metrics and stated that faults related to links and graphical user interface contributed a lot to a total number of faults. They used Druppal, which is a large open source web content management system written in PHP as a case study and they showed that a model that was constructed based on web metrics outperformed the models that used module level metrics.

El Emam, Benlarbi, Goel, & Rai, (2001b) mentioned effect of class size on the validity of the object oriented measures. They found that after controlling the size, none of the object-oriented metrics they studied was associated with proneness anymore.

Calikli et al. (2009) proposed a framework which used the hierarchical structure information about the source code of the software product, to perform defect prediction at a functional method

level and source file level. They built the prediction model with naïve bayes classifier.

As mentioned in the previous section, 4.2., Arisholm et al. (2010) systematically compared fault prediction models based on three different modeling criteria. One of them was based on three software measurement metrics, which were process measures, object-oriented code structural measures, and code churn measures. Two more modeling criteria were machine learning and evaluation performance metrics variations. They claimed that although there is a large difference between the individual metric sets in terms of cost-effectiveness, and the process measures are among the most expensive ones to collect, including them as candidate measures significantly improves the prediction models compared with models that only include structural measures

4.3. Number and Severity of Errors

According to (Shatnawi & Li, 2008), in limited time for testing, it is better to know where the most severe error are likely to occur rather than just knowing where errors are likely to occur. Differentiating errors into different severity categories can help software engineers narrow down the areas in the design to focus their efforts on testing or refactoring specially in a limited time and budget. This knowledge can help tester narrow down the testing areas.

Szabo and Khoshgoftaar (1995) classified functions into three groups: High, Medium, and Low-risk groups. However, these studies grouped modules (classes or functions) based on the number of errors, not the severity of errors.

Zhou and Leung (2006) used the Chidamber and Kemerer metrics suite to predict two levels of error severity in a storage management system. The used KC1 data from PROMISE repository of NASA that were collected throughout the lifecycle of the project, but mainly from the development phase of the project.

5. FAULT PREDICTION CHALLENGES

In this section, we present some of the challenges that researchers may counter in the area of fault prediction.

5.1. Performance Evaluation Metrics Problems

Many statistical and machine learning techniques have been proposed to predict fault-proneness of program modules in software engineering. Choosing the "best" candidate among many available models involves performance assessment and detailed comparison, but these comparisons are not simple due to many performance evaluation metrics. Different measurements could give different evaluation results. According to (Menzies, Greenwald, et al., 2007) the space of "best" predictors is brittle; minor change in a data and other evaluation factors can make different attributes appear most useful for defect prediction and some models more acceptable than others. In some studies, the selection of the "best" model cannot be made without considering project cost characteristics, which are specific in each development environment. A modeling methodology is good if it is able to perform well on all datasets, or at least most of them. One of the famous and challenging papers which argued about choosing evaluation metrics belongs to Menzies, Greenwald, et al (2007); they stated that since some models with low precision performed well, using it as a reliable parameter for performance evaluation is not recommended. Although Zhang and Zhang (2007) criticized the paper but Menzies, Dekhtyar, et al. (2007) defended their claim. They also mentioned that if the target class (faulty/ non-faulty) is in the minority, accuracy is a poor measure as for example, a classifier could score 90 percent accuracy on a dataset with 10 percent faulty data, even if it predicts that all defective modules are defect free. So deciding about what set of performance evaluation metrics should be used for evaluating a prediction model is a very difficult and crucial task as it can have a decisive impact on the analysis results and accepting and rejecting any prediction model.

5.2. Dataset Problems

One of the main challenges in this area is how to get the data. Providing data for the study usually, play a major role, as many companies are not interested in sharing their data with others. In some works like in (Hewett, 2011), a specific company provides the data, so the results are not fully trustable. Recently, several software engineering data repositories become publicly available. Since researchers want to show the comparative study to their research, they prefer to select the dataset from these public repositories such as PROMISE repository (PROMISE, 2005), different versions of open source projects such as Eclipse (ECLIPSE) and UCI machine learning repository (UCI). Therefore, these datasets can be used as a benchmark to validate and compare the proposed prediction models. According to Catal and Diri (2009b), before 2005, more than half of the researches have used non-public datasets; however after that, with the help of PROMISE repository, the usage of public datasets reached to half because the results are more reliable and not specific to a particular company.

Some authors like Menzies, Greenwald, et al. (2007) believes despite different conclusions due to different choices in datasets, now with the help of public domain datasets, the contradiction in results can be removed. In contrast, some researchers such as (T. Hall et al., 2012), claim that, these set of NASA datasets are not completely reliable because there are not enough faulty modules presented in them and it is not possible to explore the source code.

Preparing fault data and the size of dataset are other two critical factors since it may have a major impact on evaluation results. El Emam et al. (2001b) found that after controlling dataset size, none of the object-oriented metrics they studied was associated with proneness anymore. Sometimes we cannot have enough fault data to build accurate models. For example, some project partners may not collect fault data for some project components or execution cost of metrics collection tools system may be extremely expensive. Another problem here is a number of defected modules in a training dataset; some researchers believe that if the number of faulty data is less than a specific number, the reliability of the prediction model is not confirmable.

5.3. Metrics Problems

5.3.1. General Metrics Problems

Most of the companies do not share their software metric data with other organizations so that a useful database with great amount of data cannot be formed. However, there are publicly available well-established tools for extracting metrics such as size, McCabe's cyclomatic complexity, and Halstead's program vocabulary. These tools help automating the data collection process in software projects. There are so many notions about whether different metrics could be a certain predictor of the presence and absence of a fault.

Some researchers such as (Fenton & Pfleeger, 1998) claim that size of the modules may not be always directly proportional to the number of faults which is opposite to the others beliefs (Andersson & Runeson, 2007). In addition, the value of some of static code attributes such as McCabe and Halstead as defect predictors has been widely argued. Some researchers support them (Chapman & Solomon, 2002; G. A. Hall & Munson, 2000; Halstead, 1977; Khoshgoftaar, Gao, & Szabo, 2001; McCabe, 1976; Menzies, Dekhtyar, et al., 2007; Menzies, DiStefano, Orrego, & Chapman, 2004; Nagappan & Ball, 2005) and some are against them (Fenton & Neil, 1999; Fenton & Ohlsson, 2000; Shepperd & Ince, 1994).

It should be mentioned that, the fast changing web technologies pose many challenges for software developers. We are living in era web 2 and huge software companies talks about web 3. So user satisfaction plays an important role here. Web application metrics are new in field of software fault prediction and new sets of web-related metrics should be introduced in future like the one in (Giang, et al., 2010). List of these metrics are presented in Appendix 5.

5.3.2. Metrics Extraction Problems

Software engineering practitioners including designers, developers, and managers must be able to rely on experimental results especially the one that is related to software quality and metrics. In addition, software engineering researchers should be able to rely on the tools implementing these metrics, to support them in quality assessment and assurance tasks, to allow to quantify software quality and to deliver the information needed as input for their decision-making and engineering processes (Cartwright & Shepperd, 2000). Since past few years, huge number of software metrics tools came to the picture. To safely apply the results and to use them in practice, it would be necessary that all metrics tools implement the suggested metrics the way they have been validated, but unfortunately the results of metrics extraction are not always same and differ from one tool to another so the outcome which attained based on those metrics could not be compared.

5.3.3. Metrics Selection Problems

Feature selection is identifying and extracting the most useful features of the dataset for learning, and these features are very valuable for analysis and future prediction. So by removing less important and redundant data, the performance of learning algorithm could be improved. Then nature of the training data plays the major role in classification and prediction. If the data fails to exhibit the statistical regularity that machine-learning algorithms exploit, the learning will fail. Removing the redundant data from the training set will afterwards make the process of discovering regularity much easier, faster and more accurate.

If the relationship between the software metrics measured at a certain state and the defect's properties can be formulated together, it becomes possible to predict similar defects in other parts of the code as well. Validation of software metrics could be classified as finding linear or rank correlations to determine the relationship between the metrics and some dependent feature of the system under study or it is used to groups the features and the metrics into classes and performs cross tabulations to determine the tendency of the data.

Many researchers use statistical analysis and different metrics selection approaches. Analyzed results are different and have a major impact on accepting or rejecting any prediction models. Menzies, Greenwald, et al. (2007) rank attributes from most informative to least informative and the highest ranked attribute is the one with the largest information gain. Many researchers such as Catal and Diri (2009a), and Abaei and Selamat (2013) used correlation based feature selection (CFS) to find the finest subset attributes that have a tight relationship with fault data. Khoshgoftaar, Ganesan, Allen, Ross, Munikoti, Goel, & Nandi (1997) used principal component analysis (PCA) to improve the performance of the models and to reduce multicollinearity.

5.4. Machine Learning Problems

Machine learning methods fail to predict defect densities accurately compared to when regression and statistical method are applied in datasets that do not have sufficient defective modules. Many researchers have already been explored many machine learning algorithms, but the problem is that, not many research scholars are interested to improve or make some modifications to learner classifiers to come up with a better fault prediction

model. Even hybrid algorithms and soft computing techniques are not widely used in this research area.

Another problem is when a supervised learning approach cannot be taken due to absence of module's labels. For example, some companies may not collect data for their software components and fault data due to lack of budget and experience. To solve this challenging problem, researchers focus on unsupervised and semi-supervised techniques such as clustering. Usually these techniques consist of cluster modules process followed by an evaluation phase of an expert (Zhong, Khoshgoftaar, & Seliya, 2004b). In this phase, an expert with 15 years of experience, labels each cluster as fault-prone or not fault-prone by examining representative of each cluster with the help of some statistical data such as global mean, minimum, maximum, median, 75 percentile, and 90 percentile of each metric. One of the problems with this approach is that, it is not easy to find a 15 years experienced expert who would have the experience to label each cluster. Zhong et al.'s approach (2004b) is the first attempt to solve this practical problem, but software engineering community is still in early stages for the usage of such models in the practical area. Some researchers such as Catal et al. (2009), aimed to remove the obligation of an expert assistance by using metrics threshold and develop fully automated techniques that do not require human experts.

As mentioned in section 4.1, D'Ambros et al. (2012) presented a benchmark by conducting three sets of experiment, first based on comparing the same modeling approaches across different systems, second based on observing whether differences in performance are statistically significant by using different sets of software metrics, and finally investigating the stability of approaches across different learners. Based on their experiment, they found that while some approaches perform better than others in a statistically significant manner, external validity in defect prediction is still an open problem, as generalizing results to different contexts/learners proved to be a partially unsuccessful endeavor.

6. CONCLUSION

In this chapter, we tried to give a general scheme of the steps that any researcher is faced when he/she wants to work in the software fault prediction area. Although we cannot explain every steps in details; but we reviewed almost all issues and challenging factors in this field of study. Different parameters such as software metrics, machine-learning techniques, and performance evaluation metrics were illustrated and compared to each other to highlight the factors that have effect on building the finest prediction models. We also presented some challenges, which are still remained unsolved and need further attention as future works.

ACKNOWLEDGMENT

The Universiti Teknologi Malaysia (UTM) under research grant 03H02 and Ministry of Science, Technology & Innovations Malaysia, under research grant 4S062are hereby acknowledged for some of the facilities utilized during the course of this research work.

REFERENCES

Abaei, G., Rezaei, Z., & Selamat, A. (2013). Fault prediction by utilizing self-organizing Map and Threshold. In *Proceedings of Control System, Computing and Engineering (ICCSCE), 2013 IEEE International Conference on* (pp. 465-470). Malaysia: IEEE.

Abaei, G., & Selamat, A. (2013). A survey on software fault detection based on different prediction approaches. *Vietnam Journal of Computer Science*, 1-17.

Abreu, F. B., & Carapuça, R. (1994). Object-oriented software engineering: Measuring and controlling the development process. In *Proceedings of the 4th International Conference on Software Quality* (Vol. 186). IEEE.

Alan, O., & Catal, C. (2011). Thresholds based outlier detection approach for mining class outliers: An empirical case study on software measurement datasets. *Expert Systems with Applications, 38*(4), 3440–3445. doi:10.1016/j.eswa.2010.08.130

Alsmadi, I., & Najadat, H. (2011). Evaluating the change of software fault behavior with dataset attributes based on categorical correlation. *Advances in Engineering Software, 42*(8), 535–546. doi:10.1016/j.advengsoft.2011.03.010

Andersson, C., & Runeson, P. (2007). A replicated quantitative analysis of fault distributions in complex software systems. *Software Engineering. IEEE Transactions on, 33*(5), 273–286.

Ardil, E., & Sandhu, P. S. (2010). A soft computing approach for modeling of severity of faults in software systems. *International Journal of Physical Sciences, 5*(2), 074-085.

Arisholm, E., Briand, L. C., & Johannessen, E. B. (2010). A systematic and comprehensive investigation of methods to build and evaluate fault prediction models. *Journal of Systems and Software, 83*(1), 2–17. doi:10.1016/j.jss.2009.06.055

Baisch, E., & Liedtke, T. (1997). Comparison of conventional approaches and soft-computing approaches for software quality prediction. [IEEE.]. *Proceedings of Systems, Man, and Cybernetics, 2*, 1045–1049.

Bansiya, J., & Davis, C. G. (2002). A hierarchical model for object-oriented design quality assessment. *Software Engineering. IEEE Transactions on, 28*(1), 4–17.

Basili, V. R., Briand, L. C., & Melo, W. L. (1996). A validation of object-oriented design metrics as quality indicators. *Software Engineering. IEEE Transactions on*, *22*(10), 751–761.

Bibi, S., Tsoumakas, G., Stamelos, I., & Vlahavas, I. P. (2006). Software Defect Prediction Using Regression via Classification. In *Proceedings of IEEE/ACS International Conference on Computer Systems and Applications (AICCSA 2006)* (pp. 330-336). Dubai, UAE. IEEE.

Bishnu, P. S., & Bhattacherjee, V. (2012). Software fault prediction using quad tree-based k-means clustering algorithm. *Knowledge and Data Engineering. IEEE Transactions on*, *24*(6), 1146–1150.

Boehm, B. W. (1988). Understanding and controlling software costs. *Journal of Parametrics*, *8*(1), 32–68.

Boetticher, G. (2006). Improving credibility of machine learner models in software engineering. *Advanced Machine Learner Applications in Software Engineering*, 52-72.

Calikli, G., Tosun, A., Bener, A., & Celik, M. (2009). The effect of granularity level on software defect prediction. In *Proceedings of Computer and Information Sciences* (pp. 531–536). Cyprus: IEEE. doi:10.1109/ISCIS.2009.5291866

Cartwright, M., & Shepperd, M. (2000). An empirical investigation of an object-oriented software system. *Software Engineering. IEEE Transactions on*, *26*(8), 786–796.

Catal, C. (2011). Software fault prediction: A literature review and current trends. *Expert Systems with Applications*, *38*(4), 4626–4636. doi:10.1016/j.eswa.2010.10.024

Catal, C., & Diri, B. (2007). Software defect prediction using artificial immune recognition system. In *Proceedings of the 25th Conference on IASTED International Multi-Conference: Software Engineering* (pp. 285-290). Innsburk, Austria: ACTA Press.

Catal, C., & Diri, B. (2009a). Investigating the effect of dataset size, metrics sets, and feature selection techniques on software fault prediction problem. *Information Sciences*, *179*(8), 1040–1058. doi:10.1016/j.ins.2008.12.001

Catal, C., & Diri, B. (2009b). A systematic review of software fault prediction studies. *Expert Systems with Applications*, *36*(4), 7346–7354. doi:10.1016/j.eswa.2008.10.027

Catal, C., Sevim, U., & Diri, B. (2009). Clustering and metrics thresholds based software fault prediction of unlabeled program modules. In *Proceedings of Information Technology: New Generations* (pp. 199–204). Las Vegas, NV: IEEE. doi:10.1109/ITNG.2009.12

Catal, C., Sevim, U., & Diri, B. (2011). Practical development of an Eclipse-based software fault prediction tool using Naive Bayes algorithm. *Expert Systems with Applications*, *38*(3), 2347–2353. doi:10.1016/j.eswa.2010.08.022

Chapman, M., & Solomon, D. (2002). The relationship of cyclomatic complexity, essential complexity and error rates. In *Proceedings of the NASA Software Assurance Symposium*. NASA.

Chidamber, S. R., & Kemerer, C. F. (1994). A metrics suite for object oriented design. *Software Engineering. IEEE Transactions on*, *20*(6), 476–493.

D'Ambros, M., Lanza, M., & Robbes, R. (2012). Evaluating defect prediction approaches: a benchmark and an extensive comparison. *Empirical Software Engineering*, *17*(4-5), 531–577. doi:10.1007/s10664-011-9173-9

Dejaeger, K., Verbraken, T., & Baesens, B. (2013). Toward Comprehensible Software Fault Prediction Models Using Bayesian Network Classifiers. *Software Engineering. IEEE Transactions on*, *39*(2), 237–257.

Dowd, M., McDonald, J., & Schuh, J. (2006). *The art of software security assessment: Identifying and preventing software vulnerabilities.* Pearson Education. *ECLIPSE.* Retrieved March 2013 from http://www.st.cs.uni-sb.de/softevo/bug-data/eclipse

El Emam, K., Benlarbi, S., Goel, N., & Rai, S. N. (2001a). Comparing case-based reasoning classifiers for predicting high risk software components. *Journal of Systems and Software, 55*(3), 301–320. doi:10.1016/S0164-1212(00)00079-0

El Emam, K., Benlarbi, S., Goel, N., & Rai, S. N. (2001b). The confounding effect of class size on the validity of object-oriented metrics. *Software Engineering. IEEE Transactions on, 27*(7), 630–650.

Elish, K. O., & Elish, M. O. (2008). Predicting defect-prone software modules using support vector machines. *Journal of Systems and Software, 81*(5), 649–660. doi:10.1016/j.jss.2007.07.040

Elish, M. O., Al-Yafei, A. H., & Al-Mulhem, M. (2011). Empirical comparison of three metrics suites for fault prediction in packages of object-oriented systems: A case study of Eclipse. *Advances in Engineering Software, 42*(10), 852–859. doi:10.1016/j.advengsoft.2011.06.001

Evett, M., Khoshgoftar, T., Chien, P. D., & Allen, E. (1998). GP-based software quality prediction. In *Proceedings of the Third Annual Conference Genetic Programming,* (pp. 60-65). Academic Press.

Fenton, N. E., & Neil, M. (1999). A critique of software defect prediction models. *Software Engineering. IEEE Transactions on, 25*(5), 675–689.

Fenton, N. E., & Ohlsson, N. (2000). Quantitative analysis of faults and failures in a complex software system. *Software Engineering. IEEE Transactions on, 26*(8), 797–814.

Fenton, N. E., & Pfleeger, S. L. (1998). *Software metrics: a rigorous and practical approach.* PWS Publishing Co.

Giang, L. T., Kang, D., & Bae, D. H. (2010). Software fault prediction models for web applications. In *Proceedings of Computer Software and Applications Conference Workshops (COMPSACW), 2010 IEEE 34th Annual* (pp. 51-56). Korea: IEEE.

Gill, N. S., & Grover, P. S. (2003). Component-based measurement: few useful guidelines. *ACM SIGSOFT Software Engineering Notes, 28*(6), 4–4. doi:10.1145/966221.966237

Gondra, I. (2008). Applying machine learning to software fault-proneness prediction. *Journal of Systems and Software, 81*(2), 186–195. doi:10.1016/j.jss.2007.05.035

Guo, L., Ma, Y., Cukic, B., & Singh, H. (2004). Robust prediction of fault-proneness by random forests. In *Proceedings of Software Reliability Engineering* (pp. 417–428). IEEE.

Gyimothy, T., Ferenc, R., & Siket, I. (2005). Empirical validation of object-oriented metrics on open source software for fault prediction. *Software Engineering. IEEE Transactions on, 31*(10), 897–910.

Hall, G. A., & Munson, J. C. (2000). Software evolution: code delta and code churn. *Journal of Systems and Software, 54*(2), 111–118. doi:10.1016/S0164-1212(00)00031-5

Hall, T., Beecham, S., Bowes, D., Gray, D., & Counsell, S. (2012). A systematic literature review on fault prediction performance in software engineering. *Software Engineering. IEEE Transactions on, 38*(6), 1276–1304.

Halstead, M. H. (1977). *Elements of Software Science.* Elsevier Science Inc.

Hewett, R. (2011). Mining software defect data to support software testing management. *Applied Intelligence*, *34*(2), 245–257. doi:10.1007/s10489-009-0193-8

Ince, D. (1990). Software metrics: introduction. *Information and Software Technology*, *32*(4), 297–303. doi:10.1016/0950-5849(90)90063-W

Jiang, Y., & Cukic, B. (2009). Misclassification cost-sensitive fault prediction models. In *Proceedings of the 5th international conference on predictor models in software engineering*. ACM.

Jiang, Y., Cukic, B., & Ma, Y. (2008). Techniques for evaluating fault prediction models. *Empirical Software Engineering*, *13*(5), 561–595. doi:10.1007/s10664-008-9079-3

Jiang, Y., Cukic, B., & Menzies, T. (2007). Fault prediction using early lifecycle data. In *Proceedings of Software Reliability* (pp. 237–246). IEEE.

Kamiya, T., Kusumoto, S., & Inoue, K. (1999). Prediction of fault-proneness at early phase in object-oriented development. In *Proceedings of Object-Oriented Real-Time Distributed Computing* (pp. 253–258). IEEE. doi:10.1109/ISORC.1999.776386

Kanmani, S., Uthariaraj, V. R., Sankaranarayanan, V., & Thambidurai, P. (2007). Object-oriented software fault prediction using neural networks. *Information and Software Technology*, *49*(5), 483–492. doi:10.1016/j.infsof.2006.07.005

Kaszycki, G. (1999). Using process metrics to enhance software fault prediction models. In *Proceedings of Tenth International Symposium on Software Reliability Engineering*. Boca Raton, FL: Academic Press.

Khoshgoftaar, T. M., Ganesan, K., Allen, E. B., Ross, F. D., Munikoti, R., Goel, N., & Nandi, A. (1997). Predicting fault-prone modules with case-based reasoning. In *Proceedings of Software Reliability Engineering* (pp. 27–35). IEEE.

Khoshgoftaar, T. M., Gao, K., & Szabo, R. M. (2001). An application of zero-inflated Poisson regression for software fault prediction. In *Proceedings of Software Reliability Engineering* (pp. 66–73). IEEE. doi:10.1109/ISSRE.2001.989459

Khoshgoftaar, T. M., & Seliya, N. (2002). Tree-based software quality estimation models for fault prediction. In *Proceedings of Software Metrics* (pp. 203–214). IEEE. doi:10.1109/METRIC.2002.1011339

Koprinska, I., Poon, J., Clark, J., & Chan, J. (2007). Learning to classify e-mail. *Information Sciences*, *177*(10), 2167–2187. doi:10.1016/j.ins.2006.12.005

Koru, A. G., & Liu, H. (2005a). Building effective defect-prediction models in practice. *Software, IEEE*, *22*(6), 23–29. doi:10.1109/MS.2005.149

Koru, A. G., & Liu, H. (2005b). An investigation of the effect of module size on defect prediction using static measures. *ACM SIGSOFT Software Engineering Notes*, *30*(4), 1–5.

Lessmann, S., Baesens, B., Mues, C., & Pietsch, S. (2008). Benchmarking classification models for software defect prediction: A proposed framework and novel findings. *Software Engineering. IEEE Transactions on*, *34*(4), 485–496.

Li, W. (1998). Another metric suite for object-oriented programming. *Journal of Systems and Software*, *44*(2), 155–162. doi:10.1016/S0164-1212(98)10052-3

Li, Z., Alaeddine, N., & Tian, J. (2010). Multifaceted quality and defect measurement for web software and source contents. *Journal of Systems and Software*, *83*(1), 18–28. doi:10.1016/j.jss.2009.04.055

Lorenz, M., & Kidd, J. (1994). *Object-oriented software metrics: A practical guide*. Prentice-Hall, Inc.

Mahaweerawat, A., Sophatsathit, P., & Lursinsap, C. (2007). Adaptive self-organizing map clustering for software fault prediction. In *Proceedings of Fourth international joint conference on computer science and software engineering,* (pp. 35-41). Academic Press.

Mahmood, S., Lai, R., Soo Kim, Y., Hong Kim, J., Cheon Park, S., & Suk Oh, H. (2005). A survey of component based system quality assurance and assessment. *Information and Software Technology,* *47*(10), 693–707. doi:10.1016/j.infsof.2005.03.007

Marcus, A., Poshyvanyk, D., & Ferenc, R. (2008). Using the conceptual cohesion of classes for fault prediction in object-oriented systems. *Software Engineering. IEEE Transactions on,* *34*(2), 287–300.

Martin, R. C. (2003). *Agile software development: principles, patterns, and practices.* Prentice Hall PTR.

McCabe, T. J. (1976). A complexity measure. *Software Engineering, IEEE Transactions on,* (4), 308-320.

Menzies, T., Dekhtyar, A., Distefano, J., & Greenwald, J. (2007). Problems with precision: a response to comments on 'data mining static code attributes to learn defect predictors'. *IEEE Transactions on Software Engineering,* *33*(9), 637. doi:10.1109/TSE.2007.70721

Menzies, T., DiStefano, J., Orrego, A., & Chapman, R. (2004). Assessing predictors of software defects. In *Proc. Workshop Predictive Software Models (PROMISE 2005).* PROMISE.

Menzies, T., Greenwald, J., & Frank, A. (2007). Data mining static code attributes to learn defect predictors. *Software Engineering. IEEE Transactions on,* *33*(1), 2–13.

Menzies, T., Milton, Z., Turhan, B., Cukic, B., Jiang, Y., & Bener, A. (2010). Defect prediction from static code features: Current results, limitations, new approaches. *Automated Software Engineering,* *17*(4), 375–407. doi:10.1007/s10515-010-0069-5

Mitchell, T. M. (1997). *Machine learning.* Burr Ridge, IL: McGraw Hill.

Nagappan, N., & Ball, T. (2005). Static analysis tools as early indicators of pre-release defect density. In *Proceedings of the 27th international conference on Software engineering* (pp. 580-586). ACM.

Pandey, A. K., & Goyal, N. K. (2010a). Fault prediction model by fuzzy profile development of reliability relevant software metrics. *International Journal of Computers and Applications.* doi:10.5120/1584-2124

Pandey, A. K., & Goyal, N. K. (2010b). Test effort optimization by prediction and ranking of fault-prone software modules. In *Proceedings of Reliability, Safety and Hazard (ICRESH), 2010 2nd International Conference on* (pp. 136-142). IEEE.

PROMISE Repository. (n.d.). Retrieved May 2013 from http://promise.site.uottawa.ca/SERepository/datasets-page.html

Quah, T. S., & Thwin, M. M. T. (2003). Application of neural networks for software quality prediction using object-oriented metrics. In *Proceedings of Software Maintenance* (pp. 116–125). IEEE.

Radjenović, D., Heričko, M., Torkar, R., & Živkovič, A. (2013). Software fault prediction metrics: A systematic literature review. *Information and Software Technology,* *55*(8), 1397–1418. doi:10.1016/j.infsof.2013.02.009

Rana, Z. A., Awais, M. M., & Shamail, S. (2009). An FIS for early detection of defect prone modules. In *Proceedings of Emerging Intelligent Computing Technology and Applications With Aspects of Artificial Intelligence* (pp. 144–153). Springer. doi:10.1007/978-3-642-04020-7_16

Reformat, M. (2003). A fuzzy-based meta-model for reasoning about the number of software defects. In Proceedings of Fuzzy Sets and Systems—IFSA 2003 (pp. 644-651). Springer.

Sandhu, P. S., Singh, S., & Budhija, N. (2011). Prediction of level of severity of faults in software systems using density based clustering. In *Proceedings of 2011 IEEE International Conference on Software and Computer Applications.* (Vol. 9). IEEE.

Sedigh-Ali, S., Ghafoor, A., & Paul, R. A. (2001). Metrics-guided quality management for component-based software systems. In *Proceedings of Computer Software and Applications Conference,* (pp. 303-308). IEEE.

Seliya, N., & Khoshgoftaar, T. M. (2007). Software quality analysis of unlabeled program modules with semisupervised clustering. *Systems, Man and Cybernetics, Part A: Systems and Humans. IEEE Transactions on, 37*(2), 201–211.

Shafi, S., Hassan, S. M., Arshaq, A., Khan, M. J., & Shamail, S. (2008). Software quality prediction techniques: A comparative analysis. In *Proceedings of Emerging Technologies* (pp. 242–246). IEEE. doi:10.1109/ICET.2008.4777508

Shatnawi, R., & Li, W. (2008). The effectiveness of software metrics in identifying error-prone classes in post-release software evolution process. *Journal of Systems and Software, 81*(11), 1868–1882. doi:10.1016/j.jss.2007.12.794

Shepperd, M., & Ince, D. C. (1994). A critique of three metrics. *Journal of Systems and Software, 26*(3), 197–210. doi:10.1016/0164-1212(94)90011-6

Sherer, S. A. (1995). Software fault prediction. *Journal of Systems and Software, 29*(2), 97–105. doi:10.1016/0164-1212(94)00051-N

Subramanyam, R., & Krishnan, M. S. (2003). Empirical analysis of ck metrics for object-oriented design complexity: Implications for software defects. *Software Engineering. IEEE Transactions on, 29*(4), 297–310.

Szabo, R. M., & Khoshgoftaar, T. M. (1995). An assessment of software quality in a C++ environment. In *Proceedings of Software Reliability Engineering* (pp. 240–249). IEEE. doi:10.1109/ISSRE.1995.497663

Thwin, M. M. T., & Quah, T. S. (2005). Application of neural networks for software quality prediction using object-oriented metrics. *Journal of Systems and Software, 76*(2), 147–156. doi:10.1016/j.jss.2004.05.001

Tomaszewski, P., Håkansson, J., Grahn, H., & Lundberg, L. (2007). Statistical models vs. expert estimation for fault prediction in modified code–An industrial case study. *Journal of Systems and Software, 80*(8), 1227–1238. doi:10.1016/j.jss.2006.12.548

Tosun, A., Turhan, B., & Bener, A. (2009). Validation of network measures as indicators of defective modules in software systems. In *Proceedings of the 5th international conference on predictor models in software engineering (PROMISE'09)*. ACM.

Tsamardinos, I., Brown, L. E., & Aliferis, C. F. (2006). The max-min hill-climbing Bayesian network structure learning algorithm. *Machine Learning, 65*(1), 31–78. doi:10.1007/s10994-006-6889-7

Turhan, B., & Bener, A. (2009). Analysis of Naive Bayes' assumptions on software fault data: An empirical study. *Data & Knowledge Engineering, 68*(2), 278–290. doi:10.1016/j.datak.2008.10.005

Turhan, B., Kocak, G., & Bener, A. (2008). Software defect prediction using call graph based ranking (CGBR) framework. In Proceedings of Software Engineering and Advanced Applications, (pp. 191-198). IEEE.

Turhan, B., Kocak, G., & Bener, A. (2009). Data mining source code for locating software bugs: A case study in telecommunication industry. *Expert Systems with Applications*, *36*(6), 9986–9990. doi:10.1016/j.eswa.2008.12.028

Turhan, B., Menzies, T., Bener, A. B., & Di Stefano, J. (2009). On the relative value of cross-company and within-company data for defect prediction. *Empirical Software Engineering*, *14*(5), 540–578. doi:10.1007/s10664-008-9103-7

UCI. (n.d.). *Machine Learning Repository*. Retrieved May 2013 from http://archive.ics.uci.edu/ml/datasets.html

Vandecruys, O., Martens, D., Baesens, B., Mues, C., De Backer, M., & Haesen, R. (2008). Mining software repositories for comprehensible software fault prediction models. *Journal of Systems and Software*, *81*(5), 823–839. doi:10.1016/j.jss.2007.07.034

Wilkie, F. G., & Kitchenham, B. A. (2000). Coupling measures and change ripples in C++ application software. *Journal of Systems and Software*, *52*(2), 157–164. doi:10.1016/S0164-1212(99)00142-9

Xu, Z., Khoshgoftaar, T. M., & Allen, E. B. (2000). Prediction of software faults using fuzzy nonlinear regression modeling. In *Proceedings of High Assurance Systems Engineering, 2000, Fifth IEEE International Symposium on* (pp. 281-290). IEEE.

Yin, Q., Luo, R., & Guo, P. (2011). Software Fault Prediction Framework Based on aiNet Algorithm. In *Proceedings of Computational Intelligence and Security (CIS), 2011 Seventh International Conference on* (pp. 329-333). IEEE.

Yuan, X., Khoshgoftaar, T. M., Allen, E. B., & Ganesan, K. (2000). An application of fuzzy clustering to software quality prediction. In *Proceedings of Application-Specific Systems and Software Engineering Technology* (pp. 85–90). IEEE. doi:10.1109/ASSET.2000.888052

Zhang, D. (2000). Applying machine learning algorithms in software development. In *Proceedings of 2000 Monterey Workshop on Modeling Software System Structures* (pp. 275-285). IEEE.

Zhang, X., & Zhang, H. (2007). Comments on data mining static code attributes to learn defect predictors. *IEEE Transactions on Software Engineering*, *33*(9), 635–636. doi:10.1109/TSE.2007.70706

Zhong, S., Khoshgoftaar, T. M., & Seliya, N. (2004a). Analyzing software measurement data with clustering techniques. *Intelligent Systems, IEEE*, *19*(2), 20–27. doi:10.1109/MIS.2004.1274907

Zhong, S., Khoshgoftaar, T. M., & Seliya, N. (2004b). Unsupervised Learning for Expert-Based Software Quality Estimation. In *Proceedings of High Assurance Systems Engineering, 2004, Eighth IEEE International Symposium on* (pp. 149-155). IEEE.

Zhou, Y., & Leung, H. (2006). Empirical analysis of object-oriented design metrics for predicting high and low severity faults. *Software Engineering. IEEE Transactions on*, *32*(10), 771–789.

KEY TERMS AND DEFINITIONS

Class/Module Label: Refers to faultiness or non-faultiness of either module or class.

Classifier: An algorithm that implements classification in the field of machine learning and statistical analysis.

Machine Learning Algorithm: Algorithm that learns from experience and historical data with respect to some class of tasks and performance measure, such that its performance can be improved with experience.

Performance Evaluation Metrics: A set of software measurements metrics that are used for evaluating performance of any model and comparing it with existing models.

Resources: Time, testers (manpower).

Software Fault Prediction: Estimates the reliability of the system, and investigate the effect of design and testing process over number of defects based on historical data.

Software Metrics: These are based on numerical measurements that are extracted from the software project and quantify some aspect of a software product.

Software Testing: A phase used to detect and (up to some extent) predict faults.

ENDNOTES

[1]   Defects and faults have the same meaning and may be used interchangeably in this chapter

APPENDIX 1

Table 1. Different set of metrics

Metrics Name	Use	Researchers
Method Level/Static Code	• Metrics can be collected from programs development with both structural and OO programming, so they have methods • The predicted fault-prone modules are the methods which likely to have fault during system testing or field-test • Widely used method level metrics are available in PROMISE repositories and are shown in Appendix 3	-Halstead (1977) -McCabe (1976)
Class Level/Package Level	• Only for object oriented programming • CK is the most popular class-level metrics • According to several software fault prediction studies, CBO, WMC and RFC are the most significant CK metrics for fault prediction • MOOD, QMOOD, L&K are the other class-level metrics	-Chidamber & Kemerer (CK) (1994) -Zhou & Leung, (2006) -Abreu & Carapuca (1994) -Lorenz & Kidd (1994) -Bansia & Davis (2002) -Li (1998)
Component Level	• Proposed in 2001 for the first time and are shown in Appendix4 • Researchers are still works on these kinds of metrics • There are metrics like Interface, Fault tolerance, Recoverability, Accuracy, Changeability, … are categorized based of different quality attributes such Complexity, Portability, Reliability, Functionality and Maintainability	-Gill & Grover (2003) -Sedigh-Ali, Ghafoor, & Paul (2001) - Mahmood, Lai, Soo Kim, Hong Kim, Cheon Park, & Suk Oh (2005)

File Level	• Use the metrics which collected from the source
	• file-level metrics might be:
	  o Number of times the source file was inspected prior to system test release
	  o Number of lines of code for the source file prior to coding phase (auto-generated code)
	  o Number of lines of code for the source file prior to system test release
	  o Number of lines of commented code for the source prior to code (auto-generated)
	  o Number of lines of commented code for the source file prior to system test
		-Khoshgoftaar et al. (2001)

Process Level	• Combination of requirement metrics with code metrics
	• Requirement metrics are usually gathered with ARM (Automated Requirement Measurements) from textual requirement specification documents
	• In addition to above requirement metrics, researchers may apply different process metrics such as:
	  o programmer experience level
	  o the number of defects found in reviews
	  o the amount of time that the module spent in reviews
	  o the number of test cases and unique test cases run that touched the module
		- Kaszycki (1999)
		-Jiang et al. (2007)

Quantitative Level	• Regression via classification (RvC) are used for prediction
	• Some quantities values are used such as:
	  o CPU Usage
	  o Disk Space
	  o Document Quality
	  o Number of User
	  o Average Transaction
		-Bibi, Tsoumakas, Stamelos, & Vlahavas (2006)

APPENDIX 2

Table 2. Some OO metrics explanation (Class-Level/Package Level Metrics)

Metrics	Description	Definition	Reference
AHF	*Attribute Hiding Factor*	- The ratio of the sum of the invisibilities of all attributes defined in all classes to the total number of methods in the package	*MOOD suite (Abreu & Carapuca, 1994)*
AIF	*Attribute Inheritance Factor*	- The ratio of the number of inherited (and not overridden) attributes in all classes to the total number of available methods (locally defined plus inherited) for all classes in the package	*MOOD suite (Abreu & Carapuca, 1994)*
Ca	*Afferent Coupling*	- Number of other packages that depends on classes within the package - It measures the incoming dependencies (*fan-in*)	*Martin suite (Martin, 2003)*
Ce	*Efferent Coupling*	- Number of other packages that the class in the package depend on - It measures the outgoing dependencies (*fan-out*)	*Martin suite (Martin, 2003)*
CBO	*Coupling Between Object Classes*	- Number of none-inheritance-related classes to which a class is coupled	*CK suits (Chidamber & Kemerer, 1994)*
CF	*Coupling Factor*	- The ratio of the number of class couplings to the maximum possible number of class couplings in the package	*MOOD suite (Abreu & Carapuca, 1994)*
CTA	*Coupling through data abstraction*	-The number of reference types used in the attribute declarations	*Li (1998)*
CTM	*Coupling through message passing*	-Counts the number of method call expressions made into body of the measured method	*Li (1998)*
D	*Distance*	- Perpendicular distance of the package from the idealized line - This metric is an indicator of the package's balance between abstractness and stability and the range for this metric is zero to one	*Martin suite (Martin, 2003)*
DIT	*Depth of Inheritance*	- Maximum length from a class to the root class in the inheritance tree	*CK suits (Chidamber & Kemerer, 1994)*
I	*Instability*	- The ratio of efferent coupling (Ce) to total coupling (Ce + Ca) for the package; I = Ce/(Ce + Ca) - Indicator of the package's resilience to change - The range for this metric is zero to one, with zero indicating a completely stable package and with one indicating a completely unstable package	*Martin suite (Martin, 2003)*
LCOM	*Lack of Cohesion in Methods*	- Number of pairs of methods in a class using no attributes in common, minus the number of pairs of methods that do	*CK suits (Chidamber & Kemerer, 1994)*
MHF	*Method Hiding Factor*	- The ratio of the sum of the invisibilities of all methods defined in all classes to the total number of methods in the package	*MOOD suite (Abreu & Carapuca, 1994)*
MIF	*Method Inheritance Factor*	- The ratio of the number of inherited (and not overridden) methods in all classes to the total number of available methods (locally defined plus inherited) for all classes in the package	*MOOD suite (Abreu & Carapuca, 1994)*
NC	*Number of classes*	- Number of concrete and abstract classes - It is a measure of package size	*Martin suite (Martin, 2003)*
NOC	*Number of Children*	- Number of immediate subclasses of a class	*CK suits (Chidamber & Kemerer, 1994)*
NOA	*Number of attributes*	-Counts the number of attributes	*Lorenz and Kidd (1994)*

continued on following page

Table 2. Continued

Metrics	Description	Definition	Reference
NOO	*Number of operations*	-Counts the number of operations	*Lorenz and Kidd (1994)*
NOAM	*Number of added methods*	-Counts the number of operations added by a class, Inherited and overridden operations are not counted	*Lorenz and Kidd (1994)*
NOOM	*Number of overridden methods*	-Counts the number of inherited operations, which a class overrides	*Lorenz and Kidd (1994)*
PF	*Polymorphism Factor*	- The ratio of the number of methods in the package that redefine inherited methods to the maximum number of possible distinct polymorphic situations in the package	*CK suits* (Chidamber & Kemerer, 1994)
RFC	*Response for a Class*	- Number of methods in the set of all methods that can be invoked in response to a message sent to an object of a class	*CK suits* (Chidamber & Kemerer, 1994)
WMC	*Weighted Methods per Class*	- Sum of the cyclomatic complexities of all methods defined in a class.Number of methods in each class	*CK suits* (Chidamber & Kemerer, 1994)

APPENDIX 3

Table 3. Some method-level metrics

Attributes Names	Information
Loc	McCabe's line count of code
v(g)	McCabe "cyclomatic complexity"
ev(g)	McCabe "essential complexity"
iv(g)	McCabe "design complexity"
N	Halstead total operators + operands
V	Halstead "volume"
L	Halstead "program length"
D	Halstead "difficulty"
I	Halstead "intelligence"
E	Halstead "effort"
B	Halstead "delivered bugs"
T	Halstead's time estimator
lOCode	Halstead's line count
lOComment	Halstead's count of lines of comments
lOBlank	Halstead's count of blank lines
lOCodeAndlOComment	lines of code and comments
uniq_op	unique operators
uniq_opnd	unique operands
total_op	total operators
total_opnd	total operand
branchCount	branch count of the flow graph

APPENDIX 4

Table 4. Some components-level metrics

Quality Attributes	Metrics	Description
Complexity	Interface	An estimate of the complexity of interface
Complexity	Integration	Measures of effort is required in the integration process of component bases system
Complexity	Semantics	Measures the complexity of the relationship of component to a given language
Portability	Adaptability	Opportunity to adoption to different environment
Portability	Replaceability	Opportunity and effort of using components in place of other components
Portability	Portability Compliance	Adherence to application of portability related standard
Reliability	Maturity	Capacity to avoid failure as a result of faults in a components based system
Reliability	Fault Tolerance	Ability to maintain a specified level of performance in case of faults
Reliability	Recoverability	Capacity to re-established level of performance after the faults
Functionality	Suitability	Presence of set of function for specified task
Functionality	Accuracy	Provision of agreed results or effects
Functionality	Interpretability	Capability of component based system to interact with specified system
Maintainability	Analyzability	Identification of deficiencies, failure causes, components to be modified
Maintainability	Changeability	Capability to enable a specified evolution to be implemented
Maintainability	Stability	Capability to avoid unexpected effects from evolution
Maintainability	Testability	Capability to enable validating the evolving component based system

APPENDIX 5

Table 5. Some web metrics (Giang, et al., 2010)

Metrics Name	Type	Description
LOJ	User interface	The number of lines of JavaScript defined in the source code of a module
NOFJ	User interface	The number of functions of JavaScript defined in the source code of a module
LOCSS	User interface	The number of lines of CSS defined in the source code of a module
NOIC	User interface	The number of ids and classes of CSS defined in the source code of a module
NOH	Hyperlink	The number of hyperlinks defined in the source code of a module

APPENDIX 6

Table 6. Famous performance evaluation metrics

Metrics Name	Description
Recall/PD/True Positive Rate	Proportion of faulty units correctly classified, $PD = \dfrac{TP}{\left(TP + FN\right)}$
Precision	Proportion of units correctly predicted as faulty, $TP = \dfrac{TP}{\left(TP + FP\right)}$
PF/False Positive Rate	Proportion of non-faulty units incorrectly classified, $FP = \dfrac{FP}{\left(FP + TN\right)}$
Sensitivity/True Negative Rate	Proportion of correctly classified non faulty units, $TN = \dfrac{TN}{\left(FP + TN\right)}$
F-measure	Most commonly defined as the harmonic mean of precision and recall
Accuracy	Proportion of correctly classified units, $Accuracy = \dfrac{\left(TP + TN\right)}{\left(FP + TN + TP + FN\right)}$
Misclassification Rate	Misclassification Rate = 1-Accuracy
Receiver Operating Characteristic Curve (ROC)	A graphical plot of the sensitivity (or pd) vs. 1 –specificity (or pf)
Type I error	$Type\ I\ Error = \dfrac{non\ fault\ prone\ modules\ which\ classified\ as\ fault\ prone}{total\ number\ of\ faulty\ modules}$
Type II error	$Type\ II\ Error = \dfrac{fault\ prone\ modules\ which\ classified\ as\ non\ fault\ prone}{total\ number\ of\ faulty\ modules}$
Balance	Distance from the ROC 'sweet spot' (where pd=1, pf=0), $Balance = \dfrac{\sqrt{\left(0 - PF\right)^2 + \left(0 - PD\right)^2}}{\sqrt{2}}$

APPENDIX 7

Table 7. Selected paper based on different learning algorithms

Leaning Approach	Papers
Genetic programming	• GP-Based Software Quality Prediction (Evett, et al., 1999)
Decision Tree	• Tree-Based Software Quality Estimation Models for Fault Prediction (Khoshgoftaar & Seliya, 2002) • Benchmarking Classification Models for Software Defect Prediction: A Proposed Framework and Novel Findings (Lessmann, Baesens, Mues, & Pietsch, 2008) • Investigating the Effect of Dataset Size, Metrics Sets, and Feature Selection Techniques on Software Fault Prediction Problem (Catal & Diri, 2009a) • Predicting Defect-Prone Software Modules Using Support Vector Machines (Elish & Elish, 2008) • Robust Prediction of Fault-Proneness by Random Forests (Guo, Ma, Cukic, & Singh, 2004) • Empirical Validation of Object-Oriented Metrics on Open Source Software for Fault Prediction (Gyimothy, et al., 2005) • Techniques for Evaluating Fault Prediction Models (Jiang, Cukic, & Ma, 2008) • Data Mining Static Code Attributes to Learn Defect Predictors (Menzies, Greenwald, et al., 2007) • Defect Prediction From Static Code Features: Current Results, Limitations, New Approaches (Menzies, Milton, Turhan, Cukic, Jiang, & Bener, 2010) • Mining Software Repositories for Comprehensible Software Fault Prediction Models (Vandecruys, Martens, Baesens, Mues, De Backer, & Haesen, 2008)
Random Forest	• Predicting Defect-Prone Software Modules Using Support Vector Machines (Khoshgoftaar, et al., 1997) • Investigating the Effect of Dataset Size, Metrics Sets, and Feature Selection Techniques on Software Fault Prediction Problem (Catal & Diri, 2009a) • Techniques for Evaluating Fault Prediction Models (Jiang, et al., 2008) • Misclassification Cost-Sensitive Fault Prediction Models (Jiang & Cukic, 2009) • Benchmarking Classification Models for Software Defect Prediction: A Proposed Framework and Novel Findings (Lessmann, et al., 2008) • A Survey on Software Fault Detection based on Different Prediction Approaches (Abaei & Selamat, 2013) • An Investigation of the Effect of Module Size on Defect Prediction using Static Measures (Koru & Liu, 2005b)
Neural Network	• Object-Oriented Software Fault Prediction Using Neural Networks (Kanmani, Uthariaraj, Sankaranarayanan, & Thambidurai, 2007) • Application of Neural Networks for Software Quality Prediction Using Object-Oriented Metrics (Quah & Thwin, 2003; Thwin & Quah, 2005) • Predicting Defect-Prone Software Modules Using Support Vector Machines (Khoshgoftaar, et al., 1997) • Benchmarking Classification Models for Software Defect Prediction: A Proposed Framework and Novel Findings (Lessmann, et al., 2008) • Applying Machine Learning to Software Fault-Proneness Prediction (Gondra, 2008) • Robust Prediction of Fault-Proneness by Random Forests (Guo, et al., 2004) • Techniques for Evaluating Fault Prediction Models (Jiang, et al., 2008) • Software Fault Prediction (Sherer, 1995)

continued on following page

Table 7. Continued

Leaning Approach	Papers
Naïve Bayes	• Toward Comprehensible Software Fault Prediction Models Using Bayesian Network Classifiers (Dejaeger, Verbraken, & Baesens, 2013) • Investigating the Effect of Dataset Size, Metrics Sets, and Feature Selection Techniques on Software Fault Prediction Problem (Catal & Diri, 2009a) • Practical Development of an Eclipse-Based Software Fault Prediction Tool Using Naïve Bayes Algorithm (Catal, Sevim, & Diri, 2011) • Predicting Defect-Prone Software Modules Using Support Vector Machines (Khoshgoftaar, et al., 1997) • Robust Prediction of Fault-Proneness by Random Forests (Guo, et al., 2004) • Misclassification Cost-Sensitive Fault Prediction Models (Jiang & Cukic, 2009) • Fault Prediction Using Early Lifecycle Data (Jiang, et al., 2007) • Benchmarking Classification Models for Software Defect Prediction: A Proposed Framework and Novel Findings (Lessmann, et al., 2008) • Data Mining Static Code Attributes to Learn Defect Predictors (Menzies, Greenwald, et al., 2007) • Validation of Network Measures as Indicators of Defective Modules in Software Systems (Tosun, Turhan, & Bener, 2009) • The Max-Min Hill-Climbing Bayesian Network Structure Learning Algorithm (Tsamardinos, Brown, & Aliferis, 2006) • Analysis of Naive Bayes' Assumptions on Software Fault Data: An Empirical Study (Turhan & Bener, 2009) • Software Defect Prediction Using Call Graph Based Ranking (CGBR) Framework (Turhan, Kocak, & Bener, 2008) • On the Relative Value of Cross-Company and Within-Company Data for Defect Prediction (Turhan, Menzies, Bener, & Di Stefano, 2009)
Artificial Immune Systems	• Investigating the Effect of Dataset Size, Metrics Sets, and Feature Selection Techniques on Software Fault Prediction Problem (Catal & Diri, 2009a) • Software defect prediction using artificial immune recognition system (Catal & Diri, 2007) • A Survey on Software Fault Detection based on Different Prediction Approaches (Abaei & Selamat, 2013)
Fuzzy Logic	• Comparison of Conventional Approaches and Soft-Computing Approaches for Software Quality Prediction (Baisch & Liedtke, 1997) • An Application of Fuzzy Clustering to Software Quality Prediction (Yuan, et al., 2000) • A Fuzzy-Based Meta-model for Reasoning about the Number of Software Defects (Reformat, 2003) • An FIS for Early Detection of Defect Prone Modules (Rana, Awais, & Shamail, 2009) • A soft computing approach for modeling of severity of faults in software systems (Ardil & Sandhu, 2010) • Prediction of Software Faults Using f u z z y Nonlinear Regression Modeling (Xu, Khoshgoftaar, & Allen, 2000) • Fault Prediction Model by Fuzzy Profile Development of Reliability Relevant Software Metrics (Pandey & Goyal, 2010a)
Statistical Models	• Empirical Validation of Object-Oriented Metrics on Open Source Software for Fault Prediction ((Gyimothy, et al., 2005) • Using the Conceptual Cohesion of Classes for Fault Prediction in Object-Oriented Systems (Marcus, Poshyvanyk, & Ferenc, 2008) • Statistical Models vs. Expert Estimation for Fault Prediction in Modified Code-An Industrial Case Study (Tomaszewski, Håkansson, Grahn, & Lundberg, 2007) • Validation of Network Measures as Indicators of Defective Modules in Software Systems (Tosun,,Turhan, & Bener, 2009) • Predicting Defect-Prone Software Modules Using Support Vector Machines (Khoshgoftaar, et al., 1997) • Robust Prediction of Fault-Proneness by Random Forests (Guo, et al., 2004) • Misclassification Cost-Sensitive Fault Prediction Models (Jiang & Cukic, 2009) • Techniques for Evaluating Fault Prediction Models (Jiang, et al., 2008) • Object-Oriented Software Fault Prediction Using Neural Networks (Kanmani, et al., 2007) • Prediction of Fault-Proneness at Early Phase in Object-Oriented Development (Kamiya, Kusumoto, & Inoue, 1999) • Benchmarking Classification Models for Software Defect Prediction: A Proposed Framework and Novel Findings (Lessmann, et al., 2008) • Validation of Network Measures as Indicators of Defective Modules in Software Systems (Tosun, et al., 2009) • Mining Software Repositories for Comprehensible Software Fault Prediction Models (Vandecruys, et al., 2008) • Software quality prediction techniques: A comparative analysis (Shafi, et al., 2008) • Evaluating the change of software fault behavior with dataset attributes based on categorical correlation (Alsmadi & Najadat, 2011)

continued on following page

Table 7. Continued

Leaning Approach	Papers
Support Vector Machine	• Predicting Defect-Prone Software Modules Using Support Vector Machines (Khoshgoftaar, et al., 1997) • Applying Machine Learning to Software Fault-Proneness Prediction (Gondra, 2008) • Benchmarking Classification Models for Software Defect Prediction: A Proposed Framework and Novel Findings (Lessmann, et al., 2008) • Mining Software Repositories for Comprehensible Software Fault Prediction Models (Vandecruys, et al., 2008)
Clustering Techniques	• Fault prediction by utilizing self-organizing Map and Threshold (Abaei, Rezaei, Selamat, 2013) • Software Quality Analysis of Unlabeled Program Modules with Semi-supervised Clustering (Seliya & Khoshgoftaar, 2007) • Software fault prediction using quad tree-based k-means clustering algorithm (Bishnu & Bhattacherjee, 2012) • Thresholds based outlier detection approach for mining class outliers: An empirical case study on software measurement datasets (Alan & Catal, 2011) • Clustering and Metrics Thresholds Based Software Fault Prediction of Unlabeled Program Modules (Catal, et al., 2009) • Unsupervised Learning for Expert-Based Software Quality Estimation (Zhong, Khoshgoftaar, & Seliya, 2004b) • Analyzing software measurement data with clustering techniques (Zhong et al., 2004a) • Predicting Defect-Prone Software Modules Using Support Vector Machines (Khoshgoftaar, et al., 1997) • Benchmarking Classification Models for Software Defect Prediction: A Proposed Framework and Novel Findings (Lessmann, et al., 2008) • Mining Software Repositories for Comprehensible Software Fault Prediction Models (Vandecruys, et al., 2008) • Adaptive Self-Organizing Map Clustering for Software Fault Prediction (Mahaweerawat, Sophatsathit, & Lursinsap, 2007) • Prediction of Level of Severity of Faults in Software Systems using Density Based Clustering (Sandhu, et al., 2011)

Chapter 24
Building Defect Prediction Models in Practice

Rudolf Ramler
Software Competence Center Hagenberg, Austria

Johannes Himmelbauer
Software Competence Center Hagenberg, Austria

Thomas Natschläger
Software Competence Center Hagenberg, Austria

ABSTRACT

The information about which modules of a future version of a software system will be defect-prone is a valuable planning aid for quality managers and testers. Defect prediction promises to indicate these defect-prone modules. In this chapter, building a defect prediction model from data is characterized as an instance of a data-mining task, and key questions and consequences arising when establishing defect prediction in a large software development project are discussed. Special emphasis is put on discussions on how to choose a learning algorithm, select features from different data sources, deal with noise and data quality issues, as well as model evaluation for evolving systems. These discussions are accompanied by insights and experiences gained by projects on data mining and defect prediction in the context of large software systems conducted by the authors over the last couple of years. One of these projects has been selected to serve as an illustrative use case throughout the chapter.

INTRODUCTION

Knowing which modules are likely to contain defects in advance can assist in directing software quality assurance measures such as inspection and testing to these potentially critical modules. With defect prediction, the defect-prone modules in an upcoming version of a software system can be predicted from data about previous versions. Thus, defect prediction is becoming a more and more promising aid to increase the effectiveness and efficiency of these usually costly quality assurance measures. "The net result should be systems that are of higher quality, containing fewer faults, and projects that stay more closely on schedule than would otherwise be possible." (Ostrand et al. 2005, p. 340).

DOI: 10.4018/978-1-4666-6026-7.ch024

A large number of empirical studies on various aspects of defect prediction are available, and several of these incorporate data from industrial projects (e.g., Ostrand et al. 2005, Nagappan et al. 2005, Zimmermann and Nagappan 2007, Nagappan et al. 2010, Bird et al. 2011). Yet, few studies actually provide insights on how defect prediction can be applied in an industrial setting, where defect prediction itself is subject to a trade-off between cost and quality. Among these are the study from Li et al. (2006) who report experiences from initiating field defect prediction and product test prioritization at ABB, from Weyuker (2007) illustrating the research path towards making defect prediction usable for practitioners, and Wahyudin et al. (2008) presenting a framework for conducting defect prediction as an aid for the project manager in software development organizations.

In this chapter, an overview of the state of the art in defect prediction using data mining techniques is presented and key questions that are of practical importance for establishing defect prediction in large software projects are discussed. The presented work is based on and extends the extensive body of available literature on software defect prediction (see, e.g., Catal and Diri 2009, Hall et al. 2012) as well as some previous works (Ramler and Wolfmaier 2008, Ramler et al. 2009a, Ramler et al. 2009b, Ramler and Natschläger 2011, Ramler and Himmelbauer 2013) of the authors.

The key questions derived in the next section of this chapter concern aspects such as the prediction objectives and granularity level at which predictions should be made, the sources and mining of prediction data, the properties of real-world data and approaches to deal with noise, the choice of learning algorithms and validation measures. The questions identified and subsequently (Sections 3 to 7) discussed in detail provide a valuable guidance for constructing defect prediction models in a real-world setting.

In addition to the discussion of these questions, insights and experiences gained by conducting projects on data mining and defect prediction in the context of large software systems are presented. One of these projects has been selected to serve as an illustrative use case throughout the chapter. Details about this project are provided in Section 3. In the remainder of this chapter, specific issues concerning the construction of prediction models are presented which provide guidelines on how to choose a learning algorithm (Section 4), select features from different data sources (Section 5), deal with noise and data quality issues (Section 6) and evaluate prediction models for evolving systems (Section 7). In the final section, a list of open issues and unanswered questions is highlighting areas to which future research on software defect prediction should be directed.

DATA MINING AND KNOWLEDGE DISCOVERY FOR DEFECT PREDICTION

Defect prediction is based on prediction models built from software engineering data. Thus, defect prediction can be understood as an application within the broad area of *data mining* and *knowledge discovery* which refer to general results of research, techniques and tools used to extract useful information and models from (large volumes of) data (Mariscal et al. 2010).

Defect Prediction Models

The critical essence of making predictions about defects in software systems is captured in prediction models. The approach for constructing prediction models is illustrated in Figure 1.

A prediction model is related to a software system at the level of its modules. Modules may be classes, files, components or even sub-systems of a software system. The modules of the software system are described by various *attributes* (e.g., code metrics or the number of recent changes), which have to be made available via extraction from different data sources such as metric databases or

Figure 1. Inputs and output of a defect prediction model

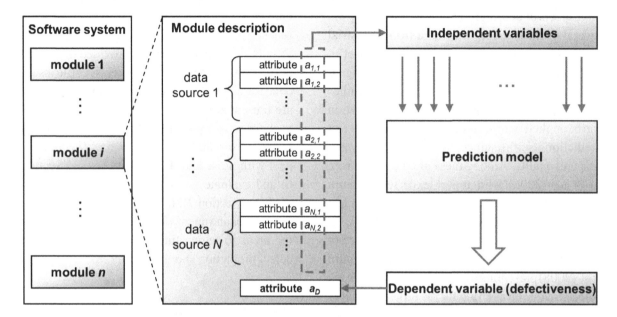

repositories of software development tools. The *attributes* are described as a vector of *independent variables* that act as predictors for the *dependent variables*, which characterize the defect-proneness of the software system's modules.

The *prediction model* defines the relationship between a vector of independent variables and the dependent variables. The prediction model is usually developed by means of supervised learning from a set of training examples, that is, the specific values of independent variables and dependent variables extracted from past versions of a software system or from comparable software systems.

The prediction model is used for predicting the defectiveness of the modules of a new version of the software system. Thereby, the input for the model may be data that has been collected throughout the development of the new version prior to its release. The model output is the predicted defectiveness of the modules at the time when the new version of the software system is released.

Predictions have to be about the future in order to be of practical use, i.e., they have to provide information about the defectiveness before this information becomes available via other sources like inspection or testing. Thus, predictions are made, for example, at the end of the development phase to predict the expected number and location of defects to support test management decisions or at release time to provide estimates on resource allocation for maintenance tasks.

Key Questions in Building Prediction Models

The *Cross-Industry Standard Process for Data Mining* (CRISP-DM; Chapman et al. 2000) describes the general issues and phases of any data mining project; see Figure 2: Business understanding, data understanding, data preparation, modeling, evaluation and deployment.

When building a defect prediction model, in each phase of the data mining process, a number of issues and key questions have to be addressed. In the following, key questions are listed that emerged throughout model construction for industrial applications. These questions are discussed and the decisions made in the context of real-world

Figure 2. Cross-industry standard process for data mining

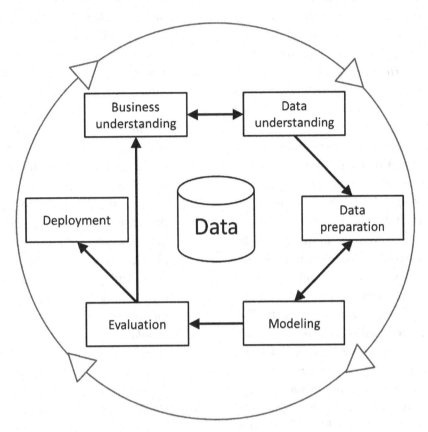

projects (Ramler et al. 2009b) are explained in the subsequent sections.

When defect prediction is introduced to a project or organization for the first time, an initial analysis cycle is recommended to prototype the construction of prediction models for gaining a better understanding of the requirements and expectations, for assessing the available data, to evaluate the prediction performance that can be achieved in the context of a project, and to collect feedback about the preliminary results from potential users, e.g., test managers, quality managers, system architects, key developers, release engineers and project managers.

- **Business understanding:** This phase focuses on understanding the objectives and needs of applying defect prediction from

a business perspective in the context of a specific project and organizational setting. When defect prediction is introduced in a real-world software project, activities like constructing models and applying defect prediction have to be fitted to established software development processes without consuming too much of the scarce resources allocated for quality assurance. In such a setting, defect prediction is prone to be considered as additional overhead that further reduces the tight budget and time on which quality managers and testers operate. In this phase, it is critical to clarify the following question by involving all stakeholders from development, testing and management: *What will the prediction model actually be used for?* This general question leads to several more specific questions that are required to characterize the basic elements involved in the development process: *How is the software system structured?, How is the evolution of the software system over different versions organized?, What quality aspects and which kinds of defects are critical?*

- **Data understanding:** The available data sources have to be explored and an inventory of the sources and the data they contain should be created. The actual data has to be extracted from the identified data sources or first needs to be collected from ongoing development activities. An initial analysis step is required in order to get familiar with the data, to identify data quality problems and to discover first insights into the data. The most prominent questions that need to be addressed in this phase are *What data sources can be used to extract defect data and attribute values?, How can the relationship between defects, modules and the versions of a software system be established?, What is the quality of the data and what issues may threaten the validity of prediction results?*

- **Data preparation:** In this phase the data sets are constructed that will be fed into the modeling tools. It should be noted that data preparation tasks are likely to be performed multiple times and not in any prescribed order. The automation of the preparation tasks is therefore a key aspect in this phase. The prerequisite, however, is a clear view about *Which of the attributes should be used as dependent and independent variables?, How should the attributes be aggregated and encoded (time range, versions, projects, etc.) for constructing the prediction model?*

- **Modeling:** Various modeling techniques are selected and applied. However, there are several learning algorithms available for calibrating a prediction model and hence the question arises: *What learning algorithm should be used to construct the prediction model?* Since this question is widely and repeatedly discussed by researchers as well as practitioners in most projects, this issue will be discussed in the following sections.

- **Evaluation:** Before proceeding to the deployment of the prediction model, it is important to thoroughly evaluate the model and to review the steps executed to construct the model in order to be sure that it properly achieves the defined business objectives. Furthermore, evaluation is also an ongoing task once the model has been deployed as part of monitoring and maintaining the quality of predictions. In this phase, an important question is *How should the performance of the prediction model be measured?* so that the desired business objective is properly reflected in this measurement.

- **Deployment:** The creation of the defect prediction model is not the final step of the project. It is necessary to integrate the resulting prediction model in a useful way in the tool set applied as part of the software development process. Depending on the requirements of the prospective users of the model, the deployment phase can be a software development project on its own. It is important for the customer to understand up front what is needed to make the constructed model applicable as part of the tool infrastructure supporting the software development processes. In general, this means that the following question has to be clarified: *How is the model integrated in the development processes and tools?* Furthermore, since the software processes are also subject to adaptations and continuous improvements, plans have to be made based on the question; *How and when should the model be adjusted or rebuilt?*

EXPLORING REAL-WORD PROJECTS: AN INDUSTRIAL CASE

The insights and experiences presented in this chapter are the cumulative result of several projects on data mining and defect prediction in the context of large software systems conducted by the authors over the last couple of years. In order to provide empirical evidence and to explain the author's findings with quantitative results, one of these projects has been selected to serve as an illustrative case throughout the remainder of this chapter. The details about this particular project and the approach used for defect prediction in the context of this project are described in the following; further results and discussions are presented in the subsequent parts of this chapter where we frequently refer to this industrial use case as the "running industrial use case".

Project Background

The project concerned the development of a large embedded software system. It has been conducted by an international company with more than 400 software engineers in development centers in Europe as well as in Asia and the U.S. The development team involved in the studied project consisted of about 40 members.

At the time when the project had been analyzed (Ramler et al. 2009b), it had already a history of about four years of developing the software system. At that time, the software system encompassed more than 700 KLOC C++ code in about 180 software components. The system has evolved to this size with an increase of about 200 KLOC per year. Since the system was first shipped, it has steadily been advanced to keep pace with a rapidly growing market and a demanding user community. Hence, over this time, not only additional features were added but also support for new hardware peripherals as well as various versions of the underlying operating system had to be developed.

The development of the software system proceeded in fixed-length iterations of six to 8 weeks. As a result of these short cycles in which the system was advanced, the project also provided new versions every six to eight weeks for system testing. In this chapter, seven consecutive versions are investigated in detail, capturing the system's evolution over about one year. Table 1 gives an overview of the increase in terms of LOC and number of components for each of the investigated versions.

The number of components per software version varies over time with an average of 156.6 components per version; the average system size is 638.9 KLOC. Throughout the iterations, the majority of these components (90% on average) are affected by development activities as the number of new or changed components shows. It can also be seen that the number of defective components ranges from 46% to 64% with an average of 58%.

Data Extraction and Preparation

Over the years of ongoing development, a number of repositories and databases had been introduced that captured different aspects of the project's history. These repositories and databases contained valuable data to derive metrics for constructing prediction models. The data actually used in the study by Ramler et al. (2009b) was extracted from five different software repositories and project databases: (1) The *issue management system* had been used to track bug reports and change requests across all development sites. Since the issue repository was hosted at a remote development site, access to the data (ca. 7.600 issue reports) had only been possible via the tool's export functionality. (2) The *release database* documented all planned, released, and maintained versions of the software system (about 180 versions in total) including the trace links to the resolved issues associated to these versions. The database's query interface was used to extract the data. (3) A commercial *versioning system* supporting multi-site develop-

Table 1. Number of total, new or changed, and defective components per analyzed version

Version	0	1	2	3	4	5	6	Avg.
Total number of components	137	147	141	154	171	165	181	156.6
Number of new or changed comp.	n.a.	141	134	142	135	156	138	141.0
Number of defective components	77	85	89	91	99	106	84	90.1
Percentage defective components	56%	58%	63%	59%	58%	64%	46%	58%
Total KLOC	539	605	565	647	682	711	723	638.9

ment had been used for storing all development artifacts. Due to the proprietary format of the repository, the change log (ca. 260.000 entries) was used as a data source. (4) The *static analysis tool* calculated code-, design-, and architecture-related metrics (ca. 200 metrics) for the software system (more than 700 KLOC C++ code), which were extracted from the tool's database. (5) The *release documentation* for all released versions (ca. 160 versions) had been stored in form of cross-linked HTML pages, which were parsed to extract the data.

Data integration is a laborious and costly endeavor. For the studied project, data integration took about one person year, i.e., 1,673 person hours (Ramler and Wolfmaier 2008). This effort does not include the costs incurred for the members of the studied projects, who provided access to the data sources and supported the analysis by clarifying questions and by providing feedback to preliminary analysis results. Including their effort would increase the total effort at least by 10%.

The effort involved in gaining relevant data from the different data sources was dedicated to, first, extracting the data from the available sources and, secondly, preparing the data for model development. The relevant data was often locked in proprietary tools and tied to specific workflows and process rules that emerged in past and ongoing infrastructure projects or improvement initiatives (e.g., a bug tracking system connected to a proprietary, non-relational database, implementing organization-specific workflows but following project-specific conventions). Once extracted in a useable format, different data sets had to be merged and transformed into metrics (e.g., the number of defects associated to a component). Great care had been taken to assure data quality over all steps from data provisioning, data profiling, data preparation, data housing to data validation. Further details about the issues encountered in integrating the data from the different repositories and databases have been reported by Ramler and Wolfmaier (2008).

Practical Considerations on Building Prediction Models and their Implications

Prediction models for test planning: For a single version, approximately 100 to 200 defects have been reported and resolved. The majority of the defects were found by the system testing group exploring every released version with manual and automated tests. In this setting, defect prediction has been proposed as an aid for managing regression test activities. With results provided by defect prediction, a quantitative basis for early estimates was available at the time when the software system was handed over from development to testing. Test planning benefits from these results – in particular, the expected number of defective components and the classification of the components as defective or non-defective – when approximating the overall test effort and when allocating testing resources to the different functional parts of the software system. Furthermore, any risk-based testing strategy (Felderer and Ramler 2013) can be supported by the prioritization of the components for testing since those components indicated as defect-prone should be tested first and with higher intensity.

Granularity of prediction: The constructed defect prediction models were used to classify the modules of the software system as likely defective or defect-free. For conducting quality assurance (QA) measures and for allocating testing resources, the 'modules' discussed by quality managers and testers were the components of the software system. In this context, components were defined as a set of related files implementing a specified functionality and the attributes measured at the level of files have been aggregated to these software components. This level of granularity was found to be a suitable abstraction from technical details such as the splitting of classes into C++ header files and implementation files (Ramler et al. 2009b). Furthermore, aggregating measurement and defect data to higher abstraction levels has been recommended in related studies (Koru and Liu 2005).

Relating defects to modules: The most critical aspect in defining and identifying modules for defect prediction is probably the relation of software modules and defect data. The results from supervised learning, i.e., the quality of the constructed prediction models, depend to a large extent on the quality of the available training data. However, providing high quality training data turned out to be a critical issue in all of the projects the authors have conducted with the industry. Most data quality issues are related to defect data, which usually shows a high likelihood to contain noise. In contrast to most other measurement data such as the size of the system in terms of the number of files, there is no 'ground truth' for the number of defects a real-world software system actually contains. At the time when the data is collected, not all of the existing defects may have been found.

Furthermore, relating known defects to modules is usually based on the changes that were made when fixing a defect. The fix for a defect may involve one or many different modules. Thus, it depends on how accurately the set of changed modules has been documented and how well it reflects the defective implementation. If other unrelated modules have been changed while fixing the defect, the derived relation of modules and defects becomes inaccurate and actually defect-free modules will be marked as defective. Since dealing with noisy data is a major issue in defect prediction (Liebchen and Sheppard 2008, Bird et al. 2009, Bachmann et al. 2010, Herzig et al. 2013), a separate section of this chapter has been devoted to this topic.

Evaluation of prediction models: There is an ongoing debate on how to assess and evaluate models for defect prediction (Jiang et al. 2008, Mende and Koschke 2009). Typically the performance of a binary prediction model is summarized by the so-called confusion matrix, which consists of the following four counts: number of defective modules predicted as defective (true positives, tp), number of non-defective modules predicted as defective (false positives, fp), number of non-defective modules predicted as non-defective (true negatives, tn) and number of defective modules predicted as non-defective (false negatives, fn). Basically one is looking for a prediction model which has high numbers of tp and tn along with low numbers of fp and fn. In this chapter, the prediction accuracy calculated as $accuracy = (tp+tn) / (tp + fp + tn + fn)$ will be used. Several more advanced measures have been suggested including the use of cost functions that relate the results to the defect prediction objective in the context of a specific project. While it is important to construct models that provide accurate prediction results, it is even more important that the models provide reliable results that can be understood by practitioners to explain a specific project situation. In most cases, prediction results are only one of many inputs when it comes to establishing a test plan or a test strategy. The overall responsibility for aligning all available inputs to a carefully balanced and viable plan still lies in the hands of the (human) test manager. Thereby the manager may refer to the prediction results as an initial starting point when establishing a new plan or they can use the results as a 'second opinion' to validate existing plans.

CHOOSING LEARNING ALGORITHMS

This section addresses the questio: *What learning algorithm should be used to construct the prediction model?* and discusses potential answers from the viewpoint of the illustrative industrial case and related studies.

Learning Algorithms used in Defect Prediction

Various types of learning algorithms have been successfully applied for defect prediction in different studies. The range of methods that has been proposed throughout the related literature ranges from statistical methods, such as linear or logistic regression (see, e.g., Hill and Lewicki 2007), to machine learning approaches, such as decision trees, neural networks, support vector machines or Bayesian networks (see, e.g., Hill and Lewicki 2007, Witten and Frank 2005) where it has been observed that the majority of applications is based on machine learning (Catal and Diri 2009).

However, there is no consensus on which learning algorithms are best suited for constructing defect prediction models. The ongoing debate is reflected by the different studies comparing methods and algorithms for defect prediction, which include Lanubile et al. (1995), Lessmann et al. (2008), Jiang et al. (2009), and Weyuker et al. (2010).

Some of these comparative studies assume that "sophisticated models are preferable to simple linear regression and correlation models because the relationship between defects (response variable) and static measures (predictor variables)" (Koru and Liu 2005, p. 24). For example, Bernstein et al. (2007) showed that non-linear prediction methods (M5 tree regression algorithm) outperformed linear methods (standard linear regression) for data sets with temporal features. However, others argue that findings concerning the superiority of one method over another are not consistent. For example, Lessmann et al. (2008) found that "the predictive accuracy of most methods does not differ significantly … This suggests that the importance of the classification model may have been overestimated in the previous research ... Given that basic models, and especially linear ones ... give similar results to more sophisticated classifiers, it is evident that most data sets are fairly well linearly separable. In other words, simple classifiers suffice to model the relationship between static code attributes and software defect." (p. 493) Consequently, they come to the conclusion that "the assessment and selection of a classification model should not be based on predictive accuracy alone but should be comprised of several additional criteria like computational efficiency, ease of use, and especially comprehensibility." (Lessmann et al. 2008, p.493).

Practical Considerations in an Industrial Context

In the studied industrial use case, the interpretation of results derived from predictions has been found as important as the predictive power of the constructed models. This is due to the facts that, first, experimentation required gaining insights into the relationship between metrics and defects as well as what combinations of metrics are relevant for constructing prediction models and, second, the discussions with quality managers and testers showed that they prefer models they can understand and interpret, which considerably increases the trust in prediction results. Thus, the decision tree learners J48 (implemented in

WEKA, Waikato Environment for Knowledge Analysis; Witten and Frank 2005) and FS-ID3 (Drobics and Bodenhofer 2002, Natschläger et al. 2004, implemented in MLF, Machine Learning Framework for Mathematica) have been selected as preferred learning algorithms in this study. Furthermore, related studies have already reported the successful application of decision trees for defect prediction (e.g., Knab et al. 2006), and the benefits of decision trees made them one of the most commonly used data mining techniques for solving classification and prediction problems.

However, to avoid bias due to selecting a particular learning algorithm (Elder 2005), all analysis is augmented with results from applying a support vector machine learner (implemented as part of the WEKA suite). Support vector machines (SVM) are a commonly used learning algorithm in many different fields. SVMs are non-linear models and have been designed especially for classification tasks to yield controllable generalization performance (Cortes and Vapnik 1995).

Note that when comparing particular methods or algorithms with respect to their prediction performance in the context of a particular application, it has to be considered that most algorithms require some amount of tuning of their meta-parameters in order to produce satisfying results. Available expertise on how to parameterize a method or an algorithm can have a considerable impact on performance and prediction results. For the results presented in this chapter, for each of the three algorithms, the same kind of cross-validation-based parameter tuning has been used in order to ensure comparable results.

From the point of view prediction accuracy, the results for the industrial case study presented in this chapter do not show a preference for a particular algorithm even though there is a slight tendency that FS-ID3 outperforms the other two in a side-by-side comparison. FS-ID3 is particularly designed to be interpretable. It is a fuzzy variant of the ID3 learning algorithm introduced by Quinlan (1986), which was designed for learning problems that are characterized by many attributes and training sets that contain many objects yet still should not need much computation. Through the use of fuzzy predicates for different types of input variables, the expressive power of decision trees has been extended in a very natural manner (Drobics and Bodenhofer 2002). As a result, the generated models contain easily interpretable phrases like 'if the value of input variable *v is large,* then …', while still maintaining numeric accuracy and predictive capabilities.

SELECTING ATTRIBUTES FROM DIFFERENT DATA SOURCES

In this section, study results, practical considerations as well as general recommendations for answering the question: *What data attributes should be used to build defect prediction models?* are presented.

Metrics and Measures Used in Defect Prediction

Fenton and Pfleeger (1998) classify software metrics with respect to *processes* described as "collections of software-related activities", *products* described as "any artifacts, deliverables or documents that result from a process activity" and *resources* described as "entities required by a process activity". Metrics from all three classes have been used as features in defect prediction (Radjenović et al. 2013).

Product metrics are computed from the – usually static – structure of the source code, the design or the requirements of the product at a particular point in time. The search for software metrics spanning the decades since the 1970s has produced numerous product-related measures (e.g., McCabe 1976, Halstead 1977, Chidamber and Kemerer 1994), with many of them evaluated by exploring their relation to software defects (e.g., Basili et al. 1996, Koru et al. 2009).

The confirmed underlying relationship between metrics and defects builds the theoretical fundament for harnessing product metrics as independent variables in defect prediction and, thus, for related empirical studies. In one of these studies, Menzies et al. (2007) demonstrated the usefulness of static, product-related metrics for constructing defect prediction models by conducting experiments with various size, structure and complexity measures derived from the NASA data sets made available via the PROMISE Data Repository. In a related study, Zimmermann et al. (2007) used 14 different size and structure metrics at the level of methods, classes, files and packages, which they aggregated to average, maximum and total numbers in order to predict defective files and packages from the Java source code of Eclipse.

Structural dependencies in software systems, e.g. captured by import/export dependencies between modules, call graphs or design-time metrics, have been used to extend the set of product-related measures in defect prediction beyond traditional size and complexity metrics. Studies that demonstrate the effectiveness of metrics and measures derived from structural dependencies in improving defect prediction results have been presented, for example, by Zimmermann and Nagappan (2007), who used complexity measures derived from dependency graphs of sub-components, components and functional areas of Windows 2003 Server to construct defect prediction models. Schröter et al. (2006) used the number of imported classes per file as an independent variable in defect prediction for Eclipse plug-ins. Their study was replicated by Zimmermann and Nagappan (2009) who contrasted the prediction results using only import dependencies to those from their comprehensive set of dependencies for Windows Server 2003, including call dependencies, data dependencies, and Windows specific dependencies such as shared registry entries.

Process metrics reflect the activities conducted in the course of software development. Thus, these metrics have the ability to capture details about the dynamics of a project's development history, in contrast to product metrics, which simply represent the results of all previous activities in a snapshot taken at a particular point in time. Process metrics are therefore considered a promising indicator for defect-prone modules, and are commonly represented by metrics and measures extracted from version management systems.

A number of studies based on change histories have been presented, for example, by Nagappan et al. (2005) predicting the defect density of components from Windows Server 2003 based on code churn metrics calculated from activity rates in the past. Hassan and Holt (2005) developed a cache-based approach incorporating heuristics like most frequently modified, most recently modified, most frequently fixed and most recently fixed subsystems using six large open source software systems. Kim et al. (2007) also used a cache-based approach on open source projects, yet with different measures such as changes showing temporal dependencies. Temporal features from the Eclipse open source project were also used for defect prediction by Bernstein et al. (2007), who combined the number of revisions and the number of reported issues within the last three months. Nagappan et al. (2010) used temporal dependencies of changes, named change bursts, for predicting defect-prone components of Windows Vista.

Other process related measures can also be encountered in studies on defect prediction. Afzal (2010) used faults-slip-through metrics from different testing levels as predictor in two large industrial projects from the telecommunication domain. Layman et al. (2008) derived in-process measures from code churn and static metrics calculated at regular time intervals.

Resource metrics: In software development, humans are a critical resource. Human factors have a huge impact on the performance, productivity and quality in software development (Boehm et al. 2009). For defect prediction, resource metrics related to the activities and interactions of programmers, testers and development teams can therefore be a rich source of features to construct prediction models. Although several studies have investigated resource metrics over the last couple of years, these types of metrics have been and still are underrepresented when compared to the numerous studies applying measures derived from products or processes (Radjenović et al. 2013).

The benefits of resource metrics have been indicated by Nagappan et al. (2008): In their study of data from Microsoft Windows Vista, they investigated metrics such as the number of engineers working on a component, the level of ownership of a component or the contributions to a component made by different organizations. They found that these metrics were useful for predicting defects and, furthermore, the prediction performance of models constructed from resource metrics was higher than those based on traditional metrics like size and complexity.

Meneely et al. (2008) conducted a case study on defect prediction for consecutive versions of a large telecommunication system. They applied social network analysis on developers (i.e., the developers are considered the nodes of the analyzed network) to derive resource-related measures mapped to files of the software system. Following the same motivation, Pinzger et al. (2008) investigated network centrality measures to identify defect-prone modules of Microsoft Windows Vista. They found that central modules are more likely to be defective than modules on the outside of the contribution network. A related concept is the ownership of a software component. Components may be owned by a single developer who is the component's sole author, or several developers may share the work on the component and, thus, the ownership. Different ownership measures were examined for Windows Vista and Windows 7 by Bird et al. (2011) and for open-source systems by Rahman and Devanbu (2011). Measures such as the proportion of ownership for the top owner and the number of low-expertise developers have a relationship with higher defect numbers while

high levels of ownership were found to be associated with fewer defects.

In contrast, the study by Ostrand et al. (2010) did not provide evidence that resource metrics will improve the prediction results over what can be achieved with product or process metrics. In this study, the metrics on the developers' fault ratio shown in previous releases were included. Similar findings were explained in a study by Ramler et al. (2010) as the combined result of all the activities from requirements engineering, design, and development to testing. New defects may be accidentally introduced as part of each of these activities, not only in development, while existing defects may as well be removed in any of these activities.

Finally, however, it should be noted that measurements of human activities represent sensitive data and the use of resource-related metrics may therefore be restricted in industry projects. The use of such data is regulated by laws and policies in many countries and within individual organizations. Even collecting resource-related data can be an infringement of these laws and policies, which limits the availability of resource metrics in practice.

Combinations and Comparisons of Metric Types

Several defect prediction studies are based on a combination of product-related and process-related measures. For example, the studies on large, closed source software systems from AT&T by Ostrand et al. (2004), Ostrand et al. (2005) and Bell et al. (2006) include, for example, the number of lines of code per file, whether or not the file had been changed in the previous release, the age of the file in number of releases, the number of defects detected in the file during the previous release. Li et al. (2006) studied defect prediction for two closed source systems from ABB Inc. based on a wide range of metrics: product-related metrics, development-related metrics, deployment-related metrics, usage-related metrics, as well as metrics related to hardware and software configurations.

A comparative study on change metrics and static code attributes from three versions of the Eclipse open source project has been conducted by Moser et al. (2008). They found that predictions using change data from the source code repository produced results that clearly outperformed predictions based on the static code attributes. Recently Rahman and Devanbu (2013) provided an extensive comparison of product and process metrics w.r.t. to performance, stability, portability and stasis. Their study is based on 85 releases of 12 open source projects. They found that product metrics are generally less useful than process metrics for constructing prediction models. They also found that code metrics show little change over time (i.e., over a series of different releases) which leads to a stagnation in predictions as the same files will be classified as defective in all releases. Arisholm and Briand (2010) used object-oriented (OO) code measures, delta measures capturing the amount of change between two releases, and process measures in their study of a closed source Java system. They concluded that what is considered as "best" measures is highly dependent on the evaluation criteria applied.

Data Sources as Drivers for Selecting Metrics

The search for the optimal attributes – i.e., the ones that have a high capability for predicting defects – often neglects that in the context of a specific project, these particular attributes may not be available or can only be made available at (unreasonably) high costs. In practice, thus, the choice of attributes serving as independent variables is mainly driven by the availability of historical project data. A number of different software repositories and corporate databases may be identified as potential data sources.

In the studied project, for example, the release database, the versioning system and a static analy-

sis repository were found suitable for extracting attributes for prediction. The dominant cost factor has been the effort required for mining these repositories and databases for attributes appropriate for defect prediction (Ramler and Wolfmaier 2008). Among several other activities, mining also involved assessing and improving data quality, since the different repositories and databases had been designed for a specific purpose other than defect prediction. As a consequence, the data quality in terms of accuracy, completeness, consistency, and timeliness was often inappropriate and needed to be improved prior to the extraction of any attributes. Furthermore, the data quality also affected the integration of heterogeneous data sources, which was hampered by partially matching data sets and substantial semantic gaps.

Yet after the indispensable step of preparing and integrating the data sources, a large number of attributes may be retrieved or calculated from a repository. Thereby, the effort involved in actually extracting the attributes is relatively low compared to the high initial effort for preparing and integrating the data source. The preparation and integration consumes an estimated share of about 80% to 90% of the total effort required for mining the repositories and project databases. For example, once exports were set up from the repository of the static analysis system tool in the studied project, about 200 code-, design-, and architecture-related metrics were available for model construction.

Due to the dominance of the initial costs for mining data sources, the question about selecting attributes for defect prediction brings about the question: "What data sources should be mined to extract attributes for defect prediction?" (Ramler et al. 2009a). Answering this question usually requires a comparative investigation of the attributes contributed by each of the mined data sources and their applicability for defect prediction.

Table 2 shows the comparison of the accuracy achieved when constructing prediction models with metrics from different data sources. The columns contain the accuracy values for predictions over six consecutive *Versions*. The rows show the *Data Sources* used to construct the prediction models. For each data source, models were constructed with each of the three *Learning Algorithms* discussed in the previous section. Dark solid cells indicate the best prediction of a version in terms of accuracy. Predictions printed in bold face are statistically not significantly different from the best predictions results for that particular version according to McNemar's test (p-level of 0.05).

The column *Overall Sum* shows the number of predictions that are best or statistically not significantly different from the best. These numbers indicate that the data sources *Static Analysis* (representing product metrics) and *Version Control* (representing process metrics) led to very similar results. Indeed, also a more detailed analysis (Ramler et al. 2009a) came to the conclusion that in this case the prediction models based on metrics extracted from the static analysis tool repository and the version control system provide the best results with a slight advantage of static analysis over version control. Models from both of these

sources clearly outperform the models constructed from *Release Management* data, which only yielded two significant results. Interestingly, the *Combination* of all metrics from all data sources did not provide models that showed a noticeable improvement in the predictions over those from the two best individual data sources.

From a practical point of view, however, it has to be mentioned that even when a repository is an appropriate data source, in practice it remains a strategic decision to include the data from this repository for model construction. The selected repositories have to be maintained as part of the project's development infrastructure also in the future and workflows and tools have to be aligned with data quality requirements from defect prediction. So, for example, the company in the studied project opted for static code metrics as the main data source, which fitted into the company's infrastructure plans, although at the point when this decision was made, the initial results did not allow to clearly favor the static code metrics over data from other sources.

Table 2. Comparison of prediction accuracy achieved with metrics from different data sources

Data Source	Learning Algorithm	Version						Overall Sum
		1	2	3	4	5	6	
Static Analysis	ID3	0.741	0.809	0.805	0.778	0.770	0.779	15
	J48	0.714	0.816	0.792	0.789	0.764	0.779	
	SVM	0.646	0.702	0.714	0.760	0.733	0.718	
Version Control	ID3	0.578	0.660	0.734	0.778	0.745	0.757	14
	J48	0.653	0.766	0.708	0.795	0.715	0.768	
	SVM	0.687	0.660	0.740	0.784	0.752	0.785	
Release Management	ID3	0.619	0.603	0.662	0.579	0.606	0.646	2
	J48	0.578	0.617	0.591	0.643	0.630	0.713	
	SVM	0.667	0.610	0.591	0.591	0.600	0.464	
Combination	ID3	0.653	0.787	0.727	0.807	0.739	0.746	16
	J48	0.639	0.759	0.734	0.749	0.727	0.646	
	SVM	0.694	0.759	0.740	0.784	0.776	0.773	

DEALING WITH NOISE AND DATA QUALITY ISSUES

This section addresses the question: *How and to what extent does the presence of noise and uncertainty in data impact the performance of defect prediction models?* As described in the previous section, the basis for defect prediction is formed by metrics and measurement data mined from software repositories and corporate databases such as versioning systems, bug tracking systems, release databases, or development logs. It is already well known that data in software engineering repositories is often of poor quality (Herzig et al. 2013, Liebchen and Shepperd 2008). Out of these findings arises the question whether one can expect to achieve reasonable defect prediction results when dealing with such noisy and incorrect data.

In the following, an overview of different kinds and causes of noise in prediction data is given. In the context of the industrial case introduced earlier, the impact of class noise on the performance of prediction models is investigated.

Causes of Noise in Prediction Data

Two types of noise can be distinguished with respect to where the noisy data is used in making predictions: attribute noise and class noise. In the following, an overview of commonly encountered causes for these types of noise is given, on the one hand by reviewing related studies on noise in software engineering data and defect prediction and on the other hand by summarizing experience gathered in the running industrial use case. A more detailed review on this topic can be found in the related study by Ramler and Himmelbauer (2013).

Attribute noise: Causes of attribute noise can mainly be assigned to one of the following two entities, *measurement data* or *modules*. Causes of attribute noise that are related to the entity *modules* have their origin either in improper granularity (class vs. file) or in an incorrect way of aggrega-

tion. Causes that have its origins in measurement data itself are: (a) *Inconsistent measurement data:* Reasons for inconsistency can be due to different metric measurement tools since different tools tend to interpret and implement metric definitions differently (Lincke et al. 2008). For example, in our case study, even a new version of the same measurement tool computed slightly different metrics, requiring to re-compute all previously retrieved metrics to ensure consistency. (b) *Imprecisely defined measurement data:* This mostly happens when data is entered manually. For example, some repositories contained manually entered data, e.g., the release database or the bug tracking system. The quality of the data in these sources varied considerably. Frequently one finds empty comment fields, typos and misspellings, as well as incorrect entries in text fields. (c) *Missing measurement data:* In general, this happens either with manually entered data or due to changes of workflows and policies throughout the project's history that lead to discontinued or disrupted datasets.

Class noise: More and more studies in the field of defect prediction address the problem of noise in classification data. In the following, examples of causes of such class noise are given that were found in related work as well as within the industrial case study considered throughout this chapter.

Report classification: Several studies investigated the issue of classification of reports in issue tracking systems. Antoniol et al. (2008) found a significant number of misclassifications of defects and non-defects since many issue reports are simply labeled as "bug" although they refer to enhancements, refactoring/restructuring activities and organizational issues. Herzig et al. (2013) manually inspected 7,401 issue reports of five open source projects to determine if the report was correctly classified as defect, feature request, improvement, documentation issue, refactoring, or other task. They were able to show that the present misclassifications of the reports have a dramatic impact on the classification of the modules – 39% of all files marked as defective actually did not have a defect.

Linking reports and changes: Bird et al. (2009) studied the quality of change logs and bug reports, and discovered that many changes and reports were not linked, sometimes even less than 50%. In cases where developers do not follow conventions to indicate a link between a report and a code change (e.g., by using specific keywords in the change log), it is not possible to automatically establish these links and the collected defect data is inherently noisy.

Relating defects to versions: For constructing a reliable prediction model, it is vital to know which defects exist in version n and which defects are introduced during the period from version n to the next version $n+1$. Bug tracking systems usually record in which version a defect has been found and to which version the fix has been applied once the defect is resolved. Yet not all defects are resolved immediately in the next version. Thus, in addition to the version the defect has been reported for, the defect is also present (i.e., open) in all versions up to the one before it has been resolved. In a previous study (Ramler 2008), the major points in the lifecycle of every defect were observed – the point where it was introduced, reported, and resolved. It was found that only 56% of the defects were resolved in the next version, 89% were fixed within two versions, and the longest time it took to fix a defect was ten versions.

Defects missed in testing: Per definition, it cannot be guaranteed that testing detects all defects in a software system, nor will the end-users be able to find and report all of the remaining defects. As a matter of fact, it is therefore not possible to establish a "ground truth" including all defects that actually exist in a particular version of a software system.

Impact of Class Noise

For the described industrial case, class noise is considered to be a crucial issue. When compared with attribute noise, class noise is expected to have the bigger impact on defect prediction performance. Great care has been applied to establish high data quality and the prediction models have been built from clean and verified datasets at the 'best of our knowledge'. Still, when these models are used to make predictions for subsequent versions, the model is fed with data that may have undergone less rigorous data analysis and preparation. Without specific measures to ensure data quality, potential misclassifications of modules may be likely in such a case, especially due to wrong or missing links between defects and modules. Overall, in the considered industrial use case, up to 20% misclassified modules are expected. Thus, when applying the prediction model on noisy data from new versions, one would like to know whether the prediction results can still be expected to be useful.

To answer this question, consider the following experiment (Ramler and Himmelbauer 2013): The basic idea is to use the same prediction models that have previously been constructed from (clean and verified) data of the versions up to n to classify the components of version $n+1$ as before. However, instead of applying these models to the clean datasets, now one evaluates the models on a large number ($N = 10,000$) of different noisy realizations of the data of version $n+1$. Here label noise is defined as an incorrect assignment of a defect to a component leading to a misclassification of the components as defective or defect-free. In the industrial use case, a simple noise model has been defined. It is based on the assumption that on the one hand, defects might be incorrectly assigned to a component with some *error probability p_1*, while on the other hand, a component that was declared defect-free might actually contain defects with some *probability p_2*. For simplicity, let us consider the case $p = p_1$

$= p_2$. Therefore, each of the N vectors of noisy data are generated by taking the original data of the test version $n+1$ and treating the classification of each component as follows: If the component is labeled defect-free, the label will be randomly changed to defective with error probability p. If the component is labeled defective, the label will be randomly changed to defect-free with probability p^k, where k is the number of defects that were assigned to the corresponding component. One can see that the more defects are assigned to a component, the lower the probability becomes that it was misclassified to be defective. The choice of the *error probability p* determines the expected noise level in the defect report data.

Whether a certain prediction model of version n still provides reasonable prediction results on noisy class data of version $n+1$ (considering a fixed noise level p) can be assessed as follows. First one evaluates the model with each of the $N =$

10,000 noisy datasets (generated with *error probability* p) and observes how often the *prediction accuracy* (i.e., the fraction of correctly classified components) remains above the *chance level* (i.e., classifying all components according to the majority class). An instance of an experiment is considered successful when the performance on test data affected by noise is better than the chance level (*accuracy > chance level*) in at least 95% of the $N = 10,000$ repetitions.

Figure 3 presents the results of the experiment for the prediction models constructed by the *FS-ID3* decision tree learner using static analysis data. The graphic shows, for each of the six test scenarios (i.e., model of *version n* for predicting *version n+1*), the empirically estimated probability that *accuracy > chance level* holds (y-axis) assuming different noise levels (x-axis; from $p = 5\%$ to $p = 50\%$ with a step size of 5%). In Figure 3, one can

Figure 3. Probability that accuracy > chance level (y-axis) for different noise levels (x-axis)

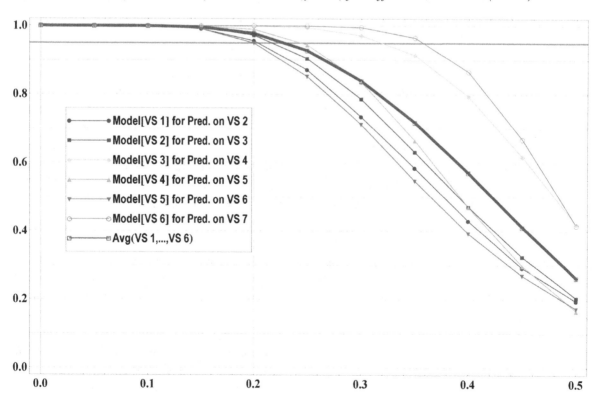

observe at which noise level the predictions remain above the threshold of 95% (red horizontal line).

The graphic shows that for a noise level of up to 20%, predictions of all examined models remain above 95%. When the noise level is increased to $p = 25\%$, four of the six models drop below the threshold. The average over all models (red bold curve) shows that also the mean probability value (92.8%) lies below 95%. Nevertheless two models, namely the model constructed from *version 3* (for predicting *version 4*) and the model from *version 6* (used to predict *version 7*), stay above 95% up to a noise level of $p = 30\%$ and $p = 35\%$, respectively. The question arises why these two scenarios are more stable than the others. The likely reason is that these two models also exhibit the highest performance gain (i.e., *model accuracy - chance level*) with respect to the accurate data.

When performing defect prediction for software systems, one always has to face noisy, incorrect data, especially also erroneous class data due to incorrect linking of defects with components. In the case of the studied industrial software system, the following findings were made (Ramler and Himmelbauer 2013): All tested models produce reliable results up to an increase in the noise level of 20% probability of incorrect linking. Two models are even capable to handle a noise level of 30% and 35%.

DEFECT PREDICTION FOR EVOLVING SYSTEMS

Maintenance and evolution put software systems in a constant state of flux. With every release, existing functionality is enhanced, defects are fixed, and new features are introduced. The growth, the evolution and the structural change of software systems (Lehman and Ramil 2001) has been covered by a number of studies, especially for open-source software (e.g., Godfrey and Qiang 2001, Koch 2007, Israeli and Feitelson 2010). The practitioners' interest in defect prediction

results is particularly focused on those parts of a software system which are more heavily modified or even new.

In the previous sections, the emphasis in evaluating the learned prediction models has been on *all modules* of the next version of the software product. However, from a practical point of view, it is interesting to investigate (a) how the models perform specifically on new and modified components of the software system and (b) how often a prediction model has to be adjusted or rebuilt in order to keep up with the changes of the underlying software system. Therefore an evaluation of previously constructed defect prediction models (a) on a subset of all components, i.e., only including new or modified components as well as (b) on the components of the future releases $n+\Delta$ with the prediction horizon $\Delta = 1, 2, ... \Delta_{max}$ in the range of the available releases assesses its generalization capabilities in a broader setting.

Predictions for New and Modified Components

First the effect of evaluating the prediction model only on new or modified modules by means of the running industrial use case is discussed. This consideration takes into account that the successful predictions observed in earlier sections may have been biased by components that remained unchanged between the version used for model construction and the version used for testing. The prediction models that have previously been constructed from data of the versions up to n (i.e., versions 0 to 5) are now used to classify *only the modified and new components* of the corresponding versions $n+1$ (i.e., versions 1 to 6).

In the studied case, most of the components from each of the analyzed versions are either new or have been modified (see Table 1). The number of new or modified components ranges from 76.2% in version 6 to 95.9% in version 1; the average over all seven analyzed versions is 90.1%. Table 3 presents the accuracy values of the predictions and the adjusted chance level for each of the versions 1 to 6 ($n+1$). Once again, all of the 18 predictions achieved an accuracy value higher than the related chance level, which corresponds to 100% successful predictions (18 successful out of 18 total predictions).

On average, the prediction accuracy is 0.740 for FS-ID3, 0.698 for J48 and 0.749 for SVM. In comparison with the accuracy values achieved when predictions are made for all the average accuracy values have slightly decreased. In contrast, the chance level per version has increased. Nevertheless, for all analyzed versions in the studied case, predictions made for new or modified components in the next version ($n+1$) are superior to guessing for any of the learning algorithms used in model construction (i.e., for all 18 predictions). For the studied case, thus, predictions specifically for new or modified components of the next version (n+1) are superior to guessing.

Predictions for Future Versions

As has been shown, successful prediction results can be produced when the prediction models constructed with data of version n are tested with data from the immediate next version $n+1$. However, since a substantial number of components is changed in every version of the software system (see Table 1), the capability to make accurate predictions may decrease for versions beyond the immediate next version, which would require the model to be updated/re-trained for each version. Therefore, in order to observe the impact on the prediction results, the prediction models that have been constructed from data of version n (i.e., versions 0 to 5) are now used to make predictions for the future versions $t=n+\Delta$ with the prediction horizon Δ. The analysis is limited to $\Delta = 1, 2, 3$ and 4 due to the amount of data available.

Table 4 presents the accuracy values of the predictions and the corresponding chance level for the versions used for testing. For reasons of

Table 3. Accuracy values of predictions for new or modified components in versions 1 to 6 (n+1) and related chance levels. Values with accuracy > chance level are printed in bold face

Version	0	1	2	3	4	5	6	Avg.
FS-ID3	-	**0.660**	**0.776**	**0.725**	**0.793**	**0.737**	**0.746**	**0.740**
J48	-	**0.624**	**0.746**	**0.739**	**0.726**	**0.712**	**0.638**	**0.698**
SVM	-	**0.702**	**0.761**	**0.746**	**0.748**	**0.763**	**0.775**	**0.749**
Chance level	-	0.589	0.649	0.592	0.664	0.635	0.507	0.606

Table 4. Accuracy values of predictions for versions n+1 to n+4 based on models created with the FS-ID3 learning algorithm. Values with accuracy > chance level are printed in bold face

Version for testing	0	1	2	3	4	5	6	Avg.
Δ=1 (n+1)	-	**0.653**	**0.787**	**0.727**	**0.807**	**0.739**	**0.746**	**0.743**
Δ=2 (n+2)	-	-	0.596	**0.714**	**0.696**	**0.764**	**0.729**	**0.700**
Δ=3 (n+3)	-	-	-	0.591	**0.626**	**0.691**	**0.702**	**0.653**
Δ=4 (n+4)	-	-	-	-	0.515	0.600	**0.630**	**0.582**
Chance level	-	0.578	0.631	0.591	0.579	0.624	0.536	-

brevity, the table shows only results for models constructed with the FS-ID3 learning algorithm. Prediction models constructed with the other two learning algorithms yield comparable results.

Each row of the table shows the prediction results for a future version from $\Delta=1$ to $\Delta=4$. Thereby, the accuracy of the predictions decreases when the distance between the versions used for model construction and the version used for testing increases, i.e. the older the constructed model is in terms of versions. An accuracy of 0.807 is achieved when the prediction for version 4 is made with the model based on the immediately preceding version 3 ($\Delta=1$). The accuracy drops to 0.696 when the model is based on version 2 and to 0.626 when it is based on version 1. Finally, when the model is constructed from version 0, the achieved accuracy (0.515) drops below the chance level (0.579). This decrease is also observable in the average accuracy values (right column in Table 4), although it should be noted that all average accuracy values are higher than the corresponding average chance levels of the versions included in the predictions.

From the viewpoint of version n used for model construction, the results show that a model based on version n achieves the highest prediction accuracy when predictions are made for the next version ($n+1$). The accuracy decreases if the versions for which predications are made are further in the future ($\Delta=2$, $\Delta=3$, ...). Four out of five predictions for versions $n+2$ have achieved an accuracy value higher than the chance level (80%) and three out of four predictions for versions $n+3$ (75%). Predictions with lower accuracy values may be attributed to variations between prediction models. Thus, depending on the specific prediction model, acceptable accuracy may as well be achieved for versions beyond the immediate next version.

One can conclude that – as shown in context of the studied case – for predictions of upcoming versions, there is an observable trend that the accuracy decreases the further a version is in the future; nevertheless these predictions still tend to be superior to guessing.

CONCLUSION AND FUTURE RESEARCH DIRECTIONS

In this chapter, several questions that correspond to key decisions in constructing prediction models are identified and discussed. These questions concern aspects such as the granularity level at which predictions should be made, the measure for a module's defectiveness, the sources of prediction data, the choice of learning algorithms, validation measures, and effects of noise.

References to the existing body of literature are given and common approaches are contrasted with observations from the authors' experience, in particular in the light of the studied industrial use case. A number of empirical studies exist that can be appreciated as examples for the various possible choices one has in answering each of the questions. Some studies even address a particular question and conclude with helpful advice.

However, the appropriate answer to each of the questions can only be given in the context of a particular prediction objective and a specific project background. The following decisions were taken in the studied industrial use case: Components have been used as prediction modules, which were classified as defective or non-defective based on the information retrieved from the issue repository. The defects actually open in a version have been determined by tracing the reported defects to all affected versions. The metrics computed from the release database, the versioning system and a static analysis tool constituted the prediction attributes, whereby the union of all metrics from the different data sources did not show a substantial improvement over the metrics from the single best source. The prediction models for a particular version n have been created from the data of their predecessor version $n-1$ using different learning algorithms. The FS-ID3 decision tree learner exhibited interpretable results in combination with a satisfactory overall prediction performance, which has been measured in terms of accuracy (in addition to precision and recall). The predictions generated by the FS-ID3 learner can – with some limitations – be used beyond the next version, i.e. for versions $n+2$, $n+3$, etc. As class noise is considered a severe problem in defect prediction, the learned models have been tested under increasing probabilities of incorrect links between bug reports and modules and it was found that the models tend to be robust up to 20% of such an error probability.

The key questions indicated in this chapter provide valuable guidance for constructing defect prediction models in a real-world setting and highlight areas for further research.

Three data sources have been combined in the form of the union of the metric sets derived from the different sources. More sophisticated ways (e.g. bagging, stacking or boosting) for constructing combinations than this relatively simple approach of using a union have been proposed in the field of statistical learning and it shall be investigated whether such approaches are suitable to build more accurate prediction models and to produce improved results when several data sources provide a wide range of attributes and, moreover, when additional metrics become available from new data sources

A simple approach to model the noise in defect report data is proposed. As a part of future research, this initial model should be extended to better cover the spectrum of different causes of noise. Furthermore, we plan to investigate how prediction models can be constructed (e.g., with alternative learning techniques, from extended data sources, or including noise reduction techniques) to be more resistant with respect to class noise.

The most critical point in improving defect prediction in the future is certainly the necessity to improve the understanding of the actual causes of defects in a software system. With an improved understanding, new measures and relationships can be introduced when constructing prediction models. We would therefore like to conclude by encouraging researchers as well as practitioners to increase the body of empirical data and studies on software defects in industrial projects as a basis for future research.

REFERENCES

Afzal, W. (2010). Using Faults-Slip-Through Metric as a Predictor of Fault-Proneness. In *Proceedings of the 17th Asia Pacific Software Engineering Conference APSEC 2010* (pp. 414-422). Los Alamitos, CA: IEEE Computer Society.

Antoniol, G., Ayari, K., Di Penta, M., Khomh, F., & Guéhéneuc, Y.-G. (2008). Is it a bug or an enhancement? A text-based approach to classify change requests. In *Proceedings of the 2008 Conference of the Centre for Advanced Studies on Collaborative Research CASCON 2008* (pp. 304-318). New York, NY: ACM.

Arisholm, E., Briand, L. C., & Johannessen, E. B. (2010). A systematic and comprehensive investigation of methods to build and evaluate fault prediction models. *Journal of Systems and Software*, *83*(1), 2–17. doi:10.1016/j.jss.2009.06.055

Bachmann, A., Bird, C., Rahman, F., Devanbu, P., & Bernstein, A. (2010). The missing links: bugs and bug-fix commits. In *Proceedings of the 18th ACM SIGSOFT International Symposium on Foundations of Software Engineering FSE-18* (pp. 97-106). New York, NY: ACM.

Basili, V. R., Briand, L. C., & Melo, W. L. (1996). A validation of object-oriented design metrics as quality indicators. *IEEE Transactions on Software Engineering*, *22*(10), 751–761. doi:10.1109/32.544352

Bell, R. M., Ostrand, T. J., & Weyuker, E. J. (2006). Looking for bugs in all the right places. In *Proceedings of the 2006 international symposium on Software testing and analysis ISSTA'06* (pp. 61-72). New York, NY: ACM.

Bernstein, A., Ekanayake, J., & Pinzger, M. (2007). Improving Defect Prediction Using Temporal Features and Non Linear Models. In *Proceedings of the 9th International Workshop on Principles of Software Evolution IWPSE'07* (pp. 11-18). New York, NY: ACM.

Bird, C., Bachmann, A., Aune, E., Duffy, J., Bernstein, A., Filkov, V., & Devanbu, P. (2009). Fair and balanced? Bias in bug-fix datasets. In *Proceedings of the 7th joint meeting of the European software engineering conference and the ACM SIGSOFT symposium on The foundations of software engineering ESEC/FSE'09* (pp. 121-130). New York, NY: ACM.

Bird, C., Nagappan, N., Murphy, B., Gall, H., & Devanbu, P. (2011). Don't touch my code! Examining the effects of ownership on software quality. In *Proceedings of the 19th ACM SIGSOFT symposium and the 13th European conference on Foundations of software engineering ESEC/FSE '11* (pp. 4-14). New York, NY: ACM.

Boehm, B. W., Abts, C., Brown, A. W., Chulani, S., Clark, B. K., & Horowitz, E. et al. (2009). *Software Cost Estimation with COCOMO II*. Upper Saddle River, NJ: Prentice Hall Press.

Catal, C., & Diri, B. (2009). A Systematic Review of Software Fault Prediction Studies. *Expert Systems with Applications*, *36*(4), 7346–7354. doi:10.1016/j.eswa.2008.10.027

Chapman, P., Clinton, J., Kerber, R., Khabaza, T., Reinartz, T., Shearer, C., & Wirth, R. (2000). *CRISPDM 1.0 step-by-step data mining guide*. Technical Report. CRISP-DM Consortium.

Chidamber, S. R., & Kemerer, C. F. (1994). A metrics suite for object oriented design. *IEEE Transactions on Software Engineering*, *20*(6), 476–493. doi:10.1109/32.295895

Cortes, C., & Vapnik, V. (1995). Support-Vector Networks. *Machine Learning*, *20*(3), 273–297. doi:10.1007/BF00994018

Cortes, C., & Vapnik, V. N. (1995). Support-Vector Networks. *Machine Learning*, *20*(3), 273–297. doi:10.1007/BF00994018

Drobics, M., & Bodenhofer, U. (2002) Fuzzy modeling with decision trees. In *Proceedings of the 2002 IEEE International Conference on Systems, Man and Cybernetics* (pp. 90–95). Los Alamitos, CA: IEEE Computer Society.

Elder, J. (2005) Top 10 data mining mistakes. In *Proceedings of the Fifth IEEE International Conference on Data Mining*. Los Alamitos, CA: IEEE Computer Society.

Felderer, M., & Ramler, R. (2013). Experiences and challenges of introducing risk-based testing in an industrial project. In D. Winkler, S. Biffl, & J. Bergsmann (Eds.), *Software Quality. Increasing Value in Software and Systems Development LNBIP 133* (pp. 10–29). Heidelberg, Germany: Springer. doi:10.1007/978-3-642-35702-2_3

Fenton, N. E., & Pfleeger, S. L. (1998). *Software Metrics: A Rigorous and Practical Approach* (2nd ed.). Boston, MA: PWS Pub. Co.

Godfrey, M., & Tu, Q. (2001). Growth, evolution, and structural change in open source software. In *Proceedings of the 4th International Workshop on Principles of Software Evolution IWPSE '01* (pp. 103-106). New York, NY: ACM.

Hall, T., Beecham, S., Bowes, D., Gray, D., & Counsell, S. (2012). A Systematic Literature Review on Fault Prediction Performance in Software Engineering. *IEEE Transactions on Software Engineering*, *38*(6), 1276–1304. doi:10.1109/TSE.2011.103

Halstead, M. H. (1977). *Elements of Software Science*. New York: Elsevier.

Hassan, A. E., & Holt, R. C. (2005). The Top Ten List: Dynamic Fault Prediction. In *Proceedings of the 21st International Conference on Software Maintenance ICSM'05* (pp. 263-272). Los Alamitos, CA: IEEE Computer Society.

Herzig, K., Just, S., & Zeller, A. (2013). It's not a bug, it's a feature: How misclassification impacts bug prediction. In *Proceedings of the 35th International Conference on Software Engineering ICSE'13* (pp. 392-401). Los Alamitos, CA: IEEE Computer Society.

Hill, T., & Lewicki, P. (2007). *STATISTICS: Methods and Applications*. Tulsa, OK: StatSoft.

Israeli, A., & Feitelson, D. G. (2010). The Linux kernel as a case study in software evolution. *Journal of Systems and Software, 83*(3), 485–501. doi:10.1016/j.jss.2009.09.042

Jiang, Y., Cukic, B., & Ma, Y. (2008). Techniques for evaluating fault prediction models. *Empirical Software Engineering, 13*(5), 561–595. doi:10.1007/s10664-008-9079-3

Jiang, Y., Lin, J., Cukic, B., & Menzies, T. (2009). Variance analysis in software fault prediction models. In *Proceedings of the 20th international conference on software reliability engineering ISSRE'09* (pp. 99-108). Los Alamitos, CA: IEEE Computer Society.

Kim, S., Zimmermann, T., Whitehead, E. J., Jr., & Zeller, A. (2007). Predicting Faults from Cached History. In *Proceedings of the 29th International Conference on Software Engineering ICSE'07* (pp. 489-498). Washington, DC: IEEE Computer Society.

Knab, P., Pinzger, M., & Bernstein, A. (2006). Predicting defect densities in source code files with decision tree learners. In *Proceedings of the international workshop on Mining software repositories MSR'06* (pp. 119-125). New York, NY: ACM.

Koch, S. (2007). Software evolution in open source projects - a large-scale investigation. *J. Software Maintenance and Evolution, 19*(6), 361–382. doi:10.1002/smr.348

Koru, A. G., & Liu, H. (2005). Building Defect Prediction Models in Practice. *IEEE Software, 22*(6), 23–29. doi:10.1109/MS.2005.149

Koru, A. G., Zhang, D., El Emam, K., & Liu, H. (2009). An Investigation into the Functional Form of the Size-Defect Relationship for Software Modules. *IEEE Transactions on Software Engineering, 35*(2), 293–304. doi:10.1109/TSE.2008.90

Lanubile, F., Lonigro, A., & Visaggio, G. (1995). Comparing models for identifying fault-prone software components. In *Proceedings of the 7th International Conference on Software Engineering and Knowledge Engineering SEKE'95* (pp. 312-319). Skokie, IL: Knowledge Systems Institute.

Layman, L., Kudrjavets, G., & Nagappan, N. (2008). Iterative identification of fault-prone binaries using in-process metrics. In *Proceedings of the Second ACM-IEEE international symposium on Empirical software engineering and measurement ESEM'08* (pp. 206-212). New York, NY: ACM.

Lehman, M. M., & Ramil, J. F. (2001). Evolution in software and related areas. In *Proceedings of the 4th International Workshop on Principles of Software Evolution IWPSE '01* (pp. 1-16). New York, NY: ACM.

Lessmann, S., Baesens, B., Mues, C., & Pietsch, S. (2008). Benchmarking Classification Models for Software Defect Prediction: A Proposed Framework and Novel Findings. *IEEE Transactions on Software Engineering, 34*(4), 485–496. doi:10.1109/TSE.2008.35

Li, P. L., Herbsleb, J., Shaw, M., & Robinson, B. (2006). Experiences and results from initiating field defect prediction and product test prioritization efforts at ABB Inc. In *Proceeding of the 28th International Conference on Software engineering ICSE'06* (pp. 413-422). New York, NY: ACM.

Liebchen, G. A., & Shepperd, M. (2008). Data sets and data quality in software engineering. In *Proceedings of the 4th International Workshop on Predictor Models in Software Engineering PROMISE'08* (pp. 39-44). New York, NY: ACM.

Lincke, R., Lundberg, J., & Löwe, W. (2008). Comparing software metrics tools. In *Proceedings of the 2008 International Symposium on Software Testing and Analysis ISSTA'08* (pp. 131-142). New York, NY: ACM.

Mariscal, G., Marban, O., & Fernandez, C. (2010). A survey of data mining and knowledge discovery process models and methodologies. *The Knowledge Engineering Review, 25*(2), 137–166. doi:10.1017/S0269888910000032

McCabe, T. J. (1976). A Complexity Measure. *IEEE Transactions on Software Engineering, 2*(4), 308–320. doi:10.1109/TSE.1976.233837

Mende, T., & Koschke, R. (2009). Revisiting the evaluation of defect prediction models. In *Proceedings of the 5th International Conference on Predictor Models in Software Engineering PROMISE'09* (pp. 7). New York, NY: ACM.

Meneely, A., Williams, L., Snipes, W., & Osborne, J. (2008). Predicting failures with developer networks and social network analysis. In *Proceedings of the 16th International Symposium on Foundations of software engineering SIGSOFT'08/FSE-16* (pp. 13-23). New York, NY: ACM.

Menzies, T., Greenwald, J., & Frank, A. (2007). Data Mining Static Code Attributes to Learn Defect Predictors. *IEEE Transactions on Software Engineering, 33*(1), 2–13. doi:10.1109/TSE.2007.256941

Moser, R., Pedrycz, W., & Succi, G. (2008). A comparative analysis of the efficiency of change metrics and static code attributes for defect prediction. In *Proceedings of the 13th international conference on Software engineering ICSE'08* (pp. 181-190). New York, NY: ACM.

Nagappan, N., & Ball, T. (2005). Use of Relative Code Churn Measures to Predict System Defect Density. In *Proceedings of 27th International Conference on Software Engineering ICSE'05* (pp. 284-292). New York, NY: ACM.

Nagappan, N., Murphy, B., & Basili, V. (2008). The influence of organizational structure on software quality: an empirical case study. In *Proceedings of the 30th international conference on Software engineering ICSE'08* (pp. 521-530). New York, NY: ACM.

Nagappan, N., Zeller, A., Zimmermann, T., Herzig, K., & Murphy, B. (2010). Change Bursts as Defect Predictors. In *Proceedings of the 21st International Symposium on Software Reliability Engineering* (pp. 309-318). Washington, DC: IEEE Computer Society.

Natschläger, T., Kossak, F., & Drobics, M. (2004). Extracting Knowledge and Computable Models from Data - Needs, Expectations, and Experience. In *Proceedings of the 13th International Conference on Fuzzy Systems* (pp. 493-498). Los Alamitos, CA: IEEE Computer Society.

Ostrand, T. J., Weyuker, E. J., & Bell, R. M. (2004). Where the Bugs Are. In *Proceedings of the International Symposium on Software Testing and Analysis ISSTA'04* (pp. 86-96). New York, NY: ACM.

Ostrand, T. J., Weyuker, E. J., & Bell, R. M. (2005). Predicting the Location and Number of Faults in Large Software Systems. *IEEE Transactions on Software Engineering, 31*, 340–355. doi:10.1109/TSE.2005.49

Ostrand, T. J., Weyuker, E. J., & Bell, R. M. (2010). Programmer-based fault prediction. In *Proceedings of the 6th International Conference on Predictive Models in Software Engineering PROMISE'10* (pp. 19). New York, NY: ACM.

Pinzger, M., Nagappan, N., & Murphy, B. (2008). Can developer-module networks predict failures? In *Proceedings of the 16th International Symposium on Foundations of software engineering SIGSOFT'08/FSE-16* (pp. 2-12). New York, NY: ACM.

Quinlan, J. R. (1986). Induction of Decision Trees. *Machine Learning*, *1*(1), 81–106. doi:10.1007/BF00116251

Radjenović, D., Heričko, M., Torkar, R., & Živkovič, A. (2013). Software fault prediction metrics: A systematic literature review. *Information and Software Technology*, *55*(8), 1397–1418. doi:10.1016/j.infsof.2013.02.009

Rahman, F., & Devanbu, P. (2011). Ownership, experience and defects: a fine-grained study of authorship. In *Proceedings of the 33rd International Conference on Software Engineering ICSE'11*, (pp. 491-500). New York, NY: ACM.

Rahman, F., & Devanbu, P. (2013). How, and why, process metrics are better. In *Proceedings of the 2013 International Conference on Software Engineering ICSE'13* (pp. 432-441). Piscataway, NJ: IEEE Press.

Ramler, R. (2008). The impact of product development on the lifecycle of defects. In *Proceedings of the 2008 Workshop on Defects in Large Software Systems DEFECTS'08* (pp. 21-25). New York, NY: ACM.

Ramler, R., & Himmelbauer, J. (2013). Noise in Bug Report Data and the Impact on Defect Prediction Results. In *Proceedings of the Joint Conference of the 23nd International Workshop on Software Measurement IWSM and the 8th International Conference on Software Process and Product Measurement Mensura* (pp. 173-180). Los Alamitos, CA: IEEE Computer Society.

Ramler, R., Klammer, C., & Natschläger, T. (2010). The usual suspects: a case study on delivered defects per developer. In *Proceedings of the 2010 International Symposium on Empirical Software Engineering and Measurement ESEM '10*. New York, NY: ACM.

Ramler, R., Larndorfer, S., & Natschläger, T. (2009a). What Software Repositories Should Be Mined for Defect Predictors? In *Proceedings of the 35th Euromicro Conference on Software Engineering and Advanced Applications SEAA'09* (pp. 181-187). Washington, DC: IEEE Computer Society.

Ramler, R., & Natschläger, T. (2011). Applying Heuristic Approaches for Predicting Defect-Prone Software Components. In *Proceedings of the 13th International Conference on Computer Aided Systems Theory EUROCAST LNCS 6927* (pp. 384-391). Heidelberg, Germany: Springer.

Ramler, R., & Wolfmaier, K. (2008). Issues and effort in integrating data from heterogeneous software repositories and corporate databases. In *Proceedings of the 2nd International Symposium on Empirical Software Engineering and Measurement ESEM'08* (pp. 330-332). New York, NY: ACM.

Ramler, R., Wolfmaier, K., Stauder, E., Kossak, F., & Natschläger, T. (2009b). Key Questions in Building Defect Prediction Models in Practice. In *Proceedings of the 10th International Conference on Product-Focused Software Process Improvement PROFES'09 LNBIP 32* (pp. 14-27). Heidelberg, Germany: Springer.

Schröter, A., Zimmermann, T., & Zeller, A. (2006). Predicting component failures at design time. In *Proceedings of the 2006 international symposium on International symposium on empirical software engineering ISESE'06* (pp. 18-27). New York, NY: ACM.

Wahyudin, D., Ramler, R., & Biffl, S. (2008). A Framework for Defect Prediction in Specific Software Project Contexts. In *Proceedings of the 3rd IFIP TC2 Central and East European Conference on Software Engineering Techniques CEE-SET 2008* (pp. 261-274). Heidelberg, Germany: Springer.

Weyuker, E. J. (2007). Software Engineering Research: From Cradle to Grave. In *Proceedings of the 6th European Software Engineering Conference and ACM SIGSOFT Symposium on the Foundations of Software Engineering ESEC-FSE'07* (pp. 305-311). New York, NY: ACM.

Weyuker, E. J., Ostrand, T. J., & Bell, R. M. (2010). Comparing the effectiveness of several modeling methods for fault prediction. *Empirical Software Engineering*, *15*(3), 277–295. doi:10.1007/s10664-009-9111-2

Witten, I. H., & Frank, E. (2005). *Data mining: practical machine learning tools and techniques*. Amsterdam: Morgan Kaufmann.

Zimmermann, T., & Nagappan, N. (2007). Predicting Subsystem Failures using Dependency Graph Complexities. In *Proceedings of the 18th International Symposium on Software Reliability ISSRE'07* (pp. 227-236). Washington, DC: IEEE Computer Society.

Zimmermann, T., & Nagappan, N. (2009). Predicting defects with program dependencies. In *Proceedings of the 3rd International Symposium on Empirical Software Engineering and Measurement ESEM'09* (pp. 435-438). Washington, DC: IEEE Computer Society.

Zimmermann, T., Premraj, R., & Zeller, A. (2007). Predicting Defects for Eclipse. In *Proceedings of the 3rd International Workshop on Predictor Models in Software Engineering PROMISE'07*. Washington, DC: IEEE Computer Society.

KEY TERMS AND DEFINITIONS

Chance Level: The chance level is the accuracy that will be reached when constantly predicting the majority class. For versions where more defective than defect-free components exist, the chance level equals the share of defective components.

Defect: A defect subsumes various kinds of faults in a software system. Defects usually manifest themselves in the code but may also be found in specifications, documentations, auxiliary code or systems, etc.

Module: The term (software) module is used as an abstraction for a part of a software system at a defined level of granularity such as classes, files or larger components of the software system.

Prediction: A prediction is the anticipation of a status or outcome in the future. The true status or outcome is unknown at the time when the prediction is made and can only be estimated with a certain degree of uncertainty.

Prediction Model: A prediction model incorporates various attributes of a software system as independent variables which describe the parts (e.g., components) of a software system and act as predictors for the dependent variables that characterize the defect-proneness of these parts of the system.

Version: A version of a software system relates the system's implementation and all related artifacts to a specific point in time, usually when an instance of the system under development is released. In this chapter, the term "version" is used interchangeably with the term "release".

Section 7
Software Management and Evolution

Chapter 25

Knowware–Based Software Engineering:
An Overview of its Origin, Essence, Core Techniques, and Future Development

RuQian Lu
Chinese Academy of Sciences, China & Peking University, China

Zhi Jin
Peking University, China & Chinese Academy of Sciences, China

ABSTRACT

The first part of this chapter reviews the origin of knowware-based software engineering. It originates from the authors' experiences in finding new techniques for knowledge-based software engineering while performing PROMIS, a continuing project series from the 1990s. The key point of PROMIS is to generate applications automatically by separating the development of domain knowledge from that of software architecture, with an important innovation of acquiring and summarizing domain knowledge automatically based on the pseudo-natural language understanding techniques. However, during PROMIS development, the authors did not find an appropriate form for the separated domain knowledge. The second part of the chapter briefly describes how the authors came to the concept of knowware. They stated that the essence of knowware is its capacity as a commercialized form of domain knowledge. It is also the third major component of IT after hardware and software. The third part of the chapter introduces the basic concepts of knowware and knowware engineering. Three life cycle models of knowware engineering and the design of corresponding knowware implementations are given. The fourth part of the chapter introduces object-oriented mixware engineering. In the fifth part of the chapter, two recent applications of knowware technique regarding smart room and Web search are reported. As a further development of PROMIS, the sixth part of the chapter discusses knowware-based redesign of its framework. In the seventh part of the chapter, the authors discuss automatic application generation and domain knowledge modeling on the J2EE platform, which combines techniques of PROMIS, knowware, and J2EE, and the development and deployment framework (i.e. PROMIS/KW**).

DOI: 10.4018/978-1-4666-6026-7.ch025

1. EXPERIMENT OF SEPARATING APPLICATION KNOWLEDGE DEVELOPMENT FROM SOFTWARE DEVELOPMENT: THE ORIGIN

The practice of software engineering shows that most failures of software development are caused by failure of requirement analysis, and the reason for that falls upon lack of good cooperation between users and software engineers. Users, usually being unable to exactly and clearly state their requirements, often change their requirements freely during the process of software developing, which makes it difficult for software engineers to perform a proper requirement analysis and to guarantee the accomplishment of the developing job successfully.

At present, requirements analysis researchers and practitioners use either formal methods or semi-formal methods with different requirement specification languages. The advantage of formal methods is that they provide strict guidance to software engineers or programmers for writing requirement specification with the assumption that user requirement is complete and precise (Chakraborty et al., 2012; Vassiliou et al., 1990; Mulopoulos et al., 1999; Kundu, 2007; Yu, 1997; Wang et. al., 2001; Castro et al., 2002; Fuxman et al., 2004); otherwise they cannot give any help, no matter how perfect they are in theory. One of the solutions to this problem is involving users into the process of software development as much as possible, so that they can realize the differences between the software under development and that they really need, or between the drafted requirement specification and their real requirements. In this way, users can find the software design deficiencies at the earliest time. However, because of the big difference between the knowledge backgrounds of software engineers and users, formal methods often cause serious problems of bad communication between them. The changing nature of requirements during software design and development process makes the situation even worse.

We believe that it is not enough to only attract users to join the development process, but we should also give the key of developing software to users, whenever it is possible. That is to let users themselves define, design, develop, maintain and modify their software. This is possible for some kinds of software, for example, management information system (Mansour et al., 2009; Jarke et al., 1990; Engels et al., 1995; Engels et al., 1992; Vilkomir et al., 2004; Bhuiyan et al., 2007; Monroe et. al., 1996). To achieve this goal, we must remove from users the burden of learning and mastering the knowledge about software development and also the burden of requirement analysis with formal methods. One way for achieving this is using knowledge. As a result, we proposed a knowledge-based software engineering method, KISSME (Knowledge Intensive Software System Manufacture Engineering), and developed a tool for supporting this method that is named as PROMIS (PROtotyping MIS)(Lu et al., 1994, 1995, 1996 (journal), 1996, 1997 (Spain), 1997, 1998, 1998 (journal), 1999, 2000, 2000 (book), 2002, 2003, 2003 (journal); Jin et al., 2003). The essence of this method is that by using a large knowledge base to support software development, users do not need to master knowledge of software development or requirements analysis of related domain. This approach is also made possible by a requirement description language BIDL (Business Information Description Language). This language is in pseudo-natural style and contains only expressions and terminology of the application domain, without any jargon from the software engineering area. Users who are not software professionals can use this language to describe their business. This description will then be transformed into the final program under the support of a domain knowledge base throughout the whole lifecycle of application development.

The following process has been used to design a pseudo natural language like BIDL:

1. Determine a set of semantic constructs of the application domain. For example, the semantic constructs for the supply-chain management could be the semantic elements concerning storage, purchase, production, service providing and business accounting and so on. One of such semantic elements may be "prescribe minimal storage".

2. Select a natural language, e.g. Chinese, as the background language.

3. Choose at least one sentence pattern from the background language for representing each semantic construct obtained in the first step. For example, for semantic element "prescribe minimal storage", a sentence pattern could be "the least storage of * must be larger than *" and one of its instances could be "the least storage of coke must be larger than 50000 tons".

4. The collection of the sentences generated by the sentence patterns is called a pseudo-natural language. And the set of all the sentence patterns form the grammar of this language, which we call as its key structure.

5. This grammar can be analyzed automatically by computer as only the key structure needs to be recognized and the * parts could be treated as parameters.

Two additional techniques should be added for allowing the automatic transformation (or automatic compiling) of knowledge. The first one is stepwise refinement, which means continually testing the knowledge base with practical examples to let its knowledge match the real world more and more precisely. The second one is to synthesize the knowledge from different sources (books, technique materials, experts or their combination), and to merge them to produce a consistent and integrated knowledge base.

We started the EAGLE (Easy Access to Global Lifecycle Engineering) project at the beginning of nineties, which aimed at realizing the KISSME approach (Lu et al., 2000). The structure of KISSME is shown in Figure 1, where DKDL (Domain Knowledge Definition Language) is a pseudo natural language for representing domain knowledge. Domain experts use it to write down their knowledge and experience. DOKB (Domain Ontology Knowledge Base) is a domain knowledge base built up on the basis of the structured ontology of corresponding application domains. ONONET (ONtology-Object-NET) is an ontology description language. The knowledge represented by ONONET comes from merging and compiling the DKDL programs (Lu & Jin, 2002, 2003). BIDL (Business Information Description Language) is an enterprise information description language. Domain users use it to describe the basic informa-

Figure 1. The architecture of PROMIS

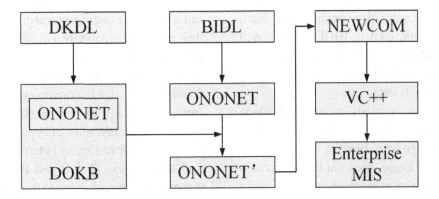

569

tion about their enterprise (Lu et al., 1994, 1995, 1996). NEWCOM is an application architecture description language, which aims at describing the network-based application architecture in Client/Server style (Lu et al., 1998).

PROMIS has two parallel processes. One is the domain knowledge acquisition process. In this process, domain experts offer their knowledge in the form of DKDL, which then is analyzed and represented in the form of ONONET and maintained in the knowledge base. The other process is to generate the application system automatically, where domain users provide their enterprise descriptions in BIDL, which then are compiled by BIDL compiler to generate the enterprise ontology in the form of ONONET. After that, with the help of domain knowledge base DOKB, the ONONET analyzer supplements the missing descriptions if necessary to make the enterprise ontology complete, which is labeled as ONONET'. Then supported by a knowledge base about information system and network structure, the application ontology in the form of ONONET' can be transformed to the application system architecture description in the form of NEWCOM, which is compiled into some high level language with ODBC interface to the underlying database.

The system developed following this technique is also called "Tian Ying" (Eagle) which can help people develop MIS. Moreover, in order to fulfill needs of different users, we offer three different versions:

Little Eagle contains an application generator and an application knowledge base. Given information about the enterprise (organization, staff, routing daily work, etc.) in BIDL form, it will generate an application automatically. Thus Little Eagle suits for users who are familiar with the domain but not software.

Medium Eagle consists of an application generator, an application knowledge base and a domain knowledge base. Besides working in the manner of Little Eagle, Medium Eagle can also generate an application automatically even when users do not provide detailed information about their target enterprise. In this case Medium Eagle acquires necessary information from the domain knowledge base. What the user has to do is only to provide the type of the wanted MIS, like "a five star hotel". Note that Medium Eagle generates only a draft of the requirement. Users can make necessary modification on the generated requirement. Thus Medium is suitable for users who are not familiar with either software or their domain.

Big Eagle contains a domain knowledge analyzer and model builder, an application generator, an application knowledge base and a set of domain knowledge bases. It does not only do what Medium Eagle does, but can also perform domain analysis whenever people meet a new domain, and build a new domain knowledge base. So it suits for professional software developers.

Eagle project gives us a lot of inspirations on both the methodology of software development and the software industry. Firstly, software knowledge and domain knowledge should be separated in the process of software development. Secondly, software developers and domain knowledge developers should be separated when we organize a development team. Thirdly, software industry and knowledge industry should be separated when developing the IT industry.

An application system usually involves lots of domain knowledge. That determines that domain experts and software engineers should cooperate well with each other during the process of system development. However, the gap caused by different knowledge backgrounds makes it difficult. If we can let software engineers and domain experts do their own jobs separately, i.e. software engineers just do their best to develop good software, and leave the job of summarizing and developing domain knowledge to domain experts. These two parts of work will be then combined in a proper way only in the last stage of system development. In this way, we can make better use of both parties' advantages. That is just like the situation that customer buys hardware from IBM and buys compatible software from a software company. We believe that it will make both the software industry and the knowledge industry to be independent and prosperous if going along this way.

The other advantage of KISSME approach is that it provides a feasible solution to the problem of "system evolution" in software engineering. Some software, e.g. MIS, is inherently subject to steady evolution because the situation of enterprise is always changing. No matter how perfect your requirements specification is, it cannot solve the problem once for ever. KISSME gives the key of developing and modifying software to users. So the users themselves can change the requirements description in BIDL according to the changing enterprise situation and let the system generate a new MIS for them. It is not necessary to ask software engineers to modify the software for them.

2. KNOWWARE AS INDEPENDENT KNOWLEDGE COMMODITY: THE ESSENCE

As stated above, one feature of Eagle is separating the development of software and the development of knowledge included in software. But Eagle did not locate a proper position for the separated knowledge. Which technique should it use for developing the knowledge? Which form should the knowledge product take after it has been devel-

oped? Can the methodology and technology, which have been adopted by scientists and engineers in software engineering, also be applied to knowledge development and knowledge product generation? If it is not fully suitable, what are the differences between them? Especially, since software is a commodity, which form should knowledge take as a product? The research trying to answer these questions leads us to the concept "knowware" (Lu, 2005 (IEEE), 2005, 2006, 2007, 2007(book), 2010; Lu&Jin, 2006, 2008). Knowware is the representation of a read only knowledge module that is independent, commercialized, suitable for computer manipulation, meeting some industrial standard, equipped with detailed documentation and embeddable in software or hardware for use. The main differences between knowware and software are listed in Table 1.

Knowware gives us a way to separate knowledge from software. That makes them two different research topics and commodities and then makes hardware, software and knowware to be a tripartite balance of forces in IT industry. Expert system and knowledge base are all similar with knowware in some sense, but they are not the same. Expert system is a kind of conventional software, because it includes a series of application program modules whose kernel is an inference engine. A traditional knowledge base is not knowware, because, firstly, it contains at least a knowledge base management program. This makes it not meeting

Table 1. Comparison between knowware and software

	Traditional software	**Knowware**
Technical content	Both domain knowledge and software techniques	Only domain knowledge
Operability	Run independently	Cannot run independently, support software running
Life circle	Mainly determined by variations of customer requirement	Mainly determined by accumulations and evolution of knowledge
Classification	Normally can be divided into system software and application software	Consist of application knowware only, "system knowware" is a software
Developer	Primly only software engineers (sometimes supported by domain experts)	Experts from various domains (sometimes supported by knowledge engineers)
Intellectual property	Software copyright	Knowledge patent

one of the prerequisites of knowware, i.e. containing knowledge only. Secondly, the representation and interface of knowledge in knowledge bases are not standardized, so they cannot be combined with other software modules in a plug-and-play style. Thirdly, general knowledge bases are not commercialized. Our goal is to make knowware a standard component, so renewing a knowware can be as easy as renewing a plug-in of a computer.

3. KNOWWARE ENGINEERING: THE CORE TECHNIQUE (1)

Software engineering can be defined as the systematic application of scientific and engineering principles to the methodology, development, operation, and maintenance of software. We define knowware engineering in a similar way. There are some similarities between the two, but many differences as well. Computer can discover knowledge with or without the help of human. That brings out an industry, i.e. the knowledge industry. If the produced knowledge is normalized, packaged and commercialized, i.e. knowware, then the collection of all the techniques used in the whole production process (including maintenance and application) is called knowware engineering. Simply speaking, knowware engineering is commercialized knowledge engineering that generates knowledge in a massive way.

Researchers have proposed many development models for software engineering, which are closely related to software life cycle, such as the waterfall model, the fountain model, the spiral model, and the rapid prototype development model, etc. Knowware engineering should have its own development models and life cycles. And as the same as for software engineering, it should have many kinds of development models and life cycles, because there are many models of obtaining, processing and applying knowledge.

In terms of the three different ways of knowledge acquisition and modeling, three development models are proposed for knowware engineering.

The first model of knowware life cycle is the smelting furnace model, furnace model for short. It is suitable for the situation when there exist plenty of knowledge sources, whose knowledge content can be captured in a batch way. Recall the mechanism of acquiring domain knowledge taken by PROMIS, we use the technique for pseudo-natural language understanding (PNLU) and let machine translate DKDL programs automatically into knowledge base in a batch way. The smelting furnace accepts and smelts these raw materials inputted, just like the blast furnace smelts iron ore. In the knowware practice, this smelting furnace is a complicated knowledge processing system with a massive and heterogeneous knowledge base containing knowledge magma. Each time when knowledge ores (books, leaflets, newspapers, technical reports, etc.) are inputted, it will undergo a process of ore dressing, where knowledge ores will be decomposed in smaller knowledge elements. These elements, though organized in some way, form the knowledge magma of the furnace. Figure 2 is an illustration of the furnace model.

The second model of knowware life cycle is the crystallization model. Its basic idea can be described as follows. Knowledge required by certain knowware is often distributed and scattered in a large information space. During knowware's life cycle, it continuously accumulates new and useful knowledge while discarding old and obsolete knowledge. Most knowledge must first be acquired, refined, analyzed, fused, and reorganized. So, knowledge surrounding us is more like a knowledge solution, and knowledge formation is more like crystallization. Owing to the huge scale of knowledge solutions, we refer to them as the knowledge sea. The demand for knowledge is just like the crystallization's center, and the knowledge in the sea precipitates and gathers around the center, so the "crystals" grow larger and larger. The structure of knowledge crystals is

Figure 2. The furnace model

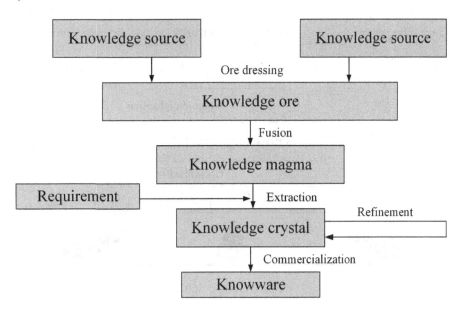

the rules and norms of knowledge representation and organization. A typical knowledge sea is the knowledge distributed in the Internet.

We need two control mechanisms to control the formation and refining process of knowledge crystal. One is knowledge pump to implement the process of knowledge gathering. A knowledge pump has to accomplish the tasks of knowledge extraction and knowledge filtering. The PNL is one kind of such knowledge pump. It can control both the content and the granularity of knowledge in the extraction process. Existing knowledge crystals can enter the knowledge sea as new knowledge particles, so that they can be used again in a new and higher level. The other is knowledge kidney, to implement the process of knowledge maintenance and knowledge renewing. The knowledge in crystals might be degraded and obsolete, new knowledge is needed to replace or modify the original knowledge.

In summary, knowledge pump and knowledge kidney cooperate to complete knowledge extraction, knowledge fusion, and knowledge reorganization. Knowware evolution depends on the evolution and update of its basis, i.e. the

knowledge crystal. Theoretically, this is an infinite process. Figure 3 shows the crystallization model.

The typical example of the crystallization model is the second-generation browser. This kind of browser can not only scrawl web pages on the Internet, but also extract knowledge from the collected web pages and synthesize it to form knowledge crystals, then finally produce knowware, or publish the knowledge in other forms, e.g. the state of art report or even encyclopedia of a specific domain.

The third model of knowware life cycle borrows a concept, i.e. the spiral model, from the model of human knowledge accumulation and evolution proposed by Nonaka and Takeuchi (1995). The spiral model describes the recursive process of knowledge transformation between tacit knowledge and explicit knowledge through a spiral of internalization, socialization, externalization and combination. That characterizes the formation and transformation of tacit and explicit knowledge, as well as individual and social knowledge. This model can also describe the formation process of expertise knowledge, and it is also a feasible way

Figure 3. The crystallization model

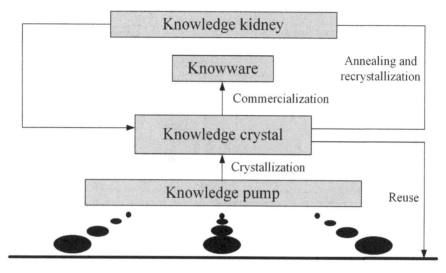

Knowledge sea

Figure 4. The spiral model

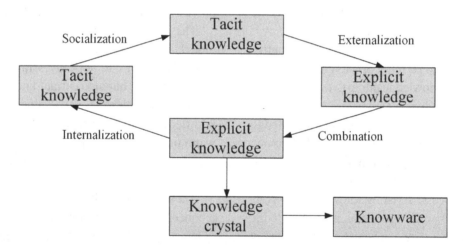

of forming knowledge crystals. Figure 4 shows the spiral model.

We call the knowledge modules generated by these three knowware engineering models the knowledge crystals. From the application view, knowledge crystals are just half-finished products and need further processing to become knowware. Table 2 shows the major differences between knowledge crystals and knowware.

As mentioned above, there is no system knowware. "System knowware" is software. We introduce a class of important software that plays the role of "system knowware". They are called knowledge middleware. Thus, knowledge middleware is a class of software tools accompanying the whole lifecycle of knowware. Table 3 lists some main functions and techniques of different kinds of knowledge middleware.

Table 2. Differences between knowledge crystals and knowware

	Knowledge crystals	Knowware
Inclusion principle	The interconnection of knowledge within a specific domain	The usefulness of knowledge under a specific requirement
Partition principle	Knowledge of different domains usually organized in different knowledge crystals	Knowledge from different crystals can be combined into a unified knowware
Representation principle	Mainly descriptive representation	Mainly procedural representation
Organization principle	Emphasize scientific principles	Emphasize efficiency in applications
Production principle	Driven by development and evolution of knowledge itself	Driven by user and market requirements
Intellectual property principle	May not have intellectual property	Always have intellectual property
Update principle	Updated as soon as the knowledge is renewed	Updated in form of replacement by a new knowware, which is generated by an evolved knowledge crystal
Update cycle	Continuous evolution	Version-wise evolution. Knowware will be renewed only after an extended accumulation and evolution of knowledge crystal

Table 3. Knowledge middleware classification

Classification	Functions	Typical techniques
Knowledge compiling middleware	Transform text knowledge into operable knowledge in a batch way	PNLU, knowledge extraction, knowledge fusion
Knowledge extracting middleware	Extract knowledge from knowledge source	Text and data mining, deep search, machine learning
Knowledge crystallizing middleware	Crystallize extracted knowledge	Ontology structuring and knowledge modeling
Knowledge updating middleware	Maintain the consistency and completeness of knowledge crystals	Truth maintenance, knowledge reduction, closed world assumption
Knowware producing middleware	Cut knowledge crystals using an Occam's shaver and integrate them according to knowware requirement	Component engineering, rapid prototyping
Knowware combining middleware	Acquire a set of basic knowware based on user requirement and assemble them into more powerful knowware	Knowledge modeling, automated architecture design, Internetware
Knowledge management middleware	Register, enroll, distribute, and protect intellectual property, and fee collection	Requirement analysis, e-commerce, web service
Update cycle	Continuous evolution	Version-wise evolution. Knowware will be renewed only after an extended accumulation and evolution of knowledge crystal

4. OBJECT ORIENTED MIXWARE (SOFTWARE + KNOWWARE) ENGINEERING: THE CORE TECHNIQUE (2)

The object-oriented programming is a most popular and widely used paradigm of software engineering. This section will show how we adapt the knowware technique to the object oriented paradigm and thus establish a framework of object oriented software—knowware co-engineering. We call the coherent integration of software and knowware modules in one functional system as a mixware and the technique delineated in this section as object oriented mixware engineering, OOME for short.

At first we would like to give some definitions.

Definition 1: An object-oriented mixware system (OOMS) is a hierarchy of objects and classes, each with a unique name. In this chapter, the hierarchy is assumed to be a tree, where the leaves are objects and other nodes are classes. The nodes are classified as software classes (objects), knowware classes (objects) and knowledge middleware classes (objects). Different kinds of classes appear as nodes of the tree in a mixed way. Any offspring node (including leaf) can inherit data parts and method parts from its ancestor nodes. □

From the definition above we can infer various conclusions. First, we don't allow multiple-inheritance. Each object or class has only one parent node. As a start, we wish the mechanism to be as simple as possible. Second, different kinds of objects/classes can inherit from each other. This will do no harm since definition 1 only prescribes the static structure of objects/classes.

A major difference between OOME and OOSE (object oriented software engineering) is that in OOME we have three different kinds of objects (classes): software objects, knowware objects and knowledge middleware objects, while in OOSE we have only one kind of objects: the software objects. Although knowledge middleware is also software in its essence, it plays a particular role in OOME. Roughly speaking, a software object is coding intensive, a knowware object is knowledge intensive, while a knowledge middleware object plays the role of bridges between these two. As a consequence, the three kinds of objects (classes) are structurally different from each other in the static sense and also behaviorally different in the dynamical sense. We will see this difference later.

Currently, we divide the life cycle of mixware engineering in three phases: object oriented mixware analysis, object oriented mixware design and object oriented mixware programming. Note that all these three phases, through look like similarly as the corresponding phases in software engineering, are much more complicated than the latter. When the software engineers start to develop a software, usually they have a clear picture in front of them, namely, for what use is the software ought to be set up. But for mixware the situation is completely different. As a career of knowledge, a knowware can be used anywhere whenever the knowledge it contains can be applied. As a consequence, different uses of knowware require often different knowledge middlewares to support it. This leads again to different configurations of the middleware. There may be two kinds of mixware developers. The first kind of developers cares only for some specific use of mixware. In this case it is relatively easy for its analysis, design and programming. The second kind of developers, which includes mainly knowware enterprises and companies, wants to have as many as possible future applications for their knowwares. They develop a mixware as a complex of knowware, software and knowledge middleware with a diversity of structures to meet the need of application diversities. In this section, we focus on the point of view of second kind of developers.

4.1 Object Oriented Mixware Analysis

The task of this phase is to analyze the application scenes of the mixware to be developed, to find and classify the classes (objects) in the application scenes and to build a prototype of the class (object) tree, or several such trees. This is only a preliminary draft of the object oriented system to be produced.

Procedure OOMA

Step1: Perform the conventional object oriented analysis as usual in software engineering to produce an inheritance tree of objects (classes), which we call stem objects (classes).

Step2: Identify the 'knowledge rich' and 'knowledge poor' objects (classes) of the tree.

Step3: Separate each knowledge rich node in two parts: the knowledge part and the coding part;

Output: A mixed inheritance tree IT consisting of the three kinds of objects (classes). ☐

Roughly, these three kinds of classes are the knowledge poor nodes (KPON), the knowledge part (KPN) and coding part (CPN) of knowledge rich nodes which will be elaborated into software classes, knowware classes and knowledge middleware classes, respectively. ☐

When doing OOMA, the following definition is relevant:

Definition 2: A stem class is called knowledge rich if it meets one or several criteria listed below:

1. *It mainly contains application knowledge rather than support knowledge. Here support knowledge means system knowledge or background knowledge, e.g. operating system is support knowledge. Utility routines are also support knowledge;*

2. *It mainly contains domain knowledge rather than software knowledge;*

3. *It mainly contains expert knowledge rather than commonsense knowledge;*

4. *It mainly contains private knowledge rather than public knowledge. Private knowledge includes expert knowledge, patent knowledge, etc.;*

5. *It mainly contains elaborated and integrated knowledge rather than fragmentary and unelaborated knowledge.* ☐

4.2 Object Oriented Mixware Design

The task of OOMD is to optimize the structure and content of the mixed inheritance tree obtained in OOMA. During this phase, the classes obtained in OOMA phase may have to be modified, enriched, combined or decomposed to ensure the best functional quality of the final system.

But the functional quality (including knowledge quality) is not the only concern of the design phase. The commercial developers may want to find more knowledge middleware which, when combined with the same knowware, will support more applications of the mixware.

Procedure OOMD

Step1: Extract all KPN nodes from the IT tree to form an independent tree KPNT. Call the IT tree without KPN nodes as IT' tree.

Step2: For each node of KPNT, generalize the knowledge contained in it, including generalizing concrete data to data types and specific data types to more general data types. Assume the resulting tree be KPNT'. Note that the number and inheritance relation of nodes are not changed in this generalization process.

Step3: Combine the tree KPNT' with IT' in the way that all (generalized) nodes of KPNT' are put back to their original places in IT' (before generalization).

Step4: Find all mismatches (inconsistencies) between knowledge contained in different knowware classes and modify them appropriately. Besides, check the (relative) completeness of knowledge contained in each knowware class and do the completion whenever it is needed.

Step5: Find all mismatches between knowledge middleware classes and knowware classes; as well as those among knowledge middleware classes themselves and modify them appropriately;

Step6: Find all mismatches between software classes on the one side, and knowledge middleware classes and knowware classes on the other side and remove them; find also all mismatches among software classes themselves and remove them.

Step7: Try to reduce the size of the new tree by combining some of father-son nodes to a single one, while keeping the combined tree free of any mismatches.

Output: A final inheritance tree MT with three kinds of classes. □

Note that step 2 is necessary for commercial production of mixware, because users' requirement tends to be specific and does not cover the potential future use of the mixware. Step 4 is necessary because the knowledge generalization of step 3 is done separately for each knowware class and mismatch may appear in this process. The ordering of design steps in this algorithm is important because mixware is a knowware centered system. The preference principle of 'knowware first', 'knowledge middlewre second' and 'software last' is crucial.

4.3 Object Oriented Mixware Programming

During this phase of development, the final representation of the classes and objects should be determined. For simplicity we consider in this subsection only objects.

Definition 3:

1. *A software object consists of two parts: data part and method part. Both parts are not empty. The data part consists of slot variables (to be instantiated with values during run time) and attributes (pre-instantiated slot variables). The method part consists of a finite set of methods to be invoked by messages.*

2. *A knowledge middleware object is an object whose data part may be empty.*

3. *A knowware object is an object whose method part is empty.* □

Definition 3 corresponds to the essence of knowware that it is just a knowledge module incapable of operating independently. A knowware object is only then functional if it is combined with an appropriate knowledge middleware object. A knowledge middleware object differs from a software object only in the content of the data part, which can be empty or not. Actually we need two forms of knowledge middleware objects: namely with or without data parts. A knowledge middleware object without data part is more flexible since it can be bound to more different knowware objects to form software objects. On the other hand, a knowledge middleware object with data part is more space efficient in case if a piece of data is shared by several knowware objects.

There are two kinds of knowledge middleware's support to knowware: the static support and the dynamic support. Structurally, any support is some kind of binding.

Definition 4:

1. The static binding is through inheritance. In the inheritance tree, any object or class inherits information from any parent class, no matter what kind these classes or objects are.

2. *The dynamic binding is through recombination. During runtime, a knowware object can be recombined with a knowledge middleware object to form a traditional software object.* □

Even the dynamic binding can be implemented in different ways, as it is shown below:

Definition 5: There are three ways of combining a knowware object with a knowledge middleware object dynamically:

1. *The call by value approach combines the two objects from the beginning of program running till the program terminates;*
2. *The call by need approach combines the two objects when the knowware object is called for. Then the binding continues until the program terminates;*
3. *The call by instance approach combines the two objects whenever the knowware object is called for. The binding is released until the next call.* □

5. KNOWWARE IN COMPLICATED ENVIRONMENT: THE APPLICATIONS

In this section we will report two practical applications of knowware. In both these two applications, the knowware is an embedded subsystem of a global system which interacts with a complicated environment.

5.1 Knowware Based Infrastructure for Rule Based Control Systems in Smart Spaces

This is a joint work of the second author Jin with Lu, Li et al. (2013), where Lu is the main contributor. An infrastructure system is constructed to control the state of a smart room. The physical conditions to be controlled include lightning, temperature, projector, etc. It consists of three parts: the knowledge reasoning part including a knowware and a reasoner running on the knowware; the external part including various elements for sensing the environment such as sensors and meters, as well as elements for exercising external control like switches and regulators; the interaction processing part playing the role of a bridge: it receives information from the sensing elements and passes it to the knowledge reasoning part. On the other hand, it also receives control instructions from the knowledge reasoning part and passes it to the external control elements. In the terminology of this chapter, the three parts of the infrastructure system belong to three categories: The category of the first part is knowware + knowledge middleware (the reasoner); that of the second one (interaction processing part) is hardware and that of the third one (interaction processing part) is software. We call such a system a complex ware (consisting of hardware, software, knowware and knowledge middleware). The structure is illustrated in Figure 5.

Now we will give a few words on the knowware. In this complicated environment, a set of logic rules is collected, integrated and compiled, which can interact with other parts of the system through the interaction processing part. Upon receiving information sensed from the environment, for example change of the temperature and the humidity, it initiates a reasoning process of the logic rules to determine the state of the environment the next steps the system ought to do.

Some example rules contained in the knowware are as follows (Lu, Li et al., 2013)):

If the room is occupied, and the room temperature is higher than 30 degrees centigrade, turn on the air conditioner to 26 degrees centigrade;

If the room is occupied, and the projector is turned off, then roll up the screen, and turn on all the lights;

Figure 5. Smart room control: A complex ware (Adapted from Lu, Huang, et al., 2012)

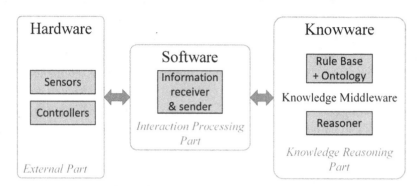

If the room is occupied, and the projector is turned on, then pull down the screen, turn off the front lights near to the screen and turn on the rear lights.

5.2 Knowware Based Automatic Generation of Domain Specific Web Portals

This is a joint work of the first author Lu with Huang et al. (2012). Yu Huang is the main implementor while Ruqian Lu is the main designer.

The motivation of this research is to create a knowware based DIY technique, which, when an appropriate knowledge request (relating to some user wanted domain) is specified, can first perform a widespread search for Web sites containing the wanted knowledge, acquire useful documents from them and develop a Web portal based on these documents. In this Web portal, all documents are classified in tree form according to the developer (and future visitor's) interest. This work is essentially knowware based and thus basically automated. Each developer needs only to do very few things. To which degree the developer has to be involved in the development process depends on how thoroughly the work is depending on the use of knowware. As it will be shown in the following, the knowwares the developer can use are structured in three levels. In this sense, the Web portal development is supported by a leveled set of knowware.

Roughly speaking, the KACTL approach consists of the following parts:

Step 1: Prepare the initial domain knowledge in form of a classification tree of interesting points according to the domain/sub domain organization;

Step 2: Take a small set of documents (say several hundred, acquired from the Web) and distribute them to the nodes of the classification tree according to how much each document matches the interesting point of some node;

Step 3: Use this set to train the classification tree as follows: for each node, calculate the frequency vectors (consisting of 'most frequent words' contained in documents assigned to this node), strength vectors (strength of a word equals to frequency of the word divided by length of the document containing it), and finally enhanced strength vectors (taking weights of son nodes into account) as characteristics of the node. We call it the labeled classification tree;

Step 4: Use a browser to scan the Web for collecting a great number (say several tens of thousands) of Web pages relating to this domain. After a necessary post-processing, the documents contained in these Web pages will be selected and distributed to the nodes of the labeled classification tree according to how they match these nodes based on their enhanced strength vectors.

Step 5: Other utility works for establishing the Web.

One can do all these five steps by oneself. One can also rely oneself to the use of knowware. There are at least three possibilities of providing knowware to easy the work of Web portal developers: the unlabeled classification tree of step 1; the labeled classification tree of step 3; the labeled classification tree with a massive set of classified documents of step 4.

A prototype system was built for the domain of cloud computing. A snapshot of part of the classification tree is shown in Figure 6.

6. PROMIS/KW, THE KNOWWARE BASED REDESIGN OF PROMIS: THE NEXT STEP (1)

In this section we give an example about knowware-based redesign of legacy systems. It is PROMIS based on knowware. Here the three knowware engineering models are all employed. To transplant the knowledge based software engineering platform PROMIS to knowware based environment, an anatomy of PROMIS technique is needed. Figure 1 shows that PROMIS can be divided into three main parts: the domain knowledge generation part, the automatic application generator with a domain knowledge base and the application system running support. The first part involves external (DKDL) and internal (ONONET) description of domain knowledge, and the transformation from the external description (Expert input) to the internal one, together with a domain ontology base (DOKB). The second part involves enterprise information description BIDL (User input), its ontology representation ONONET, and the system architecture model NEWCOM. The third part includes executable system and running support.

We call knowware-based PROMIS PROMIS/KW. Like PROMIS, PROMIS/KW also contains

three parts. The first part and the second part are similar to the corresponding parts in PROMIS, where all potential knowledge supports are replaced by knowware, while the third part supplements system evolution. Roughly speaking, the first part corresponds to the production of knowware; the second part corresponds to the application of knowware and the generation of application, and the third part the evolution of knowware.

The furnace model is suitable for the production of knowware in the first part, where the knowledge sources are summarized and dictated/written by domain experts, including regular knowledge of running a business. These 'raw materials' are input in pseudo natural language form, and the knowledge extraction middleware gets the domain knowledge with help of the key structures. This knowledge is organized in ontology form and stored in the knowledge base. Meanwhile, software engineers or programmers write a batch of basic applets and utilities and put them into the knowledge base to make it complete. When there is a need to generate a domain model, the model generation middleware will pick up corresponding domain sub-ontology including necessary applets to generate knowware, knowledge middleware and software objects respectively. So the furnace model here is not the same with the furnace model mentioned above. On the one hand, it generates not only knowware, but also knowledge middleware and the accompanying software objects, where the knowledge analysis middleware does object oriented analysis on the domain knowledge, and produces some knowware objects and knowledge middleware objects. As we stated above, knowware objects do not contain any methods. In order to utilize the knowware, one should combine it with corresponding knowledge middleware before or during running the system, depending on the preference of the system engineer. In conclusion, the representation of the domain ontology based on knowware differs from the representation in the original PROMIS.

Figure 6. Part of the classification tree of the 'cloud computing' Web portal (Cited from Lu, Huang et al., 2012)

Training Tree	Tree resulted from Algorithm 1
Cloud Computing (0)	Cloud Computing (2)
CC Concept (0)	CC Concept (10)
CC Basic Principles (8)	CC Basic Principles (0)
CC Definition (22)	CC Definition (0)
CC Discrimination Criteria (8)	CC Discrimination Criteria (1)
CC Publication (0)	CC Publication (4)
CC Journals (1)	CC Journals (0)
CC Web sites (0)	CC Web sites (0)
CC Books (3)	CC Books (5)
CC Activity (0)	CC Activity (0)
CC Conference (0)	CC Conference (0)
CC Domestic Conference (6)	CC Domestic Conference (0)
CC International Conference	CC International Conference (0)
CC Training Course (0)	CC Training Course (0)
CC Workshop (0)	CC Workshop (0)
CC Technique (7)	CC Technique (12)
CC Basic Technique (0)	CC Basic Technique (11)
CC and Map Reduce Software (1)	CC and Map Reduce Software (0)
CC and Big Table Technique (1)	CC and Big Table Technique (0)
CC and Distributed File System (1)	CC and Distributed File System (0)
CC New Technique (0)	CC New Technique (0)
CC Classification (10)	CC Classification (2)
Public Cloud (2)	Public Cloud (2)
Private Cloud (5)	Private Cloud (9)
Mixed Cloud (2)	Mixed Cloud (2)
CC Application (14)	CC Application (32)
CC and Browser (6)	CC and Browser (1)
CC and e-Commerce (5)	CC and e-Commerce (35)
CC and Mobile Communication (6)	CC and Mobile Communication (53)
CC Product (1)	CC Product (3)
CC Hardware (1)	CC Hardware (2)
CC Software (4)	CC Software (11)
CC Platform (5)	CC Platform (0)
Hadoop (2)	Hadoop (0)
GAE (0)	GAE (0)
EC2 (0)	EC2 (0)
Blue Cloud (4)	Blue Cloud (1)
CC Develop Tendency (14)	CC Develop Tendency (39)
CC Market (22)	CC Market (14)
CC Device Provider (9)	CC Device Provider (0)
CC Service Provide (12)	CC Service Provide (4)
CC Consultation Provider (2)	CC Consultation Provider (4)
CC Stock Market (7)	CC Stock Market (10)
CC Concept Stock (3)	CC Concept Stock (19)
CC Policies (3)	CC Policies (11)
CC Security (12)	CC Security (59)
CC History (5)	CC History (21)
CC Current Issues (10)	CC Current Issues (23)
CC Problems (11)	CC Problems (16)
CC Characteristics (8)	CC Characteristics (11)
CC Practice (1)	CC Practice (52)
CC Standards (2)	CC Standards (34)
CC Comments (4)	CC Comments (60)

However, the furnace model depicts the generation process of only a single piece of knowware. Whenever generating a knowware, some related knowledge elements are drawn from knowledge base and are composed. But from the view of system development practice, knowware could be reusable. We do not need to always start from knowledge magma when we want a knowware. We can build a well-structured knowware base, each time when we need new knowledge, we just have to search for it in the knowware base. In case that the needed knowware is missing, a possible solution is to compose the existing knowware to form a new one. More strictly speaking, it is to compose some parts of the existing knowware to form new knowware. That may give rise to an issue on searching and reasoning across ontologies. If even this solution does not work, external knowledge source is solicited and new knowware is constructed from scratch. There are two ways for providing knowware service, i.e. compiling or interpreting. In the compiling approach, the composing middleware operates on the selected original knowware to generate new knowware, while in the interpreting approach, it does not make any physical change to the knowware base, by just providing a view of new knowware by the related middleware (see Figure 7). The former is helpful to the knowware base reuse, but needs to reorganize the base every time when new knowware is to be generated, so the efficiency will be influenced, while the latter will consume time and space when composing new views of knowware, but performing better in some situations, especially for the running system (see the next section).

Figure 7 shows the knowware reuse cycle of the PROMIS/KW framework The knowware generation module condenses the major part of the furnace model. Domain users provide enterprise information rather then information system requirements.

It is to conclude from what we said above, that the life cycle model of knowware engineering is not fixed and unchangeable. Given a practical

Figure 7. PROMIS based on knowware

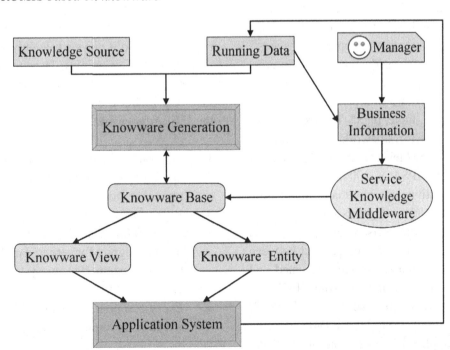

case, there may be more then one choice of life cycle models available. On the other hand, it is sometimes better to include more then one life cycle model in single knowware engineering. They may be even used in a nested way.

7. RAPID PROTOTYPING TECHNIQUE OF KNOWWARE ENGINEERING IN POST-J2EE AGE: THE NEXT STEP (2)

As pointed out in Mei et al. (2005), J2EE's emergence has three reasons. The first one is "the practice of component based software engineering", in which "component based software development, sometimes called component based software engineering, is a way of software reuse which is based on object technique, focusing on constructing software through reusable component design and construction". The second is the "deepening of enterprise computing". The enterprises "need to support several kinds of services for distribution, catalog, transaction, security, permanence, parallelism etc". The solution provided by Java is "integrating these enterprise services into containers, and invoking these services according to the configuration to satisfy the application needs". The third reason is "the widespread use of Internet which moves people to change the conventional Client/Server structure to a 3-layer architecture of representation, logic, data". The examples of implementing J2EE framework can be found in reports of PKUAS (Mei et al., 2004, 2005; Huang et al., 2004 (COMPSAC), 2004, 2006).

In this situation, our automatic application software generator must get essential improvement to fulfill the enterprise requirements in the new era. We will make a comparison between PROMIS/KW, which is virtually designed and has never been implemented, with the J2EE based version of PROMIS, which we will call PROMIS/KW*. The main idea is to let PROMIS generate J2EE-based application systems automatically.

PROMIS/KW* keeps the following principles of the original PROMIS/KW:

1. Domain knowledge automatic acquisition and domain ontology modeling based on pseudo natural language techniques;
2. Business information description based on pseudo natural language;
3. Application's function modeling based on domain (knowware) ontology base and user business information description;
4. Application's architecture modeling based on environment knowledge base, which includes knowledge about the environment where the software product will run, and system function models;
5. Automatic application generation based on architecture models;
6. Automatic application evolution based on empirical data mining and domain knowledge updating.

These six principles are all for application system automatic generation and evolution, and none of them relates to the J2EE framework. J2EE concerns only the deployment and running of the system, it does not consider automatic generation or evolution. So it plays a role only between the fifth and sixth principles. Despite of all these features, J2EE does have some influences over the six principles. Now let's see the essence of the J2EE framework:

1. Software is composed of components;
2. Deployment is divided into three layers: representation, logic and data;
3. Representation layer stores the application program for client, logic layer stores application program for server, data layer stores backup system (legacy system, database, etc.);
4. Every component is situated in containers, which is its running environment.

5. Inspecting the interaction among J2EE, PROMIS and knowware, some noticeable problems arise and need to be solved. They are:

   a. There is no place for PROMIS to play a role in J2EE's 3-layer architecture. Strictly speaking, another three layers are needed for placing PROMIS. They are foundation layer (domain knowledge base and its automatic generation), development layer (application system generation based on domain knowledge base), and evolution layer (the application evolves automatically during system running). So PROMIS/KW* has a 6-layer architecture. We could separate the generation and running parts of the application system. In this case the foundation and development layers could be removed, but evolution layer is definitely necessary.

   b. Because of the emergence of knowware and knowledge middleware, it is not clear about how to organize software, knowware and knowledge middleware into components. Should all of them be transformed into components, or just part of them? If they are transformed into components, does the union of them represent a component, or each of them becomes a component separately?

   c. The deployment of the correlated software, knowware and knowledge middleware among the multiple layers remains also an un-addressed problem.

6. Below we list a brief solution to the questions above.

7.1 The Hierarchical Structure of PROMIS/KW*

This is the biggest difference between PROMIS/KW and PROMIS/KW*. In PROMIS (PROMIS/KW included), all applications are mapped to a Client/Server architecture that is described by a program in NEWCOM language. Under the background of J2EE, PROMIS/KW* should take the 3-layer architecture including representation, logic and data. But that is not yet all. In fact the 3-layer architecture does not consider the system evolution, while PROMIS does. So what PROMIS/KW* shows is at least a 4-layer structure, in which the first three layers correspond to the three layers in J2EE, and the fourth layer is on evolution. It should be noted that although evolution does exist in PROMIS and PROMIS/KW, but they do not have a separate layer for it. As J2EE is famous for its 3-layer architecture, we accordingly treat system evolution as a single layer and call the framework with this additional layer J2EE/KW*, which is the "application system deployment" part in Figure 8, where rectangles represent knowledge,

Figure 8. The 6-layer architecture of PROMIS/KW**

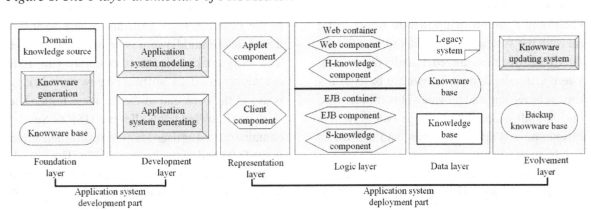

585

data or information; ellipses represent knowware or sets of knowware; trapezohedrons represent programs (software).

From this part we can see that the evolution layer contains a backup knowware base, as well as a knowware renewing system. The basis of knowware renewing lies in the data layer, where the original knowware base and system running data are kept. The monitor middleware of knowware renewing system continuously analyzes the trends of running data, extracts rules and provides them to the knowledge crystal maintenance middleware which uses this information to modify the old knowledge crystals to form new ones and to use new crystals to produce new knowware to replace the old ones. There are two choices now, i.e. to give the right of deciding how to replace the old knowware with new one to the users or to the system. If the latter is chosen, users should authorize the system and set the knowware evolution pattern as "auto". No matter which pattern is used, this can be performed in the hot deployment way. The system first interrupts all accesses to the knowware to be renewed, and saves the current running state, and finally recovers the running state and all accesses after the renewing.

Domain knowware base in the evolution layer does not need to be organized as only one piece of knowware, but as a set (a tree, a graph) of knowware. When updating the knowware base, it is not necessary to update the whole base simultaneously. In fact, only part of the base has to be changed. That is not only for reducing the cost of updating, but also for supporting the hot deployment as well. When only a subset of knowware needs to be renewed, the system need not halt to wait for the whole base to be reorganized. Usually the running system visits the domain knowware base with a domain browsing middleware. This middleware considers all isolated knowledge ontology as a unified one in a speculative way and constructs models on this basis.

But the 4-layer architecture is not sufficient to express completely the fundamental idea of PRO-

MIS. To do this, domain knowledge base automatic generation part and application system automatic generation part should be included. This is to say, two more layers are needed: the foundation layer and the development layer. The functions of these two layers cannot be substituted by the evolution layer, because the evolution layer can only improve the performance of the application system in the business intelligence aspect and it cannot make any big modification to the system architecture. Further, only knowware can be changed by the evolution layer, while all others including software and knowledge middleware cannot be changed. Also it cannot add new knowware.

In conclusion, we need six layers for the whole system. We call it PROMIS/KW**.

7.2 The Organization and Deployment of Components

Technically, the knowware-based development and the component-based development are consistent with each other. Knowware does not undermine the component based software development mechanism. On the contrary, it is the further refinement and development of the component technology. One of the critical problems is how to design the components of PROMIS/KW** in the presence of knowware and knowledge middleware. The following five solutions are worth to be considered.

The first solution is to treat knowware components as (read-only) data, and put them in data logic part. All knowledge middleware are put in the business logic part, and where to insert a knowledge middleware is decided by its type. The (S-type) knowledge middleware (the EJB container) used as software-knowware bridge is put in the back end of the business logic. The (H-type) knowledge middleware (JSP or Servlet container) used as user-knowware interface is put in the front end of the business logic. The knowledge components in the evolution layer are called R-type knowledge components. The drawback of this solution is that it separates the knowware from the knowledge middleware operating on it. Each time the knowledge middleware accesses the knowware, it has to go through the space between business logic and data logic and the container in which the knowledge middleware stays, so the efficiency will be influenced. It just suits for the situation where there are immense knowware and few accesses.

The second solution treats knowware as components. In this sense, there are three kinds of components, i.e. the software component, the knowware component and the knowledge middleware component. This solution has two disadvantages. On the one hand, pure knowware does not contain programs and should belong to the data logic part like data. So it is no good to put them in the application logic as components. On the other hand, when accessing a piece of knowware, a knowledge middleware must be involved. So it will definitely influence the efficiency to treat knowware and knowledge middleware as different components, especially in the "one container for one component" framework. Invoking any piece of knowware has to cross the containers' border that is very unworthy.

The third solution is binding knowware with the related knowledge middleware and put them in one component. It is also possible to combine part of a knowware object and part of a knowledge middleware object into a new software object, according to the needs of implementing systems. This can improve the performance. Generally the relation between knowware and knowledge middleware is neither one-to-one mapping nor one-to-many mapping, but many-to-many. So this leads to a question, i.e. which principle we should follow to bind them together? There are some possibilities:

1. Construct a graph in which knowware and knowledge middleware are vertices and the bindings between them are edges. Make each connected sub-graph as a component.

2. A component consists of a piece of knowware as the core and all the knowledge middleware operating on the knowware as the surrounding. For any knowledge middleware that relates to more than one piece of knowware, make multiple copies of the middleware so that each copy operates only on one piece of knowware. The number of components in this solution is the number of knowware pieces.

3. One way to implement the second solution is to bind all the knowledge middleware with the core knowware and then form one big object.

4. A component consists of a piece of knowledge middleware as the core and all the pieces of knowware operated on by the middleware as the surrounding. For any knowware that relates to many pieces of knowledge middleware, make multiple copies of the knowware so that each copy is operated on by only one middleware. The number of components in this solution is the number of knowledge middleware pieces.

5. One way to implement the fourth solution is to bind the core knowledge middleware with all the pieces of knowware it operates on. So a set of objects containing both knowware and knowledge middleware can be obtained.

For each particular application, the solution for constructing components should consider all factors that influence the efficiency that may be a compromise or mixture.

The fourth solution is to construct a mixed component containing part of software component and part of knowware (and knowledge middleware) component. This solution is suitable when the software function modules are closely related with the knowware modules.

The fifth solution is to combine the former four solutions together according to the real situation. For example, put the knowware with few accesses in the data logic part, while bind those with many accesses with knowledge middleware and then put them in the business logic part. This may reduce the management cost.

In principle, we will take the fifth solution.

7.3 Language for Describing Components Organization and Deployment

The original PROMIS needs a middle layer to transform a program in pseudo natural language BIDL to the target code of the application system. This middle layer is called NEWCOM (Lu et al., 1998) . It is an architecture description language for the system generated by PROMIS. PROMIS does not make an executable system directly from the application system's function model, but transform the model into an architecture description in NEWCOM and then compile this description to some target code through a NEWCOM compiler. The application system developer and its user can examine the application system's architecture and function structure in this NEWCOM layer and make necessary adjustments according to the real situation without being trapped in the details of coding. This provides the user with a means to interfere in the generating mechanism of PROMIS. Furthermore, the NEWCOM program is compiled into a program in VC++, in which the data processing part is implemented through ODBC in order to reduce the dependence on a particular database. That will make PROMIS capable of running with any database supporting ODBC. Thirdly, NEWCOM is a Client/Server based architecture description language and is suitable for describing this kind of system. Finally, the application system generated by NEWCOM enhances the data security management, and it does not only restrict the data access and operation authority, but employs the data encapsulation principle as well. NEWCOM is not just the backend of PROMIS; it is also an independent application system-developing tool and can be used to write application system directly.

In PROMIS/KW**, such an architecture description language is also needed, even though it will be very different from NEWCOM, because we take the 4-layer model instead of the 3-layer model of J2EE (although PROMIS/KW** has six layers itself, but the application system it generates can only run on the 4-layer architecture framework without the foundation layer and the development layer). We call this language NEWCOM/KW. Box 1 lists the core of NEWCOM/KW's syntax, which is overly simplified. For example, knowware is limited to be placed in the last two layers.

In Box 1, each "node" is a logic node and each logic node has its content divided in many parts. The physical distribution of each node's parts is dynamically determined at the deployment phase of the system. One logic node can be located at several physical nodes, and vice versa. Data protection is implemented through the declaration of the input and output parameters. Each input part specifies the procedures that are allowed to access this node and the authority of these accesses (read, writ, etc.). Each output part specifies which content of this node is allowed to be accessed. For example, if procedure A accesses a relation C in database B, the following two conditions must both be satisfied: A is in B's input part and C is in B's output part.

7.4 The Service Organization of PROMIS/KW**

Compared with the job J2EE has in mind (build large distributed enterprise information system), the original PROMIS is supposed to target at rather small-sized enterprise information systems. Currently, many new services are needed to support enterprise computing such as distribution, catalog, transaction, security, permanence and parallelism. Fortunately, we have J2EE supporting technique like PKUAS, so that many things need not to be done at the knowware engineering level. One important foundation of PROMIS is the domain knowledge modeling meanwhile one

Box 1. The basic syntax of NEWCOM/KW

```
<network part>  ::= NETWORK (<network name>)";"
                    [PROTOCOL  = < internet protocol name >;]
                     {<subnet part>}₁ⁿ
                     END_OF_NETWORK;
<subnet part>  ::= NETWORK (<subnet name>)";"
                    [PROTOCOL  = < network protocol name >;]
                    {<node part>}₁ⁿ
                     END_OF_NETWORK;
<node part> ::= <description layer node> | <business layer node> | <data layer node>
            | <evolution layer node>
<representation layer node> ::= REPRESENTATION(<representation layer node name>)
                                APPLET (<applet name>)
                                        [<input part>]
                                        [<procedure part>)
                                CLIENT (<user program name>)
                                        [<input part>)
                                         <user procedure part>
                                END_OF_REPRESENTATION
<business layer node> ::= BUSINESS(<business layer node name>)
                          [WEB =<WEB component name>
                                (input part)]
                                (procedure part)]₁ⁿ
                          [JSP =<JSP component name>
                                [(input part)]
                                 (procedure part)]₁ⁿ
                          [EJB =(EJB component name)
                                [(input part)]
                                 <procedure part>]₁ⁿ
                          END_OF_BUSINESS
<data layer node>  ::= DATA(<data layer node name>)
                       [DBMS=<DBMS name>
                             [(input part)]
                              (output part)
                             [<database operating part>]₁ⁿ
                              <data part>]₁ⁿ
                       [LEGACY=<legacy system name>
                              [<input part>]
                               (output part)
                              [<legacy operation name>]₁ⁿ
                               <legeacy part>]₁ⁿ
                       [KNOWWARE=<knowware name>
                                 (output part)
                                 [<knowledge middleware part>]₁ⁿ
                                  <knowware part>]₁ⁿ
                       END_OF_DATA
<evolution layer node>  ::= EVOLUTION(<evolution layer node>)
                            RUNDATA=<system running database name>
                                    [<input part>]
                                     <output part>
                                     <data part>
                            MONITOR =(monitor middleware part)
                            MINING =(mining middleware part)
                            K-CRYSTAL =(knowledge crystal name)
                                        [<input part>]
                                         (output part)
                                         (data part)
                            WRAPPING = <package middleware part>
                            KNOWWARE = <knowware set>
                            END_OF_EVOLUTION
```

major characteristic of PKUAS is to pay more attention to the application server of specific domain. However, PKUAS only puts its focus on the general techniques about how to take care of specific domain user needs. PROMIS/KW*, on the other hand, includes the domain analysis and domain modeling parts and thus provide more powerful tools for domain users to build their own enterprise information systems. In principle, we can knowwarelize all the services, and then make the online evolution of system easily.

8. RELATED WORK AND CONCLUSION

Knowledge based software engineering (KBSE) has been studied a lot in literature. It almost involves all the aspects and all the life cycle stages of software engineering. Their common characteristic is the knowledge based character. Works on KBSE have been in particular active in the realm of management information systems. This is also the area where we have started our research in KBSE. We mention the Project DAIDA (Jarke, 1990) which utilizes a software engineering database that includes knowledge of every stage from requirement specification to system implementation. It transforms the constraints of data and transactions into the abstract machine and at last into a program coded in database language DBPL. It therefore can support the design and implementation of information systems. IRIS system (Vassiliou et al., 1990) generates an information system from an object oriented requirement specification. CADDY (Engels et al., 1992 (CASE)) is a CASE tool, which can start from an extended entity-relationship model (Engels et al., 1992 (Journal)) to generate an information system. Another characteristic of KBSE is that most of its approaches start from requirements engineering (Mylopoulos et al., 1999; Kundun, 2007). Yu proposed an agent oriented modeling frame, i.e. i* (Yu, 1997), which focuses on analyzing all the

relative factors in software engineering requirement, such as goals, beliefs, competence and commitment to identify the mutual dependency relation between elements such as goals, tasks, resource (including soft resource, i.e. optimization). After that, i* framework has been combined with other software engineering techniques (Wang et al., 2001; Vilkomir et al., 2004). Another work is the Tropos methodology (Castro et al., 2002; Fuxman et al., 2004), which divides the software development process into early requirement analysis (i* framework), late requirement analysis, system architecture, and detailed design, which can be carried out by Jack programming platform. Bhuiyan et al. (2007) combined i* framework for early requirement analysis and UML technique for late requirement analysis to form a suit of requirement modeling techniques. A traditional technique of knowledge-based software engineering, the software reuse, which has the logo: "composing instead of programming", is still active (Monroe, 1996). Recently, software reuse gradually applies to the Web, and the discovery and combination of Web services is an important new technique in the new situation (MacIlraith, 2001; Bansal, 2003).

Compared with the above work, PROMIS has five main features. First, PROMIS does not start with requirements analysis, thus it does not demand the users to provide requirements, but directly starts from the information description given by users to automatically generate the model of management information systems. Secondly, PROMIS supports the thorough automation of implementing application systems, and does not need to code in advanced language in principle. Thirdly, it specially emphasizes the roles of the domain knowledge that is acquired, stored and managed separately from software engineering knowledge. Fourthly, PROMIS uses pseudo natural language technique, and that makes it easy for the domain expert to provide domain knowledge, for users to give the enterprise information description and for itself to give the key to software engineering and maintenance to users. Fifthly, PROMIS contains models for all layers from enterprise information description, to function model of application system, then to the structure model, and finally to coding. Therefore it is evolution and reuse friendly. Each time when one wants to modify, maintain or upgrade the existing system, or to develop a similar new system, one can always make use of these models with necessary changes.

In Eagle project, we emphasized separating the development of domain knowledge and software. And we found that domain knowledge should be commercialized as software had been. But we did not find a proper form at that time for the commercialized knowledge. Now we have found it. That is knowware. In 2005, the first paper on knowware was published (Lu, 2005 (Journal)). In the following research, we made further progress on the research of knowware engineering (Lu, 2005 (Journal)), knowware/software co-engineering (Lu, 2006, 2007), object-oriented knowware developing framework (Lu, 2010), knowware as service (Lu, 2007 (Book)), and the application of knowware in the information system development (Lu & Jin, 2006), etc. The paper Lu & Jin (2008) made a further development of the idea proposed in Lu & Jin (2006) and combined the software automatic generating technique in PROMIS with knowware and J2EE, and found a knowware based soft/ knowware co-developing framework. The present chapter is an extension of Lu & Jin (2008) mainly in two aspects, namely, section 3 and section 7 are new. The former extends the preliminary ideas on object oriented knowware programming drafted in Lu (2010) to a relatively complete theory and technique of object oriented mixware engineering, which includes the results in several recent keynote talks of the first author, which are not listed here. Section 7 reports new applications of knowware in two fast developing areas, i.e. smart rooms and Web search techniques. These are actually not yet all. The second contributor of the smart room work (Lu, 2013), Dr. Ge Li, has made yet other contributions on knowware application. He has created a knowware base of

software engineering knowledge and one of common medical knowledge. The medical knowware was developed in cooperation with Northeast University and has not yet been published.

We have also noticed that the knowware concept was accepted and further elaborated by other research labs (Ding, 2005, 2006, 2007 (Journal), 2007; Ding & Nadkami, 2007: Ding & Lo, 2008, 2009). Liya Ding introduced the concept of knowware system to mean a collaborating system of interacting components, where some components are knowware and others are intelligent components. In our terminology, their intelligent components are actually knowledge middleware. A knowware contains only knowledge but nothing else. Everything which helps and supports knowware to function in some software or hardware environments is knowledge middleware. A knowware system is actually a knowware development platform. We appreciate that the above authors have developed such a platform.

We should say that knowware-based software engineering is still an on-going work. Lots of efforts should be done in the future for developing the methodology, the supporting tool, the programming language, and the formal semantics. There are many challenges in front of us. One of them is to merge the methodologies and techniques developed in both software engineering and knowledge engineering to build a technical framework of software/knowware co-engineering, which is called mixware engineering in this chapter. Moreover, the experience in developing PROMIS tells us that a methodology cannot be successful without the support of a series of tools. For us, the major part of such tools may include a series of languages (e.g. domain knowledge description language and software/knowware description languages) and their implementation. We need to develop a series of J2EE based techniques and a series of PROMIS/KW** tools and languages, so that the automatic generation and evolution of application software can be realized in a J2EE based framework. Finally, the formal semantics of knowware and software/knowware co-engineering is a much bigger challenge among others. That will be one of our future directions of research.

ACKNOWLEDGMENT

This work is partially supported by the National Basic Research 973 program of China under Grant No. 2009CB320701, the Key Project of National Natural Science Foundation of China under Grant No. 61232015, and National Natural Science Foundation of China under Grant No 61073023. The authors thank MADIS Key Lab and Sino-Australian Joint Lab for Quantum Computing for their consistent support to the work described in this paper. The authors also thank Lu Yangyang for helping drawing the figures of this chapter and thank the anonymous reviewers for their valuable comments and suggestions.

REFERENCES

Bansal, S., & Vidal, J.-M. (2003). Matchmaking of Web services based on the DAML-S service model. In *Proceedings of International Joint Conference on Autonomous Agents and Multi-Agent Systems* (AAMAS'03) (pp.926—927). AAMAS.

Bhuiyan, M., Islam, M., & Krishna, S. et al. (2007). Integration of agent-oriented conceptual models and UML activity diagrams using effect annotations. [COMPSAC.]. *Proceedings of, COMPSAC07*, 171–178.

Castro, J., Kolp, M., & Mylopoulos, J. (2002). Towards requirement-driven information system engineering: the Tropos project. *Information Systems*, (27): 365–389. doi:10.1016/S0306-4379(02)00012-1

Chakraborty, A., et al. (2012). The role of requirement engineering in software development life cycle. *Journal of emerging trends in computing and information sciences, 3* (5), 723-729.

Ding, L. (2005). A model of hierarchical knowledge representation—toward knowware for computing with words. In *Proc. 6th International conference on intelligent technologies* (pp.188-197). Academic Press.

Ding, L. (2006). Knowware system for the development of intelligent systems. In *Proceedings of 7th International Conference on Intelligent Technologies* (Tech2006) (pp. 201-210). Academic Presss.

Ding, L. (2007). Design and development of knowware system. In *Proceedings of 2nd International conference on innovative computing, Information and Control* (pp. 17-21). Kumamoto.

Ding, L. (2007). A model of hierarchical knowledge representation—toward knowware for intelligent systems. *Journal of advanced computational intelligence and intelligent informatics, 11*(10), 1232- 1240.

Ding, L., & Lo, S.-L. (2008). Truth value flow inference in hybrid KBS constructed by KWS. In *Proceedings of 3rd International conference on innovative computing, information and control* (pp.311-314). Dalian, China: IEEE Computer Society.

Ding, L., & Lo, S.-L. (2009). Inference in knowware system. In *Proc. of 8th International conference on machine learning and cybernetics*, (pp. 215-220). Academic Press.

Ding, L., & Nadkami, S. (2007). Automatic construction of knowledge-based system using knowware system. In *Proc. of the 6th international conference on machine learning and cybernetics* (pp. 19-22). Academic Press.

Engels, G., Gogolla, G., & Hohenstein, U. et al. (1992). Conceptual modelling of database application using an extended ER model. *Data & Knowledge Engineering*, *9*(2), 157–204. doi:10.1016/0169-023X(92)90008-Y

Engels, G., & Lohr-Richter, P. (1992). CADDY--A highly integrated environment to support conceptual database design. In *Proc. of the 5th Int. Workshop on CASE* (pp.19 – 22). Montreal, Canada: CASE.

Fuxman, A., Liu, L., & Mylopoulos, J. et al. (2004). Specifying and analyzing early requirements in Tropos. *Requir Engin*, *9*(2), 132–150. doi:10.1007/s00766-004-0191-7

Hou, L., Jin, Z., & Wu, B. (2006). Modeling and verifying web services driven by requirements: An ontology based approach. *Sci China Ser F-Inf Sci*, *49*(6), 792–820. doi:10.1007/s11432-006-2031-5

Huang, G., Liu, T., Mei, H., et al. (2004). Towards autonomic computing middleware via reflection. In *Proceedings of 28th Annual International Computer Software and Applications Conference* (COMPSAC) (pp. 122—127). Hongkong, China: COMPSAC.

Huang, G., Mei, H., & Yang, F. (2004). Runtime software architecture based on reflective middleware. *Sci China Ser F-Inf Sci*, *47*(5), 555–576. doi:10.1360/03yf0192

Huang, G., Mei, H., & Yang, F. (2006). Runtime recovery and manipulation of software architecture of component-based systems. *Int J Auto Software Engin*, *13*(2), 251–278.

Jarke, M., Jeusfeldet, M., Mylopoulos, J., et al. (1990). *Information systems development as knowledge engineering: A review of the DAIDA project* (Technical Report MIP-9010). University of Passau.

Jin, Z., Lu, R., & Bell, D. (2003). Automatically multi-paradigm requirements modeling and analyzing: An ontology-based approach. [Series F]. *Science in China*, *46*(4), 279–297.

Kundu, S. (2007). Structuring software functional requirements for automated design and verification. [COMPSAC.]. *Proceedings of COMPSAC*, *07*, 127–134.

Lu, R. (2005). From hardware to software to knowware: IT's third liberation? *IEEE Intelligent Systems*, *20*(2), 82–85. doi:10.1109/MIS.2005.27

Lu, R. (2005). *Knowware research and fourth industry*. Paper presented at the Economic globalization and the choice of Asia. Shanghai, China.

Lu, R. (2006). Towards a software/knowware co-engineering. Invited Talk. In *Proceedings of KSEM 06*, (LNAI), (vol. 4092, pp. 23—32). Springer.

Lu, R. (2007). *Knowware, Knowware engineering and knowware/software co-engineering*. Paper presented at ICCS'07. Beijing, China.

Lu, R. (2007). *Knowware, the Third Star After Hardware and Software*. Polimetrica Publishing Co.

Lu, R. (2008). Knowware: A Commodity Form of Knowledge. In *Proceedings of RSKT 2008*, (LNAI), (vol. 5009, pp. 1-2). Springer.

Lu, R. (2010). Object-Oriented Knowware Programming and its Abstract Inheritance Semantics. In *Proc. of 2010 International Conference on Intelligent Systems and Knowledge Engineering* (pp. 1-4). Hangzhou, China: IEEE Computer Society.

Lu, R., Huang, Y., Sun, K., Chen, Z., Chen, Y., & Zhang, S. (2012). KACTL: Knowware based Automatic Construction of a Treelike Library from Web Documents. In *Proc. of International Conference on Web Systems and Applications* (WISM 2012), (LNCS), (vol. 7529, pp. 645-656). Springer.

Lu, R., & Jin, Z. (1997). A multi-agent and pseudo-natural language approach for intelligent information service. In *Proceedings of the International Conference on the Software Engineering and the Knowledge Engineering* (pp. 422-429). Madrid, Spain: Academic Press.

Lu, R., & Jin, Z. (1999). Knowledge based hierarchical software reuse. *Chinese J Adv Software Res*, *6*(1), 1–11.

Lu, R., & Jin, Z. (2000). *Domain Modeling based Software Engineering*. Boston: Kluwer Academic Publishers. doi:10.1007/978-1-4615-4487-6

Lu, R., & Jin, Z. (2002). Formal ontology: Foundation of domain knowledge sharing and reusing. *J Comp Sci Tech*, *17*(5), 535–548. doi:10.1007/BF02948822

Lu, R., & Jin, Z. (2003). Domain knowledge representation: Using an ontology language. In *Proceedings of Applied Informatics* (pp. 1302–1307). Innsbruck, Austria: IASTED/ACTA Press.

Lu, R., & Jin, Z. (2003). Automating application software generation. *Expert Systems: J Know Engin Neur Net*, *20*(2), 71–77. doi:10.1111/1468-0394.00227

Lu, R., & Jin, Z. (2006). Beyond knowledge engineering. *J Comp Sci Tech*, *21*(5), 790–799. doi:10.1007/s11390-006-0790-5

Lu, R., & Jin, Z. (2008). From knowledge based software engineering to knowware based software engineering. *Science in China Series F*, *51*(6), 638–660. doi:10.1007/s11432-008-0060-y

Lu, R., Jin, Z., & Chen, G. (2000). Ontology-oriented requirements analysis. *J Software*, *11*(8), 1009–1017.

Lu, R., Jin, Z., & Liu, L. et al. (1997). PROMIS 2.0: An intelligent case tool for MIS in the client/server application. [Xiamen.]. *Proceedings of, ISFST-97*, 399–405.

Lu, R., Jin, Z., Liu, L., et al. (1998). OSNET—A language for domain modeling. In *Proceedings of the Technology of Object-Oriented Languages and Systems* (pp.83-92). IEEE Computer Society.

Lu, R., Jin, Z., & Liu, L. et al. (1998). NEWCOM: An architecture description language in client/server style. *Journal of Complexity*, *21*(12), 1103–1111.

Lu, R., Jin, Z., & Wan, R. (1994). *PROMIS: A Knowledge-Based Approach for Automatically Prototyping Management Information Systems*. Paper presented at Avignon'94. Paris, France.

Lu, R., Jin, Z., & Wan, R. (1995). Requirement specification in pseudo language in PROMIS. In *Proc COMPSAC'95* (pp. 96—101). Dallas, TX: IEEE Computer Society.

Lu, R., Jin, Z., & Wan, R. et al. (1996). Acquiring the requirements based on domain knowledge. *J Software*, *7*(3), 137–144.

Lu, R., Jin, Z., & Xia, Y. (1996). An intelligent CASE tool for information management systems. In *Proceeding of the First International Conference on Future Computer Systems*. Academic Press.

Lu, Y., Li, G., Jin, Z., Xing, X., & Hao, Y. (2013). A knowware based infrastructure for rule based control systems in smart spaces. In *Proceedings of ICSR 2013*, (LNCS), (vol. 7925, pp. 289-294). Springer.

Maamar, Z., Mostefaoui, S.-K., & Yahyaoui, H. (2005). Toward an agent-based and context-oriented approach for Web services composition. *IEEE Transactions on Knowledge and Data Engineering*, *17*(5), 686–697. doi:10.1109/TKDE.2005.82

Mansour, O., & Ghazawneh, A. (2009). Research in Information Systems: Implications of the constant changing nature of IT capabilities in the social computing era. In *Proc. of the 32nd Information Systems Research Seminar in Scandinavia*. Academic Press.

McIlraith, S.-A., Son, T.-C., & Zeng, H.-L. (2001). Semantic Web Services. *IEEE Intelligent Systems*, *16*(2), 46–53. doi:10.1109/5254.920599

Mei, H., & Huang, G. (2004). PKUAS: An architecture-based reflective component operating platform. In *Proceedings of 10th IEEE International Workshop on Future Trends of Distributed Computing Systems* (FTDCS) (pp.163—169). Suzhou, China: FTDCS.

Mei, H., Huang, G., & Cao, D.-G. et al. (2005). Anatomy and Evaluation on J2EE Technology. *Communications of China*, *1*(4), 26–35.

Monroe, R.-J., & Gailen, D. (1996). Style based reuse for software architectures. In *Proceedings of the 1996 International Conference on Software Reuse* (pp.84—93). Academic Press.

Mu, K., Jin, Z., & Lu, R. (2011). Measuring software requirements evolution caused by inconsistency. *International Journal of Software and Informatics*, *6*(3), 419–434.

Mylopoulos, J., Chung, L., & Yu, E. (1999). From object-oriented to goal-oriented requirement analysis. *CACM*, (42), 31—37.

Nonaka, I., & Takeuchi, H. (1995). *The Knowledge Creating Company: How Japanese Companies Create Dynamics of Innovation*. Oxford University Press.

Vassiliou, Y., Marakakis, M., Katalagarianos, P., et al. (1990). IRIS: A mapping assistant for generating designs from requirements. In *Proc. of the Conf. on Advanced Information Systems Engineering* (LNCS), (vol. 436, pp. 307—338). Springer.

Vilkomir, S., Ghose, A., & Krishna, A. (2004). Combining agent-oriented conceptual modeling with formal methods. In *Proceedings of ASWEC* (pp.147—157). ASWEC.

Wang, P., Jin, Z., & Liu, L. et al. (2008). Building towards capability specifications of web services based on an environment ontology. *IEEE Transactions on Knowledge and Data Engineering*, *20*(4), 547–561. doi:10.1109/TKDE.2007.190719

Wang, X., & Lespérance, Y. (2001). Agent-oriented requirements engineering using ConGolog and i*. [AOIS.]. *Proceedings of AOIS*, *2001*, 59–78.

Yu, E. (1997). Towards modeling and reasoning support for early phase requirement engineering. In *Proceedings of 3rd IEEE International Symposium on Requirements Engineering* (pp. 226—235). IEEE.

KEY TERMS AND DEFINITIONS

Crystallization Model: A life cycle type of knowware engineering which, like the salt crystallization process from the see water, collects knowledge elements from a huge information space uninterruptedly with a knowledge pump and makes them to knowledge crystals, which will be renewed steadily by a knowledge kidney each time when fresh knowledge is coming.

Furnace Model: A life cycle type of knowware engineering which, like a smelting furnace accepting raw iron ores or used iron objects, smelting them to iron magma to cast different products, accepts different kinds of knowledge sources, decomposes them to small granule knowledge elements called knowledge magma to edit new knowledge products upon requests.

Knowledge Middleware: A class of software routines/utilities making knowware operational by supporting its development, management, transformation and application across its whole lifecycle.

Knowware: The representation of a read only knowledge module that is independent, commercialized, suitable for computer manipulation, meeting some industrial standard, equipped with detailed documentation and embeddable in software or hardware for use.

Konwware Engineering: The systematic application of scientific and engineering principles to the methodology, development, operation, and maintenance of knowware.

Mixware: A functional system generated by coherently integrating a set of knowware and software (including knowledge middleware) modules.

Spiral Model: A life cycle type of knowware engineering which, while following the basic idea of Nonaka and Takeuchi on the recursive process of knowledge transformation between tacit and explicit knowledge through a spiral of internalization, socialization, externalization and combination, emphasizes the practice driven knowledge renewal.

Chapter 26
Software Evolution Visualization:
Status, Challenges, and Research Directions

Renato Lima Novais
Federal Institute of Bahia, Brazil

Manoel Gomes de Mendonça Neto
Fraunhofer Project Center for Software and Systems Engineering at UFBA, Brazil

ABSTRACT

Software Visualization is the field of Software Engineering that aims to help people to understand software through the use of visual resources. It can be effectively used to analyze and understand the large amount of data produced during software evolution. Several Software Evolution Visualization (SEV) approaches have been proposed. The goals of the proposed approaches are varied, and they try to help programmers and managers to deal with software evolution in their daily software activities. Despite their goals, their applicability in real development scenarios is questionable. In this chapter, the authors discuss the current state of the art and challenges in software evolution visualization, presenting issues and problems related to the area, and they propose some solutions and recommendations to circumvent them. Finally, the authors discuss some research directions for the SEV domain.

INTRODUCTION

Software evolution generally deals with large amounts of data that originates from heterogeneous sources such as Software Configuration Management (SCM) repositories, Bug Tracking Systems (BTS), mailing and project discussion lists. One of the key aspects of software evolution is to build theories and models that enable us to understand the past and present, as well as predict future properties related to software maintenance activities, and hence support software maintenance tasks.

Software Visualization (SoftVis) is the field of Software Engineering (SE) that aims to help people to understand software through the use of visual resources (Diehl, 2007), and it can be

DOI: 10.4018/978-1-4666-6026-7.ch026

effectively used to analyze and understand the large amount of data produced during software evolution. For this reason, many researchers have been proposing Software Evolution Visualization (SEV) tools (Kuhn, Erni, Loretan, Nierstrasz, 2010)(Voinea, Lukkien & Telea, 2007)(Fischer & Gall, 2004)(German, Hindle & Jordan, 2006) (Cepda, Magdaleno, Murta & Werner, 2010)(Eick, Steffen & Sumner Jr, 1992). In general, these tools analyze the evolution of the software with respect to a set of software maintenance related questions.

Despite the goals of the software evolution visualization approaches, most have yet to be used in industrial environments. SEV approaches usually provide good and attractive visual metaphors, but how to use them within the software development process remains an open question. Several SEV tools are proposed as proof of concepts that is not evolved anymore.

This chapter covers Software Evolution Visualization (SEV) approaches, providing information about how SEV research is structured, synthesizing current evidence on the goals of the proposed approaches and identifying key challenges for its use in practice. This text is based on a mapping study that was carried out to analyze how the SEV area is structured (Novais et al., 2013a).

In the following sections we will discuss the current state and challenges in software evolution visualization. We will present issues and problems related to the area, and propose some solutions and recommendations to circumvent them. Finally, we will discuss some research directions for the SEV domain.

BACKGROUND

Software Visualization

Software visualization (SoftVis) can be defined as the mapping of any kind of software artifact in graphic representations (Koschke, 2003) (Roman & Cox, 1992). SoftVis is very helpful because it transforms intangible software entities and their relationships into visual metaphors that are easily interpretable by human beings. Consider coupling among software modules as an example. Using a graph as a visual metaphor, these modules can be represented as nodes and the coupling information can be represented as directed edges to build an intuitive visual metaphor for their dependency. Without a visual representation, the only way to analyze this information would be to look inside the source code or at a table of software metrics, a laborious task or one of great cognitive effort.

There are several classification taxonomies for SoftVis. Some divide SoftVis according to type of visualized object. Diehl (2007), for example, divides software visualization into visualizing the structure, behavior and evolution of the software. Structure refers to visualizing static parts of the software. Behavior refers to visualizing the execution of the software. Evolution refers to visualizing how software evolves (Diehl, 2007). SoftVis can also be classified according to the metaphors it uses to represent software. Among others, visualizations can use iconographic, pixel-based, matrix-based, graph-based and hierarchical metaphors (Keim, 2002) (Ferreira de Oliveira & Levkowitz, 2003).

Software can also be visually analyzed from different perspectives (Carneiro et al., 2008)(Carneiro, Santanna, & Mendonça, 2010)(Carneiro et al., 2010)(Carneiro & Mendonça, 2013). In this case, visualization can be classified according to the point of view it provides to engineers to explore a software system. The perspectives concern to the way in which we look to the software. In the context of software, the perspective may be represented by a set of coordinated views designed to represent a group of properties of the software.

There are several software perspectives (Novais et al., 2013a). Common perspectives in object-oriented programming are Structural, Inheritance and Coupling. Common perspectives in software evolution are Change and Authorship. For example, one might be interested in investigating software according to its structure. This structural perspective reveals how the software is organized into packages, classes and methods. The IDEs usually provide a hierarchical view for this purpose. Eclipse's package explorer is a well-known example of such a view. It uses an iconographic tree to represent the system's package and file structure. Treemap, by Johnson and Shneiderman (1991), is another well-known view that can be used to portray the Structural perspective.

Another perspective of interest in OO systems is the Inheritance perspective. It is important to visually show which classes extend others or implement certain interfaces. In this case, it is also possible to use a hierarchical view, like Treemaps. However, in order to avoid confusion, it is important to use another type of view. One example that can be used in this case is Polymetric views (Lanza & Ducasse, 2003).

The third perspective discussed here is the Coupling perspective. It represents the coupling between software entities, in this case, software modules that depend on other modules. One of the most useful views to describe this kind of information is Interactive Directed Graphs (IDG).

The fourth is the Authorship perspective. It highlights authors' activities such as how many commits they have performed or on which files they have worked. It answers questions such as "Who made these modifications to the code?"

Finally, the fifth perspective is the Changes perspective. This shows the changes made to the code. Views that address this perspective show the changes throughout the history of the piece of software. This is an inherent software evolution perspective[1].

Software Evolution Visualization

Recognition that the use of software visualization can also help to analyze software evolution is not new. Early works in the area are about 20 years old. However, in recent years a growing body of relevant work is being developed in the area.

An early work in the area was Seesoft, proposed by Eick, Steffen and Sumner Jr (1992). The Seesoft maps lines of code into a thin line on the computer screen. The color of each line indicates an attribute (or statistic, as the authors define) of interest. Seesoft was designed not only for viewing evolution. It enables developers to, for example: a) make static analysis to determine where functions are called in the code b) analyze dynamics, for profiling in which the memory used and execution time of the program are shown (Eick, Steffen & Sumner Jr 1992). For software evolution visualization, Seesoft shows the age of the source code lines. It uses colors to represent the age of the source code lines. The most recently modified lines are painted in red, the oldest in blue. There is an interpolation between these two colors to represent the lines for ages in between. In the same year, Gulla (1992) proposed a set of visualization techniques designed to improve support for maintenance of large software systems. The author used the term multi-version visualizations because visual representation containing information from several versions of the software is computed.

In 2001, Lanza proposed the Evolution Matrix to visualize the evolution of software (Lanza, 2001). Each line of the Evolution Matrix represents the whole evolution of a software class, and each row represents a version of the software. It is possible to observe some patterns in software evolution, such as the beginning of growth modules, stagnation in the development, etc. He also used an astronomy metaphor to analyze some aspects of the evolution of the classes. In this case, the evolution of the class was classified according to some types of stars (e.g. Pulsar, Supernova, Red Giant, etc.). In 10 years, this work has become the most cited within the Software Evolution Visualization community (Novais et al., 2013a).

D'Ambros, Lanza and Lungu (2009) proposed Evolution Radar, which is a visualization-based approach that integrates both file-level and module-level logical coupling information. Ripley, Sarma and van der Hoek (2007) proposed a visualization for software project awareness and evolution. Their approach presents an overview of the development activities of the entire team, providing insight into the evolution of the project based on SCM information. By same token, Storyboards is an animated visualization of software history that assists developers in spotting artifacts that are becoming more or less dependent on others (Beyer & Hassan, 2006). It tries to explain decay symptoms, highlighting refactoring candidates and spotting good structure.

Collberg et al. (2003) proposed a system for graph-based visualization of the evolution of software. This system visualizes the evolution of software using a novel graph drawing technique for visualizing large graphs with a temporal component. Vonea and Telea (2006) developed an open framework for CVS repository querying, analysis and visualization. This multi-perspective tool is an n-snapshot matrix that shows software evolution. Each column of the matrix shows the evolution of one metric.

Gonzalez et al. (2009) proposed an approach that presents a four-view design of an exploratory visualization for combined metrics-and-structure data for software evolution. The four views focus on different tasks and use-cases, showing: overview of the project commits structure and related metrics (timeline view); comparison of evolving package or class hierarchy structures over time (structure evolution view); trend analysis of metrics (metric view); and detailed code inspection (visualization of the indirect class coupling integrating source code viewing). Wu, Holt and Hassan (2004) used spectrographs to explore software evolution. The evolution spectrograph combines time, spectrum and property measurement coded in colors to characterize software evolution. The coloring technique used is to distinguish patterns easily in the evolutionary data.

Considering that the evolution data is multi-dimensional, some authors propose the use of animated visualization. The work of Langelier,

Sahraoui and Poulin (2008) is an example of this. They proposed an approach that uses animated visualization to explore the evolution of software quality.

More recently, Kuhn and Stocker (2012) proposed CodeTimeline. This is an approach that uses visualization to tell the story of the software project based on its versioning data. Notes can be used to share memories of events in the system's life cycle, such as justifications of the design used in the past. It can also be used to share more casual memories of the project team being viewed. CodeTimeline uses colors and vertical positioning to portray an authorship map of the system.

CURRENT STATE AND CHALLENGES IN SOFTWARE EVOLUTION VISUALIZATION

Issues and Problems

Several software evolution visualization approaches have been proposed in the literature. They are varied and focus on different problems. SEV has been used for: change prediction (Steinbruckner & Lewerentz, 2010)(Lungu and Lanza, 2010); authors contribution analysis (Muller et al., 2010)(Ogawa & Ma, 2010)(Voinea & Telea, 2007); defect prediction (Wu et al., 2004)(Wettel & Lanza, 2008)(Therón et al. (2007); reverse engineering (Fischer & Gall, 2006)(Balint, Marinescu, & Girba, 2006)(Beyer & Hassan, 2006); quality improvement (Goeminne & Mens, 2010)(Langelier, Sahraoui, & Poulin, 2008); process improvement (Wnuk, Regnell, & Karlsson, 2009a)(Wnuk, Regnell, & Karlsson, 2009b); identification of software anomalies (Mockus et al. 1999)(Rotschke & Krikhaar, 2002)(Fischer, Pinzger & Gall, 2003). Despite all these applications, most Software Visualization (SV) approaches are not widely used in industrial environments (Burkley, 2009). This may also be extended to software evolution visualization (SEV).

SEV approaches usually provide good and attractive visual metaphors, but how to use them within the software development process remains an open question. Most SEV tools are proposed as proof of concepts that is not evolved into robust products. The reasons for this are fourfold:

1. The proposals are not properly tied to practical software engineering goals - As any software engineering approach, software evolution visualization tools must be goal oriented (Basili et al., 2010). Many studies reported in the literature only describe their goal at a very high level of abstraction. They do not always focus on achieving real and practical software engineering goals, such as identification of candidates for refactoring (Fowler, 1999), predict buggy modules (Hata, Mizuno & Kikuno, 2012)(Giger et al., 2012), or feature modularization (Ribeiro et al., 2010)(Olszak & Jørgensen, 2012). When presenting their tools, many authors simply present examples of gained insights without giving systematic guidelines of how these insights are to be used. SEV tools must be associated with usage methodologies and guidelines.

2. They have not been evaluated thoroughly - Any SEV approach must focus on the end user and validate its usefulness in well-executed experiments or case studies. This means not proposing a new visually appealing visualization and executing a few feasibility studies on it. Unfortunately, the results we found in a mapping study show that there is little robust validation in the area (Novais et al., 2013a). Most SEV approaches are only partially validated, if validated at all.

3. There is little cooperative and comparative work in the area - Cooperative work would lead to faster improvement of existing approaches and to a deeper understanding of the area. Most of the works we found in the

literature attempt to develop new visualization approaches rather than validate or add value to existing ones. Many works found in the literature used the same open source software, e.g. Mozilla, Argo UML and Postgres. However, the authors never benchmarked their results against other approaches.

4. Approaches avoid combining different views and strategies of analysis - Most SEV approaches use only one view and many approaches would profit from combining and reusing well-established views. In order to expand the spectrum of applications, SEV approaches should combine multiple views, metrics and strategies of analysis.

Table 1 presents some software evolution visualization approaches found in the literature. For each SEV approach its general goal is presented, the evaluation type and visual strategy of analysis used, and the number of views. As can be observed, most of them have not been evaluated thoroughly, and combined few visual strategies of analysis and views.

SOLUTIONS AND RECOMMENDATIONS

Software evolution visualization tools must address practical software engineering issues therefore visualization tools should be task oriented. It is necessary to specify which SE goals they aim to reach and evaluate if they achieved those goals. Researchers should focus on answering questions like: Does my approach scale to larger real world software systems? How do my results generalize to other users, domains, and systems? Otherwise, there will always be an issue with the external validity of the proposed approach and, worse, the approach will encounter difficulties moving from state of the art to state of the practice in software engineering.

Table 1. Some SEV approaches, their goals, evaluation type used, visual strategies of analysis and number of views

SEV approaches	Goal	Evaluation Type	Visual Strategies of analysis	# of views
(Steinbruckner & Lewerentz, 2010)	change prediction	Feasibility study	Temporal Overview, Temporal Snapshot	1
(Lungu and Lanza, 2010)	change prediction	none	Temporal Overview, Temporal Snapshot	3
(Muller et al., 2010)	authors contribution analysis	Case study	Temporal Overview, Temporal Snapshot	>5
(Ogawa & Ma, 2010)	authors contribution analysis	Feasibility study	Temporal Overview	2
(Voinea & Telea, 2007)	authors contribution analysis	Feasibility study	Temporal Overview	2
(Wu et al., 2004)	defect prediction	Feasibility study	Temporal Overview, Temporal Snapshot	1
(Wettel & Lanza, 2008)	defect prediction	Feasibility study	Temporal Snapshot	2
(Therón et al. (2007)	defect prediction	Comparison with other tools	Temporal Overview	1
(Fischer & Gall, 2006)	reverse engineering	Feasibility study	Temporal Snapshot	2
(Balint, Marinescu, & Girba, 2006)	reverse engineering	Feasibility study	Temporal Overview	1
(Beyer & Hassan, 2006)	reverse engineering	Feasibility study	Temporal Snapshot	1
(Goeminne & Mens, 2010)	quality improvement	Feasibility study	Temporal Overview, Temporal Snapshot	1
(Langelier, Sahraoui, & Poulin, 2008)	quality improvement	Feasibility study	Temporal Snapshot	1
(Wnuk, Regnell, & Karlsson, 2009a)	process improvement	Feasibility study	Temporal Overview	1
(Wnuk, Regnell, & Karlsson, 2009b)	process improvement	Feasibility study	Temporal Overview	1
(Mockus et al. 1999)	identification of software anomalies	Feasibility study	Temporal Overview	1
(Rotschke & Krikhaar, 2002)	identification of software anomalies	none	Temporal Snapshot	1
(Fischer, Pinzger & Gall, 2003)	identification of software anomalies	Feasibility study	Temporal Overview, Temporal Snapshot	2

Furthermore, it is particularly important to validate the proposed approaches, especially with robust validation, such as controlled experiments or real case studies. Even though strong validation has a high cost and involves great effort, the validation is all the more worthwhile if it is associated with real software engineering goals. The best approach depends on the goal at hand.

Software evolution is a complex domain. Sometimes one needs to analyze the whole evolution of the software, while in other cases one may need to focus on specific modules. To address both cases, it is necessary to produce several views of the software. Some views can focus on representing the whole evolution of the software. Others may focus on a specific software module. The approaches should combine different views and metrics, supporting different strategies of analysis. The combination of strategies can occur in different ways. One may start from global views of the software, showing the whole evolution, and refine it into the details of chosen entities such as key packages, classes and methods. Another may start from a specific version in history, following up the analysis by providing a history-wide view of a selected module of interest. In general, approaches require the combination of different views portraying global and detailed representations of one or several versions of the software. As each view fits a specific goal, it is important to combine views in different levels of detail.

The use of common terminologies and taxonomies, such as the ones presented in (Keim, 2002) (Ferreira de Oliveira & Levkowitz, 2003) (Maletic & Collard, 2002)(Novais et al., 2013a), would facilitate the organization of the area for comparative and secondary studies on the novelty, complementarities and usefulness of the approaches.

RESEARCH DIRECTIONS

The use of visual resources to deal with the large amount of data produced by software evolution is worthwhile. However, there is much work to be done. It is always important to bear in mind the challenges previously discussed: SEV must be goal oriented and well validated to serve practical purposes. On top of this, the area should attempt to combine different data sources, metrics, views and strategies of analysis, into well-integrated SEV tools.

Following this same idea, it is important to combine visual strategies of analysis. A visual strategy of analysis defines how the evolution is visually presented for analysis (Novais and Mendonça, 2013)(Novais et al., 2013a). Due to the diverse set of software evolution comprehension tasks, it is desirable that SEV infrastructures support different strategies of analysis. There are differential and temporal strategies. Differential strategies (relative and absolute) focus on analyzing the differences between versions, while temporal strategies (overview, snapshot, and overview accumulative) describe several versions of the same visual scene.

SEV approaches should use data from different repositories. Evolutionary data can come from places as different as: software configuration management repositories, bug track systems, mailing lists, and the source code itself. Each repository provides different types of data, which are valuable for many software engineering tasks. The combination of them may lead to more powerful analyses.

By the same token, SEV approaches should use, or provide, a robust set of metrics for analysis. The user should be able choose the metrics that best fit the problem at hand. A SEV approach can suggest, as a default configuration, the use of a metric X or Y, but it should let the user choose the metrics that are displayed in its views.

At this point, one may ask how to visually portray all these data and metrics. Several works in the literature provide just one view, and try to enrich the view with all the data in the same visual scene. Excessively complex views can be produced in this case. They are attractive at first, but are difficult to use in a real world development process. To circumvent this problem, SEV approaches can combine different and simpler views in the environment. Therefore it is important to consistently combine views. Each view should provide a different perspective of the software and its evolution.

Views should also be well integrated, coordinated and interactive. From the point of view of integration, a SEV tool should provide one view as a central and reference point for the other views. When an element is identified in other views, the user should be able to easily move to the reference point. From the point of view of coordination, when an element is selected in one view, it should be highlighted in all other views. Finally, in terms of interaction, users should be able to use a set of widgets and other mechanisms to interact, request details on demand, zoom in, zoom out of selected elements shown in the views.

Any SEV approach should follow the KISS principle (Dalzell, 2009). This principle encourages simplicity. A complex visual scene can be attractive at first sight, but SEV approach designers should first focus on their use to solve practical software engineering problems. For that, designers should start by using simple visual scenes and incrementally validating and improving the proposed approaches.

Figure 1 shows an infrastructure that addresses the suggestions and recommendations presented here. First, it starts by using different software data repositories. These repositories can be Software

Configuration Management (SCM) systems, Bug Track Systems (BTS), Mailing List, or any other repositories that provide useful information for software analysis (e.g. feature mapping files (Novais et al., 2012b)(Novais et al., 2013b)). From these repositories, the SEV tool extracts valuable software evolution data. Observe that the data is not only the source code, but also any type of data related to the software under analysis. It is also important to note that the SEV tool should have a way to manually add data. This is important so as not to restrict the use of the SEV tools to a specific software repository.

After collecting and storing the raw data, the SEV tool should analyze the available data to structure the data, extract metrics, and when possible, link the data that come from different repositories. This last step is not easy. The

Figure 1. A software evolution visualization infrastructure

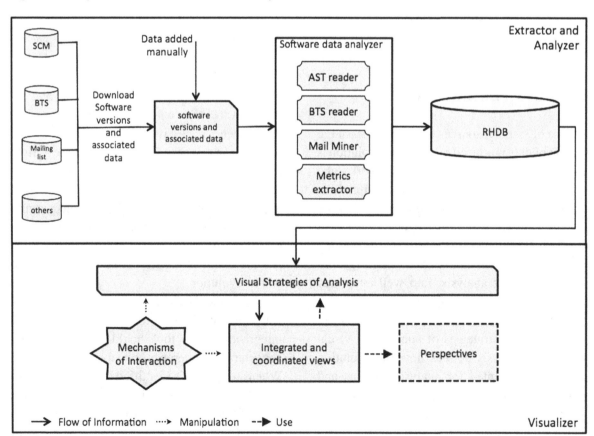

Software data analyzer has different modules: an Abstract Syntax Tree (AST) reader, a BST reader, a Mail miner, and Metrics extractor. Finally, the SEV tool may use a local own repository, called Release History Database (RHDB) for faster and easier access.

The second part of the suggested infrastructure concerns software visualization. It is important to use a set of integrated, coordinated and interactive views that address different perspectives and are able to visualize the evolution using different visual strategies of analysis. SEV tools should provide a set of mechanisms of interactions to correctly manipulate views, metrics, perspectives and strategies of analysis.

CONCLUSION

Software must evolve otherwise it dies (Lehman, 1978)(Lehman, 1980). Given this, evolution is a key topic in modern software engineering and maintenance. The evolution process produces large amounts of data that is stored in different types of data sources. All the data need to be managed. Software Visualization aims to help people to understand software through the use of visual resources. It can be effectively used to analyze and understand the large amount of data produced during software evolution.

Many researchers have proposed Software Evolution Visualization (SEV) tools. These tools aim to analyze and understand historical data with respect to a set of software maintenance goals. To address these goals the approaches usually provide interesting and attractive visual features.

However, their applicability in real development scenarios is questionable. In this text we discussed current state and challenges in software evolution visualization, presenting issues and problems related to the area, and proposed some solutions and recommendations to circumvent them. Finally, we discussed some research directions for the SEV domain.

Software evolution visualization has been used for different purposes. However, it is little used in industrial environments. This indicates that the area is failing to reach mainstream software engineering practices. Researchers have proposed many SEV approaches over the past years, but many have failed to clearly state their goals, tie them back to concrete and practical software engineering problems, and formally validate their usefulness. To circumvent these issues, a key direction may be the combination of different resources, such as data sources, metrics, perspectives, and strategies of analysis. Furthermore, a proposed multi-feature software evolution visualization approach should be incrementally built and validated.

REFERENCES

Balint, M., Marinescu, R., & Girba, T. (2006). How developers copy. In *Proceedings of the 14th IEEE International Conference on Program Comprehension*. IEEE Computer Society.

Basili, V. R., Lindvall, M., Regardie, M., Seaman, C., Heidrich, J., Münch, J., & Rombach, D. A. (2010). Trendowicz, Linking software development and business strategy through measurement. *Computer*, *43*(4), 57–65. doi:10.1109/MC.2010.108

Beyer, D., & Hassan, A. E. (2006). Evolution storyboards: Visualization of software structure dynamics. In *Proceedings of the 14th IEEE International Conference on Program Comprehension*. IEEE Computer Society.

Buckley, J. (2009). Requirements-Based Visualization Tools for Software Maintenance and Evolution. *Computer*, *42*(4), 106–108. doi:10.1109/MC.2009.127

Carneiro, G. F., Magnavita, R., Spínola, E., Spínola, F. O., & Mendonça, M. G. (2008). An Eclipse-Based Visualization Tool for Software Comprehension. In Proceedings of Sessão de Ferramentas do Simpósio Brasileiro de Engenharia de Software. Campinas.

Carneiro, G. F., & Mendonça, M. G. (2013). SourceMiner: A Multi-Perspective Software Visualization Environment. In *Proceedings of 15th International Conference on Interprise Information Systems* (ICEIS 2013), (pp. 30-42). Angers.

Carneiro, G. F., Santanna, C. N., & Mendonça, M. G. (2010). On the Design of a Multi-Perspective Visualization Environment to Enhance Software Comprehension Activities. In *Proceedings of Workshop de Manutenção Moderna de Software*. Bélem.

Carneiro, G. F., Silva, M., Santanna, C. N., Garcia, A. F., & Mendonça, M. G. (2010). Identifying Code Smells with Multiple Concern Views. In *Proceedings of Simpósio Brasileiro de Engenharia de Software*. Academic Press. doi:10.1109/SBES.2010.21

Cepda, R. S. V., Magdaleno, A. M., Murta, L. G. P., & Werner, C. M. L. (2010). Evoltrack: Improving design evolution awareness in Software development. *Journal of the Brazilian Computer Society, 16*(2), 117–131. doi:10.1007/s13173-010-0011-5

Collberg, C., Kobourov, S., Nagra, J., Pitts, J., & Wampler, K. (2003). A system for graph- based visualization of the evolution of software. In *Proceedings of the 2003 ACM symposium on Software visualization*. ACM.

D'Ambros, M., Lanza, M., & Lungu, M. (2009). Visualizing co-change information with the evolution radar. *IEEE Transactions on Software Engineering, 35*(5), 720–735. doi:10.1109/TSE.2009.17

Dalzell, T. (2009). *The Routledge Dictionary of Modern American Slang and Unconventional English*. Routledge.

Diehl, S. (2007). *Software visualization: visualizing the structure, behaviour, and evolution of software*. Springer-Verlag.

Eick, S. G., Steffen, J. L., & Sumner, E. E. Jr. (1992). Seesoft - A tool for visualizing line oriented software statistics. *IEEE Transactions on Software Engineering, 18*(11), 957–968. doi:10.1109/32.177365

Ferreira de Oliveira, M. C., & Levkowitz, H. (2003). From visual data exploration to visual data mining: a survey. *IEEE Transactions on Visualization and Computer Graphics, 9*(3), 378–394. doi:10.1109/TVCG.2003.1207445

Fischer, M., & Gall, H. (2004). Visualizing feature evolution of large-scale software based on problem and modification report data. *Journal of Software Maintenance and Evolution: Research and Practice - Analyzing the Evolution of Large-Scale Software, 16* (6), 385-403.

Fischer, M., & Gall, H. (2006). Evograph: A lightweight approach to evolutionary and structural analysis of large software systems. In *Proceedings of the 13th Working Conference on Reverse Engineering*. IEEE Computer Society.

Fischer, M., Pinzger, M., & Gall, H. (2003). Analyzing and relating bug report data for feature tracking. In *Proceedings of the 10th Working Conference on Reverse Engineering*. IEEE Computer Society.

Fowler, M. (1999). *Refactoring: Improving the Design of Existing Code*. Addison - Wesley Longman Publishing Co.

German, D., Hindle, A., & Jordan, N. (2006). Visualizing the evolution of software using softChange. *International Journal of Software Engineering and Knowledge Engineering*. doi:10.1142/S0218194006002665

Giger, E., D'Ambros, M., Pinzger, M., & Gall, H. C. (2012). Method--level bug prediction. In *Proceedings of ACM-IEEE International Symposium on Empirical Software Engineering and Measurement*. ACM/IEEE.

Goeminne, M., & Mens, T. (2010). A framework for analysing and visualising open source software ecosystems. In *Proceedings of the Joint ERCIM Workshop on Software Evolution (EVOL) and International Workshop on Principles of Software Evolution (IWPSE)*. ACM.

Gonzalez, A., Theron, R., Telea, A., & Garcia, F. J. (2009). Combined visualization of structural and metric information for software evolution analysis. In *Proceedings of the joint international and annual ERCIM workshops on Principles of software evolution (IWPSE) and software evolution (Evol) workshops*. ACM.

Gulla, B. (1992). Improved maintenance support by multi-version visualizations. In *Proceedings of Conference on Software Maintenance*. Academic Press.

Hata, H., Mizuno, O., & Kikuno, T. (2012). Bug prediction based on fine--grained module histories. In *Proceedings of 34th International Conference on Software Engineering*. ICSE.

Johson, B., & Shneiderman, B. (1991). Tree-Maps: a space-filling approach to the visualization of hierarchical information structures. In *Proceedings of the 2nd conference on Visualization '91*. IEEE Computer Society Press.

Keim, D. A. (2002). Information visualization and visual data mining. *IEEE Transactions on Visualization and Computer Graphics, 8*(1), 1–8. doi:10.1109/2945.981847

Koschke, R. (2003). Software visualization in software maintenance, reverse engineering, and re-engineering: a research survey. *Journal of Software Maintenance, 15*(2), 87–109. doi:10.1002/smr.270

Kuhn, A., Erni, D., Loretan, P., & Nierstrasz, O. (2010). Software cartography: thematic software visualization with consistent layout. *Journal of Software Maintenance, 22*(3), 191–210.

Kuhn, A., & Stocker, M. (2012). Codetimeline: Storytelling with versioning data. In *Proceedings of 34th International Conference on Software Engineering*. ICSE.

Langelier, G., Sahraoui, H., & Poulin, P. (2008). Exploring the evolution of software quality with animated visualization. In *Proceedings of the 2008 IEEE Symposium on Visual Languages and Human-Centric Computing*. IEEE Computer Society.

Lanza, M. (2001). The evolution matrix: recovering software evolution using software visualization techniques. In *Proceedings of the 4th International Workshop on Principles of Software Evolution*. ACM.

Lanza, M., & Ducasse, S. (2003). Polymetric Views – A Lightweight Visual Approach to Reverse Engineering. *IEEE Transactions on Software Engineering, 29*(9), 782–795. doi:10.1109/TSE.2003.1232284

Lehman, M. (1978). Laws of program evolution-rules and tools for programming management. In *Proceedings of Infotech State of the Art Conference, Why Software Projects Fail*. Infotech.

Lehman, M. (1980). Programs, life cycles, and laws of software evolution. *Proceedings of the IEEE, 68*(9), 1060–1076. doi:10.1109/PROC.1980.11805

Lungu, M., & Lanza, M. (2010). The small project observatory: a tool for reverse engineering software ecosystems. In *Proceedings of the 32nd ACM/IEEE International Conference on Software Engineering*. ACM.

Maletic, A. M. J. I., & Collard, M. L. (2002). A task oriented view of software visualization. In *Proceedings of VISSOFT '02: 1ST International Workshop on Visualizing Software for Understanding and Analysis*. IEEE CS Press.

Mockus, A., Eick, S. G., Graves, T. L., & Karr, A. F. (1999). On measurement and analysis of software changes. *IEEE Transactions on Software Engineering*.

Muller, C., Reina, G., Burch, M., & Weiskopf, D. (2010). Subversion statistics sifter. In *Proceedings of the 6th international conference on Advances in visual computing*. Springer-Verlag.

Novais, R., & Mendonca, M. (2013). A multistrategy software evolution visualization infrastructure. *Information and Software Technology*. doi:10.1016/j.infsof.2013.05.008

Novais, R., Torres, A., Souto, T., Mendonca, M., & Zazworka, N. (2013a). Software evolution visualization: A systematic mapping study. *Information and Software Technology, 55*(11), 1860–1883. doi:10.1016/j.infsof.2013.05.008

Novais, R. L., Carneiro, G. F., Simoes Junior, P. R. M., & Mendonça Neto, M. G. (2011a). On the use of software visualization to analyze software evolution - an interactive differential approach. In *Proceedings of 13th International Conference on Enterprise Information System*. Academic Press.

Novais, R. L., Carneiro, G. F., Simoes Junior, P. R. M., & Mendonça Neto, M. G. (2011b). An interactive differential and temporal approach to visually analyze software evolution, In *Proceedings of 6th IEEE International Workshop on Visualizing Software For Understanding and Analysis*. IEEE Computer Society Press.

Novais, R. L., Carneiro, G. F., Simoes Junior, P. R. M., & Mendonça Neto, M. G. (2012b). On the Use of Software Visualization to Analyze Software Evolution: An Interactive Differential Approach. *Lecture Notes in Business Information Processing, 102*, 241–255. doi:10.1007/978-3-642-29958-2_16

Novais, R. L., Mendonça Neto, M. G., Maron, D. L., Machado, I. C., & Lima, C. A. N. (2011c). On the use of a multiple-visualization approach to manage software bugs. [*Brazilian Workshop on Software Visualization*. São Paulo, Brazil: WBVS.]. *Proceedings of WBVS, 11*, I.

Novais, R. L., Nunes, C., Garcia, A., & Mendonça, M. (2013b). SourceMiner Evolution: A Tool for Supporting Feature Evolution Comprehension. In *Proceedings of 29th IEEE International Conference on Software Maintenance*. IEEE.

Novais, R. L., Nunes, C., Lima, C., Cirilo, E., Dantas, F., Garcia, A., & Mendonça, M. (2012a). On the proactive and interactive visualization for feature evolution comprehension: An industrial investigation. In *Proceedings of 34th International Conference on Software Engineering*. Academic Press.

Ogawa, M., & Ma, K.-L. (2010). Software evolution storylines. In *Proceedings of the 5th international symposium on Software visualization*. ACM.

Olszak, A., & Jørgensen, B. N. (2012). Modularization of Legacy Features by Relocation and Reconceptualization: How Much is Enough? In *Proceedings of 16th European Conference on Software Maintenance and Reengineering*. CSMR.

Ribeiro, M., Pacheco, H., Teixeira, L., & Borba, P. (2010). Emergent feature modularization. In *Proceedings of the ACM international conference companion on Object oriented programming systems languages and applications companion*. ACM.

Ripley, R., Sarma, A., & van der Hoek, A. (2007). A visualization for software project awareness and evolution. In *Proceedings of Visualizing Software for Understanding and Analysis*. IEEE. doi:10.1109/VISSOF.2007.4290712

Roman, G.-C., & Cox, K. C. (1992). Program visualization: the art of mapping programs to pictures. In *Proceedings of the 14th international conference on Software engineering*. ACM.

Rotschke, T., & Krikhaar, R. (2002). Architecture analysis tools to support evolution of large industrial systems. In *Proceedings International Conference on Software Maintenance*. Academic Press.

Steinbruckner, F., & Lewerentz, C. (2010). Representing development history in software cities. In *Proceedings of the 5th international symposium on Software visualization*. ACM.

Therón, R., González, A., García, F. J., & Santos, P. (2007). The use of information visualization to support software configuration management. In *Proceedings of the 11th IFIP TC 13 international conference on Human-computer interaction*. Springer-Verlag.

Voinea, L., Lukkien, J., & Telea, A. (2007). Visual assessment of software Evolution. *Science of Computer Programming*, *65*(3), 222–248. doi:10.1016/j.scico.2006.05.012

Voinea, L., & Telea, A. (2006). An open framework for cvs repository querying, analysis and visualization. In *Proceedings of the 2006 international workshop on Mining software repositories*. ACM.

Voinea, L., & Telea, A. (2007). Visual analytics: Visual data mining and analysis of software repositories. *Comput. Graph.*, *31*(3), 410–428. doi:10.1016/j.cag.2007.01.031

Wettel, R., & Lanza, M. (2008). Visual exploration of large-scale system evolution. In *Proceedings of the 2008 15th Working Conference on Reverse Engineering*. IEEE Computer Society.

Wnuk, K., Regnell, B., & Karlsson, L. (2009a). Feature transition charts for visualization of cross-project scope evolution in large-scale requirements engineering for product lines. In *Proceedings of Requirements Engineering Visualization, First International Workshop on*. Academic Press.

Wnuk, K., Regnell, B., & Karlsson, L. (2009b). What happened to our features? Visualization and understanding of scope change dynamics in a large-scale industrial setting. In *Proceedings of the 2009 17th IEEE International Requirements Engineering Conference*. IEEE Computer Society.

Wu, J., Holt, R. C., & Hassan, A. E. (2004). Exploring software evolution using spectrographs. In *Proceedings of the 11th Working Conference on Reverse Engineering*. IEEE Computer Society.

Wu, X., Murray, A., Storey, M.-A., & Lintern, R. (2004). A reverse engineering approach to support software maintenance: Version control knowledge extraction. In *Proceedings of 11th Working Conference on Reverse Engineering* (WCRE 2004). IEEE Computer Society Press.

KEY TERMS AND DEFINITIONS

Perspective: Software can also be visually analyzed from different perspectives (Carneiro et al., 2008)(Carneiro, Santanna, & Mendonça, 2010)(Carneiro et al., 2010)(Carneiro & Mendonça, 2013). The perspective in software visualization means the point of views it provides to engineers to explore a software system. The perspectives concern to the way in which we look to the software. In the context of software, the perspective may be represented by a set of coordinated views designed to represent a group of properties of the software.

Software Evolution: Software evolution is the term used to define the process that starts by the development of the software and by any step that incrementally updates the software.

Software Evolution Visualization: Software evolution visualization is the sub-area of Software Visualization that uses visual resources to visually analyze the software evolution.

Software Visualization: Software visualization is the field of Software Engineering (SE) that aims to help people to understand software through the use of visual resources (Diehl, 2007)

Visual Strategies of Analysis: A visual strategy of analysis defines how the evolution is visually presented for analysis (Novais and Mendonça, 2013)(Novais et al., 2013a). Due to the diverse set of software evolution comprehension tasks, it is desirable that SEV infrastructures support different strategies of analysis. There are differential and temporal strategies. Differential strategies (relative and absolute) focus on analyzing the differences between versions, while temporal strategies (overview, snapshot, and overview accumulative) describe several versions on the same visual scene.

ENDNOTES

[1]   In previous works we used multiple perspectives to analyze software evolution (Novais et al., 2011a) (Novais et al., 2011b)(Novais et al., 2012a)(Novais et al., 2012b) and to analyze software bugs (Novais et al., 2011c).

Compilation of References

Abaei, G., & Selamat, A. (2013). A survey on software fault detection based on different prediction approaches. *Vietnam Journal of Computer Science*, 1-17.

Abaei, G., Rezaei, Z., & Selamat, A. (2013). Fault prediction by utilizing self-organizing Map and Threshold. In *Proceedings of Control System, Computing and Engineering (ICCSCE), 2013 IEEE International Conference on* (pp. 465-470). Malaysia: IEEE.

Abbot, R. J. (1987). Knowledge abstraction. *Communications of the ACM, 30*(8), 664–671. doi:10.1145/27651.27652

Abdulla, P., & Leino, K. (2013). Tools for software verification. *International Journal on Software Tools and Technology Transfer*, *15*, 85–88. doi:10.1007/s10009-013-0270-5

Abraham, J., & Reddy, M. C. (2008). Moving patients around: a field study of coordination between clinical and non-clinical staff in hospitals. In *Proceedings of the 2008 ACM conference on Computer supported cooperative work* (pp. 225-228). ACM.

Abrahamsson, P., Warsta, J., Siponen, M. T., & Ronkainen, J. (2003). New directions on agile methods: a comparative analysis. In L.A. Clarke, L. Dillon, & W.F. Tichy (Eds.), *Proceedings of the 25th International Conference on Software Engineering*, (pp. 244-254), Portland, OR: IEEE Computer Society.

Abrahamsson, P., Salo, O., Rankainen, J., & Warsta, J. (2002). *Agile Software Development Methods - Review and Analysis (VTT Publication 478)*. Oulu, Finland: VTT Electronics.

Abram, G., & Treinish, L. (1995). An extended data-flow architecture for data analysis and visualization. In *Proceedings of the 6th Conference on Visualization* (pp. 263-270). Atlanta, GA: IEEE Computer Society.

Abran, A., Moore, J. W., Bourque, P., Dupuis, R., & Tripp, L. L. (2004). *Guide to the software engineering body of knowledge: 2004 version*. IEEE Computer Society.

Abreu, F. B., & Carapuça, R. (1994). Object-oriented software engineering: Measuring and controlling the development process. In *Proceedings of the 4th International Conference on Software Quality* (Vol. 186). IEEE.

Acuña, C., Marcos, E., de Castro, V., & Hernández, J. A. A. (2004). Web Information System for Medical Image Management. In *Proceedings of 5th International Symposium on Biological and Medical Data Analysis* (LNCS), (vol. 3337, pp. 49-59). Springer-Verlag.

Adriansyah, A., van Dongen, B., & van der Aalst, W. (2010). Towards robust conformance checking. In *Business Process Management Workshops* (pp. 122–133). Springer.

Adroin, W. R. (2000). Developing and deploying software engineering courseware in an adaptable curriculum framework. In *Proceedings of the 22nd international conference on Software engineering*. New York, NY: Academic Press.

Afzal, W. (2010). Using Faults-Slip-Through Metric as a Predictor of Fault-Proneness. In *Proceedings of the 17th Asia Pacific Software Engineering Conference APSEC 2010* (pp. 414-422). Los Alamitos, CA: IEEE Computer Society.

Agerfalk, P. J., & Fitzgerald, B. (2006). Flexible and distributed software processes: old petunias in new bowls? *Communications of the ACM, 49*(10), 27–34.

Agha, G. A. (1985). *Actors: A model of concurrent computation in distributed systems*. The MIT Press.

Agile Alliance. (n.d.). Retrieved from http://www.agilealliance.org/show/1641

Agile Manifesto. (2003). Retrieved from http://agile-manifesto.org/

Agostinho, C., Jardim-Goncalves, R., & Steiger-Garcao, A. (2011). Using neighboring domains towards setting the foundations for Enterprise Interoperability science. In *Proceedings of the International Symposium on Collaborative Enterprises* (CENT 2011). CENT.

Agrawal, R., Grandison, T., Johnson, C., & Kiernan, J. (2007). Enabling the 21st century health care information technology revolution. *Communications of the ACM*, *50*(2), 34–42. doi:10.1145/1216016.1216018

Ahmed, B. S., Zamli, K. Z., & Lim, C. P. (2012). Application of Particle Swarm Optimization to Uniform and Variable Strength Covering Array Construction. *Applied Soft Computing*, *12*, 1330–1347. doi:10.1016/j.asoc.2011.11.029

Ahn, G. J., & Sandhu, R. (2000). Role-based authorization constraints specification.[TISSEC]. *ACM Transactions on Information and System Security*, *3*(4), 207–226. doi:10.1145/382912.382913

Aiello, M., & Dustdar, S. (2006). Service Oriented Computing: Service Foundations. In *Proceedings of the Dagstuhl Seminar 2006*. Service Oriented Computing.

Alabduljalil, M. A., Tang, X., & Yang, T. (2013). Optimizing parallel algorithms for all pairs similarity search. In *Proceedings of the sixth ACM International Conference on Web Search and Data Mmining* (pp. 203-212). Rome, Italy: ACM.

Al-Ani, B., & Yusop, N. (2004). Role-playing, group work and other ambitious teaching methods in a large requirements engineering course. In *Proceedings of 11th IEEE International Conference and Workshop on the Engineering of Computer-Based Systems (ECBS '04)*. IEEE. doi:10.1109/ECBS.2004.1316712

Alan, O., & Catal, C. (2011). Thresholds based outlier detection approach for mining class outliers: An empirical case study on software measurement datasets. *Expert Systems with Applications*, *38*(4), 3440–3445. doi:10.1016/j.eswa.2010.08.130

Alexander, D. (2003). Application of monte carlo simulations to system reliability analysis. In *Proceedings of the 20th International Pump Symposium*. Houston, TX: Academic Press.

Alexander, R., Bieman, J., & Andrews, A. (2004). *Towards the systematic testing of aspect oriented pro- grams*. Tech. Rep. CS-4-105, Colorado State University.

Alford, M. W., & Lawson, J. T. (1979). *Software Requirements Engineering Methodology (Development)*. U.S. Air Force Rome Air Development Center.

Alghathbar, K. (2007). Validating the enforcement of access control policies and separation of duty principle in requirement engineering. *Information and Software Technology*, *49*(2), 142–157. doi:10.1016/j.infsof.2006.03.009

Alhroob, A., Dahal, K., & Hossain, A. (2010). Automatic test cases generation from software specifications modules. *Journal of e-Informatica Software Engineering*, *4*(1), 109-121.

Allen, F. E. (1976). A program data flow analysis procedure. *Communications of the ACM*, 137. doi:10.1145/360018.360025

Allen, R., & Garlan, D. (1997). A formal basis for architectural connection.[TOSEM]. *ACM Transactions on Software Engineering and Methodology*, *6*(3), 213–249. doi:10.1145/258077.258078

Allmaier, S. C., & Horton, G. (1997). Parallel shared-memory state-space exploration in stochastic modeling. In *Proceedings of the 4th International Symposium on Solving Irregularly Structured Problems in Parallel* (pp. 207-218). Paderborn, Germany: Springer-Verlag.

Alsewari, A.R.A., Khamis, N., & Zamli, K.Z. (2013). Greedy Interaction Elements Coverage Analysis for AI-Based T-Way Strategies. *Malaysian Journal of Computer Science, 26*.

Alsewari, A. R. A., & Zamli, K. Z. (2012). A Harmony Search Based Pairwise Sampling Strategy for Combinatorial Testing. *International Journal of the Physical Sciences, 7*, 1062–1072.

Alsewari, A. R. A., & Zamli, K. Z. (2012). Design and implementation of a harmony-search-based variable-strength t-way testing strategy with constraints support. *Information and Software Technology, 54*, 553–568. doi:10.1016/j.infsof.2012.01.002

Alsmadi, I., & Najadat, H. (2011). Evaluating the change of software fault behavior with dataset attributes based on categorical correlation. *Advances in Engineering Software, 42*(8), 535–546. doi:10.1016/j.advengsoft.2011.03.010

Alti, A., Khammaci, T., Smeda, A., & Bennouar, D. (2007). Integrating software architecture concepts into the MDA platform. In *Proceedings of ICSOFT'07* (SE), 2007. ICSOFT.

Alves, E. L. G., Machado, P. D. L., & Ramalho, F. (2008). Uma abordagem integrada para desenvolvimento e teste dirigido por modelos. In *Proceedings of the 2nd Brazilian Workshop on Systematic and Automated Software Testing* (pp. 74–83). Campinas.

Ambriola, V., Conradi, R., & Fuggetta, A. (1997). Assessing Process-centered Software Engineering Environments. *ACM Transaction on Software Engineering and Methodoloy, 283-328.*

Ameller, D. (2009). *Considering Non-functional Requirements in Model-Driven Engineering*. (Master Thesis). Universitat Politecnica de Catalunya, Departament de Llenguatges i Sistemes Informatics.

Amir, R., & Zeid, A. (2004). *A UML profile for service oriented architectures*. OOPSLA Companion. doi:10.1145/1028664.1028745

Ampatzoglou, A., & Chatzigeorgiou, A. (2007). Evaluation of object–oriented design patterns in game development. *Information and Software Technology, 49*(5), 445–454. doi:10.1016/j.infsof.2006.07.003

Ampatzoglou, A., Frantzeskou, G., & Stamelos, I. (2012). A methodology to assess the impact of design patterns on software quality. *Information and Software Technology, 54*(4), 331–346. doi:10.1016/j.infsof.2011.10.006

Anand, S., Burke, E. K., Chen, T. Y., Clark, J., Cohen, M. B., Grieskamp, W., & McMinn, P. (2013). An orchestrated survey of methodologies for automated software test case generation. *Journal of Systems and Software, 86*(8), 1978–2001. doi:10.1016/j.jss.2013.02.061

Andersson, C., & Runeson, P. (2007). A replicated quantitative analysis of fault distributions in complex software systems. *Software Engineering. IEEE Transactions on, 33*(5), 273–286.

Andrew, J., Abraham, R., Beckwith, L., Blackwell, A., Burnett, M., Erwig, M., … Widenbeck, S. (2011). The state of the art in end-user software engineering. *ACM Computing Surveys, 43*(3), 21:1-21:35.

Andrieux, A., Czajkowski, K., Dan, A., Keahey, K., Ludwig, H., & Nakata, T. et al. (2004). *Web Services Agreement Specification (WS-Agreement)*. Academic Press.

Antlr. (2005). ANTLR Parser Generator. *ANTLR v3*. Retrieved January 30, 2012, from http://www.antlr.org/files/100/www.antlr.org.html

Anton, A. (1996). Goal-based requirements analysis. In *Proceedings of the Second IEEE International Conference on Requirements Engineering (ICRE'96)* (pp. 136-144). Colorado Springs, CO: IEEE.

Antoniol, G., Ayari, K., Di Penta, M., Khomh, F., & Guéhéneuc, Y.-G. (2008). Is it a bug or an enhancement? A text-based approach to classify change requests. In *Proceedings of the 2008 Conference of the Centre for Advanced Studies on Collaborative Research CASCON 2008* (pp. 304-318). New York, NY: ACM.

AppSecEU2011 – OWASP. (n.d.). Retrieved from https://www.owasp.org/index.php/AppSecEU2011

Arabshian, K., & Troy, C. (2012). *COnTag: A Framework for Personalized Context-aware Search of Ontology-based Tagged Data*. Paper presented at the 19th International Conference on Web Services 2012. New York, NY.

Arabshian, K., Dickmann, C., & Schulzrinne, H. (2007). *Service composition in an ontology-based global service discovery system (Technical report)*. New York: Columbia University.

Arbab, F. (2004). Reo: A channel-based coordination model for component composition. *Mathematical Structures in Computer Science, 14*(3), 329–366. doi:10.1017/S0960129504004153

Arbaoui, S. et al. (2002). A comparative review of Process-Centered Software Engineering Environments. *Annals of Software Engineering,* 14.

Ardil, E., & Sandhu, P. S. (2010). A soft computing approach for modeling of severity of faults in software systems. *International Journal of Physical Sciences, 5*(2), 074-085.

Arendt, T., & Taentzer, G. (2013). A tool environment for quality assurance based on the Eclipse modeling framework. *Automated Software Engineering, 20,* 141–184. doi:10.1007/s10515-012-0114-7

Arisholm, E., Briand, L. C., & Johannessen, E. B. (2010). A systematic and comprehensive investigation of methods to build and evaluate fault prediction models. *Journal of Systems and Software, 83*(1), 2–17. doi:10.1016/j.jss.2009.06.055

Arkin, A. (2002). *Business Process Modeling Language (BPML). Business Process Management Initiative.* BPMI.

ARP4754A/ED-79A. (2010). *Guidelines for development of civil aircraft and systems.* SAE International & EUROCAE.

Arsanjani, A., Ghosh, S., Allam, A., Abdollah, T., Ganapathy, S., & Holley, K. (2008). SOMA: a method for developing service-oriented solutions. *IBM Systems Journal, 47*(3). doi:10.1147/sj.473.0377

Arshem, J. (n.d.). *Test Vector Generator Tool (TVG).* Retrieved from http://sourceforge.net/projects/tvg

ASTM E2369 – 12 Standard Specification for Continuity of Care Record (CCR). (n.d.). Retrieved from http://www.astm.org/Standards/E2369.htm

Atkinson, C., Fraunhofer, I., Kaiserslautern Paech, B., Reinhold, J., & Sander, T. (2001). Developing and applying component-based model-driven architectures. In *Proceedings of the Enterprise Distributed Object Computing Conference (EDOC '01).* Seattle, WA: EDOC.

Avery, D. (2011). The evolution of flight management systems. *IEEE Software, 28*(1), 11–13. doi:10.1109/MS.2011.17

Ayadi, N. Y., & Mohamed, B. A. (2011). An Enhanced Framework for Semantic Web Service Discovery. *Lecture Notes in Business Information Processing, 82,* 53–67. doi:10.1007/978-3-642-21547-6_5

Aydal, E. G., Paige, R. F., Chivers, H., & Brooke, P. J. (2006). Security planning and refactoring in extreme programming. In *Proceedings of Extreme Programming and Agile Processes in Software Engineering* (pp. 154-163). Springer.

Aydınoz, B. (2006). *The effect of design patterns on object–oriented metrics and software error–proneness.* (Master thesis). Middle East Technological University, Turkey.

Ayers, D., Newman, R., & Russell, S. (2005). *Tag ontology.* Retrieved from http://www.holygoat.co.uk/owl/redwood/0.1/tags/

Azham, Z., Imran, G., & Ithnin, N. (2011). Security Backlog in Scrum Security Practices. In *Proceedings of 5th Malaysian Software Engineering Conference (MySEC).* MySEC.

Bachmann, A., Bird, C., Rahman, F., Devanbu, P., & Bernstein, A. (2010). The missing links: bugs and bug-fix commits. In *Proceedings of the 18th ACM SIGSOFT International Symposium on Foundations of Software Engineering FSE-18* (pp. 97-106). New York, NY: ACM.

Bai, C. G., Hu, Q. P., Xie, M., & Ng, S. H. (2005). Software failure prediction based on a Markov Bayesian network model. *Journal of Systems and Software, 74*(3), 275–282. doi:10.1016/j.jss.2004.02.028

Baier, C., Cloth, L., Haverkort, B. R., Hermanns, H., & Katoen, J. P. (2010). Performability assessment by model checking of Markov reward models. *Formal Methods in System Design, 36*(1), 1–36. doi:10.1007/s10703-009-0088-7

Baier, C., Sirjani, M., Arbab, F., & Rutten, J. (2006). Modelling component connectors in Reo by constraint automata. *Science of Computer Programming, 61*(2), 75–113. doi:10.1016/j.scico.2005.10.008

Baisch, E., & Liedtke, T. (1997). Comparison of conventional approaches and soft-computing approaches for software quality prediction.[). IEEE.]. *Proceedings of Systems, Man, and Cybernetics, 2*, 1045–1049.

Baker, P., Dai, Z., Grabowski, J., Haugen, O., Schieferdecker, I., & Williams, C. (2007). *Model-driven testing: Using UML testing profile.* New York: Springer-Verlag New York Inc.

Balasubramaniam, R., Cao, L., Mohan, K., & Xu, P. (2006). How can distributed software development be agile? *Communications of the ACM, 49*(10), 41–46. doi:10.1145/1164394.1164418

Balint, M., Marinescu, R., & Girba, T. (2006). How developers copy. In *Proceedings of the 14th IEEE International Conference on Program Comprehension.* IEEE Computer Society.

Balsamo, S., Di Marco, A., Inverardi, P., & Simeoni, M. (2004). Model-based performance prediction in software development: a survey. *IEEE Transactions on Software Engineering, 30*(5), 295–310. doi:10.1109/TSE.2004.9

Bandara, A., Lupu, E., Russo, A., Dulay, N., Sloman, M., & Flegkas, P. (2005). *Policy refinement for DiffServ quality of service management.* Paper presented at the 2005 9th IFIP/IEEE International Symposium on Integrated Network Management. Nice, France.

Baniassad, E., & Clarke, S. (2004). Theme: An approach for aspect-oriented analysis and design. In *Proc. of 26th International Conference on Software Engineering (ICSE'04).* Edinburgh, UK: ICSE.

Bansal, S., & Vidal, J.-M. (2003). Matchmaking of Web services based on the DAML-S service model. In *Proceedings of International Joint Conference on Autonomous Agents and Multi-Agent Systems* (AAMAS'03) (pp.926—927). AAMAS.

Bansiya, J., & Davis, C. G. (2002). A hierarchical model for object-oriented design quality assessment. *Software Engineering. IEEE Transactions on, 28*(1), 4–17.

Baocai, Y., Huirong, Y., Pengbin, F., Liheng, G., & Mingli, L. (2010). *A Framework and QoS Based Web Services Discovery.* IEEE. doi:10.1109/ICSESS.2010.5552261

Baresi, L., Heckel, R., Thone, S., & Varro, D. (2003). Modeling and validation of service-oriented architectures: Application vs. style. In *Proc. ESEC/FSE 2003.* Helsinki, Finland: ESEC/FSE.

Barker, J., & Palmer, G. (2004). *Beginning C# Objects: From Concepts to Code.* Berkeley, CA: Apress, University of California at Berkeley. doi:10.1007/978-1-4302-0691-0

Barnes, R. J., Gause, D. C., & Way, E. C. (2008). Teaching the Unknown and the Unknowable in Requirements Engineering Education. In Proceedings of Requirements Engineering Education and Training.doi: doi:10.1109/REET.2008.6

Barr, M., & Wells, C. (1999). *Category Theory for Computing Science.* Les Publications CRM.

Basili, V. R., Briand, L. C., & Melo, W. L. (1996). A validation of object-oriented design metrics as quality indicators. *Software Engineering. IEEE Transactions on, 22*(10), 751–761.

Basili, V. R., Lindvall, M., Regardie, M., Seaman, C., Heidrich, J., Münch, J., & Rombach, D. A. (2010). Trendowicz, Linking software development and business strategy through measurement. *Computer, 43*(4), 57–65. doi:10.1109/MC.2010.108

Basin, D., Doser, J., & Lodderstedt, T. (2006). Model driven security: From UML models to access control infrastructures.[TOSEM]. *ACM Transactions on Software Engineering and Methodology, 15*(1), 39–91. doi:10.1145/1125808.1125810

Baumgartner, P., Fuchs, A., & Tinelli, C. (2004). *Darwin: A theorem prover for the model evolution calculus.* Paper presented at the IJCAR Workshop on Empirically Successful First Order Reasoning (ESFOR (aka S4)), Electronic Notes in Theoretical Computer Science. New York, NY.

Bawa, M., Condie, T., & Ganesan, P. (2005). LSH forest: Self-tuning indexes for similarity search. In *Proceedings of the 14th International Conference on World Wide Web* (pp. 651-660). Chiba, Japan: ACM.

Beatty, J., & Agouridas, V. (2007). Developing Requirements Engineering Skills: A Case Study in Training Practitioners. In *Proceedings of International Workshop on Requirements Engineering and Training (REET2007).* India Habitat Centre.

Becker, S., Koziolek, H., & Reussner, R. (2009). The Palladio component model for model-driven performance prediction. *Journal of Systems and Software, 82*(1), 3–22. doi:10.1016/j.jss.2008.03.066

Beck, K. (1999). *Extreme Programming Explained: Embrace Change*. Addison-Wesley.

Beck, K., & Gamma, E. (1998). Test infected: Programmers love writing tests. *Java Report, 3*(7), 37–50.

Bell, R. M., Ostrand, T. J., & Weyuker, E. J. (2006). Looking for bugs in all the right places. In *Proceedings of the 2006 international symposium on Software testing and analysis ISSTA'06* (pp. 61-72). New York, NY: ACM.

Bell, A., & Haverkort, B. R. (2001). Serial and parallel out-of-core solution of linear systems arising from generalised stochastic Petri nets. In *Procedings of High Performance Computing 2001* (pp. 181–200). Copenhagen, Denmark: Springer-Verlag.

Bell, D. E., & La Padula, L. J. (1976). *Secure computer system: Unified exposition and multics interpretation (No. MTR-2997-REV-1)*. MITRE Corp.

Bellon, S., Koschke, R., Antoniol, G., Krinke, J., & Merlo, E. (2007). Comparison and evaluation of clone detection tools. *IEEE Transactions on Software Engineering, 33*(9), 577–591. doi:10.1109/TSE.2007.70725

Bellwood, T., Clément, L., Ehnebuske, D., Hately, A., Hondo, M., Husband, Y. L., et al. (2002). *Article*. Retrieved from http://uddi.org/pubs/uddi-v3.00-published-20020719.htm

Bennett, K., Cornelius, B., Munro, M., & Robson, D. (1991). Software Maintenance. In *Software Engineer's Reference Book*. Oxford, UK: Butterworlh-Heinemann. doi:10.1016/B978-0-7506-0813-8.50027-7

Benyamina, D., Hafid, A., & Gendreau, M. (2012). Wireless Mesh Networks Design – A Survey. *IEEE Communications Surveys & Tutorials, 14*(2), 299–310. doi:10.1109/SURV.2011.042711.00007

Berchtold, S., Böhm, C., Braunmüller, B., Keim, D. A., & Kriegel, H.-P. (1997). Fast parallel similarity search in multimedia databases. In *Proceedings of the 1997 ACM SIGMOD International Conference on Management of Data* (pp. 1-12). Tucson, AZ: ACM.

Berenbach, B. (2005). A hole in the curriculum. In *Proceedings of Workshop on Requirements Engineering Education and Training*. Paris: Academic Press.

Berg, K., Conejero, J. M., & Chitchyan, R. (2005). *AOSD ontology 1.0: Public ontology of aspect orientation*. Tech. Rep. AOSD-Europe-UT-01, Report of the EU Network of Excellence on AOSD.

Berhe, S., Demurjian, S., Saripalle, R., Agresta, T., Liu, J., Cusano, A., & Gedarovich, J. (2010). Secure, obligated and coordinated collaboration in health care for the patient-centered medical home. In *Proceedings of AMIA Annual Symposium*. American Medical Informatics Association.

Berhe, S. (2011). *A framework for secure, obligated, co-ordinated and dynamic collaboration that extends NIST RBAC*. University of Connecticut.

Berhe, S., Demurjian, S., & Agresta, T. (2009). Emerging trends in health care delivery: towards collaborative security for NIST RBAC. In *Data and Applications Security XXIII* (pp. 283–290). Springer. doi:10.1007/978-3-642-03007-9_19

Berhe, S., Demurjian, S., Gokhale, S., Pavlich-Mariscal, J., & Saripalle, R. (2011). Leveraging UML for security engineering and enforcement in a collaboration on duty and adaptive workflow model that extends NIST RBAC. In *Data and Applications Security and Privacy XXV* (pp. 293–300). Springer. doi:10.1007/978-3-642-22348-8_25

Berling, T., & Runeson, P. (2003). Efficient Evaluation of Multifactor Dependent System Performance Using Fractional Design. *IEEE Transactions on Software Engineering, 29*, 769–781. doi:10.1109/TSE.2003.1232283

Bernardi, S., Campos, J., & Merseguer, J. (2011). Timing-failure risk assessment of UML design using Time Petri Net bound techniques. *Industrial Informatics. IEEE Transactions on, 7*(1), 90–104.

Bernauer, M., Kappel, G., & Kramler, G. (2004). *Representing XML schema in UML–A Comparison of Approaches*. Springer.

Berners-Lee, T., Fielding, R., & Masinter, L. (1998). *Uniform Resource Identifiers (URI), Generic Syntax, IETF RFC 2396*. Retrieved from http://www.ietf.org/rfc/rfc2396.txt

Bernstein, A., Ekanayake, J., & Pinzger, M. (2007). Improving Defect Prediction Using Temporal Features and Non Linear Models. In *Proceedings of the 9th International Workshop on Principles of Software Evolution IWPSE'07* (pp. 11-18). New York, NY: ACM.

Berre, A. et al. (2007). The ATHENA Interoperability Framework. In *Enterprise Interoperability II* (pp. 569–580). London, UK: Springer. doi:10.1007/978-1-84628-858-6_62

Berry, R. F. (1992). Computer Bench Mark Evaluation and Design of Experiments: A Case Study. *IEEE Transactions on Computers*, *41*, 1279–1289. doi:10.1109/12.166605

Bettini, C., Brdiczka, O., Henricksen, K., Indulska, J., Nicklas, D., Ranganathan, A., & Riboni, D. (2009). A Survey of Context Modelling and reasoning Techniques. *Pervasive and Mobile Computing*. PMID:20161031

Beyer, D., & Hassan, A. E. (2006). Evolution storyboards: Visualization of software structure dynamics. In *Proceedings of the 14th IEEE International Conference on Program Comprehension*. IEEE Computer Society.

Bézivin, J., Buttner, F., Gagolla, M., & Jouault, F. Kurtev, & Lindow, A. (2006). Model Transformations? Transformation Models? Berlin: Springer-Verlag.

Bézivin, J., Rumpe, B., Schürr, A., & Tratt, L. (2005). *Mandatory Example Specification*. Paper presented at CFP of the Model Transformations in Practice Workshop at MoDELS 2005. Montego Bay, Jamaica.

Bhattacharya, I., Kashyap, S. R., & Parthasarathy, S. (2005). Similarity searching in peer-to-peer databases. In *Proceedings of the 25th IEEE International Conference on Distributed Computing Systems* (pp. 329-338). Columbus, OH: IEEE Computer Society.

Bhuiyan, M., Islam, M., & Krishna, S. et al. (2007). Integration of agent-oriented conceptual models and UML activity diagrams using effect annotations.[COMPSAC.]. *Proceedings of*, *COMPSAC07*, 171–178.

Bibi, S., Tsoumakas, G., Stamelos, I., & Vlahavas, I. P. (2006). Software Defect Prediction Using Regression via Classification. In *Proceedings of IEEE/ACS International Conference on Computer Systems and Applications (AICCSA 2006)* (pp. 330-336). Dubai, UAE. IEEE.

Bieman, J. M., Alexander, R., Munger, P. W., III, & Meunier, E. (2002). Software design quality: Style and substance. In *Proceedings of ICSE Workshop on Software Quality*. Orlando, FL: ACM.

Bieman, J. M., Straw, G., Wang, H., Munger, P. W., & Alexander, R. T. (2003). Design patterns and change proneness: An examination of five evolving systems. In *Proceedings of the 9th International Software Metrics Symposium* (pp. 40–49). Sydney, Australia: IEEE.

Biermann, E., Ermel, C., & Taentzer, G. (2008). *Precise Semantics of EMF Model Trans- formations by Graph Transformation*. Academic Press.

Billington, J., Christensen, S., van Hee, K. M., Kindler, E., Kummer, O., & Petrucci, L. (2003). The Petri net markup language: concepts technology, and tools. In *Proceedings of International Conference on Applications and Theory of Petri Nets – ATPN 2003*, (LNCS), (vol. 2679, pp. 483–505). Springer.

Bingham, B., Bingham, J., Paula, F. M. D., Erickson, J., Singh, G., & Reitblatt, M. (2010). Industrial strength distributed explicit state model checking. In *Proceedings of the 2010 9th International Workshop on Parallel and Distributed Methods in Verification, and second International Workshop on High Performance Computational Systems Biology* (pp. 28-36). Enschede, The Netherlands: IEEE Computer Society.

Bird, C., Bachmann, A., Aune, E., Duffy, J., Bernstein, A., Filkov, V., & Devanbu, P. (2009). Fair and balanced? Bias in bug-fix datasets. In *Proceedings of the 7th joint meeting of the European software engineering conference and the ACM SIGSOFT symposium on The foundations of software engineering ESEC/FSE'09* (pp. 121-130). New York, NY: ACM.

Bird, C., Nagappan, N., Murphy, B., Gall, H., & Devanbu, P. (2011). Don't touch my code! Examining the effects of ownership on software quality. In *Proceedings of the 19th ACM SIGSOFT symposium and the 13th European conference on Foundations of software engineering ESEC/FSE '11* (pp. 4-14). New York, NY: ACM.

Bishnu, P. S., & Bhattacherjee, V. (2012). Software fault prediction using quad tree-based k-means clustering algorithm. *Knowledge and Data Engineering. IEEE Transactions on*, *24*(6), 1146–1150.

Bispo, C. P., Maciel, R. S. P., David, J., Ribeiro, I., & Conceição, R. (2010). Applying a Model-Driven Process for a Collaborative Service-Oriented Architecture. In *Proceedings of the 14th International Conference on Computer Supported Cooperative Work in Design* (pp. 378-383). Shangai, China: Academic Press.

Bloom, B. H. (1970). Space/time trade-offs in hash coding with allowable errors. *Communications of the ACM, 13*(7), 422–426. doi:10.1145/362686.362692

Blum, B. I. (1996). *Beyond Programming to a New Era of Design*. New York: Oxford University Press.

Boehm, B. (1981). *Software Engineering Economics*. Prentice Hall.

Boehm, B. W. (1988). Understanding and controlling software costs. *Journal of Parametrics, 8*(1), 32–68.

Boehm, B. W., Abts, C., Brown, A. W., Chulani, S., Clark, B. K., & Horowitz, E. et al. (2009). *Software Cost Estimation with COCOMO II*. Upper Saddle River, NJ: Prentice Hall Press.

Boetticher, G. (2006). Improving credibility of machine learner models in software engineering. *Advanced Machine Learner Applications in Software Engineering*, 52-72.

Bollati, V. A., Vara, J. M., Jimenez, A., & Marcos, E. (2013). Applying MDE to the (semi-) automatic development of model transformations. *Information and Software Technology, 55*(4), 699–718. doi:10.1016/j.infsof.2012.11.004

Bonomi, F., Mitzenmacher, M., Panigrahy, R., Singh, S., & Varghese, G. (2006). An improved construction for counting Bloom filters. In *Proceedings of the 14th Conference on Annual European Symposium* (vol. 14, pp. 684-695). Zurich, Switzerland: Springer-Verlag.

Booch, G. (1987). *Software Engineering with Ada*. Redwood, CA: Benjamin-Cummings.

Boroday, S. Y. (1998). Determining Essential Arguments of Boolean Functions. In *Proceedings of the Conference on Industrial Mathematics* (ICIM '98). Taganrog, Russia: ICIM.

Bosch, J. (1998). Adapting object-oriented components. In *Object-Oriented Technologys* (pp. 379–383). Springer. doi:10.1007/3-540-69687-3_77

Bouquet, F., Grandpierre, C., Legeard, B., & Peureux, F. (2008). A test generation solution to automate software testing. In *Proceedings of the 3rd international workshop on Automation of software test* (pp. 45-48). Leipzig, Germany: Academic Press.

Bourrillion, K., & Levy, J. (2014). *Guava project*. Retrieved February 4, 2014, from https://code.google.com/p/guava-libraries/

BPEL 2.0 Specification – OASIS. (2011). Retrieved from http://docs.oasis-open.org/wsbpel/

BPMN 1.1 – OMG Final Adopted Specification. (2008). Retrieved from http://www.omg.org/docs/formal/08-01-17.pdf

Brambilla, M. (2006). Generation of WebML Web application models from business process specifications. In *Proceedings of 6th International Conference on Web Engineering* (ICWE'06). ACM.

Brambilla, M., Cabot, J., & Wimmer, M. (2012). *Model-driven software Engineering in Practice*. Morgan & Claypool Publichers.

Bravetti, M., & Zavattaro, G. (2009). A theory of contracts for strong service compliance. *Journal of Mathematical Structures in Computer Science, 19*(3), 601–638. doi:10.1017/S0960129509007658

Breu, S., & Krinke, J. (2004). *Automated Software Engineering, 2004. Proceedings. 19th International Conference on*. IEEE.

Brogi, A., & Ciancarini, P. (1991). The concurrent language, shared prolog.[TOPLAS]. *ACM Transactions on Programming Languages and Systems, 13*(1), 99–123. doi:10.1145/114005.102807

Brooks, F. (1995). Mythical man-month: Essays on software engineering (20th Ann. Ed.). Reading, MA: Addison-Wesley.

Brosch, F., Koziolek, H., & Buhnova, B. (2011). Architecture-Based Reliability Prediction with the Palladio Component Model. *IEEE Transactions on Software Engineering, 38*(6), 1319–1339. doi:10.1109/TSE.2011.94

Brosch, F., Koziolek, H., Buhnova, B., & Reussner, R. (2010). Parameterized reliability prediction for component-based software architectures. In *Research into Practice–Reality and Gaps* (pp. 36–51). Springer. doi:10.1007/978-3-642-13821-8_5

Brown, W. J., Malveau, R. C., McCormick, H. W. S., & Mowbray, T. J. (1998). *AntiPatterns: Refactoring software architectures, and projects in crisis*. Hoboken, NJ: John Wiley and Sons, Inc.

Broy, M. (2004). Model Driven, Architecture-Centric Modeling in Software Development. In *Proceedings of 9th Intl. Conf. in Engineering Complex Computer Systems* (ICECCS'04), (pp. 3-12). IEEE Computer Society.

Brunswick, J. (2008). *Extending the Business Value of SOA through Business Process Management, Architect: SOA and BPM*. Academic Press.

Bryce, R. C., & Colbourn, C. J. (2009). A Density-based Greedy Algorithm for Higher Strength Covering Arrays. *Software Testing, Verification, and Reliability, 19*, 37–53. doi:10.1002/stvr.393

Buckley, J. (2009). Requirements-Based Visualization Tools for Software Maintenance and Evolution. *Computer, 42*(4), 106–108. doi:10.1109/MC.2009.127

Budinsky, F., Brodsky, S. A., & Merks, E. (2003). *Eclipse Modeling Framework*. Pearson Education.

Burger, S., Hummel, O., & Heinisch, M. (2013). Airbus cabin software. *IEEE Software, 30*(1), 21–25. doi:10.1109/MS.2013.2

Burr, K., & Young, W. (1998). Combinatorial Test Techniques: Table Based Automation, Test Generation and Code Coverage. In *Proceedings of the International Conference on Software Testing Analysis & Review (STAR)*. San Diego, CA: STAR.

Busi, N., Gorrieri, R., & Zavattaro, G. (2000). On the expressiveness of Linda coordination primitives. *Information and Computation, 156*(1), 90–121. doi:10.1006/inco.1999.2823

Buss, A., Papadopoulos, H. I., Pearce, O., & Smith, T. (2010). STAPL: Standard template adaptive parallel library. In *Proceedings of the 3rd Annual Haifa Experimental Systems Conference* (pp. 1-10). Haifa, Israel: ACM.

Butler Group. (2003). *Application Development Strategies*. Author.

Butler, J., MacCallum, I., Kleber, M., Shlyakhter, I. A., Belmonte, M. K., & Lander, E. S. et al. (2008). ALLPATHS: De novo assembly of whole-genome shotgun microreads. *Genome Research, 18*(5), 810–820. doi:10.1101/gr.7337908 PMID:18340039

Cabri, G., Leonardi, L., & Zambonelli, F. (2000). MARS: A programmable coordination architecture for mobile agents. *Internet Computing, IEEE, 4*(4), 26–35. doi:10.1109/4236.865084

Cáceres, P., de Castro, V., Vara, J. M., & Marcos, E. (2006). Model transformations for hypertext modeling on web information systems. In *Proceedings of 2006 ACM symposium on Applied computing – SAC'06*. ACM.

Calikli, G., Tosun, A., Bener, A., & Celik, M. (2009). The effect of granularity level on software defect prediction. In *Proceedings of Computer and Information Sciences* (pp. 531–536). Cyprus: IEEE. doi:10.1109/ISCIS.2009.5291866

Callele, D., & Makaroff, D. (2006). Teaching requirements engineering to an unsuspecting audience. *ACM SIGCSE Bulletin, 38*(1), 433–437. doi:10.1145/1124706.1121475

Canal, C., Murillo, J. M., & Poizat, P. (2005). Coordination and adaptation techniques for software entities. In *Object-oriented technology* (pp. 133–147). Springer. doi:10.1007/978-3-540-30554-5_13

Canal, C., Pimentel, E., & Troya, J. M. (2001). Compatibility and inheritance in software architectures. *Science of Computer Programming, 41*(2), 105–138. doi:10.1016/S0167-6423(01)00002-8

Capmbell, D. (1997). *Implementing algorithmic skeletons for generative communication with linda*. Report-University of York Department of Computer Science YCS.

Carnegie Mellon University Software Engineering Institute. (n.d.). *Capability Maturity Model Integration (CMMI®) for Development, Version 1.2* (CMU/SEI-2006-TR-008, ESC-TR-2006-008). Retrieved from www.sei.cmu.edu

Carneiro, G. F., & Mendonça, M. G. (2013). SourceMiner: A Multi-Perspective Software Visualization Environment. In *Proceedings of 15th International Conference on Interprise Information Systems* (ICEIS 2013), (pp. 30-42). Angers.

Carneiro, G. F., Magnavita, R., Spínola, E., Spínola, F. O., & Mendonça, M. G. (2008). An Eclipse-Based Visualization Tool for Software Comprehension. In Proceedings of Sessão de Ferramentas do Simpósio Brasileiro de Engenharia de Software. Campinas.

Carneiro, G. F., Santanna, C. N., & Mendonça, M. G. (2010). On the Design of a Multi-Perspective Visualization Environment to Enhance Software Comprehension Activities. In *Proceedings of Workshop de Manutenção Moderna de Software*. Bélem.

Carneiro, G. F., Silva, M., Santanna, C. N., Garcia, A. F., & Mendonça, M. G. (2010). Identifying Code Smells with Multiple Concern Views. In *Proceedings of Simpósio Brasileiro de Engenharia de Software*. Academic Press. doi:10.1109/SBES.2010.21

Carriero, N., & Gelernter, D. (1989). Linda in context. *Communications of the ACM*, *32*(4), 444–458. doi:10.1145/63334.63337

Carrozza, G., Faella, M., Fucci, F., Pietrantuono, R., & Russo, S. (2013). Engineering air traffic control systems with a model-driven approach. *IEEE Software*, *30*(3), 42–48.

Cartwright, M., & Shepperd, M. (2000). An empirical investigation of an object-oriented software system. *Software Engineering. IEEE Transactions on*, *26*(8), 786–796.

Casadei, M., & Omicini, A. (2009). Situated tuple centres in ReSpecT. In *Proceedings of the ACM Symposium on Applied Computing* (pp. 1361-1368). ACM.

Caselli, S., Conte, G., & Marenzoni, P. (1995). Parallel state space exploration for GSPN models. In *Proceedings of the 16th International Conference on Application and Theory of Petri Nets* (pp. 181-200). Turin, Italy: Springer-Verlag.

Cass, A. G., Lerner, B. S., Sutton, S. M., McCall, E. K., Wise, A., & Osterweil, L. J. (2000). Little-JIL/Juliette: A Process Definition Language and Interpreter. In *Proceedings of the 22nd International Conference on Software Engineering*. Limerick, Ireland: Academic Press.

Castro, J., Kolp, M., & Mylopoulos, J. (2002). Towards requirements-driven information systems engineering: the Tropos Project. *Information Systems*, *27*(6), 365–389. doi:10.1016/S0306-4379(02)00012-1

Catal, C., & Diri, B. (2007). Software defect prediction using artificial immune recognition system. In *Proceedings of the 25th Conference on IASTED International Multi-Conference: Software Engineering* (pp. 285-290). Innsburk, Austria: ACTA Press.

Catal, C. (2011). Software fault prediction: A literature review and current trends. *Expert Systems with Applications*, *38*(4), 4626–4636. doi:10.1016/j.eswa.2010.10.024

Catal, C., Sevim, U., & Diri, B. (2009). Clustering and metrics thresholds based software fault prediction of unlabeled program modules. In *Proceedings of Information Technology: New Generations* (pp. 199–204). Las Vegas, NV: IEEE. doi:10.1109/ITNG.2009.12

Catal, C., Sevim, U., & Diri, B. (2011). Practical development of an Eclipse-based software fault prediction tool using Naive Bayes algorithm. *Expert Systems with Applications*, *38*(3), 2347–2353. doi:10.1016/j.eswa.2010.08.022

CDA – Hl7book. (n.d.). Retrieved from http://hl7book.net/index.php?title=CDA

Cepda, R. S. V., Magdaleno, A. M., Murta, L. G. P., & Werner, C. M. L. (2010). Evoltrack: Improving design evolution awareness in Software development. *Journal of the Brazilian Computer Society*, *16*(2), 117–131. doi:10.1007/s13173-010-0011-5

Chakraborty, A., et al. (2012). The role of requirement engineering in software development life cycle. *Journal of emerging trends in computing and information sciences, 3* (5), 723-729.

Chandler, D. (2007). *Semiotics: the basics*. New York: Routledge.

Chandra, A. K. et al. (1983). On Sets of Boolean n-Vectors with All k-Projections Surjective. *Acta Informatica*, *20*, 103–111. doi:10.1007/BF00264296

Chang, G., Suihuai, Y., Gangjun, Y., & Weiwei, W. (2009). A collaborative requirements elicitation approach based on scenario. In *Proceedings of IEEE 10th International Conference on Computer-Aided Industrial Design & Conceptual Design,* (pp. 2213-2216). Wenzhou, China: IEEE Computer Society.

Chapman, M., & Solomon, D. (2002). The relationship of cyclomatic complexity, essential complexity and error rates. In *Proceedings of the NASA Software Assurance Symposium*. NASA.

Chapman, P., Clinton, J., Kerber, R., Khabaza, T., Reinartz, T., Shearer, C., & Wirth, R. (2000). *CRISPDM 1.0 step-by-step data mining guide*. Technical Report. CRISP-DM Consortium.

Chatzigeorgiou, A., Tsantalis, N., & Stephanides, G. (2006). Application of graph theory to OO software engineering. In *Proceedings of the 2006 International Workshop on Interdisciplinary Software Engineering Research* (pp. 29–36). Shanghai, China: ACM.

Che Pa, N., & Mohd Zin, A. (2011). Requirement Elicitation: Identifying the Communication Challenges between Developer and Customer. *International Journal on New Computer Architecture and their Applications, 1,* 371-383.

Chen, D. (2006). Enterprise interoperability framework. In *Open Interop Workshop on Enterprise Modelling and Ontologies for Interoperability*. Academic Press.

Chen, D., & Daclin, N. (2007). Barriers driven methodology for enterprise interoperability. In Establishing the Foundation of Collaborative Networks (pp. 453-460). Springer US.

Chen, X., Jin, Z., & Yi, L. (2007). An ontology of problem frames for guiding problem frame specification. In Z. Zhang, & J. Siekmann (Eds.), *Knowledge Science, Engineering and Management, Second International Conference,* (pp. 384-395). Berlin: Springer-Verlag.

Chen, D., Doumeingts, G., & Vernadat, F. (2008). Architectures for enterprise integration and interoperability: Past, present and future. *Computers in Industry, 59*(7), 647–659. doi:10.1016/j.compind.2007.12.016

Chen, P. P. (1976). The entity-relationship model-toward a unified view of data. *ACM Transactions on Database Systems, 1*(1), 9–36. doi:10.1145/320434.320440

Cheung, L., Roshandel, R., Medvidovic, N., & Golubchik, L. (2008). Early prediction of software component reliability. In *Proceedings of the 30th international conference on Software engineering* (pp. 111–120). ACM.

Cheung, S. C., et al. (2006). A Combinatorial Methodology for RFID Benchmarking. In *Proceedings of the 3rd RFID Academic Convocation in conjunction with the China International RFID Technology Development Conference & Exposition*. Shanghai, China: RFID.

Cheung, R. C. (1980). A User-Oriented Software Reliability Model. *IEEE Transactions on Software Engineering, SE-6*(2), 118–125. doi:10.1109/TSE.1980.234477

Chiang, Y.-J., & Silva, C. T. (1999). External memory techniques for isosurface extraction in scientific visualization. In J. M. Abello, & J. S. Vitter (Eds.), *External memory algorithms* (pp. 247–277). American Mathematical Society.

Chidamber, S. R., & Kemerer, C. F. (1994). A metrics suite for object oriented design. *Software Engineering. IEEE Transactions on, 20*(6), 476–493.

Chikhi, R., & Rizk, G. (2012). Space-efficient and exact de Bruijn graph representation based on a Bloom filter. In *Proceedings of the 12th International Conference on Algorithms in Bioinformatics* (pp. 236-248). Ljubljana, Slovenia: Springer-Verlag.

Cho, I. H., McGregor, J. D., & Krause, L. (1998). A protocol based approach to specifying interoperability between objects. In *Proceedings of Technology of Object-Oriented Languages* (pp. 84–96). IEEE.

Chua, F. F., Hao, Y., & Soo, D. K. (2007). *A Visualization Framework for Web Service Discovery and Selection Based on Quality of Service*. Paper presented at the Asia-Pacific Services Computing Conference 2007. Shanghai, China.

Chu-Carroll, M. C., & Sprenkle, S. (2000). Coven: Brewing better collaboration through software configuration management. *Software Engineering Notes, 25*(6), 88–97. doi:10.1145/357474.355058

Chung, L., Nixon, B. A., Yu, E., & Mylopoulos, J. (2000). *Non-Functional Requirements in Software Engineering*. New York: Springer Science. doi:10.1007/978-1-4615-5269-7

Ciancone, A., Drago, M. L., Filieri, A., Grassi, V., Koziolek, H., & Mirandola, R. (2013). The KlaperSuite framework for model-driven reliability analysis of component-based systems. *Software & Systems Modeling*, 1–22.

Ciardo, G., Gluckman, J., & Nicol, D. (1998). Distributed state-space generation of discrete-state stochastic models. *INFORMS Journal on Computing*, *10*(1), 82–93. doi:10.1287/ijoc.10.1.82

Ciardo, G., Miner, A. S., & Wan, M. (2009). Advanced features in SMART: the stochastic model checking analyzer for reliability and timing. *ACM SIGMETRICS Performance Evaluation Review*, *36*(4), 58–63. doi:10.1145/1530873.1530885

Cignoni, P., Montani, C., Rocchini, C., & Scopigno, R. (2003). External memory management and simplification of huge meshes. *IEEE Transactions on Visualization and Computer Graphics*, *9*(4), 525–537. doi:10.1109/TVCG.2003.1260746

Cinque, M., Cotroneo, D., & Pecchia, A. (2009). A Logging Approach for Effective Dependability Evaluation of Complex Systems. In *Proceedings of the 2009 Second International Conference on Dependability* (pp. 105-110). IEEE Computer Society.

Clarke, S., Harrison, W., Ossher, H., & Tarr, P. (1999). Subject-oriented design. In *Towards Improved Alignment of Requirements, Design and Code* (pp. 325–337). New York: ACM.

Clavel, M., Durán, F., Eker, S., Lincoln, P., Martı-Oliet, N., Meseguer, J., et al. (2003). *Maude 2.0 Manual*. Retrieved from http://maude.cs.uiuc.edu

Cleland-Huang, J. (2013). Are requirements alive and kicking? *IEEE Software*, *30*(3), 13–15.

Coad, P., & Yourdon, E. (1991). *Object-Oriented Analysis*. Upper Saddle River, NJ: Yourdon Press.

Cockburn, A. (2002). *Agile Software Development*. Boston, MA: Addison Wesley.

Cockburn, A. (2004). *Crystal Clear: A Human-Powered Methodology for Small Teams*. Addison-Wesley.

Cockburn, A. (2006). *Agile Software Development: The Cooperative Game*. Addison-Wesley.

Cohen, M. B. (2004). *Designing Test Suites for Software Interaction Testing*. (PhD Thesis). University of Auckland, Auckland, New Zealand.

Cohen, M. B., et al. (2003). Constructing Test Suites for Interaction Testing. In *Proceedings of the 25th IEEE International Conference on Software Engineering*. IEEE Computer Society.

Cohen, D. M. et al. (1997). The AETG System: An Approach to Testing based on Combinatorial Design. *IEEE Transactions on Software Engineering*, *23*, 437–443. doi:10.1109/32.605761

Cohen, M. B., Colbourn, C. J., & Ling, A. C. H. (2008). Constructing Strength Three Covering Arrays with Augmented Annealing. *Discrete Mathematics*, *308*, 2709–2722. doi:10.1016/j.disc.2006.06.036

Collberg, C., Kobourov, S., Nagra, J., Pitts, J., & Wampler, K. (2003). A system for graph- based visualization of the evolution of software. In *Proceedings of the 2003 ACM symposium on Software visualization*. ACM.

Colman, A., & Han, J. (2005). *Coordination systems in role-based adaptive software*. Paper presented at the 7th International Conference on Coordination Models and Languages, COORDINATION 2005. Namur, Belgium.

Compare, D., Inverardi, P., & Wolf, A. L. (1999). Uncovering architectural mismatch in component behavior. *Science of Computer Programming*, *33*(2), 101–131. doi:10.1016/S0167-6423(98)00006-9

Connecticut Crash Data Repository (Beta). (n.d.). Retrieved from http://www.ctcrash.uconn.edu/

Connecticut Transportation Safety Research Center | Connecticut Transportation Institute. (n.d.). Retrieved from http://www.cti.uconn.edu/connecticut-transportation-safety-research-center/

Connor, A. M., Buchan, J., & Petrova, K. (2009). Bridging the Research-Practice Gap in Requirements Engineering through Effective Teaching and Peer Learning. In *Proceedings of Sixth International Conference on Information Technology: New Generations*. doi: 10.1109/ITNG.2009.134

Cook, J. J., & Zilles, C. B. (2009). Characterizing and optimizing the memory footprint of de novo short read DNA sequence assembly. In *Proceedings of the IEEE International Symposium on Performance Analysis of Systems and Software* (pp. 143-152). Boston, MA: IEEE Computer Society.

Corkill, D. D. (1991). Blackboard systems. *AI Expert, 6*(9), 40–47.

Cortellessa, V., Di Marco, A., & Inverardi, P. (2011). Model-Based Software Performance Analysis. *Analysis*, 65–78.

Cortellessa, V., Goseva-Popstojanova, K., Appukkutty, K., Guedem, A. R., Hassan, A., Elnaggar, R., & Ammar, H. H. (2005). Model-based performance risk analysis. *Software Engineering. IEEE Transactions on, 31*(1), 3–20.

Cortes, C., & Vapnik, V. (1995). Support-Vector Networks. *Machine Learning, 20*(3), 273–297. doi:10.1007/BF00994018

Cottenier, T., Berg, A., & Elrad, T. (2007). The motorola WEAVR: Model weaving in a large industrial context. In *Proc. of the 6th Int. Conf. on Aspect-Oriented Software Development (AOSD'07)*. Vancouver, Canada: AOSD.

Coughlan, J., Lycett, M., & Macredie, R. D. (2003). Communication Issues in Requirements Elicitation: A Content Analysis of Stakeholder Experiences. *Information and Software Technology, 45*, 525–537. doi:10.1016/S0950-5849(03)00032-6

Coughlan, J., & Macredie, M. (2002). Effective Communication in Requirements Elicitation: A Comparison of Methodologies. *Requirements Engineering, 7*, 47–60. doi:10.1007/s007660200004

Cruz, J. C., & Ducasse, S. (1999). A group based approach for coordinating active objects. In *Coordinatio Languages and Models* (pp. 355–370). Springer. doi:10.1007/3-540-48919-3_25

Cui, Z., Wang, L., Liu, X., Bu, L., Zhao, J., & Li, X. (2013). Verifying aspect-oriented activity diagrams against crosscutting properties. *International Journal of Software Engineering and Knowledge Engineering, 23*(5). doi:10.1142/S0218194013400123

Curbera, F., Duftler, M., Khalaf, R., Nagy, W., Mukhi, N., & Weerawarana, S. (2002). Unraveling the Web services web: An introduction to SOAP, WSDL, and UDDI. *Internet Computing, IEEE, 6*, 86–93. doi:10.1109/4236.991449

Czerwonka, J. (2006). Pairwise testing in real world: Practical extensions to test case generator. In *Proceedings of 24th Pacific Northwest Software Quality Conference*. Portland, OR: Academic Press.

D'Ambros, M., Lanza, M., & Lungu, M. (2009). Visualizing co-change information with the evolution radar. *IEEE Transactions on Software Engineering, 35*(5), 720–735. doi:10.1109/TSE.2009.17

D'Ambros, M., Lanza, M., & Robbes, R. (2012). Evaluating defect prediction approaches: a benchmark and an extensive comparison. *Empirical Software Engineering, 17*(4-5), 531–577. doi:10.1007/s10664-011-9173-9

Daenen, K., Theeten, B., Vanderfeesten, D., Vrancken, B., Waegeman, E., & Moons, J. et al. (2010). The personal internet. *Bell Labs Technical Journal, 15*(1), 3–21. doi:10.1002/bltj.20421

Dalzell, T. (2009). *The Routledge Dictionary of Modern American Slang and Unconventional English*. Routledge.

Damian, D., Al-Ani, B., Cubranic, D., & Robles, L. (2005). Teaching Requirements Engineering in Global Software Development: A report on a three-University collaboration. In *Proceedings of Workshop on Requirements Engineering Education and Training*. Paris: Academic Press.

Daneva, M., Van Der Veen, E., Amrit, C., Ghaisas, S., Sikkel, K., & Kumar, R. et al. (2012). Agile requirements prioritization in large-scale outsourced system projects: An empirical study. *Journal of Systems and Software, 86*(5), 1333–1353. doi:10.1016/j.jss.2012.12.046

Daniele, L. M., Silva, E., Pires, L. F., & Sinderen, M. (2009). A SOA-Based Platform-Specific Framework for Context-Aware Mobile Applications. *Lecture Notes in Business Information Processing, 38*, 25–37. doi:10.1007/978-3-642-04750-3_3

Daniels, D. (2011). Thoughts from the DO-178C Committee. In *Proceedings of 6th IET International Conference on System Safety*. IET.

Dardenne, A., van Lamsweerde, A., & Fickas, S. (2003). Goal-directed Requirements Acquisition. *Science of Computer Programming, 20*(1-2), 3–50. doi:10.1016/0167-6423(93)90021-G

Davis, A. M., Hickey, A. M., & Chamillard, A. T. (2005). Moving Beyond the Classroom: Integrating Requirements Engineering Research & Education to Improve Practice. In *Proceedings of Workshop on Requirements Engineering Education and Training*. Paris: Academic Press.

Davis, A., Dieste, O., Hickey, A., Juristo, N., & Moreno, A. M. (2006a). Effectiveness of Requirements Elicitation Techniques: Empirical Results Derived from a Systematic Review. In *Proceedings of Requirements Engineering, 14th IEEE International Conference* (pp. 179-188). IEEE. http://dx.doi.org/10.1109/RE.2006.17

Davis, A. (1988). A Taxonomy for the early stages of the software development life cycle. *Journal of Systems and Software, 8*(4), 297–311. doi:10.1016/0164-1212(88)90013-1

Davis, C. J., Fuller, R. M., Tremblay, M. C., & Berndt, D. J. (2006b). Communication Challenges in Requirements Elicitation and The Use of the Repertory Grid Technique. *Journal of Computer Information Systems, 47*, 78–86.

De Castro, V., Marcos, E., & Sanz, M. L. (2006). A model driven method for service composition modelling: A case study. *International Journal on Web Engineering Technology, 2*(4), 335–353. doi:10.1504/IJWET.2006.010419

De Castro, V., Marcos, E., & Vara, J. M. (2011). Applying CIM-to-PIM model transformations for the service-oriented development of information systems. *Information and Software Technology, 53*(19), 87–105. doi:10.1016/j.infsof.2010.09.002

De Castro, V., Marcos, E., & Wieringa, R. (2009). Towards a service-oriented MDA-based approach to the alignment of business processes with IT systems: From the business model to a web service composition model. *International Journal of Cooperative Information Systems, 18*(2), 225–260. doi:10.1142/S0218843009002038

De la Rosa Algarín, A., Demurjian, S. A., Berhe, S., & Pavlich-Mariscal, J. A. (2012). A security framework for XML schemas and documents for healthcare. In *Proceedings of 2012 IEEE International Conference on Bioinformatics and Biomedicine Workshops (BIBMW)* (pp. 782-789). IEEE.

De la Rosa Algarín, A., Ziminski, T. B., Demurjian, S. A., Kuykendall, R., & Rivera Sánchez, Y. (2013). Defining and enforcing XACML role-based security policies within an XML security framework. In *Proceedings of 9th International Conference on Web Information Systems and Technologies* (pp. 16-25). Academic Press.

De la Rosa Algarín, A., Demurjian, S. A., Ziminski, T. B., Rivera Sanchez, Y. K., & Kuykendall, R. (2013). Securing XML with role-based access control: case study in health care. In A. Ruiz Martínez, F. Pereñíguez García, & R. Marín López (Eds.), *Architectures and Protocols for Secure Information Technology* (pp. 334–365). Academic Press. doi:10.4018/978-1-4666-4514-1.ch013

De Nicola, R., Ferrari, G. L., & Pugliese, R. (1998). KLAIM: A kernel language for agents interaction and mobility. *Software Engineering. IEEE Transactions on, 24*(5), 315–330.

De Vries, W., Meyer, J. C., De Boer, F., & Van der Hoek, W. (2009). A coordination language for agents interacting in distributed plan-execute cycles. *International Journal of Reasoning-based Intelligent Systems, 1*(1), 4–17. doi:10.1504/IJRIS.2009.026713

Deavours, D. D., & Sanders, W. H. (1997). An efficient disk-based tool for solving very large Markov models. *Performance Evaluation, 33*(1), 67–84. doi:10.1016/S0166-5316(98)00010-8

Deissenboeck, F., Hummel, B., Juergens, E., Pfaehler, M., & Schaetz, B. (2010). *Model clone detection in practice*. Paper presented at the 4th International Workshop on Software Clones (IWSC '10). Cape Town, South Africa.

Dejaeger, K., Verbraken, T., & Baesens, B. (2013). Toward Comprehensible Software Fault Prediction Models Using Bayesian Network Classifiers. *Software Engineering. IEEE Transactions on, 39*(2), 237–257.

Delgado, J. (2013). Service Interoperability in the Internet of Things. In *Internet of Things and Inter-cooperative Computational Technologies for Collective Intelligence* (pp. 51–87). Springer. doi:10.1007/978-3-642-34952-2_3

Delling, D., Katz, B., & Pajor, T. (2012). Parallel computation of best connections in public transportation networks. *Journal of Experimental Algorithmics, 17*, 4.1-:4.26.

deMarco, T. (1979). *Structured Analysis and System Specification*. Prentice Hall.

Dementiev, R., Kettner, L., & Sanders, P. (2008). STXXL: Standard template library for XXL data sets. *Journal of Software- Practice & Experience, 38*(6), 589-637.

Design Platform, A. R. I. S. (2007). *Getting Started with BPM*. Springer.

Devedzic, V. (2002). Understanding ontological engineering. *Communications of the ACM, 45*(4), 136–144. doi:10.1145/505248.506002

Dey, A. K., & Abowd, G. D. (2001). Towards a better understanding of context and context awareness. In *Proceedings of the workshop on the What, Who, Where, When and how of Context Awareness*. ACM Press.

Di Penta, M., Cerulo, L., Guéhéneuc, Y. G., & Antoniol, G. (2008). An empirical study of the relationships between design pattern roles and class change proneness. In *Proceedings of 24th IEEE International Conference on software Maintenance* (pp. 217–226). Beijing, China: IEEE.

Diaz, G., & Rodriguez, I. (2009). Automatically deriving choreography-conforming systems of services. In *Proceedings of IEEE International Conference on Services Computing* (pp. 9-16). IEEE Computer Society Press.

Didonet Del Fabro, M., Bézivin, J., & Valduriez, P. (2006). *Weaving Models with the Eclipse AMW plugin*. Paper presented at the Eclipse Modelling Symposium, Eclipse Summit Europe. Esslingen, Germany.

Didonet Del Fabro, M., & Valduriez, P. (2008). Towards the efficient development of model transformations using model weaving and matching transformations. *Software & Systems Modeling, 8*(3), 305–324. doi:10.1007/s10270-008-0094-z

Diehl, S. (2007). *Software visualization: visualizing the structure, behaviour, and evolution of software*. Springer-Verlag.

Dikmans, L. (2008). *Transforming BPMN into BPEL: Why and How*. Oracle Technology network.

Ding, L. (2005). A model of hierarchical knowledge representation—toward knowware for computing with words. In *Proc. 6th International conference on intelligent technologies* (pp.188-197). Academic Press.

Ding, L. (2006). Knowware system for the development of intelligent systems. In *Proceedings of 7th International Conference on Intelligent Technologies* (Tech2006) (pp. 201-210). Academic Presss.

Ding, L. (2007). A model of hierarchical knowledge representation—toward knowware for intelligent systems. *Journal of advanced computational intelligence and intelligent informatics, 11*(10), 1232- 1240.

Ding, L. (2007). Design and development of knowware system. In *Proceedings of 2nd International conference on innovative computing, Information and Control* (pp. 17-21). Kumamoto.

Ding, L., & Lo, S.-L. (2008). Truth value flow inference in hybrid KBS constructed by KWS. In *Proceedings of 3rd International conference on innovative computing, information and control* (pp.311-314). Dalian, China: IEEE Computer Society.

Ding, L., & Lo, S.-L. (2009). Inference in knowware system. In *Proc. of 8th International conference on machine learning and cybernetics*, (pp. 215-220). Academic Press.

Ding, L., & Nadkami, S. (2007). Automatic construction of knowledge-based system using knowware system. In *Proc. of the 6th international conference on machine learning and cybernetics* (pp. 19-22). Academic Press.

Dinges, P., & Agha, G. (2012). Scoped synchronization constraints for large scale actor systems. In *Coordination Models and Languages* (pp. 89–103). Springer. doi:10.1007/978-3-642-30829-1_7

Dingle, N. J., Knottenbelt, W. J., & Suto, T. (2009). PIPE2: A tool for the performance evaluation of generalised stochastic Petri nets. *SIGMETRICS Performance Evaluation Review, 36*(4), 34–39. doi:10.1145/1530873.1530881

Distefano, S., Paci, D., Puliafito, A., & Scarpa, M. (2004). UML design and software performance modeling. [Springer.]. *Proceedings of Computer and Information Sciences-ISCIS*, *2004*, 564–573.

Distefano, S., Scarpa, M., & Puliafito, A. (2011). From UML to Petri Nets: The PCM-Based Methodology. *IEEE Transactions on Software Engineering*, *37*(1), 65–79. doi:10.1109/TSE.2010.10

Dowd, M., McDonald, J., & Schuh, J. (2006). *The art of software security assessment: Identifying and preventing software vulnerabilities*. Pearson Education. *ECLIPSE*. Retrieved March 2013 from http://www.st.cs.uni-sb.de/softevo/bug-data/eclipse

Drobics, M., & Bodenhofer, U. (2002) Fuzzy modeling with decision trees. In *Proceedings of the 2002 IEEE International Conference on Systems, Man and Cybernetics* (pp. 90–95). Los Alamitos, CA: IEEE Computer Society.

DSDM Consortium. (n.d.). Retrieved from http://www.dsdm.org/

Duala-Ekoko, E., & Robillard, M. P. (2007). Tracking code clones in evolving software. In *Proceedings of the 29th International Conference on Software Engineering* (ICSE '07). Minneapolis, MN: ICSE.

Dubois, E., Hagelstein, J., Lahou, E., Rifaut, A., & Williams, F. (1986). A knowledge representation language for requirements engineering. *Proceedings of the IEEE*, *74*(10), 1431–1444. doi:10.1109/PROC.1986.13644

Ducasse, S., & Richner, T. (1997). Executable connectors: Towards reusable design elements. *ACM SIGSOFT Software Engineering Notes*, *22*(6), 483–499. doi:10.1145/267896.267928

Dumer. (1989). Asymptotically Optimal Codes Correcting Memory Defects of Fixed Multiplicity. *Problemy Peredachi Informatskii, 25*, 3–20.

Dunietz, I. S., et al. (1997). Applying Design of Experiments to Software Testing. In *Proceedings of the International Conference on Software Engineering (ICSE '97)*. ACM Press.

Durisic, D., Nilsson, M., Staron, M., & Hansson, J. (2013). Measuring the impact of changes to the complexity and coupling properties of automotive software systems. *Journal of Systems and Software*, *86*, 1275–1293. doi:10.1016/j.jss.2012.12.021

Dzidek, W., Arisholm, E., & Briand, L. (2008). A realistic empirical evaluation of the costs and benefits of UML in software maintenance. *IEEE Transactions on Software Engineering*, *34*(3), 407–431. doi:10.1109/TSE.2008.15

Eastep, J., Wingate, D., & Agarwal, A. (2011). Smart data structures: An online machine learning approach to multicore data structures. In *Proceedings of the 8th ACM International Conference on Autonomic Computing* (pp. 11-20). Karlsruhe, Germany: ACM.

Eberlein. (1997). *Requirements Acquisition and Specification for Telecommunication Services*. (PhD Thesis). University of Wales, Swansea, UK.

Ebert, C. (2008). A brief history of software technology. *IEEE Software*, *25*(6), 22–25. doi:10.1109/MS.2008.141

Eclipse. (2013). Retrieved from http://www.eclipse.org/

Edelkamp, S., & Schrodl, S. (2000). Localizing A*. In *Proceedings of the 7th National Conference on Artificial Intelligence and 12th Conference on Innovative Applications of Artificial Intelligence* (pp. 885-890). Austin, TX: The MIT Press.

Edelkamp, S., & Sulewski, D. (2010). Efficient explicit-state model checking on general purpose graphics processors. In *Proceedings of the 17th International SPIN Conference on Model Checking Software* (pp. 106-123). Enschede, The Netherlands: Springer-Verlag.

Egyed, A. (2011). Automatically detecting and tracking inconsistencies in software design models. *IEEE Transactions on Software Engineering*, *37*(2), 188–204. doi:10.1109/TSE.2010.38

Ehrig, H., & Mahr, B. (1985). *Fundamentals of Algebraic Specification 1: Equations and Initial Semantics*. Springer-Verlag. doi:10.1007/978-3-642-69962-7

Ehrig, H., & Mahr, B. (1990). *Fundamentals of algebraic specification 2: module specifications and constraints*. Springer-Verlag. doi:10.1007/978-3-642-61284-8

Ehrig, H., Mahr, B., & Orejas, F. (1992). Introduction to algebraic specification: Part 1: Formal methods for software development. *The Computer Journal, 35*, 468–477. doi:10.1093/comjnl/35.5.468

Eick, S. G., Steffen, J. L., & Sumner, E. E. Jr. (1992). Seesoft - A tool for visualizing line oriented software statistics. *IEEE Transactions on Software Engineering, 18*(11), 957–968. doi:10.1109/32.177365

EIF. (2010). *European Interoperability Framework (EIF) for European Public Services, Annex 2 to the Communication from the Commission to the European Parliament, the Council, the European Economic and Social Committee and the Committee of Regions 'Towards interoperability for European public services'*. Retrieved July 26, 2013, from http://ec.europa.eu/isa/documents/isa_annex_ii_eif_en.pdf

Elder, J. (2005) Top 10 data mining mistakes. In *Proceedings of the Fifth IEEE International Conference on Data Mining*. Los Alamitos, CA: IEEE Computer Society.

Elish, K. O., & Elish, M. O. (2008). Predicting defect-prone software modules using support vector machines. *Journal of Systems and Software, 81*(5), 649–660. doi:10.1016/j.jss.2007.07.040

Elish, M. O., Al-Yafei, A. H., & Al-Mulhem, M. (2011). Empirical comparison of three metrics suites for fault prediction in packages of object-oriented systems: A case study of Eclipse. *Advances in Engineering Software, 42*(10), 852–859. doi:10.1016/j.advengsoft.2011.06.001

Ellims, M., Ince, D., & Petre, M. (2008). The Effectiveness of T-Way Test Data Generation. *Springer LNCS 5219. SAFECOMP, 2008*, 16–29.

Emmerich, W., Aoyama, M., & Sventek, J. (2008). The impact of research on the development of middleware technology. *ACM Transactions on Software Engineering and Methodology, 17*(4), 19:1-19:48.

EN 50128. (2011). *Railway applications - Communication, signalling and processing systems - Software for railway control and protection systems*. CENELEC.

Engels, G., & Lohr-Richter, P. (1992). CADDY--A highly integrated environment to support conceptual database design. In *Proc. of the 5th Int. Workshop on CASE* (pp.19 – 22). Montreal, Canada: CASE.

Engels, G., Schäfer, W., Balzer, R., & Gruhn, V. (2001). Process-centered software engineering environments: academic and industrial perspectives. In *Proceedings of the 23rd International Conference on Software Engineering (ICSE '01)* (pp. 671-673). Washington, DC: IEEE Computer Society.

Engels, G., Gogolla, G., & Hohenstein, U. et al. (1992). Conceptual modelling of database application using an extended ER model. *Data & Knowledge Engineering, 9*(2), 157–204. doi:10.1016/0169-023X(92)90008-Y

ENISA. (n.d.). Retrieved from http://www.enisa.europa.eu/

Erl, T. (2005). *Service-Oriented Architecture: Concepts, Technology, and Design*. Upper Saddle River, NJ: Prentice Hall PTR.

Ernst, N. A., Borgida, A., Jureta, I. J., & Mylopoulos, J. (2013). Agile requirements engineering via paraconsistent reasoning. *Information Systems*.

ESA ECSS--E--40 Part 1B. (2003). *Software - Part 1: Principles and requirements*. European Space Agency (ESA).

ESA ECSS--E--40 Part 2B. (2005). *Software — Part 2: Document requirements definitions (DRDs)*. European Space Agency (ESA).

ESA PSS-05-0. (1991). *ESA software engineering standards. Issue 2*. European Space Agency (ESA). (superseded).

Estefan, J. A., Laskey, K., McCabe, F. G., & Thornton, D. (2008). *Reference Architecture for Service Oriented Architecture Version 1.0*. Academic Press.

Euzenat, J., & Shvaiko, P. (2007). *Ontology matching*. Berlin: Springer.

Evett, M., Khoshgoftar, T., Chien, P. D., & Allen, E. (1998). GP-based software quality prediction. In *Proceedings of the Third Annual Conference Genetic Programming*, (pp. 60-65). Academic Press.

FAA Job Aid. (1998). *Conducting software project reviews prior to certification*. Federal Aviation Authority (FAA). (Revised 2004)

Fabra, J., & Álvarez, P. (2010). BPEL2DENEB: translation of BPEL processes to executable high-level petri nets. In *Proceedings of Fifth International Conference on Internet and Web Applications and Services – ICIW 2010*. IEEE Computer Society Press.

Fabra, J., Álvarez, P., & Ezpeleta, J. (2007). DRLinda: a distributed message broker for collaborative interactions among business processes. In *Proceedings of 8th International Conference on Electronic Commerce and Web Technologies – EC-Web'07* (LNCS), (vol. 4655, pp. 212-221). Springer Verlag.

Fabra, J., Álvarez, P., Bañares, J., & Ezpeleta, J. (2006). A framework for the development and execution of horizontal protocols in open BPM systems. In *Proceedings of 4th International Conference on Business Process Management – BPM 2006* (LNCS). Springer Verlag.

Fabra, J., Álvarez, P., Bañares, J., & Ezpeleta, J. (2011). DENEB: a platform for the development and execution of interoperable dynamic web processes. *Concurrency and Computation*. doi:10.1002/cpe.1795 PMID:23335858

Fan, L., Cao, P., Almeida, J., & Broder, A. Z. (2000). Summary cache: A scalable wide-area web cache sharing protocol. *IEEE/ACM Transactions on Networking*, 8(3), 281–293. doi:10.1109/90.851975

FDA. (1998). *Guidance for FDA reviewers and industry. Guidance for the content of pre-market submissions for software contained in medical devices. Version 1*. U.S. Department of health and human services, Food and Drink Administration (FDA), Center for devices and radiological health (CDRH), Office of device evaluation. (Updated 2005)

Feijs, L. M. (1999). Modelling Microsoft COM using π-calculus. In *Proceedings of FM'99—Formal Methods* (pp. 1343-1363). Springer.

Felderer, M., & Ramler, R. (2013). Experiences and challenges of introducing risk-based testing in an industrial project. In D. Winkler, S. Biffl, & J. Bergsmann (Eds.), *Software Quality. Increasing Value in Software and Systems Development LNBIP 133* (pp. 10–29). Heidelberg, Germany: Springer. doi:10.1007/978-3-642-35702-2_3

Fensel, D., Lassila, O., Harmelen, F., Horrocks, I., Hendler, J., & McGuinness, J. (2000). The Semantic Web and its Languages. *IEEE Intelligent Systems*, 67–73.

Fenton, N. E., & Neil, M. (1999). A critique of software defect prediction models. *Software Engineering. IEEE Transactions on*, 25(5), 675–689.

Fenton, N. E., & Ohlsson, N. (2000). Quantitative analysis of faults and failures in a complex software system. *Software Engineering. IEEE Transactions on*, 26(8), 797–814.

Fenton, N. E., & Pfleeger, S. L. (1998). *Software Metrics: A Rigorous and Practical Approach* (2nd ed.). Boston, MA: PWS Pub. Co.

Fergerson, R. W., Noy, N. F., & Musen, M. A. (2000). The knowledge model of protégé 2000: Combining interoperability and flexibility. In R. Dieng (Ed.), *Proceedings of the 12th EKAW Conference*, (pp. 17–32). Springer-Verlag.

Ferraiolo, D. F., Sandhu, R., Gavrila, S., Kuhn, D. R., & Chandramouli, R. (2001). Proposed NIST standard for role-based access control.[TISSEC]. *ACM Transactions on Information and System Security*, 4(3), 224–274. doi:10.1145/501978.501980

Ferrari, A., Fantechi, A., Gnesi, S., & Magnani, G. (2013). Model-based development and formal methods in the railway industry. *IEEE Software*, 30(3), 28–34.

Ferreira de Oliveira, M. C., & Levkowitz, H. (2003). From visual data exploration to visual data mining: a survey. *IEEE Transactions on Visualization and Computer Graphics*, 9(3), 378–394. doi:10.1109/TVCG.2003.1207445

Fiadeiro, J. L. (2005). *Categories for Software Engineering*. Springer.

Fielding, R. T. (2000). *Architectural Styles and the Design of Network-Based Software Architectures*. (Ph.D. Thesis). University of California, Irvine, CA.

Filman, R. E., Elrad, T., Clarke, S., & Aksit, M. (2005). *Aspect-Oriented Software Development*. Boston: Addison-Wesley.

Firduas, A., & Ghani, I. (2013b). *2nd International Conference on Informatics, Environment, Energy and Applications*. IEEA.

Firduas, A., Ghani, I., & Jeong, S. R. (2013a). *A Systematic Literature Review on Secure Software Development using Feature Driven Development (FDD) Agile Model.* Paper presented at the KSII The 8th Asia Pacific International Conference on Information Science and Technology. Korea.

Fischer, M., & Gall, H. (2004). Visualizing feature evolution of large-scale software based on problem and modification report data. *Journal of Software Maintenance and Evolution: Research and Practice - Analyzing the Evolution of Large-Scale Software, 16* (6), 385-403.

Fischer, M., & Gall, H. (2006). Evograph: A lightweight approach to evolutionary and structural analysis of large software systems. In *Proceedings of the 13th Working Conference on Reverse Engineering.* IEEE Computer Society.

Fischer, M., Pinzger, M., & Gall, H. (2003). Analyzing and relating bug report data for feature tracking. In *Proceedings of the 10th Working Conference on Reverse Engineering.* IEEE Computer Society.

Fleisch, E., & Mattern, F. (2005). *Das Internet der Dinge. Ubiquitous Computing und RFID in der Praxis: Visionen, Technologien, Anwendungen, Handlungsanleitungen.* Springer-Verlag. doi:10.1007/3-540-28299-8

Fogaras, D., & Rácz, B. (2005). Scaling link-based similarity search. In *Proceedings of the 14th International Conference on World Wide Web (pp.* 641-650). Chiba, Japan: ACM.

Forbes, M. et al. (2008). Refining the In-Parameter-Order Strategy for Constructing Covering Arrays. *Journal of Research of the National Institute of Standards and Technology, 113,* 287–297. doi:10.6028/jres.113.022

Foster, I., Kesselman, C., Nick, J., & Tuecke, S. (2002). *The Physiology of the Grid: An Open Grid Services Architecture for Distributed Systems Integration.* Open Grid Service Infrastructure WG, Global Grid Forum.

Foster, I., & Kesselman, C. (1998). *The Grid: Blueprint for a New Computing Infrastructure.* Morgan Kauffmann.

Fowler, M. (1999). *Refactoring: Improving the Design of Existing Code.* Addison - Wesley Longman Publishing Co.

Fowler, M. (2005). *The new methodology.* Retrieved June 18, 2013 from http://www.martinfowler.com/articles/newMethodology.html

Fox, J. (2005). A formal foundation for aspect oriented software development. In *Proceedings of Memoria del XIV Con- greso Internacional de Computation CIC.* IPN.

France, R., & Rumpe, B. (2007). Model-driven development of complex software: A research roadmap. In *Proceedings of Future of Software 2007 (FOSE'07)* (pp. 35-54). Washington, DC: IEEE Computer Society.

France, R., Ray, I., Georg, G., & Ghosh, S. (2004). Aspect-oriented approach to early design modelling. In *Proc. of the 6th Int. Conf. on Aspect Oriented Software Development (AOSD'07).* Vancouver, Canada: IEE Proceedings Software.

Freeman, E., Hupfer, S., & Arnold, K. (1999). *JavaSpaces principles, patterns, and practice.* Addison-Wesley Professional.

Frye, C. (2006). BPM inside the belly of the SOA whale. *Web Services News,* 1–3.

Fushida, K., Kawaguchi, S., & Iida, H. (2007). A method to investigate software evolutions using design pattern detection tool. In *Proceedings of the 1st International Workshop on Software Patterns and Quality* (pp. 11–16). Academic Press.

Fuxman, A., Liu, L., & Mylopoulos, J. et al. (2004). Specifying and analyzing early requirements in Tropos. *Requir Engin, 9*(2), 132–150. doi:10.1007/s00766-004-0191-7

Gabrysiak, G. Seibel, & Neumann. (2010). Teaching requirements engineering with virtual stakeholders without software engineering knowledge. In *Proceedings of 5th International Workshop on Requirements Engineering Education and Training (REET).* doi:10.1109/REET.2010.5633109

Galitz, W. O. (2007). *The Essential Guide to User Interface Design: An Introduction to GUI Design Principles and Techniques.* Wiley.

Galper, A. R., & Brutlag, D. L. (1990). *Parallel similarity Search and Alignment with the Dynamic Programming Method (Tech. Rep.).* Academic Press.

Gamma, E., Helm, R., Johnson, R., & Vlissides, J. (1995). *Design patterns: Elements of reusable object–oriented software*. Reading, MA: Addison–Wesley.

Gamma, E., Johnson, R., Vlissides, J., & Helm, R. (1994). *Design patterns: Elements of reusable object-oriented software*. Reading, MA: Addison-Wesley Professional.

GAMP4. (2001). Good Automated Manufacturing Practice (GAMP) Guide for Validation of Automated Systems (4th ed.). International Society for Pharmaceutical Engineering (ISPE) (Updated as GAMP5 in 2008).

Gane, C., & Sarson T. (1977). *Structured Systems Analysis: Tools and Techniques*. McDonnell Douglas Systems Integration Company.

Ganek, A. G., & Corbi, T. A. (2003). The dawning of the autonomic computing era. *IBM Systems Journal*, *42*(1), 5–18. doi:10.1147/sj.421.0005

Gang, Z., Xin, P., Zhenchang, X., & Wenyun, Z. (2012). *Cloning practices: Why developers clone and what can be changed*. Paper presented at the 28th IEEE International Conference on Software Maintenance (ICSM). Trento, Italy.

Garlan, D., Cheng, S.-W., Huang, A.-C., Schmerl, B., & Steenkiste, P. (2004). Rainbow: Architecture-based self-adaptation with reusable infrastructure. *Computer*, *37*(10), 46–54. doi:10.1109/MC.2004.175

Garousi, V., Briand, L. C., & Labiche, Y. (2008). A UML-based quantitative framework for early prediction of resource usage and load in distributed real-time systems. *Software & Systems Modeling*, *8*(2), 275–302. doi:10.1007/s10270-008-0099-7

Gaspari, M., & Zavattaro, G. (1999). A Process Algebraic Specication of the New Asynchronous CORBA Messaging Service? In *Proceedings of ECOOP'99—Object-Oriented Programming* (pp. 495-518). Springer.

Geimer, M., & Wolf, F. (2010). The Scalasca performance toolset architecture. *Concurrency and Computation*, 702–719.

Gelernter, D., & Carriero, N. (1992). Coordination languages and their significance. *Communications of the ACM*, *35*(2), 96–107. doi:10.1145/129630.376083

German, D., Hindle, A., & Jordan, N. (2006). Visualizing the evolution of software using softChange. *International Journal of Software Engineering and Knowledge Engineering*. doi:10.1142/S0218194006002665

Gesbert, D., Kiani, S. G., & Gjendemsjo, A. (2007). Adaptation, coordination, and distributed resource allocation in interference-limited wireless networks. *Proceedings of the IEEE*, *95*(12), 2393–2409. doi:10.1109/JPROC.2007.907125

GesIMED System. (2008). Retrieved from http://ariadna.escet.urjc.es/gesimed/

Ge, X., Paige, R. F., Polack, F., & Brooke, P. (2007). Extreme programming security practices. In *Agile Processes in Software Engineering and Extreme Programming* (pp. 226–230). Springer. doi:10.1007/978-3-540-73101-6_42

Giang, L. T., Kang, D., & Bae, D. H. (2010). Software fault prediction models for web applications. In *Proceedings of Computer Software and Applications Conference Workshops (COMPSACW), 2010 IEEE 34th Annual* (pp. 51-56). Korea: IEEE.

Gibson, J. P. (2000). Formal requirements engineering: Learning from the students. In *Proceedings of Software Engineering Conference*. Academic Press.

Giesecke, S. (2007). Generic modeling of code clones. Dagstuhl, Germany: Internationales Begegnungs und Forschungszentrum Informatik (IBFI).

Giger, E., D'Ambros, M., Pinzger, M., & Gall, H. C. (2012). Method--level bug prediction. In *Proceedings of ACM-IEEE International Symposium on Empirical Software Engineering and Measurement*. ACM/IEEE.

Gilb, T. (1976). *Software Metrics*. Studentlitteratur AB.

Gill, N. S., & Grover, P. S. (2003). Component-based measurement: few useful guidelines. *ACM SIGSOFT Software Engineering Notes*, *28*(6), 4–4. doi:10.1145/966221.966237

Gionis, A., Indyk, P., & Motwani, R. (1999). Similarity search in high dimensions via hashing. In *Proceedings of the 25th International Conference on Very Large Data Bases* (pp. 518-529). Edinburgh, UK: Morgan Kaufmann Publishers Inc.

Git. (n.d.). Retrieved from http://git-scm.com/

Godfrey, M., & Tu, Q. (2001). Growth, evolution, and structural change in open source software. In *Proceedings of the 4th International Workshop on Principles of Software Evolution IWPSE '01* (pp. 103-106). New York, NY: ACM.

Goeminne, M., & Mens, T. (2010). A framework for analysing and visualising open source software ecosystems. In *Proceedings of the Joint ERCIM Workshop on Software Evolution (EVOL) and International Workshop on Principles of Software Evolution (IWPSE)*. ACM.

Goguen, J. A. (1991). A categorical manifesto. In *Mathematical Structures in Computer Science* (pp. 49–67). Academic Press.

Goguen, J. A. (1992). Order-sorted algebra 1: Equational deduction for multiple inheritance, overloading, exceptions and partial operations. *Theoretical Computer Science, 105*, 217–273. doi:10.1016/0304-3975(92)90302-V

Gokhale, S. (2007). Architecture-Based Software Reliability Analysis: Overview and Limitations. *IEEE Transactions on Dependable and Secure Computing, 4*(1), 32–40. doi:10.1109/TDSC.2007.4

Gokhale, S. S. (2005). A simulation approach to structure-based software reliability analysis. *IEEE Transactions on Software Engineering, 31*(8), 643–656. doi:10.1109/TSE.2005.86

Gokhale, S. S., & Trivedi, K. S. (2006). Analytical Models for Architecture-Based Software Reliability Prediction: A Unification Framework. *IEEE Transactions on Reliability, 55*(4), 578–590. doi:10.1109/TR.2006.884587

Gokhale, S. S., Wong, W., Horgan, J. R., & Trivedi, K. S. (2004). An analytical approach to architecture-based software performance and reliability prediction. *Performance Evaluation, 58*(4), 391–412. doi:10.1016/j.peva.2004.04.003

Goldberg, A. V., & Werneck, R. F. (2005). Computing point-to-point shortest paths from external memory. In *Proceedings of the 7h Workshop on Algorithm Engineering and Experiments* (pp. 26-40). Vancouver, Canada: SIAM.

Goldman, M., & Katz, S. (2006). Modular generic verification of LTL properties for aspects. In *Proc. of Foundations of Aspect Languages Workshop* (FOAL06), (pp. 17–24). Bonn, Germany: FOAL.

Gomaa, H. (2005). Architecture-Centric Evolution in Software Product Lines. In *Proceedings of ECOOP'2005 Workshop on Architecture-Centric Evolution* (ACE'2005). Glasgow, UK: ACE.

Gomes, R., Maciel, R., Silva, B., Silva, F., & Magalhães, A. (2011). MoDErNE: Model Driven Process Centered Software Engineering Environment. In *Proceedings of the II Brazilian Conference on Software: Theory and Practice, Tools Session*. São Paulo. Brazil: Academic Press.

Gondra, I. (2008). Applying machine learning to software fault-proneness prediction. *Journal of Systems and Software, 81*(2), 186–195. doi:10.1016/j.jss.2007.05.035

Gonzalez, A., Theron, R., Telea, A., & Garcia, F. J. (2009). Combined visualization of structural and metric information for software evolution analysis. In *Proceedings of the joint international and annual ERCIM workshops on Principles of software evolution (IWPSE) and software evolution (Evol) workshops*. ACM.

Grady, J. O. (2006). *Systems Requirements Analysis*. Amsterdam: Elsevier.

Graham, S., Karmarkar, A., Mischkinsky, J., Robinson, I., & Sedukhin, I. (2005). *Web Services Resource Framework 1.2*. OASIS WSRF-TC.

Grassi, V., Mirandola, R., & Sabetta, A. (2007). Filling the gap between design and performance/reliability models of component-based systems: A model-driven approach. *Journal of Systems and Software, 80*(4), 528–558. doi:10.1016/j.jss.2006.07.023

Graydon, P., Habli, I., Hawkins, R., Kelly, T., & Knight, J. (2012). Arguing Conformance. *IEEE Software, 29*(3), 50–57. doi:10.1109/MS.2012.26

Grindal, M., Offutt, J., & Andler, S. (2005). Combination Testing Strategies: a Survey. *Software Testing, Verification, and Reliability, 15*, 167–199. doi:10.1002/stvr.319

Gronback, R. C. (2009). *Eclipse Modeling Project: A Domain-Specific Language (DSL) Toolkit*. Addison-Wesley Professional.

Gruhn, V. (2002). Process-Centered Software Engineering Environments: A Brief History and Future Challenges. *Annals of Software Engineering, 14*, 363–382. doi:10.1023/A:1020522111961

Gu, X., Shi, H., & Ye, J. (2008). A Hierarchical Service Discovery Framework for Ubiquitous Computing. In *Proceedings of Third International Conference on Pervasive Computing and Applications*. ICPCA.

Gudaitis, M. S., Lamont, G. B., & Terzuoli, A. J. (1995). Multicriteria vehicle route-planning using parallel A * search. In *Proceedings of the 1995 ACM Symposium on Applied Computing* (pp. 171-176). Nashville, TN: ACM.

Gueheneuc, Y. G., Sahraoui, H., & Zaidi, F. (2004). Fingerprinting design patterns. In *Proceedings of the 11th Working Conference on Reverse Engineering* (pp. 172–181). Delft, The Netherlands: IEEE.

Gueheneuc, Y. G., & Antoniol, G. (2008). Demima: A multilayered approach for design pattern identification. *IEEE Transactions on Software Engineering, 34*(5), 667–684. doi:10.1109/TSE.2008.48

Guelfi, N., & Mammar, A. (2006). A formal framework to generate XPDL specifications from UML activity diagrams. In *Proceedings of 2006 ACM symposium on Applied computing – SAC'06*. ACM.

Guelfi, N., et al. (2003). DRIP Catalyst: An MDE/MDA Method for Fault-tolerant Distributed Software Families Development. In *Proceedings of the Workshop on Best Practices for Model Driven Software Development*. Academic Press.

Gulla, B. (1992). Improved maintenance support by multi-version visualizations. In *Proceedings of Conference on Software Maintenance*. Academic Press.

Guo, L., Ma, Y., Cukic, B., & Singh, H. (2004). Robust prediction of fault-proneness by random forests. In *Proceedings of Software Reliability Engineering* (pp. 417–428). IEEE.

Gyimothy, T., Ferenc, R., & Siket, I. (2005). Empirical validation of object-oriented metrics on open source software for fault prediction. *Software Engineering. IEEE Transactions on, 31*(10), 897–910.

Hall, G. A., & Munson, J. C. (2000). Software evolution: code delta and code churn. *Journal of Systems and Software, 54*(2), 111–118. doi:10.1016/S0164-1212(00)00031-5

Hall, J. G., Rapanotti, L., & Jackson, M. (2005). Problem frame semantics for software development. *Journal of Software and Systems Modeling, 4*(2), 189–198. doi:10.1007/s10270-004-0062-1

Hall, T., Beecham, S., Bowes, D., Gray, D., & Counsell, S. (2012). A systematic literature review on fault prediction performance in software engineering. *Software Engineering. IEEE Transactions on, 38*(6), 1276–1304.

Halpin, T. (1998). Object role modeling (ORM/NIAM). In P. Bernus, K. Mertins, & G. Schmidt (Eds.), *Handbook of Architectures of Information Systems* (pp. 81–101). Berlin: Springer-Verlag.

Halstead, M. H. (1977). *Elements of Software Science*. Elsevier Science Inc.

Hamlet, D. (2009). Tools and experiments supporting a testing-based theory of component composition.[TOSEM]. *ACM Transactions on Software Engineering and Methodology, 18*(3), 12. doi:10.1145/1525880.1525885

Han, M., Thiery, T., & Song, X. (2006). Managing exceptions in the medical workflow systems. In *Proceedings of the 28th international conference on Software engineering* (pp. 741-750). ACM.

Han, S., & Xie, T. (2012). Performance debugging in the large via mining millions of stack traces. In *Proceedings of the 2012 International Conference on Software Engineering* (pp. 145--155). IEEE.

Hanson, J. E., Nandi, P., & Kumaran, S. (2002). Conversation support for business pro- cess integration. In *Proceedings of Sixth International Enterprise Distributed Object computing Conference – EDOC'02*. IEEE Computer Society.

Harel, D. (1987). Statecharts: A visual formalism for complex systems. *Science of Computer Programming, 8*(3), 231–274. doi:10.1016/0167-6423(87)90035-9

Harel, D., Kozen, D., & Tiuryn, J. (2000). *Dynamic Logic*. The MIT Press.

Harmon, P. (2004). The OMG's model driven architecture and BPM. *Business Process Trends*, 1–3.

Hartman, A., Klinger, T., & Raskin, L. (2005). *WHITCH: IBM Intelligent Test Configuration Handler*. IBM Haifa and Watson Research Laboratories.

Hartman, A., & Raskin, L. (2004). Problems and Algorithms for Covering Arrays. *Discrete Mathematics, 284*, 149–156. doi:10.1016/j.disc.2003.11.029

Hartmann, J., Vieira, M., & Axel Ruder, H. (2004). *UML-based test generation and execution* (White paper). Siemens Corporate Research.

Hartwick, J., & Barki, H. (2001). Communication as a Dimension of User Participation. *IEEE Transactions on Professional Communication, 44*, 21–36. doi:10.1109/47.911130

Haruna, S. (2012). A Unified Theory of the Behaviour of Profit-maximising, Labour-managed and Joint-Stock Firms Operating under Uncertainty: A Comment. *The Economic Journal, 95*(380), 1093–1094. doi:10.2307/2233269

Hasheminejad, S. M. H., & Jalili, S. (2012). Design patterns selection: An automatic two–phase method. *Journal of Systems and Software, 85*(2), 408–424. doi:10.1016/j.jss.2011.08.031

Hassan, A. E., & Holt, R. C. (2005). The Top Ten List: Dynamic Fault Prediction. In *Proceedings of the 21st International Conference on Software Maintenance ICSM'05* (pp. 263-272). Los Alamitos, CA: IEEE Computer Society.

Hata, H., Mizuno, O., & Kikuno, T. (2012). Bug prediction based on fine--grained module histories. In *Proceedings of 34th International Conference on Software Engineering*. ICSE.

Hatclif, J., Leavens, G., Leino, K., Müller, P., & Parkinson, M. (2012). Behavioral interface specification languages. *ACM Computing Surveys, 44*(3), 16:1-6:58.

Haverkort, B., Bell, A., & Bohnenkamp, H. (1999). On the efficient sequential and distributed generation of very large Markov chains from stochastic Petri nets. In *Proceedings of the 8th International Workshop on Petri Nets and Performance Models* (pp. 12-21). Zaragoza, Spain: Presnsas Universitarias de Zaragoza.

Havey, M. (2005). *Essential Business Process Modeling*. O'Reilly Media, Inc.

Hay, D. C. (2003). *Requirements Analysis: From Business Views to Architecture*. Upper Saddle River, NJ: Prentice Hall.

Health Information Privacy. (n.d.). Retrieved from http://www.hhs.gov/ocr/privacy/

Heckel, R., Küster, J., Thöne, S., & Voigt, H. (2003). *Towards a UML Profile for Service-Oriented Architectures*. Paper presented at the Workshop on Model Driven Architecture: Foundations and Applications (MDAFA '03). Enschede, The Netherlands.

Helmy, W., Kamel, A., & Hegazy, O. (2012). Requirements Engineering Methodology in Agile Environment. [IJCSI]. *International Journal of Computer Science Issues, 9*(5), 293–300.

Henderson-Sellers, B., & Edwards, J. M. (1990). Object oriented systems life cycle. *Communications of the ACM, 33*(9), 142–159. doi:10.1145/83880.84529

Hentenryck, P. V., & Saraswat, V. (1996). Strategic directions in constraint programming. *ACM Computing Surveys, 28*(4).

Herbsleb, J. D., Atkins, D. L., Boyer, D. G., Handel, M., & Finholt, T. A. (2002). Introducing instant messaging and chat into the workplace. In *Proceedings of the ACM Conference on Computer-Human Interaction (CHI)* (pp. 171-178). Minneapolis, MN: ACM.

Herbsleb, J. D., & Mockus, A. (2003). An empirical study of speed and communication in globally distributed software development. *IEEE Transactions on Software Engineering, 29*(6), 481–494. doi:10.1109/TSE.2003.1205177

Hermann, K. (1999). Difficulties in the transition from OO analysis to design. *IEEE Software, 16*(5), 94–102. doi:10.1109/52.795107

Herzig, K., Just, S., & Zeller, A. (2013). It's not a bug, it's a feature: How misclassification impacts bug prediction. In *Proceedings of the 35th International Conference on Software Engineering ICSE'13* (pp. 392-401). Los Alamitos, CA: IEEE Computer Society.

Heuzeroth, D., Holl, T., Hogstrom, G., & Lowe, W. (2003). Automatic design pattern detection. In *Proceedings of the 11th IEEE International Workshop on Program Comprehension* (pp. 94–103). Portland, OR: IEEE.

Hewett, R. (2011). Mining software defect data to support software testing management. *Applied Intelligence, 34*(2), 245–257. doi:10.1007/s10489-009-0193-8

Hickey, A. M., & Davis, A. M. (2004). A Unified Model of Requirements Elicitation. *Journal of Management Information Systems, 20*, 65–84.

Hierons, R., Bogdanov, K., Bowen, J., Cleaveland, R., Derrick, J., Dick, J., ... Zedan, H. (2009). Using formal specifications to support testing. *ACM Computing Surveys, 41*(2), 9:1-9:76.

Highsmith, J., & Cockburn, A. (2001). Agile software development: the business of innovation. *Computer, 34*(9), 120–122. doi:10.1109/2.947100

Hill, J. (2010). Context-based Analysis of System Execution Traces for Validating Distributed Real-time and Embedded System Quality-of-Service Properties. In *Proceedings 16th IEEE International Conference on Embedded and Real-Time Computing Systems and Applications (RTCSA)* (pp. 92-101). Macau: IEEE.

Hill, J., & Schmidt, D. (2009). Unit Testing Non-functional Concerns of Component-based Distributed Systems. In *Proceedings of the 2nd International Conference on Software Testing, Verification, and Validation* (pp. 406-415). Denver, CO: IEEE.

Hill, T., & Lewicki, P. (2007). *STATISTICS: Methods and Applications*. Tulsa, OK: StatSoft.

Hoffmann, A. (2008). Teaching Soft Facts in Requirements Engineering Using Improvisation Theatre Techniques. In *Proceedings of Third international workshop on Multimedia and Enjoyable Requirements Engineering - Beyond Mere Descriptions and with More Fun and Games*. Barcelona: Academic Press.

Holzmann, G. J. (1988). An improved protocol reachability analysis technique. *Software, Practice & Experience, 18*(2), 137–161. doi:10.1002/spe.4380180203

Home – SMART Platforms. (n.d.). Retrieved from http://smartplatforms.org/

Honda, K., Vasconcelos, V. T., & Kubo, M. (1998). Language primitives and type discipline for structured communication-based programming. In *Programming Languages and Systems* (pp. 122–138). Springer. doi:10.1007/BFb0053567

Hong, D., Gu, T., & Baik, J. (2011). A UML model based white box reliability prediction to identify unreliable components. In *Proceedings of Secure Software Integration & Reliability Improvement Companion (SSIRI-C), 2011 5th International Conference on* (pp. 152-159). IEEE.

Horn, P. (2001). *Autonomic computing: IBM's perspective on the state of information technology*. Academic Press.

Hou, D., Jacob, F., & Jablonski, P. (2009). *Proactively managing copy-and-paste induced code clones*. Paper presented at the IEEE International Conference on Software Maintenance (ICSM 2009). Edmonton, Canada.

Hou, L., Jin, Z., & Wu, B. (2006). Modeling and verifying web services driven by requirements: An ontology based approach. *Sci China Ser F-Inf Sci, 49*(6), 792–820. doi:10.1007/s11432-006-2031-5

Hrastnik, P. (2004). Execution of business processes based on web services. *International Journal of Electronic Business, 2*(5), 550–556. doi:10.1504/IJEB.2004.005886

Hsu, C. J., & Huang, C. Y. (2011). An adaptive reliability analysis using path testing for complex component-based software systems. *Reliability. IEEE Transactions on, 60*(1), 158–170.

Hsueh, N. L., Wen, L. C., Ting, D. H., Chu, W., Chang, C. H., & Koong, C. S. (2011). An approach for evaluating the effectiveness of design patterns in software evolution. In *Proceedings of the 35th Annual Computer Software and Applications Conference Workshops* (pp. 315–320). Munich, Germany: IEEE.

Hsueh, N. L., Chu, P. H., & Chu, W. (2008). A quantitative approach for evaluating the quality of design patterns. *Journal of Systems and Software, 81*(8), 1430–1439. doi:10.1016/j.jss.2007.11.724

Huang, G., Liu, T., Mei, H., et al. (2004). Towards autonomic computing middleware via reflection. In *Proceedings of 28th Annual International Computer Software and Applications Conference* (COMPSAC) (pp. 122—127). Hongkong, China: COMPSAC.

Huang, G., Mei, H., & Yang, F. (2004). Runtime software architecture based on reflective middleware. *Sci China Ser F-Inf Sci, 47*(5), 555–576. doi:10.1360/03yf0192

Huang, G., Mei, H., & Yang, F. (2006). Runtime recovery and manipulation of software architecture of component-based systems. *Int J Auto Software Engin, 13*(2), 251–278.

Huebscher, M. C., & McCann, J. A. (2008). A survey of autonomic computing—degrees, models, and applications.[CSUR]. *ACM Computing Surveys, 40*(3), 7–13. doi:10.1145/1380584.1380585

Huijs, C., Sikkel, K., & Wieringa, R. (2005). Mission 2 Solution: Requirements Engineering Education as Central Theme in the BIT Programme. In *Proceedings of Workshop on Requirements Engineering Education and Training*. Paris: Academic Press.

Humprey, W., & Kelner, M. (1989). *Software Modeling: Principles of Entity Process Models*. Carnegie Mellon University.

Hunt, J. (2006). *Agile software construction*. New York: Springer.

Huston, B. (2001). The effects of design pattern application on metric scores. *Journal of Systems and Software, 58*(3), 261–269. doi:10.1016/S0164-1212(01)00043-7

Hutchinson, J., Rouncefield, M., & Whittle, J. (2011). Model-driven Engineering practices in industry. In *Proceedings of the 33rd International Conference on Software Engineering (ICSE '11)* (pp. 633-642). Waikiki, HI: IEEE.

Hutchinson, J., Whittle, J., Rouncefield, M., & Kristoffersen, S. (2011). Empirical assessment of MDE in industry. In *Proceedings of the 33rd International Conference on Software Engineering (ICSE '11)* (pp. 471-480). Waikiki, HI: ICSE.

Ibáñez, M. J., Álvarez, P., & Ezpeleta, J. (2008). Checking necessary conditions for control and data flow compatibility between business and interaction logics in web processes. In *Proceedings of 6th IEEE European Conference on Web Services*, (pp. 92–101). IEEE.

Ibáñez, M. J., Álvarez, P., & Ezpeleta, J. (2008). Flow and data compatibility for the correct interaction among web processes. In *Proceedings of International Conference on Intelligent Agents, Web Technologies and Internet Commerce – IAWTIC 08*, (pp. 716–722). IAWTIC.

Ibáñez, M., Álvarez, P., Bañares, J., & Ezpeleta, J. (2011). Control and data flow compatibility in the interaction between dynamic business processes. *Concurrency and Computation, 23*(1), 57–85. doi:10.1002/cpe.1595

Idury, R. M., & Waterman, M. S. (1995). A new algorithm for DNA sequence assembly. *Journal of Computational Biology, 2*(2), 291–306. doi:10.1089/cmb.1995.2.291 PMID:7497130

IEC 61508-3. (1998). *Functional safety of electrical/electronic/programmable electronic safety-related systems - Part 3: Software requirements*. International Electrotechnical Commission (IEC). (Second Ed.: 2010)

IEEE. (1990). *IEEE Standard Glossary for Software Engineering Terminology*. IEEE Standard 610.12-1990.

IEEE. (2008). *IEEE Standard for Software and System Test Documentation (IEEE Std 829-2008)*. IEEE Computer Society.

Immonen, A., & Niemelä, E. (2007). Survey of reliability and availability prediction methods from the viewpoint of software architecture. *Software & Systems Modeling, 7*(1), 49–65. doi:10.1007/s10270-006-0040-x

Ince, D. (1990). Software metrics: introduction. *Information and Software Technology, 32*(4), 297–303. doi:10.1016/0950-5849(90)90063-W

Inverardi, P., & Tivoli, M. (2001). Automatic synthesis of deadlock free connectors for com/dcom applications. *ACM SIGSOFT Software Engineering Notes, 26*(5), 121–131. doi:10.1145/503271.503227

Isa, M. A., Jawawi, D. N. A., & Zaki, M. Z. (n.d.). Model-driven estimation approach for system reliability using integrated tasks and resources. *Software Quality Journal*, 1-37.

ISO. (2011). *CEN EN/ISO 11354-1, Advanced Automation Technologies and their Applications, Part 1: Framework for Enterprise Interoperability*. Geneva, Switzerland: International Standards Office.

ISO/IEC TR 15504-1. (1998/1999). *Information technology -- Software process assessment (parts 1 to 9)*, International Standards Organization(ISO)/International Electrotechnical Commission (IEC) (Different parts have been updated in the past decade).

ISO/IEC/IEEE. (2010). Systems and software engineering – Vocabulary. International Standard ISO/IEC/IEEE 24765:2010(E). First Ed. (pp. 186). Geneva, Switzerland.

Israeli, A., & Feitelson, D. G. (2010). The Linux kernel as a case study in software evolution. *Journal of Systems and Software, 83*(3), 485–501. doi:10.1016/j.jss.2009.09.042

ISSECO – Secure Software Engineering. (n.d.). Retrieved from http://www.isseco.org/

Jackson, B. G., Regennitter, M., Yang, X., Schnable, P. S., & Aluru, S. (2010). Parallel de novo assembly of large genomes from high-throughput short reads. In *Proceedings of the 27th IEEE International Symposium on Parallel & Distributed Processing* (pp. 1-10). Atlanta, GA: IEEE Computer Society.

Jackson, M. (2008). Automated software engineering: supporting understanding. *Automated Software Engineering, 15*(3-4), 275–281. doi:10.1007/s10515-008-0034-8

Jackson, M. A. (2001). *Problem Frames: Analyzing and Structuring Software Development Problems.* Boston, MA: Addison-Wesley.

Jacobson, I. (1992). *Object-oriented software engineering: A use case driven approach.* Addison-Wesley.

Jacobson, I., & Christerson, M. (1995). A growing consensus on use cases. *Journal of Object-Oriented Programming, 8*(1), 15–19.

Jacobson, J., & Ng, P. (2005). *Aspect-Oriented Software Development with Use Cases.* Addison-Wesley.

Jakkilinki, R., Sharda, N., & Ahmad, I. (2005). Ontology-Based Intelligent Tourism Information Systems: An overview of Development Methodology and Applications. In *Proceedings of Tourism Enterprise Strategies – 2005.* Melbourne, Australia: Academic Press.

Jardim-Goncalves, R., Agostinho, C., & Steiger-Garcao, A. (2012). A reference model for sustainable interoperability in networked enterprises: towards the foundation of EI science base. *International Journal of Computer Integrated Manufacturing, 25*(10), 855–873. doi:10.1080/0951192X.2011.653831

Jardim-Goncalves, R., Grilo, A., Agostinho, C., Lampathaki, F., & Charalabidis, Y. (2013). Systematisation of Interoperability Body of Knowledge: the foundation for Enterprise Interoperability as a science. *Enterprise Information Systems, 7*(1), 7–32. doi:10.1080/17517575.2012.684401

Jardim-Goncalves, R., Popplewell, K., & Grilo, A. (2012). Sustainable interoperability: The future of Internet based industrial enterprises. *Computers in Industry, 63*(8), 731–738. doi:10.1016/j.compind.2012.08.016

Jarke, M., Jeusfeldet, M., Mylopoulos, J., et al. (1990). *Information systems development as knowledge engineering: A review of the DAIDA project* (Technical Report MIP-9010). University of Passau.

Jarzabek, S., & Xue, Y. (2010). *Are clones harmful for maintenance?* Paper presented at the 4th International Workshop on Software Clones (IWSC '10). Cape Town, South Africa.

Javed, A., Strooper, P., & Watson, G. (2007). Automated generation of test cases using modeldriven architecture. In *Proceedings of the 2nd International Workshop on Automation of Software Test (AST).* Minneapolis, MN: AST.

Jenkins, B. (n.d.). *Jenny Test Tool.* Retrieved from http://www.burtleburtle.net./bob/math/jenny.html

Jensen, R. Jensen, & Sonder, P. (2006). Architecture and Design in eXtreme Programming. Introducing 'Developer Stories' (LNCS), (vol. 4044, pp. 133–142). Berlin: Springer.

Jeong, B., Lee, D., Cho, H., & Lee, J. (2008). A novel method for measuring semantic similarity for XML schema matching. *Expert Systems with Applications, 34*, 1651–1658. doi:10.1016/j.eswa.2007.01.025

JhotDraw. (2012). *JHotDraw 7.* Retrieved from http://www.randelshofer.ch/oop/jhotdraw/files/120/jhotdraw.html

Jiang, L. (2005). *A framework for the requirements engineering process development.* (Ph.D. Thesis). University of Calgary, Calgary, Canada.

Jiang, L., Eberlein, A., & Far, B. H. (2005). Combining Requirements Engineering Techniques–Theory and Case Study. In *Proceedings of 12th IEEE International Conference and Workshops on the Engineering of Computer-Based Systems (ECBS'05).* doi:10.1109/ECBS.2005.25

Jiang, L., Misherghi, G., Su, Z., & Glondu, S. (2007). *DECKARD: Scalable and Accurate Tree-based Detection of Code Clones.* Paper presented at the 29th international conference on Software Engineering (ICSE '07). Minneapolis, MN.

Jiang, P., Ji, Y., Wang, X., Zhu, J., & Cheng, Y. (2013). Design of a Multiple Bloom Filter for Distributed Navigation Routing. *IEEE Transactions on Systems, Man, and Cybernetics: Systems, (99),* 1-7.

Jiang, P., Mair, Q., & Newman, J. (2003). Using UML to design distributed collaborative workflows: from UML to XPDL. In *Proceedings of IEEE International Workshops on Enabling Technologies.* IEEE.

Jiang, Y., & Cukic, B. (2009). Misclassification cost-sensitive fault prediction models. In *Proceedings of the 5th international conference on predictor models in software engineering.* ACM.

Jiang, Y., Lin, J., Cukic, B., & Menzies, T. (2009). Variance analysis in software fault prediction models. In *Proceedings of the 20th international conference on software reliability engineering ISSRE'09* (pp. 99-108). Los Alamitos, CA: IEEE Computer Society.

Jiang, Y., Cukic, B., & Ma, Y. (2008). Techniques for evaluating fault prediction models. *Empirical Software Engineering, 13*(5), 561–595. doi:10.1007/s10664-008-9079-3

Jiang, Y., Cukic, B., & Menzies, T. (2007). Fault prediction using early lifecycle data. In *Proceedings of Software Reliability* (pp. 237–246). IEEE.

Jing, C., Zhengang, N., Liying, L., & Fei, Y. (2009). Research and Application on Bloom Filter in Routing Planning for Indoor Robot Navigation System. In *Proceedings of Pacific-Asia Conference on Circuits, Communications and Systems (PACCS '09)* (pp. 244-247). Chengdu, China: IEEE Computer Society.

Jin, Z., Lu, R., & Bell, D. (2003). Automatically multi-paradigm requirements modeling and analyzing: An ontology-based approach.[Series F]. *Science in China, 46*(4), 279–297.

Johnson, E., & Gannon, D. (1997). HPC++: Experiments with the parallel standard template library. In *Proceedings of 11th international conference on Supercomputing* (pp. 124-131). Vienna, Austria: ACM.

Johnson, R. (2002). *Expert One-on-One J2EE Design & Development.* Wrox Press Ltd.

Johson, B., & Shneiderman, B. (1991). Tree-Maps: a space-filling approach to the visualization of hierarchical information structures. In *Proceedings of the 2nd conference on Visualization '91.* IEEE Computer Society Press.

Jones, C. (2003). Variations in software development practices. *IEEE Software, 20*(6), 22–27. doi:10.1109/MS.2003.1241362

Jones, N., & Müller-Olm, M. (2011). Preface to a special section on verification, model checking, and abstract interpretation. *International Journal on Software Tools and Technology Transfer, 13,* 491–493. doi:10.1007/s10009-011-0214-x

Joseph, S. (2011). A Model for Reliability Estimation of Software based Systems by Integrating Hardware and Software. *Science and Technology,* 26–29.

Jouault, F., & Kurtev, I. (2005). Transforming models with ATL. In *Proceedings of MoDELS Satellite Events,* (pp. 128–138). MoDELS.

Jouault, F., Allilaire, F., Bézivin, J., & Kurtev, I. (2008). ATL: A model transformation tool. *Science of Computer Programming, 72,* 1–2, 31–39. doi:10.1016/j.scico.2007.08.002

Juergens, E. (2011). *Research in Cloning Beyond Code: A First Roadmap.* Paper presented at the 5th International Workshop on Software Clones (IWSC '11). Waikiki, HI.

Julia, H. A., et al. (2009). *Making the business Case for Software Assurance.* Retrieved in 15 Apr 2010 from http://repository.cmu.edu/sei/29/

Julia, H. A. (Ed.). (2008). *Software Security Engineering: A Guide for Project Manager.* Addison Wesley Professional.

Kaminsky, A. (2007). Parallel Java: A Unified API for Shared Memory and Cluster Parallel Programming in 100% Java. In *Proceedings of 21st IEEE International Parallel and Distributed Processing Symposium (IPDPS 2007)* (pp. 1-8). Long Beach, CA: IEEE Computer Society.

Kamiya, T., Kusumoto, S., & Inoue, K. (1999). Prediction of fault-proneness at early phase in object-oriented development. In *Proceedings of Object-Oriented Real-Time Distributed Computing* (pp. 253–258). IEEE. doi:10.1109/ISORC.1999.776386

Kamiya, T., Kusumoto, S., & Inoue, K. (2002). CCFinder: a multilinguistic token-based code clone detection system for large scale source code. *IEEE Transactions on Software Engineering*, *28*(7), 654–670. doi:10.1109/TSE.2002.1019480

Kamoun, F. (2007). A roadmap towards the convergence of business process management and service oriented architecture. *Ubiquity*, 1–1.

Kandt, R. (2009). Experiences in improving flight software development processes. *IEEE Software*, *26*(3), 58–64. doi:10.1109/MS.2009.66

Kang, M. H., Park, J. S., & Froscher, J. N. (2001). Access control mechanisms for inter-organizational workflow. In *Proceedings of the 6th ACM symposium on Access control models and technologies* (pp. 66-74). ACM.

Kanmani, S., Uthariaraj, V. R., Sankaranarayanan, V., & Thambidurai, P. (2007). Object-oriented software fault prediction using neural networks. *Information and Software Technology*, *49*(5), 483–492. doi:10.1016/j.infsof.2006.07.005

Kapser, C. J., & Godfrey, M. W. (2006). Supporting the analysis of clones in software systems. *Journal of Software Maintenance and Evolution: Research and Practice*, *18*(2), 61–82. doi:10.1002/smr.327

Kapser, C. J., & Godfrey, M. W. (2008). Cloning considered harmful considered harmful: patterns of cloning in software. *Empirical Software Engineering*, *13*(6), 645–692. doi:10.1007/s10664-008-9076-6

Karlsson, B. (2005). *Beyond the C++ Standard Library: An Introduction to Boost*. Reading, MA: Addison-Wesley.

Karlstrom, D. (2002). *Introducing Extreme Programming - An Experience Report*. Paper presented at the Third International Conference on eXtreme Programming and Agile Processes in Software Engineering. New York, NY.

Kaszycki, G. (1999). Using process metrics to enhance software fault prediction models. In *Proceedings of Tenth International Symposium on Software Reliability Engineering*. Boca Raton, FL: Academic Press.

Katz, E., & Katz, S. (2008). Incremental analysis of interference among aspects. In *Proc. of Foundations of Aspect Languages Workshop* (FOAL08). Brussels, Belgium: FOAL.

Katz, S. (2005). *A survey of verification and static analysis for aspects*. Tech. Rep. Part of Milestone M8.1. Formal Methods Laboratory of AOSD-Europe.

Kavakli, E., & Loucopoulos, P. (2003). Goal driven requirements engineering: evaluation of current methods. In *Proceedings of the 8th CAiSE/IFIP8.1 Workshop on Evaluation of Modeling Methods in Systems Analysis and Design, EMMSAD*. Velden, Austria: EMMSAD.

Kavakli, V. (2002). Goal oriented requirements engineering: a unifying framework. *Requirements Engineering Journal*, *6*(4), 237–251. doi:10.1007/PL00010362

Kawaguchi, S., Yamashina, T., Uwano, H., Fushida, K., Kamei, Y., Nagura, M., & Iida, H. (2009). *SHINOBI: A Tool for Automatic Code Clone Detection in the IDE*. Paper presented at the 16th Working Conference on Reverse Engineering, 2009. New York, NY.

Keim, D. A. (2002). Information visualization and visual data mining. *IEEE Transactions on Visualization and Computer Graphics*, *8*(1), 1–8. doi:10.1109/2945.981847

Keller, A., & Ludwig, H. (2003). The WSLA framework: Specifying and monitoring service level agreements for web services. *Journal of Network and Systems Management*, *11*(1), 57–81. doi:10.1023/A:1022445108617

Kenny, P., Parsons, T., Gratch, J., & Rizzo, A. (2008). Virtual humans for assisted health care. In *Proceedings of the 1st international conference on PErvasive Technologies Related to Assistive Environments*. ACM.

Kephart, J. O., & Chess, D. M. (2003). The vision of autonomic computing. *Computer, 36*(1), 41–50. doi:10.1109/MC.2003.1160055

Khakpour, N., Khosravi, R., Sirjani, M., & Jalili, S. (2010). *Formal analysis of policy-based self-adaptive systems.* Paper presented at the 25th Annual ACM Symposium on Applied Computing. Sierre, Switzerland.

Khakpour, N., Jalili, S., Talcott, C., Sirjani, M., & Mousavi, M. R. (2010). PobSAM: policy-based managing of actors in self-adaptive systems. *Electronic Notes in Theoretical Computer Science, 263*, 129–143. doi:10.1016/j.entcs.2010.05.008

Khalid, A., Haye, M. A., Khan, M. J., & Shamail, S. (2009). Survey of Frameworks, Architectures and Techniques in Autonomic Computing. In *Proceedings of 2009 5th International Conference on Autonomic and Autonomous Systems* (pp. 220-225). Valencia, Spain: IEEE Computer Society.

Khatchadourian, R., Dovland, J., & Soundarajan, N. (2008). Enforcing behavioral constraints in evolving aspect-oriented programs. In *Proceedings of the 7th International Workshop on Foundations of Aspect- Oriented Languages* (FOAL'08). Brussels, Belgium: FOAL.

Khomh, F., & Gueheneuc, Y. G. (2008). Do design patterns impact software quality positively? In *Proceedings of the 12th European Conference on Software Maintenance and Reengineering* (pp. 274–278). Athens, Greece: IEEE.

Khomh, F., Gueheneuc, Y. G., & Antoniol, G. (2009). Playing roles in design patterns: An empirical descriptive and analytic study. In *Proceedings of the 25th International Conference on Software Maintenance* (pp. 83–92). Edmonton, Canada: IEEE.

Khomh, F., Gueheneuc, Y. G., & Team, P. (2008). *An empirical study of design patterns and software quality* (Technical report 1315). University of Montreal.

Khoshgoftaar, T. M., Ganesan, K., Allen, E. B., Ross, F. D., Munikoti, R., Goel, N., & Nandi, A. (1997). Predicting fault-prone modules with case-based reasoning. In *Proceedings of Software Reliability Engineering* (pp. 27–35). IEEE.

Khoshgoftaar, T. M., Gao, K., & Szabo, R. M. (2001). An application of zero-inflated Poisson regression for software fault prediction. In *Proceedings of Software Reliability Engineering* (pp. 66–73). IEEE. doi:10.1109/ISSRE.2001.989459

Khoshgoftaar, T. M., & Seliya, N. (2002). Tree-based software quality estimation models for fault prediction. In *Proceedings of Software Metrics* (pp. 203–214). IEEE. doi:10.1109/METRIC.2002.1011339

Khosla, S., & Maibaum, T. (1987). The prescription and description of state based systems. In B. Banieqbal, H. Barringer, & A. Pnueli (Eds.), *Temporal Logic in Specification, (LNCS), (* (Vol. 398, pp. 243–294). London, UK: Springer-Verlag. doi:10.1007/3-540-51803-7_30

Kiczales, G., Lamping, J., Mendhekar, A., Maeda, C., Lopes, C. V., Loingtier, J., & Irwin, J. (1997). Aspect oriented programming. In *Proceedings of the 11th European Conference on Object-Oriented Programming ECOOP.* Jyväskylä, Finland: Springer.

Kiczales, G., Lamping, J., Mendhekar, A., Maeda, C., Lopes, C., Loingtier, J. M., & Irwin, J. (1997). *Aspect-oriented programming.* Springer.

Kilicay-Ergin, & Laplante. (2013). An Online Graduate Requirements Engineering Course. *IEEE Transactions on Education, 56*(2), 208–216. doi:10.1109/TE.2012.2208461

Kim, D., & Shen, W. (2007). An Approach to Evaluating Structural Pattern Conformance of UML Models. In *Proceedings of ACM Symposium on Applied Computing* (pp. 1404-1408). ACM Press.

Kim, S., Zimmermann, T., Whitehead, E. J., Jr., & Zeller, A. (2007). Predicting Faults from Cached History. In *Proceedings of the 29th International Conference on Software Engineering ICSE'07* (pp. 489-498). Washington, DC: IEEE Computer Society.

Klaib, M. F. J., et al. (2008). G2Way– A backtracking strategy for pairwise test data generation. In *Proceedings of the 15th Asia-Pacific Software Engineering Conference (APSEC 08)*. Beijing, China: APSEC.

Klaib, M., et al. (2008). G2Way A Backtracking Strategy for Pairwise Test Data Generation. In *Proceeding of the 15th Asia-Pacific Software Engineering Conference APSEC '08'* (pp. 463-470). APSEC.

Knab, P., Pinzger, M., & Bernstein, A. (2006). Predicting defect densities in source code files with decision tree learners. In *Proceedings of the international workshop on Mining software repositories MSR'06* (pp. 119-125). New York, NY: ACM.

Knottenbelt, W. J. (2000). *Performance Analysis of Large Markov Models.* (Unpublished PhD Thesis). Imperial College of Science, Technology and Medicine.

Knottenbelt, W. J., & Harrison, P. G. (1999). Distributed Disk-based Solution Techniques for Large Markov Models. In *Proceedings of 3rd International Workshop on the Numerical Solution of Markov Chains* (pp. 58-75). Zaragoza, Spain: Presnsas Universitarias de Zaragoza.

Koch, N. (2006). Transformation Techniques in the Model-Driven Development Process of UWE. In *Proceedings of the 6th International Conference on Web Engineering.* Palo Alto, CA: ACM.

Koch, S. (2007). Software evolution in open source projects - a large-scale investigation. *J. Software Maintenance and Evolution, 19*(6), 361–382. doi:10.1002/smr.348

Kokash, N., & Arbab, F. (2009). Formal Behavioral Modeling and Compliance Analysis for Service-Oriented Systems. In Formal Methods for Components and Objects, (LNCS), (vol. 5751, pp. 21-41). Springer-Verlag.

Koprinska, I., Poon, J., Clark, J., & Chan, J. (2007). Learning to classify e-mail. *Information Sciences, 177*(10), 2167–2187. doi:10.1016/j.ins.2006.12.005

Ko, R. K., Lee, S. S., & Lee, E. W. (2009). Business process management (BPM) standards: a survey. *Business Process Management Journal, 15*(5). doi:10.1108/14637150910987937

Korkala, M., Abrhamsson, P., & Kyllonen, P. (2006). A case study on the impact of customer communication on defects in agile software development. [AGILE.]. *Proceedings of AGILE, 2006*, 76–88.

Koru, A. G., Zhang, D., El Emam, K., & Liu, H. (2009). An Investigation into the Functional Form of the Size-Defect Relationship for Software Modules. *IEEE Transactions on Software Engineering, 35*(2), 293–304. doi:10.1109/TSE.2008.90

Koschke, R., Falke, R., & Frenzel, P. (2006). *Clone detection using abstract syntax suffix trees.* Paper presented at the 13th Working Conference on Reverse Engineering (WCRE '06). Benevento.

Koschke, R. (2003). Software visualization in software maintenance, reverse engineering, and re-engineering: a research survey. *Journal of Software Maintenance, 15*(2), 87–109. doi:10.1002/smr.270

Koschke, R., Baxter, I. D., Michael Conradt, M., & Cordy, J. R. (2012). *Software Clone Management Towards Industrial Application.* Dagstuhl, Germany: Academic Press.

Kotek, J. (2013). *MapDB.* Retrieved February 18, 2014, from http://www.mapdb.org/

Kovitz, B. (2003). Viewpoints: hidden skills that support phased and agile requirements engineering. *Requirements Engineering, 8*(2), 135–141. doi:10.1007/s00766-002-0162-9

Krafzig, D., Banke, K., & Slama, D. (2004). *Enterprise SOA Service Oriented Architecture Best Practices.* Upper Saddle River, NJ: Prentice Hall PTR.

Kramer, J., & Magee, J. (2007). Self-managed systems: An architectural challenge. In *Proceedings of the Conference on The Future of Software Engineering* (pp. 259-268). Minneapolis, MN: IEEE Computer Society.

Krishnamurthy, P., Buhler, J., Chamberlain, R., Franklin, M., Gyang, K., & Jacob, A. et al. (2007). Biosequence similarity search on the mercury system. *The Journal of VLSI Signal Processing Systems for Signal, Image, and Video Technology, 49*(1), 101–121. doi:10.1007/s11265-007-0087-0 PMID:18846267

Kritikos, K., & Plexousakis, D. (2006). Semantic QoS Metric Matching. In *Proc. of European Conf. on Web Services.* IEEE Computer.

Krka, I., Edwards, G., Cheung, L., Golubchik, L., & Medvidovic, N. (2009). A comprehensive exploration of challenges in architecture-based reliability estimation. [Springer.]. *Proceedings of Architecting Dependable Systems, VI*, 202–227.

Kruchten, P. (2004). *The rational unified process: an introduction*. Pearson Education Inc.

Krüger, I. H., & Mathew, R. (2004). Systematic Development and Exploration of Service-Oriented Software Architectures.[WICSA.]. *Proceedings of WICSA, 2004*, 177–187.

Krug, S. (2005). *Don't Make Me Think: A Common Sense Approach to Web Usability* (2nd ed.). New Riders.

Kuhn, A., & Stocker, M. (2012). Codetimeline: Storytelling with versioning data. In *Proceedings of 34th International Conference on Software Engineering*. ICSE.

Kuhn, A., Erni, D., Loretan, P., & Nierstrasz, O. (2010). Software cartography: thematic software visualization with consistent layout. *Journal of Software Maintenance, 22*(3), 191–210.

Kuhn, D. R., Wallace, D. R., & Gallo, A. M. (2004). Software Fault Interactions and Implications for Software Testing. *IEEE Transactions on Software Engineering, 30*, 418–421. doi:10.1109/TSE.2004.24

Kuhn, R., Lei, Y., & Kacker, R. (2008). Practical Combinatorial Testing: Beyond Pairwise. *IEEE IT Professional, 10*, 19–23. doi:10.1109/MITP.2008.54

Kummer, O., Wienberg, F., Duvigneau, M., Köhler, M., Moldt, D., & Rölke, H. (2003). Renew – the reference net workshop. In *Proceedings of 24th International Conference on Application and Theory of Petri Nets – ATPN 2003*, (pp. 99–102). ATPN.

Kummer, O. (2001). Introduction to Petri nets and reference nets. *Sozionik Aktuell, 1*, 1–9.

Kundeti, V. K., Rajasekaran, S., Dinh, H., Vaughn, M., & Thapar, V. (2010). Efficient parallel and out of core algorithms for constructing large bi-directed de Bruijn graphs. *BMC Bioinformatics, 11*(1), 560. doi:10.1186/1471-2105-11-560 PMID:21078174

Kundu, D., Sarma, M., Samanta, D., & Mall, R. (2009). System testing for object-oriented systems with test case prioritization. *Software Testing. Verification and Reliability, 19*(4), 297–333. doi:10.1002/stvr.407

Kundu, S. (2007). Structuring software functional requirements for automated design and verification. [COMPSAC.]. *Proceedings of COMPSAC, 07*, 127–134.

Kwiatkowska, M. Z., & Mehmood, R. (2002). Out-of-core solution of large linear systems of equations arising from stochastic modelling. In *Proceedings of the Second Joint International Workshop on Process Algebra and Probabilistic Methods, Performance Modeling and Verification* (pp. 135-151). Copenhagen, Denmark: Springer-Verlag.

Lai-Shun, Z., Yan, H., & Zhong-Wen, L. (2011). Building Markov chain-based software reliability usage model with UML. In *Proceedings of Communication Software and Networks (ICCSN), 2011 IEEE 3rd International Conference on* (pp. 548-551). IEEE.

Laitinen, K. (1992). Document classification for software quality systems. *ACM SIGSOFT Software Engineering Notes, 17*(4), 32–39. doi:10.1145/141874.141882

Laitinen, K. (1996). Estimating understandability of software documents. *ACM SIGSOFT Software Engineering Notes, 21*(4), 81–92. doi:10.1145/232069.232092

Lalanda, P., McCann, J. A., & Diaconescu, A. (2013). *Autonomic computing: Principles, design and implementation*. Berlin: Springer. doi:10.1007/978-1-4471-5007-7

Lamancha, B. P., Reales, P., Polo, M., & Caivano, D. (2013). Model-Driven Test Code Generation. In *Evaluation of Novel Approaches to Software Engineering* (Vol. 275, pp. 155–168). Berlin: Springer. doi:10.1007/978-3-642-32341-6_11

Lamanna, D. D., Skene, J., & Emmerich, W. (2003). SLAng: A language for defining service level agreements. In *Proceedings of the 9th IEEE Workshop on Future Trends of Distributed Computing Systems* (pp. 100-106). San Juan, Puerto Rico: IEEE Computer Society.

Lami, G. (2005). Teaching Requirements Engineering in the Small: an Under-graduate Course Experience. In *Proceedings of Workshop on Requirements Engineering Education and Training*. Paris: Academic Press.

Lamsweerde, A. (2000). Requirements engineering in the year 2000: a research perspective. In *Proceedings of the 22nd International Conference on Software Engineering* (pp. 5-19). New York: ACM.

Lamsweerde, A. (2001). Goal-oriented requirements engineering: a guided tour. In *Proceedings of the 5th IEEE International Symposium on Requirements Engineering* (pp. 249-262). Toronto, Canada: IEEE.

Lange, D. B., & Nakamura, Y. (1995). Interactive visualization of design patterns can help in framework understanding. *ACM Sigplan Notices*, *30*(10), 342–357. doi:10.1145/217839.217874

Langelier, G., Sahraoui, H., & Poulin, P. (2008). Exploring the evolution of software quality with animated visualization. In *Proceedings of the 2008 IEEE Symposium on Visual Languages and Human-Centric Computing*. IEEE Computer Society.

Lano, K., & Kolahdouz-Rahimi, S. (2013). Constraint-based specification of model transformations. *IEEE Software*, *30*(3), 25–27.

Lanubile, F., Lonigro, A., & Visaggio, G. (1995). Comparing models for identifying fault-prone software components. In *Proceedings of the 7th International Conference on Software Engineering and Knowledge Engineering SEKE'95* (pp. 312-319). Skokie, IL: Knowledge Systems Institute.

Lanza, M. (2001). The evolution matrix: recovering software evolution using software visualization techniques. In *Proceedings of the 4th International Workshop on Principles of Software Evolution*. ACM.

Lanza, M., & Ducasse, S. (2003). Polymetric Views – A Lightweight Visual Approach to Reverse Engineering. *IEEE Transactions on Software Engineering*, *29*(9), 782–795. doi:10.1109/TSE.2003.1232284

Larrucea, X., & Benguria, G. (2006). Applying a Model Driven Approach to an E-Business Environment. In *Proceedings of the XV Jornadas de Ingeniería del Software y Bases de Datos* (JISBD 2006). Barcelona: JISBD.

Larrucea, X., Combelles, A., & Favaro, J. (2013). Safety-critical software. Guest editors' introduction. *Journal of Systems and Software*, *86*, 412–436.

Lauesen, S. (2002). *Software Requirements: Styles and Techniques*. US: Addison-Wesley.

Läufer, K., Baumgartner, G., & Russo, V. (2000). Safe Structural Conformance for Java. *The Computer Journal*, *43*(6), 469–481. doi:10.1093/comjnl/43.6.469

Layman, L., Kudrjavets, G., & Nagappan, N. (2008). Iterative identification of fault-prone binaries using in-process metrics. In *Proceedings of the Second ACM-IEEE international symposium on Empirical software engineering and measurement ESEM'08* (pp. 206-212). New York, NY: ACM.

Lazic, L. J., & Velasevic, D. (2004). Applying Simulation and Design of Experiments to the Embedded Software Testing Process. *Software Testing, Verification, and Reliability*, *14*, 257–282. doi:10.1002/stvr.299

LeBlanc. Sobel, Diaz-Herrera, & Hilburn. (2006). Software engineering 2004: curriculum guidelines for undergraduate degree programs in software engineering. In *Proceedings of ACM/IEEE-CS Joint Task Force on Computing Curricula*. IEEE Computer Society.

Lee, K. L., & Stotts, D. (2012). Composition of bioinformatics model federations using communication aspects. In *Proceedings of Bioinformatics and Biomedicine (BIBM), 2012 IEEE International Conference on* (pp. 1-5). IEEE.

Leffingwell & Widrig. (2000). *Managing Software Requirements: A Unified Approach*. Addison-Wesley.

Lehman, M. (1978). Laws of program evolution-rules and tools for programming management. In *Proceedings of Infotech State of the Art Conference, Why Software Projects Fail*. Infotech.

Lehman, M. M., & Ramil, J. F. (2001). Evolution in software and related areas. In *Proceedings of the 4th International Workshop on Principles of Software Evolution IWPSE '01* (pp. 1-16). New York, NY: ACM.

Lehman, M. (1980). Programs, life cycles, and laws of software evolution. *Proceedings of the IEEE*, *68*(9), 1060–1076. doi:10.1109/PROC.1980.11805

Lei, Y., et al. (2007). IPOG: A General Strategy for T-Way Software Testing. In *Proceedings of the 14th Annual IEEE International Conference and Workshops on the Engineering of Computer-Based Systems (ECBS2007)*. IEEE Computer Society.

Lei, Y. et al. (2008). IPOG/IPOG-D: Efficient Test Generation for Multi-way Combinatorial Testing. *Software Testing, Verification, and Reliability, 18*, 125–148. doi:10.1002/stvr.381

Lemos, O. A. L., Ferrari, F. C., Masiero, P. C., & Lopes, C. V. (2006). Testing aspect-oriented programming point-cut descriptors. In *Proceedings of the 2nd workshop on Testing aspect-oriented programs, in conjunction with the International Symposium on Software Testing and Analysis (ISSTA'06)*. Portland, MN: ISSTA.

Lessmann, S., Baesens, B., Mues, C., & Pietsch, S. (2008). Benchmarking classification models for software defect prediction: A proposed framework and novel findings. *Software Engineering. IEEE Transactions on, 34*(4), 485–496.

Leveson, N. G. (1995). *Safeware, system safety and computers*. Addison-Wesley.

Levoy, M. (2011). *The Stanford 3D scanning repository*. Retrieved September 2, 2013, from http://www-graphics. stanford.edu/data/3Dscanrep/

Leymann, F. (2001). *Web Services Flow Language (WSFL 1.0)*. IBM.

Li, P. L., Herbsleb, J., Shaw, M., & Robinson, B. (2006). Experiences and results from initiating field defect prediction and product test prioritization efforts at ABB Inc. In *Proceeding of the 28th International Conference on Software engineering ICSE'06* (pp. 413-422). New York, NY: ACM.

Li, S., & Juan, Z. (2009). *The WSMO-QoS Semantic Web Service Discovery Framework*. Paper presented at the International Conference on Computational Intelligence and Software Engineering, CiSE 2009. New York, NY.

Li, X., Kang, H., Harrington, P., & Thomas, J. (2006). *Autonomic and trusted computing paradigms*. Paper presented at the Thrid International Conference on Autonomic and Trusted Computing. Wuhan, China.

Li, Y., Cui, W., Li, D., & Zhang, R. (2011). Research based on OSI model. In *Proceedings of IEEE 3rd International Conference on Communication Software and Networks* (pp. 554-557). IEEE Computer Society Press.

Li, Y., Kamousi, P., Han, F., Yang, S., Yan, X., & Suri, S. (2012). Memory efficient de Bruijn graph construction. *CoRR*.

Liang, Y., Zhou, X., Yu, Z., Wang, H., & Guo, B. (2012). A context-aware multimedia service scheduling framework in smart homes. *EURASIP Journal on Wireless Communications and Networking*. doi:10.1186/1687-1499-2012-67

Liebchen, G. A., & Shepperd, M. (2008). Data sets and data quality in software engineering. In *Proceedings of the 4th International Workshop on Predictor Models in Software Engineering PROMISE'08* (pp. 39-44). New York, NY: ACM.

Liebrand, M., Ellis, H., Phillips, C., Demurjian, S., Ting, T. C., & Ellis, J. (2003). Role Delegation for a Resource-Based Security Model. In Research directions in data and applications security (pp. 37-48). Springer US.

Liker, J. K. (2004). *The Toyota Way*. McGraw-Hill.

Li, L., Li, X., He, T., & Xiong, J. (2013). Extenics-based Test Case Generation for UML Activity Diagram. *Procedia Computer Science, 17*, 1186–1193. doi:10.1016/j.procs.2013.05.151

Lima, A., et al. (2006). Gerência Flexível de Processos de Software com o Ambiente WebAPSEE. In *Proceedings of the 20th Brazilian Symposium on Software Engineering*. Florianópolis, Brasil: Academic Press.

Lincke, R., Lundberg, J., & Löwe, W. (2008). Comparing software metrics tools. In *Proceedings of the 2008 International Symposium on Software Testing and Analysis ISSTA'08* (pp. 131-142). New York, NY: ACM.

Linzhang, W., Jiesong, Y., Xiaofeng, Y., Jun, H., Xuandong, L., & Guoliang, Z. (2004). Generating test cases from UML activity diagram based on gray-box method. In *Proceedings of Software Engineering Conference*, (vol. 55, pp. 284-291). IEEE.

Li, T., Yang, D., & Lian, X. (2012). Road crosses high locality sorting for navigation route planning. *Recent Advances in Computer Science and Information Engineering, 124*, 497–502. doi:10.1007/978-3-642-25781-0_74

Liu, L., & Yu, E. (2001). From requirements to architectural design – using goals and scenarios. In *Proceedings of from Software Requirements to Architectures Workshop (STRAW 2001)* (pp. 22-30). Toronto, Canada: ACM.

Liu, Y., Schmidt, B., & Maskell, D. L. (2011). Parallelized short read assembly of large genomes using de Bruijn graphs. *BMC Bioinformatics, 12*, 354. doi:10.1186/1471-2105-12-354 PMID:21867511

Li, W. (1998). Another metric suite for object-oriented programming. *Journal of Systems and Software, 44*(2), 155–162. doi:10.1016/S0164-1212(98)10052-3

Li, Z., Alaeddine, N., & Tian, J. (2010). Multi-faceted quality and defect measurement for web software and source contents. *Journal of Systems and Software, 83*(1), 18–28. doi:10.1016/j.jss.2009.04.055

Lodderstedt, T., Basin, D., & Doser, J. (2002). SecureUML: A UML-based modeling language for model-driven security. In ≪UML≫ 2002—The Unified Modeling Language (pp. 426-441). Springer.

Lo, J. H., Huang, C. Y., Chen, I. Y., Kuo, S. Y., & Lyu, M. R. (2005). Reliability assessment and sensitivity analysis of software reliability growth modeling based on software module structure. *Journal of Systems and Software, 76*(1), 3–13. doi:10.1016/j.jss.2004.06.025

López Sanz, M., Marcos, E., Vara, J.M., Bollati, V., & Verde, J. (2012). *ArchiMeDeSTool: Especificación e Implementación de Modelos para el framework ArchiMeDeS*. Reg. No.M-009008/2012. Date: 03/12/2012

López-Sanz, M., & Marcos, E. (2012). ArchiMeDeS: A model-driven framework for the specification of service-oriented architectures. *Inf. Syst. 37*(3), 257-268. DOI=10.1016/j.is.2011.11.002

López-Sanz, M., Vara, J. M., Marcos, E., & Cuesta, C. E. (2011). A Model-Driven Approach to Weave Architectural Styles into Service-Oriented Architectures. *International Journal on Cooperative Information Systems, 20*(2), 201–220. doi:10.1142/S0218843011002201

Lorenz, M., & Kidd, J. (1994). *Object-oriented software metrics: A practical guide*. Prentice-Hall, Inc.

Loucopoulos, P., & Kavakli, V. (1997). Enterprise knowledge management and conceptual modeling. In *Proceedings of Workshop on Conceptual Modeling: Current Issues and Future Directions* (pp. 45-79). Los Angeles, CA: Springer-Verlag.

Loutas, N., Kamateri, E., Bosi, F., & Tarabanis, K. (2011). Cloud computing interoperability: the state of play. In *Proceedings of International Conference on Cloud Computing Technology and Science* (pp. 752-757). IEEE Computer Society Press.

Lu, R. (2005). *Knowware research and fourth industry*. Paper presented at the Economic globalization and the choice of Asia. Shanghai, China.

Lu, R. (2006). Towards a software/knowware co-engineering. Invited Talk. In *Proceedings of KSEM 06*, (LNAI), (vol. 4092, pp. 23—32). Springer.

Lu, R. (2007). *Knowware, Knowware engineering and knowware/software co-engineering*. Paper presented at ICCS'07. Beijing, China.

Lu, R. (2008). Knowware: A Commodity Form of Knowledge. In *Proceedings of RSKT 2008*, (LNAI), (vol. 5009, pp. 1-2). Springer.

Lu, R. (2010). Object-Oriented Knowware Programming and its Abstract Inheritance Semantics. In *Proc. of 2010 International Conference on Intelligent Systems and Knowledge Engineering* (pp. 1-4). Hangzhou, China: IEEE Computer Society.

Lu, R., & Jin, Z. (1997). A multi-agent and pseudo-natural language approach for intelligent information service. In *Proceedings of the International Conference on the Software Engineering and the Knowledge Engineering* (pp. 422-429). Madrid, Spain: Academic Press.

Lu, R., Huang, Y., Sun, K., Chen, Z., Chen, Y., & Zhang, S. (2012). KACTL: Knowware based Automatic Construction of a Treelike Library from Web Documents. In *Proc. of International Conference on Web Systems and Applications* (WISM 2012), (LNCS), (vol. 7529, pp. 645-656). Springer.

Lu, R., Jin, Z., & Wan, R. (1994). *PROMIS: A Knowledge-Based Approach for Automatically Prototyping Management Information Systems.* Paper presented at Avignon'94. Paris, France.

Lu, R., Jin, Z., & Wan, R. (1995). Requirement specification in pseudo language in PROMIS. In *Proc COMPSAC'95* (pp. 96—101). Dallas, TX: IEEE Computer Society.

Lu, R., Jin, Z., & Xia, Y. (1996). An intelligent CASE tool for information management systems. In *Proceeding of the First International Conference on Future Computer Systems*. Academic Press.

Lu, R., Jin, Z., Liu, L., et al. (1998). OSNET—A language for domain modeling. In *Proceedings of the Technology of Object-Oriented Languages and Systems* (pp.83-92). IEEE Computer Society.

Lu, Y., Li, G., Jin, Z., Xing, X., & Hao, Y. (2013). A knowware based infrastructure for rule based control systems in smart spaces. In *Proceedings of ICSR 2013*, (LNCS), (vol. 7925, pp. 289-294). Springer.

Lublinsky, B. (2007). *Defining SOA as an architectural style: Align your business model with technology.* Retrieved from http://www-128.ibm.com/developerworks/webservices/library/ar-soastyle/index.html

Lucia, A. D., Deufemia, V., Gravino, C., & Risi, M. (2009). Design pattern recovery through visual language parsing and source code analysis. *Journal of Systems and Software*, *82*(7), 1177–1193. doi:10.1016/j.jss.2009.02.012

Luigi, A., Iera, A., & Morabito, G. (2010). The Internet of Things: A survey. *Computer Networks*, *54*(15), 2787–2805. doi:10.1016/j.comnet.2010.05.010

Lungu, M., & Lanza, M. (2010). The small project observatory: a tool for reverse engineering software ecosystems. In *Proceedings of the 32nd ACM/IEEE International Conference on Software Engineering*. ACM.

Luo, Z., et al. (2006). RFID Middleware Benchmarking. In *Proceedings of the 3rd RFID Academic Convocation in conjunction with the China International RFID Technology Development Conference & Exposition*. Shanghai, China: RFID.

Lupu, E. C., & Sloman, M. (1999). Conflicts in policy-based distributed systems management. *IEEE Transactions on Software Engineering*, *25*(6), 852–869. doi:10.1109/32.824414

Lu, R. (2005). From hardware to software to knowware: IT's third liberation? *IEEE Intelligent Systems*, *20*(2), 82–85. doi:10.1109/MIS.2005.27

Lu, R. (2007). *Knowware, the Third Star After Hardware and Software.* Polimetrica Publishing Co.

Lu, R., & Jin, Z. (1999). Knowledge based hierarchical software reuse. *Chinese J Adv Software Res*, *6*(1), 1–11.

Lu, R., & Jin, Z. (2000). *Domain Modeling based Software Engineering.* Boston: Kluwer Academic Publishers. doi:10.1007/978-1-4615-4487-6

Lu, R., & Jin, Z. (2002). Formal ontology: Foundation of domain knowledge sharing and reusing. *J Comp Sci Tech*, *17*(5), 535–548. doi:10.1007/BF02948822

Lu, R., & Jin, Z. (2003). Automating application software generation. *Expert Systems: J Know Engin Neur Net*, *20*(2), 71–77. doi:10.1111/1468-0394.00227

Lu, R., & Jin, Z. (2003). Domain knowledge representation: Using an ontology language. In *Proceedings of Applied Informatics* (pp. 1302–1307). Innsbruck, Austria: IASTED/ACTA Press.

Lu, R., & Jin, Z. (2006). Beyond knowledge engineering. *J Comp Sci Tech*, *21*(5), 790–799. doi:10.1007/s11390-006-0790-5

Lu, R., & Jin, Z. (2008). From knowledge based software engineering to knowware based software engineering. *Science in China Series F*, *51*(6), 638–660. doi:10.1007/s11432-008-0060-y

Lu, R., Jin, Z., & Chen, G. (2000). Ontology-oriented requirements analysis. *J Software*, *11*(8), 1009–1017.

Lu, R., Jin, Z., & Liu, L. et al. (1997). PROMIS 2.0: An intelligent case tool for MIS in the client/server application.[Xiamen.]. *Proceedings of, ISFST-97*, 399–405.

Lu, R., Jin, Z., & Liu, L. et al. (1998). NEWCOM: An architecture description language in client/server style. *Journal of Complexity*, *21*(12), 1103–1111.

Lu, R., Jin, Z., & Wan, R. et al. (1996). Acquiring the requirements based on domain knowledge. *J Software, 7*(3), 137–144.

Lyu, M. R. (2007). Software reliability engineering: A roadmap. In *Proceedings of 2007 Future of Software Engineering* (pp. 153–170). IEEE Computer Society.

Ma, Q., Hao, W., Ying, L., Guotong, X., & Feng, L. (2008). *A Semantic QoS-Aware Discovery Framework for Web Services.* Paper presented at the International Conference on Web Services 2008. New York, NY.

Maamar, Z., Mostefaoui, S.-K., & Yahyaoui, H. (2005). Toward an agent-based and context-oriented approach for Web services composition. *IEEE Transactions on Knowledge and Data Engineering, 17*(5), 686–697. doi:10.1109/TKDE.2005.82

Maani, K. E., & Cavana, R. Y. (2007). *Systems Thinking, Systems Dynamics – Managing Change and Complexity.* Pearson Education NZ.

Machado, P., & Sampaio, A. (2010). Automatic Test-Case Generation. In *Testing Techniques in Software Engineering* (Vol. 6153, pp. 59–103). Berlin: Springer. doi:10.1007/978-3-642-14335-9_3

Maciel, R. S. P., & Ferraz, C. (2005). InterDoc: Reference Architecture for Interoperable Services in Collaborative Writing Environments. In *Proceedings of 9th International Conference on Computer Supported Cooperative Work in Design (CSCWD 2005)* (pp. 289-295). Coventry, UK: CSCWD.

Maciel, R., Gomes, R., & Silva, B. (2011). On the Use of Model-Driven Test Process Specification and Enactment by Metamodelling Foundation. In *Proceedings of the International Conference Applied Computing* (pp. 51-58). Rio de Janeiro, Brazil: Academic Press.

Maciel, R., Silva, B. C., & Mascarenhas, L. A. (2006). An Edoc-based Approach for Specific Middleware Services Development. In *Proceedings of the 4th Workshop on Computer Based Systems* (pp. 135–143). Postdam, Germany: Academic Press.

Maciel, R., Silva, B., Magalhães, A. P., & Rosa, N. (2009). An integrated approach for model driven process modeling and enactment. In *Proceedings of the XXIII Software Engineering Brazilian Symposium* (pp. 104-114). Fortaleza, Brazil: Academic Press.

Maciel, R., Gomes, R., Magalhães, A., Silva, B., & Queiroz, J. (2013). Supporting model-driven development using a process-centered engineering environment. *Automated Software Engineering, 20,* 427–461. doi:10.1007/s10515-013-0124-0

Mäder, P., Jones, P., Zhang, Y., & Cleland-Huang, J. (2013). Strategic traceability for safety-critical projects. *IEEE Software, 30*(3), 58–66. doi:10.1109/MS.2013.60

Madhavji, N. H., & Miller, J. (2005). Investigation-based Requirements Engineering Education. In *Proceedings of Workshop on Requirements Engineering Education and Training.* Paris: Academic Press.

Magalhães, A. P., David, J. M. N., Maciel, R. S. P., Silva, B. C., & Silva, F. A. (2011). Modden: An Integrated Approach for Model Driven Development and Software Product Line Processes. In *Proceedings of the V Brazilian Symposium on Software Components, Architectures and Reuse (SBCARS 2011)* (pp. 21-30). Sao Paulo, Brazil: SBCARS.

Magee, J., Kramer, J., & Giannakopoulou, D. (1999). Behaviour analysis of software architectures. In Software Architecture (pp. 35-49). Springer US.

Mahaweerawat, A., Sophatsathit, P., & Lursinsap, C. (2007). Adaptive self-organizing map clustering for software fault prediction. In *Proceedings of Fourth international joint conference on computer science and software engineering,* (pp. 35-41). Academic Press.

Mahmood, S., Lai, R., Soo Kim, Y., Hong Kim, J., Cheon Park, S., & Suk Oh, H. (2005). A survey of component based system quality assurance and assessment. *Information and Software Technology, 47*(10), 693–707. doi:10.1016/j.infsof.2005.03.007

Maity, S., & Nayak, A. (2005). Improved Test Generation Algorithms for Pairwise Testing. In *Proceedings of the 16th IEEE International Symposium on Software Reliability Engineering (ISSRE 2005).* IEEE Computer Society.

Maletic, A. M. J. I., & Collard, M. L. (2002). A task oriented view of software visualization. In *Proceedings of VISSOFT '02: 1ST International Workshop on Visualizing Software for Understanding and Analysis*. IEEE CS Press.

Malik, N. (2009). Toward an Enterprise Business Motivation Model. *The Architecture Journal*, *19*, 10–16.

Mandl, R. (1985). Orthogonal Latin Squares: An Application of Experiment Design to Compiler Testing. *Communications of the ACM*, *28*, 1054–1058. doi:10.1145/4372.4375

Mania, D., & Murphy, J. (2002). Developing performance models from non-intrusive monitoring traces. In Proceeding of Information Technology and Telecommunications (IT&T). IT&T.

Manna, Z., & Pnueli, A. (1992). *The Temporal Logic of Reactive and Concurrent Systems: Specification*. Springer-Verlag. doi:10.1007/978-1-4612-0931-7

Mansor, A. A., Kadir, W. M. W., & Elias, H. (2011). Policy-based approach for dynamic architectural adaptation: A case study on location-based system. In *Proceedings of Software Engineering (MySEC), 2011 5th Malaysian Conference in* (pp. 171-176). IEEE.

Mansor, A., Kadir, W. M. N. W., Anwar, T., & Elyas, H. (2012). Policy-based Approach to Detect and Resolve Policy Conflict for Static and Dynamic Architecture. *Journal of Theoretical and Applied Information Technology*, *37*(2), 268–278.

Mansour, O., & Ghazawneh, A. (2009). Research in Information Systems: Implications of the constant changing nature of IT capabilities in the social computing era. In *Proc. of the 32nd Information Systems Research Seminar in Scandinavia*. Academic Press.

Marcos, E., Acuña, C. J., & Cuesta, C. E. (2006). Integrating software architecture into a MDA framework. In *Proceedings of 3rd European Workshop on Software Architecture – EWSA* (LNCS), (vol. 4344, pp. 127-143). Springer.

Marcus, A., Poshyvanyk, D., & Ferenc, R. (2008). Using the conceptual cohesion of classes for fault prediction in object-oriented systems. *Software Engineering. IEEE Transactions on*, *34*(2), 287–300.

Mariscal, G., Marban, O., & Fernandez, C. (2010). A survey of data mining and knowledge discovery process models and methodologies. *The Knowledge Engineering Review*, *25*(2), 137–166. doi:10.1017/S0269888910000032

Marler, R. T., & Arora, J. S. (2004). Survey of multi-objective optimization methods for engineering. *Structural and Multidisciplinary Optimization*, *26*(6), 369–395. doi:10.1007/s00158-003-0368-6

Martin, J. (1991). *Rapid Application Development*. Prentice-Hall.

Martin, J.-P. (1992). *Qualité du logiciel et système qualité, l'industrialisation par la certification*. Masson.

Martin, R. C. (2003). *Agile software development: principles, patterns, and practices*. Prentice Hall PTR.

Martı-Oliet, N., & Meseguer, J. (2002). Rewriting logic: Roadmap and bibliography. *Theoretical Computer Science*, *285*(2), 121–154. doi:10.1016/S0304-3975(01)00357-7

Mashkoor, A., & Jacquot, J.-P. (2011). Utilizing Event-B for domain engineering: a critical analysis. *Requirements Engineering*, *16*, 191–207. doi:10.1007/s00766-011-0120-5

Mattsson, A., Lundell, B., Lings, B., & Fitzgerald, B. (2009). Linking model-driven development and software architecture: A case study. *IEEE Transactions on Software Engineering*, *35*(1), 83–93. doi:10.1109/TSE.2008.87

Maurer, F., & Hellmann, T. D. (2013). People-Centered Software Development: An Overview of Agile Methodologies. In *Proceedings of Software Engineering* (pp. 185–215). Berlin: Springer-Verlag. doi:10.1007/978-3-642-36054-1_7

McCabe, T. J. (1976). A Complexity Measure. *IEEE Transactions on Software Engineering*, *2*(4), 308–320. doi:10.1109/TSE.1976.233837

McConnell, S. (1996). *Rapid Development: Taming Wild Software Schedules*. Microsoft Press.

McGibbon, T. (1999). *A business case for software process improvement revised - measuring return on investment from software engineering and management*. Air Force Research Laboratory contract no. SP0700-98-4000.

McIlraith, S.-A., Son, T.-C., & Zeng, H.-L. (2001). Semantic Web Services. *IEEE Intelligent Systems, 16*(2), 46–53. doi:10.1109/5254.920599

McNatt, W. B., & Bieman, J. M. (2001). Coupling of design patterns: Common practices and their benefits. In *Proceedings of the 25th Annual International Computer Software and Applications Conference* (pp. 574–579). Chicago, IL: IEEE.

Meagher, D., Hashmi, M., & Tuohey, W. (2006, November-December). Regulatory considerations and business implications for automated system suppliers. *Pharmaceutical Engineering*, 24-36.

MediaWiki. (n.d.). Retrieved from http://www.mediawiki.org/wiki/MediaWiki

Medjahed, B., Bouguettaya, A., & Elmagarmid, A. K. (2003). Composing Web services on the Semantic Web. *The VLDB Journal, 12*, 333–351. doi:10.1007/s00778-003-0101-5

Meedeniya, I., Moser, I., Aleti, A., & Grunske, L. (2011). Architecture-based reliability evaluation under uncertainty. In *Proceedings of the Joint ACM SIGSOFT Conference--QoSA and ACM SIGSOFT symposium--ISARCS on Quality of software architectures--QoSA and architecting critical systems--ISARCS* (pp. 85-94). ACM.

Mei, H., & Huang, G. (2004). PKUAS: An architecture-based reflective component operating platform. In *Proceedings of 10th IEEE Interna tional Workshop on Future Trends of Distributed Computing Systems* (FTDCS) (pp.163—169). Suzhou, China: FTDCS.

Mei, H., Huang, G., & Cao, D.-G. et al. (2005). Anatomy and Evaluation on J2EE Technology. *Communications of China, 1*(4), 26–35.

Mellor, S. et al. (2004). *MDA Distilled*. Addison Wesley.

Mellor, S. J., & Balcer, M. (2002). *Executable UML: A Foundation for Model-driven Architectures*. Addison-Wesley Longman Publishing Co.

Mellor, S. J., Clark, A. N., & Futagami, T. (2003). Model-driven development. *IEEE Software, 20*, 14–18. doi:10.1109/MS.2003.1231145

Melonfire, C. (2007). *Five common errors in requirements analysis (and how to avoid them)*. Retrieved 25th Nov. 2011, from http://www.techrepublic.com/article/five-common-errors-in-requirements-analysis-and-how-to-avoid-them/6146544

Melsted, P., & Pritchard, J. K. (2011). Efficient counting of k-mers in DNA sequences using a Bloom filter. *BMC Bioinformatics*, 333. doi:10.1186/1471-2105-12-333 PMID:21831268

Memon, A. M., & Soffa, M. L. (2003). Regression Testing of GUIs. In *Proceedings of the 9th European Software Engineering Conference (ESEC) and the 11th ACM SIGSOFT International Symposium on the Foundations of Software Engineering (FSE-11)*. ACM Press.

Memon, R. N., Ahmad, R., & Salim, S. S. (2010). Problems in requirements engineering education: a survey. In *Proceedings of FIT '10*. FIT.

Memon, R. N., Salim, S. S., & Ahmad, R. (2013). *Analysis and classification of problems associated with requirements engineering education: Towards an integrated view*. Arabian Journal for Science and Engineering.

Mende, T., & Koschke, R. (2009). Revisiting the evaluation of defect prediction models. In *Proceedings of the 5th International Conference on Predictor Models in Software Engineering PROMISE'09* (pp. 7). New York, NY: ACM.

Meneely, A., Williams, L., Snipes, W., & Osborne, J. (2008). Predicting failures with developer networks and social network analysis. In *Proceedings of the 16th International Symposium on Foundations of software engineering SIGSOFT'08/FSE-16* (pp. 13-23). New York, NY: ACM.

Menzies, T., DiStefano, J., Orrego, A., & Chapman, R. (2004). Assessing predictors of software defects. In *Proc. Workshop Predictive Software Models (PROMISE 2005)*. PROMISE.

Menzies, T., Dekhtyar, A., Distefano, J., & Greenwald, J. (2007). Problems with precision: a response to comments on 'data mining static code attributes to learn defect predictors'. *IEEE Transactions on Software Engineering, 33*(9), 637. doi:10.1109/TSE.2007.70721

Menzies, T., Greenwald, J., & Frank, A. (2007). Data mining static code attributes to learn defect predictors. *Software Engineering. IEEE Transactions on, 33*(1), 2–13.

Menzies, T., Milton, Z., Turhan, B., Cukic, B., Jiang, Y., & Bener, A. (2010). Defect prediction from static code features: Current results, limitations, new approaches. *Automated Software Engineering, 17*(4), 375–407. doi:10.1007/s10515-010-0069-5

Meredith, J., Ahern, S., Pugmire, D., & Sisneros, R. (2012). EAVL: The Extreme-scale Analysis and Visualization Library. In *Proceedings of the Eurographics Symposium on Parallel Graphics and Visualization (EGPGV)* (pp. 21-30). Cagliari, Italy: Eurographics Association.

Mernik, M., Heering, J., & Sloane, A. M. (2005). When and how to develop domain-specific languages. *ACM Computing Surveys, 37*(4), 316–344. doi:10.1145/1118890.1118892

Merseguer, J., & Campos, J. (2004). Software performance modelling using UML and petri nets. *Lecture Notes in Computer Science, 2965*, 265–289. doi:10.1007/978-3-540-24663-3_13

Meseguer, J., & Talcott, C. (2006). Semantic models for distributed object reflection. In *Proceedings of ECOOP 2002—Object-Oriented Programming* (pp. 1-36). Springer.

Meseguer, J. (1992). Conditional rewriting logic as a unified model of concurrency. *Theoretical Computer Science, 96*(1), 73–155. doi:10.1016/0304-3975(92)90182-F

Meseguer, J., & Talcott, C. (2002). Semantic models for distributed object reflection. *Lecture Notes in Computer Science*, 1–36. doi:10.1007/3-540-47993-7_1

Michel, P., & Wiels, V. (1997). A framework for modular formal specification and verification. In *Proceedings of Formal Methods Europe 97*. Academic Press. doi:10.1007/3-540-63533-5_28

Microsoft SharePoint – collaboration software – Office.com. (n.d.). Retrieved from http://office.microsoft.com/en-us/sharepoint/

Miller, J., & Mukerji, J. (2003). *MDA Guide Version 1.0.1, Document number omg/2003- 06-01.* Retrieved from http://www.omg.com/mda

Miller, J., & Mukerji, J. (2003). *MDA Guide Version 1.0.1 (omg/03-06-01). Object Management Group.* OMG.

Mingsong, C., Xiaokang, Q., & Xuandong, L. (2006). Automatic test case generation for UML activity diagrams. In *Proceedings of the 2006 International Workshop on Automation of Software Test* (pp. 2-8). New York, NY: ACM.

Minsky, N. (2005). *Law governed interaction (lgi): A distributed coordination and control mechanism.* Department of Computer Science, Rutgers University.

Mishra, D., Mishra, A., & Yazici, A. (2008). Successful Requirement Elicitation by Combining Requirement Engineering Techniques. In *First International Conference on the Applications of Digital Information and Web Technologies, 2008. ICADIWT 2008.* (pp.258-263). Ostrava: IEEE Computer Society. http://dx.doi.org/10.1109/ICADIWT.2008.4664355

Mitchell, T. M. (1997). *Machine learning.* Burr Ridge, IL: McGraw Hill.

MMUCC Guideline – Model Minimum Uniform Crash Criteria. (2012). Retrieved from http://mmucc.us/sites/default/files/MMUCC_4th_Ed.pdf

Mockus, A., Eick, S. G., Graves, T. L., & Karr, A. F. (1999). On measurement and analysis of software changes. *IEEE Transactions on Software Engineering.*

Mod, A., & Murphy, J. (2001). Performance monitoring of Java component-oriented distributed applications. In *Proc. IEEE 9th International Conference on Software, Telecommunications and Computer Networks (SoftCOM)* (pp. 9-12). IEEE.

Mohagheghi, P., & Dehlen, V. (n.d.). Where Is the Proof? - A Review of Experiences from Applying MDE in Industry. In *Proceedings of the 4th European conference on Model Driven Architecture,* (pp. 432-443). Berlin, Germany: Springer-Verlag.

Mohamed, A., & Zulkernine, M. (2010). A taxonomy of software architecture-based reliability efforts. In *Proceedings of the 2010 ICSE Workshop on Sharing and Reusing Architectural Knowledge* (pp. 44-51). ACM.

Compilation of References

Mohan, & Chenoweth. (2011). Teaching requirements engineering to undergraduate students. In *Proceedings of the 42nd ACM Technical Symposium on Computer Science Education*. Dallas, TX: ACM.

Mohanta, S., Vinod, G., Ghosh, A. K., & Mall, R. (2010). An approach for early prediction of software reliability. *ACM SIGSOFT Software Engineering Notes*, *35*(6), 1–9. doi:10.1145/1874391.1874403

Mohd Zin, A., & Che Pa, N. (2009). Measuring Communication Gap in Software Requirements Elicitation Process. In *Proceedings of 8th WSEAS International Conference on Software Engineering, Parallel and Distributed Systems* (pp. 66-71). Cambridge, UK: World Scientific and Engineering Academy and Society (WSEAS).

Monfelt, Y., Pilemalm, S., Hallberg, J., & Yngström, L. (2011). The 14-layered framework for including social and organizational aspects in security management. *Information Management & Computer Security*, *19*(2), 124–133. doi:10.1108/09685221111143060

Monroe, R.-J., & Gailen, D. (1996). Style based reuse for software architectures. In *Proceedings of the 1996 International Conference on Software Reuse* (pp.84—93). Academic Press.

Morris, E., et al. (2004). *System of Systems Interoperability (SOSI), final report*. Retrieved July 26, 2013, from http://www.sei.cmu.edu/reports/04tr004.pdf

Mos, A. A. (2001). Performance monitoring of Java component-oriented distributed applications. In *Proceedings of IEEE 9th International Conference on Software, Telecommunications and Computer Networks (SoftCOM)* (pp. 9--12). IEEE.

Moser, R., Pedrycz, W., & Succi, G. (2008). A comparative analysis of the efficiency of change metrics and static code attributes for defect prediction. In *Proceedings of the 13th international conference on Software engineering ICSE'08* (pp. 181-190). New York, NY: ACM.

Mostefaoui, F. (2008). *Un cadre formel pour le développement orienté aspect: Modélisation et vérification des interactions dues aux aspects*. (Ph.D. thesis). Université de Montréal.

Mouelhi, T., Fleurey, F., Baudry, B., & Le Traon, Y. (2008). A model-based framework for security policy specification, deployment and testing. In *Model Driven Engineering Languages and Systems* (pp. 537–552). Springer. doi:10.1007/978-3-540-87875-9_38

Moy, Y., Ledinot, E., Delseny, H., Wiels, V., & Monate, B. (2013). Testing or formal verification: DO-178C alternatives and industrial experience. *IEEE Software*, *30*(3), 50–57. doi:10.1109/MS.2013.43

Mubarak-Ali, A.-F., Syed-Mohamed, S. M., & Sulaiman, S. (2011). *An Enhanced Generic Pipeline Model for Code Clone Detection*. Paper presented at the 5th Malaysian Software Engineering Conference (MySEC). Kuala Lumpur, Malaysia.

Mu, K., Jin, Z., & Lu, R. (2011). Measuring software requirements evolution caused by inconsistency. *International Journal of Software and Informatics*, *6*(3), 419–434.

Mukesh, S., & Niranjan, G. (1994). *Advanced Concepts in Operating Systems*. McGraw-Hill, Inc.

Mulla, N., & Girase, S. (2012). Comparison of Various Elicitation Techniques and Requirement Prioritisation Techniques. *International Journal of Engineering Research & Technology*, *1*, 1–7.

Muller, C., Reina, G., Burch, M., & Weiskopf, D. (2010). Subversion statistics sifter. In *Proceedings of the 6th international conference on Advances in visual computing*. Springer-Verlag.

Muqeem, M., & Beg, M. R. (2012). NVC Based Model for Selecting Effective Requirement Elicitation Technique. [IJSEA]. *International Journal of Software Engineering & Applications*, *3*, 157–165. doi:10.5121/ijsea.2012.3513

Murata, T. (1989). Petri nets: properties, analysis and applications. *Proceedings of the IEEE*, *77*, 541–580. doi:10.1109/5.24143

Murphy, A. L., Picco, G. P., & Roman, G.-C. (2006). LIME: A coordination model and middleware supporting mobility of hosts and agents.[TOSEM]. *ACM Transactions on Software Engineering and Methodology*, *15*(3), 279–328. doi:10.1145/1151695.1151698

Musa, J. D. (1993). Operational profiles in software-reliability engineering. *Software, IEEE, 10*(2), 14–32. doi:10.1109/52.199724

Mussa, M., Ouchani, S., Sammane, W., & Hamou-Lhadj, A. (2009). A survey of model-driven testing techniques. In *Proceedings of Ninth International Conference on Quality Software* (pp. 167-172). Jeju, South Korea: Academic Press.

Musser, D. R., Derge, G. J., & Saini, A. (2001). *Stl Tutorial and Reference Guide: C++ Programming with the Standard Template Library*. Boston: Addison-Wesley.

Mylopoulos, J., Chung, L., & Yu, E. (1999). From object-oriented to goal-oriented requirement analysis. *CACM*, (42), 31—37.

Mylopoulos, J. (1992). Conceptual modeling and telos. In P. Locoupoulos, & R. Zicari (Eds.), *Conceptual Modeling, Databases and CASE* (pp. 49–68). New York: John Wiley and Sons.

Mylopoulos, J., Borgida, A., & Yu, E. (1997). Representing software engineering knowledge. *Automated Software Engineering, 4*(3), 291–317. doi:10.1023/A:1008627026003

Nagappan, N., & Ball, T. (2005). Static analysis tools as early indicators of pre-release defect density. In *Proceedings of the 27th international conference on Software engineering* (pp. 580-586). ACM.

Nagappan, N., & Ball, T. (2005). Use of Relative Code Churn Measures to Predict System Defect Density. In *Proceedings of 27th International Conference on Software Engineering ICSE'05* (pp. 284-292). New York, NY: ACM.

Nagappan, N., Murphy, B., & Basili, V. (2008). The influence of organizational structure on software quality: an empirical case study. In *Proceedings of the 30th international conference on Software engineering ICSE'08* (pp. 521-530). New York, NY: ACM.

Nagappan, N., Zeller, A., Zimmermann, T., Herzig, K., & Murphy, B. (2010). Change Bursts as Defect Predictors. In *Proceedings of the 21st International Symposium on Software Reliability Engineering* (pp. 309-318). Washington, DC: IEEE Computer Society.

Nagaraj, K., Killian, C., & Neville, J. (2012). Structured comparative analysis of systems logs to diagnose performance problems. In *Proceedings of Symposium on Networked Systems Design and Implementation*. USENIX Association.

Nagy, I., Bergmans, L., & Aksit, M. (2004). Declarative aspect composition. In *Software-engineering Properties of Languages for Aspect Technologies, SPLAT!* Lancaster, UK: AOSD.

Najm, E., Nimour, A., & Stefani, J. B. (1999). Infinite types for distributed object interfaces. In Formal Methods for Open Object-Based Distributed Systems (pp. 353-369). Springer US.

Nakajima, S., & Tamai, T. (2004). Lightweight formal analysis of aspect oriented models. In *Proceedings of Workshop on Aspect Oriented Modeling at UML*. UML.

Nakajo, T., & Kume, H. (1991). A case history analysis of software error cause-effect relationships. *Transactions on Software Engineering, 17*(8), 830–838. doi:10.1109/32.83917

Nationwide Health Information Network (NHIN). (n.d.). Retrieved from http://www.nist.gov/healthcare/testing/nhin.cfm

Natschläger, T., Kossak, F., & Drobics, M. (2004). Extracting Knowledge and Computable Models from Data - Needs, Expectations, and Experience. In *Proceedings of the 13th International Conference on Fuzzy Systems* (pp. 493-498). Los Alamitos, CA: IEEE Computer Society.

Naumann, J. D., & Jenkins, A. M. (1982). Prototyping: The New Paradigm for Systems Development. *Management Information Systems Quarterly, 6*(3). doi:10.2307/248654

Nawrocki, J., Jasiński, M., Walter, B., & Wojciechowski, A. (2002). Extreme programming modified: Embrace requirements engineering practices. In *Proceedings of the 10th Anniversary IEEE Joint International Conference on Requirements Engineering (RE'02)* (pp. 303-310). IEEE Computer Society.

Nevalainen, R., Halminen, J., Harju, H., & Johansson, M. (2010). Certification of Software in Safety-Critical I&C Systems of Nuclear Power Plants. In P. Tsvetkov (Ed.), *Nuclear Power*. InTech. doi:10.5772/9909

Nguyen, L., Armarego, J., & Swatman, P. (2002). Understanding Requirements Engineering: a Challenge for Practice and Education. *School Working Papers Series 2002.*

Nogueira, L., Pinho, L. M., & Coelho, J. (2012). A feedback-based decentralised coordination model for distributed open real-time systems. *Journal of Systems and Software, 85*(9), 2145–2159. doi:10.1016/j.jss.2012.04.033

Nonaka, I., & Takeuchi, H. (1995). *The Knowledge Creating Company: How Japanese Companies Create Dynamics of Innovation.* Oxford University Press.

Nouh, M., Ziarati, R., Mouheb, D., Alhadidi, D., Debbabi, M., Wang, L., & Pourzandi, M. (2010). Aspect weaver: A model transformation approach for uml models. In Proceedings of *the 2010 Conference of the Center for Advanced Studies on Collaborative Research (CASCON '10).* ACM Press.

Novais, R. L., Carneiro, G. F., Simoes Junior, P. R. M., & Mendonça Neto, M. G. (2012b). On the Use of Software Visualization to Analyze Software Evolution: An Interactive Differential Approach. *Lecture Notes in Business Information Processing, 102,* 241–255. doi:10.1007/978-3-642-29958-2_16

Novais, R. L., Mendonça Neto, M. G., Maron, D. L., Machado, I. C., & Lima, C. A. N. (2011c). On the use of a multiple-visualization approach to manage software bugs.[*Brazilian Workshop on Software Visualization.* São Paulo, Brazil: WBVS.]. *Proceedings of WBVS, 11,* I.

Novais, R., & Mendonca, M. (2013). A multi-strategy software evolution visualization infrastructure. *Information and Software Technology.* doi:10.1016/j.infsof.2013.05.008

Nuseibeh, B., & Easterbrook, S. (2000). Requirements engineering: a roadmap. In *Proceedings of the Conference on the Future of Software Engineering, (ICSE 2000)* (pp. 35-46). Limerick, Ireland: ACM.

Nwana, H. S., Lee, L. C., & Jennings, N. R. (1996). Coordination in software agent systems. *British Telecom Technical Journal, 14*(4), 79–88.

OASIS. (2007). *Reference Model for Service Oriented Architecture, Committee Draft 1.0.* Retrieved from http://www.oasis-open.org/committees/download.php/16587/wd-soa-rm-cd1ED.pdf

Oberle, D., Volz, R., Motik, B., & Staab, S. (2004). An extensible ontology software environment. In *Handbook on Ontologies.* Springer. doi:10.1007/978-3-540-24750-0_15

Object Management Group. (2010). Retrieved from http://www.omg.org/

Ogawa, M., & Ma, K.-L. (2010). Software evolution storylines. In *Proceedings of the 5th international symposium on Software visualization.* ACM.

Oguz, F., & Sengün, A. (2011). Mystery of the unknown: revisiting tacit knowledge in the organizational literature. *Journal of Knowledge Management, 15*(3), 445–461. doi:10.1108/13673271111137420

Olszak, A., & Jørgensen, B. N. (2012). Modularization of Legacy Features by Relocation and Reconceptualization: How Much is Enough? In *Proceedings of 16th European Conference on Software Maintenance and Reengineering.* CSMR.

OMG & MDA. (2011). *The Architecture of Choice for a Changing World.* Retrieved from http://www.omg.org/mda/productssuccess.htm

OMG BPMN 2.0 – OMG Formal Specification. (2011). Retrieved from http://www.omg.org/spec/BPMN/2.0/

OMG Service Oriented Architecture SIG – ABSIG. (2009). Retrieved from http://soa.omg.org/

OMG. (2001). *Model Driven Architecture. A technical perspective.* OMG document-ormsc/01-07-01.

OMG. (2003). *MDA Guide: Version 1.0.1.* Retrieved from omg/2003-06-01

OMG. (2005). *UML 2.0 Testing Profile, Final Adopted Specification Version 1.0.* Retrived July, 2005, from http://www.omg.org/spec/UTP/1.0/IEEE 2008

OMG. (2008). *Software Process Engineering Metamodel Specification, Version 2.0.* OMG.

OMG. (2009). *Service Oriented Architecture Modeling Language (SoaML), FTF Beta 2*. Retrieved from http://www.omg.org/spec/SoaML/1.0/Beta2/PDF/

OMG. (n.d.). *Deployment and Configuration Adopted Submission*. Retrieved from www.omg.org

Omicini, A., & Zambonelli, F. (1998). TuCSoN: a coordination model for mobile information agents. In *Proceedings of the 1st Workshop on Innovative Internet Information Systems* (Vol. 138). Academic Press.

Omicini, A., & Zambonelli, F. (1999). Tuple centres for the coordination of Internet agents. In *Proceedings of the 1999 ACM symposium on Applied computing* (pp. 183-190). ACM.

Omicini, A. (2001). *Coordination of Internet agents: Models, technologies, and applications*. Springer. doi:10.1007/978-3-662-04401-8

Omicini, A., & Viroli, M. (2011). Coordination models and languages: From parallel computing to self-organisation. *The Knowledge Engineering Review*, *26*(1), 53–59. doi:10.1017/S026988891000041X

Open mHealth – Home. (n.d.). Retrieved from http://openmhealth.org/

Open, U. P. (2008). *OpenUP component – MDD*. Retrieved from http://www.eclipse.org/epf/openup_component/mdd.php

OpenHealthTools – Home. (n.d.). Retrieved from http://www.openhealthtools.org/index.htm

O'Rourke, C., Fishman, N., & Selkow, W. (2003). *Enterprise architecture using the Zachman framework*. Boston: Course Technology.

Ostadzadeh, S., & Fereidoon, S. (2011). An Architectural Framework for the Improvement of the Ultra-Large-Scale Systems Interoperability. In *Proceedings of International Conference on Software Engineering Research and Practice*. Las Vegas, NV: Academic Press.

Ostrand, T. J., Weyuker, E. J., & Bell, R. M. (2004). Where the Bugs Are. In *Proceedings of the International Symposium on Software Testing and Analysis ISSTA'04* (pp. 86-96). New York, NY: ACM.

Ostrand, T. J., Weyuker, E. J., & Bell, R. M. (2010). Programmer-based fault prediction. In *Proceedings of the 6th International Conference on Predictive Models in Software Engineering PROMISE'10* (pp. 19). New York, NY: ACM.

Ostrand, T. J., Weyuker, E. J., & Bell, R. M. (2005). Predicting the Location and Number of Faults in Large Software Systems. *IEEE Transactions on Software Engineering*, *31*, 340–355. doi:10.1109/TSE.2005.49

OWASP. (2013). Retrieved on 10 August 2013, https://www.owasp.org

Pachauri, A. (2013). Automated test data generation for branch testing using genetic algorithm: An improved approach using branch ordering, memory and elitism. *Journal of Systems and Software*, *86*(8), 1191–1208. doi:10.1016/j.jss.2012.11.045

Pacheco, C., & Garcia, I. (2012). A Systematic Literature Review of Stakeholder Identification Methods in Requirements Elicitation. *Journal of Systems and Software*, *85*, 2171–2181. doi:10.1016/j.jss.2012.04.075

Paetch, F., Eberlin, A., & Maurer, F. (2003). Requirement engineering and agile software development. In *Proceedings of the Twelfth IEEE International Workshops on Enabling Technologies (WETICE'03)* (pp. 308-313). IEEE Computer Society.

Paine, J. (2007). *Make category theory intuitive!* Retrieved from http://www.j-paine.org/make_category_theory_intuitive.html

Palmer, N. (2006). Understanding the BPMN–XPDL–BPEL value chain. *Business Integration Journal*, 54–55.

Pandey, A. K., & Goyal, N. K. (2010b). Test effort optimization by prediction and ranking of fault-prone software modules. In *Proceedings of Reliability, Safety and Hazard (ICRESH), 2010 2nd International Conference on* (pp. 136-142). IEEE.

Pandey, A. K., & Goyal, N. K. (2010a). Fault prediction model by fuzzy profile development of reliability relevant software metrics. *International Journal of Computers and Applications*. doi:10.5120/1584-2124

Papadopoulos, G. A., & Arbab, F. (1998). Coordination models and languages. *Advances in Computers*, *46*, 329–400. doi:10.1016/S0065-2458(08)60208-9

Papazoglou, M., Traverso, P., Dustdar, S., & Leymann, F. (2008). Service-Oriented Computing. Research Roadmap. *International Journal of Cooperative Information Systems*, *17*(2), 223–255. doi:10.1142/S0218843008001816

Parnas, D. (2006). Agile methods and GSD: the wrong solution to an old but real problem. *Communications of the ACM*, *49*(10), 27–34.

Parnas, D. L. (1972). On the criteria to be used in decomposing systems into modules. *Communications of the ACM*, *15*(12), 1053–1058. doi:10.1145/361598.361623

Parsons, T., Mos, A., & Murphy, J. (2006). Non-intrusive end-to-end runtime path tracing for J2EE systems. *IEE Proceedings. Software*. doi:10.1049/ip-sen:20050069

Păsăreanu, C. (2011). New results in software model checking and analysis. *International Journal on Software Tools and Technology Transfer*, *13*, 1–2. doi:10.1007/s10009-010-0178-2

Path Language, X. M. L. XPath. (1999). *Version 1.0*. Retrieved from http://www.w3.org/TR/xpath/

Paulk, M., Weber, C., Curtis, B., & Chrissis, M. (1995). *The Capability Maturity Model: Guidelines for improvement of the software process*. Addison-Wesley.

Pautasso, C., Zimmermann, O., & Leymann, F. (2008). *RESTful Web Services vs. Big Web Services: Making the Right Architectural Decision*. Paper presented at 17th International World Wide Web Conference (WWW2008). Bejing, China.

Pavlich-Mariscal, J. A., Demurjian, S. A., & Michel, L. D. (2010). A framework for security assurance of access control enforcement code. *Computers & Security*, *29*(7), 770–784. doi:10.1016/j.cose.2010.03.004

Pavlich-Mariscal, J. A., Demurjian, S. A., & Michel, L. D. (2010). A framework of composable access control features: Preserving separation of access control concerns from models to code. *Computers & Security*, *29*(3), 350–379. doi:10.1016/j.cose.2009.11.005

Pawlak, R., Duchien, L., Florin, G., Legond-Aubry, F., Seinturier, L., & Martelli, L. (2002). A UML notation for aspect oriented software design. In *Proc. of the 1st Workshop on Aspect Oriented Modeling with UML* (AOSD'02). Enschede, The Netherlands: AOSD.

Peiris, M., & Hill, J. (2013). Auto-Constructing Dataflow Models from System Execution Traces. In *Proceedings of 16th IEEE International Symposium on Object/Component/Service-Oriented Real-Time Distributed Computing*. Paderborn, Germany: IEEE.

Pell, J., Hintze, A., Canino-Koning, R., Howe, A., Tiedje, J. M., & Brown, C. T. (2012). Scaling metagenome sequence assembly with probabilistic de Bruijn graphs. In *Proceedings of the National Academy of Sciences* (pp. 13:272-213:277). PNAS.

Peristeras, V., & Tarabanis, K. (2006). The Connection, Communication, Consolidation, Collaboration Interoperability Framework (C4IF) For Information Systems Interoperability. *International Journal of Interoperability in Business Information Systems*, *1*(1), 61–72.

Petrenko, A., Simao, A., & Maldonado, J. (2012). Model-based testing of software and systems: Recent advance and challenges. *International Journal on Software Tools and Technology Transfer*, *14*, 383–386. doi:10.1007/s10009-012-0240-3

Petri, C. A. (1962). *Kommunikation mit Automaten*. (PhD Dissertation). University of Bonn.

Petriu, D. B., & Woodside, M. (2007). An intermediate metamodel with scenarios and resources for generating performance models from UML designs. *Software & Systems Modeling*, *6*(2), 163–184. doi:10.1007/s10270-006-0026-8

Petterson, J. (1977). Petri nets. *ACM Computing Surveys*, *9*(3), 223–252. doi:10.1145/356698.356702

Pevzner, P. A., Tang, H., & Waterman, M. S. (2001). An Eulerian path approach to DNA fragment assembly. In *Proceedings of the National Academy of Sciences* (pp. 9748-9753). PNAS.

Pietrantuono, R., Russo, S., & Trivedi, K. S. (2010). Software Reliability and Testing Time Allocation: An Architecture-Based Approach. *IEEE Transactions on Software Engineering, 36*(3), 323–337. doi:10.1109/TSE.2010.6

Pike, G., & Alakuijala, J. (2013). *CityHash*. Retrieved June, 2013, from https://code.google.com/p/cityhash/

Pinzger, M., Nagappan, N., & Murphy, B. (2008). Can developer-module networks predict failures? In *Proceedings of the 16th International Symposium on Foundations of software engineering SIGSOFT'08/FSE-16* (pp. 2-12). New York, NY: ACM.

Pitta, D. A., & Fowler, D. (2005). Online consumer communities and their value to new product developers. *Journal of Product and Brand Management, 14*(5), 283–291. doi:10.1108/10610420510616313

Popp, G., Jurjens, J., Wimmel, G., & Breu, R. (2003). Security-critical system development with extended use cases. In *Proceedings of Software Engineering Conference,* (pp. 478-487). IEEE.

Poppendieck, M., & Poppendieck, T. (2003). *Lean Software Development: An Agile Toolkit*. Addison-Wesley.

Poppendieck, M., & Poppendieck, T. (2006). *Implementing Lean Software Development: From Concept to Cash*. Addison-Wesley.

Popplewell, K. (2011). Towards the definition of a science base for enterprise interoperability: A European perspective. *Journal of Systemics, Cybernetics, and Informatics, 9*(5), 6–11.

Pothon, F. (2012). *DO-178C/ED-12C versus DO-178B/ED-12B: Changes and Improvements*. ACG Solutions.

Prasanna, M., & Chandran, K. R. (2009). Automatic test case generation for UML Object diagrams using Genetic Algorithm. *Int. J. Advance. Soft Comput. Appl, 1*(1), 19–32.

Pratt. (2013). *Pratt & Whitney Canada*. Retrieved from http://www.pwc.ca/

Prechelt, L., Unger, B., Tichy, W. F., Brossler, P., & Votta, L. G. (2001). A controlled experiment in maintenance: Comparing design patterns to simpler solutions. *IEEE Transactions on Software Engineering, 27*(12), 1134–1144. doi:10.1109/32.988711

PROMISE Repository. (n.d.). Retrieved May 2013 from http://promise.site.uottawa.ca/SERepository/datasets-page.html

Qaisar, Z. H., Anwar, N., & Rehman, S. U. (2013). Using UML Behavioral Model to Support Aspect Oriented Model. *Journal of Software Engineering and Applications, 6.*

Qi, Y., & Guo-Xing, S. (2007). *Context-Aware Service Discovery in Pervasive Computing Environments*. Paper presented at the Third International Conference on Semantics, Knowledge and Grid, 2007. New York, NY.

Quah, T. S., & Thwin, M. M. T. (2003). Application of neural networks for software quality prediction using object-oriented metrics. In *Proceedings of Software Maintenance* (pp. 116–125). IEEE.

Queralt, A., & Teniente, E. (2012). Verification and validation of UML conceptual schemas with OCL constraints. *ACM Transactions on Software Engineering and Methodology, 21* (2), 13:1-13:41.

Quinlan, J. R. (1986). Induction of Decision Trees. *Machine Learning, 1*(1), 81–106. doi:10.1007/BF00116251

Radjenović, D., Heričko, M., Torkar, R., & Živkovič, A. (2013). Software fault prediction metrics: A systematic literature review. *Information and Software Technology, 55*(8), 1397–1418. doi:10.1016/j.infsof.2013.02.009

Rahman, F., & Devanbu, P. (2011). Ownership, experience and defects: a fine-grained study of authorship. In *Proceedings of the 33rd International Conference on Software Engineering ICSE'11,* (pp. 491-500). New York, NY: ACM.

Rahman, F., & Devanbu, P. (2013). How, and why, process metrics are better. In *Proceedings of the 2013 International Conference on Software Engineering ICSE'13* (pp. 432-441). Piscataway, NJ: IEEE Press.

Ramler, R. (2008). The impact of product development on the lifecycle of defects. In *Proceedings of the 2008 Workshop on Defects in Large Software Systems DEFECTS'08* (pp. 21-25). New York, NY: ACM.

Ramler, R., & Himmelbauer, J. (2013). Noise in Bug Report Data and the Impact on Defect Prediction Results. In *Proceedings of the Joint Conference of the 23nd International Workshop on Software Measurement IWSM and the 8th International Conference on Software Process and Product Measurement Mensura* (pp. 173-180). Los Alamitos, CA: IEEE Computer Society.

Ramler, R., & Natschläger, T. (2011). Applying Heuristic Approaches for Predicting Defect-Prone Software Components. In *Proceedings of the 13th International Conference on Computer Aided Systems Theory EUROCAST LNCS 6927* (pp. 384-391). Heidelberg, Germany: Springer.

Ramler, R., & Wolfmaier, K. (2008). Issues and effort in integrating data from heterogeneous software repositories and corporate databases. In *Proceedings of the 2nd International Symposium on Empirical Software Engineering and Measurement ESEM'08* (pp. 330-332). New York, NY: ACM.

Ramler, R., Klammer, C., & Natschläger, T. (2010). The usual suspects: a case study on delivered defects per developer. In *Proceedings of the 2010 International Symposium on Empirical Software Engineering and Measurement ESEM '10*. New York, NY: ACM.

Ramler, R., Larndorfer, S., & Natschläger, T. (2009a). What Software Repositories Should Be Mined for Defect Predictors? In *Proceedings of the 35th Euromicro Conference on Software Engineering and Advanced Applications SEAA'09* (pp. 181-187). Washington, DC: IEEE Computer Society.

Ramler, R., Wolfmaier, K., Stauder, E., Kossak, F., & Natschläger, T. (2009b). Key Questions in Building Defect Prediction Models in Practice. In *Proceedings of the 10th International Conference on Product-Focused Software Process Improvement PROFES'09 LNBIP 32* (pp. 14-27). Heidelberg, Germany: Springer.

Ramsin, R., & Paige, R. (2008). Process-centered review of object oriented software development methodologies. *ACM Computing Surveys, 40* (1), 3:1-3:89.

Rana, Z. A., Awais, M. M., & Shamail, S. (2009). An FIS for early detection of defect prone modules. In *Proceedings of Emerging Intelligent Computing Technology and Applications With Aspects of Artificial Intelligence* (pp. 144–153). Springer. doi:10.1007/978-3-642-04020-7_16

Ran, S. P. (2003). A model for Web services discovery with QoS. *ACM SIGecom Exchanges, 4*(1), 1–10. doi:10.1145/844357.844360

Reeves, J. W. (1992). What is software design?, *C++ Journal, 2*(2).

Reformat, M. (2003). A fuzzy-based meta-model for reasoning about the number of software defects. In Proceedings of Fuzzy Sets and Systems—IFSA 2003 (pp. 644-651). Springer.

Regev, G., Gause, D. C., & Wegmann, A. (2009). Experiential learning approach for requirements engineering education. *Requirements Engineering, 14*(4), 269–287. doi:10.1007/s00766-009-0084-x

Reisig, W., Fahland, D., Lohmann, N., Massuthe, P., Stahl, C., Weinberg, D., et al. (2006). Analysis techniques for service models. In *Proceedings of Second International Symposium on Leveraging Applications of Formal Methods, Verification and Validation, 2006* (ISoLA 2006). IEEE Computer Society. Dijkman, R. (2010). BPMN 2.0 execution semantics formalized as graph rewrite rules. In *Proceedings of BPMN 2010*. BPMN.

Ren, K., Wang, C., & Wang, Q. (2012). Toward secure and effective data utilization in public cloud. *IEEE Network, 26*(6), 69–74. doi:10.1109/MNET.2012.6375896

Rennie, M. W., & Misic, V. B. (2004). *Towards a Service-Based Architecture Description Language (TR 04/08)*. University of Manitoba.

Ren, S., Yu, Y., Chen, N., Marth, K., Poirot, P. E., & Shen, L. (2006). Actors, roles and coordinators—a coordination model for open distributed and embedded systems. In *Coordination Models and Languages* (pp. 247–265). Springer. doi:10.1007/11767954_16

Reorda, M. S., Peng, Z., & Violanate, M. (2005). *System-Level Test and Validation of Hardware/Software Systems*. Springer-Verlag. doi:10.1007/1-84628-145-8

Reussner, R. H. (2001). Enhanced component interfaces to support dynamic adaption and extension. In *Proceedings of the 34ᵗʰ Annual Hawaii International Conference on* (pp. 10-20). IEEE.

Reza, M., & Raman, R. (2012). An Analytical Review of Process-Centered Software Engineering Environments. In *Proceedings of the 19th International Conference and Workshops on Engineering of Computer-Based Systems* (pp. 64-73). Novi Sabi, Serbia: Academic Press.

Ribeiro, M., Pacheco, H., Teixeira, L., & Borba, P. (2010). Emergent feature modularization. In *Proceedings of the ACM international conference companion on Object oriented programming systems languages and applications companion*. ACM.

Ripley, R., Sarma, A., & van der Hoek, A. (2007). A visualization for software project awareness and evolution. In *Proceedings of Visualizing Software for Understanding and Analysis*. IEEE. doi:10.1109/VISSOF.2007.4290712

Robertson, S., & Robertson, J. (1999). *Mastering the requirements process*. ACM Press.

Robertson, S., & Robertson, J. (1999). *Mastering the Requirements Process*. Harlow, UK: Addison-Wesley.

Rohr, M., Giesecke, S., Hasselbring, W., Hiel, M., Heuvel, W.-J. V. D., & Weigand, H. (2006). A classification scheme for self-adaptation research. In *Proceedings of International Conference on Self-Organization and Autonomous Systems*. Erfurt, Germany: Academic Press.

Rohr, M., van Hoorn, A., Hasselbring, W., Lübcke, M., & Alekseev, S. (2010). Workload-intensity-sensitive timing behavior analysis for distributed multi-user software systems. In *Proceedings of the first joint WOSP/SIPEW international conference on Performance engineering* (pp. 87-92). ACM.

Rolland, C., & Prakash, N. (2000). From conceptual modelling to requirements engineering. *Annals of Software Engineering*, *10*(1-4), 151–176. doi:10.1023/A:1018939700514

Roman, G.-C., & Cox, K. C. (1992). Program visualization: the art of mapping programs to pictures. In *Proceedings of the 14th international conference on Software engineering*. ACM.

Ropponen, J., & Lyytinen, K. (2000). Components of software development risk: How to address them? A Project Manager survey. *IEEE Transactions on Software Engineering*, *26*(2), 98–112. doi:10.1109/32.841112

Rosca, D. (2000). An active/collaborative approach in teaching requirementsengineering. In Proceedings of 30th Annual Frontiers in Education. doi: doi:10.1109/FIE.2000.897606

Roser, S., & Bauer, B. (2005). A categorization of collaborative business process modeling techniques. In *Proceedings of Seventh IEEE International Conference on E-Commerce Technology Workshops – CECW'05*. IEEE Computer Society.

Ross, A., Rhodes, D., & Hastings, D. (2008). Defining changeability: Reconciling flexibility, adaptability, scalability, modifiability, and robustness for maintaining system lifecycle value. *Systems Engineering*, *11*(3), 246–262. doi:10.1002/sys.20098

Rossi, D., Cabri, G., & Denti, E. (2001). Tuple-based technologies for coordination. In *Coordination of Internet agents* (pp. 83–109). Springer. doi:10.1007/978-3-662-04401-8_4

Rotschke, T., & Krikhaar, R. (2002). Architecture analysis tools to support evolution of large industrial systems. In *Proceedings International Conference on Software Maintenance*. Academic Press.

Rottenstreich, O., Kanizo, Y., & Keslassy, I. (2012). The variable-increment counting Bloom filter. In *Proceedings of the 31st Annual IEEE International Conference on Computer Communications* (pp. 1880-1888). Orlando, FL: IEEE Computer Society.

Roy, C. K., & Cordy, J. R. (2007). A Survey on Software Clone Detection Research. School of Computing TR 2007-541, Queen's University, 115.

RTCA/DO-178B. (1992). *Software considerations in airborne systems and equipment Certification*. RTCA Inc. [EUROCAE document number: ED-12B]

RTCA/DO-178C. (2011). *Software considerations in airborne systems and equipment Certification*. RTCA Inc. [EUROCAE document number: ED-12C]

RTCA/DO-248C. (2011). *Supporting Information for DO-178C and DO-278A*. RTCA Inc. [EUROCAE document number: ED-94C]

RTCA/DO-330. (2011). *Software Tool Qualification Considerations*. RTCA Inc.[EUROCAE document number: ED-215]

RTCA/DO-331. (2011). *Model-Based Development and Verification Supplement to DO-178C and DO-278*. RTCA Inc. [EUROCAE document number: ED-218]

RTCA/DO-332. (2011). *Object-Oriented Technology and Related Techniques Supplement to DO-178C and DO-278A*. RTCA Inc. [EUROCAE document number: ED-217]

RTCA/DO-333. (2011). *Formal Methods Supplement to DO-178C and DO-278A*. RTCA Inc. [EUROCAE document number: ED-216]

Rubinstein, M. F., & Firstenberg, I. R. (1999). *The Minding Organisation*. John Wiley & Sons.

Rumbaugh, J., Blaha, M., Premerlani, W., Eddy, F., & Lorensen, W. (1991). *Object-Oriented Modeling and Design*. Upper Saddle River, NJ: Prentice-Hall.

Saad, R. T., Zilio, S. D., & Berthomieu, B. (2010). A general lock-free algorithm for parallel state space construction. In *Proceedings of the 2010 9th International Workshop on Parallel and Distributed Methods in Verification, and second International Workshop on High Performance Computational Systems Biology* (pp. 8-16). Enschede, The Netherlands: IEEE Computer Society.

Sabas, A. (2012). *A Categorical Framework for the Specification and the Verification of Aspect Oriented Systems*. (Ph.D. thesis). Université de Montréal.

Sabetzadeh, M. (2008). *Merging and Consistency Checking of Distributed Models*. (Ph.D. thesis). University of Toronto.

SableCc. (2009). SableCC. *SableCC*. Retrieved Jan 30, 2012, from http://sablecc.org/

Sachpazidis, I., & Sakas, G. (2008). Medication intake assessment. In *Proceedings of the 1st international conference on Pervasive Technologies Related to Assistive Environments*. ACM.

Safyallah, H., & Sartipi, K. (2006). Dynamic Analysis of Software Systems using Execution Pattern Mining. In *Proceedings of the 14th IEEE International Conference on Program Comprehension* (pp. 84--88). IEEE.

Salehie, M., & Tahvildari, L. (2009). Self-adaptive software: Landscape and research challenges. *ACM Transactions on Autonomous and Adaptive Systems*, 4(2), 1–42. doi:10.1145/1516533.1516538

Salfner, F., Lenk, M., & Malek, M. (2010). A survey of online failure prediction methods.[CSUR]. *ACM Computing Surveys*, 42(3), 10. doi:10.1145/1670679.1670680

Salonen, E., & Piilil, R. (2012). *Find the bug, Fix the bug, Do it fewer times (TimeToPic)*. Retrieved from http://www.timetopic.net/Pages/default.aspx

Saltzer, J. H., & Schroeder, M. D. (1975). The protection of information in computer systems. *Proceedings of the IEEE*, 63(9), 1278–1308. doi:10.1109/PROC.1975.9939

Samba, D., Lbath, R., & Coulette, B. (2011). Specification and Implementation of SPEM4MDE, a metamodel for MDE software processes. In *Proceedings of the 23rd International Conference on Software Engineering Knowledge Engineering (SEKE'2011)* (pp. 646-653). Miami Beach, FL: SEKE.

Samuel, P., Mall, R., & Kanth, P. (2007). Automatic test case generation from UML communication diagrams. *Information and Software Technology*, 49(2), 158–171. doi:10.1016/j.infsof.2006.04.001

Sánchez Cuadrado, J., García Molina, J., & Menarguez Tortosa, M. (2006). *RubyTL: A Practical, Extensible Transformation Language*. Paper presented at the European Conference on Model Driven Architecture - Foundations and Applications (ECMDA-FA 2006). Bilbao, Spain.

Sanders, P., Schultes, D., & Vetter, C. (2008). Mobile route planning. In *Proceedings of ESA 2008* (LNCS), (vol. 5193, pp. 732-743). Berlin: Springer.

Sandhu, P. S., Singh, S., & Budhija, N. (2011). Prediction of level of severity of faults in software systems using density based clustering. In *Proceedings of 2011 IEEE International Conference on Software and Computer Applications*. (Vol. 9). IEEE.

Sandhu, P., Singh, P., & Verma, A. A. (2008). Evaluating quality of software systems by design patterns detection. In *Proceedings of International Conference on Advanced Computer Theory and Engineering* (pp. 3–7). Singapore: IEEE.

Sandy, K. (2006). *BPM Think Tank. EbizQ*. Retrieved from http://www.ebizq.net/blogs/column2/archives/bpmthinktank2006/

Santos, L. O. B. S., & Eduardo, G. ,. Alves, S., Lu'ıs, F., P., & Marten, V. S. (2009). *Towards a Goal-Based Service Framework for Dynamic Service Discovery and Composition*. Paper presented at the Sixth International Conference on Information Technology: New Generations 2009. New York, NY.

Sato, N., & Trivedi, K. S. (2007). Accurate and efficient stochastic reliability analysis of composite services using their compact Markov reward model representations. In *Proceedings of Services Computing* (pp. 114–121). IEEE. doi:10.1109/SCC.2007.21

Sawant, V., & Shah, K. (2011). Construction of test cases from UML models. In *Technology Systems and Management* (Vol. 145, pp. 61–68). Berlin: Springer Heidelberg. doi:10.1007/978-3-642-20209-4_9

Scheinholtz, L. A. (2007). What Are Employers Really Looking For? In *Proceedings of Requirements Engineering Education and Training*. Academic Press.

Scheu, H., & Marquardt, W. (2011). Sensitivity-based coordination in distributed model predictive control. *Journal of Process Control, 21*(5), 715–728. doi:10.1016/j.jprocont.2011.01.013

Schilit, B. N., Adams, N. W. R., & Roy, W. (1994). Context-Aware Computing Applications. In *Proceedings of the 1994 First Workshop on Mobile Computing Systems and Applications*. IEEE Computer Society.

Schmidt, D.C. (2006). Model-driven engineering. *IEEE Computer, 39* (2).

Schmidt, D. (1993). *The ADAPTIVE Communication Environment: An object-oriented network programming toolkit for developing communication software*. Academic Press.

Schneidewind, N. F. (2009). Analysis of object-oriented software reliability model development. *Innovations in Systems and Software Engineering, 5*(4), 243–253. doi:10.1007/s11334-009-0097-0

Schroeder, P. J., & Korel, B. (2000). Black-box Test Reduction Using Input-Output Analysis. In *Proceedings of the International Symposium on Software Testing and Analysis (ISSTA'00)*. Portland, OR: ISSTA.

Schroeder, P. J., Faherty, P., & Korel, B. (2002). Generating Expected Results for Automated Black-Box Testing. In *Proceedings of 17th IEEE International Conference on Automated Software Engineering (ASE'02)*. Edinburgh, UK: IEEE.

Schröter, A., Zimmermann, T., & Zeller, A. (2006). Predicting component failures at design time. In *Proceedings of the 2006 international symposium on International symposium on empirical software engineering ISESE'06* (pp. 18-27). New York, NY: ACM.

Schwaber, K., & Beedle, M. (2001). *Agile Software Development with Scrum*. Prentice Hall.

Schwaber, K., & Beedle, M. (2002). *Agilè Software Development with Scrum* (International Ed.). Pearson.

Sedigh-Ali, S., Ghafoor, A., & Paul, R. A. (2001). Metrics-guided quality management for component-based software systems. In *Proceedings of Computer Software and Applications Conference,* (pp. 303-308). IEEE.

SEI. (1991). Software Engineering Institute Requirements Engineering Project. In *Proceedings of Requirements Engineering and Analysis Workshop*. Carnegie Mellon University.

Selic, B. (2003). The pragmatics of Model-driven Development. *IEEE Software, 20*(5), 19–25. doi:10.1109/MS.2003.1231146

Selic, B. (2008). MDA manifestations upgrade. *The European Journal for the Informatics Professional, 9*(2), 12–16.

Selic, B. (2008). Personal reflections on automation, programming culture, and model-based software engineering. *Automated Software Engineering, 15*(3-4), 379–391. doi:10.1007/s10515-008-0035-7

Seliya, N., & Khoshgoftaar, T. M. (2007). Software quality analysis of unlabeled program modules with semisupervised clustering. *Systems, Man and Cybernetics, Part A: Systems and Humans. IEEE Transactions on, 37*(2), 201–211.

Senapathi, M., & Srinivasan, A. (2012). Understanding post-adoptive agile usage: An exploratory cross-case analysis. *Journal of Systems and Software, 85*(6), 1255–1268. doi:10.1016/j.jss.2012.02.025

Senge, P. M. (1990). *The Fifth Discipline – The Art & Practice of the Learning Organization.* Currency Doubleday.

Seroussi, G., & Bshouty, N. H. (1988). Vector Sets for Exhaustive Testing of Logic Circuits. *IEEE Transactions on Information Theory, 34*, 513–522. doi:10.1109/18.6031

Shafi, S., Hassan, S. M., Arshaq, A., Khan, M. J., & Shamail, S. (2008). Software quality prediction techniques: A comparative analysis. In *Proceedings of Emerging Technologies* (pp. 242–246). IEEE. doi:10.1109/ICET.2008.4777508

Shaker, P., & Peters, D. K. (2005). An introduction to aspect oriented software development. In *Proc. of Newfoundland Electrical and Computer Engineering Conference.* IEEE.

Shalloway, A., & Trott, J. (2005). *Design patterns explained: A new perspective on object–oriented design.* Reading, MA: Addison–Wesley.

Shanthi, A. V. K., & Kumar, D. G. M. (2011). Automated test cases generation for object oriented software. *Indian Journal of Computer Science and Engineering, 2*(4).

Sharma, V., & Trivedi, K. (2007). Quantifying software performance, reliability and security: An architecture-based approach. *Journal of Systems and Software, 80*(4), 493–509. doi:10.1016/j.jss.2006.07.021

Shatnawi, R., & Li, W. (2008). The effectiveness of software metrics in identifying error-prone classes in post-release software evolution process. *Journal of Systems and Software, 81*(11), 1868–1882. doi:10.1016/j.jss.2007.12.794

Shehab, M., Bertino, E., & Ghafoor, A. (2005). Secure collaboration in mediator-free environments. In *Proceedings of the 12th ACM conference on Computer and communications security* (pp. 58-67). ACM.

Shepperd, M., & Ince, D. C. (1994). A critique of three metrics. *Journal of Systems and Software, 26*(3), 197–210. doi:10.1016/0164-1212(94)90011-6

Sherer, S. A. (1995). Software fault prediction. *Journal of Systems and Software, 29*(2), 97–105. doi:10.1016/0164-1212(94)00051-N

Shiba, T., Tsuchiya, T., & Kikuno, T. (2004). Using Artificial Life Techniques to Generate Test Cases for Combinatorial Testing. In *Proceedings of the 28th Annual International Computer Software and Applications Conference (COMPSAC'04).* IEEE Computer Society.

Shlaer, S., & Mellor, S. J. (1992). *Object Lifecycles: Modeling the World in States.* Upper Saddle River, NJ: Yourdon Press.

Shneiderman, B., Plaisant, C., Cohen, M., & Jacobs, S. (2009). *Designing the User Interface: Strategies for Effective Human-Computer Interaction* (5th ed.). Prentice Hall.

Shull, F. (2012). Disbanding the process police: new visions for assuring compliance. *IEEE Software, 29*(3), 3–6. doi:10.1109/MS.2012.58

Sikora, E., Tenbergen, B., & Pohl, K. (2012). Industry needs and research directions in requirements engineering for embedded systems. *Requirements Engineering, 17*, 57–78. doi:10.1007/s00766-011-0144-x

Silva, B. C., Magalhães, A. P., Maciel, R. S. P., Martins, N., & Nogueira, L. (2009). Transforms: Um Ambiente de Apoio a Modelagem e Execução de Processos de Software Dirigido por Modelos. In *Proceedings of the XXIII Brazilian Symposium on Software Engineering, Tools Session.* Fortaleza, Brazil: Academic Press.

Silverás, B. (2011). *BPMS Watch.* Retrieved from http://www.brsilver.com/

Sim, S. E., & Gallardo-Valencia, R. E. (2013). Performative and lexical knowledge sharing in agile requirements. In *Managing requirements knowledge* (pp. 199–219). Berlin: Springer-Verlag. doi:10.1007/978-3-642-34419-0_9

Singh, L. K. (2011). Software Reliability Early Prediction in Architectural Design Phase: Overview and Limitations. *Journal of Software Engineering and Applications, 4*(3), 181–186. doi:10.4236/jsea.2011.43020

Singler, J., Sanders, P., & Putze, F. (2007). MCSTL: The multi-core standard template library. In *Proceedings of the 13th International Euro-Par Conference on Parallel Processing* (pp. 682-694). Rennes, France: Springer-Verlag.

Skipper, M. C. (2004). *Formal Models for Aspect-Oriented Software Development*. (Ph.D. thesis). Imperial College London.

Slaughter, S., Harter, D., & Krishnan, M. (1998). Evaluating the cost of software quality. *Communications of the ACM, 41*(8), 67–73. doi:10.1145/280324.280335

Smaalders, B. (2006). Performance anti-patterns. *Queue - Performance, 4*(1), 44-50.

Smith, J. M., & Stotts, D. (2003). SPQR: Flexible automated design pattern extraction from source code. In *Proceedings of the 18th IEEE International Conference on Automated Software Engineering* (pp. 215–224). Montreal, Canada: IEEE.

Smith, M., Friese, T., & Freisleben, B. (2006). Model driven development of service-oriented grid applications. In *Proceedings of the Advanced International Conference on Telecommunications and International Conference on Internet and Web Applications and Services* (AICT-ICIW'06). AICT-ICIW.

Smith, R., & Gotel, O. (2007). RE-O-POLY: A Game to Introduce Lightweight Requirements Engineering Good Practices. In *Proceedings of International Workshop on Requirements Engineering and Training*. India Habitat Center.

Sommerville, I. (2004). *Software Engineering* (7th ed.). Addison-Wesley.

Sommerville, I. (2006). *Software engineering*. Addison-Wesley.

Song, J., & Kang, W. H. (2009). System reliability and sensitivity under statistical dependence by matrix-based system reliability method. *Structural Safety, 31*(2), 148–156. doi:10.1016/j.strusafe.2008.06.012

Souza, V. E. S. (2012). *Requirements-based software system adaptation*. (Unpublished PhD Thesis). University of Trento.

Spinellis, D. (2010). UML everywhere. *IEEE Software, 27*(5), 90–91. doi:10.1109/MS.2010.131

Spyrou, S., Bamidis, P. D., Maglaveras, N., Pangalos, G., & Pappas, C. (2008). A methodology for reliability analysis in health networks. *Information Technology in Biomedicine. IEEE Transactions on, 12*(3), 377–386.

SQUARE | Cybersecurity Engineering | The CERT Division. (n.d.). Retrieved from http://www.cert.org/cybersecurity-engineering/products-services/square.cfm

Stamper, R., Liu, K., Hafkamp, M., & Ades, Y. (2000). Understanding the roles of signs and norms in organizations - A semiotic approach to information systems design. *Journal of Behaviour & Information Technology, 19*(1), 15–27. doi:10.1080/014492900118768

Stein, D., Hanenberg, S., & Unland, R. (2002). A UML-based aspect oriented design notation for aspect. In *Proceedings of Aspect Oriented Software Development (AOSD 2002)*. AOSD.

Steinberg, D., Budinsky, F., Paternostro, M., & Merks, E. (2008). *EMF: Eclipse Modeling Framework*. Addison-Wesley Professional.

Steinbruckner, F., & Lewerentz, C. (2010). Representing development history in software cities. In *Proceedings of the 5th international symposium on Software visualization*. ACM.

Stern, U., & Dill, D. L. (1995). Improved probabilistic verification by hash compaction. In *Proceedings of the IFIP WG 10.5 Advanced Research Working Conference on Correct Hardware Design and Verification Methods* (pp. 206-224). Frankfurt, Germany: Springer-Verlag.

Stevens, B., & Mendelsohn, E. (1998). Efficient Software Testing Protocols. In *Proceedings of the 8th IBM Centre for Advanced Studies Conference (CASCON '98)*. IBM Press.

Storzer, M., Krinke, J., & Breu, S. (2003). Trace analysis for aspect application. In Proceedings of Analysis of Aspect Oriented Software (AAOS). ECOOP.

Strang, T., & Linnhoff-Popien, C. (2004). A Context-Modelling survey. In *Proceedings of First International Workshop on Advanced Context Modelling, Reasoning and Management*. UbiComp.

Subramanyam, R., & Krishnan, M. S. (2003). Empirical analysis of ck metrics for object-oriented design complexity: Implications for software defects. *Software Engineering. IEEE Transactions on, 29*(4), 297–310.

Sun, Y., Meng, X., Liu, S., & Pan, P. (2006). Flexible workflow incorporated with RBAC. In *Computer Supported Cooperative Work in Design II* (pp. 525–534). Springer. doi:10.1007/11686699_53

Suraci, V., Mignanti, S., & Aiuto, A. (2007). *Context-aware Semantic Service Discovery.* Paper presented at the 16th IST, Mobile and Wireless Communications Summit. New York, NY.

Suto, T., Bradley, J. T., & Knottenbelt, W. J. (2006). Performance trees: A new approach to quantitative performance specification. In *Proceedings of the 14th IEEE International Symposium on Modeling, Analysis, and Simulation of Computer and Telecommunication Systems* (pp. 303-313). Monterey, CA: IEEE Computer Society.

Su, X., Liu, H., Wu, Z., Yang, X., & Zuo, D. (2011). SA based software deployment reliability estimation considering component dependence. *Journal of Electronics (China), 28*(1), 118–125. doi:10.1007/s11767-011-0561-5

Svahnberg, M., & Gorschek, T. (2005). Multi-perspective Requirements Engineering Education with focus on Industry Relevance. In *Proceedings of the Workshop on Requirements Engineering Education & Training.* Paris: Academic Press.

Swain, S. K., & Mohapatra, D. P. (2010). Test case generation from Behavioral UML Models. *International Journal of Computers and Applications, 6*(8), 5–11. doi:10.5120/1098-1436

Szabo, R. M., & Khoshgoftaar, T. M. (1995). An assessment of software quality in a C++ environment. In *Proceedings of Software Reliability Engineering* (pp. 240–249). IEEE. doi:10.1109/ISSRE.1995.497663

Szyperski, C. (1998). *Component software: Beyond object-oriented programming.* Harlow, UK: Addison-Wesley.

Talcott, C. L. (2006). Coordination models based on a formal model of distributed object reflection. *Electronic Notes in Theoretical Computer Science, 150*(1), 143–157. doi:10.1016/j.entcs.2005.12.028

Tamames, J. A. H., Acuña, C. J., de Castro, V., Marcos, E., Sanz, M. L., & Malpica, N. (2007). Web-PACS for multicenter clinical trials. *IEEE Transactions on Information Technology in Biomedicine, 11*(1), 87–93. doi:10.1109/TITB.2006.879601 PMID:17249407

Tang, D. T., & Chen, C. L. (1984). Iterative Exhaustive Pattern Generation for Logic Testing. *IBM Journal of Research and Development, 28,* 212–219. doi:10.1147/rd.282.0212

Teodoro, G., Valle, E., Mariano, N., Torres, R., & Meira, W. J. (2011). Adaptive parallel approximate similarity search for responsive multimedia retrieval. In *Proceedings of the 20th ACM International Conference on Information and Knowledge Management* (pp. 495-504). Glasgow, UK: ACM.

Thatte, S. (2001). *XLANG: Web Services for Business Process Design.* Microsoft.

Thayer, R. H., Bailin, S. C., & Dorfman, M. (1997). *Software Requirements Engineerings.* IEEE Computer Society Press.

Therón, R., González, A., García, F. J., & Santos, P. (2007). The use of information visualization to support software configuration management. In *Proceedings of the 11th IFIP TC 13 international conference on Human-computer interaction.* Springer-Verlag.

Thwin, M. M. T., & Quah, T. S. (2005). Application of neural networks for software quality prediction using object-oriented metrics. *Journal of Systems and Software, 76*(2), 147–156. doi:10.1016/j.jss.2004.05.001

Tigris.org: Open Source Software Engineering. (n.d.). Retrieved from http://www.tigris.org/

Tiwari, S., Rathore, S. S., & Gupta, A. (2012). Selecting Requirement Elicitation Techniques for Software Projects. In *Proceedings of Sixth International Conference on Software Engineering (CONSEG),* (pp. 1-10). IEEE Computer Society. http://dx.doi.org/10.1109/CONSEG.2012.6349486.

Tolone, W., Ahn, G. J., Pai, T., & Hong, S. P. (2005). Access control in collaborative systems.[CSUR]. *ACM Computing Surveys, 37*(1), 29–41. doi:10.1145/1057977.1057979

Tomaszewski, P., Håkansson, J., Grahn, H., & Lundberg, L. (2007). Statistical models vs. expert estimation for fault prediction in modified code–An industrial case study. *Journal of Systems and Software*, *80*(8), 1227–1238. doi:10.1016/j.jss.2006.12.548

Torres-Jimenez, J., & Rodriguez-Tello, E. (2012). New bounds for binary covering arrays using simulated annealing. *Information Sciences*, *185*, 137–152. doi:10.1016/j.ins.2011.09.020

Tosun, A., Turhan, B., & Bener, A. (2009). Validation of network measures as indicators of defective modules in software systems. In *Proceedings of the 5th international conference on predictor models in software engineering (PROMISE'09)*. ACM.

Tran, V. X., Tsuji, H., & Masuda, R. (2009). A new QoS ontology and its QoS-based ranking algorithm for Web services. *Simulation Modelling Practice and Theory*, *17*, 1378–1398. doi:10.1016/j.simpat.2009.06.010

Tsamardinos, I., Brown, L. E., & Aliferis, C. F. (2006). The max-min hill-climbing Bayesian network structure learning algorithm. *Machine Learning*, *65*(1), 31–78. doi:10.1007/s10994-006-6889-7

Tsantalis, N., Chatzigeorgiou, A., Stephanides, G., & Halkidis, S. T. (2006). Design pattern detection using similarity scoring. *IEEE Transactions on Software Engineering*, *32*(11), 896–909. doi:10.1109/TSE.2006.112

Tsur, S., Abiteboul, S., Agrawal, R., Dayal, U., Klein, J., & Weikum, G. (2001). Are Web Services the Next Revolution in e-Commerce? (Panel). In *Proceedings of the 27th International Conference on Very Large Data Bases*. Morgan Kaufmann Publishers Inc.

Tuohey, W. (2002). Benefits and effective application of software engineering standards. *Software Quality Journal*, *10*, 47–68. doi:10.1023/A:1015772816632

Turhan, B., Kocak, G., & Bener, A. (2008). Software defect prediction using call graph based ranking (CGBR) framework. In Proceedings of Software Engineering and Advanced Applications, (pp. 191-198). IEEE.

Turhan, B., & Bener, A. (2009). Analysis of Naive Bayes' assumptions on software fault data: An empirical study. *Data & Knowledge Engineering*, *68*(2), 278–290. doi:10.1016/j.datak.2008.10.005

Turhan, B., Kocak, G., & Bener, A. (2009). Data mining source code for locating software bugs: A case study in telecommunication industry. *Expert Systems with Applications*, *36*(6), 9986–9990. doi:10.1016/j.eswa.2008.12.028

Turhan, B., Menzies, T., Bener, A. B., & Di Stefano, J. (2009). On the relative value of cross-company and within-company data for defect prediction. *Empirical Software Engineering*, *14*(5), 540–578. doi:10.1007/s10664-008-9103-7

Turk, T. (2009). *The effect of software design patterns on object–oriented software quality and maintainability*. (Master thesis). Middle East Technological University, Turkey.

Turner, J. A. (1987). Understanding the elements of system design. In R. J. Boland Jr, & R. A. Hirschheim (Eds.), *Critical Issues in Information Systems Research* (pp. 97–111). New York: John Wiley.

UCI. (n.d.). *Machine Learning Repository*. Retrieved May 2013 from http://archive.ics.uci.edu/ml/datasets.html

Ueda, Y., Kamiya, T., Kusumoto, S., & Inoue, K. (2006). Code clone analysis environment for supporting software development and maintenance. *Electronics and Communications in Japan (Part III Fundamental Electronic Science)*, *89*(11), 10–18. doi:10.1002/ecjc.20279

Unified Modeling Language (UML). (2011). Retrieved from http://www.uml.org/

Upson, C., Thomas Faulhaber, J., Kamins, D., Laidlaw, D. H., Schlegel, D., & Vroom, J. et al. (1989). The application visualization system: A computational environment for scientific visualization. *IEEE Computer Graphics and Applications*, *9*(4), 30–42. doi:10.1109/38.31462

Uschold, M., King, M., Moralee, S., & Zorgios, Y. (1998). The enterprise ontology. *The Knowledge Engineering Review*, *13*(1), 31–89. doi:10.1017/S0269888998001088

UTS. (2011, May). Retrieved from http://www.handbook.uts.edu.au/subjects/32550.html

Valis, D., & Bartlett, L. (2010). The failure phenomenon: a critique. *International Journal of Performance Engineering*, *6*(2), 181–190.

van Breugel, F., & Koshkina, M. (2006). *Models and Verification of BPEL*. Retrieved from http://www.cse.yorku.ca/franck/ research/drafts/tutorial.pdf

van der Aalst, W. M. P. (2004). Business process management demystified: a tutorial on models, systems and standards for workflow management. In Lectures on Concurrency and Petri Nets (LNCS), (vol. 3098, pp. 1-65). Springer-Verlag.

van der Aalst, W. M. P. (2000). Workflow verification: finding control-flow errors using petri-net-based techniques. In *Business Process Management, Models, Techniques, and Empirical Studies*. Springer-Verlag.

van der Aalst, W. M. P., & ter Hofstede, A. H. M. (2005). YAWL: Yet another workflow language. *Information Systems*, *30*(4), 245–275. doi:10.1016/j.is.2004.02.002

van Genuchten, M., van Dijk, C., Scholten, H., & Vogel, D. (2001). Using group support systems for software inspections. *IEEE Software*, *18*(3), 60–65. doi:10.1109/52.922727

Vandecruys, O., Martens, D., Baesens, B., Mues, C., De Backer, M., & Haesen, R. (2008). Mining software repositories for comprehensible software fault prediction models. *Journal of Systems and Software*, *81*(5), 823–839. doi:10.1016/j.jss.2007.07.034

Vara, J. M., Vela, B., Bollati, V. A., & Marcos, E. (2009). Supporting model-driven development of object-relational database schemas: a case study. In *Proceedings of 2nd International Conference on Theory and Practice of Model Transformations – ICMT'09*. Springer-Verlag.

Vara, J. M., & Marcos, E. (2012). A framework for model-driven development of information systems: Technical decisions and lessons learned. *Journal of Systems and Software*, *85*(10), 2368–2384. doi:10.1016/j.jss.2012.04.080

Vassiliou, Y., Marakakis, M., Katalagarianos, P., et al. (1990). IRIS: A mapping assistant for generating designs from requirements. In *Proc. of the Conf. on Advanced Information Systems Engineering* (LNCS), (vol. 436, pp. 307—338). Springer.

Vela, B., & Marcos, E. (2003). Extending UML to represent XML schemas. *CAiSE Short Paper Proceedings* (Vol. 74).

Verner, L. (2004). BPM: the promise and the challenge. *Queue*, *2*(1), 82–91. doi:10.1145/984458.984503

Versionone. (2006). *3rd Annual Survey:2008, The State of Agile Development*. Retrieved October 13, 2012, from http://www.versionone.com

Viega, J., & McGraw, G. (2001). *Building secure software: how to avoid security problems the right way*. Pearson Education.

Vilkomir, S., Ghose, A., & Krishna, A. (2004). Combining agent-oriented conceptual modeling with formal methods. In *Proceedings of ASWEC* (pp.147—157). ASWEC.

Voeten, J., Hendriks, T., Theelen, B., Schuddemat, J., Suermondt, W. T., Gemei, J., & van Huët, C. (2011). Predicting Timing Performance of Advanced Mechatronics Control Systems. In *Proceedings of Computer Software and Applications Conference Workshops (COMPSACW), 2011 IEEE 35th Annual* (pp. 206-210). IEEE.

Vo, H. T., Silva, C. T., Scheidegger, L. F., & Pascucci, V. (2012). Simple and efficient mesh layout with space-filling curves. *Journal of Graphics Tools*, *6*(1), 25–39. doi:10.1080/2151237X.2012.641828

Voinea, L., & Telea, A. (2006). An open framework for cvs repository querying, analysis and visualization. In *Proceedings of the 2006 international workshop on Mining software repositories*. ACM.

Voinea, L., Lukkien, J., & Telea, A. (2007). Visual assessment of software Evolution. *Science of Computer Programming*, *65*(3), 222–248. doi:10.1016/j.scico.2006.05.012

Voinea, L., & Telea, A. (2007). Visual analytics: Visual data mining and analysis of software repositories. *Comput. Graph.*, *31*(3), 410–428. doi:10.1016/j.cag.2007.01.031

Vokac, M. (2004). Defect frequency and design patterns: An empirical study of industrial code. *IEEE Transactions on Software Engineering*, *30*(12), 904–917. doi:10.1109/TSE.2004.99

Vokac, M., Tichy, W., Sjoberg, D. I., Arisholm, E., & Aldrin, M. (2004). A controlled experiment comparing the maintainability of programs designed with and without design patterns—A replication in a real programming environment. *Empirical Software Engineering*, *9*(3), 149–195. doi:10.1023/B:EMSE.0000027778.69251.1f

W3C. (2004). *Web Services Architecture (WSA)*. Retrieved from http://www.w3.org/TR/ws-arch/

W3C. (2007). *Web Services Description Language (WSDL) Version 2.0 Part 1: Core Language*. Retrieved from http://www.w3.org/TR/2007/REC-wsdl20-20070626

W3C. (2008). *Web Content Accessibility Guidelines (WCAG) 2.0*. Retrieved 16 August 2013, from http://www.w3.org/TR/WCAG/

W3C. (2011). *Web Service Standards*. Retrieved from http://www.w3.org/2011/07/wspas-pr.html

Wada, H., Suzuki, J., & Oba, K. (2006). Modeling Non-Functional Aspects in Service Oriented Architecture. In *Proc. of the 2006 IEEE International Conference on Service Computing*. Chicago, IL: IEEE.

Wahono, R. S. (2003). Analyzing requirements engineering problems. In *Proceedings of IECI Japan Workshop*. IECI.

Wahyudin, D., Ramler, R., & Biffl, S. (2008). A Framework for Defect Prediction in Specific Software Project Contexts. In *Proceedings of the 3rd IFIP TC2 Central and East European Conference on Software Engineering Techniques CEE-SET 2008* (pp. 261-274). Heidelberg, Germany: Springer.

Walker, D., Zdancewic, S., & Ligatti, J. (2003). A theory of aspects. In *Proceedings of the 8th ACM SIGPLAN International Conference on Functional Programming (ICFP'03)*. ACM Press.

Walsh, A. E. (2002). *Ebxml: The Technical Reports*. Prentice Hall.

Wang, H., & Liu, K. (2012). User oriented trajectory similarity search. In *Proceedings of the ACM SIGKDD International Workshop on Urban Computing* (pp. 103-110). Beijing, China: ACM.

Wang, H., & Zhang, D. (2003). MDA-based Development of E-Learning System. In *Proceedings of the 27th International Computer Software and Applications Conference* (pp. 684-689). IEEE Press.

Wang, W., Tolk, A., & Wang, W. (2009). The levels of conceptual interoperability model: Applying systems engineering principles to M&S. In *Spring Simulation Multiconference*. Society for Computer Simulation International.

Wang, Z. Y., Nie, C. H., & Xu, B. W. (2007). Generating Combinatorial Test Suite for Interaction Relationship. In *Proceeding of the 4th International Workshop on Software Quality Assurance (SOQUA2007)*. Dubrovnik, Croatia: SOQUA.

Wang, Z. Y., Xu, B. W., & Nie, C. H. (2008). Greedy Heuristic Algorithms to Generate Variable Strength Combinatorial Test Suite. In *Proceedings of the 8th International Conference on Quality Software*. Oxford, UK: Academic Press.

Wang, C., Ren, K., Yu, S., & Urs, K. M. R. (2012). Achieving usable and privacy-assured similarity search over outsourced cloud data. [Orlando, FL: IEEE Computer Society.]. *Proceedings - IEEE INFOCOM, 2012*, 451–459.

Wang, C., Zheng, X., & Tu, X. (2012). A Coordination Space Based Resource-Centered Dynamic Coordination Approach to Software Systems. In *Proceedings of Advances in Computer Science and Information Engineering* (pp. 655–660). Academic Press. doi:10.1007/978-3-642-30126-1_103

Wang, P., Jin, Z., & Liu, L. et al. (2008). Building towards capability specifications of web services based on an environment ontology. *IEEE Transactions on Knowledge and Data Engineering*, *20*(4), 547–561. doi:10.1109/TKDE.2007.190719

Wang, X., & Lespérance, Y. (2001). Agent-oriented requirements engineering using ConGolog and i*.[AOIS.]. *Proceedings of AOIS, 2001*, 59–78.

Wang, X., Wu, Z., & Zhao, M. (2008). The relationship between developers and customers in agile methodology. In *Proceedings of Computer Science and Information Technology* (pp. 566–572). IEEE. doi:10.1109/ICCSIT.2008.9

Want, R., Hpper, A., Falcao, V., & Gibbons, J. (1992). The Active Badge Location System. *ACM Transactions on Information Systems*, 91–102. doi:10.1145/128756.128759

Watson, A. (2008). A brief history of MDA, upgrade. *The European Journal for the Informatics Professional*, *9*(2), 7–11.

Watt, D. A., & Brown, D. (2001). *Java collections: An introduction to abstract data types, data structures and algorithms*. New York, NY: John Wiley & Sons, Inc.

Weber, S., Emrich, A., Broschart, J., Ras, E., & Ünalan, Ö. (2009). Supporting Software Development Teams with a Semantic Process and Artifact-oriented Collaboration Environment. In *Proceedings of the Collaboration and Knowledge Sharing in Software Development Teams*. Kaiserslautern, Germany: Academic Press.

Wegner, P. (1997). Why interaction is more powerful than algorithms. *Communications of the ACM*, *40*(5), 80–91. doi:10.1145/253769.253801

Welsh, J., & Han, J. (1994). Software documents: concepts and tools. *Software - Concepts and Tools, 15*(1), 12-25.

Welsh, M., & Culler, D. (1999). Jaguar: Enabling efficient communication and I/O in Java. *Concurrency (Chichester, England)*, *12*(7), 519–538. doi:10.1002/1096-9128(200005)12:7<519::AID-CPE497>3.0.CO;2-M

Wendorff, P. (2001). Assessment of design patterns during software reengineering: Lessons learned from a large commercial project. In *Proceedings of the 5th European Conference on Software Maintenance and Reengineering Conference* (pp. 77–84). Lisbon, Portugal: IEEE.

Wettel, R., & Lanza, M. (2008). Visual exploration of large-scale system evolution. In *Proceedings of the 2008 15th Working Conference on Reverse Engineering*. IEEE Computer Society.

Wewetzer, C., Scheuermann, B., Lübke, A., & Mauve, M. (2009). Content registration in VANETs - saving bandwidth through node cooperation. In *Proceedings of the 34th IEEE Conference on Local Computer Networks* (pp. 661-668). Zurich, Switzerland: IEEE Computer Society.

Weyuker, E. J. (2007). Software Engineering Research: From Cradle to Grave. In *Proceedings of the 6th European Software Engineering Conference and ACM SIGSOFT Symposium on the Foundations of Software Engineering ESEC-FSE'07* (pp. 305-311). New York, NY: ACM.

Weyuker, E. J., Ostrand, T. J., & Bell, R. M. (2010). Comparing the effectiveness of several modeling methods for fault prediction. *Empirical Software Engineering*, *15*(3), 277–295. doi:10.1007/s10664-009-9111-2

White, L., & Almezen, H. (2000). Generating Test Cases for GUI Responsibilities Using Complete Interaction Sequences. In *Proceedings of the International Symposium on Software Reliability Engineering*. IEEE Computer Society Press.

White, S. (2004). *Process Modelling Notations and Workflow Patterns*. IBM Corporation.

White, S. A. (2005). *Using BPMN to Model a BPEL Process*. IBM Corp.

Whittle, J., & Jayaraman, P. K. (2007). Mata: A tool for aspect-oriented modeling based on graph transformation. In *Proceedings of MoDELS Workshops 2007*. Nashville, TN: MoDELS.

Wiegers, K. E. (2004). *In Search of Excellent Requirements*. Retrieved from www.processimpact.com

Wiegers, K. E. (2003). *Software Requirements* (2nd ed.). Redmond, WA: Microsoft Press.

Wiels, V. (1997). *Modularité pour la conception et la validation formelles de systèmes*. (Ph.D. thesis). ENSAE-ONERA/CERT/DERI, Toulouse, France.

Wilkie, F. G., & Kitchenham, B. A. (2000). Coupling measures and change ripples in C++ application software. *Journal of Systems and Software*, *52*(2), 157–164. doi:10.1016/S0164-1212(99)00142-9

Williams, A. W. (2000). Determination of Test Configurations for Pair-Wise Interaction Coverage. In *Proceedings of the 13th International Conference on the Testing of Communicating Systems (Testcom 2000)*. Ottawa, Canada: Testcom.

Williams, A. W., & Probert, R. L. (2001). A Measure for Component Interaction Test Coverage. In *Proceedings of the ACSI/IEEE International Conference on Computer Systems and Applications (AICCSA 2001)*. IEEE Computer Society.

Williams, A. W., Ho, J. H., & Lareau, A. (2003). *TConfig Test Tool Version 2.1. School of Information Technology and Engineering (SITE)*. University of Ottawa. Retrieved from http://www.site.uottawa.ca/~awilliam

Witkowski, C. M. (1983). A parallel processor algorithm for robot route planning. In *Proceedings of the 8th International Joint Conference on Artificial Intelligence* (pp. 827-829). Karlsruhe, Germany: Morgan Kaufmann Publishers Inc.

Witten, I. H., & Frank, E. (2005). *Data mining: practical machine learning tools and techniques*. Amsterdam: Morgan Kaufmann.

Wnuk, K., Regnell, B., & Karlsson, L. (2009a). Feature transition charts for visualization of cross-project scope evolution in large-scale requirements engineering for product lines. In *Proceedings of Requirements Engineering Visualization, First International Workshop on*. Academic Press.

Wnuk, K., Regnell, B., & Karlsson, L. (2009b). What happened to our features? Visualization and understanding of scope change dynamics in a large-scale industrial setting. In *Proceedings of the 2009 17th IEEE International Requirements Engineering Conference*. IEEE Computer Society.

Wohlin, C., & Regnell, B. (1999). Achieving industrial relevance in software engineering education. In *Proceedings of 12th Conference on* Software Engineering Education and Training. New Orleans, LA: Academic Press.

Wolf, F., & Mohr, B. (2003). Automatic performance analysis of hybrid MPI/OpenMP applications. *Journal of Systems Architecture*, 702–719.

Wolper, P., & Leroy, D. (1993). Reliable hashing without collision detection. In *Proceedings of the 5th International Conference on Computer Aided Verification* (pp. 59-70). Elounda, Greece: Springer-Verlag.

Woodcock, J., Larsen, P., Bicarregui, J., & Fitzgerald, J. (2009). Formal methods: practice and experience. *ACM Computing Surveys, 41*(4), 19:1-19:36.

Wright, G. H. V. (1951). Deontic logic. *Mind, 60*, 1–15. doi:10.1093/mind/LX.237.1

Wright, J., Smith, J., & Shuller, S. (2009). *Development Technologies Introduction*. Software Development Technologies.

Wu, J., Holt, R. C., & Hassan, A. E. (2004). Exploring software evolution using spectrographs. In *Proceedings of the 11th Working Conference on Reverse Engineering*. IEEE Computer Society.

Wu, X., Murray, A., Storey, M.-A., & Lintern, R. (2004). A reverse engineering approach to support software maintenance: Version control knowledge extraction. In *Proceedings of 11th Working Conference on Reverse Engineering* (WCRE 2004). IEEE Computer Society Press.

Wyckoff, P., McLaughry, S. W., Lehman, T. J., & Ford, D. A. (1998). T spaces. *IBM Systems Journal, 37*(3), 454–474. doi:10.1147/sj.373.0454

Wylie, B., Wolf, F., Mohr, B., & Geimer, M. (2007). Integrated runtime measurement summarization and selective event tracing for scalable parallel execution performance diagnosis. *Applied Parallel Computing. State of the Art in Scientific Computing*, 460--469.

Xu, D., Alsmadi, I., & Xu, W. (2007). Model checking aspect oriented design specification. In *Proceedings of 31st Annual International Computer Software and Applications Conference*. Beijing, China: Compsac.

Xu, D., Xu, W., & Nygard, K. (2005). A state-based approach to testing aspect oriented programs. In *Proc. of the 17th International Conference on Software Engineering and Knowledge Engineering*, (pp. 188–197). Academic Press.

Xu, Z., Khoshgoftaar, T. M., & Allen, E. B. (2000). Prediction of software faults using fuzzy nonlinear regression modeling. In *Proceedings of High Assurance Systems Engineering, 2000, Fifth IEEE International Symposium on* (pp. 281-290). IEEE.

Xu, D., & Wong, W. E. (2008). Testing aspect-oriented programs with UML design models. *International Journal of Software Engineering and Knowledge Engineering, 18,* 413–437. doi:10.1142/S0218194008003672

Yacoub, S. M., & Ammar, H. H. (2002). A Methodology for Architecture-Level Reliability Risk Analysis. *IEEE Transactions on Software Engineering, 28*(6), 529–547. doi:10.1109/TSE.2002.1010058

Yacoub, S., Cukic, B., & Ammar, H. H. (2004). A Scenario-Based Reliability Analysis Approach for Component-Based Software. *IEEE Transactions on Reliability, 53*(4), 465–480. doi:10.1109/TR.2004.838034

Yang, J., Evans, D., & Bhardwaj, D. (2006). Perracotta: mining temporal API rules from imperfect traces. In *Proceedings of the 28th international conference on Software engineering* (pp. 282--291). ACM.

Yan, J., & Zhang, J. (2008). A Backtracking Search Tool for Constructing Combinatorial Test Suites. *Journal of Systems and Software, 81,* 1681–1693. doi:10.1016/j.jss.2008.02.034

Yao, S. J., Chen, C. X., Dang, L. M., & Liu, W. (2008). Design of QoS ontology about dynamic web service selection. *Computer Engineering and Design, 29*(6), 1500–1548.

Yellin, D. M., & Strom, R. E. (1997). Protocol specifications and component adaptors. [TOPLAS]. *ACM Transactions on Programming Languages and Systems, 19*(2), 292–333. doi:10.1145/244795.244801

Yilmaz, C., Cohen, M. B., & Porter, A. (2006). Covering Arrays for Efficient Fault Characterization in Complex Configuration Spaces. *IEEE Transactions on Software Engineering, 31,* 20–34. doi:10.1109/TSE.2006.8

Yin, Q., Luo, R., & Guo, P. (2011). Software Fault Prediction Framework Based on aiNet Algorithm. In *Proceedings of Computational Intelligence and Security (CIS), 2011 Seventh International Conference on* (pp. 329-333). IEEE.

Yoo, J., Jee, E., & Cha, S. (2009). Formal modeling and verification of safety-critical software. *IEEE Software, 26*(3), 42–49. doi:10.1109/MS.2009.67

Younis, M. I., & Zamli, K. Z. (2009). ITTW: T-Way Minimization Strategy Based on Intersection of Tuples. In *Proceedings of the IEEE Symposium in Industrial Electronics and Applications (ISIEA 2009)*. IEEE Press.

Younis, M. I., Zamli, K. Z., & Isa, N. A. M. (2009). YZ Strategy for IC Testing. In *Proceedings of the 7th International Conference on Robotics, Vision, Signal Processing, & Power Applications (RoViSP 2009)*. Langkawi, Malyasia: RoViSP.

Younis, M. I., & Zamli, K. Z. (2010). MC-MIPOG: A Parallel t-Way Test Generation Strategy for Multicore Systems. *ETRI Journal, 32,* 73–82. doi:10.4218/etrij.10.0109.0266

Yourdon, E., & Constantine, L. (1979). *Structured Design.* Prentice Hall.

Yu, E. S. K. (1997). Towards modeling and reasoning support for early-phase requirements engineering. In *Proceedings of Third IEEE International Symposium on Requirements Engineering RE97* (pp. 226-235). Annapolis, MD: IEEE Computer Society.

Yu, E. S. K. (2001). Agent-oriented modeling: software versus the world. In M.J. Wooldridge, G. Weiss, & P. Ciancarini (Eds.), *Agent-Oriented Software Engineering: Proceedings of the Second International Workshop (AOSE-2001)*, (LNCS), (vol. 2222, pp. 206-225). Berlin: Springer-Verlag.

Yu, E. S. K., & Mylopoulos, J. (1994). Understanding why in software process modeling, analysis, and design. In *Proceedings of the 16th international Conference on Software Engineering* (pp. 159-168). Sorrento, Italy: IEEE Computer Society Press.

Yu, L., & Tai, K. C. (1998). In-parameter-order: a test generation strategy for pairwise testing. In *Proceedings of The 3rd IEEE International Symposium on High-Assurance Systems Engineering*. IEEE Computer Society.

Yuan, Q., Wu, J., Liu, C., & Zhang, Z. (2008). A model driven approach toward business process test case generation. In *Proceedings of the 10th International Symposium on Web Site Evolution (WSE)* (pp. 41–44). Beijing, China: WSE.

Yuan, X., Khoshgoftaar, T. M., Allen, E. B., & Ganesan, K. (2000). An application of fuzzy clustering to software quality prediction. In *Proceedings of Application-Specific Systems and Software Engineering Technology* (pp. 85–90). IEEE. doi:10.1109/ASSET.2000.888052

Yue, T., Briand, L., & Labiche, Y. (2011). A systematic review of transformation approaches between user requirements and analysis models. *Requirements Engineering, 16,* 75–99. doi:10.1007/s00766-010-0111-y

Yusop, N., Mehboob, Z., & Zowghi, D. (2007). The Role of Conducting Stakeholder Meetings in Requirements Engineering Training. In *Proceedings of Requirements Engineering Education & Training.* Academic Press.

Zamli, K. Z. et al. (2011). Design And Implementation of A T-Way Test Data Generation Strategy with Automated Execution Tool Support. *Information Sciences, 181,* 1741–1758. doi:10.1016/j.ins.2011.01.002

Zamli, K. Z., Mat Isa, N. A., & Khamis, N. (2005). The Design And Implementation Of The VRPML Support Environments. *Malaysian Journal of Computer Science, 18*(1), 57–69.

Zave, P., & Jackson, M. (1997). Four dark corners of requirements engineering. *ACM Transactions on Software Engineering and Methodology, 6*(1), 1–30. doi:10.1145/237432.237434

Zdun, U., & Dustdar, S. (2007). Model-Driven Integration of Process-Driven SOA Models. *International Journal of Business Process Integration and Management.*

Zekaoui, L. (2006). *Mixed Covering Arrays on Graphs and Tabu Search Algorithms.* (MSc Thesis). University of Ottawa, Ottawa, Canada.

Zerbino, D. R., & Birney, E. (2008). Velvet: Algorithms for de novo short read assembly using de Bruijn graphs. *Genome Research, 18*(5), 821–829. doi:10.1101/gr.074492.107 PMID:18349386

Zeshan, F., & Radziah, M. (2012). Medical Ontology in the Dynamic Healthcare Environment. *Procedia Computer Science, 10,* 340–348. doi:10.1016/j.procs.2012.06.045

Zhang, D. (2000). Applying machine learning algorithms in software development. In *Proceedings of 2000 Monterey Workshop on Modeling Software System Structures* (pp. 275-285). IEEE.

Zhang, T., Ying, S., Cao, S., & Jia, X. (2006). A Modeling Framework for Service-Oriented Architecture. In *Proceedings of the Sixth International Conference on Quality Software* (QSIC 2006), (pp. 219-226). QSIC.

Zhang, X., & Zhang, H. (2007). Comments on data mining static code attributes to learn defect predictors. *IEEE Transactions on Software Engineering, 33*(9), 635–636. doi:10.1109/TSE.2007.70706

Zhao, J., Lingshuang, S., Zhiwen, C., & Bing, X. (2010). *A Flexible Multi-Source Web Service's QoS Acquisition Framework and Implementation.* Paper presented at the Symposia and Workshops on Ubiquitous, Autonomic and Trusted Computing 2010. New York, NY.

Zhao, Y., Tang, H., & Ye, Y. (2012). RAPSearch2: A fast and memory-efficient protein similarity search tool for next-generation sequencing data. *Bioinformatics (Oxford, England), 28*(1), 125–126. doi:10.1093/bioinformatics/btr595 PMID:22039206

Zheng, J., & Harper, K. E. (2010). Concurrency design patterns, software quality attributes and their tactics. In *Proceedings of the 3rd International Workshop on Multicore Software Engineering* (pp. 40–47). Cape Town, South Africa: ACM.

Zhong, S., Khoshgoftaar, T. M., & Seliya, N. (2004b). Unsupervised Learning for Expert-Based Software Quality Estimation. In *Proceedings of High Assurance Systems Engineering, 2004, Eighth IEEE International Symposium on* (pp. 149-155). IEEE.

Zhong, S., Khoshgoftaar, T. M., & Seliya, N. (2004a). Analyzing software measurement data with clustering techniques. *Intelligent Systems, IEEE, 19*(2), 20–27. doi:10.1109/MIS.2004.1274907

Zhou, Y., & Leung, H. (2006). Empirical analysis of object-oriented design metrics for predicting high and low severity faults. *Software Engineering. IEEE Transactions on, 32*(10), 771–789.

Zhu, Y., & Xiao-Hua, M. (2010). *A Framework for Service Discovery in Pervasive Computing*. Paper presented at the 2nd International Conference on Information Engineering and Computer Science (ICIECS). New York, NY.

Zhu, H. (2008). Role-based systems are autonomic. In *Proceedings of Cognitive Informatics* (pp. 144–152). IEEE.

Zimmermann, T., & Nagappan, N. (2007). Predicting Subsystem Failures using Dependency Graph Complexities. In *Proceedings of the 18th International Symposium on Software Reliability ISSRE'07* (pp. 227-236). Washington, DC: IEEE Computer Society.

Zimmermann, T., & Nagappan, N. (2009). Predicting defects with program dependencies. In *Proceedings of the 3rd International Symposium on Empirical Software Engineering and Measurement ESEM'09* (pp. 435-438). Washington, DC: IEEE Computer Society.

Zimmermann, T., Premraj, R., & Zeller, A. (2007). Predicting Defects for Eclipse. In *Proceedings of the 3rd International Workshop on Predictor Models in Software Engineering PROMISE'07*. Washington, DC: IEEE Computer Society.

Zio, E. (2009). Reliability engineering: Old problems and new challenges. *Reliability Engineering & System Safety, 94*(2), 125–141. doi:10.1016/j.ress.2008.06.002

Zisman, A. (2007). A static verification framework for secure peer-to-peer applications. In *Internet and Web Applications and Services* (pp. 8–8). IEEE. doi:10.1109/ICIW.2007.11

Zowghi, D. (2009). Teaching Requirements Engineering to the Baháí Students in Iran who are Denied of Higher Education. In *Proceedings of Fourth International Workshop on Requirements Engineering Education and Training* (REET). IEEE Computer Society.

About the Contributors

Imran Ghani is a Senior Lecturer at Faculty of Computing, Universiti Teknologi Malaysia (UTM), Johor Campus. He received his Master of Information Technology Degree from UAAR (Pakistan), M.Sc Computer Science from UTM (Malaysia), and Ph.D. from Kookmin University (South Korea). His research focus includes studying agile software development practices, semantics techniques, content-based, collaborative filtering techniques, Semantic Web services, semantics-based software testing, business IT, enterprise architecture, and software architecture.

Wan Mohd Nasir Wan Kadir is an Associate Professor of Software Engineering in the Faculty of Computing, Universiti Teknologi Malaysia (UTM). He received his BSc. from UTM, MSc. from UMIST, and Ph.D. in the field of Software Engineering (SE) from University of Manchester. He has been with UTM since 1997. He was the Head of SE Department from 2005 to 2009, and currently, he is the Deputy Dean of the Faculty of Computing. He is the Co-Editor-In-Chief of *Int. Journal of Innovative Computing* (IJIC) and *Int. Journal of SE and Technology* (IJSET). He is also the Chairman of MySEC'06, and a member of pro-tem committee of Malaysian SE Interest Group (MySEIG). He serves as a Program Committee member of ICSEA (2008-2010), APSEC (2008-2013), ICSOFT (2009-2010), ENASE (2009-2011), and MySEC (2006-2013). His research interests include adaptable software architecture, software evolution, service-oriented computing, model-driven development, software testing, and software measurement.

Mohammad Nazir Ahmad is currently working in the Faculty of Computing at the Universiti Teknologi Malaysia. He is a founder of the Applied Ontology and Conceptual Modeling Special Interest Group (AOCO-SIG). Nazir holds a PhD from the University of Queensland. He is a member of the Association for Information Systems (AIS) and the International Association for Ontology and its Applications (IAOA).

* * *

Golnoush Abaei received her B.E. in Software Engineering from Islamic Azad University, Central Branch, Tehran, Iran and the master's degree, MCA (Master of Computer Application) from University of Mysore, Mysore, Karnataka state, India. Now she is a Ph.D candidate in University Technology Malaysia. She had worked in several software companies as a programmer, software tester, project manager and system analyst for almost four years before she started her masters. She worked in faculty of software engineering in Shahab e Danesh institute of higher education in Iran. Her research interests are software testing, software defect prediction, and soft computing.

Rodina Ahmad is an Associate Professor in University Malaya, Malaysia. She holds a PhD in software engineering from UKM, Malaysia and her Masters from Rensselaer Polytechnic Institute, USA and Bachelors from University of Hartford, USA. Her research interest lies in empirical studies of requirements engineering, and organizational Analysis (Requirements elicitation, analysis, modelling, prioritization, and evolution).

Sabrina Ahmad received Bachelor of Information Technology (Hons) from Universiti Utara Malaysia and MSc. in Real-time Software Engineering from Universiti Teknologi Malaysia. She obtained Ph.D in Computer Science from The University of Western Australia. Her specialization is in requirements engineering and focusing on improving software quality. She is currently a Senior Lecturer at the Faculty of Information and Communication Technology, Universiti Teknikal Malaysia Melaka. Her research interests include software engineering, software requirements, quality metrics, defect management and process model. She is a member of Innovative Software System and Services Research Group and Computational Intelligence and Technologies Lab in Universiti Teknikal Malaysia Melaka. She is Certified Professional Requirements Engineering (IREB CPRE -FL) and Certified Information Technology Architect (IASA CITA-F).

A. De la Rosa Algarín is a Ph.D. student of Computer Science and Engineering at the University of Connecticut, with research interests including: information and knowledge-level security and privacy enforcement, document-level information security, identity-inferred access control, knowledge modeling, and ontology engineering. He holds two majors, one in Computer Science and another in Mathematics, from the University of Puerto Rico.

AbdulRahman A. Alsewari obtained his BEng in Computer Engineering from the Military Engineering College, Baghdad in 2002, his MEng in Electronic System Design Engineering from the Universiti Sains Malaysia in 2009, and his PhD in Software Engineering from Universiti Sains Malaysia in 2012. He was a lecturer and a head of IT department in the Faculty of Engineering and Information Technology, Dar-Alsalam International University for Science and Technology Sana'a, Yemen. Currently, he is a senior lecturer in the Faculty of Computer Systems and Software Engineering. His research interests include Optimization Algorithm, Software Engineering, and Software Testing.

Pedro Álvarez received his Ph.D. in computer science engineering from the University of Zaragoza (Spain) in 2004. He has worked as a Lecture Professor at this University since 2000 and belongs to the Group of Complex and Heterogeneous Systems Integration (GIDHE). His research interests include service-based applications, business processes, and scientific workflows. More specifically, his research work focuses on integration problems of this type of distributed systems and the use of formal models (Petri nets, Linda-based coordination, etc.) for solving them. He has co-authored several publications in national and international conferences and journals and has participated in several research projects.

Adila Firdaus Bt Arbain earned her Bachelor's Degree in Software Engineering. Currently, she is doing Ph. D in Computer Science. Her research interests include agile methodologies and secure software development.

Hishammuddin Asmuni is a Senior Lecturer at the Faculty of Computing in Universiti Teknologi Malaysia. He received his first degree in Computer Science at the Universiti Malaya in 1996 and later obtained his MSc degree in Computer Science from Universiti Teknologi Malaysia in 1999 specializing in the area of Software Engineering. After teaching for four years, he pursued his PhD at the University of Nottingham, United Kingdom in Computer Science specializing in the area of Artificial Intelligence in 2008. His current research interest includes optimization techniques particularly in parallel bio-inspired algorithm and software testing. He has also published in many reputable journals and learned conferences.

Zulkarnain Azham earned his Bachelor's Degree in Software Engineering, Master's Degree in Computer Science (Information Security). Currently, he is doing Ph. D in Computer Science. His research focus is on information security.

Maslita Abd Aziz is a senior lecturer at Faculty of Information and Communication Technology, UTeM. She finished her first degree at Universiti Utara Malaysia (UUM) with BSc in Information Technology (with Hons.) and later her MSc from Rochester Institute of Technology, New York, USA with MSc in Information Technology (with Hons) specializing in Software Development and Management. Her research interests are in semantic network and information retrieval, specifically on code retrieval of how to assist programmers during system development or learning the language. She is also interested in improving teaching and learning approach of programming language especially for novice learner. She is a member of Innovative Software System and Services Research Group and Computational Intelligence and Technologies Lab in Universiti Teknikal Malaysia Melaka. She is an active member as an InfoSys instructor in Malaysia.

S. Berhe is an Assistant Research Professor in Computer Science and Engineering at the University of Connecticut with research focuses mainly on fine-grained extending role-based access control to support collaborative access control as applied to the care and treatment of patients in clinical and emergent settings. Previously, he was a post-doc in the Biomedical Informatics Department at the Columbia University Medical School. Dr. Berhe has one book chapter and ten refereed conference/workshop/journal articles.

Verónica A. Bollati is a Visiting Professor at the Department of Computing Languages and Systems at the Rey Juan Carlos University sited in Madrid, Spain. She received her M.Sc. degree in Information Systems from the National Technological University, Argentina in 2002 and she got her PhD in Computer Science by the Rey Juan Carlos University in 2011. She is a member of the Kybele Research Group where leads the Model-Driven Engineering research line. Her research interests include Model-Driven Engineering, Model Transformations and Languages, Software Engineering, Tool Development, Services Engineering, etc. She has co-authored several publications in national and international conferences and journals and has participated in several research projects.

Michel Boyer is an associate professor in computer science at The University of Montreal. His research interests include theoretical computer science, and quantum information science.

Valeria de Castro is an Associate Professor at the Department of Computing Languages and Systems at the Rey Juan Carlos University sited in Madrid, Spain. She received her M.Sc. degree in Information Systems from the National Technological University, Argentina in 2002 and she got her PhD in Computer Science at the Rey Juan Carlos University in 2007. She is a member of the Kybele Research Group where she leads the Service Engineering research line. Her research interests include Services Engineering, Service-Oriented Development, Web Engineering, and Model Driven Engineering. She has co-authored several publications in national and international conferences and journals and has participated in several research projects.

João Pedro Dantas Bittencourt de Queiroz is a System Analyst at Brazilian Federal Institution. He is a MSc Student in Computer Science at Federal University of Bahia and also graduated in Computer Science at Federal University of Bahia. His current research interests include model-driven software development, service-oriented architecture and business processes modeling. He has also worked with computer graphics and augmented reality applied to medicine.

José C. Delgado is an Associate Professor at the Computer Science and Engineering Department of the Instituto Superior Técnico (Lisbon University), in Lisbon, Portugal, where he earned the Ph.D. degree in 1988. He lectures courses in the areas of Computer Architecture, Information Technology and Service Engineering. He has performed several management roles in his faculty, namely Director of the Taguspark campus, near Lisbon, and Coordinator of the B.Sc. and M.Sc. in Computer Science and Engineering at that campus. He has been the coordinator of and researcher in several research projects, both national and European. As an author, his publications include a book, several book chapters and more than 50 papers in international refereed conferences and journals.

S. A. Demurjian is a Full Professor and Director of Graduate Studies in Computer Science and Engineering at the University of Connecticut, and co-Director of Research Informatics for the Biomedical Informatics Division, with research interests of: secure-software engineering, security for biomedical applications, and security-Web architectures. Dr. Demurjian has over 150 archival publications, in the following categories: a book, 2 edited collections, 54 journal articles and book chapters, and 98 refereed conference/workshop articles.

Javier Fabra holds an Associate Professor position in the Department of Computer Science and Systems Engineering at the University of Zaragoza. He received his Ph.D. in computer science from the University of Zaragoza, Spain, in 2010. Javier Fabra belongs to the Group of Complex and Heterogeneous Systems Integration (GIDHE), where his main research areas focus on service-oriented computing and architectures, business processes and interoperability issues in distributed and flexible systems by means of the application of high-level Petri nets. He has co-authored several publications in national and international conferences and journals and has participated in several research projects.

Ramon Araújo Gomes is a System Analyst at a Brazilian National Organization. He is a MSc Student in Computer Science at Federal University of Bahia and also graduated in Computer Science at Federal University of Bahia. His current research interests include model driven software development, software testing, and business processes modeling.

James H. Hill is an Assistant Professor of Computer Science at Indiana University-Purdue University Indianapolis (IUPUI). At IUPUI, he is the co-director of the Software Engineering and Distributed Systems Group. His areas of research include domain-specific modeling, system emulation, real-time software instrumentation, and performance analytics via system execution traces. He has published over 50 peer-review publications in these areas. Lastly, is the lead architecture of the CUTS system execution modeling tool set (cuts.cs.iupui.edu), and OASIS middleware (oasis.cs.iupui.edu).

Johannes Himmelbauer is an industrial researcher of the Data Analysis Systems group at the Software Competence Center Hagenberg, Austria. His research interests include general machine learning and data mining techniques, in particular in the area of knowledge discovery. Amongst others, he has led projects for machine learning in steel production and in the area of regional health insurance funds. He studied Technical Mathematics at the Johannes Kepler University of Linz and holds an M.Sc. (2002) from the Johannes Kepler University of Linz, Austria.

Weichih Huang received his B.S. (2004) degree in National Taiwan Normal University and MS (2006) degree in National Tsing Hua University. He was a software engineer in Billion, based in Taiwan, from 2007 to 2011. Currently, he is a PhD student supervised by Dr. William Knottenbelt at Imperial College London. His research interests include self-adaptive software systems and embedded systems.

Mohd Adham Isa received the M.Sc in Computer Science from University Teknologi Malaysia in 2009. He is obtained his PhD degree in the same institution. His current research interests are software quality analysis, software modeling, and software measurement.

Dayang Norhayati Abang Jawawi is an associate professor in the Department of Software Engineering, Faculty of Computer Science and Information Systems, Universiti Teknologi Malaysia (UTM). She received her B.Sc. in Software Engineering from Sheffield Hallam University, UK, and conducted her M.Sc. and Ph.D. research in Software Engineering from Universiti Teknologi Malaysia. Her research interests are in software reuse, software quality and software testing. Currently, she is Head of the Software Engineering Department, Faculty of Computer Science and Information Systems, UTM, and a member of the Software Engineering Research Group (SERG), K-Economy, UTM. Most of her research projects focus on rehabilitation and mobile robotics, real-time embedded systems, and precision farming applications.

Seung Ryul Jeong received the Ph.D. degree from the University of South Carolina. He is a full professor of management information systems and the Graduate School of Business Information Technology at the Kookmin University, Seoul, South Korea. His research interests include BPM, Project Management, ERP, IS audit, and Software Processes.

Zhi Jin is a professor of Computer Science at the Peking University, Beijing, China. She received the MS degree in computer science in 1987 and the PhD degree in 1992, both from Changsha Institute of Technology, China. Her research interests include software requirements engineering and knowledge engineering. She has published 2 books and more than 100 referred journal/conference papers in these areas. She has won various nation-class awards/honors in China, including the Natural Science Foundation for Distinguished Young Scholars of China (2006), and the Zhongchuang Software Talent Award (1997).

Emaliana Kasmuri received Bachelor of Science Computer (Hons) and MSc. in Real-time Software Engineering from Universiti Teknologi Malaysia. She is currently a lecturer at the Faculty of Information and Communication Technology, Universiti Teknikal Malaysia Melaka. Her research interests include software engineering and mobile application development. She is a member Computational Intelligence and Technologies Lab in Universiti Teknikal Malaysia Melaka. Certified Sun Java Programmer (SCJP) and Certified Information Technology Architect (IASA CITA-F).

William Knottenbelt is a Reader in Applied Performance Modelling in the Department of Computing at Imperial College London, where he became a Lecturer in 2000. His research interests are related to the performance modelling of systems using high-level formalisms such as stochastic Petri Nets, stochastic process algebras and queueing networks. His research has been supported by three EPSRC research grants as Principal Investigator.

Marcos López-Sanz received his PhD in Computer Science from the Rey Juan Carlos University with a work on service-oriented model-driven specification of software architectures. He also received an MSc in Computer Science from the same University. His research interests include Software Architecture, Model-Driven Engineering, Service-Orientation, Software Engineering of Distributed Systems and Grid Computing, Database Design, etc. He currently belongs to the Kybele Research Group and works as a visiting teacher for the Rey Juan Carlos University. He received his BSc in IT Systems from the Polytechnic University of Madrid. He is co-author of numerous journal articles and conference papers, and has participated in many joint research projects.

Ruqian Lu is a professor of computer science of the Institute of Mathematics, Academy of Mathematics and Systems Science. He is a fellow of Chinese Academy of Sciences. His research interests include artificial intelligence, knowledge engineering and knowledge based software engineering. He has published more than 100 papers and 10 books. He has won two first class awards from the Academia Sinica and a National second-class prize from the Ministry of Science and Technology. He has also won the sixth Hua Loo-keng Mathematics Prize.

Rita Suzana Pitangueira Maciel is adjunct professor from Computer Science Department at Federal University of Bahia Brazil, holds a Master and a Doctoral degree in Computer Science, and her current research interests include model driven software development, service-oriented architecture and business processes modeling. Additionally, she has practiced application software engineering for ten years in industry.

Abdelhamid Abdelhadi Mansor is currently working as an Assistant Professor in Computer Science Department – Faculty of Mathematical Sciences University of Khartoum, Sudan. In 2000, he graduated from Faculty of Mathematical Sciences – University of Khartoum with a BSc (Honors) in Computer Science & Statistics. In 2002, he received his MSc. Degree in Networks and Computer Architecture from Faculty of Electrical Engineering – University of Khartoum, Sudan. He has a PhD. in the field of Software Engineering from the Universtiti Technologi Malaysia. His research interests include Software Engineering, distributed systems, Adaptive software system and Service-Oriented Architecture.

Esperanza Marcos is a Full Professor at the Department of Computing Languages and Systems at the Rey Juan Carlos University, Madrid, Spain. She is the leader of the Kybele Research Group. Kybele's main research interests include Service Engineering, Software Engineering, Model-Driven Engineering, Information Systems Development, and Philosophical Foundations on Information Systems Engineering. Prof. Marcos received a PhD in Computer Sciences from Polytechnic University of Madrid (Spain) in 1997. She is co-author of several books and she has published several book's chapters and articles in journals and conferences. Prof. Marcos has participated and managed several research projects.

Ana Patrícia F. Magalhães Mascarenhas is graduated in informatics and holds master degree in Mechatronic Systems in Federal University of Bahia where she is now a PhD. student in Computer Science. She is assistant professor from Computer Science Department at University of Bahia State. Her current researches include model driven software development, specially related to model transformations, and software development processes. She has also worked for ten years in industry.

Rafia Naz Memon received her Bachelor's in Software Engineering in 2006 and Masters of Information Technology in 2008 from MUET, Pakistan. She holds a Ph.D. in software engineering from UM, Malaysia and serving as an Assistant Professor at QUEST, Pakistan. Her research interest lies in requirements engineering and software engineering education.

Manoel Mendonça is a Professor of Computer Science at the Federal University of Bahia (UFBA). Prof. Mendonça holds a Ph.D. in computer science from the University of Maryland at College Park (UMCP), a M.Sc. in computer engineering from UNICAMP (Brazil), and a bachelor in electrical engineering from UFBA. From 1994 to 1997, he was a visiting scientist and was awarded a doctoral fellowship from IBM Toronto Laboratory's Centre for Advanced Studies. From 1997 to 2000, he worked as a Faculty Research Associate at UMCP and as a scientist at the Fraunhofer Center Maryland. He joined Salvador University (Brazil) as a Professor in 2000. There he headed the university's Computing Research Center and helped to create the first computer science master and doctoral programs at his home state of Bahia. From 2008 to 2009, he was the president of the Special Commission for Software Engineering of the Brazilian Computer Society (SBC). He joined UFBA in 2009. There, he has headed the computer science graduate program and software engineering lab. Since 2012, he is the Director of the Fraunhofer Center for Software and Systems Engineering at UFBA. Dr. Mendonça has published over 100 technical papers. His main research interests are on software engineering and information visualization. He is a member of SBC and ACM, and a senior member of IEEE.

John-Jules Ch. Meyer is a full professor of Computer Science at Utrecht University where he heads the Intelligent Systems Group. His current research interests include artificial intelligence, and intelligent agents in particular, from theory to applications. He is a Fellow of the European Coordinating Committee for Artificial Intelligence.

Radziah Mohamad is a senior lecturer in the Faculty of Computing, Universiti Teknologi Malaysia. She received her Bachelor of Software Engineering from Sheffield Hallam University, UK, MS, and PhD from Universiti Teknologi Malaysia. She is the referee for many scientific journals like *IET Software* and *Malaysian Journal of Computer Science*.

Roy Morien has worked in the IT industry since January 1975, and has been a University academic since February 1985. He has qualifications in Corporate Administration and Law, Accounting, Business Management and Information Systems. During his nearly 30-year career as a University academic, he has published and presented at numerous conferences primarily on the subject of System Development methodologies, with a special interest in 'lightweight' methodologies. However, his interests lie in both Education and Information Systems, and the nexus between business studies and computer studies. His knowledge and understanding of Agile Methods can be traced back to his earliest days of teaching and applying systems development methods, usually on the topics of Software Prototyping, Rapid Application Development (RAD), and evolutionary and incremental approaches to system development. His academic career includes teaching in the area of Information Systems and Database development in Australia, Indonesia, Singapore, Hong Kong, and Thailand. He is currently an academic editor at Naresuan University in Thailand.

Al-Fahim Mubarak-Ali received his Bachelor of Computer Science (Software Engineering) degree from Universiti Malaysia Pahang, Malaysia in 2009 and Master of Science (Computer Science) degree from Universiti Sains Malaysia, Malaysia in 2012. Currently, he is pursuing his PhD in the area of Software Engineering in Universiti Teknologi Malaysia, Malaysia.

Noor Azilah Muda received MSc. in Software Engineering from Universiti Teknologi Malaysia. Her specialization is in soft computing area particularly in pattern recognition problems. She is currently a Senior Lecturer at the Faculty of Information and Communication Technology, Universiti Teknikal Malaysia Melaka. Her research interests include artificial immune system, data management, and software engineering. She is a member of Computational Intelligence and Technologies Lab (CIT) research group in Universiti Teknikal Malaysia Melaka. She recently has certified in IREB Certified Professional for Requirements Engineering (CPRE-FL), and since 2005, she is one of the IBM Certified Database Associates DB2 Universal Database V8.1 Family.

Thomas Natschläger is a key researcher and head of the Data Analysis Systems group at the Software Competence Center Hagenberg, Austria. His research interests include general machine learning and data mining techniques (in particular interpretable data analysis methods), recurrent neural networks and prediction systems. Amongst others, he has lead projects for machine learning in discrete manufacturing, machine learning in steel production and optimization of local weather forecasts. He studied Telematik at the Technical University of Graz and holds a M.Sc. (1996, Technical University of Graz) and a PhD (1999, Technical University of Graz) and was an associate professor at the Technical University of Graz (1999-2003).

Renato Novais is an effective professor at Federal Institute of Bahia (IFBA). He holds a D.Sc. degree in Computer Science from Federal University of Bahia. During his Doctorate, he spent a period as a visiting scientist in Fraunhofer Center for Experimental Software Engineering, MD, USA. His main research areas are software visualization, software evolution, experimental software engineering, software maintenance and reengineering, and software comprehension.

Oluwagbemi Oluwatolani is a Nigerian who holds B.Sc. and M.Sc. degrees in Computer Science. She is currently pursuing her PhD degree in Computer Science at Universiti Teknologi Malaysia. As a Lecturer cum Researcher with over 5 years research and teaching experience, she has published about 20 articles in reputable journals and learned conferences, which are indexed in major computer science repositories. Her research interest is Software Processes and Testing.

J. Pavlich-Mariscal is an Associate Professor of the Pontificia Universidad Javeriana (Colombia). His research interests are access control, model driven development, code generation, and CASE tools. He has several publications about access control in conferences and journals, and has developed software for the Universidad Católica del Norte (Chile), and the Connecticut Departments of Insurance and Transportation, among others.

Manjua Peiris is a PhD student in Department of Computer Science at Indiana University-Purdue University Indianapolis (IUPUI). He is a research assistant in Software Engineering and Distributed Systems research Group. His areas of research include using system execution traces for performance analysis and developing techniques to detect software performance anti-patterns using system execution traces. He has received the BSc degree in Computer Science and Engineering (with first class honors) in 2006 from university of Moratuwa Sri Lanka and MS degree in Computer Science from Purdue University, Indianapolis in 2013.

Srini Ramaswamy earned his Ph.D. degree in Computer Science from the Center for Advanced Computer Studies (CACS) at the University of Louisiana at Lafayette in 1994. He is a member of the Society for Computer Simulation International, Computing Professionals for Social Responsibility, a Senior member of the IEEE and a Senior member of the Association of Computing Machinery (ACM). He is an active member of IEEE SMCS Technical Committee on Distributed Intelligent Systems and also serves as an Associate Editor for the *IEEE Transactions on Systems, Man and Cybernetics, Part C: Applications and Reviews*. In the local community, Dr. Srini Ramaswamy is currently leading Industrial Software Systems research at ABB, the Swiss Multinational Fortune 500 company at its India Corporate Research Center (INCRC) in Bangalore, India.

Rudolf Ramler is a key researcher at the Software Competence Center Hagenberg, Austria. His research interests include software testing, quality management, and software analysis. He has managed research projects on testing Web-based systems, test management, as well as the development of tools for test automation and quality monitoring. Rudolf works as a consultant in industry projects and is a lecturer at the Upper Austrian University of Applied Sciences at Hagenberg, the Johannes Kepler University of Linz, and the Vienna University of Technology. He holds an M.Sc. (2001) from the Johannes Kepler University of Linz, Austria.

Eran Rubin is currently a lecturer at the Faculty of Technology Management at the Holon Institute of Technology (HIT). His research interests include Information Systems' value and impact, decision support systems, and systems analysis and design. Dr. Rubin has published in various journals including *Information and Management, Journal of Business Finance and Accounting, Electronic Commerce Research and Applications*, and *Requirements Engineering*. He received his PhD in Management Information Systems from the University of British Columbia.

Hillel Rubin is a Professor at the Faculty of Civil and Environment Engineering at Technion – Israel Institute of Technology, Haifa, Israel. His research interests concern Water Resources and Environmental Engineering and Systems. He received all his academic degrees at Technion, and served for several years as a visiting professor in various American Universities like University of Florida, University of Michigan, University of NY at Buffalo. Dr. Rubin has published more than 100 scientific articles in refereed journals.

Arsène Sabas is a research scientist at CanmetENERGY-Natural Resources Canada. He received his PhD in computer science from The University of Montreal. His research interests include software engineering, agent-oriented software engineering, formal methods, aspect-oriented systems, and real time multi-agents systems.

Siti Salwa Salim is a Professor in University Malaya, Malaysia. She holds a PhD in software engineering from Manchester University, UK, Masters from UM, Malaysia and Bachelors from Wichita State University, US. Her research interest lies in requirements engineering, human computer interaction, computer-supported cooperative work, component-based software development, and affective computing.

Ali Selamat has received a B.Sc. (Hons.) in IT from Teesside University, U.K. and M.Sc. in Distributed Multimedia Interactive Systems from Lancaster University, U.K. in 1997 and 1998, respectively. He has received a Dr. Eng. degree from Osaka Prefecture University, Japan in 2003. Currently, he is the Dean of Research Alliance in Knowledge Economy (K-Economy RA) UTM. He is also a professor at the Software Engineering Department, Faculty of Computing UTM. He is currently a treasurer of IEEE Malaysia Computer Society Chapter and also the auditor of IEEE Malaysia Section. He is the editors of *International Journal of Digital Content Technology and its Applications* (JDCTA), *International Journal of Advancements in Computing Technology* (IJACT), and *International Journal of Intelligent, Information and Database Systems* (IJIIDS). His research interests include software engineering, software agents, Web engineering, information retrievals, pattern recognitions, genetic algorithms, neural networks, and soft-computing.

Subash Shankar is an associate professor of Computer Science at Hunter College and the Graduate Center of the City University of New York. His research interests include formal methods, applied logic, software engineering, and programming languages.

Shahida Sulaiman is an associate professor of the Faculty of Computing, Universiti Teknologi Malaysia (UTM). She holds a PhD in Computer Science and Masters in Computer Science (Software Engineering in Real Time Systems). Her expertise includes software design, software maintenance, software visualisation and documentation, and knowledge management.

Sharifah Mashita Syed-Mohamad is a senior lecturer of the School of Computer Sciences, Universiti Sains Malaysia (USM). She received her PhD in software engineering from the University of Technology, Sydney, Australia in 2012. Her research interests include software reliability, software testing, software maintenance, agile development, and empirical research.

William G. Tuohey, PhD, MSc, worked for many years in the European Space industry, and on civil aviation software. He had key technical roles in development of simulation software and, particularly, of on-board attitude and orbit spacecraft control software in a number of scientific satellite missions. Since 2000, he has lectured on software engineering, operations research, and applied statistics in the School of Computing in Dublin City University. His research interests are in software engineering and applied mathematics. As well as having continued concern for the effective application of software standards for critical systems, he is particularly interested in application of mathematics to improve aspects of software engineering practice.

Linda Westfall is the president of Westfall Team, Inc., which provides software engineering, software quality engineering, and software project management training and consulting services. Linda has more than 35 years of experience in real time software and has worked as a software engineer, tester, systems analyst, process engineer, quality engineer, and manager. Linda is a past chair of the ASQ Software Division and has served as the Division's Program Chair and Certification Chair and on the ASQ National Certification Board. Linda was a significant contributor to the 3rd and 4th edition of the PMI's PMBOK® Guide and participated in exam development for the Professional Engineer (PE) in software engineering. Linda is a PE in software engineering, an ASQ Fellow, and is an ASQ CSQE, CMQ/OE, CQA, a PMI PMP, and a Certified Scrum Master and Product Owner. Linda is the author of *The Certified Software Quality Engineer Handbook*.

Virginie Wiels is a research engineer at ONERA - the French Aerospace Lab. She is deputy director of the Information Modeling and Processing Department. Her research interests include formal methods, software certification, and critical embedded systems.

Zhenchang Xing is an assistant professor in the School of Computer Engineering, Nanyang Technological University. He received his PhD in Computer Science from University of Alberta, Canada in 2008. His research currently focuses on innovative human-oriented software development infrastructure and tools, sustainable software maintenance and reengineering, and reliable and secure system operation.

Nor Izzaty Yasin earned her Bachelor's Degree in Software Engineering. Her research focus is on agile methodologies and secure software development.

Mohammed I. Younis obtained his BSc in computer engineering from the University of Baghdad in 1997, his MSc degree from the same university in 2001, and his PhD in Software Engineering from Universiti Sains Malaysia in 2010. He is a senior lecturer with the Computer Engineering Department, College of Engineering, University of Baghdad. He has been also a member of the Iraqi Union of Engineers since 1997. His research interests include software engineering, parallel and distributed computing, algorithm design, networking and security, cryptography, embedded systems, and RFID development.

Liguo Yu is an associate professor at Computer Science Department, Indiana University South Bend. He received his Ph.D. degree in computer science from Vanderbilt University in 2004. He received his MS degree from Institute of Metal Research, Chinese Academy of Science and his BS degree in Physics from Jilin University. Before joining Indiana University South Bend, he was a visiting assistant professor at Tennessee Tech University. His research areas include software coupling, software maintenance and software evolution, empirical software engineering, and open-source development. He is also interested in social network analysis, knowledge management, and complex system.

Kamal Z. Zamli obtained his BSc in electrical engineering from Worcester Polytechnic Institute, USA, in 1992, his MSc degree in real-time software engineering from Universiti Teknologi Malaysia in 2000, and his PhD in software engineering from University of Newcastle upon Tyne, UK, in 2003. Professor Dr. Kamal is currently dean of the Research in the Department of Research and Innovation. He is a senior lecturer in the Faculty of Computer Systems and Software Engineering, Universiti Malaysia Pahang. His research interests include software engineering, t-way testing, and algorithm design.

Furkh Zeshan is an Assistant Professor in the Department of Computer Science, COMSATS Institute of Information Technology (CIIT), Lahore, Pakistan. He received his PhD from Universiti Teknologi Malaysia. His specialization includes service-oriented computing, Embedded and Real-Time computing and agent-oriented software engineering.

Index